Marketing Research

Marketing Research

An Applied Orientation

Sixth Edition

Naresh K. Malhotra

Georgia Institute of Technology

Prentice Hall

Boston   Columbus   Indianapolis   New York   San Francisco   Upper Saddle River

Amsterdam   Cape Town   Dubai   London   Madrid   Milan   Munich   Paris   Montreal   Toronto

Delhi   Mexico City   Sao Paulo   Sydney   Hong Kong   Seoul   Singapore   Taipei   Tokyo

Editorial Director: Sally Yagan
Acquisitions Editor: James Heine
Product Development Manager: Ashley Santora
Director of Marketing: Patrice Lumumba Jones
Senior Marketing Manager: Anne Fahlgren
Marketing Assistant: Susan Osterlitz
Senior Managing Editor: Judy Leale
Production Project Manager: Kelly Warsak
Permissions Project Manger: Charles Morris
Senior Operations Supervisor: Arnold Vila
Operations Specialist: Ben Smith
Art Director: Steven Frim
Cover Designer: Steven Frim
Cover Art: Steven Frim
Interior Text: Jill Little

Creative Director: Christy Mahon
IRC Manager, Rights and Permissions: Zina Arabia
Manager, Visual Research: Beth Brenzel
Photo Researcher: Kathy Ringrose
Image Permission Coordinator: Angelique Sharps
Manager, Cover Visual Research & Permissions:
  Karen Sanatar
Media Director: Lisa Rinaldi
Lead Media Project Manager: Denise Vaughn
Full-Service Project Management: Jennifer
  Welsch/BookMasters, Inc.
Composition: Integra Software Services
Printer/Binder: Edwards Brothers
Cover Printer: Lehigh-Phoenix Color
Text Font: 10/12 Times

Credits and acknowledgments borrowed from other sources and reproduced, with permission, in this textbook appear on appropriate page within text.

SAS logo is provided courtesy of SAS Institute. Copyright © SAS Institute, Inc., Cary NC. All Rights Reserved. Used with permission. SAS and all other SAS Institute Inc. product or service names are registered trademarks or trademarks of SAS Institute Inc. in the USA and other countires. ® indicates USA registration.

Microsoft® and Windows® are registered trademarks of the Microsoft Corporation in the U.S.A. and other countries. Screen shots and icons reprinted with permission from the Microsoft Corporation. This book is not sponsored or endorsed by or affiliated with the Microsoft Corporation.

Library of Congress Cataloging-in-Publication Data

Malhotra, Naresh K.
  Marketing research : an applied orientation / Naresh K. Malhotra—6th ed.
    p. cm.
Includes bibliographical references and index.
ISBN 978-0-13-608543-0 (casebound : alk. paper)
  1. Marketing research.   2. Marketing research—Methodology.   I. Title.
HF5415.2.M29 2010
658.8'3—dc22

                                                2009011023

10 9 8 7 6 5 4 3 2 1

Prentice Hall
is an imprint of

www.pearsonhighered.com

ISBN 10:   0-13-608543-1
ISBN 13: 978-0-13-608543-0

To the memory of my father,
Mr. H. N. Malhotra
and
To my mother, Mrs. Satya Malhotra

and

To my wife Veena and children Ruth and Paul

The love, encouragement, and support of my parents, wife,
and children have been exemplary.

"The greatest of these is love."

I Corinthians 13:13

"But God showed how much He loved us by having Christ die for us,
even though we were sinful."

Romans 5:8
The Holy Bible

Brief Contents

Contents

Foreword

The world of business is moving more rapidly than ever, meaning the intelligent and thoughtful use of research is critical to keeping pace. Undoubtedly the most successful people will have a broad base of education, high levels of communication skills, and creative approaches to the opportunities racing toward us. It is a significant achievement when a textbook such as Dr. Malhotra's allows the classroom to become a source of these skills.

This text has already proven its worth as one of the most successful in the field, with well over 140 universities using it in the United States and eight foreign-language and several different English-language editions in print. It is unsurpassed in presenting the fundamentals that allow you to become a researcher and intelligent user of research. The real-life examples, titled Real Research, bring you closer to the world businesspeople face daily. At every step, you can relate to the ongoing Department Store Project, the Dell Running Case, and the practical vignettes that bring the educational material to a realistic and practical level. These materials are complemented by Active Research, Experiential Research, and Decision Research exercises that offer additional hands-on experience. The text's grasp of the leading edge of research is evident in its integration of modern tools of research such as the Internet, computer analytic software, and the latest management practices. The demonstration movies, screen captures, and step-by-step instructions for running SPSS and SAS programs provide the most extensive help available for learning these statistical packages.

We at Burke, Inc., are pleased to be asked to contribute again to a new edition. We have shared our experiences as well as our philosophies, technical skill, and thoughts about the future of research. This sixth edition of *Marketing Research: An Applied Orientation* provides the foundation we believe every student should have. We are confident you will find its combination of theory, practice, and sound advice to be of great value to you.

Michael Baumgardner, Ph.D.
President and CEO, Burke, Inc.

Preface

The Sixth Edition—Helping You Learn Marketing Research

Marketing research is an integral part of marketing. Its task is to assess information needs and provide management with relevant, accurate, reliable, valid, and current information to aid marketing decision making (see Figure 1.2). Companies use marketing research to stay competitive and to avoid high costs of poor decisions based on unsound information.

If you are a marketing major, understanding your consumers, suppliers, channel partners, employees, and competitors and the environment is your foundation for developing effective marketing programs. You gain that understanding by conducting marketing research. This book and course will help you succeed in your marketing career.

If you are not a marketing major, any company or organization you work for will use marketing research information for making decisions. You will want to understand how to generate such information and how to evaluate its relevance, accuracy, and usefulness. The research process we describe in this book is very general and applies to any area of management, not just marketing. Only the context in which we illustrate it is marketing. Therefore, this course and this book will help you be more effective in your job, regardless of the specific area in which you work.

Since research is best learned by doing, this book emphasizes a hands-on, do-it-yourself approach. You will have many opportunities to see how marketing research affects management decisions in chapter features including Real Research, Active Research, Experiential Research, Decision Research, Project Research, cases, video cases, and extensive review questions, problems, Internet and computer exercises, and activities (role playing, fieldwork, and group discussions). The data analysis chapters illustrate in detail each step in running SPSS and SAS, and we've provided four distinct ways in which you can learn these programs on your own. SPSS and SAS files are provided for all data sets; outputs, demonstration movies, and screen captures are posted on the Web site. *This book provides students the most extensive help available to learn SPSS and SAS.* Thus, we prepared this textbook and all the additional materials to help you understand the fundamental principles of marketing research and how to apply them in real-life marketing situations.

New for the Sixth Edition

The sixth edition contains major revisions suggested in surveys of professors (users and nonusers) and students, critical reviews, and detailed evaluations. Significant changes include:

1. *Updating.* New and updated material starts with Chapter 1 and continues throughout the text.
2. *A New Chapter.* A new Chapter 22, "Structural Equation Modeling and Path Analysis," completes our coverage of popular data analysis techniques. It explains structural equation modeling and path analysis from an intuitive perspective and presents the techniques in a simple and easy to understand manner, retaining the text's applied and managerial orientation.
3. *New Concept Maps.* Concept maps in each chapter connect concepts in a downward-branching hierarchical structure, with labeled arrows that articulate flows and relationships. The contribution of concept maps to learning is well documented; find more information at the Institute for Human and Machine Cognition Web site at www.ihmc.us.
4. *New Running Case About Dell.* Case 1.1 begins a new running case that features Dell Computers, using the actual questionnaire and real data collected by a prominent marketing research firm. This case is another way to see the linkages between chapters and trace the entire marketing research process throughout the book. Case questions conclude each chapter; answers appear in the *Instructor's Manual.*
5. *New Critical Thinking Cases.* Three new comprehensive cases with critical thinking and case questions are structured around principles for research, instructional strategies,

Socratic questioning, critical reading and writing, higher order thinking, and assessment as propounded by the Foundation for Critical Thinking (www.criticalthinking.org). These cases are 2.1 American Idol, 2.2 Baskin-Robbins, and 2.3 Akron Children's Hospital. Solutions appear in the *Instructor's Manual*.

6. *New Video Cases.* Each chapter, except the data analysis chapters, is followed by a video case, with questions pertaining to that chapter and all the preceding chapters. These cases are drawn from the Prentice Hall video library but have been written, with relevant discussion questions, from a marketing research perspective. Each can be used with or without the video.

7. *New Cases with Real Questionnaire and Data.* Two new cases contain real questionnaires and data sets. Although the true identity of these firms has been disguised for proprietary reasons, the data sets are real and were obtained in actual surveys conducted by marketing research companies. The cases new to the sixth edition are Case 3.1: AT&T Wireless: Ma Bell Becomes Ma Again and Case 4.1: JPMorgan Chase: Chasing Growth Through Mergers and Acquisitions. Cases 3.1, 3.2, and 3.3 deal only with data analysis; Cases 4.1 and 4.2 are comprehensive and their questions relate to every chapter of the book. All these cases include actual questionnaires and real data.

8. *Added Emphasis on SAS.* Relevant chapters contain a special section on SAS Learning Edition, along with another on SPSS Windows, that illustrate the relevant programs and the steps required to run them. We have provided SPSS and SAS files for all input data sets featured in the data analysis chapters (Chapters 14 through 22), input data sets that appear in Internet and Computer Exercises, input data sets for cases (Cases 3.1, 3.2, 3.3, 4.1, and 4.2), and the corresponding output files. While the SAS steps are illustrated for the Learning Edition, these steps will also work for the SAS Enterprise Guide.

9. *New SPSS and SAS Computerized Demonstration Movies.* We have created computerized demonstration movies illustrating step-by-step instructions for each data analysis procedure—SPSS and SAS—available for downloading from the Web site for this book (see Exhibit 14.2).

10. *New SPSS and SAS Screen Captures.* In addition to the demonstration movies, we have also provided screen captures with notes illustrating step-by-step instructions for running each data analysis procedure presented in the book using SPSS as well as SAS. These are on the text Web site for downloading.

11. *SPSS and SAS Step-by-Step Instructions.* Each chapter contains separate step-by-step SPSS and SAS instructions for conducting the data analysis presented in that chapter. While the SAS steps are illustrated for the Learning Edition, these steps will also work for the SAS Enterprise Guide.

12. *New and Updated Examples.* New examples have been added, some old ones deleted, and the remaining ones updated as appropriate.

13. *New Web Site Materials.* To keep the book concise, we have placed some material on the instructor Web site (Instructor Resource Center) and the student Web site.

14. *Updated References.* Each chapter contains many references dated 2008 or later. Of course, the classic references have been retained.

Integrated Learning Package

If you take advantage of the following special features, you should find this textbook interesting and even fun.

1. *Balanced orientation.* We've blended scholarship with a highly applied and managerial orientation showing how marketing researchers apply concepts and techniques and how managers use their findings to improve marketing practice. In each chapter, we talk about real marketing research firms, large and small.

2. *Real-life examples.* Real-life examples (Real Research) describe the kind of marketing research firms used to address a specific managerial problem and the decisions they based on the findings.

3. *Hands-on approach.* You'll find more real-life scenarios and exercises in every chapter. Active Research features ask you to do some research on the Internet and play the roles of a marketing researcher and a marketing manager. Experiential Research features let you

experience the research concepts in each chapter. Decision Research presents a real-life marketing situation in which you assume the role of a consultant and recommend marketing research and marketing management decisions.

4. *Running project.* A running example in every chapter is based on an actual department store project I conducted, although several aspects have been disguised. You will participate by conducting some research and analysis.

5. *Critical thinking emphasis.* You can practice your critical thinking skills including Socratic questioning, critical reading and writing, and higher order thinking and assessment in the three comprehensive critical thinking cases, end-of-chapter review questions, applied problems, and group discussions.

6. *Concept maps.* Concept maps help you visualize the interrelated concepts in each chapter.

7. *Extensive Internet coverage.* We'll show you how to integrate the Internet into each step of the marketing research process and you'll have plenty of opportunities to do Internet research.

8. *International focus.* Every chapter has a section titled International Marketing Research or an example illustrating a data analysis technique in an international setting. Chapter 24 introduces advanced concepts in international marketing research.

9. *Ethics focus.* Ethical issues are pervasive in marketing research. Every chapter has a section titled Ethics in Marketing Research or an example of a data analysis technique that raises an ethical question. We'll talk about ethics from the perspectives of the four stakeholders: the client, the marketing research firm, the respondents, and the general public.

10. *Focus on technology.* Technological developments have shaped the way in which marketing research is conducted and we talk about these throughout the book.

11. *Contemporary focus.* We apply marketing research to current topics such as customer value, satisfaction, loyalty, customer equity, brand equity and management, innovation, entrepreneurship, return on marketing, relationship marketing, and socially responsible marketing throughout the text.

12. *Statistical software.* We illustrate data analysis procedures with respect to SPSS, SAS, MINITAB, Excel, and other popular programs, but we emphasize SPSS and SAS. Separate SPSS Windows and SAS Learning Edition sections in the relevant chapters discuss the programs and the steps you need to run them. While the SAS steps are illustrated for the Learning Edition, these steps will also work for the SAS Enterprise Guide.

    The Web site includes all the SPSS and SAS data sets used in each data analysis chapter and the corresponding output files, the SPSS and SAS data sets for the relevant Internet and Computer Exercises, and cases. You can also download the SPSS and SAS demonstration movies and screen captures.

13. *Video Instruction.* Each chapter of the book, except the data analysis chapters, is followed by a video case and questions written from a marketing research perspective. You can study these cases with or without the videos.

14. *Comprehensive cases with real data.* At the end of the book, you'll find two comprehensive cases, relevant questionnaires, and statistical data files, with case questions that test your understanding of each chapter of the book. These cases (Case 4.1, JPMorgan Chase, and Case 4.2, Wendy's) will let you see the interrelatedness of all the marketing research concepts discussed in the book. The data are the actual, original data, although the identities of the actual firms have been changed. There are three additional data analysis cases with actual questionnaire and real data (Cases 3.1 AT&T, 3.2 IBM, and 3.3 Kimberly-Clark).

15. *Running case about Dell.* Case 1.1 is a running case about Dell that features the actual questionnaire and real data. This case is another way to see the linkages between chapters and trace the entire marketing research process through the book.

16. *Harvard Business School cases.* To show you how managers integrate marketing research with marketing management decisions, the book includes six Harvard Business School cases, with comprehensive marketing research questions that cover each chapter of the book (except the data analysis chapters).

17. *Live research: Conducting a marketing research project.* If your instructor wishes to implement a marketing research project, we give specific steps in each chapter.

18. *Acronyms.* Acronyms are the most popular mnemonic technique college students use. Each chapter thus contains one or more helpful acronyms that summarize important concepts.

19. *Extensive exercises and activities.* Extensive exercises and activities, which include questions, problems, Internet and computer exercises, role playing, fieldwork, and group discussion, conclude each chapter. Here you'll find ample opportunities for learning and testing yourself on the concepts in the chapter.

20. *Learning aids.* We offer a complete set of learning aids, including a Web site that can be found at www.pearsonhighered.com/malhotra.

21. *AACSB learning standards.* At the end of each chapter, we supply exercises that help you meet the AACSB learning standards with respect to

- Communication
- Ethical reasoning
- Analytic skills
- Use of information technology
- Multiculture and diversity
- Reflective thinking

You Can Learn SPSS and SAS on Your Own!

Many students complain that they spend a substantial amount of time learning SPSS or SAS. We have addressed this situation. The sixth edition provides four ways in which you can learn SPSS and SAS on your own: (1) detailed step-by-step instructions appear in the chapter, (2) you can download (from the Web site for this book) computerized demonstration movies illustrating these step-by-step instructions, (3) you can download screen captures with notes illustrating these step-by-step instructions, and (4) you can refer to the *Study Guide and Technology Manual*, a supplement that accompanies this book. *Thus, we provide the most extensive help available anywhere to learn SPSS and SAS!*

Tips for Using This Textbook

Here are a few tips on how to use this book to master the material.

- *Read the chapter.* Start by reading the chapter. Be sure to look at the objectives and read the overview so you will know what is in the chapter. Some students mistakenly think this step isn't important; don't skip it.
- *Review the key terms.* Read through these new terms to be sure you understand each one. Key terms are often targets of quiz and exam questions.
- *Answer the review questions.* Go through the review questions and try to answer them without looking in the chapter. When you are finished, go back and see whether you got them all correct. For those you couldn't answer; go back and locate the correct information in the chapter.
- *Do the problems.* Pick several problems you believe would be interesting. Spend some time thinking about the question and the concepts each problem explores. You can make these problems fun to do as you analyze the concepts at a deeper level.
- *Attempt the Internet and computer exercises.* These exercises give you practice in analyzing both qualitative data (that you will search on the Web) and quantitative data (that you can download from the Web site for this book).
- *Try one of the cases or video cases.* The cases and video cases provide an excellent summary of the material presented in the chapter. Read one and answer each of the questions at the end. (You do not need to see the video to answer the video case questions, but you can view it on the Companion Website for this text by visiting www.pearsonhighered.com/malhotra).
- *Have some fun with critical thinking.* Go to one of the critical thinking cases (2.1 American Idol, 2.2 Baskin-Robbins, and 2.3 Akron Children's Hospital). These cases are comprehensive and contain questions on all the chapters except the data analysis chapters. Use what you've learned, along with the case information, to answer the critical thinking questions as well as the technical questions. Doing these cases will help you understand and apply the concepts in real-life situations from a critical thinking perspective.

How to Prepare for Exams

If you've followed the tips, you're almost ready for the exam. A brief review of the key terms and a scan of the chapter is all you need. If not, here is a sequence of activities that will help you learn the material.

- Read the chapter.
- Review the concept maps.
- Review the key terms.
- Answer the review questions.
- Read the chapter overview.
- Read the chapter summary.
- Go through the chapter and locate all the bold and italic words. Read the context of each term to make sure you understand it.
- Start at the beginning of the chapter and read the topic sentence of each paragraph. These provide a good summary of that paragraph.
- Reread the chapter summary.

Congratulations! You are now ready for the exam. Relax; you'll do well.

Student Supplements and Value Packs

The book is supported by a useful set of supplements to further enhance your learning.

1. *A Functional and Useful Web site.* Access this site at www.pearsonhighered.com/malhotra. It contains:

   - Data for Case 1.1 Dell; Cases 3.1 AT&T, 3.2 IBM, and 3.3 Kimberly-Clark; and Cases 4.1 JPMorgan Chase and 4.2 Wendy's, given in the book (SPSS and SAS).
   - Data files for all the Internet and Computer Exercises (SPSS and SAS).
   - Data file for the data set(s) used in each data analysis chapter (SPSS and SAS). The corresponding output files are also provided.
   - SPSS and SAS computerized demonstration movies.
   - SPSS and SAS screen captures.
   - Videos for all the video cases.
   - Additional materials that supplement the topic discussed in the book.

2. *Student Version of SPSS.* You can obtain a student version of SPSS as an optional value package with this book.

3. *Study Guide and Technology Manual.* This supplement will help deepen your learning and is available in print format. I have personally written this manual to ensure that it is closely geared to the book and that it facilitates student learning.

4. *CourseSmart E-textbooks Online: The Largest eTextbook Store on the Internet!* Developed for students looking to save money on required or recommended textbooks, CourseSmart eTextbooks Online saves students up to 50 percent off the suggested list price of the print text. Students simply select their eText by title or author and purchase immediate access to the content for the duration of the course, using any major credit card. With a CourseSmart eText, students can search for specific keywords or page numbers, make notes online, print out reading assignments that incorporate lecture notes, and bookmark important passages for later review. For more information, or to purchase a CourseSmart eTextbook, visit www.coursesmart.com.

Acknowledgments

Many people have been extremely helpful in writing this textbook. I would like to acknowledge Professor Arun K. Jain (State University of New York at Buffalo), who taught me marketing research in a way I will never forget. My students, particularly former doctoral students (James Agarwal, Imad Baalbaki, Ashutosh Dixit, Dan McCort, Rick McFarland, Charla Mathwick, Gina Miller, Mark Peterson, Jamie Pleasant, Cassandra Wells, and Ashutosh Patil) as well as other doctoral students (Mark Leach and Tyra Mitchell) have been very helpful in many ways.

I particularly want to acknowledge the assistance of Mark Leach and Gina Miller in writing the ethics sections and chapter, Mark Peterson in writing the computer applications, and James Agarwal with the international marketing research examples in the earlier two editions. MBA students David Ball, Joshua Pitts, and Madhavi Akella provided helpful research assistance. The students in my marketing research courses have provided useful feedback as the material was class-tested for several years.

My colleagues at Georgia Tech, especially Fred Allvine, have been very supportive. I also want to thank Ronald L. Tatham, former chairman, Burke, Inc., for his encouragement and support, as well as Michael Baumgardner, the current president and CEO of Burke. William D. Neal, founder and senior executive officer of SDR, Inc., has been very helpful and supportive over the years. Ken Athaide, senior vice president, Marketing Strategies International, and the other practitioners have also contributed to this book. Pamela Prentice of SAS was very helpful with the SAS additions incorporated in the sixth edition.

The reviewers have offered many constructive and valuable suggestions. I gratefully acknowledge the help of the following, among others:

Reviewers for the Sixth Edition

Manoj Agarwal, Binghamton University

Arun K. Jain, University at Buffalo

Sanjay S. Mehta, Sam Houston State University

Richard G. Netemeyer, University of Virginia

Cecelia Wittmayer, Dakota State University

Reviewers for the Fifth Edition

Robert W. Armstrong, University of North Alabama

John Thomas Drea, Western Illinois University

Perry Haan, Franklin University

Mark Hill, Montclair State University

Mary Jean Koontz, Golden Gate University

Haim Mano, University of Missouri, St. Louis

David W. Pan, Northeastern State University

Audhesh Paswan, University of North Texas

Scott D. Swain, Boston University

Reviewers for the Fourth Edition

Gerald Cavallo, Fairfield University–Connecticut

Curt Dommeyer, California State University–Northridge

Charles Hofacker, Florida State University

Yong-Soon Kang, Binghamton University–SUNY

John Tsalikis, Florida International University

Reviewers for the Third Edition

Tom Anastasti, Boston University

Joel Herche, University of the Pacific

Subash Lonial, University of Louisville

Paul Sauer, Canisius College

John Weiss, Colorado State University

Reviewers for the Second Edition

Rick Andrews, University of Delaware

Holland Blades, Jr., Missouri Southern State College

Sharmila Chatterjee, Santa Clara University

Rajshekhar Javalgi, Cleveland State University

Mushtaq Luqmani, Western Michigan University

Jeanne Munger, University of Southern Maine

Audesh Paswan, University of South Dakota

Venkatram Ramaswamy, University of Michigan

Gillian Rice, Thunderbird University

Paul L. Sauer, Canisius College

Hans Srinivasan, University of Connecticut

Reviewers for the First Edition

David M. Andrus, Kansas State University

Joe Ballenger, Stephen F. Austin State University

Joseph D. Brown, Ball State University

Thomas E. Buzas, Eastern Michigan University

Rajendar K. Garg, Northeastern Illinois University

Lawrence D. Gibson, Consultant

Ronald E. Goldsmith, Florida State University

Rajshekhar G. Javalgi, Cleveland State University

Charlotte H. Mason, University of North Carolina

Kent Nakamoto, University of Colorado

Thomas J. Page, Jr., Michigan State University

William S. Perkins, Pennsylvania State University

Sudhi Seshadri, University of Maryland at College Park

David Shani, Baruch College

The team at Prentice Hall provided outstanding support. Special thanks are due to Sally Yagan, editorial director; James Heine, acquisitions editor; Ashley Santora, product development manager; Anne Fahlgren, senior marketing manager; Kelly Warsak, project manager; Karin Williams, editorial assistant; and Teri Stratford, photo researcher. Special recognition is due to the several field representatives and salespeople who have done an outstanding job.

I acknowledge with great respect my mother, Mrs. Satya Malhotra, and my departed father, Mr. H. N. Malhotra. Their love, encouragement, support, and the sacrificial giving of themselves have been exemplary. My heartfelt love and gratitude go to my wife, Veena, and my children, Ruth and Paul, for their faith, hope, and love.

Above all, I want to acknowledge and thank my Savior and Lord, Jesus Christ, for the many miracles He has performed in my life. This book is, truly, the result of His grace—"This is the Lord's doing; it is marvelous in our eyes" (Psalm 118:23). It is also an answer to prayers—"And whatsoever ye shall ask in my name, that will I do, that the Father may be glorified in the Son. If ye shall ask any thing in my name, I will do *it*" (John 14:13–14).

Naresh K. Malhotra

Author Biography

Naresh K. Malhotra is Regents Professor (highest academic rank in the University System of Georgia) in the College of Management, Georgia Institute of Technology. He has been listed in Marquis' *Who's Who in America* continuously since 1997, and in *Who's Who in the World* since 2000. He received the prestigious Academy of Marketing Science CUTCO/Vector Distinguished Marketing Educator Award in 2005. He is also the winner of numerous awards and honors for research, teaching, and service to the profession, including the Academy of Marketing Science, Outstanding Marketing Teaching Excellence Award, 2003.

Dr. Malhotra was Chairman, Academy of Marketing Science Foundation, 1996 to 1998; President, Academy of Marketing Science, 1994 to 1996; and Chairman, Board of Governors, 1990 to 1992. He is a Distinguished Fellow of the Academy and Fellow of the Decision Sciences Institute. The founding editor of *Review of Marketing Research,* he was an associate editor of *Decision Sciences* for 18 years and section editor, Health Care Marketing Abstracts, *Journal of Health Care Marketing.* He has served on the editorial boards of more than a dozen journals, including *Journal of Marketing Research, Journal of Marketing, Journal of Consumer Research,* and *Journal of the Academy of Marketing Science.*

Marketing Research: An Applied Orientation has been translated into Chinese, Spanish, Russian, Portuguese, Hungarian, French, Bahasa Indonesian, and Japanese. It has also been published in several English-language editions including North American, International, European, Indian, and one for Australia and New Zealand. Dr. Malhotra's *Basic Marketing Research: A Decision-Making Approach,* Third Edition, was published by Prentice Hall in 2008. This book has also been translated into a number of languages.

In the 1987 AMA Educators' Proceedings, Professor Malhotra was ranked number one based on articles published in the *Journal of Marketing Research* during 1980 to 1985. He also holds the all-time record for the maximum number of publications in the *Journal of Health Care Marketing.* He was ranked number one based on publications in the *Journal of the Academy of Marketing Science* (*JAMS*) from its inception through Volume 23, 1995, and during the ten-year period 1986–1995 (*JAMS,* 24(4) (Fall 1996): 297). He was several times ranked number one based on publications in the *International Marketing Review,* including from 1996 to 2006 based on a study by Xu et al. published in the *Asia Pacific Journal of Management* (2008). In a landmark study by West et al. (2008) examining publications in the top four marketing journals (*JMR, JM, JAMS,* and *JCR*) over a 25-year period from 1977 to 2002, Professor Malhotra earned three top-three rankings: ranked number three based on publications in all the four journals combined, ranked number three based on publications in *JMR,* and ranked number one based on publications in *JAMS.*

Dr. Malhotra has published more than 100 papers in major refereed journals, including in *Journal of Marketing Research, Journal of Consumer Research, Marketing Science, Management Science, Journal of Marketing, Journal of Academy of Marketing Science, Journal of Retailing, Journal of Health Care Marketing*, and leading journals in statistics, management science, information systems, and psychology. He has also published numerous refereed articles in the proceedings of major national and international conferences. Several of his articles have received best paper research awards. Dr. Malhotra has consulted for business, nonprofit, and government organizations in the United States and abroad and has served as an expert witness in legal and regulatory proceedings with special expertise in data analysis and statistical methods.

An ordained minister of the Gospel and a member and Deacon of First Baptist Church, Atlanta, Dr. Malhotra lives in the Atlanta area with his wife, Veena, and children, Ruth and Paul.

Part I

Introduction and Early Phases of Marketing Research

In this part, we define and classify marketing research and set out a six-step marketing research process. We discuss the nature and scope of marketing research and explain its role in decision support systems. We describe the marketing research industry and the many exciting career opportunities in this field. We discuss problem definition, the first and the most important step, in detail. Finally, we describe the development of an approach to the problem, the second step in the marketing research process, and discuss in detail the various components of the approach. The perspective given in these chapters should be useful to both marketing decision makers and researchers.

" The role of a marketing researcher must include consulting skills, technical proficiency, and sound management. The focus of the role is to provide information to identify marketing problems and solutions in such a way that action can be taken. "

Michael Baumgardner, President and CEO, Burke, Inc.

Objectives   [After reading this chapter, the student should be able to:]

1. Define marketing research and distinguish between problem identification and problem-solving research.

2. Describe a framework for conducting marketing research as well as the six steps of the marketing research process.

3. Understand the nature and scope of marketing research and its role in designing and implementing successful marketing programs.

4. Explain how the decision to conduct marketing research is made.

5. Discuss the marketing research industry and the types of research suppliers, including internal, external, full-service, and limited-service suppliers.

6. Describe careers available in marketing research and the backgrounds and skills needed to succeed in them.

7. Explain the role of marketing research in decision support systems in providing data, marketing models, and specialized software.

8. Acquire an appreciation of the international dimension and the complexity involved in international marketing research.

9. Gain an understanding of the ethical aspects of marketing research and the responsibilities each of the marketing research stakeholders have to themselves, one another, and the research project.

Introduction to Marketing Research

Overview

Marketing research comprises one of the most important and fascinating facets of marketing. In this chapter, we give a formal definition of marketing research and classify marketing research into two areas: problem identification and problem-solving research. We provide several real-life examples to illustrate the basic concepts of marketing research. We describe the marketing research process and the six steps that are involved in conducting research and discuss the nature of marketing research, emphasizing its role of providing information for marketing decision making. Next, we provide an overview of marketing research suppliers who collectively constitute the marketing research industry, along with guidelines for selecting a supplier. The demand for well-executed marketing research leads to many exciting career opportunities, which we describe. We show that marketing research is also an integral part of marketing information systems or decision support systems.

For the purpose of illustration, we examine a department store patronage project, which was an actual marketing research project conducted by the author, and use it as a running example throughout the book. The scope of this project has been expanded in the sixth edition to include questions, and we also make available the relevant data for analysis. These "Project Research" sections appear in each chapter. The topic of international marketing research is introduced and discussed systematically in the subsequent chapters. The ethical aspects of marketing research and the responsibilities each of the marketing research stakeholders have to themselves, one another, and the research project are presented and developed in more detail throughout the text. This chapter includes several Internet and hands-on applications of marketing research in the form of "Active Research," "Experiential Research," and "Decision Research" illustrations with exercises, other emphases that pervade the entire book. For instructors wishing to implement a real-life marketing research project, we include a section titled "Live Research: Conducting a Marketing Research Project." Perhaps there is no better way to present an overview than to give a few examples that provide a flavor of the varied nature of marketing research.

Real Research

Boeing: Taking Flight

The Boeing Company (www.boeing.com) has been the premier manufacturer of commercial jetliners for more than 40 years and provides products and services to customers in 145 countries. Headquartered in Chicago, Boeing had about 12,000 commercial jetliners in service worldwide as of 2009, which is roughly 75 percent of the world fleet. Boeing Commercial Airplanes (BCA) is the division of Boeing that develops and sells airplanes in the commercial segment. Although the airplane manufacturing industry is an oligopoly with only a few players, the competition is intense and the stakes are high. The division understands that it is important to continuously monitor the dynamic marketplace and understand the needs and priorities of BCA customers (airlines) and their customers (people who fly). To achieve this purpose, BCA employs marketing research on a regular basis.

Boeing recently entrusted Harris Interactive (www.harrisinteractive.com) with a study of this type. Harris Interactive, one of the largest market research firms in the world, is based in Rochester, New York. It is best known for *The Harris Poll* and for pioneering Internet-based research methods. Boeing commissioned a study to determine the aircraft preferences of fliers. "We presented respondents with real-life air travel scenarios to better understand the attitudes and feelings that led to their choices," said Dr. David Bakken, senior vice president of marketing sciences, Harris Interactive. "What we found was that travelers taking very long flights generally prefer the more convenient and flexible experience provided by smaller planes."

Based on extensive marketing research, Boeing launched the newest members of its 737 family, thereby bringing more economical solutions to airlines, a better flight experience to passengers, and improved environmental performance to the world.

The study was a survey based on 913 interviews conducted in the United Kingdom, Tokyo, and Hong Kong with international travelers (age 18 and over) who had taken at least one recent eight-hour or longer flight. Interviews were conducted between November 2003 and February 2004 using a two-stage methodology. Respondents were first screened and qualified by telephone or via in-person interviews, and then they completed an online survey at home or work or at a central interviewing location. In each region, Harris polled equal numbers of Premium Class Business, Economy Business, and Economy Leisure travelers. Some key findings:

- More than 60 percent preferred a single-deck, 250-passenger airplane to a double-deck, 550-passenger airplane for nonstop flights.
- Seven out of 10 travelers preferred a nonstop trip on a single-deck, 250-passenger airplane to a trip involving a connecting flight on a double-deck, 550-passenger airplane with an on-board lounge.
- Travelers in all the classes of service from all three regions believed smaller airplanes would provide a better experience with check-in, boarding, disembarking, baggage claim, and customs/immigration than the 550-seat aircraft.

From Boeing's point of view, these were important insights. The company is responding with enhanced products. Based on these findings and subsequent product research that involved in-depth interviews and surveys of airlines, BCA developed a new version of the Boeing 737, which caters to the 100- to 215-seat market. The new concept is focused on bringing more economical solutions to airlines, a better flight experience to passengers, and improved environmental performance to the world. The newest members of the Boeing 737 family—the 737-600/-700/-800/-900 models—continue the 737's preeminence as the world's most popular and reliable commercial jet transport. Meeting the market demands, the 737 family has won orders for more than 5,200 airplanes, an amazing feat even for Boeing.[1] ∎

Real Research   ## Satmetrix Puts Customer Metrics in Real Time

Many of the nation's largest corporations are realizing that the information they can get from clients and customers through marketing research can best be used if it is provided each day. How about each minute? This is the basis upon which a company called Satmetrix (www.satmetrix.com), a customer feedback solution company, operates—real time. The Satmetrix Customer Relationship program is designed to maximize the impact of customer interactions by continuously gathering and transforming customer dialogues into potential actions that can be taken to increase sales and customer satisfaction. This program is focused on feeding the voice of the customers back into the organization. Not only can customers go online and submit complaints and suggestions to the company, but Satmetrix also hosts live chat sessions for users of certain products. All of this is done with the aim of capturing the true words and emotions of consumers, and in turn using this information to improve or develop products and services. Satmetrix capitalizes on the need for "live" marketing research.

As of 2009, the Internet continues to revolutionize the marketing research process. With the use of online services, there is no need for extra data input that traditional research methods require. Satmetrix itself is not the traditional full-service supplier of marketing research. As a standardized limited-service provider, the company does not get involved with every aspect of the research process. The approach, design, and data preparation are the same for each customer, and these are the parts of the research process with which the company is involved.

Their service, however, aids clients in identifying any problems with products through customer feedback and with problem solving, especially if customers give suggestions. For example, network station NBC (www.nbc.com) takes advantage of Satmetrix services to obtain feedback from viewers. It helps the network to learn what viewers are looking for, their likes, and their dislikes. Ideally, the feedback is used and television shows are altered to more closely suit viewers' tastes and desires, thus leading to an increased number of people tuning in to watch the shows. NBC found, for example, that viewers wanted a sitcom that was lighthearted, clever, and humorous; therefore, *Kath and Kim*, a remake of the popular Australian comedy by the same name, was launched on October 9, 2008. Viewer feedback provided by Satmetrix has been instrumental in composing and modifying scripts and storylines. As a result, in 2009, *Will and Grace* was a top-rated comedy show on NBC.[2] ■

Real Research   ## Scion: The Illustrious Offspring of Toyota

Toyota has had tremendous success with both the Toyota and Lexus brands of cars. The Lexus brand was created to sell cars more luxurious than those previously offered by Toyota and to cater to the older, more affluent crowd. However, the company noticed an opportunity in the younger, "Generation Y" crowd (those born between 1977 and 1995), where Toyota had a relatively smaller market share. More than 65 million Americans fall into this demographic category. Cars bought by this group are less expensive and more youth-oriented. Chief rivals within this competitive landscape include Honda, Volkswagen, BMW, Mazda, Ford, and Chevrolet.

Focus groups and surveys by Toyota targeted at the teen through thirties age group suggested that Toyota had the image of being "my parents' car." Needless to say, sales to this diverse and elusive age group were small. Toyota then began a secret project, code-named "Genesis," to research the under-30 market to find out what features they wanted in their cars and to determine their buying habits. The members of the study looked at existing Toyota models such as the Echo, the Celica, and the MR2 Spyder and found that the Generation Y crowd perceived these cars as having no cohesive theme and carrying Toyota's older image. Several cars were brought to the United States that were being used in Japan to see what kind of reaction they would elicit. The cars that created the most buzz ultimately were modified for American preferences and resulted in a third line of cars for Toyota, aptly named "Scion" (www.scion.com). The Scion name means "offspring of an illustrious family" and illustrates the fact that they are a spin-off from Toyota.

Now that Toyota had the cars and the strategy, they had to build their brand and market the new cars to this new audience. Toyota hired marketing firm ATTIK (www.attik.com) to help with this task. They conducted qualitative market research through traditional focus groups and clinics as well as quantitative research through Internet surveys and youth panels. They also implemented case studies by asking people to study their younger friends' preferences and to report their findings. The results of this market research revealed that the Generation Y crowd values individuality and expression, diversity, and style. Because they are more prone to disdain commercialism and can be swayed more effectively by word-of-mouth communications, Scion chose not to advertise through traditional channels such as network television or magazines. Rather, they decided to market the Scion through guerrilla tactics such as live concerts and events with a music or arts focus catered toward this younger crowd.

Scion took the results of their market research and applied them to their business strategy. In 2003, the first Scions were available for sale. Three different models were designed to attract a wide spectrum of younger buyers, such as the Scion xB, which is a boxy, compact sports utility vehicle. All Scions came loaded with options that were desirable to the target buyer, such as 160-watt stereos, cell phone holders, plush seats, and plenty of customization options. They implemented a no-haggling, easy-to-understand pricing structure to make the buying process more enjoyable for many of these first-time buyers.

More than 90 percent of Scion owners have never owned a Toyota car before, and the median age of Scion owners is 34, much lower than the average ages of Toyota and Lexus owners (49 and 54, respectively). Since 2006, Scion has been partnering with Nielsen Online's BuzzMetrics service (www.nielsen-online.com) to use information from consumer-generated media (CGM) in formulating their market strategies. CGM is important to Scion because that's where their customers are and where they are most likely to see and engage in the brand. There are many blogs, Web sites, and social networking sites for discussions for customers to get more information and see how other customers like the product. All the three models (tC, xB, and xD) continued to do well through 2008, until the recession hit.

Although Toyota appears to have figured out through market research the secret to attracting younger buyers, they cannot simply be content. The tricky younger generation is fickle. Therefore, Scion and Toyota must continually rely on market research to meet the ever-changing demands of younger buyers.[3] ■

Real Research   Fast . . . Fruit?

Average consumers have become more concerned with health and nutrition. Obesity lawsuits have been filed against fast-food giants that have offered only fatty, greasy burgers and fries. As a result, many fast-food chains are now offering healthier alternatives, such as salads and fresh fruit, as well as decreasing serving sizes.

It seems that this shift toward healthier fare is paying off for fast-food chains. According to the Quick-Track® research study conducted by market research firm Sandelman & Associates (www.sandelman.com) in 2009, Americans were satisfied with fast food. The Quick-Track is a syndicated market research project conducted quarterly to track key consumer behavioral and attitudinal measures for all major fast-food and pizza chains in individual markets. In this study, each quarter 400 respondents are surveyed in each market via a combination of telephone and Internet interviews in more than 100 markets representing a wide range of demographics. Telephone respondents are selected via a computer-generated random sample of listed and unlisted telephone numbers, and online respondents are selected from a panel of more than 5 million Internet users.

Respondents were asked their opinions of past visits to each fast-food restaurant chain within the last three months. They were asked to rate their opinions on the overall restaurant experience as well as on 12 specific attributes such as food, service, cleanliness, and value. The responses were scored on a scale with 1 = Poor and 5 = Excellent. To ensure reliability and representation of the population, only chains with a minimum of 150 responses were considered.

The three most important attributes for respondents were cleanliness (77 percent rated it as extremely important), food taste and flavor (74 percent), and order accuracy (66 percent). The availability of healthy and nutritious food is increasing in importance among respondents, with 40 percent rating it as extremely important (up from 34 percent in 2003). The overall increase in satisfaction with fast-food chains can be attributed to the chains' responsiveness to customer demands for food quality, taste, health, and nutrition.

One example of how fast-food chains respond to the consumer's desire for healthier, tasty food offerings is to provide fresh fruit as a menu option. Wendy's, for example, is now offering fresh fruit bowls as an entrée or as a dessert. McDonald's is offering a fruit and walnut salad, and IHOP is selling fruit plate entrees. These are not isolated examples in the food industry. According to marketing research firm NPD Group (www.npd.com), fruit consumption in restaurants has increased by more than 10 percent from 2006 to 2009. Kerrii Anderson, president of Wendy's, commented that now's the time for fruit, because people are looking for different and new tastes and for healthier alternatives.[4] ■

These examples illustrate the crucial role played by marketing research in designing and implementing successful marketing programs.[5] Note that marketing research is being used by all kinds of organizations, such as Boeing, NBC, Toyota, and fast-food restaurants (McDonald's, Wendy's, IHOP). Furthermore, marketing research has become global (Harris Interactive), real time (Satmetrix), responsive (Toyota), and much more integrated with marketing and product development (McDonald's, Wendy's, IHOP). These examples illustrate only a few of the methods used to conduct marketing research: telephone, personal, and online surveys; focus groups; in-depth interviews; and the use of the Internet as a source of information. This book will

Marketing research has helped fast-food chains like McDonald's identify and respond to consumers' desire for healthier food.

introduce you to the full complement of marketing research techniques and illustrate their applications in formulating effective marketing strategies. Perhaps the role of marketing research can be better understood in light of its definition.

Definition of Marketing Research

The American Marketing Association formally defines marketing research as the following:

> Marketing research is the function that links the consumer, customer, and public to the marketer through information—information used to identify and define marketing opportunities and problems; generate, refine, and evaluate marketing actions; monitor marketing performance; and improve understanding of marketing as a process.
>
> Marketing research specifies the information required to address these issues, designs the method for collecting information, manages and implements the data collection process, analyzes the results, and communicates the findings and their implications.[6]

As of 2009, the American Marketing Association's Web site, MarketingPower (www. marketingpower.com), supplies marketing professionals with information on marketing careers, "Best Practices" articles, and industry trends. For the purpose of this book, which emphasizes the need for information for decision making, marketing research is defined as follows:

marketing research
The systematic and objective identification, collection, analysis, dissemination, and use of information for the purpose of assisting management in decision making related to the identification and solution of problems (and opportunities) in marketing.

> **Marketing research** is the systematic and objective identification, collection, analysis, dissemination, and use of information for the purpose of improving decision making related to the identification and solution of problems and opportunities in marketing.

Several aspects of this definition are noteworthy. First, marketing research is systematic. Thus, systematic planning is required at all stages of the marketing research process. The procedures followed at each stage are methodologically sound, well documented, and, as much as possible, planned in advance. Marketing research uses the scientific method in that data are collected and analyzed to test prior notions or hypotheses.

Marketing research attempts to provide accurate information that reflects a true state of affairs. It is objective and should be conducted impartially. Although research is always influenced by the researcher's philosophy, it should be free from the personal or political biases of the researcher or the management. Research that is motivated by personal or political gain involves a breach of professional standards. Such research is deliberately biased so as to result in predetermined findings. The motto of every researcher should be, "Find it and tell it like it is."

Marketing research involves the identification, collection, analysis, dissemination, and use of information. Each phase of this process is important. We identify or define the marketing research problem or opportunity and then determine what information is needed to investigate it. Because every marketing opportunity translates into a research problem to be investigated, the terms "problem" and "opportunity" are used interchangeably here. Next, the relevant information sources are identified and a range of data collection methods varying in sophistication and complexity are evaluated for their usefulness. The data are collected using the most appropriate method; they are analyzed and interpreted, and inferences are drawn. Finally, the findings, implications, and recommendations are provided in a format that allows the information to be used for marketing decision making and to be acted upon directly. The next section elaborates on this definition by classifying different types of marketing research.[7]

A Classification of Marketing Research

Our definition states that organizations engage in marketing research for two reasons: (1) to identify and (2) to solve marketing problems. This distinction serves as a basis for classifying marketing research into problem-identification research and problem-solving research, as shown in Figure 1.1.

problem-identification research
Research that is undertaken to help identify problems that are not necessarily apparent on the surface and yet exist or are likely to arise in the future.

Problem-identification research is undertaken to help identify problems that are, perhaps, not apparent on the surface and yet exist or are likely to arise in the future. Examples of problem-identification research include market potential, market share, brand or company image, market characteristics, sales analysis, short-range forecasting, long-range forecasting, and business trends research. A survey of companies conducting marketing research indicated that 97 percent of those who responded were conducting market potential, market share, and market characteristics

FIGURE 1.1

**A Classification
of Marketing
Research**

research. About 90 percent also reported that they were using other types of problem-identification research. Research of this type provides information about the marketing environment and helps diagnose a problem. For example, a declining market potential indicates that the firm is likely to have a problem achieving its growth targets. Similarly, a problem exists if the market potential is increasing but the firm is losing market share. The recognition of economic, social, or cultural trends, such as changes in consumer behavior, may point to underlying problems or opportunities.[8]

**problem-solving
research**
Research undertaken
to help solve specific
marketing problems.

Once a problem or opportunity has been identified, **problem-solving research** is undertaken to arrive at a solution. The findings of problem-solving research are used in making decisions that will solve specific marketing problems. Most companies conduct problem-solving research.[9] Table 1.1 shows the different types of issues that are addressed by problem-solving research, including segmentation, product, pricing, promotion, and distribution research.

Classifying marketing research into two main types is useful from a conceptual as well as a practical viewpoint. However, problem-identification research and problem-solving research go

TABLE 1.1
Problem-Solving Research

Segmentation Research

determine basis of segmentation

establish market potential and responsiveness for various segments

select target markets and create lifestyle profiles, demography, media, and product image characteristics

Product Research	**Promotional Research**
test concept	optimal promotional budget
optical product design	sales promotion relationship
package tests	optimal promotional mix
product modification	copy decisions
brand positioning and repositioning	media decisions
test marketing	creative advertising testing
control store tests	claim substantiation
	evaluation of advertising effectiveness

Pricing Research	**Distribution Research**
importance of price in brand selection	type of distribution
pricing policies	attitudes of channel members
product line pricing	intensity of wholesale and retail coverage
price elasticity of demand	channel margins
response to price changes	location of retail and wholesale outlets

hand in hand, and a given marketing research project may combine both types of research. This was illustrated in the opening Boeing example. The consumer surveys identified potential demand for smaller planes (problem identification). Subsequent product research led to the introduction of the new versions of the Boeing 737, which cater to the 100- to 215-seat market (problem solving). Kellogg's provides another example.

Real Research

Crunchy Nut Red Adds Color to Kellogg's Sales

Kellogg's (www.kelloggs.com), marketing its products in more than 180 countries as of 2009, experienced a slump in the market and faced the challenge of reviving low cereal sales. Through problem-identification research, Kellogg's was able to identify the problem and, through problem-solving research, develop several solutions to increase cereal sales.

Kellogg's performed several tasks to identify the problem. The researchers spoke to decision makers within the company, interviewed industry experts, conducted analysis of available data, performed some qualitative research, and surveyed consumers about their perceptions and preferences for cereals. Several important issues or problems were identified by this research. Current products were being targeted to kids, bagels and muffins were winning for favored breakfast foods, and high prices were turning consumers to generic brands. Some other information also came to light during the research. Adults wanted quick foods that required very little or no preparation. These issues helped Kellogg's identify the problem. It was not being creative in introducing new products to meet the needs of the adult market.

After defining the problem, Kellogg's went to work on solutions. It developed and tested several new flavors of cereals using mall intercept interviews with adult consumers. Based on the results, Kellogg's introduced new flavors that were more suited to the adult palate but were not the tasteless varieties of the past. For example, in 2008 it introduced Kellogg's Nutri-Grain Cereal Bar Blackberry. This new cereal bar is filled with blackberries. The new cereal bar was supported by an ad campaign and major in-store promotions.

Through creative problem-identification research followed by problem-solving research, Kellogg's has not only seen an increase in sales, but also increased consumption of cereal at times other than just breakfast.[10] ∎

ACTIVE RESEARCH

NFL Is Tickled Pink

Visit www.nfl.com. Use a search engine as well as your library's online databases to obtain information on women's attitudes toward the National Football League (NFL).

As the marketing director of the NFL, what marketing strategies would you formulate to target female fans? The NFL would like to appeal to more female fans. What kind of marketing research would you recommend?

Problem-identification and problem-solving research not only go hand in hand, as shown by the Kellogg's example, but they also follow a common marketing research process.

The Marketing Research Process

marketing research process
A set of six steps that defines the tasks to be accomplished in conducting a marketing research study. These include problem definition, development of an approach to the problem, research design formulation, fieldwork, data preparation and analysis, and report preparation and presentation.

We conceptualize the **marketing research process** as consisting of six steps. Each of these steps is discussed in great detail in the subsequent chapters; thus, the discussion here is brief.

Step 1: Problem Definition

The first step in any marketing research project is to define the problem. In defining the problem, the researcher should take into account the purpose of the study, the relevant background information, the information needed, and how it will be used in decision making. Problem definition involves discussion with the decision makers, interviews with industry experts, analysis of secondary data, and, perhaps, some qualitative research, such as focus groups. Once the problem has been precisely defined, the research can be designed and conducted properly. (See Chapter 2.)

Step 2: Development of an Approach to the Problem

Development of an approach to the problem includes formulating an objective or theoretical framework, analytical models, research questions, and hypotheses and identifying the information needed. This process is guided by discussions with management and industry experts, analysis of secondary data, qualitative research, and pragmatic considerations. (See Chapter 2.)

Step 3: Research Design Formulation

A research design is a framework or blueprint for conducting the marketing research project. It details the procedures necessary for obtaining the required information, and its purpose is to design a study that will test the hypotheses of interest, determine possible answers to the research questions, and provide the information needed for decision making. Conducting exploratory research, precisely defining the variables, and designing appropriate scales to measure them are also a part of the research design. The issue of how the data should be obtained from the respondents (for example, by conducting a survey or an experiment) must be addressed. It is also necessary to design a questionnaire and a sampling plan to select respondents for the study. More formally, formulating the research design involves the following steps:

1. Definition of the information needed
2. Secondary data analysis
3. Qualitative research
4. Methods of collecting quantitative data (survey, observation, and experimentation)
5. Measurement and scaling procedures
6. Questionnaire design
7. Sampling process and sample size
8. Plan of data analysis

These steps are discussed in detail in Chapters 3 through 12.

Step 4: Fieldwork or Data Collection

Data collection involves a field force or staff that operates either in the field, as in the case of personal interviewing (in-home, mall intercept, or computer-assisted personal interviewing), from an office by telephone (telephone or computer-assisted telephone interviewing), through mail (traditional mail and mail panel surveys with prerecruited households), or electronically (e-mail or Internet). Proper selection, training, supervision, and evaluation of the field force help minimize data-collection errors. (See Chapter 13.)

Step 5: Data Preparation and Analysis

Data preparation includes the editing, coding, transcription, and verification of data. Each questionnaire or observation form is inspected or edited and, if necessary, corrected. Number or letter codes are assigned to represent each response to each question in the questionnaire. The data from the questionnaires are transcribed or keypunched onto magnetic tape or disks, or input directly into the computer. The data are analyzed to derive information related to the components of the marketing research problem and, thus, to provide input into the management decision problem. (See Chapters 14 through 21.)

Step 6: Report Preparation and Presentation

The entire project should be documented in a written report that addresses the specific research questions identified; describes the approach, the research design, data collection, and data analysis procedures adopted, and presents the results and the major findings. The findings should be presented in a comprehensible format so that management can readily use them in the decision-making process. In addition, an oral presentation should be made to management using tables, figures, and graphs to enhance clarity and impact. (See Chapter 23.) The Internet is also being used to disseminate marketing research results and reports, which can be posted on the Web and made available to managers on a worldwide basis.

Although we have described the research process as a sequence of steps, it should be noted that these steps are interdependent and iterative. Thus, at each step, the researcher should not only look back at the previous steps but also look ahead to the following steps. As indicated by the Marriott example, our description of the marketing research process is fairly typical of the research being done by major corporations.

Real Research   Marketing Research at Marriott Corporation

Marriott International, Inc. (www.marriott.com) is a leading worldwide hospitality company. Its heritage can be traced to a root beer stand opened in Washington, D.C., in 1927 by J. Willard and Alice S. Marriott. As of 2009, Marriott International has nearly 3,000 lodging properties located in the United States and 69 other countries and territories. Its brands include Marriott, Renaissance, Courtyard, Residence Inn, Fairfield Inn, Towneplace Suites, Springhill Suites, and Ramada International.

Marketing research at Marriott is done at the corporate level through the Corporate Marketing Services (CMS). Its goals include providing Marriott managers with the information that they need to better understand the market and the customer.

CMS does many different types of research. It uses quantitative and qualitative research approaches such as telephone and mail surveys, focus groups, and customer intercepts to gain more information on market segmentation, product testing, price sensitivity of consumers, consumer satisfaction, and the like.

The process of research at Marriott is a simple stepwise progression. The first steps are to better define the problem to be addressed and the objectives of the client unit and to develop an approach to the problem. The next step is to design the study by formulating a formal research design. CMS must decide whether to do its own research or to buy it from an outside organization, and in that case, decide whether to use multiple firms. Once a decision is made, the data are collected and analyzed. Then CMS presents the study findings to the client unit in a formal report. The final step in the research process is to conduct a constant dialogue between the client and CMS. During this stage, CMS may help explain the implications of the research findings, assist in decision making, or make suggestions for future research.[11] ∎

The Role of Marketing Research in Marketing Decision Making

The nature and role of marketing research can be better understood in light of the basic marketing paradigm depicted in Figure 1.2.

FIGURE 1.2

The Role of Marketing Research

The emphasis in marketing is on the identification and satisfaction of customer needs. In order to determine customer needs and to implement marketing strategies and programs aimed at satisfying those needs, marketing managers need information. They need information about customers, competitors, and other forces in the marketplace. In recent years, many factors have increased the need for more and better information. As firms have become national and international in scope, the need for information on larger and more distant markets has increased. As consumers have become more affluent and sophisticated, marketing managers need better information on how they will respond to products and other marketing offerings. As competition has become more intense, managers need information on the effectiveness of their marketing tools. As the environment changes more rapidly, marketing managers need more timely information.[12]

The task of marketing research is to assess the information needs and provide management with relevant, accurate, reliable, valid, current, and actionable information. Today's competitive marketing environment and the ever-increasing costs attributed to poor decision making require marketing research to provide sound information. Sound decisions are not based on gut feeling, intuition, or even pure judgment. In the absence of sound information, an incorrect management decision may be made, as illustrated by the case of Johnson & Johnson baby aspirin.

Real Research   ## J & J's Gentleness Could Not Handle Pain

Johnson & Johnson (www.jnj.com) is considered to be the world's most broadly based manufacturer of health care products with more than 250 operating companies in 57 countries as of 2009. Despite its success in the industry, Johnson & Johnson's attempt to use its company name on baby aspirin proved to be unsuccessful. Johnson & Johnson baby products are perceived as gentle, but gentleness is not what people want in a baby aspirin. Although baby aspirin should be safe, gentleness per se is not a desirable feature. Rather, some people perceived that a gentle aspirin might not be effective enough. This is an example of what intuitively seemed to be a natural move but without proper marketing research turned out to be an incorrect decision.[13] ■

As indicated by the Johnson & Johnson example, marketing managers make numerous strategic and tactical decisions in the process of identifying and satisfying customer needs. As shown in Figure 1.2, they make decisions about potential opportunities, target market selection, market segmentation, planning and implementing marketing programs, marketing performance, and control. These decisions are complicated by interactions among the controllable marketing variables of product, pricing, promotion, and distribution. Further complications are added by uncontrollable environmental factors such as general economic conditions, technology, public policies and laws, the political environment, competition, and social and cultural changes. Another factor in this mix is the complexity of the various customer groups: consumers, employees, shareholders, suppliers. Marketing research helps the marketing manager link the marketing variables with the environment and the customer groups. It helps remove some of the uncertainty by providing relevant information about the marketing variables, environment, and consumers. In the absence of relevant information, consumers' response to marketing programs cannot be predicted reliably or accurately. Ongoing marketing research programs provide information on controllable and uncontrollable factors and consumers; this information enhances the effectiveness of decisions made by marketing managers.[14]

Traditionally, marketing researchers were responsible for assessing information needs and providing the relevant information, whereas marketing decisions were made by the managers. However, these roles are changing. Marketing researchers are becoming more involved in decision making, whereas marketing managers are becoming more involved with research. This trend can be attributed to better training of marketing managers, the Internet and other advances in technology, and a shift in the marketing research paradigm in which more and more marketing research is being undertaken on an ongoing basis rather than in response to specific marketing problems or opportunities.

In essence, marketing research must add value to marketing decision making, indeed to the entire organization. It should be emphasized that marketing managers do not work in isolation from other functions in the organization. Rather, the marketing orientation embodies a cross-functional perspective to meet consumer needs and attain long-term profitability. Therefore, marketing research should interface with the other functions in the organization such as manufacturing, research and development, finance, accounting, and other functional areas as may be relevant in a given project.

FIGURE 1.3

Power Decisions' Methodology

Source: www.powerdecisions. com. Used with permission of Power Decisions Group.

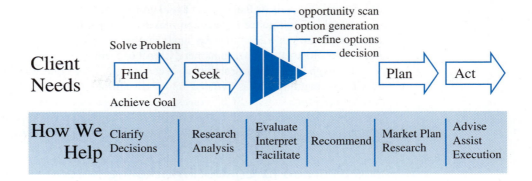

As illustrated by the examples in the chapter overview and by the Power Decisions example, marketing and marketing research are becoming more and more integrated.[15] Power Decisions (www.powerdecisions.com) is a market research company focused on marketing strategy. Using market research and decision clarification tools, they help clients benefit from the right marketing research information for uncovering marketing strategy solutions that work. Power Decisions researches, evaluates, and facilitates its clients' market entry and market share growth. Figure 1.3 is a pictorial representation of Power Decisions' methodology.

A food-processing company approached Power Decisions for opportunity scanning and brand development. The client was a well-respected private-label food processor that held a strong position in Western markets. Top grocery chains stocked much of its canned vegetables line—it was known for packing quality product at competitive prices. The private-label business, however, grew more price competitive and profits began to erode. A proprietary brand strategy was required to deliver higher profits through restored margins.

Power Decisions' role was to guide an 18-month multistage effort to discover the most appropriate product categories to pursue. They undertook a major consumer research product concept testing study, which consisted of the following steps:

- Scanned and evaluated more than 40 product groups, recommending a shortlist of product category candidates.
- Conducted a consumer research study to find a set of canned food products with low consumer satisfaction and high interest in a new brand.
- Made a trade-off analysis to calculate the price–quality blends that had the best chance of success.
- Worked closely with the client product development team as they formulated test runs of the final food product chosen to ensure that the test formulations held true to the product attributes formula derived from consumer research.

The final stage was to manage the brand name development, package design, initial ad campaign, and test market plan. As a result, the new brand containing the blend of ingredients desired most by consumers was successfully introduced at a premium price level. The brand fast gained both trade and consumer acceptance and was later expanded to other products and institutional markets.[16]

As shown by the experience of Power Decisions, marketing research can greatly enhance the information available to management. Marketing research also plays a special role in obtaining competitive intelligence.

Marketing Research and Competitive Intelligence

competitive intelligence

The process of enhancing marketplace competitiveness through a greater understanding of a firm's competitors and the competitive environment.

Competitive intelligence (CI) may be defined as the process of enhancing marketplace competitiveness through a greater understanding of a firm's competitors and the competitive environment. This process is unequivocally ethical. It involves the legal collection and analysis of information regarding the capabilities, vulnerabilities, and intentions of business competitors, conducted by using information databases and other "open sources" and through ethical marketing research inquiry.

CI enables senior managers in companies of all sizes to make informed decisions about everything from marketing, research and development (R&D), and investing tactics to long-term business strategies. Effective CI is a continuous process involving the legal and ethical collection of information, analysis that doesn't avoid unwelcome conclusions, and controlled dissemination of actionable intelligence to decision makers. Competitive intelligence is a crucial part of the emerging knowledge economy. By analyzing rivals' moves, CI allows companies to anticipate market developments rather than merely react to them.

Although marketing research plays a central role in the collection, analysis, and dissemination of CI information, CI has evolved into a discipline of its own. The Society of Competitive Intelligence Professionals (SCIP) consists of members conducting CI for large and small companies, providing management with early warning of changes in the competitive landscape. For more information on competitive intelligence, go to SCIP's Web page at www.scip.org.

The Decision to Conduct Marketing Research

Marketing research can be beneficial in a variety of situations, but the decision to conduct research is not automatic. Rather, this decision should be guided by a number of considerations, including the costs versus the benefits, the resources available to conduct the research, the resources available to implement the research findings, and management's attitude toward research. Marketing research should be undertaken when the expected value of information it generates exceeds the costs of conducting the marketing research project. In general, the more important the decision confronting management and the greater the uncertainty or risk facing them, the greater the value of information obtained. Formal procedures are available for quantifying the expected value as well as the costs of a marketing research project. Although in most instances the value of information exceeds the costs, there are instances when the reverse may be true. A pie manufacturer, for example, wanted to understand consumers' purchase of pies in convenience stores. I advised against a major marketing research project when we discovered that less than 1 percent of the sales were coming from convenience stores and that this situation was unlikely to change in the next five years.

Resources, especially time and money, are always limited. However, if either time or money is not available in adequate amounts to conduct a quality project, that project probably should not be undertaken. It is better not to do a formal project than undertake one in which the integrity of the research is compromised because of lack of resources. Likewise, a firm may lack the resources to implement the recommendations arising from the findings of marketing research. In that case, spending the resources to conduct the research may not be warranted. And if management does not have a positive attitude toward research, then it is likely that the project report will gather dust after the project is conducted. However, there may be exceptions to this guideline. I conducted a project for a retail chain with management that was hostile toward the project, but the research was commissioned and funded by the parent organization. Although the store management was opposed to the findings, which reflected negatively on the store chain, the parent company did implement my recommendations.

There are other instances that may argue against conducting a marketing research project. If the required information is already available within the organization, or the decision for which the research is to be conducted has already been made, or the research is going to be used for gaining political ends, then the value of information generated is greatly reduced and the project is generally not warranted. However, if the decision is made to conduct marketing research, then management may also rely on marketing research suppliers and services to obtain the specific information needed.[17]

The Marketing Research Industry

The marketing research industry consists of suppliers who provide marketing research services. Marketing research suppliers and services provide most of the information needed for making marketing decisions. Most of the big suppliers have several subsidiaries and divisions that encompass various areas of marketing research. Nevertheless, it is useful to classify marketing research suppliers and services. Broadly, research suppliers can be classified as internal or external (see Figure 1.4). An **internal supplier** is a marketing research department within the firm. Many firms, particularly the big ones, ranging from automobile companies (GM, Ford, Chrysler) to consumer products firms (Procter & Gamble, Colgate Palmolive, Coca-Cola) to banks (JPMorgan Chase, Bank of America), maintain in-house marketing research departments. The marketing research department's place in the organizational structure may vary considerably.

internal supplier
Marketing research departments located within a firm.

FIGURE 1.4

Marketing Research Suppliers and Services

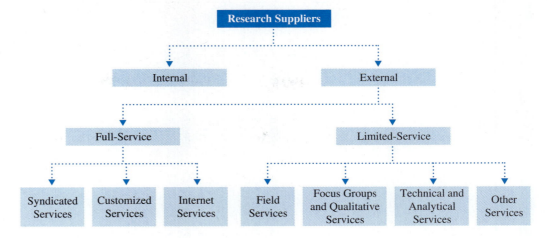

At one extreme, the research function may be centralized and located at the corporate head-quarters. At the other extreme is a decentralized structure in which the marketing research function is organized along divisional lines. In a decentralized scheme, the company may be organized into divisions by products, customers, or geographical regions, with marketing research personnel assigned to the various divisions. These personnel generally report to a division manager rather than to a corporate-level executive. In addition, between these two extremes, there are different types of organizations. The best organization for a firm depends on its marketing research needs and the structure of marketing and other functions, although in recent years there has been a trend toward centralization and a trimming of the marketing research staff. Internal suppliers often rely on external suppliers to perform specific marketing research tasks.

External suppliers are outside firms hired to supply marketing research data. These external suppliers, which collectively comprise the **marketing research industry**, range from small (one or a few persons) operations to very large global corporations.[18] Table 1.2 lists the top 50 U.S. research suppliers.[19] External suppliers can be classified as full-service or limited-service suppliers. **Full-service suppliers** offer the entire range of marketing research services, from problem definition, approach development, questionnaire design, sampling, data collection, data analysis, and interpretation, to report preparation and presentation. The services provided by these suppliers can be further broken down into syndicated services, customized services, and Internet services (see Figure 1.4).

Syndicated services collect information of known commercial value that they provide to multiple clients on a subscription basis. Surveys, panels, scanners, and audits are the main means by which these data are collected. For example, the Nielsen Television Index by Nielsen Media Research (www.nielsenmedia.com) provides information on audience size and demographic characteristics of households watching specific television programs. The Nielsen Company (www.nielsen.com) provides scanner volume tracking data, such as those generated by electronic scanning at checkout counters in supermarkets. The NPD Group (www.npd.com) maintains one of the largest consumer panels in the United States. Quick-Track, conducted by Sandelman & Associates in the "Fast . . . Fruit" opening example, is another illustration of a syndicated service. Syndicated services are discussed in more detail in Chapter 4.[20]

Customized services offer a wide variety of marketing research services customized to suit a client's specific needs. Each marketing research project is treated uniquely. Some marketing research firms that offer these services include Burke, Inc. (www.burke.com), Synovate (www.synovate.com), and TNS (www.tns-global.com). The survey conducted by Harris Interactive for Boeing in the opening example constituted customized research.

Internet services are offered by several marketing research firms, including some that have specialized in conducting marketing research on the Internet. For example, Greenfield Online Research Center Inc. in Westport, Connecticut (www.greenfieldonline.com), a subsidiary of The Greenfield Consulting firm (www.greenfieldgroup.com), offers a broad range of customized qualitative and quantitative online marketing research for consumer, business-to-business, and professional markets. Using large, proprietary databases, studies are conducted within the company's secure Web site. Jupiter Research (www.jupiterresearch.com) offers research and consulting services that focus on consumer online behavior and interactive technologies.

external suppliers
Outside marketing research companies hired to supply marketing research data or services.

marketing research industry
The marketing research industry consists of external suppliers who provide marketing research services.

full-service suppliers
Companies that offer the full range of marketing research activities.

syndicated services
Companies that collect and sell common pools of data designed to serve information needs shared by a number of clients.

customized services
Companies that tailor the research procedures to best meet the needs of each client.

Internet services
Companies that have specialized in conducting marketing research on the Internet.

TABLE 1.2
Top 50 U.S. Market Research Firms

U.S. 2007	Rank 2006	Organization	Headquarters	Web site	U.S. Research Revenue[1] ($, in millions)	Worldwide Research Revenue[1] ($, in millions)	Percent Non-U.S. Revenue
1	1	The Nielsen Co.	New York	nielsen.com	$2,173.0	$4,220.0	48.5%
2	2	IMS Health Inc.	Norwalk, Conn.	imshealth.com	801.0	2,192.6	63.5
3	3	Kantar Group*	Fairfield, Conn.	kantargroup.com	526.8	1,551.4	66.0
4	5	Westat Inc.	Rockville, MD	westat.com	467.8	467.8	—
5	4	IRI	Chicago	infores.com	441.0	702.0	37.2
6	6	TNS U.S.	New York	tnsglobal.com	379.8	2,137.2	82.2
7	7	Arbitron Inc.	New York	arbitron.com	338.5	352.1	3.9
8	8	GfK AG USA	Nuremberg, Germany	gfk.com	319.7	1,603.00	80.1
9	9	Ipsos	New York	ipsos-na.com	281.2	1,270.30	77.9
10	10	Synovate	London	synovate.com	250.4	867.0	71.1
11	11	Maritz Research	Fenton, Mo.	maritzresearch.com	187.4	223.3	16.1
12	13	J.D. Power and Associates*	Westlake Village, Calif.	jdpower.com	184.5	260.5	29.2
13	12	Harris Interactive Inc.	Rochester, N.Y.	harrisinteractive.com	161.0	227.0	29.1
14	14	The NPD Group Inc.	Port Washington, N.Y.	npd.com	160.4	211.1	24.0
15	—	Opinion Research/Guideline Group	Omaha, Neb.	infousa.com	124.7	206.7	39.7
	15	Opinion Research Corp.	Princeton, N.J.	opinionresearch.com	97.5	179.5	45.7
	38	Guideline Inc.	New York	guideline.com	26.8	26.8	—
16	18	comScore Inc.	Reston, Va.	comscore.com	77.0	87.2	11.7
17	20	Market Strategies Inc.	Livonia, Mich.	marketstrategies.com	75.7	80.4	5.8
	20	Market Strategies Inc.	Livonia, Mich.	marketstrategies.com	53.4	58.1	8.1
	37	Flake-Wilkerson Market Insights	Little Rock, Ark.	fw-mi.com	22.3	22.3	—
18	17	Lieberman Research Worldwide	Los Angeles	lrwonline.com	71.0	87.4	18.8
19	—	Abt Associates Inc.	Cambridge, Mass.	abtassociates.com	55.1	55.1	—
	19	Abt Associates Inc.	Cambridge, Mass.	abtassociates.com	33.0	33.0	—
	41	Abt SRBI Inc.	New York	srbi.com	22.1	22.1	—
20	23	OTX	Los Angeles	otxresearch.com	50.8	54.5	6.8
21	21	Burke, Inc.	Cincinnati	burke.com	47.0	53.1	11.5
22	22	MVL Group Inc.	Jupiter, Fla.	mvlgroup.com	42.3	42.3	—
23	26	Knowledge Networks Inc.	Menlo Park, Calif.	knowledgenetworks.com	37.3	37.3	—
23	25	National Research Corp.	Lincoln, Neb.	nationalresearch.com	37.3	41.3	9.7
25	24	Directions Research Inc.	Cincinnati	directionsresearch.com	37.2	37.2	—

Rank	Prev. Rank	Company	Headquarters	Website	U.S. Revenue	Worldwide Revenue	% Non-U.S.
26	40	Phoenix Marketing International	Rhinebeck, N.Y.	phoenixmi.com	33.5	34.9	4.0
27	34	Lieberman Research Group	Great Neck, N.Y.	liebermanresearch.com	30.1	30.1	—
28	27	ICR/Int'l Communications Research	Media, Pa.	icrsurvey.com	28.8	29.7	3.0
29	28	Morpace Inc.	Farmington Hills, Mich.	morpace.com	28.7	33.2	13.6
30	33	MarketCast	Los Angeles	marketcastonline.com	25.1	25.1	—
31	36	Data Development Worldwide	New York	datadw.com	25.0	25.3	1.2
32	39	C&R Research Services Inc.	Chicago	crresearch.com	23.6	23.6	—
33	32	Informa Research Services Inc.	Calabasas, Calif.	informars.com	23.5	23.5	—
34	31	National Analysts Worldwide	Philadelphia	nationalanalysts.com	23.3	23.3	—
35	44	Service Management Group	Kansas City, Mo.	servicemanagement.com	22.4	23.0	2.6
36	34	Market Probe Inc.	Milwaukee	marketprobe.com	21.7	41.4	47.6
37	—	Hitwise	New York	hitwise.com	21.6	49.9	56.7
38	42	Walker Information	Indianapolis	walkerinfo.com	21.2	25.5	16.9
39	43	KS&R Inc.	Syracuse, N.Y.	ksrinc.com	17.1	21.0	18.6
40	47	Bellomy Research Inc.	Winston-Salem, N.C.	bellomyresearch.com	16.7	16.7	—
41	46	MarketVision Research Inc.	Cincinnati	marketvisionresearch.com	16.4	16.4	—
42	28	Public Opinion Strategies	Alexandra, Va.	pos.org	15.5	15.5	—
43	—	Compete Inc.	Boston	compete.com	14.9	14.9	—
44	45	Savitz Research Companies	Dallas	savitzresearch.com	14.8	14.8	—
45	48	RDA Group Inc.	Bloomfield Hills, Mich.	rdagroup.com	13.7	16.8	18.5
46	—	Gongos Research Inc.	Auburn Hills, Mich.	gongos.com	13.3	13.3	—
47	—	Q Research Solutions Inc.	Old Bridge, N.J.	whoisq.com	13.0	13.2	1.5
48	49	Marketing Analysts Inc.	Charleston, S.C.	marketinganalysts.com	12.8	13.6	5.9
49	50	RTi Market Research & Brand Strategy	Stamford, Conn.	rtiresearch.com	12.2	12.2	—
50	—	The Link Group	Atlanta	the-link-group.com	11.9	13.3	10.5
		Total			$7,828.7	$17,638.0	55.6%
		All other (150 CASRO companies not included in the Top 50)[2]			$774.3	$870.1	11.0%
		Total (200 companies)			$8,603.0	$18,508.1	53.5%

*Estimated by Top 50 [1]U.S. and worldwide revenue may include nonresearch activities for some companies that are significantly higher. See individual company profiles for details. [2]Total revenue of 150 survey research companies that provide financial information on a confidential basis to the Council of American Survey Research Organizations (CASRO).

Source: Council of American Survey Research Organizations (CASRO) American Marketing Association.

limited-service suppliers
Companies that specialize in one or a few phases of the marketing research project.

field services
Companies whose primary service offering is their expertise in collecting data for research projects.

focus groups and qualitative services
Services related to facilities, recruitment, and other services for focus groups and other forms of qualitative research, such as one-on-one depth interviews.

technical and analytical services
Services related to design issues and computer analysis of quantitative data, such as those obtained in large surveys.

Limited-service suppliers specialize in one or a few phases of the marketing research project, as illustrated by the Satmetrix example in the chapter overview. Services offered by such suppliers are classified as field services, focus groups and qualitative research, technical and analytical services, and other services. **Field services** collect data through mail, personal, telephone, or electronic interviewing, and firms that specialize in interviewing are called *field service organizations*. These organizations may range from small proprietary organizations that operate locally to large multinational organizations. Some organizations maintain extensive interviewing facilities across the country for interviewing shoppers in malls. Some firms that offer field services are Field Facts, Inc. (www.fieldfacts.com) and Field Work Chicago, Inc. (www.fieldwork.com).

Focus groups and qualitative services provide facilities and recruitment of respondents for focus groups and other forms of qualitative research such as one-on-one depth interviews. Some firms may provide additional services such as moderators and prepare focus group reports. Examples of such firms include Jackson Associates (www.jacksonassociates.com) and The Opinion Suites (www.opinionsuites.com). **Technical and analytical services** are offered by firms that specialize in design issues and computer analysis of quantitative data, such as those obtained in large surveys. Firms such as SDR of Atlanta (www.sdr-consulting.com) offer sophisticated data analysis using advanced statistical techniques. Sawtooth Technologies (www.sawtooth.com) provides software for research data collection and analysis. Microcomputers and statistical software packages enable firms to perform data analysis in-house. However, the specialized data analysis expertise of outside suppliers is still in demand.

Other services include branded marketing research products and services developed to address specific types of marketing research problems. For example, Survey Sampling International (www.surveysampling.com) specializes in sampling design and distribution. Some firms focus on specialized services such as research in ethnic markets (Hispanic, African, multicultural). Examples in this category include Hispanic Consumer Research (www.hispanic-consumer-research.com) and Multicultural Insights (www.multicultural-insights.com).

There are certain guidelines that should be followed when selecting a research supplier, whether it is a full-service or a limited-service supplier.

Selecting a Research Supplier

A firm that cannot conduct an entire marketing research project in-house must select an external supplier for one or more phases of the project. The firm should compile a list of prospective suppliers from such sources as trade publications, professional directories, and word of mouth. When deciding on criteria for selecting an outside supplier, a firm should ask itself why it is seeking outside marketing research support. For example, a small firm that needs one project investigated may find it economically efficient to employ an outside source. A firm may not have the technical expertise to undertake certain phases of a project, or political conflict-of-interest issues may determine that a project be conducted by an outside supplier.

When developing criteria for selecting an outside supplier, a firm should keep some basics in mind. What is the reputation of the supplier? Do they complete projects on schedule? Are they known for maintaining ethical standards? Are they flexible? Are their research projects of high quality? What kind and how much experience does the supplier have? Has the firm had experience with projects similar to this one? Do the supplier's personnel have both technical and nontechnical expertise? In other words, in addition to technical skills, are the personnel assigned to the task sensitive to the client's needs, and do they share the client's research ideology? Do they have Professional Researcher Certification offered by the Marketing Research Association (www.mra-net.org)? Can they communicate well with the client? You can also find checklists for qualifying marketing research suppliers at the Web sites of prominent marketing research associations (e.g., www.esomar.org).

A competitive bidding process often is used in selecting external suppliers, particularly for large jobs. Often an organization commissioning research to external suppliers will issue a request for proposal (RFP), request for information (RFI), request for application (RFA), invitation to bid (ITB), or a similar call, inviting suppliers to submit bids. You can locate actual RFPs on the Internet by doing a Google advanced search using "RFP" and "Marketing Research." Some marketing research firms, such as Marketing Research Services, Inc. (www.mrsi.com), will post an RFP format on their Web sites that prospective clients can use to issue RFPs. Awarding projects based on lowest price is not a good rule of thumb. The completeness of the research proposal and the criteria discussed earlier must all be factored into the hiring decision. Moreover, long-term contracts with research suppliers are preferable to selection on a project-by-project basis. Remember that the cheapest bid is not always the best one. Competitive bids should be obtained and compared on the basis of quality as well as price. A good practice is to get a written bid or contract before beginning the project. Decisions about marketing research suppliers, just like other management decisions, should be based on sound information.

The Internet is very efficient for identifying marketing research firms that supply specific services. Using a search engine, such as Yahoo!, several research firms can be identified, and it is easy to find information on the suppliers at their Web sites. Many sites include information on company history, products, clients, and employees. For example, www.greenbook.org lists thousands of market research companies, and specific firms can be conveniently located using their search procedures. Career opportunities are available with marketing research suppliers as well as with marketing and advertising firms.

ACTIVE RESEARCH

Redesigning Yahoo!

Visit www.greenbook.org and identify all the marketing research firms in your local area that conduct Internet-based surveys.

As the research director for Yahoo!, you need to select a marketing research firm that specializes in researching consumers shopping on the Internet. Make a list of five such firms. Which one will you select and why?

As the director of marketing, how would you use information on consumer shopping on the Internet in redesigning the Yahoo! Web site?

Careers in Marketing Research

Promising career opportunities are available with marketing research firms (e.g., the Nielsen Co., Burke, Inc., The Kantar Group). Equally appealing are careers in business and nonbusiness firms and agencies with in-house marketing research departments (e.g., Procter & Gamble, Coca-Cola, GM, the Federal Trade Commission, United States Census Bureau). Advertising agencies (e.g., BBDO International, J. Walter Thompson, Young & Rubicam) also conduct substantial marketing research and employ professionals in this field. Some of the positions available in marketing research include vice president of marketing research, research director, assistant director of research, project manager, statistician/data processing specialist, senior analyst, analyst, junior analyst, fieldwork director, and operational supervisor. Figure 1.5 lists job titles in marketing research and describes their accompanying responsibilities.[21]

The most common entry-level position in marketing research for people with bachelor's degrees (e.g., BBA) is an operational supervisor. These people are responsible for supervising a well-defined set of operations, including fieldwork, data editing, and coding, and may be involved in programming and data analysis. In the marketing research industry, however, there is a growing preference for people with master's degrees. Those with MBA or equivalent degrees are likely to be employed as project managers. In marketing research firms such as TNS, the project manager works with the account director in managing the day-to-day operations of a marketing research project. The typical entry-level position in a business firm would be junior research analyst (for BBAs) or research analyst (for MBAs). The junior analyst and the research analyst learn about the particular industry and receive training from a senior staff member, usually the marketing research manager. The junior analyst position includes a training program to prepare individuals for the responsibilities of a research analyst, including coordinating with the marketing department and sales force to develop goals for product exposure. The research analyst responsibilities include checking all data for accuracy, comparing and contrasting new research with established norms, and analyzing primary and secondary data for the purpose of market forecasting.

As these job titles indicate, people with a variety of backgrounds and skills are needed in marketing research. Technical specialists such as statisticians obviously need strong backgrounds in statistics and data analysis. Other positions, such as research director, call for managing the work of others and require more general skills.

FIGURE 1.5

Selected Marketing Research Job Descriptions

1. **Vice President of Marketing Research:** This is the senior position in marketing research. The VP is responsible for the entire marketing research operation of the company and serves on the top management team. The VP sets the objectives and goals of the marketing research department.
2. **Research Director:** Also a senior position, the director has the overall responsibility for the development and execution of all the marketing research projects.
3. **Assistant Director of Research:** This person serves as an administrative assistant to the director and supervises some of the other marketing research staff members.
4. **(Senior) Project Manager:** This person has overall responsibility for the design, implementation, and management of research projects.
5. **Statistician/Data Processing Specialist:** This person serves as an expert on theory and application of statistical techniques. Responsibilities include experimental design, data processing, and analysis.
6. **Senior Analyst:** This person participates in the development of projects and directs the operational execution of the assigned projects. A senior analyst works closely with the analyst, junior analyst, and other personnel in developing the research design and data collection. The senior analyst prepares the final report. The primary responsibility for meeting time and cost constraints rests with the senior analyst.
7. **Analyst:** An analyst handles the details involved in executing the project. The analyst designs and pretests the questionnaires and conducts a preliminary analysis of the data.
8. **Junior Analyst:** The junior analyst handles routine assignments such as secondary data analysis, editing and coding of questionnaires, and simple statistical analysis.
9. **Fieldwork Director:** This person is responsible for the selection, training, supervision, and evaluation of interviewers and other fieldworkers.
10. **Operational Supervisor:** This person is responsible for supervising operations such as fieldwork, data editing, and coding, and may be involved in programming and data analysis.

For descriptions of other marketing research positions and current salaries, visit www.marketresearchcareers.com. Marketing research is a growing industry offering attractive employment opportunities. The 2008 *Annual Survey of Market Research Professionals* (www.marketresearchcareers.com) revealed important trends for those interested in a career in market research.

- More than half of all research firms expect to hire professionals in 2008, seeking to fill between two to four positions.
- In spite of the tough economy, the average raise for market research professionals in 2008 was expected to be 4 percent.
- Demand for entry level, project managers, and market research managers will be substantial throughout 2008.

To prepare for a career in marketing research, you should:

- Take all the marketing courses you can.
- Take courses in statistics and quantitative methods.
- Acquire Internet and computer skills. Knowledge of programming languages is an added asset.
- Take courses in psychology and consumer behavior.
- Acquire effective written and verbal communication skills.
- Think creatively. Creativity and common sense command a premium in marketing research.

Marketing researchers should be liberally educated so that they can understand the problems confronting managers and address them from a broad perspective.[22] The following example shows what makes a successful marketing researcher and marketing manager.

Real Research

Eric Kim at Samsung and Intel

Eric Kim earned an undergraduate degree in physics at Harvey Mudd College in Claremont, California; a master's in engineering at UCLA; and an MBA at Harvard. He learned his current craft at such places as Lotus Development Corp., D&B, and Spencer Trask Software Group, a technology-focused venture-capital firm in New York City. Spencer Trask CEO Kevin Kimberlin remembers Kim as the rare executive who knows software and electronics and is also skilled in marketing and marketing research—and in closing tough deals.

When Kim arrived at Samsung in 1999, he realized that the basic problem lay in the brand image and that the Samsung brand was perceived to be inferior to other brands with comparable products. To confirm his intuition and dig out specific, actionable issues, he conducted marketing research involving focus groups, depth interviews, and surveys of channel partners and customers. The research revealed that brand image was fuzzy and inconsistent from market to market. One reason was that it employed a gaggle of 55 ad agencies. Kim consolidated advertising, assigning Madison Avenue's Foote, Cone & Belding Worldwide to coordinate Samsung's global marketing. Kim made another smart move by sponsoring big-ticket events like the Salt Lake City Olympics in 2002, gaining quick, cost-effective global exposure. When Kim left Samsung in 2004, the company had earned $12.04 billion in net profits that year while many other retail-tech stars had fizzled, and business in the United States had more than tripled since 1999.

On November 4, 2004, Intel poached Samsung executive Eric Kim and used him to invigorate its advertising and inject more consumer values into the chip giant's brand, according to an internal communication by president Paul Otellini. Kim's secret lies in his broad-based education and very good knowledge of marketing and marketing research. As of 2009, Eric Kim was general manager of Intel's digital home group.[23] ■

The Role of Marketing Research in MIS and DSS

Earlier, we defined marketing research as the systematic and objective identification, collection, analysis, and dissemination of information for use in marketing decision making.[24] The information obtained through marketing research and sources such as internal records and marketing intelligence becomes an integral part of the firm's marketing information system (MIS). A **marketing information system (MIS)** is a formalized set of procedures for generating, analyzing, storing, and distributing information to marketing decision makers on an ongoing basis. Note that the definition of MIS is similar to that of marketing research, except that an MIS provides information continuously rather than on the basis of ad hoc research studies. The design of an MIS focuses on each decision maker's responsibilities, style, and information needs. Information gathered from various sources, such as invoices and marketing intelligence, including marketing research, is combined and presented in a format that can be readily used in decision making. More information can be obtained from an MIS than from ad hoc marketing research projects, but an MIS is limited in the amount and nature of information it provides and the way this information can be used by the decision maker. This is because the information is rigidly structured and cannot be easily manipulated.

Developed to overcome the limitations of an MIS, decision support systems (DSS) enable decision makers to interact directly with databases and analysis models. **Decision support systems (DSS)** are integrated systems including hardware, communications network, database, model base, software base, and the DSS user (decision maker) that collect and interpret information for decision making. Marketing research contributes research data to the database, marketing models and analytical techniques to the model base, and specialized programs for analyzing marketing data to the software base. A DSS differs from an MIS in various ways (see Figure 1.6).[25] A DSS combines the use of models or analytical techniques with the traditional

marketing information system (MIS)
A formalized set of procedures for generating, analyzing, storing, and distributing pertinent information to marketing decision makers on an ongoing basis.

decision support systems (DSS)
Information systems that enable decision makers to interact directly with both databases and analysis models. The important components of a DSS include hardware and a communications network, database, model base, software base, and the DSS user (decision maker).

FIGURE 1.6

Management Information Systems Versus Decision Support Systems

MIS	DSS
• Structured Problems	• Unstructured Problems
• Use of Reports	• Use of Models
• Rigid Structure	• User-Friendly Interaction
• Information Displaying Restricted	• Adaptability
• Can Improve Decision Making by Clarifying Raw Data	• Can Improve Decision Making by Using "What-If" Analysis

access and retrieval functions of an MIS. A DSS is easier to use in an interactive mode and can adapt to changes in the environment as well as to the decision-making approach of the user. In addition to improving efficiency, a DSS can also enhance decision-making effectiveness by using "what if" analysis.[26] DSS have been further developed to expert systems that utilize artificial intelligence procedures to incorporate expert judgment.

Real Research

DSS Give FedEx an Exceptional Edge

Federal Express (www.fedex.com), with 2008 revenues of $37.953 billion, has grown into a network of companies, offering just the right mix of transportation, e-commerce, and business solutions. The FedEx worldwide network links you to more than 220 countries and territories, often within 24 to 48 hours. A major ingredient in FedEx's success has been the advanced worldwide decision support systems that provide information on customers. Such information includes detailed aspects of every shipment such as ordering, billing, tracking, and tracing.

As one example of the several strategic ways in which the DSS are used, FedEx has implemented highly sophisticated "Segment Management Marketing" (SMM). FedEx has developed a "value quotient" formula that allows marketers to analyze individual customers on a case-by-case analysis. This value quotient includes weights for strategic/competitive values of customers and profitability through a survey of 30 questions. The objectives help define the weight given to an individual customer and provide a more strategic perspective than simply using profit to pinpoint the value of a customer. FedEx has defined 14 highly specific customer segments based on consumer attitudes relating to price, reliability, urgency, safety of product, tracking, and proof of delivery. The current SMM, which is a part of the company's DSS, includes family classifications and segments to help marketers further understand the customers they serve. Thus, FedEx has taken a very aggressive information-oriented approach to competition that will be the key to continued success.[27] ■

ACTIVE RESEARCH

Sony's Digital Quest

Visit www.sony.com and search the Internet using a search engine as well as your library's online databases to find information on the market for digital cameras.

As the marketing manager for Sony digital cameras, your objective is to switch more traditional photographers to the digital camera. What information from the company's DSS would you find helpful in achieving this goal?

What kind of marketing research would you undertake to obtain the information identified by the DSS?

The marketing research process outlined earlier in this chapter, which is followed by companies such as FedEx, was also adopted in the department store project.

The Department Store Patronage Project

A department store patronage project that I conducted is used as a running example throughout this text to illustrate concepts and data analysis procedures. The purpose of this project was to assess the relative strengths and weaknesses of a major department store relative to a group of direct and indirect competitors. This store will be referred to as Sears; the true identity of the actual store has been disguised. The goal was to formulate marketing programs designed to boost the declining sales and profits of Sears. Ten major stores, including prestigious department stores (e.g., Saks Fifth Avenue, Neiman-Marcus), national chains (e.g., JCPenney), discount stores (e.g., Kmart, Wal-Mart), and some regional chains (e.g., Kohl's) were considered in this study. A questionnaire was designed and administered, using in-home personal interviews, to a convenience sample of 271 households drawn from a major metropolitan area. A six-point scale was used (subjects were asked to check a number from 1 to 6) whenever ratings were obtained. The following information was solicited:

1. Familiarity with the 10 department stores
2. Frequency with which household members shopped at each of the 10 stores

3. Relative importance attached to each of the eight factors selected as the choice criteria utilized in selecting a department store. These factors were quality of merchandise, variety and assortment of merchandise, returns and adjustment policy, service of store personnel, prices, convenience of location, layout of store, and credit and billing policies.
4. Evaluation of the 10 stores on each of the eight factors of the choice criteria
5. Preference ratings for each store
6. Rankings of the 10 stores (from most preferred to least preferred)
7. Degree of agreement with 21 lifestyle statements
8. Standard demographic characteristics (age, education, etc.)
9. Name, address, and telephone number

The study helped the sponsor to determine consumer perceptions of and preferences for the department stores. Areas of weakness were identified in terms of specific factors influencing the consumers' choice criteria and in terms of specific product categories. Appropriate marketing programs were designed to overcome these weaknesses. Finally, a positioning strategy was developed to attain a desirable store image.

This study is used as a running example throughout this book. Examples titled "Project Research" that illustrate the various concepts and also provide opportunities for hands-on research are featured in each chapter. The data analysis chapters also provide you access to the actual data collected in this project.

Project Research | ## Marketing and Marketing Research at Sears

Project Activities

Visit www.sears.com and search the Internet to identify relevant information on Sears' marketing strategy. Answer the following questions.

1. What are the marketing opportunities and problems confronting Sears?
2. What role can marketing research play in helping Sears address these marketing opportunities and problems?
3. What type of marketing research would be needed to help Sears decide whether it should aggressively expand in rural areas in the United States? ■

International Marketing Research

The United States accounts for only about 40 percent of the marketing research expenditures worldwide. About 40 percent of all marketing research is conducted in Western Europe and about 10 percent in Japan. Most of the research in Europe is done in the United Kingdom, Germany, France, Italy, and Spain. Japan is the clear leader in the Asia–Pacific region, followed by Australia, China, Korea, and Taiwan. Brazil and Mexico lead the Central and South American markets in terms of marketing research expenditures.[28] With the globalization of markets, marketing research has assumed a truly international character and this trend is likely to continue. Several U.S. firms conduct international marketing research, including Nielsen, IMS Health, Information Resources, and the Kantar Group (see Table 1.2). Foreign-based firms include Infratest and GfK, both of Germany.

Conducting international marketing research (research for truly international products), foreign research (research carried out in a country other than the country of the research-commissioning organization), or multinational research (research conducted in all or all important countries where the company is represented) is much more complex than domestic marketing research. All research of this kind, including cross-cultural research, will be discussed under the broad rubric of international marketing research. The opening Boeing example illustrated some of the complexities involved in conducting this type of research. The environment prevailing in the countries, cultural units, or international markets that are being researched influences the way the six steps of the marketing research process should be performed. These environmental factors and their impact on the marketing research process are discussed in detail in subsequent chapters. In addition, Chapter 24 is devoted exclusively to this topic.

Globalization of companies is the trend of today. Whether going online or setting up physical operations in a foreign country, research must be conducted so that relevant environmental factors are taken into consideration when going global. Many companies have faced global disaster because they did not take into account the differences between their country and the country with which they wished to do business.

Companies that are basing their business on the Web can run into problems. Many times the content on the Web page may be interpreted in a way that was unintended, such as in the case of a car manufacturer in Mexico. The Web page showed a hiker standing next to a car. In Mexico, hikers are poor people and they do not own cars. You also want local content to accommodate multiple languages in areas such as India, where one region may have 20 different languages. Companies must take these environmental factors into account in order to gain sales and customers in other countries.

Despite the complexity involved, international marketing research is expected to grow at a faster rate than domestic research. A major contributing factor is that markets for many products in the United States are approaching saturation. In contrast, the markets for these products in other countries are in the early stages of development, and marketing research can play a crucial role in penetrating the market, as illustrated by the success of Starbucks in Japan.

Real Research   ## Starbucks: Buck-Up in Japan

A very well-known example of ingenious marketing for the Japanese marketplace is the success of Starbucks Coffee Shops in Japan. Starbucks is able to market cups of coffee at high-level prices, which was inconceivable before Starbucks began with a shop in Ginza, Tokyo, in 1996. Starbucks Coffee Japan, Ltd., is a U.S./Japan joint venture, which has achieved success through store design and constant branding to create a sophisticated atmosphere attracting sophisticated, modern Japanese women, who generally didn't go to coffee shops. Starbucks' success, of course, comes from its accurate understanding of the intricate marketing issues at stake by conducting marketing research.

When Starbucks entered the Japanese market, it wanted a detailed assessment of its options. Intage Inc. (www.intage.co.jp), a Tanashi-Shi, Tokyo-based full-service marketing research and consulting firm, conducted analyses on consumer behavior and preferences. The survey utilized Intage's Central Location Testing Facilities in downtown Tokyo and also mail survey methodology, as well as resources from the research company's Business Information Services. The survey provided some important information to Starbucks. They understood that their intended customer segments were willing to pay in the ballpark of 250 yen (US$2.08) for espresso and 280 yen (US$2.33) for caffe latte. The survey also revealed that the customers wanted plenty of food items on the menu, including sandwiches and salads. The survey in general gave the company an idea of acceptable consumer price range, differences in prices, and packaging. This played an important part in the success of Starbucks Japan. As of 2009, Starbucks operated more than 4,500 coffeehouses in 47 countries.[29] ∎

Marketing research played an important role in the success of Starbucks Coffee Shops in Japan.

Ethics in Marketing Research

Several aspects of marketing research have strong ethical implications. As explained earlier, marketing research is generally conducted by commercial (i.e., for-profit) firms that are either independent research organizations (external suppliers) or departments within corporations (internal suppliers). Most marketing research is conducted for clients representing commercial firms. The profit motive may occasionally cause researchers or clients to compromise the objectivity or professionalism associated with the marketing research process.

Marketing research has often been described as having four stakeholders: (1) the marketing researcher, (2) the client, (3) the respondent, and (4) the public. These stakeholders have certain responsibilities to one another and to the research project. For example, see the respondent bill of rights on the Web site of the Council for Marketing and Opinion Research (www.cmor.org). Ethical issues arise when the interests of these stakeholders are in conflict and when one or more of the stakeholders are lacking in their responsibilities.[30] For example, if the researcher does not follow appropriate marketing research procedures, or if the client misrepresents the findings in the company's advertising, ethical norms are violated. Ethical issues can arise at each step of the marketing research process and Table 1.3 gives an overview. Ethical issues are best resolved by

---

TABLE 1.3
An Overview of Ethical Issues in the Marketing and Research Process

I. Problem Definition
- Using surveys as a guise for selling or fundraising
- Personal agendas of the researcher or client
- Conducting unnecessary research

II. Developing an Approach
- Using findings and models developed for specific clients or projects for other projects
- Soliciting proposals to gain research expertise without pay

III. Research Design
- Formulating a research design more suited to the researcher's rather than the client's needs
- Using secondary data that are not applicable or have been gathered through questionable means
- Disguising the purpose of the research
- Soliciting unfair concessions from the researcher
- Not maintaining anonymity of respondents
- Disrespecting privacy of respondents
- Misleading respondents
- Disguising observation of respondents
- Embarrassing or putting stress on respondents
- Using measurement scales of questionable reliability and validity
- Designing overly long questionnaires, overly sensitive questions, piggybacking
- Using inappropriate sampling procedures and sample size

IV. Fieldwork
- Increasing (dis)comfort level of respondents
- Following (un)acceptable fieldwork procedures

V. Data Preparation and Analysis
- Identifying and discarding unsatisfactory respondents
- Using statistical techniques when the underlying assumptions are violated
- Interpreting the results and making incorrect conclusions and recommendations

VI. Report Preparation and Presentation
- Incomplete reporting
- Biased reporting
- Inaccurate reporting

the stakeholders behaving honorably. Codes of conduct, such as the American Marketing Association code of ethics, are available to guide behavior and help resolve ethical dilemmas. We give the URLs of important marketing research associations, and you are encouraged to review their codes of conduct.

<table>
<tr><td>

Experiential Research

</td><td>

Marketing Research Associations Online

Domestic

AAPOR: American Association for Public Opinion Research (www.aapor.org)
AMA: American Marketing Association (www.marketingpower.com)
ARF: The Advertising Research Foundation (www.arfsite.org)
CASRO: The Council of American Survey Research Organizations (www.casro.org)
MRA: Marketing Research Association (www.mra-net.org)
QRCA: Qualitative Research Consultants Association (www.qrca.org)
RIC: Research Industry Coalition (www.researchindustry.org)
CMOR: Council for Marketing and Opinion Research (www.cmor.org)

International

ESOMAR: European Society for Opinion and Marketing Research (www.esomar.nl)
MRS: The Market Research Society (U.K.) (www.marketresearch.org.uk)
MRSA: The Market Research Society of Australia (www.mrsa.com.au)
PMRS: The Professional Marketing Research Society (Canada) (www.pmrs-aprm.com)

Compare the ethical guidelines for conducting marketing research posted at the following Web sites: CASRO: The Council of American Survey Research Organizations (www.casro.org), CMOR: Council for Marketing and Opinion Research (www.cmor.org), and ESOMAR: European Society for Opinion and Marketing Research (www.esomar.nl).

Which organization has the most stringent set of guidelines?
Which organization's ethical guidelines are the most complete?
What is missing from the guidelines of all three organizations? ■

</td></tr>
</table>

The Internet can be useful to marketing researchers in many ways. A variety of marketing research information related to the client company, its competitors, the industry, and relevant marketing, economic, governmental, and environmental information can be obtained by conducting a search using popular search engines: AltaVista (www.altavista.com), AOL Search (www.search.aol.com), Ask Jeeves (www.askjeeves.com), FAST search (www.alltheweb.com), Google (www.google.com), Lycos (www.lycos.com), MSN Search (search.msn.com), Netscape Search (search.netscape.com), WebCrawler (www.webcrawler.com), and Yahoo! (www.yahoo.com). KnowThis (www.knowthis.com) is a specialty search engine for a virtual marketing library. Important sources of marketing research information on the Internet include bulletin boards, newsgroups, and blogs. A newsgroup is an Internet site (e.g., http://groups.google.com) where people can read and post messages pertaining to a particular topic. Blogs or Web logs can be used to obtain information on a variety of topics and to recruit respondents for surveys. Although you can find blogs on most search engines, special engines such as Blog Search Engine (www.blogsearchengine.com) have been designed for blog searches.

The Internet can be used to help find a job in marketing research. Research Info at www.researchinfo.com offers a research employment board where job postings and job wanted ads are placed. The Internet is quickly becoming a useful tool in the identification, collection, analysis, and dissemination of information related to marketing research. Throughout this book, we show how the six steps of the marketing research process are facilitated by the use of the Internet.

<table>
<tr><td>

Decision Research

</td><td>

Samsonite: It's in the Bag

The Situation

Samsonite is one of the world's largest designers, manufacturers, and distributors of luggage. They sell their products using a number of quality brand names, including Samsonite® and American Tourister®, and are a leader in the highly fragmented global luggage industry. Through aggressive

</td></tr>
</table>

Samsonite must make use of marketing research to continually introduce successful new products in the marketplace.

product development and marketing, President and Chief Executive Officer Marcello Bottoli hoped to increase the company's market share from 36 percent in 2005 to 40 percent in 2010. Mr. Bottoli recognizes the importance of new product development and that Samsonite must continually introduce successful new products in the marketplace.

The Marketing Research Decision

1. What type of marketing research should Samsonite undertake to successfully introduce new products and increase market share?
2. Discuss the role of the type of research you recommend in enabling Marcello Bottoli to increase Samsonite's market share.

The Marketing Management Decision

1. How should Marcello Bottoli build an aggressive marketing strategy?
2. Discuss how the marketing management decision action that you recommend to Marcello Bottoli is influenced by the research that you suggested earlier and by the findings of that research.[31] ■

SPSS Windows and SAS

In this book, we feature SPSS programs (www.spss.com), not merely as a statistical package, but as an integrative package that can be used in the various stages of the marketing research process. We illustrate the use of SPSS for defining the problem, developing an approach, formulating the research design, and conducting data collection, data preparation and analysis, and report preparation and presentation. In addition to the BASE module, we also feature other SPSS programs such as Decision Time, What If?, Maps, Data Entry, SamplePower, Missing Values, TextSmart, and SmartViewer. Data analysis is also illustrated with three other software packages: SAS (www.sas.com), MINITAB (www.minitab.com), and EXCEL (www.microsoft.com), with special emphasis being placed on SAS.[32]

Help for running the SPSS and SAS programs used in the data analysis chapters (Chapters 14 to 22) is provided in four ways: (1) detailed step-by-step instructions are given in each of these chapters, (2) you can download (from the Web site for this book) computerized demonstration movies illustrating these step-by-step instructions, (3) you can download screen captures with notes illustrating these step-by-step instructions, and (4) you can refer to the *Study Guide and Technology Manual*, a supplement that accompanies this book. Thus, this book provides the most comprehensive instructions for running SPSS and SAS available anywhere.

Summary

Marketing research involves the identification, collection, analysis, dissemination, and use of information. It is a systematic and objective process designed to identify and solve marketing problems. Thus, marketing research can be classified as problem-identification research and problem-solving research. The marketing research process consists of six steps that must be followed systematically. Figure 1.7 is a concept map for the marketing research process. The role of marketing research is to assess information needs and provide relevant information in order to improve marketing decision making. However, the decision to undertake marketing research is not an automatic one but must be carefully considered.

Marketing research may be conducted internally or may be purchased from external suppliers, referred to as the marketing research industry. Full-service suppliers provide the entire range of marketing research services from problem definition to report preparation and presentation. The services provided by these suppliers can be classified as syndicated, standardized, customized, or Internet services. Limited-service suppliers specialize in one or a few phases of the marketing research project. Services offered by these suppliers can be classified as field services, focus groups and qualitative services, technical and analytical services, and other services.

Due to the need for marketing research, attractive career opportunities are available with marketing research firms, business and nonbusiness firms, agencies with marketing research departments, and advertising agencies. Information obtained using marketing research becomes an integral part of the MIS and DSS. Marketing research contributes to the DSS by providing research data to the database, marketing models and analytical techniques to the model base, and specialized marketing research programs to the software base. International marketing research is much more complex than domestic research as the researcher must consider the environment prevailing in the international markets that are being researched. The ethical issues in marketing research involve four stakeholders: (1) the marketing researcher, (2) the client, (3) the respondent, and (4) the public. The Internet can be used at every step of the marketing research process. SPSS Windows is an integrative package that can greatly facilitate marketing research.

FIGURE 1.7

A Concept Map for the Marketing Research Process

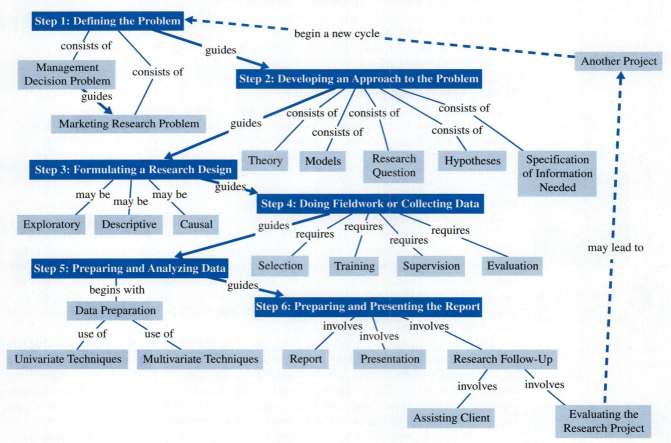

Key Terms and Concepts

marketing research, 7
problem-identification research, 7
problem-solving research, 8
marketing research process, 9
competitive intelligence, 13
internal supplier, 14
external suppliers, 15

marketing research industry, 15
full-service suppliers, 15
syndicated services, 15
customized services, 15
Internet services, 15
limited-service suppliers, 18
field services, 18

focus groups and qualitative
    services, 18
technical and analytical services, 18
marketing information system
    (MIS), 21
decision support systems (DSS), 21

Suggested Cases, Video Cases, and HBS Cases

Running Case with Real Data

1.1 Dell

Comprehensive Critical Thinking Cases

2.1 American Idol   2.2 Baskin-Robbins   2.3 Akron Children's Hospital

Comprehensive Cases with Real Data

4.1 JPMorgan Chase   4.2 Wendy's

Video Cases

| 1.1 Burke | 2.1 Accenture | 3.1 NFL | 8.1 P&G | 10.1 Dunkin' Donuts |
| 11.1 Motorola | 12.1 Subaru | 13.1 Intel | 23.1 Marriott | |

Comprehensive Harvard Business School Cases

Case 5.1: The Harvard Graduate Student Housing Survey (9-505-059)
Case 5.2: BizRate.Com (9-501-024)
Case 5.3: Cola Wars Continue: Coke and Pepsi in the Twenty-First Century (9-702-442)
Case 5.4: TiVo in 2002 (9-502-062)
Case 5.5: Compaq Computer: Intel Inside? (9-599-061)
Case 5.6: The New Beetle (9-501-023)

Live Research: Conducting a Marketing Research Project

1. Compile background information on the client organization.
2. Discuss the marketing organization and operations of the client.
3. Explain how the project results will help the client make specific marketing decisions.
4. Organize the class. This may require forming project teams. The entire class could be working on the same project with each team working on all aspects of the project or assign each team a specific responsibility, for example, a specific component of the problem or a specific aspect of the project, e.g., collection and analysis of secondary data. Each student should participate in primary data collection. Alternatively, the class could be working on multiple projects with specific teams assigned to a specific project. The approach is flexible and can handle a variety of organizations and formats.
5. Develop a project schedule clearly specifying the deadlines for the different steps.
6. Explain how the teams will be evaluated.
7. Select one or two students to be project coordinators.

Acronym

The role and salient characteristics of marketing research may be described by the acronym

Research:

R ecognition of information needs
E ffective decision making
S ystematic and objective
E xude/disseminate information
A nalysis of information
R ecommendations for action
C ollection of information
H elpful to managers

Exercises

Questions

1. Describe the task of marketing research.
2. What decisions are made by marketing managers? How does marketing research help in making these decisions?
3. Define marketing research.
4. Describe one classification of marketing research.
5. Describe the steps in the marketing research process.
6. How should the decision to conduct research be made?
7. Explain one way to classify marketing research suppliers and services.
8. What are syndicated services?
9. What is the main difference between a full-service and a limited-service supplier?
10. What are technical and analytical services?
11. List five guidelines for selecting an external marketing research supplier.
12. What career opportunities are available in marketing research?
13. Discuss three ethical issues in marketing research that relate to (1) the client, (2) the supplier, and (3) the respondent.
14. What is a marketing information system?
15. How is a DSS different from an MIS?

Problems

1. Look through recent issues of newspapers and magazines to identify five examples of problem-identification research and five examples of problem-solving research.
2. List one kind of marketing research that would be useful to each of the following organizations:
   a. Your campus bookstore
   b. The public transportation authority in your city
   c. A major department store in your area
   d. A restaurant located near your campus
   e. A zoo in a major city

Internet and Computer Exercises

1. Visit the Web sites of the top three marketing research firms in Table 1.2. Write a report on the services offered by these firms. Use the framework of Figure 1.4. What statements can you make about the structure of the marketing research industry?
2. Visit the Web site of Sears (www.sears.com). Write a report about the retailing and marketing activities of Sears. This will help you better understand the department store patronage project that is used as a running example throughout this book.
3. Visit the Bureau of Labor Statistics at www.bls.gov. What is the employment potential for marketing researchers?
4. Examine recent issues of magazines such as *Marketing News, Quirk's Marketing Research Review,* and *Marketing Research: A Magazine of Management and Applications* to identify one application in each of the following areas:
   a. Identification of information needs
   b. Collection of information
   c. Analysis of information
   d. Provision of information (report preparation)

Activities

Role Playing

1. You are the research director for a major bank. You are to recruit a junior analyst who would be responsible for collecting and analyzing secondary data (data already collected by other agencies that are relevant to your operations). With a fellow student playing the role of an applicant for this position, conduct the interview. Does this applicant have the necessary background and skills? Reverse the roles and repeat the exercise.
2. You are a project director working for a major research supplier. You have just received a telephone call from an irate respondent who believes that an interviewer has violated her privacy by calling at an inconvenient time. The respondent expresses several ethical concerns. Ask a fellow student to play the role of this respondent. Address the respondent's concerns and pacify her.

Fieldwork

1. Using your local newspaper and national newspapers such as *USA Today,* the *Wall Street Journal,* or the *New York Times,* compile a list of career opportunities in marketing research.

2. Interview someone who works for a marketing research supplier. What is this person's opinion about career opportunities in marketing research? Write a report of your interview.
3. Interview someone who works in the marketing research department of a major corporation. What is this person's opinion about career opportunities available in marketing research? Write a report of your interview.

Note: The interviews in Fieldwork exercises 2 and 3 can be conducted in person, by telephone, or online.

Group Discussion

In small groups of four or five, discuss the following issues.

1. What type of institutional structure is best for a marketing research department in a large business firm?
2. What is the ideal educational background for someone seeking a career in marketing research? Is it possible to acquire such a background?
3. Can ethical standards be enforced in marketing research? If so, how?

Dell Running Case

Review the Dell case, Case 1.1, and questionnaire given toward the end of the book. Answer the following questions.

1. Discuss the role that marketing research can play in helping Dell maintain and build on its leadership position in the personal computers market.
2. What problem-identification research should Dell undertake?
3. What problem-solving research should Dell undertake?
4. Would you like to pursue a marketing research career with Dell? Explain.

VIDEO CASE 1.1   Burke: Learning and Growing Through Marketing Research

Alberta Burke, who previously worked in P&G's marketing department, founded Burke, Inc., in 1931. At that time, there were few formalized marketing research companies, not only in the United States, but also in the world. As of 2009, Burke, based in Cincinnati, Ohio, is a marketing research and decision-support company that helps its clients to understand their business practices and make them more efficient. Burke's employee owners add value to research and consulting assignments by applying superior thinking to help clients solve business problems. Burke is 100 percent employee owned. This video case traces the evolution of marketing research and how Burke implements the various phases of the marketing research process.

The Evolution of Marketing Research

The first recorded marketing research took place more than a century ago, in 1895 or 1896. By telegram, a professor sent questions to advertising agencies about the future of advertising. He got back about 10 responses and wrote a paper describing what was happening. In the first years, most of the marketing research done was a spin-off of the Bureau of Census data, and the analysis was basically limited to counting.

The next wave of marketing research came in the early 1930s, often done by ladies in white gloves who knocked on doors and asked about cake mixes. The primary methodology was door-to-door surveys; the telephone was not a very widely utilized service at that time.

Then came World War II, which saw the introduction of the psychological side of marketing research. Through the 1950s and 1960s, television became an integral part of life, and with that came television advertising. Testing of television commercials became the hot area of marketing research in the 1960s and 1970s. Another fundamental change happening at that time was when the marketing research industry made a shift from just generating and testing new ideas and sharing them with clients to working more with clients on how to use those ideas to make decisions.

In the 1980s and 1990s, Burke moved a notch higher by developing processes to provide further value add. It began working with customers to identify the basic decision that needed to be made and then determine what information would be required to make that decision. The marketing research industry started developing processes that generated information to be used as input into management decision making.

The marketing research industry has come a long way from the telegrams of 1895. As of 2009, the industry is trying to find creative ways to research consumers using methods such as telephone interviews, mall intercepts, Web interviews, mobile phone surveys, and multimode methods. As Debbi Wyrick, a senior account executive at Burke, notes, when people can respond in more than one way—responding in the way that is most efficient for them—it increases the chance of getting a response.

To stay on the cutting edge, Burke conducts meta-research (research about how to do research). Recently, Burke was concerned as to whether the length of an online (Internet) survey has an adverse impact on the completion rate. In an effort to find out, Burke fielded two Internet surveys. One was brief (10 questions taking an average of 5 minutes to complete), and the other was longer (20 questions taking about 20 minutes to complete). The completion rate for the short survey was 35 percent, whereas it was only 10 percent for the longer survey. Burke now designs shorter Internet surveys so as to reduce the proportion of people who drop off without completing the survey.

How Burke Implements the Marketing Research Process

We briefly describe Burke's approach to defining the marketing research problem, developing an approach, research design, data collection and analysis, and report preparation and presentation.

Define the Marketing Research Problem and Develop an Approach

The simplest way to find out when a company needs help is when it has to make a decision. Any time there is a go or no go, a yes or no, or a decision to be made, Burke asks what information can help reduce the risk associated with the decision. Burke then talks with the company to develop the information that might help to reduce that risk.

The first step is to define the marketing research problem, and a lot of discovery takes place at this stage. The account executive (AE) will sit down with a client and try to determine whether what the client believes is the problem really is the problem, or whether Burke needs to change or broaden the scope of the problem. Discussions with the key decision makers (DM) might reveal that the company has been focusing on too narrow an issue or that it has been focusing on the wrong problem altogether.

Burke believes that defining the marketing research problem is critical to a successful research project. The company finds out what the symptoms are and works with the client to identify the underlying causes. Considerable effort is devoted to examining the background or the environmental context of the problem. In at least half the cases, when they go through the process of exploring the problem, the problem will change. It will gain a new scope or direction. This process results in a precise definition of the marketing research problem, including an identification of its specific components.

Once the problem has been defined, Burke develops a suitable approach. The problem definition is refined to generate more specific research questions and sometimes hypotheses. Because of its vast experience, Burke has developed a variety of analytical models that are customized to the identified problem. This process also results in the identification of information that will help the client solve its problem.

Research Design Formulation

In formulating the research design, Burke places special emphasis on qualitative research, survey methods, questionnaire design, and sampling design.

QUALITATIVE RESEARCH One of the pitfalls that Burke encounters comes with qualitative research. Qualitative research is nice because it is immediate. The information generated tends to be extremely rich and in the customer's words. Burke gets to see what kinds of answers are being given and what kinds of questions and concerns customers or potential customers might have. However, one of the dangers is thinking that all customers or potential customers might view products or service offerings in the same manner; that is, generalizing the findings of qualitative research to the larger population. Burke also can conduct focus groups online.

SURVEY METHODS Although Burke uses a variety of methods, telephone studies represent about 70 percent of its surveys. Other methods used include mall intercept, mail, and Internet or Web-based surveys. Burke carefully selects the method that is best suited to the problem. Burke predicts that telephone surveys will decrease, whereas Internet surveys will increase. If Burke is trying to interview customers around the globe, it sends an e-mail invitation to respondents to complete the survey via the Web. Burke likes the Internet's ability to show pictures of a particular product or concept to the survey respondents.

QUESTIONNAIRE DESIGN In designing the questionnaire, Burke pays particular attention to the content and wording of the questions. Some questions are well defined and can be easily framed; for other issues, the exact questions to ask might not be clear. The simpler the question and the more clear it is who the target respondents are, the better the information generated.

SAMPLING DESIGN Burke has a sampling department that consults with the senior account management team and account executives to determine the proper sample to use. The sampling frame is defined in terms of who the respondents are who can answer the questions that need to be addressed. The target population is defined by the marketing research problem and the research questions. Burke often buys the sampling lists from outside firms that specialize in this area. Burke is concerned about using a representative sample so that the results can be generalized to the target population (e.g., all the target consumers as opposed to only the consumers included in the sample).

Data Collection and Analysis

Once the information has been collected, it will reside either in a computer-related format or a paper format that is entered into a computer format. The results are tabulated and analyzed via computers. Through the "Digital Dashboard" product, Burke not only has the ability to disseminate the results to clients when the project is finished, but also to show them the data as they are being collected. Burke breaks down the data analysis by relevant groups. You might see information by total respondents, and you might see information broken out by gender or business size. Essentially, Burke looks at different breaks in the data to try to understand what is happening, if there are differences based on different criteria, and, if so, how to make decisions based on that information. In addition, Burke likes the data to be categorized into usable units such as time, frequency, or location instead of the vague responses that respondents sometimes give.

Report Preparation and Presentation

Clients need information much faster than they have in the past because decisions need to be made much more quickly. Organizing large meetings to present data analysis results is no longer practical. Most of the time, Burke reports and delivers data over the Web. The report documents the entire research process. It discusses the management decision problem, the marketing research problem, the approach and research design, the information obtained to help management make the decision, and the recommendations.

The report-writing process starts from the first conversation with the client, and it is written as the research proceeds, not simply when the project is almost done. The report focuses on improving management's decision making. Burke's goal is to help clients have better decision-making abilities so that the clients are more valuable to their respective companies. Burke emphasizes this focus by reminding its clients, "Here are the management decision and marketing research problems we agreed upon. Here's the information we gathered. Here's the decision it points to." Burke might even add, "This is what we recommend you do."

Burke believes that a successful research project often leads to a subsequent research project; the research process is more of a circular process. It does not typically have a finite beginning and end. Once you solve a problem, there is always another one to work on.

Conclusion

The field of marketing research has evolved in sophistication, scope, and importance over the years. Advances in technology have improved processes and methodologies,

providing higher value-added services. Burke has a strong identity and a long, rich legacy in market research—since 1931—and hence it is an apt representative of the marketing research industry. This case also demonstrates key aspects of the marketing research process, from problem definition to collecting data to analyzing data and presenting the macro-analysis report. Burke is continually undertaking efforts to improve the marketing research process, and this is what helps Burke and its clients learn and grow.

Questions

1. Describe the evolution of marketing research. How has the role of marketing research changed as the field has evolved?
2. What is Burke's view of the role of marketing research?
3. Visit www.burke.com and write a report about the various marketing research services offered.
4. What is Burke's view of the importance of defining the marketing research problem?
5. What is Burke's view of the marketing research process? How does it compare with the one given in Chapter 1?
6. If Burke were to offer you a position as an account executive with the responsibility of providing marketing research services to P&G, would you accept this position? Why or why not?

Reference

See www.burke.com, accessed February 15, 2009.

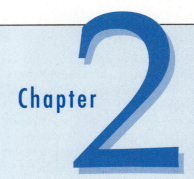

"Defining the marketing research problem is one of the most important tasks in a marketing research project. It is also one of the most difficult.

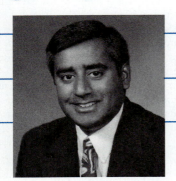

Ken Athaide, Senior Vice President,
Marketing Strategies International

Objectives [After reading this chapter, the student should be able to:]

1. Understand the importance of and the process used for defining the marketing research problem.

2. Describe the tasks involved in problem definition, including discussions with decision makers, interviews with industry experts, secondary data analysis, and qualitative research.

3. Discuss the environmental factors affecting the definition of the research problem: past information and forecasts, resources and constraints, objectives of the decision maker, buyer behavior, legal environment, economic environment, and marketing and technological skills of the firm.

4. Clarify the distinction between the management decision problem and the marketing research problem.

5. Explain the structure of a well-defined marketing research problem, including the broad statement and the specific components.

6. Discuss in detail the various components of the approach: objective/ theoretical framework, analytical models, research questions, hypotheses, and specification of information needed.

7. Acquire an appreciation of the complexity involved and gain an understanding of the procedures for defining the problem and developing an approach in international marketing research.

8. Understand the ethical issues and conflicts that arise in defining the problem and developing the approach.

Defining the Marketing Research Problem and Developing an Approach

Overview

This chapter covers the first two of the six steps of the marketing research process described in Chapter 1: defining the marketing research problem and developing an approach to the problem. Defining the problem is the most important step, because only when a problem has been clearly and accurately identified can a research project be conducted properly. Defining the marketing research problem sets the course of the entire project. In this chapter, we allow the reader to appreciate the complexities involved in defining a problem by identifying the factors to be considered and the tasks involved. Additionally, we provide guidelines for appropriately defining the marketing research problem and avoiding common types of errors. We also discuss in detail the components of an approach to the problem: objective/theoretical framework, analytical models, research questions, hypotheses, and specification of the information needed. The special considerations involved in defining the problem and developing an approach in international marketing research are discussed. Several ethical issues that arise at this stage of the marketing research process are considered.

We introduce our discussion with an example from Harley-Davidson, which needed specific information about its customers.

Real Research

Harley Goes Whole Hog

The motorcycle manufacturer Harley-Davidson (www.harleydavidson.com) made such an important comeback in the early 2000s that there was a long waiting list to get a bike. In 2007, Harley-Davidson's revenues exceeded $6 billion with a market share of about 50 percent in the heavyweight category. Although distributors urged Harley-Davidson to build more motorcycles, the company was skeptical about investing in new production facilities.

The years of declining sales taught top management to be more risk averse than risk prone. Harley-Davidson was now performing well again, and investing in new facilities meant taking risks. Would the demand follow in the long run or would customers stop wanting Harleys when the next fad came along? The decrease in motorcycles' quality linked to Harley's fast growth had cost the company all its bad years. Top management was afraid that the decision to invest was too early. On the other hand, investing would help Harley-Davidson expand and possibly become the clear market leader in the heavyweight segment. Discussions with industry experts indicated that brand loyalty was a major factor influencing the sales and repeat sales of motorcycles. Secondary data revealed that the vast majority of motorcycle owners also owned automobiles such as cars, SUVs, and trucks. Focus groups with motorcycle owners further indicated that motorcycles were not used primarily as a means of basic transportation but as a means of recreation. The focus groups also highlighted the role of brand loyalty in motorcycle purchase and ownership.

Forecasts called for an increase in consumer spending on recreation and entertainment well into the year 2015. Empowered by the Internet, consumers in the twenty-first century had become increasingly sophisticated and value conscious. Yet brand image and brand loyalty played a significant role in buyer behavior with well-known brands continuing to command a premium. Clearly, Harley-Davidson had the necessary resources and marketing and technological skills to achieve its objective of being the dominant motorcycle brand on a global basis.

This process and the findings that emerged helped define the management decision problem and the marketing research problem. The management decision problem was: Should Harley-Davidson invest to produce more motorcycles? The marketing research problem was to determine if customers would be

A correct definition of the marketing research problem and an appropriate approach helped Harley-Davidson make the right decision to invest in its production facilities.

loyal buyers of Harley-Davidson in the long term. Specifically, the research had to address the following questions:

1. Who are the customers? What are their demographic and psychographic characteristics?
2. Can different types of customers be distinguished? Is it possible to segment the market in a meaningful way?
3. How do customers feel regarding their Harleys? Are all customers motivated by the same appeal?
4. Are the customers loyal to Harley-Davidson? What is the extent of brand loyalty?

One of the research questions (RQs) examined and its associated hypotheses (Hs) were:

RQ: Can the motorcycle buyers be segmented based on psychographic characteristics?
H1:   There are distinct segments of motorcycle buyers.
H2:   Each segment is motivated to own a Harley for a different reason.
H3:   Brand loyalty is high among Harley-Davidson customers in all segments.

   This research was guided by the theory that brand loyalty is the result of positive beliefs, attitude, affect, and experience with the brand. Both qualitative research and quantitative research were conducted. First, focus groups of current owners, would-be owners, and owners of other brands were conducted to understand their feelings about Harley-Davidson. Then 16,000 surveys were mailed to get the psychological, sociological, and demographic profiles of customers and also their subjective appraisal of Harley.
   Some of the major findings were as follows:

- Seven categories of customers could be distinguished: (1) the adventure-loving traditionalist, (2) the sensitive pragmatist, (3) the stylish status seeker, (4) the laid-back camper, (5) the classy capitalist, (6) the cool-headed loner, and (7) the cocky misfit. Thus, H1 was supported.
- All customers, however, had the same desire to own a Harley: It was a symbol of independence, freedom, and power. This uniformity across segments was surprising, contradicting H2.
- All customers were long-term loyal customers of Harley-Davidson, supporting H3.

   Based on these findings, the decision was taken to invest and in this way to increase the number of Harleys built in the future.[1] ∎

This example shows the importance of correctly defining the marketing research problem and developing an appropriate approach.

Importance of Defining the Problem

problem definition
A broad statement of the general problem and identification of the specific components of the marketing research problem.

Although each step in a marketing research project is important, problem definition is the most important step. As mentioned in Chapter 1, for the purpose of marketing research, problems and opportunities are treated interchangeably. **Problem definition** involves stating the general problem and identifying the specific components of the marketing research problem. Only when the marketing research problem has been clearly defined can research be designed and conducted properly. Of all the tasks in a marketing research project, none is more vital to the ultimate fulfillment of a client's needs than a proper definition of the research problem. All the effort, time, and money spent from this point on will be wasted if the problem is misunderstood or ill defined.[2] As stated by Peter Drucker, the truly serious mistakes are made not as a result of wrong answers but because of asking the wrong questions. This point is worth remembering, because inadequate problem definition is a leading cause of failure of marketing research projects. Further, better communication and more involvement in problem definition are the most frequently mentioned ways of improving the usefulness of research. These results lead to the conclusion that the importance of clearly identifying and defining the marketing research problem cannot be overstated. I cite an episode from personal experience to illustrate this point.

Real Research   Chain Restaurant Study

One day, I received a telephone call from a research analyst who introduced himself as one of our alumni. He was working for a restaurant chain in town and wanted help in analyzing the data he had collected while conducting a marketing research study. When we met, he presented me with a copy of the questionnaire and asked how he should analyze the data. My first question to him was, "What is the problem being addressed?" When he looked perplexed, I explained that data analysis was not an independent exercise. Rather, the goal of data analysis is to provide information related to the problem components. I was surprised to learn that he did not have a clear understanding of the marketing research problem and that a written definition of the problem did not exist. So, before proceeding any further, I had to define the marketing research problem. Once that was done, I found that much of the data collected were not relevant to the problem. In this sense, the whole study was a waste of resources. A new study had to be designed and implemented to address the problem identified. ■

Further insights on the difficulty involved in appropriately defining the problem are provided by the problem definition process.[3]

The Process of Defining the Problem and Developing an Approach

The problem definition and approach development process is shown in Figure 2.1. The tasks involved in problem definition consist of discussions with the decision makers, interviews with industry experts and other knowledgeable individuals, analysis of secondary data, and sometimes qualitative research. These tasks help the researcher to understand the background of the problem by analyzing the environmental context. Certain essential environmental factors bearing on the problem should be evaluated. Understanding the environmental context facilitates the identification of the management decision problem. Then the management decision problem is translated into a marketing research problem. Based on the definition of the marketing research problem, an appropriate approach is developed. The components of the approach consist of an objective/theoretical framework, analytical models, research questions, hypotheses, and specification of the information needed. Further explanation of the problem definition process begins with a discussion of the tasks involved.

Tasks Involved

Discussions with Decision Makers

Discussions with decision makers (DM) are extremely important. The DM needs to understand the capabilities and limitations of research.[4] Research provides information relevant to management decisions, but it cannot provide solutions because solutions require managerial judgment. Conversely, the researcher needs to understand the nature of the decision managers face and what they hope to learn from the research.

To identify the management problem, the researcher must possess considerable skill in interacting with the DM. Several factors may complicate this interaction. Access to the DM may be difficult, and some organizations have complicated protocols for access to top executives. The organizational status of the researcher or the research department may make it difficult to reach the key DM in the early stages of the project. Finally, there may be more than one key DM and

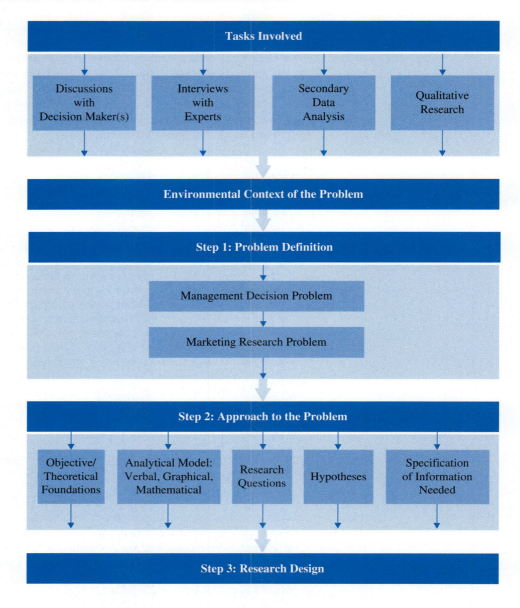

meeting with them collectively or individually may be difficult. Despite these problems, it is necessary that the researcher interact directly with the key decision makers.[5]

problem audit
A comprehensive examination of a marketing problem to understand its origin and nature.

The **problem audit** provides a useful framework for interacting with the DM and identifying the underlying causes of the problem. The problem audit, like any other type of audit, is a comprehensive examination of a marketing problem with the purpose of understanding its origin and nature.[6] The problem audit involves discussions with the DM on the following issues that are illustrated with a problem facing McDonald's:

1. The events that led to the decision that action is needed, or the history of the problem. McDonald's, a long-time leader in the fast-food industry, was losing market share in 2003 and 2004 to competitors such as Burger King, Wendy's, and Subway in some of the key markets. This problem came into sharper focus as these competitors launched new products and aggressive promotional campaigns, whereas the recent campaigns of McDonald's were not as successful.

2. The alternative courses of action available to the DM. The set of alternatives may be incomplete at this stage, and qualitative research may be needed to identify the more innovative courses of action. The alternatives available to the management of McDonald's include introducing new sandwiches and menu items, reducing prices, opening more restaurants, launching special promotions, and increasing advertising.

3. The criteria that will be used to evaluate the alternative courses of action. For example, new product offerings might be evaluated on the basis of sales, market share, profitability, return on investment, and so forth. McDonald's will evaluate the alternatives based on contributions to market share and profits.

4. The potential actions that are likely to be suggested based on the research findings. The research findings will likely call for a strategic marketing response by McDonald's.

5. The information that is needed to answer the DM's questions. The information needed includes a comparison of McDonald's and its major competitors on all the elements of the marketing mix (product, pricing, promotion, and distribution) in order to determine relative strengths and weaknesses.

6. The manner in which the DM will use each item of information in making the decision. The key decision makers will devise a strategy for McDonald's based on the research findings and their intuition and judgment.

7. The corporate culture as it relates to decision making.[7] In some firms, the decision-making process is dominant; in others, the personality of the DM is more important. Awareness of corporate culture may be one of the most important factors that distinguishes researchers who affect strategic marketing decisions from those who do not. The corporate culture at McDonald's calls for a committee approach in which critical decisions are made by key decision makers.

It is important to perform a problem audit because the DM, in most cases, has only a vague idea of what the problem is. For example, the DM may know that the firm is losing market share but may not know why, because DMs tend to focus on symptoms rather than on causes. Inability to meet sales forecasts, loss of market share, and decline in profits are all symptoms. The researcher should treat the underlying causes, not merely address the symptoms. For example, loss of market share may be caused by a superior promotion by the competition, inadequate distribution of the company's products, or any number of other factors. Only when the underlying causes are identified can the problem be successfully addressed, as exemplified by the effort of store brand jeans.

Real Research   Look Who's Picking Levi's Pocket

For years, teenagers have considered store label jeans "uncool." Although the lower price tag of store brand jeans, such as JCPenney's Arizona brand jeans or the Gap's in-house brand, has long appealed to value-conscious parents, teenagers have preferred big brand names such as Levi's, Lee, and Wrangler. The big-name brands have historically dominated the $12 billion industry as a result. Through marketing research problem audits, the private labels determined that the real cause for their low market share was lack of image. Therefore, the marketing research problem was defined as enhancing their image in the eyes of the target market—the lucrative teenage segment.

Arizona jeans and Gap's in-house brands have led the charge among the "generics" in changing their image. These store brand jeans, along with other store label jeans, now target the teenage market with "cutting edge" advertising. Their advertisements feature rock bands such as Aerosmith along with high-tech imagery to attract teenagers. The brands also promote their trendy Web sites—areas where their target market should go and visit to be "cool."

Gap jeans have also scored big. The chain's strategy has been to distance their store brand jeans from the store itself. Teenagers think of the Gap as a place where older people or their parents shop, thus making it "uncool." Gap's marketing campaign now aims to separate their store name and image from their jeans that are aimed at teens. This is the opposite of a more typical or traditional brand name leveraging strategy. The results, according to the research services firm TRU (www.teenresearch.com), are that "Teens are not putting it together that this is the house brand."

The results for the store brand jeans have been quite successful. According to the marketing research firm NPD Group, private label jeans' market share has risen in the 2000s. Levi's, the market leader, has seen their market share drop over the same time period. Levi's drop is also indicative for the big brand names nationwide. These impressive results are encouraging other stores to consider introducing their own label jeans to capture a portion of the teenage market.[8] ■

As in the case of the private label jeans, a problem audit, which involves extensive interaction between the DM and the researcher, can greatly facilitate problem definition by determining the underlying causes. The interaction between the researcher and the DM is facilitated when one or more people in the client organization serve as a liaison and form a team with the marketing researcher. In order to be fruitful, the interaction between the DM and the researcher should be characterized by the seven Cs:

1. *Communication.* Free exchange of ideas between the DM and researcher is essential.
2. *Cooperation.* Marketing research is a team project in which both parties (DM and researcher) must cooperate.
3. *Confidence.* The interaction between the DM and the researcher should be guided by mutual trust.
4. *Candor.* There should not be any hidden agendas, and an attitude of openness should prevail.
5. *Closeness.* Feelings of warmth and closeness should characterize the relationship between the DM and the researcher.
6. *Continuity.* The DM and the researcher must interact continually rather than sporadically.
7. *Creativity.* The interaction between the DM and the researcher should be creative rather than formulaic.

ACTIVE RESEARCH

Sprite: The Third Largest Soft Drink Brand

Visit www.coca-cola.com and www.sprite.com and obtain as much information about the marketing program of Sprite as you can. Write a brief report.

As the brand manager for Sprite, the third largest soft drink brand, you are concerned about improving the performance of the brand. Identify possible symptoms that indicate to you that the performance of Sprite is below expectations.

You are conducting marketing research for Sprite to help improve the performance of the brand. Identify possible underlying causes that might be contributing to the lack of performance.

Interviews with Industry Experts

In addition to discussions with the DM, interviews with industry experts, individuals knowledgeable about the firm and the industry, may help formulate the marketing research problem.[9] These experts may be found both inside and outside the firm. If the notion of experts is broadened to include people very knowledgeable about the general topic being investigated, then these interviews are also referred to as an **experience survey** or the **key-informant technique**. Another variation of this in a technological context is the **lead-user survey** that involves obtaining information from the lead users of the technology. Typically, expert information is obtained by unstructured personal interviews, without administering a formal questionnaire. It is helpful, however, to prepare a list of topics to be covered during the interview. The order in which these topics are covered and the questions to ask should not be predetermined but decided as the interview progresses. This allows greater flexibility in capturing the insights of the experts. The purpose of interviewing experts is to help define the marketing research problem rather than to develop a conclusive solution. Unfortunately, two potential difficulties may arise when seeking advice from experts:

1. Some individuals who claim to be knowledgeable and are eager to participate may not really possess expertise.
2. It may be difficult to locate and obtain help from experts who are outside the client organization.

For these reasons, interviews with experts are more useful in conducting marketing research for industrial firms and for products of a technical nature, where it is relatively easy to identify and approach the experts. This method is also helpful in situations where little information is available from other sources, as in the case of radically new products. The Internet can be searched to find industry experts outside of the client's organization. By going to industry sites and newsgroups (e.g., groups.google.com), you can find access to many knowledgeable industry experts. You could also do searches on the topic at hand and follow up on any postings or FAQs. Experts can provide valuable insights in modifying or repositioning existing products, as illustrated by the repositioning of Diet Cherry Coke.

experience survey
Interviews with people very knowledgeable about the general topic being investigated.

key-informant technique
Another name for experience surveys, i.e., interviews with people very knowledgeable about the general topic being investigated

lead-user survey
Interviews with lead users of the technology.

Real Research   Cherry Picking: The Repositioning of Diet Cherry Coke

As of 2009, Coca-Cola (www.coca-cola.com) is still the world's leading manufacturer, marketer, and distributor of nonalcoholic beverages to more than 200 countries, with more than 2,800 beverage products. Sales of Diet Cherry Coke had been languishing, however, down from more than 8 million cases sold in the peak years. Coke system bottlers had begun to cut back distribution of Diet Cherry Coke. Faced with this issue, Coca-Cola had to determine the cause of such a decline in sales. When industry experts were consulted, the real problem was identified: Diet Cherry Coke was not positioned correctly. These experts emphasized that brand image was a key factor influencing soft drink sales, and Diet Cherry Coke was perceived as conventional and old-fashioned, an image inconsistent with that of Cherry Coke. Hence, the marketing research problem was identified as measuring the image and positioning of Diet Cherry Coke. The research undertaken confirmed the diagnosis of the industry experts and provided several useful insights.

Based on the research results, the product was repositioned to align it more closely to the image of Cherry Coke. The aim was to target younger drinkers. The packaging was remade to also be more consistent with the Cherry Coke packaging. Bolder, edgy graphics were used to appeal to the youth segment. Finally, Diet Cherry Coke was placed with Cherry Coke in a teen-targeted promotional giveaway. Positioning Diet Cherry Coke as a youthful soft drink and targeting the teenage segment led to a turnaround and increased sales. Sales have shown an upward trajectory since thanks to the industry experts who helped identify the real problem.[10] ■

The Diet Cherry Coke example points to the key role of industry experts. However, information obtained from the DM and the industry experts should be supplemented with the available secondary data.

ACTIVE RESEARCH

Wal-Mart: The Largest Retailer!

Visit www.walmart.com and search the Internet using a search engine as well as your library's online databases to identify the challenges and opportunities facing Wal-Mart, the largest retailer in the United States.

Visit groups.google.com and survey the postings in retailing newsgroups to identify an expert in retailing. Interview this expert (via telephone or online) to identify the challenges and opportunities facing Wal-Mart.

As the CEO of Wal-Mart, what marketing strategies would you formulate to overcome these challenges and capitalize on the opportunities?

Secondary Data Analysis

secondary data
Data collected for some purpose other than the problem at hand.

primary data
Data originated by the researcher specifically to address the research problem.

Secondary data are data collected for some purpose other than the problem at hand. **Primary data**, on the other hand, are originated by the researcher for the specific purpose of addressing the research problem. Secondary data include information made available by business and government sources, commercial marketing research firms, and computerized databases. Secondary data are an economical and quick source of background information. Analysis of available secondary data is an essential step in the problem definition process: Primary data should not be collected until the available secondary data have been fully analyzed. Given the tremendous importance of secondary data, this topic will be discussed in detail in Chapter 4, which also further discusses the differences between secondary and primary data.

It is often helpful to supplement secondary data analysis with qualitative research.

Qualitative Research

qualitative research
An unstructured, exploratory research methodology based on small samples intended to provide insight and understanding of the problem setting.

Information obtained from the DM, industry experts, and secondary data may not be sufficient to define the research problem. Sometimes qualitative research must be undertaken to gain an understanding of the problem and its underlying factors. **Qualitative research** is unstructured, exploratory in nature, based on small samples, and may utilize popular qualitative techniques such as focus groups (group interviews), word association (asking respondents to indicate their first responses to stimulus words), and depth interviews (one-on-one interviews that probe the respondents' thoughts in detail). Other exploratory research techniques, such as pilot surveys and

pilot surveys
Surveys that tend to be less structured than large-scale surveys in that they generally contain more open-ended questions and the sample size is much smaller.

case studies
Case studies involve an intensive examination of a few selected cases of the phenomenon of interest. Cases could be customers, stores, or other units.

case studies, may also be undertaken to gain insights into the phenomenon of interest. **Pilot surveys** tend to be less structured than large-scale surveys in that they generally contain more open-ended questions and the sample size is much smaller. **Case studies** involve an intensive examination of a few selected cases of the phenomenon of interest. The cases could be consumers, stores, firms, or a variety of other units such as markets, Web sites, and so on. The data are obtained from the company, external secondary sources, and by conducting lengthy unstructured interviews with people knowledgeable about the phenomenon of interest. In the department store project, valuable insights into factors affecting store patronage were obtained in a case study comparing the five best stores with the five worst stores.

Exploratory research is discussed in more detail in Chapter 3, and qualitative research techniques are discussed in detail in Chapter 5.

Although research undertaken at this stage may not be conducted in a formal way, it can provide valuable insights into the problem, as illustrated by Harley-Davidson in the opening example. Industry experts indicated the importance of brand loyalty, which also emerged as a major factor in focus groups. Secondary data revealed that most motorcycle owners also owned automobiles such as cars, SUVs, and trucks. Focus groups further indicated that motorcycles were used primarily as a means of recreation, and all these factors were useful in defining the problem as determining if customers would be loyal buyers of Harley-Davidson in the long term. Procter & Gamble (P&G) provides another illustration of the role of qualitative research in defining the marketing research problem.

Real Research

P&G's Peep into Privacy

P&G, the maker of Tide laundry detergent, Pampers diapers, and Crest toothpaste, is sending video crews and cameras into about 80 households around the world, hoping to capture, on tape, life's daily routines and procedures in all their boring glory. P&G thinks the exercise will yield a mountain of priceless insights into consumer behavior that more traditional methods—focus groups, interviews, home visits—may have missed. People tend to have selective memories when talking to a market researcher. They might say, for example, that they brush their teeth every morning or indulge in just a few potato chips when in fact they often forget to brush and eat the whole bag.

Videotaping, P&G hopes, will help it get at the whole truth. Initially, the study followed families in the United Kingdom, Italy, Germany, and China. After a subject family agrees to participate, one or two ethnographer-filmmakers arrive at the home when the alarm clock rings in the morning and stay until bedtime, usually for a four-day stretch. To be as unobtrusive as possible, the crew might at certain times leave the camera alone in a room with the subjects or let them film themselves. There are ground rules. If friends come over, the subjects must inform them that they are being filmed. The subjects and filmmakers agree on boundaries ahead of time: Most bedroom and bathroom activities aren't taped. A small London research firm, Everyday Lives Ltd. (www.edlglobal.net), runs the program for P&G.

Of course, P&G is acting on the information obtained by such research to come up with innovative products that cater to the market needs. For example, some of the movies at customers' homes revealed that one of the biggest challenges faced by working mothers is their hectic mornings. In between getting the kids off to school and juggling a host of other duties, they still want to make sure they leave the house looking their best. So P&G defined the marketing research problem as determining the potential for multipurpose products that could help this segment of customers by making their makeup routine easier. Subsequent research led to the launch of multipurpose products such as a CoverGirl cosmetic that is a moisturizer, foundation, and sunscreen all rolled into one.[11] ■

environmental context of the problem
Consists of the factors that have an impact on the definition of the marketing research problem, including past information and forecasts, resources and constraints of the firm, objectives of the decision maker, buyer behavior, legal environment, economic environment, and marketing and technological skills of the firm.

The insights gained from qualitative research, along with discussions with decision makers, interviews with industry experts, and secondary data analysis, help the researcher to understand the environmental context of the problem.

Environmental Context of the Problem

To understand the background of a marketing research problem, the researcher must understand the client's firm and industry. In particular, the researcher should analyze the factors that have an impact on the definition of the marketing research problem. These factors, encompassing the **environmental context of the problem**, include past information and forecasts pertaining to the

FIGURE 2.2

Factors to Be Considered in the Environmental Context of the Problem

Past Information and Forecasts

Resources and Constraints

Objectives

Buyer Behavior

Legal Environment

Economic Environment

Marketing and Technological Skills

industry and the firm, resources and constraints of the firm, objectives of the decision maker, buyer behavior, legal environment, economic environment, and marketing and technological skills of the firm, as shown in Figure 2.2. Each of these factors is discussed briefly.[12]

Past Information and Forecasts

Past information and forecasts of trends with respect to sales, market share, profitability, technology, population, demographics, and lifestyle can help the researcher understand the underlying marketing research problem. Where appropriate, this kind of analysis should be carried out at the industry and firm levels. For example, if a firm's sales have decreased but industry sales have increased, the problems will be very different than if the industry sales have also decreased. In the former case, the problems are likely to be specific to the firm.[13]

Past information and forecasts can be valuable in uncovering potential opportunities and problems. The following example shows how marketers can exploit potential opportunities by correctly assessing potential demand.

Real Research   Smarte Carte Becomes Smart with Marketing Research

Smarte Carte, Inc. (www.smartecarte.com), with its headquarters in St. Paul, Minnesota, is the leader in baggage cart, locker, and stroller services at more than 1,000 airports, train stations, bus terminals, shopping centers, and entertainment facilities around the world. The company recently developed a new locker using "smart" technology. They wanted to know which would be the ideal markets for this new product and sought the help of Emerge Marketing (www.emergemarketing.com).

Expanding into new markets requires knowledge of each market's size and growth potential, barriers to entry, and competitors. Using qualitative research (like focus groups and depth interviews) and secondary research methods (like Census Bureau information and Nielsen ratings), Emerge Marketing developed baseline information for a number of possible market segments. Based on the key requirements identified for each market, it was found that the new locker technology would be a good fit for amusement parks, ski areas, and water parks. The study had revealed that the features offered by the new product suited the needs of these markets segments the best. Moreover, the competitive picture was most favorable in these segments. Thus, the problem definition was narrowed to determining the demand potential for the new technology in these three segments (amusement parks, ski areas, and water parks). Further research was then conducted to quantify the market in terms of potential sales in these segments so that Smarte Carte could develop products, manufacturing capabilities, and budgets accordingly. Based on the study, Smarte Carte fine-tuned the product for these three markets. For example, keyless electronic storage lockers were developed with the water parks in mind. Visitors could lock their valuables in this locker and then enjoy their rides without having to worry about the safety of their locker keys.[14] ■

ACTIVE RESEARCH

The Lunch on the Go Crowd

Obtain from secondary sources data on the sales of restaurants for the past year and sales forecasts for the next two to five years.

How would you obtain this information using the Internet?

You are the marketing manager for Houston's restaurants. You come across information stating that more and more people are having lunch on the go and that this trend is expected to continue for the next five years. What kind of problems and opportunities does this information suggest?

This example illustrates the usefulness of past information and forecasts, which can be especially valuable if resources are limited and there are other constraints on the organization.

Resources and Constraints

To formulate a marketing research problem of appropriate scope, it is necessary to take into account both the resources available, such as money and research skills, and the constraints on the organization, such as cost and time. Proposing a large-scale project that would cost $100,000 when only $40,000 has been budgeted obviously will not meet management approval. In many instances, the scope of the marketing research problem may have to be reduced to accommodate budget constraints. This might be done, as in the department store project, by confining the investigation to major geographical markets rather than conducting the project on a national basis.

It is often possible to extend the scope of a project appreciably with only a marginal increase in costs. This can considerably enhance the usefulness of the project, thereby increasing the probability that management will approve it. Time constraints can be important when decisions must be made quickly.[15] A project for Fisher-Price, a major toy manufacturer, involving mall intercept interviews in six major cities (Chicago, Fresno, Kansas City, New York, Philadelphia, and San Diego) had to be completed in six weeks. Why this rush? The results had to be presented at an upcoming board meeting where a major (go/no go) decision was to be made about a new product introduction.[16]

Other constraints, such as those imposed by the client firm's personnel, organizational structure and culture, or decision-making styles, should be identified to determine the scope of the research project. However, constraints should not be allowed to diminish the value of the research to the decision maker or compromise the integrity of the research process. If a research project is worth doing, it is worth doing well. In instances where the resources are too limited to allow a high-quality project, the firm should be advised not to undertake formal marketing research. For this reason, it becomes necessary to identify resources and constraints, a task that can be better understood when examined in the light of the objectives of the organization and the decision maker.

Objectives

objectives
Goals of the organization and of the decision maker must be considered in order to conduct successful marketing research.

Decisions are made to accomplish **objectives**. The formulation of the management decision problem must be based on a clear understanding of two types of objectives: (1) the organizational objectives (the goals of the organization), and (2) the personal objectives of the decision maker (DM). For the project to be successful, it must serve the objectives of the organization and of the DM. This, however, is not an easy task.

The decision maker rarely formulates personal or organizational objectives accurately. Rather, it is likely that these objectives will be stated in terms that have no operational significance, such as "to improve corporate image." Direct questioning of the DM is unlikely to reveal all of the relevant objectives. The researcher needs skill to extract these objectives. An effective technique is to confront the decision makers with each of the possible solutions to a problem and ask whether they would follow that course of action. If a "no" answer is received, use further probing to uncover objectives that are not served by the course of action.

Buyer Behavior

buyer behavior
A body of knowledge that tries to understand and predict consumers' reactions based on an individual's specific characteristics.

Buyer behavior is a central component of the environmental context. In most marketing decisions, the problem can ultimately be traced to predicting the response of buyers to specific actions by the marketer. An understanding of the underlying buyer behavior can provide valuable insights into the problem. The buyer behavior factors that should be considered include:

1. The number and geographical location of the buyers and nonbuyers
2. Demographic and psychological characteristics
3. Product consumption habits and the consumption of related product categories
4. Media consumption behavior and response to promotions
5. Price sensitivity
6. Retail outlets patronized
7. Buyer preferences

The following example shows how an understanding of the relevant buyer behavior helps in identifying the causes underlying a problem.

Real Research

How "Got Milk?" Got Sales

Milk sales had declined in the 1980s and early 1990s, and the milk industry needed to find a way to increase sales. An advertising company was hired by the California Milk Processor Board, which in turn hired M/A/R/C Research (www.marcresearch.com) to conduct a telephone tracking survey of Californians over age 11. To identify the cause of low milk sales, the research company sought to understand the underlying behavior of consumers toward milk. Through extensive focus groups, household observations, and telephone surveys, M/A/R/C was able to understand consumer behavior underlying milk consumption. This research revealed how people used milk, what made them want it, with what foods they used it, and how they felt when they were deprived of it. They found that 88 percent of milk is consumed at home and that milk was not the central drink of the average person, but it was used in combination with certain foods such as cereal, cakes, pastries, and so forth. However, milk was strongly missed when there was none around. The advertising agency, Goodby, Silverstein & Partners, developed an ad campaign around consumer behavior with respect to milk and launched the well-known "milk mustache" campaign with the "Got Milk?" tag line. This creative advertising was a real attention getter, showing celebrities from Joan Lunden to Rhea Perlman and Danny DeVito sporting the famous white mustache. Through marketing research and the advertising campaign, milk sales increased and continued to be stable through 2009. But beyond sales, "Got Milk?" has become part of the American language. Some consumers have even said that their kids walk into the kitchen with a cookie asking for a "glass of got milk?"[17] ■

An understanding of the consumer behavior underlying milk consumption was critical to identifying the real causes that led to the decline in milk consumption.

Source: National Fluid Milk Processor Promotion Board.

The decline in milk consumption could be attributed to changes in the sociocultural environment, which include demographic trends and consumer tastes. In addition, the legal environment and the economic environment can have an impact on the behavior of consumers and the definition of the marketing research problem.

Legal Environment

legal environment
Regulatory policies and norms within which organizations must operate.

The **legal environment** includes public policies, laws, government agencies, and pressure groups that influence and regulate various organizations and individuals in society. Important areas of law include patents, trademarks, royalties, trade agreements, taxes, and tariffs. Federal laws have an impact on each element of the marketing mix. In addition, laws have been passed to regulate specific industries. The legal environment can have an important bearing on the definition of the marketing research problem, as can the economic environment.

Economic Environment

economic environment
The economic environment consists of income, prices, savings, credit, and general economic conditions.

Along with the legal environment, another important component of the environmental context is the **economic environment**, which is comprised of purchasing power, gross income, disposable income, discretionary income, prices, savings, credit availability, and general economic conditions. The general state of the economy (rapid growth, slow growth, recession, or stagflation) influences the willingness of consumers and businesses to take on credit and spend on big-ticket items. Thus, the economic environment can have important implications for marketing research problems.

Marketing and Technological Skills

A company's expertise with each element of the marketing mix, as well as its general level of marketing and technological skills, affects the nature and scope of the marketing research project. For example, the introduction of a new product that requires sophisticated technology may not be a viable course if the firm lacks the skills to manufacture or market it.

A firm's marketing and technological skills greatly influence the marketing programs and strategies that can be implemented. At a broader level, other elements of the technological environment should be considered. Technological advances, such as the continuing development of computers, have had a dramatic impact on marketing research. To illustrate, computerized checkout lanes allow supermarkets to monitor daily consumer demand for products and make the scanner data available to the researcher. It is possible to obtain precise information on retail sales, not only of the firm's brands but also of competing brands. The speed and accuracy of data collection enable the researcher to investigate intricate problems such as the daily changes in market share during a promotion.

Many of the factors to be considered in the environmental context of the problem can be researched via the Internet. Past information and forecasts of trends can be found by searching for the appropriate information with search engines. For client-specific information, the user can go to the company home page and get the information from there. Investor Communication Solutions (www.broadridge.com) is an effective way to research a company and find information on financial reports, company news, corporate profiles, or annual reports. Finally, you can go to sites such as Yahoo! Business or Finance or www.quicken.com to find analysts' views of the company. Firms such as D&B (www.dnb.com) create company databases that can be accessed through a subscription or reports that can be purchased on a one-time basis.

Environmental Context and Problem Definition

After gaining an adequate understanding of the environmental context of the problem, the researcher can define the management decision problem and the marketing research problem. This process was illustrated in the opening Harley-Davidson example. Forecasts called for an increase in consumer spending on recreation and entertainment well into the year 2015. Empowered by the Internet, consumers in the twenty-first century became increasingly sophisticated and value conscious. Yet brand image and brand loyalty played a significant role in buyer behavior with well-known brands continuing to command a premium. Clearly, Harley-Davidson had the necessary resources and marketing and technological skills to achieve its objective of being the dominant motorcycle brand on a global basis. The management decision problem was: Should Harley-Davidson invest to produce more motorcycles? The marketing research problem was to determine if the customers would be loyal buyers of Harley-Davidson in the long term. The following section provides further understanding of the management decision problem and the marketing research problem.

Management Decision Problem and Marketing Research Problem

management decision problem
The problem confronting the decision maker. It asks what the decision maker needs to do.

marketing research problem
A problem that entails determining what information is needed and how it can be obtained in the most feasible way.

The **management decision problem** asks what the DM needs to do, whereas the **marketing research problem** asks what information is needed and how it can best be obtained (Table 2.1). Research can provide the necessary information to make a sound decision.[18] The management decision problem is action oriented. It is concerned with the possible actions the DM can take. How should the loss of market share be addressed? Should the market be segmented differently? Should a new product be introduced? Should the promotional budget be increased? In contrast, the marketing research problem is information oriented. It involves determining what information is needed and how that information can be obtained effectively and efficiently. Whereas the management decision problem focuses on symptoms, the marketing research problem focuses on underlying causes.

Consider, for example, the loss of market share for a particular product line. The DM's decision problem is how to recover this loss. Alternative courses of action include modifying existing products, introducing new products, changing other elements in the marketing mix, and segmenting the market. Suppose the DM and the researcher (R) believe that the problem is caused by inappropriate segmentation of the market and want research to provide information on this issue. The research problem would then become the identification and evaluation of an alternative basis for segmenting the market. Note that this process is interactive. The department store project example illustrates further the distinction between the management decision problem and the marketing research problem as well as the interactive nature of the problem definition process.

Project Research   Defining the Problem

DM: We have seen a decline in the patronage of our store.

R: How do you know that?

DM: Well, it is reflected in our sales and market share.

R: Why do you think your patronage has declined?

DM: I wish I knew!

R: What about competition?

DM: I suspect we are better than competition on some factors and worse than them on others.

R: How do the customers view your store?

DM: I think most of them view it positively, although we may have a weak area or two.

After a series of dialogues with the DM and other key managers, analysis of secondary data, and qualitative research, the problem was identified as follows:

Management Decision Problem

What should be done to improve the patronage of Sears?

Marketing Research Problem

Determine the relative strengths and weaknesses of Sears vis-à-vis other major competitors with respect to factors that influence store patronage. ■

TABLE 2.1	
Management Decision Problems Versus the Marketing Research Problem	
Management Decision Problem	Marketing Research Problem
Asks what the decision maker needs to do	Asks what information is needed and how it should be obtained
Action oriented	Information oriented
Focuses on symptoms	Focuses on the underlying causes

The following examples further distinguish between the management decision problem and the marketing research problem:

MANAGEMENT DECISION PROBLEM	MARKETING RESEARCH PROBLEM
Should a new product be introduced?	To determine consumer preferences and purchase intentions for the proposed new product
Should the advertising campaign be changed?	To determine the effectiveness of the current advertising campaign
Should the price of the brand be increased?	To determine the price elasticity of demand and the impact on sales and profits of various levels of price changes

conceptual map
A way to link the broad statement of the marketing research problem to the management decision problem.

While distinct, the marketing research problem has to be closely linked to the management decision problem. A good way to link the broad statement of the marketing research problem with the management decision problem is through the use of a conceptual map. A **conceptual map** involves the following three components:

Management wants to *(take an action)*.

Therefore, we should study *(topic)*.

So that we can explain *(question)*.

The first line states the rationale for the question and the project. This is the management decision problem. The second line of the conceptual map declares what broader topic is being investigated. The third line implies the question being investigated—the who/how/why that needs to be explained. Thus, the second and third lines define the broad marketing research problem. An example of the conceptual map for AT&T follows:

Management wants to (develop retention programs that will retain 90 percent of heavy users of wireless services and lead to 10 percent higher sales over the next 2 years).

Therefore, we should study (heavy-user loyalty).

So that we can explain (what will be the most important variables in retaining these customers over the next 2 years).

As can be seen, the preceding example provides valuable definitions of the management decision problem and the broad marketing research problems that are closely linked. The problem is now focused on a segment of customers (heavy users) and one behavior of these customers (staying with the company over the next 2 years). Measurable results, such as "90 percent retention of heavy users," are included, as well as a company goal (10 percent increase in sales over the next 2 years). This distinction and linkage between the management decision problem and the marketing research problem helps us in understanding how the marketing research problem should be defined.

Defining the Marketing Research Problem

The general rule to be followed in defining the marketing research problem is that the definition should (1) allow the researcher to obtain all the information needed to address the management decision problem, and (2) guide the researcher in proceeding with the project. Researchers make two common errors in problem definition. The first arises when the research problem is defined

FIGURE 2.3

Proper Definition of the Marketing Research Problem

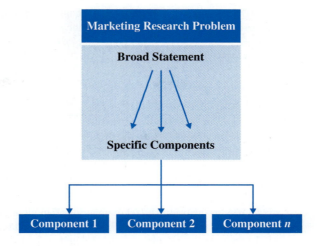

broad statement
The initial statement of the marketing research problem that provides an appropriate perspective on the problem.

specific components
The second part of the marketing research problem definition. The specific components focus on the key aspects of the problem and provide clear guidelines on how to proceed further.

too broadly. A broad definition does not provide clear guidelines for the subsequent steps involved in the project. Some examples of overly broad marketing research problem definitions are (1) develop a marketing strategy for the brand, (2) improve the competitive position of the firm, or (3) improve the company's image. These are not specific enough to suggest an approach to the problem or a research design.

The second type of error is just the opposite: The marketing research problem is defined too narrowly. A narrow focus may preclude consideration of some courses of action, particularly those that are innovative and may not be obvious. It may also prevent the researcher from addressing important components of the management decision problem. For example, in a project conducted for a major consumer products firm, the management problem was how to respond to a price cut initiated by a competitor. The alternative courses of action initially identified by the firm's research staff were (1) decrease the price of the firm's brand to match the competitor's price cut; (2) maintain price but increase advertising heavily; (3) decrease the price somewhat, without matching the competitor's price, and moderately increase advertising. None of these alternatives seemed promising. When outside marketing research experts were brought in, the problem was redefined as improving the market share and profitability of the product line. Qualitative research indicated that in blind tests consumers could not differentiate products offered under different brand names. Furthermore, consumers relied on price as an indicator of product quality. These findings led to a creative alternative: Increase the price of the existing brand and introduce two new brands—one priced to match the competitor and the other priced to undercut it. This strategy was implemented, leading to an increase in market share and profitability.

The likelihood of committing either type of error in problem definition can be reduced by stating the marketing research problem in broad, general terms and identifying its specific components (see Figure 2.3). The **broad statement** provides perspective on the problem and acts as a safeguard against committing the second type of error. The **specific components** focus on the key aspects of the problem and provide clear guidelines on how to proceed further, thereby reducing the likelihood of the first type of error. Examples of appropriate marketing research problem definitions follow.

Project Research   Marketing Research Problem Definition

In the department store project, the marketing research problem is to determine the relative strengths and weaknesses of Sears, vis-à-vis other major competitors, with respect to factors that influence store patronage. Specifically, research should provide information on the following questions.

1. What criteria do households use when selecting department stores?
2. How do households evaluate Sears and competing stores in terms of the choice criteria identified in question 1?
3. Which stores are patronized when shopping for specific product categories?
4. What is the market share of Sears and its competitors for specific product categories?

5. What is the demographic and psychographic profile of the customers of Sears? Does it differ from the profile of customers of competing stores?
6. Can store patronage and preference be explained in terms of store evaluations and customer characteristics? ■

Real Research   Major League Baseball Majors in Research

Major League Baseball (MLB, www.mlb.com) wanted to evaluate the effect of the size and frequency of its nonprice promotions for MLB games. The management decision problem was: Should MLB teams continue with nonprice promotions? The broad marketing research problem was defined as determining the impact of nonprice promotions on attendance at MLB games. Specifically, this research should answer the following questions.

1. What is the overall effect of nonprice promotions on attendance?
2. What is the marginal impact on attendance of additional promotional days?
3. Are nonprice promotions effective in building long-term loyalty?
4. What are the demographic and psychographic characteristics of people who respond to nonprice promotions?

Analysis of a data set containing 1,500 observations revealed that nonprice promotion increases single game attendance by about 14 percent. Additionally, increasing the number of promotions has a negative effect on the marginal impact of each promotion. The loss from this "watering down" effect, however, is outweighed by the gain from having an extra promotion day. Promotion most influences occasional attendees but does not engender long-term loyalty.

Based on these findings, strategic decisions were taken to improve overall revenue by continuing the nonprice promotions, especially during the off-season and games for which sales projections were not impressive. The research results also led to the decision to spread out promotions to reduce the watering-down effect. A correct definition of the problem led to useful findings that when implemented resulted in increased revenues.[19] ■

In the MLB example, the broad statement of the problem focused on gathering information about the effect of nonprice promotions, and the specific components identified the particular items of information that should be obtained. This was also true in the opening Harley-Davidson example, where a broad statement of the marketing research problem was followed by four specific components. Problem definition in the department store project followed a similar pattern.

Once the marketing research problem has been broadly stated and its specific components identified, the researcher is in a position to develop a suitable approach.

A proper definition of the marketing research problem led to research that resulted in the correct use of non-price promotions for MLB games.

Components of the Approach

In the process of developing an approach, we must not lose sight of the goal—the outputs. The outputs of the approach development process should include the following components: objective/theoretical framework, analytical models, research questions, hypotheses, and specification of information needed (see Figure 2.1). Each of these components is discussed in the following sections.

Objective/Theoretical Framework

theory
A conceptual scheme based on foundational statements, or axioms, that are assumed to be true.

objective evidence
Unbiased evidence that is supported by empirical findings.

In general, research should be based on objective evidence and supported by theory. A **theory** is a conceptual scheme based on foundational statements called *axioms*, which are assumed to be true. **Objective evidence** (evidence that is unbiased and supported by empirical findings) is gathered by compiling relevant findings from secondary sources. Likewise, an appropriate theory to guide the research might be identified by reviewing academic literature contained in books, journals, and monographs. The researcher should rely on theory to determine which variables should be investigated. Furthermore, theoretical considerations provide information on how the variables should be operationalized and measured, as well as how the research design and sample should be selected. A theory also serves as a foundation on which the researcher can organize and interpret the findings. "Nothing is so practical as a good theory."[20]

Theory also plays a vital role in influencing the research procedures adopted in basic research. However, applying a theory to a marketing research problem requires creativity on the part of the researcher. A theory may not specify adequately how its abstract constructs (variables) can be embodied in a real-world phenomenon. Moreover, theories are incomplete. They deal with only a subset of variables that exist in the real world. Hence, the researcher must also identify and examine other, nontheoretical, variables.[21]

The department store patronage project illustrates how theory can be used to develop an approach. Review of the retailing literature revealed that the modeling of store patronage in terms of choice criteria had received considerable support.[22] Furthermore, as many as 42 choice criteria had been identified in the literature, and guidelines on operationalizing these variables were provided. This provided an initial pool from which the final eight characteristics included in the questionnaire were selected. Theoretical considerations also suggested that store behavior could be examined via a survey of respondents familiar with department store shopping. The theoretical framework also serves as a foundation for developing an appropriate analytical model.

Analytical Model

analytical model
An explicit specification of a set of variables and their interrelationships designed to represent some real system or process in whole or in part.

verbal models
Analytical models that provide a written representation of the relationships between variables.

graphical models
Analytical models that provide a visual picture of the relationships between variables.

mathematical models
Analytical models that explicitly describe the relationships between variables, usually in equation form.

An **analytical model** is a set of variables and their interrelationships designed to represent, in whole or in part, some real system or process. Models can have many different forms. The most common are verbal, graphical, and mathematical structures. In **verbal models**, the variables and their relationships are stated in prose form. Such models may be mere restatements of the main tenets of a theory. **Graphical models** are visual. They are used to isolate variables and to suggest directions of relationships but are not designed to provide numerical results. They are logical preliminary steps to developing mathematical models. **Mathematical models** explicitly specify the relationships among variables, usually in equation form. These models can be used as guides for formulating the research design and have the advantage of being amenable to manipulation.[23] The different models are illustrated in the context of the department store project.

Project Research   Model Building

Verbal Model

A consumer first becomes aware of a department store. That person then gains an understanding of the store by evaluating the store in terms of the factors comprising the choice criteria. Based on the evaluation, the consumer forms a degree of preference for the store. If preference is strong enough, the consumer will patronize the store.

Graphical Model

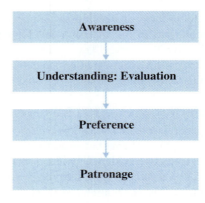

Mathematical Model

$$y = a_0 + \sum_{i=1}^{n} a_i x_i$$

where

y = degree of preference
a_0, a_i = model parameters to be estimated statistically
x_i = store patronage factors that constitute the choice criteria ■

As can be seen from this example, the verbal, graphical, and mathematical models depict the same phenomenon or theoretical framework in different ways. The phenomenon of store patronage stated verbally is represented for clarity through a figure (graphical model) and is put in equation form (mathematical model) for ease of statistical estimation and testing. Graphical models are particularly helpful in conceptualizing an approach to the problem. In the opening Harley-Davidson example, the underlying theory was that brand loyalty is the result of positive beliefs, attitude, affect, and experience with the brand. This theory may be represented by the following graphical model.

The verbal, graphical, and mathematical models complement each other and help the researcher identify relevant research questions and hypotheses.

Research Questions

research questions
Research questions are refined statements of the specific components of the problem.

Research questions (RQs) are refined statements of the specific components of the problem. Although the components of the problem define the problem in specific terms, further detail may be needed to develop an approach. Each component of the problem may have to be broken down into subcomponents or research questions. Research questions ask what specific information is required with respect to the problem components. If the research questions are answered by the research, then the information obtained should aid the decision maker. The formulation of the research questions should be guided not only by the problem definition, but also by the theoretical framework and the analytical model adopted. For a given problem component, there are likely to be several research questions, as in the case of the department store project.

Project Research   Research Questions

The fifth component of the research problem was the psychological profile of Sears' customers. In the context of psychological characteristics, several research questions were asked about the customers of Sears.

- Do they exhibit store loyalty?
- Are they heavy users of credit?

- Are they more conscious of personal appearance as compared to customers of competing stores?
- Do they combine shopping with eating out?

The research questions were then further refined by precisely defining the variables and determining how they were to be operationalized. To illustrate, how should the use of Sears credit be measured? It could be measured in any of the following ways.

1. Whether the customer holds a Sears credit card
2. Whether the customer uses the Sears credit card
3. The number of times the Sears credit card was used in a specified time period
4. The dollar amount charged to the Sears credit card during a specified time period ■

The theoretical framework and the analytical model play a significant role in the operationalization and measurement of variables specified by the research questions. Whereas in the department store project, the literature reviewed did not provide any definitive measure of store credit, the mathematical model could incorporate any of the alternative measures. Thus, it was decided to include all four measures of store credit in the study. Research questions may be further refined into one or more hypotheses.

Hypotheses

hypothesis
An unproven statement or proposition about a factor or phenomenon that is of interest to the researcher.

A **hypothesis** (H) is an unproven statement or proposition about a factor or phenomenon that is of interest to the researcher. It may, for example, be a tentative statement about relationships between two or more variables as stipulated by the theoretical framework or the analytical model. Often, a hypothesis is a possible answer to the research question. Hypotheses go beyond research questions because they are statements of relationships or propositions rather than merely questions to which answers are sought. Whereas research questions are interrogative, hypotheses are declarative and can be tested empirically (see Chapter 15). An important role of a hypothesis is to suggest variables to be included in the research design. The relationship among the marketing research problem, research questions, and hypotheses, along with the influence of the objective/theoretical framework and analytical models, is described in Figure 2.4 and illustrated by the following example from the department store project.[24]

Project Research | Hypotheses

The following hypotheses were formulated in relation to the research question on store loyalty:[25]

H1: Customers who are store loyal are less knowledgeable about the shopping environment.
H2: Store-loyal customers are more risk averse than are nonloyal customers.

These hypotheses guided the research by ensuring that variables measuring knowledge of the shopping environment and propensity to take risks were included in the research design. ■

Unfortunately, it may not be possible to formulate hypotheses in all situations. Sometimes sufficient information is not available to develop hypotheses. At other times, the most reasonable statement of a hypothesis may be a trivial restatement of the research question. For example:

RQ: Do customers of Sears exhibit store loyalty?
H: Customers of Sears are loyal.

FIGURE 2.4

Development of Research Questions and Hypotheses

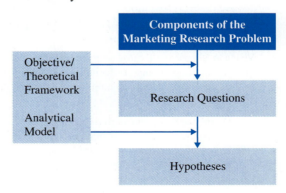

Hypotheses are an important part of the approach to the problem. When stated in operational terms, as H1 and H2 in the department store example, they provide guidelines on what, and how, data are to be collected and analyzed. When operational hypotheses are stated using symbolic notation, they are commonly referred to as *statistical hypotheses*. A research question may have more than one hypothesis associated with it, as in the Harley-Davidson example and the one that follows.

Real Research   ## The Taste of Comfort

In the midst of an insecure global environment in 2009, nothing was more comforting than trusted, familiar foods and treats. Do certain foods provide comfort under different situations in people's lives? For instance, does chicken soup make people feel better on a rainy day or when they have a cold, partially because they may have eaten chicken soup during the same situations when they were growing up? Marketing research was conducted to investigate comfort foods. The specific research questions and the associated hypotheses were:

RQ1: What foods are considered to be comfort foods?
H1:   Potato chips are considered comfort food.
H2:   Ice cream is considered comfort food.
RQ2: When do people eat comfort foods?
H3:   People eat comfort foods when they are in a good mood.
H4:   People eat comfort foods when they are in a bad mood.
RQ3: How do people become attached to comfort foods?
H5:   People are attached to comfort foods that are consistent with their personality.
H6:   People are attached to comfort foods because of past associations.

In-depth telephone interviews were conducted with 411 people across the United States. The purpose was to find out what people's favorite comfort foods were and how these products became comfort foods. From the qualitative answers, a 20-minute quantitative phone survey was developed for a larger sample size of 1,005.

The results showed that America's favorite comfort food is potato chips, followed by ice cream, cookies, and candy. Thus, both H1 and H2 were supported. Many respondents also considered natural, homemade, or even "healthy" foods such as meats, soups, and vegetables comfort foods. The psychological comfort of these foods may provide a powerful impact on people's food choices just as the taste does for snack foods.

People are also more likely to eat comfort foods when they are in good moods than sad: jubilant (86 percent), celebrating (74 percent), got the blues (39 percent), the blahs (52 percent), and lonely (39 percent). Thus, H3 had stronger support than H4, although both were supported.

The results also showed that past associations with products and personality identification are the two main reasons why foods become comfort foods, thus supporting H5 and H6. Foods often remind people of specific events during their lives, which is why they eat them for comfort. Some foods also help people form their identities because the products are consistent with their personality. For instance, meat and potatoes are staples for the macho, all-American male, which may explain why many males do not want to try healthier soy products.

The more marketers know about the psychology behind foods, at both the associative and personality levels, the better they will be at establishing new brands, as well as packaging and advertising existing brands that are already considered comfort foods and have their own brand personalities. For example, Frito-Lay's Baked Lays brand of low-fat potato chips has been very successful. Frito-Lay combined the fact that chips are fun to eat with the wave of health-conscious people in the United States. The slogan for the new brand was "Taste the Fun, Not the Fat," which affects one's concept of wanting a fun lifestyle. The fun product continues to be comforting while reducing people's guilt by its low fat content.[26] ∎

Experiential Research   ## Marketing Research Begins at Home (or Near the Campus)

Visit a local business located near your campus. Interview the business owner or manager and identify some of the marketing challenges facing this business. Also, interview an expert in this industry. Search and analyze secondary data pertaining to this business and the industry and identify the environmental context of the problem.

1. Define the management decision problem.
2. Define the marketing research problem.
3. Develop a graphical model explaining the consumer choice process leading to the patronage of this business or its competitors.
4. Develop an appropriate research question and hypothesis. ∎

Specification of Information Needed

By focusing on each component of the problem and the analytical framework and models, research questions, and hypotheses, the researcher can determine what information should be obtained in the marketing research project. It is helpful to carry out this exercise for each component of the problem and make a list specifying all the information that should be collected. Let us consider the department store project and focus on the components of the problem identified earlier in this chapter to determine the information that should be obtained from the respondents selected for the survey.

Project Research   ## Specification of Information Needed

Component 1

This component involves the criteria households use to select a department store. Based on the process outlined earlier in this chapter, the researcher identified the following factors as part of the choice criteria: quality of merchandise, variety and assortment of merchandise, returns and adjustment policy, service of store personnel, prices, convenience of location, layout of store, credit and billing policies. The respondents should be asked to rate the importance of each factor as it influences their store selection.

Component 2

This component is concerned with competition. The researcher identified nine department stores as competitors of Sears based on discussions with management. The respondents should be asked to evaluate Sears and its nine competitors on the eight choice criteria factors.

Component 3

Specific product categories are the focus of this component. Sixteen different product categories were selected, including women's dresses, women's sportswear, lingerie and body fashion, junior merchandise, men's apparel, cosmetics, jewelry, shoes, sheets and towels, furniture and bedding, and draperies. The respondents should be asked whether they shop at each of the 10 stores for each of the 16 product categories.

Component 4

No additional information needs to be obtained from the respondents.

Component 5

Information on the standard demographic characteristics should be obtained from the respondents. Based on the process outlined earlier in this chapter, the researcher identified the following psychographic characteristics as relevant: store loyalty, credit use, appearance consciousness, and combining shopping with eating. Information on these variables should also be obtained from the respondents.

Component 6

No additional information needs to be obtained from the respondents.

Project Activities

Review the discussion of the Sears project given in this chapter.

1. Do you think that the marketing research problem is appropriately defined, given the management decision problem facing Sears? Why or why not?
2. Develop an alternative graphical model of how consumers select a department store.
3. Develop two research questions and two hypotheses corresponding to components 1 to 4 and 6 of the marketing research problem. ■

International Marketing Research

The precise definition of the marketing research problem is more difficult in international marketing research than in domestic marketing research. Unfamiliarity with the environmental factors of the country where the research is being conducted can greatly increase the difficulty of understanding the problem's environmental context and uncovering its causes.

Real Research   Heinz Ketchup Could Not Catch Up in Brazil

In 2009, Heinz (www.heinz.com) was selling products in more than 200 countries and sales were topping $10 billion with approximately 60 percent of revenue coming from overseas. Despite good track records inland and overseas, H. J. Heinz Co. failed in Brazil, a market that seemed to be South America's biggest and most promising. Heinz entered into a joint venture with Citrosuco Paulista, a giant orange juice exporter, because of the future possibility of buying the profitable company. Yet the sales of its products, including ketchup, did not take off. Where was the problem? A problem audit revealed that the company lacked a strong local distribution system. Heinz lost control of the distribution because it worked on consignment. Distribution could not reach 25 percent penetration. The other related problem was that Heinz concentrated on neighborhood shops because this strategy was successful in Mexico. However, the problem audit revealed that 75 percent of the grocery shopping in São Paulo is done in supermarkets and not the smaller shops. Although Mexico and Brazil may appear to have similar cultural and demographic characteristics, consumer behavior can vary greatly. A closer and intensive look at the Brazilian food distribution system and the behavior of consumers could have averted this failure. Heinz, however, is looking more closely at Asia, especially China, where the company markets baby food and where 22 million babies are born every year.[27] ■

As the Heinz example illustrates, many international marketing efforts fail, not because research was not conducted, but because the relevant environmental factors were not taken into account. Generally, this leads to a definition of the problem that is too narrow. Consider, for example, the consumption of soft drinks. In many Asian countries such as India, water is consumed with meals, and soft drinks are generally served to guests and on special occasions. Therefore, the management decision problem of increasing the market share of a soft drink brand would translate to a different marketing research problem in India than in the United States. Before defining the problem, the researcher must isolate and examine the impact of the **self-reference criterion** (SRC), or the unconscious reference to one's own cultural values. The following steps help researchers account for environmental and cultural differences when defining the problem in an international marketing context:[28]

self-reference criterion
The unconscious reference to one's own cultural values.

Step 1   Define the marketing research problem in terms of domestic environmental and cultural factors. This involves an identification of relevant American (domestic country) traits, economics, values, needs, or habits.

Step 2   Define the marketing research problem in terms of foreign environmental and cultural factors. Make no judgments. This involves an identification of the related traits, economics, values, needs, or habits in the proposed market culture. This task requires input from researchers familiar with the foreign environment.

Step 3   Isolate the self-reference criterion (SRC) influence on the problem and examine it carefully to see how it complicates the problem. Examine the differences between steps 1 and 2. The SRC can be seen to account for these differences.

Step 4   Redefine the problem without the SRC influence and address it for the foreign market situation. If the differences in step 3 are significant, the impact of the SRC should be carefully considered.

Consider the broad problem of the Coca-Cola Company trying to increase its penetration of the soft drink market in India. In step 1, the problem of increasing the market penetration in the United States would be considered. In the United States, virtually all households consume soft drinks, and the problem would be to increase the soft drink consumption of existing consumers. Furthermore, soft drinks are regularly consumed with meals and as thirst quenchers. So the problem of increasing marketing penetration would involve getting the consumers to consume more soft drinks with meals and at other times. In India, on the other hand (step 2), a much smaller percentage of households consume soft drinks, and soft drinks are not consumed with meals. Thus, in step 3, the SRC can be identified as the American notion that soft drinks are an all-purpose, all-meal beverage. In step 4, the problem in the Indian context can be defined as how to get a greater percentage of the Indian consumers to consume soft drinks (Coca-Cola products) and how to get them to consume soft drinks (Coca-Cola products) more often for personal consumption.

While developing theoretical frameworks, models, research questions, and hypotheses, remember that differences in the environmental factors, especially the sociocultural environment, may lead to differences in the formation of perceptions, attitudes, preferences, and choice behavior. For example, orientation toward time varies considerably across cultures. In Asia, Latin America, and the Middle East, people are not as time conscious as Westerners. This influences their perceptions of and preferences for convenience foods such as frozen foods and prepared dinners. In developing an approach to the problem, the researcher should consider the equivalence of consumption and purchase behavior and the underlying factors that influence them. This is critical to the identification of the correct research questions, hypotheses, and information needed.

Real Research   Surf Superconcentrate Faces a Super Washout in Japan

As of 2009, Unilever (www.unilever.com) sold consumer products in 150 countries. As much as 85 percent of their profits came from overseas, with 7 percent of their profits being attributed to Asia and the Pacific. Unilever attempted to break into the Japanese detergent market with Surf Superconcentrate. It achieved 14.5 percent of the market share initially during test marketing, which fell down to a shocking 2.8 percent when the product was introduced nationally. Where did they go wrong? Surf was designed to have a distinctive premeasured packet as in tea-bag-like sachets, joined in pairs because convenience was an important attribute to Japanese consumers. It also had a "fresh smell" appeal. However, Japanese consumers noticed that the detergents did not dissolve in the wash, partly because of weather conditions and also because of the popularity of low-agitation washing machines. Surf was not designed to work in the new washing machines. Unilever also found that the "fresh smell" positioning of new Surf had little relevance because most consumers hung their wash out in the fresh air. The research approach was certainly not without flaw as Unilever failed to identify critical attributes that are relevant in the Japanese detergent market. Furthermore, it identified factors such as "fresh smell" that had no relevance in the Japanese context. Appropriate qualitative research such as focus groups and depth interviews across samples from the target market could have revealed the correct characteristics or factors leading to a suitable research design.

Despite weak performance in the Japanese market, Surf continued to perform well in several markets including India through 2009. Surf, launched in 1952, is the third-biggest-selling product in the washing detergent market behind Unilever's Persil and Procter & Gamble's Ariel.[29] ∎

Ethics in Marketing Research

Ethical issues arise if the process of defining the problem and developing an approach is compromised by the personal agendas of the client (DM) or the researcher. This process is adversely affected when the DM has hidden objectives such as gaining a promotion or justifying a decision that has been already made. The DM has the obligation to be candid and disclose to the researcher all the relevant information that will enable a proper definition of the marketing research problem. Likewise, the researcher is ethically bound to define the problem so as to further the best interests of the client, rather than the interests of the research firm. At times this may mean making the interests of the research firm subservient to those of the client, leading to an ethical dilemma.

Real Research   Ethical or More Profitable?

A marketing research firm is hired by a major consumer electronics company (e.g., Philips) to conduct a large-scale segmentation study with the objective of improving market share. The researcher, after following the process outlined in this chapter, determines that the problem is not market segmentation but distribution. The company appears to be lacking an effective distribution system, which is limiting market share. However, the distribution problem requires a much simpler approach that will greatly reduce the cost of the project and the research firm's profits. What should the researcher do? Should the research firm conduct the research the client wants rather than the research the client needs? Ethical guidelines indicate that the research firm has an obligation to disclose the actual problem to the client. If, after the distribution problem has been discussed, the client still desires the segmentation research, the research firm should feel free to conduct the study. The reason is that the researcher cannot know for certain the motivations underlying the client's behavior.[30] ∎

Several ethical issues are also pertinent in developing an approach. When a client solicits proposals, not with the intent of subcontracting the research, but with the intent of gaining the expertise of research firms without pay, an ethical breach has occurred. If the client rejects the proposal of a research firm, then the approach specified in that proposal should not be implemented by the client, unless the client has paid for the development of the proposal. Likewise, the research firm has the ethical obligation to develop an appropriate approach. If the approach is going to make use of models developed in another context, then this should be communicated to the client. For example, if the researcher is going to use a customer satisfaction model developed previously for an insurance company in a customer satisfaction study for a bank, then this information should be disclosed. Proprietary models and approaches developed by a research firm are the property of that firm and should not be reused by the client in subsequent studies without the permission of the research firm.

Such ethical situations would be satisfactorily resolved if both the client and the researcher adhered to the seven Cs: communication, cooperation, confidence, candor, closeness, continuity, and creativity, as discussed earlier. This would lead to a relationship of mutual trust that would check any unethical tendencies.

Decision Research Kellogg's: From Slumping to Thumping

The Situation

Kellogg's is the world's leading producer of cereal and a leading producer of convenience foods, including cookies, crackers, toaster pastries, cereal bars, frozen waffles, meat alternatives, pie crusts, and cones, with 2007 annual sales of $11.776 billion and a market share of more than 30 percent. David Mackay, chairman and CEO of Kellogg's, takes pride in being a part of the Kellogg Company because of the consistency of the decisions that are made within the company to promote the long-term growth of their business as well as serve the needs of their people and communities.

With such a large share of the market, one would think that Kellogg's is untouchable. However, Kellogg's faced a slump in the market. Its cereal sales were declining and it had to face the challenge of getting out of its slump. Kellogg's therefore turned to marketing research to identify the problem and develop several solutions to increase cereal sales.

To identify the problem, Kellogg's used several tasks to help them in the process. The researchers spoke to decision makers within the company, interviewed industry experts, conducted analysis of available data, and performed some qualitative research. Several important issues came out of this preliminary research. Current products were being targeted to kids. Bagels and muffins were winning for favored breakfast foods. High prices were turning consumers to generic brands. Some other information also came to light during the research. Adults want quick foods that require very little or no preparation.

Marketing research helped Kellogg's address a slump in sales by introducing successful new products and increasing market share.

The Marketing Research Decision

1. What is the management decision problem facing Kellogg's?
2. Define an appropriate marketing research problem that Kellogg's needs to address.
3. Discuss the role of the type of marketing research problem you have identified in enabling David Mackay to increase the sales of Kellogg's.

The Marketing Management Decision

1. David Mackay is wondering what changes Kellogg's should make to increase market share. What marketing strategies should be formulated?
2. Discuss how the marketing management decision action that you recommend to David Mackay is influenced by the research that you suggested earlier and by the findings of that research.[31] ■

SPSS Windows

In defining the problem and developing an approach, the researcher can use Decision Time and What If? software distributed by SPSS. Forecasts of industry and company sales, and other relevant variables, can be aided by the use of Decision Time. Once the data are loaded into Decision Time, the program's interactive wizard asks you three simple questions. Based on the answers, Decision Time selects the best forecasting method and creates a forecast.

What If? uses the forecast by Decision Time to enable the researcher to explore different options to get a better understanding of the problem situation. The researcher can generate answers to questions such as: How will an increase in advertising affect the sales of the product? How will a decrease (increase) in price affect the demand? How will an increase in the sales force affect the sales by region? And so on.

Forecasts and what-if analyses can help the researcher to isolate the underlying causes, identify the relevant variables that should be investigated, and formulate appropriate research questions and hypotheses.

Summary

Defining the marketing research problem is the most important step in a research project. It is a difficult step, because frequently management has not determined the actual problem or has only a vague notion about it. The researcher's role is to help management identify and isolate the problem. Figure 2.5 is a concept map for problem definition.

The tasks involved in formulating the marketing research problem include discussions with management, including the key decision makers, interviews with industry experts, analysis of secondary data, and qualitative research. These tasks should lead to an understanding of the environmental context of the problem. The environmental context of the problem should be analyzed and certain essential factors evaluated. These factors include past information and forecasts about the industry and the firm, objectives of the DM, buyer behavior, resources and constraints of the firm, the legal and economic environment, and marketing and technological skills of the firm.

Analysis of the environmental context should assist in the identification of the management decision problem, which should then be translated into a marketing research problem. The management decision problem asks what the DM needs to do, whereas the marketing research problem asks what information is needed and how it can be obtained effectively and efficiently. The researcher should avoid defining the marketing research problem either too broadly or too narrowly. An appropriate way of defining the marketing research problem is to make a broad statement of the problem and then identify its specific components.

Developing an approach to the problem is the second step in the marketing research process. The components of an approach consist of an objective/theoretical framework, analytical models, research questions, hypotheses, and specification of information needed. It is necessary that the approach developed be based on objective or empirical evidence and be grounded in theory. The relevant variables and their interrelationships may be neatly summarized via an analytical model. The most common kinds of model structures are verbal, graphical, and mathematical. The research questions are refined statements of the specific components of the problem that ask what specific information is required with respect to the problem components. Research questions may be further refined into hypotheses. Finally, given the problem definition, research questions, and hypotheses, the information needed should be specified. Figure 2.6 is a concept map for developing an approach to the problem.

When defining the problem in international marketing research, the researcher must isolate and examine the impact

FIGURE 2.5

A Concept Map for Problem Definition

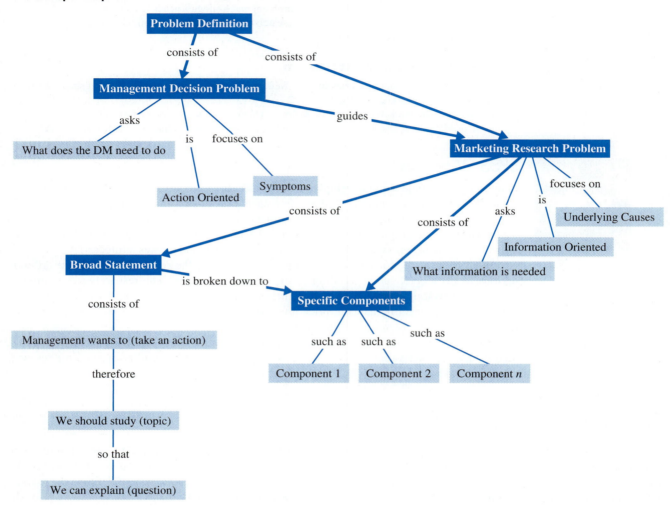

of the self-reference criterion (SRC), or the unconscious reference to one's own cultural values. Likewise, when developing an approach, the differences in the environment prevailing in the domestic market and the foreign markets should be carefully considered. Several ethical issues that have an impact on the client and the researcher can arise at this stage but can be resolved by adhering to the seven Cs: communication, cooperation, confidence, candor, closeness, continuity, and creativity.

Key Terms and Concepts

problem definition, 36
problem audit, 38
experience survey, 40
key-informant technique, 40
lead-user survey, 40
secondary data, 41
primary data, 41
qualitative research, 41
pilot surveys, 42
case studies, 42

environmental context of the
   problem, 42
objectives, 44
buyer behavior, 45
legal environment, 46
economic environment, 46
management decision problem, 47
marketing research problem, 47
conceptual map, 48
broad statement, 49

specific components, 49
theory, 51
objective evidence, 51
analytical model, 51
verbal models, 51
graphical models, 51
mathematical models, 51
research questions, 52
hypothesis, 53
self-reference criterion, 56

FIGURE 2.6

A Concept Map for Approach to the Problem

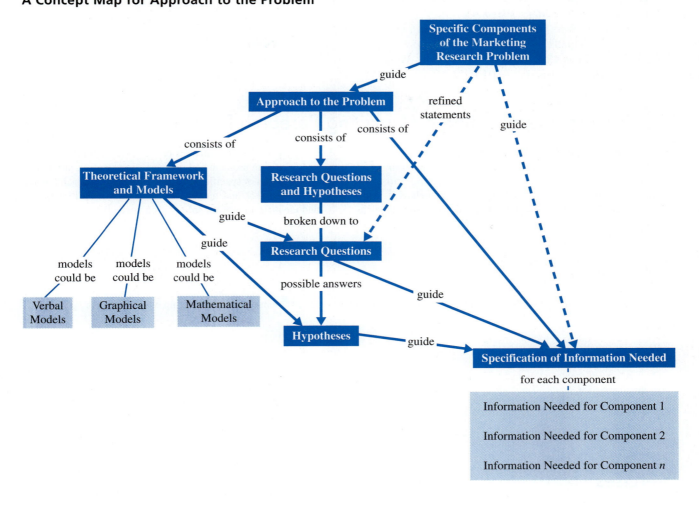

Suggested Cases, Video Cases, and HBS Cases

Running Case with Real Data

1.1 Dell

Comprehensive Critical Thinking Cases

2.1 American Idol   2.2 Baskin-Robbins   2.3 Akron Children's Hospital

Comprehensive Cases with Real Data

4.1 JPMorgan Chase   4.2 Wendy's

Video Cases

2.1 Accenture	3.1 NFL	4.1 Mayo Clinic	5.1 Nike
8.1 P&G	9.1 eGO	10.1 Dunkin' Donuts	11.1 Motorola
12.1 Subaru	13.1 Intel	23.1 Marriott	24.1 Nivea

Comprehensive Harvard Business School Cases

Case 5.1: The Harvard Graduate Student Housing Survey (9-505-059)
Case 5.2: BizRate.Com (9-501-024)
Case 5.3: Cola Wars Continue: Coke and Pepsi in the Twenty-First Century (9-702-442)
Case 5.4: TiVo in 2002 (9-502-062)
Case 5.5: Compaq Computer: Intel Inside? (9-599-061)
Case 5.6: The New Beetle (9-501-023)

Live Research: Conducting a Marketing Research Project

1. Invite the client to discuss the project with the class.
2. Have the class (or different teams) analyze the environmental context of the problem: past information and forecasts, resources and constraints, objectives, buyer behavior, legal environment, economic environment, and marketing and technological skills.
3. Jointly with the client make a presentation about the management decision problem and the marketing research problem.
4. Ask the class or specific teams to develop an approach (analytical framework and models, research questions, hypotheses, and identification of the information needed).

Acronym

The factors to be considered while analyzing the environmental context of the problem may be summed up by the acronym

Problem:

P ast information and forecasts
R esources and constraints
O bjectives of the decision maker
B uyer behavior
L egal environment
E conomic environment
M arketing and technological skills

Exercises

Questions

1. What is the first step in conducting a marketing research project?
2. Why is it important to define the marketing research problem appropriately?
3. What are some reasons why management is often not clear about the real problem?
4. What is the role of the researcher in the problem definition process?
5. What is a problem audit?
6. What is the difference between a symptom and a problem? How can a skillful researcher differentiate between the two and identify a true problem?
7. What are some differences between a management decision problem and a marketing research problem?
8. What are the common types of errors encountered in defining a marketing research problem? What can be done to reduce the incidence of such errors?
9. How are the research questions related to components of the problem?
10. What are the differences between research questions and hypotheses?
11. Is it necessary for every research project to have a set of hypotheses? Why or why not?
12. What are the most common forms of analytical models?
13. Give an example of an analytical model that includes all the three major types.
14. Describe a microcomputer software program that can be used to assist the researcher in defining the research problem.

Problems

1. State the research problems for each of the following management decision problems.
   a. Should a new product be introduced?
   b. Should an advertising campaign that has run for three years be changed?
   c. Should the in-store promotion for an existing product line be increased?
   d. What pricing strategy should be adopted for a new product?
   e. Should the compensation package be changed to motivate the sales force better?
2. State management decision problems for which the following research problems might provide useful information.
   a. Estimate the sales and market share of department stores in a certain metropolitan area.
   b. Determine the design features for a new product that would result in maximum market share.
   c. Evaluate the effectiveness of alternative TV commercials.

    d. Assess current and proposed sales territories with respect to their sales potential and workload.

    e. Determine the prices for each item in a product line so as to maximize total sales for the product line.

3. Identify five symptoms facing marketing decision makers and a plausible cause for each one.

4. For the first component of the department store project, identify the relevant research questions and develop suitable hypotheses. (Hint: Closely follow the example given in this chapter for the fifth component of the department store project.)

5. Suppose you are doing a project for Delta Air Lines. Identify, from secondary sources, the attributes or factors passengers consider when selecting an airline.

Internet and Computer Exercises

1. You are a consultant to Coca-Cola USA working on a marketing research project for Diet Coke.

    a. Use the online databases in your library to compile a list of articles related to the Coca-Cola Company, Diet Coke, and the soft drink industry published during the past year.

    b. Visit the Coca-Cola and PepsiCo Web sites and compare the information available on diet soft drinks.

    c. Based on the information collected from the Internet, write a report on the environmental context surrounding Diet Coke.

2. Select any firm. Using secondary sources, obtain information on the annual sales of the firm and the industry for the last 10 years. Use a spreadsheet package, such as Excel, or any microcomputer or mainframe statistical package to develop a graphical model relating the firm's sales to the industry sales.

3. Visit the Web sites of competing sneaker brands (e.g., Nike, Reebok, New Balance). From an analysis of information available at these sites, determine the factors of the choice criteria used by consumers in selecting a sneaker brand.

4. Bank of America wants to know how it can increase its market share and has hired you as a consultant. Read the 10-K reports for Bank of America and three competing banks at www.sec.gov/edgar.shtml and analyze the environmental context of the problem.

Activities

Role Playing

1. Ask a fellow student to play the role of decision maker (DM) for a local soft drink firm contemplating the introduction of a lemon-lime soft drink. This product would be positioned as a "change of pace" soft drink to be consumed by all soft drink users, including heavy cola drinkers. You act the role of a researcher. Hold discussions with the DM and identify the management decision problem. Translate the management problem into a written statement of the research problem. Does the DM agree with your definition? Develop an approach to the research problem that you have identified.

2. You are vice president of marketing for American Airlines and would like to increase your share of the business market. Make a list of relevant objectives for American Airlines. As the DM, what are your personal objectives?

Fieldwork

1. Set up an appointment and visit a bookstore, a restaurant, or any business located on or near the university campus. Hold discussions with the decision maker. Can you identify a marketing research problem that could be fruitfully addressed?

2. Consider the field trip described in question 1. For the problem you have defined, develop an analytical model, research question, and the appropriate hypotheses. Discuss these with the decision maker you visited earlier.

Group Discussion

1. Form a small group of five or six people to discuss the following statement: "Correct identification and appropriate definition of the marketing research problem are more crucial to the success of a marketing research project than sophisticated research techniques." Did your group arrive at a consensus?

2. We are all aware that the Coca-Cola Company changed its flagship brand of 99 years to New Coke and subsequently returned to the old favorite, Coca-Cola Classic. Working in a group of four, read as much material as you can on this "marketing bungle." Identify the decision problem Coke management faced. As a team of researchers, define the marketing research problem and its specific components.

3. Form a different group of five or six to discuss the following: "Theoretical research and applied research should not be mixed. Hence, it is wrong to insist that the approach to an applied marketing research problem be grounded in theory."

Dell Running Case

Review the Dell case, Case 1.1, and the questionnaire provided toward the end of the book.

1. Conduct an Internet search on Dell and briefly describe the environmental context of the problem surrounding the company.

2. Define the management decision problem facing Dell as it seeks to maintain and build on its leadership position in the personal computers market.

3. Define an appropriate marketing research problem that corresponds to your definition of the management decision problem.

4. Present a graphical model describing consumers' selection of a personal computer brand.

5. Formulate three research questions, with one or more hypotheses associated with each.

Video Cases

VIDEO CASE 2.1   Accenture: The Accent Is in the Name

As of 2009, Accenture (www.accenture.com) is the largest consulting firm in the world and one of the largest computer services and software companies on the *Fortune* Global 500 list. It has more than 170,000 employees in 49 countries and reported revenues of $25.68 billion for the fiscal year ended August 31, 2008. Through its network of businesses, the company enhances its consulting, technology, and outsourcing expertise through alliances, affiliated companies, venture capital, and other capabilities. Accenture delivers innovations that help clients across all industries quickly realize their visions. With more than 110 offices in about 50 countries, Accenture can quickly mobilize its broad and deep global resources to accelerate results for clients. The company has extensive experience in 18 industry groups in key business areas, including customer relationship management, supply chain management, business strategy, technology, and outsourcing. Accenture's clients include 89 of the *Fortune* Global 100 and more than half of the *Fortune* Global 500.

Accenture was originally named Andersen Consulting and was created in 1989 as a part of Arthur Andersen. In 2000, Andersen Consulting won the right to divorce itself from Arthur Andersen after the parent company broke contractual agreements, moving into areas of service where Andersen Consulting was already an established leader. However, it then had to change its name. This was an extremely significant event, because Andersen Consulting had built up considerable brand equity in its name, partly by spending approximately $7 billion over 10 years on building the name. In addition, the new name would need to be trademarked in 47 countries. Thus, the name change became a top priority, and the company focused much of its time and effort on this task.

The first task was to pick a new name. The company challenged its employees to come up with suggestions for a new name by creating an internal contest, which resulted in a list of more than 2,500 entries. After extensive marketing research on various names, which included surveys of target customers, it decided to go with the name Accenture. Marketing research revealed that the "Acc" in the name connotes accomplishment and accessibility, and

the name sounds like "adventure." The company settled on this name because it believed this name conveyed the message that it was focused on the future. It also spent a considerable amount of time creating a new logo. The final version of the logo was the company's name accented with a greater than (>) symbol placed above the letter t, which it believed stressed its focus on the future.

Another task, which occurred simultaneously, was to get the word out and prepare the target market for the brand change. The company began running ads notifying everyone that its name would change at the beginning of 2001. Accenture has a well-defined group of companies that comprise the target market, and it had to focus its efforts on them. A teaser advertisement created by Young and Rubicam with the old signature torn through at the corner of the ad and typing in "Renamed. Redefined. Reborn 01.01.01" set the stage for the change. Marketing research revealed that 01.01.01, the launch date of the new brand, had a resonance with the computer industry, because 0 and 1 are the two digits of the binary world of computers.

Finally, on January 1, 2001, the company announced its new name to the world. The initial campaign illustrated the change by the slogan, "Renamed. Redefined. Reborn." Accenture used this opportunity not only to present the new name, but also to sell its services and help people understand what it had to offer. In the end, Accenture spent a total of $175 million to rebrand itself, but it did not stop there. In February it began a new campaign titled, "Now it gets interesting." This campaign took the perspective that despite all the incredible changes that have occurred recently due to technology, even more challenges lie ahead. The commercials showed how Accenture could help clients capitalize on these challenges. The success of this campaign was evidenced by the increased traffic on the company's Web site. This is very important to Accenture, because it believes that if it can get somebody to visit its site, it has a better opportunity to tell the whole story. Next came the "I Am Your Idea" theme. This campaign was followed by "High Performance. Delivered," which was still running in 2009. It also featured Tiger Woods with the tag line, "We know what it takes to be a Tiger."

Accenture has been successful in transferring the brand equity to its new name. Marketing research revealed that it has approximately 50 percent awareness with the public, which is essentially the same number it had under the old name. Accenture's marketing goes far beyond the name, because it is constantly challenged as the product it offers changes.

Conclusion

The case describes the marketing research conducted by Andersen Consulting to change its name, while at the same time maintain the brand equity and the goodwill of its previous name. Andersen Consulting was able to successfully transition to a new name and a new identity, reflecting the new realities of the market and Accenture's positioning in it. Finding a new name is only the beginning; repositioning a global brand today requires good marketing research, creative marketing, big budgets, and awareness of the next business trends. Such efforts will help Accenture to further strengthen the accent in its name by building brand equity.

Questions

1. Discuss the role of marketing research in helping Andersen Consulting select a new name (Accenture).
2. Define Accenture's target market. Discuss the role of marketing research in helping Accenture understand the needs of its target customers.
3. Accenture would like to increase preference and loyalty to its services. Describe the management decision problem.
4. Define a suitable marketing research problem corresponding to the management decision problem that you identified in question 3.
5. Develop a graphical model explaining how a *Fortune* 500 firm would select a consulting organization.
6. Develop two research questions, each with two hypotheses, based on the marketing research problem you defined in question 4.

References

1. See www.accenture.com, accessed February 10, 2009.
2. Todd Wasserman, "Accenture Accents Idea Campaign," *Brandweek* (September 30, 2002): 4.

Part II Research Design Formulation

A research design (step 3) is formulated after the problem has been defined (step 1) and the approach developed (step 2). This part of the text describes in detail exploratory, descriptive, and causal research designs. Exploratory research involves secondary data and qualitative research, while descriptive research makes use of survey and observation methods. The major methodology used in causal designs is experimentation. We describe the primary scales of measurement and the comparative and noncomparative scaling techniques commonly used. We present several guidelines for designing questionnaires and explain the procedures, techniques, and statistical considerations involved in sampling. Managers and researchers should find this material helpful.

"A research design is the heart and soul of a marketing research project. It outlines how the marketing research project will be conducted and guides data collection, analysis, and report preparation."

Seth Ginsburg, Owner and Chief Consultant,
Sethburg Communications

Objectives   [After reading this chapter, the student should be able to:]

1. Define research design, classify various research designs, and explain the differences between exploratory and conclusive designs.

2. Compare and contrast the basic research designs: exploratory, descriptive, and causal.

3. Describe the major sources of errors in a research design, including random sampling error and the various sources of nonsampling error.

4. Discuss managerial aspects of coordinating research projects, particularly budgeting and scheduling.

5. Describe the elements of a marketing research proposal and show how it addresses the steps of the marketing research process.

6. Explain research design formulation in international marketing research.

7. Understand the ethical issues and conflicts that arise in formulating a research design.

Research Design

Overview

Chapter 2 discussed how to define a marketing research problem and develop a suitable approach. These first two steps are critical to the success of the entire marketing research project. Once they have been completed, attention should be devoted to designing the formal research project by formulating a detailed research design (see Figure 2.1 in Chapter 2).

This chapter defines and classifies research designs. We describe the two major types of research designs: exploratory and conclusive. We further classify conclusive research designs as descriptive or causal and discuss both types in detail. We then consider the differences between the two types of descriptive designs, cross-sectional and longitudinal, and identify sources of errors. We cover budgeting and scheduling of a research project and present guidelines for writing a marketing research proposal. The special considerations involved in formulating research designs in international marketing research are discussed. Several ethical issues that arise at this stage of the marketing research process are considered. The reader can develop a better appreciation of the concepts presented in this chapter by first considering the following example, which illustrates exploratory and conclusive research designs.

Real Research

More Than Just Causes

In a study of cause-related marketing, exploratory research in the form of secondary data analysis and focus groups was conducted to identify the social causes that American businesses should be concerned about. The following causes were identified as salient: child care, drug abuse, public education, hunger, crime, the environment, medical research, and poverty.

Then conclusive research in the form of a descriptive cross-sectional survey was undertaken to quantify how and why cause-related marketing influences consumers' perceptions of companies and brands and to determine the relative salience of the causes identified in the exploratory research. A random sample of 2,000 Americans was surveyed by telephone. About 61 percent of respondents said that when price and quality are equal, they would switch brands or stores to companies that support good causes that help on the local or national level. The survey also revealed that 68 percent of consumers would pay more for a product that is linked to a good cause. Company support of good causes produces a more positive image and greater trust of the company, according to 66 percent of those surveyed. The relative salience of the social causes that businesses should address is presented in the following table.

Social Issues Businesses Should Work the Hardest to Solve

Social Issue	Percent Saying It Is a Major Concern
Public education	33
Crime	32
Environment	30
Poverty	24
Medical research	23
Hunger	23
Child care	22
Drug abuse	18

Exploratory research followed by conclusive research helped Starbucks realize that the environment was an important cause influencing consumers' perceptions of companies and brands.

In keeping with these findings, Starbucks (www.starbucks.com) decided to help the environment by providing a new "eco-friendly" coffee cup, composting coffee grounds, and recycling burlap bags. The company also has initiatives to help small coffee bean farmers, local community programs, and charitable giving. There are even employee incentives and awards for volunteering for these causes. One of the newest social programs is to match employee volunteer hours with dollars to the same organization. Starbucks, in conjunction with international specialty coffee organizations such as the Colombian Coffee Federation and the Specialty Coffee Association of America, advised many environmental organizations about growing earth-friendly coffee. An extensive set of guidelines was established, called the "Conservation Principles for Coffee Production." Thus, Starbucks has differentiated its brand and enhanced its image in a way that checkbook philanthropy never could.[1] ■

As this example indicates, at a broad level, two main types of research designs are employed in marketing research: exploratory and conclusive. An understanding of the fundamentals of research design and its components enables the researcher to formulate a design that is appropriate for the problem at hand.

Research Design: Definition

research design
A framework or blueprint for conducting the marketing research project. It specifies the details of the procedures necessary for obtaining the information needed to structure and/or solve marketing research problems.

A **research design** is a framework or blueprint for conducting the marketing research project. It details the procedures necessary for obtaining the information needed to structure or solve marketing research problems. Although a broad approach to the problem has already been developed, the research design specifies the details—the nuts and bolts—of implementing that approach. A research design lays the foundation for conducting the project. A good research design will ensure that the marketing research project is conducted effectively and efficiently. Typically, a research design involves the following components, or tasks:

1. Define the information needed (Chapter 2).
2. Design the exploratory, descriptive, and/or causal phases of the research (Chapters 3–7).
3. Specify the measurement and scaling procedures (Chapters 8 and 9).
4. Construct and pretest a questionnaire (interviewing form) or an appropriate form for data collection (Chapter 10).
5. Specify the sampling process and sample size (Chapters 11 and 12).
6. Develop a plan of data analysis (Chapter 14).

Each of these components will be discussed in great detail in the subsequent chapters. First, we must further our understanding of research design with a classification of the different types.

Research Design: Classification

exploratory research
One type of research design, which has as its primary objective the provision of insights into and comprehension of the problem situation confronting the researcher.

Research designs may be broadly classified as exploratory or conclusive (see Figure 3.1). The differences between exploratory and conclusive research are summarized in Table 3.1. The primary objective of **exploratory research** is to provide insights into, and an understanding of,

FIGURE 3.1

**A Classification
of Marketing
Research Designs**

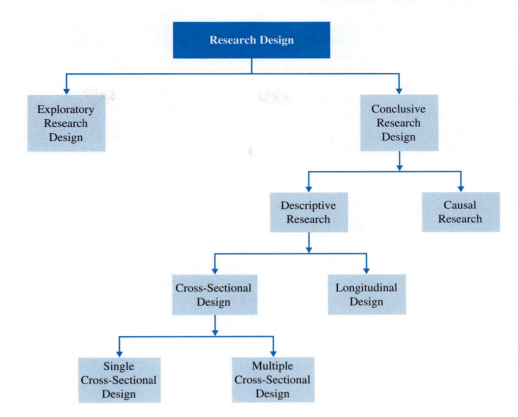

the problem confronting the researcher.[2] Exploratory research is used in cases when you must define the problem more precisely, identify relevant courses of action, or gain additional insights before an approach can be developed. The information needed is only loosely defined at this stage, and the research process that is adopted is flexible and unstructured. For example, it may consist of personal interviews with industry experts. The sample, selected to generate maximum insights, is small and nonrepresentative. The primary data are qualitative in nature and are analyzed accordingly. Given these characteristics of the research process, the findings of exploratory research should be regarded as tentative or as input to further research. Typically, such research is followed by further exploratory or conclusive research. Sometimes, exploratory research, particularly qualitative research, is all the research that is conducted. In these cases, caution should be exercised in utilizing the findings obtained. Exploratory research will be discussed in more detail in the next section.

The insights gained from exploratory research might be verified or quantified by conclusive research, as in the opening example. The importance of salient social causes that businesses should address, identified through exploratory research, was determined through a survey

TABLE 3.1

Differences Between Exploratory and Conclusive Research

	Exploratory	Conclusive
Objective:	To provide insights and understanding	To test specific hypotheses and examine relationships
Characteristics:	Information needed is defined only loosely. Research process is flexible and unstructured. Sample is small and nonrepresentative. Analysis of primary data is qualitative.	Information needed is clearly defined. Research process is formal and structured. Sample is large and representative. Data analysis is quantitative.
Findings/Results:	Tentative	Conclusive
Outcome:	Generally followed by further exploratory or conclusive research	Findings used as input into decision making

(conclusive research) that showed that public education was the most important cause of concern to 33 percent of the respondents. The objective of conclusive research is to test specific hypotheses and examine specific relationships. This requires that the researcher clearly specify the information needed.[3] **Conclusive research** is typically more formal and structured than exploratory research. It is based on large, representative samples, and the data obtained are subjected to quantitative analysis. The findings from this research are considered to be conclusive in nature in that they are used as input into managerial decision making. (However, it should be noted that from the perspective of the philosophy of science, nothing can be proven and nothing is conclusive.) As shown in Figure 3.1, conclusive research designs may be either descriptive or causal, and descriptive research designs may be either cross-sectional or longitudinal. Each of these classifications is discussed further, beginning with exploratory research.

conclusive research
Research designed to assist the decision maker in determining, evaluating, and selecting the best course of action to take in a given situation.

ACTIVE RESEARCH

Holiday Inn: All in the Family

Visit www.ichotelsgroup.com and write a report about the various hotel brands owned by Holiday Inn.

What type of research would you conduct for determining a coherent marketing strategy for the various hotel brands owned by Holiday Inn?

As vice president of marketing for Holiday Inn, discuss the role that exploratory and conclusive research can play in determining a coherent marketing strategy for the various hotel brands owned by Holiday Inn, such as Holiday Inn Hotels and Resorts, Holiday Inn Select, Holiday Inn SunSpree Resorts, and Holiday Inn Family Suites Resorts.

Exploratory Research

As its name implies, the objective of exploratory research is to explore or search through a problem or situation to provide insights and understanding (Table 3.2). Exploratory research could be used for any of the following purposes:

- Formulate a problem or define a problem more precisely.
- Identify alternative courses of action.
- Develop hypotheses.
- Isolate key variables and relationships for further examination.[4]
- Gain insights for developing an approach to the problem.
- Establish priorities for further research.

The opening example in the overview section illustrated the use of exploratory research to identify the social causes that American businesses should be concerned about. This

---

TABLE 3.2

A Comparison of Basic Research Designs

	Exploratory	Descriptive	Causal
Objective:	Discovery of ideas and insights	Describe market characteristics or functions	Determine cause-and-effect relationships
Characteristics:	Flexible, versatile	Marked by the prior formulation of specific hypotheses	Manipulation of one or more independent variables
	Often the front end of total research design	Preplanned and structured design	Measure the effect on dependent variable(s)
			Control of other mediating variables
Methods:	Expert surveys	Secondary data: quantitative analysis	Experiments
	Pilot surveys Case studies	Surveys	
	Secondary data: qualitative analysis	Panels	
	Qualitative research	Observation and other data	

research identified the following causes as salient: child care, drug abuse, public education, hunger, crime, the environment, medical research, and poverty. In general, exploratory research is meaningful in any situation where the researcher does not have enough understanding to proceed with the research project. Exploratory research is characterized by flexibility and versatility with respect to the methods because formal research protocols and procedures are not employed. It rarely involves structured questionnaires, large samples, and probability sampling plans. Rather, researchers are alert to new ideas and insights as they proceed. Once a new idea or insight is discovered, they may redirect their exploration in that direction. That new direction is pursued until its possibilities are exhausted or another direction is found. For this reason, the focus of the investigation may shift constantly as new insights are discovered. Thus, the creativity and ingenuity of the researcher play a major role in exploratory research. Yet the abilities of the researcher are not the sole determinants of good exploratory research. Exploratory research can greatly benefit from use of the following methods (see Table 3.2):

Survey of experts (discussed in Chapter 2)

Pilot surveys (discussed in Chapter 2)

Case studies (discussed in Chapter 2)

Secondary data analyzed in a qualitative way (discussed in Chapter 4)

Qualitative research (discussed in Chapter 5)

The use of exploratory research in defining the problem and developing an approach was discussed in Chapter 2. The advantages and disadvantages of exploratory research are further discussed in Chapter 4 ("Secondary Data") and Chapter 5 ("Qualitative Research"). To aid the reader in visualizing the applications of exploratory research, we now consider the department store project, which employed the following types of exploratory studies:

- A review of academic and trade literature to identify the relevant store characteristics (choice criteria), demographic and psychographic factors that influence consumer patronage of department stores
- Interviews with retailing experts to determine trends, such as emergence of new types of outlets and shifts in consumer patronage patterns (e.g., shopping on the Internet)
- A comparative analysis of the five best and five worst stores of the same chain to gain some idea of the factors that influence store performance
- Focus groups to determine the factors that consumers consider important in selecting department stores

The following example further illustrates exploratory research.

Real Research   ## Waterpik Picks a Winning Product

Waterpik Technologies (www.waterpik.com) began in 1962. As of 2009, it is a leading developer, manufacturer, and marketer of health care products for the entire family. Waterpik wants to retain its market position by introducing innovative products that satisfy the needs of its customers. In 2003, based on initial research and evaluation of trends, Waterpik made the decision to concentrate on developing new showerhead product platform concepts that provide the best showering experience and value.

The company hired Innovation Focus (www.innovationfocus.com), an internationally recognized consulting firm driven to help clients develop and implement profitable ideas for growth. By using a unique mix of creative and analytical marketing research, Innovation Focus helped Waterpik to find the right answers to their questions and finally come up with a successful product.

The exploratory research phase was kicked off with a trends meeting with Waterpik marketing professionals to list and prioritize key consumer wants and needs. This was followed by a technology session with Waterpik engineers to uncover applicable technologies and the company's internal competencies. These meetings set the foundation for conducting detailed marketing research. To get a variety of perspectives and to speed up the process, Innovation Focus decided to conduct what was named an innovation session. The session had 21 participants, including consumers, external designers and marketers, and Waterpik specialists. More than 140 concepts were generated. This was followed by validation and concept refinement sessions with more consumers using a descriptive survey. And the winner (the final product) emerged through this process.

Two years after the first session, Waterpik was ready to introduce its new product. The showerhead had seven unique and adjustable settings that addressed consumers' interest in being able to adjust the coverage, force, and shape of the shower spray. Mist and pressure control features were also incorporated to allow the users to "turn their shower into a spa." Powered by marketing research, Waterpik was able to hit the ground running with its new product.[5] ■

Note that Waterpik did not rely exclusively on exploratory research. Once new product concepts were identified, they were further tested by descriptive research in the form of consumer surveys. This example points to the importance of descriptive research in obtaining more conclusive findings.

Descriptive Research

descriptive research
A type of conclusive research that has as its major objective the description of something—usually market characteristics or functions.

As the name implies, the major objective of **descriptive research** is to describe something—usually market characteristics or functions (see Table 3.2). Descriptive research is conducted for the following reasons:

1. To describe the characteristics of relevant groups, such as consumers, salespeople, organizations, or market areas. For example, we could develop a profile of the "heavy users" (frequent shoppers) of prestigious department stores like Saks Fifth Avenue and Neiman Marcus.
2. To estimate the percentage of units in a specified population exhibiting a certain behavior. For example, we might be interested in estimating the percentage of heavy users of prestigious department stores who also patronize discount department stores.
3. To determine the perceptions of product characteristics. For example, how do households perceive the various department stores in terms of salient factors of the choice criteria?
4. To determine the degree to which marketing variables are associated. For example, to what extent is shopping at department stores related to eating out?
5. To make specific predictions. For example, what will be the retail sales of Neiman Marcus (specific store) for fashion clothing (specific product category) in the Dallas area (specific region)?

The example at the beginning of the chapter employed descriptive research in the form of a survey undertaken to quantify the salience of the different social causes for businesses. As this example shows, descriptive research assumes that the researcher has much prior knowledge about the problem situation.[6] In the opening example, the relevant social causes had already been identified through exploratory research before the descriptive survey was conducted. In fact, a major difference between exploratory and descriptive research is that descriptive research is characterized by the prior formulation of specific hypotheses. Thus, the information needed is clearly defined. As a result, descriptive research is preplanned and structured. It is typically based on large representative samples. A formal research design specifies the methods for selecting the sources of information and for collecting data from those sources. A descriptive design requires a clear specification of the who, what, when, where, why, and way (the six Ws) of the research. (It is interesting to note that news reporters use similar criteria for describing a situation.) We illustrate this in the context of the department store patronage project.

Project Research   The Six Ws

1. Who—Who should be considered a patron of a particular department store? Some of the possibilities are:
   a. Anyone who enters the department store, whether or not she or he purchases anything
   b. Anyone who purchases anything from the store
   c. Anyone who makes purchases at the department store at least once a month
   d. The person in the household most responsible for department store shopping

2. What—What information should be obtained from the respondents? A wide variety of information could be obtained, including:
   a. Frequency with which different department stores are patronized for specific product categories
   b. Evaluation of the various department stores in terms of the salient choice criteria
   c. Information pertaining to specific hypotheses to be tested
   d. Psychographics and lifestyles, media consumption habits, and demographics
3. When—When should the information be obtained from the respondents? The available options include:
   a. Before shopping
   b. While shopping
   c. Immediately after shopping
   d. Some time after shopping to allow time for evaluation of their shopping experience
4. Where—Where should the respondents be contacted to obtain the required information? Possibilities include contacting the respondents:
   a. In the store
   b. Outside the store but in the shopping mall
   c. In the parking lot
   d. At home
5. Why—Why are we obtaining information from the respondents? Why is the marketing research project being conducted? Possible reasons could be to:
   a. Improve the image of the sponsoring store
   b. Improve patronage and market share
   c. Change the product mix
   d. Develop a suitable promotional campaign
   e. Decide on the location of a new store
6. Way—In what way are we going to obtain information from the respondents? The possible ways could be:
   a. Observation of respondents' behavior
   b. Personal interviews
   c. Telephone interviews
   d. Mail interviews
   e. Electronic (e-mail or Internet) interviews ■

These and other similar questions should be asked until the information to be obtained has been clearly defined.

In summary, descriptive research, in contrast to exploratory research, is marked by a clear statement of the problem, specific hypotheses, and detailed information needs. The survey conducted in the department store patronage project, which involved personal interviews, is an example of descriptive research. Other examples of descriptive studies are:

- Market studies, which describe the size of the market, buying power of the consumers, availability of distributors, and consumer profiles
- Market share studies, which determine the proportion of total sales received by a company and its competitors
- Sales analysis studies, which describe sales by geographic region, product line, type and size of the account
- Image studies, which determine consumer perceptions of the firm and its products
- Product usage studies, which describe consumption patterns
- Distribution studies, which determine traffic flow patterns and the number and location of distributors
- Pricing studies, which describe the range and frequency of price changes and probable consumer response to proposed price changes
- Advertising studies, which describe media consumption habits and audience profiles for specific television programs and magazines

In the opening example, descriptive research in the form of a survey was undertaken to quantify the relative salience of various social causes to American businesses: child care, drug abuse, public education, hunger, crime, the environment, medical research, and poverty.

All these examples demonstrate the range and diversity of descriptive research studies. A vast majority of marketing research studies involve descriptive research, which incorporates the following major methods:

- Secondary data analyzed in a quantitative as opposed to a qualitative manner (discussed in Chapter 4)
- Surveys (Chapter 6)
- Panels (Chapters 4 and 6)
- Observational and other data (Chapter 6)

cross-sectional design
A type of research design involving the collection of information from any given sample of population elements only once.

Although the methods shown in Table 3.2 are typical, it should be noted that the researcher is not limited to these methods. For example, surveys can involve the use of exploratory (open-ended) questions, or causal studies (experiments) are sometimes administered by surveys. Descriptive research using the methods of Table 3.2 can be further classified into cross-sectional and longitudinal research (Figure 3.1).

single cross-sectional design
A cross-sectional design in which one sample of respondents is drawn from the target population and information is obtained from this sample once.

Cross-Sectional Designs

The cross-sectional study is the most frequently used descriptive design in marketing research. **Cross-sectional designs** involve the collection of information from any given sample of population elements only once. They may be either single cross-sectional or multiple cross-sectional (Figure 3.1). In **single cross-sectional designs**, only one sample of respondents is drawn from the target population, and information is obtained from this sample only once. These designs are also called *sample survey research designs*.

Real Research

Internet Health Care Services

Harris Interactive, with revenues of $238.7 million for the year ended June 30, 2008, is a worldwide market research and consulting firm that uses the Internet to conduct market research. Harris Interactive (www.harrisinteractive.com) conducted a study to determine the needs for online health care services and the best way to meet them. The research design consisted of an exploratory phase followed by a descriptive cross-sectional online survey of 1,000 U.S. health care consumers over the age of 18.

According to the survey, a visit to the doctor's office is not enough for most consumers. The average time a doctor spends with a patient has decreased to 15 minutes, which reduces the overall interpersonal health care communication. The survey revealed that consumers demand a range of options for accessing their doctors and nurses, which includes face-to-face, online, and telephone communication:

- 86 percent of respondents wanted to schedule appointments by phone with a person.
- 89 percent would like online or phone access to a nurse triage to help manage a chronic medical condition with availability after office hours.
- 40 percent expressed frustration at having to see their physicians in person to get answers to simple health care questions.
- 86 percent wanted electronic medical reminders.
- 83 percent wanted lab test procedures and results to be available online.
- 69 percent wanted online charts for monitoring chronic conditions.

In response to such findings, Kaiser Permanente (www.kaiserpermanente.org) redesigned its Web site in 2008 to enable members to access drug and medical encyclopedias, request appointments, ask confidential questions or get advice from nurses and pharmacists, and share health concerns with other members and physicians in discussion groups. The Kaiser site also provides access to information on health plan benefit options, local health education classes, physician directories, and directions to facilities. Members of the Kaiser site also have information on specific doctors and facilities at their fingertips. Alternative health care communication methods like Kaiser's will support the physician–patient relationship and make a physician's practice and the entire HMO more competitive when consumers make their decisions about doctors and health care providers.[7] ■

multiple cross-sectional design
A cross-sectional design in which there are two or more samples of respondents, and information from each sample is obtained only once.

In **multiple cross-sectional designs**, there are two or more samples of respondents, and information from each sample is obtained only once. Often, information from different samples is obtained at different times over long intervals. The following examples illustrate single and multiple cross-sectional designs. Multiple cross-sectional designs allow comparisons at the aggregate level but not at the individual respondent level. Because a different sample is taken each time a survey is conducted, there is no way to compare the measures on an individual respondent across surveys. One type of multiple cross-sectional design of special interest is cohort analysis.

cohort analysis
A multiple cross-sectional design consisting of a series of surveys conducted at appropriate time intervals. The cohort refers to the group of respondents who experience the same event within the same time interval.

COHORT ANALYSIS **Cohort analysis** consists of a series of surveys conducted at appropriate time intervals, where the cohort serves as the basic unit of analysis. A cohort is a group of respondents who experience the same event within the same time interval.[8] For example, a birth (or age) cohort is a group of people who were born during the same time interval, such as 1951 through 1960. The term *cohort analysis* refers to any study in which there are measures of some characteristics of one or more cohorts at two or more points in time.

It is unlikely that any of the individuals studied at time one will also be in the sample at time two. For example, the age cohort of people between 8 and 19 years old was selected and their soft drink consumption was examined every 10 years for 30 years. In other words, every 10 years a different sample of respondents was drawn from the population of those who were then between 8 and 19 years old. This sample was drawn independently of any previous sample drawn in this study from the population of 8 to 19 years old. Obviously, people who were selected once were unlikely to be included again in the same age cohort (8 to 19 years old), as these people would be much older at the time of subsequent sampling. This study showed that this cohort had increased consumption of soft drinks over time. Similar findings were obtained for other age cohorts (20 to 29, 30 to 39, 40 to 49, and 50+). Further, the consumption of each cohort did not decrease as the cohort aged. These results are presented in Table 3.3, in which the consumption of the various age cohorts over time can be determined by reading down the diagonal. These findings contradicted the common belief that the consumption of soft drinks will decline with the graying of America. This common but erroneous belief was based on single cross-sectional studies. Note that if any column of Table 3.3 is viewed in isolation as a single cross-sectional study (reading down the column), the consumption of soft drinks declines with age, fostering the erroneous belief.[9]

Cohort analysis is also used to predict changes in voter opinions during a political campaign. Well-known marketing researchers like Louis Harris (www.harrisinteractive.com) or George Gallup (www.gallup.com), who specialize in political opinion research, periodically question cohorts of voters (people with similar voting patterns during a given interval) about their voting preferences to predict election results. Thus, cohort analysis is an important cross-sectional design. The other type of descriptive design is longitudinal design.

TABLE 3.3

Consumption of Soft Drinks by Various Age Cohorts (Percentage Consuming on a Typical Day)

Age	1950	1960	1969	1979	
8–19	52.9	62.6	73.2	81.0	
20–29	45.2	60.7	76.0	75.8	C8
30–39	33.9	46.6	67.7	71.4	C7
40–49	23.2	40.8	58.6	67.8	C6
50+	18.1	28.8	50.0	51.9	C5
		C1	C2	C3	C4

C1: cohort born prior to 1900   C5: cohort born 1931–40
C2: cohort born 1901–10   C6: cohort born 1941–49
C3: cohort born 1911–20   C7: cohort born 1950–59
C4: cohort born 1921–30   C8: cohort born 1960–69

Longitudinal Designs

longitudinal design
A type of research design involving a fixed sample of population elements that is measured repeatedly. The sample remains the same over time, thus providing a series of pictures that, when viewed together, portray a vivid illustration of the situation and the changes that are taking place over time.

In **longitudinal designs**, a fixed sample (or samples) of population elements is measured repeatedly on the same variables. A longitudinal design differs from a cross-sectional design in that the sample or samples remain the same over time. In other words, the same people are studied over time and the same variables are measured. In contrast to the typical cross-sectional design, which gives a snapshot of the variables of interest at a single point in time, a longitudinal study provides a series of pictures that give an in-depth view of the situation and the changes that take place over time. For example, the question, "How did the American people rate the performance of George W. Bush immediately after the war in Afghanistan?" would be addressed using a cross-sectional design. However, a longitudinal design would be used to address the question, "How did the American people change their view of Bush's performance during the war in Afghanistan?"

panel
A sample of respondents who have agreed to provide information at specified intervals over an extended period.

Sometimes, the term *panel* or *true panel* is used interchangeably with the term *longitudinal design*. A **panel** consists of a sample of respondents, generally households that have agreed to provide information at specified intervals over an extended period. Syndicated firms maintain panels, and panel members are compensated for their participation with gifts, coupons, information, or cash. Panels are discussed further in Chapter 4. A panel design can be used to understand and monitor changes in women's attitudes toward golf, as illustrated in the following example.

Real Research

Women's Golf Apparel Market Is in "Full Swing"

In 2008, there were about 26.2 million golfers in the United States, and of that number, women comprised 25 percent and represented one of the few growing segments in the long-stagnant golf market. Although women comprise a smaller percentage of all U.S. golfers, they purchase more than 50 percent of all golf products, excluding golf clubs, according to the Women's Sports Foundation. This trend has led traditional golf brands to introduce women's lines and open women's-only golf stores around the country to cater to the needs of neglected female golfers.

To meet this growing demand, TimeOut, a division of King Louie International (www.kinglouie. com/timeoutforher), now offers a full line of LPGA-licensed clothing. In order to ascertain what this large mass of women golfers expects and wants in their golf clothing, TimeOut created Fairway Forum, a panel of female golf enthusiasts that provides insight into women's apparel tastes. Women who have been recruited to this panel participate in focus groups and surveys. Because the women belong to the panel, multiple surveys measuring essentially the same variables can be conducted on the same set of respondents, thus implementing a longitudinal design.

What TimeOut has learned is that with the passage of time women are becoming more and more serious about their golf game and wish more LPGA events were televised. Additionally, TimeOut discovered that women are extremely eager for new brands to hit the market, as traditional brands do not offer enough selection to meet their tastes. These women do not want to wear reformulated versions of men's golf apparel nor do they want to scamper about the course in "cutesy" clothing, and finally, these women do not want to encounter other women wearing the same outfit. These ladies are hungry for more variety and are demanding it in the marketplace.

This research further indicated that female golfers want apparel that is both functional and attractive. For example, they want deep pockets to keep balls in while going around the course. The forum also helped determine some of the underlying psychological factors that women link with their apparel. Although these women want to be treated as athletes, they also want to be treated with respect, and these feelings have become more intense over time. TimeOut's Fairway Forum panel has been an excellent help in assisting sporting goods and apparel manufacturers in designing clothing to meet the needs of this growing and changing golf segment. The demand for women's golf apparel has grown over time, exceeding $250 million per year in 2009.[10] ■

Data obtained from panels not only provide information on market shares that are based on an extended period of time but also allow the researcher to examine changes in market share over time.[11] As the following section explains, these changes cannot be determined from cross-sectional data.

Longitudinal designs implemented by using TimeOut's Fairway Forum panel have enabled manufacturers to design suitable clothing for women golfers.

Relative Advantages and Disadvantages of Longitudinal and Cross-Sectional Designs

The relative advantages and disadvantages of longitudinal versus cross-sectional designs are summarized in Table 3.4. A major advantage of longitudinal design over the cross-sectional design is the ability to detect change at the individual level, i.e., for an individual respondent. This is possible because of repeated measurement of the same variables on the same sample.

Tables 3.5 and 3.6 demonstrate how cross-sectional data can mislead researchers about changes over time. The cross-sectional data reported in Table 3.5 reveal that purchases of Brands A, B, and C remain the same in time periods 1 and 2. In each survey, 20 percent of the respondents purchased Brand A; 30 percent, Brand B; and 50 percent, Brand C. The longitudinal data presented in Table 3.6 show that substantial change, in the form of brand-switching, occurred in the study period. For example, only 50 percent (100/200) of the respondents who purchased Brand A in period 1 also purchased it in period 2. The corresponding repeat purchase figures for Brands B and C are, respectively, 33.3 percent (100/300) and 55 percent (275/500). Hence, during this interval, Brand C experienced the greatest loyalty and Brand B the least. Table 3.6 provides valuable information on brand loyalty and brand switching. (Such a table is called a *turnover table* or a *brand-switching matrix.*[12])

TABLE 3.4		
Relative Advantages and Disadvantages of Longitudinal and Cross-Sectional Designs		
Evaluation Criteria	Cross-Sectional Design	Longitudinal Design
Detecting change	−	+
Large amount of data collection	−	+
Accuracy	−	+
Representative sampling	+	−
Response bias	+	−
Note: A + indicates a relative advantage over the other design, whereas a − indicates a relative disadvantage.		

TABLE 3.5		
Cross-Sectional Data May Not Show Change		
	Time Period	
Brand Purchased	Period 1 Survey	Period 2 Survey
Brand A	200	200
Brand B	300	300
Brand C	500	500
Total	1,000	1,000

Longitudinal data enable researchers to examine changes in the behavior of individual units and to link behavioral changes to marketing variables, such as changes in advertising, packaging, pricing, and distribution. Since the same units are measured repeatedly, variations caused by changes in the sample are eliminated and even small changes are apparent.

Another advantage of panels is that relatively large amounts of data can be collected. Because panel members are usually compensated for their participation, they are willing to participate in lengthy and demanding interviews. Yet another advantage is that panel data can be more accurate than cross-sectional data. A typical cross-sectional survey requires the respondent to recall past purchases and behavior; these data can be inaccurate because of memory lapses. Panel data, which rely on continuous recording of purchases in a diary, place less reliance on the respondent's memory. A comparison of panel and cross-sectional survey estimates of retail sales indicates that panel data give more accurate estimates.[13]

The main disadvantage of panels is that they may not be representative. Nonrepresentativeness may arise because of:

1. *Refusal to cooperate.* Many individuals or households do not wish to be bothered with the panel operation and refuse to participate. Consumer panels requiring members to keep a record of purchases have a cooperation rate of 60 percent or less.
2. *Mortality.* Panel members who agree to participate may subsequently drop out because they move away or lose interest. Mortality rates can be as high as 20 percent per year.[14]
3. *Payment.* Payment may cause certain types of people to be attracted, making the group unrepresentative of the population.

Another disadvantage of panels is response bias. New panel members are often biased in their initial responses. They tend to increase the behavior being measured, such as food purchasing. This bias decreases as the respondent overcomes the novelty of being on the panel, so it can be reduced by initially excluding the data of new members. Seasoned panel members may also give biased responses because they believe they are experts or want to look good or give the "right" answer. Bias also results from boredom, fatigue, and incomplete diary or questionnaire entries.[15]

TABLE 3.6				
Longitudinal Data May Show Substantial Change				
Brand Purchased in Period 1	Brand Purchased in Period 2			
	Brand A	Brand B	Brand C	Total
Brand A	100	50	50	200
Brand B	25	100	175	300
Brand C	75	150	275	500
Total	200	300	500	1,000

Causal Research

causal research
A type of conclusive research where the major objective is to obtain evidence regarding cause-and-effect (causal) relationships.

Causal research is used to obtain evidence of cause-and-effect (causal) relationships (see Table 3.2). Marketing managers continually make decisions based on assumed causal relationships. These assumptions may not be justifiable, and the validity of the causal relationships should be examined via formal research.[16] For example, the common assumption that a decrease in price will lead to increased sales and market share does not hold in certain competitive environments. Causal research is appropriate for the following purposes:

1. To understand which variables are the cause (independent variables) and which variables are the effect (dependent variables) of a phenomenon
2. To determine the nature of the relationship between the causal variables and the effect to be predicted

Like descriptive research, causal research requires a planned and structured design. Although descriptive research can determine the degree of association between variables, it is not appropriate for examining causal relationships. Such an examination requires a causal design, in which the causal or independent variables are manipulated in a relatively controlled environment. A relatively controlled environment is one in which the other variables that may affect the dependent variable are controlled or checked as much as possible. The effect of this manipulation on one or more dependent variables is then measured to infer causality. The main method of causal research is experimentation.[17]

Because of its complexity and importance, a separate chapter (Chapter 7) has been devoted to causal designs and experimental research. However, we give some examples here. In the context of the department store patronage project, a researcher wishes to determine whether the presence and helpfulness of salespeople (causal variable) will influence the sales of housewares (effect variable). A causal design could be formulated in which two groups of otherwise comparable housewares departments of a particular chain are selected. For four weeks, trained salespeople are stationed in one group of housewares departments but not in the other. Sales are monitored for both groups, while controlling for other variables. A comparison of sales for the two groups will reveal the effect of salespeople on housewares sales in department stores. Alternatively, instead of selecting two groups of stores, the researcher could select only one set of department stores and carry out this manipulation for two comparable time periods: Salespeople are present in one time period and absent in the other. As another example, consider the research conducted by Microsoft.

Real Research

Microsoft : Experimenting with Usability

Microsoft performs meticulous usability research to enhance and develop its product portfolio in a way that is most beneficial to the customer. Usability research is aimed at increasing user comfort by making the product more intuitive to learn and remember. Microsoft Usability Group is an important part of this effort. The group was conceived in 1988 to integrate user feedback into the design of the Microsoft development process and thereby into the end products.

The key to the success (high awareness and high sales) of Office 2007 (www.microsoft.com) was that the product was carefully designed and tested by the Usability Group. In a controlled experiment, one group of computer users was asked to work with Office 2007. Two other carefully matched groups worked with the previous versions of Office: one with Office 2003 and the other with Office XP. All three groups rated the products on ease of use, capabilities, and the ability to enhance a computer user's experience. Office 2007 was rated significantly better than the previous versions on all factors, leading to the introduction of this version.[18] ■

In the Microsoft experiment, the causal (independent) variable was the Office suite, which was manipulated to have three levels: XP, 2003, and 2007. The effect (dependent) variables were ease of use, capabilities, and the ability to enhance a computer user's experience. The influence of other variables, such as user expertise and experience with Microsoft Office, had to be controlled. Although the preceding example distinguished causal research from other types of research, causal research should not be viewed in isolation. Rather, the exploratory, descriptive, and causal designs often complement each other.

ACTIVE RESEARCH

Taco Bell: Thinking Outside the Bun

Visit www.tacobell.com and search the Internet using a search engine as well as your library's online databases to obtain information on the advertising for Taco Bell. Write a brief report.

As the advertising manager, how would you determine whether the advertising budget for Taco Bell for the next year should be increased, decreased, or remain the same as the current budget?

Design an experiment to determine whether the advertising budget for Taco Bell for the next year should be increased, decreased, or remain the same as the current budget. Identify the independent, the dependent, and the control variables.

Experiential Research

Gallup(ing) Research

Visit www.gallup.com and examine some of the recent projects conducted by Gallup. You will have to read through some of the reports posted on this Web site.

What type of exploratory research was conducted in these projects? Which methods were used?
What type of descriptive research was conducted in these projects? Which methods were used?
Did any project use an experimental design? If yes, identify the cause, effect, and control variables.
In which project was the research design most appropriate? Why? ■

Relationships Among Exploratory, Descriptive, and Causal Research

We have described exploratory, descriptive, and causal research as major classifications of research designs, but the distinctions among these classifications are not absolute. A given marketing research project may involve more than one type of research design and thus serve several purposes. Which combination of research designs should be employed depends on the nature of the problem. We offer the following general guidelines for choosing research designs:

1. When little is known about the problem situation, it is desirable to begin with exploratory research. Exploratory research is appropriate when the problem needs to be defined more precisely, alternative courses of action identified, research questions or hypotheses developed, and key variables isolated and classified as dependent or independent.
2. Exploratory research is the initial step in the overall research design framework. It should, in most instances, be followed by descriptive or causal research. For example, hypotheses developed via exploratory research should be statistically tested using descriptive or causal research. This was illustrated in the cause-related marketing example given in the "Overview" section. Exploratory research in the form of secondary data analysis and focus groups was conducted to identify the social causes that American businesses should be concerned about. Then a descriptive cross-sectional survey was undertaken to quantify the relative salience of these causes.
3. It is not necessary to begin every research design with exploratory research. It depends upon the precision with which the problem has been defined and the researcher's degree of certainty about the approach to the problem. A research design could well begin with descriptive or causal research. To illustrate, a consumer satisfaction survey that is conducted quarterly need not begin with or include an exploratory phase each quarter.

4. Although exploratory research is generally the initial step, it need not be. Exploratory research may follow descriptive or causal research. For example, descriptive or causal research results in findings that are hard for managers to interpret. Exploratory research may provide more insights to help understand these findings.

The relationship among exploratory, descriptive, and causal research is further illustrated by the department store patronage project.

Project Research   ## Exploring and Describing Store Patronage

In the department store patronage project, exploratory research, including secondary data analysis and qualitative research, was first conducted to define the problem and develop a suitable approach. This was followed by a descriptive study consisting of a survey in which a questionnaire was constructed and administered by personal interviews.

Suppose the patronage study was to be repeated after a year to determine if any changes had taken place. At that point, exploratory research would probably be unnecessary and the research design could begin with descriptive research.

Assume that the survey is repeated a year later and some unexpected findings are obtained. Management wonders why the store's ratings on in-store service have declined when the sales staff has increased. Exploratory research in the form of focus groups might be undertaken to probe the unexpected findings. The focus groups may reveal that while the salespeople are easy to find, they are not perceived to be friendly or helpful. This may suggest the need for training the sales staff.

Project Activities

1. Suppose Sears was interested in examining changes in department store shopping as people grow from 30 to 40 to 50 to 60 years old. What type of research design should be adopted?
2. How can Sears make use of causal research? Identify two scenarios in which such a design would be appropriate. ■

The department store patronage project involved the use of exploratory and descriptive research but not causal research. This reflects the fact that exploratory and descriptive research are frequently used in commercial marketing research but causal research is not as popular. However, it is possible to combine exploratory, descriptive, and causal research as demonstrated by Citibank.

Real Research   ## Citibank Groups Exploratory, Descriptive, and Causal Research

As of 2009, Citigroup (www.citigroup.com) was a leading provider of a range of financial products and services, including banking, in more than 100 countries. In order to maintain its leadership position, Citigroup must continually research target customers to better cater to their needs. Marketing research at Citibank (www.citibank.com), a division of Citigroup, is typical in that it is used to measure consumer awareness of products, monitor their satisfaction and attitudes associated with the product, track product usage, and diagnose problems as they occur. To accomplish these tasks Citibank makes extensive use of exploratory, descriptive, and causal research.

Often it is advantageous to offer special financial packages to specific groups of customers, in this case for senior citizens. Citibank followed the following seven-step process to help in the design.

Step 1   A task force was created to better define the market parameters to include all the needs of the many Citibank branches. A final decision was made to include Americans 55 years of age or older, retired, and in the upper half of the financial strata of that market.

Step 2   Exploratory research in the form of secondary data analysis of the mature or older market was then performed and a study of competitive products was conducted. Exploratory qualitative research involving focus groups was also carried out in order to determine the needs and desires of the market and the level of satisfaction with the current products. In the case of senior citizens, a great deal of diversity was found in the market. This was determined to be due to such factors as affluence, relative age, and the absence or presence of a spouse.

Step 3 The next stage of exploratory research was brainstorming. This involved the formation of many different financial packages targeted for the target market. In this case, a total of 10 ideas were generated.

Step 4 The feasibility of each of the 10 ideas generated in step 3 was then tested. The following list of questions was used as a series of hurdles that the ideas had to pass to continue on to the next step.

- Can the idea be explained in a manner that the target market will easily understand?
- Does the idea fit into the overall strategy of Citibank?
- Is there an available description of a specific target market for the proposed product?
- Does the research conducted so far indicate a potential match for target market needs, and is the idea perceived to have appeal to this market?
- Is there a feasible outline of the tactics and strategies for implementing the program?
- Have the financial impact and cost of the program been thoroughly evaluated and determined to be in line with company practices?

In this study, only one idea generated from the brainstorming session made it past all the listed hurdles and on to step 5.

Step 5 A creative work plan was then generated. This plan was to emphasize the competitive advantage of the proposed product as well as better delineate the specific features of the product.

Step 6 The previous exploratory research was now followed up with descriptive research in the form of mall intercept surveys of people in the target market range. The survey showed that the list of special features was too long, and it was decided to drop the features more commonly offered by competitors.

Step 7 Finally, the product was test-marketed in six of the Citibank branches within the target market. Test marketing is a form of causal research. Given successful test-marketing results, the product was introduced nationally.[19] ■

The Internet can facilitate the implementation of different types of research designs. During the exploratory phase of the research, forums, chat rooms, or newsgroups can be used to generally discuss a topic with anyone who visits the chat room. Newsgroups focus on a particular topic and function like bulletin boards. Internet users stop by a newsgroup to read messages left by others and to post their own responses or comments. Newsgroups or chat rooms could be used to set up more formal focus groups with experts or individuals representing the target audience in order to obtain initial information on a subject. In Chapter 5, we discuss the use of the Internet for conducting focus groups in more detail. Chapter 6 covers the use of the Internet for descriptive research, while the use of the Internet for causal research is discussed in Chapter 7.

Many descriptive studies utilize secondary data, which we describe in Chapter 4; surveys, which are discussed in Chapter 6; and panels, which are discussed in Chapters 4 and 6. The use of the Internet for causal research designs is discussed in Chapter 7. The Internet, in its capacity as a source of information, can be useful in uncovering secondary data and collecting primary data needed in conclusive research.

ACTIVE RESEARCH

Wells Fargo: Banking on Online Banking

Visit www.wellsfargo.com and search the Internet using a search engine as well as your library's online databases to obtain information on consumers' attitudes toward online banking.

The Wells Fargo Bank would like to determine consumers' attitudes toward online banking and hopes to repeat this project annually. What type of research design would you implement and why?

As the CEO of Wells Fargo, how would you use information about consumers' attitudes toward online banking in improving the competitiveness of your bank?

Regardless of the kind of research design employed, the researcher should attempt to minimize the potential sources of error.

Potential Sources of Error

total error
The variation between the true mean value in the population of the variable of interest and the observed mean value obtained in the marketing research project.

random sampling error
The error due to the particular sample selected being an imperfect representation of the population of interest. It may be defined as the variation between the true mean value for the sample and the true mean value of the population.

nonsampling error
Nonsampling errors are errors that can be attributed to sources other than sampling, and they can be random or nonrandom.

Several potential sources of error can affect a research design. A good research design attempts to control the various sources of error. These errors are discussed in great detail in subsequent chapters, but it is pertinent at this stage to give brief descriptions.

The **total error** is the variation between the true mean value in the population of the variable of interest and the observed mean value obtained in the marketing research project. For example, the average annual income of the target population is $75,871, as determined from the latest census records, but the marketing research project estimates it as $67,157 based on a sample survey. As shown in Figure 3.2, total error is composed of random sampling error and nonsampling error.

Random Sampling Error

Random sampling error occurs because the particular sample selected is an imperfect representation of the population of interest. Random sampling error is the variation between the true mean value for the population and the true mean value for the original sample. For example, the average annual income of the target population is $75,871, but it is only $71,382 for the original sample, as determined from the mail panel records that are believed to be accurate. Random sampling error is discussed further in Chapters 11 and 12.

Nonsampling Error

Nonsampling errors can be attributed to sources other than sampling, and they may be random or nonrandom. They result from a variety of reasons, including errors in problem definition, approach, scales, questionnaire design, interviewing methods, and data preparation and analysis. For example, the researcher designs a poor questionnaire, which contains

FIGURE 3.2

Potential Sources of Error in Research Designs

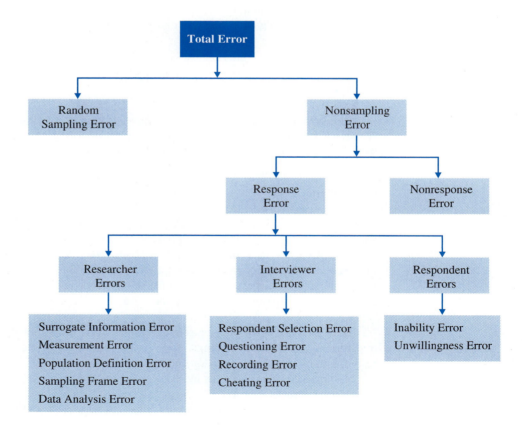

nonresponse error
A type of nonsampling error that occurs when some of the respondents included in the sample do not respond. This error may be defined as the variation between the true mean value of the variable in the original sample and the true mean value in the net sample.

response error
A type of nonsampling error arising from respondents who do respond, but give inaccurate answers or their answers are misrecorded or misanalyzed. It may be defined as the variation between the true mean value of the variable in the net sample and the observed mean value obtained in the marketing research project.

several questions that lead the respondents to give biased answers. Nonsampling errors consist of nonresponse errors and response errors.

NONRESPONSE ERROR **Nonresponse error** arises when some of the respondents included in the sample do not respond. The primary causes of nonresponse are refusals and not-at-homes (see Chapter 12). Nonresponse will cause the net or resulting sample to be different in size or composition from the original sample. Nonresponse error is defined as the variation between the true mean value of the variable in the original sample and the true mean value in the net sample. For example, the average annual income is $71,382 for the original sample but $69,467 for the net sample, both determined from the mail panel records that are believed to be accurate.

RESPONSE ERROR **Response error** arises when respondents give inaccurate answers or their answers are misrecorded or misanalyzed. Response error is defined as the variation between the true mean value of the variable in the net sample and the observed mean value obtained in the marketing research project. For example, the average annual income is $69,467 for the net sample, but is estimated as $67,157 in the marketing research project. Response errors can be made by researchers, interviewers, or respondents.[20]

Errors made by the researcher include surrogate information, measurement, population definition, sampling frame, and data analysis errors.

Surrogate information error may be defined as the variation between the information needed for the marketing research problem and the information sought by the researcher. For example, instead of obtaining information on consumer choice of a new brand (needed for the marketing research problem), the researcher obtains information on consumer preferences since the choice process cannot be easily observed.

Measurement error may be defined as the variation between the information sought and the information generated by the measurement process employed by the researcher. While seeking to measure consumer preferences, the researcher employs a scale that measures perceptions rather than preferences.

Population definition error may be defined as the variation between the actual population relevant to the problem at hand and the population as defined by the researcher. The problem of appropriately defining the population may be far from trivial, as illustrated by the case of affluent households.

Real Research | ## How Affluent Is Affluent?

In a recent study, the population of the affluent households was defined in four different ways: (1) households with income of $50,000 or more; (2) the top 20 percent of households, as measured by income; (3) households with net worth over $250,000; and (4) households with spendable discretionary income 30 percent higher than that of comparable households. The number and characteristics of the affluent households varied depending upon the definition, underscoring the need to avoid population definition error.[21] ∎

As may be surmised, the results of this study would have varied markedly depending upon the way the population of affluent households was defined.

Sampling frame error may be defined as the variation between the population defined by the researcher and the population as implied by the sampling frame (list) used. For example, the telephone directory used to generate a list of telephone numbers does not accurately represent the population of potential consumers because of unlisted, disconnected, and new numbers in service.

Data analysis error encompasses errors that occur while raw data from questionnaires are transformed into research findings. For example, an inappropriate statistical procedure is used, resulting in incorrect interpretation and findings.

Response errors made by the interviewer include respondent selection, questioning, recording, and cheating errors.

Respondent selection error occurs when interviewers select respondents other than those specified by the sampling design or in a manner inconsistent with the sampling design.

For example, in a readership survey, a nonreader is selected for the interview but is classified as a reader of the *Wall Street Journal* in the 15- to 19-years category in order to meet a difficult quota requirement.

Questioning error denotes errors made in asking questions of the respondents or in not probing when more information is needed. For example, while asking questions an interviewer does not use the exact wording given in the questionnaire.

Recording error arises due to errors in hearing, interpreting, and recording the answers given by the respondents. For example, a respondent indicates a neutral response (undecided), but the interviewer misinterprets that to mean a positive response (would buy the new brand).

Cheating error arises when the interviewer fabricates answers to a part or all of the interview. For example, an interviewer does not ask the sensitive questions related to respondent's debt but later fills in the answers based on personal assessment.

Response errors made by the respondent are comprised of inability and unwillingness errors.

Inability error results from the respondent's inability to provide accurate answers. Respondents may provide inaccurate answers because of unfamiliarity, fatigue, boredom, faulty recall, question format, question content, and other factors. For example, a respondent cannot recall the brand of yogurt purchased four weeks ago.

Unwillingness error arises from the respondent's unwillingness to provide accurate information. Respondents may intentionally misreport their answers because of a desire to provide socially acceptable answers, avoid embarrassment, or please the interviewer. For example, a respondent intentionally misreports reading *Time* magazine in order to impress the interviewer.

These sources of error are discussed in more detail in the subsequent chapters; what is important here is that there are many sources of error. In formulating a research design, the researcher should attempt to minimize the total error, not just a particular source. This admonition is warranted by the general tendency among students and unsophisticated researchers to control sampling error with large samples. Increasing the sample size does decrease sampling error, but it may also increase nonsampling error by increasing interview errors.

Nonsampling error is likely to be more problematic than sampling error. Sampling error can be calculated, whereas many forms of nonsampling error defy estimation. Moreover, nonsampling error has been found to be the major contributor to total error, whereas random sampling error is relatively small in magnitude.[22] The point is that total error is important. A particular type of error is important only in that it contributes to total error.

Sometimes, researchers deliberately increase a particular type of error to decrease the total error by reducing other errors. For example, suppose a mail survey is being conducted to determine consumer preferences for purchasing fashion clothing from department stores. A large sample size has been selected to reduce sampling error. A response rate of 30 percent may be expected. Given the limited budget for the project, the selection of a large sample size does not allow for follow-up mailings. However, past experience indicates that the response rate could be increased to 45 percent with one follow-up and to 55 percent with two follow-up mailings. Given the subject of the survey, nonrespondents are likely to differ from respondents in terms of salient variables. Hence, it may be desirable to reduce the sample size to make money available for follow-up mailings. While decreasing the sample size will increase random sampling error, the two follow-up mailings will more than offset this loss by decreasing nonresponse error.

Once a suitable research design has been formulated, the researcher is in a position to prepare a budget and schedule for the project, both of which are needed to prepare a proposal for the client.

Budgeting and Scheduling the Project

budgeting and scheduling
Management tools needed to help ensure that the marketing research project is completed within the available resources.

Once a research design, appropriately controlling the total error, has been specified, the budgeting and scheduling decisions should be made. **Budgeting and scheduling** help to ensure that the marketing research project is completed within the available resources—financial, time, personnel, and other. By specifying the time parameters within which each

critical path method (CPM)
Management technique of dividing a research project into component activities, determining the sequence of these components and the time each activity will require.

program evaluation and review technique (PERT)
A more sophisticated critical path method that accounts for the uncertainty in project completion times.

graphical evaluation and review technique (GERT)
A sophisticated critical path method that accounts for both the completion probabilities and the activity costs.

marketing research proposal
The official layout of the planned marketing research activity for management. It describes the research problem, the approach, the research design, data collection methods, data analysis methods, and reporting methods.

task should be completed and the costs of each task, the research project can be effectively managed. A useful approach for managing a project is the **critical path method (CPM)**, which involves dividing the research project into component activities, determining the sequence of these activities, and estimating the time required for each activity. These activities and time estimates are diagrammed in the form of a network flowchart. The critical path, the series of activities whose delay will hold up the project, can then be identified.

An advanced version of CPM is the **program evaluation and review technique (PERT)**, which is a probability-based scheduling approach that recognizes and measures the uncertainty of the project completion times.[23] An even more advanced scheduling technique is the **graphical evaluation and review technique (GERT)**, in which both the completion probabilities and the activity costs can be built into a network representation.

Marketing Research Proposal

Once the research design has been formulated and budgeting and scheduling of the project accomplished, a written research proposal should be prepared. The **marketing research proposal** contains the essence of the project and serves as a contract between the researcher and management. The research proposal covers all phases of the marketing research process. It describes the research problem, the approach, the research design, and how the data will be collected, analyzed, and reported. It gives a cost estimate and a time schedule for completing the project. Although the format of a research proposal may vary considerably, most proposals address all steps of the marketing research process and contain the following elements.

1. *Executive Summary.* The proposal should begin with a summary of the major points from each of the other sections, presenting an overview of the entire proposal.
2. *Background.* The background to the problem, including the environmental context, should be discussed.
3. *Problem Definition/Objectives of the Research.* Normally, a statement of the problem, including the specific components, should be presented. If this statement has not been developed (as in the case of problem identification research), the objectives of the marketing research project should be clearly specified.
4. *Approach to the Problem.* At a minimum, a review of the relevant academic and trade literature should be presented, along with some kind of an analytical model. If research questions and hypotheses have been identified, then these should be included in the proposal.
5. *Research Design.* The research design adopted, whether exploratory, descriptive, or causal, should be specified. Information should be provided on the following components: (1) kind of information to be obtained, (2) method of administering the questionnaire (mail, telephone, personal or electronic interviews), (3) scaling techniques, (4) nature of the questionnaire (type of questions asked, length, average interviewing time), and (5) sampling plan and sample size.
6. *Fieldwork/Data Collection.* The proposal should discuss how the data will be collected and who will collect it. If the fieldwork is to be subcontracted to another supplier, this should be stated. Control mechanisms to ensure the quality of data collected should be described.
7. *Data Analysis.* The kind of data analysis that will be conducted (simple cross-tabulations, univariate analysis, multivariate analysis) and how the results will be interpreted should be described.
8. *Reporting.* The proposal should specify whether intermediate reports will be presented and at what stages, what will be the form of the final report, and whether a formal presentation of the results will be made.
9. *Cost and Time.* The cost of the project and a time schedule, broken down by phases, should be presented. A CPM or PERT chart might be included. In large projects, a payment schedule is also worked out in advance.
10. *Appendices.* Any statistical or other information that is of interest only to a few people should be contained in appendices.

Preparing a research proposal has several advantages. It ensures that the researcher and management agree about the nature of the project and helps sell the project to management. Because preparation of the proposal entails planning, it helps the researcher conceptualize and execute the marketing research project.

International Marketing Research

While conducting international marketing research, it is important to realize that given the environmental differences (see Chapter 24), the research design appropriate for one country may not be suitable in another. Consider the problem of determining household attitudes toward major appliances in the United States and Saudi Arabia. While conducting exploratory research in the United States, it is appropriate to conduct focus groups jointly with male and female heads of households. However, it would be inappropriate to conduct such focus groups in Saudi Arabia. Given the traditional culture, the wives are unlikely to participate freely in the presence of their husbands. It would be more useful to conduct one-on-one depth interviews, including both male and female heads of households in the sample.

Real Research   There's No Place Like Home

GfK (www.gfk.it), a European custom marketing research company, conducted a two-year, two-part study to determine the new trends in European youth and culture—what matters to European teenagers, and how international marketers should approach them. Exploratory research in the form of focus groups was conducted first to identify issues that are salient to European youth. The issues identified in focus groups were quantified by conducting a descriptive longitudinal survey. The survey was conducted in two parts spanning 16 different European countries, including Denmark, Norway, Sweden, the United Kingdom, Germany, Italy, Spain, and France, among others.

In each country, four groups of respondents were selected; 14–16-year-old girls, 14–16-year-old boys, 17–20-year-old girls, and 17–20-year-old boys. A descriptive survey was designed and administered in personal, face-to-face settings. Given the European youth culture, it was felt that the teens would feel more comfortable and be able to provide more candid responses in a personal setting. A total of 523 young people participated. Two years later, the same people were contacted in 9 of the 16 countries, with a total of 305 people participating.

The results showed that tastes and opinions of teenagers in Europe have been changing dramatically over the past few years and particularly during the last two years. It was discovered that European teens did not trust big companies. The concept of home included not only the family and actual home dwelling, but a sense of belonging and community, especially with friends. It is a symbol of coziness and warmth. The European teens did not see their families much during the week. Instead, friends filled this home function. Finally, they did put a lot of stock in a brand that has been around for a long time, feeling that if the brand has proven its existence over time, it must be good and worthy of its long stay.

The results proved very beneficial for McDonald's (www.mcdonalds.com) in developing their international advertising aimed at this market. McDonald's new campaign did not focus on its big-company status but localized its advertising to make it seem to be the local hamburger hangout joint for teens. Meeting up with friends at the local McDonald's made the McDonald's "home." It appeared to be fun, and the teens wanted to be there. Additionally, McDonald's focused on the longevity and stability of the brand. It will always be around as a fun place where teens can hang out with their friends and have fun for a low price. The campaign resulted in increased market share in the lucrative European teenage market. As of 2009, McDonald's derived more than 35 percent of its total sales from Europe.[24] ∎

In many countries, particularly developing countries, consumer panels have not been developed, making it difficult to conduct descriptive longitudinal research. Likewise, in many countries the marketing support infrastructure (i.e., retailing, wholesaling, advertising, and promotional infrastructure) is lacking, making it infeasible to implement a causal design involving a field experiment. In formulating a research design, considerable effort is required

By using cross-sectional and longitudinal surveys, McDonald's has determined what appeals to European youth and positioned itself accordingly.

to ensure the equivalence and comparability of secondary and primary data obtained from different countries. In the context of collecting primary data, qualitative research, survey methods, scaling techniques, questionnaire design, and sampling considerations are particularly important. These topics are discussed in more detail in subsequent chapters.

Ethics in Marketing Research

During the research design stage, not only are the concerns of the researcher and the client involved, but the rights of the respondents must also be respected. Although there usually isn't any direct contact between the respondent and the other stakeholders (client and researcher) during research design, this is the stage when decisions with ethical ramifications, such as using hidden video or audio tape recorders, are made.

The basic question of the type of research design that should be adopted (i.e., descriptive or causal, cross-sectional or longitudinal) has ethical overtones. For example, when studying brand-switching in toothpaste purchases, a longitudinal design is the only actual way to assess changes in an individual respondent's brand choice. A research firm that has not conducted many longitudinal studies may try to justify the use of a cross-sectional design. Is this ethical?

The researchers must ensure that the research design utilized will provide the information needed to address the marketing research problem that has been identified. The client should have the integrity not to misrepresent the project and should describe the constraints under which the researcher must operate and not make unreasonable demands. Longitudinal research takes time. Descriptive research might require interviewing customers. If time is an issue, or if customer contact has to be restricted, the client should make these constraints known at the start of the project. Finally, the client should not take undue advantage of the research firm to solicit unfair concessions for the current project by making false promises of future research contracts.

Real Research   Big Brother or Big Bully?

Ethical dilemmas may arise due to the strong desire of marketing research firms to become suppliers to large business firms that are heavy users of marketing research. Take, for example, Visa, Coca-Cola, or Ford Motor Company. Such firms have large marketing research budgets and regularly hire external marketing research suppliers. These large clients can manipulate the price for the current study or demand unreasonable concessions in the research design (e.g., the examination of additional variables, more focus groups, a larger, more targeted sample for the survey, or additional data analyses) by suggesting the potential for the marketing research firm to become a regular supplier. This may be considered just business, but it becomes unethical when there is no intention to follow up with a larger study or to use the research firm in the future.[25] ■

Equally important, the responsibilities to the respondents must not be overlooked. The researcher should design the study so as not to violate the respondents' right to safety, right to privacy, or right to choose. Furthermore, the client must not abuse its power to jeopardize the anonymity of the respondents. These respondent-related issues are discussed in more detail in Chapters 4, 5, 6, and 7.

Decision Research   NASCAR: Changing the Redneck Image

The Situation

The sound of engines roaring . . . the voices of screaming fans . . . the beating of hearts pumping . . . the excitement of NASCAR! The National Association of Stock Car Auto Racing (NASCAR) is a company unlike any other. Although it generates excitement in fans all across the nation, NASCAR has been stereotyped as only appealing to Southerners with lower incomes who work in laborer-type jobs. Brian France, CEO of NASCAR, wanted to increase its audience and change its stereotyped image.

NASCAR conducted exploratory research to identify ways to penetrate the nonrace market, reach younger fans, and build its brand image across the nation. Extensive focus groups revealed that: (1) NASCAR had a rural sports image, (2) this image was not necessarily negative, and (3) companies that supported sports were viewed positively.

The Marketing Research Decision

1. Do you think the research design adopted by NASCAR was appropriate? Why or why not?
2. What research designs would you recommend?
3. Discuss the role of the type of research design you recommend in enabling Brian France to change the image of NASCAR.

The Marketing Management Decision

1. Brian France realizes that it is crucial for NASCAR to project the right image. However, he wonders what that image is. What advice would you give him?
2. Discuss how the course of action you recommend to Brian France is influenced by the research that you suggested earlier and by the findings of that research.[26] ■

Marketing research has helped NASCAR shed the image of a sport that appealed only to Southerners with lower incomes and blue-collar occupations and establish the image of a national sport that builds excitement for everyone.

Summary

A research design is a framework or blueprint for conducting the marketing research project. It specifies the details of how the project should be conducted. Research designs may be broadly classified as exploratory or conclusive. The primary purpose of exploratory research is to provide insights into the problem. Conclusive research is conducted to test specific hypotheses and examine specific relationships. The findings from conclusive research are used as input into managerial decision making. Conclusive research may be either descriptive or causal. Figure 3.3 is a concept map for research design.

The major objective of descriptive research is to describe market characteristics or functions. A descriptive design requires a clear specification of the who, what, when, where, why, and way of the research. Descriptive research can be further classified into cross-sectional and longitudinal research. Cross-sectional designs involve the collection of information from a sample of population elements at a single point in time. In contrast, in longitudinal designs repeated measurements are taken on a fixed sample. Causal research is designed for the primary purpose of obtaining evidence about cause-and-effect (causal) relationships.

A research design consists of six components. Error can be associated with any of these components. The total error is composed of random sampling error and nonsampling error. Nonsampling error consists of nonresponse and response errors. Response error encompasses errors made by researchers, interviewers, and respondents. A written marketing research proposal including all the elements of the marketing research process should be prepared. In formulating a research design when conducting international marketing research, considerable effort is required to ensure the equivalence and comparability of secondary and primary data obtained from different countries.

In terms of ethical issues, the researchers must ensure that the research design utilized will provide the information sought, and that the information sought is the information needed by the client. The client should have the integrity not to misrepresent the project and should describe the situation that the researcher must operate within and not make unreasonable demands. Every precaution should be taken to ensure the respondents' or subjects' right to safety, right to privacy, or right to choose.

FIGURE 3.3

A Concept Map for Research Design

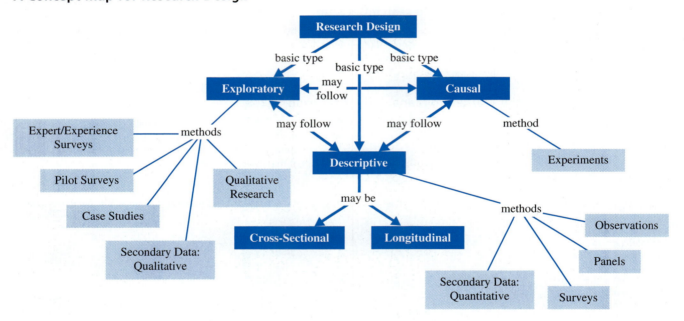

Key Terms and Concepts

Suggested Cases, Video Cases, and HBS Cases

Running Case with Real Data

1.1 Dell

Comprehensive Critical Thinking Cases

2.1 American Idol   2.2 Baskin-Robbins   2.3 Akron Children's Hospital

Comprehensive Cases with Real Data

4.1 JPMorgan Chase   4.2 Wendy's

Video Cases

3.1 NFL   4.1 Mayo Clinic   7.1 AFLAC   8.1 P&G   9.1 eGO

12.1 Subaru   13.1 Intel   23.1 Marriott   24.1 Nivea

Comprehensive Harvard Business School Cases

Case 5.1: The Harvard Graduate Student Housing Survey (9-505-059)
Case 5.2: BizRate.Com (9-501-024)
Case 5.3: Cola Wars Continue: Coke and Pepsi in the Twenty-First Century (9-702-442)
Case 5.4: TiVo in 2002 (9-502-062)
Case 5.5: Compaq Computer: Intel Inside? (9-599-061)
Case 5.6: The New Beetle (9-501-023)

Live Research: Conducting a Marketing Research Project

1. Each team presents to the class the type of research design they think is appropriate.

2. As a class, select the research design for this project.
3. It is helpful to invite the client to this session.

Acronym

The components of a research design may be summarized by the acronym

Design:

D ata analysis plan
E xploratory, descriptive, causal design
S caling and measurement
I nterviewing forms: questionnaire design
G enerate the information needed
N Sample size and plan

Exercises

Questions

1. Define research design in your own words.
2. How does formulating a research design differ from developing an approach to a problem?
3. Differentiate between exploratory and conclusive research.
4. What are the major purposes for which descriptive research is conducted?
5. List the six Ws of descriptive research and give an example of each.
6. Compare and contrast cross-sectional and longitudinal designs.
7. Describe cohort analysis. Why is it of special interest?
8. Discuss the advantages and disadvantages of panels.
9. What is a causal research design? What is its purpose?
10. What is the relationship among exploratory, descriptive, and causal research?
11. List the major components of a research design.
12. What potential sources of error can affect a research design?
13. Why is it important to minimize total error rather than any particular source of error?

Problems

1. Sweet Cookies is planning to launch a new line of cookies and wants to assess the market size. The cookies have a mixed chocolate-pineapple flavor and will be targeted at the premium end of the market. Discuss the six Ws of a descriptive research design that may be adopted.
2. Express each of the following types of error as an equation:
   a. Total error
   b. Random sampling error
   c. Nonresponse error
   d. Response error
3. Welcome Inc. is a chain of fast-food restaurants located in major metropolitan areas in the South. Sales have been growing very slowly for the last two years. Management has decided to add some new items to the menu, but first they want to know more about their customers and their preferences.
   a. List two hypotheses.
   b. What kind of research design is appropriate? Why?

Internet and Computer Exercises

1. Visit the Greenfield Online Research Center (www.greenfieldonline.com).
   a. What surveys are currently being conducted by Greenfield?
   b. How are the respondents being recruited for these surveys?
   c. Discuss the different type of errors likely to arise, given the way the respondents are being recruited.
2. Visit the Web page of three of the marketing research firms listed in Table 1.2. What types of research designs have been implemented recently by these firms?
3. Obtain one of the CPM/PERT programs. Using this program, develop a schedule for the research project described in role-play exercise 2 that follows.
4. You are conducting an image study for Carnival Cruise Lines. As part of exploratory research, analyze the messages posted to the newsgroup rec.travel.cruises to determine the factors that consumers use in evaluating cruise companies.

Activities

Role Playing

1. Assume the role of marketing manager of Sweet Cookies, Inc., and have your partner assume the role of a researcher hired by the firm (see problem 1). Discuss the issue and formulate the appropriate:
   a. management decision problem
   b. marketing research problem
   c. research design
2. You are a manager in charge of a marketing research project. Your goal is to determine what effects different levels of advertising have on consumption behavior. Based on the results of the project, you will recommend the amount of money to be budgeted for advertising different products next year. Your supervisor will require strong justification for your recommendations, so your research design has to be as sound as possible. However, your resources (time, money, and labor) are limited. Develop a research project to address this problem. Focus on the kind of research designs you would use, why you would use them, and how you would conduct the research.

Fieldwork

1. Contact a few marketing research organizations and ask them about the kind of research designs they have used during the last year and the nature of the problems addressed. Write a report on your findings.

Group Discussion

1. "If the research budget is limited, exploratory research can be dispensed with." Discuss this quote.
2. As a small group, discuss the following statement: "The researcher should always attempt to develop an optimal design for every marketing research project."
3. "There are many potential sources of error in a research project. It is impossible to control all of them. Hence, marketing research contains many errors, and we cannot be confident of the findings." Discuss these statements as a small group. Did your group arrive at a consensus?

Dell Running Case

Review the Dell case, Case 1.1, and the questionnaire given toward the end of the book.

1. How can Dell make use of exploratory research to understand how household consumers buy personal computers and related equipment?
2. Describe one way in which Dell can make use of descriptive research.

3. Describe one way in which Dell can make use of causal research.
4. Dell would like to determine consumer response to a new lightweight tablet PC that it has developed. What research design would you recommend?

VIDEO CASE 3.1 National Football League: The King of Professional Sports

The National Football League (www.nfl.com) is considered the king of all professional sports in the United States. It was formed by 11 teams in 1920 as the American Professional Football Association and adopted the name National Football League in 1922. The league currently consists of 32 teams from American cities and regions, divided evenly into two conferences (AFC and NFC), with four, four-team divisions. The NFL governs and promotes the game, sets and enforces rules, and regulates team ownership. It generates revenue mostly through sponsorships, licensing of merchandise, and selling national broadcasting rights. It has been extremely successful because it is advertiser-friendly. The teams operate as separate businesses but share a percentage of their revenue. NFL revenues amounted to $5.86 billion in 2006, and the average player salary was $1.4 million in the same period.

Players are tough, strong, and fiercely competitive on the field, but remove their helmets and a softer side emerges. Marketing research has documented the positive impact of cause-related marketing on corporate image. The NFL has a strong tradition of public service and is an active contributor to various social causes. Bettering communities and helping others ties into the basic team concept and is an extension of the NFL's philosophy. NFL players strongly believe and encourage others to get involved, whether it is time or money or anything else—even the smallest of gestures can make a big difference to someone else.

Focus groups and surveys have shown that community involvement is particularly important for an organization that depends on the community for support. The NFL has a rich history of giving, and each of the 32 teams has its own community relations initiatives. The fact that there are around 1,600 players in the league indicates the far-reaching capabilities of this powerful organization. According to Joe Browne, Executive Vice President of Communications and Public Affairs, the NFL views its public service activities as giving something back to its customers—the fans who attend the games and watch them on TV. The NFL has worked with a number of non-profit and charitable organizations over the years, with

each team taking on a different issue, such as the Philadelphia Eagles building community playgrounds. Each year the Eagles take time off from the world of sports and business and build a playground in the Philadelphia area. The New England Patriots help deliver Thanksgiving dinners to those in need, and the Pittsburgh Steelers visit the elderly—football players reaching out to make a difference.

Back in 1974, the league formed a partnership with the United Way, a national network of more than 1,300 locally governed organizations that work to create lasting positive changes in communities and people's lives. This partnership is still in existence today and has encouraged fans to give back to society. Consequently, fundraising for United Way has soared from $800 million to $4 billion. The relationship between United Way and the NFL has blossomed into a charitable enterprise that touches 30 million people each year by providing funds and programs to the needy. The NFL's ongoing ad campaigns remind fans that football players are regular guys who want to do good in the community where they work and live. The effectiveness of these ad campaigns is evaluated by undertaking surveys that measure people's awareness, perceptions, preferences, intentions, and behaviors toward the NFL and comparing them against benchmarks.

Based on marketing research, the NFL's marketing strategy has two pillars: football and community. Football is its product, something that the NFL does best. Community means giving back to the community in exchange for all its support and love. The support of the community is tremendous, with 18 million tickets sold each season and more than 120 million people watching NFL games on TV each week. Then, there is the huge impact of the Super Bowl—an event that has been the top-rated show each year, seen by more viewers than any other program, an exposure that has proven to be an effective messaging medium. The tremendous reach and power of TV commercials helped the NFL's "join the team" initiative get a spectacular start with thousands of eager fans calling up NFL teams across the country ready to join the team. The NFL believes that charity and being a good corporate citizen are essential to achieve success in business. This makes the entire entity stronger. By giving back to its customers, the NFL shows that it cares about them.

The NFL's impact on the community extends way beyond the games played on Sundays and Monday nights, because there is a special bond that fans feel with each of the teams in the league. Consumer perception and attitudinal surveys have consistently shown that the NFL is held in high regard, and the League tries hard to maintain these positive perceptions. It realizes that at the end of the day, the NFL is an energy, a symbol that represents American tradition, which if not maintained would wither away.

Joe Browne describes people's relationship with the NFL as a love affair in which the NFL and the teams have to give this love back to the people for supporting them so well. That's what the NFL does through its various programs such as NFL charities, the NFL football fund, and the disaster relief fund that the NFL established after 9/11 to give back to the families of those killed in New York and Washington. There is charity on the field, too; each time a player is fined, the money is used to help fund various causes. Fans can get into the game by going to the auctions section on the NFL Web site, because all of the proceeds go to players' charities. According to Beth Colleton, Director of Community Affairs, NFL stands for quality, tradition, and integrity—all of which come together to define Americana. The NFL captures the American energy like no other—an energy that continues to ignite goodwill with each passing season.

Conclusion

The NFL has used marketing research to foster immense goodwill and influence to make a difference to the community. The strong public service feeling at the NFL and the active involvement by NFL players in various social initiatives and programs bear testimony to how seriously the NFL takes its responsibility toward society and the immensely positive impact it has on society, all supported by marketing research. Continued reliance on marketing research can help the NFL to remain the king of professional sports.

Questions

1. Football is a male-dominated sport. Discuss the role that marketing research can play in helping the NFL more effectively market the league to women.
2. The NFL would like to increase its penetration of the women segment. Define the management decision problem.
3. What is the main competition faced by the NFL?
4. Define an appropriate marketing research problem corresponding to the management decision problem in question 2.
5. Develop three appropriate research questions, each with suitable hypotheses.
6. What type of research design would you recommend for investigating the marketing research problem?

References
1. "In a League of Its Own," www.economist.com/business/displaystory.cfm?story_id=6859210, accessed February 6, 2009.
2. "NFL Team Values/Revenues, Ranked," www.forbes.com/lists/2006/30/06nfl_NFL-Team-Valuations_land.html, accessed January 2, 2008.
3. "NFL Studies What Women Want," www.reuters.com/article/MediaMarketing06/idUSN2933923020061129, accessed January 2, 2008.
4. "Making Sure Ads Play to Women, Too," www.boston.com/sports/football/patriots/articles/2004/01/28/making_sure_ads_play_to_women_too/?page=1, accessed January 2, 2008.
5. "Why the NFL Struggles to Attract Female Fans," www.dmwmedia.com/news/2006/12/05/why-the-nfl-struggles-to-attract-female-fans, accessed January 2, 2008.

Chapter 4

> "Secondary data analysis of reputable studies is a cost-effective way to provide useful context, dimensionality, and insight into the formulation or exploration of a research problem."

Robert L. Cohen, Ph.D., President and CEO, Scarborough Research

Objectives

[After reading this chapter, the student should be able to:]

1. Define the nature and scope of secondary data and distinguish secondary data from primary data.

2. Analyze the advantages and disadvantages of secondary data and their uses in the various steps of the marketing research process.

3. Evaluate secondary data using specifications, error, currency, objectives, nature, and dependability criteria.

4. Describe in detail the different sources of secondary data, including internal sources and external sources in the form of published materials, computerized databases, and syndicated services.

5. Discuss in detail the syndicated sources of secondary data, including household/consumer data obtained via surveys, purchase and media panels, and electronic scanner services, as well as institutional data related to retailers, wholesalers, and industrial/service firms.

6. Explain the need to use multiple sources of secondary data and describe single-source data.

7. Discuss applications of secondary data in computer mapping.

8. Identify and evaluate the sources of secondary data useful in international marketing research.

9. Understand the ethical issues involved in the use of secondary data.

Exploratory Research Design: Secondary Data

Overview

Chapter 1 discussed the Internet as a source of marketing research information. Analysis of secondary data helps define the marketing research problem and develop an approach (Chapter 2). Also, before the research design for collecting primary data is formulated (Chapter 3), the researcher should analyze the relevant secondary data. In some projects, particularly those with limited budgets, research may be largely confined to the analysis of secondary data, since some routine problems may be addressed based only on secondary data.

This chapter discusses the distinction between primary and secondary data. The advantages and disadvantages of secondary data are considered and criteria for evaluating secondary data are presented, along with a classification of secondary data. Internal secondary data are described and major sources of external secondary data, such as published materials, online and offline databases, and syndicated services, are also discussed. We consider applications of secondary data in computer mapping. The sources of secondary data useful in international marketing research are discussed. Several ethical issues that arise in the use of secondary data are identified. Finally, we discuss the use of the Internet and computers in identifying and analyzing secondary data.[1]

We begin by citing several examples to give you a flavor of secondary data.

Real Research

Boston Market: Some Place Like Home

According to secondary data, home meal replacement (HMR) will be the family dining business of the twenty-first century. HMR is portable, high-quality food that's meant for takeout, and it is the fastest-growing and most significant opportunity in the food industry today. According to Nielsen's consumer panel data (www.nielsen.com), 55 percent of respondents purchased a meal for at-home consumption several times a month. Convenience and type of food were the two most influential factors when purchasing HMR. Also, 77 percent of the respondents preferred their meals ready to eat.

Secondary data indicating huge demand for home meal replacement spurred Boston Market to become the leader in this segment.

Another recent study by consultants McKinsey & Co. (www.mckinsey.com) projects that virtually all growth in food sales will come from food service, defined as food prepared at least partially away from home. Estimates of total HMR market size, as well as future potential, vary widely. Numbers ranging from $25 billion to $100 billion have been given for the year 2010. It is the most important trend to hit the food industry since the advent of frozen food.

Most industry experts say the trend started when Boston Market (www.bostonmarket.com) came to town, attracting consumers with promises of food just like mom used to make. Boston Market is now the HMR leader. The company constantly monitors HMR-related data available from secondary sources and uses them as inputs into its research and marketing programs. Currently, Boston Market is using such data to test new products that could be introduced in 2010. Such product tests being conducted include prepackaged "take and go" lunch boxes, expanded catering services, enhanced drive-through operations, call-ahead pick-up services, and signature meals.[2] ∎

Real Research

High Touch Goes High Tech

According to the U.S. Department of Labor, more than 50 percent of the American workforce was over 40 years old by 2005. By 2015, women will account for about 50 percent of the workforce. There will also be a decline in the number of young (age 16–24) workers available to fill entry-level positions. This potential shortage of young workers has caused many fast-food restaurants to switch from a "high touch" to a "high tech" service orientation. Many of the services formerly rendered by workers are now performed by consumers by using high-tech equipment. The use of touch screen kiosks is becoming a popular trend that provides a new avenue to cut labor costs and increase customer service. Fast-food companies that are deploying this new technology include Taco Bell, Arby's, and Pizza Hut.[3] ∎

As these examples illustrate, research and consulting firms (Nielsen, McKinsey & Co.) and government departments (U.S. Department of Labor) are only a few of the sources from which secondary data may be obtained. The nature and role of secondary data become clear when we understand the distinction between primary and secondary data.

Primary Versus Secondary Data

primary data
Data originated by the researcher for the specific purpose of addressing the research problem.

secondary data
Data collected for some purpose other than the problem at hand.

Primary data are originated by a researcher for the specific purpose of addressing the problem at hand. The collection of primary data involves all six steps of the marketing research process (Chapter 1). Obtaining primary data can be expensive and time consuming. The department store patronage project cited in Chapter 1 is an example of primary data collection.

Secondary data are data that have already been collected for purposes other than the problem at hand. These data can be located quickly and inexpensively. In the department store patronage project, secondary data on the criteria used by households to select department stores were obtained from marketing journals (*Journal of Retailing*, *Journal of Marketing*, *Journal of the Academy of Marketing Science*, and *Journal of Marketing Research*). Several other examples of secondary data were provided in the preceding section. The differences between primary and secondary data are summarized in Table 4.1. As compared to primary data, secondary data are collected rapidly and easily, at a relatively low cost, and in a short time.

These differences between primary and secondary data lead to some distinct advantages and uses of secondary data.

TABLE 4.1

A Comparison of Primary and Secondary Data

	Primary Data	Secondary Data
Collection purpose	For the problem at hand	For other problems
Collection process	Very involved	Rapid and easy
Collection cost	High	Relatively low
Collection time	Long	Short

Advantages and Uses of Secondary Data

As can be seen from the foregoing discussion, secondary data offer several advantages over primary data. Secondary data are easily accessible, relatively inexpensive, and quickly obtained. Some secondary data, such as those provided by the U.S. Bureau of the Census, are available on topics for which it would not be feasible for a firm to collect primary data. Although it is rare for secondary data to provide all the answers to a nonroutine research problem, such data can be useful in a variety of ways.[4] Secondary data can help you:

1. Identify the problem.
2. Better define the problem.
3. Develop an approach to the problem.
4. Formulate an appropriate research design (for example, by identifying the key variables).
5. Answer certain research questions and test some hypotheses.
6. Interpret primary data more insightfully.

Given these advantages and uses of secondary data, we state the following general rule:

Examination of available secondary data is a prerequisite to the collection of primary data. Start with secondary data. Proceed to primary data only when the secondary data sources have been exhausted or yield marginal returns.

The rich dividends obtained by following this rule are illustrated by examples we have given in the introduction to this chapter. These examples show that analysis of secondary data can provide valuable insights and lay the foundation for conducting primary data analysis. However, the researcher should be cautious in using secondary data, because they have some limitations and disadvantages.

Disadvantages of Secondary Data

Because secondary data have been collected for purposes other than the problem at hand, their usefulness to the current problem may be limited in several important ways, including relevance and accuracy. The objectives, nature, and methods used to collect the secondary data may not be appropriate to the present situation. Also, secondary data may be lacking in accuracy, or they may not be completely current or dependable. Before using secondary data, it is important to evaluate them on these factors. These factors are discussed in more detail in the following section.

ACTIVE RESEARCH

Nike: Celebrating Celebrity Endorsements

Search the Internet using a search engine as well as your library's online databases to obtain information on the use of celebrity endorsements in marketing.

You are conducting a marketing research project to determine the effectiveness of celebrity endorsements in Nike advertising. What type of secondary data would you examine?

As the marketing director of Nike, how would you use secondary data on celebrity endorsements to determine whether you should continue to contract celebrities to endorse the Nike brand?

Criteria for Evaluating Secondary Data

The quality of secondary data should be routinely evaluated, using the criteria of Table 4.2, which are discussed in the following sections.

Specifications: Methodology Used to Collect the Data

The specifications or the methodology used to collect the data should be critically examined to identify possible sources of bias. Such methodological considerations include size and nature of the sample, response rate and quality, questionnaire design and administration, procedures used

TABLE 4.2		
Criteria for Evaluating Secondary Data		
Criteria	Issues	Remarks
Specifications/ Methodology	Data collection method	Data should be reliable, valid, and generalizable to the problem at hand.
	Response rate	
	Quality of data	
	Sampling technique	
	Sample size	
	Questionnaire design	
	Fieldwork	
	Data analysis	
Error/Accuracy	Examine errors in: approach, research design, sampling, data collection, data analysis, reporting	Assess accuracy by comparing data from different sources.
Currency	Time lag between collection and publication	Census data are periodically updated by syndicated firms.
	Frequency of updates	
Objective	Why were the data collected?	The objective will determine the relevance of the data.
Nature	Definition of key variables	Reconfigure the data to increase their usefulness, if possible.
	Units of measurement	
	Categories used	
	Relationships examined	
Dependability	Expertise, credibility, reputation, and trustworthiness of the source	Data should be obtained from an original rather than an acquired source.

for fieldwork, and data analysis and reporting procedures. These checks provide information on the reliability and validity of the data and help determine whether they can be generalized to the problem at hand. The reliability and validity can be further ascertained by an examination of the error, currency, objectives, nature, and dependability associated with the secondary data.

Real Research

Rating the Television Ratings Methodology

WTVJ-TV, an NBC affiliate in Miami, uses the syndicated services of Nielsen Media Research (www.nielsenmedia.com), which provides television ratings and audience estimates. The television station feels that the data provided by Nielsen Media Research have been skewed because the methodology used was flawed. Specifically, they claim that Nielsen Media Research is putting too many meters into the homes of families who speak only Spanish, which is underestimating their ratings. The problem is that the station is English speaking, and while 46 percent of its viewers are Hispanic, they all speak English. By placing more Nielsen meters in homes that do not speak English, the information is not representative of the Miami community or the station's viewers. Also, since many decisions are based on the information provided by Nielsen, such as programming, advertising, and media buys, it is important that the station have accurate and reliable information about the market.

Just the reverse has been argued in other areas. On July 8, 2004, the company introduced Nielsen's local people meters (LPMs) in Los Angeles. The LPM rating system was gradually installed in other major markets and went live in Cleveland on August 28, 2008. The meters electronically record what programs are being watched—and who is watching them. Some networks and a coalition of community groups, called Don't Count Us Out, complained that the Nielsen sample audience underrepresents Latinos and African Americans, producing faulty results.

Although many support the actions of Nielsen Media Research and feel that the data do represent the community, the complaint still raises a very important question: Can a company be confident that the information it receives is generated using appropriate methodology?[5] ■

Error: Accuracy of the Data

The researcher must determine whether the data are accurate enough for the purposes of the current study. Secondary data can have a number of sources of error, or inaccuracy, including errors in the approach, research design, sampling, data collection, analysis, and reporting stages of the project. Moreover, it is difficult to evaluate the accuracy of secondary data, because the researcher did not participate in the research. One approach is to find multiple sources of data and compare those using standard statistical procedures.

The accuracy of secondary data can vary, particularly if they relate to phenomena that are subject to change. Moreover, data obtained from different sources may not agree. In these cases, the researcher should verify the accuracy of secondary data by conducting pilot studies or by other appropriate methods. Often, by exercising creativity, this can be done without much expense or effort.

Real Research

Detailing E-Tailing Revenues

In order to determine e-commerce sales, many research firms such as Forrester Research, ComScore, Nielsen Online, and the U.S. Commerce Department conduct studies. All four organizations have distinct methodologies of collecting and analyzing data to report results. The Forrester Research firm polls 5,000 online consumers every month during the first nine working days of each month. Responses from those polled consumers are adjusted to represent the U.S. population. Differing from Forrester Research, Nielsen Online's EcommercePulse polls a larger sample of 36,000 Internet users monthly and tracks how much money those consumers spend online. Differing once again is the U.S. Commerce Department, which randomly chooses 11,000 merchants to fill out survey forms about online sales. Finally, ComScore uses a passive response system that collects data from 1.5 million Internet users, allowing ComScore to track their Internet traffic through the company's servers.

For the calendar year 2007, Forester Research reported $175 billion in online sales, the Commerce Department reported $127 billion, and ComScore reported $122.8 billion. Unlike Forrester, the Commerce Department and ComScore exclude sales of travel services, event tickets, and auctions. Such huge differences in online sales create problems for e-commerce companies, and even Federal Reserve Chairman Ben Bernanke has addressed this issue as a major problem. Comparing e-tail sales figures available from different sources can give marketing researchers an idea of the degree of error that may be present in the data. According to a study by Forrester Research, the e-commerce transactions are expected to reach $335 billion annually by 2012. The forecasts from the other sources vary considerably with Commerce Department forecasting e-commerce sales of only 218.4 billion by 2012.[6] ∎

Currency: When the Data Were Collected

Secondary data may not be current, and the time lag between data collection and publication may be long, as is the case with much census data. Moreover, the data may not be updated frequently enough for the purpose of the problem at hand. Marketing research requires current data; therefore, the value of secondary data is diminished as they become dated. For instance, while the 2000 Census of Population data are comprehensive, they may not be applicable to a metropolitan area whose population has changed rapidly since the census. Fortunately, several marketing research firms update census data periodically and make the current information available on a syndicated basis.

Objective: The Purpose for Which the Data Were Collected

Data are invariably collected with some objective in mind, and a fundamental question to ask is why the data were collected in the first place. The objective for collecting data will ultimately determine the purpose for which that information is relevant and useful. Data collected with a specific objective in mind may not be appropriate in another situation. As explained in more detail later in the chapter, scanner volume tracking data are collected with the objective of examining aggregate movement of brands, including shifts in market shares. Such data on sales of orange juice, for example, would be of limited value in a study aimed at understanding how households select specific brands.

Nature: The Content of the Data

The nature, or content, of the data should be examined with special attention to the definition of key variables, the units of measurement, categories used, and the relationships examined. If the key variables have not been defined or are defined in a manner inconsistent with the researcher's definition, then the usefulness of the data is limited. Consider, for example, secondary data on consumer preferences for TV programs. To use this information, it is important to know how preference for programs was defined. Was it defined in terms of the program watched most often, the one considered most needed, most enjoyable, most informative, or the program of greatest service to the community?

Likewise, secondary data may be measured in units that may not be appropriate for the current problem. For example, income may be measured by individual, family, household, or spending unit, and could be gross or net after taxes and deductions. Income may be classified into categories that are different from research needs. If the researcher is interested in high-income consumers with gross annual household incomes of over $90,000, secondary data with income categories of less than $15,000, $15,001–$35,000, $35,001–$50,000, and more than $50,000 will not be of much use. Determining the measurement of variables such as income may be a complex task. Finally, the relationships examined should be taken into account in evaluating the nature of data. If, for example, actual behavior is of interest, then data inferring behavior from self-reported attitudinal information may have limited usefulness. Sometimes it is possible to reconfigure the available data, for example, to convert the units of measurement, so that the resulting data are more useful to the problem at hand.

Dependability: How Dependable Are the Data?

An overall indication of the dependability of data may be obtained by examining the expertise, credibility, reputation, and trustworthiness of the source. This information can be obtained by checking with others who have used the information provided by the source. Data published to promote sales, to advance specific interests, or to carry on propaganda should be viewed with suspicion. The same may be said of data published anonymously or in a form that attempts to hide the details of the data collection methodology and process. It is also pertinent to examine whether the secondary data came from an original source, one that generated the data, or an acquired source, one that procured the data from an original source. For example, the Census of Population is an original source, whereas the Statistical Abstracts of the United States is an acquired source. As a general rule, secondary data should be secured from an original, rather than an acquired source. There are at least two reasons for this rule. First, an original source is the one that specifies the details of the data collection methodology. Second, an original source is likely to be more accurate and complete than a secondary source.

Real Research   ## Flying High on Secondary Data

Money magazine published the results of a study conducted to uncover the airline characteristics consumers consider most important. In order of importance, these characteristics are safety, price, baggage handling, on-time performance, customer service, ease of reservations and ticketing, comfort, frequent flyer programs, and food. *Money* magazine then ranked the 10 largest U.S. airlines according to these characteristics.

This article would be a useful source of secondary data for American Airlines in conducting a market research study to identify characteristics of its service that should be improved. However, before using the data, American should evaluate them according to several criteria.

First, the methodology used to collect the data for this article should be examined. This *Money* magazine article includes a section that details the methodology used in the study. *Money* used a poll of 1,017 frequent fliers to determine important airline characteristics. The results of the survey had a 3 percent margin of error. American would need to decide whether a sample size of 1,017 was generalizable to the population, and whether an error of 3 percent is acceptable. In addition, American should evaluate what type of response or nonresponse errors might have occurred in the data collection or analysis process.

The currency of the data and the objective of the study would be important to American Airlines in deciding whether to utilize this article as a source of secondary data. This study was conducted before the merger of Delta and Northwest, which was announced in 2008. Perhaps airline passengers' criteria have changed since these events, which would diminish the usefulness of this study. The objective of the study was to rate airlines along choice criteria for a popular business magazine. The results are not likely to be biased toward any particular airline, because the magazine does not have a vested interest in any of the airline companies.

American would also need to look at the nature and dependability of the data. For instance, it would need to look at how the nine choice criteria are defined. For example, price is measured in terms of fare per mile. This may not be useful to American if it did not want to quantify price in that manner. In regard to dependability, American would need to research the reputation of *Money* magazine and of ICR, the company *Money* hired to administer the survey. American also needs to consider the fact that *Money* used some secondary research in its study. For instance, it used reports from the National Transportation Safety Board data on airline accidents and incident reports from the Federal Aviation Administration to rank the safety performance of the 10 airlines. It is always better to get information from the original source. Thus, American might want to acquire these reports and do its own safety ranking. This would be more reliable than getting this information from the *Money* magazine report.

The *Money* magazine article might be useful as a starting place for the marketing research project by American Airlines. For instance, it might be useful in formulating the problem definition. However, because of the article's limitations in regard to currency, nature, and dependability, this source should be supplemented by other sources of secondary research, as well as primary research.[7] ■

ACTIVE RESEARCH

Gallup Polls: On a Gallup

Visit www.gallup.com. Examine the information on how Gallup polls are conducted.

As the CEO of Home Depot, you come across a Gallup poll that states that more and more women are shopping for home improvement products and services. How will you use this information to improve the competitiveness of Home Depot?

By applying the criteria we have considered, evaluate the quality of Gallup polls.

Classification of Secondary Data

Figure 4.1 presents a classification of secondary data. Secondary data may be classified as either internal or external. **Internal data** are those generated within the organization for which the research is being conducted. This information may be available in a ready-to use-format, such as information routinely supplied by the management decision support system. On the other hand, these data may exist within the organization but may require considerable processing before they are useful to the researcher. For example, a variety of information can be found on sales invoices. Yet this information may not be easily accessible; further processing may be required to extract it. **External data** are those generated by sources outside the organization. These data may exist in the form of published material, computerized databases, or information made available by syndicated services. Before collecting external secondary data, it is useful to analyze internal secondary data.

internal data
Internal data are data available within the organization for which the research is being conducted.

external data
Data that originate external to the organization.

FIGURE 4.1

A Classification of Secondary Data

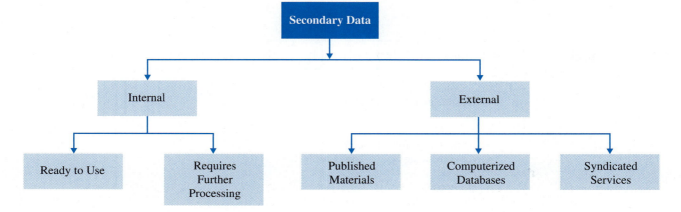

Internal Secondary Data

Internal sources should be the starting point in the search for secondary data. Since most organizations have a wealth of in-house information, some data may be readily available and may provide useful insights. For example, sales and cost data are compiled in the regular accounting process. When internal data on sales showed Reebok (www.reebok.com) that Internet sales were a mere 0.7 percent of their total sales but were rousing bad feelings among retailers, the company discontinued online selling. It is also possible to process routinely collected sales data to generate a variety of useful information, as illustrated by the department store example.

Project Research   Internal Secondary Data

Extensive analysis was conducted on internal secondary data in the department store patronage project. This provided several rich insights. For example, sales were analyzed to obtain:

- Sales by product line
- Sales by major department (e.g., menswear, housewares)
- Sales by specific stores
- Sales by geographical region
- Sales by cash versus credit purchases
- Sales in specific time periods
- Sales by size of purchase
- Sales trends in many of these classifications ∎

Secondary internal data have two significant advantages. They are easily available and inexpensive. In fact, internal secondary sources are generally the least costly of any source of marketing research information, yet these data often are not fully exploited. However, this trend is changing with the increased popularity of database marketing.

Database Marketing

database marketing
Database marketing involves the use of computers to capture and track customer profiles and purchase detail.

Database marketing involves the use of computers to capture and track customer profiles and purchase detail. This secondary information serves as the foundation for marketing programs or as an internal source of information related to customer behavior. For many companies, the first step in creating a database is to transfer raw sales information, such as that found on sales call reports or on invoices, to a microcomputer. This consumer purchase information is then enhanced by overlaying it with demographic and psychographic information for the same customers, available from syndicated firms such as Donnelley Marketing (www.donnelleymarketing.com) and Experian (www.experian.com). This information can then be analyzed in terms of a customer's activity over the life of the business relationship. A profile of heavy versus low users, signs of change in the usage relationships, or significant "customer life cycle" events such as anniversaries can be identified and acted upon. These databases provide the essential tool needed to nurture, expand, and protect the customer relationship.[8]

Real Research   Type of Individual/Household Level Data Available from Syndicated Firms

I. Demographic Data
- Identification (name, address, telephone)
- Sex
- Marital status
- Names of family members
- Age (including ages of family members)
- Income
- Occupation
- Number of children present

- Home ownership
- Length of residence
- Number and make of cars owned

II. Psychographic Lifestyle Data
- Interest in golf
- Interest in snow skiing
- Interest in book reading
- Interest in running
- Interest in bicycling
- Interest in pets
- Interest in fishing
- Interest in electronics
- Interest in cable television

There are also firms such as D&B (www.dnb.com) and American Business Information, a division of InfoUSA (www.infousa.com), that collect demographic data on businesses. ■

CRM (customer relationship management) is a unique type of database-driven marketing. As part of its CRM system, Chrysler (www.chrysler.com) implemented what they call Personal Information Centers. These PICs, as they are called, offer car owners an individualized Web site that creates direct links with the marketing research team. These PICs collect data on all aspects of buying a car, giving the company the ability to engage in customized marketing. If a prospect, on his or her completed online survey, indicated handling of minivans to be a concern, separate data could be included on a brochure sent only to that prospect. These data would show how the Chrysler minivan stood up against the competition in the minivan market. Chrysler believes that the customer relationship begins when a prospect first contacts the company and doesn't stop when a buyer purchases a vehicle. With this in mind, the company uses its CRM system to constantly track buyers' and prospects' opinions and desires. Its CRM has enabled the company to maintain its leadership in the automobile market. In 2007, private equity concern Cerberus Capital Management bought Chrysler for about $7.4 billion—or about one-fifth of the $37 billion Daimler paid in 1998.[9]

Database marketing can lead to quite sophisticated and targeted marketing programs, as illustrated in the following example.

Real Research   Caterpillar: The Pillar of Database Marketing

Besides their famous earthmoving equipment, Caterpillar builds $2 billion per year of large truck engines, the kind that are found everywhere in the big 18-wheelers on the road. These trucks are always custom built by the truck manufacturers, who are really assemblers, such as Peterbilt. In the beginning, Caterpillar had no database, and their executives had a lot of questions: "What truck fleets are we not calling on? What fleets should test our two new engines? How can we get a marketing strategy that can be measured? How do we adjust to the coming downturn in sales?"

To try to answer these questions, Alan Weber and Frank Weyforth, two database marketing veterans, got Caterpillar truck marketing to chip in money for a project. They used part of the money to give laptops to the 260 Caterpillar sales force with this provision: "You get paid for sales, but only if the customer name and other data are entered into the laptop database." It worked. When they began, they had data on only 58,000 customers and 11,000 fleets of 10 trucks or more.

There were four internal databases in Caterpillar that were not compatible with one another. To get the data, the team combined the internal databases, appended data from the National Motor Carriers directory, D&B and TRW data, and trade publication lists. After two years of work, they had a file of 110,000 customers, 8,000 mid-range fleets, and 34,000 heavy-duty fleets: the universe of all heavy trucks in America. Next they did some serious modeling. Using the data they assembled on SIC code, truck owner vocations, engine models, number of trucks, and trucking category, they were able to predict which noncustomers were most likely to buy. They grouped their customers and prospects into 83 heavy-duty groups and 34 mid-range groups.

With the data available, they estimated customer lifetime value. Sales, service, usage, and engine model combined determined that value for customers. Prospect value was determined by the group to which each prospect had been assigned. They determined, from this analysis, the high-value customers and prospects that should be targeted.

Weber and Weyforth developed a set of different messages that could be sent to each customer and prospect. Messages that stressed retention were different from messages that were designed for conquest. During the first year with the new database, they were able to sign up 500 conquest fleets. They sold an average of 50 to 100 engines per fleet at about $15,000 per engine. The total increased sales that could be attributed to the new database system were approximately $500 million. They successfully launched the two new engines that had been part of the original goal. Caterpillar market share went up by 5 percent and continued to grow through 2009.[10] ■

Most large organizations have intranets, which greatly facilitate the search for and access to internal secondary data. The Procter & Gamble Company, for example, has developed powerful intranet applications that enable its managers worldwide to search for past and current research studies and a wide variety of marketing-related information on the basis of keywords. Once located, the information can be accessed online. Sensitive information can be secured electronically with user names and passwords.

Published External Secondary Sources

Sources of published external secondary data include federal, state, and local governments, nonprofit organizations (e.g., Chambers of Commerce), trade associations and professional organizations, commercial publishers, investment brokerage firms, and professional marketing research firms. In fact, so much data are available that the researcher can be overwhelmed. Therefore, it is important to classify published sources. (See Figure 4.2.) Published external sources may be broadly classified as general business data or government data. General business sources are comprised of guides, directories, indexes, and statistical data. Government sources may be broadly categorized as census data and other publications.

General Business Data

Businesses publish a lot of information in the form of books, periodicals, journals, newspapers, magazines, reports, and trade literature. Moody's (www.moodys.com) and Standard and Poor's (www.standardandpoors.com) provide information on U.S. and foreign companies. Another useful source for industrial brand and trade information is ThomasNet (www.thomasnet.com). Valuable marketing and marketing research information may be obtained from www.SecondaryData.com.

A variety of business-related sites can provide sales leads, mailing lists, business profiles, and credit ratings for American businesses. Many sites supply information on businesses within a specific industry. For example, you can gain access to the full-text *American Demographics* and *Marketing Tools* publications at www.marketingtools.com. All of American Marketing Association's publications can be searched by using keywords at www.marketingpower.com. Encyclopedia Britannica provides free online access to the entire 32 volumes (www.britannica.com). Data on American manufacturers and key decision makers can be obtained from Harris InfoSource (www.harrisinfo.com). Another good source is USAData.com. Guides, indexes, and directories can help in locating information available from general business sources. Sources are also available for identifying statistical data. A brief description of each of these resource categories follows.

FIGURE 4.2

A Classification of Published Secondary Sources

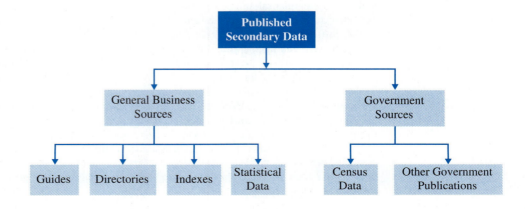

GUIDES Guides are an excellent source of standard or recurring information. A guide may help identify other important sources of directories, trade associations, and trade publications. Guides are one of the first sources a researcher should consult. Some of the most useful are the *American Marketing Association Bibliography Series, Business Information Sources, Data Sources for Business and Market Analysis*, and *Encyclopedia of Business Information Sources*. You can find guides on the Internet. @BRINT (www.brint.com) is a guide to business technology management and knowledge management sites with editorial comments.

DIRECTORIES Directories are helpful for identifying individuals or organizations that collect specific data. Some of the important directories include *Directories in Print, Consultants and Consulting Organizations Directory, Encyclopedia of Associations, FINDEX: The Directory of Market Research Reports,* Fortune *500 Directory, Million Dollar Directory: Leading Public and Private Companies, Standard Directory of Advertisers,* and *Thomas Register of American Manufacturers.* You can also find directories on the Internet, for example the Google directory at www.google.com/dirhp and the Yahoo! directory at dir.yahoo.com.

INDEXES It is possible to locate information on a particular topic in several different publications by using an index. Indexes can, therefore, increase the efficiency of the search process. You can also find indexes on the Internet, for example the *Librarian's Internet Index* at www.lii.org. CI Resource Index (www.ciseek.com) contains sites for competitive intelligence information. Several were used in the department store project.

Project Research   Data Search

In addition to reviewing the theoretical literature, as discussed in Chapter 2, it was also necessary to identify the nonacademic sources of secondary data related to the factors considered in selecting department stores and other aspects of store patronage. The *Business Periodical Index*, the *Wall Street Journal Index*, and the *New York Times Index* were used to generate a list of relevant articles that had appeared in the last five years. The *Business Periodical Index* classifies articles by specific industries and firms, making it easy to locate articles of interest. Several articles obtained in this manner proved useful. One pointed to the tendency of people to combine shopping with eating out. Therefore, as discussed in Chapter 2, a specific research question was framed to investigate this behavior.

Project Activities

Identify the sources of secondary data that will help Sears do the following:

1. Increase penetration of the Hispanic population.
2. Project domestic retail sales growth to the year 2015.
3. Identify the impact of lifestyle changes on department store sales.
4. Evaluate the effectiveness of Sears' advertising. ■

As illustrated by this example, indexes greatly facilitate a directed search of the relevant literature. Several indexes are available for both academic and business sources. Some of the more useful business indexes are *Business Periodical Index, Business Index, Predicasts F & S Index: United States, Social Sciences Citation Index,* and the *Wall Street Journal Index.*

American business information can be obtained by visiting various business-related sites that provide sales leads and mailing lists, business profiles, and credit ratings. You can find reports on different industries at research firms' sites, such as www.jupiterresearch.com, www.forrester.com, www.idc.com, and www.greenfield.com, to name a few. However, other general publications also publish research results, such as www.wsj.com, www.businessweek.com, www.business20.com, and www.nytimes.com.

NONGOVERNMENTAL STATISTICAL DATA Business research often involves compiling statistical data reflecting market or industry factors. A historic perspective of industry participation and growth rates can provide a context for market share analysis. Market statistics related to population demographics, purchasing levels, television viewership, and product usage are just some of the types of nongovernmental statistics available from secondary sources. Important sources of nongovernmental statistical data include *A Guide to Consumer Markets, Predicasts*

Basebook, Predicasts Forecasts, Sales and Marketing Management Survey of Buying Power, Standard & Poor's Statistical Service, and *Standard Rate and Data Service.*

Government Sources

The U.S. government also produces large amounts of secondary data. Its publications may be divided into census data and other publications.[11]

CENSUS DATA The U.S. Bureau of the Census is the world's largest source of statistical data. Its monthly catalog lists and describes its various publications.[12] More convenient, however, is the *Guide to Economic Census.* Census data are useful in a variety of marketing research projects. The demographic data collected by the Census Bureau includes information about household types, sex, age, marital status, and race. Consumption detail related to automobile ownership, housing characteristics, work status, and practices as well as occupations are just a few of the categories of information available. What makes this demographic information particularly valuable to marketers is that these data can be geographically categorized at various levels of detail. These data can be summarized at various levels: city block, block group, census tract, metropolitan statistical area (MSA), consolidated metropolitan statistical area (CMSA), region (Northeast, Midwest, South, and West), or they can be aggregated for the nation as a whole. Census tracts have a population of more than 4,000 and are defined by local communities. In urban areas, the MSAs have a population of at least 50,000 and comprise counties containing a central city. In addition, census data are available by civil divisions, such as wards, cities, counties, and states.

The quality of census data is high and the data are often extremely detailed. Furthermore, one can purchase computer tapes or diskettes from the Bureau of the Census for a nominal fee and recast this information in a desired format.[13] Many private sources update the census data at a detailed geographic level for the between-census years.[14] Important census data include Census of Housing, Census of Manufacturers, Census of Population, Census of Retail Trade, Census of Service Industries, and Census of Wholesale Trade.

Real Research

The Changing Color of the American Marketplace

According to Census 2000, there are 105.5 million households within the United States that included 281.4 million people. Census 2000 revealed a great deal on the makeup of our population, including that 3.6 percent is Asian American, 12.3 percent is African American, and 12.5 percent is Hispanic American. This means that there are more than 10.2 million Asian Americans, more than 34.7 million African Americans, and more than 35.3 million Hispanic Americans living within the United States. In 2009, in some areas the minorities indeed comprised the majority of the population. From 2000 to 2010, the minority groups are expected to grow at a much faster pace than the rest of the population.

Such a dramatic difference in growth seriously changes the retailing landscape. Marketing companies must embrace these trends and determine how to best configure their marketing mix to meet the needs of these varying cultures. Their inclusion in the research process and marketing plans will be crucial to the long-term success of many organizations.

Mazda North America, though it had been making efforts to sell with diversity in mind, decided to put more money and effort into targeting Hispanic, Asian, and African Americans in the years 2010 to 2015. Univision, a Hispanic television network, is using these results to pitch to CEOs to put more money into ethnic entertainment. Understanding that the Asian American, African American, and Hispanic American markets are not only different markets but also different cultures, each with vastly different histories, will fuel America's growth for the next decade.[15] ∎

OTHER GOVERNMENT PUBLICATIONS In addition to the census, the federal government collects and publishes a great deal of statistical data. The more useful publications are *Business America, Business Conditions Digest, Business Statistics, Index to Publications, Statistical Abstract of the United States,* and *Survey of Current Business.* The second example in the "Overview" section showed how statistics from the U.S. Department of Labor helped fast-food restaurants switch from a high touch to a high tech orientation.

Extensive business statistics can be obtained from FedStats (www.fedstats.gov) and Stat-USA (www.stat-usa.gov). FedStats compiles statistical information from more than 100 agencies. The U.S. Department of Commerce can be reached at www.doc.gov. The Bureau of Census information can be reached via the Department of Commerce (www.doc.gov) or directly at www.census.gov.

The Bureau of Labor Statistics provides useful information, especially Consumer Expenditure Surveys (www.bls.gov). A wide range of economic statistics can be obtained from the Bureau of Economic Analysis (www.bea.doc.gov). Information about public companies can be obtained from the EDGAR Database of Corporate Information that contains SEC filings (www.sec.gov/edgar.shtml). Information about small businesses can be obtained at www.sbaonline.sba.gov. Two of the most useful sources for locating government organizations are the U.S. Government Manual and the Congressional Directory; both can be located at www.gpoaccess.gov. These government sites can provide valuable information to the marketing researcher.

Experiential Research

U.S. Census Bureau

The 2000 census of the United States provides insight into the demographic profile of not only the United States in full, but also smaller U.S. regions, such as states and MSAs. Go to the home page for the U.S. Census Bureau (www.census.gov) and do the following:

1. Find the population clocks on the U.S. Census Bureau's home page. What is the current population estimate for the United States? For the world?
2. Find "state and county quick facts." Compare your home state's "population percentage change from 1990 to 2000" with that of the United States in full. Which grew faster?
3. Find out how many "singles without children living at home" were counted in your zip code in the 2000 census. Look on the left side of the home page, select "American FactFinder," and follow the steps shown. ■

Most published information is also available in the form of computerized databases.

Computerized Databases

online databases
Databases, stored in computers, that require a telecommunications network to access.

Computerized databases consist of information that has been made available in computer-readable form for electronic distribution. In the 2000s, the number of databases, as well as the vendors providing these services, has grown phenomenally.[16] Thus, a classification of computerized databases is helpful.

Internet databases
Internet databases can be accessed, searched, and analyzed on the Internet. It is also possible to download data from the Internet and store it in the computer or an auxiliary storage device.

Classification of Computerized Databases

Computerized databases may be classified as online, Internet, or offline, as shown in Figure 4.3. **Online databases** consist of a central data bank, which is accessed with a computer via a telecommunications network. **Internet databases** can be accessed, searched, and analyzed on the Internet. It is also possible to download data from the Internet and store it in the computer or an auxiliary storage device.[17] **Offline databases** make the information available on diskettes and CD-ROM disks. Thus, offline databases can be accessed at the user's location without the use of an external telecommunications network. For example, the U.S. Bureau of the Census makes

offline databases
Databases that are available on diskette or CD-ROM.

FIGURE 4.3

A Classification of Computerized Databases

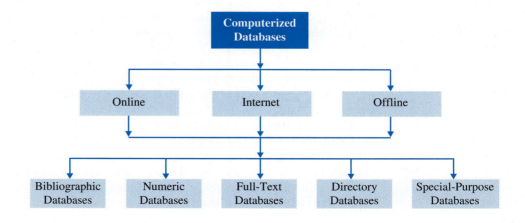

computer data files available on CD-ROM disks. These disks contain detailed information organized by census track or zip code. In the department store patronage project, this type of information was used in sample selection.[18] As indicated by the following example, several vendors are providing data in various forms.

| **Real Research** | InfoUSA: Here, There, and Everywhere |

InfoUSA (www.infousa.com) is a leading provider of sales and marketing support data. The company gathers data from multiple sources, including:

- 5,200 Yellow Page and Business White Page directories
- 17 million phone calls to verify information. Every business is called one to four times a year.
- County courthouse and Secretary of State data
- Leading business magazines and newspapers
- Annual reports
- 10Ks and other SEC filings
- New business registrations and incorporations
- Postal service information, including National Change of Address, ZIP+4 carrier route, and Delivery Sequence files

The underlying database on which all these products are based contains information on 210 million U.S. consumers and 14 million businesses, as of 2009. The products derived from these databases include sales leads, mailing lists, business directories, mapping products, and also delivery of data on the Internet.[19] ■

bibliographic databases
Databases composed of citations to articles in journals, magazines, newspapers, marketing research studies, technical reports, government documents, and the like. They often provide summaries or abstracts of the material cited.

numeric databases
Numeric databases contain numerical and statistical information that may be important sources of secondary data.

full-text databases
Databases containing the complete text of secondary source documents comprising the database.

directory databases
Directory databases provide information on individuals, organizations, and services.

Online, Internet, and offline databases may be further classified as bibliographic, numeric, full-text, directory, or special-purpose databases. **Bibliographic databases** are composed of citations to articles in journals, magazines, newspapers, marketing research studies, technical reports, government documents, and the like.[20] They often provide summaries or abstracts of the material cited. Examples of bibliographic databases include ABI/Inform and the Predicasts Terminal System. Another bibliographic database, Management Contents, provided by the Dialog Corporation, was used to enhance the literature search in the department store patronage project.

Numeric databases contain numerical and statistical information, such as survey and time-series data. Economic and industry data lend themselves to time-series presentations, which are developed when the same variables are measured over time. Such data are particularly relevant for assessing market potential, making sales forecasts, or setting sales quotas. The American Statistics Index (ASI) provides abstracts and indexes of federal government statistical publications. Global Financial Data (www.globalfinancialdata.com) provides historical data on securities, dividends, and exchange rates.

Commercially updated census data are another example of numeric databases. Several sources provide updated, current-year and 5-year projections on population statistics collected in the latest census. A variety of geographic categorization schemes, including census tract, zip code, and Nielsen's Designated Market Areas or Selling Areas, can be used as keys for searching these databases. Claritas, now know as Nielsen's Claritas (www.claritas.com), is one firm that provides updated demographic information annually.

Full-text databases contain the complete text of the source documents comprising the database. Vu/Text Information Systems, Inc., provides electronic full-text delivery and search capabilities for a number of newspapers (e.g., *Washington Post, Boston Globe, Miami Herald*). The LexisNexis service provides full-text access to hundreds of business databases, including selected newspapers, periodicals, company annual reports, and investment firm reports.

Directory databases provide information on individuals, organizations, and services. Economic Information Systems, Inc., through its database EIS Nonmanufacturing Establishments, provides information on location, headquarters, name, percentage of industry sales, industry classification, and employment size class for about 200,000 nonmanufacturing establishments that employ 20 or more people. As another example, the national electronic Yellow Pages directories of manufacturers, wholesalers, retailers, professionals, and service

special-purpose databases

Databases that contain information of a specific nature, e.g., data on a specialized industry.

organizations provide the names, addresses, and North American Industrial Classification codes of numerous organizations.

Finally, there are **special-purpose databases**. For example, the Profit Impact of Market Strategies (PIMS) database is an ongoing database of research and analysis on business strategy conducted by the Strategic Planning Institute in Cambridge, Massachusetts. This database comprises more than 250 companies, which provide data on more than 2,000 businesses.[21] Virtually all libraries of major universities maintain computerized databases of management and related literature that students can access free of charge.

Although computerized databases are numerous and varied, their sheer number can be overwhelming and locating a particular database may seem difficult. How, then, do you locate specific bibliographic, numeric, full-text, directory, or special-purpose databases? Directories of databases provide the needed help.

Directories of Databases

There are numerous sources of information on databases. Perhaps the best way to obtain information about databases is to consult a directory. The *Gale Directory of Databases* (www.gale.cengage.com) is published every six months. Volume 1 covers online databases and Volume 2 covers CD-ROMs and other offline databases. Some of the other useful directories that are periodically updated are:

Directory of On-line Databases Santa Monica, CA: Cuadra Associates, Inc. (www.cuadra.com)

Encyclopedia of Information System and Services Detroit: Gale Research Company

Syndicated Sources of Secondary Data

syndicated services (sources)

Information services offered by marketing research organizations that provide information from a common database to different firms that subscribe to their services.

In addition to published data or data available in the form of computerized databases, syndicated sources constitute the other major source of external secondary data. **Syndicated services**, also referred to as *syndicated sources*, are companies that collect and sell common pools of data of known commercial value, designed to serve information needs shared by a number of clients (see Chapter 1). These data are not collected for the purpose of marketing research problems specific to individual clients, but the data and reports supplied to client companies can be personalized to fit particular needs. For example, reports could be organized on the basis of the clients' sales territories or product lines. Using syndicated services is frequently less expensive than collecting primary data. Figure 4.4 presents a classification of syndicated services. Syndicated services can be classified based on the unit of measurement (households/consumers or institutions). Household/consumer data may be obtained from surveys, purchase and media panels, or electronic scanner services. Information obtained through surveys consists of values and lifestyles, advertising evaluation, or general information related to preferences, purchase, consumption, and other aspects of behavior. Panels emphasize information on purchases or media consumption. Electronic scanner services might provide scanner data only, scanner data linked to panels, or scanner data linked to panels and (cable) TV. When institutions are the unit of measurement, the data may be obtained from retailers, wholesalers, or industrial firms. An overview of the various syndicated sources is given in Table 4.3 on page 115. Each of these sources will be discussed.

Syndicated Data from Households

Surveys

surveys

Interviews with a large number of respondents using a predesigned questionnaire.

Various syndicated services regularly conduct **surveys**, which involve interviews with a large number of respondents using a predesigned questionnaire. Often these surveys are conducted on samples drawn from panels. Panels were discussed in Chapter 3 in the context of longitudinal research designs. Panels are samples of respondents who provide specified information at regular intervals over an extended period of time. These respondents may be organizations, households,

FIGURE 4.4
A Classification of Syndicated Services

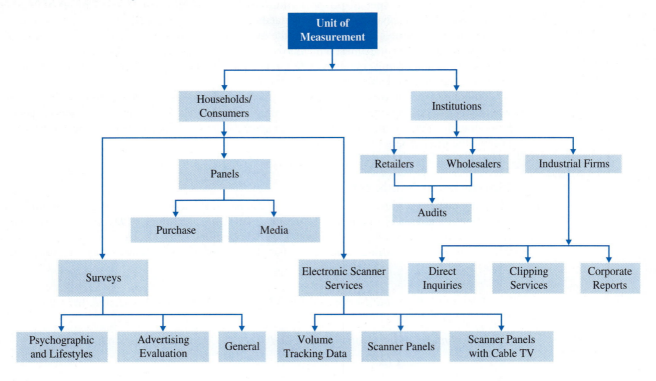

or individuals, although household panels are most common. Comprehensive demographic, lifestyle, and product-ownership data are collected only once as each respondent is admitted into the panel. The panel is used as a respondent pool from which the research organization can draw either representative or targeted samples based on the relevant background characteristics of the panel members. Response rates to panel surveys, including mail panels, are substantially improved over the random sampling process because of the commitment panel members make to participate in surveys.

syndicated panel surveys
Syndicated panel surveys measure the same group of respondents over time but not necessarily on the same variables.

psychographics
Quantified psychological profiles of individuals.

lifestyles
A lifestyle may be defined as a distinctive pattern of living that is described by the activities people engage in, the interests they have, and the opinions they hold of themselves and the world around them (AIOs).

Syndicated panel surveys measure the same group of respondents over time but not necessarily on the same variables. A large pool of respondents is recruited to participate on the panel. From this pool, different subsamples of respondents may be drawn for different surveys. Any of the survey techniques may be used, including telephone, personal, mail, or electronic interviewing. The content and topics of the surveys vary and cover a wide range. Also known as *omnibus panels*, these panels are used to implement different cross-sectional designs at different points in time, generally for different surveys. For example, eNation involves five weekly online omnibus surveys of 1,000 American adults using Synovate's (www.synovate.com) Global Opinion Panels. Synovate has other omnibus panels including TeleNation with two national telephone surveys each week that total 2,000 interviews. Omnibus panels are different from the panels using longitudinal designs discussed in Chapter 3. It may be recalled that in a longitudinal design, repeated measurements on the same variables are made on the same sample, and such panels are also referred to as *true panels* to distinguish them from omnibus panels. Surveys may be broadly classified on the basis of their content as psychographics and lifestyles, advertising evaluation, or general surveys.

PSYCHOGRAPHICS AND LIFESTYLES **Psychographics** refer to the psychological profiles of individuals and to psychologically based measures of lifestyle. **Lifestyles** refer to the distinctive modes of living of a society or some of its segments. Together, these measures are generally referred to as Activities, Interests, and Opinions, or simply AIOs. The following example provides an application.

TABLE 4.3

Overview of Syndicated Services

Type	Characteristics	Advantages	Disadvantages	Uses
Surveys	Surveys conducted at regular intervals	Most flexible way of obtaining data; information on underlying motives	Interviewer errors; respondent errors	Market segmentation; advertising theme selection, and advertising effectiveness
Purchase Panels	Households provide specific information regularly over an extended period of time; respondents asked to record specific behaviors as they occur	Recorded purchase behavior can be linked to the demographic/ psychographic characteristics	Lack of representativeness; response bias; maturation	Forecasting sales, market share, and trends; establishing consumer profiles, brand loyalty, and switching; evaluating test markets, advertising, and distribution
Media Panels	Electronic devices automatically recording behavior, supplemented by a diary	Same as purchase panel	Same as purchase panel	Establishing advertising rates; selecting media program or air time; establishing viewer profiles
Scanner Volume Tracking Data	Household purchases recorded through electronic scanners in supermarkets	Data reflect actual purchases; timely data; less expensive	Data may not be representative; errors in recording purchases; difficult to link purchases to elements of marketing mix other than price	Price tracking, modeling; effectiveness of in-store promotion
Scanner Panels with Cable TV	Scanner panels of households that subscribe to cable TV	Data reflect actual purchases; sample control; ability to link panel data to household characteristics	Data may not be representative; quality of data limited	Promotional mix analyses; copy testing; new-product testing; positioning
Audit Services	Verification of product movement by examining physical records or performing inventory analysis	Relatively precise information at the retail and wholesale levels	Coverage may be incomplete; matching of data on competitive activity may be difficult	Measurement of consumer sales and market share competitive activity; analyzing distribution patterns; tracking of new products
Industrial Product Syndicated Services	Data banks on industrial establishments created through direct inquiries of companies, clipping services, and corporate reports	Important source of information on industrial firms; particularly useful in initial phases of the project	Data are lacking in terms of content, quantity, and quality	Determining market potential by geographic area; defining sales territories; allocating advertising budget

Real Research   Campbell Makes Sure AIOs Are in Its Alphabet Soup

Yankelovich Research and Consulting Services (www.yankelovich.com) provides the Yankelovich Monitor, a survey that contains data on lifestyles and social trends. The survey is conducted at the same time each year among a nationally projectable sample of 2,500 adults, 16 years of age or older, including a special sample of 300 college students living on campus. The sample is based on the most recent census data. Interviews are conducted in person at the respondent's home and take approximately 1.5 hours to complete. In addition, a questionnaire that takes about one hour to complete is left behind for the respondents to answer and mail

When syndicate data showed an adult craving for foods that cater to a healthy appetite, Campbell introduced their Chunky Soup.

back. Advertising agencies use the Yankelovich Monitor to discern changes in lifestyles and design advertising themes that reflect these trends. When the Monitor showed an adult craving for foods that cater to a healthy appetite, Campbell (campbellsoup.com) introduced their Chunky Soup by using the NFL as a sponsor and stars Kurt Warner and Donovan McNabb in many of their commercials. These commercials showed that even soup can be hearty enough for the "big boys," in hopes of reaching a target market of adults who want a soup that can fill them up. The 2006 Winter Olympics featured advertisements that showed Olympic athletes trying to keep themselves warm and satisfied by eating Campbell's soup. The company also used Sarah Hughes, Olympic Gold Medalist, as an ambassador for its Campbell's Labels for Education™ program.[22] ■

SRI Consulting, partner of SRI International and formerly Stanford Research Institute (www.future.sri.com), conducts an annual survey of consumers that is used to classify persons into VALS-2 (Values and Lifestyles) types for segmentation purposes.[23] Information on specific aspects of consumers' lifestyles is also available. GfK Custom Research North America (www.gfkamerica.com) conducts an annual survey of 5,000 consumers who participate in leisure sports and recreational activities. Several firms conduct surveys to compile demographic and psychographic information at the household, sub-zip (e.g., 30306-3035), and zip-code level, which is then made available on a subscription basis. Such information is particularly valuable for client firms seeking to enhance internally generated customer data for database marketing.

ADVERTISING EVALUATION The purpose of advertising evaluation surveys is to assess the effectiveness of advertising using print and broadcast media. A well-known survey is the Gallup and Robinson Magazine Impact Research Service (MIRS) (www.gallup-robinson.com). In the MIRS, ads are tested using an at-home in-magazine context among widely dispersed samples. The system offers standardized measures with flexible design options. Test ads may naturally appear in the magazine or are inserted as tip-ins. It provides strong, validated measures of recall, persuasion, and ad reaction with responsive scheduling. Such results are particularly important to heavy advertisers, such as Procter & Gamble, General Motors, Sears, PepsiCo, Eastman Kodak, and McDonald's, who are greatly concerned about how well their advertising dollars are spent.[24]

Evaluation of effectiveness is even more critical in the case of TV advertising. Television commercials are evaluated using either the recruited audience method or the in-home viewing method. In the former method, respondents are recruited and brought to a central viewing facility, such as a theater or mobile viewing laboratory. The respondents view the commercials and provide data regarding knowledge, attitudes, and preferences related to the product being advertised and the commercial itself. In the in-home viewing method, consumers evaluate commercials at home in their normal viewing environment. New commercials can be pretested at the network level or in local markets distributed via DVDs. A survey of viewers is then conducted to assess the effectiveness of the commercials. Gallup & Robinson, Inc. (www.gallup-robinson.com) offers testing of television commercials using both these methods.

These methods are also used for testing the effectiveness of advertising in other media such as magazines, radio, newspapers, and direct mail. Experian Simmons (www.smrb.com) conducts four different surveys with a large sample of respondents so that magazine, TV, newspaper, and radio media exposure can be monitored. Mediamark Research & Intelligence (www.mediamark.com) is another firm that makes available information on the consumption of media, products, and services by household. Its Starch Readership Survey specializes in measuring audience levels for print media. Starch annually measures exposure and readership levels for nearly 1,000 issues of consumer, business, and industrial publications. Personal interviews are conducted with a sample of more than 100,000 respondents.

A recognition method is used in which the respondents are shown advertisements in recently published magazines. Each individual is questioned about each ad. Based on the response to an ad, the individual is classified into one of the following four levels of recognition: (1) Nonreader: The individual has not seen the advertisement; (2) Noted: The individual remembers seeing the advertisement in this issue; (3) Associated: The individual has seen the advertisement and recognizes the brand or advertiser's name; and (4) Read most: The individual read 50 percent or more of the written material in the advertisement.

These data are summarized for each advertisement in each magazine. From these statistics, Starch can generate overall readership percentages, readership per advertising dollar (based on current advertising rates), and advertisement rank within product categories. This type of data can be used to compare advertisements across current or past issues as well as against averages for the product category. This information is very useful to companies that advertise heavily in print media, such as American Airlines, Gucci, and GM, for evaluating the effectiveness of their advertising.

GENERAL SURVEYS Surveys are also conducted for a variety of other purposes, including examination of purchase and consumption behavior. For example, Harris Interactive's (www.harrisinteractive.com) ShopperInsight is an Internet-based survey of 26,000 primary household shoppers nationwide asking for their reasons why they have chosen a particular supermarket, drugstore, or mass merchandiser. Shoppers are asked to rate their shopping experience based on 30 key factors that influence their choice of retailer, from checkout lines to store cleanliness, hours, and location. In addition, attributes such as product pricing and selection are evaluated across 45 individual product categories for every supermarket, drugstore, and mass merchandiser. These findings can help merchandisers like Wal-Mart gauge their strengths and weaknesses. For example, the findings from a recent survey reinforced Wal-Mart's strategy of providing everyday low prices versus having frequent promotions on special items. The results showed that Wal-Mart's prices were 3.8 percent lower than Target, its closest competitor.

USES OF SURVEYS Since a wide variety of data can be obtained, survey data have numerous uses. They can be used for market segmentation, as with psychographics and lifestyles data, and for establishing consumer profiles. Surveys are also useful for determining product image, measurement and positioning, and conducting price perception analysis. Other notable uses include advertising theme selection and evaluation of advertising effectiveness.

Real Research   CARAVAN Survey

Opinion Research Corporation (www.opinionresearch.com) is a research and consulting firm that helps organizations worldwide to improve their marketing performance. One of its service offerings, CARAVAN®, is a twice-weekly telephone survey, each conducted among a national probability sample of 1,000 adults. An online version is also offered.

One of the clients was national restaurant chain like Chili's. It needed to determine the general public's reaction to a proposed new advertising campaign. The campaign would include a celebrity endorsement involving a sports personality in a television commercial as well as an in-store promotion centered on that celebrity. Through CARAVAN, the restaurant chain was able to gain valuable insights into the potential impact of the ad campaign. The questions asked in the survey were designed to understand if the whole campaign would be appealing to the target market segment (young families, in this case). It also covered questions that probed if the celebrity's image matched with the perceived image of the restaurant chain and the values it stood for. Thus the survey enabled the study of the potential impact of the ad campaign on the public's opinion and their future visits to the restaurant chain. ■

ADVANTAGES AND DISADVANTAGES OF SURVEYS Surveys are the most flexible means of obtaining data from respondents. The researcher can focus on only a certain segment of the population—for example, teenagers, owners of vacation homes, or housewives between the ages of 30 and 40. Surveys are the primary means of obtaining information about consumers' motives, attitudes, and preferences. A variety of questions can be asked, and visual aids, packages, products, or other props can be used during the interviews. Properly analyzed, survey data can be manipulated in many ways so that the researcher can look at intergroup differences, examine the effects of independent variables such as age or income, or even predict future behavior.

On the other hand, survey data may be limited in several significant ways. The researcher has to rely primarily on the respondents' self-reports. There is a gap between what people say and what they actually do. Errors may occur because respondents remember incorrectly or give socially desirable responses. Furthermore, samples may be biased, questions poorly phrased, interviewers not properly instructed or supervised, and results misinterpreted.

Purchase and Media Panels

Often, survey data can be complemented with data obtained from purchase and media panels. While panels are also maintained for conducting surveys, the distinguishing feature of purchase and media panels is that the respondents record specific behaviors as they occur. Previously, behavior was recorded in a diary, and the diary was returned to the research organization every one to four weeks. Paper diaries have been gradually replaced by electronic diaries. Now, most of the panels are online and the behavior is recorded electronically, either entered online by the respondents or recorded automatically by electronic devices. Panel members are compensated for their participation with gifts, coupons, information, or cash. The content of information recorded is different for purchase panels and media panels.

purchase panels
A data-gathering technique in which respondents record their purchases online or in a diary.

PURCHASE PANELS In **purchase panels**, respondents record their purchases of a variety of different products, as in the NPD Panel.

Real Research   Information in These Diaries (Panels) Is No Secret

The NPD Group (www.npd.com) is a leading provider of essential market information collected and delivered online for a wide range of industries and markets and has over 1600 clients, ranging from *Fortune* 100 leaders to smaller businesses as of 2009. NPD combines information obtained via surveys with that recorded by respondents about their behaviors to generate reports on consumption behaviors, industry sales, market share, and key demographic trends. NPD consumer information is collected from their Online Panel about a wide range of product categories, including fashion, food, fun, house and home, tech and auto. Respondents provide detailed information regarding the brand and amount purchased, price paid, whether any special deals were involved, the store where purchased, and intended use. The composition of the panel

A study using the NPD online panel indicated that women actually like shopping for swimwear.

is representative of the U.S. population as a whole. For example, a recent study conducted by NPD revealed that women actually like shopping for swimwear. According to the survey, women rated their overall shopping experience for swimwear as excellent or very good, with 69 percent of satisfied shoppers being in the age range of 35–44. The results also showed that the biggest purchasing influences for a retail buyer are point-of-purchase display and the hang-tag description on the suit, while for a catalog buyer the catalog layout is important. These findings have obvious implications for the marketing of swimwear. Another recent study identified the top five women's accessory purchases as (1) handbag/purse, (2) costume/fashion jewelry, (3) fashion hair accessory, (4) sunglasses, and (5) gloves/mittens. Such findings help department stores in determining the product mix for women's departments.[25] ∎

Other organizations that maintain purchase panels include the NFO World Group (www.nfow.com). This group maintains a number of panels, including a large interactive panel. NFO Special Panels, such as the Baby Panel, provide access to highly targeted groups of consumers. Each quarter, approximately 2,000 new mothers and 2,000 expectant mothers join the NFO Baby Panel.

media panels
A data-gathering technique that is comprised of samples of respondents whose television viewing behavior is automatically recorded by electronic devices, supplementing the purchase information recorded online or in a diary.

MEDIA PANELS In **media panels**, electronic devices automatically record viewing behavior, thus supplementing a diary or an online panel. Perhaps the most familiar media panel is Nielsen Television Index by Nielsen Media Research (www.nielsenmedia.com), which provides television ratings and audience estimates. The heart of the Nielsen Media Research national ratings service is an electronic measurement system called the Nielsen People Meter. These meters are placed in a sample of 11,000 households in the United States, randomly selected and recruited by Nielsen Media so as to be representative of the population. The People Meter is placed on each TV in the sample household. The meter measures two things—what program or channel is being tuned in and who is watching. Household tuning data for each day are stored in the in-home metering system until they are automatically retrieved by Nielsen Media Research's computers each night. Nielsen Media Research's Operations Center in Dunedin, Florida, processes this information each night for release to the television industry and other customers the next day.

To measure the audiences for local television, Nielsen Media Research gathers viewing information using TV diaries, booklets in which samples of viewers record their television viewing during a measurement week. They conduct diary measurement for each of the 210 television markets in the country four times each year, during February, May, July, and November. The diary requests that viewers write down not only who watched, but what program and what channel they watched. Once the diaries are filled out, viewers mail them back to Nielsen Media Research and the information is transferred into computers in order to calculate ratings.

Using these data, Nielsen estimates the number and percentage of all TV households viewing a given show. This information is also disaggregated by 10 demographic and socioeconomic characteristics, such as household income, education of head of house, occupation of head of house, household size, age of children, age of women, and geographical location. The Nielsen Television Index is useful to firms such as AT&T, Kellogg Company, JCPenney, Pillsbury, and Unilever in selecting specific TV programs on which to air their commercials.[26]

In April 2007, Nielsen Media Research introduced the new commercial-minute ratings that allow advertising agencies, advertisers, and programmers to develop individualized minute-by-minute ratings of national commercials by demographic group for all national television programs. Another index by the same company is the Nielsen Homevideo Index®, NHI. The NHI was established in 1980 and provides a measurement of cable, pay cable, VCRs, DVD players, satellite dishes, and other new television technologies. The data are collected through the use of People Meters, set-tuning meters, and paper diaries.

In addition to the Nielsen Television Index, other services provide media panels. Arbitron maintains local and regional radio and TV diary panels. Arbitron's (www.arbitron.com) Portable People Meter is a panel-based measure of multimedia, including TV, radio, satellite radio, and the Web.[27] In the ScanAmerica peoplemeter ratings system, an electronic meter automatically collects continuous detailed measures of television set tuning for every set in the home. TV BehaviorGraphics™, by Simmons Market Research Bureau (www.smrb.com), is a behavioral targeting system used to identify the best prospects for products and services based on consumers' viewing of broadcast and cable television programs. The system was developed through an integration process that merges the Nielsen National Television Index (NTI) with the

Simmons National Consumer Survey (NCS). It consists of a multisegment cluster system that classifies consumers into distinct groups based on their television viewing behavior. The system, which is used by the top advertising agencies and television media, is available to subscribers. Syndicated services also collect the same type of audience data for radio. Radio audience statistics are typically collected using diaries two to four times per year

Given the growing popularity of the Internet, syndicated services are also geared to this medium. Nielsen Online (www.nielsen-online.com) tracks and collects Internet usage in real time from over 50,000 home and work users. It reports site and e-commerce activity: number of visits to properties, domains, and unique sites; rankings by site and by category; time and frequency statistics; traffic patterns; and e-commerce transactions. It also reports banner advertising: audience response to banners, creative content, frequency, and site placement. This service has been launched in collaboration with Nielsen.

Real Research   Hitwise: Monitoring Web Site Hits

Hitwise (www.hitwise.com) is a leading provider of online competitive intelligence services. Every day, the company monitors more than 25 million Internet users and interacts with more than 450,000 Web sites across industry categories in several countries. Hitwise benchmarks its clients' online presence to competing Web sites. Client firms use this information to optimize their online investment in affiliate programs, marketing, online advertising, content development, and lead generation. For example, Heinz is one of the clients that has hugely benefited from the services offered by Hitwise. Heinz had created nearly 57 varieties of microsites for its brands at the peak of the dot.com craze. However, today, thanks to Hitwise, Heinz has learned specific online activity is only relevant for core brands such as ketchup, baby food, and beans. For other brands, brand value is delivered via the corporate site.

The Hitwise methodology is as follows. Hitwise provides daily rankings of Web sites in more than 160 industry and interest categories. It also offers a range of online tools allowing subscribers to analyze and track competing Web sites. Subscribers can also track Internet usage patterns. Hitwise monitors Internet Service Provider (ISP) networks and other data sources for this purpose (visits that any Web site receives from the ISP's subscribers). The figures from ISPs are aggregated to calculate a site's ranking. Hitwise extracts from the partner ISP's networks a list of the Web sites visited and ranks them according to a range of industry standard metrics, including page requests, visits, and average visit length. Hitwise also extracts Click-Stream data, which analyzes the movements of visitors between sites to provide subscribers with information on traffic to and from competing sites. To ensure representative sampling, a geographically diverse range of ISP networks in metropolitan and regional areas, representing all types of Internet usage including home, work, educational, and public access, are monitored.[28] ■

USES OF PURCHASE AND MEDIA PANELS Purchase panels provide information useful for forecasting sales, estimating market shares, assessing brand loyalty and brand-switching behavior, establishing profiles of specific user groups, measuring promotional effectiveness, and conducting controlled store tests. Media panels yield information helpful for establishing advertising rates by radio and TV networks, selecting appropriate programming, and profiling viewer or listener subgroups. Advertisers, media planners, and buyers find panel information to be particularly useful.

ADVANTAGES AND DISADVANTAGES OF PURCHASE AND MEDIA PANELS As compared to sample surveys, purchase and media panels offer certain distinct advantages.[29] Panels can provide longitudinal data (data can be obtained from the same respondents repeatedly). People who are willing to serve on panels may provide more and higher-quality data than sample respondents. In purchase panels, information is recorded at the time of purchase, eliminating recall errors.[30] Information recorded by electronic devices is accurate because it eliminates human errors.

The disadvantages of purchase and media panels include lack of representativeness, maturation, and response biases. Most panels are not representative of the U.S. population. They underrepresent certain groups such as minorities and those with low education levels. This problem is further compounded by refusal to respond and attrition of panel members. Over time maturation sets in, and the panel members must be replaced (see Chapter 7). Response biases may occur, since simply being on the panel may alter behavior. Since purchase or media data are entered by hand, recording errors are also possible (see Chapter 3).

Electronic Scanner Services

scanner data
Data obtained by passing merchandise over a laser scanner that reads the UPC code from the packages.

Although information provided by surveys and purchase and media panels is useful, electronic scanner services are becoming increasingly popular. **Scanner data** reflect some of the latest technological developments in the marketing research industry. Scanner data are collected by passing merchandise over a laser scanner, which optically reads the bar-coded description (the universal product code or UPC) printed on the merchandise. This code is then linked to the current price held in the computer memory and used to prepare a sales slip. Information printed on the sales slip includes descriptions as well as prices of all items purchased. Checkout scanners, which are now used in many retail stores, are revolutionizing packaged-goods marketing research.

volume tracking data
Scanner data that provides information on purchases by brand, size, price, and flavor or formulation.

Three types of scanner data are available: volume tracking data, scanner panels, and scanner panels with cable TV. **Volume tracking data** provide information on purchases by brand, size, price, and flavor or formulation, based on sales data collected from the checkout scanner tapes. This information is collected nationally from a sample of supermarkets with electronic scanners. Scanner services providing volume tracking data include National Scan Track (Nielsen, www.nielsen.com) and InfoScan (Information Resources, Inc., usa.infores.com). IRI's InfoScan tracking service collects scanner data weekly from more than 34,000 supermarket, drug, and mass merchandiser outlets across the United States. InfoScan store tracking provides detailed information on sales, share, distribution, pricing, and promotion.[31]

scanner panels
Scanner data where panel members are identified by an ID card allowing each panel member's purchases to be stored with respect to the individual shopper.

In **scanner panels**, each household member is given an ID card that can be read by the electronic scanner at the cash register. The scanner panel member simply presents the ID card at the checkout counter each time she or he shops. In this way, consumer identity is linked to products purchased as well as the time and day of the shopping trip, and the firm can build a shopping record for that individual. Alternatively, some firms provide handheld scanners to panel members. These members scan their purchases once they are home. The Nielsen Consumer Panel, called Homescan, is used to record the purchases of approximately 300,000 households throughout the world. The consumer scans the bar codes on purchases with a handheld scanner, which records the price, promotions, and quantity of each item. The information in the handheld scanner is then transmitted to Nielsen through telephone lines. Nielsen uses the information from the scanner and additional information gathered from the consumer to determine such things as consumer demographics, quantity and frequency of purchases, percentage of households purchasing, shopping trips and expenditures, price paid, and usage information. Manufacturers and retailers use this information to better understand the purchasing habits of consumers. The Boston Market example given in the "Overview" section provided an illustration. According to Nielsen's consumer panel data, 55 percent of respondents purchased a meal for at-home consumption several times a month.[32]

scanner panels with cable TV
The combination of a scanner panel with manipulations of the advertising that is being broadcast by cable television companies.

An even more advanced use of scanning, **scanner panels with cable TV**, combines scanner panels with new technologies growing out of the cable TV industry. Households on these panels subscribe to one of the cable TV systems in their market. By means of a cable TV "split," the researcher targets different commercials into the homes of the panel members. For example, half the households may see test commercial A during the 6:00 P.M. newscast while the other half see test commercial B. These panels allow researchers to conduct fairly controlled experiments in a relatively natural environment. IRI's BehaviorScan system contains such a panel.[33]

Real Research

Using Total TV Households for Testing Total Advertising

Based on cereal consumption research conducted in 2008, more than 90 percent of consumers eat cereal for breakfast and per capita consumption is very high. Results also indicated that cereal was the favorite breakfast item, and was eaten regularly by three out of four adults. Therefore, General Mills (www.generalmills.com) has been promoting Total cereal on national television but is concerned about the effectiveness of its commercials.

Technology has been developed that allows transmission of advertising into participating households without the use of a cable TV system. Since the panel members can be selected from all available (total) TV households, not just those with cable TV, the bias of cable-only testing is eliminated. Using this type of system, General Mills can test which one of four test commercials for Total cereal results in the highest sales. Four groups of panel members are selected, and each receives a different test commercial. These households are monitored via scanner data to determine which group purchased the most Total cereal.[34] ■

This example shows how scanner services incorporate advanced marketing research technology, which results in some advantages over survey and purchase panel data.

USES OF SCANNER DATA   Scanner data are useful for a variety of purposes.[35] National volume tracking data can be used for tracking sales, prices, distribution, modeling, and analyzing early warning signals. Scanner panels with cable TV can be used for testing new products, repositioning products, analyzing promotional mix, and making advertising decisions, including budget, copy and media, and pricing. These panels provide marketing researchers with a unique controlled environment for the manipulation of marketing variables.

ADVANTAGES AND DISADVANTAGES OF SCANNER DATA   Scanner data have an obvious advantage over surveys and purchase panels, since they reflect purchasing behavior that is not subject to interviewing, recording, memory, or expert biases. The record of purchases obtained by scanners is complete and unbiased by price sensitivity, since the panelist is not required to be overly conscious of price levels and changes. Another advantage is that in-store variables like pricing, promotions, and displays are part of the data set. The data are also likely to be current and can be obtained quickly. Finally, scanner panels with cable TV provide a highly controlled testing environment.

A major weakness of scanner data is lack of representativeness. National volume tracking data may not be projectable onto the total population, because only large supermarkets have scanners. Also, certain types of outlets, such as food warehouses and mass merchandisers, are excluded. Likewise, scanners have limited geographical dispersion and coverage.

The quality of scanner data may be limited by several factors. All products may not be scanned. For example, a clerk may use the register to ring up a heavy item to avoid lifting it. If an item does not scan on the first try, the clerk may key in the price and ignore the bar code. Sometimes a consumer purchases many flavors of the same item, but the clerk scans only one package and then rings in the number of purchases. Thus, the transaction is inaccurately recorded. With respect to scanner panels, the system provides information on TV sets in use rather than actual viewing behavior. Although scanner data provide behavioral and sales information, they do not provide information on underlying attitudes, preferences, and reasons for specific choices.

ACTIVE RESEARCH

J.D. Power: Powering Ford Vehicles

Visit www.jdpower.com and write a brief report about the latest vehicle dependability study findings and methodology.

As the CEO of Ford Motor Company, what marketing strategies would you adopt to increase the dependability and image of Ford vehicles?

How can you make use of the J.D. Power vehicle dependability study and other secondary and syndicated data to help Ford Motor Company to increase the dependability and image of its vehicles?

Syndicated Data from Institutions

Retailer and Wholesaler Audits

As Figure 4.4 shows, syndicated data are available for retailers and wholesalers as well as industrial firms. The most popular means of obtaining data from retailers and wholesalers is an audit. An **audit** is a formal examination and verification of product movement traditionally carried out by auditors who make in-person visits to retail and wholesale outlets and examine physical records or analyze inventory. Retailers and wholesalers who participate in the audit receive basic reports and cash payments from the audit service. Audit data focus on the products or services sold through the outlets or the characteristics of the outlets themselves, as illustrated by the following example. With the advent of scanner data, the need to perform audits has greatly decreased. Although audits are still being conducted, many do not collect data manually but make use of computerized information.

An example of the traditional audit is the Nielsen Convenience Track, which is a retail audit of convenience stores in 30 local markets (www.nielsen.com). Another example is the National

audit
A data collection process derived from physical records or by performing inventory analysis. Data are collected personally by the researcher or by representatives of the researcher, and the data are based on counts, usually of physical objects other than people.

Retail Census by GfK Audits & Surveys (www.gfkauditsandsurveys.com) that provides updated measurements of product distribution in all types of retail and service outlets. Conducted annually since its inception in 1953, it is based on a national probability sample of approximately 30,000 outlets of all kinds throughout the country in more than 500 different geographic areas. The audit is conducted by personal store visits, making GfK Audits & Surveys' Retail Census the largest annual product availability measurement in the United States. For high speed and accuracy, the in-store auditors use handheld computers to capture UPC information electronically. Nielsen Convenience Track can integrate convenience store data with data from other channels, including grocery, drug, and mass merchandisers.

Wholesale audit services, the counterpart of retail audits, monitor warehouse withdrawals. Participating operators, which include supermarket chains, wholesalers, and frozen-food warehouses, typically account for more than 80 percent of the volume in the area.

USES OF AUDIT DATA The uses of retail and wholesale audit data include (1) determining the size of the total market and the distribution of sales by type of outlet, region, or city; (2) assessing brand shares and competitive activity; (3) identifying shelf space allocation and inventory problems; (4) analyzing distribution problems; (5) developing sales potentials and forecasts; and (6) developing and monitoring promotional allocations based on sales volume. Thus, audit data were particularly helpful in obtaining information on the environmental context of the problem in the department store patronage project.

ADVANTAGES AND DISADVANTAGES OF AUDIT DATA Audits provide relatively accurate information on the movement of many different products at the wholesale and retail levels. Furthermore, this information can be broken down by a number of important variables, such as brand, type of outlet, and size of market.

However, audits have limited coverage. Not all markets or operators are included. Also, audit information may not be timely or current, particularly compared to scanner data. Typically, there is a two-month gap between the completion of the audit cycle and the publication of reports. Another disadvantage is that, unlike scanner data, audit data cannot be linked to consumer characteristics. In fact, there may even be a problem in relating audit data to advertising expenditures and other marketing efforts. Some of these limitations are overcome in electronic (online) audits, as the following example illustrates.

Real Research Online Audits for Tracking Online Shopping

Since 1997, Ashford.com offers a big selection and low prices for watches and jewelry. Obviously, for an online retailer, the holidays are a particularly important period. It is a time when many people shop online, so sales can really soar. Ashford.com was able to use electronic audit data about how their purchasers shop and how much they are buying.

Nielsen Online (www.nielsen-online.com) constructed a Holiday E-Commerce Index, which measured Web shopping in eight different categories. Rather than gathering descriptive research about the customers from the customers, Nielsen Online gathered the data from the stores where the customers shopped. Because the orders were placed online, the store computers were able to track the purchases with ease. This computer tracking was then used to gather the purchasing information from the stores and accumulated into a report format. The survey told Ashford.com that a large portion of their customers were purchasing from the Web site while at work. This trend applied around the Web, as 46 percent of holiday online shopping was conducted during work hours versus the 54 percent that was conducted from consumers' homes. Nielsen Online determined that Ashford.com's customers were shopping during the lunch hour or in small, 10–15 minute clips throughout the day.

Additionally, Nielsen Online demonstrated that online sales across the Web increased greatly in the first week of December as the holidays approached. Ashford.com's sales increased 385 percent during this period, so they did extremely well compared to other online companies. This information told Ashford.com that they should make sure their site is up and working during the workday. Promotions should be offered and flashed on the screen during this time. Additionally, the company might want to start advertising in corporate settings. Newspapers like the *Wall Street Journal* and other corporate Web sites would be good places to advertise. Online retailers like Ashford.com must take advantage of electronic audits and other types of marketing research in order to offer the products that online consumers want.[36] ■

Industry Services

Industry services provide syndicated data about industrial firms, businesses, and other institutions. Financial, operating, and employment data are also collected by these syndicated research services for almost every North American Industry Classification System (NAICS) industrial category. These data are collected by making direct inquiries; from clipping services that monitor newspapers, the trade press, or broadcasts; and from corporate reports. The range and sources of syndicated data available for industrial goods firms are more limited than those available for consumer goods firms. Services available include D&B International Business Locator (www.dnb.com); *Fortune* Datastore, which contains databases such as the *Fortune* 500, *Fortune* 1000, Global 500, and the fastest-growing companies database (www.fortune.com); and Standard & Poor's Information Services, which includes Corporate Profiles (www.standardpoor.com).

The D&B International Business Locator provides one-click access to more than 28 million public/private companies in more than 200 countries. After finding a business, the locator will provide key business data, including full address information, NAIC/line of business details, business size (sales, net worth, employees), names of key principals and identification of this location's headquarters, and domestic parent company and/or global parent company.

USES OF INDUSTRY SERVICES Information provided by industrial services is useful for sales management decisions including identifying prospects, defining territories, setting quotas, and measuring market potential by geographic areas. It can also aid in advertising decisions such as targeting prospects, allocating advertising budgets, selecting media, and measuring advertising effectiveness. This kind of information is also useful for segmenting the market and designing custom products and services for important segments.

ADVANTAGES AND DISADVANTAGES OF INDUSTRY SERVICES Industry services represent an important source of secondary information on industrial firms. The information they provide can be valuable in the initial phases of a marketing project. However, they are limited in the nature, content, quantity, and quality of information.

Combining Information from Different Sources: Single-Source Data

It is desirable to combine secondary information obtained from different sources. Combining data allows the researcher to compensate for the weakness of one method with the strengths of another. One outcome of the effort to combine data from different sources is **single-source data**. Single-source research follows a person's TV, reading, and shopping habits. After recruiting a test panel of households, the research firm meters each home's TV sets and surveys family members periodically on what they read. Their grocery purchases are tracked by UPC scanners. For background, most systems also track retail data, such as sales, advertising, and promotion. Thus, single-source data provide integrated information on household variables, including media consumption and purchases, and marketing variables, such as product sales, price, advertising, promotion, and in-store marketing effort.[37]

Information Resources, Inc. (www.infores.com) collects consumer purchase information from a nationally representative household panel of approximately 70,000 recruited households with coverage at the regional, national, and individual market level. It is designed to supply strategic direction to marketers by focusing on the consumer dynamics that drive brand and category performance. Complete multi-outlet purchase information on these households is tracked electronically. Panel households use a simple in-home scanning device, called a ScanKey, to record their purchases from all outlets. Panelists are not required to record any causal information except for manufacturer coupons. Price reductions are recorded by scanner, and features and displays are captured by IRI's in-store personnel, ensuring an accurate and unbiased record of sales. Other examples of single-source data include CACI Marketing Systems (www.caci.com), MRI Cable Report by Mediamark Research (www.mediamark.com), and PRIZM by Claritas (www.claritas.com). The MRI Cable Report integrates information on cable television with demographic and product usage information. PRIZM combines census data, consumer surveys about shopping and lifestyles, and purchase data to identify segments. An application of single-source data is illustrated by the Campbell Soup Company.

Real Research

Soaps Shed a "Guiding Light" on V-8 Consumption

CBS's *Guiding Light* celebrated its 71st anniversary on January 25, 2008, making it the longest running drama ever. In 2008, both *Guiding Light* and ABC's *General Hospital* were popular in terms of overall soap opera viewership (www.soapzone.com).

The Campbell Soup Company (www.campbell.com) used single-source data to target its advertising for V8 juice (www.v8juice.com). By obtaining single-source data on product consumption, media consumption, and demographic characteristics, Campbell found that demographically similar TV audiences consume vastly different amounts of V8. For example, on an index of 100 for the average household's V-8 consumption, *General Hospital* had a below-average 80 index, while *Guiding Light* had an above-average 120 index. These results were surprising, because *General Hospital* actually had a slightly higher percentage of women 25 to 54 years old, the demographic group most predisposed to buy V8, and so would be expected to be a better medium to reach V8 drinkers. Using this information, Campbell rearranged its advertising schedule to raise the average index. As of 2008, the V8 (www.v8juice.com) line consisted of V8 100% Vegetable Juices, V8 Splash Juice Drinks, and V8 V-Fusion Juices, that are a blend of vegetable and fruit juices.[38] ■

computer mapping

Maps that solve marketing problems are called thematic maps. They combine geography with demographic information and a company's sales data or other proprietary information and are generated by a computer.

Computer Mapping

The V8 example shows the usefulness of combining secondary information from different sources. As another example, **computer mapping** combines geography with demographic information and a company's sales data or other proprietary information to develop thematic maps. Marketers now routinely make decisions based on these color-coded maps. Mapping systems allow users to download geographically detailed demographic data supplied by vendors. The user can then draw a map that color codes neighborhoods in Dallas, for example, by the relative density of households headed by 35- to 45-year-olds with incomes of $50,000 or more. These systems allow users to add proprietary information to the downloaded data.

Real Research

Claritas: Empowering Verizon's Marketing Research

Verizon Communications Inc., headquartered in New York, is a leader in delivering broadband and other wireline and wireless communication services, serving more than 80 million customers nationwide.

When company executives recently decided to converge its local phone service with wireless, Internet, and long-distance services, they needed a way to identify the best customers and choicest markets for building a combined wireless and wireline network. And they needed to do so while being mindful of government restrictions against using phone customer data to market other communications services.

Computer mapping combines geography with demographic and other proprietary data to generate thematic maps.

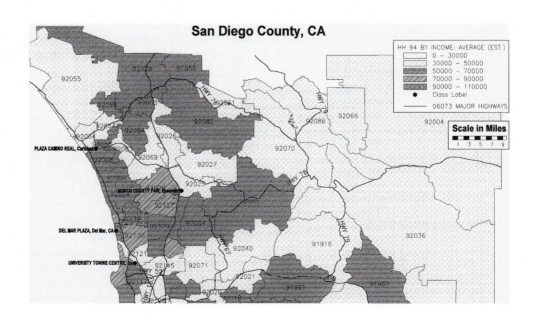

Verizon approached Nielsen Claritas (www.claritas.com) for help in formulating a marketing plan. Claritas provided those capabilities with geodemographic tools, proprietary surveys, and in-depth market analysis. Its industry-specific survey, Convergence Audit™, provided detailed profiles of consumers who use long-distance, paging, Internet, and cell phone services.

The PRIZM segmentation system from Claritas classified Verizon customers by consumer demographic and lifestyle characteristics into target groups for the various telephony services. Verizon also employed the Compass™ (also from Claritas) marketing analysis system to analyze its wireless markets and identify those markets with the highest potential for buying wireline services.

Verizon identified 19 of 62 PRIZM clusters that are fertile ground for a converged wireless–wireline network. The company then used Compass to rank its wireless markets by concentration of target group clusters. In high-ranking markets like Little Rock, Arkansas; Charlotte, North Carolina; and Jacksonville, Florida, Verizon conducted direct marketing campaigns of bundled services to wireless customers. "In two days, we prioritized 54 markets so we had a battle plan on where to go first," says Mickey Freeman, staff manager of strategic marketing. "Claritas gave us a common logic to look at the similarities and differences of each of our markets."[39] ■

Another application of secondary data is provided by the Buying Power Index.

Buying Power Index

Sales & Marketing Management's annual *Survey of Buying Power* (www.surveyofbuying power.com) provides data to help you analyze each of your U.S. markets, whether they are cities, counties, metro areas, or states. It features statistics, rankings, and projections for every county and media market in the United States with demographics broken out by age, race, city, county, and state; information on retail spending; and projections for future growth in these areas. All of the rankings are divided into 323 metro markets (geographic areas set by the Census Bureau) and 210 media markets (television or broadcast markets determined by Nielsen Media Research), all furnished by Claritas, Inc.

There are also statistics that are unique to the *Survey*. Effective buying income (EBI) is a measurement of disposable income, and the buying power index (BPI), for which the *Survey* is best known, is a unique measure of spending power that takes population, EBI, and retail sales into account to determine a market's ability to buy—the higher the index, the better.

Experiential Research

Nielsen Online

Nielsen Online reports on nearly 70 percent of the world's Internet usage to give a broad view of the online world. The company focuses its research on Internet usage in the following countries: Australia, Brazil, France, Germany, Italy, Japan, Spain, Switzerland, the United Kingdom, and the United States.

Go to Nielsen Online's home page at www.nielsen-online.com. On the top menu bar, select "Resources" and then select "Free Data and Rankings." Under "Internet Audience Metrics," to view results for a country, double-click on the country name. For the following exercises, choose "Home Panel" and "Web Usage Data" to view the most recent month's results for each country. (If the Web site has been restructured, follow a similar procedure.) Record your findings about each country's "PC Time Per Person" in a table.

1. Which country posts the most "PC Time Per Person"?
2. Which country posts the least "PC Time Per Person"?
   Now choose "Global Index Chart" in order to view the latest month's Global Internet Index: Average Usage.
3. What is the average "PC Time Spent per Month" for the set of countries?
4. Which countries were above the average for "PC Time Spent per Month" for the latest month?
5. Which countries were below the average for "PC Time Spent per Month" for the latest month? ■

International Marketing Research

A wide variety of secondary data are available for international marketing research.[40] As in the case of domestic research, the problem is not one of lack of data but of the plethora of information available, and it is useful to classify the various sources. Secondary international data are available from both domestic government and nongovernment sources (see Figure 4.5). The most important government sources are the Department of Commerce (www.commerce.gov), the Agency for

FIGURE 4.5

Sources of International Secondary Data

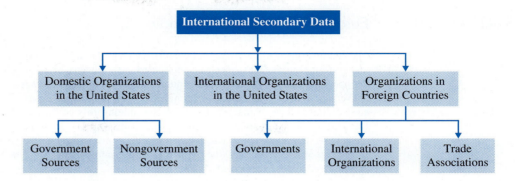

International Development (www.usaid.gov), the Small Business Administration (www.sba.gov), the Export-Import Bank of the United States (www.exim.gov), the Department of Agriculture (www.usda.gov), the Department of State (www.state.gov), the Department of Labor (www.dol.gov), and the Port Authority of New York and New Jersey (www.panynj.gov). The Department of Commerce offers not only a number of publications but also a variety of other services, such as the foreign buyer program, matchmaker events, trade missions, export contact list service, the foreign commercial service, and custom statistical service for exporters. The National Trade Data Bank (www.stat-usa.gov) provides useful information about exporting to and importing from countries around the world. Another very useful source is the CIA World Factbook (www.cia.gov).

Nongovernment organizations, including international organizations located in the United States, can also provide information about international markets. These data sources include the United Nations (www.un.org), the Organization for Economic Cooperation and Development (www.oecd.org), the International Monetary Fund (www.imf.org), the World Bank (www.worldbank.org), the International Chambers of Commerce (www.iccwbo.org), the Commission of the European Union to the United States (www.eurunion.org), and the Japanese External Trade Organization (www.jetro.org). Finally, locally sourced secondary data are available from foreign governments, international organizations located abroad, trade associations, and private services, such as syndicated firms. To illustrate, the following sites provide useful country information:

Australia (www.nla.gov.au)

France (www.insee.fr)

Japan (www.stat.go.jp/english)

Norway (www.ssb.no)

United Kingdom (www.statistics.gov.uk)

While conducting a review of the literature, one could use directories, indexes, books, commercially produced reference material, and magazines and newspapers.

Evaluation of secondary data is even more critical for international than for domestic projects. Different sources report different values for a given statistic, such as GDP, because of differences in the way the unit is defined. Measurement units may not be equivalent across countries. In France, for example, workers are paid a thirteenth monthly salary each year as an automatic bonus, resulting in a measurement construct that is different from other countries.[41] The accuracy of secondary data may also vary from country to country. Data from highly industrialized countries like the United States are likely to be more accurate than those from developing countries. Business and income statistics are affected by the taxation structure and the extent of tax evasion. Population censuses may vary in frequency and year in which the data are collected. In the United States, the census is conducted every 10 years, whereas in the People's Republic of China there was a 29-year gap between the censuses of 1953 and 1982. However, this situation is changing fast. Several syndicated firms are developing huge sources of international secondary data.

Real Research   Euroconsumers Go for Spending Splash

The Gallup organization (www.gallup.com), which specializes in survey research obtaining both lifestyle and psychographic data, recently conducted interviews with more than 22,500 adults across the European Community. Their results point to an exploding consumer durable market, particularly for convenience items, such as remote controlled TVs, microwave ovens, VCRs, and cellular phones. The educational level and the standard of living among this consumer group are generally improving. Europeans are also displaying higher levels of discretionary purchasing, demonstrated in a growing demand for travel packages, which continued to be strong through the year 2008, until the recession hit In the personal-care market, the number of European women using perfume is declining, offset by a growing demand for deodorants.

This type of syndicated data is useful to marketers such as Motorola, AT&T, and RCA, which are looking to develop European markets. For example, when renting an apartment in Germany, the renter must install all the major appliances and lighting fixtures. Whirlpool has developed value packages offering significant savings on appliances that are carefully targeted at apartment renters.[42] ■

Ethics in Marketing Research

The researcher is ethically obligated to ensure the relevance and usefulness of secondary data to the problem at hand. The secondary data should be evaluated by the criteria discussed earlier in this chapter. Only data judged to be appropriate should be used. It is also important that the data were collected using procedures that are morally appropriate. Data can be judged unethical if they were gathered in a way that harms the respondents or invades their privacy. Ethical issues also arise if the users of secondary data are unduly critical of the data that do not support their interests and viewpoints.

Real Research   The Ethical Pill Can Be Bitter to Swallow

ABC, NBC, CBS, some advertising agencies, and major advertisers are at odds with Nielsen Media Research's (www.nielsenmedia.com) television ratings. They criticize Nielsen's sampling scheme and intrusive data recording methodologies. A central issue in the criticisms of Nielsen is that the Big Three have received declining viewership ratings. As of 2009, prime-time viewership to the seven broadcast networks has declined. The top four broadcast networks (ABC, CBS, NBC, and Fox) each had across-the-board audience declines. according to Nielsen Media Research data.

Rather than accept the idea that the broadcast network audience is shrinking, the networks would prefer a more flattering assessment of their audiences. Ratings translate directly into advertising revenues. The more viewers a television show draws, the higher fees a network can charge for airing advertising at that spot. Advertising charges can differ dramatically between time slots, so accurate (or aggressive) viewer ratings are desirable from the network's perspective.

In defense of the networks, monopolies tend to resist innovation and lack incentive to improve processes. Complacency rules, as long as the money keeps coming. As a professional marketing research supplier, however, Nielsen Media Research is ethically bound to provide accurate and representative data—to the best of its ability. Users also have the ethical responsibility of not criticizing secondary data simply because the data do not support their own viewpoints. Eventually network executives will have to swallow the bitter pill of reality that cable TV, direct-broadcast satellite TV, and the Internet are all gaining ground over broadcast television viewership. Network executives find it difficult to swallow this pill.[43] ■

Given the limitations of secondary data, it is often necessary to collect primary data in order to obtain the information needed to address the management decision problem. The use of secondary data alone when the research problem requires primary data collection could raise ethical concerns. Such concerns are heightened when the client is being billed a fixed fee for the project and the proposal submitted to get the project did not adequately specify the data collection methodology. On the other hand, in some cases it may be possible to obtain the information needed from secondary sources alone, making it unnecessary to collect primary data. The unnecessary collection of expensive primary data, when the research problem can be addressed based on secondary data alone, may be unethical. These ethical issues become more salient if the research firm's billings go up, but at the expense of the client.

Decision Research   Tommy Hilfiger: Keeping Abreast of the Market to Remain a Hi-Flier

The Situation

From the blacktop to the golf course, designer Tommy Hilfiger has the streets covered. His namesake casual wear is worn by rap, rock, teen, and sports stars and fans, and, these days, many of them are women. Tommy designs, sources, makes, and markets men's and women's sportswear and denim wear, as well as athletic wear, children's wear, and accessories. Through extensive licensing deals (almost 40 product lines), Tommy also offers products such as fragrances, belts, bedding, home furnishings, and cosmetics. As of 2009, the company's clean-cut clothing is sold in major department and specialty stores as well as some 180 Tommy Hilfiger shops and outlets. With such a large empire, it is no wonder that Fred Gehring, CEO and president of Tommy Hilfiger, is always kept busy trying to make sure the company does not forget the most important aspect of its business—satisfying consumers' needs!

Selling apparel will never be an easy job. "Just when you think you've figured out exactly what your customers want, everything changes—sometimes overnight," says apparel expert Richard Romer, executive vice president for The CIT Group/Commercial Services, a New York–based credit protection and lending services provider for apparel manufacturers. "Basically, changes in apparel occur every other year: long skirts to short skirts, and back to long." The apparel market's constant state of flux forces catalogers and other marketers to constantly reevaluate the market they're targeting, and then reinvent their companies, their offerings, and their catalogs.

The Marketing Research Decisions

1. What sources of secondary data should Tommy Hilfiger consult to keep informed about apparel fashion trends?
2. What sources of syndicated data would be useful?
3. Discuss the role of the type of research you recommend in enabling Fred Gehring and Tommy Hilfiger to keep abreast of apparel fashion trends.

The Marketing Management Decision

1. In order to enhance the appeal of Tommy Hilfiger clothing to the fashion-conscious consumer, what marketing actions should Fred Gehring take?
2. Discuss how the marketing management decision action that you recommend to Fred Gehring is influenced by the secondary sources of data that you suggested earlier and by the content of information they provide.[44] ■

Marketing research enables Tommy Hilfiger to keep abreast of apparel fashion trends and the changing preferences of its target market.

SPSS Windows

SPSS Maps integrates seamlessly with SPSS base menus, enabling you to map a variety of data. You can choose from six base thematic maps, or create other maps by combining map options. Maps can be further customized using the SPSS Syntax Editor. Such maps can be used for a variety of purposes, including interpreting sales and other data geographically to determine where the biggest customers are located, displaying sales trends for specific geographic locations, using buying trend information to determine the ideal location for new company stores, and so on.

Summary

In contrast to primary data, which originate with the researcher for the specific purpose of the problem at hand, secondary data are data originally collected for other purposes. Secondary data can be obtained quickly and are relatively inexpensive. However, they have limitations and should be carefully evaluated to determine their appropriateness for the problem at hand. The evaluation criteria consist of specifications, error, currency, objectivity, nature, and dependability.

A wealth of information exists in the organization for which the research is being conducted. This information constitutes internal secondary data. External data are generated by sources outside the organization. These data exist in the form of published (printed) material, online, Internet, and offline databases, or information made available by syndicated services. Published external sources may be broadly classified as general business data or government data. General business sources comprise guides, directories, indexes, and statistical data. Government sources may be broadly categorized as census data and other data. Computerized databases may be online, Internet, or offline. These databases may be further classified as bibliographic, numeric, full-text, directory, or specialized databases. Figure 4.6 is a concept map for secondary data.

Syndicated services or sources are companies that collect and sell common pools of data designed to serve a number of clients. Syndicated services can be classified based on the unit of measurement (households/consumers or institutions). Household/consumer data may be obtained via surveys, purchase and media panels, or electronic scanner services. When

FIGURE 4.6

A Concept Map for Secondary Data

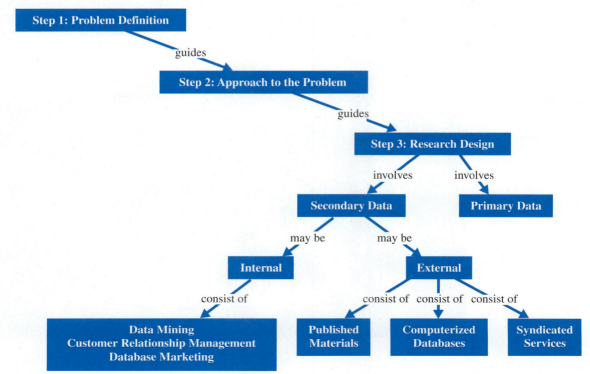

FIGURE 4.7

A Concept Map for Syndicated Data

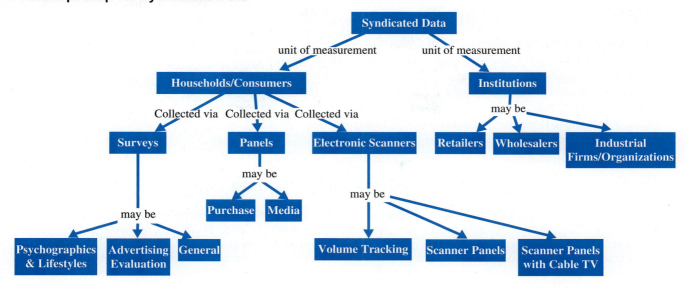

institutions are the unit of measurement, the data may be obtained from retailers, wholesalers, or industrial firms. It is desirable to combine information obtained from different secondary sources. Figure 4.7 is a concept map for syndicated data.

There are several specialized sources of secondary data useful for conducting international marketing research.

However, the evaluation of secondary data becomes even more critical as the usefulness and accuracy of these data can vary widely. Ethical dilemmas that can arise include the unnecessary collection of primary data, the use of only secondary data when primary data are needed, the use of secondary data that are not applicable, and the use of secondary data that have been gathered through morally questionable means.

Key Terms and Concepts

primary data, 100
secondary data, 100
internal data, 105
external data, 105
database marketing, 106
online databases, 111
Internet databases, 111
offline databases, 111
bibliographic databases, 112
numeric databases, 112

full-text databases, 112
directory databases, 112
special-purpose databases, 113
syndicated services (sources), 113
surveys, 113
syndicated panel surveys, 114
psychographics, 114
lifestyles, 114
purchase panels, 118
media panels, 119

scanner data, 121
volume tracking data, 121
scanner panels, 121
scanner panels with cable TV, 121
audit, 122
industry services, 124
single-source data, 124
computer mapping, 125

Suggested Cases, Video Cases, and HBS Cases

Running Case with Real Data

  1.1 Dell

Comprehensive Critical Thinking Cases

  2.1 American Idol   2.2 Baskin-Robbins   2.3 Akron Children's Hospital

Comprehensive Cases with Real Data

  4.1 JPMorgan Chase   4.2 Wendy's

Video Cases

4.1 Mayo Clinic	7.1 AFLAC	8.1 P&G	9.1 eGO
12.1 Subaru	13.1 Intel	23.1 Marriott	24.1 Nivea

Comprehensive Harvard Business School Cases

Case 5.1: The Harvard Graduate Student Housing Survey (9-505-059)
Case 5.2: BizRate.Com (9-501-024)
Case 5.3: Cola Wars Continue: Coke and Pepsi in the Twenty-First Century (9-702-442)
Case 5.4: TiVo in 2002 (9-502-062)
Case 5.5: Compaq Computer: Intel Inside? (9-599-061)
Case 5.6: The New Beetle (9-501-023)

Live Research: Conducting a Marketing Research Project

1. Assign one or more teams the responsibility of collecting and analyzing secondary data, including those available on the Internet.
2. For example, one team could search the library's electronic database, another could search government sources, and another team could visit the library and work with a reference librarian to identify the relevant sources.
3. It is worthwhile to visit the Web sites of syndicated firms to identify the relevant information, some of which can be obtained without cost.
4. If the project is supported by a budget, then relevant information can be purchased from syndicated sources.

Acronym

The criteria used for evaluating secondary data may be described by the acronym

Second:

S pecifications: methodology used to collect the data
E rror: accuracy of the data
C urrency: when the data were collected
O bjective: purpose for which data were collected
N ature: content of the data
D ependability: overall, how dependable are the data

Exercises

Questions

1. What are the differences between primary and secondary data?
2. Why is it important to obtain secondary data before primary data?
3. Differentiate between internal and external secondary data.
4. What are the advantages of secondary data?
5. What are the disadvantages of secondary data?
6. What are the criteria to be used when evaluating secondary data?
7. List the various sources of published secondary data.
8. What are the different forms of computerized databases?
9. What are the advantages of computerized databases?
10. List and describe the various syndicated sources of secondary data.
11. What is the nature of information collected by surveys?
12. How can surveys be classified?
13. Explain what a panel is. What is the difference between purchase panels and media panels?
14. What are relative advantages of purchase and media panels over surveys?
15. What kinds of data can be gathered through electronic scanner services?
16. Describe the uses of scanner data.
17. What is an audit? Discuss the uses, advantages, and disadvantages of audits.
18. Describe the information provided by industrial services.
19. Why is it desirable to use multiple sources of secondary data?

Problems

1. Obtain automobile industry sales and sales of major automobile manufacturers for the last five years from secondary sources. (Hint: See Chapter 23, Table 23.1).
2. Select an industry of your choice. Using secondary sources, obtain industry sales and the sales of the major firms in that industry for the past year. Estimate the market shares of each major firm. From another source, obtain information on the market shares of these same firms. Do the two estimates agree?

Internet and Computer Exercises

1. Conduct an online data search to obtain background information on an industry of your choice (e.g., sporting goods). Your search should encompass both qualitative and quantitative information.

2. Visit the Web site of a company of your choice. Suppose the management decision problem facing this company was to expand its share of the market. Obtain as much secondary data from the Web site of this company and other sources on the Internet as are relevant to this problem.

3. Visit the Web site of the Bureau of Census (see one of the URLs given in the book). Write a report about the secondary data available from the Bureau that would be useful to a fast-food firm such as McDonald's for the purpose of formulating domestic marketing strategy.

4. Visit www.census.gov/statab. Use State Rankings and Vital Statistics to identify the top six states for marketing products to the elderly.

5. For the department store patronage project, Sears would like you to summarize the retail sales in the United States by visiting www.census.gov.

6. Visit www.npd.com and write a description of the panels maintained by NPD.

7. Visit www.nielsen.com and write a report about the various services offered by Nielsen.

Activities

Role Playing

1. You are the marketing research manager of a local bank. Management has asked you to assess the demand potential for checking accounts in your metropolitan area. What sources of secondary data should you consult? What kind of information would you expect to obtain from each source? Ask a group of fellow students to play the role of management and explain to them the role of secondary data in this project.

2. You are the group product manager for Procter & Gamble in charge of laundry detergents. How would you make use of information available from a store audit? Ask another student to play the role of vice president of marketing. Explain to your boss the value of store audit information related to laundry detergents.

Fieldwork

1. Make a trip to your local library. Write a report explaining how you would use the library to collect secondary data for a marketing research project assessing the demand potential for Cross soft-tip pens. Please be specific.

Group Discussion

1. Discuss the significance and limitations of the government census data as a major source of secondary data.

2. Discuss the growing use of computerized databases.

3. Discuss how the Nielsen TV ratings can affect the price advertisers pay for a commercial broadcast during a particular time.

Dell Running Case

Review the Dell case, Case 1.1, and questionnaire given toward the end of the book. Answer the following questions.

1. Search the Internet to find information on the latest U.S. market share of Dell and other PC marketers.

2. Search the Internet to obtain information on Dell's marketing strategy. Do you agree with Dell's marketing strategy? Why or why not?

3. Visit the U.S. Census Bureau at www.census.gov. As Dell seeks to increase its penetration of U.S. households, what information available from the U.S. Census Bureau is helpful?

4. What information available from syndicated firms would be useful to Dell as it seeks to increase its penetration of U.S. households?

5. How can Dell make use of lifestyle information available from syndicated services?

6. What information is available on consumer technology usage from syndicated firms? How can Dell make use of this information? Hint: Visit www.npd.com, and under "Industries" select "Consumer Technology."

7. What information available from www.nielsen-online.com can help Dell evaluate the effectiveness of its Web site?

VIDEO CASE 4.1   The Mayo Clinic: Staying Healthy with Marketing Research

William and Charles Mayo began practicing medicine in the 1880s in Rochester, Minnesota. They were quickly recognized as extremely talented surgeons, and they gained so many patients that they were forced to think about expanding their practice. Around the turn of the century, the Mayo brothers began inviting others to join their practice. The partnerships that the Mayos entered into created one of the first private group practices of medicine in the United States. In 1919, the Mayo brothers turned their partnership into a not-for-profit, charitable organization known as the Mayo Foundation. All proceeds beyond operating expenses were to be contributed to education, research, and patient care. The Mayo Clinic (www.mayoclinic.org) has been operating in this fashion ever since. The Mayo Clinic's primary value is, "The needs of the patient come first." Its mission is, "Mayo will provide the best care to every patient every day through integrated clinical practice, education, and research."

As of 2008, more than 3,300 physicians and scientists and more than 52,000 allied health staff worked at the original Mayo Clinic in Rochester and newer clinics in Jacksonville, Florida, and Phoenix/Scottsdale, Arizona. Collectively, the three clinics treat more than half a million people each year. Philanthropy is a big part of the Mayo Clinic. From the Mayos' donations in 1919, philanthropy has been deeply rooted in the Mayo Clinic's operations. In 2006, 87,000 donors provided $230 million in contributions, private grants, and endowments. These donations are used heavily in research and education, and Mayo's capital expansion depends on these investments. Total revenues for 2006 were $6.29 billion, up from $5.81 billion in 2005. Net income from current activities was $117.4 million, down from $195.9 million in 2005. Patient care is the largest form of revenue, bringing in $5.3 billion in 2006. The Mayo Clinic continues to donate huge amounts of money to education and research. In 2006, Mayo contributed $314 million to research and education.

The majority of its business is brought in because of the positive experiences that patients have at the Mayo Clinic. This is a result of the care the Mayo Clinic provides as well as the environment it has created. Collaboration throughout the Mayo Clinic has resulted in excellent care, better methods, and innovation, while also being mindful of the environment in which the care takes place. Marketing research revealed that the clinic environment is an important part of the patient's experience. Therefore, Mayo breaks the mold of a plain, static look with the addition of soothing music and elaborate art, believing that this adds to the patients' experience and helps them to heal faster.

Over the years, the Mayo Clinic has become a name that the public trusts despite the lack of any advertising. It has a strong reputation as a research center, a specialty care provider, and a school of medicine. Explaining the Mayo Clinic's success and how it became the top choice for people in need of care, John la Forgia, chair of the Department of Public Affairs at the Mayo Clinic, says that a key differentiator for the Mayo Clinic is its ability to diagnose and treat ailments that other clinics and doctors cannot; the patient then goes home and tells others his or her story, creating immense goodwill and word-of-mouth publicity for the Mayo Clinic.

What helps Mayo achieve strong brand recognition is its emphasis on marketing research. A significant portion of marketing research is devoted to brand management. Marketing research is used to continuously monitor consumer perceptions and evaluations of the Mayo Clinic. According to John la Forgia, the Mayo Clinic's Office of Brand Management serves two basic functions. The first is operating as a clearinghouse for external perceptions. The second is to provide physicians with an understanding of the brand as they branch out into new areas. A brand-equity research project found that the Mayo Clinic was considered to be the best practice in the country. It also found that 84 percent of the public is aware of the Mayo Clinic, and that they associate words such as *excellence, care,* and *compassion* with it.

The other part of its strategy is the enhancement of the brand. To accomplish this, the Mayo Clinic relies on marketing research to monitor the perceptions of its patients, the public, donors, the medical staff, and other constituencies.

A recent marketing research study revealed that consumers' choice of a health care organization is determined by their evaluation of the alternative health care organizations on the following salient attributes: (1) doctors, (2) medical technology, (3) nursing care, (4) physical facilities, (5) management, and (6) ethics. Since then, the Mayo Clinic has sought to emphasize these factors.

In the service industry, the onus of maintaining a good reputation and name depends largely on the way the service is delivered. Thus, it is most important for Mayo to keep delivering the product and not lose sight of the fact that Mayo is a health care provider and all of the brand equity it has in the minds of Americans depends on its continued delivery of excellent health care. Mayo Clinic marketers say that keeping the brand strong well into the future will depend primarily upon patients' day-to-day experiences, which can be enhanced by marketing research identifying patient needs and developing medical programs to meet those needs.

Conclusion

Through an unflinching focus on patient care, cutting-edge research in medical science, and reliance on marketing research, the Mayo Clinic has been able to carve a special place for itself in the hearts and minds of people and build a strong brand.

Questions

1. The Mayo Clinic would like to further strengthen their brand image and equity. Define the management decision problem.
2. Define the marketing research problem corresponding to the management decision problem you have defined in question 1.
3. What type of research design should be adopted? Why?
4. Describe the sources of secondary data that would be helpful in determining consumer preferences for health care facilities.

References

1. www.mayoclinic.org, accessed February 20, 2009.
2. www.wikipedia.org, accessed February 20, 2009.
3. Misty Hathaway and Kent Seltman, "International Market Research at the Mayo Clinic," *Marketing Health Services* (Winter 2001): 19.
4. Daniel Fell, "Taking U.S. Health Services Overseas," *Marketing Health Services* (Summer 2002): 21.

> " I have degrees in mathematics, but have become an enthusiastic user of qualitative research because of the rich insights I have gained with well-done qualitative research. "

Mary Klupp, Director, Ford Credit Global Consumer Insights,
Ford Motor Company, Dearborn, MI

Objectives   [After reading this chapter, the student should be able to:]

1. Explain the difference between qualitative and quantitative research in terms of the objectives, sampling, data collection and analysis, and outcomes.

2. Understand the various forms of qualitative research, including direct procedures such as focus groups and depth interviews, and indirect methods such as projective techniques.

3. Describe focus groups in detail, with emphasis on planning and conducting focus groups and their advantages, disadvantages, and applications.

4. Describe depth interview techniques in detail, citing their advantages, disadvantages, and applications.

5. Explain projective techniques in detail and compare association, completion, construction, and expressive techniques.

6. Discuss the considerations involved in conducting qualitative research in an international setting.

7. Understand the ethical issues involved in conducting qualitative research.

8. Discuss the use of the Internet and computers in obtaining and analyzing qualitative data.

Exploratory Research Design: Qualitative Research

Overview

Like secondary data analysis (see Chapter 4), qualitative research is a major methodology used in exploratory research (Chapter 3). Researchers undertake qualitative research to define the problem or develop an approach (Chapter 2). In developing an approach, qualitative research is often used for generating hypotheses and identifying variables that should be included in the research. In cases where conclusive or quantitative research is not done, qualitative research and secondary data comprise the major part of the research project. This is the case in many business-to-business marketing research projects. In this chapter, we discuss the differences between qualitative and quantitative research and the role of each in the marketing research project. We present a classification of qualitative research and cover the major techniques, focus groups, and depth interviews, in detail. We also consider the indirect procedures, called *projective techniques*, with emphasis on association, completion, construction, and expressive techniques. The analysis of qualitative data is explained in some detail. The considerations involved in conducting qualitative research when researching international markets are discussed. Several ethical issues that arise in qualitative research are identified. The chapter also discusses the use of the Internet and computers in qualitative research. The following examples give the flavor of qualitative research and its applications in marketing research.

Real Research

"Show and Tell" Focus Groups Tell "Baby-Boomer" Values

Baby boomers are a large consumer target for many products, and "show and tell" focus groups are providing the needed insight into the core values these boomers hold close to their hearts.

The show and tell focus groups work in this manner. Participants are asked to bring in three or four items that represent their ideal environment. The items can be pictures or souvenirs; it does not matter as long as the participants are able to explain why they chose the items and how they fit into their ideal environment. Examples might include a father bringing in a good-luck fishing lure that his father gave to his grandchildren as a present or an elementary teacher bringing a copy of the book she has finally decided to write. Group discussion is then centered around these items. What qualitative research has uncovered about the baby boomers can be described by five specific themes:

1. Quality family life is a major concern. The ability to have a positive impact on the lives of their children is extremely important, as is a tight-knit family unit that is supportive of each other. The home is very important.
2. Long-term friendships help round out their identity outside of the workplace and home. Keeping in touch with friends is an integral element of the boomer lifestyle.
3. Taking the time to get away from the hassles of everyday life in the form of "getaway vacations" with family and friends helps to maintain firm understanding of what is important in life and recharge dying batteries.
4. Spiritual and physical fitness are important in leading a full, well-balanced life.
5. There is no such thing as a mid-life crisis. Life is too short to dwell on successes or failures.

This type of research is invaluable in designing advertising and promotional campaigns. It provides the necessary foundation for appealing to those values that are most important to the boomers and to those values that are most likely to stimulate their buying behavior. For example, the 2009 Honda Pilot SUV was marketed with the tag line "You'll be ready for anything in the 2009 Pilot." Honda emphasized both the exterior and interior features of the vehicle, so you can rough it in the middle of nowhere and still enjoy some of the comforts of home.[1] ■

Based on focus groups and survey research, the 2009 Honda Pilot targeted the baby boomers with an emphasis on the home and getaway adventures.

Real Research

Feelings, Nothing More Than Feelings

Qualitative research in the form of focus groups and individual depth interviews is used to discover what sensory feelings are important for customers. Such feelings cannot be uncovered by quantitative research. Depth interviews are conducted one-on-one and allow extensive probing of each respondent. Thus, it is possible to uncover underlying feelings (as well as values, beliefs, and attitudes). Several examples show how identifying consumers' sensory feelings are crucial in designing products.

- **Ford:** Ford (www.ford.com) decided to redesign one of its Taurus models. They remodeled the dashboard buttons, the rear fenders, and so on. They decided to change the door latches. However, there was a problem with the sound when somebody closed the door. It sounded weird. The latch made two thumps, which gave the impression to the user that something was wrong, even if there was no problem at all. Although consumers may not be aware of their own perceptions, they are very sensitive to sounds a car makes.
- **Whirlpool:** Whereas one might think that the perfect product would not make any noise, the case of Whirlpool (www.whirlpool.com) denies it. Whirlpool launched a new refrigerator, a quieter one. However, customers called the company to complain about "the softer, water-gurgling sounds" of the model. People had the impression that the new refrigerator was the noisiest they had ever heard when it was actually the quietest ever manufactured.
- **Estee Lauder:** The cosmetics industry provides a lot of examples of qualitative research because cosmetics are an intimate product. For example, Estee Lauder (www.esteelauder.com) changed the shape of its blue compact so it appeals more to the customer. The shape was redesigned by rounding the edges to make it softer and thus create a link with the round shape of a woman's body.[2] ■

These examples illustrate the rich insights into the underlying behavior of consumers that can be obtained by using qualitative procedures.

Primary Data: Qualitative Versus Quantitative Research

As was explained in Chapter 4, primary data are originated by the researcher for the specific purpose of addressing the problem at hand. Primary data may be qualitative or quantitative in nature, as shown in Figure 5.1. The distinction between qualitative and quantitative research closely parallels the distinction between exploratory and conclusive research discussed in Chapter 3. The differences between the two research methodologies are summarized in Table 5.1.[3]

FIGURE 5.1

A Classification of Marketing Research Data

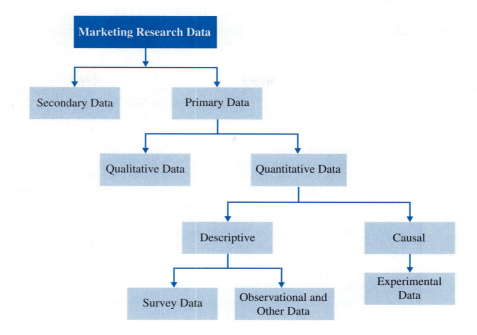

qualitative research
An unstructured, exploratory research methodology based on small samples that provides insights and understanding of the problem setting.

quantitative research
A research methodology that seeks to quantify the data and, typically, applies some form of statistical analysis.

Qualitative research provides insights and understanding of the problem setting, while **quantitative research** seeks to quantify the data and, typically, applies some form of statistical analysis. Whenever a new marketing research problem is being addressed, quantitative research must be preceded by appropriate qualitative research. Sometimes qualitative research is undertaken to explain the findings obtained from quantitative research. However, the findings of qualitative research are misused when they are regarded as conclusive and are used to make generalizations to the population of interest.[4] It is a sound principle of marketing research to view qualitative and quantitative research as complementary, rather than in competition with each other.[5] Qualitative researchers can be located through the Qualitative Research Consultants Association (www.qrca.org), which is the largest body of independent qualitative research consultants in the world.

The story goes that Alfred Politz, a strong proponent of quantitative research, and Ernest Dichter, a strong proponent of qualitative research, were having their usual debate about the merits of the two methods. Politz stressed the importance of large-scale, projectable samples. Dichter answered: "But, Alfred, ten thousand times nothing is still nothing!" As Dichter argued, mere quantification, when the underlying behavior of interest is not well understood, will not lead to meaningful results. However, qualitative and quantitative research in combination can provide rich insights that can help in formulating successful marketing strategies, as in the case of Kellogg's Pop-Tarts Yogurt Blasts.

TABLE 5.1		
Qualitative Versus Quantitative Research		
	Qualitative Research	Quantitative Research
Objective	To gain a qualitative understanding of the underlying reasons and motivations	To quantify the data and generalize the results from the sample to the population of interest
Sample	Small number of nonrepresentative cases	Large number of representative cases
Data collection	Unstructured	Structured
Data analysis	Nonstatistical	Statistical
Outcome	Develop an initial understanding	Recommend a final course of action

Real Research

Kellogg's: Pop-Tarts Yogurt Blasts Blast Competition

Kellogg's was in the process of developing a new extension of its popular Pop-Tarts product with a yogurt component. They wanted to determine the best name for this new product and approached BuzzBack for help. They had four possible options and wanted to find out which one mothers and children (the primary purchasers of Pop-Tarts) liked the best and why.

BuzzBack Market Research (www.buzzback.com), a provider of online marketing research services, surveyed 175 mothers and their children (children under 13 years of age must have parental permission to participate in any online research study, according to regulations set by the Children's Online Privacy Protection Act of 1998). This survey took place over a weekend. The respondents were asked their name choices as well as their packaging preferences. The survey included both qualitative and quantitative data because Kellogg's wanted to find out *why* each respondent preferred a certain name so they could tailor their marketing campaign to fit those reasons.

The results of the survey indicated that both mothers and their children preferred Pop-Tarts Yogurt Blasts as the new name for the product. The qualitative data also suggested that they were fond of this new product because it offered a tasty, nutritional twist to the traditional Pop-Tart product.

The product was launched with great success in June 2003 and was available in both strawberry and blueberry flavors. The suggested retail cost was $2.09 for an 8-count box. That year, Pop-Tarts were the number one brand in toaster pastries and one of Kellogg's largest brands in the United States, despite increasingly strong competition in the toaster pastry market. Sales of Pop-Tarts continued to be strong through 2009.[6] ■

ACTIVE RESEARCH

Nine West Going West: Penetrating the Women's Shoes Market

Visit www.ninewest.com and search the Internet using a search engine as well as your library's online databases to obtain information on the marketing strategy of Nine West.

As the marketing manager, what marketing strategies would you formulate in helping Nine West increase its penetration of the women's shoes market?

How would you use qualitative and quantitative research in helping Nine West increase its penetration of the women's shoes market?

Although the Kellogg's example suggests the rationale behind qualitative research, we consider this topic in more detail.

Rationale for Using Qualitative Research

There are several reasons to use qualitative research. It is not always possible, or desirable, to use fully structured or formal methods to obtain information from respondents (see Chapter 3). People may be unwilling or unable to answer certain questions. People are unwilling to give truthful answers to questions that invade their privacy, embarrass them, or have a negative impact on their ego or status. Examples of such sensitive questions include: "Have you recently purchased sanitary napkins? Drugs for nervous tension? Pills for anxiety?" Second, people may be unable to provide accurate answers to questions that tap their subconscious. The values, emotional drives, and motivations residing at the subconscious level are disguised from the outer world by rationalization and other ego defenses. For example, a person may have purchased an expensive sports car to overcome feelings of inferiority. However, if asked, "Why did you purchase this sports car?" he may say, "I got a great deal," "My old car was falling apart," or "I need to impress my customers and clients." In such cases, the desired information can be best obtained through qualitative research. As illustrated in the "Feelings" examples in the "Overview" section, qualitative research is also very useful for discovering which sensory feelings are important to customers.[7]

direct approach
One type of qualitative research in which the purposes of the project are disclosed to the respondent or are obvious, given the nature of the interview.

A Classification of Qualitative Research Procedures

A classification of qualitative research procedures is presented in Figure 5.2. These procedures are classified as either direct or indirect, based on whether the true purpose of the project is known to the respondents. A **direct approach** is not disguised. The purpose of the

FIGURE 5.2

A Classification of Qualitative Research Procedures

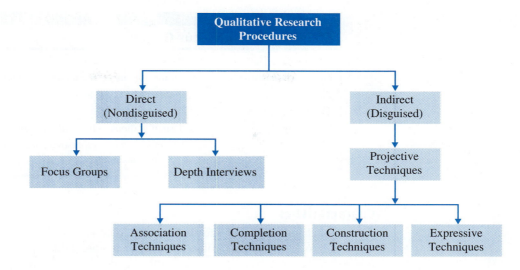

---

indirect approach
A type of qualitative research in which the purposes of the project are disguised from the respondents.

project is disclosed to the respondents or is otherwise obvious to them from the questions asked. Focus groups and depth interviews are the major direct techniques. In contrast, research that takes an **indirect approach** disguises the true purpose of the project. Projective techniques, the commonly used indirect techniques, consist of association, completion, construction, and expressive techniques. Each of these techniques is discussed in detail, beginning with focus groups.

Focus Group Interviews

focus group
An interview conducted by a trained moderator among a small group of respondents in an unstructured and natural manner.

A **focus group** is an interview conducted by a trained moderator in a nonstructured and natural manner with a small group of respondents. The moderator leads the discussion. The main purpose of focus groups is to gain insights by listening to a group of people from the appropriate target market talk about issues of interest to the researcher. The value of the technique lies in the unexpected findings often obtained from a free-flowing group discussion.

Focus groups are the most important qualitative research procedure. They are so popular that many marketing research practitioners consider this technique synonymous with qualitative research.[8] Several hundred facilities around the country now conduct focus groups several times a week, and the typical focus group costs the client about $4,000. Given their importance and popularity, we describe the salient characteristics of focus groups in detail.[9]

A typical focus group session.

TABLE 5.2	
Characteristics of Focus Groups	
Group size	8 to 12
Group composition	Homogeneous; respondents prescreened
Physical setting	Relaxed, informal atmosphere
Time duration	1 to 3 hours
Recording	Use of audiocassettes and videotapes
Moderator	Observational, interpersonal, and communication skills of the moderator

Characteristics

The major characteristics of a focus group are summarized in Table 5.2. A focus group generally includes 8 to 12 members. Groups of fewer than 8 are unlikely to generate the momentum and group dynamics necessary for a successful session. Likewise, groups of more than 12 may be too crowded and may not be conducive to a cohesive and natural discussion.[10]

A focus group should be homogeneous in terms of demographic and socioeconomic characteristics. Commonalty among group members avoids interactions and conflicts among group members on side issues.[11] Thus, a women's group should not combine married homemakers with small children, young unmarried working women, and elderly divorced or widowed women since their lifestyles are substantially different. Moreover, the participants should be carefully screened to meet certain criteria. The participants must have had adequate experience with the object or issue being discussed. People who have already participated in numerous focus groups should not be included. These so-called professional respondents are atypical and their participation leads to serious validity problems.[12]

The physical setting for the focus group is also important. A relaxed, informal atmosphere encourages spontaneous comments. Light refreshments should be served before the session and made available throughout. Although a focus group may last from 1 to 3 hours, a duration of 1.5 to 2 hours is typical. This period of time is needed to establish rapport with the participants and explore, in depth, their beliefs, feelings, ideas, attitudes, and insights regarding the topics of concern. Focus group interviews are invariably recorded, often on videotape, for subsequent replay, transcription, and analysis. Videotaping has the advantage of recording facial expressions and body movements, but it can increase the costs significantly. Frequently, clients observe the session from an adjacent room using a one-way mirror. Video transmission technology enables the clients to observe focus group sessions live from a remote location. For example, Stamford, Connecticut–based FocusVision Network, Inc. (www.focusvision.com) offers such a videoconferencing system.

The moderator plays a key role in the success of a focus group. The moderator must establish rapport with the participants, keep the discussion moving forward, and probe the respondents to elicit insights. In addition, the moderator may have a central role in the analysis and interpretation of the data. Therefore, the moderator should possess skill, experience, knowledge of the discussion topic, and an understanding of the nature of group dynamics. The key qualifications of the moderator are summarized in the accompanying Real Research example.

Real Research   Key Qualifications of Focus Group Moderators

1. **Kindness with firmness:** The moderator must combine a disciplined detachment with understanding empathy in order to generate the necessary interaction.
2. **Permissiveness:** The moderator must be permissive yet alert to signs that the group's cordiality or purpose is disintegrating.
3. **Involvement:** The moderator must encourage and stimulate intense personal involvement.
4. **Incomplete understanding:** The moderator must encourage respondents to be more specific about generalized comments by exhibiting incomplete understanding.
5. **Encouragement:** The moderator must encourage unresponsive members to participate.

FIGURE 5.3

Procedure for Planning and Conducting Focus Groups

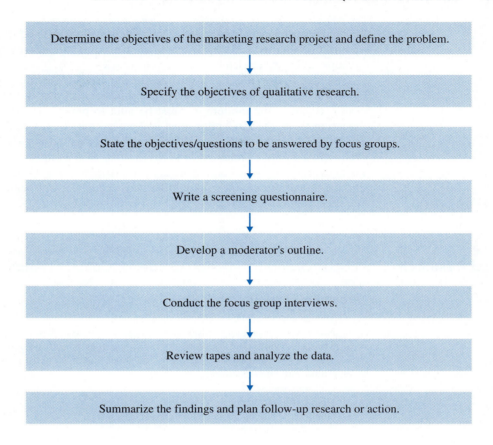

Determine the objectives of the marketing research project and define the problem.

Specify the objectives of qualitative research.

State the objectives/questions to be answered by focus groups.

Write a screening questionnaire.

Develop a moderator's outline.

Conduct the focus group interviews.

Review tapes and analyze the data.

Summarize the findings and plan follow-up research or action.

6. Flexibility: The moderator must be able to improvise and alter the planned outline amid the distractions of the group process.
7. Sensitivity: The moderator must be sensitive enough to guide the group discussion at an intellectual as well as emotional level.[13] ∎

Planning and Conducting Focus Groups

The procedure for planning and conducting focus groups is described in Figure 5.3. Planning begins with an examination of the objectives of the marketing research project. In most instances, the problem has been defined by this stage, and if so, the general statement as well as the specific components of the problem should be carefully studied. Given the problem definition, the objectives of the qualitative research should be clearly specified, as illustrated by the department store patronage project.

Project Research   Qualitative Research Objectives

In the department store study, the objectives of qualitative research were as follows:

1. Identify the relevant factors (choice criteria) used by households in selecting department stores.
2. Identify what consumers consider to be competing stores for specific product categories.
3. Identify the psychological characteristics of consumers that are likely to influence store patronage behavior.
4. Identify any other aspects of consumer choice behavior that may be relevant to store patronage. ∎

Note that these objectives are closely tied to the components of the department store problem defined in Chapter 2. The objectives must be specified before conducting any qualitative research, be it focus groups, depth interviews, or projective techniques.

The next step is to develop a detailed list of objectives for the focus group. This may take the form of a list of questions the researcher would like answered. Then a questionnaire to screen potential participants is prepared. Typical information obtained from the questionnaire includes product familiarity and knowledge, usage behavior, attitudes toward and participation in focus groups, and standard demographic characteristics.

A detailed moderator's outline for use during the focus group interview should be constructed. This involves extensive discussions among the researcher, client, and moderator. Because the moderator must be able to pursue important ideas when participants mention them, the moderator must understand the client's business, the focus group objectives, and how the findings will be used. Use of a moderator's outline reduces some of the reliability problems inherent in focus groups, such as those caused by different moderators not covering the same content areas in comparable ways. Given its importance, we illustrate how a moderator's outline should be constructed for determining why consumers upgrade cellular handsets.[14]

Real Research   Focus Group Discussion Guide for Cellular Handsets

Preamble (5 minutes)

- Thanks and welcome
- Nature of a focus group (informal, multiway, expansive, all views, disagree)
- May ask obvious questions—humor me (sometimes *actually* obvious, sometimes not)
- There are no right or wrong answers—all about finding out what people think
- Audio and video recording
- Colleagues viewing
- Help self to refreshments
- Going to be talking about cellular phone handsets
- Questions or concerns?

Intros and Warm-Up (3 minutes)

Like to go round the room and have you introduce yourselves . . .
- First name
- Best thing about having a cellular phone
- Worst thing about having a cellular phone

Cellular Environment (5 minutes)

- When you're out and about, what do you take with you?
- Let's start with the things you *always* take with you.

  FLIPCHART

- And what are the things you *often* take with you?

  FLIPCHART

Cellular Usage (10 minutes)

- I'd like to understand a bit about how you typically use your cellular phone . . .
- How many calls do you typically make or receive in a week?
- What are some of the most common types of outgoing calls you make?

  BRIEFLY EXPLORE

- What are the most common types of incoming calls you receive?
- If we were to take away your cellular phone, what difference would that make to your life?

  BRIEFLY EXPLORE

Past Handset Purchase (15 minutes)

- Thinking now about your current handset, I'd like to talk about two different things . . .
- First, how you actually went about the process of choosing the handset and, second, any criteria you had for the handset itself . . .

Past Handset Selection Process

- So thinking first only about *how* you went about choosing your handset, *not* any features you wanted, how did you go about choosing one?

EXPLORE PROCESS

Past Handset Criteria

- Ok, so now tell me what you actually looked for in a handset.

EXPLORE

Usage of Handset Features (10 minutes)

- Thinking now about handset features, I'd like to start by making a list of all the handset features you can think of—anything the handset can do, any settings you can change, etc.
- We'll talk in a minute about which features you actually use, but I want to start with a list of everything your handset *could* do.

FLIPCHART

- Which features have you *ever* used, even if only once?

FLIPCHART

- Are there any settings you only changed once, but are really glad you could change?
- Why?

EXPLORE

- And which features do you use regularly?
- Why?

EXPLORE

Desired Features (3 minutes)

- Are there any features your handset *doesn't* have, but you wish that it did?

EXPLORE

Motivations for Replacement (10 minutes)

- You've all been invited here because you've replaced your handset at least once . . .
- What motivated you to replace your handset?

EXPLORE

- Was the handset replacement tied to your switching or renewing your operator contract, i.e., contract with your wireless service provider?
- What do you think are some of the reasons that people would replace their handsets?

EXPLORE

Triggers to Past Upgrade (10 minutes)

- You've all been invited here because you've upgraded your handset at least once . . .
- What was it that made you want to upgrade to a better handset?

UNPROMPTED FIRST

- What were *all* the factors involved in that decision?
- What was the single *biggest* reason?

EXPLORE

Barriers to Past Upgrade (5 minutes)

- How long was it from the first time you ever considered upgrading, however briefly, until the time you actually went ahead and bought the new handset?
- What were *all* the reasons you didn't do it immediately?

EXPLORE

- What was the *main* reason for leaving it a while?

EXPLORE

Triggers and Barriers to Future Upgrade (15 minutes)

- What about the future—when do you think you will next upgrade your handset?

  EXPLORE

- What would spur you to do that?
- Is there a killer feature that would have you upgrade immediately?

  EXPLORE

- How would you go about choosing your next handset?

  EXPLORE

- And what will you actually look for in your next handset?

  EXPLORE

Closing Exercise (10 minutes)

- Finally, I'd like your creativity for a few minutes—to come up with ideas . . .
- Don't worry about whether it's a good idea or a bad idea.
- The only word I'm going to ban is "free"!
- Supposing a handset manufacturer wanted to encourage you to upgrade tomorrow . . .
- What could they do?
- Just call out anything at all that occurs to you—obvious, profound, serious, silly, whatever . . .

  EXPLORE AND REFINE

- Thank the respondents and close the session. ■

After a detailed outline is formulated, participants are recruited and the focus group interview conducted. During the interview, the moderator must (1) establish rapport with the group; (2) state the rules of group interaction; (3) set objectives; (4) probe the respondents and provoke intense discussion in the relevant areas; and (5) attempt to summarize the group's response to determine the extent of agreement.

Following the group discussion, either the moderator or an analyst reviews and analyzes the results. The analyst not only reports specific comments and findings but also looks for consistent responses, new ideas, concerns suggested by facial expressions and body language, and other hypotheses that may or may not have received confirmation from all of the participants.

Because the number of participants is small, frequencies and percentages are not usually reported in a focus group summary. Instead, reports typically include expressions like "most participants thought" or "participants were divided on this issue." Meticulous documentation and interpretation of the session lays the groundwork for the final step: taking action. In the case of consumer research, this usually means doing additional research, as illustrated in the Mall of Atlanta (the actual name of the mall has been disguised) topline report that gives a summary of the focus group objectives, procedures, findings, and implications.

Real Research   Mall of Atlanta Focus Group Topline Report

Focus Group Objectives

The Mall of Atlanta focus groups were conducted to understand shopping mall expectations of the youth segment, to determine this group's perceptions of the recent weekend visit, and to analyze the perceived brand identity of the mall based on the individual's experience.

Method and Procedures

Reactions were solicited for the Mall of Atlanta experience from 60 youth visitors (30 males and 30 females) who attended the mall on the weekend prior to the group discussion (i.e., Labor Day Weekend). Six focus groups were conducted, each with 10 respondents. The current focus groups were conducted at a local focus group facility on September 16, 2008. The youth were given $30 and instructed to visit the mall during September 5–7; however, no other instructions or explanations were given to the youth. They were not aware that they would be participating in a discussion group when they visited the mall.

Summary of Findings
Mall Visit Experience

- For entertainment, participants typically engage in movies (theater and rental), sports (spectator and participatory), drinks, or just "hanging out" with friends. They typically need only three or four hours to experience the mall, and try to hold costs to under $30, except for a special occasion.
- Examples of special occasions include dinner, concerts, theater, museums, and theme malls. Most often, the theme mall is a destination like Mall of Georgia, Universal Studios, or Sea World. However, many have visited Mall of Atlanta more than once, and a few have been Mall of Atlanta "Crown Customers" who shop at the Mall of Atlanta loyally.
- Visitors were pleasantly surprised and delighted with the mall's entertainment, the surprisingly short lines in the children's area, the first-class magic show, and winning a large stuffed animal.
- When asked to describe feelings surrounding the experience, most were very positive—*"excited to go," "feel like a kid again," "didn't feel like I should have to go to work tomorrow,"* and *"friendly, fun to share the experience with others in attendance."* The only negatives were *"tired," "hot,"* and *"yucky."*
- On the other hand, visitors were frustrated to find a lack of signage and maps, a "deserted" feeling resulting from the lack of hosts or guides, and the dry, dirty look of some areas in the mall.
- Visitors were asked to suggest necessary changes in the mall:
  - Crowds. They can be daunting, and there must be a way to make them more palatable, such as drinking fountains, benches, misters, ceiling fans that work, or entertainment. Made comparisons to Mall of Georgia, which respondents said had more space and better groomed patrons.
  - Dress code. Complaints that many people were showing a lot of skin, but hardly anyone looked like Britney Spears or Ricky Martin. Who wants the bowling alley crowd to dress this way? Several agreed there should be a "no shirt, no shoes, no service" policy.
  - Information. Booths placed in visible spots throughout the mall would be helpful. Visitors agreed that maps were very hard to find, and that perhaps handing them out in line at the entrance of the mall would help.

Brand Identity Versus Mall of Georgia
PERSONALITY

- *Mall of Atlanta.* Definitely male, but surprisingly, not a teen. Middle-aged or older, a little tired, moody. Blue-collar worker, not very smart, wearing "gimme" T-shirt and cap. Drives a big old American car, may have money problems. A follower rather than a leader.
- *Mall of Georgia.* Both female and male, perhaps that loving, indulgent aunt and uncle who shower you with experiences you don't get at home. Dressed classically in khakis and a polo shirt. Nurturing, approachable, well-rounded, and affluent. Like this person better than the Mall of Atlanta personality because it's more fun.

BRAND VALUE To many, Mall of Atlanta was described as "just a bunch of shops and rides." Other malls like Mall of Georgia encompass a complete entertainment experience. Several "long-timers" remember a time when Mall of Atlanta included the experience of regional history and of other cultures. What made it unique in the past is gone now, as the specific areas have become less distinct and not associated with as much meaning. As a result, there was a general feeling that the value had declined.

Implications

In general, the results of this latest in the series of focus groups, focusing on youth perceptions, are similar to those from previous focus groups with nonyouth. Respondents view the Mall of Atlanta as more of a "working person's" mall. However, the young respondents' perceptions of the Mall of Atlanta were markedly more negative when compared to the Mall of Georgia than any other segment of customers included in this series of quarterly focus groups begun two years ago. Perhaps Mall of Georgia's remodeling, which was completed last year, has become more salient in the minds of Mall of Atlanta's young customers because of the youths' higher use of informal "buzz" (word-of-mouth). More research on this topic using a large sample survey is needed. ■

Six focus groups were conducted in the Mall of Atlanta project. The number of focus groups that should be conducted on a single subject depends on (1) the nature of the issue, (2) the number of distinct market segments, (3) the number of new ideas generated by each successive group, and (4) time and cost. Resources permitting, one should conduct additional discussion groups until the moderator can anticipate what will be said. This usually happens after three or four groups are conducted on the same topic.[15] It is recommended that at least two groups be conducted.[16] Properly conducted focus groups can generate important hypotheses that can serve as a basis for conducting quantitative research, as the following example indicates.

Real Research

Making Kool-Aid Cool!

Kool-Aid (www.koolaid.com) is a well-known product among moms and kids and is used in many households throughout America. Despite this, Kool-Aid sales had begun to decline. Kraft Foods wanted to find out why heavy users had slowed down their consumption of the product and how they could get Kool-Aid back into people's lifestyles.

Kool-Aid conducted focus groups, classifying the groups by product usage ranging from heavy users to light users. They found out a great deal about the different users. The heavy users like to drink Kool-Aid all year round and all family members drink it, not just the children. The heavy users also add more than just water to the mix; they add ingredients such as fruits, fruit juice, and club soda and drink Kool-Aid at home. On the other hand, the light users perceive Kool-Aid as a summer drink for kids. They are also more likely to head out of the house for socializing, and since Kool-Aid is not ready made and portable, they do not use it often. Hence the following hypotheses were formulated:

H1: The heavy users like and drink Kool-Aid all year round.
H2: Among the heavy users, all members of the family drink Kool-Aid.
H3: The heavy users regularly drink Kool-Aid at home.
H4: Among the light users, the kids are primary users of Kool-Aid.
H5: The light users drink Kool-Aid primarily away from home.

A follow-up quantitative survey using telephone interviews supported these hypotheses. Therefore, Kool-Aid developed and tested different advertising executions for the heavy and light users. The heavy users were targeted with an execution showing people of all ages drinking Kool-Aid together in a home or a backyard. This is where the "How do you like your Kool-Aid" slogan came from, showing family and friends talking about the different ways they drink their Kool-Aid. The light users were targeted with advertising showing children and adults at a community dog wash enjoying summer fun and drinking Kool-Aid out of thermoses. This campaign was very successful in arresting the loss of Kool-Aid sales. As of 2009, more than 575 million gallons of Kool-Aid are consumed in a year, including 225 million gallons during the summer season.[17] ■

Other Variations in Focus Groups

Focus groups can use several variations of the standard procedure. One variation was illustrated in the opening example where participants were asked to bring in three or four items that represent their ideal environment in order to encourage them to reveal their underlying beliefs and attitudes. Other variations include:

Two-way focus group. This allows one target group to listen to and learn from a related group. In one application, physicians viewed a focus group of arthritis patients discussing the treatment they desired. A focus group of these physicians was then held to determine their reactions.

Dual-moderator group. This is a focus group interview conducted by two moderators. One moderator is responsible for the smooth flow of the session, and the other ensures that specific issues are discussed.

Dueling-moderator group. Here there are also two moderators, but they deliberately take opposite positions on the issues to be discussed. This allows the researcher to explore both sides of controversial issues.

Respondent-moderator group. In this type of focus group, the moderator asks selected participants to play the role of moderator temporarily to improve group dynamics.

Client-participant groups. Client personnel are identified and made part of the discussion group. Their primary role is to offer clarifications that will make the group process more effective.

Mini-groups. These groups consist of a moderator and only 4 or 5 respondents. They are used when the issues of interest require more extensive probing than is possible in the standard group of 8 to 12.

telesessions
A focus group technique using a telecommunications network.

Telesession groups. **Telessessions** are focus group sessions that are conducted by phone, using the conference call technique.

Electronic group interviewing (EGI). Keypads and other electronic devices are used to gauge group opinion. When the moderator wants to poll the focus group participants on a certain issue, respondents express their opinions using the keypad on a scale of 0 to 10 or 0 to 100, and the results are instantly displayed on a large video screen.

Online focus groups are emerging as an important form of focus groups and are discussed in detail in the following section. We conclude our section on focus groups with a discussion of the advantages and disadvantages.

Advantages of Focus Groups

Focus groups offer several advantages over other data-collection techniques. These may be summarized by the 10 S's:[18]

1. *Synergism*: Putting a group of people together will produce a wider range of information, insight, and ideas than will individual responses secured privately.
2. *Snowballing*: A bandwagon effect often operates in a group interview, in that one person's comment triggers a chain reaction from the other participants.
3. *Stimulation*: Usually after a brief introductory period, the respondents want to express their ideas and expose their feelings as the general level of excitement over the topic increases in the group.
4. *Security*: Because the participants' feelings are similar to those of other group members, they feel comfortable and are therefore willing to express their ideas and feelings.
5. *Spontaneity*: Since participants are not required to answer specific questions, their responses can be spontaneous and unconventional and should therefore provide an accurate idea of their views.
6. *Serendipity*: Ideas are more likely to arise out of the blue in a group than in an individual interview.
7. *Specialization*: Because a number of participants are involved simultaneously, use of a highly trained, but expensive, interviewer is justified.
8. *Scientific scrutiny*: The group interview allows close scrutiny of the data-collection process, in that observers can witness the session and it can be recorded for later analysis.
9. *Structure*: The group interview allows for flexibility in the topics covered and the depth with which they are treated.
10. *Speed*: Since a number of individuals are being interviewed at the same time, data collection and analysis proceed relatively quickly.

Disadvantages of Focus Groups

The disadvantages of focus groups may be summarized by the five M's:

1. *Misuse*: Focus groups can be misused and abused by considering the results as conclusive rather than exploratory.
2. *Misjudge*: Focus group results can be more easily misjudged than the results of other data-collection techniques. Focus groups are particularly susceptible to client and researcher biases.
3. *Moderation*: Focus groups are difficult to moderate. Moderators with all the desirable skills are rare. The quality of the results depends heavily on the skills of the moderator.
4. *Messy*: The unstructured nature of the responses makes coding, analysis, and interpretation difficult. Focus group data tend to be messy.
5. *Misrepresentation*: Focus group results are not representative of the general population and are not projectable. Consequently, focus group results should not be the sole basis for decision making.

When properly conducted and used, focus groups have numerous applications.

Applications of Focus Groups

Focus groups are being used extensively for profit, nonprofit, and all types of organizations.[19] They can be used in almost any situation requiring some preliminary understanding and insights, as illustrated in the baby-boomer, Kellogg's Pop-Tarts, and Kool-Aid examples. We will discuss some substantive and methodological applications that represent the wide range of use of this technique. Focus groups can be used to address substantive issues such as:

1. Understanding consumers' perceptions, preferences, and behavior concerning a product category
2. Obtaining impressions of new product concepts
3. Generating new ideas about older products
4. Developing creative concepts and copy material for advertisements
5. Securing price impressions
6. Obtaining preliminary consumer reaction to specific marketing programs

The methodological applications of focus groups include:

1. Defining a problem more precisely
2. Generating alternative courses of action
3. Developing an approach to a problem
4. Obtaining information helpful in structuring consumer questionnaires
5. Generating hypotheses that can be tested quantitatively
6. Interpreting previously obtained quantitative results

Experiential Research

Gatorade: From a Sports Drink to a Lifestyle Drink

Management would like to transform Gatorade from a sports drink to a lifestyle drink. Visit www.gatorade.com and search the Internet using a search engine as well as your library's online databases to obtain information on the marketing strategy of Gatorade energy drinks.

1. Prepare a focus group discussion guide for determining the reasons why people consume Gatorade drinks and what would lead them to consume more Gatorade.
2. Conduct a focus group of 8 to 12 students using your discussion guide.
3. Prepare a focus group topline report for Gatorade management. ■

Online Focus Group Interviews

As in the case of traditional focus groups, online focus group participation is by invitation only. The respondents are prerecruited, generally from an online list of people who have expressed an interest in participating. A screening questionnaire is administered online to qualify the respondents. Those who qualify are invited to participate in a focus group; they receive a time, a URL, a room name, and a password via e-mail. Generally, four to six people participate in the online group. There are fewer people in an online focus group than in a face-to-face meeting because too many voices can confuse the discussion.

Before the focus group begins, participants receive information about the focus group that covers such things as how to express emotions when typing. Electronic emotion indicators are produced using keyboard characters and are standard in their use on the Internet. For example, :-) and :-(are examples of smiling and sad faces. The emotions are usually inserted in the text at the point at which the emotion is felt. Emotions can also be expressed using a different font or color. There is a wide range of emotions to choose from, such as: I'm frowning, I'm laughing to myself, I'm embarrassed, I'm mad now, I'm responding passionately now, and so on. This is then followed by the response. The participants can also preview information about the focus group topic by visiting a Web site and reading information or downloading and viewing an actual TV ad on their PCs. Then, just before the focus group begins, participants visit a Web site where they log on and get some last-minute instructions.

When it is time for the group, they move into a Web-based chat room. They go to the focus group location (URL) and click on the "Enter Focus Room" item. To enter, they must supply the room name, user name, and password that was e-mailed to them earlier. In the chat room, the moderator and the participants type to each other in real time. The general practice is for the moderators to always pose their questions in all capital letters and the respondents are asked to use upper and lower case. The respondents are also asked to always start their response with the question number, so the moderator can quickly tie the response to the proper question. This makes it fast and easy to transcribe a focus group session. The group interaction lasts for about an hour. A raw transcript is available as soon as the group is completed, and a formatted transcript is available within 48 hours. The whole process is much faster than the traditional method. Examples of companies that provide online focus groups include comScore SurveySite (www.comscore.com), Harris Interactive (www.harrisinteractive.com), and Burke (www.burke.com).

New forms of online focus groups continue to emerge. For example, online bulletin board focus groups involve the moderator and the respondents over an extended period of time, from a few days to a few weeks. Thus, respondents can think and respond at their own convenience. An example is SurveySite's FocusSite for holding an in-depth discussion among 25 or more participants over an extended period of time. Participants enter the discussion several times over a 1- to 2-day period, depending on research objectives. The extended time period allows respondents to react to, and build upon, each other's ideas in a way that is often not possible during a typical focus group session that lasts from 1 to 3 hours.

Advantages of Online Focus Groups

People from all over the country or even the world can participate, and the client can observe the group from the convenience of the home or office. Geographical constraints are removed and time constraints are lessened. Unlike traditional focus groups, you have the unique opportunity to contact group participants again at a later date, to revisit issues, or introduce them to modifications in material presented in the original focus group. The Internet enables the researcher to reach segments that are usually hard to interview: doctors, lawyers, professionals, working mothers, and others who lead busy lives and are not interested in taking part in traditional focus groups.

Moderators may also be able to carry on side conversations with individual respondents, probing deeper into interesting areas. People are generally less inhibited in their responses and are more likely to fully express their thoughts. A lot of online focus groups go well past their allotted time since so many responses are expressed. Finally, as there is no travel, videotaping, or facilities to arrange, the cost is much lower than for traditional focus groups. Firms are able to keep costs between one-fifth and one-half the cost of traditional focus groups.[20]

Disadvantages of Online Focus Groups

Only people that have and know how to use a computer can be surveyed online. Since the name of an individual on the Internet is often private, actually verifying that a respondent is a member of a target group is difficult. This is illustrated in a cartoon in *The New Yorker*, where two dogs are seated at a computer and one says to the other, "On the Internet, nobody knows you are a dog!" To overcome this limitation, other traditional methods such as telephone calls are used for recruitment and verification of respondents. Body language, facial expressions, and tone of voice cannot be obtained and electronic emotions obviously do not capture as full a breadth of emotion as videotaping.

Another factor that must be considered is the lack of general control over the respondent's environment and their potential exposure to distracting external stimuli. Since online focus groups could potentially have respondents scattered all over the world, the researchers and moderator(s) have no idea what else the respondents may be doing while participating in the group. Only audio and visual stimuli can be tested. Products cannot be touched (e.g., clothing) or smelled (e.g., perfumes). It is difficult to get the clients as involved in online focus groups as they are in observing traditional focus groups. Table 5.3 presents a comparison of online and traditional focus groups.

TABLE 5.3

Online Versus Traditional Focus Groups

Characteristic	Online Focus Groups	Traditional Focus Groups
Group size	4 to 6 participants	8 to 12 participants
Group composition	Anywhere in the world	Drawn from the local area
Time duration	1 to 1.5 hours	1 to 3 hours
Physical setting	Researcher has little control	Under the control of the researcher
Respondent identity	Difficult to verify	Can be easily verified
Respondent attentiveness	Respondents can engage in other tasks	Attentiveness can be monitored
Respondent recruiting	Easier. Can be recruited online, by e-mail, by panel, or by traditional means	Recruited by traditional means (telephone, mail, mail panel)
Group dynamics	Limited	Synergistic, snowballing (bandwagon) effect
Openness of respondents	Respondents are more candid due to lack of face-to-face contact	Respondents are candid, except for sensitive topics
Nonverbal communication	Body language cannot be observed Emotions expressed by using symbols	Easy to observe body language and emotions
Use of physical stimuli	Limited to those that can be displayed on the Internet	A variety of stimuli (products, advertising, demonstrations, and so on) can be used
Transcripts	Available immediately	Time-consuming and expensive to obtain
Observers' communication with moderator	Observers can communicate with the moderator on a split-screen	Observers can manually send notes to the focus-group room
Unique moderator skills	Typing, computer usage, familiarity with chat-room slang	Observational
Turnaround time	Can be set up and completed in a few days	Takes many days for setup and completion
Client travel costs	None	Can be expensive
Client involvement	Limited	High
Basic focus-group costs	Much less expensive	More expensive due to facility rental, food, video/audio taping, and transcript preparation

Uses of Online Focus Groups

There are instances in which traditional focus groups will continue to be preferred. For instance, you really can't explore highly emotional issues or subject matters online. Since the reach for online focus groups is currently limited to people with Internet access, online focus groups are not appropriate for every research situation. However, they are very suitable for companies that use the Internet to sell products or services and want to either gain market share or gather intelligence. Applications include banner ads, copy testing, concept testing, usability testing, multimedia evaluation, and comparisons of icons or graphic images. Another potential use for online focus groups or surveys is for corporations that want to gather feedback on workplace issues like downsizing, job changes, and diversity. Employees can be referred to a Web site where they can participate anonymously in discussions with management. Companies such as CyberDialogue (www.cyberdialogue.com) specialize in online focus groups, e-mail surveys, and Web surveys.

Real Research   Enhancing the Utility of Sports Utility Vehicles

One industry that has taken advantage of online focus groups is the automobile industry, specifically Nissan North America. While designing the Xterra sports utility vehicle (SUV), Nissan conducted several online focus groups to get feedback on designs, as well as find out what their target market wanted to see in an SUV. The market, consisting of young, active, athletic people, was eager to participate. They wanted an SUV that could carry sporting and camping equipment inside the vehicle or on racks, but they wanted it to be offered at a reasonable price. The focus groups discussed topics such as the features they were looking for, such as racks on the top and the back of the SUV, four doors, a sporty design, trendy colors, and lots of room inside the vehicle. Nissan delivered in all of these areas, and has been successful. The 2001 Xterra being named the top SUV for 2001 by AAA demonstrates the company's success.

Online focus groups revealed that many automobile buyers wanted custom-built vehicles. Therefore, in 2002 Nissan become the first major automaker to announce Web-enabled, build-to-order manufacturing. While other major automakers like Ford and GM offer Web vehicle services, Nissan claims that its Web engine configuration is similar to Dell's custom manufacturing Web engine. In 2009, Nissan offered its customization technology on all Xterra models that are made in Nissan's Tennessee plant.[21] ■

Experiential Research

Online Qualitative Research

Another online qualitative research technique is an online bulletin board on which recruited respondents post their responses to discussion items over a longer period of time, such as several days. (These are also called *multiday moderated threaded discussions*.) Online capabilities can also be used to allow clients to remotely monitor traditional focus groups (through streaming video) or online focus groups. The following Web sites illustrate these online capabilities.

1. To experience the steps involved in designing and analyzing online bulletin board research, go to www.2020research.com, select Online Research and then QualBoard, and then "QualBoards Interactive—View the Flash Demo." To advance this overview, use the buttons at the bottom of the screen.
2. To experience how a sponsor of an online focus group can monitor the actual focus group as if from behind the one-way mirror in the back room of the focus group facility, go to www.activegroup.net and select Products, then ActiveGroup, then "Demo." You will have to provide an e-mail address and a one-word user name to activate the streaming video.
3. Visit e-FocusGroups (www.e-focusgroups.com) and click on online. Then click on "click here to see Respondent View" to get a view of what the respondents see in an online focus group. Click on "click here to see Client View" to view what the clients see in an online focus group. Write a brief report.
4. Visit comScore SurveySite (www.comscore.com) and write a report on FocusSite, comScore SurveySite's qualitative online methodology. ■

Depth Interviews

depth interview
An unstructured, direct, personal interview in which a single respondent is probed by a highly skilled interviewer to uncover underlying motivations, beliefs, attitudes, and feelings on a topic.

Depth interviews are another method of obtaining qualitative data. We describe the general procedure for conducting depth interviews and then illustrate some specific techniques. The advantages, disadvantages, and applications of depth interviews are also discussed.

Characteristics

Like focus groups, depth interviews are an unstructured and direct way of obtaining information, but unlike focus groups, depth interviews are conducted on a one-on-one basis. A depth interview is an unstructured, direct, personal interview in which a single respondent is probed by a highly skilled interviewer to uncover underlying motivations, beliefs, attitudes, and feelings on a topic.[22]

A depth interview may take from 30 minutes to more than one hour. To illustrate the technique in the context of the department store example, the interviewer begins by asking a general question such as, "How do you feel about shopping at department stores?" The interviewer then encourages the subject to talk freely about his or her attitudes toward department stores. After asking the initial question, the interviewer uses an unstructured format. The subsequent direction of the interview is determined by the respondent's initial reply, the interviewer's probes for elaboration, and the respondent's answers. Suppose the respondent replies to the initial question by saying, "Shopping isn't fun anymore." The interviewer might then pose a question such as, "Why isn't it fun anymore?" If the answer is not very revealing ("Fun has just disappeared from shopping"), the interviewer may ask a probing question, such as, "Why was it fun before and what has changed?"

Although the interviewer attempts to follow a rough outline, the specific wording of the questions and the order in which they are asked is influenced by the subject's replies. Probing is of critical importance in obtaining meaningful responses and uncovering hidden issues. Probing is done by asking such questions as, "Why do you say that?" "That's interesting, can you tell me more?" or "Would you like to add anything else?"[23] Probing is further discussed in Chapter 13 on fieldwork. The value of information uncovered by probing is shown in the following example.

Real Research   ## Probing for Intelligence

In a study designed to come up with new credit card features, respondents merely listed features of existing credit cards when questioned in a structured way. Then depth interviews were employed to probe the respondents. For example, the interviewer asked respondents to ask themselves, "What is important to me? What problems do I have? How do I wish I could live? What is my ideal world?" As a result of this method, consumers relayed information they had previously been unaware of and several new credit card features surfaced. The study uncovered the need for an "intelligent" credit card that could perform such tasks as keeping track of credit card and bank balances, investments, and emergency telephone numbers. Another concern of credit card users is the bulging wallet and annoyance from carrying too many credit cards. Research results found from such a focus group can help credit card companies offer new features while attracting new customers and satisfying existing customers. For example, in 2002 PrivaSys and First Data teamed up to introduce a battery-powered electronic credit card with an internal chip capable of holding an American Express card, MasterCard, gas cards, and other debit cards all on one single piece of plastic that is the same size and shape as one credit card. As of 2009, PrivaSys (www.privasys.com) had developed additional smart-card technologies to help card issuers to reduce fraud and provide substantial differentiation while delivering cardholders additional security and convenience.[24] ∎

As this example indicates, probing is effective in uncovering underlying or hidden information. Probing is an integral part of depth interviews and is used in all depth-interviewing techniques.

Techniques

laddering
A technique for conducting depth interviews in which a line of questioning proceeds from product characteristics to user characteristics.

Three depth-interviewing techniques that have recently gained popularity are laddering, hidden issue questioning, and symbolic analysis. In **laddering**, the line of questioning proceeds from product characteristics to user characteristics. This technique allows the researcher to tap into the consumer's network of meanings. Laddering provides a way to probe into consumers' deep underlying psychological and emotional reasons that affect their purchasing decisions. When determining why a person buys a product, researchers want to know more than simply "quality" and "low price." Therefore, to examine the in-depth underlying motivators a laddering technique should be used.

Laddering requires interviewers to be trained in specific probing techniques in order to develop a meaningful "mental map" of the consumer's view of a target product. The ultimate goal is to combine mental maps of consumers who are similar, which will lead to the reasons why people purchase particular products. Probing is used to go beyond the initial responses interview participants give to a question. When asked why they prefer a product, responses are initially attribute-related. Examples of these responses would include color, taste, price, size, and product name. Each attribute, consequence, and value of the underlying motivators is found by "climbing the ladder" to the real reasons for purchasing products. The line of questioning generally proceeds from product characteristics to user characteristics. Following initial responses with "why" questions leads to much more useful information for the marketer:

hidden issue questioning
A type of depth interview that attempts to locate personal sore spots related to deeply felt personal concerns.

QUESTION: Why do you buy Maybelline cosmetics?

ANSWER: "I buy Maybelline cosmetics because it is a good brand name at a reasonable price."

QUESTION: Why are reasonably priced cosmetics so important to you?

ANSWER: "Well, buying a quality product that isn't high priced makes me feel good about myself because I am spending my money wisely."

symbolic analysis
A technique for conducting depth interviews in which the symbolic meaning of objects is analyzed by comparing them with their opposites.

In **hidden issue questioning**, the focus is not on socially shared values but rather on personal "sore spots"; not on general lifestyles but on deeply felt personal concerns. **Symbolic analysis** attempts to analyze the symbolic meaning of objects by comparing them with their opposites. To learn what something is, the researcher attempts to learn what it is not. The logical opposites of a product that are investigated are nonusage of the product, attributes of an imaginary "non-product," and opposite types of products. The three techniques are illustrated with the following example.

Real Research

Hidden Issues and Hidden Dimensions in Air Travel

In this study, the researcher was investigating attitudes toward airlines among male middle managers.

Laddering. Each airline attribute, such as wide-body aircrafts, was probed (why do you like to travel in wide-body aircrafts?) to determine why it was important (I can get more work done), and then that reason was probed (I accomplish more), and so on (I feel good about myself). Laddering indicated that managers preferred advanced seat reservations, wide-body aircraft, and first-class cabin seating (product characteristics), which resulted in greater physical comfort. This enabled them to get more work done while on the flight, leading to a sense of accomplishment and higher self-esteem (user characteristics). This technique showed that an advertising campaign like the old United Airlines campaign, "You're The Boss," which bolsters the self-esteem of the managers, is worthy of consideration.

Hidden issue questioning. Respondents were questioned about fantasies, work lives, and social lives to identify hidden life issues. The answers indicated that glamorous, historic, elite, "masculine camaraderie," competitive activities, like Grand Prix car racing, fencing, and World War II airplane dogfighting, were of personal interest to the managers. These interests could be tapped with an advertising campaign like the one by Lufthansa German Airlines featuring a World War I–type "Red Baron" spokesperson. That campaign communicated the aggressiveness, high status, and competitive heritage of the airline.

Symbolic analysis. Questions asked included, "What would it be like if you could no longer use airplanes?" Responses like, "Without planes, I would have to rely on e-mail, letters, and telephone calls" were received. This suggests that what airlines sell to the managers is face-to-face communication. Thus, an effective ad might be one that guarantees that the airline will do the same thing for a manager that Federal Express does for a package.

Information revealed by these techniques can be used to effectively position an airline and to design appropriate advertising and communication strategies. Marketing environment, following the rise of oil prices in 2008, had been very challenging for airline companies. Using these techniques, in 2009 American Airlines was administering the Business ExtrAA program that offered more variety, more choice, and more flexibility than any other airline incentive program for businesses. Programs such as this one helped American to avoid the Chapter 11 bankruptcy that plagued other major airlines such as United, Delta, Northwest, and US Airways.[25] ■

Using the depth interview technique, American Airlines developed the Business ExtrAA program that offered more variety, more choice, and more flexibility than other airline incentive programs for businesses.

The interviewer's role is critical to the success of the depth interview. The interviewer should (1) avoid appearing superior and put the respondent at ease; (2) be detached and objective, yet personable; (3) ask questions in an informative manner; (4) not accept brief "yes" or "no" answers; and (5) probe the respondent.

Advantages and Disadvantages of Depth Interviews

Depth interviews can uncover greater depth of insights than focus groups. Also, depth interviews attribute the responses directly to the respondent, unlike focus groups, where it is often difficult to determine which respondent made a particular response. Depth interviews result in free exchange of information that may not be possible in focus groups because there is no social pressure to conform to group response.

Depth interviews suffer from many of the disadvantages of focus groups and often to a greater extent. Skilled interviewers capable of conducting depth interviews are expensive and difficult to find. The lack of structure makes the results susceptible to the interviewer's influence, and the quality and completeness of the results depend heavily on the interviewer's skills. The data obtained are difficult to analyze and interpret, and the services of skilled psychologists are typically required for this purpose. The length of the interview combined with high costs means that the number of depth interviews in a project will be small. A relative comparison of focus groups and depth interviews is given in Table 5.4. Despite these disadvantages, depth interviews do have some applications.

Applications of Depth Interviews

As with focus groups, the primary use of depth interviews is for exploratory research to gain insights and understanding. However, unlike focus groups, depth interviews are used infrequently in marketing research. Nevertheless, depth interviews can be effectively employed in special problem situations, such as those requiring:[26]

1. Detailed probing of the respondent (automobile purchase)
2. Discussion of confidential, sensitive, or embarrassing topics (personal finances, loose dentures)
3. Situations where strong social norms exist and the respondent may be easily swayed by group response (attitude of college students toward sports)

TABLE 5.4
Focus Groups Versus Depth Interviews

Characteristic	Focus Groups	Depth Interviews
Group synergy and dynamics	+	−
Peer pressure/group influence	−	+
Client involvement	+	−
Generation of innovative ideas	+	−
In-depth probing of individuals	−	+
Uncovering hidden motives	−	+
Discussion of sensitive topics	−	+
Interviewing respondents who are competitors	−	+
Interviewing respondents who are professionals	−	+
Scheduling of respondents	−	+
Amount of information	+	−
Bias in moderation and interpretation	+	−
Cost per respondent	+	−
Time (interviewing and analysis)	+	−

Note: A + indicates a relative advantage over the other procedure, a − indicates a relative disadvantage.

4. Detailed understanding of complicated behavior (department store shopping)
5. Interviews with professional people (industrial marketing research)
6. Interviews with competitors, who are unlikely to reveal the information in a group setting (travel agents' perceptions of airline package travel programs)
7. Situations where the product consumption experience is sensory in nature, affecting mood states and emotions (perfumes, bath soap)

Real Research

Climbing the Ladder to PlayStation 3 Success

The laddering technique was used to determine consumer attitudes and purchasing motivations toward the Sony PlayStation 3 (www.us.playstation.com). The key laddering insights for this product included:

- My friends come over and we spend an evening working together through a game or playing against each other.
- Challenging games require more critical thinking and decision making. It feels more like a puzzle rather than a game.
- Some games are suited to adults only, so I don't feel like I am playing a "kid's game," but taking part in a high-quality gaming experience.

Marketing implications from this information on the Sony PlayStation 3 include:

- Set up gaming kiosks in nightclubs in large cities such as Los Angeles and New York to attract adults.
- Advertise through sitcoms such as *Friends* with Joey and Chandler playing games on a PlayStation 3.
- Target magazines such as *Wired* and *Sports Illustrated* with more mature ads.

With such a high demand for Sony products, the company realizes that it must continue to learn more about consumer behavior patterns. The insights generated from laddering serve as a departure point for further research and hypothesis testing that can help develop new ideas for products, distribution, pricing, or promotion.[27] ■

ACTIVE RESEARCH

Life Takes Visa?

Search the Internet using a search engine as well as your library's online databases to obtain information on why people use credit cards.

Conduct two depth interviews for determining the reasons why people use credit cards.

As the marketing manager for Visa, how would you use information on the reasons why people use credit cards to increase your market share?

grounded theory
An inductive and more structured approach in which each subsequent depth interview is adjusted based on the cumulative findings from previous depth interviews with the purpose of developing general concepts or theories.

protocol interview
In a protocol interview, a respondent is placed in a decision-making situation and asked to verbalize the process and the activities that he or she would undertake to make the decision.

The PlayStation 3 example illustrates the value of depth interviews in uncovering the hidden responses that underlie the clichés elicited in ordinary questioning. A special way in which depth interviews are used is grounded theory. **Grounded theory** uses an inductive and more structured approach in which each subsequent depth interview is adjusted based on the cumulative findings from previous depth interviews with the purpose of developing general concepts or theories. Sometimes historical records are also analyzed. This approach is useful in designing new products or modifying existing products and developing advertising and promotion strategies. Another variation of depth interview is protocol interview. In a **protocol interview**, a respondent is placed in a decision-making situation and asked to verbalize the process and the activities that he or she would undertake to make the decision.

Projective Techniques

Both focus groups and depth interviews are direct approaches in which the true purpose of the research is disclosed to the respondents or is otherwise obvious to them. Projective techniques are different from these techniques in that they attempt to disguise the purpose of the research.

projective technique
An unstructured and indirect form of questioning that encourages the respondents to project their underlying motivations, beliefs, attitudes, or feelings regarding the issues of concern.

A **projective technique** is an unstructured, indirect form of questioning that encourages respondents to project their underlying motivations, beliefs, attitudes, or feelings regarding the issues of concern.[28] In projective techniques, respondents are asked to interpret the behavior of others rather than describe their own behavior. In interpreting the behavior of others, respondents indirectly project their own motivations, beliefs, attitudes, or feelings into the situation. Thus, respondents' attitudes are uncovered by analyzing their responses to scenarios that are deliberately unstructured, vague, and ambiguous. The more ambiguous the situation, the more respondents project their emotions, needs, motives, attitudes, and values, as demonstrated by work in clinical psychology on which projective techniques are based.[29] As in psychology, these techniques are classified as association, completion, construction, and expressive. Each of these classifications is discussed.[30]

Association Techniques

association techniques
A type of projective technique in which the respondent is presented with a stimulus and asked to respond with the first thing that comes to mind.

word association
A projective technique in which respondents are presented with a list of words, one at a time. After each word, they are asked to give the first word that comes to mind.

In **association techniques**, an individual is presented with a stimulus and asked to respond with the first thing that comes to mind. **Word association** is the best known of these techniques. In word association, respondents are presented with a list of words, one at a time, and asked to respond to each with the first word that comes to mind. The words of interest, called *test words*, are interspersed throughout the list, which also contains some neutral, or filler, words to disguise the purpose of the study. For example, in the department store study, some of the test words might be: "location," "parking," "shopping," "quality," and "price." The subject's response to each word is recorded verbatim, and responses are timed so that respondents who hesitate or reason out (defined as taking longer than 3 seconds to reply) can be identified. The interviewer, not the respondent, records the responses. This controls for the time required for the respondent to write the response.

The underlying assumption of this technique is that association allows respondents to reveal their inner feelings about the topic of interest. Responses are analyzed by calculating (1) the frequency with which any word is given as a response; (2) the amount of time that elapses before a response is given; and (3) the number of respondents who do not respond at all to a test word within a reasonable period of time. Those who do not respond at all are judged to have an emotional involvement so high that it blocks a response. It is often possible to classify the associations as favorable, unfavorable, or neutral. An individual's pattern of responses and the details of the response are used to determine the person's underlying attitudes or feelings on the topic of interest, as shown in the following example.

Real Research

Dealing with Dirt

Word association was used to study women's attitudes toward detergents. Following is a list of stimulus words used and the responses of two women of similar age and household status. The sets of responses are quite different, suggesting that the women differ in personality and in their attitudes toward housekeeping. Mrs. M's associations suggest that she is resigned to dirt. She sees dirt as inevitable and does not want to do much about it. She does not do hard cleaning, nor does she get pleasure from her family. Mrs. C sees dirt too, but is energetic, factual-minded, and less emotional. She is actively ready to combat dirt and uses soap and water as her weapons.

Stimulus	Mrs. M	Mrs. C
washday	everyday	ironing
fresh	and sweet	clean
pure	air	soiled
scrub	don't; husband does	clean
filth	this neighborhood	dirt
bubbles	bath	soap and water
family	squabbles	children
towels	dirty	wash

These findings suggest that the market for detergents could be segmented on the basis of attitudes. In 2009, P&G was the laundry detergent market leader, offering a number of different brands. Research findings similar to those discussed here have helped P&G appropriately position its various detergent brands for different attitudinal segments, leading to increased sales. For example, by focusing on fragrance, P&G increased Gain's annual sales to more than $1 billion in the year ended June 30, 2009. That made Gain number 2, behind P&G's Tide, which dominated the market with 44 percent of sales.[31] ∎

There are several variations to the standard word association procedure illustrated here. Respondents may be asked to give the first two, three, or four words that come to mind rather than only the first word. This technique can also be used in controlled tests, as contrasted with free association. In controlled tests, respondents might be asked, "What department stores come to mind first when I mention high-quality merchandise?" More detailed information can be obtained from completion techniques, which are a natural extension of association techniques.

Completion Techniques

completion technique
A projective technique that requires the respondent to complete an incomplete stimulus situation.

In **completion techniques**, the respondent is asked to complete an incomplete stimulus situation. Common completion techniques in marketing research are sentence completion and story completion.

sentence completion
A projective technique in which respondents are presented with a number of incomplete sentences and asked to complete them.

SENTENCE COMPLETION   **Sentence completion** is similar to word association. Respondents are given incomplete sentences and asked to complete them. Generally, they are asked to use the first word or phrase that comes to mind, as illustrated in the department store patronage project.

Project Research   Sentence Completion

In the context of the store patronage study, the following incomplete sentences may be used.

A person who shops at Sears is

_____

A person who receives a gift certificate good for Macy's would be

_____

JCPenney is most liked by

_____

When I think of shopping in a department store, I

_____ ∎

This example illustrates one advantage of sentence completion over word association: Respondents can be provided with a more directed stimulus. Sentence completion may provide more information about the subjects' feelings than word association. However, sentence completion is not as disguised, and many respondents may be able to guess the purpose of the study. A variation of sentence completion is paragraph completion, in which the respondent completes a paragraph beginning with the stimulus phrase. A further expanded version of sentence completion and paragraph completion is story completion.

story completion
A projective technique in which the respondents are provided with part of a story and required to give the conclusion in their own words.

STORY COMPLETION   In **story completion**, respondents are given part of a story—enough to direct attention to a particular topic but not to hint at the ending. They are required to give the conclusion in their own words. The respondents' completion of this story will reveal their underlying feelings and emotions, as in the following example.

Real Research   Pantyhose Have Horror Stories?

Stories? Horror stories? That is one thing that DuPont (www.dupont.com), a manufacturer of pantyhose material, overlooked when doing research to find out what customers like. DuPont conducted the same research that all other companies conduct, including focus groups and surveys. Unfortunately, it wasn't enough.

The problem with focus groups was the respondents' unwillingness to respond. Some felt ashamed or just weren't interested in the subject. In other cases, customers had feelings and opinions they just weren't comfortable discussing directly. Then story completion was used.

Respondents were asked to bring in pictures and tell stories describing certain feelings, opinions, and reactions to wearing pantyhose. To their surprise, many women showed up and had a lot to say. Women were freer in expressing their ideas. One woman brought in a picture of a spilled ice-cream sundae, capturing the rage she feels when she spots a run in her hose. Others brought in a picture of a Mercedes and Queen Elizabeth.

The analysis indicated that those women felt more attractive and sexy to men when they wear pantyhose. The problem wasn't necessarily that women don't like to wear pantyhose, but more that they have a feeling associated with wearing pantyhose, and when pantyhose get a run, tear, or other defect, women lose the associated feeling they have (such as attractive, sexy, sensual). It was that pantyhose needed to be more durable and long-lasting, so when women wear them all day, they can survive the "wear and tear" that may occur.

Thus, DuPont was able to see what consumers' true feelings were about its products. When these findings were confirmed in a telephone survey, DuPont modified its pantyhose material to fit the consumers' needs. Furthermore, stocking manufacturers have begun to use these findings, tailoring ads to appeal less to women's executive personas and more toward their sexy, cocktail-dress side.

As of 2009, DuPont remains the world's largest maker of pantyhose material, and its marketing research efforts have proven successful, thanks to its intensive use of qualitative research.[32] ■

Construction Techniques

construction technique
A projective technique in which the respondent is required to construct a response in the form of a story, dialogue, or description.

Construction techniques are closely related to completion techniques. Construction techniques require the respondent to construct a response in the form of a story, dialogue, or description. In a construction technique, the researcher provides less initial structure to the respondent than in a completion technique. The two main construction techniques are (1) picture response and (2) cartoons.

PICTURE RESPONSE The roots of **picture response techniques** can be traced to the Thematic Apperception Test (TAT), which consists of a series of pictures of ordinary as well as unusual events. In some of these pictures, the persons or objects are clearly depicted, while in others they are relatively vague. The respondent is asked to tell stories about these pictures. The respondent's interpretation of the pictures gives indications of that individual's personality. For example, an individual may be characterized as impulsive, creative, unimaginative, and so on. The name "Thematic Apperception Test" is used because themes are elicited based on the subject's perceptual interpretation (apperception) of pictures.

picture response technique
A projective technique in which the respondent is shown a picture and asked to tell a story describing it.

In marketing research uses of picture response techniques, respondents are shown a picture and asked to tell a story describing it. The responses are used to evaluate attitudes toward the topic and describe the respondents. In a variation of this technique, such as Zaltman's Metaphor Elicitation Technique, the respondents are asked to bring 12 to 15 pictures of their choice to the interview and then asked to describe the salient content of each picture. The picture descriptions reveal the underlying values, attitudes, and beliefs of the respondents. In another variation called *photo sort*, respondents are provided with a photo deck portraying different types of people. Respondents sort the photos to connect the people in the photos with the brands that they would use. A photo sort for Visa revealed that the credit card had a middle-of-the road, female image. Therefore, Visa renewed its relationship with the National Football League through 2010 to attract more males. Another variation of this technique requires the respondents to draw pictures or drawings to express their feelings about the brand or object being investigated. Another illustration of the picture response technique is provided by the example on some consumers' preference for high-fat food rich in calories.

Real Research   "Gimme a Double Shake and a Lard on White"

The light and healthy craze seems to be dying down for one segment of the population. In response to direct questioning, consumers are hesitant to say they want food that is bad for them. However, this finding emerged in a picture response test in which the respondents were asked to describe a picture depicting people consuming high-fat food rich in calories. A significant number of the respondents defended the behavior of the people in the picture, explaining that the increased stress in everyday life has caused people to turn from tasteless rice cakes to comfort foods loaded with the ingredients that make life worth living.

FIGURE 5.4

A Cartoon Test

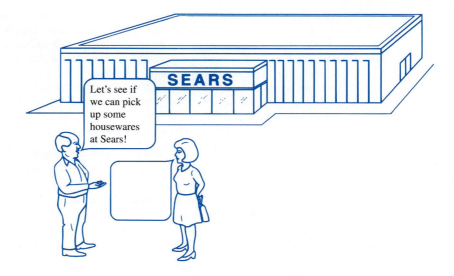

cartoon tests
Cartoon characters are shown in a specific situation related to the problem. The respondents are asked to indicate the dialogue that one cartoon character might make in response to the comments of another character.

expressive techniques
Projective techniques in which the respondent is presented with a verbal or visual situation and asked to relate the feelings and attitudes of other people to the situation.

role playing
Respondents are asked to assume the behavior of someone else.

Many marketers have capitalized upon this finding by introducing products that contain large amounts of fat and calories. Pepperidge Farm recently introduced its own bid for the comfort food market: no-calories-barred soft-baked cookies with about 40 percent of the calories coming from fat. The new line is already the third biggest seller for the company.

Fast-food restaurants like McDonald's also rolled out several new products that were extremely high in fat and calories for the New Tastes Menu. McDonald's new products included the fried Chicken Parmesan sandwich smothered with cheese and tomato sauce, and a portable breakfast sandwich that had a sausage patty surrounded by two pancakes.[33] ■

CARTOON TESTS In **cartoon tests**, cartoon characters are shown in a specific situation related to the problem. The respondents are asked to indicate what one cartoon character might say in response to the comments of another character. The responses indicate the respondents' feelings, beliefs, and attitudes toward the situation. Cartoon tests are simpler to administer and analyze than picture response techniques. An example is shown in Figure 5.4.

Expressive Techniques

In **expressive techniques**, respondents are presented with a verbal or visual situation and asked to relate the feelings and attitudes of other people to the situation. The respondents express not their own feelings or attitudes, but those of others. The two main expressive techniques are role playing and third-person technique.

ROLE PLAYING In **role playing**, respondents are asked to play the role or assume the behavior of someone else. The researcher assumes that the respondents will project their own feelings into the role. These can then be uncovered by analyzing the responses, as shown in the department store patronage project.[34]

Real Research   What Is Privacy?

When focus groups revealed that privacy was a major concern of apartment residents, an apartment builder became concerned with how people view privacy. The research company, Cossette Communication Group (www.cossette.com), used the role-playing technique to gain the required information. Respondents were asked to play the role of an architect and design their own apartment homes using the boards provided. After the homes were designed, a series of research questions were asked. These questions addressed how the participants perceived privacy. For example, the respondents were asked how much space was needed between rooms to make them feel that their privacy would not be invaded, and how much sound should be audible through walls. The marketing research company felt that it would be more effective to have subjects become involved in a role-playing activity followed by questions on why they did what they did, rather than simply asking subjects what they would do in a certain situation. "We had people show us what privacy meant to them, rather than assuming they could explain it to us in words." The results helped the building company in designing and building apartments so that occupants would be more comfortable and feel more private. Walls between bedrooms were made to absorb more sound so that voices would not carry as easily. Additionally, bedrooms were set further apart instead of directly adjacent to each other. Apartments were built so that bedrooms were on opposite sides of the building. This way, roommates would not feel that their privacy was being compromised. The construction company benefited greatly from Cossette's creative methods of research, as demonstrated by the increased customer satisfaction that resulted from individuals feeling more confident about maintaining their privacy.[35] ■

third-person technique

A projective technique in which the respondent is presented with a verbal or visual situation and asked to relate the beliefs and attitudes of a third person to the situation.

THIRD-PERSON TECHNIQUE In **third-person technique**, the respondent is presented with a verbal or visual situation and asked to relate the beliefs and attitudes of a third person rather than directly expressing personal beliefs and attitudes. This third person may be a friend, neighbor, colleague, or a "typical" person. Again, the researcher assumes that the respondent will reveal personal beliefs and attitudes while describing the reactions of a third party. Asking the individual to respond in the third person reduces the social pressure to give an acceptable answer, as the following example shows.

Real Research   ## What Will the Neighbors Say?

A study was performed for a commercial airline to understand why some people do not fly. When the respondents were asked, "Are you afraid to fly?" very few people said yes. The major reasons given for not flying were cost, inconvenience, and delays caused by bad weather. However, it was suspected that the answers were heavily influenced by the need to give socially desirable responses. Therefore, a follow-up study was done. In the second study, the respondents were asked, "Do you think your neighbor is afraid to fly?" The answers indicated that most of the neighbors who traveled by some other means of transportation were afraid to fly.

The fear of flying increased after the highjackings of September 11, 2001. The Air Transport Association (ATA) reported that passenger enplanements, the number of ticketed passengers that board the airplane, were down. However, Continental Airlines, which addressed the fear of flying by stressing heightened security measures and enhanced cabin comforts for passengers, suffered a much lower drop in passenger enplanements.[36] ■

Note that asking the question in the first person ("Are you afraid to fly?") did not elicit the true response. Phrasing the same question in the third person ("Do you think your neighbor is afraid to fly?") lowered the respondent's defenses and resulted in truthful answers. In a popular version of the third-person technique, the researcher presents the respondent with a description of a shopping list and asks for a characterization of the purchaser.[37]

We conclude our discussion of projective techniques by describing their advantages, disadvantages, and applications.

Advantages and Disadvantages of Projective Techniques

Projective techniques have a major advantage over the unstructured direct techniques (focus groups and depth interviews): They may elicit responses that subjects would be unwilling or unable to give if they knew the purpose of the study. At times, in direct questioning, the respondent may intentionally or unintentionally misunderstand, misinterpret, or mislead the researcher. In these cases, projective techniques can increase the validity of responses by disguising the purpose. This is particularly true when the issues to be addressed are personal, sensitive, or subject to strong social norms. Projective techniques are also helpful when underlying motivations, beliefs, and attitudes are operating at a subconscious level.[38]

Projective techniques suffer from many of the disadvantages of unstructured direct techniques, but to a greater extent. These techniques generally require personal interviews with highly trained interviewers. Skilled interpreters are also required to analyze the responses. Hence, they tend to be expensive. Furthermore, there is a serious risk of interpretation bias. With the exception of word association, all techniques are open ended, making the analysis and interpretation difficult and subjective. Some projective techniques, such as role playing, require respondents to engage in unusual behavior. In such cases, the researcher may assume that respondents who agree to participate are themselves unusual in some way. Therefore, they may not be representative of the population of interest.

Applications of Projective Techniques

Projective techniques are used less frequently than unstructured direct methods (focus groups and depth interviews). A possible exception may be word association, which is used commonly to test brand names and occasionally to measure attitudes about particular products, brands, packages, or advertisements. As the examples have shown, projective techniques can be used in a variety of situations. The usefulness of these techniques is enhanced when the following guidelines are observed.

1. Projective techniques should be used because the required information cannot be accurately obtained by direct methods.
2. Projective techniques should be used for exploratory research to gain initial insights and understanding.
3. Given their complexity, projective techniques should not be used naively.

As a result, it is desirable to compare findings generated by projective techniques with the findings of the other techniques that permit a more representative sample. Table 5.5 gives a relative comparison of focus groups, depth interviews, and projective techniques. Given these comparisons, the various qualitative techniques should not be viewed as mutually exclusive. They can often be used in combination to yield valuable information, as illustrated by the following example.

Real Research   Just the Facts, Please

Just The Facts, Inc. (JTF, www.just-the-facts.com) consults with clients in areas such as competitive intelligence and marketing research. In one of the projects in the education field, for example, four suburban high school districts and a community college had created a student careers program. However, the student interest level and image of the program was not encouraging involvement or achieving significant participation among the intended target audience.

TABLE 5.5

A Comparison of Focus Groups, Depth Interviews, and Projective Techniques

Criteria	Focus Groups	Depth Interviews	Projective Techniques
Degree of structure	Relatively high	Relatively medium	Relatively low
Probing of individual respondents	Low	High	Medium
Moderator bias	Relatively medium	Relatively high	Low to high
Interpretation bias	Relatively low	Relatively medium	Relatively high
Uncovering subconscious information	Low	Medium to high	High
Discovering innovative information	High	Medium	Low
Obtaining sensitive information	Low	Medium	High
Involve unusual behavior/questioning	No	To a limited extent	Yes
Overall usefulness	Highly useful	Useful	Somewhat useful

JTF Consulting Associates were given the assignment of determining why participation levels were so low, and what could be done to improve the program's appeal. They conducted focus groups, depth interviews, and sentence completion techniques with those involved in the program: teachers, guidance counselors, students, parents, and administrators.

The focus groups were conducted with teachers, counselors, students, and parents to generate new ideas. Depth interviews were conducted with administrators since it was difficult to assemble them in groups. Additional insights were obtained from students by also administering the sentence completion technique. The analysis showed that the actual problem was in the image of the program as much as in its quality. The target audience (student community) did not perceive the program to be useful in finding a suitable job. It was found that the program needed repositioning through effective marketing and PR efforts. A strategic marketing plan, advertising, and promotional tactics were formulated on the basis of the study. The coordinators of the program responded with a strong PR campaign in the local media. They also conducted reach-out programs at schools and the community college. The entire program was relaunched, addressing the needs of the various audiences. Finally, JTF was also asked to develop new informational brochures and a videotape to help communicate the renewed direction and image of the program.[39] ■

Project Research — Project Activities

1. Discuss the role of qualitative research in the Sears project.
2. Given the qualitative research objectives, develop a focus group discussion guide.
3. Illustrate the use of laddering, hidden issue questioning, and symbolic analysis in conducting depth interviews for Sears.
4. How can expressive techniques be used to determine underlying attitudes toward Sears? ■

ACTIVE RESEARCH

Projecting Cosmetic Usage

Visit www.clinique.com and search the Internet using a search engine as well as your library's online databases to obtain information on the underlying reasons why women use cosmetics.

As the brand manager for Clinique, how would you use information on the reasons why women use cosmetics to formulate marketing strategies that would increase your market share?

Which, if any, of the projective techniques would you use to determine the reasons why women use cosmetics?

Analysis of Qualitative Data

Compared to quantitative research, where numbers and what they stand for are the units of analysis, qualitative data analysis uses words as the units of analysis and is guided by fewer universal rules and standard procedures. The goal in qualitative research is to decipher, examine, and interpret meaningful patterns or themes that emerge out of the data. The "meaningfulness" of patterns and themes is determined by the research question at hand.

There are three general steps that should be followed when analyzing qualitative data.[40]

1. *Data reduction.* In this step, the researcher chooses which aspects of the data are emphasized, minimized, or set aside for the project at hand.
2. *Data display.* In this step, the researcher develops a visual interpretation of the data with the use of such tools as a diagram, chart, or matrix. The display helps to illuminate patterns and interrelationships in the data.
3. *Conclusion drawing and verification.* In this step, the researcher considers the meaning of analyzed data and assesses its implications for the research question at hand.

These steps are illustrated in the following example.

Real Research   Effectively Communicating Campus News: A Qualitative Analysis

Suppose that a researcher collects qualitative data using focus groups with a sample of graduate college students to provide insight on the following research question:

> What are the most effective ways of communicating important campus news
> (e.g., death of faculty member, payment deadlines, campus power outage) to
> graduate college students?

Following the steps laid out earlier, after collecting the data, the researcher would first want to choose which aspects of the data are pertinent to the research question at hand. To do this, he or she would highlight particular pieces or "chunks" of the focus group transcripts that shed light on the research issue. For example, in this case the researcher may decide that it is important to consider (a) the ways that the respondents recall receiving important news in the past, (b) the respondents' opinions on what means of communication they feel are most effective, and (c) the respondents' explanations for why they feel these are the most effective ways of communication. The transcripts would then be coded to reflect these categories of interest. After coding the data, the researcher may want to visually display the data in order to make the findings more clear. An example of this is shown by the following chart:

Respondent	(a) Past Communications	(b) Most Effective	(c) Why
A	• E-mail • Informal interchanges • Telephone	• E-mail	• News is communicated in almost "real time"
B	• E-mail • Student newspaper • Campus Web page	• E-mail • Campus Web page	• Easy to keep a record of the news for future reference
C	• Informal interchanges • Telephone • Campus mail	• Campus mail	• Work on campus • Do not have Internet access at home

In order to draw conclusions from the data, it is important not only to know what the respondents felt were the most effective ways of communication, but also why they felt that way. For example, by asking why, we see that respondent C has a logical explanation for why he did not name e-mail as an effective means of communication for him. In addition, even though both respondents A and B named e-mail as an effective way to communicate information, they both had markedly different reasons for doing so. These types of insights are more difficult to obtain with quantitative research that uses a survey or an experiment. ■

Software Packages

Software packages are available that can be used to assist in the analysis of qualitative data. There are six main types: word processors, word retrievers, text-base managers, code-and-retrieve programs, code-based theory builders, and conceptual network builders. It is important to remember that although these packages may help in the manipulation of relevant text segments, they cannot determine meaningful categories for coding or define important themes and factors; these steps are the responsibility of the researcher. In addition, because large investments in both time and money are needed to purchase and learn how to use the software, researchers should take the time to consider whether a software package is needed, given the scope of the project.

If you do decide to purchase and use a software package to aid in your qualitative analysis, then it is important to be aware of the specific things that various programs can do for you. These include:

1. Coding. Programs can help you segment or "chunk" your data and assign codes to key words or to "chunks."
2. Memoing/Annotation. Programs can allow you to make side notes that correspond to sections of your data. These side notes can help to provide meaning to the data.

3. Data Linking. Programs can help you keep track of relationships between different parts of the database, including your transcripts, codes, and memos.
4. Search and Retrieval. Programs can allow you to search for specific words or strings of words using Boolean requests.
5. Conceptual/Theory Development. Programs can help you develop a theory with the use of rule-based hypothesis testing or by building semantic networks.
6. Data Display. Programs can show results onscreen or even with split screens.
7. Graphics Editing. Programs can help you create and edit networks composed of nodes connected by links.

Some of the most popular software packages are XSight and NVivo (www. qsrinter-national.com), ATLAS.ti (www.atlasti.com), CATPACII (www.terraresearch.com), and Ethnograph (www.qualisresearch.com). These Web sites offer information about the software packages and also sample demonstration copies.

Experiential Research

Qualitative Data Analysis Software

Visit the Web sites of XSight and NVivo (www.qsrinternational.com), ATLAS.ti (www.atlasti.com), CATPACII (www.terraresearch.com), and Ethnograph (www.qualisresearch.com) and download the sample demonstration copies for any two of the software packages. Compare and contrast the two with respect to the following questions:

1. Evaluate the "user friendliness" of the two packages. How hard is the program to learn? How easy is the program to use? Do you think the time and effort required to gain an understanding of the program is worth it?
2. Evaluate the availability and usefulness of the support material available on the Web site. How good are the manuals or other documentation? Are tutorials and other technical support available and easy to navigate?
3. Do the programs allow you to produce visual displays such as matrix displays, semantic networks, or hierarchical diagrams? ■

International Marketing Research

Because the researcher is often not familiar with the foreign product market to be examined, qualitative research is crucial in international marketing research. In the initial stages of cross-national research, qualitative research can provide insights into the problem and help in developing an approach by generating relevant research questions and hypotheses, models, and characteristics that influence the research design. Thus, qualitative research may reveal the differences between the foreign and domestic markets. Focus groups can be used in many settings, particularly in industrialized countries. However, professional standards and practices may vary from the United States. For example, in Mexico it is considered acceptable for recruiters to invite family and friends to participate in a focus group. In some countries like India and Bolivia, due to lack of proper facilities, focus groups are held in hotels with closed-circuit monitoring. The moderator should not only be trained in focus group methodology but should also be familiar with the language, culture, and patterns of social interaction prevailing in that country. The focus group findings should be derived not only from the verbal contents but also from nonverbal cues like voice intonations, inflections, expressions, and gestures.[41]

The size of the focus group could also vary. For example, in Asia seven respondents produce the highest level of interaction among group members. In some regions, such as in the Middle or Far East, people are hesitant to discuss their feelings in a group setting. In other countries such as Japan, people think it is impolite to disagree with others publicly. In these cases, depth interviews should be used. Moreover, qualitative data that are generated should be interpreted in the context of the culture. The following example highlights the importance of cultural differences in qualitative research.

Real Research   ## Bugs Bug British

Culture is a very important determinant of how qualitative research, such as focus groups, should be conducted. In focus group discussions in Britain, it is not easy to make a housewife admit her house has cockroaches. To do this, the moderator must reassure her that everyone else has the problem too. In France, just the opposite occurs: The respondents start to chatter away about cockroaches within seconds of sitting down. These cultural attitudes greatly influence which qualitative research techniques should be used, how they should be implemented, and how the data should be interpreted.[42] ∎

The use of projective techniques in international marketing research should be carefully considered. Association techniques (word association), completion techniques (sentence completion, story completion), and expressive techniques (role playing, third-person technique) involve the use of verbal cues. Construction techniques (picture response and cartoon tests) employ nonverbal stimuli (pictures). Whether verbal or nonverbal stimuli are used, the equivalence of meaning across the cultures should be established. This can be a difficult task if the sociocultural environments in which the research is conducted vary greatly. Establishing the equivalence of pictures can be particularly problematic. Line drawings are subject to fewer problems of interpretation than photographs. The specific techniques that are used and how the results are communicated should take into account the cultural aspects and the nature of the problem being addressed, as illustrated in the following example.

Real Research   ## Video Safaris

Pierre Bélisle, who heads Bélisle Marketing (www.pbelisle.com), buys into the idea that "If you want to understand how a lion hunts, don't go to the zoo. Go to the jungle." A recent project by Bélisle Marketing demonstrated that the trophies from such "safaris" can be brought back more easily and less expensively than ever before, thanks to current video technology.

Canada Post, Canada's national postal system, sought feedback from consumers on a redesign of its retail post offices. They appointed Bélisle Marketing to perform this task. The client sought to explore the strengths and any weaknesses of the redesign as expressed in a prototype transformation of a flagship store. It seemed clear that only an expedition to this location could answer the client's information needs. The qualitative portion of the design included on-location, task-based interviews during working hours, on-location mini-groups after hours, and traditional in-facility focus groups with a field trip to the outlet. Bélisle Marketing felt that a traditional written report would be inadequate to display the findings of this research. They therefore proposed that the on-location interviews and mini-groups be videotaped and that a video report be produced instead of a traditional written report.

The results were powerful. The report told in detail what the customers wanted. For example, Canada Post got to know where exactly the customers wanted the post boxes to be positioned and which would be the ideal location for the counter. They also understood how a self-service weighing machine would help the customer to weigh and post an envelope without help from the staff. Canada Post has decided to roll out the new design to more outlets, along with many modifications suggested in the video.[43] ∎

The usual limitations of qualitative techniques also apply in the international context, perhaps to a greater extent. It is often difficult to find trained moderators and interviewers overseas. The development of appropriate coding, analysis, and interpretation procedures poses additional difficulties.

Ethics in Marketing Research

When conducting qualitative research, ethical issues related to the respondents and the general public are of primary concern. These issues include disguising the purpose of the research and the use of deceptive procedures, videotaping and recording the proceedings, the comfort level of the respondents, and misusing the findings of qualitative research.[44]

All indirect procedures require disguising the purpose of the research, at least to some extent. Often, a cover story is used to camouflage the true purpose. This can violate the respondents' right to know and also result in psychological harm. For example, respondents may be

Qualitative research helped
Canada Post, Canada's
national postal system,
redesign its outlets to
better meet the needs of
its customers.

upset if, after responding to a series of completion techniques, they discovered that they had spent their time on a trivial issue such as what should be the color of the can of a new orange drink, when they had been recruited to participate in a study on nutrition. To minimize such negative effects, the respondents should be informed up front that the true purpose of the research is being disguised so as not to bias the responses. After completing the research tasks, debriefing sessions should be held in which the respondents are informed about the true purpose and given opportunities to make comments or ask questions. Deceptive procedures that violate respondents' right to privacy and informed consent should be avoided, for example, allowing clients to observe focus groups or in-depth interviews by introducing them as colleagues helping with the project.

An ethical dilemma involves videotaping or recording the focus group or the depth interview. Video- or audiotaping the respondents without their prior knowledge or consent raises ethical concerns. Ethical guidelines suggest that respondents should be informed and their consent obtained prior to the start of the proceedings, preferably at the time of recruitment. Furthermore, at the end of the meeting, participants should be asked to sign a written statement conveying their permission to use the recording. This statement should disclose the true purpose of the research and all people who will have access to the recording. Participants should be given an opportunity to refuse to sign. The tapes should be edited to completely omit the identity and comments of the respondents who have refused.

Another concern that needs to be addressed is the comfort level of the respondents. During qualitative research, particularly during in-depth interviews, respondents should not be pushed beyond a point so as to make them uncomfortable. Respect for the respondent's welfare should warrant restraint on the part of the moderator or interviewer. If a respondent feels uncomfortable and does not wish to answer more questions on a particular topic, the interviewer should not aggressively probe further. A final issue relates to the general public and deals with the ethics of using qualitative research results for questionable purposes, as in the political campaigns profiled in the following example.

Real Research   Focusing on Mudslinging in Presidential Campaigns

The ethics of negative or "attack" ads has been under debate for some time. However, the focus has shifted from the ads themselves to the ethics of employing marketing research techniques to design the ad message. Nowhere, perhaps, is this phenomenon more prevalent than in political "mudslinging" presidential campaigns. In particular, the George H. W. Bush campaign against Michael Dukakis has been cited. In designing negative ads about Dukakis, the Bush campaign leaders tested negative information about

Dukakis in focus groups. The idea was to develop some insight into how the American public would react if this negative information were released in the form of advertisements. Negative issues that elicited very negative emotions from the focus groups were chosen to be incorporated into Bush's political advertising. The result? Painted " . . . as an ineffectual, weak, liberal, do-gooder lacking in common sense . . . ," Dukakis lost the election by a wide margin. Similar (mis)use of qualitative research was observed in the 1992 and 1996 presidential elections that Bill Clinton won in part by negatively attacking the Republicans. In the 2000 presidential election, Al Gore unfairly attacked George W. Bush as lacking in experience when focus groups revealed that experience was an important criterion for voters. The 2004 presidential elections were also cited for negative attacks by both parties, particularly by John Kerry on George W. Bush, again based on focus group and survey findings on issues such as Iraq and the economy. Perhaps, the 2008 presidential election is unsurpassed in terms of negative attacks by both Barack Obama and John McCain based on the perceived weaknesses of the opponent identified through focus groups and other qualitative research procedures.[45] ■

Decision Research | Lotus Development Corporation: Developing Its Web Site

The Situation

Mike Rhodin is president and CEO of Lotus Development Corporation (www.lotus.com), which is one of the brands of the IBM Software group. Lotus is a company that recognizes the need for individuals and businesses to work together and therefore redefines the concept of conducting business through practical knowledge management, e-business, and other groundbreaking ways of connecting the world's ideas, thinkers, buyers, sellers, and communities via the Internet. As of 2009, Lotus markets its products in more than 80 countries worldwide through direct and extensive business partner channels. The company also provides numerous professional consulting, support, and education services through the Lotus Professional Services organization. To stay ahead of the competitors, Rhodin wishes to increase their site's number of hits and wants Lotus to maintain a Web site that is going to best meet the needs of its customers.

Lotus conducts focus groups of customers and business partners every four months to determine users' reaction to its Web site. This routine of focus groups recognizes the fact that Web sites are products with very short life cycles and need ongoing attention to keep them up-to-date. The focus groups evaluate Lotus' Web site and the sites of other companies. Some objectives for the focus groups include identifying factors that lead Internet users to visit a Web site, identifying what factors entice visitors to return often to a Web site, and identifying users' technological capabilities.

The use of focus groups allows Lotus to actively collect some information that is not collected passively. Passive counters can keep track of the number of visitors to a Web site, as well as the number of visitors who actually use the site. For example, Lotus can monitor the number of visitors who use its chat rooms that pertain to specific products. However, just knowing that the number of visitors is changing does not provide a company with insights concerning why there is a decrease or increase in visitors. Focus groups are ways to gain those insights.

From focus groups, Lotus learned that customers wanted improved navigation and a higher level of consistency. In the past, the emphasis was on making sure that information was delivered quickly to customers. Focus groups revealed that the company needed to further develop the site to make it easier for Web site visitors to navigate through all of that information.

The Marketing Research Decision

1. Do you think that Lotus' use of focus groups was appropriate?
2. What type of research designs would you recommend and why?
3. Discuss the role of the type of research you recommend in enabling Mike Rhodin to design an effective Web site.

The Marketing Management Decision

1. What should Mike Rhodin do to increase the traffic and enhance the experience of visitors to the Web site?
2. Discuss how the marketing management decision action that you recommend to Mike Rhodin is influenced by the research design that you suggested earlier and by the findings of that research.[46] ■

Summary

Qualitative and quantitative research should be viewed as complementary. Qualitative research methods may be direct or indirect. In direct methods, respondents are able to discern the true purpose of the research, while indirect methods disguise the purpose of the research. The major direct methods are focus groups and depth interviews. Focus groups are conducted in a group setting, whereas depth interviews are done one-on-one. Focus group interviews are the most widely used qualitative research technique.

The indirect techniques are called projective techniques because they aim to project the respondent's motivations, beliefs, attitudes, and feelings onto ambiguous situations. The projective techniques may be classified as association (word association), completion (sentence completion, story completion), construction (picture response, cartoon tests), and expressive (role playing, third person) techniques. Projective techniques are particularly useful when respondents are unwilling or unable to provide the required information by direct methods. Figure 5.5 is a concept map for qualitative research.

Qualitative research can reveal the salient differences between the domestic and foreign markets. Whether focus groups or depth interviews should be conducted and how the findings should be interpreted depends heavily on the cultural differences. When conducting qualitative research, the researcher and the client must respect the respondents. This should include protecting the anonymity of respondents, honoring all statements and promises used to ensure participation, and conducting research in a way that does not embarrass or harm the respondents. Focus groups, depth interviews, and projective techniques can also be conducted via the Internet. Microcomputers and mainframes can be used to select and screen respondents and in coding and analyzing qualitative data.

Key Terms and Concepts

qualitative research, 139
quantitative research, 139
direct approach, 140
indirect approach, 141
focus group, 141
telesessions, 149
depth interview, 153
laddering, 154

hidden issue questioning, 154
symbolic analysis, 154
grounded theory, 157
protocol interview, 157
projective technique, 158
association techniques, 158
word association, 158
completion techniques, 159

sentence completion, 159
story completion, 159
construction technique, 160
picture response technique, 160
cartoon tests, 161
expressive techniques, 161
role playing, 161
third-person technique, 162

FIGURE 5.5

A Concept Map for Qualitative Research

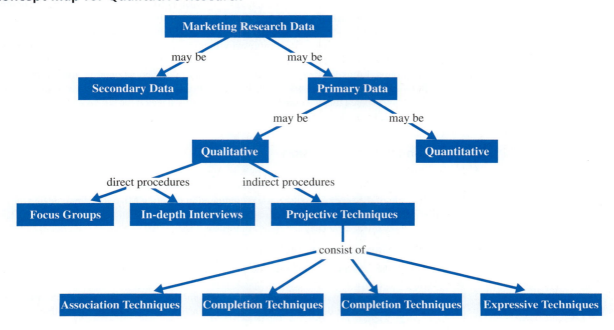

Suggested Cases, Video Cases, and HBS Cases

Running Case with Real Data

1.1 Dell

Comprehensive Critical Thinking Cases

2.1 American Idol   2.2 Baskin-Robbins   2.3 Akron Children's Hospital

Comprehensive Cases with Real Data

4.1 JPMorgan Chase   4.2 Wendy's

Video Cases

5.1 Nike   6.1 Starbucks   8.1 P&G   10.1 Dunkin' Donuts

11.1 Motorola   12.1 Subaru   13.1 Intel   23.1 Marriott   24.1 Nivea

Comprehensive Harvard Business School Cases

Case 5.1: The Harvard Graduate Student Housing Survey (9-505-059)
Case 5.2: BizRate.Com (9-501-024)
Case 5.3: Cola Wars Continue: Coke and Pepsi in the Twenty-First Century (9-702-442)
Case 5.4: TiVo in 2002 (9-502-062)
Case 5.5: Compaq Computer: Intel Inside? (9-599-061)
Case 5.6: The New Beetle (9-501-023)

Live Research: Conducting a Marketing Research Project

1. In most projects, it would be important to conduct some form of qualitative research.
2. Assign different teams different responsibilities, for example, interviewing key decision makers, interviewing industry experts, conducting depth interviews with consumers, doing a focus group, and so on.

Acronyms

The key characteristics of a focus group may be described by the acronym

Focus Groups:

F ocused (on a particular topic)
O utline prepared for discussion
C haracteristics of the moderator
U nstructured
S ize: 8–12
G roup composition: homogeneous
R ecorded: audiocassettes and videotapes
O bservation: one-way mirror
U ndisguised
P hysical setting: relaxed
S everal sessions needed: 1–3 hours each

The main features of a depth interview may be summarized by the acronym

Depth:

D epth of coverage
E ach respondent individually interviewed
P robe the respondent
T alented interviewer required
H idden motives may be uncovered

The main characteristics of projective techniques may be described by the acronym

Projective:

P roject the underlying motivations, beliefs, attitudes
R elationship: association techniques
O vercome respondent's unwillingness or inability to answer
J udgment required in interpretation of responses
E xpressive techniques
C onstruction, completion techniques
T hematic: themes are elicited
I ndirect
V ague situations are used as stimuli
E xploratory in nature

Exercises

Questions

1. What are the primary differences between qualitative and quantitative research techniques?
2. What is qualitative research and how is it conducted?
3. Differentiate between direct and indirect qualitative research. Give an example of each.
4. Why is the focus group the most popular qualitative research technique?
5. Why is the focus group moderator so important in obtaining quality results?
6. What are some key qualifications of focus group moderators?
7. Why should the researcher guard against using professional respondents?
8. Give two ways in which focus groups can be misused.
9. What is the difference between a dual moderator and a dueling-moderator group?
10. What is the conference call technique? What are the advantages and disadvantages of this technique?
11. What is a depth interview? Under what circumstances is it preferable to focus groups?

12. What are the major advantages of depth interviews?
13. What are projective techniques? What are the four types of projective techniques?
14. Describe the term *association technique*. Give an example of a situation in which this technique is especially useful.
15. When should projective techniques be employed?

Problems

1. Following the methods outlined in the text, develop a plan for conducting a focus group to determine consumers' attitudes toward and preferences for imported automobiles. Specify the objectives of the focus group, write a screening questionnaire, and develop a moderator's outline.
2. Suppose Baskin Robbins wants to know why some people do not eat ice cream regularly. Develop a cartoon test for this purpose.

Internet and Computer Exercises

1. The Coca-Cola Company has asked you to conduct Internet focus groups with heavy users of soft drinks. Explain how you would identify and recruit such respondents.
2. Could a depth interview be conducted via the Internet? What are the advantages and disadvantages of this procedure over conventional depth interviews?
3. Visit the Web site of the Qualitative Research Consultants Association (www.qrca.org). Write a report about the current state of the art in qualitative research.

4. *Tennis* magazine would like to recruit participants for online focus groups. How would you make use of a newsgroup (Usenet: rec.sport.tennis) to recruit participants?
5. Obtain the CATPACII program discussed in the text. Use it to analyze the data from depth interviews that you have conducted with three fellow students (as the respondents) to determine attitude toward sports.

Activities

Role Playing

1. You are a marketing research consultant hired to organize focus groups for an innovative German-style fast-food restaurant. What kind of people would you select to participate in focus groups? What screening criteria would you use? What questions would you ask?
2. As a marketing researcher, persuade your boss (a fellow student) not to bypass quantitative research once the qualitative research has been conducted.

Fieldwork

1. The campus athletic center is trying to determine why more students do not use its facilities. Conduct a series of focus groups to determine what could be done to attract more students to the athletic center. Based on the focus group results, generate the relevant hypotheses.
2. A cosmetics firm would like to increase its penetration of the female student market. It hires you as a consultant to obtain an understanding and preliminary insights into the attitudes, purchases, and use of cosmetics by female students. Conduct at least five depth interviews. Employ the construction technique as well. Do your findings from the two techniques agree? If not, try to reconcile the discrepancy.

Group Discussion

1. In a group of 5 or 6, discuss whether qualitative research is scientific.
2. "If the focus group findings confirm prior expectations, the client should dispense with quantitative research." Discuss this statement in a small group.
3. As a small group of 5 or 6, discuss the following statement: "Quantitative research is more important than qualitative research because it results in statistical information and conclusive findings."

Dell Running Case

Review the Dell case, Case 1.1, and questionnaire given toward the end of the book.

1. In gaining an understanding of the consumer decision-making process for personal computer purchases, would focus groups or depth interviews be more useful? Explain.
2. Develop a focus group discussion guide for understanding the consumer decision-making process for personal computer purchases.
3. Can projective techniques be useful to Dell as it seeks to increase its penetration of U.S. households? Which projective technique(s) would you recommend?
4. Devise word association techniques to measure consumer associations that might affect attitudes toward personal computer purchases.
5. Design sentence completion techniques to uncover underlying motives for personal computer purchases.

Video Cases

VIDEO CASE 5.1 Nike: Associating Athletes, Performance, and the Brand

Nike is the largest seller of athletic footwear, athletic apparel, and other athletic gear in the world, with about 30 percent market share worldwide. Nike markets its products under its own brand, as well as Nike Golf, Nike Pro, Air Jordan, Team Starter, and subsidiaries, including Bauer, Cole Haan, Hurley International, and Converse. As of 2009, the company sells its products through a mix of independent distributors, licensees, and subsidiaries in approximately 120 countries worldwide. Nike has grown from an $8,000 company in 1963 to a company with revenues of $19.65 billion for the year ended May 31, 2008.

In 2008, Nike spent an enormous amount of money, more than a billion dollars, on advertising, endorsements, and sales promotion. In order to make sure that this money is being spent properly, Nike relies on marketing research. It has shown a history of innovation and inspiration in its marketing and is quick to adapt to the changing consumer and the world of sports. Nike has used marketing research in understanding where the future growth lies. A recent example is Nike's shift from marketing in the more traditional sports (basketball and running) to other sports (golf and soccer), where it has not been as strong. Marketing research surveys revealed that the awareness of Nike among soccer and golf players was low, and Nike decided to work on increasing these numbers. Nike has decided that the money needed for licenses in its strong areas can be better spent in other areas where Nike does not have the brand awareness.

Today, the Nike Swoosh is recognized around the world. This is the result of more than 40 years of work and innovation. It signed the first athletes to wear its shoes in 1973. Early on, Nike realized the importance of associating athletes with its products. The partnerships help relate the excellence of the athlete with the perception of the brand. Through focus groups and surveys, Nike discovered the pyramid influence, which shows that the mass market can be influenced by the preferences of a small group of top athletes. After it realized this effect, Nike began to spend millions on celebrity endorsements. The association with the athlete also helps dimensionalize the company and what it believes in. With Nike, this was, and remains, extremely important. It wants to convey a message that the company's goal is to bring innovation to every athlete in the world. Nike also uses the athletes to design new products by attempting to meet their individual goals.

Explaining Nike's strategy of celebrity endorsements, Trevor Edwards, vice president of U.S. Brand Management, says that the sports figures, such as Ronaldo, Michael Jordan, and Tiger Woods, who have endorsed Nike brands all have represented excellence in some way. Nevertheless, the athletes also have a personal side, such as their drive to win or their ability to remain humble. All these qualities speak something about the Nike brand; this not only benefits the brand, but also helps to define what the Nike brand is and what it stands for.

The company also realized that in order to achieve its lofty growth goals, it must appeal to multiple market segments. Based on marketing research, Nike divided the market into three different groups: the ultimate athlete, the athletics participant, and the consumer who is influenced by sports culture. The first segment is the professional athletes. The second constituency is the participants, those who participate in sports and athletic activities but do not see themselves as athletes or as being part of the larger sport. The third segment comprises those who influence others and are influenced by the world of sports. These three different constituencies form three different consumer segments, and Nike uses very different strategies for each.

Nike has always been an aggressive user of marketing research and this has been shown in its attack on the European market. It decided to concentrate on different sports in order to reach European consumers. Americans love baseball. And football. And basketball. But Europe's favorite game is soccer. Nike placed its focus on major sporting events (World Cups and Olympics) and celebrity athletes that are relevant to the European consumer. Marketing research in the form of focus groups and survey research revealed that the best positioning for Nike shoes was one that enhanced performance in the sport. Through massive advertising campaigns, it has been able to change the perception of its products from fashion to performance, and in the process increase sales dramatically.

Another technique Nike has used is to specifically design a product line for a certain market. Nike uses marketing research to determine the lifestyles and product usage characteristics of a particular market segment and then designs products for that segment. An example is the Presto line, which was designed for a certain youth lifestyle. Nike focused on the lifestyle and designed the products around this group. It also used marketing research to determine the most effective media to communicate with the target market.

Because of these methods, the Nike logo is recognized by 97 percent of U.S. citizens, and its sales have soared as a result. However, Nike faces a new concern: that it has lost its traditional image of being a smaller, innovative company. It also faces future obstacles in maintaining brand equity and brand meaning. Continued reliance on marketing research will help Nike to meet these challenges, associate its brand with top athletes and performance, and enhance its image.

Conclusion

Nike used marketing research to build its brand into one of the most well-known and easily recognized brands in the world. Nike's strategy of celebrity endorsements, its expansion into Europe, and the resulting stronger association with soccer are some of the steps taken by Nike to grow its brand. In the coming years, as Nike expands to newer markets and capitalizes newer opportunities, it will have to continue its reliance on marketing research and continue to associate athletes, performance, and the brand.

Questions

1. Nike would like to increase its share of the athletic shoe market. Define the management decision problem.
2. Define an appropriate marketing research problem corresponding to the management decision problem you have identified.
3. Develop a graphical model explaining consumers' selection of a brand of athletic shoes.
4. How can qualitative research be used to strengthen Nike's image? Which qualitative research technique(s) should be used and why?

References

1. www.nike.com, accessed February 15, 2009.
2. Hoover's, A D&B Company, http://premium.hoovers.com.gate.lib.buffalo.edu/subscribe/co/factsheet.xhtml?ID=rcthcfhfshkyjc, accessed May 31, 2007.

"The key to good descriptive research is knowing exactly what you want to measure and selecting a survey method in which every respondent is willing to cooperate and capable of giving you complete and accurate information efficiently.

Jeff Miller, Chief Operating Officer, Burke, Inc.

Objectives [After reading this chapter, the student should be able to:]

1. Discuss and classify survey methods and describe the various telephone, personal, mail, and electronic interviewing methods.

2. Identify the criteria for evaluating survey methods, compare the different methods, and evaluate which is best suited for a particular research project.

3. Explain and classify the different observation methods used by marketing researchers and describe personal observation, mechanical observation, audit, content analysis, and trace analysis.

4. Identify the criteria for evaluating observation methods, compare the different methods, and evaluate which, if any, is suited for a particular research project.

5. Describe the relative advantages and disadvantages of observational methods and compare them to survey methods.

6. Discuss the considerations involved in implementing surveys and observation methods in an international setting.

7. Understand the ethical issues involved in conducting survey and observation research.

Descriptive Research Design: Survey and Observation

Overview

In previous chapters, we have explained that once the marketing research problem has been defined (step 1 of the marketing research process) and an appropriate approach developed (step 2), the researcher is in a position to formulate the research design (step 3). As was discussed in Chapter 3, the major types of research designs are exploratory and conclusive. Exploratory designs employ secondary data analysis (Chapter 4) and qualitative research (Chapter 5) as the major methodologies. Conclusive research designs may be classified as causal or descriptive. Causal designs will be explained in Chapter 7.

In this chapter, we focus on the major methods employed in descriptive research designs: survey and observation. As was explained in Chapter 3, descriptive research has as its major objective the description of something—usually market characteristics or functions. Survey, or communication, methods may be classified by mode of administration as traditional telephone interviews, computer-assisted telephone interviews, personal in-home interviews, mall-intercept interviews, computer-assisted personal interviews, mail interviews, mail panels, e-mail, and Internet surveys. We describe each of these methods and present a comparative evaluation of all the survey methods. Next, we consider the major observational methods: personal observation, mechanical observation, audit, content analysis, and trace analysis. The relative advantages and disadvantages of observation over survey methods are discussed. The considerations involved in conducting survey and observation research when researching international markets are discussed. Several ethical issues that arise in survey research and observation methods are identified. To begin our discussion, here are some examples of these methods.

Real Research

Who Will Be the Next President?

Internet surveys are gaining in popularity, and the November 2000 U.S. elections provided market researchers with a unique opportunity to test online survey methods, their accuracy, and also their ability to predict elections. Harris Interactive (www.harrisinteractive.com) took the initiative to conduct online

Internet polls accurately predicted Barack Obama as the winner in the 2008 presidential election.

research in 73 different political races, including nationwide votes for president, statewide votes in 38 states, and several senatorial and gubernatorial elections. Interactive online interviews were conducted between October 31 and November 6, 2000, with a total of 240,666 adults who were characterized as likely voters. The results turned out to be almost identical to those found in the nationwide Harris Interactive telephone poll, which happened to be the only other poll to have Bush and Gore tied in its final prediction, with the following results:

2000 Presidential Elections: The Nationwide Vote

	Gore %	Bush %	Nader %	Errors Bush/Gore Spread %	Nader %
Election Results	48	48	3	—	—
Harris Interactive (Online)	47	47	4	0	1
Harris Interactive (Phone)	47	47	5	0	2
CBS	45	44	4	1	1
Gallup/CNN/USA Today	46	48	4	2	1
Pew Research	47	49	4	2	1
IBD/CSM/TIPP	46	48	4	2	1
Zogby	48	46	5	2	2
ICR/Politics Now	44	46	7	2	4
NBC/WSJ	44	47	3	3	0
ABC/WashPost	45	48	3	3	0
Battleground	45	50	4	5	1
Rasmussen (Automated Telephone)	49	40	4	9	1

Notes:
1. Undecided and others omitted.
2. The National Council on Published Polls (NCPP) has calculated the error on the spread as being half the difference between the actual spread (i.e., the result) and the spread in the poll. We show it here as the difference (i.e., our estimates of error are twice those shown by NCPP).

Source: Courtesy of National Council on Published Polls.

The accuracy of the other 72 races turned out to be quite high as well. The accuracy of these online polls in predicting the results of 73 races proved that well-designed Internet surveys can reliably predict elections. Likewise, Internet polls were also accurate in predicting the votes and George W. Bush as the winner in the 2004 presidential election and in predicting Obama as the winner of the 2008 presidential election. Therefore, the popularity of Internet surveys for election polling and other uses is expected to continue to grow.[1] ∎

Real Research ## Marketing Research: The Japanese Way

Japanese companies rely heavily on personal observation as a means of obtaining information. When Canon Cameras (www.canon.com) was losing market share in the United States to Minolta, Canon decided that its distributor, Bell & Howell, was not giving adequate support. However, Canon did not use data from a broad survey of consumers or retailers to make this decision. Instead, it relied on personal observation and sent three managers to the United States to look into the problem.

Canon's head of the team, Tatehiro Tsuruta, spent almost six weeks in America. On entering a camera store, he would act just like a customer. He would note how the cameras were displayed and how the clerks served customers. He observed that the dealers were not enthusiastic about Canon. He also observed that it would not be advantageous for Canon to use drugstores and other discount outlets. This led Canon to open its own sales subsidiary, resulting in increased sales and market share. Its own sales subsidiary was also a major asset in expanding the sales of its digital cameras in the early 2000s. As of 2009, Canon sold its products in more than 115 countries worldwide through direct sales and resellers with about 75 percent of its sales generated outside Japan.[2] ∎

Telephone and Internet interviews, as well as other survey methods, are becoming increasingly popular for predicting election results and have many other applications. Observation methods are employed less frequently, but they too have important uses in marketing research, as indicated by the Canon example.

Survey Methods

survey method

A structured questionnaire given to a sample of a population and designed to elicit specific information from respondents.

structured data collection

Use of a formal questionnaire that presents questions in a prearranged order.

fixed-alternative questions

Questions that require respondents to choose from a set of predetermined answers.

The **survey method** of obtaining information is based on the questioning of respondents. Respondents are asked a variety of questions regarding their behavior, intentions, attitudes, awareness, motivations, and demographic and lifestyle characteristics. These questions may be asked verbally, in writing, or via computer, and the responses may be obtained in any of these forms. Typically, the questioning is structured. *Structured* here refers to the degree of standardization imposed on the data collection process. In **structured data collection**, a formal questionnaire is prepared and the questions are asked in a prearranged order; thus the process is also direct. Whether research is classified as direct or indirect is based on whether the true purpose is known to the respondents. As explained in Chapter 5, a direct approach is nondisguised in that the purpose of the project is disclosed to the respondents or is otherwise obvious to them from the questions asked.

The structured-direct survey, the most popular data collection method, involves administering a questionnaire. In a typical questionnaire, most questions are **fixed-alternative questions** that require the respondent to select from a predetermined set of responses. Consider, for example, the following question designed to measure attitude toward department stores:

	Disagree				*Agree*
Shopping in department stores is fun.	1	2	3	4	5

The survey method has several advantages. First, the questionnaire is simple to administer. Second, the data obtained are reliable because the responses are limited to the alternatives stated. The use of fixed-response questions reduces the variability in the results that may be caused by differences in interviewers. Finally, coding, analysis, and interpretation of data are relatively simple.[3]

Disadvantages are that respondents may be unable or unwilling to provide the desired information. For example, consider questions about motivational factors. Respondents may not be consciously aware of their motives for choosing specific brands or shopping at specific department stores. Therefore, they may be unable to provide accurate answers to questions about their motives. Respondents may be unwilling to respond if the information requested is sensitive or personal. Also, structured questions and fixed-response alternatives may result in loss of validity for certain types of data such as beliefs and feelings. Finally, wording questions properly is not easy (see Chapter 10 on questionnaire design). Yet, despite these disadvantages, the survey approach is by far the most common method of primary data collection in marketing research, as illustrated by the political polling example in the "Overview" section and the example of Ariba.

Real Research

Survey Supports Customer Support

Ariba (www.ariba.com), a B2B software provider, utilizes both the Internet and sophisticated computer applications to collect survey data. Ariba has integrated its Vantive Enterprise Customer Relationship Management platform (a proprietary software system) with the Web Survey System from CustomerSat.com. With this setup, Ariba has the ability to gain real-time feedback, track trends, and obtain immediate notification of unsatisfied customers. Other advantages that Ariba receives from this system are the ability to distribute positive data figures to build company morale and to implement best practices procedures as a result of the data.

The system works by administering an online survey to each customer (respondent) who asks for customer support. This survey not only gathers specifics about the problem the customer is experiencing but also data that can be used to make executive decisions down the road (e.g., current product needs, what customers like/dislike). The system then analyzes the responses and routes the respondent to an appropriate specialist. Customers can rate and comment on their customer support experience within 24 hours of the case being closed. Ariba can use this survey data not only to improve its customer support system but also to utilize the non-problem-related data to make executive decisions about the direction and offerings of the company. As a result of implementing this system, Ariba's growth has been phenomenal.[4] ∎

Survey methods can be classified based on the mode used to administer the questionnaire. These classification schemes help distinguish among survey methods.

Survey Methods Classified by Mode of Administration

Survey questionnaires may be administered in four major modes: (1) telephone interviews, (2) personal interviews, (3) mail interviews, and (4) electronic interviews (see Figure 6.1). Telephone interviews may be further classified as traditional telephone interviews or computer-assisted telephone interviews (CATI). Personal interviews may be conducted in the home, as mall-intercept interviews, or as computer-assisted personal interviews (CAPI). The third major method, mail interviewing, takes the form of ordinary mail surveys or surveys conducted using mail panels. Finally, electronic interviews can be conducted via e-mail or administered on the Internet. Of these methods, telephone interviews are the most popular, followed by personal interviews and mail surveys. The use of electronic methods, especially Internet surveys, is growing at a fast pace. We now describe each of these methods.

Telephone Methods

As stated earlier, telephone interviews can be typed as traditional and computer assisted.

Traditional Telephone Interviews

Traditional telephone interviews involve phoning a sample of respondents and asking them a series of questions. The interviewer uses a paper questionnaire and records the responses with a pencil. Advances in telecommunications and technology have made nationwide telephone interviewing from a central location practical. Consequently, the use of local telephone interviewing has decreased in recent years.[5]

Computer-Assisted Telephone Interviewing

Computer-assisted telephone interviewing from a central location is far more popular than the traditional telephone method. Computer-assisted telephone interviewing (CATI) uses a computerized questionnaire administered to respondents over the telephone. A computerized questionnaire may be generated using a mainframe computer, a minicomputer, or a personal computer. The interviewer sits in front of a computer terminal and wears a mini-headset. The computer replaces a paper and pencil questionnaire, and the mini-headset substitutes for a telephone. Upon command, the computer dials the telephone number to be called. When contact is made, the interviewer reads questions posed on the computer screen and records the respondent's answers directly into the computer's memory bank.

FIGURE 6.1

A Classification of Survey Methods

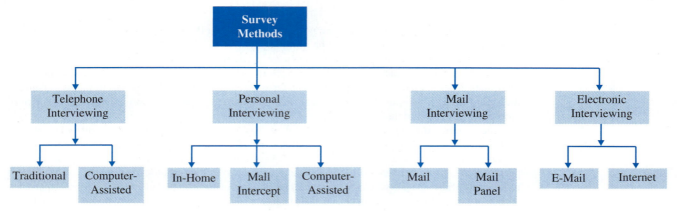

In computer-assisted telephone interviewing, the computer systematically guides the interviewer.

The computer systematically guides the interviewer. Only one question at a time appears on the screen. The computer checks the responses for appropriateness and consistency. It uses the responses as they are obtained to personalize the questionnaire. The data collection flows naturally and smoothly. Interviewing time is reduced, data quality is enhanced, and the laborious steps in the data-collection process, coding questionnaires and entering the data into the computer, are eliminated. Because the responses are entered directly into the computer, interim and update reports on data collection or results can be provided almost instantaneously. The Harris Interactive phone survey in the polling example in the "Overview" section made use of CATI, as does the following example.

Real Research Telephone Surveys: The Hallmark of Hallmark

Because females control more than half of the purchasing decisions in their homes, Hallmark Inc. (www.hallmark.com) did some research on this target market—women. Qualitative research revealed the importance of girlfriends in the life of women. A national telephone survey was conducted asking women ages 18–39 how they first became acquainted with their girlfriends, and how often they kept in touch with their girlfriends. Respondents were asked to rate how likely (or unlikely) they were to share secrets, surprises, disagreements with spouses, and personal (pregnancy) information with their girlfriends. The results showed that 45 percent of women felt that there was an occasion on which they would rather share the information with a female friend than a male friend. It was also found that 81 percent of women "calmly discuss topics when they have a difference in opinion with their girlfriends." Both of these percentages illustrate a higher probability for females to share information and engage in correspondence.

Forty-two percent of the women in the study stated that they have one woman they consider their "best friend." Thirty-three percent of women live within 10 miles of their best friend, and 28 percent live more than 100 miles away from their best friends. Based on this information, Hallmark launched its new line of cards, "Hallmark Fresh Ink," that enable women to keep in touch with their girlfriends. Knowing that females were their target market and how much they kept in touch with one another enabled the company to launch a successful new line. Telephone surveys have become the hallmark of Hallmark's marketing research, enabling the company to formulate successful marketing strategies. As of 2009, Hallmark held more than 50 percent of the market share in the United States for greeting cards sales, and their cards were sold in over 43,000 retail outlets. They also published products in more than 30 languages that were sold in over 100 countries.[6] ∎

Several software packages, such as Ci3 by Sawtooth Software (www.sawtoothsoftware.com), are available for conducting CATI. Computer-automated telephone surveys (CATS) systems are capable of dialing and interviewing respondents without any human intervention, other than the digital recording of questions to be asked during the phone survey.

Delta Air Lines: Surveying Airline Preferences

Visit www.delta.com and search the Internet using a search engine as well as your library's online databases to obtain information on consumers' preferences for selecting an airline for domestic travel.

As the marketing manager for Delta Air Lines, how would you use information on consumers' airline preferences for domestic travel to formulate marketing strategies that would increase your market share?

What are the advantages and disadvantages of telephone interviewing in conducting a survey to obtain information on consumers' airline preferences for domestic travel? Would you recommend this method for administering a survey for Delta Air Lines?

Personal Methods

Personal interviewing methods may be categorized as in-home, mall-intercept, or computer-assisted.

Personal In-Home Interviews

In personal in-home interviews, respondents are interviewed face-to-face in their homes. The interviewer's task is to contact the respondents, ask the questions, and record the responses. In recent years, the use of personal in-home interviews has declined due to its high cost. Nevertheless, they are still used, particularly by syndicated firms (see Chapter 4), such as Mediamark Research, Inc. (MRI).

Real Research   Mediamark: Benchmarking U.S. Households

Mediamark (www.mediamark.com) conducts an ongoing, comprehensive study of the adult population of the United States called the National Study. This study, conducted continuously since 1979, surveys the demographics, product usage, and media exposure of all persons age 18 and over in the contiguous 48 states.

Respondents are selected on a strict area probability basis. A computer list of more than 90 million households is merged with other sources necessary to construct a properly stratified sample. The sample is composed of three sections: a sample of metropolitan areas; nonmetropolitan counties; and each of 10 major U.S. markets: New York, Los Angeles, Chicago, Philadelphia, San Francisco, Boston, Detroit, Washington, D.C., Cleveland, and Dallas/Ft. Worth. These markets are more heavily sampled to allow MRI to prepare reliable media and marketing estimates on a local market basis.

Fieldwork is done in two waves per year, each lasting six months and consisting of approximately 13,000 interviews. Two different methods are used to question the respondent:

1. First, an in-home interview is used to collect demographics and data related to media exposure (including magazines, newspapers, radio, television, cable, Internet, and outdoor).
2. At the end of the interview, the fieldworker leaves behind a self-completing questionnaire booklet covering personal and household usage of some 500 product categories and services and 6,000 brands.

Fieldwork is conducted by LHK Partners Inc., Newtown Square, Pennsylvania (www.partnersinc.com). Each fieldworker is thoroughly trained in interviewing techniques as well as in methods of gaining access to respondents and establishing rapport.

A wide range of techniques is used to elicit the full cooperation of respondents. Listed households are informed by mail ahead of time that they will be contacted by an interviewer. Up to six separate attempts are made to contact difficult-to-reach respondents. Households presenting language barriers are reassigned to specifically qualified interviewers, as are refusals and other unusual cases.

The personal interview takes, on average, 60–65 minutes to complete. At its conclusion, the questionnaire booklet is presented and a $20 payment is offered as an incentive for its completion. The interviewer then makes an appointment to return at a later date to pick it up.

Over the years, the National Study has become a source of valuable information on consumers for firms in a variety of industries.[7] ■

A mall-intercept interview in progress.

Despite their many applications, the use of personal in-home interviews is declining, while mall intercepts are becoming more frequent.

Mall-Intercept Personal Interviews

In mall-intercept personal interviews, respondents are intercepted while they are shopping in malls and brought to test facilities in the malls. The interviewer then administers a questionnaire as in the in-home personal survey. The advantage of mall-intercept interviews is that it is more efficient for the respondent to come to the interviewer than for the interviewer to go to the respondent.[8] This method has become increasingly popular and there are several hundred permanent mall research facilities. As the following example shows, mall intercepts are especially appropriate when the respondents need to see, handle, or consume the product before they can provide meaningful information.

Real Research   Same Name, New Number

Stepping into the new millennium, AT&T (www.att.com) had moved from just providing long-distance phone service to offering cable, wireless cellular service, and Internet services. However, most people still viewed the firm purely as an old-fashioned, boring telephone company. Therefore, the company wanted to create a new image of being fun and trendy. Their ad agency, Young & Rubicam (www.yr.com), had the idea of using the logo of AT&T, the blue and white globe, and animate it to be the "spokesperson" in the ads. In order to determine if the logo was recognizable enough, AT&T hired SE Surveys, a New York research firm. The researchers conducted 500 mall-intercept personal interviews in 15 markets to address AT&T's problem. Mall-intercept interviewing was selected over other survey methods so that the respondents could be shown a picture of the AT&T logo before responding. The consumers were asked if they recognized the logo, which was pictured without the company name. The survey results showed that 75 percent of the entire sample recognized the logo as being representative of AT&T without any help, whereas 77 percent of the 18–24-year-olds and 80 percent of the "high-value, active networkers" recognized the logo. High-value, active networkers are those who spend $75 or more on wireless services or long-distance.

Given these positive results, commercials were made that showed the animated logo bouncing about the screen, demonstrating how AT&T's various services can help an individual or a business. Since then, awareness and perceptions of AT&T's services have continued to remain high. On March 5, 2006, it was announced that AT&T would acquire BellSouth for $67 billion. Significant synergies were expected to generate earnings per share growth in 2010.[9] ■

A handheld computer can replace paper questionnaires used in in-home and mall-intercept interviewing. Using pen-based computing technology, this system uses the display memory as a software keypad.

Computer-Assisted Personal Interviewing (CAPI)

In computer-assisted personal interviewing (CAPI), the third form of personal interviewing, the respondent sits in front of a computer terminal and answers a questionnaire on the computer screen by using the keyboard or a mouse. There are several user-friendly electronic packages that design questions that are easy for the respondent to understand. Help screens and courteous error messages are also provided. The colorful screens and on- and off-screen stimuli add to the respondent's interest and involvement in the task. This method has been classified as a personal interview technique since an interviewer is usually present to serve as a host or hostess and to guide the respondent as needed. CAPI has been used to collect data at shopping malls, product clinics, conferences, and trade shows. One popular way in which CAPI is administered is through the use of kiosks.

Real Research   ### TouchScreen: Surveys with the Touch of a Screen

---

TouchScreen Research (www.touchscreenresearch.com.au) is Australia's leading supplier of touch screen survey software and associated hardware. They have helped a number of clients, including ANZ Bank and Eli Lilly, in collecting market research data. TouchScreen kiosks have also proven extremely popular in Australia because of their sleek and practical design as well as their effectiveness in collecting pertinent data.

One of the satisfied clients is Exhibitions and Trade Fairs (ETF), who organized Melbourne and Sydney 2005 Money Expos. ETF introduced visitors in these expos to the Touch Screen Survey Kiosks. ETF, as organizer of this event, was able to identify the benefits of conducting surveys at each of the expos. The data extracted from the surveys provided ETF with specific information such as type and demographics of the visitors who attended the expo, how visitors became aware of the event, and what interest factors attracted visitors to attend. For example, the survey revealed to ETF that the media exposure through PBL Media Group, ACP's *Money* magazine, and Channel 9 were very effective from a publicity standpoint. Also, the "one stop shop" approach, bringing mortgage and investment loans, retirement planning, and superannuation/managed funds all under the same roof, was another feature of the expo that attracted visitors.

What was more remarkable was the turnaround time. Within 72 hours of the expo closing its doors, TouchScreen Research was able to provide ETF with a PDF file that contained an easy-to-read, well-collated, and comprehensive survey findings. ETF was able to utilize these findings for the purpose of providing valuable selling points when speaking with potential exhibitors and sponsors as well as for planning and strategizing its marketing activities and planning its visitor campaign. It was also able to identify specific target areas for future exhibitions based on this data.[10] ■

Computer-assisted personal interviewing (CAPI), such as that using touch screens, is becoming more popular around the world.

TABLE 6.1
Some Decisions Related to the Mail Interview Package

Outgoing Envelope

Outgoing envelope: size, color, return address

Postage

Method of addressing

Cover Letter

Sponsorship	Signature
Personalization	Postscript
Type of appeal	

Questionnaire

Length	Layout
Content	Color
Size	Format
Reproduction	Respondent anonymity

Return Envelope

Type of envelope

Postage

Incentives

Monetary versus nonmonetary

Prepaid versus promised amount

Mail Methods

Mail interviews, the third major form of survey administration, can be conducted via ordinary mail or the mail panel.

Mail Interviews

In the traditional mail interview, questionnaires are mailed to preselected potential respondents. A typical mail interview package consists of the outgoing envelope, cover letter, questionnaire, return envelope, and possibly an incentive. The respondents complete and return the questionnaires. There is no verbal interaction between the researcher and the respondent.[11]

However, before data collection can begin, the respondents need to be at least broadly identified. Therefore, an initial task is to obtain a valid mailing list. Mailing lists can be compiled from telephone directories, customer rosters, or association membership rolls, or purchased from publication subscription lists or commercial mailing list companies.[12] Regardless of its source, a mailing list should be current and closely related to the population of interest. The researcher must also make decisions about the various elements of the mail interview package (see Table 6.1). Mail surveys are used for a variety of purposes, including measurement of consumer preferences, as illustrated by the following example.

Real Research

Mint to Be Together

The Mint Museum of Art (www.mintmuseum.org) is located in Charlotte, North Carolina, and has a reputation as one of the Southeast's leading cultural institutions. Due to recent changes in the area's population, the Mint began to wonder if its diverse and vast collection was the best way to present art to the public, and just who this public was. Additionally, the Mint wanted to create a Mint Museum of Craft + Design, but they were not sure if this is what the public would want, or if they would understand the concept. So they hired InterActive Research of Atlanta.

InterActive Research created a two-phase study to discover the information desired by the Mint. The goal of the research was to measure awareness, usage, and attitudes toward the existing museum, as well as the plan for the new Museum of Craft + Design. The first phase of the study was qualitative and consisted of 15 focus groups, followed by a quantitative phase that was composed of a detailed questionnaire mailed to approximately 10,000 Charlotte-area residents; 1,300 responses were returned.

The results showed that the Mint was perceived as elitist. Respondents also felt that the current collection was too diverse and did not present a coherent theme. People supported the Craft + Design idea of the new museum, but they felt a large educational initiative was needed to inform the public about what exactly this entailed. Pricing and parking were seen as two barriers that currently prevented people from attending, so it was decided this needed to be kept in mind when developing the new building. Entrance fees of $5 to $7 were found to be acceptable, but people didn't think they would pay to go to the new museum if it cost more than that. The research also implied that the museum should consider offering a joint membership in both of its museums to encourage attendance. Many of these research findings were implemented as of 2008. Based on the research results provided, the Mint decided to consolidate its current collection into a more focused theme—Art in the Americas—and organize it in chronological order. It will occasionally have a European piece, but most of the art will have originated in either North or South America. The maximum admission price was $6 per person and tickets purchased were good for admission to both the Mint Museum of Art and the Mint Museum of Craft + Design as long as they were used on the same day.[13] ∎

ACTIVE RESEARCH

Restaurant Dining: A Casual Affair?

Visit www.outback.com and search the Internet using a search engine as well as your library's online databases to obtain information on consumers' preferences for casual restaurants.

As the marketing manager for Outback, how would you use information on consumers' preferences for casual restaurants to formulate marketing strategies that would increase your sales and market share?

What are the advantages and disadvantages of mail/mail panel/fax in conducting a survey to obtain information on consumers' preferences for casual restaurants? Which, if any, of these methods would you recommend for conducting a survey for Outback?

Mail Panels

mail panels
A large and nationally representative sample of households who have agreed to periodically participate in mail questionnaires, product tests, and telephone surveys.

Mail panels were introduced in Chapters 3 and 4. A **mail panel** consists of a large, nationally representative sample of households that have agreed to participate in periodic mail questionnaires and product tests. The households are compensated with various incentives. Data on the panel members are updated every year. Because of the panel members' commitment, the response rates can approach 80 percent. The Consumer Opinion Panel maintained by Synovate (www.synovate.com) consists of a representative sample of more than 600,000 households in the United States and 60,000 in Canada. Several marketing research companies are moving from mail panels to online panels. The NFO World Group (www.nfow.com) claims that one out of every 200 households is a member of their online consumer panel.

Mail panels can be used to obtain information from the same respondents repeatedly. Thus, they can be used to implement a longitudinal design.

Electronic Methods

As mentioned earlier, electronic surveys can be conducted by e-mail or administered on the Internet or the Web.

E-Mail Interviews

To conduct an e-mail survey, a list of e-mail addresses is obtained. The survey is written within the body of the e-mail message. The e-mails are sent out over the Internet. E-mail surveys use pure text (ASCII) to represent questionnaires and can be received and responded to by anyone with an e-mail address, whether or not they have access to the Web. Respondents type the answers to either closed-ended or open-ended questions at designated places, and click on "reply." Responses are data entered and tabulated. Note that data entry is typically required.

E-mail surveys have several limitations. Given the technical limitations of most e-mail systems, questionnaires cannot utilize programmed skip patterns, logic checks, or randomization. The limited intelligence of ASCII text cannot keep a respondent from, say, choosing both "yes" and "no" to a question where only one response is meaningful. Skipping instructions (e.g., "If the answer to question 5 is yes, go to question 9") must appear explicitly, just as on paper. These factors can reduce the quality of data from an e-mail survey and can require post-survey data cleaning. Another limitation is that some e-mail software products limit the length of the body of an e-mail message.

Internet Interviews

hypertext markup language
Hypertext markup language (HTML) is the language of the Web.

In contrast to e-mail surveys, Internet or Web surveys use **hypertext markup language** (HTML), the language of the Web, and are posted on a Web site. Respondents may be recruited over the Internet, from potential respondent databases maintained by the marketing research firm, from an Internet panel, or they can be recruited by conventional methods (mail, telephone). Respondents are asked to go to a particular Web location to complete the survey. Many times, respondents are not recruited; they happen to be visiting the Web site where the survey is posted (or other popular Web sites) and they are invited to participate in the survey. Either all or every *i*th Web site visitor is allowed to participate. Web surveys offer several advantages as compared to e-mail surveys. It is possible in HTML, but not in ASCII text, to construct buttons, check boxes, and data entry fields that prevent respondents from selecting more than one response where only one is intended, or from otherwise typing where no response is required. Skip patterns can be programmed and performed automatically as in CATI or CAPI. It is possible to validate responses as they are entered. Finally, additional survey stimuli such as graphs, images, animations, and links to other Web pages may be integrated into or around the survey. The responses are collected in an adjoining database. The data require some processing before they can be tabulated or used in a statistical package. All these factors contribute to higher quality data. The Harris Interactive Online survey in the polling example in the "Overview" section was an example of an Internet survey. As indicated by the Harris Interactive Online survey example, other studies have also shown that the results obtained from Internet surveys can be very close to those obtained by using the traditional methods.

Internet panels are gaining in popularity and can be an efficient source of obtaining Internet samples (as discussed in more detail in Chapter 11). In fact, many marketing research suppliers and syndicated firms have replaced their traditional mail panels with Internet panels. Internet panels take less time and cost less to build and maintain as compared to mail panels. Several companies offer Internet panels that may be used by other researchers to draw Internet samples by paying the appropriate fee. Such firms include Harris Interactive (www.harrisinteractive.com), Survey Sampling International (www.surveysampling.com), and Greenfield Online (www.greenfieldonline.com).

Limitations of e-mail surveys include the need for possible cleanup from the messages; limited forms that must be strictly adhered to by the user to ensure no cleanup is required; and e-mail system compatibility issues. Another drawback is spam. About half of all e-mail traffic is spam that is annoying. The Can Spam Act that became effective January 2, 2004, has been largely ineffective in curbing Spam.

For Internet or Web surveys that recruit respondents who are browsing or by placing banner ads, there is inherent self-selection bias. This can be alleviated by using a validated sample, where individuals are preselected from a set of e-mail addresses and sent an invitation to the Web site. Web surveys do offer an advantage over e-mail surveys because they can have graphics and sound, can be sent over a secured server, and provide instantaneous feedback. Web surveys can also employ alert systems that can trigger when certain thresholds are met. For instance, if a hotel site reaches its trigger limit for subpar performance, a manager can be immediately notified and can act quickly. Problems, of course, with any Web survey include the fact that bias may be introduced if the respondents answer more than once, and, also for nonvalidated samples, statistical representativeness may be an issue.

Basically, Internet research can be just as representative and effective as other traditional methods, especially as the Internet population continues to grow. Problems of conducting research over the Internet must be effectively addressed and resolved, just as the problems with traditional research have been and continue to be.[14]

Real Research

Sony: Internet Surveys Capture Music Download Market Shares

No company involved with the music industry can ignore the online music market. It is a growing and highly dynamic industry segment. Sony (www.sony.com) is conscious of this fact and has developed an innovative means to determine the views of the lead users of the Internet to capture the pulses of this market.

"It just happens that I'm a member of Sony's PS3 [Playstation Web site] Voice of the Elite," says Joseph Laszlo, a diehard netizen and gamer. Voice of the elite (VOTE) is a Web-based survey run by Sony on the Playstation Web site. The access to the survey is restricted to select members of the PS Web site who are also serious gamers.

Aside from making the respondent feel a bit important, Sony's surveys are often very interesting. They share some of their results with the respondents, which often provides new insights. Sony regularly shares a result from an earlier survey as part of a current one; this is a good practice for this kind of ongoing loyalty/market research program since everyone wants to know how his or her opinion matches that of the panel.

One of the recent surveys was directed toward understanding the online music industry from the user's point of view. Sony asked its pool of loyal PS3 gamers, "Where do you go online to download music?" Results were as follows: iTunes: 18.8 percent; Napster: 8.6 percent; MusicMatch: 7.8 percent; Rhapsody: 2.9 percent; Buymusic: 2.2 percent; eMusic: 1.7 percent; Other [presumably including the illegal services]: 31.4 percent; and None: 26.6 percent.

Sony receives considerable revenues in the form of royalties from legal music downloads. Naturally, Sony's strategy is to promote legal online music downloading and reduce illegal downloading. To this end, Sony provides access to online music stores through its official Web site (www.sonymusic.com). The survey results presented here gave some interesting insights used to design this service. It suggests that among the very savvy Internet users (assuming gamers are very savvy), iTunes has a large lead, but not as large as you might expect, and that the Napster brand has indeed helped a relative latecomer carve out a number two position among the legal services, at least with this segment of the online population. The options for downloading provided in the Sony site were in good part decided by the results of the survey. Even the positioning of the sites in the list reflects the survey results, with iTunes and Napster finding their way to the top of the list.[15] ∎

Several Web-based services are available for fielding online surveys. CreateSurvey (www.createsurvey.com) and Zoomerang (www.zoomerang.com) let you create and administer online surveys at their sites. The Survey System (www.surveysystem.com) is a software package available for working with telephone, online, and printed questionnaires. It handles all phases of survey projects, from creating questionnaires through data entry, interviewing, e-mail, or Web page Internet surveys, to producing tables, graphics, and text reports. EFM Feedback (www.vovici.com), Web Online Surveys (web-online-surveys.com), and SurveyPro (www.apian.com) are other popular software for creating Web-based and other surveys.

Experiential Research

Experiencing Survey Research

1. Use CreateSurvey (www.createsurvey.com) and Zoomerang (www.zoomerang.com) to create a survey questionnaire to measure students' satisfaction with the campus newspaper. Compare the two sites in terms of (1) ease of creating a survey, (2) flexibility of asking different type of questions, and (3) overall satisfaction.
2. Visit the Web sites of any two of the following survey software companies: EFM Feedback (www.vovici.com), Web Online Surveys (web-online-surveys.com), and SurveyPro (www.apian.com). If you had to recommend the purchase of survey software, which one of the two would you recommend and why?
3. To experience how a sponsor of an Internet survey can monitor results during the field portion of the project, go to http://us.lightspeedpanel.com, read the Lightspeed Mini-poll question, and select "View Results."
4. Visit Greenfield Online (www.greenfieldonline.com) and take an online survey. Note that you will first have to become a member of the panel to take a survey. Write a brief report about your experience.
5. Visit comScore SurveySite (www.comscore.com) and write a report on SurveySite's methodology for e-mail surveys, pop-up surveys, and domain departure surveys. ∎

Remember, however, that not all survey methods are appropriate in a given situation. Therefore, the researcher should conduct a comparative evaluation to determine which methods are appropriate.

A Comparative Evaluation of Survey Methods

Table 6.2 compares the different survey methods across a variety of factors. For any particular research project, the relative importance attached to these factors will vary. These factors may be broadly classified as task, situational, and respondent factors. Task factors relate to tasks that have to be performed to collect the data and to the topic of the survey. These factors consist of diversity of questions and flexibility, use of physical stimuli, sample control, quantity of data, and response rate. The situational factors comprise control of the data-collection environment, control of field force, potential for interviewer bias, speed, and cost. The respondent factors pertain to survey respondents and include perceived anonymity, social desirability, obtaining sensitive information, low incidence rate, and respondent control. We discuss in detail the evaluation of the different survey methods on each of these factors.

Task Factors

The demand that the task to be performed places on the respondents and the data collection process influences the survey method that should be used. The nature of the task involved has an impact on the diversity of questions and flexibility, use of physical stimuli, sample control, quantity of data, and response rate.

DIVERSITY OF QUESTIONS AND FLEXIBILITY The diversity of questions that can be asked in a survey and the flexibility of data collection depend upon the degree of interaction the respondent has with the interviewer and the questionnaire, as well as the ability to actually see the questions. A wide variety of questions can be asked in a personal interview because the respondents can see the questionnaire and an interviewer is present to clarify ambiguities. Because the respondent and the interviewer meet face to face, the interviewer can administer complex questionnaires, explain and clarify difficult questions, and even utilize unstructured techniques. Thus, in-home, mall-intercept, and CAPI allow for high diversity. Flexibility is also high, especially in the case of in-home and mall-intercept interviews but is decreased somewhat in CAPI due to limited interaction with the interviewer. In Internet surveys, multimedia capabilities can be utilized and so the ability to ask a diversity of questions is moderate to high, despite the absence of an interviewer. Moreover, a certain amount of interactivity can be built into the questionnaire enhancing the flexibility. In mail surveys, mail panels, and e-mail surveys, less diversity and flexibility are possible, as the survey is essentially self-administered by the respondent and there is no interviewer present to offer any clarifications. However, the lack of interaction with the interviewer is moderated by the ability to see the questionnaire. Therefore, these methods receive a moderate rating. In traditional telephone interviews and CATI, the respondent cannot see the questions while answering and this limits the diversity of questions. For example, in a telephone interview or CATI, one could not ask respondents to rank 15 brands of automobiles in terms of preference. However, in CATI, as in the case of CAPI and Internet surveys, the researcher can personalize the questionnaire and handle complex skip patterns (directions for skipping questions in the questionnaire based on the subject's responses), thereby providing some flexibility and resulting in a low to moderate rating.

An often-overlooked benefit of Internet survey research is the ease with which an Internet survey can be quickly modified. For example, early data returns may suggest additional questions that should be asked. Changing or adding questions on the fly would be nearly impossible with a mail questionnaire and difficult with personal or telephone questionnaires, but can be achieved in a matter of minutes with some Internet survey systems.

USE OF PHYSICAL STIMULI Often it is helpful or necessary to use physical stimuli such as the product, a product prototype, commercials, or promotional displays during the interview. For the most basic example, a taste test involves tasting the product. In other cases, photographs, maps, or other audiovisual cues are helpful. In these cases, personal interviews conducted at central

TABLE 6.2
A Comparative Evaluation of Survey Methods

Criteria	Telephone CATI	In-Home Interviews	Mall-Intercept Interviews	CAPI	Mail Surveys	Mail Panels	E-Mail	Internet
Task Factors								
Diversity of questions and flexibility	Low to moderate	High	High	Moderate to high	Moderate	Moderate	Moderate	Moderate to high
Use of physical stimuli	Low	Moderate to high	High	High	Moderate	Moderate	Low	Moderate
Sample control	Moderate to high	Potentially high	Moderate	Moderate	Low	Moderate to high	Low	Low to moderate
Quantity of data	Low	High	Moderate	Moderate	Moderate	High	Moderate	Moderate
Response rate	Moderate	High	High	High	Low	High	Low	Very low
Situational Factors								
Control of data collection environment	Moderate	Moderate to high	High	High	Low	Low	Low	Low
Control of field force	Moderate	Low	Moderate	Moderate	High	High	High	High
Potential for interviewer bias	Moderate	High	High	Low	None	None	None	None
Speed	High	Moderate	Moderate to high	Moderate to high	Low	Low to moderate	High	Very high
Cost	Moderate	High	Moderate to high	Moderate to high	Low	Low to moderate	Low	Low
Respondent Factors								
Perceived anonymity of the respondent	Moderate	Low	Low	Low	High	High	Moderate	High
Social desirability	Moderate	High	High	Moderate to high	Low	Low	Moderate	Low
Obtaining sensitive information	High	Low	Low	Low to moderate	High	Moderate to high	Moderate	High
Low incidence rate	High	Low	Low	Low	Moderate	Moderate	Moderate	High
Respondent control	Low to moderate	Low	Low	Low	High	High	High	Moderate to high

locations (mall-intercept and CAPI) score high and are preferable to in-home interviews. Mail surveys and mail panels are moderate on this dimension, because sometimes it is possible to mail the facilitating aids or even product samples. Internet surveys are also moderately suitable. Because they are Web-based, the questionnaires can include multimedia elements such as prototype Web pages and advertisements. The use of physical stimuli is limited in traditional telephone interviews, CATI, and also in e-mail surveys.

sample control

The ability of the survey mode to reach the units specified in the sample effectively and efficiently.

SAMPLE CONTROL **Sample control** is the ability of the survey mode to reach the units specified in the sample effectively and efficiently.[16] At least in principle, in-home personal interviews offer the best sample control. It is possible to control which sampling units are interviewed, who is interviewed, the degree of participation of other members of the household, and many other aspects of data collection. In practice, to achieve a high degree of control the researcher has to overcome several problems. It is difficult to find respondents at home during the day because most people work outside the home. Also, for safety reasons, interviewers are reluctant to venture into certain neighborhoods, and people have become cautious of responding to strangers at their doors.

Mall-intercept and CAPI allow only a moderate degree of sample control. Although the interviewer has control over which respondents to intercept, the choice is limited to mall shoppers, and frequent shoppers have a greater probability of being included. Also, potential respondents can intentionally avoid or initiate contact with the interviewer. Compared to mall-intercept, CAPI offers slightly better control, because sampling quotas can be set and respondents randomized automatically.

sampling frame

A representation of the elements of the target population. It consists of a list or set of directions for identifying the target population.

Moderate to high sampling control can be achieved with traditional telephone interviews and CATI. Telephones offer access to geographically dispersed respondents and hard-to-reach areas. These procedures depend upon a **sampling frame**—a list of population units with their telephone numbers.[17] The sampling frames normally used are telephone directories, but telephone directories are limited in that (1) not everyone has a phone, (2) some people have unlisted phones, and (3) directories do not reflect new phones in service or recently disconnected phones. While the telephone has achieved an almost total penetration of households in the United States, there are some variations by region and within regions. The percentage of households with unlisted numbers is about 31 percent and varies considerably by geographical region. In large metropolitan areas, it may be as high as 60 percent. The total of unpublished numbers and new phones in service since the directory was published can account for as much as 40 percent of total telephone households in some metropolitan areas.[18]

random digit dialing (RDD)

A technique used to overcome the bias of unpublished and recent telephone numbers by selecting all telephone number digits at random.

The **random digit dialing (RDD)** technique is used to overcome the bias of unpublished and recent numbers. RDD consists of selecting all 10 (area code, prefix or exchange, suffix) telephone number digits at random. This approach gives all households with telephones an approximately equal chance of being included in the sample, but it suffers from limitations. It is costly and time-consuming to implement, since not all possible telephone numbers are in service: Although there are 10 billion possible telephone numbers, there are only about 100 million actual household telephone numbers. Also, RDD does not distinguish between telephone numbers that are of interest and those that are not (in a consumer survey, for example, business and government numbers are not of interest). There are several variations of RDD that reduce wasted effort. One variation randomly selects a working exchange and adds a block of four-digit random numbers. In **random digit directory designs** a sample of numbers is drawn from the directory. These numbers are modified to allow unpublished numbers a chance of being included in the sample. The popular approaches for modification of numbers include (1) adding a constant to the last digit, (2) randomizing the last *r* digits, and (3) a two-stage procedure. These procedures are described and illustrated in Figure 6.2. Of these three methods, adding a constant to the last digit, particularly plus-one sampling, results in high contact rates and representative samples.[19]

random digit directory designs

A research design for telephone surveys in which a sample of numbers is drawn from the telephone directory and modified to allow unpublished numbers a chance of being included in the sample.

Mail surveys require a list of addresses of individuals or households eligible for inclusion in the sample. Mail surveys can reach geographically dispersed respondents in hard-to-reach areas.[20] However, mailing lists are sometimes unavailable, outdated, or incomplete. Typically, telephone and street directories are used for a listing of the general population. Problems with these types of lists have been discussed already. Catalogs of mailing lists contain thousands of lists that can be purchased. Another factor outside the researcher's control is whether the questionnaire is

FIGURE 6.2

**Random Digit
Directory Designs**

Addition of a Constant to the Last Digit

An integer between 1 and 9 is added to the telephone number selected from the directory. In plus-one sampling the number added to the last digit is 1.

Number selected from directory: 404–953–3004 (area code-exchange-block). Add 1 to the last digit to form 404–953–3005. This is the number to be included in the sample.

Randomization on the *r* Last Digits

Replace the *r* (*r* = 2, 3, or 4) last digits with an equal number of randomly selected digits.

Number selected from directory: 212–881–1124. Replace the last four digits of block with randomly selected numbers 5, 2, 8, and 6 to form 212–881–5286.

Two-Stage Procedure

The first stage consists of selecting an exchange and telephone number from the directory. In the second stage, the last three digits of the selected number are replaced with a three-digit random number between 000 and 999.

Cluster 1

Selected exchange: 202–636
Selected number: 202–636–3230
Replace the last three digits (230) with randomly selected 389 to form 202–636–3389.
Repeat this process until the desired number of telephone numbers from this cluster is obtained.

answered and who answers it. Some subjects refuse to respond because of lack of interest or motivation; others cannot respond because they are illiterate. For these reasons, the degree of sample control in mail surveys is low.[21]

Mail panels, on the other hand, provide moderate to high control over the sample. They provide samples matched to U.S. Bureau of the Census statistics on key demographic variables. It is also possible to identify specific user groups within a panel and to direct the survey to households with specific characteristics. Specific members of households in the panel can be questioned. Finally, low-incidence groups, groups that occur infrequently in the population, can be reached with panels, but there is a question of the extent to which a panel can be considered to be representative of the entire population.

Not all populations are candidates for Internet survey research. The general consumer population is often a poor fit, because many U.S. households do not regularly use Internet services. Although the respondents can be screened to meet qualifying criteria and quotas imposed, the ability to meet quotas is limited by the number and characteristics of respondents who visit the Web site. However, there are some exceptions to this broad statement. For example, computer products purchasers and users of Internet services are both ideal populations. Business and professional users of Internet services are also an excellent population to reach with Internet surveys. Over 90 percent of businesses are currently estimated to have Internet connections. It can be difficult to prevent respondents from completing the Internet survey multiple times. Thus, sample control is low to moderate for Internet surveys targeted at the general population. E-mail surveys suffer from many of the limitations of mail surveys and thus offer low sample control.

QUANTITY OF DATA In-home personal interviews allow the researcher to collect large amounts of data. The social relationship between the interviewer and the respondent, as well as the home environment, motivates the respondent to spend more time in the interview. Less effort is required of the respondent in a personal interview than in a telephone or mail interview. The interviewer records answers to open-ended questions and provides visual aids to help with lengthy and complex scales. Some personal interviews last for as long as 75 minutes. In contrast to in-home interviews, mall intercept and CAPI provide only moderate amounts of data. Because these interviews are conducted in shopping malls and other central locations, the respondents' time is more limited. Typically, the interview time is 30 minutes or less.

For example, in recent mall-intercept interviews conducted by General Foods, the interview time was limited to 25 minutes.[22]

Mail surveys also yield moderate amounts of data. Fairly long questionnaires can be used, since short questionnaires have not been shown to generate higher response rates than long ones, up to a certain limit. The same is true for e-mail and Internet surveys, although the Internet is a better medium in this respect. Mail panels, on the other hand, can generate large amounts of data because of the special relationship between the panel members and the sponsoring organization. For example, the author has used the Synovate (www.synovate.com) panel to administer a questionnaire that took more than an hour to complete.

Traditional telephone interviews and CATI result in the most limited quantities of data. They tend to be shorter than other surveys, because respondents can easily terminate the telephone conversation at their own discretion. These interviews commonly last about 15 minutes, although longer interviews may be conducted when the subject matter is of interest to the respondents. Studies indicate that respondents tend to underestimate the length of telephone interviews by as much as 50 percent. This suggests that telephone interviews may be conducted for a longer duration than is currently the practice.

response rate
The percentage of the total attempted interviews that are completed.

RESPONSE RATE Survey **response rate** is broadly defined as the percentage of the total attempted interviews that are completed. Personal, in-home, mall-intercept and computer-assisted interviews yield the highest response rate (typically between 60 to 80 percent). Problems caused by not-at-homes can often be resolved by calling back at different times. Telephone interviews, traditional and CATI, yield moderate response rates between 40 and 60 percent. These modes also suffer from not-at-homes or no-answers. Higher response rates are obtained by callbacks. Many telephone surveys attempt to call back at least three times.

Mail surveys have poor response rates. In a cold mail survey of randomly selected respondents, without any pre- or post-mailing contact, the response rate is typically less than 15 percent if there is no incentive. Such low response rate can lead to serious bias (nonresponse bias) because whether a person responds to a mail survey is related to his or her interest in the topic. The magnitude of **nonresponse bias** increases as the response rate decreases.[23] However, use of appropriate response-inducement procedures can increase the response rate in mail surveys to about 80 percent. Response rates in mail panels are high, typically in the 60–80 percent range, because of assured respondent cooperation.

nonresponse bias
When actual respondents differ from those who refuse to participate.

Internet surveys have the poorest response rates, even lower than e-mail surveys. This is due to the fact that some respondents may have access to e-mail but not to the Web, and accessing the Web requires more effort and skill. Furthermore, respondents generally need to be connected to the Internet while completing a Web survey; they may not be offline, as with e-mail surveys. If the respondents are prerecruited, they have to log onto a Web site. Many are unwilling to undertake this effort.

A comprehensive, though dated, review of the literature covering 497 response rates in 93 journal articles found weighted average response rates of 81.7, 72.3, and 47.3 percent for, respectively, personal, telephone, and mail surveys.[24] However, response rates have decreased in recent times. The same review also found that response rates increase with:

- either prepaid or promised monetary incentives
- increase in the amount of monetary incentive
- nonmonetary premiums and rewards (pens, pencils, books)
- preliminary notification
- foot-in-the door techniques

critical request
The target behavior that is being researched.

These are multiple request strategies. The first request is relatively small, and all or most people agree to comply. The small request is followed by a larger request, called the **critical request**, which is actually the target behavior.

- personalization (sending letters addressed to specific individuals)
- follow-up letters

A further discussion of improving response rates is found in Chapter 12.

Situational Factors

In any practical situation, the researcher has to balance the need to collect accurate and high-quality data with the budget and time constraints. The situational factors that are important include control of the data collection environment, control of field force, potential for interviewer bias, speed, and cost. The first three factors have an impact on the accuracy and quality of data while the latter two dictate constraints that have to be met.

CONTROL OF THE DATA COLLECTION ENVIRONMENT The degree of control a researcher has over the environment in which the respondent answers the questionnaire is another factor that differentiates the various survey modes. Personal interviews conducted at central locations (mall intercept and CAPI) offer the greatest degree of environmental control. For example, the researcher can set up a special facility for demonstrating the product. In-home personal interviews offer moderate to high control because the interviewer is present. Traditional telephone and CATI offer moderate control. The interviewer cannot see the environment in which the interview is being conducted, but he or she can sense the background conditions and encourage the respondent to be attentive and involved. In mail surveys and panels, e-mail, and Internet surveys, the researcher has little control over the environment, as the interview is self-administered by the respondents in an environment they choose.

field force
The field force is made up of both the actual interviewers and the supervisors involved in data collection.

CONTROL OF FIELD FORCE The **field force** consists of interviewers and supervisors involved in data collection. Because they require no such personnel, mail surveys, mail panels, e-mail, and Internet surveys eliminate field force problems. Traditional telephone interviews, CATI, mall intercept, and CAPI all offer moderate degrees of control because the interviews are conducted at a central location, making supervision relatively simple. In-home personal interviews are problematic in this respect. Since many interviewers work in many different locations, continual supervision is impractical.[25]

POTENTIAL FOR INTERVIEWER BIAS An interviewer can bias the results of a survey by the manner in which he or she (1) selects respondents (interviewing somebody else when required to interview the male head of household), (2) asks research questions (omitting questions), and (3) records answers (recording an answer incorrectly or incompletely). The extent of the interviewer's role determines the potential for bias.[26] In-home and mall-intercept personal interviews are highly susceptible to interviewer bias given the face-to-face interaction between the interviewer and the respondent. Traditional telephone interviews and CATI are less susceptible, although the potential is still there; there is interaction but it is not face-to-face. For example, with inflection and tone of voice, interviewers can convey their own attitudes and thereby suggest answers. Computer-assisted personal interviews have a low potential for bias. Mail surveys, mail panels, e-mail, and Internet surveys are free of it.

SPEED The Internet is by far the fastest method of obtaining data from a large number of respondents. First, there is the speed with which a questionnaire can be created, distributed to respondents, and the data returned. Since printing, mailing, and data keying delays are eliminated, the researcher can have data in hand within hours of writing an Internet questionnaire. Data are obtained in electronic form, so statistical analysis software can be programmed to process standard questionnaires and return statistical summaries and charts automatically. The e-mail survey is also fast, although slower than the Internet since greater time is needed to compile an e-mail list and data entry is also required.

Traditional telephone interviews and CATI are also fast ways of obtaining information. When a central telephone facility is used, several hundred telephone interviews can be done per day. Data for even large national surveys can be collected in two weeks or less. Next in speed, with moderate to high rating, are mall-intercept and computer-assisted interviews that reach potential respondents in central locations. In-home personal interviews, with a moderate rating, are slower, because there is dead time between interviews while the interviewer travels to the next respondent. To expedite data collection, interviews can be conducted in different markets or regions simultaneously. Mail surveys are typically the slowest. It usually takes several weeks to receive completed questionnaires; follow-up mailings take even longer. In a recent study comparing two survey methods, the mean number of days respondents took for the e-mail surveys was a mere 4.3, compared with 18.3 for the mail survey. Mail panels are faster than mail surveys, with a low to moderate rating, because little follow-up is required.[27]

COST For large samples, the cost of Internet surveys is the lowest. Printing, mailing, keying, and interviewer costs are eliminated, and the incremental costs of each respondent are typically low, so studies with large numbers of respondents can be done at substantial savings compared to mail, telephone, or personal surveys. However, when the sample size is small, the programming costs can be substantial and other low-cost methods such as mail and e-mail surveys should also be considered. Personal interviews tend to be the most expensive mode of data collection per completed response. In general, Internet, e-mail, mail surveys, mail panel, traditional telephone, CATI, CAPI, mall-intercept, and personal in-home interviews require progressively larger field staff and greater supervision and control. Hence, the cost increases in this order. However, relative costs depend on the subject of inquiry and the procedures adopted.[28]

Respondent Factors

Since surveys are generally targeted at specific respondent groups, the respondent characteristics should also be considered while selecting a survey method. These factors include perceived anonymity, social desirability, obtaining sensitive information, low incidence rate, and respondent control.

perceived anonymity
The respondent's perceptions that their identities will not be discerned by the interviewer or the researcher.

PERCEIVED ANONYMITY **Perceived anonymity** refers to the respondents' perceptions that the interviewer or the researcher will not discern their identities. Perceived anonymity of the respondent is high in mail surveys, mail panels, and Internet surveys because there is no contact with an interviewer while responding. It is low in personal interviews (in-home, mall intercept, and computer-assisted) due to face-to-face contact with the interviewer. Traditional telephone interviews and CATI fall in the middle as the contact with the interviewer is not face-to-face. It is also moderate with e-mail. Although there is no contact with the interviewer, respondents know that their names can be located on the return e-mail.

social desirability
The tendency of the respondents to give answers that may not be accurate but that may be desirable from a social standpoint.

SOCIAL DESIRABILITY/SENSITIVE INFORMATION **Social desirability** is the tendency of the respondents to give answers that are socially acceptable, whether or not they are true. Because mail surveys, mail panels, and Internet surveys do not involve any social interaction between the interviewer and the respondent, they are least susceptible to social desirability. Evidence suggests that such methods are good for obtaining sensitive information such as that related to financial or personal behavior. Traditional telephone interviews and CATI are moderately good at avoiding socially desirable responses. They are good for obtaining sensitive information, because the respondents have the perception that they are not committing to anything in writing over the telephone.[29] E-mail is only moderately good for controlling social desirability and obtaining sensitive information, given the respondents' awareness that their names can be located on the return e-mail. Personal interviews, whether in-home, mall intercept, or computer-assisted, are limited in this respect, although the problem is somewhat mitigated in the case of computer-assisted interviews due to limited interaction with the interviewer.[30]

As can be seen, perceived anonymity, social desirability, and obtaining sensitive information are interrelated criterion. With some exceptions, social desirability is the mirror image of perceived anonymity. When perceived anonymity is high, social desirability is low and vice versa. With some exceptions, obtaining sensitive information is directly related to perceptions of anonymity. Respondents are more willing to give sensitive information when they perceive that their responses will be anonymous.

incidence rate
Incidence rate refers to the rate of occurrence or the percentage of persons eligible to participate in the study.

LOW INCIDENCE RATE **Incidence rate** refers to the rate of occurrence or the percentage of persons eligible to participate in the study. As will be discussed in more detail in Chapter 12, incidence rate determines how many contacts need to be screened for a given sample size requirement. There are times when the researcher is faced with a situation where the incidence rate of the survey respondents is low. This is generally the case when the population represents a niche or a highly targeted market, rather than the general population. Suppose a study of cosmetics for Avon calls for a sample of females age 18 to 27 who have used a cosmetic foundation at least twice in the past week. Estimates show that such people who would qualify to participate in the study represent only 5 percent of the population. Thus, only 1 in every 20 people in the general population would qualify, resulting in a lot of wasted effort if the general population is sampled. In such cases, a survey method should be selected that can locate the qualified respondents efficiently and minimize waste. The telephone interview can be very effective (high rating) as a method of screening potential respondents to determine eligibility. All it takes is a phone call. The three personal methods (in-home, mall intercept, and CAPI) are all inefficient because the interviewer has to make personal contact with potential respondents. Three of the self-administered methods (mail, mail panel, and e-mail) are moderate in terms of efficiency as all three are relatively low cost and can be used to contact a large number of potential respondents so the desired sample size of qualified respondents is obtained. The Internet, however, is very good in this respect (high rating). In an Internet survey, screening questions can be used to weed out ineligible respondents quickly and efficiently.

RESPONDENT CONTROL Methods that allow respondent control over the interviewing process will solicit greater cooperation and are therefore desirable. Two aspects of control are particularly important to the respondents. The first is control over when to answer the survey, and the flexibility to even answer it in parts at different times, especially if the survey is long. The second aspect of control pertains to the ability of the respondent to regulate the rate at which she answers the survey, i.e., the flexibility to answer the survey at her own pace. Three of the self-administered methods, namely mail, mail panel, and e-mail, are the best (high rating) in terms of imparting this control to respondents. Some control is lost in Internet surveys, because in random pop-up surveys the respondents do not have the flexibility of answering at a later time. However, Internet surveys can be designed to allow respondents to come back and complete them, resulting in moderate to high rating. Telephone surveys are low to moderate as the pace is regulated by the interviewer, and although the telephone call can be rescheduled, the respondent must commit to a specific time. All the three personal methods, namely in-home, mall intercept, and CAPI, are low on this factor as the pace is regulated by the interviewer, and generally the interview cannot be rescheduled.

Some Other Survey Methods

We have covered the basic survey methods. Other survey methods are also used, which are variations of these basic methods. The more popular of these other methods are described in Table 6.3.

TABLE 6.3
Additional Survey Methods

Method	Advantages/Disadvantages	Comment
Completely automated telephone surveys (CATS)	Same as CATI	Useful for short, in-bound surveys initiated by respondent.
Wireless phone interview (voice-based format)	Same as CATI	Useful for point-of-purchase survey if respondent cooperation is obtained.
Wireless phone interview (text-based format)	Same as e-mail	Useful for point-of-purchase survey if respondent cooperation is obtained.
In-office interview	Same as in-home interview	Useful for interviewing busy managers.
Central location interview	Same as mall-intercept interview	Examples include trade shows, conferences, exhibitions, purchase-intercepts.
Kiosk-based computer interview	Same as CAPI	See www.intouchsurvey.com for more information.
Fax interview	Same as mail survey, except higher response rate	Useful in some business surveys.
Drop-off survey	Same as mail survey, except higher cost and higher response rate	Useful for local-market surveys.

Selection of Survey Methods

As is evident from Table 6.2 and the preceding discussion, no survey method is superior in all situations. Depending upon such factors as information requirements, budgetary constraints (time and money), and respondent characteristics, none, one, two, or even all methods may be appropriate.[31] Remember that the various data-collection modes are not mutually exclusive. Rather, they can be employed in a complementary fashion to build on each other's strengths and compensate for each other's weaknesses. The researcher can employ these methods in combination and develop creative methods. To illustrate, in a classic project, interviewers distributed the product, self-administered questionnaires, and returned envelopes to respondents. Traditional telephone interviews were used for follow-up. Combining the data-collection modes resulted in telephone cooperation from 97 percent of the respondents. Furthermore, 82 percent of the questionnaires were returned by mail.[32] In the chapter introduction, we illustrated how election polling successfully used telephone and Internet interviewing. However, caution should be exercised when using different methods in the same domestic marketing research project (also called the use of mixed-mode surveys). The method used may affect the responses obtained and hence the responses obtained by different methods may not be comparable. The results of studies examining the effect of survey methods on respondents are not very consistent. The following department store project example illustrates the selection of a survey mode, whereas the P&G example illustrates the use of a combination of survey methods.

Project Research | ## Personal In-Home Interviews

In the department store project, personal in-home interviews were utilized, for a number of reasons. Many diverse questions were asked. Some questions were complex and a relatively large amount of data had to be collected. The information obtained was not sensitive or threatening. Trained students were used as interviewers, thereby reducing the cost. Another critical consideration was that the personal interviews could be conducted without subcontracting the data collection to a field service organization.

Telephone methods were not chosen due to the complexity of the questions and amount of data needed. Mall intercept and CAPI were not appropriate either, because so much data were needed. The use of a central location facility would have necessitated subcontracting with a field service organization. Mail surveys were ruled out due to low response rate and complexity of the information needed. Mail panels were inappropriate given the complexity of information needed; a self-administered questionnaire was not considered to be appropriate. Electronic methods were not chosen because many people in the target market did not have access to e-mail or the Internet when the survey was conducted. ■

Real Research | ## P&G's Tide: Getting the Buzz with Nielsen BuzzMetrics

Nielsen BuzzMetrics' (www.nielsenbuzzmetrics.com) BrandPulse suite of products—BrandPulse and BrandPulse Insight—measure consumer-generated media to help companies understand consumer needs, reactions, and issues. BrandPulse helps answer basic and fundamental questions about the volume, spread, and influence of word-of-mouth practices and consumer-to-consumer recommendations on a company or brand. BrandPulse Insight provides the latest information on hot consumer trends, up-to-the-minute data about growing consumer concerns, safety/quality issues, or sudden shifts in consumer opinions. It generates verifiable data about the online consumers who are best suited to influence and shape word-of-mouth behavior.

Tide (www.tide.com), one of the most popular consumer brands in the world from P&G, wanted to boost its consumer image for a variety of reasons. Tide's feedback system needed to spread information and brand data more quickly to receive complete data and identify niche markets. Tide chose BrandPulse suite to redesign its feedback system. Tide is now capturing and assimilating on one platform consumer feedback from all incoming sources, including word of mouth. Tide's Web site has a whole new look and feel, with consumers receiving instant self-service answers to many of their queries about Tide products and issues. Those requiring follow-up are automatically routed to the appropriate consumer relations representative. Consumers with stain questions are linked to Tide's "Stain Detective," and when appropriate, other consumers are offered surveys, study opportunities, coupons, or special promotions. All functions are powered by Nielsen BuzzMetrics' tools but maintain the look and feel of Tide's Web site. Such proactive gathering of information helps in the development of new products as well. This is reflected in the number of product improvements Tide has made. P&G had modified this product 22 times in its 21 years of existence. It also makes modifications to cater to market segments such as geographies. For example, a Tide bar was introduced in the Indian market after considering the opinion of its Indian users.[33] ■

Observation Methods

observation
The recording of behavioral patterns of people, objects, and events in a systematic manner to obtain information about the phenomenon of interest.

Observation methods are the second type of methodology used in descriptive research. **Observation** involves recording the behavioral patterns of people, objects, and events in a systematic manner to obtain information about the phenomenon of interest. The observer does not question or communicate with the people being observed. Information may be recorded as the events occur or from records of past events. Observational methods may be structured or unstructured, direct or indirect. Furthermore, observation may be conducted in a natural or contrived environment.[34]

Structured Versus Unstructured Observation

structured observation
Observation techniques where the researcher clearly defines the behaviors to be observed and the methods by which they will be measured.

unstructured observation
Observation that involves a researcher monitoring all relevant phenomena without specifying the details in advance.

In **structured observation**, the researcher specifies in detail what is to be observed and how the measurements are to be recorded. An example would be an auditor performing inventory analysis in a store. This reduces the potential for observer bias and enhances the reliability of the data. Structured observation is appropriate when the marketing research problem has been clearly defined and the information needed has been specified. In these circumstances, the details of the phenomenon to be observed can be clearly identified. Structured observation is suitable for use in conclusive research.

In **unstructured observation**, the observer monitors all aspects of the phenomenon that seem relevant to the problem at hand, for example, observing children playing with new toys. This form of observation is appropriate when the problem has yet to be formulated precisely and flexibility is needed in observation to identify key components of the problem and to develop hypotheses. In unstructured observation, potential for observer bias is high. For this reason, the observation findings should be treated as hypotheses to be tested, rather than as conclusive findings. Thus, unstructured observation is most appropriate for exploratory research.

Disguised Versus Undisguised Observation

In disguised observation, the respondents are unaware that they are being observed. Disguise enables respondents to behave naturally, since people tend to behave differently when they know they are being observed. Disguise may be accomplished by using one-way mirrors, hidden cameras, or inconspicuous mechanical devices. Observers may be disguised as shoppers or sales clerks or in other appropriate roles.

In undisguised observation, the respondents are aware that they are under observation. For example, they may be aware of the presence of the observer. Researchers disagree on how much effect the presence of an observer has on behavior. One viewpoint is that the observer effect is minor and short-lived. The other position is that the observer can seriously bias the behavior patterns.[35]

Natural Versus Contrived Observation

natural observation
Observing behavior as it takes place in the environment.

contrived observation
The behavior is observed in an artificial environment.

Natural observation involves observing behavior as it takes place in the environment. For example, one could observe the behavior of respondents eating fast food at Burger King. In **contrived observation**, respondents' behavior is observed in an artificial environment, such as a test kitchen set up in a shopping mall.

The advantage of natural observation is that the observed phenomenon will more accurately reflect the true phenomenon. The disadvantages are the cost of waiting for the phenomenon to occur and the difficulty of measuring the phenomenon in a natural setting.

The Canon Cameras example in the "Overview" section presented an example of unstructured, disguised observation in a natural setting.

Observation Methods Classified by Mode of Administration

As shown in Figure 6.3, observation methods may be classified by mode of administration as personal observation, mechanical observation, audit, content analysis, and trace analysis.

FIGURE 6.3

A Classification of Observation Methods

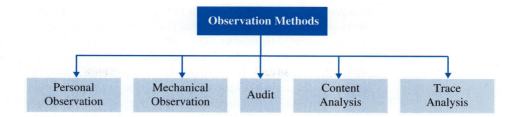

Personal Observation

personal observation
An observational research strategy in which human observers record the phenomenon being observed as it occurs.

In **personal observation**, a researcher observes actual behavior as it occurs, as in the Canon Cameras example in the "Overview" section. The observer does not attempt to control or manipulate the phenomenon being observed. The observer merely records what takes place. For example, a researcher might record traffic counts and observe traffic flows in a department store. This information could aid in designing store layout and determining location of individual departments, shelf locations, and merchandise displays. Companies like Microsoft also make use of personal observation in learning about the software needs of users.[36] Another example is provided in the context of the department store project.

Project Research   License Plate Personal Observation

In the department store project, license plate observations could be used to establish the primary trading area of a shopping mall. These observations help marketers determine where their customers live. In a license plate study, observers record the license plate numbers of the automobiles in a parking lot. These numbers are fed into a computer and paired with automobile registration data. This results in a map of customers located by census tract or zip codes. Such a map, along with other demographic data, can help a department store chain determine new locations, decide on billboard space, and target direct marketing efforts. License plate observation studies cost less ($5,000 to $25,000) and are believed to be quicker and more reliable than direct communication methods such as interviews with shoppers. ■

Mechanical Observation

mechanical observation
An observational research strategy in which mechanical devices rather than human observers record the phenomenon being observed.

In **mechanical observation**, mechanical devices, rather than human observers, record the phenomenon being observed. These devices may or may not require the respondents' direct participation. They are used for continuously recording ongoing behavior for later analysis.

Of the mechanical devices that do not require respondents' direct participation, the Nielsen audimeter is best known. The audimeter is attached to a television set to continually record what channel the set is tuned to. Recently, people meters have been introduced. People meters attempt to measure not only the channels to which a set is tuned but also who is watching.[37] Arbitron has developed the portable people meter, a device worn by people that measures their TV and radio programming during their waking hours. The PreTesting Company (www.pretesting.com) uses the People Reader that unobtrusively records reading material and reader's eye movements to determine the reader's habits, the stopping power, and the brand recall associated with different size ads.

Other common examples include turnstiles that record the number of people entering or leaving a building, and traffic counters placed across streets to determine the number of vehicles passing certain locations. On-site cameras (still, motion picture, or video) are increasingly used by retailers to assess package designs, counter space, floor displays, and traffic flow patterns. Technological advances such as the universal product code (UPC) have made a major impact on mechanical observation. The UPC system, together with optical scanners, allows for mechanized information collection regarding consumer purchases by product category, brand, store type, price, and quantity (see scanner data in Chapter 4).

The Internet can be a very good source for observation and can provide valuable information. The observations can be made in a variety of ways. The primary observations can be made by the number of times the Web page is visited. The time spent on the page can also be measured by advanced techniques of starting the timer when the person visiting the page clicks on a certain icon and stopping the timer when the person clicks on the next button. Further, various other links can be provided by the researcher on the Web page, and it can be observed to see which links are accessed more often. This will provide the researcher with important information about the information needs of the individuals and also the interests of the target segment. The analysis of the links from where the company site is being approached by the individuals will provide the market researcher with important information regarding the consumers' related interests, and an in-depth analysis of the link sites will provide information on advertising, competitors, consumers, and target market demographics and psychographics.

Web-based tracking of Internet users is one exciting and controversial electronic observation technique. Web surfers are served cookies. The cookie is a group of letters and numbers stored in a Web surfer's browser that identify the user. It is a sophisticated means by which a Web site can collect information on visitors. Often this process takes place without the Web surfer's knowledge. Companies and individuals that host Web sites use cookies to collect marketing research information on visitors. Cookies follow the traveler through the Web site and record the pages accessed by the visitor and the number of minutes spent on each page. Your name, address, phone number, and access site can be collected by the cookie and saved into a database if the visitor enters any information. During a follow-up visit, the cookie accesses this information and has the ability to repeat it to the visitor. In essence, the cookie collects data on the user during every visit to the site. The online advertising company DoubleClick (www.doubleclick.com) uses the information obtained from cookies to target advertising. For example, if a user visits an airline site and then a hotel site, that individual will be targeted with Delta Air Lines and Marriott advertisements. Such practices are controversial because they raise privacy concerns amongst individuals and policy makers.

In contrast to the Internet, many mechanical observation devices do require active respondent involvement. These mechanical devices may be classified into five groups: (1) eye-tracking monitors, (2) pupilometers, (3) psychogalvanometers, (4) voice pitch analyzers, and (5) devices measuring response latency. Eye-tracking equipment, such as oculometers, eye cameras, or eye view minuters, records the gaze movements of the eye. These devices can be used to determine how a respondent reads an advertisement or views a TV commercial and for how long the respondent looks at various parts of the stimulus. Such information is directly relevant to assessing advertising effectiveness. The pupilometer measures changes in the diameter of the pupils of the respondent's eyes. Respondents are asked to look at a screen on which an advertisement or other stimulus is projected. Image brightness and distance from the respondents' eyes are held constant. Changes in pupil size are interpreted as changes in cognitive (thinking) activity resulting from exposure to the stimulus. The underlying assumption is that increased pupil size reflects interest and positive attitudes toward the stimulus.[38]

psychogalvanometer
An instrument that measures a respondent's galvanic skin response.

galvanic skin response
Changes in the electrical resistance of the skin that relate to a respondent's affective state.

voice pitch analysis
Measurement of emotional reactions through changes in the respondent's voice.

response latency
The amount of time it takes to respond.

The **psychogalvanometer** measures **galvanic skin response** (GSR) or changes in the electrical resistance of the skin.[39] The respondent is fitted with small electrodes that monitor electrical resistance and is shown stimuli such as advertisements, packages, and slogans. The theory behind this device is that physiological changes such as increased perspiration accompany emotional reactions. Excitement leads to increased perspiration, which increases the electrical resistance of the skin. From the strength of the response, the researcher infers the respondent's interest level and attitudes toward the stimuli.

Voice pitch analysis measures emotional reactions through changes in the respondent's voice. Changes in the relative vibration frequency of the human voice that accompany emotional reaction are measured with audio-adapted computer equipment.[40]

Response latency is the time a respondent takes before answering a question. It is used as a measure of the relative preference for various alternatives.[41] Response time is thought to be directly related to uncertainty. Therefore, the longer a respondent takes to choose between two alternatives, the closer the alternatives are in terms of preference. On the other hand, if the respondent makes a quick decision, one alternative is clearly preferred. With the increased popularity of computer-assisted data collection, response latency can be recorded accurately and without the respondent's awareness.

Technological developments are giving rise to new ways of observation. Tools such as functional magnetic resonance imaging (fMRI) that were originally developed to see brain tumors are now being used to see how someone reacts to different stimulants. The use of these devices allows a researcher to place an item such as brand in front of a person and see exactly what part of the brain the product affects and how strongly. These tools help measure the emotional and thought processes associated with decision making and highlight how the brain functions during a decision-making process. By discovering what elements trigger positive brain responses, marketers may be able to devise more appealing products or more effective advertising campaigns.

Use of eye-tracking monitors, pupilometers, psychogalvanometers, and voice pitch analyzers assumes that physiological reactions are associated with specific cognitive and affective responses. This has yet to be clearly demonstrated. Furthermore, calibration of these devices to measure physiological arousal is difficult and they are expensive to use. Another limitation is that respondents are placed in an artificial environment and know that they are being observed.

Real Research

Mirro: "Nonsticking" Itself from a Sticky Situation

In 2004, Global Home Products LLC purchased the Mirro, Regal, and WearEver brands and combined them to form The WearEver Company (www.wearever.com). Mirro manufactures inexpensive cookware and conducted exploratory research to try to increase market share by introducing a new product. The objective of the research was to determine what characteristics could be added to their kitchenware in order to be more beneficial to the user. The company hired Metaphase design group (www.metaphase.com) to conduct observational market research by using in-house personal meetings with female heads of households. The cities that Metaphase targeted were St. Louis, Boston, and San Francisco. All in-house observations were videotaped for later analysis. The results showed that the most problematic activities involving kitchenware were its pouring characteristics, its storage problems, and its difficulty to clean. More specifically, the company found, "Pouring was a problem, as was moving food in and out of the pan. And people didn't know what to do with their lids while they were cooking. They complained about the mess that lids leave when you have to set them on the counter or on the stove top." Metaphase also noted that most consumers were unhappy with the ability of "nonstick" pans to not stick.

After analyzing the results, Mirro, along with Metaphase, designed a new pot, Allegro, that had a square top with a circular bottom. The square top allowed for easier storage, the ability to pour more carefully, and added volume. All three of these features were directly related to the exploratory research results that the company obtained. The results of the new product were explained by president Gerry Paul: "Allegro sales have topped expectations, and production has finally caught up with the overwhelming demand generated by the early infomercials. Consumer reaction is very good."[42] ■

Audit

In an audit, the researcher collects data by examining physical records or performing inventory analysis. Audits have two distinguishing features. First, data are collected personally by the researcher. Second, the data are based upon counts, usually of physical objects. Retail and wholesale audits conducted by marketing research suppliers were discussed in the context of secondary data (see Chapter 4). Here we focus on the role of audits in collecting primary data. In this respect, an important audit conducted at the consumer level, generally in conjunction with one of the survey methods, is the pantry audit. In a **pantry audit**, the researcher takes an inventory of brands, quantities, and package sizes in a consumer's home, perhaps in the course of a personal interview. Pantry audits greatly reduce the problem of untruthfulness or other forms of response bias. However, obtaining permission to examine consumers' pantries can be difficult, and the fieldwork is expensive. Furthermore, the brands in the pantry may not reflect the most preferred brands or the brands purchased most often. For these reasons, audits are most common at the retail and wholesale level, and these audits were discussed in Chapter 4.

pantry audit
A type of audit where the researcher inventories the brands, quantities, and package sizes of products in a consumer's home.

Content Analysis

content analysis
The objective, systematic, and quantitative description of the manifest content of a communication.

Content analysis is an appropriate method when the phenomenon to be observed is communication, rather than behavior or physical objects. It is defined as the objective, systematic, and quantitative description of the manifest content of a communication.[43] It includes observation as well as analysis. The unit of analysis may be words (different words or types of words in the message), characters (individuals or objects), themes (propositions), space and time measures (length or duration of the message), or topics (subject of the message). Analytical categories for classifying the units are developed and the communication is broken down according to prescribed rules. Marketing research applications involve observing and analyzing the content or message of advertisements, newspaper articles, television and radio programs, and the like. For example, the frequency of appearance of blacks, women, and members of other minority groups in mass media has been studied using content analysis. Suppose we wanted to examine how the portrayal of women in U.S. magazine advertising has changed, positively or negatively, over the 10-year period from 1998 to 2008. We could select a sample of 100 magazines that were in circulation in 1998 as well as in 2008. We could select 10 advertisements featuring women for each of these magazines, from different issues of each magazine, for 1998 as well as 2008. This will give us a sample of 1,000 advertisements for each year. We could then develop positive as well as negative categories for classifying the advertisements based on how they have portrayed the role of women. The number and percentage of advertisements falling in the positive and negative categories could then be compared. The analysis might look something like this:

Categories	1998		2008	
	Number	Percentage	Number	Percentage
Positive				
Intelligent	100	10	150	15
Contributes to society	200	20	350	35
Positive role model	150	15	200	20
Total Positive	450	45	700	70
Negative				
Sex symbol	350	35	150	15
Looked down upon	200	20	150	15
Total Negative	550	55	300	30
Grand Total	1,000	100	1,000	100

This analysis indicates that the positive portrayal of women in U.S. magazine advertising has gone up dramatically, increasing from 45 percent in 1998 to 70 percent in 2008. The greatest increase is in the contribution to society category, which has increased from 20 percent in 1998 to 35 percent in 2008. On the other hand, the negative portrayal of women as sex symbols has markedly decreased from 35 percent in 1998 to 15 percent in 2008.

In the department store patronage project, content analysis may be used to analyze magazine advertisements of the sponsoring and competing stores to compare their projected images. Content analysis has also been used in cross-cultural advertising research, as in the following example.

Real Research

Cross-Cultural Content Makes Ad Agencies Content

As of 2009, the United States accounts for half of the world's advertising expenditures, followed by Japan, which accounts for 10 percent. Content analysis was used to compare the information content in American and Japanese magazine advertising. Six categories of magazines (general, women's, men's, professional, sports, and entertainment) were chosen from each country. Advertisements from these magazines were selected for analysis, resulting in a total of 1,440 advertisements: 832 from American magazines and 608 from Japanese magazines. Three judges independently noted whether each advertisement was informative or uninformative, which criteria for information content were satisfied by the advertisement, the size of the ad, and the product category being advertised. Japanese magazine advertising was found to be consistently more informative than U.S. magazine advertising. For example, more than 85 percent of the Japanese ads analyzed satisfied at least one criterion for information content and thus were perceived to be informative, compared to only 75 percent of the American ads. Likewise, Japanese ads had an average of 1.7 information cues per ad, compared to 1.3 cues per ad for the American ads. This information is useful for multinational companies and advertising agencies including Young & Rubicam, Saatchi & Saatchi Worldwide, McCann Erickson Worldwide, Ogilvy & Mather Worldwide, BBDO Worldwide, and others with global operations conducting cross-cultural advertising campaigns.[44] ∎

Content analysis can involve tedious coding and analysis. However, microcomputers and mainframes can be used to facilitate coding and analysis. The manifest content of the object can be computer coded. The observed frequencies of category codes can be aggregated and compared on the criteria of interest using computers. Although content analysis has not been widely used in marketing research, the technique offers great potential. For example, it could be profitably employed in the analysis of open-ended questions.

Trace Analysis

trace analysis
An approach in which data collection is based on physical traces, or evidence, of past behavior.

An observation method that can be inexpensive if used creatively is trace analysis. In **trace analysis**, data collection is based on physical traces, or evidence, of past behavior. These traces may be left intentionally or unintentionally by the respondents. To illustrate, in the context of the department store patronage project, store charge card slips are traces shoppers leave behind, which can be analyzed to examine their store credit usage behavior.

Several other innovative applications of trace analysis have been made in marketing research.

- The selective erosion of tiles in a museum indexed by the replacement rate was used to determine the relative popularity of exhibits.
- The number of different fingerprints on a page was used to gauge the readership of various advertisements in a magazine.
- The position of the radio dials in cars brought in for service was used to estimate share of listening audience of various radio stations. Advertisers used the estimates to decide on which stations to advertise.
- The age and condition of cars in a parking lot were used to assess the affluence of customers.
- The magazines people donated to charity were used to determine people's favorite magazines.
- Internet visitors leave traces that can be analyzed to examine browsing and usage behavior by using cookies.

Real Research

Have a Cookie!

Many users do not realize it, but they have been served a cookie or two while on the Internet. A cookie is not a culinary delight in this case. It is a sophisticated means by which a Web site can collect information on visitors. Often this process takes place without the knowledge of the Web surfer.

The cookie is a group of letters and numbers stored in a Web surfer's browser that identify the user. Companies and individuals that host Web sites use cookies to collect marketing research information on visitors. Cookies follow the traveler through the Web site and record the pages accessed by the visitor and the number of minutes spent on each page. Your name, address, phone number, and access site can be collected by the cookie and saved into a database if you enter any information. During a follow-up visit, the cookie accesses this information and has the ability to repeat it to you. In essence, the cookie collects data on the user during every visit to the site.

Expedia (www.expedia.com) uses cookies to collect information about site traffic. The information helps marketing personnel at the travel site to collect demographics on the reader. Also, the company can monitor "hits" on particular topics and gain valuable feedback on user interest. Data collection is based upon visitor behavior. This disguised technique enables Expedia to monitor use patterns and to eliminate socially acceptable response bias. Information collected in this manner has been used to modify editorial content and format to make the Web site more appealing and useful to visitors.[45] ■

Although trace analysis has been creatively applied, it has limitations. Current evidence indicates that it should be used only when no other approach is possible. Moreover, ethical issues, such as the use of cookies, should be duly addressed.

ACTIVE RESEARCH

Observing the Popularity of Theme Park Exhibits

Visit www.disney.com and search the Internet using a search engine as well as your library's online databases to obtain information on the criteria that consumers use for selecting theme parks.

If Disney World wants to determine how many people visit its theme parks on a daily basis and which are the most popular exhibits, can the observation method be used? If yes, which observation method would you use?

As the marketing manager for Disney World, how would you use information on criteria that consumers use for selecting theme parks to formulate marketing strategies that would increase your attendance and market share?

A Comparative Evaluation of Observation Methods

A comparative evaluation of the observation methods is given in Table 6.4. The different observation methods are evaluated in terms of the degree of structure, degree of disguise, ability to observe in a natural setting, observation bias, measurement and analysis bias, and additional general factors.

Structure relates to the specification of what is to be observed and how the measurements are to be recorded. As can be seen from Table 6.4, personal observation is low, trace analysis is medium, and audit and content analysis are high on the degree of structure. Mechanical observation can vary widely from low to high depending upon on the methods used. Methods such as optical scanners are very structured in that the characteristics to be measured, for example, characteristics of items purchased scanned in supermarket checkouts, are precisely defined. Thus, these methods are high in the degree of structure. In contrast, mechanical methods such as use of hidden cameras to observe children at play with toys tend to be unstructured.

The degree of disguise is low in the case of audits because it is difficult to conceal the identity of auditors. Personal observation offers a medium degree of disguise because there are limitations on the extent to which the observer can be disguised as a shopper, sales clerk, employee, and so forth. Trace analysis and content analysis offer a high degree of disguise as the data are collected "after the fact," that is, after the phenomenon to be observed has taken place. Some mechanical observations, such as hidden cameras, offer excellent disguise whereas the use of others, such as the use of psychogalvanometers, is very difficult to disguise.

The ability to observe in a natural setting is low in trace analysis because the observation takes place after the behavior has occurred. It is medium in the case of content analysis because the communication being analyzed is only a limited representation of the natural phenomenon. Personal observation and audits are excellent on this score as human observers can observe people or objects in a variety of natural settings. Mechanical observation methods vary from low (e.g., use of psychogalvanometers) to high (e.g., use of turnstiles).

Observation bias is low in the case of mechanical observation because a human observer is not involved. It is also low for audits. Although the auditors are humans, the observation usually takes place on objects and the characteristics to be observed are well defined, leading to low observation bias. Observation bias is medium for trace analysis and content analysis. In both these methods, human observers are involved, and the characteristics to be observed are not that well defined. However, the observers typically do not interact with human respondents during the observation process, thus lessening the degree of bias. It is high for personal observation due to the use of human observers who interact with the phenomenon being observed.

Data analysis bias is low for audits and content analysis because the variables are precisely defined, the data are quantitative, and statistical analysis is conducted. Trace analysis has a medium degree of bias because the definition of variables is not very precise. Mechanical observation methods can have a low (e.g., scanner data) to medium (e.g., hidden camera) degree of analysis bias depending on the method. Unlike personal observation, the bias in mechanical observation is limited to the medium level due to improved measurement and classification, because the phenomenon to be observed can be recorded continuously using mechanical devices.

TABLE 6.4
A Comparative Evaluation of Observation Methods

Criteria	Personal Observation	Mechanical Observation	Audit	Content Analysis	Trace Analysis
Degree of structure	Low	Low to high	High	High	Medium
Degree of disguise	Medium	Low to high	Low	High	High
Ability to observe in natural setting	High	Low to high	High	Medium	Low
Observation bias	High	Low	Low	Medium	Medium
Analysis bias	High	Low to medium	Low	Low	Medium
General remarks	Most flexible	Can be intrusive	Expensive	Limited to communications	Method of last resort

In addition, personal observation is the most flexible. Human observers can observe a wide variety of phenomena in a wide variety of settings. Some mechanical observation methods such as use of psychogalvanometers can be very intrusive, leading to artificiality and bias. Audits using human auditors tend to be expensive. Content analysis is well suited for and limited to the observation of communications. As mentioned earlier, trace analysis is a method of last resort. The application of these criteria will lead to the identification of an appropriate method, if observation is at all suitable in the given situation.

Project Research   ## Project Activities

1. Do you think that the use of personal in-home interviews was the best method in the Sears project? Why or why not?
2. If the Sears survey were to be conducted today, which survey method should be used and why?
3. Discuss the use of personal and mechanical observation methods to determine consumer preferences for department stores. ■

A Comparison of Survey and Observation Methods

Only about 1 percent of the marketing research projects rely solely on observational methods to obtain primary data.[46] This implies that observational methods have some major disadvantages as compared to survey methods. Yet these methods offer some advantages that make their use in conjunction with survey methods quite fruitful.

Relative Advantages of Observation

The greatest advantage of observational methods is that they permit measurement of actual behavior rather than reports of intended or preferred behavior. There is no reporting bias, and potential bias caused by the interviewer and the interviewing process is eliminated or reduced. Certain types of data can be collected only by observation. These include behavior patterns that the respondent is unaware of or unable to communicate. For example, information on babies' toy preferences is best obtained by observing babies at play, because they are unable to express themselves adequately. Moreover, if the observed phenomenon occurs frequently or is of short duration, observational methods may be cheaper and faster than survey methods.

Relative Disadvantages of Observation

The most serious disadvantage of observation is that the reasons for the observed behavior may not be determined because little is known about the underlying motives, beliefs, attitudes, and preferences. For example, people observed buying a brand of cereal may or may not like it themselves. They may be purchasing that brand for someone else in the household. Another limitation of observation is that selective perception (bias in the researcher's perception) can bias the data. In addition, observation is often time-consuming and expensive, and it is difficult to observe certain forms of behavior such as personal activities. Finally, in some cases the use of observational methods may be unethical, as in monitoring the behavior of people without their knowledge or consent.

To sum up, observation has the potential to provide valuable information when properly used. From a practical standpoint, it is best to view observation methods as a complement to survey methods, rather than as being in competition with them. The following example illustrates this point.

Real Research   ## How Do You Like Your Beef?

When people shop for meat at the grocery store, they tend to stick with what they know. This is what was found when marketing research was conducted for the National Cattlemen's Beef Association (NCBA). The research was performed to help the NCBA (www.beef.org) figure out why the sales of certain cuts of beef had been dropping by 20 percent over a period of 4 years. The research used mechanical observation and customer interviews. The researchers stationed themselves at the meat cases of stores in order to record the buying behavior of consumers. The consumers were videotaped while shopping for beef. These observations showed that many consumers were not purchasing certain cuts of beef even when they looked good and were less fattening than the more popular sirloin or ground beef. When these consumers were asked why they didn't buy certain cuts of beef, the overwhelming response was that they didn't know how to cook them.

The NCBA took several steps to address this situation. Appropriate cooking instructions for the cut of meat are now clearly printed on the package. Additionally, the NCBA worked with grocers to change the store layout to display beef according to the cooking method. There are labels above each section that state not only the nutritional facts, but also the ways in which a cut of beef may be prepared. Small recipe cards have also been placed alongside the beef cuts.

The demand for beef and cattle held steady during the tough economic environment of 2008. In fact, the good news for the beef industry was that the demand for live cattle was up 1.5 percent for January–July 2008 compared to the same months of 2007.[47] ■

Ethnographic Research

Ethnographic research is the study of human behavior in its natural context and involves observation of behavior and setting along with depth interviews. Sometimes audio and visual recordings are also obtained. Thus, both the questioning and observation methods are combined to understand the behavior of consumers. The following example illustrates this method.

Real Research   PortiCo Documents with Documentaries

PortiCo Research (www.porticoresearch.com) specializes in observing individuals, questioning them in depth, recording them on videos, and selling these tapes for tens of thousands of dollars to its major clients, such as Honda, Delta, Lipton, and Procter & Gamble. They have fine-tuned the method of collecting ethnographic data and have made it into a very profitable business.

PortiCo's specialty is total immersion in the lives of consumers in an effort to document how they make purchasing decisions. Research teams of anthropologists, social psychologists, and ethnographers (professionals who comparatively study people) go into the subjects' homes with videographers. The teams tape the subjects in their homes and also go shopping with them to watch what they buy and ask questions on the reasons for their purchases. After filming, employees of PortiCo transcribe the findings of the videos and analyze them for their clients. The analysis is based on the research problem that the client has set out to solve or get more information about. For example, PortiCo did a large study for Lipton to find out people's attitudes toward tea. With the results of the study, Lipton would find out whether or not to invest more in advertising, develop new flavors, or market more iced tea instead of hot tea. The findings showed that Americans don't drink very much hot tea, especially because of the presence of caffeinated coffee in the marketplace. If and when they do drink hot tea, it is normally flavored, herbal tea. Most of Lipton's hot tea is not in special flavors. However, they have recently begun to bring herbal teas to market. The study did find, however, that American consumers like iced tea. As a result of the findings, Lipton has done a lot of creative developments in the area of iced tea. They pushed the marketing of Brisk Iced Tea in the can, which is now the number one selling brand of ready-to-drink iced tea. Also, Lipton has created a Cold Brew Blend tea bag in both family size, to make a whole pitcher, and single-glass size, for one serving. This tea bag allows iced tea to be brewed with cold water instead of having to use boiling water. Therefore, consumers can enjoy their tea faster with much less hassle. These marketing efforts, guided by the findings of PortiCo Research, have resulted in increased sales and market share for Lipton.[48] ■

Other Methods

mystery shopping
Trained observers pose as consumers and shop at company- or competitor-owned stores to collect data about customer–employee interaction and other marketing variables.

In addition to ethnographic research, there are also a variety of other methods that combine the use of questioning and observation. One such method that is commonly used is **mystery shopping**. Trained observers pose as consumers and shop at company- or competitor-owned stores to collect data about customer–employee interaction and other marketing variables, such as prices, displays, layout, and so on. The mystery shoppers question the store employees, mentally take note of the answers, and observe the variables of interest. For more information on mystery shopping and firms that provide this service, visit www.mysteryshop.org.

International Marketing Research

Given the differences in the economic, structural, informational and technological, and sociocultural environments, the feasibility and popularity of the different interviewing methods vary widely. Table 6.5 provides an illustration of how cultural and environmental factors may have an impact on

TABLE 6.5
The Impact of Cultural and Environmental Factors on the Selection of Survey Methods

- A survey that takes 20 minutes in the United States could take more than twice as long in Germany. The German language is not as concise as English, and Germans like to talk more than Americans do. For similar reasons, the interviewing time could be longer in other countries as well, such as in Brazil.

- Telephone directories are unreliable in some countries (e.g., some African nations, such as Sierra Leone), because they are updated infrequently.

- The incidence of unlisted telephones can vary widely across countries and across segments. For example, in Colombia, the numbers of some members of the elite and upper classes are never listed.

- In some countries, such as Japan, China, Thailand, Malaysia, and those in Southeast Asia, telephone interviews are considered rude. In contrast, in some South American countries, such as Argentina and Peru, the response rates to telephone surveys is high given the low levels of telemarketing and the element of surprise in receiving an unexpected long-distance or local call.

- Traditional personal interviewing methods remain popular in some European countries (e.g., Switzerland, Sweden, France), Asian countries (e.g., China, India, Hong Kong), African countries (e.g., Nigeria, Kenya), and South American countries (e.g., Colombia, Mexico) due to the prevalence of face-to-culture.

- Low literacy rates and/or the lack of a reliable postal system in rural areas might make mail surveys infeasible in some countries (e.g., Ghana, Ivory Coast, El Salvador, Uruguay, Paraguay).

- Mall interviews are limited due to the lack of shopping malls in many developing countries and some developed countries (e.g., Germany). In addition, domestic laws might prohibit or make it more difficult to interview people while shopping.

- Telephone penetration is low in some countries, particularly in rural areas. In some countries, such as Cambodia, multiple families might share a phone line because of high phone rates.

- In countries with high cellular/mobile phone penetration and low hard/wired-line penetration (e.g., Thailand, Malaysia), the use of traditional phone surveys is unappealing.

- Poor access to computers and the Internet makes the use of electronic interviewing infeasible in some countries (e.g., rural populations in Africa, Asia, and South America).

the use of survey methods. This table points out that it is unlikely that a single data-collection methodology will be effective in a multicountry research study. For instance, mail surveys are popular in the United States and Canada. However, mail surveys in Europe are less popular and rare in most other parts of the world. Several reasons account for this difference, including lower literacy rates, excessive time for mail to reach its destination, and cultures where people do not believe in writing replies that will be read by a stranger.

A similar problem occurs with telephone surveys. Phone interviewing has grown in Europe recently, but is still not widely used outside the United States. Response rates for mail and telephone surveys are much lower in marketing studies abroad. Face-to-face interview techniques remain the most popular internationally used marketing field research techniques. It is very important to instruct field workers who are collecting the data on how they may be affecting the results of a face-to-face study in an international setting. In selecting interviewers, it is also useful to consider the nationalities of the interviewer compared with the participants because of cultural relations that may bias the responses.

Selection of appropriate interviewing methods is much more difficult because of the challenges of conducting research in foreign countries. Given the differences in the economic, structural, informational and technological, and sociocultural environment, the feasibility and popularity of the different interviewing methods vary widely. In the United States and Canada, the telephone has achieved almost total penetration of households. As a result, telephone interviewing is the dominant mode of questionnaire administration. The same situation exists in some European countries, such as Sweden. However, in many of the other European countries, telephone penetration is still not complete. In developing countries, only a very few households have telephones.

In-home personal interviews are the dominant mode of collecting survey data in many European countries such as Switzerland, newly industrialized countries (NICs), and developing countries. Although mall intercepts are being conducted in some European countries, such as Sweden, they are not popular in Europe or developing countries. In contrast, central location/street interviews constitute the dominant method of collecting survey data in France and the Netherlands.

TABLE 6.6

A Comparative Evaluation of Survey Methods for International Marketing Research

Criteria	Telephone	Personal	Mail	Electronic
High sample control	+	+	−	−
Difficulty in locating respondents at home	+	−	+	+
Inaccessibility of homes	+	−	+	+
Unavailability of a large pool of trained interviewers	+	−	+	+
Large population in rural areas	−	+	−	−
Unavailability of maps	+	−	+	+
Unavailability of current telephone directory	−	+	−	+
Unavailability of mailing lists	+	+	−	+
Low penetration of telephones	−	+	+	−
Lack of an efficient postal system	+	+	−	+
Low level of literacy	−	+	−	−
Face-to-face communication culture	−	+	−	−
Poor access to computers and Internet	?	+	?	−

Note: A + denotes an advantage, and a − denotes a disadvantage.

Because of low cost, mail interviews continue to be used in most developed countries where literacy is high and the postal system is well developed: United States, Canada, Denmark, Finland, Iceland, Norway, Sweden, and The Netherlands, for example. In Africa, Asia, and South America, however, the use of mail surveys and mail panels is low because of illiteracy and the large proportion of the population living in rural areas. Mail panels are extensively used only in a few countries outside the United States, such as Canada, the United Kingdom, France, Germany, and The Netherlands. However, the use of panels may increase with the advent of new technology. Likewise, although a Web site can be accessed from anywhere in the world, access to the Web or e-mail is limited in many countries, particularly developing countries. Hence, the use of electronic surveys is not feasible, especially for interviewing households. European marketing research firms have been slower to adopt electronic interviewing as Internet penetration in Europe has lagged that in the United States. The different methods of survey administration in international marketing research are discussed in more detail in Chapter 24.

Selection of Survey Methods

No questionnaire administration method is superior in all situations. Table 6.6 presents a comparative evaluation of the major modes of collecting quantitative data in the context of international marketing research. In this table, the survey methods are discussed only under the broad headings of telephone, personal, mail, and electronic (e-mail, Internet) interviews. The use of CATI, CAPI, and mail panels depends heavily on the state of technological development in the country. Likewise, the use of mall-intercept interviewing is contingent upon the dominance of shopping malls in the retailing environment. The same is true for e-mail and Internet surveys, which rely on access to computers and the Internet. The major methods of interviewing should be carefully evaluated on the criteria given in Table 6.6, as shown.

Another very important consideration in selecting the methods of administering questionnaires is to ensure equivalence and comparability across countries. Different methods may have different reliabilities in different countries. In collecting data from different countries, it is desirable to use survey methods with equivalent levels of reliability, rather than the same method, as illustrated in the following example.[49]

Real Research   Using Dominant Survey Methods to Gain Dominant Market Share

With worldwide sales accounting for about 50 percent of its total, Reebok is marketed in more than 170 countries as of 2009. Currently, Reebok is seeking to expand in Europe and would like to institute strong marketing programs to sell street sneakers to the European masses. A survey of consumer preferences for sneakers is to be undertaken in three countries: Sweden, France, and Switzerland.

By using the dominant mode of interviewing in each country, Reebok can accurately assess the preferences of Europeans for street sneakers.

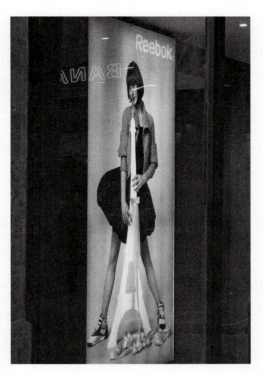

Comparability of results can best be achieved by using the dominant mode of interviewing in each country: telephone interviews in Sweden, central location/street interviews in France, and in-home personal interviews in Switzerland.[50] ■

As in the case of surveys, the selection of an appropriate observation method in international marketing research should also take into account the differences in the economic, structural, informational and technological, and sociocultural environment.

Ethics in Marketing Research

The use of survey research as a guise for selling (called *sugging* in the trade language) or fundraising (*frugging*) is unethical. Another ethical issue that is salient in survey and observation research is respondents' anonymity. Researchers have an obligation to not disclose respondents' names to outside parties, including the client. This is all the more critical if the respondents were promised anonymity in order to obtain their participation. The client is not entitled to the names of respondents. Only when respondents are notified in advance and their consent is obtained prior to administering the survey can their names be disclosed to the client. Even in such situations, the researcher should have the assurance that the client will not use respondents' names in sales efforts or misuse them in other ways. The following example highlights the battle being waged by the marketing research industry in the ethical arena.

Real Research

The Signal Is Busy for Telephone Research

The Council for Marketing and Opinion Research (CMOR) (www.cmor.org) recently identified the "major threats to research vitality." At the top of the list was telephone research due to concern over proposed legislation. About half of the states have introduced bills to regulate unsolicited telephone calls and the remaining are considering similar legislation. A California law, designed to limit eavesdropping, makes it illegal to listen in on an extension, and this might limit supervisory monitoring of telephone interviewers.

Another issue facing the marketing research industry is image; the general public does not distinguish between telephone research and telemarketing. This identity crisis is exacerbated by the action of some firms to commit "sugging" or "frugging," industry terms for selling or fundraising, respectively, under the guise of a survey.

All of these barriers have raised the cost of telephone research and make it difficult for researchers to obtain representative samples. Recent statistics released by CMOR confirm that the industry still faces an increasing trend in the number of people refusing to participate in surveys each year. The study surveyed 3,700 U.S. consumers, and nearly 45 percent stated they had refused to participate in a survey during the last year. CMOR's definition of a survey refusal does not include cases where consumers avoid phone calls by means of caller ID or answering machines. Such factors would actually push the true refusal rate much higher. Consumers' concern about privacy is the number one reason survey refusal rate is so high. In addition, the widespread use of the Internet and publicized awareness of fraudulent use has made consumers more hesitant about participating in interviews. The study also reveals that only 30 percent of respondents "agree" or "strongly agree" that researchers can be trusted to protect consumers' right to privacy. CMOR is fighting back and has hired the Washington law firm of Covington and Burling to lobby Congress and coordinate state-level lobbying. Another action under consideration is a "seal of approval" from the CMOR to raise the public's perceptions of responsible research firms. The battle to save telephone research must be waged; all it takes is a phone call.[51] ■

Researchers should not place respondents in stressful situations. Disclaimers such as "there are no right or wrong answers; we are only interested in your opinion" can relieve much of the stress inherent in a survey.

Often the behavior of people is observed without their knowledge because informing the respondents may alter their behavior.[52] However, this can violate respondents' privacy. One guideline is that people should not be observed for research in situations where they would not expect to be observed by the public. However, observing people in public places like a mall or a grocery store is appropriate if certain procedures are followed. Notices should be posted in these areas stating that they are under observation for marketing research purposes. After the data have been collected, the researcher should obtain the necessary permission from the respondents. If any of the respondents refuse to grant permission, the observation records pertaining to them should be destroyed. These guidelines should also be applied when using cookies on the Internet.[53]

Decision Research   Microsoft: Small Businesses Represent a Big Market

---

The Situation

Statistics from the U.S. Small Business Administration show that in 2009 small businesses generated about 50 percent of all U.S. sales and contributed 50 percent of private GDP. They also employed more than 50 percent of the U.S. workforce. Microsoft Corporation is impressed with these statistics because they indicate that small businesses may represent a big market for its products. It wonders whether the needs of small businesses are different from those of large businesses. Steve Ballmer, the CEO, would like to develop specialized products for the small businesses. Some of these products could include a Web site just for small businesses; the Microsoft Small Business Council (which provides information to help small businesses use technology); the Microsoft Small Business Technology Partnership Board (an educational resource); the BackOffice Small Business Server; and a Small Business Edition of Microsoft Works.

The Marketing Research Decision

1. If a survey is to be conducted to determine small businesses' preferences for software products, which survey method would you recommend and why?
2. Discuss the role of the type of research you recommend in enabling Steve Ballmer to determine small businesses' preferences for software products.

The Marketing Management Decision

1. Steve Ballmer is wondering what Microsoft should do to effectively meet the needs of small businesses. What is your recommendation?
2. Discuss how the marketing management decision action that you recommend to Steve Ballmer is influenced by the type of survey that you suggested earlier and by the findings of that survey.[54] ■

Summary

The two basic means of obtaining primary quantitative data in descriptive research are survey and observation. Survey involves the direct questioning of respondents; observation entails recording respondent behavior. Figure 6.4 gives a concept map for quantitative descriptive data.

Surveys involve the administration of a questionnaire and may be classified, based on the method or mode of administration, as (1) traditional telephone interviews, (2) CATI, (3) in-home personal interviews, (4) mall-intercept interviews, (5) CAPI, (6) mail surveys, (7) mail panels, (8) e-mail surveys, and (9) Internet surveys. Of these methods, traditional telephone interviews and CATI are the most popular in USA. However, each method has some general advantages and disadvantages. The various methods may be

FIGURE 6.4

A Concept Map for Quantitative Descriptive Data

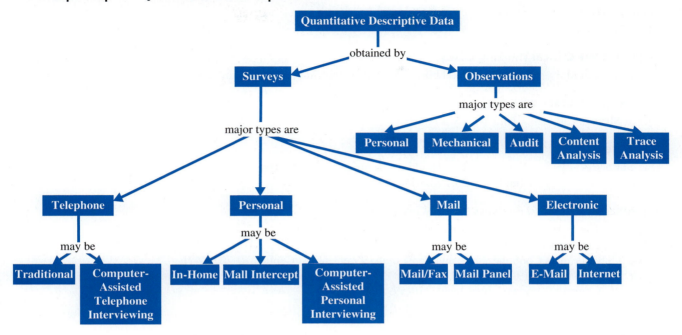

compared in terms of task, situational, and respondent factors. Task factors relate to tasks that have to be performed to collect the data and to the topic of the survey. These factors consist of diversity of questions and flexibility, use of physical stimuli, sample control, quantity of data, and response rate. The situational factors comprise control of the data-collection environment, control of field force, potential for interviewer bias, speed, and cost. The respondent factors pertain to survey respondents and include perceived anonymity, social desirability, obtaining sensitive information, low incidence rate, and respondent control. Although these data-collection methods are usually thought of as distinct and competitive, they should not be considered mutually exclusive. It is possible to employ them productively in combination.

Observational methods may be classified as structured or unstructured, disguised or undisguised, and natural or contrived. The major methods are personal observation, mechanical observation, audit, content analysis, and trace analysis. As compared

to surveys, the relative advantages of observational methods are (1) they permit measurement of actual behavior, (2) there is no reporting bias, and (3) there is less potential for interviewer bias. Also, certain types of data can be obtained best, or only, by observation. The relative disadvantages of observation are (1) very little can be inferred about motives, beliefs, attitudes, and preferences; (2) there is the potential for observer bias; (3) most methods are time-consuming and expensive; (4) it is difficult to observe some forms of behavior; and (5) there is the potential for being unethical. Observation is rarely used as the sole method of obtaining primary data, but it can be usefully employed in conjunction with survey methodology.

In collecting data from different countries, it is desirable to use survey methods with equivalent levels of reliability, rather than the same method. Respondents' anonymity should be protected and their names should not be turned over to the clients. People should not be observed without their consent for research in situations where they would not expect to be observed by the public.

Key Terms and Concepts

survey method, 179
structured data collection, 179
fixed-alternative questions, 179
mail panels, 186
hypertext markup language, 187
sample control, 191
sampling frame, 191
random digit dialing (RDD), 191
random digit directory designs, 191
response rate, 193
nonresponse bias, 193

critical request, 193
field force, 194
perceived anonymity, 195
social desirability, 195
incidence rate, 195
observation, 198
structured observation, 198
unstructured observation, 198
natural observation, 198
contrived observation, 198
personal observation, 199

mechanical observation, 199
psychogalvanometer, 200
galvanic skin response, 200
voice pitch analysis, 200
response latency, 200
pantry audit, 201
content analysis, 201
trace analysis, 203
mystery shopping, 206

Suggested Cases, Video Cases, and HBS Cases

Running Case with Real Data

1.1 Dell

Comprehensive Critical Thinking Cases

2.1 American Idol   2.2 Baskin-Robbins   2.3 Akron Children's Hospital

Comprehensive Cases with Real Data

4.1 JPMorgan Chase   4.2 Wendy's

Video Cases

6.1 Starbucks	8.1 P&G	10.1 Dunkin' Donuts	11.1 Motorola
12.1 Subaru	13.1 Intel	23.1 Marriott	24.1 Nivea

Comprehensive Harvard Business School Cases

Case 5.1: The Harvard Graduate Student Housing Survey (9-505-059)
Case 5.2: BizRate.Com (9-501-024)
Case 5.3: Cola Wars Continue: Coke and Pepsi in the Twenty-First Century (9-702-442)
Case 5.4: TiVo in 2002 (9-502-062)
Case 5.5: Compaq Computer: Intel Inside? (9-599-061)
Case 5.6: The New Beetle (9-501-023)

Live Research: Conducting a Marketing Research Project

As a class, discuss the various survey methods and select one that is appropriate for the project. In addition to the criteria given in this chapter, certain practical constraints may have to be considered if the students have to collect data. Examples include the following:

1. There should be a budget for making long-distance calls if a telephone survey is to be done beyond the local calling area.
2. A CATI system may not be available, and so the telephone method may be limited to the traditional telephone.
3. Students will not be allowed to conduct mall-intercept interviews unless permission is obtained from the mall management.

Some malls have signed exclusive contracts with marketing research firms for data collection.

4. It may not be practical to do in-home personal interviews covering a large geographic area, even in the local region.
5. There may not be enough time for a mail survey and a mail panel may be prohibitively expensive.
6. E-mail addresses may not be available or may be very difficult to get.
7. Mechanical observation devices may be impractical to obtain and use.

Acronyms

The classification of survey methods by mode of administration may be described by the acronym

Methods:

M ail panels
E lectronic methods: e-mail and Internet surveys
T elephone interviews
H ome (in-home personal) interviewing
O n-site mall interviews
D irect mail interviews
S oftware for CATI and CAPI

In using observational methods, you must WATCH the respondents' behavior. These methods may be described by the acronym

Watch:

W alkie-talkie: mechanical observation
A udit
T race analysis
C ontent analysis
H uman (personal) observation

Exercises

Questions

1. Explain briefly how the topics covered in this chapter fit into the framework of the marketing research process.
2. What are the advantages and disadvantages of the structured-direct survey method?
3. Name the major modes for obtaining information via a survey.
4. What are the relevant factors for evaluating which survey method is best suited to a particular research project?
5. What would be the most appropriate survey method for a project in which control of field force and cost are critical factors?

6. Name the types of mechanical observation and explain how they work.
7. Explain how content analysis could be employed in the analysis of open-ended questions. Comment on the relative advantages and disadvantages of using such a method.
8. Why is trace analysis used as a means of last resort?
9. What are the relative advantages and disadvantages of observation?

Problems

1. Describe a marketing research problem in which both survey and observation methods could be used for obtaining the information needed.

2. Collect 30 advertisements featuring women from recent issues of popular magazines. Do a content analysis of these ads to examine the different roles in which women are portrayed in advertising.
3. The campus food service would like to determine how many people eat in the student cafeteria. List the survey methods in which this information could be obtained. Which method is best?

Internet and Computer Exercises

1. Ask your instructor or other faculty members if you could serve as a respondent in a computer-assisted personal interview. Then answer the same questionnaire in a pencil and paper format. Compare the two experiences.
2. Use simple spreadsheet software, such as EXCEL, or any appropriate computer program, to conduct the content analysis described in problem 2.
3. Locate an Internet survey for which you would qualify as a respondent. Answer this survey. How would you evaluate this survey based on the criteria factors of Table 6.2?
4. Locate an Internet survey. Examine the content of the questionnaire carefully. What are relative advantages and disadvantages of administering the same survey using CATI or mall-intercept interviewing?
5. Design an e-mail survey to measure students' attitudes toward credit cards. E-mail the survey to 10 students. Summarize, in a qualitative way, the responses received. Are student attitudes toward credit cards positive or negative?
6. Visit the Gallup organization's Web site at www.gallup.com. What survey methods have been used by Gallup in some of the recent surveys posted at this site? Why were these survey methods selected?

Activities

Role Playing

1. You work for a high-tech company and are asked to do a study of people's responses to your advertising. Specifically, your boss wants to know which ads in a series are especially appealing or interesting to consumers. Your recommendations will be used to determine the product's copy mix. Explain how you will obtain this information. What methods will you use and why? Be specific.
2. You have been hired by the campus bookstore to determine how students make purchase decisions while shopping. You are to use the method of personal observation. Disguise yourself as a shopper and observe the behavior of other students in the bookstore. Write a report about your findings.

Fieldwork

1. Visit a local marketing research firm engaged in survey research. Take a tour of their CATI facilities. Write a report describing how this firm conducts CATI.
2. Contact a marketing research firm with mall-intercept interviewing facilities. Arrange to visit these facilities when mall-intercept interviews are being conducted. Write a report about your experience.

Group Discussion

1. As a small group, discuss the ethical issues involved in disguised observation. How can such issues be addressed?
2. "With advances in technology, observation methods are likely to become popular." Discuss this statement as a small group.

Dell Running Case

Review the Dell case, Case 1.1, and questionnaire given toward the end of the book.

1. The Dell survey was administered by posting it on a Web site and sending an e-mail invitation to respondents. Evaluate the advantages and disadvantages of this method. Do you think that this was the most effective method?
2. Compare the various survey methods for conducting the Dell survey.

3. Can Dell make use of the observation method to determine consumers' preferences for PCs and notebook computers? If yes, which observation method would you recommend and why?
4. Visit a store selling PCs and notebooks (e.g., Best Buy, Staples, etc.). If this store wants to conduct a survey to determine consumer preferences for PCs and notebook computers, which survey method would you recommend and why?

VIDEO CASE 6.1 Starbucks: Staying Local While Going Global Through Marketing Research

Named after the first mate in the novel *Moby Dick*, Starbucks is the largest coffeehouse company in the world. As of August 2007, there were 6,566 company-operated stores and 3,729 licensed stores in the United States, and 1,613 company-operated stores and 2,488 joint venture and licensed stores outside the United States. The company's objective is to establish Starbucks as the most recognized and respected brand in the world. It expects to achieve this by continuing with rapid expansion of retail stores and growing its specialty sales and other operations. It will also continually pursue other opportunities to leverage the Starbucks brand through new products and new distribution channels that meet consumer needs determined by marketing research.

Over the last two decades, Starbucks has revitalized the coffee industry. The inspiration behind Starbucks was conceived when CEO Howard Schultz visited Italy. At that time, Starbucks was a coffee company, and people were very passionate about the coffee, but in Milan Howard saw the passion around the coffeehouse experience. In Milan, Howard went from one espresso bar to the next and saw how people at the coffeehouses knew each other. These people were getting their daily coffees, but they also were making daily connections with other people, with the baristas, and with the artistry; the folks making the drinks were connecting with their customers and knew them personally. From this experience, Howard recognized that although Starbucks was passionate about the coffee, it also had the opportunity to be equally passionate about the coffeehouse experience.

Marketing research determined four strategic pillars for expressing the Starbucks brand. The four pillars are (1) the coffee, which is Starbucks' foundation and which gives Starbucks its credibility; (2) some of the finest products that are associated with the coffee experience; (3) the warm, welcoming, and inspiring environment; and (4) community involvement. Even though the coffee and the products are important, the key to Starbucks' success has been the latter two. It has designed an environment that is warm and welcoming and provides an experience that makes the company a part of the community or local culture. It has been able to achieve this success by emphasizing the Starbucks culture.

Starbucks also draws upon customers for ideas by conducting extensive marketing research. Many of its products and services are a direct result of suggestions from patrons or local employees. Much more than most companies, consumers touch and influence the corporation. Many innovations and retail items resulted directly from customers' feedback obtained by conducting marketing research and by suggestions made to the baristas. From customized CD music collections to sales of sandwiches, gums, and chocolates—all were a result of customer recommendations. Many stores even offer wireless Internet access in response to customer demand. Through its baristas, Starbucks found that people were interested in an iced Starbucks and the blended Starbucks, and thus the Frappuccino was born—an idea that came from customers and the baristas rather than corporate headquarters.

This local connection with customers and the consequent brand building have allowed Starbucks to move into other successful venues—from coffee bean sales at grocery stores to partnerships with United Airlines, Marriott, Pepsi, Kraft, and others. Starbucks has some of the best coffee in the world, but it was missing from grocery stores, which is where most coffee is purchased. Syndicated data from Nielsen showed that grocery stores sell two-thirds of the coffee in the United States, and Starbucks has been able to enter this lucrative market. It has also used partnerships in other industries to increase revenues.

In the past few years, Starbucks has been aggressively expanding its global footprint by entering newer markets and strengthening its position in countries it already has a presence. Growing a brand overseas, however, can be different from doing so in Starbucks' home market. According to Thomas Yang, former senior vice president of International Marketing, this difference in different growth behavior in different countries can be attributed to Starbucks' different stages of development in the United States and different parts of the world. In international markets, Starbucks is at the brand development and establishment stage, allowing consumers to discover what the brand is about and what the Starbucks experience is about. In contrast, Starbucks has had a presence in North America since 1971. In the United States, the Starbucks experience is pretty well-known and understood, and thus it is in a different stage.

Starbucks has been extremely successful in achieving its objectives. It has been able to maintain a local feel despite massive growth around the globe. It has done this by stressing its culture and placing the focus on its employees and customers through marketing research. Starbucks hopes to continue staying local while going global through marketing research.

Conclusion

Starbucks has gone from a small local coffee start-up in the 1970s to the largest coffeehouse company in the world. This success has largely been due to the strong connection it has been able to foster with its consumers and maintain a local charm and feel in its stores even as it continues to expand globally at breakneck speed. This strong connection has also enabled Starbucks to gather useful feedback and marketing research information from customers leading to

the introduction of several successful new products and penetration into new global markets.

Questions

1. Use the Internet to identify secondary sources of information pertaining to coffee consumption in the United States.
2. What are consumers looking for in a coffeehouse experience? How do they view the Starbucks coffeehouse experience? How can Starbucks determine answers to these questions?
3. A survey is to be conducted to determine the image coffee drinkers have of Starbucks and other coffee chains. Which survey method should be used and why?
4. Starbucks is thinking of introducing a new gourmet coffee with a strong aroma. Can the observation method be used to determine the consumer reaction to this coffee prior to national introduction? If so, which observation method should be used?

References

1. www.starbucks.com, accessed February 15, 2009.
2. Steven Gray and Kate Kelly, "Starbucks Plans to Make Debut in Movie Business," *Wall Street Journal* (January 12, 2006): A1, A8.
3. Bob Keefe, "Starbucks to Offer CD-Burning Capabilities at Stores in Future," *Knight Ridder Tribune Business News* (June 28, 2004): 1.

Chapter 7

" While experiments cannot prove causality,

experimentation is the best method

for making causal inferences. "

Lynd Bacon, CEO and Founder, Sighthound Solutions, Inc.

Objectives [After reading this chapter, the student should be able to:]

1. Explain the concept of causality as defined in marketing research and distinguish between the ordinary meaning and the scientific meaning of causality.

2. Define and differentiate the two types of validity: internal validity and external validity.

3. Discuss the various extraneous variables that can affect the validity of results obtained through experimentation and explain how the researcher can control extraneous variables.

4. Describe and evaluate experimental designs and the differences among preexperimental, true experimental, quasi-experimental, and statistical designs.

5. Compare and contrast the use of laboratory versus field experimentation and experimental versus nonexperimental designs in marketing research.

6. Describe test marketing and its various forms: standard test market, controlled test market, simulated test market, electronic and other forms of test marketing.

7. Understand why the internal and external validity of field experiments conducted overseas is generally lower than in the United States.

8. Describe the ethical issues involved in conducting causal research and the role of debriefing in addressing some of these issues.

Causal Research Design: Experimentation

Overview

We introduced causal designs in Chapter 3, where we discussed their relationship to exploratory and descriptive designs and defined experimentation as the primary method employed in causal designs. This chapter explores the concept of causality further. We identify the necessary conditions for causality, examine the role of validity in experimentation, and consider the extraneous variables and procedures for controlling them. We present a classification of experimental designs and consider specific designs, along with the relative merits of laboratory and field experiments. An application in the area of test marketing is discussed in detail. The considerations involved in conducting experimental research when researching international markets are discussed. Several ethical issues that arise in experimentation are identified. The chapter also discusses the use of the Internet and computers in causal research.

Real Research

It's in the Bag

LeSportsac, Inc. (www.lesportsac.com) filed a suit against Kmart Corporation (www.kmart.com) after Kmart introduced a "di Paris sac" line of bags, which LeSportsac claimed looked like its bags. According to LeSportsac, Kmart led consumers to believe that they were purchasing LeSportsac bags when they were not. To prove its point, LeSportsac undertook causal research.

Two groups of women were selected. One group was shown two LeSportsac lightweight soft-sided bags from which all tags were removed and all words and designs were printed over within the distinctive LeSportsac ovals. The second group of women were shown two "di Paris sac" bags with the brand name visible and bearing the tags and labels these bags carry in Kmart stores. Information was obtained from both groups of women to learn whether or not these women perceived a single company or source and/or brand identification of the masked bags, what identifications they made, if any, and the reasons they gave for doing so. The sample consisted of 200 women in each group selected by mall-intercept interviews conducted in Chicago, Los Angeles, and New York. Rather than utilizing a probability sample, the respondents were selected in accordance with age quotas.

In its lawsuit against Kmart, LeSportsac designed an experiment to demonstrate that Kmart misled consumers to believe that they were purchasing LeSportsac bags when they were not.

The study indicated that many consumers could not distinguish the origin of the two makes of bags, supporting the position of LeSportsac. This experiment helped LeSportsac convince the court of appeals to affirm the issuance of an injunction against Kmart. Kmart agreed to stop selling its "di Paris sac." LeSportsac was founded in 1974 and as of 2009 its products are sold in more than 20 countries worldwide, including the United States, Italy, the United Kingdom, France, Sweden, Japan, Hong Kong, Korea, Taiwan, Singapore, Australia, Colombia, and Saudi Arabia.[1] ■

Real Research

POP Buys

Rite Aid Drug Co. (www.riteaid.com) conducted an experiment to examine the effectiveness of in-store radio advertisements to induce point-of-purchase (POP) buys. Twenty statistically compatible drugstores were selected based on store size, geographical location, traffic flow count, and age. Half of these were randomly selected as test stores, whereas the other half served as control stores. The test stores aired the radio advertisements, whereas the control stores' POP radio systems were removed. Tracking data in the form of unit volume and dollar sales were obtained for seven days before the experiment, during the course of the four-week experiment, and seven days after the experiment. The products monitored varied from inexpensive items to small kitchen appliances. Results indicated that sales of the advertised products in the test stores at least doubled. Based on this evidence, Rite Aid concluded that in-store radio advertising was highly effective in inducing POP buys and decided to continue it.

In 2009, Point of Purchase Advertising International (www.popai.com) reported a study to determine the effectiveness of POP advertising. The study found that only 30 percent of drugstore shoppers read retailer advertisements, picked up an in-store circular, or arrived at the store with a shopping list. However, 34 percent of shoppers questioned after leaving the store could recall seeing or hearing advertisements or announcements made inside the store. Anheuser-Busch, Pepsi/Frito-Lay, Pfizer, Procter & Gamble, and Ralston-Purina sponsored this study. All these companies sell products that can benefit from point-of-purchase advertising, and based on these results decided to increase their POP promotional budget.[2] ■

Concept of Causality

causality
When the occurrence of X increases the probability of the occurrence of Y.

Experimentation is commonly used to infer causal relationships. The concept of **causality** requires some explanation. The scientific concept of causality is complex. "Causality" means something very different to the average person on the street than to a scientist.[3] A statement such as "X causes Y" will have different meanings to an ordinary person and to a scientist, as seen in the accompanying table.

Ordinary Meaning	Scientific Meaning
X is the only cause of Y.	X is only one of a number of possible causes of Y.
X must always lead to Y. (X is a deterministic cause of Y).	The occurrence of X makes the occurrence of Y more probable (X is a probabilistic cause of Y).
It is possible to prove that X is a cause of Y.	We can never prove that X is a cause of Y. At best, we can infer that X is a cause of Y.

The scientific meaning of causality is more appropriate to marketing research than is the everyday meaning. Marketing effects are caused by multiple variables, and the relationship between cause and effect tends to be probabilistic. Moreover, we can never prove causality (i.e., demonstrate it conclusively); we can only infer a cause-and-effect relationship. In other words, it is possible that the true causal relation, if one exists, may not have been identified. We further clarify the concept of causality by discussing the conditions for causality.

Conditions for Causality

Before making causal inferences, or assuming causality, three conditions must be satisfied. These are (1) concomitant variation, (2) time order of occurrence of variables, and (3) elimination of other possible causal factors. These conditions are necessary but not sufficient to demonstrate causality. No one of these three conditions, or all three conditions combined, can demonstrate decisively that a causal relationship exists.[4]

Concomitant Variation

concomitant variation
A condition for inferring causality that requires that a cause, *X*, and an effect, *Y*, occur together or vary together as predicted by the hypothesis under consideration.

Concomitant variation is the extent to which a cause, *X*, and an effect, *Y*, occur together or vary together in the way predicted by the hypothesis under consideration. Evidence pertaining to concomitant variation can be obtained in a qualitative or quantitative manner.

For example, in the qualitative case, the management of a department store believes that sales are highly dependent upon the quality of in-store service. This hypothesis could be examined by assessing concomitant variation. Here, the causal factor *X* is in-store service, and the effect factor *Y* is sales. A concomitant variation supporting the hypothesis would imply that stores with satisfactory in-store service would also have satisfactory sales. Likewise, stores with unsatisfactory service would exhibit unsatisfactory sales. If, on the other hand, the opposite pattern was found, we would conclude that the hypothesis is untenable.

For a quantitative example, consider a random survey of 1,000 respondents regarding purchase of fashion clothing from department stores. This survey yields the data in Table 7.1. The respondents have been classified into high- and low-education groups based on a median or even split. This table suggests that the purchase of fashion clothing is influenced by education level. Respondents with high education are likely to purchase more fashion clothing. Seventy-three percent of the respondents with high education have a high purchase level, whereas only 64 percent of those with low education have a high purchase level. Furthermore, this is based on a relatively large sample of 1,000 people.

Based on this evidence, can we conclude that high education causes high purchase of fashion clothing? Certainly not! All that can be said is that association makes the hypothesis more tenable; it does not prove it. What about the effect of other possible causal factors such as income? Fashion clothing is expensive, so people with higher incomes can buy more of it. Table 7.2 shows the relationship between purchase of fashion clothing and education for different income segments. This is equivalent to holding the effect of income constant. Here again, the sample has been split at the median to produce high- and low-income groups of equal size. Table 7.2 shows that the difference in purchase of fashion clothing between high- and low-education respondents has been reduced considerably. This suggests that the association indicated by Table 7.1 may be spurious.

We could give similar examples to show why the absence of initial evidence of concomitant variation does not imply that there is no causation. It is possible that considering a third variable may crystallize an association that was originally obscure. The time order of the occurrence of variables provides additional insights into causality.

TABLE 7.1
Evidence of Concomitant Variation Between Purchase of Fashion Clothing and Education

Education - X	Purchase of Fashion Clothing - Y		
	High	Low	Total
High	363 (73%)	137 (27%)	500 (100%)
Low	322 (64%)	178 (36%)	500 (100%)

TABLE 7.2
Purchase of Fashion Clothing by Income and Education

	Low Income				High Income		
	Purchase				Purchase		
Education	High	Low	Total	Education	High	Low	Total
High	122 (61%)	78 (39%)	200 (100%)	High	241 (80%)	59 (20%)	300 (100%)
Low	171 (57%)	129 (43%)	300 (100%)	Low	151 (76%)	49 (24%)	200 (100%)

Time Order of Occurrence of Variables

The time order of occurrence condition states that the causing event must occur either before or simultaneously with the effect; it cannot occur afterwards. By definition, an effect cannot be produced by an event that occurs after the effect has taken place. However, it is possible for each event in a relationship to be both a cause and an effect of the other event. In other words, a variable can be both a cause and an effect in the same causal relationship. To illustrate, customers who shop frequently in a department store are more likely to have the charge or credit card for that store. Also, customers who have the charge card for a department store are more likely to shop there frequently.

Consider the in-store service and sales of a department store. If in-store service is the cause of sales, then improvements in service must be made before, or at least simultaneously with, an increase in sales. These improvements might consist of training or hiring more sales personnel. Then, in subsequent months, the sales of the department store should increase. Alternatively, the sales might increase simultaneously with the training or hiring of additional sales personnel. On the other hand, suppose a store experienced an appreciable increase in sales and then decided to use some of that money to retrain its sales personnel, leading to an improvement in service. In this case, in-store service cannot be a cause of increased sales. Rather, just the opposite hypothesis might be plausible.

Absence of Other Possible Causal Factors

The absence of other possible causal factors means that the factor or variable being investigated should be the only possible causal explanation. In-store service may be a cause of sales if we can be sure that changes in all other factors affecting sales, such as pricing, advertising, level of distribution, product quality, competition, and so on were held constant or otherwise controlled.

In an after-the-fact examination of a situation, we can never confidently rule out all other causal factors. In contrast, with experimental designs, it is possible to control for some of the other causal factors. It is also possible to balance the effects of some of the uncontrolled variables so that only random variations resulting from these uncontrolled variables will be measured. These aspects are discussed in more detail later in this chapter. The difficulty of establishing a causal relationship is illustrated by the following example.

Real Research   Which Comes First?

Recent statistical data show that consumers increasingly make buying decisions in the store while they are shopping. Some studies indicate that as much as 80 percent of buying decisions are made at point of purchase (POP). POP buying decisions have increased concurrently with increased advertising efforts in the stores. These include radio advertisements, ads on shopping carts and grocery bags, ceiling signs, and shelf displays. It is estimated that brand and retail owners spent more than $1 billion in 2008 trying to influence the consumer at the point of purchase. It is difficult to ascertain from these data whether the increased POP decision making is the result of increased advertising efforts in the store, or whether the increase in store advertising results from attempts to capture changing consumer attitudes toward purchasing and to capture sales from the increase in POP decision making. It is also possible that both variables may be causes and effects in this relationship.[5] ∎

If, as the preceding example indicates, it is difficult to establish cause-and-effect relationships, what is the role of evidence obtained in experimentation?

Role of Evidence

Evidence of concomitant variation, time order of occurrence of variables, and elimination of other possible causal factors, even if combined, still do not demonstrate conclusively that a causal relationship exists. However, if all the evidence is strong and consistent, it may be reasonable to conclude that there is a causal relationship. Accumulated evidence from several investigations increases our confidence that a causal relationship exists. Confidence is further enhanced if the evidence is interpreted in light of intimate conceptual knowledge of the problem situation. Controlled experiments can provide strong evidence on all three conditions.

ACTIVE RESEARCH

> **Internet Information**
>
> As the head of the Federal Trade Commission, what are your concerns about the increased availability of information on the Internet?
>
> Search the Internet using a search engine as well as your library's online databases to obtain information on Internet usage by consumers.
>
> What conditions are necessary for you to conclude that consumer use is causing greater availability of information on the Internet?

independent variables
Variables that are manipulated by the researcher and whose effects are measured and compared.

test units
Individuals, organizations, or other entities whose response to independent variables or treatments is being studied.

dependent variables
Variables that measure the effect of the independent variables on the test units.

extraneous variables
Variables, other than the independent variables, that influence the response of the test units.

experiment
The process of manipulating one or more independent variables and measuring their effect on one or more dependent variables, while controlling for the extraneous variables.

experimental design
The set of experimental procedures specifying (1) the test units and sampling procedures, (2) independent variables, (3) dependent variables, and (4) how to control the extraneous variables.

Definitions and Concepts

In this section, we define some basic concepts and illustrate them using examples, including the LeSportsac and Rite Aid examples given at the beginning of this chapter.

INDEPENDENT VARIABLES **Independent variables** are variables or alternatives that are manipulated (i.e., the levels of these variables are changed by the researcher) and whose effects are measured and compared. These variables, also known as *treatments*, may include price levels, package designs, and advertising themes. In the two examples given at the beginning of this chapter, the treatments consisted of LeSportsac versus the "di Paris sac" bags in the first example and in-store radio advertising (present versus absent) in the second.

TEST UNITS **Test units** are individuals, organizations, or other entities whose response to the independent variables or treatments is being examined. Test units may include consumers, stores, or geographic areas. The test units were women in the LeSportsac case and stores in the Rite Aid example.

DEPENDENT VARIABLES **Dependent variables** are the variables that measure the effect of the independent variables on the test units. These variables may include sales, profits, and market shares. The dependent variable was brand or source identification in the LeSportsac example and sales in the Rite Aid example.

EXTRANEOUS VARIABLES **Extraneous variables** are all variables other than the independent variables that affect the response of the test units. These variables can confound the dependent variable measures in a way that weakens or invalidates the results of the experiment. Extraneous variables include store size, store location, and competitive effort. In the Rite Aid example, store size, geographical location, traffic flow count, and age of the stores were extraneous variables that had to be controlled.

EXPERIMENT An **experiment** is formed when the researcher manipulates one or more independent variables and measures their effect on one or more dependent variables, while controlling for the effect of extraneous variables.[6] Both the LeSportsac and Rite Aid research projects qualify as experiments based on this definition.

EXPERIMENTAL DESIGN An **experimental design** is a set of procedures specifying (1) the test units and how these units are to be divided into homogeneous subsamples, (2) what independent variables or treatments are to be manipulated, (3) what dependent variables are to be measured, and (4) how the extraneous variables are to be controlled.[7]

Real Research | Taking Coupons at Face Value

An experiment was conducted to test the effects of the face value of coupons on the likelihood of coupon redemption, controlling for the frequency of brand usage. Personal interviews were conducted in greater New York area with 280 shoppers who were entering or leaving a supermarket. Subjects were randomly assigned to two treatment groups. One group was offered 15-cent coupons and the other 50-cent coupons for four products: Tide detergent, Kellogg's Corn Flakes, Aim toothpaste, and Joy liquid detergent. During the interviews, the respondents answered questions about which brands they used and how likely they were to cash coupons of the given face value the next time they shopped. An interesting finding was that higher face value coupons produced higher likelihood of redemption among infrequent or nonbuyers of the promoted brand but had little effect on regular buyers. America's love affair with the coupon continued in 2007 as 257 billion coupons were distributed within newspaper free-standing inserts (FSIs). According to the annual Marx FSI Trend Report, this represented a 1.5 percent increase in comparison to 2006. This represented over $320 billion in consumer incentives.[8] ■

In the preceding experiment, the independent variable that was manipulated was the value of the coupon (15-cent coupon versus 50-cent coupon). The dependent variable was the likelihood of cashing the coupon. The extraneous variable that was controlled was brand usage. The test units were individual shoppers. The experimental design required the random assignment of test units (shoppers) to treatment groups (15-cent coupon or 50-cent coupon).

Definition of Symbols

To facilitate our discussion of extraneous variables and specific experimental designs, we define a set of symbols that are commonly used in marketing research.

X = the exposure of a group to an independent variable, treatment, or event, the effects of which are to be determined

O = the process of observation or measurement of the dependent variable on the test units or group of units

R = the random assignment of test units or groups to separate treatments

In addition, the following conventions are adopted:

- Movement from left to right indicates movement through time.
- Horizontal alignment of symbols implies that all those symbols refer to a specific treatment group.
- Vertical alignment of symbols implies that those symbols refer to activities or events that occur simultaneously.

For example, the symbolic arrangement

$$X \quad O_1 \quad O_2$$

means that a given group of test units was exposed to the treatment variable (X) and the response was measured at two different points in time, O_1 and O_2.

Likewise, the symbolic arrangement

$$R \quad X_1 \quad O_1$$
$$R \quad X_2 \quad O_2$$

means that two groups of test units were randomly assigned to two different treatment groups at the same time, and the dependent variable was measured in the two groups simultaneously.

Validity in Experimentation

When conducting an experiment, a researcher has two goals: (1) draw valid conclusions about the effects of independent variables on the study group, and (2) make valid generalizations to a larger population of interest. The first goal concerns internal validity; the second, external validity.[9]

Internal Validity

internal validity
A measure of accuracy of an experiment. It measures whether the manipulation of the independent variables, or treatments, actually caused the effects on the dependent variable(s).

Internal validity refers to whether the manipulation of the independent variables or treatments actually caused the observed effects on the dependent variables. Thus, internal validity examines whether the observed effects on the test units could have been caused by variables other than the treatment. If the observed effects are influenced or confounded by extraneous variables, it is difficult to draw valid inferences about the causal relationship between the independent and dependent variables. Internal validity is the basic minimum that must be present in an experiment before any conclusion about treatment effects can be made. Without internal validity, the experimental results are confounded. Control of extraneous variables is a necessary condition for establishing internal validity.

External Validity

external validity
A determination of whether the cause-and-effect relationships found in the experiment can be generalized.

External validity refers to whether the cause-and-effect relationships found in the experiment can be generalized. In other words, can the results be generalized beyond the experimental situation, and if so, to what populations, settings, times, independent variables, and dependent variables can the results be projected?[10] Threats to external validity arise when the specific set of experimental conditions does not realistically take into account the interactions of other relevant variables in the real world.

It is desirable to have an experimental design that has both internal and external validity, but in applied marketing research often we have to trade one type of validity for another.[11] To control for extraneous variables, a researcher may conduct an experiment in an artificial environment. This enhances internal validity, but it may limit the generalizability of the results, thereby reducing external validity. For example, fast-food chains test customers' preferences for new formulations of menu items in test kitchens. Can the effects measured in this environment be generalized to fast-food outlets? (Further discussion on the influence of artificiality on external validity may be found in the section of this chapter on laboratory versus field experimentation.) Regardless of these deterrents to external validity, if an experiment lacks internal validity, it may not be meaningful to generalize the results. Factors that threaten internal validity may also threaten external validity, the most serious of these being extraneous variables.

Extraneous Variables

In this section, we classify extraneous variables in the following categories: history, maturation, testing, instrumentation, statistical regression, selection bias, and mortality.

History

history (H)
Specific events that are external to the experiment but occur at the same time as the experiment.

Contrary to what the name implies, **history (H)** does not refer to the occurrence of events before the experiment. Rather, history refers to specific events that are external to the experiment but occur at the same time as the experiment. These events may affect the dependent variable. Consider the following experiment,

$$O_1 \quad X_1 \quad O_2$$

where O_1 and O_2 are measures of sales of a department store chain in a specific region, and X_1 represents a new promotional campaign. The difference $(O_2 - O_1)$ is the treatment effect. Suppose the experiment revealed that there was no difference between O_2 and O_1. Can we then conclude that the promotional campaign was ineffective? Certainly not! The promotional campaign (X_1) is not the only possible explanation of the difference between O_2 and O_1. The campaign might well have been effective. What if general economic conditions declined during the experiment, and the local area was particularly hard hit by layoffs and plant closings (history)? Conversely, even if there was some difference between O_2 and O_1, it may be incorrect to conclude that the campaign was effective if history was not controlled, because the experimental effects might have been confounded by history. The longer the time interval between observations, the greater the possibility that history will confound an experiment of this type.

Maturation

maturation (MA)
An extraneous variable attributable to changes in the test units themselves that occur with the passage of time.

Maturation (MA) is similar to history except that it refers to changes in the test units themselves. These changes are not caused by the impact of independent variables or treatments but occur with the passage of time. In an experiment involving people, maturation takes place as people become older, more experienced, tired, bored, or uninterested. Tracking and market studies that span several months are vulnerable to maturation because it is difficult to know how respondents are changing over time.

Maturation effects also extend to test units other than people. For example, consider the case in which the test units are department stores. Stores change over time in terms of physical layout, decor, traffic, and composition.

Testing Effects

Testing effects are caused by the process of experimentation. Typically, these are the effects on the experiment of taking a measure on the dependent variable before and after the presentation of the treatment. There are two kinds of testing effects: (1) main testing effect (MT) and (2) interactive testing effect (IT).

main testing effect (MT)
An effect of testing occurring when a prior observation affects a latter observation.

The **main testing effect (MT)** occurs when a prior observation affects a latter observation. Consider an experiment to measure the effect of advertising on attitudes toward a certain brand. The respondents are given a pretreatment questionnaire measuring background information and attitude toward the brand. They are then exposed to the test commercial embedded in an appropriate program. After viewing the commercial, the respondents again answer a questionnaire measuring, among other things, attitude toward the brand. Suppose that there is no difference between the pre- and posttreatment attitudes. Can we conclude that the commercial was ineffective? An alternative explanation might be that the respondents tried to maintain consistency between their pre- and posttreatment attitudes. As a result of the main testing effect, posttreatment attitudes were influenced more by pretreatment attitudes than by the treatment itself. The main testing effect may also be reactive, causing the respondents to change their attitudes simply because these attitudes have been measured. The main testing effect compromises the internal validity of the experiment.

interactive testing effect (IT)
An effect in which a prior measurement affects the test unit's response to the independent variable.

In the **interactive testing effect (IT)**, a prior measurement affects the test unit's response to the independent variable. Continuing with our advertising experiment, when people are asked to indicate their attitudes toward a brand, they become aware of that brand: They are sensitized to that brand and become more likely to pay attention to the test commercial than people who were not included in the experiment. The measured effects are then not generalizable to the population; therefore, the interactive testing effects influence the experiment's external validity.[12]

Instrumentation

instrumentation (I)
An extraneous variable involving changes in the measuring instrument or in the observers or scores themselves.

Instrumentation (I) refers to changes in the measuring instrument, in the observers, or in the scores themselves. Sometimes, measuring instruments are modified during the course of an experiment. In the advertising experiment, if a newly designed questionnaire was used to measure the posttreatment attitudes, this could lead to variations in the responses obtained. Consider an experiment in which dollar sales are being measured before and after exposure to an in-store display (treatment). If there is a nonexperimental price change between O_1 and O_2, this results in a change in instrumentation because dollar sales will be measured using different unit prices. In this case, the treatment effect $(O_2 - O_1)$ could be attributed to a change in instrumentation.

Instrumentation effects are likely when interviewers make pre- and posttreatment measurements. The effectiveness of interviewers can be different at different times.

Statistical Regression

statistical regression (SR)
An extraneous variable that occurs when test units with extreme scores move closer to the average score during the course of the experiment.

Statistical regression (SR) effects occur when test units with extreme scores move closer to the average score during the course of the experiment. In the advertising experiment, suppose that some respondents had either very favorable or very unfavorable attitudes. On posttreatment measurement, their attitudes might have moved toward the average. People's attitudes change continuously. People with extreme attitudes have more room for change, so variation is more likely. This has a confounding effect on the experimental results, because the observed effect (change in attitude) may be attributable to statistical regression rather than to the treatment (test commercial).

Selection Bias

selection bias (SB)
An extraneous variable attributable to the improper assignment of test units to treatment conditions.

Selection bias (SB) refers to the improper assignment of test units to treatment conditions. This bias occurs when selection or assignment of test units results in treatment groups that differ on the dependent variable before the exposure to the treatment condition. If test units self-select their own groups or are assigned to groups on the basis of the researchers' judgment, selection bias is possible. For example, consider a merchandising experiment in which two different merchandising displays (old and new) are assigned to different department stores. The stores in the two groups may not be equivalent to begin with. They may vary with respect to a key characteristic, such as store size. Store size is likely to affect sales regardless of which merchandising display was assigned to a store.

Mortality

mortality (MO)
An extraneous variable attributable to the loss of test units while the experiment is in progress.

Mortality (MO) refers to the loss of test units while the experiment is in progress. This happens for many reasons, such as test units refusing to continue in the experiment. Mortality confounds results because it is difficult to determine if the lost test units would respond in the same manner to the treatments as those that remain. Consider again the merchandising display experiment. Suppose that during the course of the experiment, three stores in the new display treatment condition drop out. The researcher could not determine whether the average sales for the new display stores would have been higher or lower if these three stores had continued in the experiment.

The various categories of extraneous variables are not mutually exclusive. They can occur jointly and also interact with each other. To illustrate, testing—maturation—mortality refers to a situation where, because of pretreatment measurement, the respondents' beliefs and attitudes change over time and there is a differential loss of respondents from the various treatment groups.

Controlling Extraneous Variables

Extraneous variables represent alternative explanations of experimental results. They pose a serious threat to the internal and external validity of an experiment. Unless they are controlled for, they affect the dependent variable and thus confound the results. For this reason, they are also called **confounding variables**. There are four ways of controlling extraneous variables: randomization, matching, statistical control, and design control.

confounding variables
Synonymous with extraneous variables, used to illustrate that extraneous variables can confound the results by influencing the dependent variable.

Randomization

randomization
One method of controlling extraneous variables that involves randomly assigning test units to experimental groups by using random numbers. Treatment conditions are also randomly assigned to experimental groups.

Randomization refers to the random assignment of test units to experimental groups by using random numbers. Treatment conditions are also randomly assigned to experimental groups. For example, respondents are randomly assigned to one of three experimental groups. One of the three versions of a test commercial, selected at random, is administered to each group. As a result of random assignment, extraneous factors can be represented equally in each treatment condition. Randomization is the preferred procedure for ensuring the prior equality of experimental groups.[13] However, randomization may not be effective when the sample size is small, because randomization merely produces groups that are equal on average. It is possible, though, to check whether randomization has been effective by measuring the possible extraneous variables and comparing them across the experimental groups.

Matching

matching
One method of controlling extraneous variables that involves matching test units on a set of key background variables before assigning them to the treatment conditions.

Matching involves comparing test units on a set of key background variables before assigning them to the treatment conditions. In the merchandising display experiment, stores could be matched on the basis of annual sales, size, or location. Then one store from each matched pair would be assigned to each experimental group.

Matching has two drawbacks. First, test units can be matched on only a few characteristics, so the test units may be similar on the variables selected but unequal on others. Second, if the matched characteristics are irrelevant to the dependent variable, then the matching effort has been futile.[14]

Statistical Control

statistical control
One method of controlling extraneous variables by measuring the extraneous variables and adjusting for their effects through statistical methods.

Statistical control involves measuring the extraneous variables and adjusting for their effects through statistical analysis. This was illustrated in Table 7.2, which examined the relationship (association) between purchase of fashion clothing and education, controlling for the effect of income. More advanced statistical procedures, such as analysis of covariance (ANCOVA), are also available. In ANCOVA, the effects of the extraneous variable on the dependent variable are removed by an adjustment of the dependent variable's mean value within each treatment condition. (ANCOVA is discussed in more detail in Chapter 16.)

design control
One method of controlling extraneous variables that involves using specific experimental designs.

Design Control

Design control involves the use of experiments designed to control specific extraneous variables. The types of controls possible by suitably designing the experiment are illustrated in the following example.

Real Research

Experimenting with New Products

Controlled-distribution electronic test markets are used increasingly to conduct experimental research on new products. This method makes it possible to control for several extraneous factors that affect new product performance and manipulate the variables of interest. It is possible to ensure that a new product: (1) obtains the right level of store acceptance and all commodity volume distribution, (2) is positioned in the correct aisle in each store, (3) receives the right number of facings on the shelf, (4) has the correct everyday price, (5) never has out-of-stock problems, and (6) obtains the planned level of trade promotion, display, and price features on the desired time schedule. Thus, a high degree of internal validity can be obtained.[15] ∎

preexperimental designs
Designs that do not control for extraneous factors by randomization.

The preceding example shows that controlled-distribution electronic test markets can be effective in controlling for specific extraneous variables. Extraneous variables can also be controlled by adopting specific experimental designs, as described in the next section.

true experimental designs
Experimental designs distinguished by the fact that the researcher can randomly assign test units to experimental groups and also randomly assign treatments to experimental groups.

A Classification of Experimental Designs

Experimental designs may be classified as preexperimental, true experimental, quasi-experimental, or statistical (Figure 7.1). **Preexperimental designs** do not employ randomization procedures to control for extraneous factors. Examples of these designs include the one-shot case study, the one-group pretest-posttest design, and the static group. In **true experimental designs**, the researcher can randomly assign test units and treatments to experimental groups. Included in this category are the pretest-posttest control group design, the posttest-only control group design, and the Solomon four-group design. **Quasi-experimental designs** result when the researcher is unable to achieve full manipulation of scheduling or allocation of treatments to test units but can still apply part of the apparatus of true experimentation. Two such designs are time series and multiple time series designs. A **statistical design** is a series of basic experiments that allows for statistical control and analysis of external variables. The basic designs used in statistical designs include preexperimental, true experimental, and quasi-experimental. Statistical designs are classified on the basis of their characteristics and use. The important statistical designs include randomized block, Latin square, and factorial. These designs are illustrated in the context of measuring the effectiveness of a test commercial for a department store.[16]

quasi-experimental designs
Designs that apply part of the procedures of true experimentation but lack full experimental control.

statistical design
Designs that allow for the statistical control and analysis of external variables.

FIGURE 7.1

A Classification of Experimental Designs

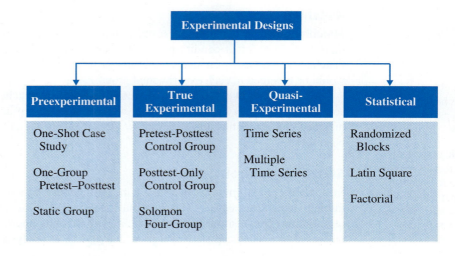

Preexperimental Designs

These designs are characterized by an absence of randomization. Three specific designs are described: the one-shot case study, the one-group pretest-posttest design, and the static group.

One-Shot Case Study

one-shot case study
A preexperimental design in which a single group of test units is exposed to a treatment X, and then a single measurement on the dependent variable is taken.

Also known as the after-only design, the **one-shot case study** may be symbolically represented as

$$X \quad O_1$$

A single group of test units is exposed to a treatment X, and then a single measurement on the dependent variable is taken (O_1). There is no random assignment of test units. Note that the symbol R is not used, because the test units are self-selected or selected arbitrarily by the researcher.

The danger of drawing valid conclusions from an experiment of this type can be easily seen. It does not provide a basis of comparing the level of O_1 to what would happen when X was absent. Also, the level of O_1 might be affected by many extraneous variables, including history, maturation, selection, and mortality. Lack of control for these extraneous variables undermines the internal validity. For these reasons, the one-shot case study is more appropriate for exploratory than for conclusive research.

Project Research — One-Shot Case Study

A one-shot case study to measure the effectiveness of a test commercial for a department store, for example, Sears, would be conducted as follows. Telephone interviews are conducted with a national sample of respondents who report watching a particular TV program the previous night. The program selected is the one that contains the test (Sears) commercial (X). The dependent variables (Os) are unaided and aided recall. First, unaided recall is measured by asking the respondents whether they recall seeing a commercial for a department store, for example, "Do you recall seeing a commercial for a department store last night?" If they recall the test commercial, details about commercial content and execution are solicited. Respondents who do not recall the test commercial are asked about it specifically, for example, "Do you recall seeing a commercial for Sears last night?" (aided recall). The results of aided and unaided recall are compared to norm scores to develop an index for interpreting the scores. ■

One-Group Pretest-Posttest Design

one-group pretest-posttest design
A preexperimental design in which a group of test units is measured twice.

The **one-group pretest-posttest design** may be symbolized as

$$O_1 \quad X \quad O_2$$

In this design, a group of test units is measured twice. There is no control group. First, a pretreatment measure is taken (O_1), then the group is exposed to the treatment (X). Finally, a posttreatment measure is taken (O_2). The treatment effect is computed as $O_2 - O_1$, but the validity of this conclusion is questionable because extraneous variables are largely uncontrolled. History, maturation, testing (both main and interactive testing effects), instrumentation, selection, mortality, and regression could possibly be present.

Project Research — One-Group Pretest-Posttest Design

A one-group pretest-posttest design to measure the effectiveness of a test commercial for a department store, for example, Sears, would be implemented as follows. Respondents are recruited to central theater locations in different test cities. At the central location, respondents are first administered a personal interview to measure, among other things, attitudes toward the store, Sears (O_1). Then they watch a TV program containing the test (Sears) commercial (X). After viewing the TV program, the respondents are again administered a personal interview to measure attitudes toward the store, Sears (O_2). The effectiveness of the test commercial is measured as $O_2 - O_1$. ■

Static Group Design

static group
A preexperimental design in which there are two groups: the experimental group (EG), which is exposed to the treatment, and the control group (CG). Measurements on both groups are made only after the treatment, and test units are not assigned at random.

The **static group** is a two-group experimental design. One group, called the *experimental group (EG)*, is exposed to the treatment, and the other, called the *control group (CG)*, is not. Measurements on both groups are made only after the treatment, and test units are not assigned at random. This design may be symbolically described as

$$EG: \quad X \quad O_1$$
$$CG: \qquad \quad O_2$$

The treatment effect would be measured as $O_1 - O_2$. Note that this difference could also be attributed to at least two extraneous variables (selection and mortality). Because test units are not randomly assigned, the two groups (EG and CG) may differ before the treatment, and selection bias may be present. There may also be mortality effects, because more test units may withdraw from the experimental group than from the control group. This would be particularly likely to happen if the treatment was unpleasant.

In practice, a control group is sometimes defined as the group that receives the current level of marketing activity, rather than a group that receives no treatment at all. The control group is defined this way because it is difficult to reduce current marketing activities, such as advertising and personal selling, to zero.

Project Research Static Group

A static group comparison to measure the effectiveness of a test commercial for a department store would be conducted as follows. Two groups of respondents would be recruited on the basis of convenience. Only the experimental group would be exposed to the TV program containing the test (Sears) commercial. Then, attitudes toward the department store (Sears) of both the experimental and control group respondents would be measured. The effectiveness of the test commercial would be measured as $O_1 - O_2$. ■

True Experimental Designs

The distinguishing feature of the true experimental designs, as compared to preexperimental designs, is randomization. In true experimental designs, the researcher randomly assigns test units to experimental groups and treatments to experimental groups. True experimental designs include the pretest-posttest control group design, the posttest-only control group design, and the Solomon four-group design.

Pretest-Posttest Control Group Design

pretest-posttest control group design
A true experimental design in which the experimental group is exposed to the treatment but the control group is not. Pretest and posttest measures are taken on both groups.

In the **pretest-posttest control group design**, test units are randomly assigned to either the experimental or the control group, and a pretreatment measure is taken on each group. Then, the experimental group is exposed to the treatment (X). Finally, a posttreatment measure is taken on each of the experimental and control groups. This design is symbolized as

$$EG: \quad R \quad O_1 \quad X \quad O_2$$
$$CG: \quad R \quad O_3 \qquad \quad O_4$$

The treatment effect (*TE*) is measured as

$$(O_2 - O_1) - (O_4 - O_3)$$

This design controls for most extraneous variables. Selection bias is eliminated by randomization. The other extraneous effects are controlled as follows:

$$O_2 - O_1 = TE + H + MA + MT + IT + I + SR + MO$$
$$O_4 - O_3 = H + MA + MT + I + SR + MO$$
$$= EV \text{ (Extraneous Variables)}$$

where the symbols for the extraneous variables are as defined previously. The experimental result is obtained by

$$(O_2 - O_1) - (O_4 - O_3) = TE + IT$$

Interactive testing effect is not controlled, because of the effect of the pretest measurement on the reaction of units in the experimental group to the treatment.

As this example shows, the pretest-posttest control group design involves two groups and two measurements on each group. A simpler design is the posttest-only control group design.

Project Research | Pretest-Posttest Control Group

In the context of measuring the effectiveness of a test commercial for a department store, for example, Sears, a pretest-posttest control group design would be implemented as follows. A sample of respondents would be selected at random. Half of these would be randomly assigned to the experimental group, and the other half would form the control group. Respondents in both groups would be administered a questionnaire to obtain a pretest measurement on attitudes toward the department store (Sears). Only the respondents in the experimental group would be exposed to the TV program containing the test commercial. Then, a questionnaire would be administered to respondents in both groups to obtain posttest measures on attitudes toward the store (Sears). ■

Posttest-Only Control Group Design

posttest-only control group design
A true experimental design in which the experimental group is exposed to the treatment but the control group is not and no pretest measure is taken.

The **posttest-only control group design** does not involve any premeasurement. It may be symbolized as

$$\begin{array}{llll} \text{EG:} & R & X & O_1 \\ \text{CG:} & R & & O_2 \end{array}$$

The treatment effect is obtained by

$$TE = O_1 - O_2$$

This design is fairly simple to implement. Because there is no premeasurement, the testing effects are eliminated, but this design is sensitive to selection bias and mortality. It is assumed that the two groups are similar in terms of pretreatment measures on the dependent variable, because of the random assignment of test units to groups. However, because there is no pretreatment measurement, this assumption cannot be checked. This design is also sensitive to mortality. It is difficult to determine whether those in the experimental group who discontinue the experiment are similar to their counterparts in the control group. Yet another limitation is that this design does not allow the researcher to examine changes in individual test units.

It is possible to control for selection bias and mortality through carefully designed experimental procedures. Examination of individual cases is often not of interest. On the other hand, this design possesses significant advantages in terms of time, cost, and sample size requirements. It involves only two groups and only one measurement per group. Because of its simplicity, the posttest-only control group design is probably the most popular in marketing research. Note that, except for premeasurement, the implementation of this design is very similar to that of the pretest-posttest control group design.

Project Research | Posttest-Only Control Group

To measure the effectiveness of a test commercial for a department store, the posttest-only control group design would be implemented as follows. A sample of respondents would be selected at random. The sample would be randomly split, with half the subjects forming the experimental group and the other half constituting the control group. Only the respondents in the experimental group would be exposed to the TV program containing the test (Sears) commercial. Then, a questionnaire would be administered to both groups to obtain posttest measures on attitudes toward the department store (Sears). The difference in the attitudes of the experimental group and the control group would be used as a measure of the effectiveness of the test commercial. ■

Solomon four-group design

A true experimental design that explicitly controls for interactive testing effects, in addition to controlling for all the other extraneous variables.

In this example, the researcher is not concerned with examining the changes in the attitudes of individual respondents. When this information is desired, the Solomon four-group design should be considered. The **Solomon four-group design** overcomes the limitations of the pretest-posttest control group and posttest-only control group designs in that it explicitly controls for interactive testing effect, in addition to controlling for all the other extraneous variables (EV). However, this design has practical limitations: It is expensive and time-consuming to implement. Hence, it is not considered further.[17]

In all true experimental designs, the researcher exercises a high degree of control. In particular, the researcher can control when the measurements are taken, on whom they are taken, and the scheduling of the treatments. Moreover, the researcher can randomly select the test units and randomly expose test units to the treatments. In some instances, the researcher cannot exercise this kind of control, and then quasi-experimental designs should be considered.

ACTIVE RESEARCH

Fox News: Outfoxing Rivals

Visit www.foxnews.com and search the Internet using a search engine as well as your library's online databases to obtain information on consumers' preferences for network news channels.

Fox News wants to determine which one of three new formats it should implement. Would you recommend a preexperimental or a true experimental design? Which specific design would you recommend?

As the marketing manager of Fox News, how would you use information on consumers' preferences for network news channels to formulate marketing strategies that would increase your audience and market share?

Quasi-Experimental Designs

A quasi-experimental design results under the following conditions. First, the researcher can control when measurements are taken and on whom they are taken. Second, the researcher lacks control over the scheduling of the treatments and also is unable to expose test units to the treatments randomly.[18] Quasi-experimental designs are useful because they can be used in cases when true experimentation cannot, and because they are quicker and less expensive. However, because full experimental control is lacking, the researcher must take into account the specific variables that are not controlled. Popular forms of quasi-experimental designs are time series and multiple time series designs.

Time Series Design

time series design

A quasi-experimental design that involves periodic measurements on the dependent variable for a group of test units. Then, the treatment is administered by the researcher or occurs naturally. After the treatment, periodic measurements are continued in order to determine the treatment effect.

The **time series design** involves a series of periodic measurements on the dependent variable for a group of test units. The treatment is then administered by the researcher or occurs naturally. After the treatment, periodic measurements are continued to determine the treatment effect. A time series experiment may be symbolized as

$$O_1 \quad O_2 \quad O_3 \quad O_4 \quad O_5 \quad X \quad O_6 \quad O_7 \quad O_8 \quad O_9 \quad O_{10}$$

This is a quasi-experiment, because there is no randomization of test units to treatments, and the timing of treatment presentation, as well as which test units are exposed to the treatment, may not be within the researcher's control.

Taking a series of measurements before and after the treatment provides at least partial control for several extraneous variables. Maturation is at least partially controlled, because it would not affect O_5 and O_6 alone but would influence other observations. By similar reasoning, main testing effect, instrumentation, and statistical regression are controlled as well. If the test units are selected randomly or by matching, selection bias can be reduced. Mortality may pose a problem, but it can be largely controlled by paying a premium or offering other incentives to respondents.

The major weakness of the time series design is the failure to control history. Another limitation is that the experiment may be affected by the interactive testing effect, because multiple measurements are being made on the test units. Nevertheless, time series designs are useful. The effectiveness of a test commercial (X) may be examined by broadcasting the commercial a predetermined number of times and examining the data from a preexisting test panel. Although the marketer can control the scheduling of the test commercial, it is uncertain when or whether the panel members are exposed to it. The panel members' purchases before, during, and after the campaign are examined to determine whether the test commercial has a short-term effect, a long-term effect, or no effect.

Multiple Time Series Design

multiple time series design
A time series design that includes another group of test units to serve as a control group.

The **multiple time series design** is similar to the time series design except that another group of test units is added to serve as a control group. Symbolically, this design may be described as

$$EG: \quad O_1 \quad O_2 \quad O_3 \quad O_4 \quad O_5 \quad X \quad O_6 \quad O_7 \quad O_8 \quad O_9 \quad O_{10}$$
$$CG: \quad O_{11} \quad O_{12} \quad O_{13} \quad O_{14} \quad O_{15} \qquad O_{16} \quad O_{17} \quad O_{18} \quad O_{19} \quad O_{20}$$

If the control group is carefully selected, this design can be an improvement over the simple time series experiment. The improvement lies in the ability to test the treatment effect twice: against the pretreatment measurements in the experimental group and against the control group. To use the multiple time series design to assess the effectiveness of a commercial, the test panel example would be modified as follows. The test commercial would be shown in only a few of the test cities. Panel members in these cities would comprise the experimental group. Panel members in cities where the commercial was not shown would constitute the control group.

Real Research

Splitting Commercials Shows Their Strength

A multiple time series design was used to examine the buildup effect of increased advertising. The data were obtained from the Nielsen BASES (www.bases.com) split-cable TV advertising field experiment. In the split-cable system, one group of households was assigned to the experimental panel and an equivalent group to the control panel. The two groups were matched on demographic variables. Data were collected for 76 weeks. Both panels received the same level of advertising for the first 52 weeks for the brand in question. For the next 24 weeks, the experimental panel was exposed to twice as much advertising as the control panel. The results indicated that the buildup effect of advertising was immediate with a duration of the order of the purchase cycle. Information of this type can be useful in selecting advertising timing patterns (allocating a set of advertising exposures over a specified period to obtain maximum impact).

A recent experimental study showed a new approach to relating advertising exposures of TV media schedules to sales-related market performance. These measures included cumulative sales volume, number of purchases, penetration, and repeat-purchase patterns. The approach was derived from a matched split-cable experimental design methodology. Consumer panel companies such as BASES can provide the data needed to implement such an approach. In the future, it is expected that companies like Nielsen BASES will be at the forefront of using technological advances to measure consumer advertising exposure and purchase behavior simultaneously.[19] ∎

In concluding our discussion of preexperimental, true experimental, and quasi-experimental designs, we summarize in Table 7.3 the potential sources of invalidity that may affect each of these designs. In this table, a minus sign indicates a definite weakness, a plus sign indicates that the factor is controlled, a question mark denotes a possible source of concern, and a blank means that the factor is not relevant. It should be remembered that potential sources of invalidity are not the same as actual errors.

Statistical Designs

Statistical designs consist of a series of basic experiments that allow for statistical control and analysis of external variables. In other words, several basic experiments are conducted simultaneously. Thus, statistical designs are influenced by the same sources of invalidity that affect the basic designs being used. Statistical designs offer the following advantages:

TABLE 7.3
Sources of Invalidity of Experimental Designs

	Source of Invalidity								
	Internal								External
Design	History	Maturation	Testing	Instrumentation	Regression	Selection	Mortality		Interaction of testing and of X
Preexperimental designs:									
One-shot case study X O	−	−				−	−		
One-group pretest–posttest design O X O	−	−	−	−	?				−

Static group comparison
  X   O
      O
	+	?	+	+	+	−	−		

True experimental designs:									
Pretest–posttest control R O X O R O O	+	+	+	+	+	+	+		−
Posttest-only control group design R X O R O	+	+	+	+	+	+	+		+
Quasi-experimental designs:									
Time series O O O X O O O	−	+	+	?	+	+	+		−
Multiple time series O O O X O O O O O O O O O	+	+	+	+	+	+	+		−

Note: A + indicates a relative advantage, whereas a − indicates a relative disadvantage.

1. The effects of more than one independent variable can be measured.
2. Specific extraneous variables can be statistically controlled.
3. Economical designs can be formulated when each test unit is measured more than once.

   The most common statistical designs are the randomized block design, the Latin square design, and the factorial design.

Randomized Block Design

A **randomized block design** is useful when there is only one major external variable, such as sales, store size, or income of the respondent, that might influence the dependent variable. The test units are blocked, or grouped, on the basis of the external variable. The researcher must be able to identify and measure the blocking variable. By blocking, the researcher ensures that the various experimental and control groups are matched closely on the external variable.

As this example illustrates, in most marketing research situations, external variables, such as sales, store size, store type, location, income, occupation, and social class of the respondent, can influence the dependent variable. Therefore, generally speaking, randomized block designs are more useful than completely random designs. Their main limitation is that the researcher can control for only one external variable. When more than one variable must be controlled, the researcher must use Latin square or factorial designs.

Project Research   ## Randomized Block Design

Let us extend the department store (Sears) test commercial example to measure the impact of humor on the effectiveness of advertising.[20] Three test commercials, A, B, and C, have, respectively, no humor, some humor, and high levels of humor. Which of these would be the most effective? Management feels that the respondents' evaluation of the commercials will be influenced by the extent of their store patronage, so store patronage is identified as the blocking variable, and the randomly selected respondents are classified into four blocks (heavy, medium, light, or nonpatrons of the department store). Respondents from each block are randomly assigned to the treatment groups (test commercials A, B, and C). The results reveal that the some-humor commercial (B) was the most effective overall (see Table 7.4). ■

Latin Square Design

A **Latin square design** allows the researcher to statistically control two noninteracting external variables as well as to manipulate the independent variable. Each external or blocking variable is divided into an equal number of blocks or levels. The independent variable is also divided into the same number of levels. A Latin square is conceptualized as a table (see Table 7.5), with the

TABLE 7.4
An Example of a Randomized Block Design

Block No.	Store Patronage	Treatment Groups		
		Commercial A	Commercial B	Commercial C
1	Heavy	A	B	C
2	Medium	A	B	C
3	Low	A	B	C
4	None	A	B	C

Note: A, B, and C denote three test commercials, which have, respectively, no humor, some humor, and high humor.

TABLE 7.5
An Example of Latin Square Design

Store Patronage	Interest in the Store		
	High	Medium	Low
High	B	A	C
Medium	C	B	A
Low and none	A	C	B

Note: A, B, and C denote the three test commercials, which have, respectively, no humor, some humor, and high humor.

rows and the columns representing the blocks in the two external variables. The levels of the independent variable are then assigned to the cells in the table. The assignment rule is that each level of the independent variable should appear only once in each row and each column, as shown in Table 7.5.

Project Research   Latin Square Design

To illustrate the Latin square design, suppose that in the previous example, in addition to controlling for store patronage, the researcher also wanted to control for interest in the store (defined as high, medium, or low). To implement a Latin square design, store patronage would also have to be blocked at three rather than four levels (e.g., by combining the low and nonpatrons into a single block). Assignments of the three test commercials could then be made as shown in Table 7.5. Note that each of the commercials, A, B, and C, appears once, and only once, in each row and each column. ■

Although Latin square designs are popular in marketing research, they are not without limitations. They require an equal number of rows, columns, and treatment levels, which is sometimes problematic. Note that in the previous example, the low and nonpatrons had to be combined to satisfy this requirement. Also, only two external variables can be controlled simultaneously. An additional variable can be controlled with an expansion of this design into a *Graeco-Latin square*. Finally, Latin squares do not allow the researcher to examine interactions of the external variables with each other or with the independent variable. To examine interactions, factorial designs should be used.

Factorial Design

factorial design
A statistical experimental design that is used to measure the effects of two or more independent variables at various levels and to allow for interactions between variables.

A **factorial design** is used to measure the effects of two or more independent variables at various levels. Unlike the randomized block design and the Latin square, factorial designs allow for interactions between variables.[21] An interaction is said to take place when the simultaneous effect of two or more variables is different from the sum of their separate effects. For example, an individual's favorite drink might be coffee and favorite temperature level might be cold, but this individual might not prefer cold coffee, leading to an interaction.

A factorial design may also be conceptualized as a table. In a two-factor design, each level of one variable represents a row and each level of another variable represents a column. Multidimensional tables can be used for three or more factors. Factorial designs involve a cell for every possible combination of treatment variables. Suppose that in the previous example, in addition to examining the effect of humor, the researcher was also interested in simultaneously examining the effect of amount of store information. Further, the amount of store information was also varied at three levels (high, medium, and low). As shown in Table 7.6, this would require $3 \times 3 = 9$ cells. Thus, nine different commercials would be produced, each having a specific level of store information and amount of humor. The respondents would be randomly selected and randomly assigned to the nine cells. Respondents in each cell would receive a specific treatment combination. For example, respondents in the upper left-hand corner cell would view a commercial that had no humor and low store information. The results revealed a significant interaction between the two factors or variables. Respondents in the low amount of store information condition preferred the high humor commercial (C). However, those in the high amount of store

TABLE 7.6		
An Example of a Factorial Design		
Amount of Store Information	Amount of Humor	
	No Humor	Medium Humor	High Humor
Low	A	B	C
Medium	D	E	F
High	G	H	I

information condition preferred the no humor commercial (G). Note that although Table 7.6 may appear somewhat similar to Table 7.4, the random assignment of respondents and data analysis are very different for the randomized block design and the factorial design.[22]

The main disadvantage of a factorial design is that the number of treatment combinations increases multiplicatively with an increase in the number of variables or levels. In our example of Table 7.6, if the amount of humor and store information had five levels each instead of three, the number of cells would have jumped from 9 to 25. All the treatment combinations are required if all the main effects and interactions are to be measured. If the researcher is interested in only a few of the interactions or main effects, *fractional factorial designs* may be used. As their name implies, these designs consist of only a fraction, or portion, of the corresponding full factorial design.

Experiential Research

Experimenting with Price Sensitivity

Canon wants to determine consumers' price sensitivity for its new advanced digital camera and hires you as a consultant.

1. Visit www.bestbuy.com and identify the price ranges of the digital cameras by Canon and other brands.
2. Search the Internet using a search engine as well as your library's online databases to obtain information on consumers' price sensitivity for digital cameras.
3. To determine consumers' price sensitivity for Canon's new advanced digital camera, design an appropriate experiment. Would you recommend a true experimental design? If yes, which one?
4. As the marketing manager for Canon Cameras, how would you use information on consumers' price sensitivity for digital cameras to formulate pricing strategies that would increase your market share? ■

Laboratory Versus Field Experiments

laboratory environment
An artificial setting for experimentation in which the researcher constructs the desired conditions.

field environment
An experimental location set in actual market conditions.

Experiments may be conducted in laboratory or field environments. A **laboratory environment** is an artificial one, which the researcher constructs with the desired conditions specific to the experiment. The term **field environment** is synonymous with actual market conditions. The Rite Aid example in the "Overview" section presented a field experiment. Our experiment to measure the effectiveness of a test commercial could be conducted in a laboratory environment by showing the test commercial embedded in a TV program to respondents in a test theater. The same experiment could also be conducted in a field environment by running the test commercial on actual TV stations. The differences between the two environments are summarized in Table 7.7.

Laboratory experiments have some advantages over field experiments. The laboratory environment offers a high degree of control because it isolates the experiment in a carefully monitored environment. Therefore, the effects of history can be minimized. A laboratory experiment

TABLE 7.7
Laboratory Versus Field Experiments

Factor	Laboratory	Field
Environment	Artificial	Realistic
Control	High	Low
Reactive error	High	Low
Demand artifacts	High	Low
Internal validity	High	Low
External validity	Low	High
Time	Short	Long
Number of units	Small	Large
Ease of implementation	High	Low
Cost	Low	High

also tends to produce the same results if repeated with similar subjects, leading to high internal validity. Laboratory experiments tend to use a small number of test units, last for a shorter time, be more restricted geographically, and be easier to conduct than field experiments. Hence, they are generally less expensive as well.

As compared to field experiments, laboratory experiments suffer from some disadvantages. The artificiality of the environment may cause reactive error, in that the respondents react to the situation itself, rather than to the independent variable.[23] Also, the environment may cause **demand artifacts**, a phenomenon in which the respondents attempt to guess the purpose of the experiment and respond accordingly. For example, while viewing the test commercial, the respondents may recall pretreatment questions about the brand and guess that the commercial is trying to change their attitudes toward the brand.[24] Finally, laboratory experiments are likely to have lower external validity than field experiments. Because a laboratory experiment is conducted in an artificial environment, the ability to generalize the results to the real world may be diminished.

It has been argued that artificiality, or lack of realism, in a laboratory experiment need not lead to lower external validity. One must be aware of the aspects of the laboratory experiment that differ from the situation to which generalizations are to be made. External validity will be reduced only if these aspects interface with the independent variables explicitly manipulated in the experiment, as is often the case in applied marketing research. However, another consideration is that laboratory experiments allow for more complex designs than field experiments. Hence, the researcher can control for more factors or variables in the laboratory setting, increasing external validity.[25]

The researcher must consider all of these factors when deciding whether to conduct laboratory or field experiments. Field experiments are less common in marketing research than laboratory experiments, although laboratory and field experiments play complementary roles.[26]

The Internet can also be a useful vehicle for conducting causal research. Different experimental treatments can be displayed at different Web sites. Respondents can then be recruited to visit these sites and respond to a questionnaire that obtains information on the dependent and extraneous variables. Thus, the Internet can provide a mechanism for controlled experimentation, although in a laboratory type of environment. Let us continue with the example of testing advertising effectiveness considered in this chapter. Different advertisements or commercials can be posted at different Web sites. Matched or randomly selected respondents can be recruited to visit these sites, with each group visiting only one site. If any pretreatment measures have to be obtained, the respondents answer a questionnaire posted on the site. Then they are exposed to a particular advertisement or a commercial at that site. After viewing the advertisement or commercial, the respondents answer additional questions, providing posttreatment measures. Control groups can also be implemented in a similar way. Thus, all types of experimental designs that we have considered can be implemented in this manner.

Experimental Versus Nonexperimental Designs

In Chapter 3, we discussed three types of research designs: exploratory, descriptive, and causal. Of these, only causal designs are truly appropriate for inferring cause-and-effect relationships. Although descriptive survey data are often used to provide evidence of "causal" relationships, these studies do not meet all the conditions required for causality. For example, it is difficult in descriptive studies to establish the prior equivalence of the respondent groups with respect to both the independent and dependent variables. On the other hand, an experiment can establish this equivalence by random assignment of test units to groups. In descriptive research, it is also difficult to establish time order of occurrence of variables. However, in an experiment, the researcher controls the timing of the measurements and the introduction of the treatment. Finally, descriptive research offers little control over other possible causal factors.

We do not wish to undermine the importance of descriptive research designs in marketing research. As we mentioned in Chapter 3, descriptive research constitutes the most popular research design in marketing research, and we do not want to imply that it should never be used to examine causal relationships. Indeed, some authors have suggested procedures for drawing causal inferences from descriptive (nonexperimental) data.[27] Rather, our intent is to alert the reader to the limitations of descriptive research for examining causal relationships. Likewise, we also want to make the reader aware of the limitations of experimentation.[28]

---

demand artifacts
The respondents attempt to guess the purpose of the experiment and respond accordingly.

Project Research | Project Activities

The book illustrates the use of various experimental designs in determining the effectiveness of a test commercial for a department store such as Sears.

1. If Sears is to determine the effectiveness of a proposed new television advertising campaign, which experimental design would you recommend and why?
2. Should the results of the survey proposed for Sears in Chapter 6 be used to make causal inferences? Why or why not? ■

Limitations of Experimentation

Experimentation is becoming increasingly important in marketing research, but there are limitations of time, cost, and administration of an experiment.

Time

Experiments can be time-consuming, particularly if the researcher is interested in measuring the long-term effects of the treatment, such as the effectiveness of an advertising campaign. Experiments should last long enough so that the posttreatment measurements include most or all the effects of the independent variables.

Cost

Experiments are often expensive. The requirements of experimental group, control group, and multiple measurements significantly add to the cost of research.

Administration

Experiments can be difficult to administer. It may be impossible to control for the effects of the extraneous variables, particularly in a field environment. Field experiments often interfere with a company's ongoing operations, and obtaining cooperation from the retailers, wholesalers, and others involved may be difficult. Finally, competitors may deliberately contaminate the results of a field experiment.

Application: Test Marketing

test marketing
An application of a controlled experiment done in limited, but carefully selected, test markets. It involves a replication of the planned national marketing program for a product in the test markets.

test markets
A carefully selected part of the marketplace that is particularly suitable for test marketing.

standard test market
A test market in which the product is sold through regular distribution channels. For example, no special considerations are given to products simply because they are being test-marketed.

Test marketing, also called *market testing*, is an application of a controlled experiment, done in limited but carefully selected parts of the marketplace called **test markets**. It involves a replication of a planned national marketing program in the test markets. Often, the marketing mix variables (independent variables) are varied in test marketing, and the sales (dependent variable) are monitored so that an appropriate national marketing strategy can be identified. The two major objectives of test marketing are (1) to determine market acceptance of the product, and (2) to test alternative levels of marketing mix variables. Test marketing is being practiced by both consumer-product and industrial-product companies. Test-marketing procedures may be classified as standard test markets, controlled and minimarket tests, simulated test marketing, electronic test marketing, virtual test marketing, and Web-enabled test marketing.

Standard Test Market

In a **standard test market**, test markets are selected and the product is sold through regular distribution channels. Typically, the company's own sales force is responsible for distributing the product. Sales personnel stock the shelves, restock, and take inventory at regular intervals. One or more combinations of marketing mix variables (product, price, distribution, and promotional levels) are employed.

Designing a standard test market involves deciding what criteria are to be used for selecting test markets, how many test markets to use, and the duration of the test. Test markets must be carefully selected. Some commonly used test markets are Charlotte, North Carolina, Indianapolis, Indiana, Kansas City, Missouri, Nashville, Tennessee, Rochester, New York, and Sacramento and Stockton, California. These cities are desirable test markets because each is considered to be fairly representative of a large segment of the U.S. population. For a list of other test market cities visit the USA Web site of the Acxiom Corporation (www.acxiom.com). The criteria for selection of test markets are described in the literature.[29] In general, the more test markets that can be used, the better. If resources are limited, at least two test markets should be used for each program variation to be tested. However, where external validity is important, at least four test markets should be used.

The duration of the test depends on the repurchase cycle for the product, the probability of competitive response, cost considerations, the initial consumer response, and company philosophy. The test should last long enough for repurchase activity to be observed. This indicates the long-term impact of the product. If competitive reaction to the test is anticipated, the duration should be short. The cost of the test is also an important factor. The longer a test, the more it costs, and at some point the value of additional information is outweighed by its costs. Recent evidence suggests that tests of new brands should run for at least 10 months. An empirical analysis found that the final test market share was reached in 10 months 85 percent of the time and in 12 months 95 percent of the time.[30] Test marketing can be very beneficial to a product's successful introduction, but is not without risk.

Real Research

Test Marketing: Wow!

Olestra, marketed under the name Olean, developed and researched by Procter & Gamble (www.pg.com) over 25 years at a cost of more than $200 million, is an amazing new cooking oil that adds zero calories and no fat to the snacks people love. Frito-Lay's (www.fritolay.com) Max chips with Olean were test-marketed in three cities in 31 supermarkets. Researchers collected sales data and customer reports of any effects that they associated with eating Frito-Lay's Max chips. The key findings were encouraging: (1) Sales exceeded expectations; both the initial purchase and repurchase rates were very high; (2) most people responded positively that snacks made with Olean offered a good way to reduce fat in their diets; and (3) the reporting rate of any side effects was lower than the small reporting rate anticipated prior to FDA approval.

Because the initial findings were encouraging, it was decided to expand the test marketing to Columbus, Ohio, and Indianapolis, Indiana. The product in these test markets was changed in packaging design, price, and the name, called WOW!, which better described the product with its great taste and no- and low-fat/calorie-reduced attributes versus the Max product name used in the initial test markets. The test market results were again positive. Based on favorable results, the decision was made to launch nationally Frito-Lay's WOW! line of Ruffles, Lay's, and Doritos chips, all made with Olestra. Subsequently, consumer focus on reduced calories has led Frito-Lay to change the name and packaging

Test marketing played a crucial role in Frito-Lay's decision to launch nationally the "WOW!" line of Ruffles, Lay's, and Doritos chips, all made with Olestra. Subsequently, the WOW! Name was changed to the Light line of Lay's.

of the WOW! Products—the company's line of snacks cooked in Olestra—to the Light line of Lay's, Ruffles, Doritos, and Tostitos to more effectively communicate the product's reduced calories. The new packaging was in stores as of 2005 and sales continued to be strong trough 2009.[31] ■

A standard test market constitutes a one-shot case study. In addition to the problems associated with this design, test marketing faces two unique problems. First, competitors often take actions such as increasing their promotional efforts to contaminate the test-marketing program. When Procter & Gamble test-marketed its hand-and-body lotion, Wondra, the market leader, Chesebrough-Ponds, started a competitive buy-one-get-one-free promotion for its flagship brand, Vaseline Intensive Care lotion. This encouraged consumers to stock up on Vaseline Intensive Care lotion, and as a result, Wondra did poorly in the test market. In spite of this, Procter & Gamble launched the Wondra line nationally. Ponds again countered with the same promotional strategy. Today, Wondra has about 4 percent of the market, and Vaseline Intensive Care has 22 percent.[32]

Another problem is that while a firm's test marketing is in progress, competitors have an opportunity to beat it to the national market. Hills Bros. High Yield Coffee was test-marketed and introduced nationally, but only after Procter & Gamble introduced Folger's Flakes. Procter & Gamble skipped test-marketing Folger's Flakes and beat Hills Bros. to the national market. P&G also launched Ivory shampoo without test marketing.

Sometimes it is not feasible to implement a standard test market using the company's personnel. Instead, the company must seek help from an outside supplier, in which case a controlled test market may be an attractive option.

Controlled Test Market

controlled test market
A test-marketing program conducted by an outside research company in field experimentation. The research company guarantees distribution of the product in retail outlets that represent a predetermined percentage of the market.

In a **controlled test market**, the entire test-marketing program is conducted by an outside research company. The research company guarantees distribution of the product in retail outlets that represent a predetermined percentage of the market. It handles warehousing and field sales operations, such as shelf stocking, selling, and inventory control. The controlled test market includes both minimarket (or forced distribution) tests and the smaller controlled store panels. This service is provided by a number of research firms, including Nielsen (www.nielsen.com).

Simulated Test Market

simulated test market
A quasi–test market in which respondents are preselected, then interviewed and observed on their purchases and attitudes toward the product.

Also called a laboratory test or test market simulation, a **simulated test market** yields mathematical estimates of market share based on initial reaction of consumers to a new product. The procedure works as follows. Typically, respondents are intercepted in high-traffic locations, such as shopping malls, and prescreened for product usage. The selected individuals are exposed to the proposed new product concept and given an opportunity to buy the new product in a real-life or laboratory environment. Those who purchase the new product are interviewed about their evaluation of the product and repeat-purchase intentions. The trial and repeat-purchase estimates so generated are combined with data on proposed promotion and distribution levels to project a share of the market.

Simulated test markets can be conducted in 16 weeks or less. The information they generate is confidential and the competition cannot get hold of it. They are also relatively inexpensive. Whereas a standard test market can cost as much as $1 million, simulated test markets cost less than 10 percent as much. One of the major firms supplying this service is Nielsen BASES (www.bases.com). Simulated test markets are becoming increasingly popular.[33]

Electronic, Virtual, and Web-Enabled Test Markets

An electronic test market combines consumer scanner panel, store distribution, and household-level media delivery in designated markets. An example would be services offered by Information Resources, Inc., using BehaviorScan, which combines scanner panels with broadcasting system (see Chapter 4). A virtual test market uses a computer simulation of an interactive shopping experience in three dimensions. Web-enabled test markets involve product tests using online distribution, i.e., the product being tested is offered solely through a dedicated Web site. Because of its lower costs, Web-enabled test marketing is gaining in popularity. It is being used by consumer packaged goods companies like Procter & Gamble and General Mills.

International Marketing Research

If field experiments are difficult to conduct in the United States, the challenge they pose is greatly increased in the international arena. In many countries, the marketing, economic, structural, information, and technological environment (see Chapter 24) is not developed to the extent that it is in the United States. For example, in many countries, the TV stations are owned and operated by the government with severe restrictions on television advertising. This makes field experiments manipulating advertising levels extremely difficult. Consider, for example, M&M/Mars that has set up massive manufacturing facilities in Russia and advertises its candy bars on television. Yet the sales potential has not been realized. Is Mars advertising too much, too little, or just right? Although the answer could be determined by conducting a field experiment that manipulated the level of advertising, such causal research is not feasible, given the tight control of the Russian government on television stations. Despite their troubles, Mars has continued to invest in Russia. On April 28, 2008, Mars announced plans to acquire the Wm. Wrigley Jr. Company, the chewing gum concern, for about $23 billion, in part to cater to fast growing markets in Russia, India, and China.

Likewise, the lack of major supermarkets in the Baltic states makes it difficult for P&G to conduct field experiments to determine the effect of in-store promotions on the sales of its detergents. In some countries in Asia, Africa, and South America, a majority of the population lives in small towns and villages. Yet basic infrastructures such as roads, transportation, and warehouse facilities are lacking, making it difficult to achieve desired levels of distribution. Even when experiments are designed, it is difficult to control for the time order of occurrence of variables and the absence of other possible causal factors, two of the necessary conditions for causality. Because the researcher has far less control over the environment, control of extraneous variables is particularly problematic. Furthermore, it may not be possible to address this problem by adopting the most appropriate experimental design, as environmental constraints may make that design infeasible.

Thus, the internal and external validity of field experiments conducted overseas is generally lower than in the United States. By pointing to the difficulties of conducting field experiments in other countries, we do not wish to imply that such causal research cannot or should not be conducted. Some form of test marketing is generally possible, as the following example indicates.

Real Research

Flawless Quality and Exclusivity at $100,000 Each

Watchmaker Lange Uhren GmbH (www.alange-soehne.com) has succeeded in the struggling eastern German economy of 2008–2009. The reason is their marketing savvy supported by marketing research. Simulated test marketing was done in the United States, Japan, and France to determine an effective positioning and pricing strategy for the watches. In each country, the price and the positioning strategy were varied and consumer response assessed. The results, which were similar across countries, indicated that a prestige positioning with a premium price would be most effective. The eastern Germany area was well known for superior craftsmanship prior to the rise of communism. Lange Uhren used a well-trained workforce and the new marketing platform to rekindle this tradition. The new positioning strategy is based on flawless quality and exclusivity, which are portrayed uniquely in each cultural context. The watches are sold by only a few retailers worldwide for as much as $100,000 each. The precious wristwatches that bear the "A. Lange & Söhne" signature have their roots in the grand history of Saxony.

German jewelry industry officials were "cautiously optimistic" when discussing the 2010 to 2015 industry outlook. Officials believed that there would be an increase in demand from European Union–member states for German-made jewelry such as watches. Europe is the primary sales market for German-made goods and, as of 2009, accounts for an estimated 70 percent of all jewelry and watch exports. Given these predictions and statistics, Lange Uhren is well positioned to continue its success in this industry.[34] ∎

Ethics in Marketing Research

It is often necessary to disguise the purpose of the experiment in order to produce valid results. Consider, for example, a project conducted to determine the effectiveness of television commercials for Kellogg's Rice Krispies cereal. The respondents are recruited and brought to a central facility. They are told that they will be watching a television program on nutrition and then will be asked some questions. Interspersed in the program is the commercial for Rice Krispies (test commercial), as well as commercials for some other products (filler commercials). After viewing the program and the commercials, the respondents are administered a questionnaire. The questionnaire obtains evaluations on the program content, the test commercial, and some of the filler commercials. Note that the evaluations of the program content and the filler commercials are not of interest but are obtained to reinforce the nature of the disguise. If the respondents knew the true purpose was to determine the effectiveness of the Rice Krispies commercial, their responses might be biased.

Disguising the purpose of the research should be done in a manner that does not violate the rights of the respondents. One way to handle this ethical dilemma is to inform the respondents, at the beginning, that the experiment has been disguised. They should also be given a description of the research task and told that they can leave the experiment at any time. After the data have been collected, the true purpose of the study and the nature of the disguise should be fully explained to the respondents and they should be given an opportunity to withdraw their information. The procedure is called **debriefing**. Disclosure in this way does not bias the results. There is evidence indicating that data collected from subjects informed of the disguise and those not informed are similar.[35] Debriefing can alleviate stress and make the experiment a learning experience for the respondents. However, if not properly handled, debriefing itself can be stressful. In the Rice Krispies cereal example, respondents may find it disheartening that they spent their time on a trivial task, evaluating a cereal commercial. The researcher should anticipate and address this issue in the debriefing session.

One further ethical concern is the responsibility of the researcher to use an appropriate experimental design for the problem so as to control errors caused by extraneous variables. As the following example illustrates, determining the most appropriate experimental design for the problem requires not only an initial evaluation but also continuous monitoring.

debriefing
After the experiment, informing test subjects what the experiment was about and how the experimental manipulations were performed.

Real Research   Correcting Errors Early: A Stitch in Time Saves Nine

For the fiscal year ending May 31, 2008, Nike (www.nike.com) reported record revenues of $18.6 billion, a $2.3 billion increase over the previous year's earnings. Nike's revenue rose as demand grew across all regions and the weak dollar helped boost the value of overseas sales. A marketing research firm specializing in advertising research is examining the effectiveness of a television commercial for Nike athletic shoes. A one-group pretest-posttest design was used. Attitudes held by the respondents toward Nike athletic shoes were obtained prior to being exposed to a sports program and several commercials, including the one for Nike. Attitudes were again measured after viewing the program and the commercials. Initial evaluation based on a small sample found the one-group pretest-posttest design adopted in this study to be susceptible to demand artifacts: Respondents attempt to guess the purpose of the experiment and respond accordingly. Because time and financial constraints make redesigning the study difficult at best, the research continues without correction. Continuing a research project after knowing errors were made in the early stages is not ethical behavior. Experimental design problems should be disclosed immediately to the client. Decisions on whether to redesign the study or accept the flaw should be made jointly by the researcher and the client.[36] ■

Decision Research   Levi's: Fading Jeans and Market Share

The Situation

As of 2009, Levi's (www.levi.com) is a leading global apparel company, with sales in more than 110 countries. It has been a long-standing company with more than 150 years of being in the clothing business. Although one may think this long history can only result in good things, Levi's heritage has been its worst enemy. John Anderson, the president and chief executive officer for Levi Strauss & Co., had to work to revamp Levi's antique image and make the brand appealing to younger generations in efforts to boost its declining sales. In the last five years, Anderson saw worldwide sales drop 40 percent, losing market share to competitors like the Gap, and trendier ones such as Calvin Klein, Tommy Hilfiger, and Diesel. Another problem for Anderson came from store brand jeans, such as JCPenney's Arizona brand jeans or the Gap's in-house brand, which have changed their image and launched an

Experimental research can help Levi's determine the power of its national brand as compared to an in-house brand like Gap or a store brand like JCPenney's Arizona jeans.

assault on big brand names like Levi's. These store brand jeans, along with other store label jeans, now target the teenage market with "cutting edge" advertising. American trade publication *Brand Strategy* estimated that the brand has lost about 50 percent of the younger consumer market share worldwide between 1999 and 2008.

To compete with these brands and maintain leadership, Levi's, the market leader, is considering introducing their own line of private-label jeans to capture a larger portion of the teenage market. John Anderson wonders, "How powerful is a national brand like Levi's compared to an in-house brand like Gap or a store brand like JCPenney's Arizona jeans?"

The Marketing Research Decision

1. If you were John Anderson, what type of research would you want to conduct to help arrive at an answer?
2. Please explain how you would implement the type of research you have recommended.
3. Discuss the role of the type of research you recommend in enabling John Anderson to determine the power of a national brand like Levi's compared to an in-house brand like Gap or a store brand like JCPenney's Arizona jeans.

The Marketing Management Decision

1. What should Levi's do to compete with in-house and store brands of jeans?
2. Discuss how the marketing management decision action that you recommend is influenced by the research that you suggested earlier and by the findings of that research.[37] ∎

Summary

The scientific notion of causality implies that we can never prove that X causes Y. At best, we can only infer that X is one of the causes of Y in that it makes the occurrence of Y probable. Three conditions must be satisfied before causal inferences can be made: (1) concomitant variation, which implies that X and Y must vary together in a hypothesized way; (2) time order of occurrence of variables, which implies that X must precede Y; and (3) elimination of other possible causal factors, which implies that competing explanations must be ruled out. Experiments provide the most convincing evidence of all three conditions. An experiment is formed when one or more independent variables are manipulated or controlled by the researcher, and their effect on one or more dependent variables is measured. Figure 7.2 gives a concept map for experiments.

In designing an experiment, it is important to consider internal and external validity. Internal validity refers to

whether the manipulation of the independent variables actually caused the effects on the dependent variables. External validity refers to the generalizability of experimental results. For the experiment to be valid, the researcher must control the threats imposed by extraneous variables, such as history, maturation, testing (main and interactive testing effects), instrumentation, statistical regression, selection bias, and mortality. There are four ways of controlling extraneous variables: randomization, matching, statistical control, and design control.

Experimental designs may be classified as preexperimental, true experimental, quasi-experimental, or statistical. An experiment may be conducted in a laboratory environment or under actual market conditions in a real-life setting. Only causal designs encompassing experimentation are appropriate for inferring cause-and-effect relationships.

Although experiments have limitations in terms of time, cost, and administration, they are becoming increasingly

FIGURE 7.2

A Concept Map for Experiments

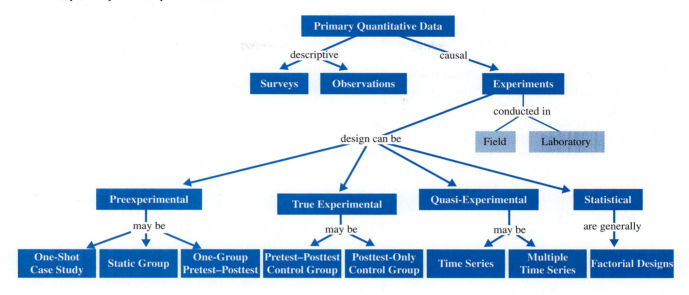

popular in marketing. Test marketing is an important application of experimental design.

The internal and external validity of field experiments conducted overseas is generally lower than in the United States. The level of development in many countries is lower, and the researcher lacks control over many of the marketing variables. The ethical issues involved in conducting causal research include disguising the purpose of the experiment. Debriefing can be used to address some of these issues. The Internet and computers are very useful in the design and implementation of experiments.

Key Terms and Concepts

causality, 218
concomitant variation, 219
independent variables, 221
test units, 221
dependent variables, 221
extraneous variables, 221
experiment, 221
experimental design, 221
internal validity, 222
external validity, 223
history (H), 223
maturation (MA), 223
main testing effect (MT), 224
interactive testing effect (IT), 224
instrumentation (I), 224
statistical regression (SR), 224

selection bias (SB), 224
mortality (MO), 225
confounding variables, 225
randomization, 225
matching, 225
statistical control, 225
design control, 226
preexperimental designs, 226
true experimental designs, 226
quasi-experimental designs, 226
statistical design, 226
one-shot case study, 227
one-group pretest-posttest design, 227
static group, 228
pretest-posttest control group
  design, 228

posttest-only control group design, 229
Solomon four-group design, 230
time series design, 230
multiple time series design, 231
randomized block design, 233
Latin square design, 233
factorial design, 234
laboratory environment, 235
field environment, 235
demand artifacts, 236
test marketing, 237
test markets, 237
standard test market, 237
controlled test market, 239
simulated test market, 239
debriefing, 241

Suggested Cases, Video Cases, and HBS Cases

Running Case with Real Data

1.1 Dell

Comprehensive Critical Thinking Cases

2.1 American Idol   2.2 Baskin-Robbins   2.3 Akron Children's Hospital

Comprehensive Cases with Real Data

4.1 JPMorgan Chase   4.2 Wendy's

Video Cases

7.1 AFLAC   8.1 P&G   11.1 Motorola   12.1 Subaru   23.1 Marriott

Comprehensive Harvard Business School Cases

Case 5.1: The Harvard Graduate Student Housing Survey (9-505-059)
Case 5.2: BizRate.Com (9-501-024)
Case 5.3: Cola Wars Continue: Coke and Pepsi in the Twenty-First Century (9-702-442)
Case 5.4: TiVo in 2002 (9-502-062)
Case 5.5: Compaq Computer: Intel Inside? (9-599-061)
Case 5.6: The New Beetle (9-501-023)

Live Research: Conducting a Marketing Research Project

If an experiment is to be conducted, the choice of an experimental design may have to be tempered by several considerations:

1. It may not be possible to control for certain extraneous variables.
2. There may be only limited flexibility to manipulate the independent variables, for example, advertising or sales effort cannot be reduced to the zero level.

3. Random assignment of test units to the treatment conditions may not be possible.
4. The choice of dependent variables may be limited by measurement considerations.

Acronym

The extraneous factors that threaten the internal and external validity of the experiment may be described by the acronym

Threats:

T   esting
H   istory
R   egression
E   rrors in measurement: instrumentation
A   ging: maturation
T   ermination of test units: mortality
S   election bias

Exercises

Questions

1. What are the requirements for inferring a causal relationship between two variables?
2. Differentiate between internal and external validity.
3. List any five extraneous variables and give an example to show how each can reduce internal validity.
4. Describe the various methods for controlling extraneous sources of variation.
5. What is the key characteristic that distinguishes true experimental designs from preexperimental designs?
6. List the steps involved in implementing the posttest-only control group design. Describe the design symbolically.
7. What is a time series experiment? When is it used?
8. How is a multiple time series design different from a basic time series design?

9. What advantages do statistical designs have over basic designs?
10. What are the limitations of the Latin square design?
11. Compare laboratory and field experimentation.
12. Should descriptive research be used for investigating causal relationships? Why or why not?
13. What is test marketing? What are the major types of test marketing?
14. What is the main difference between a standard test market and a controlled test market?
15. Describe how simulated test marketing works.

Problems

1. A pro-life group wanted to test the effectiveness of an antiabortion commercial. Two random samples, each of 250 respondents, were recruited in Atlanta. One group was shown

the antiabortion commercial. Then, attitudes toward abortion were measured for respondents in both groups.
   a. Identify the independent and dependent variables in this experiment.
   b. What type of design was used?
   c. What are the potential threats to internal and external validity in this experiment?
2. In the experiment just described, suppose the respondents had been selected by convenience rather than randomly. What type of design would result?
3. Consider the following table in which 500 respondents have been classified based on product use and income.

| Product | Income | | |
Use	High	Medium	Low
High	40	30	40
Medium	35	70	60
Low	25	50	150

   a. Does this table indicate concomitant variation between product use and income?
   b. Describe the relationship between product use and income, based on the table.

4. State the type of experiment being conducted in the following situations. In each case, identify the potential threat to internal and external validity.
   a. A major distributor of office equipment is considering a new sales presentation program for its salespeople. The largest sales territory is selected, the new program is implemented, and the effect on sales is measured.
   b. Procter & Gamble wants to determine if a new package design for Tide is more effective than the current design. Twelve supermarkets are randomly selected in Chicago. In six of them, randomly selected, Tide is sold in the new packaging. In the other six, the detergent is sold in the old package. Sales for both groups of supermarkets are monitored for three months.
5. Describe a specific situation for which each of the following experimental designs is appropriate. Defend your reasoning.
   a. One-group pretest-posttest design
   b. Pretest-posttest control group design
   c. Posttest-only control group design
   d. Multiple time series design
   e. Factorial design

Internet and Computer Exercises

1. Survey the relevant literature and write a short paper on the role of the computer in controlled experiments in marketing research.
2. Design an experiment for determining the effectiveness of online coupons based on relevant information obtained from www.coupons-online.com.
3. Coca-Cola has developed three alternative package designs for its flagship product, Coke. Design an Internet-based experiment to determine which, if any, of these new package designs is superior to the current one.

4. Microsoft has developed a new version of its spreadsheet EXCEL but is not sure what the user reaction will be. Design an Internet-based experiment to determine user reaction to the new and the previous versions of EXCEL.
5. Explain how you would implement a posttest-only control group design on the Internet to measure the effectiveness of a new print ad for the Toyota Camry.

Activities

Role Playing

1. You are a marketing research manager for the Coca-Cola Company. The company would like to determine whether it should increase, decrease, or maintain the current level of advertising dollars spent on Coke Classic. Design a field experiment to address this issue.
2. What potential difficulties do you see in conducting the experiment just described? What assistance would you require from the Coca-Cola management to overcome these difficulties?

Fieldwork

1. Select two different perfume advertisements for any brand of perfume. Design and conduct an experiment to determine

which ad is more effective. Use a student sample with 10 students being exposed to each ad (treatment condition). Develop your own measures of advertising effectiveness in this context.

Group Discussion

1. "Whereas one cannot prove a causal relationship by conducting an experiment, experimentation is unscientific for examining cause-and-effect relationships." Discuss this statement as a small group.

Dell Running Case

Review the Dell case, Case 1.1, and questionnaire given toward the end of the book.

1. Is causal research necessary in this case? If so, which experimental designs would you recommend and why? If not, describe a scenario in which it would be.

2. If a mall-intercept interview is used and Dell conducts causal research without randomizing respondents, which preexperimental design would you recommend?
3. Can you think of any way in which the static group design can be randomized to increase its validity?

Video Cases

VIDEO CASE 7.1   AFLAC: Marketing Research Quacks Like a Duck

AFLAC Incorporated (www.aflac.com) sells supplemental health and life insurance. In the United States, AFLAC is known for its policies that "pay cash" to supplement or replace a policyholder's income when an accident or sickness prevents the policyholder from working. In 1989, the Columbus, Georgia, company, American Family Life Assurance Company, adopted the acronym AFLAC. At that point, the company had very little brand recognition; the name AFLAC meant nothing to potential customers. To boost brand recognition, AFLAC undertook extensive marketing research and emerged with the symbol of the duck. As of 2009, AFLAC boasts 90 percent brand recognition. This is so high that it actually rivals Coke, the company with the highest brand recognition, at 95 percent. Even children (age 8 to 13) are familiar with the AFLAC name, ranking it in the company of Pepsi, Old Navy, and M&M's. This is important, because as children grow up and start to buy insurance, the AFLAC name will be at the front of their minds.

Marketing research was at the forefront of the campaign. First, the decision was made to simply try to use ads to increase brand recognition rather than sell insurance. This decision came from focus groups and survey research that found customers would think that they did not need whatever type of insurance was being advertised, whether life, health, home, or so on. Instead, research indicated that customers would respond to insurance ads better if they simply raised the recognition of the brand. Then, salespeople would do the job of educating potential customers about the need for different types of insurance products.

After the decision was made to just raise brand awareness with ads, a specific campaign had to be created. Again, marketing research played a major role. From the start, it was decided that the ads that tested the best were going to be the ads that would be used. The research said that test customers viewing the ads preferred the AFLAC duck much more than any other ad viewed. But where did the duck come from? During the ad development process, one of the ad agency (the Kaplan Thaler Group) researchers just began to say the word "AFLAC" over and over again. Eventually, it was noticed that this word, said a certain way, sounded like a quacking duck. This led to the duck commercials. The risk in these commercials was that AFLAC was making fun of the fact that no one knew about the brand name, and humor in advertising does not always appeal to people who want a more serious tone. What if the people had seen the television commercial and thought, "How stupid!" or "A life insurance company should be more serious than that." Therefore, the duck commercials were tested against alternatives in experimental design situations. The test audiences loved the duck commercials and rated them the most memorable out of all the possibilities (AFLAC's main objective). Thus, the duck was born.

The campaign has been nothing but a success. Not only has AFLAC's brand recognition soared, but the company's sales have as well. Before the duck campaign, AFLAC's annual sales were growing in the 10 to 15 percent range. Post duck, AFLAC's sales are growing at an annual rate of 24 percent. Surprisingly, the growth is not limited to the United States. In fact, 70 percent of AFLAC's profits are from clients in Japan. The duck is now a world phenomenon, and AFLAC has marketing research to thank.

Conclusion

The case describes the crucial role of marketing research in designing the right advertising campaign and the resulting impact on brand recognition. The extraordinary growth in AFLAC's name recognition within just a few years of the launch of a new advertising campaign speaks volumes about the marketing research that was conducted to test the duck commercials.

Questions

1. If AFLAC wants to forecast the demand for supplemental health and life insurance, what type of research design should be adopted and why?
2. Identify sources of secondary data that would be useful in forecasting the demand for supplemental health and life insurance.

3. Identify sources of syndicated data that would be useful in fore-casting the demand for supplemental health and life insurance.
4. AFLAC wants to test a duck commercial against a nonduck commercial to determine which ad generates more favorable attitudes toward AFLAC. What type of experimental design would you recommend? Why would you recommend this type of design?
5. If a duck commercial is to be tested against two nonduck commercials to determine which ad generates more favorable attitudes toward AFLAC, what type of experimental design would you recommend?

References

1. http://aflac.com/us/en/Default.aspx, accessed February 20, 2009.
2. www.wikipedia.org, accessed February 20, 2009.
3. Suzanne Vranica, "AFLAC Duck's Paddle to Stardom: Creativity on the Cheap," *Wall Street Journal* (July 30, 2004): B1–B2.
4. Tony Adams, "Sales in Japan Help AFLAC Raise First-Quarter Net Earnings by Almost 33 Percent," *Knight Ridder Tribune Business News* (April 28, 2004): 1.

"When we analyze research results, we must believe that the measurements provide realistic representations of opinions and behaviors and properly capture how a respondent's data relate to all other respondents.

Greg Van Scoy, Senior Vice President, Client Services, Burke, Inc.

Objectives

[After reading this chapter, the student should be able to:]

1. Introduce the concepts of measurement and scaling and show how scaling may be considered an extension of measurement.

2. Explain the characteristics of description, order, distance, and origin and how they define the level of measurement of a scale.

3. Discuss the primary scales of measurement and differentiate nominal, ordinal, interval, and ratio scales.

4. Classify and discuss scaling techniques as comparative and noncomparative, and describe the comparative techniques of paired comparison, rank order, constant sum, and Q-sort scaling.

5. Discuss the considerations involved in implementing the primary scales of measurement in an international setting.

6. Understand the ethical issues involved in selecting scales of measurement.

7. Discuss the use of the Internet and computers in implementing the primary scales of measurement.

Measurement and Scaling: Fundamentals and Comparative Scaling

Overview

Once the type of research design has been determined (Chapters 3 through 7) and the information to be obtained specified, the researcher can move on to the next phase of the research design: deciding on measurement and scaling procedures. In this chapter, we describe the concepts of scaling and measurement and explain the fundamental scale characteristics of description, order, distance, and origin. We discuss four primary scales of measurement: nominal, ordinal, interval, and ratio. We next describe both comparative and noncomparative scaling techniques and explain comparative techniques in detail. Noncomparative techniques are covered in Chapter 9. The considerations involved in implementing the primary scales of measurement when researching international markets are discussed. Several ethical issues that arise in measurement and scaling are identified. The chapter also discusses the use of the Internet and computers in implementing the primary scales of measurement.

Real Research

The World's and America's Most Admired Companies

The value of the World's Most Admired Companies rankings, as with *Fortune's* list of America's most admired, lies in their having been bestowed by the people who are closest to the action: senior executives and outside directors in each industry, and financial analysts who are in a position to study and compare the competitors in each field. *Fortune* asked them to rate companies on the eight criteria used to rank America's most admired: innovativeness, overall quality of management, value as a long-term investment, responsibility to the community and the environment, ability to attract and keep talented people, quality of products or services, financial soundness, and wise use of corporate assets. For global ranking, *Fortune* added another criterion to reflect international scope: a company's effectiveness in doing business globally. A company's overall ranking is based on the average of the scores of all criteria attributes. The 2008 top two World's Most Admired Companies were Apple and General Electric, in that order. The 2008 America's Most Admired Companies were:

ID	Company	Rank
A	Apple, U.S.	1
B	General Electric, U.S.	2
C	Toyota Motor, Japan	3
D	Berkshire Hathaway, U.S.	4
E	Procter & Gamble, U.S.	5
F	FedEx, U.S.	6
G	Johnson & Johnson, U.S.	7
H	Target, U.S.	8
I	BMW, Germany	9
J	Microsoft, U.S.	10

Source: List of Top Ten Companies from The World's Most Admired Companies®, March 17, 2008. *FORTUNE*, © Time Inc. All rights reserved.

In this example, the ID alphabets used to identify the companies represent a nominal scale. Thus, "E" denotes Procter & Gamble and "F" refers to FedEx. The ranks represent an ordinal scale. Thus, Johnson & Johnson, ranked 7, received higher evaluations than Target, ranked 8. The company score, the average rating on all the criteria attributes, represents an interval scale. These scores are not shown in the table. Finally, the annual revenue for these companies, also not shown, represents a ratio scale.[1] ■

Apple was the world's and America's most admired company in 2008.

Measurement and Scaling

measurement

The assignment of numbers or other symbols to characteristics of objects according to certain prespecified rules.

Measurement means assigning numbers or other symbols to characteristics of objects according to certain prespecified rules.[2] Note that what we measure is not the object, but some characteristic of it. Thus, we do not measure consumers—only their perceptions, attitudes, preferences, or other relevant characteristics. In marketing research, numbers are usually assigned for one of two reasons. First, numbers permit statistical analysis of the resulting data. Second, numbers facilitate the communication of measurement rules and results.

The most important aspect of measurement is the specification of rules for assigning numbers to the characteristics. The assignment process must be isomorphic: There must be one-to-one correspondence between the numbers and the characteristics being measured. For example, the same dollar figures are assigned to households with identical annual incomes. Only then can the numbers be associated with specific characteristics of the measured object, and vice versa. In addition, the rules for assigning numbers should be standardized and applied uniformly. They must not change over objects or time.

scaling

The generation of a continuum upon which measured objects are located.

Scaling may be considered an extension of measurement. **Scaling** involves creating a continuum upon which measured objects are located. To illustrate, consider a scale from 1 to 100 for locating consumers according to the characteristic "attitude toward department stores." Each respondent is assigned a number from 1 to 100 indicating the degree of (un)favorableness, with 1 = extremely unfavorable, and 100 = extremely favorable. Measurement is the actual assignment of a number from 1 to 100 to each respondent. Scaling is the process of placing the respondents on a continuum with respect to their attitude toward department stores. In the opening example of most admired companies, the assignment of numbers to reflect the annual revenue was an example of measurement. The placement of individual companies on the annual revenue continuum was scaling.

Scale Characteristics and Levels of Measurement

All the scales that we use in marketing research can be described in terms of four basic characteristics. These characteristics are description, order, distance, and origin, and together they define the level of measurement of a scale. The level of measurement denotes what properties of an object the scale is measuring or not measuring. An understanding of the scale characteristics is fundamental to understanding the primary type of scales.

Description

description
The unique labels or descriptors that are used to designate each value of the scale. All scales possess description.

By **description**, we mean the unique labels or descriptors that are used to designate each value of the scale. Some examples of descriptors are as follows: 1. Female, 2. Male; 1 = Strongly disagree, 2 = Disagree, 3 = Neither agree nor disagree, 4 = Agree, and 5 = Strongly agree; and the number of dollars earned annually by a household. To amplify, Female and Male are unique descriptors used to describe values 1 and 2 of the gender scale. It is important to remember that all scales possess this characteristic of description. Thus, all scales have unique labels or descriptors that are used to define the scale values or response options.

Order

order
The relative sizes or positions of the descriptors. Order is denoted by descriptors such as greater than, less than, and equal to.

By **order**, we mean the relative sizes or positions of the descriptors. There are no absolute values associated with order, only relative values. Order is denoted by descriptors such as "greater than," "less than," and "equal to." For example, a respondent's preference for three brands of athletic shoes is expressed by the following order, with the most preferred brand being listed first and the least preferred brand last.

Nike

Reebok

Adidas

For this respondent, the preference for Nike is greater than the preference for Reebok. Likewise, the preference for Adidas is less than the preference for Reebok. Respondents who check the same age category, say 35 to 49, are considered to be equal to each other in terms of age, and greater than respondents in the 20 to 34 age group. All scales do not possess the order characteristic. In the gender scale (1. Female, 2. Male) considered earlier, we have no way of determining whether a female is greater than or less than a male. Thus, the gender scale does not possess order.

Distance

distance
The characteristic of distance means that absolute differences between the scale descriptors are known and may be expressed in units.

The characteristic of **distance** means that absolute differences between the scale descriptors are known and may be expressed in units. A five-person household has one person more than a four-person household, which in turn has one person more than a three-person household. Thus, the following scale possesses the distance characteristic.

Number of persons living in your household _____

Notice, that a scale that has distance also has order. We know that a five-person household is greater than the four-person household in terms of the number of persons living in the household. Likewise, a three-person household is less than a four-person household. Thus, distance implies order but the reverse may not be true.

Origin

origin
The origin characteristic means that the scale has a unique or fixed beginning or true zero point.

The **origin** characteristic means that the scale has a unique or fixed beginning or true zero point. Thus, an exact measurement of income by a scale such as: What is the annual income of our household before taxes? $ _____ has a fixed origin or a true zero point. An answer of zero would mean that the household has no income at all. A scale that has origin also has distance (and order and description). Many scales used in marketing research do not have a fixed origin or true zero point, as in the disagree-agree scale considered earlier under description. Notice that such a scale was defined as 1 = Strongly disagree, 2 = Disagree, 3 = Neither agree nor disagree, 4 = Agree, and 5 = Strongly agree. However, 1 is an arbitrary origin or starting point. This scale could just as easily have been defined as 0 = Strongly disagree, 1 = Disagree, 2 = Neither agree nor disagree, 3 = Agree, and 4 = Strongly agree, with 0 as the origin. Alternatively, shifting the origin to -2 will result in an equivalent scale: -2 = Strongly disagree, -1 = Disagree, 0 = Neither agree nor disagree, 1 = Agree, and 2 = Strongly agree. All these three forms of the agree-disagree scale, with the origin at 1, 0, or -2, are equivalent. Thus, this scale does not have a fixed origin or a true zero point and consequently does not possess the characteristic of origin.

You may have observed that description, order, distance, and origin represent successively higher-level characteristics, with origin being the highest-level characteristic. Description is the most basic characteristic that is present in all scales. If a scale has order, it also has description. If a scale has distance, it also has order and description. Finally, a scale that has origin also has distance, order, and description. Thus, if a scale has a higher-level characteristic, it also has all the lower-level characteristics. However, the reverse may not be true, i.e., if a scale has a lower-level characteristic, it may or may not have a higher-level characteristic. With an understanding of scale characteristics, we are ready to discuss the primary type of scales.

Primary Scales of Measurement

There are four primary scales of measurement: nominal, ordinal, interval, and ratio.[3] These scales are illustrated in Figure 8.1, and their properties are summarized in Table 8.1 and discussed in the following sections.

Nominal Scale

nominal scale
A scale whose numbers serve only as labels or tags for identifying and classifying objects. When used for identification, there is a strict one-to-one correspondence between the numbers and the objects.

A **nominal scale** is a figurative labeling scheme in which the numbers serve only as labels or tags for identifying and classifying objects. The only characteristic possessed by these scales is description. For example, the numbers assigned to the respondents in a study constitute a nominal scale. When a nominal scale is used for the purpose of identification, there is a strict one-to-one correspondence between the numbers and the objects. Each number is assigned to only one object and each object has only one number assigned to it. Common examples include Social Security numbers and numbers assigned to football players. In marketing research, nominal scales are used for identifying respondents, brands, attributes, stores, and other objects.

When used for classification purposes, the nominally scaled numbers serve as labels for classes or categories. For example, you might classify the control group as group 1 and the experimental group as group 2. The classes are mutually exclusive and collectively exhaustive. The objects in each class are viewed as equivalent with respect to the characteristic represented by the nominal number. All objects in the same class have the same number and no two classes have the same number. However, a nominal scale need not involve the assignment of numbers; alphabets or symbols could be assigned as well. In the opening example, alphabets were assigned to denote specific companies.

The numbers in a nominal scale do not reflect the amount of the characteristic possessed by the objects. For example, a high Social Security number does not imply that the person is in some way superior to those with lower Social Security numbers or vice versa. The same applies to numbers

FIGURE 8.1

An Illustration of Primary Scales of Measurement

Scale				
Nominal	Numbers Assigned to Runners	 7	11	3 Finish
Ordinal	Rank Order of Winners	Third Place	Second Place	First Place Finish
Interval	Performance Rating on a 0-to-10 Scale	8.2	9.1	9.6
Ratio	Time to Finish, in Seconds	15.2	14.1	13.4

TABLE 8.1
Primary Scales of Measurement

Scale	Basic Characteristics	Common Examples	Marketing Examples	Permissible Statistics Descriptive	Permissible Statistics Inferential
Nominal	Numbers identify and classify objects	Social Security numbers, numbering of football players	Brand numbers, store types, sex classification	Percentages, mode	Chi-square, binomial test
Ordinal	Numbers indicate the relative positions of the objects but not the magnitude of differences between them	Quality rankings, rankings of teams in a tournament	Preference rankings, market position, social class	Percentile, median	Rank-order correlation, Friedman ANOVA
Interval	Differences between objects can be compared; zero point is arbitrary	Temperature (Fahrenheit, centigrade)	Attitudes, opinions, index numbers	Range, mean, standard deviation	Product-moment correlations, t-tests, ANOVA, regression, factor analysis
Ratio	Zero point is fixed; ratios of scale values can be computed	Length, weight	Age, income, costs, sales, market shares	Geometric mean, harmonic mean	Coefficient of variation

assigned to classes. The only permissible operation on the numbers in a nominal scale is counting. Only a limited number of statistics, all of which are based on frequency counts, are permissible. These include percentages, mode, chi-square, and binomial tests (see Chapter 15). It is not meaningful to compute an average Social Security number, the average sex of the respondents in a survey, or the number assigned to an average department store, as in the following example.

Project Research   Nominal Scale

In the department store project, numbers 1 through 10 were assigned to the 10 stores considered in the study (see Table 8.2). Thus store number 9 referred to Sears. This did not imply that Sears was in any way superior or inferior to Neiman Marcus, which was assigned the number 6. Any reassignment of the numbers, such as transposing the numbers assigned to Sears and Neiman Marcus, would have no effect on the numbering system, because the numerals did not reflect any characteristics of the stores. It is meaningful to

TABLE 8.2
Illustration of Primary Scales of Measurement

Nominal Scale No.	Nominal Scale Store	Ordinal Scale Preference Rankings	Interval Scale Preference Ratings 1–7	Interval Scale Preference Ratings 11–17	Ratio Scale $ Spent Last 3 Months
1.	Nordstrom	7 79	5	15	0
2.	Macy's	2 25	7	17	200
3.	Kmart	8 82	4	14	0
4.	Kohl's	3 30	6	16	100
5.	JCPenney	1 10	7	17	250
6.	Neiman-Marcus	5 53	5	15	35
7.	Marshalls	9 95	4	14	0
8.	Saks Fifth Avenue	6 61	5	15	100
9.	Sears	4 45	6	16	0
10.	Wal-Mart	10 115	2	12	10

make statements such as "75 percent of the respondents patronized store 9 (Sears) within the last month." Although the average of the assigned numbers is 5.5, it is not meaningful to state that the number of the average store is 5.5. ■

Ordinal Scale

ordinal scale
A ranking scale in which numbers are assigned to objects to indicate the relative extent to which some characteristic is possessed. Thus it is possible to determine whether an object has more or less of a characteristic than some other object.

An **ordinal scale** is a ranking scale in which numbers are assigned to objects to indicate the relative extent to which the objects possess some characteristic. An ordinal scale allows you to determine whether an object has more or less of a characteristic than some other object, but not how much more or less. Thus, an ordinal scale indicates relative position, not the magnitude of the differences between the objects. The object ranked first has more of the characteristic as compared to the object ranked second, but whether the object ranked second is a close second or a poor second is not known. The ordinal scales possess description and order characteristics but do not possess distance (or origin). Common examples of ordinal scales include quality rankings, rankings of teams in a tournament, socioeconomic class, and occupational status. In marketing research, ordinal scales are used to measure relative attitudes, opinions, perceptions, and preferences. In the opening example, the rank order of the most admired companies represented an ordinal scale. Apple with a rank of 1, was America's most admired company. Measurements of this type include "greater than" or "less than" judgments from the respondents.

In an ordinal scale, as in a nominal scale, equivalent objects receive the same rank. Any series of numbers can be assigned that preserves the ordered relationships between the objects. For example, ordinal scales can be transformed in any way as long as the basic ordering of the objects is maintained.[4] In other words, any monotonic positive (order-preserving) transformation of the scale is permissible, because the differences in numbers are void of any meaning other than order (see the following example). For these reasons, in addition to the counting operation allowable for nominal scale data, ordinal scales permit the use of statistics based on centiles. It is meaningful to calculate percentile, quartile, median (Chapter 15), rank order correlation (Chapter 17), or other summary statistics from ordinal data.

Project Research   Ordinal Scale

Table 8.2 gives a particular respondent's preference rankings. Respondents ranked 10 department stores in order of preference by assigning rank 1 to the most preferred store, rank 2 to the second most preferred store, and so on. Note that JCPenney (ranked 1) is preferred to Macy's (ranked 2), but how much it is preferred we do not know. Also, it is not necessary that we assign numbers from 1 to 10 to obtain a preference ranking. The second ordinal scale, which assigns a number 10 to JCPenney, 25 to Macy's, 30 to Kohl's, and so on, is an equivalent scale, as it was obtained by a monotonic positive transformation of the first scale. The two scales result in the same ordering of the stores according to preference. ■

ACTIVE RESEARCH

United Flying for Customer Satisfaction

Visit www.united.com and search the Internet using a search engine as well as your library's online databases to obtain information on customer satisfaction with airlines.

As the marketing director for United Airlines, what marketing strategies would you formulate to enhance satisfaction?

How would you use nominal and ordinal scales to measure customer satisfaction with the major airlines such as United and its competitors?

interval scale
A scale in which the numbers are used to rate objects such that numerically equal distances on the scale represent equal distances in the characteristic being measured.

Interval Scale

In an **interval scale**, numerically equal distances on the scale represent equal values in the characteristic being measured. An interval scale contains all the information of an ordinal scale, but it also allows you to compare the differences between objects. The difference between any two scale values is identical to the difference between any other two adjacent values of an interval scale. There is a constant or equal interval between scale values. The difference between 1 and 2 is the same as the difference between 2 and 3, which is the same as the difference between 5 and 6. The distance between descriptors is known. A common example in everyday life is a temperature scale. In marketing research, attitudinal data obtained from rating scales are often treated as interval data. In the opening example of the most admired companies, the ratings on all the criteria attributes represented an interval scale.[5]

In an interval scale, the location of the zero point is not fixed, i.e., these scales do not possess the origin characteristic. Both the zero point and the units of measurement are arbitrary. Hence, any positive linear transformation of the form $y = a + bx$ will preserve the properties of the scale. Here, x is the original scale value, y is the transformed scale value, b is a positive constant, and a is any constant. Therefore, two interval scales that rate objects A, B, C, and D as 1, 2, 3, and 4, or as 22, 24, 26, and 28, are equivalent. Note that the latter scale can be derived from the former by using a = 20 and b = 2 in the transforming equation. Because the zero point is not fixed, it is not meaningful to take ratios of scale values. As can be seen, the ratio of D to B values changes from 2:1 to become 7:6 when the scale is transformed. Yet ratios of differences between scale values are permissible. In this process, the constants a and b in the transforming equation drop out in the computations. The ratio of the difference between D and B to the difference between C and B is 2:1 in both the scales.

Project Research

Interval Scale

In Table 8.2, a respondent's preferences for the 10 stores are expressed on a 7-point rating scale. We can see that although Sears received a preference rating of 6 and Wal-Mart a rating of 2, this does not mean that Sears is preferred three times as much as Wal-Mart. When the ratings are transformed to an equivalent 11-to-17 scale (next column), the ratings for these stores become 16 and 12, and the ratio is no longer 3 to 1. In contrast, the ratios of preference differences are identical on the two scales. The ratio of the preference difference between JCPenney and Wal-Mart to the preference difference between Neiman Marcus and Wal-Mart is 5 to 3 on both the scales. ∎

Statistical techniques that may be used on interval scale data include all of those that can be applied to nominal and ordinal data. In addition, you can calculate the arithmetic mean, standard deviation (Chapter 15), product moment correlations (Chapter 17), and other statistics commonly used in marketing research. However, certain specialized statistics such as geometric mean, harmonic mean, and coefficient of variation are not meaningful on interval scale data.

As a further illustration, Federation Internationale de Football Association (FIFA) uses ordinal and interval scaling to rank football teams of various countries.

Real Research

Scaling the Football World

According to Federation Internationale de Football Association's (FIFA) (www.fifa.com) September 2008 men's rankings, Spain was at the top with 1,565 points and Italy was in the second spot with 1,339 points. The top 10 countries in men's football (known as soccer in the United States) are shown.

Ranking as of September 2008

ID	Team	Rank	Points
A	Spain	1	1,565
B	Italy	2	1,339
C	Germany	3	1,329
D	Netherlands	4	1,295
E	Croatia	5	1,266
F	Brazil	6	1,252
G	Argentina	7	1,230
H	Czech Republic	8	1,134
I	Portugal	9	1,120
J	Turkey	10	1,033

The alphabets assigned to countries constitute a nominal scale, and the rankings represent an ordinal scale, whereas the points awarded denote an interval scale. Thus country G refers to Argentina, which was ranked 7 and received 1,230 points. Note that the alphabets assigned to denote the countries simply serve the purpose of identification and are not in any way related to their football-playing capabilities. Such information can be obtained only by looking at the ranks. Thus, Croatia, ranked 5, played better than Turkey, ranked 10. The lower the rank, the better the performance. The ranks do not give any information on the magnitude of the differences between countries, which can be obtained only by looking at the points. Based on the points awarded, it can be seen that Italy, with 1,339 points, played only marginally better than Germany, with 1,329 points. The points help us to discern the magnitude of difference between countries receiving different ranks.[6] ■

Ratio Scale

A **ratio scale** possesses all the properties of the nominal, ordinal, and interval scales and, in addition, an absolute zero point. Thus, ratio scales possess the characteristic of origin (and distance, order, and description). Thus, in ratio scales we can identify or classify objects, rank the objects, and compare intervals or differences. It is also meaningful to compute ratios of scale values. Not only is the difference between 2 and 5 the same as the difference between 14 and 17, but also 14 is seven times as large as 2 in an absolute sense. Common examples of ratio scales include height, weight, age, and money. In marketing, sales, costs, market share, and number of customers are variables measured on a ratio scale. In the opening example, the rate of return of the most admired companies, not shown, could be represented on a ratio scale.

Ratio scales allow only proportionate transformations of the form $y = bx$, where b is a positive constant. One cannot add an arbitrary constant, as in the case of an interval scale. An example of this transformation is provided by the conversion of yards to feet ($b = 3$). The comparisons between the objects are identical whether made in yards or feet.

All statistical techniques can be applied to ratio data. These include specialized statistics such as geometric mean, harmonic mean, and coefficient of variation.

The four primary scales (discussed here) do not exhaust the measurement-level categories. It is possible to construct a nominal scale that provides partial information on order (the partially ordered scale). Likewise, an ordinal scale can convey partial information on distance, as in the case of an ordered metric scale. A discussion of these scales is beyond the scope of this text.[7]

Project Research | Ratio Scale

In the ratio scale illustrated in Table 8.2, a respondent is asked to indicate the dollar amounts spent in each of the 10 stores during the last two months. Note that whereas this respondent spent $200 in Macy's and only $10 in Wal-Mart, this person spent 20 times as much in Macy's as Wal-Mart. Also, the zero point is fixed, because 0 means that the respondent did not spend anything at that store. Multiplying these numbers by 100 to convert dollars to cents results in an equivalent scale.

Project Activities

In the context of the Sears project, develop questions to measure each of the following variables and identify the level of measurement in each question.

1. Marital status of respondent
2. Age of respondent
3. Annual household income before taxes
4. Familiarity with Sears
5. Importance of price in selecting a department store
6. Number of bank credit cards owned ■

ACTIVE RESEARCH

Coaching Consumer Preferences for Coach

Visit www.coach.com and search the Internet using a search engine as well as your library's online databases to obtain information on consumer preferences for leather goods.

How would you use interval and ratio scales to measure consumer preferences for leather goods?

As the marketing director for Coach, how would you use information on consumer preferences for leather goods to increase your market share?

FIGURE 8.2

A Classification of Scaling Techniques

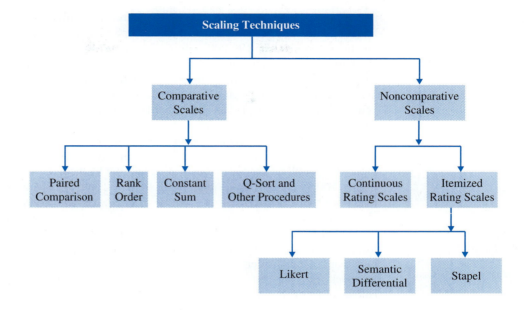

A Comparison of Scaling Techniques

comparative scales
One of two types of scaling techniques in which there is direct comparison of stimulus objects with one another.

The scaling techniques commonly employed in marketing research can be classified into comparative and noncomparative scales (see Figure 8.2). **Comparative scales** involve the direct comparison of stimulus objects. For example, respondents might be asked whether they prefer Coke or Pepsi. Comparative scale data must be interpreted in relative terms and have only ordinal or rank order properties. For this reason, comparative scaling is also referred to as nonmetric scaling. As shown in Figure 8.2, comparative scales include paired comparisons, rank order, constant sum scales, Q-sort, and other procedures.

The major benefit of comparative scaling is that small differences between stimulus objects can be detected. As they compare the stimulus objects, respondents are forced to choose between them. In addition, respondents approach the rating task from the same known reference points. Consequently, comparative scales are easily understood and can be applied easily. Other advantages of these scales are that they involve fewer theoretical assumptions, and they also tend to reduce halo or carryover effects from one judgment to another. The major disadvantages of comparative scales include the ordinal nature of the data and the inability to generalize beyond the stimulus objects scaled. For instance, to compare RC Cola to Coke and Pepsi, the researcher would have to do a new study. These disadvantages are substantially overcome by the noncomparative scaling techniques.

noncomparative scales
One of two types of scaling techniques in which each stimulus object is scaled independently of the other objects in the stimulus set.

In **noncomparative scales**, also referred to as *monadic* or *metric scales*, each object is scaled independently of the others in the stimulus set. The resulting data are generally assumed to be interval or ratio scaled.[8] For example, respondents may be asked to evaluate Coke on a 1-to-6 preference scale (1 = not at all preferred, 6 = greatly preferred). Similar evaluations would be obtained for Pepsi and RC Cola. As can be seen in Figure 8.2, noncomparative scales can be continuous rating or itemized rating scales. The itemized rating scales can be further classified as Likert, semantic differential, or Stapel scales. Noncomparative scaling is the most widely used scaling technique in marketing research. Given its importance, Chapter 9 is devoted to noncomparative scaling. The rest of this chapter focuses on comparative scaling techniques.

Comparative Scaling Techniques

Paired Comparison Scaling

paired comparison scaling
A comparative scaling technique in which a respondent is presented with two objects at a time and asked to select one object in the pair according to some criterion. The data obtained are ordinal in nature.

As its name implies, in **paired comparison scaling**, a respondent is presented with two objects and asked to select one according to some criterion. The data obtained are ordinal in nature. Respondents may state that they shop in JCPenney more than in Sears, like Total cereal better than Kellogg's Product 19, or like Crest more than Colgate. Paired comparison scales are frequently used when the stimulus objects are physical products. Coca-Cola is reported to have conducted more than 190,000 paired comparisons before introducing New Coke.[9] Paired comparison scaling is the most widely used comparative scaling technique.

Figure 8.3 shows paired comparison data obtained to assess a respondent's shampoo preferences. As can be seen, this respondent made 10 comparisons to evaluate five brands. In general, with n brands, $[n(n - 1)/2]$ paired comparisons are required to include all possible pairings of objects.[10]

Paired comparison data can be analyzed in several ways.[11] The researcher can calculate the percentage of respondents who prefer one stimulus to another by summing the matrices of Figure 8.3 for all the respondents, dividing the sum by the number of respondents, and multiplying by 100. Simultaneous evaluation of all the stimulus objects is also possible. Under the assumption of transitivity, it is possible to convert paired comparison data to a rank order. **Transitivity of preference** implies that if brand A is preferred to B, and brand B is preferred to C, then brand A is preferred to C. To arrive at a rank order, the researcher determines the number of times each brand is preferred by summing the column entries in Figure 8.3. Therefore, this respondent's rank order of preference, from most to least preferred, is Head and Shoulders, Jhirmack, Finesse, Pert, and Vidal Sassoon. It is also possible to derive an interval scale from paired comparison data using the Thurstone case V procedure. Refer to the appropriate literature for a discussion of this procedure.[12]

Several modifications of the paired comparison technique have been suggested. One involves the inclusion of a neutral/no difference/no opinion response. Another extension is graded paired comparisons. In this method, respondents are asked which brand in the pair is preferred and how much it is preferred. The degree of preference may be expressed by how much more the respondent is willing to pay for the preferred brand. The resulting scale is a dollar metric scale. Another modification of paired comparison scaling is widely used in obtaining similarity judgments in multidimensional scaling (see Chapter 21).

Paired comparison scaling is useful when the number of brands is limited, because it requires direct comparison and overt choice. However, with a large number of brands, the number of comparisons becomes unwieldy. Other disadvantages are that violations of the assumption of transitivity may occur, and order in which the objects are presented may bias the results. Paired comparisons bear little resemblance to the marketplace situation that involves selection from multiple alternatives. Also, respondents may prefer one object to certain others, but they may not like it in an absolute sense.

transitivity of preference

An assumption made in order to convert paired comparison data to rank order data. It implies that if brand A is preferred to brand B and brand B is preferred to brand C, then brand A is preferred to brand C.

FIGURE 8.3

Obtaining Shampoo Preferences Using Paired Comparisons

Instructions

We are going to present you with 10 pairs of shampoo brands. For each pair, please indicate which one of the two brands of shampoo in the pair you would prefer for personal use.

Recording Form

	Jhirmack	*Finesse*	*Vidal Sassoon*	*Head & Shoulders*	*Pert*
Jhirmack		0	0	1	0
Finesse	1[a]		0	1	0
Vidal Sassoon	1	1		1	1
Head & Shoulders	0	0	0		0
Pert	1	1	0	1	
Number of times preferred[b]	3	2	0	4	1

[a] A 1 in a particular box means that the brand in that column was preferred over the brand in the corresponding row. A 0 means that the row brand was preferred over the column brand.
[b] The number of times a brand was preferred is obtained by summing the 1's in each column.

Real Research

Paired Comparison Scaling

The most common method of taste testing is paired comparison. The consumer is asked to sample two different products and select the one with the most appealing taste. The test is done in private, either in homes or other predetermined sites. A minimum of 1,000 responses is considered an adequate sample.

Ocean Spray (www.oceanspray.com), North America's top producer of bottled and canned juices/juice drinks, makes extensive use of taste tests in developing new products. Respondents are asked to sample new drinks presented in pairs, evaluate them on taste and flavor, and choose the one they like more than the other.

Taste tests showed that several consumers preferred white cranberries to the strong, tart taste of red cranberries. Therefore, in early 2002, Ocean Spray added White Cranberry drinks, made with natural white cranberries harvested a few weeks earlier than the red variety, and Juice Spritzers, lightly carbonated juice drinks, to its product line in an effort to appeal to a broader range of consumers. After conducting taste tests, Ocean Spray introduced in 2004 an innovative new product that combines the goodness of fruit juice with the cool, refreshing taste of tea that consumers crave when the weather heats up. When taste tests showed a clear preference over competing energy drinks, in 2008 Ocean Spray introduced Cranergy™, a new juice drink that delivers natural energy. Cranergy was available in two flavors—Cranberry Lift and Raspberry Cranberry Lift.[13] ■

Experiential Research

Which Is It? Coke or Pepsi

Which cola drink would be the most popular among your friends in a taste test? Develop a script for testing for preference between two cola drinks: Coke and Pepsi. Make sure the drinks are chilled to the same temperature and poured into three groups of identical cups. Each person will select a cup from the first group, taste the cola, eat a cracker, and take a swallow of water. Repeat this when tasting from the second and third groups. (The first group might be Pepsi, the second group Coke, and the third group Pepsi.) After tasting from each of the three cola sample groups, have the respondents complete the survey form you created. To avoid a biasing effect from the order of presentation of the samples, it will be important for half of the respondents to have a rotated order of presentation: The first group Coke, the second group Pepsi, and the third group Coke. Conduct the taste test on 30 respondents/students.

1. How many respondents correctly identified the two identical samples of cola?
2. Of those who correctly identified the two identical samples of cola, which cola was preferred: Coke or Pepsi?
3. Of those who correctly identified the two identical samples of cola, how many had no preference between Coke and Pepsi?
4. In sum, who would you say is the winner in your taste test: Coke or Pepsi? Or, is it too close to tell? ■

Rank Order Scaling

rank order scaling
A comparative scaling technique in which respondents are presented with several objects simultaneously and asked to order or rank them according to some criterion.

After paired comparisons, the most popular comparative scaling technique is rank order scaling. In **rank order scaling**, respondents are presented with several objects simultaneously and asked to order or rank them according to some criterion. For example, respondents may be asked to rank brands of toothpaste according to overall preference. As shown in Figure 8.4, these rankings are typically obtained by asking the respondents to assign a rank of 1 to the most preferred brand, 2 to the second most preferred, and so on, until a rank of n is assigned to the least preferred brand. Like paired comparison, this approach is also comparative in nature, and it is possible that the respondent may dislike the brand ranked 1 in an absolute sense. Furthermore, rank order scaling also results in ordinal data. See Table 8.2, which uses rank order scaling to derive an ordinal scale.

Rank order scaling is commonly used to measure preferences for brands as well as attributes. Rank order data are frequently obtained from respondents in conjoint analysis (see Chapter 21), because rank order scaling forces the respondent to discriminate among the stimulus objects. Moreover, as compared to paired comparisons, this type of scaling process more closely resembles the shopping environment. It also takes less time and eliminates intransitive responses. If there are n stimulus objects, only $(n - 1)$ scaling decisions need be made in rank order scaling. However, in paired comparison scaling, $[n(n - 1)/2]$ decisions would be required. Another advantage is that most respondents easily understand the instructions for ranking. The major disadvantage is that this technique produces only ordinal data.

FIGURE 8.4

Preference for Toothpaste Brands Using Rank Order Scaling

Instructions

Rank the various brands of toothpaste in order of preference. Begin by picking out the one brand that you like most and assign it a number 1. Then find the second most preferred brand and assign it a number 2. Continue this procedure until you have ranked all the brands of toothpaste in order of preference. The least preferred brand should be assigned a rank of 10.

No two brands should receive the same rank number.

The criterion of preference is entirely up to you. There is no right or wrong answer. Just try to be consistent.

	Brand	*Rank Order*
1.	Crest	_____
2.	Colgate	_____
3.	Aim	_____
4.	Gleem	_____
5.	Sensodyne	_____
6.	Ultra Brite	_____
7.	Close Up	_____
8.	Pepsodent	_____
9.	Plus White	_____
10.	Stripe	_____

Finally, under the assumption of transitivity, rank order data can be converted to equivalent paired comparison data, and vice versa. Figure 8.3 illustrated this point. It is possible to derive an interval scale from rankings using the Thurstone case V procedure. Other approaches for deriving interval scales from rankings have also been suggested.[14] The following example shows how rank order scaling is used to determine the world's top brands.

Real Research

World's Best-Known Brands

To be a strong competitor in today's American marketplace, companies rely heavily on brand recognition. When consumers recognize a company or a product as a household name, preferably for good reasons rather than as a result of bad publicity, brand equity is increased. Interbrand (www.interbrand.com) is a company dedicated to identifying, building, and expressing the right idea for a brand. *Business Week*/Interbrand publish an annual ranking and value of the world's best-known brands. Here are the top five for 2008:[15] ■

The World's Five Most Valuable Brands

Brand	Rank	2008 Brand Value ($ Billions)
Coca-Cola	1	66.667
IBM	2	59.031
Microsoft	3	59.007
GE	4	53.086
Nokia	5	35.942

Another example of rank order scaling was America's most admired companies given in the "Overview" section.

Constant Sum Scaling

constant sum scaling
A comparative scaling technique in which respondents are required to allocate a constant sum of units such as points, dollars, chits, stickers, or chips among a set of stimulus objects with respect to some criterion.

In **constant sum scaling**, respondents allocate a constant sum of units, such as points, dollars, or chips, among a set of stimulus objects with respect to some criterion. As shown in Figure 8.5, respondents may be asked to allocate 100 points to attributes of a toilet soap in a way that reflects

FIGURE 8.5

Importance of Toilet Soap Attributes Using a Constant Sum Scale

Instructions

Below are eight attributes of toilet soaps. Please allocate 100 points among the attributes so that your allocation reflects the relative importance you attach to each attribute. The more points an attribute receives, the more important the attribute is. If an attribute is not at all important, assign it zero points. If an attribute is twice as important as some other attribute, it should receive twice as many points.

Form

| | *Average Responses of Three Segments* | | |
Attribute	Segment I	Segment II	Segment III
1. Mildness	8	2	4
2. Lather	2	4	17
3. Shrinkage	3	9	7
4. Price	53	17	9
5. Fragrance	9	0	19
6. Packaging	7	5	9
7. Moisturizing	5	3	20
8. Cleaning power	13	60	15
Sum	100	100	100

the importance they attach to each attribute. If an attribute is unimportant, the respondent assigns it zero points. If an attribute is twice as important as some other attribute, it receives twice as many points. The sum of all the points is 100. Hence, the name of the scale.

The attributes are scaled by counting the points assigned to each one by all the respondents and dividing by the number of respondents. These results are presented for three groups, or segments, of respondents in Figure 8.5. Segment I attaches overwhelming importance to price. Segment II considers basic cleaning power to be of prime importance. Segment III values lather, fragrance, moisturizing, and cleaning power. Such information cannot be obtained from rank order data unless they are transformed into interval data. Note that the constant sum also has an absolute zero—10 points are twice as many as 5 points, and the difference between 5 and 2 points is the same as the difference between 57 and 54 points. For this reason, constant sum scale data are sometimes treated as metric. Although this may be appropriate in the limited context of the stimuli scaled, these results are not generalizable to other stimuli not included in the study. Hence, strictly speaking, the constant sum should be considered an ordinal scale because of its comparative nature and the resulting lack of generalizability. It can be seen that the allocation of points in Figure 8.5 is influenced by the specific attributes included in the evaluation task.

The main advantage of the constant sum scale is that it allows for fine discrimination among stimulus objects without requiring too much time. However, it has two primary disadvantages. Respondents may allocate more or fewer units than those specified. For example, a respondent may allocate 108 or 94 points. The researcher must modify such data in some way or eliminate this respondent from analysis. Another potential problem is rounding error if too few units (e.g., points) are used. On the other hand, the use of a large number of units may be too taxing on the respondent and cause confusion and fatigue.

ACTIVE RESEARCH

Lexus: Luminescence of Luxury

Visit www.lexus.com and search the Internet using a search engine as well as your library's online databases to obtain information on consumer purchase intentions for luxury cars.

As the marketing manager for Lexus, how would you use information on consumer purchase intentions for luxury cars to increase your sales?

Would you use a comparative scaling technique to measure consumer purchase intentions for luxury cars? If yes, which technique?

Q-sort scaling
A comparative scaling technique that uses a rank order procedure to sort objects based on similarity with respect to some criterion.

Q-Sort and Other Procedures

Q-sort scaling was developed to discriminate quickly among a relatively large number of objects. This technique uses a rank order procedure in which objects are sorted into piles based on similarity with respect to some criterion. For example, respondents are given 100 attitude statements on individual cards and asked to place them into 11 piles, ranging from "most highly agreed with" to "least highly agreed with." The number of objects to be sorted should not be less than 60 nor more than 140; 60 to 90 objects is a reasonable range. The number of objects to be placed in each pile is prespecified, often to result in a roughly normal distribution of objects over the whole set.

Another comparative scaling technique is magnitude estimation.[16] In this technique, numbers are assigned to objects such that ratios between the assigned numbers reflect ratios on the specified criterion. For example, respondents may be asked to indicate whether they agree or disagree with each of a series of statements measuring attitude toward department stores. Then they assign a number between 0 to 100 to each statement to indicate the intensity of their agreement or disagreement. Providing this type of number imposes a cognitive burden on the respondents. Finally, mention must be made of Guttman scaling, or scalogram analysis, which is a procedure for determining whether a set of objects can be ordered into an internally consistent, unidimensional scale.

International Marketing Research

In the four primary scales, the level of measurement increases from nominal to ordinal to interval to ratio scale. This increase in measurement level is obtained at the cost of complexity. From the viewpoint of the respondents, nominal scales are the simplest to use, whereas the ratio scales are the most complex. Respondents in many developed countries, due to higher education and consumer sophistication levels, are quite used to providing responses on interval and ratio scales. However, it has been argued that opinion formation may not be well crystallized in some developing countries. Hence, these respondents experience difficulty in expressing the gradation required by interval and ratio scales. Preferences can, therefore, be best measured by using ordinal scales. In particular, the use of binary scales (e.g., preferred/not preferred), the simplest type of ordinal scale, has been recommended.[17] For example, when measuring preferences for jeans in the United States, Levi Strauss & Co. could ask consumers to rate their preferences for wearing jeans on specified occasions using a 7-point interval scale. However, consumers in Papua New Guinea could be shown a pair of jeans and simply asked whether or not they would prefer to wear it for a specific occasion (e.g., when shopping, working, relaxing on a holiday, etc.). The advantage of selecting the primary scales to match the profile of the target respondents is well illustrated by the Japanese survey of automobile preferences in Europe.

Real Research   ## Car War—Japan Making a Spearhead

For the first time, European journalists had given their car-of-the-year award to a Japanese model— Nissan's new British-made Micra, a $10,000 subcompact. This came as a big blow to the European automakers that have been trying to keep the Japanese onslaught at bay. "They will change the competitive balance," warns Bruce Blythe, Ford of Europe Inc.'s head of business strategy. How did the Japanese do it?

Nissan conducted a survey of European consumers' preferences for automobiles using interval scales to capture the magnitude of preference differences. The use of interval scales enabled Nissan to compare the differences between automobile features and determine which features were preferred. The findings revealed distinct consumer preferences. So the Japanese made inroads by transplanting their production and building technical centers in Europe to customize their cars to local styling tastes and preferences. Nissan introduced new models in Europe in 2009 in hopes of lifting recent sagging sales in that market. The European automakers need to be on guard against such fierce competition.[18] ∎

Using interval scales to measure European consumers' automobile preferences, Nissan has developed award-winning models such as the British-made Micra.

It should also be noted that comparative scales, except for paired comparisons, require comparisons of multiple stimulus objects and are, therefore, taxing on the respondents. In contrast, in noncomparative scales, each object is scaled independently of others in the stimulus set, that is, objects are scaled one at a time. Hence, noncomparative scales are simpler to administer and more appropriate in cultures where the respondents are less educated or unfamiliar with marketing research.

Experiential Research

Qualtrics Question Library and Primary Scales

Access to Qualtrics is included with this book. Use the Qualtrics question library to electronically develop the following scales.

1. Gender measured on a nominal scale
2. Age measured on an ordinal scale
3. Age measured on a ratio scale
4. Income measured on an ordinal scale

Design your own question to measure income on an interval scale. ■

Ethics in Marketing Research

The researcher has the responsibility to use the appropriate type of scales to get the data needed to answer the research questions and test the hypotheses. Take, for example, a newspaper such as the *Wall Street Journal* wanting information on the personality profiles of its readers and nonreaders. Information on the personality characteristics might best be obtained by giving respondents (readers and nonreaders) several cards, each listing one personality characteristic. The respondents are asked to sort the cards and to rank-order the personality characteristics, listing, in order, those they believe describe their personality best first and those that do not describe themselves last. This process will provide rich insight into the personality characteristics by allowing respondents to compare and shuffle the personality cards. However, the resulting data are ordinal and cannot be easily used in multivariate analysis. To examine differences in the personality characteristics of readers and nonreaders and relate them to marketing strategy variables, interval scale data are needed. It is the obligation of the researcher to obtain the data that are most appropriate, given the research questions, as the following example illustrates.

Real Research

Scaling Ethical Dilemmas

In a study designed to measure ethical judgments of marketing researchers, scale items from a previously developed and tested scale were used. After a pretest was conducted on a convenience sample of 65 marketing professionals, however, it became apparent that some original scale items were worded in a way that did not reflect current usage. Therefore, these items were updated. For example, an item that was gender specific, such as, "He pointed out that . . . " was altered to read "The project manager pointed out that. . . . " Subjects were requested to show their approval or disapproval of the stated action (item) of a marketing research director with regard to specific scenarios. Realizing that a binary or dichotomous scale would be too restrictive, approval or disapproval was indicated by having respondents supply interval-level data via 5-point scales with descriptive anchors of 1 = disapprove, 2 = disapprove somewhat, 3 = neither approve or disapprove, 4 = approve somewhat, and 5 = approve. In this way, scaling dilemmas were resolved.[19] ■

After the data have been collected, they should be analyzed correctly. If nominal scaled data are gathered, then statistics permissible for nominal scaled data must be used. Likewise, when ordinal scaled data are collected, statistical procedures developed for use with interval or ratio data should not be used. Conclusions based on the misuse of statistics are misleading. Using the previous personality example, if it were decided to gather data by the rank order technique described, ordinal data would be collected. If, after collection, the client wishes to know how the readers and the nonreaders differed, the researcher should treat these data correctly and use nonmetric techniques for analysis (discussed in Chapter 15). When the researcher lacks the expertise to identify and use the appropriate statistical techniques, help should be sought from other sources, for example, from statisticians.

Decision Research

New Balance: Attaining a Balance in Marketing Strategy

The Situation

The U.S. athletic footwear market is likely to grow slowly during 2008–2012, characterized by good volume sales and falling prices, according to a recently published report from Mintel International (www.mintel.com). It projects annual growth of less than 3 percent, before inflation. This is due to factors such as overly complex manufacturer/retailer relationships that sap brand loyalty and foster excessive bargain hunting, a slow growth economy, and competition from brown shoe manufacturers as the previously distinct line between athletic and brown shoes becomes blurred. Alongside this, weak retail pricing is likely to lead to more of a two-tier market—an upscale shoe market for those most dedicated to athletic shoes (young males) and those with higher levels of discretionary income, and a mass market for the rest of the nation. One bright spot revealed by Mintel's consumer research is that respondents overwhelmingly agree that they are willing to "spend money on good sneakers."

Jim Davis, CEO of New Balance Athletic Shoe, Inc., is trying to appeal to those consumers Mintel's research is talking about. New Balance rose quickly starting in the mid-1990s to be the third-largest seller of athletic shoes. Its strategy mirrored Nike's in launching the largest possible number of shoe styles and selling primarily through specialty athletic shoe stores and sporting goods stores. A big difference, however, was that New Balance created an upscale brand image that aimed to attract a greater number of 35- to 64-year-olds. Times are changing, however, and New Balance is learning that it must also change to keep improving its market growth and profits.

The Marketing Research Decision

1. New Balance would like to determine consumer preferences for its brand as compared to Nike, Reebok, and Adidas. Which scaling technique should be used?
2. Discuss the role of the type of scaling technique you recommend in enabling Jim Davis to determine consumer preferences for New Balance as compared to Nike, Reebok, and Adidas and increase the market share of New Balance.

Scaling techniques can help New Balance increase its market share and determine consumer preferences for its brand as compared to Nike, Reebok, and Adidas.

The Marketing Management Decision

1. In order to increase the market share of New Balance, what should Jim Davis do?
2. Discuss how the marketing management decision action that you recommend to Jim Davis is influenced by the scaling technique that you suggested earlier and by the findings of that research.[20] ■

SPSS Windows

Using SPSS Data Entry, the researcher can design any of the primary type of scales: nominal, ordinal, interval, or ratio. Either the question library can be used or customized scales can be designed. Moreover, paired comparison, rank order, and constant sum scales can be easily implemented. We show the use of SPSS Data Entry to design ordinal scales to measure education and income (Figure 8.6). This software is not included but may be purchased separately from SPSS.

FIGURE 8.6

Ordinal Scales for Measuring Education and Income

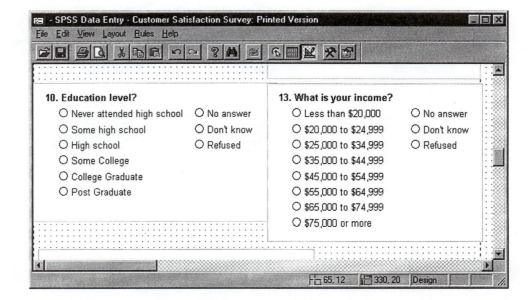

Summary

Measurement is the assignment of numbers or other symbols to characteristics of objects according to set rules. Scaling involves the generation of a continuum upon which measured objects are located. The fundamental scale characteristics are description, order, distance, and origin. Description means the unique labels or descriptors that are used to designate each value of the scale. Order means the relative sizes or positions of the descriptors. Order is denoted by descriptors such as greater than, less than, and equal to. The characteristic of distance means that absolute differences between the scale descriptors are known and may be expressed in units. The origin characteristic means that the scale has a unique or fixed beginning or true zero point. Description is the most basic characteristic that is present in every scale. If a scale has order, it also has description. If a scale has distance, it also has order and description. Finally, a scale that has origin also has distance, order, and description.

The four primary scales of measurement are nominal, ordinal, interval, and ratio. Figure 8.7 presents a concept map for primary scales. Of these, the nominal scale is the most basic in that the numbers are used only for identifying or classifying objects and the only characteristic possessed is description. In the ordinal scale, the next-higher-level scale, the numbers indicate the relative position of the objects but not the magnitude of difference between them. Thus, only the order and description characteristics are present. The interval scale has the characteristic of distance, in addition to order and description. Therefore, it permits a comparison of the differences between the objects. However, as it has an arbitrary zero point, it is not meaningful to calculate ratios of scale values on an interval scale. The highest level of measurement is represented by the ratio scale in which the zero point is fixed. The researcher can compute ratios of scale values using this scale. The ratio scale incorporates all the properties of the lower-level scales and also has the origin characteristic.

Scaling techniques can be classified as comparative or noncomparative. Comparative scaling involves a direct comparison of stimulus objects. Comparative scales include paired comparisons, rank order, constant sum, and the Q-sort. The data obtained by these procedures have only ordinal properties.

Respondents in many developed countries, due to higher education and consumer sophistication levels, are quite used to providing responses on interval and ratio scales. However, in developing countries, preferences can be best measured by using ordinal scales. Ethical considerations require that the appropriate type of scales be used in order to get the data needed to answer the research questions and test the hypotheses. The Internet, as well as several specialized computer programs, are available to implement the different types of scales.

FIGURE 8.7

A Concept Map for Primary Scales

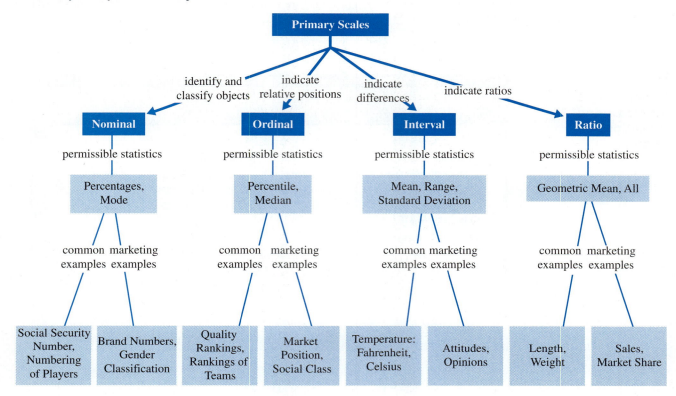

Key Terms and Concepts

measurement, 250
scaling, 250
description, 251
order, 251
distance, 251
origin, 251

nominal scale, 252
ordinal scale, 254
interval scale, 254
ratio scale, 256
comparative scales, 257
noncomparative scales, 257

paired comparison scaling, 257
transitivity of preference, 258
rank order scaling, 259
constant sum scaling, 260
Q-sort scaling, 262

Suggested Cases, Video Cases, and HBS Cases

Running Case with Real Data

1.1 Dell

Comprehensive Critical Thinking Cases

2.1 American Idol   2.2 Baskin-Robbins   2.3 Akron Children's Hospital

Comprehensive Cases with Real Data

4.1 JPMorgan Chase   4.2 Wendy's

Video Cases

8.1 P&G   10.1 Dunkin' Donuts   12.1 Subaru   23.1 Marriott

Comprehensive Harvard Business School Cases

Case 5.1: The Harvard Graduate Student Housing Survey (9-505-059)
Case 5.2: BizRate.Com (9-501-024)
Case 5.3: Cola Wars Continue: Coke and Pepsi in the Twenty-First Century (9-702-442)
Case 5.4: TiVo in 2002 (9-502-062)
Case 5.5: Compaq Computer: Intel Inside? (9-599-061)
Case 5.6: The New Beetle (9-501-023)

Live Research: Conducting a Marketing Research Project

1. As a class, discuss the level of measurement (nominal, ordinal, interval, or ratio) that is appropriate for the key variables.
2. Discuss which, if any, of the comparative techniques are appropriate.

3. Consider the practical constraints. For example, if a certain level of measurement has been used to measure a variable in the past (e.g., ordinal preference), the same may have to be used again in the project to allow a comparison of the findings with past results.

Acronyms

The four primary types of scales may be described by the acronym

Four:

F igurative: nominal scale
O rdinal scale
U nconstrained zero point: interval scale
R atio scale

The different comparative and noncomparative scales may be represented by the acronym

Scales:

S emantic differential scale
C onstant sum scale
A rranged in order: rank order scale
L ikert scale
E ngaged: paired comparison scale
S tapel scale

Exercises

Questions

1. What is measurement?
2. What are the basic characteristics of a scale?
3. What are the primary scales of measurement?
4. Describe the differences between a nominal and an ordinal scale.
5. What are the implications of having an arbitrary zero point in an interval scale?
6. What are the advantages of a ratio scale over an interval scale? Are these advantages significant?
7. What is a comparative rating scale?
8. What is a paired comparison?
9. What are the advantages and disadvantages of paired comparison scaling?
10. Describe the constant sum scale. How is it different from the other comparative rating scales?
11. Describe the Q-sort methodology.

Problems

1. Identify the type of scale (nominal, ordinal, interval, or ratio) being used in each of the following. Please explain your reasoning.
   a. I like to solve crossword puzzles.

Disagree				*Agree*
1	2	3	4	5

   b. How old are you? _____

   c. Please rank the following activities in terms of your preference by assigning ranks 1 (most preferred) to 5 (least preferred).
   i. Reading magazines _____
   ii. Watching television _____
   iii. Dating _____
   iv. Shopping _____
   v. Eating out _____
   d. What is your Social Security number? _____
   e. On an average weekday, how much time do you spend doing your homework and class assignments?
   i. Less than 15 minutes _____
   ii. 15 to 30 minutes _____
   iii. 31 to 60 minutes _____
   iv. 61 to 120 minutes _____
   v. More than 120 minutes _____
   f. How much money did you spend last month on entertainment? _____

2. Suppose each of the questions a through f in problem 1 was administered to 100 respondents. Identify the kind of analysis that should be done for each question to summarize the results.

Internet and Computer Exercises

1. Visit the Web sites of two marketing research firms conducting surveys. Analyze one survey of each firm to critically evaluate the primary type of scales being used.
2. Surf the Internet to find two examples of each of the four primary types of scales. Write a report describing the context in which these scales are being used.
3. Search the Internet to identify the five top-selling automobile brands during the last calendar year. Rank-order these brands according to sales.

4. Marshalls and Wal-Mart are two of the stores considered in the department store project. Develop a series of paired comparison scales comparing these two stores on store image characteristics. Identify the relevant store image characteristics by visiting the Web sites of these two stores (www.marshalls.com, www.wal-mart.com). How do the store image characteristics that you have identified compare to those used in the department store project (see Chapter 2)?

Activities

Role Playing

1. You are a marketing research analyst with the Coca-Cola Company. After missing the mark in changing the formulation of Coke, management has become wary of taste tests. You are asked to write a technical report on the uses and limitations of taste tests and make a recommendation about whether taste tests should be used in the future research conducted by the Coca-Cola Company. Present your report to a group of students representing Coca-Cola management.

Fieldwork

1. Develop three comparative (paired comparison, rank order, and constant sum) scales to measure attitude toward five popular brands of toothpaste (Crest, Colgate, Aim, Pepsodent, and Ultra Brite). Administer each scale to five students. No student should be administered more than one scale. Note the time it takes each student to respond. Which scale was the easiest to administer? Which scale took the shortest time?
2. Develop a constant sum scale to determine preferences for restaurants. Administer this scale to a pilot sample of 20 students to determine their preferences for some of the popular restaurants in your city. Based on your pilot study, which restaurant is most preferred?

Group Discussion

1. "A brand could receive the highest median rank on a rank order scale of all the brands considered and still have poor sales." Discuss.

Dell Running Case

Review the Dell case, Case 1.1, and questionnaire given toward the end of the book.

1. What primary scales of measurement have been employed in the Dell questionnaire? Illustrate each type.
2. Access to Qualtrics is included with this book. What primary scales are available using Qualtrics? How can Dell make use of these scales?
3. Use the Qualtrics question library to illustrate the use of rank order and constant sum scales in a customer perception survey by Dell.

Video Cases

VIDEO CASE 8.1 — Procter & Gamble: Using Marketing Research to Build Brands

As of 2009, Procter & Gamble (www.pg.com) delivered products under 300 brands to nearly 5 billion consumers in more than 180 countries around the world. P&G employed about 138,000 employees in approximately 80 countries worldwide. Its net sales amounted to $83.5 billion in 2008. The company began operations in the United States in 1837 and has continued to expand its global operations. The stated purpose of the company is to "provide products and services of superior quality and value that improve the lives of the world's consumers."

Over time, P&G has proven to be an innovator in creating brands and understanding consumers by making extensive use of marketing research. Building brands has been a cornerstone of P&G's success. The marketers at P&G use marketing research to determine a brand's equity and then make sure everyone understands it, because it drives every decision made about the brand. P&G always thinks about the consumer and why a particular product is relevant to the consumer. P&G always asks *"What is in this for the consumer?"* This strategy has served the company well. It believes in catering to the consumer. With that in mind, P&G has spent a tremendous amount of effort, innovation, and money on marketing research.

A focus group talking about a product is simply not enough; the marketers at P&G dig deeper to try to really understand consumer behaviors. Leonara Polonsky, the marketing director at P&G, describes the intensity with which P&G pursues its marketing research efforts. Some of these efforts include shopping with consumers and spending several hours in consumers' homes. In fact, Polonsky describes her own experience at spending time at consumers' homes in Caracas, making coffee with them and trying to understand how these consumers think about coffee. This marketing research initiative is an innovative approach that puts the consumer at the center of everything P&G does. P&G now thinks much more holistically about the consumer's entire experience related to its brands, and so it pays much more attention, for example, to the in-store experience.

P&G's basic marketing principles have not changed, but its methods of targeting and identifying consumers have changed to meet the increasingly complicated consumer base. In the early days, P&G would mass market through television and other sources, because this was the most effective strategy at the time. P&G has changed its key strategy from mass marketing to *consumer* targeting. According to Jim Stengel, P&G's Global Marketing Director, targeting is the future of brand marketing and brand building, because the better a company understands its market the better its marketing will be.

One of the areas that P&G constantly researches is the consumers' in-store experience, viewing it as another way of connecting with consumers and making their experience better. One of the ways it does this is by partnering with retailers to develop in-store experiences to please consumers, which has become more difficult because consumers have less time and higher expectations.

P&G realizes that it is no longer possible to shout at consumers. It has to talk to them when they want to listen, and it is the consumers who chose the time and the place for this communication. That time and place, today, is increasingly becoming the Internet. An excellent example is the Pampers Web site, where caregivers can get helpful parenting information. The Pampers site is P&G's way of connecting with consumers on their terms. All parents want information about babies, and Pampers provides information about babies. The Pampers' Web site is not about selling diapers, but about helping parents understand their babies and answer questions about them. In the process, P&G also collects valuable marketing research information.

Sometimes new-product plans result from Internet marketing research. P&G has discovered that Internet research offers a more representative feel for consumer reactions, and P&G is leveraging the Internet to understand consumers. This was the case when P&G decided to launch Crest White Strips not on television, but on the Internet. The Crest White Strips product launch was one of the most successful product launches in history.

The Pampers brand also presents an example of understanding brand equity; the brand has recently been redefined from one about absorption to one about baby development. Focus groups and surveys revealed that parents are very emotionally involved in the development of their babies. This simple but deep change from a functional equity to a broad emotional one has resulted in a whole different look for Pampers diapers, a whole different look in the advertising, a different media plan, and a totally new product plan.

P&G is always conducting marketing research to discover new ways to reach out to consumers, sometimes by developing new products and introducing new product categories. P&G invented disposable diapers, home dry-cleaning, and the very popular cleaning tool the Swiffer, which was designed after extensive marketing research. P&G marketing has been innovative and pioneering over the years, and one would expect the same from it in the future.

Conclusion

The case presents P&G's strong culture of understanding its consumers by conducting marketing research and innovating to meet their needs and desires. P&G, with its long and rich legacy, has continuously evolved newer ways to connect with consumers and gain insights into their behavior. P&G has been adept at adopting newer technologies, such as the Internet, and leveraging marketing research to enhance its understanding of its consumers. P&G is constantly using marketing research to solve the problems of today and to build brands that will continue to be leaders tomorrow.

Questions

1. Discuss the role that marketing research can play in helping P&G build its various brands.
2. P&G is considering further increasing its market share. Define the management decision problem.
3. Define an appropriate marketing research problem based on the management decision problem you have identified.
4. Formulate an appropriate research design to address the marketing research problem you have defined.
5. Use the Internet to determine the market shares of the major toothpaste brands for the last calendar year.
6. What type of syndicate data will be useful in addressing the marketing research problem?
7. Discuss the role of qualitative research in helping P&G to increase its share of the toothpaste market.
8. P&G has developed a new toothpaste that provides tooth and gum protection for 24 hours after each brushing. It would like to determine consumers' response to this new toothpaste before introducing it in the marketplace. If a survey is to be conducted to determine consumer preferences, which survey method should be used and why?
9. What role can causal research play in helping P&G increase its market share?
10. Illustrate the use of the primary type of scales in measuring consumer preferences for toothpaste brands.
11. If marketing research to determine consumer preferences for toothpaste brands were to be conducted in Latin America, how would the research process be different?
12. Discuss the ethical issues involved in researching consumer preferences for toothpaste brands.

References

1. www.pg.com, accessed February 20, 2009.
2. Chris Isidore, "P&G to Buy Gillette for $57B," http://money.cnn.com/2005/01/28/news/fortune500/pg_gillette, accessed September 3, 2005.
3. Jack Neff, "Humble Try: P&G's Stengel Studies Tactics of Other Advertisers—and Moms—in Bid to Boost Marketing Muscle," *Advertising Age* (February 18, 2002): 3.

> **"** It is important that we establish reliability and validity of our scales. Otherwise, we cannot believe in our data. **"**

Chet Zalesky, President, CMI

Objectives [After reading this chapter, the student should be able to:]

1. Describe the noncomparative scaling techniques, distinguish between continuous and itemized rating scales, and explain Likert, semantic differential, and Stapel scales.

2. Discuss the decisions involved in constructing itemized rating scales with respect to the number of scale categories, balanced versus unbalanced scales, odd or even number of categories, forced versus nonforced choice, degree of verbal description, and the physical form of the scale.

3. Discuss the criteria used for scale evaluation and explain how to assess reliability, validity, and generalizability.

4. Discuss the considerations involved in implementing noncomparative scales in an international setting.

5. Understand the ethical issues involved in developing noncomparative scales.

6. Discuss the use of the Internet and computers in implementing continuous and itemized rating scales.

Measurement and Scaling: Noncomparative Scaling Techniques

Overview

As discussed in Chapter 8, scaling techniques are classified as comparative or noncomparative. The comparative techniques, consisting of paired comparison, rank order, constant sum, and Q-sort scaling, were discussed in the last chapter. The subject of this chapter is noncomparative techniques, which are comprised of continuous and itemized rating scales. We discuss the popular itemized rating scales, the Likert, semantic differential, and Stapel scales, as well as the construction of multi-item rating scales. We show how scaling techniques should be evaluated in terms of reliability and validity and consider how the researcher selects a particular scaling technique. Mathematically derived scales are also presented. The considerations involved in implementing noncomparative scales when researching international markets are discussed. Several ethical issues that arise in rating scale construction are identified. The chapter also discusses the use of the Internet and computers in developing continuous and itemized rating scales.

Real Research

New York City Transit in Transit

The New York City Transit (NYCT) (www.mta.nyc.ny.us/nyct/subway) does not have a wholly captive audience, as some people believe. Many people do not use the mass transit system when they have a choice. A much needed rate hike brought fears that more people would avoid taking the bus or subway. Therefore, research was undertaken to uncover ways to increase ridership.

In a telephone survey, respondents were asked to rate different aspects of the transit system using five-point Likert scales. Likert scales were chosen because they are easy to administer over the telephone and the respondents merely indicate their degree of (dis)agreement (1 = strongly disagree, 5 = strongly agree).

The results showed that personal safety was the major concern on subways. New Yorkers were afraid to use a subway station in their own neighborhoods. NYCT was able to respond to riders' concerns by increasing police presence, having a more visible NYCT staff, increasing lighting, and repositioning walls, columns, and stairways for better visibility throughout the station.

Telephone surveys also revealed that cleanliness of subway stations and subway cars is related to the perception of crime. In response, NYCT was able to concentrate more on ways to maintain a cleaner appearance. Action was also taken to reduce the number of homeless people and panhandlers. They are asked to leave, and sometimes transportation to shelters is provided.

Results of marketing research efforts have helped NYCT improve perceptions surrounding the system, leading to increased ridership. As of 2008, the New York subway system has 468 stations—the largest number of public transit subway stations for any system in the world.[1] ■

Noncomparative Scaling Techniques

noncomparative scale
One of two types of scaling techniques in which each stimulus object is scaled independently of the other objects in the stimulus set.

Respondents using a **noncomparative scale** employ whatever rating standard seems appropriate to them. They do not compare the object being rated either to another object or to some specified standard, such as "your ideal brand." They evaluate only one object at a time, and for this reason noncomparative scales are often referred to as *monadic scales*. Noncomparative techniques consist of continuous and itemized rating scales, which are described in Table 9.1 and discussed in the following sections.

Using Likert scales, the New York City Transit was able to determine people's perceptions of the subway system and address their concerns, leading to increased ridership.

TABLE 9.1
Basic Noncomparative Scales

Scale	Basic Characteristics	Examples	Advantages	Disadvantages
Continuous rating scale	Place a mark on a continuous line	Reaction to TV commercials	Easy to construct	Scoring can be cumbersome unless computerized
Itemized Rating Scales				
Likert scale	Degree of agreement on a 1 (strongly disagree) to 5 (strongly agree) scale	Measurement of attitudes	Easy to construct, administer, and understand	More time consuming
Semantic differential	Seven-point scale with bipolar labels	Brand, product, and company images	Versatile	Controversy as to whether the data are interval
Stapel scale	Unipolar ten-point scale, −5 to +5, without a neutral point (zero)	Measurement of attitudes and images	Easy to construct; administered over telephone	Confusing and difficult to apply

continuous rating scale
Also referred to as a *graphic rating scale*, this measurement scale has the respondents rate the objects by placing a mark at the appropriate position on a line that runs from one extreme of the criterion variable to the other.

Continuous Rating Scale

In a **continuous rating scale**, also referred to as a *graphic rating scale*, respondents rate the objects by placing a mark at the appropriate position on a line that runs from one extreme of the criterion variable to the other. Thus, the respondents are not restricted to selecting from marks previously set by the researcher. The form of the continuous scale may vary considerably. For example, the line may be vertical or horizontal; scale points, in the form of numbers or brief descriptions, may be provided; and, if provided, the scale points may be few or many. Three versions of a continuous rating scale are illustrated.

Project Research   Continuous Rating Scales

How would you rate Sears as a department store?

Version 1

Probably the worst - - - - - - - I - Probably the best

Version 2

Probably the worst - - - - - - - I - Probably the best

          0   10   20   30   40   50   60   70   80   90   100

Version 3

                   Very bad   Neither good   Very good
                                      nor bad

Probably the worst - - - - - - - I - Probably the best

          0   10   20   30   40   50   60   70   80   90   100 ■

Once the respondent has provided the ratings, the researcher divides the line into as many categories as desired and assigns scores based on the categories into which the ratings fall. In the department store project example, the respondent exhibits an unfavorable attitude toward Sears. These scores are typically treated as interval data. Thus, continuous scales possess the characteristics of description, order, and distance, as discussed in Chapter 8.

The advantage of continuous scales is that they are easy to construct. However, scoring is cumbersome and unreliable. Moreover, continuous scales provide little new information. Hence, their use in marketing research has been limited. Recently, however, with the increased popularity of computer-assisted personal interviewing (CAPI), Internet surveys, and other technologies, their use is becoming more frequent. Continuous rating scales can be easily implemented in CAPI or on the Internet. The cursor can be moved on the screen in a continuous fashion to select the exact position on the scale that best describes the respondent's evaluation. Moreover, the scale values can be automatically scored by the computer, thus increasing the speed and accuracy of processing the data.

Real Research

Continuous Measurement and Analysis of Perceptions: The Perception Analyzer

The Perception Analyzer (www.perceptionanalyzer.com) by MSInteractive is a computer-supported, interactive feedback system composed of wireless or wired handheld dials for each participant, a console (computer interface), and special software that edits questions, collects data, and analyzes participant responses. Members of focus groups use it to record their emotional response to television commercials, instantly and continuously. Each participant is given a dial and instructed to continuously record his or her reaction to the material being tested. As the respondents turn the dials, the information is fed to a computer. Thus, the researcher can determine the second-by-second response of the respondents as the commercial is run. Furthermore, this response can be superimposed on the commercial to see the respondents' reactions to the various frames and parts of the commercial.

The analyzer was recently used to measure responses to a series of "slice-of-life" commercials for McDonald's. The researchers found that mothers and daughters had different responses to different aspects

Companies such as McDonald's have used the Perception Analyzer to measure consumers' reactions to commercials, company videos, and other audio/visual materials.

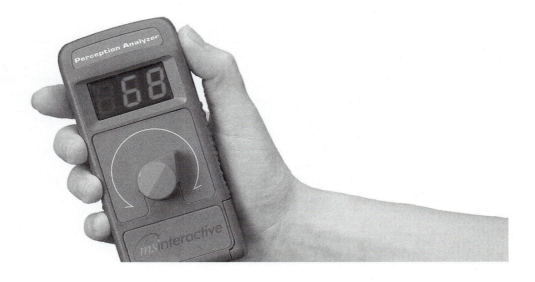

of the commercial. Using the emotional response data, the researchers could determine which commercial had the greatest emotional appeal across mother-daughter segments. McDonald's marketing efforts proved successful with 2008 revenues of $23.52 billion.[2] ■

ACTIVE RESEARCH

Developing Hit Movies: Not a Mickey Mouse Business

Visit www.disney.com and search the Internet using a search engine as well as your library's online databases to obtain information on consumer movie viewing habits and preferences.

How would you measure audience reaction to a new movie slated for release by the Walt Disney Company?

As the marketing director for Disney movies, how would you develop "hit" movies?

---

itemized rating scale
A measurement scale having numbers and/or brief descriptions associated with each category. The categories are ordered in terms of scale position.

Itemized Rating Scales

In an **itemized rating scale**, the respondents are provided with a scale that has a number or brief description associated with each category. The categories are ordered in terms of scale position, and the respondents are required to select the specified category that best describes the object being rated. Itemized rating scales are widely used in marketing research and form the basic components of more complex scales, such as multi-item rating scales. We first describe the commonly used itemized rating scales, the Likert, semantic differential, and Stapel scales, and then examine the major issues surrounding the use of these scales.

Likert scale
A measurement scale with five response categories ranging from "strongly disagree" to "strongly agree," which requires the respondents to indicate a degree of agreement or disagreement with each of a series of statements related to the stimulus objects.

Likert Scale

Named after its developer, Rensis Likert, the **Likert scale** is a widely used rating scale that requires the respondents to indicate the degree of agreement or disagreement with each of a series of statements about the stimulus objects.[3] Typically, each scale item has five response categories, ranging from "strongly disagree" to "strongly agree." We illustrate with a Likert scale for evaluating attitudes toward Sears in the context of the department store project.

Project Research

Likert Scale

Instructions

Listed here are different opinions about Sears. Please indicate how strongly you agree or disagree with each by using the following scale:

1 = Strongly disagree
2 = Disagree
3 = Neither agree nor disagree
4 = Agree
5 = Strongly agree

		Strongly disagree	Disagree	Neither agree nor disagree	Agree	Strongly agree
1.	Sears sells high-quality merchandise.	1	2X	3	4	5
2.	Sears has poor in-store service.	1	2X	3	4	5
3.	I like to shop at Sears.	1	2	3X	4	5
4.	Sears does not offer a good mix of different brands within a product category.	1	2	3	4X	5
5.	The credit policies at Sears are terrible.	1	2	3	4X	5
6.	Sears is where America shops.	1X	2	3	4	5
7.	I do not like the advertising done by Sears.	1	2	3	4X	5
8.	Sears sells a wide variety of merchandise.	1	2	3	4X	5
9.	Sears charges fair prices.	1	2X	3	4	5 ■

The data are typically treated as interval. Thus, the Likert scale possesses the characteristics of description, order, and distance. To conduct the analysis, each statement is assigned a numerical score, ranging either from -2 to $+2$ or 1 to 5. The analysis can be conducted on an item-by-item basis (profile analysis), or a total (summated) score can be calculated for each respondent by summing across items. Suppose the Likert scale in the department store example was used to measure attitudes toward Sears as well as JCPenney. Profile analysis would involve comparing the two stores in terms of the average respondent ratings for each item, such as quality of merchandise, in-store service, and brand mix. The summated approach is most frequently used and, as a result, the Likert scale is also referred to as a *summated scale*.[4] When using this approach to determine the total score for each respondent on each store, it is important to use a consistent scoring procedure so that a high (or low) score consistently reflects a favorable response. This requires that the categories assigned to the negative statements by the respondents be scored by reversing the scale when analyzing the data. Note that for a negative statement, an agreement reflects an unfavorable response, whereas for a positive statement, agreement represents a favorable response. Accordingly, a "strongly agree" response to a favorable statement and a "strongly disagree" response to an unfavorable statement would both receive scores of 5. In the scale shown here, if a higher score is to denote a more favorable attitude, the scoring of items 2, 4, 5, and 7 will be reversed. Thus, the respondent in the department store project example has an attitude score of 22. The reason for having both positive and negative statements is to control the tendency of some respondents to mark one or the other end of the scale without reading the items. Each respondent's total score for each store is calculated. A respondent will have the most favorable attitude toward the store with the highest score. The procedure for developing summated Likert scales is described later in the section on multi-item scales.

The Likert scale has several advantages. It is easy to construct and administer. Respondents readily understand how to use the scale, making it suitable for mail, telephone, personal or electronic interviews. Therefore, this scale was used in the NYCT telephone survey in the opening example. The major disadvantage of the Likert scale is that it takes longer to complete than other itemized rating scales because respondents have to read each statement. Sometimes, it may be difficult to interpret the response to a Likert item, especially if it is an unfavorable statement. In our example, the respondent disagrees with statement number 2 that Sears has poor in-store service. In reversing the score of this item prior to summing, it is assumed that this respondent would agree with the statement that Sears has good in-store service. This, however, may not be true; the disagreement merely indicates that the respondent would not make statement number 2. The following example shows another use of a Likert scale in marketing research.

Real Research   ## How Concerned Are You About Your Online Privacy?

In spite of the enormous potential of e-commerce, its share compared to the total portion of the economy still remains small: less than 3 percent worldwide as of 2009. The lack of consumer confidence in online privacy is a major problem hampering the growth of e-commerce. A recent report showed that practically all Americans (94.5 percent), including Internet users and non-Internet users, are concerned about "the privacy of their personal information when or if they buy online." Therefore, the author and his colleagues have developed a scale for measuring Internet users' information privacy concerns. This is a 10-item, three-dimensional scale. The three dimensions are control, awareness, and collection. Each of the 10 items is scored on a 7-point Likert-type agree-disagree scale. The scale has been shown to have good reliability and validity. This scale should enable online marketers and policy makers to measure and address Internet users' information privacy concerns, which should result in increased e-commerce.[5] Due to space constraints we show only the items used to measure awareness.

Awareness (of Privacy Practices)

We used 7-point scales anchored with "strongly disagree" and "strongly agree."

1. Companies seeking information online should disclose the way the data are collected, processed, and used.
2. A good consumer online privacy policy should have a clear and conspicuous disclosure.
3. It is very important to me that I am aware and knowledgeable about how my personal information will be used. ∎

Semantic Differential Scale

semantic differential
A 7-point rating scale with endpoints associated with bipolar labels that have semantic meaning.

The **semantic differential** is a 7-point rating scale with endpoints associated with bipolar labels that have semantic meaning. In a typical application, respondents rate objects on a number of itemized, 7-point rating scales bounded at each end by one of two bipolar adjectives, such as "cold" and "warm."[6] We illustrate this scale by presenting a respondent's evaluation of Sears on five attributes.

The respondents mark the blank that best indicates how they would describe the object being rated.[7] Thus, in our example, Sears is evaluated as somewhat weak, reliable, very old-fashioned, warm, and careful. The negative adjective or phrase sometimes appears at the left side of the scale and sometimes at the right. This controls the tendency of some respondents, particularly those with very positive or very negative attitudes, to mark the right- or left-hand sides without reading the labels. The methods for selecting the scale labels and constructing a semantic differential scale have been described elsewhere by the author. A general semantic differential scale for measuring self-concepts, person concepts, and product concepts is shown.

Project Research Semantic Differential Scale

Instructions

This part of the study measures what certain department stores mean to you by having you judge them on a series of descriptive scales bounded at each end by one of two bipolar adjectives. Please mark (X) the blank that best indicates how accurately one or the other adjective describes what the store means to you. Please be sure to mark every scale; do not omit any scale.

Form

Sears is:

Powerful	:—:—:—:—:-X-:—:—: Weak
Unreliable	:—:—:—:—:—:-X-:—: Reliable
Modern	:—:—:—:—:—:—:-X-: Old-fashioned
Cold	:—:—:—:—:—:-X-:—: Warm
Careful	:—:-X-:—:—:—:—:—: Careless ■

Real Research A Semantic Differential Scale for Measuring Self-Concepts, Person Concepts, and Product Concepts[8]

1.	Rugged	:—:—:—:—:—:—:	Delicate
2.	Excitable	:—:—:—:—:—:—:	Calm
3.	Uncomfortable	:—:—:—:—:—:—:	Comfortable
4.	Dominating	:—:—:—:—:—:—:	Submissive
5.	Thrifty	:—:—:—:—:—:—:	Indulgent
6.	Pleasant	:—:—:—:—:—:—:	Unpleasant
7.	Contemporary	:—:—:—:—:—:—:	Noncontemporary
8.	Organized	:—:—:—:—:—:—:	Unorganized
9.	Rational	:—:—:—:—:—:—:	Emotional
10.	Youthful	:—:—:—:—:—:—:	Mature
11.	Formal	:—:—:—:—:—:—:	Informal
12.	Orthodox	:—:—:—:—:—:—:	Liberal
13.	Complex	:—:—:—:—:—:—:	Simple
14.	Colorless	:—:—:—:—:—:—:	Colorful
15.	Modest	:—:—:—:—:—:—:	Vain ■

Individual items on a semantic differential scale may be scored on either a -3 to $+3$ or a 1-to-7 scale. The resulting data are commonly analyzed through profile analysis. In profile analysis, means or median values on each rating scale are calculated and compared by plotting or statistical analysis. This helps determine the overall differences and similarities among the objects. To assess differences across segments of respondents, the researcher can compare mean responses of different segments. Although the mean is most often used as a summary statistic, there is some controversy as to whether the data obtained should be treated as an interval scale.[9] On the other hand, in cases when the researcher requires an overall comparison of objects, such as to determine store preference, the individual item scores are summed to arrive at a total score. As in the case of the Likert scale, the scores for the negative items are reversed before summing.

Its versatility makes the semantic differential a popular rating scale in marketing research. It has been widely used in comparing brand, product, and company images. It has also been used to develop advertising and promotion strategies and in new product development studies.[10] Several modifications of the basic scale have been proposed.

Stapel Scale

Stapel scale
A scale for measuring attitudes that consists of a single adjective in the middle of an even-numbered range of values, from −5 to +5, without a neutral point (zero).

The **Stapel scale**, named after its developer, Jan Stapel, is a unipolar rating scale with 10 categories numbered from −5 to +5, without a neutral point (zero).[11] This scale is usually presented vertically. Respondents are asked to indicate how accurately or inaccurately each term describes the object by selecting an appropriate numerical response category. The higher the number, the more accurately the term describes the object, as shown in the department store project. In this example, Sears is evaluated as not having high quality and having somewhat poor service.

Project Research

Stapel Scale

Instructions

Please evaluate how accurately each word or phrase describes each of the department stores. Select a plus number for the phrases you think describe the store accurately. The more accurately you think the phrase describes the store, the larger the plus number you should choose. You should select a minus number for phrases you think do not describe it accurately. The less accurately you think the phrase describes the store, the larger the minus number you should choose. You can select any number, from +5 for phrases you think are very accurate, to −5 for phrases you think are very inaccurate.

Form

SEARS

+5	+5
+4	+4
+3	+3
+2	+2X
+1	+1
HIGH QUALITY	**POOR SERVICE**
−1	−1
−2X	−2
−3	−3
−4	−4
−5	−5 ■

The data obtained by using a Stapel scale are generally treated as interval and can be analyzed in the same way as semantic differential data. The Stapel scale produces results similar to the semantic differential. The Stapel scale's advantages are that it does not require a pretest of the adjectives or phrases to ensure true bipolarity, and it can be administered over the telephone. However, some researchers believe the Stapel scale is confusing and difficult to apply. Of the three itemized rating scales considered, the Stapel scale is used least. However, this scale merits more attention than it has received.

ACTIVE RESEARCH

The Diet Craze: Attitude Toward Diet Soft Drinks

Visit www.dietcoke.com and search the Internet using a search engine as well as your library's online databases to obtain information on consumers' attitudes toward diet drinks.

As the brand manager for Diet Coke, how would you use information on consumer attitudes to segment the market?

How would you use each of the three itemized scales to measure consumers' attitudes toward Diet Coke and other diet soft drinks? Which scale do you recommend?

Noncomparative Itemized Rating Scale Decisions

As is evident from the discussion so far, noncomparative itemized rating scales need not be used as originally proposed but can take many different forms. The researcher must make six major decisions when constructing any of these scales.

1. The number of scale categories to use
2. Balanced versus unbalanced scale
3. Odd or even number of categories
4. Forced versus nonforced choice
5. The nature and degree of the verbal description
6. The physical form of the scale

Number of Scale Categories

Two conflicting considerations are involved in deciding the number of scale categories. The greater the number of scale categories, the finer the discrimination among stimulus objects that is possible. On the other hand, most respondents cannot handle more than a few categories. Traditional guidelines suggest that the appropriate number of categories should be seven plus or minus two: between five and nine.[12] Yet there is no single optimal number of categories. Several factors should be taken into account in deciding on the number of categories.

If the respondents are interested in the scaling task and are knowledgeable about the objects, a larger number of categories may be employed. On the other hand, if the respondents are not very knowledgeable or involved with the task, fewer categories should be used. Likewise, the nature of the objects is also relevant. Some objects do not lend themselves to fine discrimination, so a small number of categories is sufficient. Another important factor is the mode of data collection. If telephone interviews are involved, many categories may confuse the respondents. Likewise, space limitations may restrict the number of categories in mail questionnaires.

How the data are to be analyzed and used should also influence the number of categories. In situations where several scale items are added together to produce a single score for each respondent, five categories are sufficient. The same is true if the researcher wishes to make broad generalizations or group comparisons. If, however, individual responses are of interest or the data will be analyzed by sophisticated statistical techniques, seven or more categories may be required. The size of the correlation coefficient, a common measure of relationship between variables (Chapter 17), is influenced by the number of scale categories. The correlation coefficient decreases with a reduction in the number of categories. This, in turn, has an impact on all statistical analysis based on the correlation coefficient.[13]

Balanced Versus Unbalanced Scales

balanced scale
A scale with an equal number of favorable and unfavorable categories.

In a **balanced scale**, the number of favorable and unfavorable categories are equal; in an unbalanced scale, they are unequal.[14] Examples of balanced and unbalanced scales are given in Figure 9.1. In general, the scale should be balanced in order to obtain objective data. However, if the distribution of responses is likely to be skewed, either positively or negatively, an unbalanced scale with more categories in the direction of skewness may be appropriate. If an unbalanced scale is used, the nature and degree of unbalance in the scale should be taken into account in data analysis.

FIGURE 9.1

Balanced and Unbalanced Scales

Balanced Scale		Unbalanced Scale	
Jovan Musk for Men is		Jovan Musk for Men is	
Extremely good	_____	Extremely good	_____
Very good	_____	Very good	_____
Good	_____	Good	_____
Bad	_____	Somewhat good	_____
Very bad	_____	Bad	_____
Extremely bad	_____	Very bad	_____

Odd or Even Number of Categories

With an odd number of categories, the middle scale position is generally designated as neutral or impartial. The presence, position, and labeling of a neutral category can have a significant influence on the response. The Likert scale is a balanced rating scale with an odd number of categories and a neutral point.[15]

The decision to use an odd or even number of categories depends on whether some of the respondents may be neutral on the response being measured. If a neutral or indifferent response is possible from at least some of the respondents, an odd number of categories should be used. If, on the other hand, the researcher wants to force a response or believes that no neutral or indifferent response exists, a rating scale with an even number of categories should be used. A related issue is whether the scale should be forced or nonforced.

Forced Versus Nonforced Scales

forced rating scales
A rating scale that forces the respondents to express an opinion because "no opinion" or "no knowledge" option is not provided.

On **forced rating scales**, the respondents are forced to express an opinion, because a "no opinion" option is not provided. In such a case, respondents without an opinion may mark the middle scale position. If a sufficient proportion of the respondents do not have opinions on the topic, marking the middle position will distort measures of central tendency and variance. In situations where the respondents are expected to have no opinion, as opposed to simply being reluctant to disclose it, the accuracy of data may be improved by a nonforced scale that includes a "no opinion" category.[16]

Nature and Degree of Verbal Description

The nature and degree of verbal description associated with scale categories varies considerably and can have an effect on the responses. Scale categories may have verbal, numerical, or even pictorial descriptions. Furthermore, the researcher must decide whether to label every scale category, some scale categories, or only extreme scale categories. Surprisingly, providing a verbal description for each category may not improve the accuracy or reliability of the data. Yet an argument can be made for labeling all or many scale categories to reduce scale ambiguity. The category descriptions should be located as close to the response categories as possible.

The strength of the adjectives used to anchor the scale may influence the distribution of the responses. With strong anchors (1 = completely disagree, 7 = completely agree), respondents are less likely to use the extreme scale categories. This results in less variable and more peaked response distributions. Weak anchors (1 = generally disagree, 7 = generally agree), in contrast, produce uniform or flat distributions. Procedures have been developed to assign values to category descriptors so as to result in balanced or equal-interval scales.[17]

Physical Form or Configuration

A number of options are available with respect to scale form or configuration. Scales can be presented vertically or horizontally. Categories can be expressed by boxes, discrete lines, or units on a continuum and may or may not have numbers assigned to them. If numerical values are used, they may be positive, negative, or both. Several possible configurations are presented in Figure 9.2.

Two unique rating scale configurations used in marketing research are the thermometer scale and the smiling face scale. For the thermometer scale, the higher the temperature, the more favorable the evaluation. Likewise, happier faces indicate more favorable evaluations. These scales are especially useful for children.[18] Examples of these scales are shown in Figure 9.3.

FIGURE 9.2

Rating Scale Configurations

A variety of scale configurations may be employed to measure the gentleness of Cheer detergent. Some examples include:

Cheer detergent is:

1. Very harsh — — — — — — — Very gentle

2. Very harsh 1 2 3 4 5 6 7 Very gentle

3. ☐ Very harsh
☐
☐
☐ Neither harsh nor gentle
☐
☐
☐ Very gentle

4. —— —— —— —— —— —— ——
Very harsh | Harsh | Somewhat harsh | Neither harsh nor gentle | Somewhat gentle | Gentle | Very gentle

5. [−3] [−2] [−1] [0] [+1] [+2] [+3]
Very harsh | | | Neither harsh nor gentle | | | Very gentle

Table 9.2 summarizes the six decisions in designing rating scales. Table 9.3 presents some commonly used scales. Although we show these scales as having five categories, the number of categories can be varied depending upon the judgment of the researcher.

Project Research   Project Activities

1. Develop Likert, semantic differential, and Stapel scales for measuring customer satisfaction toward Sears.
2. Illustrate the six itemized rating scale decisions of Table 9.2 in the context of measuring customer satisfaction toward Sears. ■

TABLE 9.2
Summary of Itemized Rating Scale Decisions

1. Number of categories	Although there is no single, optimal number, traditional guidelines suggest that there should be between five and nine categories.
2. Balanced versus unbalanced	In general, the scale should be balanced to obtain objective data.
3. Odd or even number of categories	If a neutral or indifferent scale response is possible from at least some of the respondents, an odd number of categories should be used.
4. Forced versus nonforced	In situations where the respondents are expected to have no opinion, the accuracy of data may be improved by a nonforced scale.
5. Verbal description	An argument can be made for labeling all or many scale categories. The category descriptions should be located as close to the response categories as possible.
6. Physical form	A number of options should be tried and the best one selected.

FIGURE 9.3

Some Unique Rating Chart Configurations

Thermometer Scale

Instructions

Please indicate how much you like McDonald's hamburgers by coloring in the thermometer with your blue pen. Start at the bottom and color up to the temperature level that best indicates how strong your preference is for McDonald's hamburgers.

Form

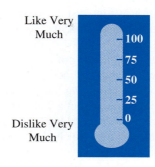

Smiling Face Scale

Instructions

Please tell me how much you like the Barbie Doll by pointing to the face that best shows how much you like it. If you did not like the Barbie Doll at all, you would point to Face 1. If you liked it very much, you would point to Face 5. Now tell me, how much did you like the Barbie Doll?

Form

ACTIVE RESEARCH

Dressing Consumers: Measuring Preferences for Dress Shoes

Visit www.rockport.com and search the Internet using a search engine as well as your library's online databases to obtain information on consumers' preferences for dress shoes.

Develop an itemized scale to measure consumers' preferences for dress shoes and justify your rating scale decisions.

As the marketing manager for Rockport, how would you use information on consumers' preferences for dress shoes to increase your sales?

TABLE 9.3

Some Commonly Used Scales in Marketing

Construct	Scale Descriptors				
Attitude	Very Bad	Bad	Neither Bad Nor Good	Good	Very Good
Importance	Not at All Important	Not Important	Neutral	Important	Very Important
Satisfaction	Very Dissatisfied	Dissatisfied	Neither Dissatisfied nor Satisfied	Satisfied	Very Satisfied
Purchase Intent	Definitely Will Not Buy	Probably Will Not Buy	Might or Might Not Buy	Probably Will Buy	Definitely Will Buy
Purchase Frequency	Never	Rarely	Sometimes	Often	Very Often

Multi-Item Scales

multi-item scales
A multi-item scale consists of multiple items, where an item is a single question or statement to be evaluated.

construct
A specific type of concept that exists at a higher level of abstraction than do everyday concepts.

A **multi-item scale** consists of multiple items, where an item is a single question or statement to be evaluated. The Likert, semantic differential, and Stapel scales presented earlier to measure attitudes toward Sears are examples of multi-item scales. Note that each of these scales has multiple items. The development of multi-item rating scales requires considerable technical expertise.[19] Figure 9.4 is a paradigm for constructing multi-item scales. The researcher begins by developing the construct of interest. A **construct** is a specific type of concept that exists at a higher level of abstraction than do everyday concepts, such as brand loyalty, product involvement, attitude, satisfaction, and so forth. Next, the researcher must develop a theoretical definition of the construct that states the meaning of the central idea or concept of interest. For this, we need an underlying theory of the construct being measured. A theory is necessary not only for constructing the scale but also for interpreting the resulting scores. For example, brand loyalty may be defined as the consistent repurchase of a brand prompted by a favorable attitude toward the brand. The construct must be operationalized in a way that is consistent with the theoretical definition. The operational definition specifies which observable characteristics will be measured and the process of assigning value to the construct. For example, in the context of toothpaste purchases, consumers will be characterized as brand loyal if they exhibit a highly favorable attitude (top quartile) and have purchased the same brand on at least four of the last five purchase occasions.

The next step is to generate an initial pool of scale items. Typically, this is done based on theory, analysis of secondary data, and qualitative research. From this pool, a reduced set of potential scale items is generated by the judgment of the researcher and other knowledgeable individuals. Some qualitative criterion is adopted to aid their judgment. The reduced set of items is still too large to constitute a scale. Thus, further reduction is achieved in a quantitative manner.

FIGURE 9.4

Development of a Multi-Item Scale

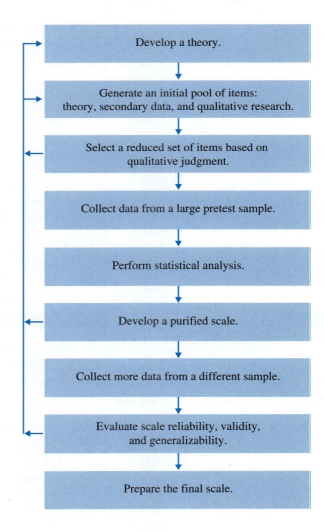

Develop a theory.

Generate an initial pool of items: theory, secondary data, and qualitative research.

Select a reduced set of items based on qualitative judgment.

Collect data from a large pretest sample.

Perform statistical analysis.

Develop a purified scale.

Collect more data from a different sample.

Evaluate scale reliability, validity, and generalizability.

Prepare the final scale.

Data are collected on the reduced set of potential scale items from a large pretest sample of respondents. The data are analyzed using techniques such as correlations, exploratory factor analysis, confirmatory factor analysis, cluster analysis, discriminant analysis, and statistical tests discussed later in this book. As a result of these statistical analyses, several more items are eliminated, resulting in a purified scale. The purified scale is evaluated for reliability and validity by collecting more data from a different sample (see the following section). On the basis of these assessments, a final set of scale items is selected. As can be seen from Figure 9.4, the scale development process is an iterative one with several feedback loops.[20]

Real Research

Measuring Technical Sophistication with a Technically Sophisticated Scale

The following multi-item scale measures the technical sophistication of a product line.[21]

1.	Technical	1	2	3	4	5	6	7	Nontechnical
2.	Low engineering content	1	2	3	4	5	6	7	High engineering content
3.	Fast changing	1	2	3	4	5	6	7	Slowly changing
4.	Unsophisticated	1	2	3	4	5	6	7	Sophisticated
5.	Commodity	1	2	3	4	5	6	7	Customized
6.	Unique	1	2	3	4	5	6	7	Common
7.	Complex	1	2	3	4	5	6	7	Simple

Items 1, 3, 6, and 7 are reversed when scoring. This scale can be used in industrial marketing to measure the technical sophistication of a customer's product line and suggest changes to improve technical quality. ■

Experiential Research

Measuring Satisfaction Using the Qualtrics Question Library

Access to Qualtrics is included with this book. Use the Qualtrics question library to electronically develop the following satisfaction scales.

1. Five-point Likert (type) balanced scale
2. Five-point Likert (type) unbalanced scale
3. Seven-point Likert (type) balanced scale
4. Seven-point semantic differential scale
5. Five-point smiling faces scale ■

Scale Evaluation

A multi-item scale should be evaluated for accuracy and applicability.[22] As shown in Figure 9.5, this involves an assessment of reliability, validity, and generalizability of the scale. Approaches

FIGURE 9.5

Evaluation of a Multi-Item Scale

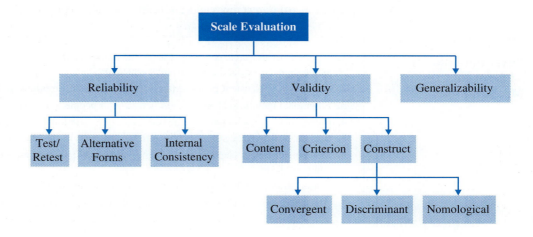

measurement error
The variation in the information sought by the researcher and the information generated by the measurement process employed.

true score model
A mathematical model that provides a framework for understanding the accuracy of measurement.

systematic error
Systematic error affects the measurement in a constant way and represents stable factors that affect the observed score in the same way each time the measurement is made.

random error
Measurement error that arises from random changes or differences in respondents or measurement situations.

reliability
The extent to which a scale produces consistent results if repeated measurements are made on the characteristic.

test-retest reliability
An approach for assessing reliability in which respondents are administered identical sets of scale items at two different times under as nearly equivalent conditions as possible.

to assessing reliability include test-retest reliability, alternative-forms reliability, and internal consistency reliability. Validity can be assessed by examining content validity, criterion validity, and construct validity.

Before we can examine reliability and validity, we need an understanding of measurement accuracy, because it is fundamental to scale evaluation.

Measurement Accuracy

As was mentioned in Chapter 8, a measurement is a number that reflects some characteristic of an object. A measurement is not the true value of the characteristic of interest but rather an observation of it. A variety of factors can cause **measurement error**, which results in the measurement or observed score being different from the true score of the characteristic being measured (see Figure 9.6). The **true score model** provides a framework for understanding the accuracy of measurement. According to this model,

$$X_O = X_T + X_S + X_R$$

where

X_O = the observed score or measurement
X_T = the true score of the characteristic
X_S = systematic error
X_R = random error

Note that the total measurement error includes the systematic error, X_S, and the random error, X_R. **Systematic error** affects the measurement in a constant way. It represents stable factors that affect the observed score in the same way each time the measurement is made, such as mechanical factors (see Figure 9.6). **Random error**, on the other hand, is not constant. It represents transient factors that affect the observed score in different ways each time the measurement is made, such as transient personal or situational factors. The distinction between systematic and random error is crucial to our understanding of reliability and validity.

Reliability

Reliability refers to the extent to which a scale produces consistent results if repeated measurements are made.[23] Systematic sources of error do not have an adverse impact on reliability, because they affect the measurement in a constant way and do not lead to inconsistency. In contrast, random error produces inconsistency, leading to lower reliability. Reliability can be defined as the extent to which measures are free from random error, X_R. If $X_R = 0$, the measure is perfectly reliable.

Reliability is assessed by determining the proportion of systematic variation in a scale. This is done by determining the association between scores obtained from different administrations of the scale. If the association is high, the scale yields consistent results and is therefore reliable. Approaches for assessing reliability include the test-retest, alternative-forms, and internal consistency methods.

TEST-RETEST RELIABILITY In **test-retest reliability**, respondents are administered identical sets of scale items at two different times under as nearly equivalent conditions as possible. The time interval

FIGURE 9.6

Potential Sources of Error in Measurement

1. Other relatively stable characteristics of the individual that influence the test score, such as intelligence, social desirability, and education
2. Short-term or transient personal factors, such as health, emotions, fatigue
3. Situational factors, such as the presence of other people, noise, and distractions
4. Sampling of items included in the scale: addition, deletion, or changes in the scale items
5. Lack of clarity of the scale, including the instructions or the items themselves
6. Mechanical factors, such as poor printing, overcrowding of items in the questionnaire, and poor design
7. Administration of the scale, such as differences among interviewers
8. Analysis factors, such as differences in scoring and statistical analysis

between tests or administrations is, typically, two to four weeks. The degree of similarity between the two measurements is determined by computing a correlation coefficient (see Chapter 17). The higher the correlation coefficient, the greater the reliability.

There are several problems associated with the test-retest approach to determining reliability. First, it is sensitive to the time interval between testing. Other things being equal, the longer the time interval, the lower the reliability. Second, the initial measurement may alter the characteristic being measured. For example, measuring respondents' attitudes toward low-fat milk may cause them to become more health conscious and develop a more positive attitude toward low-fat milk. Third, it may be impossible to make repeated measurements (for example, the research topic may be the respondent's initial reaction to a new product). Fourth, the first measurement may have a carryover effect to the second or subsequent measurements. Respondents may attempt to remember answers they gave the first time. Fifth, the characteristic being measured may change between measurements. For example, favorable information about an object between measurements may make a respondent's attitude more positive. Finally, the test-retest reliability coefficient can be inflated by the correlation of each item with itself. These correlations tend to be higher than correlations between different scale items across administrations. Hence, it is possible to have high test-retest correlations because of the high correlations between the same scale items measured at different times even though the correlations between different scale items are quite low. Because of these problems, a test-retest approach is best applied in conjunction with other approaches, such as alternative forms.[24]

alternative-forms reliability
An approach for assessing reliability that requires two equivalent forms of the scale to be constructed and then the same respondents are measured at two different times.

ALTERNATIVE-FORMS RELIABILITY In **alternative-forms reliability**, two equivalent forms of the scale are constructed. The same respondents are measured at two different times, usually two to four weeks apart, with a different scale form being administered each time. The scores from the administration of the alternative-scale forms are correlated to assess reliability.[25]

There are two major problems with this approach. First, it is time-consuming and expensive to construct an equivalent form of the scale. Second, it is difficult to construct two equivalent forms of a scale. The two forms should be equivalent with respect to content. In a strict sense, this requires that the alternative sets of scale items should have the same means, variances, and intercorrelations. Even if these conditions are satisfied, the two forms may not be equivalent in content. Thus, a low correlation may reflect either an unreliable scale or nonequivalent forms.

internal consistency reliability
An approach for assessing the internal consistency of the set of items when several items are summated in order to form a total score for the scale.

INTERNAL CONSISTENCY RELIABILITY **Internal consistency reliability** is used to assess the reliability of a summated scale where several items are summed to form a total score. In a scale of this type, each item measures some aspect of the construct measured by the entire scale, and the items should be consistent in what they indicate about the characteristic. This measure of reliability focuses on the internal consistency of the set of items forming the scale.

split-half reliability
A form of internal consistency reliability in which the items constituting the scale are divided into two halves and the resulting half scores are correlated.

The simplest measure of internal consistency is **split-half reliability**. The items on the scale are divided into two halves and the resulting half scores are correlated. High correlations between the halves indicate high internal consistency. The scale items can be split into halves based on odd- and even-numbered items or randomly. The problem is that the results will depend on how the scale items are split. A popular approach to overcoming this problem is to use the coefficient alpha.

coefficient alpha
A measure of internal consistency reliability that is the average of all possible split-half coefficients resulting from different splittings of the scale items.

The **coefficient alpha**, or Cronbach's alpha, is the average of all possible split-half coefficients resulting from different ways of splitting the scale items. This coefficient varies from 0 to 1, and a value of 0.6 or less generally indicates unsatisfactory internal consistency reliability. An important property of coefficient alpha is that its value tends to increase with an increase in the number of scale items. Therefore, coefficient alpha may be artificially, and inappropriately, inflated by including several redundant scale items.[26] Another coefficient that can be employed in conjunction with coefficient alpha is coefficient beta. Coefficient beta assists in determining whether the averaging process used in calculating coefficient alpha is masking any inconsistent items.

Some multi-item scales include several sets of items designed to measure different aspects of a multidimensional construct. For example, store image is a multidimensional construct that includes quality of merchandise, variety and assortment of merchandise, returns and adjustment policy, service of store personnel, prices, convenience of location, layout of the store, and credit and billing policies. Hence, a scale designed to measure store image would contain items measuring each of these dimensions. Because these dimensions are somewhat independent, a measure of internal consistency computed across dimensions would be inappropriate. However, if several items are used to measure each dimension, internal consistency reliability can be computed for each dimension.

Real Research	The Technology Behind Technology Opinion Leadership

In a study of technology adoption, opinion leadership was measured using the following 7-point Likert-type scales (1 = strongly agree, 7 = strongly disagree).

Opinion Leadership

1. My opinions on hardware/software products seem not to count with other people.
2. When other people choose to adopt a hardware/software product, they turn to me for advice.
3. Other people select hardware/software products rarely based on what I have suggested to them.
4. I often persuade other people to adopt the hardware/software products that I like.
5. Other people rarely come to me for advice about choosing hardware/software products.
6. I often influence other people's opinions about hardware/software products.

The alpha value for opinion leadership was 0.88, indicating good internal consistency. It was found that early adopters of technology products tend to be younger males who are opinion leaders, seek novel information, and have a lot of computer experience. Information technology companies like Microsoft need to ensure positive reactions from early product adopters and should focus marketing efforts on these individuals in the new product introduction stage.[27] ∎

Validity

validity
The extent to which differences in observed scale scores reflect true differences among objects on the characteristic being measured, rather than systematic or random errors.

The **validity** of a scale may be defined as the extent to which differences in observed scale scores reflect true differences among objects on the characteristic being measured, rather than systematic or random error. Perfect validity requires that there be no measurement error ($X_O = X_T$, $X_R = 0$, $X_S = 0$). Researchers may assess content validity, criterion validity, or construct validity.[28]

content validity
A type of validity, sometimes called *face validity*, that consists of a subjective but systematic evaluation of the representativeness of the content of a scale for the measuring task at hand.

CONTENT VALIDITY   Content validity, sometimes called *face validity*, is a subjective but systematic evaluation of how well the content of a scale represents the measurement task at hand. The researcher or someone else examines whether the scale items adequately cover the entire domain of the construct being measured. Thus, a scale designed to measure store image would be considered inadequate if it omitted any of the major dimensions (quality, variety and assortment of merchandise, etc.). Given its subjective nature, content validity alone is not a sufficient measure of the validity of a scale, yet it aids in a common-sense interpretation of the scale scores. A more formal evaluation can be obtained by examining criterion validity.

criterion validity
A type of validity that examines whether the measurement scale performs as expected in relation to other variables selected as meaningful criteria.

CRITERION VALIDITY   Criterion validity reflects whether a scale performs as expected in relation to other variables selected as meaningful criteria (criterion variables). Criterion variables may include demographic and psychographic characteristics, attitudinal and behavioral measures, or scores obtained from other scales. Based on the time period involved, criterion validity can take two forms: concurrent and predictive validity.

Concurrent validity is assessed when the data on the scale being evaluated and on the criterion variables are collected at the same time. To assess concurrent validity, a researcher may develop short forms of standard personality instruments. The original instruments and the short versions would be administered simultaneously to a group of respondents and the results compared. To assess predictive validity, the researcher collects data on the scale at one point in time and data on the criterion variables at a future time. For example, attitudes toward cereal brands could be used to predict future purchases of cereals by members of a scanner panel. Attitudinal data are obtained from the panel members, and then their future purchases are tracked with scanner data. The predicted and actual purchases are compared to assess the predictive validity of the attitudinal scale.

construct validity
A type of validity that addresses the question of what construct or characteristic the scale is measuring. An attempt is made to answer theoretical questions of why a scale works and what deductions can be made concerning the theory underlying the scale.

CONSTRUCT VALIDITY   Construct validity addresses the question of what construct or characteristic the scale is, in fact, measuring. When assessing construct validity, the researcher

convergent validity
A measure of construct validity that measures the extent to which the scale correlates positively with other measures of the same construct.

discriminant validity
A type of construct validity that assesses the extent to which a measure does not correlate with other constructs from which it is supposed to differ.

attempts to answer theoretical questions about why the scale works and what deductions can be made concerning the underlying theory. Thus, construct validity requires a sound theory of the nature of the construct being measured and how it relates to other constructs. Construct validity is the most sophisticated and difficult type of validity to establish. As Figure 9.5 shows, construct validity includes convergent, discriminant, and nomological validity.

Convergent validity is the extent to which the scale correlates positively with other measures of the same construct. It is not necessary that all these measures be obtained by using conventional scaling techniques. **Discriminant validity** is the extent to which a measure does not correlate with other constructs from which it is supposed to differ. It involves demonstrating a lack of correlation among differing constructs. **Nomological validity** is the extent to which the scale correlates in theoretically predicted ways with measures of different but related constructs. A theoretical model is formulated that leads to further deductions, tests, and inferences. Gradually, a nomological net is built in which several constructs are systematically interrelated. We illustrate construct validity in the context of a multi-item scale designed to measure self-concept.[29]

Real Research

To Thine Own Self Be True

The following findings would provide evidence of construct validity for a multi-item scale to measure self-concept.

nomological validity
A type of validity that assesses the relationship between theoretical constructs. It seeks to confirm significant correlations between the constructs as predicted by theory.

- High correlations with other scales designed to measure self-concepts and with reported classifications by friends (convergent validity)
- Low correlations with unrelated constructs of brand loyalty and variety seeking (discriminant validity)
- Brands that are congruent with the individual's self-concept are more preferred, as postulated by the theory (nomological validity)
- A high level of reliability ■

Notice that a high level of reliability was included as an evidence of construct validity in this example. This illustrates the relationship between reliability and validity.

Relationship Between Reliability and Validity

The relationship between reliability and validity can be understood in terms of the true score model. If a measure is perfectly valid, it is also perfectly reliable. In this case $X_O = X_T$, $X_R = 0$, and $X_S = 0$. Thus, perfect validity implies perfect reliability. If a measure is unreliable, it cannot be perfectly valid, because at a minimum $X_O = X_T + X_R$. Furthermore, systematic error may also be present, i.e., $X_S \neq 0$. Thus, unreliability implies invalidity. If a measure is perfectly reliable, it may or may not be perfectly valid, because systematic error may still be present ($X_O = X_T + X_S$). Although lack of reliability constitutes negative evidence for validity, reliability does not in itself imply validity. Reliability is a necessary, but not sufficient, condition for validity.

Generalizability

generalizability
The degree to which a study based on a sample applies to a universe of generalizations.

Generalizability refers to the extent to which one can generalize from the observations at hand to a universe of generalizations. The set of all conditions of measurement over which the investigator wishes to generalize is the universe of generalization. These conditions may include items, interviewers, situations of observation, and so on. A researcher may wish to generalize a scale developed for use in personal interviews to other modes of data collection, such as mail and telephone interviews. Likewise, one may wish to generalize from a sample of items to the universe of items, from a sample of times of measurement to the universe of times of measurement, from a sample of observers to a universe of observers, and so on.[30]

In generalizability studies, measurement procedures are designed to investigate the universes of interest by sampling conditions of measurement from each of them. For each universe of interest, an aspect of measurement called a *facet* is included in the study. Traditional reliability methods can be viewed as single-facet generalizability studies. A test-retest correlation is concerned with whether scores obtained from a measurement scale are generalizable to the universe scores across all times of possible measurement. Even if the test-retest correlation is high, nothing can be said about the generalizability of the scale to other universes. To generalize to other universes, generalizability theory procedures must be employed.

Choosing a Scaling Technique

In addition to theoretical considerations and evaluation of reliability and validity, certain practical factors should be considered in selecting scaling techniques for a particular marketing research problem.[31] These include the level of information (nominal, ordinal, interval, or ratio) desired, the capabilities of the respondents, the characteristics of the stimulus objects, method of administration, the context, and cost.

As a general rule, using the scaling technique that will yield the highest level of information feasible in a given situation will permit the use of the greatest variety of statistical analyses. Also, regardless of the type of scale used, whenever feasible, several scale items should measure the characteristic of interest. This provides more accurate measurement than a single-item scale. In many situations, it is desirable to use more than one scaling technique or to obtain additional measures using mathematically derived scales.

Mathematically Derived Scales

All the scaling techniques discussed in this chapter require the respondents to evaluate directly various characteristics of the stimulus objects. In contrast, mathematical scaling techniques allow researchers to infer respondents' evaluations of characteristics of stimulus objects. These evaluations are inferred from the respondents' overall judgments of the objects. Two popular mathematically derived scaling techniques are multidimensional scaling and conjoint analysis. These techniques are discussed in detail in Chapter 21.

International Marketing Research

In designing the scale or response format, respondents' educational or literacy levels should be taken into account.[32] One approach is to develop scales that are pan-cultural, or free of cultural biases. Of the scaling techniques we have considered, the semantic differential scale may be said to be pan-cultural. It has been tested in a number of countries and has consistently produced similar results.

Real Research   Copying the Name Xerox

Xerox (www.xerox.com) was a name well received in the former Soviet Union for the past 30 years. In fact, the act of copying documents was called Xeroxing, a term coined after the name of the company. It was a brand name people equated with quality. However, with the disintegration of the Soviet Union into the Commonwealth of Independent States (CIS), sales of Xerox started to fall. The management initially considered this problem to be the result of intense competition with strong competitors such as Canon, Ricoh Co., Mitsubishi Electric Corp., and Minolta Camera Co. First attempts at making the product more competitive did not help. Subsequently, marketing research was undertaken to measure the image of Xerox and its competitors. Semantic differential scales were used, because this type of scale is considered pan-cultural. The bipolar labels used were carefully tested to ensure that they had the intended semantic meaning in the Russian language and context.

The results of the study revealed that the real problem was a growing negative perception of Russian customers toward Xerox products. What could have gone wrong? The problem was not with Xerox, but with several independent producers of copying machines that had illegally infringed on Xerox's trademark rights. With the disintegration of the Soviet Union, the protection of these trademarks was unclear and trademark infringement kept growing. As a result, customers developed a misconception that Xerox was selling low-quality products. Among other courses of action, Xerox ran a corporate campaign on the national Russian TV and radio networks as well as in local print media. The campaign emphasized

Xerox's leadership position in the commonwealth countries where quality demands were very high. This was a positive step in removing some misconceptions of Russian consumers toward Xerox. Xerox also registered its trademark separately in each republic. Xerox saw its revenues grow substantially in Russia and other CIS countries. As of 2008, Xerox Corporation was a $17 billion technology and services enterprise helping businesses deploy Smarter Document Management[SM] strategies and finding better ways to work.[33] ■

Although the semantic differential worked well in the Russian context, an alternative approach is to develop scales that use a self-defined cultural norm as a base referent. For example, respondents may be required to indicate their own anchor point and position relative to a culture-specific stimulus set. This approach is useful for measuring attitudes that are defined relative to cultural norms (e.g., attitude toward marital roles). In developing response formats, verbal rating scales appear to be the most suitable. Even less-educated respondents can readily understand and respond to verbal scales. Special attention should be devoted to determining equivalent verbal descriptors in different languages and cultures. The endpoints of the scale are particularly prone to different interpretations. In some cultures, "1" may be interpreted as best, whereas in others, it may be interpreted as worst, regardless of how it is scaled. In such cases, it might be desirable to avoid numbers and to just use boxes that the respondent can check (worst ☐☐☐☐☐☐ best). It is important that the scale endpoints and the verbal descriptors be employed in a manner that is consistent with the culture.

Finally, in international marketing research, it is critical to establish the equivalence of scales and measures used to obtain data from different countries. This topic is complex and is discussed in some detail in Chapter 24.

Ethics in Marketing Research

The researcher has the ethical responsibility to use scales that have reasonable reliability, validity, and generalizability. The findings generated by scales that are unreliable, invalid, or not generalizable to the target population are questionable at best and raise serious ethical issues. Moreover, the researcher should not bias the scales so as to slant the findings in any particular direction. This is easy to do by biasing the wording of the statements (Likert-type scales), the scale descriptors, or other aspects of the scales. Consider the use of scale descriptors. The descriptors used to frame a scale can be chosen to bias results in a desired direction, for example, to generate a positive view of the client's brand or a negative view of a competitor's brand. To project the client's brand favorably, respondents are asked to indicate their opinion of the brand on several attributes using 7-point scales anchored by the descriptors "extremely poor" to "good." In such a case, respondents are reluctant to rate the product extremely poorly. In fact, respondents who believe the product to be only mediocre will end up responding favorably. Try this yourself. How would you rate BMW automobiles on the following attributes?

Reliability	Horrible	1	2	3	4	5	6	7	Good
Performance	Very poor	1	2	3	4	5	6	7	Good
Quality	One of the worst	1	2	3	4	5	6	7	Good
Prestige	Very low	1	2	3	4	5	6	7	Good

Did you find yourself rating BMW cars positively? Using this same technique, it is possible to negatively bias evaluations of competitors' brands by providing a mildly negative descriptor (somewhat poor) against a strong positive descriptor (extremely good).

Thus, we see how important it is to use balanced scales with comparable positive and negative descriptors. When this guideline is violated, responses are biased and should be interpreted accordingly. The researcher has a responsibility to both the client and respondents to ensure the applicability and usefulness of the scale. Similarly, client companies have a responsibility to treat their customers and the general public in an ethical manner. The following example proposes an appropriate scale for evaluating the conduct of direct marketers.

Real Research A Direct Measure of the Ethics of Direct Marketers

Many types of businesses are marketing to people over the phone, by e-mail, by text messages, and by direct mail without any consideration for the individuals they are trying to persuade to purchase their products. Many direct-marketing companies, including insurance, health care, and telecommunication companies, have paid billions of dollars in fines for unethical marketing practices. Denny Hatch has proposed the following honesty scale for companies using direct marketing.

1. Overall, my offer is, in Dick Benson's words, "scrupulously honest."
   0   1   2   3   4   5

2. I would be proud to make this offer to my mother or my daughter.
   0   1   2   3   4   5

3. My guarantee is clearly stated and ironclad. I will live up to it.
   0   1   2   3   4   5

4. I believe from my toes to my nose every promise I make in the offer.
   0   1   2   3   4   5

5. All the type in my promotion is easy to read and the copy is clear.
   0   1   2   3   4   5

6. All testimonials are absolutely real and have been freely given.
   0   1   2   3   4   5

7. Merchandise will arrive at the time promised. I do not live on float.
   0   1   2   3   4   5

8. I slavishly adhere to all industry opt-in/opt-out guidelines.
   0   1   2   3   4   5

9. I make it very easy to cancel or return the merchandise.
   0   1   2   3   4   5

10. I issue prompt refunds to unsatisfied customers.
   0   1   2   3   4   5

This is a self-rate scale of 0 to 5, where 0 is failing and 5 is excellent. Direct marketers should apply this to themselves to find out just how ethical their practices are. If your score is less than 50, you are not being scrupulously honest.[34] ∎

Decision Research Monster: The Monster of Career Networks

The Situation

When you think of the word "monster," what do you think? Scary creatures under your bed? Elmo and Grover from *Sesame Street*? The Walt Disney movie titled *Monsters, Inc.*? These days, the word "monster" also refers to the online job search company that has connected millions of job searchers with employers. This company (www.monster.com) was founded in 1994 by Jeff Taylor, and Sal Iannuzzi was appointed chairman and CEO in 2007. It is the leading online global careers network and the world's number one hiring management resource. As of 2008, its clients included more than 90 of the *Fortune* 100 and approximately 490 of the *Fortune* 500 companies. The company had operations in 36 countries around the world. No wonder this company has added a whole new meaning to the word *monster*.

Monster makes heavy use of marketing research techniques in a unique way. Unlike companies such as Nielsen that conduct marketing research for different companies, Monster researches companies that are in need of employees to fill their positions and provides the service of matching job searchers to these companies. Although Monster is doing well, more and more companies have followed in Monster's footsteps and have entered the arena of providing job search services. These competing companies include HotJobs (hotjobs.yahoo.com), Kforce (www.kforce.com), eJobs (www.ejobs.com), and eCareers (www.ecareers.org). With all of these different services available, the market is beginning to become saturated with Internet recruiting Web sites. It is important for Monster, now more than ever, to differentiate itself from the competition.

The use of appropriate scaling techniques can help Monster match the companies' job specifications with the skills and qualifications of job applicants.

The Marketing Research Decision

1. The success of Monster lies in matching the companies' job specifications with the skills and qualifications of job applicants. What scaling techniques should Monster use to measure companies' job specifications and job applicants' skills and qualifications?
2. Discuss the role of the type of scaling technique you recommend in enabling Sal Iannuzzi to match companies' job specifications and job applicants' skills and qualifications and thereby increase the market share of Monster.

The Marketing Management Decision

1. What should Sal Iannuzzi do to gain market share over competitors?
2. Discuss how the marketing management decision action that you recommend to Sal Iannuzzi is influenced by the scaling technique that you suggested earlier and by the findings of that research.[35] ■

SPSS Windows

Using SPSS Data Entry, the researcher can design any of the three noncomparative scales: Likert, semantic differential, or Stapel. Moreover, multi-item scales can be easily accommodated. Either the question library can be used or customized scales can be designed. We show the use of SPSS Data Entry to design Likert-type scales for rating salespeople and product characteristics in Figure 9.7.

FIGURE 9.7

Likert-Type Scales for Rating Salespeople and Product Characteristics

```
📠 Manual examples.sav - SPSS Data Entry - Scale Button Matrices                    _□✕
File  Edit  View  Data  Rules  Help
```

Please rate your sales representative on the following characteristics:

	Excellent	Very Good	Good	Fair	Poor
Helpfulness	❑	❑	❑	❑	❑
Promptfulness	❑	❑	❑	❑	❑
Knowledge of product	❑	❑	❑	❑	❑

Please rate the importance of the following product characteristics:

	Important				Not Important
Reliability	1	2	3	4	5
Price	1	2	3	4	5
Range of features	1	2	3	4	5

```
                                    1/1   Skip & Fill On   Auto Check: On   Entry
```

Summary

In noncomparative scaling, each object is scaled independently of the other objects in the stimulus set. The resulting data are generally assumed to be interval or ratio scaled. Figure 9.8 gives a concept map for noncomparative scales. Noncomparative rating scales can be either continuous or itemized. The itemized rating scales are further classified as Likert, semantic differential, or Stapel scales. The data from all these three types of scale are typically treated as interval scale. Thus, these scales possess the characteristics of description, order, and distance, as discussed in Chapter 8. When using noncomparative itemized rating scales, the researcher must decide on the number of scale categories, balanced versus unbalanced scales, odd or even number of categories, forced versus nonforced scales, nature and degree of verbal description, and the physical form or configuration.

Multi-item scales consist of a number of rating scale items. These scales should be evaluated in terms of reliability and validity. Reliability refers to the extent to which a scale produces consistent results if repeated measurements are made. Approaches to assessing reliability include test-retest, alternative-forms, and internal consistency. Validity, or accuracy of measurement, may be assessed by evaluating content validity, criterion validity, and construct validity.

The choice of particular scaling techniques in a given situation should be based on theoretical and practical considerations. As a general rule, the scaling technique used should be the one that will yield the highest level of information feasible. Also, multiple measures should be obtained.

In international marketing research, special attention should be devoted to determining equivalent verbal descriptors in different languages and cultures. The researcher has a responsibility to both the client and respondents to ensure the applicability and usefulness of the scales. The Internet and computers are useful for developing and testing continuous and itemized rating scales, particularly multi-item scales.

FIGURE 9.8

A Concept Map for Noncomparative Scales

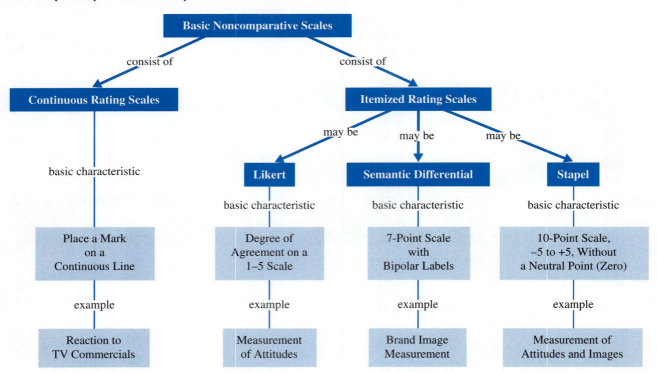

Key Terms and Concepts

noncomparative scale, 273
continuous rating scale, 274
itemized rating scale, 276
Likert scale, 276
semantic differential, 278
Stapel scale, 279
balanced scale, 280
forced rating scales, 281
multi-item scales, 284
construct, 284

measurement error, 286
true score model, 286
systematic error, 286
random error, 286
reliability, 286
test-retest reliability, 286
alternative-forms
    reliability, 287
internal consistency
    reliability, 287

split-half reliability, 287
coefficient alpha, 287
validity, 288
content validity, 288
criterion validity, 288
construct validity, 288
convergent validity, 289
discriminant validity, 289
nomological validity, 289
generalizability, 289

Suggested Cases, Video Cases, and HBS Cases

Running Case with Real Data

1.1 Dell

Comprehensive Critical Thinking Cases

2.1 American Idol   2.2 Baskin-Robbins   2.3 Akron Children's Hospital

Comprehensive Cases with Real Data

4.1 JPMorgan Chase   4.2 Wendy's

Video Cases

12.1 Subaru   23.1 Marriott   24.1 Nivea

Comprehensive Harvard Business School Cases

Case 5.1: The Harvard Graduate Student Housing Survey (9-505-059)
Case 5.2: BizRate.Com (9-501-024)
Case 5.3: Cola Wars Continue: Coke and Pepsi in the Twenty-First Century (9-702-442)
Case 5.4: TiVo in 2002 (9-502-062)
Case 5.5: Compaq Computer: Intel Inside? (9-599-061)
Case 5.6: The New Beetle (9-501-023)

Live Research: Conducting a Marketing Research Project

1. Continuous measures are generally more difficult to implement.
2. As a class, discuss the type of itemized rating scales (Likert, semantic differential, or Stapel) that are appropriate for the key variables.
3. Discuss multi-item scales and the issues of reliability and validity.

4. Consider the practical constraints. For example, if a certain type of scale has been used to measure a variable in the past (e.g., a 10-point Likert-type scale to measure customer satisfaction), the same may have to be used again in the project to allow a comparison of the findings with past results.

Acronym

The rating scale decisions may be described by the acronym

Rating:

R esponse option: forced vs. nonforced
A ttractive vs. unattractive number of categories: balanced vs. unbalanced
T otal number of categories
I mpartial or neutral category: odd vs. even number of categories
N ature and degree of verbal description
G raphics: physical form and configuration

Exercises

Questions

1. What is a semantic differential scale? For what purposes is this scale used?
2. Describe the Likert scale.
3. What are the differences between the Stapel scale and the semantic differential? Which scale is more popular?
4. What are the major decisions involved in constructing an itemized rating scale?
5. How many scale categories should be used in an itemized rating scale? Why?
6. What is the difference between balanced and unbalanced scales?
7. Should an odd or even number of categories be used in an itemized rating scale?
8. What is the difference between forced and nonforced scales?
9. How do the nature and degree of verbal description affect the response to itemized rating scales?
10. What are multi-item scales?
11. Describe the true score model.
12. What is reliability?
13. What are the differences between test-retest and alternative-forms reliability?
14. Describe the notion of internal consistency reliability.
15. What is validity?
16. What is criterion validity? How is it assessed?
17. How would you assess the construct validity of a multi-item scale?
18. What is the relationship between reliability and validity?
19. How would you select a particular scaling technique?

Problems

1. Develop a Likert, a semantic differential, and a Stapel scale for measuring store loyalty.
2. Develop a multi-item scale to measure students' attitudes toward internationalization of the management curriculum. How would you assess the reliability and validity of this scale?
3. Develop a Likert scale for measuring the attitude of students toward the Internet as a source of general information. Administer your scale to a small sample of 30 students and refine it.
4. The following scale was used in a recent study to measure attitudes toward new technology: Please tell me how much you agree or disagree with the following statements as they describe how you view new technology. Use a scale of 1 to 5, where 1 = strongly disagree and 5 = strongly agree.

   I'm a person who avoids new technology.
   I'm a technology buff who keeps up with the latest equipment.
   I take a "wait-and-see" approach to new technology until it is proven.
   I'm the kind of person friends turn to for advice on buying new technology.

   a. How would you score this scale to measure attitudes toward new technology?
   b. Develop an equivalent semantic differential scale to measure attitudes toward new technology.
   c. Develop an equivalent Stapel scale to measure attitudes toward new technology.
   d. Which scale form is most suited for a telephone survey?

Internet and Computer Exercises

1. Design Likert scales to measure the usefulness of Ford Motor Company's Web site. Visit the site at www.ford.com and rate it on the scales that you have developed.
2. Design semantic differential scales to measure the perception of FedEx overnight delivery service and compare it to that offered by UPS. Relevant information may be obtained by visiting the Web sites of these two companies (www.fedex.com, www.ups.com).
3. Visit the Office of Scales Research Web site (www.siu.edu/departments/coba/osr). (If this Web site has moved, search www.siu.edu). Identify one application of the Likert scale and one application of the semantic differential scale. Write a report describing the context in which these scales have been used.
4. Visit the Web sites of two marketing research firms conducting surveys. Analyze one survey of each firm to critically evaluate the itemized rating scales being used.
5. Surf the net to find two examples each of Likert, semantic differential, and Stapel scales. Write a report describing the context in which these scales are being used.

Activities

Role Playing

1. You work in the marketing research department of a firm specializing in developing decision support systems (DSS) for the health care industry. Your firm would like to measure the attitudes of hospital administrators toward DSS. The interviews would be conducted by telephone. You have been asked to develop an appropriate scale for this purpose. Management would like you to explain and justify your reasoning in constructing this scale.

Fieldwork

1. Develop a semantic differential scale to measure the images of two major airlines that fly to your city. Administer this scale to a pilot sample of 20 students. Based on your pilot study, which airline has a more favorable image?

Group Discussion

1. "It really does not matter which scaling technique you use. As long as your measure is reliable, you will get the right results." Discuss this statement as a small group.
2. "One need not be concerned with reliability and validity in applied marketing research." Discuss this statement as a small group.

Dell Running Case

Review the Dell case, Case 1.1, and questionnaire given toward the end of the book. Go to the Web site for this book and download the Dell data file.

1. Perform the following operations:
   a. Reverse the scoring of the second and the third items under the Innovativeness scale.
   b. Sum the Market Maven items (q10_1 to q10_4) to form a Total Market Maven Score.
   c. Sum the Innovativeness items (q10_5 to q10_10) to form a Total Innovativeness Score. Note that you will have to reverse the scores for the negatively worded items (q10_6 and q10_7) before summing.
   d. Sum the Opinion Leadership items (q10_11 to q10_13) to form a Total Opinion Leadership Score.
   e. Compute Cronbach's alpha for each of these three sets of items.
2. Design Likert, semantic differential, and Stapel scales to measure consumers' preferences for Dell computers.

VIDEO CASE 9.1   eGO: Reinventing Wheels

eGO Vehicles, based in Nashville, Tennessee, was founded in 1999 by its then-president and CEO, Andrew Kallfelz. It produces light, electric vehicles and claims to be the leading manufacturer of "fun, easy-to-ride, eco-friendly personal transportation." eGO cycles do not require gas or oil and produce zero emissions. They run entirely on electricity and have a range of 20 to 25 miles while traveling at 20 to 25 miles per hour. The company is constantly monitoring market conditions to find opportunities to expand globally, for example, shifting its production site from the United States to Taiwan.

Based on marketing research in the form of focus groups, surveys, and personal observations, the eGO cycle was conceptualized to perform almost any errand one can think of. Although the concept seemed promising, taking the product from the design to the marketplace presented several challenges and hurdles. The first challenge was the design of the cycle. The team at eGO was very particular about the cycle not having a motorcycle-like look and feel. In addition, the team did not want the technology and the engine to be visible. Andrew Kallfelz described the designing goal as "Make

it almost like a magic carpet." The cycles are distinctive looking. The designers sought such distinctiveness. They did not want people to think, "Oh, a motorcycle" (bad for the environment), or "Oh, a bike" (you have to pedal). The idea was to have a mode of transportation to make small trips without using three tons of steel to do it. After a year and a half of product testing, the eGO cycle gained the approval of the National Highway and Transportation Safety Agency. With this approval, eGO was able to register the cycle in every state.

The eGO is a new and different concept and its looks should—and do—reflect that. This specific niche provides eGO with its greatest strength and its greatest challenge. Although consumers might want the product, no distribution channels were available. Bike stores did not want a nonbike product taking up floor space, and motorcycle shops did not want a bicycle in their stores.

The solution to this problem was found through marketing research. eGO needed to find how to distribute the product and with whom to distribute the product through. Marketing research showed that customers wanted to test the cycle even though it was unavailable in many stores. eGO responded by bringing the bikes to football games, shows, and events for people to test drive. In addition, research showed that articles in trade journals and appearances on popular television shows would help customers become more familiar with the product without actually seeing it firsthand. eGO's bikes have appeared in *Time* and on TV programs such as *Good Morning America* and the *Today Show.* eGO believes these appearances provide customers with the assurance they need to pay $1,400 on their credit cards to a Web site to buy a product they have never seen. A survey of existing eGO owners revealed that the vehicle is used for commuting, recreation, business, and errands. Finally, research showed these products would also be successful in markets where golf carts are already used for transportation and in resort areas for rentals.

The team at eGO found, to great pleasure, that the cycle was an instant hit, turning heads and fast becoming the topic of hot discussion—in effect marketing itself. Jim Hamman, founder and vice president of marketing and sales, recounts ". . . it (eGO cycle) would create a discussion everywhere you went. People would be talking out of their cars to you at a stop sign and ask where did you get that? How does it work? How much is it? It created such a buzz that there was certainly something there." Strong customer reaction led to strong demand, and in a short span of 2 years eGO grew its orders from zero to hundreds of products shipped globally each month.

The eGO Cycle2, already in its second version, is eGO's core product. It comes in three models; features vary based on local requirements and marketing research. For instance, three options are available in the U.S. market as of 2009: the eGO Cycle 2 classic, SE, and LX. For the European marketplace, the brand name was changed to Helios and three different models are available. The price for an eGO Cycle ranges from $1,399 to $1,999. The price is determined by the model and the country of purchase by applying product and geographic price segmentation. The pricing strategy takes into account not only product costs, but also consumer price sensitivity (elasticity of demand) based on marketing research.

The eGO's energy costs do not exceed half a cent per mile. Warranties are provided for the battery (6 months), the chassis (10 years), and all other parts for up to one year. Furthermore, customers are able to individualize their eGO Cycle. Across all models one can customize the cycle and choose from four colors upon request. This customization strategy was adopted after marketing research revealed strong desire of consumers to have a role in configuring the cycle. eGO also offers additional accessories, such as eGO clothing.

With no established marketing or distribution model to follow, eGO had to develop its own model and perfect it as it went along, learning from experience and feedback. The direct marketing and direct distribution model has been the mainstay of eGO's marketing and distribution process, although it is slow and time-consuming and requires a lot of creativity. The eGO Cycle is sold by authorized dealers, and accessories can be purchased online. In cases where there is no authorized dealer available in non–U.S. markets, eGO provides shipping as an exception. In North America, distributors are only found in the United States, but plans for Canadian dealers are in the works. The expansion into the Asia–Pacific (APAC) region only covers Japan, Korea, Taiwan, and Australia. Since 2004, contract dealers have sold eGO cycles in seven European countries, including the Czech Republic, Germany and the United Kingdom.

According to "Electric Bikes Worldwide Reports" (2007) the eGO Vehicles Company is on the right track and is likely to succeed and cope with future challenges. This is certainly due to the company's ability to quickly adapt and sense consumer needs as determined by marketing research. First, eGO Vehicle produces a core model of an electric bike that can comply with local restrictions as well as local consumer tastes. Second, the manufacturing site has been relocated to Taiwan, where industry concentration takes place. Thus, various location advantages can be exploited because the environment enforces innovation, knowledge, and expertise as well as cheaper production costs.

Conclusion

The case presents an engaging example of marketing a new, innovative, and in some ways, unconventional, product. The case demonstrates how the marketing effort at eGO overcame challenges such as lack of established media to reach customers and novelty of the product to develop eGO's brand equity and establish its brand image. Strategies and initiatives such as marketing research, customer feedback, direct marketing, and online sales are exemplary for any small startup trying to establish a strong market image for its product or service.

Questions

1. eGO would like to increase its U.S. sales. Define the management decision problem.
2. Define the marketing research problem corresponding to the management decision problem you identified.
3. What type of research design do you think the company adopted in conducting marketing research to determine consumer preferences for eGO vehicles?
4. Can eGO make use of a panel? If so, what type of a panel for what purpose?
5. How would you use the Internet to determine men's preferences for electric vehicles?
6. What sources of syndicated data would be useful to eGO in projecting future demand for its vehicles?
7. Are focus groups or depth interviews better for determining the factors that underlie consumer preferences for eGO?
8. If a survey is to be conducted to determine consumer preferences for eGO, which survey method should be used and why?
9. Illustrate the use of nominal, ordinal, interval and ratio scales for measuring consumer preferences for eGO.
10. Illustrate the use of Likert, semantic differential, and Stapel scales for measuring consumer preferences for eGO.

References

1. www.egovehicles.com, accessed April 8, 2009.
2. eGO Vehicles, "Consumer Purchase Criteria for Personal Electric Vehicles," http://egovehicles.com/fileadmin/user_upload/PDFs/technical_note_60.pdf, accessed April 8, 2007.
3. F. E. Jamerson and E. Benjamin, "Electric Bikes Worldwide Reports," 8th ed., www.ebwr.com, accessed May 8, 2007.

"Pretesting a questionnaire is absolutely essential for success. All legitimate researchers understand this and won't dare waste the public's time or their own effort with a questionnaire that hasn't been pretested."

Diane Bowers, President, Council of American Survey Research Organizations (CASRO), Port Jefferson, New York

Objectives [After reading this chapter, the student should be able to:]

1. Explain the purpose of a questionnaire and its objectives of asking questions that the respondents can and will answer, encouraging respondents, and minimizing response error.

2. Describe the process of designing a questionnaire, the steps involved, and guidelines that must be followed at each step.

3. Discuss the observational form of data collection and specify the who, what, when, where, why, and way of behavior to be observed.

4. Discuss the considerations involved in designing questionnaires for international marketing research.

5. Understand the ethical issues involved in questionnaire design.

6. Discuss the use of the Internet and computers in designing questionnaires.

Questionnaire and Form Design

Overview

Questionnaire or form design is an important step in formulating a research design. Once the researcher has specified the nature of the research design (Chapters 3 through 7) and determined the scaling procedures (Chapters 8 and 9), a questionnaire or an observational form can be developed. This chapter discusses the importance of questionnaires and observational forms. Next, we describe the objectives of a questionnaire and the steps involved in designing questionnaires. We provide several guidelines for developing sound questionnaires. We also consider the design of observation forms. The considerations involved in designing questionnaires when conducting international marketing research are discussed. Several ethical issues that arise in questionnaire design are identified.

Real Research

The Consensus on Census 2000 Questionnaires

Every 10 years, the United States Census Bureau (www.census.gov) conducts a survey to determine how many people are in the country, as well as the various demographics of these individuals. This survey is done using questionnaires. Because the forms have been long and hard to understand in the past, there has been a decline in mail responses for the census. As a result, the questionnaires were redesigned for the 2000 census. The goal was to make them more user friendly and shorter in hopes of increasing the response rates.

As a result of improved design, mail response rates to the Census 2000 questionnaires were about 10 percent higher than in 1990.

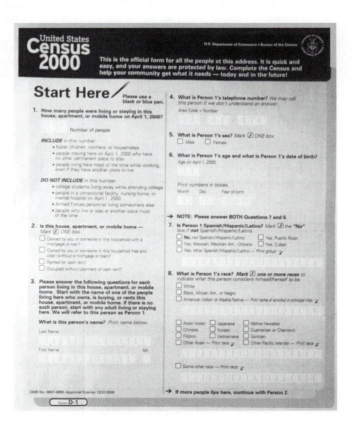

The questionnaire was considerably shortened. Whereas the 1990 short form contained 12 subjects, the 2000 short form had only 7 subjects (name, sex, age, relationship, Hispanic origin, and race for each household member, as well as whether the home was owned or rented). Likewise, the long form for 2000 had 34 subjects instead of 38 for 1990.

Once the content of the questionnaire was determined, it was time to work on the structure and actual wording of the statements. The hard part of the process was making the questions short enough to keep respondents interested, but long enough to obtain the necessary data. Each question had to be clearly defined using unambiguous words. A review was conducted of the 1990 census questions to determine which ones needed to be revised. After determining the content, structure, wording, and sequence of questions, the Bureau looked to a New York design firm, Two Twelve Associates (www.twotwelve.com), to improve form and layout and develop visual imagery for the questionnaire, including a logo and slogan.

The revised questionnaire was thoroughly pretested. The most extensive pretest was the 1996 National Content Survey (formally known as the U.S. Census 2000 Test), which was designed to test new and revised question wording, formatting, and sequencing.

During actual data collection, a card was first mailed before the questionnaire was sent and respondents were given the option to request the questionnaire in English, Spanish, Chinese, Korean, Vietnamese, or Tagalog. Then the questionnaire package was sent in an official envelope with the Census logo on the front. A note on the envelopes reminded the recipients that their response was required by law.

As a result of the user-friendly format of the 2000 questionnaires, mail response rates were about 10 percent higher than in 1990. The consensus was that the 2000 questionnaires were much improved over those used a decade earlier. The Bureau has continued to redesign the Census questionnaire. The American Community Survey is a nationwide survey designed to provide communities a fresh look at how they are changing. It will replace the decennial long form in future censuses and is a critical element in the Census Bureau's reengineered 2010 census.[1] ■

Real Research ## comScore SurveySite for Web Site Evaluation

Online marketers and Web site designers are increasingly concerned with what design features and experiences make visitors return to a site. An equally important concern is knowing what features and experiences are *undesirable* so that they can avoid including them in their site. comScore SurveySite (www.comscore.com), an online marketing research company, conducted an extensive study to address these questions.

It recruited 87 American and Canadian Web sites to participate in the study. Each site was equipped with a feedback icon so visitors could participate in a standardized survey that asked evaluative questions about the visit. The questionnaire consisted of 12 questions that fell into two broad areas: design/technical evaluation and emotional experience during the site visit. The design/technical questions were kept simple so that even respondents who were not technically savvy could answer them. These questions were asked first, in part A, and followed a logical order. Then, in part B, questions related to emotional experience were asked. All the questions were asked using 7-point rating scales except one, which was open ended. That question asked respondents what factors were most important in their decisions to return or not return to the site. The final part, part C, obtained Web usage and demographic information. The questionnaire had been extensively pretested before it was used in the study.

The results of the survey found that content was the most important factor in determining whether or not a site would receive repeat visitors. Correspondingly, "frivolous content" was the most cited reason for not returning to a site. The second most important factor in determining the repeat visit rate was whether or not the respondent found the visit enjoyable. Enjoyment may mean that visitors found the information they were looking for. Next, quality of the organization of the site and its degree of uniqueness also influence repeat visit rates. Based on the results of this survey, marketers and site designers should consider content, layout, and uniqueness when developing Web sites. Doing so will help improve the number of repeat visitors to their site.[2] ■

Questionnaires and Observation Forms

As was discussed in Chapters 5 and 6, survey and observation are the two basic methods for obtaining quantitative primary data in descriptive research. Both of these methods require some procedure for standardizing the data-collection process so that the data obtained are internally consistent and can be analyzed in a uniform and coherent manner. If 40 different interviewers conduct personal interviews or make observations in different parts of the country, the data they collect will not be comparable unless they follow specific guidelines and ask questions and record answers in a standard way. A standardized questionnaire or form will ensure comparability of the data, increase speed and accuracy of recording, and facilitate data processing.

Experiential Research

How Important Is a Questionnaire?

Sprite is the third most popular soft drink brand, behind Coke and Pepsi. College students are heavy users of soft drinks.

1. As the brand manager for Sprite, what information do you need to target this segment?
2. Search the Internet, as well as your library's online databases, to obtain information that will assist the brand manager of Sprite in targeting the student segment.
3. You and a fellow student each interview a different respondent (another student) to determine preferences for soft drinks, without constructing a questionnaire. How comparable are the data each of you obtained? Next develop a formal questionnaire jointly and each of you administer it to another respondent. Are the data you two obtained more comparable than before? What does this teach you about the importance of a questionnaire? ■

Questionnaire Definition

questionnaire

A structured technique for data collection that consists of a series of questions, written or verbal, that a respondent answers.

A **questionnaire**, whether it is called a *schedule, interview form*, or *measuring instrument*, is a formalized set of questions for obtaining information from respondents. Typically, a questionnaire is only one element of a data-collection package that might also include (1) fieldwork procedures, such as instructions for selecting, approaching, and questioning respondents (see Chapter 13); (2) some reward, gift, or payment offered to respondents; and (3) communication aids, such as maps, pictures, advertisements, and products (as in personal interviews) and return envelopes (in mail surveys). Regardless of the form of administration, a questionnaire is characterized by some specific objectives.

Objectives of a Questionnaire

Any questionnaire has three specific objectives. First, it must translate the information needed into a set of specific questions that the respondents can and will answer. Developing questions that respondents can and will answer and that will yield the desired information is difficult. Two apparently similar ways of posing a question may yield different information. Hence, this objective is a challenge.

Second, a questionnaire must uplift, motivate, and encourage the respondent to become involved in the interview, to cooperate, and to complete the interview. Incomplete interviews have limited usefulness at best. In designing a questionnaire, the researcher should strive to minimize respondent fatigue, boredom, incompleteness, and nonresponse. A well-designed questionnaire can motivate the respondents and increase the response rate, as illustrated by the Census 2000 questionnaire in the opening example.

Third, a questionnaire should minimize response error. The potential sources of error in research designs were discussed in Chapter 3, where response error was defined as the error that arises when respondents give inaccurate answers or their answers are misrecorded or misanalyzed. A questionnaire can be a major source of response error. Minimizing this error is an important objective of questionnaire design.

Questionnaire Design Process

The great weakness of questionnaire design is lack of theory. Because there are no scientific principles that guarantee an optimal or ideal questionnaire, questionnaire design is a skill acquired through experience. It is an art rather than a science. Stanley Payne's *The Art of Asking Questions*, published in 1951, is still a basic work in the field.[3] This section presents guidelines useful to beginning researchers in designing questionnaires. Although these rules can help you avoid major mistakes, the fine-tuning of a questionnaire comes from the creativity of a skilled researcher.

FIGURE 10.1

**Questionnaire
Design Process**

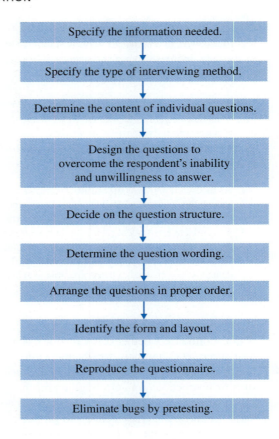

Specify the information needed.

Specify the type of interviewing method.

Determine the content of individual questions.

Design the questions to overcome the respondent's inability and unwillingness to answer.

Decide on the question structure.

Determine the question wording.

Arrange the questions in proper order.

Identify the form and layout.

Reproduce the questionnaire.

Eliminate bugs by pretesting.

Questionnaire design will be presented as a series of steps (see Figure 10.1). These steps are (1) specify the information needed, (2) specify the type of interviewing method, (3) determine the content of individual questions, (4) design the questions to overcome the respondent's inability and unwillingness to answer, (5) decide on the question structure, (6) determine the question wording, (7) arrange the questions in proper order, (8) identify the form and layout, (9) reproduce the questionnaire, and (10) pretest the questionnaire. We will present guidelines for each step. In practice, the steps are interrelated and the development of a questionnaire will involve some iteration and looping. For example, the researcher may discover that respondents misunderstand all the possible wordings of a question. This may require a loop back to the earlier step of deciding on the question structure.[4]

Specify the Information Needed

The first step in questionnaire design is to specify the information needed. This is also the first step in the research design process. Note that as the research project progresses, the information needed becomes more and more clearly defined. It is helpful to review components of the problem and the approach, particularly the research questions, hypotheses, and the information needed. To further ensure that the information obtained fully addresses all the components of the problem, the researcher should prepare a set of dummy tables. A dummy table is a blank table used to catalog data. It describes how the analysis will be structured once the data have been collected.

It is also important to have a clear idea of the target population. The characteristics of the respondent group have a great influence on questionnaire design. Questions that are appropriate for college students may not be appropriate for housewives. Understanding is related to respondent socioeconomic characteristics. Furthermore, poor understanding is associated with a high incidence of uncertain or no-opinion responses. The more diversified the respondent group, the more difficult it is to design a single questionnaire that is appropriate for the entire group.

Type of Interviewing Method

An appreciation of how the type of interviewing method influences questionnaire design can be obtained by considering how the questionnaire is administered under each method (see Chapter 6). In personal interviews, respondents see the questionnaire and interact face to face with the interviewer. Thus, lengthy, complex, and varied questions can be asked. In telephone interviews, the respondents interact with the interviewer, but they do not see the questionnaire. This limits the type of questions that can be asked to short and simple ones (see the department store project). Mail questionnaires are self-administered, so the questions must be simple and detailed instructions must be provided. In computer-assisted interviewing (CAPI and CATI), complex skip patterns and randomization of questions to eliminate order bias can be easily accommodated. Internet questionnaires share many of the characteristics of CAPI, but e-mail questionnaires have to be simpler. Questionnaires designed for personal and telephone interviews should be written in a conversational style.

In the department store project example, ranking 10 stores is too complex a task to be administered over the telephone. Instead, the simpler rating task, where the stores are rated one at a time, is selected to measure preferences. Note the use of cards to facilitate the ranking task in the personal interview. Interviewer instructions (typed in capital letters) are much more extensive in the personal interview. Another difference is that whereas the respondent records the ranks in mail and electronic surveys, the interviewer records the store names in the personal interview. The type of interviewing method also influences the content of individual questions.

Project Research   Effect of Interviewing Method on Questionnaire Design

Mail Questionnaire

Please rank-order the following department stores in order of your preference to shop at these stores. Begin by picking out the one store that you like most and assign it a number 1. Then find the second most preferred department store and assign it a number 2. Continue this procedure until you have ranked all the stores in order of preference. The least preferred store should be assigned a rank of 10. No two stores should receive the same rank number. The criterion of preference is entirely up to you. There is no right or wrong answer. Just try to be consistent.

	STORE	RANK ORDER
1.	Nordstrom	_____
2.	Macy's	_____
3.	Kmart	_____
4.	Kohl's	_____
5.	JCPenney	_____
6.	Neiman Marcus	_____
7.	Marshalls	_____
8.	Saks Fifth Avenue	_____
9.	Sears	_____
10.	Wal-Mart	_____

Telephone Questionnaire

I will read to you the names of some department stores. Please rate them in terms of your preference to shop at these stores. Use a 10-point scale, where 1 denotes not so preferred and 10 denotes greatly preferred. Numbers between 1 and 10 reflect intermediate degrees of preference. Again, please remember that the higher the number, the greater the degree of preference. Now, please tell me your preference to shop at . . . (READ ONE STORE AT A TIME)

STORE	NOT SO PREFERRED									GREATLY PREFERRED
1. Nordstrom	1	2	3	4	5	6	7	8	9	10
2. Macy's	1	2	3	4	5	6	7	8	9	10
3. Kmart	1	2	3	4	5	6	7	8	9	10
4. Kohl's	1	2	3	4	5	6	7	8	9	10
5. JCPenney	1	2	3	4	5	6	7	8	9	10
6. Neiman Marcus	1	2	3	4	5	6	7	8	9	10
7. Marshalls	1	2	3	4	5	6	7	8	9	10
8. Saks Fifth Avenue	1	2	3	4	5	6	7	8	9	10
9. Sears	1	2	3	4	5	6	7	8	9	10
10. Wal-Mart	1	2	3	4	5	6	7	8	9	10

Personal Questionnaire

(HAND DEPARTMENT STORE CARDS TO THE RESPONDENT) Here is a set of department store names, each written on a separate card. Please examine these cards carefully. (GIVE RESPONDENT TIME) Now, please examine these cards again and pull out the card that has the name of the store you like the most, that is, your most preferred store for shopping. (RECORD THE STORE NAME AND KEEP THIS CARD WITH YOU) Now, please examine the remaining nine cards. Of these remaining nine stores, what is your most preferred store for shopping? (REPEAT THIS PROCEDURE SEQUENTIALLY UNTIL THE RESPONDENT HAS ONLY ONE CARD LEFT)

	STORE RANK	NAME OF THE STORE
1.	1	_____
2.	2	_____
3.	3	_____
4.	4	_____
5.	5	_____
6.	6	_____
7.	7	_____
8.	8	_____
9.	9	_____
10.	10	_____

Electronic Questionnaire

This question for e-mail and Internet questionnaires will be very similar to that for the mail questionnaire; in all these methods, the questionnaire is self-administered by the respondent. ■

Individual Question Content

Once the information needed is specified and the type of interviewing method decided, the next step is to determine individual question content: what to include in individual questions.

Is the Question Necessary?

Every question in a questionnaire should contribute to the information needed or serve some specific purpose. If there is no satisfactory use for the data resulting from a question, that question should be eliminated. As illustrated in the opening example, a hard look at the 1990 Census of Population short form resulted in the elimination of questions pertaining to five subjects.

In certain situations, however, questions may be asked that are not directly related to the information that is needed. It is useful to ask some neutral questions at the beginning of the questionnaire to establish involvement and rapport, particularly when the topic of the questionnaire is sensitive or controversial. Sometimes filler questions are asked to disguise the purpose or sponsorship of the project. Rather than limiting the questions to the brand of interest, questions about competing brands may also be included to disguise the sponsorship. For example, a survey on personal computers sponsored by HP may also include filler questions related to Dell and Apple. Questions unrelated to the immediate problem may sometimes be included to generate client support for the project. At times, certain questions may be duplicated for the purpose of assessing reliability or validity.[5]

Are Several Questions Needed Instead of One?

Once we have ascertained that a question is necessary, we must make sure that it is sufficient to get the desired information. Sometimes, several questions are needed to obtain the required information in an unambiguous manner. Consider the question,

> "Do you think Coca-Cola is a tasty and refreshing soft drink?"   (Incorrect)

double-barreled question

A single question that attempts to cover two issues. Such questions can be confusing to respondents and result in ambiguous responses.

A "yes" answer will presumably be clear, but what if the answer is "no"? Does this mean that the respondent thinks that Coca-Cola is not tasty, that it is not refreshing, or that it is neither tasty nor refreshing? Such a question is called a **double-barreled question**, because two or more questions are combined into one. To obtain the required information unambiguously, two distinct questions should be asked:

> "Do you think Coca-Cola is a tasty soft drink?" and
> "Do you think Coca-Cola is a refreshing soft drink?"   (Correct)

Another example of multiple questions embedded in a single question is the "why" question. In the context of the department store study, consider the question,

> "Why do you shop at Nike Town?"   (Incorrect)

The possible answers may include "to buy athletic shoes," "it is more conveniently located than other stores," and "it was recommended by my best friend." Each of these answers relates to a different question embedded in the "why" question. The first answer tells why the respondent shops in the athletic merchandise store, the second answer reveals what the respondent likes about Nike Town as compared to other stores, and the third answer tells how the respondent learned about Nike Town. The three answers are not comparable and any one answer may not be sufficient. Complete information may be obtained by asking two separate questions:

> "What do you like about Nike Town as compared to other stores?" and
> "How did you first happen to shop in Nike Town?"   (Correct)

Most "why" questions about the use of a product or choice alternative involve two aspects: (1) attributes of the product, and (2) influences leading to knowledge of it.[6]

ACTIVE RESEARCH

Old Navy: Quality and Style Are Never Old

Visit www.oldnavy.com and conduct an Internet search using a search engine and your library's online database to obtain information on Old Navy's marketing program.

As the CEO of Old Navy, what would you do to improve consumers' perceptions of the quality of your brand?

Formulate a double-barreled question to determine consumer perceptions of the quality and style of Old Navy clothing. Then reformulate this question to obtain unambiguous answers.

Overcoming Inability to Answer

Researchers should not assume that respondents can provide accurate or reasonable answers to all questions. The researcher should attempt to overcome the respondents' inability to answer. Certain factors limit the respondents' ability to provide the desired information. The respondents may not be informed, may not remember, or may be unable to articulate certain types of responses.

Is the Respondent Informed?

Respondents are often asked about topics on which they are not informed. A husband may not be informed about monthly expenses for groceries and department store purchases if it is the wife who makes these purchases, or vice versa. Research has shown that respondents will often answer questions even though they are uninformed, as the following example shows.

Real Research

The Complaint About Consumer Complaints

In one study, respondents were asked to express their degree of agreement or disagreement with the following statement: "The National Bureau of Consumer Complaints provides an effective means for consumers who have purchased a defective product to obtain relief." As many as 96.1 percent of the lawyers and 95 percent of the general public who responded expressed an opinion. Even with a "don't know" option in the response set, 51.9 percent of the lawyers and 75.0 percent of the public still expressed an opinion about the National Bureau of Consumer Complaints. Why should these high response rates be problematic? Because there is no such entity as the National Bureau of Consumer Complaints![7] ■

filter questions
An initial question in a questionnaire that screens potential respondents to ensure they meet the requirements of the sample.

In situations where not all respondents are likely to be informed about the topic of interest, **filter questions** that measure familiarity, product use, and past experience should be asked before questions about the topics themselves.[8] Filter questions enable the researcher to filter out respondents who are not adequately informed.

The department store questionnaire included questions related to 10 different department stores, ranging from prestigious stores to discount stores. It was likely that many respondents would not be sufficiently informed about all the stores, so information on familiarity and frequency of patronage was obtained for each store (see Chapter 1). This allowed for separate analysis of data on stores about which the respondents were not informed. A "don't know" option appears to reduce uninformed responses without reducing the overall response rate or the response rate for questions about which the respondents have information. Hence, this option should be provided when the researcher expects that respondents may not be adequately informed about the subject of the question.[9]

Can the Respondent Remember?

Many things that we might expect everyone to know are remembered by only a few. Test this out on yourself. Can you answer the following?

> What is the brand name of the shirt you were wearing two weeks ago?
> What did you have for lunch a week ago?
> What were you doing a month ago at noon?
> How many gallons of soft drinks did you consume during the last four weeks?   (Incorrect)

These questions are incorrect because they exceed the ability of the respondents to remember. Evidence indicates that consumers are particularly poor at remembering quantities of products consumed. In situations where factual data were available for comparison, it was found that consumer reports of product usage exceeded actual usage by 100 percent or more.[10] Thus, soft drink consumption may be better obtained by asking:

> How often do you consume soft drinks in a typical week?
>
> i. _____ Less than once a week
> ii. _____ 1 to 3 times per week
> iii. _____ 4 to 6 times per week
> iv. _____ 7 or more times per week   (Correct)

telescoping
A psychological phenomenon that takes place when an individual telescopes or compresses time by remembering an event as occurring more recently than it actually occurred.

The inability to remember leads to errors of omission, telescoping, and creation. *Omission* is the inability to recall an event that actually took place. **Telescoping** takes place when an individual telescopes or compresses time by remembering an event as occurring more recently than it actually occurred.[11] For example, a respondent reports three trips to the supermarket in the last two weeks when, in fact, one of these trips was made 18 days ago. *Creation* error takes place when a respondent "remembers" an event that did not actually occur.

The ability to remember an event is influenced by (1) the event itself, (2) the time elapsed since the event, and (3) the presence or absence of events that would aid memory. We tend to remember events that are important or unusual or that occur frequently. People remember their wedding anniversary and birthday. Likewise, more recent events are remembered better. A grocery shopper is more likely to remember what was purchased on the last shopping trip as compared to what was bought three shopping trips ago.

Research indicates that questions that do not provide the respondent with cues to the event, and rely on unaided recall, can underestimate the actual occurrence of an event. For example, unaided recall of soft drink commercials could be measured by questions like, "What brands of soft drinks do you remember being advertised last night on TV?" The aided recall approach attempts to stimulate the respondent's memory by providing cues related to the event of interest. The aided recall approach would list a number of soft drink brands and then ask, "Which of these brands were advertised last night on TV?" In presenting cues, the researcher must guard against biasing the responses by employing several successive levels of stimulation. The influence of stimulation on responses can then be analyzed to select an appropriate level of stimulation.

Can the Respondent Articulate?

Respondents may be unable to articulate certain types of responses. For example, if asked to describe the atmosphere of the department store they would prefer to patronize, most respondents may be unable to phrase their answers. On the other hand, if the respondents are provided with alternative descriptions of store atmosphere, they will be able to indicate the one they like the best. If the respondents are unable to articulate their responses to a question, they are likely to ignore that question and may refuse to respond to the rest of the questionnaire. Thus respondents should be given aids, such as pictures, maps, and descriptions, to help them articulate their responses.

Overcoming Unwillingness to Answer

Even if respondents are able to answer a particular question, they may be unwilling to do so, either because too much effort is required, the situation or context may not seem appropriate for disclosure, no legitimate purpose or need for the information requested is apparent, or the information requested is sensitive.

Effort Required of the Respondents

Most respondents are unwilling to devote a lot of effort to provide information. Hence, the researcher should minimize the effort required of the respondents. Suppose the researcher is interested in determining from which departments in a store the respondent purchased merchandise on the most recent shopping trip. This information can be obtained in at least two ways. The researcher could ask the respondent to list all the departments from which merchandise was purchased on the most recent shopping trip, or the researcher could provide a list of departments and ask the respondent to check the applicable ones:

> Please list all the departments from which you purchased merchandise
> on your most recent shopping trip to a department store.   (Incorrect)

In the list that follows, please check all the departments from which you purchased merchandise on your most recent shopping trip to a department store.

1.	Women's dresses	_____
2.	Men's apparel	_____
3.	Children's apparel	_____
4.	Cosmetics	_____
	.	
	.	
	.	
17.	Jewelry	_____
18.	Other (please specify)	_____	(Correct)

The second option is preferable, because it requires less effort from respondents.

Context

Some questions may seem appropriate in certain contexts but not in others. For example, questions about personal hygiene habits may be appropriate when asked in a survey sponsored by the American Medical Association, but not in one sponsored by a fast-food restaurant. Respondents are unwilling to respond to questions that they consider inappropriate for the given context. Sometimes, the researcher can manipulate the context in which the questions are asked so that the questions seem appropriate. For example, before asking for information on personal hygiene in a survey for a fast-food restaurant, the context could be manipulated by making the following statement. "As a fast-food restaurant, we are very concerned about providing a clean and hygienic environment for our customers. Therefore, we would like to ask you some questions related to personal hygiene."

Legitimate Purpose

Respondents are also unwilling to divulge information that they do not see as serving a legitimate purpose. Why should a firm marketing cereals want to know their age, income, and occupation? Explaining why the data are needed can make the request for the information seem legitimate and increase the respondents' willingness to answer. A statement such as, "To determine how the consumption of cereal and preferences for cereal brands vary among people of different ages, incomes, and occupations, we need information on . . ." can make the request for information seem legitimate.

Sensitive Information

Respondents are unwilling to disclose, at least accurately, sensitive information because this may cause embarrassment or threaten the respondent's prestige or self-image. If pressed for the answer, respondents may give biased responses, especially during personal interviews (see Chapter 6, Table 6.2).[12] Sensitive topics include money, family life, political and religious beliefs, and involvement in accidents or crimes. The techniques described in the following section can be adopted to increase the likelihood of obtaining information that respondents are unwilling to give.

Increasing the Willingness of Respondents

Respondents may be encouraged to provide information that they are unwilling to give by the following techniques.[13]

1. Place sensitive topics at the end of the questionnaire. By then, initial mistrust has been overcome, rapport has been created, the legitimacy of the project has been established, and respondents are more willing to give information.
2. Preface the question with a statement that the behavior of interest is common. For example, before requesting information on credit card debt, say, "Recent studies show that most Americans are in debt." This technique, called the *use of counterbiasing statements*, is further illustrated by the following example.[14]

Real Research   Public Versus Private

A recent poll conducted by Gallup (www.gallup.com) sought to obtain information on whether personal information about political candidates or ordinary citizens should be disclosed to the public. This question was prefaced with the following statement: "The question of where to draw the line on the matter of privacy has been much debated, with some saying that the standards should be different for candidates for important public office than for ordinary citizens." This statement increased the willingness of the people to respond. ■

3. Ask the question using the third-person technique (see Chapter 5): Phrase the question as if it referred to other people.
4. Hide the question in a group of other questions that respondents are willing to answer. The entire list of questions can then be asked quickly.
5. Provide response categories rather than asking for specific figures. Do not ask, "What is your household's annual income?" Instead, ask the respondent to check the appropriate income category: under $25,000, $25,001–$50,000, $50,001–$75,000, or over $75,000. In personal interviews, give the respondents cards that list the numbered choices. The respondents then indicate their responses by number.

6. Use randomized techniques. In these techniques, respondents are presented with two questions, one sensitive and the other a neutral question with a known probability of a "yes" response (e.g., "Is your birthday in March?"). They are asked to select one question randomly, for example, by flipping a coin. The respondent then answers the selected question "yes" or "no," without telling the researcher which question is being answered. Given the overall probability of a "yes" response, the probability of selecting the sensitive question, and the probability of a "yes" response to the neutral question, the researcher can determine the probability of a "yes" response to the sensitive question using the law of probability. However, the researcher cannot determine which respondents have answered "yes" to the sensitive question.[15]

Choosing Question Structure

A question may be unstructured or structured. In the following sections, we define unstructured questions and discuss their relative advantages and disadvantages and then consider the major types of structured questions: multiple choice, dichotomous, and scales.[16]

Unstructured Questions

unstructured questions
Open-ended questions that respondents answer in their own words.

Unstructured questions are open-ended questions that respondents answer in their own words. They are also referred to as *free-response* or *free-answer* questions. The following are some examples:

- What is your occupation?
- What do you think of people who patronize discount department stores?
- Who is your favorite political figure?

Open-ended questions are good as first questions on a topic. They enable the respondents to express general attitudes and opinions that can help the researcher interpret their responses to structured questions. Unstructured questions have a much less biasing influence on response than structured questions. Respondents are free to express any views. Their comments and explanations can provide the researcher with rich insights. Hence, unstructured questions are useful in exploratory research.

A principal disadvantage is that potential for interviewer bias is high. Whether the interviewers record the answers verbatim or write down only the main points, the data depend on the skills of the interviewers. Tape recorders should be used if verbatim reporting is important.

Another major disadvantage of unstructured questions is that the coding of responses is costly and time-consuming.[17] The coding procedures required to summarize responses in a format useful for data analysis and interpretation can be extensive. Implicitly, unstructured or open-ended questions give extra weight to respondents who are more articulate. Also, unstructured questions are not suitable for self- or computer-administered questionnaires (mail, mail panel, CAPI, e-mail, and Internet), because respondents tend to be more brief in writing than in speaking.

Precoding can overcome some of the disadvantages of unstructured questions. Expected responses are recorded in multiple-choice format, although the question is presented to the respondents as an open-ended question. Based on the respondent's reply, the interviewer selects the appropriate response category. This approach may be satisfactory when the respondent can easily formulate the response, and it is easy to develop precoded categories because the response alternatives are limited. For example, this approach may be used to obtain information on ownership of appliances. It has also been used successfully in business surveys, as shown by the following example.

Real Research

Assessing Access Attitudes

A major telecommunications firm conducted a national telephone survey to determine the attitudes of businesses toward telecommunication services . One of the questions was asked as an open-ended question with precoded responses.[18]

Which company or companies is your business presently using for long-distance telephone service? If more than one, please indicate the names of all the companies. (ASK AS AN OPEN-ENDED QUESTION. ALLOW FOR MULTIPLE RESPONSES AND SCORE AS FOLLOWS.)

1. _____ VERIZON
2. _____ SPRINT NEXTEL
3. _____ QWEST
4. _____ AT&T
5. _____ Regional Bell operating co. (insert name)
6. _____ Other (specify)
7. _____ Don't know/no answer ∎

In general, open-ended questions are useful in exploratory research and as opening questions. Otherwise, their disadvantages outweigh their advantages in a large survey.[19]

Structured Questions

structured questions
Questions that prespecify the set of response alternatives and the response format. A structured question could be multiple choice, dichotomous, or a scale.

Structured questions specify the set of response alternatives and the response format. A structured question may be multiple choice, dichotomous, or a scale.

MULTIPLE-CHOICE QUESTIONS   In multiple-choice questions, the researcher provides a choice of answers and respondents are asked to select one or more of the alternatives given. Consider the following question.

Do you intend to buy a new car within the next six months?

_____ Definitely will not buy
_____ Probably will not buy
_____ Undecided
_____ Probably will buy
_____ Definitely will buy
_____ Other (please specify)

Several of the issues discussed in Chapter 9 with respect to itemized rating scales also apply to multiple-choice answers. Two additional concerns in designing multiple-choice questions are the number of alternatives that should be included and order or position bias.

The response alternatives should include the set of all possible choices. The general guideline is to list all alternatives that may be of importance and include an alternative labeled "Other (please specify)," as shown here. The response alternatives should be mutually exclusive. Respondents should also be able to identify one, and only one, alternative, unless the researcher specifically allows two or more choices (for example, "Please indicate all the brands of soft drinks that you have consumed in the past week"). If the response alternatives are numerous, consider using more than one question to reduce the information-processing demands on the respondents.

order or position bias
A respondent's tendency to check an alternative merely because it occupies a certain position or is listed in a certain order.

Order or position bias is the respondents' tendency to check an alternative merely because it occupies a certain position or is listed in a certain order. Respondents tend to check the first or the last statement in a list, particularly the first. For a list of numbers (quantities or prices), there is a bias toward the central value on the list. To control for order bias, several forms of the questionnaire should be prepared with the order in which the alternatives are listed varied from form to form. Unless the alternatives represent ordered categories, each alternative should appear once in each of the extreme positions, once in the middle, and once somewhere in between.[20]

Multiple-choice questions overcome many of the disadvantages of open-ended questions, because interviewer bias is reduced and these questions are administered quickly. Also, coding and processing of data are much less costly and time-consuming. In self-administered questionnaires, respondent cooperation is improved if the majority of the questions are structured.

Multiple-choice questions are not without disadvantages. Considerable effort is required to design effective multiple-choice questions. Exploratory research using open-ended questions may be required to determine the appropriate response alternatives. It is difficult to obtain information on alternatives not listed. Even if an "Other (please specify)" category is included, respondents tend to choose among the listed alternatives. In addition, showing respondents the list of possible answers produces biased responses. There is also the potential for order bias.[21]

dichotomous question
A structured question with only two response alternatives, such as yes and no.

DICHOTOMOUS QUESTIONS   A **dichotomous question** has only two response alternatives: yes or no, agree or disagree, and so on. Often, the two alternatives of interest are supplemented by a neutral alternative, such as "no opinion," "don't know," "both," or "none."[22] The question asked before about intentions to buy a new car as a multiple-choice question can also be asked as a dichotomous question.

Do you intend to buy a new car within the next six months?

_____ Yes
_____ No
_____ Don't know

The decision to use a dichotomous question should be guided by whether the respondents approach the issue as a yes-or-no question. Although decisions are often characterized as series of binary or dichotomous choices, the underlying decision-making process may reflect uncertainty, which can best be captured by multiple-choice responses. For example, two individuals may be equally likely to buy a new car within the next six months if the economic conditions remain favorable. However, one individual, who is being optimistic about the economy, will answer "yes," whereas the other, feeling pessimistic, will answer "no."

Another issue in the design of dichotomous questions is whether to include a neutral response alternative. If it is not included, respondents are forced to choose between "yes" and "no" even if they feel indifferent. On the other hand, if a neutral alternative is included, respondents can avoid taking a position on the issue, thereby biasing the results. We offer the following guidelines. If a substantial proportion of the respondents can be expected to be neutral, include a neutral alternative. If the proportion of neutral respondents is expected to be small, avoid the neutral alternative.

The general advantages and disadvantages of dichotomous questions are very similar to those of multiple-choice questions. Dichotomous questions are the easiest type of questions to code and analyze, but they have one acute problem: The response can be influenced by the wording of the question. To illustrate, the statement, "Individuals are more to blame than social conditions for crime and lawlessness in this country," produced agreement from 59.6 percent of the respondents. However, on a matched sample that responded to the opposite statement, "Social conditions are more to blame than individuals for crime and lawlessness in this country," 43.2 percent (as opposed to 40.4 percent) agreed.[23] To overcome this problem, the question should be framed in one way on one-half of the questionnaires and in the opposite way on the other half. This is referred to as the *split ballot technique.*

SCALES   Scales were discussed in detail in Chapters 8 and 9. To illustrate the difference between scales and other kinds of structured questions, consider the question about intentions to buy a new car. One way of framing this using a scale is as follows:

Do you intend to buy a new car within the next six months?

Definitely will not buy	Probably will not buy	Undecided	Probably will buy	Definitely will buy
1	2	3	4	5

This is only one of several scales that could be used to ask this question (see Chapters 8 and 9). As shown in the following example, a survey may contain different types of questions.

Real Research   ## Question Structure in GAP

The Global Airline Performance (GAP) study is a survey conducted to measure the opinions of air travelers on 22 airlines departing from 30 airports across the world. It reaches 240,000 passengers each year and is conducted in seven languages. This survey uses different types of structured questions, including multiple choice, dichotomous, and scales, as illustrated in the following.[24]

Q. How did you make your reservation? (Please pick ONE only)

_____ Airline Web site
_____ Airline phone reservations or ticket office
_____ Through travel agent
_____ Other

Q. Are you using an e-ticket (electronic paperless ticket) on this trip?

_____ Yes
_____ No

Q. Based on your experience of today's flight, would you select this airline for your next trip on this route?

_____ Definitely would (5)
_____ Probably would (4)
_____ Might/might not (3)
_____ Probably not (2)
_____ Definitely not (1) ■

ACTIVE RESEARCH

Estée Lauder: The Sweet Smell of Perfume

Conduct an Internet search using a search engine and your library's online database to obtain information on consumers' attitudes toward perfumes.

As the marketing chief for Estée Lauder perfumes, how would you instill positive consumer attitudes toward your brands?

Obtain information on consumers' attitudes toward Estée Lauder perfumes using an unstructured, a multiple-choice, a dichotomous, and a scaling question.

Choosing Question Wording

Question wording is the translation of the desired question content and structure into words that respondents can clearly and easily understand. Deciding on question wording is perhaps the most critical and difficult task in developing a questionnaire, as illustrated by the Census 2000 questionnaire in the opening example. If a question is worded poorly, respondents may refuse to answer it or may answer it incorrectly. The first condition, known as *item nonresponse*, can increase the complexity of data analysis.[25] The second condition leads to response error, discussed earlier (see also Chapter 3). Unless the respondents and the researcher assign exactly the same meaning to the question, the results will be seriously biased.[26]

To avoid these problems, we offer the following guidelines: (1) define the issue, (2) use ordinary words, (3) use unambiguous words, (4) avoid leading questions, (5) avoid implicit alternatives, (6) avoid implicit assumptions, (7) avoid generalizations and estimates, and (8) use positive and negative statements.

Define the Issue

A question should clearly define the issue being addressed. Beginning journalists are admonished to define the issue in terms of who, what, when, where, why, and way (the six Ws).[27] These can also serve as guidelines for defining the issue in a question. (See Chapter 3 for an application of these guidelines to descriptive research.) Consider the following question:

Which brand of shampoo do you use? (Incorrect)

On the surface, this may seem to be a well-defined question, but we may reach a different conclusion when we examine it under the microscope of who, what, when, and where. "Who" in this question refers to the respondent. It is not clear, though, whether the researcher is referring to the brand the respondent uses personally or the brand used by the household. "What" is the brand of shampoo. However, what if more than one brand of shampoo is being used? Should the respondent mention the most preferred brand, the brand used most often, the brand used most recently, or the brand that comes to mind first? "When" is not clear; does the researcher mean last time, last week, last month, last year, or ever? As for "where," it is implied that the shampoo is used at home, but this is not stated clearly. A better wording for this question would be:

Which brand or brands of shampoo have you personally used at home during the last month? In case of more than one brand, please list all the brands that apply. (Correct)

Use Ordinary Words

Ordinary words should be used in a questionnaire and they should match the vocabulary level of the respondents.[28] When choosing words, keep in mind that the average person in the United States has a high school, not a college, education. For certain respondent groups, the education level is even lower. For example, the author did a project for a major telecommunications firm that operates primarily in rural areas. The average educational level in these areas is less than high school, and many respondents had only fourth- to sixth-grade education. Technical jargon should also be avoided. Most respondents do not understand technical marketing words. For example, instead of asking,

"Do you think the distribution of soft drinks is adequate?"   (Incorrect)
ask,
"Do you think soft drinks are readily available when you want to buy them?"   (Correct)

Use Unambiguous Words

The words used in a questionnaire should have a single meaning that is known to the respondents. A number of words that appear to be unambiguous have different meanings to different people.[29] These include "usually," "normally," "frequently," "often," "regularly," "occasionally," and "sometimes." Consider the following question:

In a typical month, how often do you shop in department stores?

_____ Never
_____ Occasionally
_____ Sometimes
_____ Often
_____ Regularly   (Incorrect)

The answers to this question are fraught with response bias, because the words used to describe category labels have different meanings for different respondents. Three respondents who shop once a month may check three different categories: occasionally, sometimes, and often. A much better wording for this question would be the following:

In a typical month, how often do you shop in department stores?

_____ Less than once
_____ 1 or 2 times
_____ 3 or 4 times
_____ More than 4 times   (Correct)

Note that this question provides a consistent frame of reference for all respondents. Response categories have been objectively defined, and respondents are no longer free to interpret them in their own way.

Additionally, all-inclusive or all-exclusive words may be understood differently by different people. Some examples of such words are "all," "always," "any," "anybody," "ever," and "every." Such words should be avoided. To illustrate, "any" could mean "every," "some," or "one only" to different respondents, depending on how they look at it.

In deciding on the choice of words, researchers should consult a dictionary and thesaurus and ask the following questions of each word used:

1. Does it mean what we intended?
2. Does it have any other meanings?
3. If so, does the context make the intended meaning clear?
4. Does the word have more than one pronunciation?
5. Is there any word of similar pronunciation that might be confused with this word?
6. Is a simpler word or phrase suggested?

The U.S. Census Bureau took great pains to use ordinary and unambiguous words in the Census 2000 questionnaires, which not only improved the response rate but also resulted in more accurate data (see opening example).

Avoid Leading or Biasing Questions

leading question
A question that gives the respondent a clue as to what answer is desired or leads the respondent to answer in a certain way.

acquiescence bias (yea-saying)
This bias is the result of some respondents' tendency to agree with the direction of a leading question (yea-saying).

A **leading question** is one that clues the respondent to what answer is desired or leads the respondent to answer in a certain way. Some respondents have a tendency to agree with whatever way the question is leading them to answer. This tendency is known as **yea-saying** and results in a bias called **acquiescence bias**. Consider the following question:

Do you think that patriotic Americans should buy imported automobiles when that would put American labor out of work?

_____ Yes
_____ No
_____ Don't know   (Incorrect)

This question would lead respondents to a "No" answer. After all, how can patriotic Americans put American labor out of work? Therefore, this question would not help determine the preferences of Americans for imported versus domestic automobiles. A better question would be:

Do you think that Americans should buy imported automobiles?

_____ Yes
_____ No
_____ Don't know   (Correct)

Bias may also arise when respondents are given clues about the sponsor of the project. Respondents tend to respond favorably toward the sponsor. The question, "Is Colgate your favorite toothpaste?" is likely to bias the responses in favor of Colgate. A more unbiased way of obtaining this information would be to ask, "What is your favorite toothpaste brand?" Likewise, the mention of a prestigious or nonprestigious name can bias the response, as in, "Do you agree with the American Dental Association that Colgate is effective in preventing cavities?" An unbiased question would be to ask, "Is Colgate effective in preventing cavities?"[30]

Avoid Implicit Alternatives

implicit alternative
An alternative that is not explicitly expressed.

An alternative that is not explicitly expressed in the options is an **implicit alternative**. Making an implied alternative explicit may increase the percentage of people selecting that alternative, as in the two following questions.

1. Do you like to fly when traveling short distances?   (Incorrect)
2. Do you like to fly when traveling short distances,
   or would you rather drive?   (Correct)

In the first question, the alternative of driving is only implicit, but in the second question, it is explicit. The first question is likely to yield a greater preference for flying than the second question.

Questions with implicit alternatives should be avoided unless there are specific reasons for including them.[31] When the alternatives are close in preference or large in number, the alternatives at the end of the list have a greater chance of being selected. To overcome this bias, the split ballot technique should be used to rotate the order in which the alternatives appear.

Avoid Implicit Assumptions

Questions should not be worded so that the answer is dependent upon implicit assumptions about what will happen as a consequence. Implicit assumptions are assumptions that are not stated in the question, as in the following example.[32]

1. Are you in favor of a balanced budget?   (Incorrect)
2. Are you in favor of a balanced budget if it would result in an increase
   in the personal income tax?   (Correct)

Implicit in question 1 are the consequences that will arise as a result of a balanced budget. There might be a cut in defense expenditures, increase in personal income tax, cut in social programs, and so on. Question 2 is a better way to word this question. Question 1's failure to make its assumptions explicit would result in overestimating the respondents' support for a balanced budget.

Avoid Generalizations and Estimates

Questions should be specific, not general. Moreover, questions should be worded so that the respondent does not have to make generalizations or compute estimates. Suppose we were interested in households' annual per capita expenditure on groceries. If we asked respondents

"What is the annual per capita expenditure on groceries in your household?"   (Incorrect)

they would first have to determine the annual expenditure on groceries by multiplying the monthly expenditure on groceries by 12 or the weekly expenditure by 52. Then they would have to divide the annual amount by the number of persons in the household. Most respondents would be unwilling or unable to perform these calculations. A better way of obtaining the required information would be to ask the respondents two simple questions:

"What is the monthly (or weekly) expenditure on groceries in your household?"
and
"How many members are there in your household?"   (Correct)

The researcher can then perform the necessary calculations.

Dual Statements: Positive and Negative

Many questions, particularly those measuring attitudes and lifestyles, are worded as statements to which respondents indicate their degree of agreement or disagreement. Evidence indicates that the response obtained is influenced by the directionality of the statements: whether they are stated positively or negatively. In these cases, it is better to use dual statements, some of which are positive and the others negative. Two different questionnaires could be prepared. One questionnaire would contain half negative and half positive statements in an interspersed way. The direction of these statements would be reversed in the other questionnaire. An example of dual statements was provided in the summated Likert scale in Chapter 9 designed to measure attitudes toward Sears; some statements about Sears were positive whereas others were negative.

ACTIVE RESEARCH

FedEx: The Big Caters to the Small

Visit www.fedex.com and conduct an Internet search using a search engine and your library's online database to obtain information on the overnight package delivery market. Write a brief report.

As the marketing director for FedEx, how would you penetrate the important small business market for overnight package delivery?

Evaluate the wording of the following question asked of small business owners/CEOs: "If FedEx were to introduce a new overnight delivery service for small businesses, how likely are you to adopt it?"

Determining the Order of Questions

Opening Questions

The opening questions can be crucial in gaining the confidence and cooperation of respondents. The opening questions should be interesting, simple, and nonthreatening. Questions that ask respondents for their opinions can be good opening questions, because most people like to express their opinions. Sometimes such questions are asked even though they are unrelated to the research problem and their responses are not analyzed.[33]

Real Research   Opening Opinion Question Opens the Door to Cooperation

The American Chicle Youth Poll was commissioned by the American Chicle Group, Pfizer Company (www.pfizer.com), and conducted by GfK NOP (www.gfkamerica.com). A nationwide cross-section of 1,000 American young people, age 8 to 17 and attending school, was interviewed. The questionnaire contained a simple opening question asking an opinion about living in the local town or city.

To begin with, I'd like to know, how much do you like living in this (town/city)? Would you say you like it a *lot*, a *little*, or *not too much?*

A lot   _____
A little   _____
Not too much   _____
Don't know   _____ ■

In some instances, it is necessary to screen or qualify the respondents, or determine whether the respondent is eligible to participate in the interview. In these cases, the qualifying questions serve as the opening questions.

Project Research

Opening Question

In the department store project, the questionnaire was to be answered by the male or female head of the household who did most of the shopping in department stores. The first question asked was, "Who in your household does most of the shopping in department stores?" Thus the opening question helped in identifying the eligible respondents. It also gained cooperation because of its simple and nonthreatening nature. ■

Type of Information

The type of information obtained in a questionnaire may be classified as (1) basic information, (2) classification information, and (3) identification information. Basic information relates directly to the research problem. **Classification information**, consisting of socioeconomic and demographic characteristics, is used to classify the respondents and understand the results. **Identification information** includes name, postal address, e-mail address, and telephone number. Identification information may be obtained for a variety of purposes, including verifying that the respondents listed were actually interviewed, remitting promised incentives, and so on. As a general guideline, basic information should be obtained first, followed by classification and, finally, identification information. The basic information is of greatest importance to the research project and should be obtained first, before we risk alienating the respondents by asking a series of personal questions. The questionnaire given in problem 7 (see exercises for this chapter) incorrectly obtains identification (name) and some classification (demographic) information in the beginning.

classification information
Socioeconomic and demographic characteristics used to classify respondents.

identification information
A type of information obtained in a questionnaire that includes name, postal address, e-mail address, and phone number.

Difficult Questions

Difficult questions or questions that are sensitive, embarrassing, complex, or dull should be placed late in the sequence. After rapport has been established and the respondents become involved, they are less likely to object to these questions. Thus in the department store project, information about credit card debt was asked at the end of the section on basic information. Likewise, income should be the last question in the classification section, and telephone number the final item in the identification section.

Effect on Subsequent Questions

Questions asked early in a sequence can influence the responses to subsequent questions. As a rule of thumb, general questions should precede specific questions. This prevents specific questions from biasing responses to general questions. Consider the following sequence of questions:

Q1: "What considerations are important to you in selecting
    a department store?"   (Incorrect)
Q2: "In selecting a department store, how important is convenience
    of location?"   (Correct)

Note that the first question is general, whereas the second is specific. If these questions were asked in the reverse order, respondents would be clued about convenience of location and would be more likely to give this response to the general question.

Going from general to specific is called the **funnel approach**. The funnel approach is particularly useful when information has to be obtained about respondents' general choice behavior and their evaluations of specific products.[34] Sometimes the inverted funnel approach may be useful. In this approach, questioning begins with specific questions and concludes with the general questions. The respondents are compelled to provide specific

funnel approach
A strategy for ordering questions in a questionnaire in which the sequence starts with general questions that are followed by progressively specific questions in order to prevent specific questions from biasing general questions.

information before making general evaluations. This approach is useful when respondents have no strong feelings or have not formulated a point of view.

Logical Order

Questions should be asked in a logical order. All of the questions that deal with a particular topic should be asked before beginning a new topic. When switching topics, brief transitional phrases should be used to help respondents switch their train of thought.

branching questions
Question used to guide an interviewer through a survey by directing the interviewer to different spots on the questionnaire depending on the answers given.

Branching questions should be designed carefully.[35] **Branching questions** direct respondents to different places in the questionnaire based on how they respond to the question at hand. These questions ensure that all possible contingencies are covered. They also help reduce interviewer and respondent error and encourage complete responses. Skip patterns based on the branching questions can become quite complex. A simple way to account for all contingencies is to prepare a flowchart of the logical possibilities and then develop branching questions and instructions based on it. A flowchart used to assess the use of credit in store purchases is shown in Figure 10.2.

Placement of branching questions is important, and the following guidelines should be followed: (1) The question being branched (the one to which the respondent is being directed) should be placed as close as possible to the question causing the branching, and (2) the branching questions should be ordered so that the respondents cannot anticipate what additional information will be required. Otherwise, the respondents may discover that they can avoid detailed questions by giving certain answers to branching questions. For example, the respondents should first be asked if they have seen any of the listed commercials before they are asked to evaluate commercials. Otherwise, the respondents will quickly discover that

FIGURE 10.2

Flowchart for Questionnaire Design

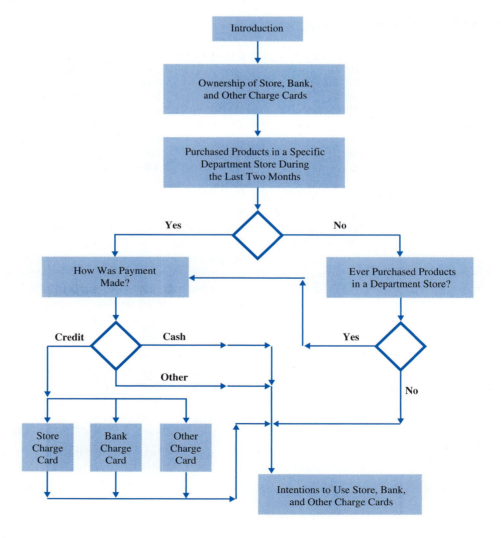

stating they have seen a commercial leads to detailed questions about that commercial and that they can avoid detailed questions by stating that they have not seen the commercial.

ACTIVE RESEARCH

Flat Panel Television Sets: The Market Is Anything but Flat

Conduct an Internet search using a search engine and your library's online database to obtain information on consumers' perceptions, preferences, and purchase intentions for flat panel television sets.

Specify the information needed and the order in which you would obtain information on consumers' perceptions, preferences, and purchase intentions for Samsung flat panel television sets.

As the vice president for marketing, what marketing strategies would you formulate to increase Samsung's penetration of the flat panel television market?

Form and Layout

The format, spacing, and positioning of questions can have a significant effect on the results, as illustrated by the Census 2000 questionnaire in the opening example. This is particularly important for self-administered questionnaires. Experiments on mail questionnaires for census of population revealed that questions at the top of the page received more attention than those placed at the bottom. Instructions printed in red made little difference except that they made the questionnaire appear more complicated to the respondents.

Project Research   ## Form and Layout

In the department store project, the questionnaire was divided into several parts. Part A contained the qualifying question, information on familiarity, frequency of shopping, evaluation of the 10 stores on each of the eight factors of the choice criteria, and preference ratings for the 10 stores. Part B contained questions on the relative importance attached to each factor of the choice criteria and the preference rankings of the 10 stores. Part C obtained information on lifestyles. Finally, part D obtained standard demographic and identification information. Identification information was obtained along with classification information, rather than in a separate part, so as to minimize its prominence. Dividing the questionnaire into parts in this manner provided natural transitions. It also alerted the interviewer and the respondent that, as each part began, a different kind of information was being solicited. ∎

It is a good practice to divide a questionnaire into several parts. Several parts may be needed for questions pertaining to the basic information. The questions in each part should be numbered, particularly when branching questions are used. Numbering of questions also makes the coding of responses easier. The questionnaires should preferably be precoded. In **precoding**, the codes to enter in the computer are printed on the questionnaire. Typically, the code identifies the line number and the column numbers in which a particular response will be entered. Note that when CATI or CAPI is used, the precoding is built into the software. Coding of questionnaires is explained in more detail in Chapter 14 on data preparation. Here we give an example of a precoded questionnaire. To conserve space, only part of the questionnaire is reproduced.

precoding
In questionnaire design, assigning a code to every conceivable response before data collection.

Real Research   ## Example of a Precoded Survey from *The American Lawyer* Magazine (www.americanlawyer.com)

The American Lawyer
A Confidential Survey of Our Subscribers

1. Considering all the times you pick it up, about how much time, in total, do you spend in reading or looking through a typical issue of *The American Lawyer?*

Less than 30 minutes	☐ -1	1 1/2 hours to 1 hour 59 minutes	☐ -4
30 to 59 minutes	☐ -2	2 hours to 2 hours 59 minutes	☐ -5
1 hour to 1 hour 29 minutes	☐ -3	3 hours or more	☐ -6

2. After you have finished reading an issue of *The American Lawyer,* what do you usually do with it?

Save entire issue for firm library . . . . ☐ -1	Place in a waiting room/public area . . . . ☐ -5
Save entire issue for home use . . . . ☐ -2	Discard it . . . . ☐ -6
Pass it along to others in my company . . . . ☐ -3	Other _____ ☐ -7
Clip and save items of interest . . . . ☐ -4	(Please specify)

3. *Not including yourself,* how many other people, on the average, would you estimate read or look through your personal copy (not the office copy) of *The American Lawyer*?

Number of additional readers per copy:

One . . . . ☐ -1	Five . . . . ☐ -5	10–14 . . . . ☐ -9
Two . . . . ☐ -2	Six . . . . ☐ -6	15 or more . . . . ☐ -x
Three . . . . ☐ -3	Seven . . . . ☐ -7	None . . . . ☐ -0
Four . . . . ☐ -4	8–9 . . . . ☐ -8	

Source: www.americanlawyer.com. ■

The questionnaires themselves should be numbered serially. This facilitates the control of questionnaires in the field as well as the coding and analysis. Numbering makes it easy to account for the questionnaires and to determine if any have been lost. A possible exception to this rule is mail questionnaires. If these are numbered, respondents assume that a given number identifies a particular respondent. Some respondents may refuse to participate or may answer differently under these conditions. However, recent research suggests that this loss of anonymity has little, if any, influence on the results.[36]

Reproduction of the Questionnaire

How a questionnaire is reproduced for administration can influence the results. For example, if the questionnaire is reproduced on poor-quality paper or is otherwise shabby in appearance, the respondents will think the project is unimportant and the quality of response will be adversely affected. Therefore, the questionnaire should be reproduced on good-quality paper and have a professional appearance.

When a printed questionnaire runs to several pages, it should take the form of a booklet rather than a number of sheets of paper clipped or stapled together. Booklets are easier for the interviewer and the respondents to handle and do not come apart with use as do clipped and stapled papers. They allow the use of double-page format for questions and look more professional.

Each question should be reproduced on a single page (or double-page spread). A researcher should avoid splitting a question, including its response categories. Split questions can mislead the interviewer or the respondent into thinking that the question has ended at the end of a page. This will result in answers based on incomplete questions.

Vertical response columns should be used for individual questions. It is easier for interviewers and respondents to read down a single column rather than sideways across several columns. Sideways formatting and splitting, done frequently to conserve space, should be avoided. This problem can be observed in *The American Lawyer* questionnaire.

The tendency to crowd questions together to make the questionnaire look shorter should be avoided. Overcrowded questions with little blank space between them can lead to errors in data collection and yield shorter and less informative replies. Moreover, they give the impression that the questionnaire is complex and can result in lower cooperation and completion rates. Although shorter questionnaires are more desirable than longer ones, the reduction in size should not be obtained at the expense of crowding.

Directions or instructions for individual questions should be placed as close to the questions as possible. Instructions relating to how the question should be administered or answered by the respondent should be placed just before the question. Instructions concerning how the answer should be recorded or how the probing should be done should be placed after the question (for more information on probing and other interviewing procedures, see Chapter 13). It is a common practice to distinguish instructions from questions by using distinctive type, such as capital letters. (See the department store project in the section titled "Effect of Interviewing Method on Questionnaire Design.")

Although color does not influence response rates to questionnaires, it can be employed advantageously in some respects. Color coding is useful for branching questions. The next question to which the respondent is directed is printed in a color that matches the space in which the answer to the branching question was recorded. Surveys directed at different respondent groups can be reproduced on different colored paper. In a mail survey conducted for a major telecommunications firm, the business questionnaire was printed on white paper, whereas the household questionnaire was printed on yellow paper.

The questionnaire should be reproduced in such a way that it is easy to read and answer. The type should be large and clear. Reading the questionnaire should not impose a strain. Several technologies allow researchers to obtain better print quality and simultaneously reduce costs. One effort along these lines resulted in a lowering of printing costs from $1,150 to $214.[37]

Pretesting

pretesting
The testing of the questionnaire on a small sample of respondents for the purpose of improving the questionnaire by identifying and eliminating potential problems.

Pretesting refers to the testing of the questionnaire on a small sample of respondents to identify and eliminate potential problems. Even the best questionnaire can be improved by pretesting. As a general rule, a questionnaire should not be used in the field survey without adequate pretesting. A pretest should be extensive, as illustrated by the Census 2000 questionnaire in the opening example. All aspects of the questionnaire should be tested, including question content, wording, sequence, form and layout, question difficulty, and instructions. The respondents in the pretest should be similar to those who will be included in the actual survey in terms of background characteristics, familiarity with the topic, and attitudes and behaviors of interest.[38] In other words, respondents for the pretest and for the actual survey should be drawn from the same population.

Pretests are best done by personal interviews, even if the actual survey is to be conducted by mail, telephone, or electronic means, because interviewers can observe respondents' reactions and attitudes. After the necessary changes have been made, another pretest could be conducted by mail, telephone, or electronic means if those methods are to be used in the actual survey. The latter pretests should reveal problems peculiar to the interviewing method. To the extent possible, a pretest should involve administering the questionnaire in an environment and context similar to that of the actual survey.

A variety of interviewers should be used for pretests. The project director, the researcher who developed the questionnaire, and other key members of the research team should conduct some pretest interviews. This will give them a good feel for potential problems and the nature of the expected data. Regular interviewers, however, should conduct most of the pretest interviews. It is good practice to employ both experienced and new interviewers. The experienced interviewers can easily perceive uneasiness, confusion, and resistance in the respondents. New interviewers can help the researcher identify interviewer-related problems. Ordinarily, the pretest sample size is small, varying from 15 to 30 respondents for the initial testing, depending on the heterogeneity of the target population. The sample size can increase substantially if the pretesting involves several stages or waves.

Protocol analysis and debriefing are two commonly used procedures in pretesting. In protocol analysis, the respondent is asked to "think aloud" while answering the questionnaire. Typically, the respondent's remarks are tape-recorded and analyzed to determine the reactions invoked by different parts of the questionnaire. Debriefing occurs after the questionnaire has been completed. Respondents are told that the questionnaire they just completed was a pretest and the objectives of pretesting are described to them. They are then asked to describe the meaning of each question, to explain their answers, and to state any problems they encountered while answering the questionnaire.

Editing involves correcting the questionnaire for the problems identified during pretesting. After each significant revision of the questionnaire, another pretest should be conducted, using a different sample of respondents. Sound pretesting involves several stages. One pretest is a bare minimum. Pretesting should be continued until no further changes are needed.

Finally, the responses obtained from the pretest should be coded and analyzed. The analysis of pretest responses can serve as a check on the adequacy of the problem definition and the data and analysis required to obtain the necessary information. The dummy tables prepared before developing the questionnaire will point to the need for the various sets of data. If the response to a question cannot be related to one of the preplanned dummy tables, either those data are superfluous, or some relevant analysis has not been foreseen. If part of a dummy table remains empty, a necessary question may have been omitted. Analysis of pretest data helps to ensure that all data collected will be utilized and that the questionnaire will obtain all the necessary data.[39] Table 10.1 summarizes the questionnaire design process in the form of a checklist.

TABLE 10.1
Questionnaire Design Checklist

Step 1   Specify the information needed.

    1. Ensure that the information obtained fully addresses all the components of the problem. Review components of the problem and the approach, particularly the research questions, hypotheses, and the information needed.

    2. Prepare a set of dummy tables.

    3. Have a clear idea of the target population.

Step 2   Specify the type of interviewing method.

    1. Review the type of interviewing method determined based on considerations discussed in Chapter 6.

Step 3   Determine the content of individual questions.

    1. Is the question necessary?

    2. Are several questions needed instead of one to obtain the required information in an unambiguous manner?

    3. Do not use double-barreled questions.

Step 4   Design the questions to overcome the respondent's inability and unwillingness to answer.

    1. Is the respondent informed?

    2. If respondents are not likely to be informed, filter questions that measure familiarity, product use, and past experience should be asked before questions about the topics themselves.

    3. Can the respondent remember?

    4. Avoid errors of omission, telescoping, and creation.

    5. Questions that do not provide the respondent with cues can underestimate the actual occurrence of an event.

    6. Can the respondent articulate?

    7. Minimize the effort required of the respondents.

    8. Is the context in which the questions are asked appropriate?

    9. Make the request for information seem legitimate.

   10. If the information is sensitive:

      a. Place sensitive topics at the end of the questionnaire.

      b. Preface the question with a statement that the behavior of interest is common.

      c. Ask the question using the third-person technique.

      d. Hide the question in a group of other questions that respondents are willing to answer.

      e. Provide response categories rather than asking for specific figures.

      f. Use randomized techniques, if appropriate.

Step 5   Decide on the question structure.

    1. Open-ended questions are useful in exploratory research and as opening questions.

    2. Use structured questions whenever possible.

    3. In multiple-choice questions, the response alternatives should include the set of all possible choices and should be mutually exclusive.

    4. In a dichotomous question, if a substantial proportion of the respondents can be expected to be neutral, include a neutral alternative.

    5. Consider the use of the split ballot technique to reduce order bias in dichotomous and multiple-choice questions.

    6. If the response alternatives are numerous, consider using more than one question to reduce the information-processing demands on the respondents.

Step 6   Determine the question wording.

    1. Define the issue in terms of who, what, when, where, why, and way (the six Ws).

    2. Use ordinary words. Words should match the vocabulary level of the respondents.

    3. Avoid ambiguous words: usually, normally, frequently, often, regularly, occasionally, sometimes, etc.

    4. Avoid leading questions that clue the respondent to what the answer should be.

    5. Avoid implicit alternatives that are not explicitly expressed in the options.

    6. Avoid implicit assumptions.

    7. Respondents should not have to make generalizations or compute estimates.

    8. Use positive and negative statements.

(continued)

TABLE 10.1

Questionnaire Design Checklist *(continued)*

Step 7   Arrange the questions in proper order.

1. The opening questions should be interesting, simple, and nonthreatening.
2. Qualifying questions should serve as the opening questions.
3. Basic information should be obtained first, followed by classification, and, finally, identification information.
4. Difficult, sensitive, or complex questions should be placed late in the sequence.
5. General questions should precede the specific questions.
6. Questions should be asked in a logical order.
7. Branching questions should be designed carefully to cover all possible contingencies.
8. The question being branched should be placed as close as possible to the question causing the branching, and the branching questions should be ordered so that the respondents cannot anticipate what additional information will be required.

Step 8   Identify the form and layout.

1. Divide a questionnaire into several parts.
2. Questions in each part should be numbered.
3. The questionnaire should be precoded.
4. The questionnaires themselves should be numbered serially.

Step 9   Reproduce the questionnaire.

1. The questionnaire should have a professional appearance.
2. Booklet format should be used for long questionnaires.
3. Each question should be reproduced on a single page (or double-page spread).
4. Vertical response columns should be used.
5. Grids are useful when there are a number of related questions that use the same set of response categories.
6. The tendency to crowd questions to make the questionnaire look shorter should be avoided.
7. Directions or instructions for individual questions should be placed as close to the questions as possible.

Step 10   Eliminate bugs by pretesting.

1. Pretesting should be done always.
2. All aspects of the questionnaire should be tested, including question content, wording, sequence, form and layout, question difficulty, and instructions.
3. The respondents in the pretest should be similar to those who will be included in the actual survey.
4. Begin the pretest by using personal interviews.
5. Pretest should also be conducted by mail, telephone, or electronic interviewing if those methods are to be used in the actual survey.
6. A variety of interviewers should be used for pretests.
7. The pretest sample size is small, varying from 15 to 30 respondents for the initial testing.
8. Use protocol analysis and debriefing to identify problems.
9. After each significant revision of the questionnaire, another pretest should be conducted, using a different sample of respondents.
10. The responses obtained from the pretest should be coded and analyzed.

Computer and Internet Questionnaire Construction

Software is available for designing questionnaires administered over the Internet or other modes (e.g., telephone, personal interviews, or mail). Although we describe the use of the software for constructing Internet questionnaires, the functions are essentially similar for questionnaires constructed by other modes. The software will help develop and disseminate the questionnaire, and, in many cases, retrieve and analyze the collected data, and prepare a report. The software can automatically perform a variety of tasks such as:

- *Personalization.* The respondent's name and personal responses are automatically inserted into key questions.
- *Incorporate complex skip patterns.* The software can check many conditions and responses to determine which question should be asked next.

- *Randomize response choices.* The order of presentation of response options in multiple-choice questions can be randomized for each respondent to control for order bias.
- *Consistency checks.* Consistency checks can be programmed to identify inconsistent responses while the interview is still in progress so that corrective action may be taken if necessary.
- *Add new response categories as the interviewing progresses.* If many respondents give a particular response to the "Other, please specify" category, that response will be automatically converted into a check-off category and added to the set of prespecified response options.

In addition, these software programs have a variety of features that facilitate questionnaire construction.

Question List. The user can select a variety of formats from a menu of question types such as open ended, multiple choice, scales, dichotomous questions, and so forth. Moreover, one can use buttons, drop-down boxes (closed position or open position), check boxes, or open-ended scrolling text boxes.

Question Libraries. The user can select predefined questions or save questions used often in the question library. For example, the question library may contain predefined questions for measuring satisfaction, purchase intention, and other commonly used constructs in marketing.

Questionnaire Appearance. The user can select the background color and graphics of the questionnaire from a range of available templates or create a customized template using the template manager.

Preview. You can preview the questionnaire as it is being developed to examine the content, interactivity, type of questions, and background design and make any changes that may be needed.

Publish. This user can create the HTML questionnaire, post it to a unique Web page, create a database to collect the data on the hosting server, and obtain a unique URL to which respondents can be directed.

Notification. The user can create, personalize, send, and track e-mail–based invitations to participate in the survey.

As each respondent completes the survey, the data are transferred over the Web to the data file on the host server. The data can be downloaded and analyzed at any time, even when the survey is running. Thus, results can be examined in real-time. Some commonly used questionnaire software are SurveyTime (www.surveytime.com), SurveyPro (www.surveypro.com), Surveyz (www.surveyz.com), and PerfectSurveys (www.perfectsurveys.com). Other popular packages include EFM Feedback (www.vovici.com) and SSI Web by Sawtooth Software (www.sawtoothsoftware.com). With this book you have access to Qualtrics (www.qualtrics.com), which will enable you to electronically design questionnaires.

Several Web sites allow users to create and file their own questionnaires for free. CreateSurvey (www.createsurvey.com) allows anyone to create and administer online surveys to whomever they want. It distributes the survey, monitors participation and participants, and then collects and analyzes the data, all for free, because it is sponsored by Web advertising. However, CreateSurvey does not provide respondents. Users do this at their discretion. For instance, they can create a Web page and have the survey as a link from the Web page or send out an e-mail with the link asking people to participate in the survey. Another Web-based service is Zoomerang (www.zoomerang.com) by MarketTools (www.markettools.com).

A number of Web sites housed in universities offer valuable resources, such as scales and question libraries, for constructing questionnaires. Some helpful sites include the Interuniversity Consortium for Political and Social Research at the University of Michigan (www.icpsr.umich.edu); the Roper Center at the University of Connecticut (www.ropercenter.uconn.edu); the Survey Research Library at Florida State University (www.fsu.edu/~survey); and the Odum Institute, which houses the Louis Harris Data Center at the University of North Carolina, Chapel Hill (www.irss.unc.edu).[40]

Observational Forms

Forms for recording observational data are easier to construct than questionnaires. The researcher need not be concerned with the psychological impact of the questions and the way they are asked. The researcher need only develop a form that identifies the required information clearly, makes it easy for the fieldworker to record the information accurately, and simplifies the coding, entry, and analysis of data.

Observational forms should specify the who, what, when, where, why, and way of behavior to be observed. In the department store project, an observational form for the study of purchases would include space for all of the following information.

Project Research   Observation

Who: Purchasers, browsers, males, females, parents with children, children alone

What: Products/brands considered, products/brands purchased, size, price of package inspected, influence of children or other family members

When: Day, hour, date of observation

Where: Inside the store, checkout counter, or type of department within the store

Why: Influence of price, brand name, package size, promotion, or family members on the purchase

Way: Personal observer disguised as sales clerk, undisguised personal observer, hidden camera, or obtrusive mechanical device

Project Activities

1. Given the information obtained in the Sears project in Chapter 1, construct an appropriate questionnaire.
2. Critically evaluate the questionnaire you have constructed using the principles discussed in this chapter.
3. Do you think that the required information can be obtained by observation? If yes, design an appropriate observation form. ■

The form and layout as well as the reproduction of observational forms should follow the same guidelines discussed for questionnaires. A well-designed form permits fieldworkers to record individual observations, but not to summarize observations because that could lead to error. Finally, like questionnaires, observational forms also require adequate pretesting.

International Marketing Research

The questionnaire or research instrument should be adapted to the specific cultural environment and should not be biased in terms of any one culture. This requires careful attention to each step of the questionnaire design process. The information needed should be clearly specified. It is important to take into account any differences in underlying consumer behavior, decision-making process, psychographic, lifestyle, and demographic variables. In the context of demographic characteristics, information on marital status, education, household size, occupation, income, and dwelling unit may have to be specified differently for different countries, as these variables may not be directly comparable across countries. For example, household definition and size vary greatly, given the extended family structure in some countries and the practice of two or even three families living under the same roof.

Although personal interviewing is the dominant survey method in international marketing research, different interviewing methods may be used in different countries. Hence, the questionnaire may have to be suitable for administration by more than one method. For ease of comprehension and translation, it is desirable to have two or more simple questions rather than a single complex question. In overcoming the inability to answer, the variability in the extent to which respondents in different cultures are informed about the subject matter of the survey should be taken into account. Respondents in some countries, for example, in the Far East and the CIS (former Soviet Union), may not be as well informed as those in the United States.

The use of unstructured or open-ended questions may be desirable if the researcher lacks knowledge about the determinants of response in other countries. Unstructured questions also reduce cultural bias, because they do not impose any response alternatives. However, unstructured questions are more affected by differences in educational levels than structured questions. They should be used with caution in countries with high illiteracy rates. Unstructured and structured questions can be employed in a complementary way to provide rich insights, as in the following example.

Real Research

The Theme: Singapore's Theme Restaurants

Singapore is comprised of more than 60 surrounding islets and has a population of 4.6 million people as of 2008 (www.visitsingapore.com). Globally, it is known for its diverse restaurant industry. Out of the 27,000 food-service establishments, 21 percent are classified as restaurants. A study was conducted on the following four theme restaurants in Singapore: Hard Rock Café, Planet Hollywood, Celebrities Asia, and House of Mao (visit www.asiacuisine.com.sg for a description of these restaurants).

The questionnaire was pretested with 20 diners who had eaten at all four of the theme restaurants. Some revisions were made to the questionnaire based on the comments from those people. The survey was then administered to 300 participants in a questionnaire format that was designed to find out the participants' perceptions of the theme restaurants. The participants were chosen at random using a mall-intercept method and by asking the participants if they had been a customer in a theme restaurant in the past year. If their answer was yes, they were asked to participate and then fill out a four-page survey. The survey was divided into two sections: Section A asked about the participant's general perception of the theme restaurants, and section B asked the respondent to rate each of the four restaurants on a 5-point scale on nine different attributes. Respondents were also asked several open-ended questions at the end of the questionnaire, such as if they thought more theme restaurants would open in Singapore in the future and if they thought these restaurants would be successful.

Most respondents felt more theme restaurants would open in Singapore and most were neutral about their success. House of Mao received the highest rating in theme concept, and Hard Rock Café received the highest rating in overall experience meeting expectations. Hard Rock Café had the best overall ratings on the nine attributes. Based on this survey, there is room for growth in the theme restaurant industry in Singapore.[41] ■

The questionnaire may have to be translated for administration in different cultures. The researcher must ensure that the questionnaires in different languages are equivalent. The special procedures designed for this purpose are discussed in Chapter 24.

Pretesting of the questionnaire is complicated in international research, because the linguistic equivalence must be pretested. Two sets of pretests are recommended. The translated questionnaire should be pretested on monolingual subjects in their native language. The original and translated versions should also be administered to bilingual subjects. The pretest data from administration of the questionnaire in different countries or cultures should be analyzed and the pattern of responses compared to detect any cultural biases.

Ethics in Marketing Research

Several ethical issues related to the researcher–respondent relationship and the researcher–client relationship may have to be addressed in questionnaire design. Of particular concern are the use of overly long questionnaires, asking sensitive questions, combining questions of more than one client in the same questionnaire or survey (piggybacking), and deliberately biasing the questionnaire.

Respondents are volunteering their time and should not be overburdened by soliciting too much information. The researcher should avoid overly long questionnaires. An overly long questionnaire may vary in length or completion time depending upon variables such as the topic of the survey, the effort required, the number of open-ended questions, the frequency of use of complex scales, and the method of administration. According to the guidelines of the Professional Marketing Research Society of Canada (www.pmrs-aprm.com), with the exception of in-home personal interviews, questionnaires that take more than 30 minutes to complete are generally considered "overly long." Personal in-home interviews can take up to 60 minutes without over-loading the respondents. Overly long questionnaires are burdensome on the respondents and adversely affect the quality of responses. Similarly, questions that are confusing, exceed the respondents' ability, are difficult, or are otherwise improperly worded should be avoided.

Sensitive questions deserve special attention. On one hand, candid and honest responses are needed to generate meaningful findings. On the other hand, the researcher should not invade respondents' privacy or cause them undue stress. The guidelines we have given in this chapter should be followed. To minimize discomfort, it should be made clear at the beginning of the interview that respondents are not obligated to answer any question that makes them uncomfortable.

An important researcher–client issue is piggybacking, which occurs when a questionnaire contains questions pertaining to more than one client. This is often done in omnibus panels (see Chapters 3 and 4) that different clients can use to field their questions. Piggybacking can substantially reduce costs and can be a good way for clients to collect primary data they would not be able to afford otherwise. In these cases, all clients must be aware of and consent to the arrangement. Unfortunately, piggybacking is sometimes used without the client's knowledge for the sole purpose of increasing the research firm's profit. This is unethical.

Finally, the researcher has the ethical responsibility of designing the questionnaire so as to obtain the required information in an unbiased manner. Deliberately biasing the questionnaire in a desired direction—for example, by asking leading questions—cannot be condoned. In deciding the question structure, the most appropriate rather than the most convenient option should be adopted, as illustrated by the next example. Also, the questionnaire should be thoroughly pretested before fieldwork begins, or an ethical breach has occurred.

Real Research   ## Questioning International Marketing Ethics

In designing a questionnaire, open-ended questions may be most appropriate if the response categories are not known. In a study designed to identify ethical problems in international marketing, a series of open-ended questions was used. The objective of the survey was to elicit the three most frequently encountered ethical problems, in order of priority, to Australian firms that engage in international marketing activities. After reviewing the results, the researcher tabulated and categorized them into 10 categories that occurred most often: traditional small-scale bribery; large-scale bribery; gifts, favors, and entertainment; pricing; inappropriate products or technology; tax evasion practices; illegal or immoral activities; questionable commissions to channel members; cultural differences; and involvement in political affairs. The sheer number of categories indicates that international marketing ethics should probably be questioned more closely! The use of structured questions in this case, although more convenient, would have been inappropriate, raising ethical concerns.[42] ■

Decision Research   ## Does Delta Stack Up to the Competition?

The Situation

Richard Anderson was the chief executive officer of Delta Air Lines. Under his leadership, on April 14, 2008, Delta Air Lines Inc. and Northwest Airlines Corporation announced an agreement in which the two carriers will combine in an all-stock transaction with a combined enterprise value of $17.7 billion, creating America's premier global airline.

Since 2000, the Global Airline Performance (GAP) study has teamed up P. Robert and Partners and the London-based Aviation Information and Research unit of IATA, the International Air Transport Association, to perform a two-part syndicated survey for measuring passenger satisfaction on 22 different airlines in 30 different countries. It samples 240,000 passengers each year and is conducted in seven languages. The interviewers catch the respondents at the most opportune time: while waiting to board the plane. The first part of the survey consists of 20 questions about the airline staff and their willingness to assist; the second part, one that must be sent by mail or fax, asks questions about the boarding process, service on the plane, and comfort. Delta's general manager of marketing research, Paul Lai, agrees that keeping the information fresh in the respondent's mind helps get a clearer view of how the airline can increase customer satisfaction. Another benefit of the survey is that it is ongoing so that they can track responses over time. Lai also enjoys receiving the data about other airlines so they can conduct comparative analyses and identify areas in which Delta is lagging the competition. The survey revealed to Delta and other airlines that two service issues are most important. One is the operational service such as arrival/departure times without delays. The second is more subjective and cannot be controlled as easily—airline employee and customer relations. If Paul Lai remains in tune with the surveys performed by GAP, Delta will have no problem staying ahead of the flight competition.

The Marketing Research Decision

1. Instead of using part 2 of the GAP questionnaire, Paul Lai would like to develop his own questionnaire to measure passengers' perceptions of the boarding process, service on the plane, and comfort. Develop such a questionnaire.
2. Discuss the role of the questionnaire you recommend in enabling Paul Lai to determine consumer preferences for airlines and increase market share for Delta.

Properly designed questionnaires can help Delta Airlines determine passengers' perceptions and formulate marketing programs to improve passengers' satisfaction levels.

The Marketing Management Decision

1. What should Richard Anderson do to improve Delta's in-flight services?
2. Discuss how the marketing management decision action that you recommend to Richard Anderson is influenced by the questionnaire that you suggested earlier and by the findings of that research.[43] ■

SPSS Windows

SPSS Data Entry can help the researcher in designing a questionnaire, facilitated by the drag-and-drop feature of the program.

Summary

To collect quantitative primary data, a researcher must design a questionnaire or an observation form. A questionnaire has three objectives. It must translate the information needed into a set of specific questions the respondents can and will answer. It must motivate respondents to complete the interview. It must also minimize response error.

Designing a questionnaire is an art rather than a science. The process begins by specifying (step 1) the information needed and (step 2) the type of interviewing method. The next (step 3) is to decide on the content of individual questions. The question should overcome the respondents' inability and unwillingness to answer (step 4). Respondents may be unable to answer if they are not informed, cannot remember, or cannot articulate the response. The unwillingness of the respondents to answer must also be overcome. Respondents may be unwilling to answer if the question requires too much effort, is asked in a situation or context deemed inappropriate, does not serve a legitimate purpose, or solicits sensitive information. Then comes the decision regarding the question structure (step 5). Questions can be unstructured (open ended) or structured to a varying degree. Structured questions include multiple choice, dichotomous questions, and scales.

Determining the wording of each question (step 6) involves defining the issue, using ordinary words, using unambiguous words, and using dual statements. The researcher should avoid leading questions, implicit alternatives, implicit assumptions, and generalizations and estimates. Figure 10.3 gives a concept map for question wording. Once the questions have been worded, the order in which they will appear in the questionnaire must be decided (step 7). Special consideration should be given to opening questions, type of information, difficult questions, and the effect on subsequent questions. The questions should be arranged in a logical order.

The stage is now set for determining the form and layout of the questions (step 8). Several factors are important in reproducing the questionnaire (step 9). These include appearance, use of booklets, fitting entire question on a page, response category format, avoiding overcrowding, placement of directions, color coding, easy-to-read format, and cost. Last but not least is pretesting (step 10). Important issues are the extent of pretesting, nature of respondents, type of interviewing method, type of interviewers, sample size, protocol analysis and debriefing, and editing and analysis.

FIGURE 10.3

A Concept Map for Question Wording

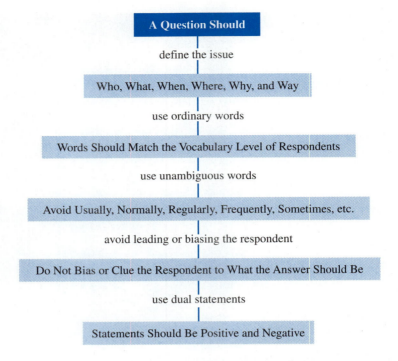

The design of observational forms requires explicit decisions about what is to be observed and how that behavior is to be recorded. It is useful to specify the who, what, when, where, why, and way of the behavior to be observed.

The questionnaire should be adapted to the specific cultural environment and should not be biased in terms of any one culture. Also, the questionnaire may have to be suitable for administration by more than one method because different interviewing methods may be used in different countries. Several ethical issues related to the researcher–respondent relationship and the researcher–client relationship may have to be addressed. The Internet and computers can greatly assist the researcher in designing sound questionnaires and observational forms.

Key Terms and Concepts

Suggested Cases, Video Cases, and HBS Cases

Running Case with Real Data

Comprehensive Critical Thinking Cases

Comprehensive Cases with Real Data

Video Cases

Comprehensive Harvard Business School Cases

Case 5.3: Cola Wars Continue: Coke and Pepsi in the Twenty-First Century (9-702-442)
Case 5.4: TiVo in 2002 (9-502-062)
Case 5.5: Compaq Computer: Intel Inside? (9-599-061)
Case 5.6: The New Beetle (9-501-023)

Live Research: Conducting a Marketing Research Project

1. Each team can develop a questionnaire following the principles discussed in the chapter. The best features of each questionnaire can be combined to develop the project questionnaire.

2. Each team should be assigned a few pretest interviews.

3. If a questionnaire has already been prepared, it should be critically evaluated in the class.

Acronyms

The objectives and steps involved in developing a questionnaire may be defined by the acronym

Questionnaire:

Objectives	Q	uestions that respondents can answer
	U	plift the respondent
	E	rror elimination
Steps	S	pecify the information needed
	T	ype of interviewing method
	I	ndividual question content
	O	vercoming inability and unwillingness to answer
	N	onstructured versus structured questions
	N	onbiased question wording
	A	rrange the questions in proper order
	I	dentify form and layout
	R	eproduction of the questionnaire
	E	liminate bugs by pretesting

The guidelines for question wording may be summarized by the acronym

Wording:

W	ho, what, when, where, why, and way
O	rdinary words
R	egularly, normally, usually, etc., should be avoided
D	ual statements (positive and negative)
I	mplicit alternatives and assumptions should be avoided
N	onleading and nonbiasing questions
G	eneralizations and estimates should be avoided

The guidelines for deciding on the order of questions may be summarized by the acronym

Order:

O	pening questions: simple
R	udimentary or basic information should be obtained first
D	ifficult questions toward the end
E	xamine the influence on subsequent questions
R	eview the sequence to ensure a logical order

The guidelines for reproducing a questionnaire may be summarized by the acronym

Reproduce:

R	esponse category format
E	ntire question on a page
P	rofessional appearance
R	educe costs
O	vercrowding should be avoided
D	irections or instructions
U	se of booklets
C	olor coding
E	asy to read

The guidelines for pretesting a questionnaire may be summarized by the acronym

Pretest:

P	rotocol analysis and debriefing
R	espondents from the same population
E	xtent: extensive
T	ype of interviewing method
E	diting and analysis
S	ample size: 15 to 30 per iteration
T	ype of interviewers

Exercises

Questions

1. What is the purpose of questionnaires and observation forms?
2. Explain how the mode of administration affects questionnaire design.
3. How would you determine whether a specific question should be included in a questionnaire?
4. What is a double-barreled question?
5. What are the reasons that respondents are unable to answer the question asked?
6. Explain the errors of omission, telescoping, and creation. What can be done to reduce such errors?
7. Explain the concepts of aided and unaided recall.

8. What are the reasons that respondents are unwilling to answer specific questions?
9. What can a researcher do to make the request for information seem legitimate?
10. Explain the use of randomized techniques in obtaining sensitive information.
11. What are the advantages and disadvantages of unstructured questions?
12. What are the issues involved in designing multiple-choice questions?
13. What are the guidelines available for deciding on question wording?
14. What is a leading question? Give an example.
15. What is the proper order for questions intended to obtain basic, classification, and identification information?
16. What guidelines are available for deciding on the form and layout of a questionnaire?
17. Describe the issues involved in pretesting a questionnaire.
18. What are the major decisions involved in designing observational forms?

Problems

1. Develop three double-barreled questions related to flying and passengers' airline preferences. Also develop corrected versions of each question.

2. List at least 10 ambiguous words that should not be used in framing questions.
3. Do the following questions define the issue? Why or why not?
   a. What is your favorite brand of toothpaste?
   b. How often do you go on a vacation?
   c. Do you consume orange juice?
      1. Yes   2. No
4. Design an open-ended question to determine whether households engage in gardening. Also develop a multiple-choice and a dichotomous question to obtain the same information. Which form is the most desirable?
5. Formulate five questions that ask respondents to provide generalizations or estimates.
6. Develop a series of questions for determining the proportion of households with children under age 10 where child abuse takes place. Use the randomized response technique.
7. A new graduate hired by the marketing research department of a major telephone company is asked to prepare a questionnaire to determine household preferences for telephone calling cards. The questionnaire is to be administered in mall-intercept interviews. Using the principles of questionnaire design, critically evaluate this questionnaire, which follows.

HOUSEHOLD TELEPHONE CALLING CARD SURVEY

1. Your name? _____

2. Age _____

3. Marital status _____

4. Income _____

5. Which, if any of the following telephone calling cards do you have?
   1. _____ AT&T   3. _____ Sprint Nextel
   2. _____ Verizon   4. _____ Others

6. How frequently do you use a telephone calling card?

   Infrequently   Very Frequently
        1   2   3   4   5   6   7

7. What do you think of the telephone calling card offered by AT&T?

   _____

8. Suppose your household were to select a telephone calling card. Please rate the importance of the following factors in selecting a card.

	Not Important				Very Important
a. Cost per call	1	2	3	4	5
b. Ease of use	1	2	3	4	5
c. Local and long-distance charges included in the same bill	1	2	3	4	5
d. Rebates and discounts on calls	1	2	3	4	5
e. Quality of telephone service	1	2	3	4	5
f. Quality of customer service	1	2	3	4	5

9. How important is it for a telephone company to offer a calling card?

   Not important   Very Important
        1   2   3   4   5   6   7

10. Do you have children living at home? _____

Thank You for Your Help.

Internet and Computer Exercises

1. HP would like to conduct an Internet survey to determine the image of HP PCs and the image of its major competitors (Apple, Dell, and Lenovo). Develop such a questionnaire. Relevant information may be obtained by visiting the Web sites of these companies (www.lenovo.com, www.applecomputer.com, www.dell.com, www.hp.com).
2. Develop the questionnaire in Fieldwork problem 1 using an electronic questionnaire design package such as the Ci3 System. Administer this questionnaire to 10 students using a microcomputer.
3. Develop the questionnaire in Fieldwork problem 2 using an electronic questionnaire design package. Compare your experiences in designing this questionnaire electronically and manually.
4. Visit the Web site of one of the online marketing research firms (e.g., Greenfield Online Research Center, Inc., at www.greenfieldonline.com). Locate a survey being currently administered at this site. Critically analyze the questionnaire using the principles discussed in this chapter.

Activities

Role Playing

1. You have just been hired as a management trainee by a firm that manufactures major appliances. Your boss has asked you to develop a questionnaire to determine how households plan to buy, purchase, and use major appliances. This questionnaire is to be used in a nationwide study. However, you feel that you do not have the expertise or the experience to construct such a complex questionnaire. Explain this to your boss (role played by a fellow student).
2. You are working as an assistant marketing research manager with a national department store chain. Management, represented by a group of students, is concerned about the extent of shoplifting by the employees. You are assigned the task of developing a questionnaire to determine the extent of shoplifting by the employees. This questionnaire would be mailed to employees nationwide. Explain your approach to designing the questionnaire to management. (Hint: Use the randomized response technique.)

Fieldwork

1. Develop a questionnaire for determining how students select restaurants. Pretest the questionnaire by administering it to 10 students using personal interviews. How would you modify the questionnaire based on the pretest?
2. Develop a questionnaire for determining household preferences for popular brands of cold cereals. Administer the questionnaire to 10 female head of households using personal interviews. How would you modify the questionnaire if it were to be administered by telephone? What changes would be necessary if it were to be administered by mail?

Group Discussion

1. "Because questionnaire design is an art, it is useless to follow a rigid set of guidelines. Rather, the process should be left entirely to the creativity and ingenuity of the researcher." Discuss as a small group.
2. Discuss as a small group the role of questionnaire design in minimizing total research error.
3. Discuss the importance of form and layout in questionnaire construction.

Dell Running Case

Review the Dell case, Case 1.1, and questionnaire given toward the end of the book.

1. Critically evaluate the Dell questionnaire using the principles discussed in this chapter.
2. Draft a questionnaire to measure students' preferences for notebook computers.
3. Evaluate the questionnaire you have developed using the principles discussed in this chapter.
4. Develop a revised questionnaire to measure students' preferences for notebook computers.
5. What did you learn in the questionnaire revision process?

Video **Cases**

VIDEO CASE 10.1 Dunkin' Donuts: Dunking the Competition

In 1950, Bill Rosenberg founded the Dunkin' Donuts chain (www.dunkindonuts.com) by opening the first location in Quincy, Massachusetts. By 1975, 1,000 locations nationwide were grossing a collective $300 million in sales. At the beginning of 2008, there were 7,988 Dunkin' Donuts stores worldwide, including 5,769 franchised restaurants in the United States and 2,219 internationally. The company clocked worldwide sales of $5.3 billion during fiscal year 2007.

This impressive growth would not have been possible without extensive marketing research and a commitment to quality. Bill Rosenberg began the culture within the company of listening to what the customer wanted and then providing it, and that tradition continues today. Marketing research in the form of focus groups and survey research revealed that customers select a coffee and donut shop based on five factors: accessibility, quality, variety, image, and affordability. The company's business is built around these factors. From research, Dunkin' Donuts found that its customers wanted a coffee and donut shop that was very accessible—close to work or home and easy to get to. To accompany its stand-alone locations, Dunkin' Donuts has opened locations in Home Depot, Wal-Mart, 7-11, and Stop & Shop stores to add to the convenience that customers desire. Every location is strategically placed and designed with these customers' preferences in mind. Because these purchases are so convenience driven, the locations can be placed close together without cannibalizing business.

Marketing research further revealed that quality translates to freshness in the donut business. Therefore, Dunkin' Donuts makes donuts at least four times a day. Upon conducting research with survey questionnaires and taste testing in many different markets, Dunkin' Donuts found the blend of coffee that customers favor the most. This coffee is brewed and then allowed to sit for no longer than 18 minutes. After the 18-minute window, the coffee is poured out, and a fresh pot is brewed. This commitment to quality was made as a result of researching what the customer desired in a cup of coffee.

The company also offers variety—52 flavors of donuts. Recently, Dunkin' Donuts has expanded its coffee line (again, due to research and taste testing) to include iced coffees, cappuccinos, lattes, espressos, and flavored coffees, such as hazelnut coffee.

Marketing research showed that customers preferred an image that related to the common person. They did not want a coffee shop that was flashy with lots of bells and whistles; they just wanted a common shop that made a great cup of coffee. Therefore, Dunkin' Donuts appeals to just about everyone. During the late 1970s and the 1980s, the ad campaign of "Fred the Baker" brought this image to life. With commercials showing him waking up in the middle of the night with a commitment to quality, he appealed to the common person. The Mercedes and the pickup truck come together in an egalitarian Dunkin' Donuts parking lot. In addition, Dunkin' Donuts is affordable. Just about any consumer can afford the Dunkin' Donuts experience. Dunkin' Donuts is much less expensive compared to Starbucks and other upscale coffee shops.

Dunkin' Donuts realizes that first and foremost its donuts and coffee need to be up to par to customers' expectations. Already the retail market leader in donuts and bagels, Dunkin' Donuts knows that it takes a commitment to marketing research to stay there. Bob Pitts, the current Technology Product Developer, demands a continuing commitment to listening to what the customers prefer. Again, this manifests itself through constant research and taste testing. The customer is a very important source of wisdom and insight at Dunkin' and customer opinion and feedback is important. Customers' preferences have not only shaped the recipes of donuts and bagels, but they have also prompted the introduction of the Dunkin' Decaf and flavored coffees such as Hazelnut and French Vanilla. The huge success of these introductions reaffirmed the importance of customers to Dunkin' Donuts and its new products. This journey of innovation has continued with the launch of indulgent coffee drinks, such as cappuccinos, lattes, and espressos. In August 2007, Dunkin' announced a partnership with Procter & Gamble. In this alliance, P&G roasts

Dunkin's packaged coffee according to Dunkin's specifications and is responsible for distribution as well as a national marketing campaign based on the coffee shop chain's current "America runs on Dunkin'" theme. The initiative helps P&G gain entry into the premium coffee market, and Dunkin' Donuts gets P&G's distribution expertise and a new source of income. The packaged coffee is available at Kroger, Wal-Mart, and other stores.

Speaking to customers and getting their insights is a crucial part of Dunkin' Donuts' marketing research strategy. The use of focus/consumer groups and market surveys for taste testing and feedback is an ongoing process. With a commanding presence in the market, reliance on marketing research has had obvious positive effects that are sure to continue in the future, and Dunkin' Donuts can continue dunking the competition.

Conclusion

Marketing research has kept Dunkin' Donuts relevant and appealing to people across the world throughout the years. Dunkin's positioning as an everyday, accessible store for everyone has helped it to foster a bond with its customers. This relationship of respect and humility has endured even as Dunkin' has expanded its product portfolio to include more varieties and target newer customers, all without alienating its existing customers. The emphasis that Dunkin' places on using marketing research to make the customers critical stakeholders who provide feedback and insight and help direct the innovation process has reaped rich benefits for Dunkin' Donuts.

Questions

1. Discuss the role that marketing research can play in helping a coffee shop such as Dunkin' Donuts formulate sound marketing strategies.
2. Dunkin' Donuts is considering further expansion in the United States. Define the management decision problem.
3. Define an appropriate marketing research problem based on the management decision problem you have identified.
4. Use the Internet to determine the market shares of the major coffee shops for the last calendar year.
5. What type of syndicate data will be useful to Dunkin' Donuts?
6. Discuss the role of qualitative research in helping Dunkin' Donuts expand further in the United States.
7. Dunkin' Donuts has developed a new line of pastries with a distinctive French taste. It would like to determine consumers' response to this new line of pastries before introducing them in the marketplace. If a survey is to be conducted to determine consumer preferences, which survey method should be used and why?
8. Design a taste test comparing Dunkin' Donuts coffees with those offered by Starbucks.
9. Develop a questionnaire for assessing consumer preferences for fast coffee shops.

References

1. www.dunkindonuts.com, accessed January 15, 2009.
2. "Dunkin' Donuts Competes with Coffee Chains with Latte Offerings in Michigan," *Knight Ridder Tribune Business News* (March 19, 2004): 1.

"Sampling is the only feasible way to collect marketing research data in most situations. This inevitably introduces sampling errors. However, sampling errors are often only a small part of the total research errors.

Chuck Chakrapani, President, Standard Research Systems

Objectives   [After reading this chapter, the student should be able to:]

1. Differentiate a sample from a census and identify the conditions that favor the use of a sample versus a census.

2. Discuss the sampling design process: definition of the target population, determination of the sampling frame, selection of sampling technique(s), determination of sample size, and execution of the sampling process.

3. Classify sampling techniques as nonprobability and probability sampling techniques.

4. Describe the nonprobability sampling techniques of convenience, judgmental, quota, and snowball sampling.

5. Describe the probability sampling techniques of simple random, systematic, stratified, and cluster sampling.

6. Identify the conditions that favor the use of nonprobability sampling versus probability sampling.

7. Understand the sampling design process and the use of sampling techniques in international marketing research.

8. Identify the ethical issues related to the sampling design process and the use of appropriate sampling techniques.

9. Explain the use of the Internet and computers in sampling design.

Sampling: Design and Procedures

Overview

Sampling is one of the components of a research design. The formulation of the research design is the third step of the marketing research process. At this stage, the information needed to address the marketing research problem has been identified and the nature of the research design (exploratory, descriptive, or causal) has been determined (Chapters 3 through 7). Furthermore, the scaling and measurement procedures have been specified (Chapters 8 and 9), and the questionnaire has been designed (Chapter 10). The next step is to design suitable sampling procedures. Sampling design involves several basic questions: (1) Should a sample be taken? (2) If so, what process should be followed? (3) What kind of sample should be taken? (4) How large should it be? and (5) What can be done to control and adjust for nonresponse errors?

This chapter introduces the fundamental concepts of sampling and the qualitative considerations necessary to answer these questions. We address the question of whether or not to sample and describe the steps involved in sampling. Next, we present nonprobability and probability sampling techniques. We discuss the use of sampling techniques in international marketing research, identify the relevant ethical issues, and describe the use of the Internet and computers for sampling. Statistical determination of sample size and the causes for, control of, and adjustments for nonresponse error are discussed in Chapter 12.

Real Research

Reviving a Lame Duck

The sale of duck stamps by the U.S. Fish and Wildlife Service (USFWS) (www.fws.gov) to pay the cost of preserving the wetlands was declining. So the USFWS brought in The Ball Group (www.ballgroup.com), a marketing research and advertising firm based in Lancaster, Pennsylvania, to conduct research to discover who else might be interested in purchasing the stamps and why these groups would want to purchase the stamps—what marketing should take place and what benefits the stamps were perceived as providing. The Ball Group decided to conduct focus groups and a telephone survey to determine the answers to these questions. The sampling process for the telephone survey was as follows. Duck stamps are available throughout the United States, and all U.S. citizens are affected by the preservation of the wetlands, so the population was defined to include all U.S. citizens. The sampling frame consisted of computer software for randomly and efficiently generating telephone numbers. The sample size, determined by resource constraints and sample size used in similar studies, was 1,000.

The steps in the sampling design process were as follows:

1. *Target population: Element:* Male or female head of household; *Sampling unit:* Working telephone numbers; *Extent:* United States; *Time:* Period of the survey
2. *Sampling frame:* Computer program for randomly and efficiently generating telephone numbers, excluding nonworking and nonhousehold numbers
3. *Sampling technique:* Simple random sampling with modification to exclude nonworking and business telephone numbers
4. *Sample size:* 1,000
5. *Execution:* Use a computer program to randomly generate a list of household telephone numbers. Select the male or female head of household using the next birthday method. Conduct the interviews using a computer-assisted telephone interviewing (CATI) system.

An appropriate sampling design helped the U.S. Fish and Wildlife Service create effective marketing strategies for the Duck Stamp program.

The result of this research showed that people did want to help the effort, but they wanted something to demonstrate their generosity. Therefore, the U.S. Fish and Wildlife Service decided to start marketing the stamps to the American public as a great way to "donate" money to help save the wetlands. For $30, in addition to receiving a stamp, purchasers also receive a certificate saying that they helped to save the wetlands. As of 2009, the duck stamp program was a great success.[1] ■

Real Research

Random Sampling and Pop-Up Surveys

comScore SurveySite is a full-service research firm based in Ontario, Canada (www.comscore.com). comScore SurveySite's mission is to provide "leading-edge and innovative Web site evaluation systems and market research to the Internet community." Its goal is to be the "undisputed leader in quality Web site research and visitor analysis." SurveySite conducted a survey to determine Canada's perception of the high-tech industry compared to the United States. Three thousand Canadian IT managers were surveyed, and the results revealed that Canadians perceive themselves to have fallen behind in technology compared to the United States. Many respondents noted that Australia was a more realistic country to compare Canada to, instead of the United States.

One research program SurveySite offers is the "Pop-Up Survey." The product counts the number of people that visit a Web site and selects visitors at a predetermined interval. For example, every 100th person to click on a client's Web site is selected based on systematic random sampling. When this happens, a small Java script pops up. The script requests the user to complete a short online survey. If the visitor clicks no, the Java script disappears and the person continues browsing. If the visitor clicks yes, a client-designed survey appears.

The advantage to this "pop-up" model is that it significantly increases the user response rate. The typical survey method offers a banner that asks visitors to take the survey. The banners, however, tend to have a very poor response rate. In general, the rate is about 0.02 percent or 1 out of every 500 visitors. The SurveySite "pop-up" dramatically improves the response rate, and it enables data collection to be reduced from weeks to days.

As a result, SurveySite's Internet research strategy has helped the Internet research firm to land corporate clients such as Timex, Delta Hotels, Toronto-Dominion Bank, Kellogg's, and Canadian Tire.[2] ■

population
The aggregate of all the elements, sharing some common set of characteristics, that comprises the universe for the purpose of the marketing research problem.

This example illustrates the various steps in the sampling design process. However, before we discuss these aspects of sampling in detail, we will address the question of whether the researcher should sample or take a census.

Sample or Census

The objective of most marketing research projects is to obtain information about the characteristics or parameters of a population. A **population** is the aggregate of all the elements that share some common set of characteristics and that comprise the universe for the purposes of the marketing research problem. The population parameters are typically numbers, such as the proportion of consumers who are loyal to a particular brand of toothpaste. Information about population parameters may be obtained by taking a census or a sample. A **census** involves a complete enumeration of the elements of a population. The population parameters can be calculated directly in a straightforward way after the census is enumerated. A **sample**, on the other hand, is a subgroup of the population selected for participation in the study. Sample characteristics, called *statistics*, are then used to make inferences about the population parameters. The inferences that link sample characteristics and population parameters are estimation procedures and tests of hypotheses. These inference procedures are considered later in Chapters 15 through 21.

Table 11.1 summarizes the conditions favoring the use of a sample versus a census. Budget and time limits are obvious constraints favoring the use of a sample. A census is both costly and time-consuming to conduct. A census is unrealistic if the population is large, as it is for most consumer products. In the case of many industrial products, however, the population is small, making a census feasible as well as desirable. For example, in investigating the use of certain machine tools by U.S. automobile manufacturers, a census would be preferred to a sample. Another reason for preferring a census in this case is that variance in the characteristic of interest is large. For example, machine tool usage of Ford will vary greatly from the usage of Honda. Small population sizes as well as high variance in the characteristic to be measured favor a census.

If the cost of sampling errors is high (e.g., if the sample omitted a major manufacturer such as Ford, the results could be misleading), a census, which eliminates such errors, is desirable. High costs of nonsampling errors, on the other hand, would favor sampling. A census can greatly increase nonsampling error to the point that these errors exceed the sampling errors of a sample. Nonsampling errors are found to be the major contributor to total error, whereas random sampling errors have been relatively small in magnitude (see Chapter 3).[3] Hence, in most cases, accuracy considerations would favor a sample over a census. This is one of the reasons that the U.S. Bureau of the Census checks the accuracy of various censuses by conducting sample surveys.[4] However, it is not always possible to reduce nonsampling error sufficiently to compensate for sampling error, as in the case of a study involving U.S. automobile manufacturers.

A sample may be preferred if the measurement process results in the destruction or contamination of the elements sampled. For example, product usage tests result in the consumption of the product. Therefore, taking a census in a study that requires households to use a new brand of cereal would not be feasible. Sampling may also be necessary to focus attention on individual cases, as in the case of depth interviews. Finally, other pragmatic considerations, such as the need to keep the study secret, may favor a sample over a census.

census
A complete enumeration of the elements of a population or study objects.

sample
A subgroup of the elements of the population selected for participation in the study.

TABLE 11.1 **Sample Versus Census**		
	Conditions Favoring the Use of	
	Sample	Census
1. Budget	Small	Large
2. Time available	Short	Long
3. Population size	Large	Small
4. Variance in the characteristic	Small	Large
5. Cost of sampling errors	Low	High
6. Cost of nonsampling errors	High	Low
7. Nature of measurement	Destructive	Nondestructive
8. Attention to individual cases	Yes	No

ACTIVE RESEARCH

Boeing: Spreading Its Wings and Flying

Conduct an Internet search using a search engine and your library's online database to determine the population of all airlines operating in the United States.

If a survey of airlines is to be conducted to determine their future plans to purchase/lease airplanes, would you take a sample or a census? Why?

As the CEO of Boeing, how would you use information on the future plans of airlines to purchase/lease airplanes to formulate your marketing strategy?

The Sampling Design Process

The sampling design process includes five steps that are shown sequentially in Figure 11.1. These steps are closely interrelated and relevant to all aspects of the marketing research project, from problem definition to the presentation of the results. Therefore, sample design decisions should be integrated with all other decisions in a research project.[5]

Define the Target Population

target population
The collection of elements or objects that possess the information sought by the researcher and about which inferences are to be made.

Sampling design begins by specifying the target population. The **target population** is the collection of elements or objects that possess the information sought by the researcher and about which inferences are to be made. The target population must be defined precisely. Imprecise definition of the target population will result in research that is ineffective at best and misleading at worst. Defining the target population involves translating the problem definition into a precise statement of who should and should not be included in the sample.

The target population should be defined in terms of elements, sampling units, extent, and time. An **element** is the object about which or from which the information is desired. In survey research, the element is usually the respondent. A **sampling unit** is an element, or a unit containing the element, that is available for selection at some stage of the sampling process. Suppose that Revlon wanted to assess consumer response to a new line of lipsticks and wanted to sample females over 18 years of age. It may be possible to sample females over 18 directly, in which case a sampling unit would be the same as an element. Alternatively, the sampling unit might be households. In the latter case, households would be sampled and all females over 18 in each selected household would be interviewed. Here, the sampling unit and the population element are different. Extent refers to the geographical boundaries, and the time factor is the time period under consideration. The opening duck stamps example showed an appropriate definition of a population. We use the department store project to provide another illustration.

element
An object that possesses the information sought by the researcher.

sampling unit
The basic unit containing the elements of the population to be sampled.

FIGURE 11.1

The Sampling Design Process

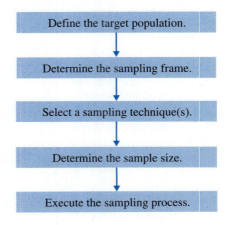

Define the target population.

↓

Determine the sampling frame.

↓

Select a sampling technique(s).

↓

Determine the sample size.

↓

Execute the sampling process.

Project Research | Target Population

The target population for the department store project was defined as follows:

Element: male or female head of the household responsible for most of the shopping at department stores
Sampling units: households
Extent: metropolitan Atlanta
Time: 2009 ■

Defining the target population may not be as easy as it was in this example. Consider a marketing research project assessing consumer response to a new brand of men's cologne. Who should be included in the target population? All men? Men who have used cologne during the last month? Men 17 or older? Should females be included, because some women buy colognes for their husbands? These and similar questions must be resolved before the target population can be appropriately defined.[6]

Determine the Sampling Frame

sampling frame
A representation of the elements of the target population. It consists of a list or set of directions for identifying the target population.

A **sampling frame** is a representation of the elements of the target population. It consists of a list or set of directions for identifying the target population. Examples of a sampling frame include the telephone book, an association directory listing the firms in an industry, a mailing list purchased from a commercial organization, a city directory, or a map. If a list cannot be compiled, then at least some directions for identifying the target population should be specified, such as random digit dialing procedures in telephone surveys (see Chapter 6). In the opening duck stamp example, the sampling frame consisted of a computer program for randomly and efficiently generating telephone numbers, excluding nonworking and nonhousehold numbers.

Often it is possible to compile or obtain a list of population elements, but the list may omit some elements of the population or include other elements that do not belong. Therefore, the use of a list will lead to sampling frame error, which was discussed in Chapter 3.[7]

In some instances, the discrepancy between the population and the sampling frame is small enough to ignore. However, in most cases, the researcher should recognize and treat the sampling frame error. This can be done in at least three ways. One approach is to redefine the population in terms of the sampling frame. If the telephone book is used as a sampling frame, the population of households could be redefined as those with a correct listing in the telephone book in a given area. Although this approach is simplistic, it does prevent the researcher from being misled about the actual population being investigated.[8]

Another way is to account for sampling frame error by screening the respondents in the data-collection phase. The respondents could be screened with respect to demographic characteristics, familiarity, product usage, and other characteristics to ensure that they satisfy the criteria for the target population. Screening can eliminate inappropriate elements contained in the sampling frame, but it cannot account for elements that have been omitted.

Yet another approach is to adjust the data collected by a weighting scheme to counterbalance the sampling frame error. This is discussed in Chapter 12 and also in Chapter 14. Regardless of which approach is adopted, it is important to recognize any sampling frame error that exists, so that inappropriate population inferences can be avoided.

Select a Sampling Technique

Bayesian approach
A selection method in which the elements are selected sequentially. The Bayesian approach explicitly incorporates prior information about population parameters as well as the costs and probabilities associated with making wrong decisions.

Selecting a sampling technique involves several decisions of a broader nature. The researcher must decide whether to use a Bayesian or traditional sampling approach, to sample with or without replacement, and to use nonprobability or probability sampling.

In the **Bayesian approach**, the elements are selected sequentially. After each element is added to the sample, the data are collected, sample statistics computed, and sampling costs determined. The Bayesian approach explicitly incorporates prior information about population parameters as well as the costs and probabilities associated with making wrong decisions. This approach is theoretically appealing. Yet it is not used widely in marketing research because much of the required information on costs and probabilities is not available. In the traditional sampling approach, the entire sample is selected before data collection begins. Because the traditional approach is most commonly used, this is the approach assumed in the following sections.

sampling with replacement
A sampling technique in which an element can be included in the sample more than once.

In **sampling with replacement**, an element is selected from the sampling frame and appropriate data are obtained. Then the element is placed back in the sampling frame. As a result, it is possible for an element to be included in the sample more than once. In **sampling without replacement**, once an element is selected for inclusion in the sample, it is removed from the sampling frame and, therefore, cannot be selected again. The calculation of statistics is done somewhat differently for the two approaches, but statistical inference is not very different if the sampling frame is large relative to the ultimate sample size. Thus the distinction is important only when the sampling frame is not large compared to the sample size.

sampling without replacement
A sampling technique in which an element cannot be included in the sample more than once.

The most important decision about the choice of sampling technique is whether to use probability or nonprobability sampling. Given its importance, the issues involved in this decision are discussed in great detail in this chapter.

If the sampling unit is different from the element, it is necessary to specify precisely how the elements within the sampling unit should be selected. In in-home personal interviews and telephone interviews, merely specifying the address or the telephone number may not be sufficient. For example, should the person answering the doorbell or the telephone be interviewed, or someone else in the household? Often, more than one person in a household may qualify. For example, both the male and female heads of household may be eligible to participate in a study examining family leisure-time activities. When a probability sampling technique is being employed, a random selection must be made from all the eligible persons in each household. A simple procedure for random selection is the next birthday method. The interviewer asks which of the eligible persons in the household has the next birthday and includes that person in the sample, as in the opening duck stamps example.

Determine the Sample Size

sample size
The number of elements to be included in a study.

Sample size refers to the number of elements to be included in the study. Determining the sample size is complex and involves several qualitative and quantitative considerations. The qualitative factors are discussed in this section, and the quantitative factors are considered in Chapter 12. Important qualitative factors that should be considered in determining the sample size include (1) the importance of the decision, (2) the nature of the research, (3) the number of variables, (4) the nature of the analysis, (5) sample sizes used in similar studies, (6) incidence rates, (7) completion rates, and (8) resource constraints.

In general, for more important decisions, more information is necessary and the information should be obtained more precisely. This calls for larger samples, but as the sample size increases, each unit of information is obtained at greater cost. The degree of precision may be measured in terms of the standard deviation of the mean. The standard deviation of the mean is inversely proportional to the square root of the sample size. The larger the sample, the smaller the gain in precision by increasing the sample size by one unit.

The nature of the research also has an impact on the sample size. For exploratory research designs, such as those using qualitative research, the sample size is typically small. For conclusive research, such as descriptive surveys, larger samples are required. Likewise, if data are being collected on a large number of variables, larger samples are required. The cumulative effects of sampling error across variables are reduced in a large sample.

If sophisticated analysis of the data using multivariate techniques is required, the sample size should be large. The same applies if the data are to be analyzed in great detail. Thus, a larger sample would be required if the data are being analyzed at the subgroup or segment level than if the analysis is limited to the aggregate or total sample.

Sample size is influenced by the average size of samples in similar studies. Table 11.2 gives an idea of sample sizes used in different marketing research studies. These sample sizes have been determined based on experience and can serve as rough guidelines, particularly when nonprobability sampling techniques are used.

Finally, the sample size decision should be guided by a consideration of the resource constraints. In any marketing research project, money and time are limited. Other constraints include the availability of qualified personnel for data collection. In the opening duck stamp example, the sample size of 1,000 was determined by resource constraints and the sample size used in similar

TABLE 11.2
Sample Sizes Used in Marketing Research Studies

Type of Study	Minimum Size	Typical Range
Problem identification research (e.g., market potential)	500	1,000–2,500
Problem-solving research (e.g., pricing)	200	300–500
Product tests	200	300–500
Test-marketing studies	200	300–500
TV/radio/print advertising (per commercial or ad tested)	150	200–300
Test-market audits	10 stores	10–20 stores
Focus groups	2 groups	6–15 groups

studies. The sample size required should be adjusted for the incidence of eligible respondents and the completion rate, as explained in the next chapter.

Execute the Sampling Process

Execution of the sampling process requires a detailed specification of how the sampling design decisions with respect to the population, sampling frame, sampling unit, sampling technique, and sample size are to be implemented. If households are the sampling unit, an operational definition of a household is needed. Procedures should be specified for vacant housing units and for callbacks in case no one is at home. Detailed information must be provided for all sampling design decisions.

Real Research

Tourism Department Telephones Birthday Boys and Girls

A telephone survey was conducted for the Florida Department of Tourism (www.myflorida.com) to gain an understanding of the travel behavior of in-state residents. In 2008, there were more than 18 million residents in Florida, ranking the state fourth in the United States after California, Texas, and New York. These households were stratified by north, central, and south Florida regions. A computerized random digit sample was used to reach these households. Households were screened to locate family members who met four qualifications:

1. Age 25 or older
2. Live in Florida at least seven months of the year
3. Have lived in Florida for at least two years
4. Have a Florida driver's license

   To obtain a representative sample of qualified individuals, a random method was used to select the respondent from within a household. All household members meeting the four qualifications were listed and the person with the next birthday was selected. Repeated callbacks were made to reach that person. The steps in the sampling design process were as follows.

1. *Target population:* Adults meeting the four qualifications (element) in a household with a working telephone number (sampling unit) in the state of Florida (extent) during the survey period (time)
2. *Sampling frame:* Computer program for generating random telephone numbers
3. *Sampling technique:* Stratified sampling. The target population was geographically stratified into three regions: north, central, and south Florida.
4. *Sample size:* 868
5. *Execution:* Allocate the sample among strata; use computerized random digit dialing; list all the members in the household who meet the four qualifications; select one member of the household using the next birthday method.[9] ■

An appropriate sampling design process enabled the Florida Department of Tourism to gain valuable insights into the travel behavior of in-state residents. The opening duck stamp example provides another illustration of the sampling design process.

Experiential Research

The New York Yankees: Yanking Families to the Game

The New York Yankees is one of America's favorite baseball teams.

1. As the marketing manager of the New York Yankees, what marketing programs will you design to target families?
2. Visit newyork.yankees.mlb.com and identify information at this site that would be useful for marketing research purposes.
3. Search the Internet, as well as your library's online databases, to obtain information that will assist the marketing manager of the New York Yankees to target families.
4. The New York Yankees want to conduct a telephone survey to determine how to attract more families to the Yankees' games. Design the sampling process.
5. If the MLB (mlb.mlb.com) is to conduct Internet surveys to determine how to increase attendance at MLB games, what sampling process would you recommend? ■

nonprobability sampling
Sampling techniques that do not use chance selection procedures. Rather, they rely on the personal judgment of the researcher.

probability sampling
A sampling procedure in which each element of the population has a fixed probabilistic chance of being selected for the sample.

A Classification of Sampling Techniques

Sampling techniques may be broadly classified as nonprobability and probability (see Figure 11.2). **Nonprobability sampling** relies on the personal judgment of the researcher rather than chance to select sample elements. The researcher can arbitrarily or consciously decide what elements to include in the sample. Nonprobability samples may yield good estimates of the population characteristics. However, they do not allow for objective evaluation of the precision of the sample results. Because there is no way of determining the probability of selecting any particular element for inclusion in the sample, the estimates obtained are not statistically projectable to the population. Commonly used nonprobability sampling techniques include convenience sampling, judgmental sampling, quota sampling, and snowball sampling.

In **probability sampling**, sampling units are selected by chance. It is possible to prespecify every potential sample of a given size that could be drawn from the population, as well as the

FIGURE 11.2
A Classification of Sampling Techniques

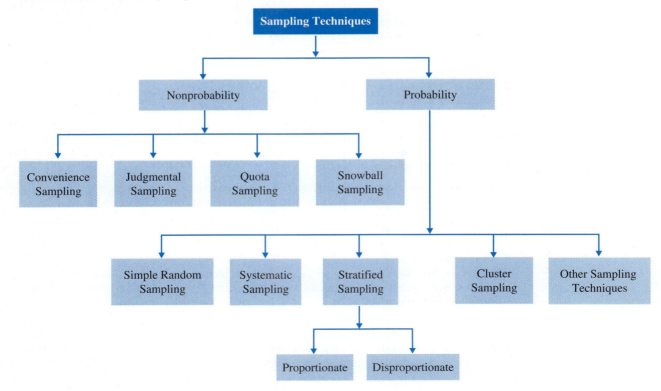

probability of selecting each sample. Every potential sample need not have the same probability of selection, but it is possible to specify the probability of selecting any particular sample of a given size. This requires not only a precise definition of the target population, but also a general specification of the sampling frame. Because sample elements are selected by chance, it is possible to determine the precision of the sample estimates of the characteristics of interest. Confidence intervals, which contain the true population value with a given level of certainty, can be calculated. This permits the researcher to make inferences or projections about the target population from which the sample was drawn. Probability sampling techniques are classified based on:

- Element versus cluster sampling
- Equal unit probability versus unequal probabilities
- Unstratified versus stratified selection
- Random versus systematic selection
- Single-stage versus multistage techniques

All possible combinations of these five aspects result in 32 different probability sampling techniques. Of these techniques, we consider simple random sampling, systematic sampling, stratified sampling, and cluster sampling in depth and briefly touch on some others. First, however, we discuss nonprobability sampling techniques.

Nonprobability Sampling Techniques

Figure 11.3 presents a graphical illustration of the various nonprobability sampling techniques. The population consists of 25 elements and we have to select a sample of size 5. A, B, C, D, and E represent groups and can also be viewed as strata or clusters.

Convenience Sampling

convenience sampling
A nonprobability sampling technique that attempts to obtain a sample of convenient elements. The selection of sampling units is left primarily to the interviewer.

Convenience sampling attempts to obtain a sample of convenient elements. The selection of sampling units is left primarily to the interviewer. Often, respondents are selected because they happen to be in the right place at the right time. Examples of convenience sampling include (1) use of students, church groups, and members of social organizations, (2) mall-intercept interviews without qualifying the respondents, (3) department stores using charge account lists, (4) tear-out questionnaires included in a magazine, and (5) "people on the street" interviews.[10]

Convenience sampling is the least expensive and least time-consuming of all sampling techniques. The sampling units are accessible, easy to measure, and cooperative. In spite of these advantages, this form of sampling has serious limitations. Many potential sources of selection bias are present, including respondent self-selection. Convenience samples are not representative of any definable population. Hence, it is not theoretically meaningful to generalize to any population from a convenience sample, and convenience samples are not appropriate for marketing research projects involving population inferences. Convenience samples are not recommended for descriptive or causal research, but they can be used in exploratory research for generating ideas, insights, or hypotheses. Convenience samples can be used for focus groups, pretesting questionnaires, or pilot studies. Even in these cases, caution should be exercised in interpreting the results. Nevertheless, this technique is sometimes used even in large surveys.

Real Research   Olympic Convenience

The International Olympic Committee (IOC—www.olympic.org) used surveys at the 2000 Summer Olympics in Sydney to find out what visitors thought about the level of commercialism in Sydney. One survey was given to a convenience sample of 200 visitors, asking them about what level of commercialism they find appropriate, whether they thought the event was too commercial, and whether company sponsorship of the Games was perceived to be positive. The survey, conducted by Performance Research (www.performanceresearch.com), revealed that 77 percent of the visitors found the presence of large corporations such as Coca-Cola (www.cocacola.com) and McDonald's (www.mcdonalds.com) to be appropriate. Furthermore, 88 percent of the visitors thought the sponsors contributed to the Olympics positively. About 33 percent said that they thought that a company's involvement in Sydney made them feel more positive about that company in general.

A Graphical Illustration of Nonprobability Sampling Techniques

1. Convenience Sampling

A	B	C	D	E
1	6	11	16	21
2	7	12	17	22
3	8	13	18	23
4	9	14	19	24
5	10	15	20	25

Group D happens to assemble at a convenient time and place. So all the elements in this group are selected. The resulting sample consists of elements 16, 17, 18, 19, and 20. Note that no elements are selected from groups A, B, C, and E.

2. Judgmental Sampling

A	B	C	D	E
1	6	11	16	21
2	7	12	17	22
3	8	13	18	23
4	9	14	19	24
5	10	15	20	25

The researcher considers groups B, C, and E to be typical and convenient. Within each of these groups one or two elements are selected based on typicality and convenience. The resulting sample consists of elements 8, 10, 11, 13, and 24. Note that no elements are selected from groups A and D.

3. Quota Sampling

A	B	C	D	E
1	6	11	16	21
2	7	12	17	22
3	8	13	18	23
4	9	14	19	24
5	10	15	20	25

A quota of one element from each group, A to E, is imposed. Within each group, one element is selected based on judgment or convenience. The resulting sample consists of elements 3, 6, 13, 20, and 22. Note that one element is selected from each column or group.

4. Snowball Sampling

	Random			
Selection		*Referrals*		
A	B	C	D	E
1	6	11	16	21
2	7	12	17	22
3	8	13	18	23
4	9	14	19	24
5	10	15	20	25

Elements 2 and 9 are selected randomly from groups A and B. Element 2 refers elements 12 and 13. Element 9 refers element 18. The resulting sample consists of elements 2, 9, 12, 13, and 18. Note that no element is selected from group E.

Performance Research continued their study of Olympic sponsorship by conducting 900 telephone, 1,500 Internet, and 300 on-site surveys using convenience samples in conjunction with the 2002 Winter Olympics in Salt Lake City, Utah. The results with respect to companies' sponsorship and involvement in the Olympics were again positive. The IOC used this information to enhance sponsorship revenues. For the 2002 Games, 30-second advertising spots were priced at roughly $600,000. Some companies that advertised were Coca-Cola, Visa, Kodak, McDonald's, Panasonic, Sports Illustrated, and Xerox. A survey was also conducted at the 2004 Olympics in Athens to assess spectators' satisfaction with the Games. A convenience sample of 1,024 persons—46 percent Greeks, 13 percent Americans, and the rest different nationalities—was used and the results indicated an overwhelming seal of approval for the Olympic Games in Athens. Surveys based on convenience samples were conducted for the 2008 Olympics in Beijing, as well. According to a survey by Survey Sampling International (surveysampling.com) more than 80 percent of Chinese citizens agreed that having the 2008 Olympic Games held in their country strengthened people's participation in sports activities.[11] ∎

Surveys based on convenience samples have indicated positive perceptions of companies sponsoring the Olympics.

Judgmental Sampling

judgmental sampling
A form of convenience sampling in which the population elements are purposely selected based on the judgment of the researcher.

Judgmental sampling is a form of convenience sampling in which the population elements are selected based on the judgment of the researcher. The researcher, exercising judgment or expertise, chooses the elements to be included in the sample, because he or she believes that they are representative of the population of interest or are otherwise appropriate. Common examples of judgmental sampling include (1) test markets selected to determine the potential of a new product, (2) purchase engineers selected in industrial marketing research because they are considered to be representative of the company, (3) bellwether precincts selected in voting behavior research, (4) expert witnesses used in court, and (5) department stores selected to test a new merchandising display system.

Project Research

Sampling Technique

In the department store study, 20 census tracts in the metropolitan area were selected based on judgment. Tracts with very poor people and those with undesirable (high-crime-rate) areas were excluded. In each tract, blocks judged to be representative or typical were selected. Finally, households located 10 houses apart from each other were selected within each block. The interviewer instructions were as follows.

"Start at the southeast corner of the designated block. Go around the entire block in a clockwise manner. After completing an interview, skip 10 households to select the next one. However, go to the next dwelling unit if you encounter any of the following situations: respondent not at home, respondent refuses to cooperate, or no qualified respondent is available. After completing a block, go to the next assigned block and follow the same procedure until you obtain the required number of completed interviews."

Project Activities

Answer the following as they pertain to the Sears project.

1. What is the target population? The sampling frame? The sample size?
2. Do you think the use of judgment sampling was appropriate? If not, which sampling technique do you recommend? ■

Judgmental sampling is low cost, convenient, and quick, yet it does not allow direct generalizations to a specific population, usually because the population is not defined explicitly. Judgmental sampling is subjective and its value depends entirely on the researcher's judgment, expertise, and creativity. It may be useful if broad population inferences are not required. As in the department store example, judgment samples are frequently used in commercial marketing research projects. An extension of this technique involves the use of quotas.

Quota Sampling

quota sampling
A nonprobability sampling technique that is a two-stage restricted judgmental sampling. The first stage consists of developing control categories or quotas of population elements. In the second stage, sample elements are selected based on convenience or judgment.

Quota sampling may be viewed as two-stage restricted judgmental sampling. The first stage consists of developing control categories, or quotas, of population elements. To develop these quotas, the researcher lists relevant control characteristics and determines the distribution of these characteristics in the target population. The relevant control characteristics, which may include sex, age, and race, are identified on the basis of judgment. Often, the quotas are assigned so that the proportion of the sample elements possessing the control characteristics is the same as the proportion of population elements with these characteristics. In other words, the quotas ensure that the composition of the sample is the same as the composition of the population with respect to the characteristics of interest. In the second stage, sample elements are selected based on convenience or judgment. Once the quotas have been assigned, there is considerable freedom in selecting the elements to be included in the sample. The only requirement is that the elements selected fit the control characteristics.[12]

Real Research

Does Metropolitan Magazine Readership Measure Up?

A study is undertaken to determine the readership of certain magazines by the adult population of a metropolitan area with a population of 350,000. A quota sample of 1,000 adults is selected. The control characteristics are sex, age, and race. Based on the composition of the adult population of the community, the quotas are assigned as follows.

Control Characteristic	Population Composition Percentage	Sample Composition Percentage	Number
Sex			
Male	48	48	480
Female	52	52	520
	100	100	1,000
Age			
18–30	27	27	270
31–45	39	39	390
46–60	16	16	160
Over 60	18	18	180
	100	100	1,000
Race			
White	59	59	590
Black	35	35	350
Other	6	6	60
	100	100	1,000

In this example, quotas are assigned such that the composition of the sample is the same as that of the population. In certain situations, however, it is desirable either to under- or oversample elements with certain characteristics. To illustrate, it may be desirable to oversample heavy users of a product so that their behavior can be examined in detail. Although this type of sample is not representative, it may nevertheless be very relevant.

Even if the sample composition mirrors that of the population with respect to the control characteristics, there is no assurance that the sample is representative. If a characteristic that is relevant to the problem is overlooked, the quota sample will not be representative. Relevant control characteristics are often omitted, because there are practical difficulties associated with including many control characteristics. Because the elements within each quota are selected based on convenience or judgment, many sources of selection bias are potentially present. The interviewers may go to selected areas where eligible respondents are more likely to be found. Likewise, they may avoid people who look unfriendly, are not well dressed, or live in undesirable locations. Quota sampling does not permit assessment of sampling error.

Quota sampling attempts to obtain representative samples at a relatively low cost. Its advantages are the lower costs and greater convenience to the interviewers in selecting elements for each quota. Recently, tighter controls have been imposed on interviewers and interviewing procedures that tend to reduce selection bias, and guidelines have been suggested for improving the quality of mall-intercept quota samples. Under certain conditions, quota sampling obtains results close to those for conventional probability sampling.[13]

Snowball Sampling

snowball sampling

A nonprobability sampling technique in which an initial group of respondents is selected randomly. Subsequent respondents are selected based on the referrals or information provided by the initial respondents. This process may be carried out in waves by obtaining referrals from referrals.

In **snowball sampling**, an initial group of respondents is selected, usually at random. After being interviewed, these respondents are asked to identify others who belong to the target population of interest. Subsequent respondents are selected based on the referrals. This process may be carried out in waves by obtaining referrals from referrals, thus leading to a snowballing effect. Even though probability sampling is used to select the initial respondents, the final sample is a nonprobability sample. The referrals will have demographic and psychographic characteristics that are more similar to the persons referring them than would occur by chance.[14]

A major objective of snowball sampling is to estimate characteristics that are rare in the population. Examples include users of particular government or social services, such as food stamps, whose names cannot be revealed; special census groups, such as widowed males under 35; and members of a scattered minority population. Snowball sampling is used in industrial buyer–seller research to identify buyer–seller pairs. The major advantage of snowball sampling is that it substantially increases the likelihood of locating the desired characteristic in the population. It also results in relatively low sampling variance and costs.[15]

Real Research   Knowledge Is Power

It is estimated that in 2009, every minute someone somewhere in the world was infected with HIV. A study was undertaken to examine the risk behavior of Indo-Chinese drug users (IDUs) in Australia. A structured questionnaire was administered to 184 IDUs age 15 to 24. Respondents were recruited using snowball sampling techniques "based on social and street networks." This technique was used because drug users know other drug users and can easily provide referrals for research purposes. Respondents were asked numerous questions regarding their drug use, injection-related risk behaviors, and perceived susceptibility to HIV. Interviews were held in Melbourne and in Sydney. Locations of interviews varied from on the streets, to restaurants and coffee shops, and even in people's homes.

The results showed that heroin was the first drug injected for 98 percent of the respondents, and 86 percent of them stated they smoked the drug prior to intravenous use. Age for the first injection varied from 11 years to 23 years, averaging 17 years. Thirty-six percent "ever shared" a needle, 23 percent of those shared with a close friend, and 1 percent shared with a partner or lover. The awareness of bloodborne viruses and related complications was low. Based on these results, the public health officials in Australia decided to launch a vigorous campaign to educate the IDUs of the risks they faced and what they could do to reduce them.[16] ■

In this example, snowball sampling was more efficient than random selection. In other cases, random selection of respondents through probability sampling techniques is more appropriate.

ACTIVE RESEARCH

Unisex Shirts: Sampling Gender Inequalities Affirmatively

Visit www.polo.com and conduct an Internet search using a search engine and your library's online database to obtain information on the marketing strategy of Polo Ralph Lauren.

As the vice president of marketing for Polo Ralph Lauren, what information would you like to have to determine whether the company should launch nationally a new line of unisex shirts it has developed?

Polo Ralph Lauren would like to determine initial consumer reaction to a new line of unisex shirts it has developed. If nonprobability sampling is to be used, which sampling technique would you recommend and why?

Probability Sampling Techniques

Probability sampling techniques vary in terms of sampling efficiency. Sampling efficiency is a concept that reflects a trade-off between sampling cost and precision. Precision refers to the level of uncertainty about the characteristic being measured. Precision is inversely related to sampling errors but positively related to cost. The greater the precision, the greater the cost, and most studies require a trade-off. The researcher should strive for the most efficient sampling design, subject to the budget allocated. The efficiency of a probability sampling technique may be assessed by comparing it to that of simple random sampling. Figure 11.4 presents a graphical illustration of the various probability sampling techniques. As in the case of nonprobability sampling, the population consists of 25 elements and we have to select a sample of size 5. A, B, C, D, and E represent groups and can also be viewed as strata or clusters.

simple random sampling (SRS)
A probability sampling technique in which each element in the population has a known and equal probability of selection. Every element is selected independently of every other element and the sample is drawn by a random procedure from a sampling frame.

Simple Random Sampling

In **simple random sampling (SRS)**, each element in the population has a known and equal probability of selection. Furthermore, each possible sample of a given size (n) has a known and equal probability of being the sample actually selected. This implies that every element is selected independently of every other element. The sample is drawn by a random procedure from a sampling

FIGURE 11.4
A Graphical Illustration of Probability Sampling Techniques

A Graphical Illustration of Probability Sampling Techniques

1. *Simple Random Sampling*

A	B	C	D	E
1	6	11	**16**	21
2	**7**	12	17	22
3	8	13	18	23
4	**9**	14	19	**24**
5	10	15	20	25

Select five random numbers from 1 to 25. The resulting sample consists of population elements 3, 7, 9, 16, and 24. Note that there is no element from Group C.

2. *Systematic Sampling*

A	B	C	D	E
1	6	11	16	21
2	**7**	**12**	**17**	**22**
3	8	13	18	23
4	9	14	19	24
5	10	15	20	25

Select a random number between 1 to 5, say 2. The resulting sample consists of population 2, $(2 + 5 =)$ 7, $(2 + 5 \times 2 =)$ 12, $(2 + 5 \times 3 =)$ 17, and $(2 + 5 \times 4 =)$ 22. Note that all the elements are selected from a single row.

3. *Stratified Sampling*

A	B	C	D	E
1	6	11	16	**21**
2	**7**	12	17	22
3	8	**13**	18	23
4	9	14	**19**	24
5	10	15	20	25

Randomly select a number from 1 to 5 from each stratum, A to E. The resulting sample consists of population elements 4, 7, 13, 19, and 21. Note that one element is selected from each column.

4. *Cluster Sampling (Two-Stage)*

A	B	C	D	E
1	6	11	16	**21**
2	**7**	12	17	22
3	8	13	**18**	**23**
4	9	14	19	24
5	10	15	**20**	25

Randomly select three clusters, B, D, and E. Within each cluster, randomly select one or two elements. The resulting sample consists of population elements 7, 18, 20, 21, and 23. Note that no elements are selected from clusters A and C.

frame. This method is equivalent to a lottery system in which names are placed in a container, the container is shaken, and the names of the winners are then drawn out in an unbiased manner.

To draw a simple random sample, the researcher first compiles a sampling frame in which each element is assigned a unique identification number. Then random numbers are generated to determine which elements to include in the sample. The random numbers may be generated with a computer routine or a table (see Table 1 shown in the Appendix of Statistical Tables). Suppose that a sample of size 10 is to be selected from a sampling frame containing 800 elements. This could be done by starting with row 1 and column 1 of Table 1, considering the three rightmost digits, and going down the column until 10 numbers between 1 and 800 have been selected. Numbers outside this range are ignored. The elements corresponding to the random numbers generated constitute the sample. Thus, in our example, elements 480, 368, 130, 167, 570, 562, 301, 579, 475, and 553 would be selected. Note that the last three digits of row 6 (921) and row 11 (918) were ignored, because they were out of range.

SRS has many desirable features. It is easily understood. The sample results may be projected to the target population. Most approaches to statistical inference assume that the data have been collected by simple random sampling. However, SRS suffers from at least four significant limitations. First, it is often difficult to construct a sampling frame that will permit a simple random sample to be drawn. Second, SRS can result in samples that are very large or spread over large geographic areas, thus increasing the time and cost of data collection. Third, SRS often results in lower precision with larger standard errors than other probability sampling techniques. Fourth, SRS may or may not result in a representative sample. Although samples drawn will represent the population well on average, a given simple random sample may grossly misrepresent the target population. This is more likely if the size of the sample is small. For these reasons, SRS is not widely used in marketing research. Procedures such as systematic sampling are more popular.

Systematic Sampling

systematic sampling
A probability sampling technique in which the sample is chosen by selecting a random starting point and then picking every *i*th element in succession from the sampling frame.

In **systematic sampling**, the sample is chosen by selecting a random starting point and then picking every *i*th element in succession from the sampling frame. The sampling interval, *i*, is determined by dividing the population size *N* by the sample size *n* and rounding to the nearest integer. For example, there are 100,000 elements in the population and a sample of 1,000 is desired. In this case, the sampling interval, *i*, is 100. A random number between 1 and 100 is selected. If, for example, this number is 23, the sample consists of elements 23, 123, 223, 323, 423, 523, and so on.[17]

Systematic sampling is similar to SRS in that each population element has a known and equal probability of selection. However, it is different from SRS in that only the permissible samples of size *n* that can be drawn have a known and equal probability of selection. The remaining samples of size *n* have a zero probability of being selected.

For systematic sampling, the researcher assumes that the population elements are ordered in some respect. In some cases, the ordering (for example, alphabetic listing in a telephone book) is unrelated to the characteristic of interest. In other instances, the ordering is directly related to the characteristic under investigation. For example, credit card customers may be listed in order of outstanding balance, or firms in a given industry may be ordered according to annual sales. If the population elements are arranged in a manner unrelated to the characteristic of interest, systematic sampling will yield results quite similar to SRS.

On the other hand, when the ordering of the elements is related to the characteristic of interest, systematic sampling increases the representativeness of the sample. If firms in an industry are arranged in increasing order of annual sales, a systematic sample will include some small and some large firms. A simple random sample may be unrepresentative because it may contain, for example, only small firms or a disproportionate number of small firms. If the ordering of the elements produces a cyclical pattern, systematic sampling may decrease the representativeness of the sample. To illustrate, consider the use of systematic sampling to generate a sample of monthly department store sales from a sampling frame containing monthly sales for the last 60 years. If a sampling interval of 12 is chosen, the resulting sample would not reflect the month-to-month variation in sales.[18]

Systematic sampling is less costly and easier than SRS, because random selection is done only once. Moreover, the random numbers do not have to be matched with individual elements as in SRS. Because some lists contain millions of elements, considerable time can be saved. This reduces the costs of sampling. If information related to the characteristic of interest is available for the population, systematic sampling can be used to obtain a more representative and reliable (lower sampling error) sample than SRS. Another relative advantage is that systematic sampling can even be used without knowledge of the composition (elements) of the sampling frame. For example, every *i*th person leaving a department store or mall can be intercepted. For these reasons, systematic sampling is often employed in consumer mail, telephone, mall-intercept, and Internet interviews.

Real Research   ## Autos.msn.com Equips Autos with Cell Phone Accessories

Autos.msn.com is a Microsoft-owned Web site (autos.msn.com) that gives auto pricing and other vehicle research information to consumers. It conducted a poll to find out if people currently use or would consider using the cell phone hands-free devices. Autos.msn.com conducted an Internet survey using systematic random sampling that popped up on a separate screen when every 50th visitor stopped at the Web site. Of the 879 individuals who were presented with the survey, 836 responded.

The results indicated that 62 percent of the respondents had never used a hands-free device, and only 54 percent were willing to use one in the future. In light of the realization that individuals are not too receptive to the idea of attaching hands-free devices to their cellular phones, it is estimated that by the year 2012, 75 percent of the vehicles in the country will be equipped with cell phone accessories. This will take place as a result of state laws that will increasingly be passed. For example, a Washington, D.C., law prohibits anyone driving in the city from talking on a cell phone without a hands-free device.[19] ■

Stratified Sampling

stratified sampling
A probability sampling technique that uses a two-step process to partition the population into subpopulations, or strata. Elements are selected from each stratum by a random procedure.

Stratified sampling is a two-step process in which the population is partitioned into subpopulations, or strata. The strata should be mutually exclusive and collectively exhaustive in that every population element should be assigned to one and only one stratum and no population elements should be omitted. Next, elements are selected from each stratum by a random procedure, usually SRS. Technically, only SRS should be employed in selecting the elements from each stratum. In practice, sometimes systematic sampling and other probability sampling procedures are employed. Stratified sampling differs from quota sampling in that the sample elements are selected probabilistically rather than based on convenience or judgment. A major objective of stratified sampling is to increase precision without increasing cost.[20]

The variables used to partition the population into strata are referred to as *stratification variables*. The criteria for the selection of these variables consist of homogeneity, heterogeneity, relatedness, and cost. The elements within a stratum should be as homogeneous as possible, but the elements in different strata should be as heterogeneous as possible. The stratification variables should also be closely related to the characteristic of interest. The more closely these criteria are met, the greater the effectiveness in controlling extraneous sampling variation. Finally, the variables should decrease the cost of the stratification process by being easy to measure and apply. Variables commonly used for stratification include demographic characteristics (as illustrated in the example for quota sampling), type of customer (credit card versus non–credit card), size of firm, or type of industry. It is possible to use more than one variable for stratification, although more than two are seldom used because of pragmatic and cost considerations. The number of strata to use is a matter of judgment, but experience suggests the use of no more than six. Beyond six strata, any gain in precision is more than offset by the increased cost of stratification and sampling.

Real Research   ## Online Retirement Plans Are On

CIGNA (www.cigna.com) provides health care and related benefits offered through the workplace. Key product lines include health care products and services, and group disability, life, and accident insurance. The company achieved revenues of $19.1 billion in 2008. CIGNA conducted a national stratified marketing research survey to learn more about online users' demands for additional Internet retirement services. CIGNA contracted Gfk NOP World (www.gfkamerica.com) to survey by telephone 659 full-time employees over the age of 18 with a quota of 80 percent of those surveyed to be participants in a retirement plan, such as a pension or 401(k) plan through their employer. The sample was stratified by income and age because of differences in the use of the Internet and possible varying concerns on retirement services. The sampling design adopted is shown in the accompanying table.

The survey revealed that results did vary by income and age, confirming the usefulness of these variables for stratification. For example, 75 percent of those with annual income less than $20,000 had not conducted at least one e-commerce Internet transaction, whereas only 30 percent of those with income of $50,000 or more had not done so. Age was an important factor in users' preferences for online retirement plan information, with those over 65 expressing the least preference.

Overall, the results of the survey showed that there is an increasing interest in employees having access to their retirement programs and funds online, which gives them greater control in their retirement planning. CIGNA used the survey results to offer AnswerNet and CIGNATrade, Web sites that allow customers to access their retirement plans and brokerage accounts, respectively. Furthermore, CIGNA and Yahoo! offered CIGNA health care members and retirement plan participants the opportunity to have personalized benefits Web sites based on the My Yahoo! interface.[21] A key to obtaining these actionable research findings was the use of an appropriate sampling design that may be represented as:

Sampling Design

Target population	Adults meeting qualifications: over 18 years old, full-time employment in the United States, working telephone number, 80 percent currently participate in retirement plan during the survey period
Sampling frame	Commercial phone list provided by GfK NOP
Sampling technique	Stratified sampling by age and income
Sample size	659
Execution	Allocate sample by strata, select random phone number from list, survey first qualified household member subject to quota requirements ■

Another important decision involves the use of proportionate or disproportionate sampling (see Figure 11.2). In proportionate stratified sampling, the size of the sample drawn from each stratum is proportionate to the relative size of that stratum in the total population. In disproportionate stratified sampling, the size of the sample from each stratum is proportionate to the relative size of that stratum and to the standard deviation of the distribution of the characteristic of interest among all the elements in that stratum. The logic behind disproportionate sampling is simple. First, strata with larger relative sizes are more influential in determining the population mean, and these strata should also exert a greater influence in deriving the sample estimates. Consequently, more elements should be drawn from strata of larger relative size. Second, to increase precision, more elements should be drawn from strata with larger standard deviations and fewer elements should be drawn from strata with smaller standard deviations. (If all the elements in a stratum are identical, a sample size of 1 will result in perfect information.) Note that the two methods are identical if the characteristic of interest has the same standard deviation within each stratum.

Disproportionate sampling requires that some estimate of the relative variation, or standard deviation of the distribution of the characteristic of interest, within strata be known. As this information is not always available, the researcher may have to rely on intuition and logic to determine sample sizes for each stratum. For example, large retail stores might be expected to have greater variation in the sales of some products as compared to small stores. Hence, the number of large stores in a sample may be disproportionately large. When the researcher is primarily interested in examining differences between strata, a common sampling strategy is to select the same sample size from each stratum.

Stratified sampling can ensure that all the important subpopulations are represented in the sample. This is particularly important if the distribution of the characteristic of interest in the population is skewed. For example, because most households have annual incomes of less than $75,000, the distribution of household incomes is skewed. Very few households have annual incomes of $200,000 or more. If a simple random sample is taken, households with incomes of $200,000 or more may not be adequately represented. Stratified sampling would guarantee that the sample contains a certain number of these households. Stratified sampling combines the simplicity of SRS with potential gains in precision. Therefore, it is a popular sampling technique.

Cluster Sampling

In **cluster sampling**, the target population is first divided into mutually exclusive and collectively exhaustive subpopulations, or clusters. Then a random sample of clusters is selected, based on a probability sampling technique such as SRS. For each selected cluster, either all the elements are

cluster sampling
First, the target population is divided into mutually exclusive and collectively exhaustive subpopulations called *clusters*. Then, a random sample of clusters is selected based on a probability sampling technique such as simple random sampling. For each selected cluster, either all the elements are included in the sample or a sample of elements is drawn probabilistically.

FIGURE 11.5

**Types of Cluster
Sampling**

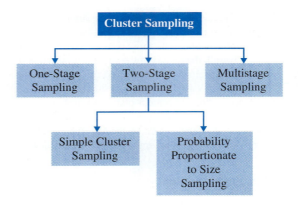

included in the sample or a sample of elements is drawn probabilistically. If all the elements in each selected cluster are included in the sample, the procedure is called *one-stage cluster sampling.* If a sample of elements is drawn probabilistically from each selected cluster, the procedure is *two-stage cluster sampling.* As shown in Figure 11.5, two-stage cluster sampling can be either simple two-stage cluster sampling involving SRS, or probability proportionate to size (PPS) sampling. Furthermore, a cluster sample can have multiple (more than two) stages, as in multistage cluster sampling.

The key distinction between cluster sampling and stratified sampling is that in cluster sampling, only a sample of subpopulations (clusters) is chosen, whereas in stratified sampling, all the subpopulations (strata) are selected for further sampling. The objectives of the two methods are also different. The objective of cluster sampling is to increase sampling efficiency by decreasing costs. The objective of stratified sampling is to increase precision. With respect to homogeneity and heterogeneity, the criteria for forming clusters are just the opposite of that for forming strata. Elements within a cluster should be as heterogeneous as possible, but clusters themselves should be as homogeneous as possible. Ideally, each cluster should be a small-scale representation of the population. In cluster sampling, a sampling frame is needed only for those clusters selected for the sample. The differences between stratified sampling and cluster sampling are summarized in Table 11.3.

area sampling
A common form of cluster sampling in which the clusters consist of geographic areas such as counties, housing tracts, blocks, or other area descriptions.

A common form of cluster sampling is **area sampling**, in which the clusters consist of geographic areas, such as counties, housing tracts, or blocks. If only one level of sampling takes place in selecting the basic elements (for example, the researcher samples blocks and then all the households within the selected blocks are included in the sample), the design is called *single-stage area sampling.* If two (or more) levels of sampling take place before the basic elements are selected (the researcher samples blocks, and then samples households within selected blocks), the design is called *two-(multi)stage area sampling.* The distinguishing feature of the one-stage area sample is that all of the households in the selected blocks (or geographic areas) are included in the sample.

There are two types of two-stage designs, as shown in Figure 11.5. One type involves SRS at the first stage (e.g., sampling blocks) as well as the second stage (e.g., sampling households within blocks). This design is called *simple two-stage cluster sampling.* In this design, the fraction of elements (e.g., households) selected at the second stage is the same for each sample cluster

TABLE 11.3

Differences Between Stratified and Cluster Sampling

Factor	Stratified Sampling	Cluster Sampling (One-Stage)
Objective	Increase precision	Decrease cost
Subpopulations	All strata are included	A sample of clusters is chosen
Within subpopulations	Each stratum should be homogeneous	Each cluster should be heterogeneous
Across subpopulations	Strata should be heterogeneous	Clusters should be homogeneous
Sampling frame	Needed for the entire population	Needed only for the selected clusters
Selection of elements	Elements selected from each stratum randomly	All elements from each selected cluster are included

(e.g., selected blocks). A marketing research project investigated the behavior of affluent consumers. A simple random sample of 800 block groups was selected from a listing of neighborhoods with average incomes exceeding $50,000 in the states ranked in the top half by income according to census data. Commercial list organizations supplied head-of-household names and addresses for approximately 95 percent of the census-tabulated homes in these 800 block groups. From the 213,000 enumerated households, 9,000 were selected by simple random sampling.[22]

This design is appropriate when the clusters are equal in size, that is, the clusters contain approximately the same number of sampling units. However, if they differ greatly in size, simple two-stage cluster sampling can lead to biased estimates. Sometimes the clusters can be made of equal size by combining clusters. When this option is not feasible, probability proportionate to size (PPS) sampling can be used.

In **probability proportionate to size sampling**, the clusters are sampled with probability proportional to size. The size of a cluster is defined in terms of the number of sampling units within that cluster. Thus, in the first stage, large clusters are more likely to be included than small clusters. In the second stage, the probability of selecting a sampling unit in a selected cluster varies inversely with the size of the cluster. Thus, the probability that any particular sampling unit will be included in the sample is equal for all units, because the unequal first-stage probabilities are balanced by the unequal second-stage probabilities. The numbers of sampling units included from the selected clusters are approximately equal. An example of this type of multistage sampling is provided by the "Truth" campaign.

probability proportionate to size sampling
A selection method in which the clusters are selected with probability proportional to size and the probability of selecting a sampling unit in a selected cluster varies inversely with the size of the cluster.

Real Research

The "Truth" Is Out with Youth Smoking

The Truth campaign (www.thetruth.com), aimed primarily at youth, consists of offering startling cigarette industry–related facts in a straightforward manner so that the viewer can make his or her own conclusions, opinions, and choices. To examine the effectiveness of this campaign, the experimenters collected data from 1997 through 2002 from the National Institute on Drug Abuse and surveys conducted by the University of Michigan. They targeted 420 randomly selected public and private schools through a multistage sampling design. In the first stage, they randomly selected geographic areas. During stage 2, they randomly selected which schools they would target, and in the final stage they randomly selected which classes would take the survey. At all stages, sample weights were used to ensure that the probability of a geographic location, school, or class was representative of their actual proportion of the population.

They selected up to 350 students from each participating school and administered the surveys during normal class hours in normal classrooms. Each respondent was asked, "How frequently have you smoked cigarettes during the past 30 days?" Responses were scored. The survey covered a total of 18,000 eighth graders, 17,000 tenth graders, and 16,000 twelfth graders per year from 1997 to 2002, with an average response rate of 89 percent, 86.2 percent, and 82.8 percent, respectively.

The results of the survey showed that the Truth campaign led to a significant decline in youth smoking prevalence nationwide. All things considered, the Truth campaign has been highly successful and is still being promoted as of 2009. As long as legislation requires tobacco companies to fund such campaigns, there will be antismoking messages aimed toward youth to prevent young smokers.[23] ∎

Cluster sampling has two major advantages: feasibility and low cost. In many situations, the only sampling frames readily available for the target population are clusters, not population elements. It is often not feasible to compile a list of all consumers in a population, given the resources and constraints. However, lists of geographic areas, telephone exchanges, and other clusters of consumers can be constructed relatively easily. Cluster sampling is the most cost-effective probability sampling technique. This advantage must be weighed against several limitations. Cluster sampling results in relatively imprecise samples, and it is difficult to form heterogeneous clusters because, for example, households in a block tend to be similar rather than dissimilar.[24] It can be difficult to compute and interpret statistics based on clusters. The strengths and weaknesses of cluster sampling and the other basic sampling techniques are summarized in Table 11.4. Exhibit 11.1 on page 357 describes the procedures for drawing probability samples.

Other Probability Sampling Techniques

In addition to the four basic probability sampling techniques, there are a variety of other sampling techniques. Most of these may be viewed as extensions of the basic techniques and

TABLE 11.4
Strengths and Weaknesses of Basic Sampling Techniques

Technique	Strengths	Weaknesses
Nonprobability Sampling		
Convenience sampling	Least expensive, least time-consuming, most convenient	Selection bias, sample not representative, not recommended for descriptive or causal research
Judgmental sampling	Low cost, convenient, not time-consuming	Does not allow generalization, subjective
Quota sampling	Sample can be controlled for certain characteristics	Selection bias, no assurance of representativeness
Snowball sampling	Can estimate rare characteristics	Time-consuming
Probability Sampling		
Simple random sampling (SRS)	Easily understood, results projectable	Difficult to construct sampling frame, expensive, lower precision, no assurance of representativeness
Systematic sampling	Can increase representativeness, easier to implement than SRS, sampling frame not necessary	Can decrease representativeness if there are cyclical patterns
Stratified sampling	Includes all important subpopulations, precision	Difficult to select relevant stratification variables, not feasible to stratify on many variables, expensive
Cluster sampling	Easy to implement, cost-effective	Imprecise, difficult to compute and interpret results

sequential sampling
A probability sampling technique in which the population elements are sampled sequentially, data collection and analysis are done at each stage, and a decision is made as to whether additional population elements should be sampled.

double sampling
A sampling technique in which certain population elements are sampled twice.

were developed to address complex sampling problems. Two techniques with some relevance to marketing research are sequential sampling and double sampling.

In **sequential sampling**, the population elements are sampled sequentially, data collection and analysis are done at each stage, and a decision is made as to whether additional population elements should be sampled. The sample size is not known in advance, but a decision rule is stated before sampling begins. At each stage, this rule indicates whether sampling should be continued or whether enough information has been obtained. Sequential sampling has been used to determine preferences for two competing alternatives. In one study, respondents were asked which of two alternatives they preferred, and sampling was terminated when sufficient evidence was accumulated to validate a preference. It has also been used to establish the price differential between a standard model and a deluxe model of a consumer durable.[25]

In **double sampling**, also called *two-phase sampling*, certain population elements are sampled twice. In the first phase, a sample is selected and some information is collected from all the elements in the sample. In the second phase, a subsample is drawn from the original sample and additional information is obtained from the elements in the subsample. The process may be extended to three or more phases, and the different phases may take place simultaneously or at different times. Double sampling can be useful when no sampling frame is readily available for selecting final sampling units but when the elements of the frame are known to be contained within a broader sampling frame. For example, a researcher wants to select households that consume apple juice in a given city. The households of interest are contained within the set of all households, but the researcher does not know which they are. In applying double sampling, the researcher would obtain a sampling frame of all households in the first phase. This would be constructed from the city directory or purchased. Then a sample of households would be drawn, using systematic random sampling to determine the amount of apple juice consumed. In the second phase, households that consume apple juice would be selected and stratified according to the amount of apple juice consumed. Then a stratified random sample would be drawn and detailed questions regarding apple juice consumption asked.[26]

EXHIBIT 11.1

Procedures for Drawing Probability Samples

Simple Random Sampling

1. Select a suitable sampling frame.
2. Assign each element a number from 1 to N (population size).
3. Generate n (sample size) different random numbers between 1 and N. This can be done using a microcomputer or mainframe software package or using a table of simple random numbers (Table 1 in the Appendix of Statistical Tables). To use Table 1, select the appropriate number of digits (e.g., if $N = 900$, select three digits). Arbitrarily select a beginning number. Then proceed either up or down until n different numbers between 1 and N have been selected. Note: discard 0, duplicate numbers, and numbers greater than N.
4. The numbers generated denote the elements that should be included in the sample.

Systematic Sampling

1. Select a suitable sampling frame.
2. Assign each element a number from 1 to N (population size).
3. Determine the sampling interval, i, $i = \dfrac{N}{n}$. If i is a fraction, round to the nearest integer.
4. Select a random number, r, between 1 and i, as explained in simple random sampling.
5. The elements with the following numbers will comprise the systematic random sample: $r, r + i, r + 2i, r + 3i, r + 4i, \ldots, r + (n - 1)i$.

Stratified Sampling

1. Select a suitable sampling frame.
2. Select the stratification variable(s) and the number of strata (H).
3. Divide the entire population into H strata. Based on the classification variable, assign each element of the population to one of the H strata.
4. In each stratum, number the elements from 1 to N_h (the population size of stratum h).
5. Determine the sample size of each stratum, n_h, based on proportionate or disproportionate stratified sampling. Note: $\displaystyle\sum_{h=1}^{H} n_h = n$
6. In each stratum, select a simple random sample of size n_h.

Cluster Sampling

We describe the procedure for selecting a simple two-stage sample, because this represents the simpler case.

1. Assign a number, from 1 to N, to each element in the population.
2. Divide the population into C clusters, of which c will be included in the sample.
3. Calculate the sampling interval, i, $i = \dfrac{N}{c}$. If i is a fraction, round to the nearest integer.
4. Select a random number, r, between 1 and i, as explained in simple random sampling.
5. Identify elements with the following numbers: $r, r + i, r + 2i, r + 3i, \ldots, r + (c - 1)i$.
6. Select the clusters that contain the identified elements.
7. Select sampling units within each selected cluster based on SRS or systematic sampling. The number of sampling units selected from each sample cluster is approximately the same and equal to $\dfrac{n}{c}$.
8. If the population of a cluster exceeds the sampling interval, i, that cluster is selected with certainty. That cluster is removed from further consideration. Calculate the new population size, N^*, number of clusters to be selected, $c^*(= c - 1)$, and the new sampling interval, i^*. Repeat this process until each of the remaining clusters has a population less than the relevant sampling interval. If b clusters have been selected with certainty, select the remaining $c - b$ clusters according to steps 1 through 7. The fraction of units to be sampled from each cluster selected with certainty is the overall sampling fraction $= n/N$. Thus, for clusters selected with certainty we would select $n_s = \dfrac{n}{N}(N_1 + N_2 + \cdots + N_b)$ units. The units selected from clusters selected under two-stage sampling will therefore be $n^* = n - n_s$.

TABLE 11.5 Choosing Nonprobability Versus Probability Sampling		
	Conditions Favoring the Use of	
Factors	Nonprobability Sampling	Probability Sampling
Nature of research	Exploratory	Conclusive
Relative magnitude of sampling and nonsampling errors	Nonsampling errors are larger	Sampling errors are larger
Variability in the population	Homogeneous (low)	Heterogeneous (high)
Statistical considerations	Unfavorable	Favorable
Operational considerations	Favorable	Unfavorable
Time	Favorable	Unfavorable
Cost	Favorable	Unfavorable

Choosing Nonprobability Versus Probability Sampling

The choice between nonprobability and probability samples should be based on considerations such as the nature of the research, relative magnitude of nonsampling versus sampling errors, variability in the population, as well as statistical and operational considerations such as costs and time (see Table 11.5). For example, in exploratory research, the findings are treated as preliminary and the use of probability sampling may not be warranted. On the other hand, in conclusive research where the researcher wishes to use the results to estimate overall market shares or the size of the total market, probability sampling is favored. Probability samples allow statistical projection of the results to a target population. For these reasons, probability sampling was used in the opening duck stamp example.

For some research problems, highly accurate estimates of population characteristics are required. In these situations, the elimination of selection bias and the ability to calculate sampling error make probability sampling desirable. However, probability sampling will not always result in more accurate results. If nonsampling errors are likely to be an important factor, then nonprobability sampling may be preferable, as the use of judgment may allow greater control over the sampling process.

Another consideration is the homogeneity of the population with respect to the variables of interest. A more heterogeneous population would favor probability sampling, because it would be more important to secure a representative sample. Probability sampling is preferable from a statistical viewpoint, because it is the basis of the most common statistical techniques.

However, probability sampling is sophisticated and requires statistically trained researchers. It generally costs more and takes longer than nonprobability sampling. In many marketing research projects, it is difficult to justify the additional time and expense and thus operational considerations favor the use of nonprobability sampling. In practice, the objectives of the study often exert a dominant influence on which sampling method will be used, as in the following example.

Real Research   Laboring Labor Statistics

The Bureau of Labor Statistics (www.bls.gov) publishes employment measurements on a monthly basis. These measurements assumed greater importance given the relatively high unemployment in 2009. The BLS traditionally used a quota sampling method, which cut off the sample when a certain number of responses were met for each type of employer in a specific industry or labor sector. In June 2000, the bureau applied a new technique for estimating jobs in the wholesale trade sector, which included suppliers for large retailers, construction contractors, hospitals, and farms. The new technique was stratified sampling that stratified employers by labor sectors. Within each stratum, employers were selected at random so that a true representation of the employment numbers could be obtained. The previously used quota method was not adapted every year to account for the actual percentage of each type of employer within the sector. For instance, the number of farming employers is decreasing, whereas hospital and medical-related employers are on the rise, which would require changes in the quota percentages. The quota method was phased out for all sectors by June 2003.

Probabilistic sampling provides better estimates of employment statistics because it selects employers at random within each labor sector. The sampling estimates can be projected to the population and sampling errors estimated. Patricia M. Getz, division chief for the bureau's Current Employment Statistics division, describes probabilistic sampling as "the recognized standard—more scientifically based."[27] ■

ACTIVE RESEARCH

Herbal Essences: Introducing New Products Is of the Essence

Conduct an Internet search using a search engine and your library's online database to determine the size of the shampoo market in the United States.

As the marketing chief of Herbal Essences, how would you determine which new products should be introduced into the market?

Herbal Essences would like to determine the demand for new shampoo. If a survey is to be conducted using probability sampling, which sampling technique should be used and why?

Uses of Nonprobability and Probability Sampling

Nonprobability sampling is used in concept tests, package tests, name tests, and copy tests, where projections to the populations are usually not needed. In such studies, interest centers on the proportion of the sample that gives various responses or expresses various attitudes. Samples for these studies can be drawn using methods such as mall-intercept quota sampling. On the other hand, probability sampling is used when there is a need for highly accurate estimates of market share or sales volume for the entire market. National market tracking studies, which provide information on product category and brand usage rates, as well as psychographic and demographic profiles of users, use probability sampling. Studies that use probability sampling generally employ telephone interviews. Stratified and systematic sampling are combined with some form of random digit dialing to select the respondents.

Internet Sampling

Issues in Online Sampling

As discussed in Chapter 6, Internet surveys (and sampling) offer many advantages. The respondents can complete the survey at their convenience. Internet surveys, like computer-assisted surveys (computer-assisted telephone interviewing, CATI, and computer-assisted personal interviewing, CAPI), can incorporate automatic skip patterns, consistency check, and other intelligent features. The data collection can be fast and inexpensive. A major issue related to Internet sampling is representativeness because of lack of computer ownership and Internet access in many households in the United States. Internet access is even more restricted in foreign countries. Furthermore, heavy users of the Internet may have a disproportionately higher probability of being included. Unrestricted Internet samples in which any visitor can participate are convenience samples and suffer from self-selection bias in that the respondents can initiate their own selection.

Sampling potential respondents who are surfing the Internet is meaningful if the sample that is generated is representative of the target population. More and more industries are meeting this criterion. In software, computers, networking, technical publishing, semiconductors, and graduate education, it is rapidly becoming feasible to use the Internet for sampling respondents for quantitative research, such as surveys. For internal customer surveys, where the client's employees share a corporate e-mail system, an intranet survey is practical even if workers have no access to the external Internet. However, sampling on the Internet may not yet be practical for many noncomputer-oriented consumer products. For example, if P&G were to do a survey of housewives to determine their preferences and usage of laundry detergents, an

Internet survey would not be a good choice as an Internet sample is unlikely to be representative of the target population.

To avoid sampling errors, the researcher must be able to control the pool from which the respondents are selected. Also, the researcher must ensure that the respondents do not respond multiple times ("stuff the ballot box"). These requirements are met by e-mail surveys, where the researcher selects specific respondents. Furthermore, the surveys can be encoded to match the returned surveys with their corresponding outbound e-mailings. This can also be accomplished with Web surveys by e-mailing invitations to selected respondents and asking them to visit the Web site where the survey is posted. In this case, the survey is posted in a hidden location on the Web, which is protected by a password. Hence, non-invited Web surfers are unable to access it.

Online Sampling Techniques

The sampling techniques commonly used on the Internet may be classified as online intercept (nonrandom and random), online recruited, and other techniques, as shown in Figure 11.6. Online recruited techniques can be further classified as panel (recruited or opt-in) or nonpanel (list rentals).

In online intercept sampling, visitors to a Web site are intercepted and given an opportunity to participate in the survey. The interception can be made at one or more Web sites, including high-traffic sites such as Yahoo! In nonrandom sampling, every visitor is intercepted. This may be meaningful if the Web site traffic is low, the survey has to be completed in a short time, and no incentive is being offered. However, this results in a convenience sample. Quotas can be imposed to improve representativeness. In random intercept sampling, the software selects visitors at random and a "pop-up" window asks whether the person wants to participate in the survey. The selection can be made based on simple random or systematic random sampling. If the population is defined as Web site visitors, then this procedure results in a probability sample (simple random or systematic, as the case may be). However, if the population is other than Web site visitors, then the resulting sample is more similar to a nonprobability sample. Nevertheless, randomization improves representativeness and discourages multiple responses from the same respondent.

Internet panels function in ways similar to non-Internet panels (discussed in Chapters 3 and 4) and share many of the same advantages and disadvantages. In recruited panels, members can be recruited online or even by traditional means (mail, telephone). Based on the researcher's judgment, certain qualifying criteria can be introduced to prescreen the respondents. They are offered incentives for participation such as sweepstake prizes, redeemable points, and other types of Internet currencies. Members typically provide detailed psychographic, demographic, Internet usage, and product consumption information at the time of joining. Opt-in panels operate similarly except that members choose to opt in as opposed to being recruited. To select a sample, the online company sends an e-mail message to those panelists who qualify based on sample specifications given by the researcher. All of the sampling techniques can be implemented using both types of Internet panels. The success of probability sampling techniques depends upon the extent to which the panel is representative of the target population. Highly

FIGURE 11.6

A Classification of Internet Sampling

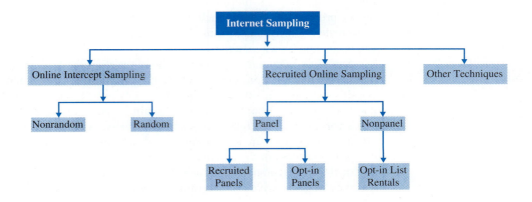

targeted samples can be achieved, e.g., teenage girls who shop in malls more than twice a month. For example, respondents for Harris Poll Online (HPOL) surveys are drawn from the multimillion-member HPOL database (www.harrisinteractive.com). E-mail addresses for respondents in the database have been obtained from a number of sources, including the HPOL registration site and HPOL banner advertisements. To maintain reliability and integrity in the sample, the following procedures are used:

- *Password protection.* Each invitation contains a password that is uniquely assigned to that e-mail address. A respondent is required to enter the password at the beginning of the survey to gain access into the survey. Password protection ensures that a respondent completes the survey only one time.
- *Reminder invitations.* To increase the number of respondents in the survey and to improve overall response rates, up to two additional reminder invitations are typically e-mailed at two- to four-day intervals to those respondents who have not yet participated in the survey.
- *Summary of the survey findings.* To increase the number of respondents in the survey and to improve overall response rates, respondents are often provided with a summary of some of the survey responses via the Internet.

Nonpanel recruited sampling methods can also be used that request potential respondents to go online to answer a survey. To illustrate, an electronics store, such as Best Buy (www.bestbuy.com), may hand its customers a flier that directs them to a specific password-protected site to respond to a questionnaire. If the population is defined as the company's customers, as in a customer satisfaction survey, and a random procedure is used to select respondents, a probability sample will be obtained. Other nonpanel approaches involve the use of e-mail lists that have been rented from suppliers. Presumably, these respondents opted in or gave permission for their e-mail addresses to be circulated. Offline techniques such as short telephone screening interviews are also used for recruiting Internet samples. Several companies routinely collect e-mail addresses in their customer relationship databases by obtaining that information from customer telephone interactions, product registration cards, on-site registrations, special promotions, and so on.

A variety of other online sampling approaches are also possible. For example, a survey invitation pops up every time a visitor makes a purchase. Furthermore, the Internet can be used to order and access samples generated by marketing research suppliers, such as Survey Samples, Inc. (SSI) (www.ssisamples.com).

ACTIVE RESEARCH

Online Sampling to Build Customer Satisfaction and Loyalty

Visit www.amazon.com and conduct an Internet search using a search engine and your library's online database to obtain information on consumers' Internet shopping behavior.

Amazon.com wants you to conduct an Internet survey to determine customer satisfaction. How would you select the sample?

As the marketing chief for Amazon.com, what marketing strategies will you adopt to enhance customer satisfaction and loyalty?

International Marketing Research

Implementing the sampling design process in international marketing research is seldom an easy task. Several factors should be considered in defining the target population. The relevant element (respondent) may differ from country to country. In the United States, children play an important role in the purchase of children's cereals. However, in countries with authoritarian child-rearing practices, the mother may be the relevant element. Women play a key role in the purchase of automobiles and other durables in the United States; in male-dominated societies, such as in the Middle East, such decisions are made by men. Accessibility also varies across countries. In Mexico, houses cannot be entered by strangers because of boundary walls and servants.

Additionally, dwelling units may be unnumbered and streets unidentified, making it difficult to locate designated households.[28]

Developing an appropriate sampling frame is a difficult task. In many countries, particularly in developing countries, reliable information about the target population may not be available from secondary sources. Government data may be unavailable or highly biased. Population lists may not be available commercially. The time and money required to compile these lists may be prohibitive. For example, in Saudi Arabia, there is no officially recognized census of population, no elections, and hence no voter registration records, and no accurate maps of population centers. In this situation, the interviewers could be instructed to begin at specified starting points and to sample every nth dwelling until the specified number of units has been sampled.

Given the lack of suitable sampling frames, the inaccessibility of certain respondents, such as women in some cultures, and the dominance of personal interviewing, probability sampling techniques are uncommon in international marketing research. Quota sampling has been used widely in the developed and developing countries in both consumer and industrial surveys. Snowball sampling is also appealing when the characteristic of interest is rare in the target population or when respondents are hard to reach. For example, it has been suggested that in Saudi Arabia graduate students be employed to hand-deliver questionnaires to relatives and friends. These initial respondents can be asked for referrals to other potential respondents, and so on. This approach would result in a large sample size and a high response rate.

The use of Internet sampling in international marketing research must consider the possibility that Internet availability and use could vary markedly among countries. Many countries may lack servers, hardware, and software, and this lack of technical infrastructure makes Internet research difficult and expensive. In addition, there may be cultural differences in attitude toward and usage of the Internet. For example, in Latin America the attitude toward Internet research is not positive due to the respondents missing social interaction with others while participating in the research.

Sampling techniques and procedures vary in accuracy, reliability, and cost from country to country. If the same sampling procedures are used in each country, the results may not be comparable. To achieve comparability in sample composition and representativeness, it may be desirable to use different sampling techniques in different countries.

Real Research   Achieving Sample Comparability Through Diversity

Research in the United States has shown that most consumers feel that a purchase is accompanied by a degree of risk when they choose among alternative brands. A study was conducted to compare the U.S. results with those from Mexico, Thailand, and Saudi Arabia. The targeted respondent in each culture was an upper-middle-income woman residing in a major city. However, differences in sampling occurred across the countries. In the United States, random sampling from the telephone directory was used. In Mexico, judgmental sampling was used by having experts identify neighborhoods where the target respondents lived; homes were then randomly selected for personal interviews. In Thailand, judgmental sampling was also used, but the survey took place in major urban centers and a store intercept technique was used to select respondents. Finally, in Saudi Arabia, convenience sampling employing the snowball procedure was used, because there were no lists from which sampling frames could be drawn and social customs prohibited spontaneous personal interviews. Thus, comparability in sample composition and representativeness was achieved by using different sampling procedures in different countries.[29] ■

Ethics in Marketing Research

The researcher has several ethical responsibilities to both the client and the respondents in the sampling process. Pertaining to the client, the researcher must develop a sampling design that is appropriate for controlling the sampling and nonsampling errors (see Chapter 3). When appropriate, probability sampling should be used. When nonprobability sampling is used, effort should be made to obtain a representative sample. It is unethical and misleading to treat nonprobability samples as probability samples and to project the results to a target population. As the following example demonstrates, appropriate definition of the population and the sampling frame and application of the correct sampling techniques are essential if the research is to be conducted and the findings used ethically.

Real Research

Systematic Sampling Reveals Systematic Gender Differences in Ethical Judgments

In an attempt to explore differences in research ethics judgments between male and female marketing professionals, data were obtained from 420 respondents. The population was defined as marketing professionals, and the sampling frame was the American Marketing Association directory. The respondents were selected based on a systematic sampling plan from the directory. Attempts were made to overcome nonresponse by not only mailing a cover letter and a stamped preaddressed return envelope along with the questionnaire, but also by promising to provide each respondent with a copy of the research study results. Results of the survey showed that female marketing professionals, in general, demonstrated higher levels of research ethics judgments than their male counterparts.[30] ■

Researchers must be sensitive to preserving the anonymity of the respondents when conducting business-to-business research, employee research, and other projects in which the population size is small. When the population size is small, it is easier to discern the identities of the respondents than when the samples are drawn from a large population. Sampling details that are too revealing or verbatim quotations in reports to the client can compromise the anonymity of the respondents. In such situations, the researcher has the ethical obligation to protect the identities of the respondents, even if it means limiting the level of sampling detail that is reported to the client and other parties.

Decision Research

MTV: The World's Most Widely Distributed TV Network

The Situation

As of 2009, MTV Networks included favorites such as MTV, VH1, Nickelodeon, Nick at Nite, Comedy Central, CMT: Country Music Television, Spike TV, TV Land, Logo, and more than 137 networks around the world. MTV Networks uses a free-flowing corporate culture and a group of power brands to earn big profits for parent Viacom (www.viacom.com).

Tom Freston, CEO of MTV, actually took MTV as a small start-up company and turned it into a cultural behemoth. Judy McGrath was named chairman and CEO of MTV Networks in July 2004. Although MTV has become a global icon, with millions of viewers all over the world glued to its programming, MTV is constantly trying to keep up with what is popular and keep its viewers watching.

MTV is always trying to find new ways to engage its target audience, 18- to 24-year-olds. This has not always been an easy task. For example, the channel had fading hits like *Beavis & Butthead* and *The Real World*. Ratings began to slip as users complained that there was no longer music on MTV. Telephone surveys were conducted with the 18- to 24-year-old group. The sample was selected by choosing households based on computerized random digit dialing. If the household had 18- to 24-year-olds, one person was selected using the next birthday method. The results of this survey showed that MTV needed a makeover.

The Marketing Research Decision

1. Because trends come and go, it is important for MTV to stay in touch with its audience and know their wants. Judy McGrath especially wants to keep in touch with the 18- to 24-year-olds through periodic surveys. What sampling technique would you recommend?
2. Discuss the role of the type of sampling technique you recommend in enabling Judy McGrath to keep in touch with the target audience.

The Marketing Management Decision

1. What should Judy McGrath do to attract the 18- to 24-year-old group to MTV?
2. Discuss how the marketing management decision action that you recommend to Judy McGrath is influenced by the sampling technique that you suggested earlier and by the findings of that research.[31] ■

Summary

Information about the characteristics of a population may be obtained by conducting either a sample or a census. Budget and time limits, large population size, and small variance in the characteristic of interest favor the use of a sample. Sampling is also preferred when the cost of sampling error is low, the cost of nonsampling error is high, the nature of measurement is destructive, and attention must be focused on individual cases. The opposite set of conditions favor the use of a census.

Sampling design begins by defining the target population in terms of elements, sampling units, extent, and time. Then the sampling frame should be determined. A sampling frame is a representation of the elements of the target population. It consists of a list or directions for identifying the target population. At this stage, it is important to recognize any sampling frame errors that may exist. The next steps involve selecting a sampling technique and determining the sample size. In addition to quantitative analysis, several qualitative considerations should be taken into account in determining the sample size. Finally, execution of the sampling process requires detailed specifications for each step in the sampling process.

Figure 11.7 gives a concept map for sampling techniques. Sampling techniques may be classified as nonprobability and probability techniques. Nonprobability sampling techniques rely on the researcher's judgment. Consequently, they do not permit an objective evaluation of the precision of the sample results, and the estimates

obtained are not statistically projectable to the population. The commonly used nonprobability sampling techniques include convenience sampling, judgmental sampling, quota sampling, and snowball sampling.

In probability sampling techniques, sampling units are selected by chance. Each sampling unit has a nonzero chance of being selected, and the researcher can prespecify every potential sample of a given size that could be drawn from the population, as well as the probability of selecting each sample. It is also possible to determine the precision of the sample estimates and inferences and make projections to the target population. Probability sampling techniques include simple random sampling, systematic sampling, stratified sampling, cluster sampling, sequential sampling, and double sampling. The choice between probability and nonprobability sampling should be based on the nature of the research, the degree of error tolerance, the relative magnitude of sampling and nonsampling errors, the variability in the population, and statistical and operational considerations.

When conducting international marketing research, it is desirable to achieve comparability in sample composition and representativeness even though this may require the use of different sampling techniques in different countries. It is unethical and misleading to treat nonprobability samples as probability samples and project the results to a target population. The Internet and computers can be used to make the sampling design process more effective and efficient.

FIGURE 11.7

A Concept Map for Sampling Techniques

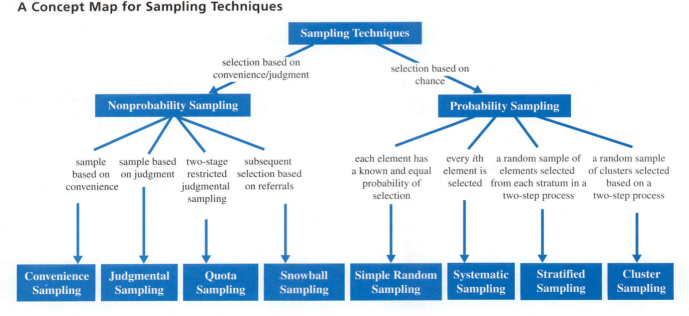

Key Terms and Concepts

population, 338
census, 339
sample, 339
target population, 340
element, 340
sampling unit, 340
sampling frame, 341
Bayesian approach, 341
sampling with replacement, 342

sampling without replacement, 342
sample size, 342
nonprobability sampling, 344
probability sampling, 344
convenience sampling, 345
judgmental sampling, 347
quota sampling, 348
snowball sampling, 349
simple random sampling (SRS), 350

systematic sampling, 351
stratified sampling, 352
cluster sampling, 353
area sampling, 354
probability proportionate to size
  sampling, 355
sequential sampling, 356
double sampling, 356

Suggested Cases, Video Cases, and HBS Cases

Running Case with Real Data

1.1 Dell

Comprehensive Critical Thinking Cases

2.1 American Idol   2.2 Baskin-Robbins   2.3 Akron Children's Hospital

Comprehensive Cases with Real Data

4.1 JPMorgan Chase   4.2 Wendy's

Video Cases

11.1 Motorola   12.1 Subaru   13.1 Intel   23.1 Marriott   24.1 Nivea

Comprehensive Harvard Business School Cases

Case 5.1: The Harvard Graduate Student Housing Survey (9-505-059)
Case 5.2: BizRate.Com (9-501-024)
Case 5.3: Cola Wars Continue: Coke and Pepsi in the Twenty-First Century (9-702-442)
Case 5.4: TiVo in 2002 (9-502-062)
Case 5.5: Compaq Computer: Intel Inside? (9-599-061)
Case 5.6: The New Beetle (9-501-023)

Live Research: Conducting a Marketing Research Project

A census may be feasible in a business-to-business (B-to-B) project where the size of the population is small, but it is infeasible in most consumer projects.

1. Define the target population (element, sampling unit, extent, and time) and discuss a suitable sampling frame.

2. Probability sampling techniques are more difficult and time-consuming to implement, and their use may not be warranted unless the results are being projected to a population of interest.

Acronym

The sampling design process and the steps involved may be represented by the acronym

Sample:

S ampling design process
A mount: sample size determination
M ethod: sampling technique selection
P opulation definition
L ist: sampling frame determination
E xecution of the sampling process

Exercises

Questions

1. What is the major difference between a sample and a census?
2. Under what conditions would a sample be preferable to a census? A census preferable to a sample?
3. Describe the sampling design process.
4. How should the target population be defined?
5. What is a sampling unit? How is it different from the population element?
6. What qualitative factors should be considered in determining the sample size?
7. What are incidence rates? How do they affect the sample size?
8. How do probability sampling techniques differ from nonprobability sampling techniques?
9. What is the least expensive and least time-consuming of all sampling techniques? What are the major limitations of this technique?
10. What is the major difference between judgmental and convenience sampling?
11. What is the relationship between quota sampling and judgmental sampling?
12. What are the distinguishing features of simple random sampling?
13. Describe the procedure for selecting a systematic random sample.
14. Describe stratified sampling. What are the criteria for the selection of stratification variables?
15. What are the differences between proportionate and disproportionate stratified sampling?
16. Describe the cluster sampling procedure. What is the key distinction between cluster sampling and stratified sampling?
17. What factors should be considered in choosing between probability and nonprobability sampling?
18. What strategies are available to adjust for nonresponse?

Problems

1. Define the appropriate target population and the sampling frame in each of the following situations:
   a. The manufacturer of a new cereal brand wants to conduct in-home product usage tests in Chicago.
   b. A national chain store wants to determine the shopping behavior of customers who have its store charge card.
   c. A local TV station wants to determine households' viewing habits and programming preferences.
   d. The local chapter of the American Marketing Association wants to test the effectiveness of its new member drive in Atlanta.
2. A manufacturer would like to survey users to determine the demand potential for a new power press. The new press has a capacity of 500 tons and costs $225,000. It is used for forming products from lightweight and heavyweight steel and can be used by automobile, construction equipment, and major appliance manufacturers.
   a. Identify the population and sampling frame that could be used.
   b. Describe how a simple random sample can be drawn using the identified sampling frame.
   c. Could a stratified sample be used? If so, how?
   d. Could a cluster sample be used? If so, how?
   e. Which sampling technique would you recommend? Why?

Internet and Computer Exercises

1. P&G would like to conduct a survey of consumer preferences for toothpaste brands in California. Stratified random sampling will be used. Visit www.census.gov to identify information that will be relevant in determining income and age strata.
2. Generate the quota sample described in Role Playing question 1 using a microcomputer.
3. Using a computer program, generate a set of 1,000 random numbers for selecting a simple random sample.
4. Visit the comScore SurveySite Web site (www.comscore.com). Examine the Internet surveys being conducted. Write a report about the sampling plans being used.

Activities

Role Playing

1. The alumni office of your university would like to conduct a survey to determine alumni attitudes toward a new fundraising program. As a consultant, you must develop a quota sample. What quota variables and levels of variables should be used? How many alumni should be included in each cell? Obtain the necessary information from the alumni office or the library on your campus and present your results to a group of students representing the alumni office.
2. You work as a marketing research manager for a major New York City bank. Management would like to know if the banking habits of different ethnic groups differ. They wonder whether, given the varied population of New York City, it is meaningful to segment the market according to ethnic background. A survey will be conducted. You have been asked to design an appropriate sampling process. Complete the assignment and make a presentation of your results to a group of students representing the bank management.

Fieldwork

1. A major software firm wants to determine the use of spreadsheets by (1) manufacturing firms, (2) service organizations, and (3) educational institutions located in the state of California. Using the resources available in your library, develop an appropriate sampling plan.
2. Visit a local marketing research firm. Determine what procedures the firm uses for sample control in telephone interviews. Summarize your findings in a report.

Group Discussion

1. "Given that the U.S. Bureau of the Census uses sampling to check on the accuracy of various censuses, a constitutional amendment should be passed replacing the decennial census with a sample." Discuss as a small group.

2. "Because nonsampling errors are greater in magnitude than sampling errors, it really does not matter which sampling technique is used." Discuss this statement.

Dell Running Case

Review the Dell case, Case 1.1, and questionnaire provided toward the end of the book.

1. As the marketing manager of Dell personal computers, what marketing programs will you design to target families?

2. Conduct an Internet search using a search engine and your library's online database to obtain information that will assist you in targeting families.

3. Dell wants to conduct a telephone survey to determine how they can attract more families to Dell PCs and notebooks. Design the sampling process.

VIDEO CASE 11.1   Motorola: Projecting the Moto Lifestyle

Starting in 1928 as the Galvin Manufacturing Corporation, Motorola (www.motorola.com) has evolved into a worldwide company with more than $30.15 billion in revenue in 2008. Today, it is a leading manufacturer and provider of wireless, semiconductor, broadband, and automotive products and services. With the wireless division, Motorola knew it needed to change. It had found through focus groups and survey research that many customers and potential customers saw Motorola's phone models as dependable, but also as dull, predictable, and boring. With the mobile phone market being flashy and consumer driven, Motorola needed answers on how to become more mainstream and popular.

To find these answers, Motorola turned to marketing research and an advertising agency named Ogilvy & Mather. Motorola and Ogilvy & Mather conducted focus groups, depth interviews, and mall-intercept surveys. Although focus groups generated some innovative ideas, depth interviews enabled the probing of emotions related to mobile phones. Mall intercepts were chosen because the respondents could be shown models of Motorola and competing brands. They found from this research that customers buying mobile phones did not buy the phone based on technical schematic selling points. Customers buy phones based on how they emotionally feel about the brand of phone and the particular style of the phone. Most customers do not understand the technical parameters of the different phone models enough to make a decision based on them. So they are choosing among cell phones based on whether the phone "fits" into their lives or by considering "Is this phone me?" This research challenged the company's management to think of cell phones not so much as engineered functional devices but as fashion accessories that help consumers make statements about who they are. It pointed Motorola into developing a marketing strategy that developed the brand name instead of pushing the features of the phone. Moreover, the brand name had to be a global one based on universal principles. Marketing research also revealed that consumers were looking for "intelligence everywhere," and therefore the brand had to be developed in that environment.

Ogilvy & Mather sought to develop the Motorola brand to represent a set of universal principles—a set of core principles that defined the brand—and then send out this idea to every country and have a localized interpretation for the idea. The result of this is that the core ethos of the brand is preserved while at the same time offering local offices the flexibility to mould the brand according to local conditions and develop the brand such that the people of that country can relate to and identify with it. For Motorola, Ogilvy developed the core idea of "intelligence everywhere." This core idea is used as the framework for all Motorola businesses around the world.

This was accomplished by creating the Moto, which is a cute name for Motorola's global-branded cell phone. The name is easy to pronounce, and it does not mean anything bad or weird anywhere in the world. It also carries a part of the Motorola name, a strong positive brand name that reminds consumers of the company's heritage. Motorola's advertising agency, Ogilvy & Mather, created a Moto lifestyle image (www.hellomoto.com). Knowing from research that customers wanted to relate to the phone and brand on a personal level, Motorola's Moto lifestyle showed the public fast, upbeat, and flashy people living and using Motorola products in an intelligent way. This created an emotional connection with customers, as they were almost saying to themselves, "That's the way I want to live." This was followed by Motodextrous ads in 2004 that projected a perfect balance between design and technology to enable people to live the Moto lifestyle with the slogan of "Intelligence Everywhere." This campaign, an obvious success, was possible due only to the marketing research conducted to find why customers buy certain brands and models of mobile phones. When marketing research indicated a big need for hands-free driving, in October 2007 the company introduced MOTOROKR T505 Bluetooth, the In-Car Speakerphone and Digital FM Transmitter, its first road-ready, music-oriented ROKR accessory and the latest addition to its portfolio of in-car solutions.

Given the high costs associated with an advertising campaign, it was well researched and backed with strong supporting evidence and data. Marketing professionals need to substantiate their spending on advertising and brand building with research data that spells out the rationale for that spending. The Moto campaign, instead of inducing customers to buy Motorola phones because of their features, appealed to consumers' lifestyle choices. The campaign positioned Motorola phones as aspirational products that embodied a certain attitude. This positioning created an emotional connection with the consumers and targeted people's desires to be associated with products that stand for qualities that they consider to be "cool"; that is, fashionable and worthy of being identified with.

The key here is to identify a set of core values the brand stands for and then be able to make the brand work in all parts of the world. The success of global brand icons such as Dove, IBM, and others has shown that a brand's strengths can indeed be leveraged across countries and cultures. Identifying this set of core values, though, is no easy task and requires extensive marketing research. From finding consumer preferences to their desires and perceptions about the brand, marketing research helps to gain insight into the consumers' mind-sets. For example, marketing research showed that style matters regardless of income or social status, an insight Motorola employed while developing the Motofone for developing countries.

Conclusion

Based on marketing research findings, the Moto campaign established Motorola as a chic and aspirational brand that helped it overcome its poor consumer image and branding problems. The Moto campaign projects Motorola's core values and its lifestyle appeals to consumers across the world. Possessing a Moto was no longer possessing a cell phone, but having a product whose core values represented the type of lifestyle the user of the phone desired and lived. With this dependence on marketing research in the forefront of Motorola's actions, it is certain to remain a global contender in the mobile phone market for years to come.

Questions

1. Discuss the role that marketing research can play in helping Motorola further build the Moto brand.
2. Management would like to continue rebuilding Motorola. They feel this can best be accomplished by increasing Motorola's U.S. marketing share. Define the management decision problem.
3. Define an appropriate marketing research problem based on the management decision problem you have identified.
4. Use the Internet to determine the market shares of the major cell phone handset manufacturers (Nokia, Motorola, Samsung, Sony/Ericsson, etc.) for the last calendar year.
5. What type of syndicate data will be useful to Motorola?
6. Discuss the role of qualitative research in helping Motorola expand its market share.
7. Do you think that the mall-intercept interviewing conducted by Motorola was the best method of administering the survey? Why or why not?
8. Discuss the role of experimentation in helping Motorola design handsets that are preferred by consumers.
9. Develop a questionnaire for assessing consumer preferences for cellular handsets.
10. What sampling plan should be adopted for the survey of question 7?
11. If Motorola were to conduct marketing research to determine consumer preferences for cellular handset manufacturers in Asia, how would the research process be different?
12. Discuss the ethical issues involved in researching consumer preferences for cellular handset manufacturers.

References

1. www.motorola.com, accessed February 15, 2009.
2. www.hellomoto.com, accessed February 15, 2009.
3. www.hoovers.com, accessed February 15, 2009.
4. www.wikipedia.org, accessed February 15, 2009.
5. www.technologyreview.com/read_article.aspx?id=17663, accessed June 4, 2007.
6. Soo Youn, "Motorola Chips Away at Nokia's Lead in Cell-Phone Market," *Knight Ridder Tribune Business News* (June 9, 2004): 1.

> " The size of the sample is determined not only by statistical calculations, but also managerial considerations including time and cost. "

*Beverly Weiman, President and CEO,
Survey Sampling International*

Objectives [After reading this chapter, the student should be able to:]

1. Define key concepts and symbols pertinent to sampling.

2. Understand the concepts of the sampling distribution, statistical inference, and standard error.

3. Discuss the statistical approach to determining sample size based on simple random sampling and the construction of confidence intervals.

4. Derive the formulas to statistically determine the sample size for estimating means and proportions.

5. Discuss the nonresponse issues in sampling and the procedures for improving response rates and adjusting for nonresponse.

6. Understand the difficulty of statistically determining the sample size in international marketing research.

7. Identify the ethical issues related to sample size determination, particularly the estimation of population variance.

Sampling: Final and Initial Sample Size Determination

Overview

In Chapter 11, we considered the role of sampling in research design formulation, described the sampling process, and presented the various nonprobability and probability sampling techniques.

This chapter focuses on the determination of sample size in simple random sampling. We define various concepts and symbols and discuss the properties of the sampling distribution. Additionally, we describe statistical approaches to sample size determination based on confidence intervals. We present the formulas for calculating the sample size with these approaches and illustrate their use. We briefly discuss the extension to determining sample size in other probability sampling designs. The sample size determined statistically is the final or net sample size; that is, it represents the completed number of interviews or observations. However, to obtain this final sample size, a much larger number of potential respondents have to be contacted initially. We describe the adjustments that need to be made to the statistically determined sample size to account for incidence and completion rates and calculate the initial sample size. We also cover the nonresponse issues in sampling, with a focus on improving response rates and adjusting for nonresponse. We discuss the difficulty of statistically determining the sample size in international marketing research, identify the relevant ethical issues, and explain the role of the Internet and computers.

Statistical determination of sample size requires knowledge of the normal distribution and the use of normal probability tables. The normal distribution is bell shaped and symmetrical. Its mean, median, and mode are identical (see Chapter 15). Information on the normal distribution and the use of normal probability tables is presented in Appendix 12A.

Real Research

Bicycling Reduces Accidents Due to Error

The sample size in *Bicycling* (www.bicycling.com) magazine's survey of U.S. retail bicycle stores was influenced by statistical considerations. The allowance for sampling error was limited to 5 percentage points.

The table that follows was used to determine the allowances that should be made for sampling error. The computed confidence intervals took into account the effect of the sample design on sampling error. These intervals indicate the range (plus or minus the figure shown) within which the results of repeated samplings in the same time period could be expected to vary, 95 percent of the time, assuming that the sample procedure, survey execution, and questionnaire used were the same.[1]

Recommended Allowance for Sampling Error of a Percentage

In Percentage Points	(At 95% Confidence Level for a Sample Size of 456)
Percentage near 10	3
Percentage near 20	4
Percentage near 30	4
Percentage near 40	5
Percentage near 50	5
Percentage near 60	5
Percentage near 70	4
Percentage near 80	4
Percentage near 90	3

Like the cyclists who read it, *Bicycling* magazine attempts to limit the error due to chance (sampling) factors.

The table should be used as follows: If a reported percentage is 43, look at the row labeled "percentages near 40." The number in this row is 5, which means that the 43 percent obtained in the sample is subject to a sampling error of plus or minus 5 percentage points. Another way of saying this is that very probably (95 times out of 100) the average of repeated samplings would be somewhere between 38 percent and 48 percent, with the most likely figure being 43 percent. A 2009 survey conducted by *Bicycling* magazine to gauge readers' interests made use of this table for estimating sampling errors. ∎

Real Research

Opinion Place Bases Its Opinions on 1,000 Respondents

Marketing research firms are now turning to the Web to conduct online research. Some leading market research companies (ASI Market Research, GfK Custom Research, Inc., and M/A/R/C Research) partnered with Digital Marketing Services (DMS), Dallas, to conduct custom research on AOL.

DMS and AOL will conduct online surveys on AOL's *Opinion Place* (www.opinionplace.com) with an average base of 1,000 respondents by survey. This sample size was determined based on statistical considerations as well as sample sizes used in similar research conducted by traditional methods. AOL will give reward points (that can be traded in for prizes) to respondents. Users will not have to submit their e-mail addresses. The surveys will help measure the response to advertisers' online campaigns. The primary objective of these research projects is to gauge consumers' attitudes and other subjective information that can help media buyers plan their campaigns.

Another advantage of online surveys is that you are sure to reach your target (sample control), and that they are quicker to turn around than traditional surveys such as mall intercepts or home interviews. They also are cheaper (DMS charges $20,000 for an online survey, whereas it costs between $30,000 and $40,000 to conduct a mall-intercept survey of 1,000 respondents). ∎

To grasp the statistical aspects of sampling, it is important to understand certain basic definitions and symbols.

Definitions and Symbols

Confidence intervals and other statistical concepts that play a central role in sample size determination are defined in the following list.

Parameter: A **parameter** is a summary description of a fixed characteristic or measure of the target population. A parameter denotes the true value that would be obtained if a census rather than a sample were undertaken.

Statistic: A **statistic** is a summary description of a characteristic or measure of the sample. The sample statistic is used as an estimate of the population parameter.

Finite population correction: The **finite population correction (fpc)** is a correction for overestimation of the variance of a population parameter, for example, a mean or proportion, when the sample size is 10 percent or more of the population size.

TABLE 12.1
Symbols for Population Parameters and Sample Statistics

Variable	Population	Sample
Mean	μ	$\overline{X}$
Proportion	π	p
Variance	σ^2	s^2
Standard deviation	σ	s
Size	N	n
Standard error of the mean	$\sigma_{\overline{x}}$	$s_{\overline{x}}$
Standard error of the proportion	σ_p	s_p
Standardized variate (z)	$\dfrac{X - \mu}{\sigma}$	$\dfrac{X - \overline{X}}{s}$
Coefficient of variation (CV)	$\dfrac{\sigma}{\mu}$	$\dfrac{s}{\overline{X}}$

Precision level: When estimating a population parameter by using a sample statistic, the **precision level** is the desired size of the estimating interval. This is the maximum permissible difference between the sample statistic and the population parameter.

Confidence interval: The **confidence interval** is the range into which the true population parameter will fall, assuming a given level of confidence.

Confidence level: The **confidence level** is the probability that a confidence interval will include the population parameter.

The symbols used in statistical notation for describing population and sample characteristics are summarized in Table 12.1.

The Sampling Distribution

sampling distribution
The distribution of the values of a sample statistic computed for each possible sample that could be drawn from the target population under a specified sampling plan.

The **sampling distribution** is the distribution of the values of a sample statistic computed for each possible sample that could be drawn from the target population under a specified sampling plan.[2] Suppose a simple random sample of five hospitals is to be drawn from a population of 20 hospitals. There are $(20 \times 19 \times 18 \times 17 \times 16)/(1 \times 2 \times 3 \times 4 \times 5)$, or 15,504 different samples of size 5 that can be drawn. The relative frequency distribution of the values of the mean of these 15,504 different samples would specify the sampling distribution of the mean.

statistical inference
The process of generalizing the sample results to the population results.

An important task in marketing research is to calculate statistics, such as the sample mean and sample proportion, and use them to estimate the corresponding true population values. This process of generalizing the sample results to the population results is referred to as **statistical inference**. In practice, a single sample of predetermined size is selected and the sample statistics (such as mean and proportion) are computed. Hypothetically, in order to estimate the population parameter from the sample statistic, every possible sample that could have been drawn should be examined. If all possible samples were actually to be drawn, the distribution of the statistic would be the sampling distribution. Although in practice only one sample is actually drawn, the concept of a sampling distribution is still relevant. It enables us to use probability theory to make inferences about the population values.

The important properties of the sampling distribution of the mean, and the corresponding properties for the proportion, for large samples (30 or more) are as follows:

normal distribution
A basis for classical statistical inference that is bell-shaped and symmetrical in appearance. Its measures of central tendency are all identical.

1. The sampling distribution of the mean is a **normal distribution** (see Appendix 12A). Strictly speaking, the sampling distribution of a proportion is a binomial. However, for large samples ($n = 30$ or more), it can be approximated by the normal distribution.

2. The mean of the sampling distribution of the mean ($\overline{X} = \dfrac{\left(\sum\limits_{i=1}^{n} X_i\right)}{n}$) or the proportion ($p = X/n$, X = the count of the characteristic of interest) equals the corresponding population parameter value, μ or π, respectively.

standard error

The standard deviation of the sampling distribution of the mean or proportion.

3. The standard deviation is called the **standard error** of the mean or the proportion to indicate that it refers to a sampling distribution of the mean or the proportion, and not to a sample or a population. The formulas are:

<table>
<tr><td align="center">Mean</td><td align="center">Proportion</td></tr>
</table>

$$\sigma_{\bar{x}} = \frac{\sigma}{\sqrt{n}} \qquad\qquad \sigma_p = \sqrt{\frac{\pi(1-\pi)}{n}}$$

4. Often the population standard deviation, σ, is not known. In these cases, it can be estimated from the sample by using the following formula:

$$s = \sqrt{\frac{\sum_{i=1}^{n}(X_i - \bar{X})^2}{n-1}}$$

or

$$s = \sqrt{\frac{\sum_{i=1}^{n} X_i^2 - \frac{\left(\sum_{i=1}^{n} X_i\right)^2}{n}}{n-1}}$$

In cases where σ is estimated by s, the standard error of the mean becomes

$$s_{\bar{x}} = \frac{s}{\sqrt{n}}$$

   Assuming no measurement error, the reliability of an estimate of a population parameter can be assessed in terms of its standard error.

5. Likewise, the standard error of the proportion can be estimated by using the sample proportion p as an estimator of the population proportion, π, as:

$$\text{est. } s_p = \sqrt{\frac{p(1-p)}{n}}$$

z value

The number of standard errors a point is away from the mean.

6. The area under the sampling distribution between any two points can be calculated in terms of **z values**. The z value for a point is the number of standard errors a point is away from the mean or proportion. The z values may be computed as follows:

$$z = \frac{\bar{X} - \mu}{\sigma_{\bar{x}}} \qquad\qquad \text{and} \qquad\qquad z = \frac{p - \pi}{\sigma_p}$$

   For example, the areas under one side of the curve between the mean and points that have z values of 1.0, 2.0, and 3.0 are, respectively, 0.3413, 0.4772, and 0.4986. (See Table 2 in the Appendix of Statistical Tables.)

7. When the sample size is 10 percent or more of the population size, the standard error formulas will overestimate the standard deviation of the population mean or proportion. Hence, these should be adjusted by a finite population correction factor defined by:

$$\sqrt{\frac{N-n}{N-1}}$$

In this case

$$\sigma_{\bar{x}} = \frac{\sigma}{\sqrt{n}}\sqrt{\frac{N-n}{N-1}} \qquad\qquad \text{and} \qquad\qquad \sigma_p = \sqrt{\frac{\pi(1-\pi)}{n}}\sqrt{\frac{N-n}{N-1}}$$

Statistical Approach to Determining Sample Size

Several qualitative factors should also be taken into consideration when determining the sample size (see Chapter 11). These include the importance of the decision, the nature of the research, the number of variables, the nature of the analysis, sample sizes used in similar studies, incidence rates, completion rates, and resource constraints. The statistically determined sample size is the net or final sample size—the sample remaining after eliminating potential respondents who do not qualify or who do not complete the interview. Depending on incidence and completion rates, the size of the initial sample may have to be much larger. In commercial marketing research, limits on time, money, and expert resources can exert an overriding influence on sample size determination. In the department store project, the sample size was determined based on these considerations.

The statistical approach to determining sample size that we consider is based on traditional statistical inference.[3] In this approach, the precision level is specified in advance. This approach is based on the construction of confidence intervals around sample means or proportions.

The Confidence Interval Approach

The confidence interval approach to sample size determination is based on the construction of confidence intervals around the sample mean or proportion using the standard error formula. This was illustrated in the opening *Bicycling* magazine example where the sampling errors were related to the sample size and to the confidence level. As another example, suppose that a researcher has taken a simple random sample of 300 households to estimate the monthly expenses for department store shopping and found that the mean household monthly expense for the sample is $182. Past studies indicate that the population standard deviation σ can be assumed to be $55.

We want to find an interval within which a fixed proportion of the sample means will fall. Suppose we want to determine an interval around the population mean that will include 95 percent of the sample means, based on samples of 300 households. The 95 percent could be divided into two equal parts, half below and half above the mean, as shown in Figure 12.1. Calculation of the confidence interval involves determining a distance below ($\overline{X}_L$) and above ($\overline{X}_U$) the population mean (μ) that contains a specified area of the normal curve.

The z values corresponding to ($\overline{X}_L$) and ($\overline{X}_U$) may be calculated as

$$z_L = \frac{\overline{X}_L - \mu}{\sigma_{\bar{x}}}$$

$$z_U = \frac{\overline{X}_U - \mu}{\sigma_{\bar{x}}}$$

where $z_L = -z$ and $z_U = +z$. Therefore, the lower value of $\overline{X}$ is

$$\overline{X}_L = \mu - z\sigma_{\bar{x}}$$

and the upper value of $\overline{X}$ is

$$\overline{X}_U = \mu + z\sigma_{\bar{x}}$$

FIGURE 12.1

95 Percent Confidence Interval

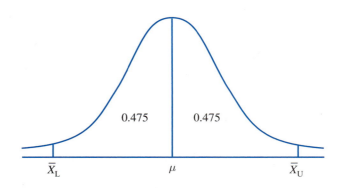

Note that μ is estimated by $\overline{X}$. The confidence interval is given by

$$\overline{X} \pm z\sigma_{\bar{x}}$$

We can now set a 95 percent confidence interval around the sample mean of \$182. As a first step, we compute the standard error of the mean:

$$\sigma_{\bar{x}} = \frac{\sigma}{\sqrt{n}} = \frac{55}{\sqrt{300}} = 3.18$$

From Table 2 in the Appendix of Statistical Tables, it can be seen that the central 95 percent of the normal distribution lies within ± 1.96 z values. The 95 percent confidence interval is given by

$$\overline{X} \pm 1.96\sigma_{\bar{x}}$$
$$= 182.00 \pm 1.96(3.18)$$
$$= 182.00 \pm 6.23$$

Thus the 95 percent confidence interval ranges from \$175.77 to \$188.23. The probability of finding the true population mean to be between \$175.77 and \$188.23 is 95 percent.

Sample Size Determination: Means

The approach used here to construct a confidence interval can be adapted to determine the sample size that will result in a desired confidence interval.[4] Suppose the researcher wants to estimate the monthly household expense for department store shopping more precisely so that the estimate will be within $\pm\$5.00$ of the true population value. What should be the size of the sample? The following steps, summarized in Table 12.2, will lead to an answer.

1. Specify the level of precision. This is the maximum permissible difference (D) between the sample mean and the population mean. In our example, $D = \pm\$5.00$.
2. Specify the level of confidence. Suppose that a 95 percent confidence level is desired.
3. Determine the z value associated with the confidence level using Table 2 in the Appendix of Statistical Tables. For a 95 percent confidence level, the probability that the population mean will fall outside one end of the interval is 0.025(0.05/2). The associated z value is 1.96.
4. Determine the standard deviation of the population. The standard deviation of the population may be known from secondary sources. If not, it might be estimated by conducting a pilot study. Alternatively, it might be estimated on the basis of the researcher's judgment. For example, the range of a normally distributed variable is approximately equal to plus or minus three standard deviations, and one can thus estimate the standard deviation by dividing the range by 6. The researcher can often estimate the range based on knowledge of the phenomenon.
5. Determine the sample size using the formula for the standard error of the mean.

$$z = \frac{\overline{X} - \mu}{\sigma_{\bar{x}}}$$

$$= \frac{D}{\sigma_{\bar{x}}}$$

or

$$\sigma_{\bar{x}} = \frac{D}{z}$$

or

$$\frac{\sigma}{\sqrt{n}} = \frac{D}{z}$$

TABLE 12.2

Sample Size Determination for Means and Proportions

Steps	Means	Proportions
1. Specify the level of precision.	$D = \pm\$5.00$	$D = p - \pi = \pm0.05$
2. Specify the confidence level (CL).	$CL = 95\%$	$CL = 95\%$
3. Determine the z value associated with the CL.	z value is 1.96	z value is 1.96
4. Determine the standard deviation of the population.	Estimate σ: $\sigma = 55$	Estimate π: $\pi = 0.64$
5. Determine the sample size using the formula for the standard error.	$n = \dfrac{\sigma^2 z^2}{D^2}$ $n = \dfrac{55^2 (1.96)^2}{5^2}$ $= 465$	$n = \dfrac{\pi (1 - \pi)z^2}{D^2}$ $n = \dfrac{0.64(1 - 0.64)(1.96)^2}{(0.05)^2}$ $= 355$
6. If the sample size represents $>= 10\%$ of the population, apply the finite population correction (fpc).	$n_c = \dfrac{nN}{N + n - 1}$	$n_c = \dfrac{nN}{N + n - 1}$
7. If necessary, reestimate the confidence interval by employing s to estimate σ.	$= \overline{X} \pm zs_{\overline{x}}$	$= p \pm zs_p$
8. If precision is specified in relative rather than absolute terms, then use these equations to determine the sample size.	$D = R\mu$ $n = \dfrac{CV^2 z^2}{R^2}$	$D = R\pi$ $n = \dfrac{z^2(1 - \pi)}{R^2\pi}$

or

$$n = \frac{\sigma^2 z^2}{D^2}$$

In our example,

$$n = \frac{55^2 (1.96)^2}{5^2}$$
$$= 464.83$$
$$= 465 \text{ (rounded to the next higher integer)}$$

It can be seen from the formula for sample size that sample size increases with an increase in the population variability, degree of confidence, and the precision level required of the estimate. Because the sample size is directly proportional to σ^2, the larger the population variability, the larger the sample size. Likewise, a higher degree of confidence implies a larger value of z, and thus a larger sample size. Both σ^2 and z appear in the numerator. Greater precision means a smaller value of D, and thus a larger sample size because D appears in the denominator.

6. If the resulting sample size represents 10 percent or more of the population, the finite population correction (fpc) should be applied.[5] The required sample size should then be calculated from the formula

$$n_c = nN/(N + n - 1)$$

where

$$n = \text{sample size without fpc}$$
$$n_c = \text{sample size with fpc}$$

7. If the population standard deviation, σ, is unknown and an estimate is used, it should be reestimated once the sample has been drawn. The sample standard deviation, s, is used as an estimate of σ. A revised confidence interval should then be calculated to determine the precision level actually obtained.

Suppose that the value of 55.00 used for σ was an estimate because the true value was unknown. A sample of $n = 465$ is drawn, and these observations generate a mean $\overline{X}$

of 180.00 and a sample standard deviation s of 50.00. The revised confidence interval then is

$$\overline{X} \pm z s_{\overline{x}}$$
$$= 180.00 \pm 1.96(50.0/\sqrt{465})$$
$$= 180.00 \pm 4.55$$

or

$$175.45 \leq \mu \leq 184.55$$

Note that the confidence interval obtained is narrower than planned, because the population standard deviation was overestimated, as judged by the sample standard deviation.

8. In some cases, precision is specified in relative rather than absolute terms. In other words, it may be specified that the estimate be within plus or minus R percentage points of the mean. Symbolically,

$$D = R\mu$$

In these cases, the sample size may be determined by

$$n = \frac{\sigma^2 z^2}{D^2}$$
$$= \frac{CV^2 z^2}{R^2}$$

where the coefficient of variation $CV = (\sigma/\mu)$ would have to be estimated.

The population size, N, does not directly affect the size of the sample, except when the finite population correction factor has to be applied. Although this may be counterintuitive, upon reflection it makes sense. For example, if all the population elements are identical on the characteristics of interest, then a sample size of 1 will be sufficient to estimate the mean perfectly. This is true whether there are 50, 500, 5,000, or 50,000 elements in the population. What directly affects the sample size is the variability of the characteristic in the population. This variability enters into the sample size calculation by way of population variance σ^2 or sample variance s^2. Also, note that the larger the sample size, the more accurate the parameter estimation (sample mean), i.e., the smaller the precision level (error) for a given level of confidence. This can be seen from the formula in step 5. A larger sample will also result in a narrower confidence interval. This can be seen from the formula for the confidence interval in step 7.

ACTIVE RESEARCH

Estimating Average Household Expenditure on Cellular Services to a T

Visit www.t-mobile.com and conduct an Internet search using a search engine and your library's online database to obtain information on the average monthly amount U.S. households spend on cellular (cell phone) services.

Assuming a confidence level of 95 percent, precision level of $10, and a standard deviation of $100, what should be the sample size to determine the average monthly household expenditure on cellular services?

As the vice president of marketing for T-Mobile, how would you use information on the average monthly household expenditure on cellular services to expand your revenues?

Sample Size Determination: Proportions

If the statistic of interest is a proportion, rather than a mean, the approach to sample size determination is similar. Suppose that the researcher is interested in estimating the proportion of households possessing a department store credit card. The following steps, also summarized in Table 12.2, should be followed.

1. Specify the level of precision. Suppose the desired precision is such that the allowable interval is set as $D = p - \pi = \pm 0.05$.

2. Specify the level of confidence. Suppose that a 95 percent confidence level is desired.
3. Determine the z value associated with the confidence level. As explained in the case of estimating the mean, this will be $z = 1.96$.
4. Estimate the population proportion π. As explained earlier, the population proportion may be estimated from secondary sources, estimated from a pilot study, or based on the judgment of the researcher. Suppose that, based on secondary data, the researcher estimates that 64 percent of the households in the target population possess a department store credit card. Hence, $\pi = 0.64$.
5. Determine the sample size using the formula for the standard error of the proportion.

$$\sigma_p = \frac{p - \pi}{z}$$

$$= \frac{D}{z}$$

$$= \sqrt{\frac{\pi(1 - \pi)}{n}}$$

or

$$n = \frac{\pi(1 - \pi)z^2}{D^2}$$

In our example,

$$n = \frac{0.64(1 - 0.64)(1.96)^2}{(0.05)^2}$$

$$= 354.04$$

$$= 355 \text{ (rounded to the next higher integer)}$$

6. If the resulting sample size represents 10 percent or more of the population, the finite population correction (fpc) should be applied. The required sample size should then be calculated from the formula:

$$n_c = nN/(N + n - 1)$$

where

n = sample size without fpc

n_c = sample size with fpc

7. If the estimate of π turns out to be poor, the confidence interval will be more or less precise than desired. Suppose that after the sample has been taken, the proportion p is calculated to have a value of 0.55. The confidence interval is then reestimated by employing s_p to estimate the unknown σ_p as

$$p \pm zs_p$$

where

$$s_p = \sqrt{\frac{p(1 - p)}{n}}$$

In our example,

$$s_p = \sqrt{\frac{0.55(1 - 0.55)}{355}}$$

$$= 0.0264$$

The confidence interval, then, is

$$= 0.55 \pm 1.96 (0.0264)$$

$$= 0.55 \pm .052$$

which is wider than that specified. This could be attributed to the fact that the sample standard deviation based on $p = 0.55$ was larger than the estimate of the population standard deviation based on $\pi = 0.64$.

If a wider interval than specified is unacceptable, the sample size can be determined to reflect the maximum possible variation in the population. This occurs when the product $\pi(1 - \pi)$ is the greatest, which happens when π is set at 0.5. This result can also be seen intuitively. Because one-half the population has one value of the characteristic and the other half the other value, more evidence would be required to obtain a valid inference than if the situation were more clear-cut and the majority had one particular value. In our example, this leads to a sample size of

$$n = \frac{0.5(0.5)(1.96)^2}{(0.05)^2}$$

$$= 384.16$$

$$= 385 \text{ rounded to the next higher integer}$$

8. Sometimes, precision is specified in relative rather than absolute terms. In other words, it may be specified that the estimate be within plus or minus R percentage points of the population proportion. Symbolically,

$$D = R\pi$$

In such a case, the sample size may be determined by

$$n = \frac{z^2(1 - \pi)}{R^2\pi}$$

Real Research   ## Statistical Sampling: Not Always an Emergency

The city of Los Angeles, California, hired PriceWaterhouseCoopers (PWC) to evaluate customer demand for nonemergency city services and investigate customer services usage patterns. The goal was to implement a new system that would alleviate some of the strain on the city's 911 phone system. A telephone survey of 1,800 randomly selected Los Angeles City residents was conducted.

The random digit dialing telephone survey was stratified into two groups of 900 each: city resident customers who had contacted the city for service in the past six months and a group of other residents. The sample size was determined by using a 95 percent confidence interval and a margin of error of 3.5 percent. At this confidence level, one would expect that if all the residents of Los Angeles were asked the same survey, that responses to the survey would change no more than ± 3.5 percent.

To confirm that the sample size of 900 was adequate, calculations for sample size determination by proportions were made as follows, using the maximum possible population variation ($\pi = 0.5$). The precision of D in this study is 0.035 for a 95 percent confidence level.

$$n = \frac{\pi(1 - \pi)z^2}{D^2}$$

$$n = [(0.5)(1 - 0.5)(1.96^2)]/(0.035)^2 = 784$$

Therefore, the 900 sample size was more than sufficient.

Findings from the telephone survey revealed that the Department of Water and Power, the Sanitation Bureau, the Bureau of Parking Violations, and the Police Department received about one-half of the city's nonemergency customer contact volume. The main method of contacting the city was by phone, which accounted for about 74 percent of the contacts, compared to 18 percent who made personal visits. Despite high Internet usage rates in Los Angeles, very few residents accessed city services through the Web. By Web enabling many of the city's services, there was a potential for large cost savings by reducing the call volume and improving customer service. The survey also identified specific services and functionality residents would like to see available online. Therefore, the city of Los Angeles launched a 311/Internet customer service to alleviate some of the strain on the city's 911 phone system. As of 2009, this service had become popular, handling a large share of the city's nonemergency customer contacts.[6] ∎

ACTIVE RESEARCH

> ### Wells Fargo: Banking on Online Banking
>
> Visit www.wellsfargo.com and conduct an Internet search using a search engine and your library's online database to obtain information on the proportion of consumers who use online banking.
>
> If about 15 percent of the people in a given area are expected to use Internet banking, what should be the sample size for a 95 percent confidence level and a 5 percent precision level?
>
> As the vice president of marketing for Wells Fargo, what information would you like to have in order to determine whether the bank should expand its online services?

There are a number of Web sites on the Internet that offer free use of sample size and confidence interval calculators, for example, Survey System (www.surveysystem.com). You can use this calculator to determine how many people you need to interview in order to get results that reflect the target population as precisely as needed. You can also find the level of precision you have in an existing sample. The Discovery Research Group also has a sample size calculator (www.drgutah.com).

Experiential Research

The Ultimate Rocky Mountain Destination

Skiing is a popular winter sport in the United States.

1. Visit www.ski.com and conduct an Internet search using a search engine and your library's online database to obtain information on the proportion of people who ski every season.
2. In a survey of the general population on skiing, what should be the sample size for a 95 percent confidence level and a 5 percent precision level? Use the estimate of the population proportion that you determined in step 1.
3. As the director of marketing for Vail Cascade Resort, Colorado, "the ultimate Rocky Mountain destination," what information would you need to formulate marketing strategies to increase your sales? ■

Multiple Characteristics and Parameters

In the preceding examples, we focused on the estimation of a single parameter. In commercial marketing research, several characteristics, not just one, are of interest in any project. The researcher is required to estimate several parameters, not just one. The calculation of sample size in these cases should be based on a consideration of all the parameters that must be estimated, as illustrated in the department store monthly expenses example.

Project Research

Sample Size Estimation

Suppose that in addition to the mean household monthly expenses for department store shopping, it was decided to estimate the mean household monthly expense for clothes and for gifts. The sample sizes needed to estimate each of the three mean monthly expenses are given in Table 12.3 and are 465 for department store shopping, 246 for clothes, and 217 for gifts. If all the three variables were equally important, the most conservative approach would be to select the largest value of $n = 465$ to determine the sample size. This will lead to each variable being estimated at least as precisely as specified. However, if the researcher were most concerned with the mean household monthly expense for clothes, a sample size of $n = 246$ could be selected.

Project Activities

1. Suppose that the researcher wants to estimate the average monthly amount households spend shopping in Sears so the estimate is within $\pm \$10$ of the true population value. Assuming a 95 percent confidence level and a standard deviation of $100, what should be the sample size?
2. If the survey were conducted using the sample size determined in question 1, would the estimates based on the sample lie within $\pm 5\%$ of the true population values? ■

TABLE 12.3
Sample Size for Estimating Multiple Parameters

	Mean Household Monthly Expense On:		
	Department Store Shopping	Clothes	Gifts
Confidence level	95%	95%	95%
z value	1.96	1.96	1.96
Precision level (D)	$5	$5	$4
Standard deviation of the population (σ)	$55	$40	$30
Required sample size (n)	465	246	217

So far, the discussion of sample size determination has been based on the methods of traditional statistical inference and has assumed simple random sampling. Next, we discuss the determination of sample size when other sampling techniques are used.

Other Probability Sampling Techniques

The determination of sample size for other probability sampling techniques is based on the same underlying principles. The researcher must specify the level of precision and the degree of confidence and estimate the sampling distribution of the test statistic.

In simple random sampling, cost does not enter directly into the calculation of sample size. However, in the case of stratified or cluster sampling, cost has an important influence. The cost per observation varies by strata or cluster and the researcher needs some initial estimates of these costs. In addition, the researcher must take into account within-strata variability or within- and between-cluster variability. Once the overall sample size is determined, the sample is apportioned among strata or clusters. This increases the complexity of the sample size formulas. The interested reader is referred to standard works on sampling theory for more information.[7] In general, to provide the same reliability as simple random sampling, sample sizes are the same for systematic sampling, smaller for stratified sampling, and larger for cluster sampling.

Adjusting the Statistically Determined Sample Size

The sample size determined statistically represents the final or net sample size that must be achieved in order to ensure that the parameters are estimated with the desired degree of precision and the given level of confidence. In surveys, this represents the number of interviews that must be completed. In order to achieve this final sample size, a much greater number of potential respondents have to be contacted. In other words, the initial sample size has to be much larger because typically the incidence rates and completion rates are less than 100 percent.[8]

incidence rate
The rate of occurrence of persons eligible to participate in the study expressed as a percentage.

Incidence rate refers to the rate of occurrence or the percentage of persons eligible to participate in the study. Incidence rate determines how many contacts need to be screened for a given sample size requirement. Suppose a study of floor cleaners calls for a sample of female heads of households age 25 to 55. Of the women between the ages of 20 and 60 who might reasonably be approached to see if they qualify, approximately 75 percent are heads of households between 25 and 55. This means that, on average, 1.33 women would be approached to obtain one qualified respondent. Additional criteria for qualifying respondents (for example, product usage behavior) will further increase the number of contacts. Suppose that an added eligibility requirement is that the women should have used a floor cleaner during the last two months. It is estimated that 60 percent of the women contacted would meet this criteria. Then the incidence rate is $0.75 \times 0.60 = 0.45$. Thus the final sample size will have to be increased by a factor of (1/0.45) or 2.22.

completion rate
The percentage of qualified respondents who complete the interview. It enables researchers to take into account anticipated refusals by people who qualify.

Similarly, the determination of sample size must take into account anticipated refusals by people who qualify. The **completion rate** denotes the percentage of qualified respondents who complete the interview. If, for example, the researcher expects an interview completion rate of 80 percent of eligible respondents, the number of contacts should be increased by a factor of 1.25. The incidence rate and the completion rate together imply that the number of potential respondents contacted, that is, the initial sample size, should be 2.22 × 1.25 or 2.77 times the sample size required. In general, if there are c qualifying factors with an incidence of $Q_1, Q_2, Q_3, \ldots, Q_c$, each expressed as a proportion,

$$\text{Incidence rate} = Q_1 \times Q_2 \times Q_3 \ldots \times Q_c$$

$$\text{Initial sample size} = \frac{\text{Final sample size}}{\text{Incidence} \times \text{Completion rate}}$$

The number of units that will have to be sampled will be determined by the initial sample size. These calculations assume that an attempt to contact a respondent will result in a determination as to whether the respondent is eligible. However, this may not be case. An attempt to contact the respondent may be inconclusive as the respondent may refuse to answer, not be at home, be busy, etc. Such instances will further increase the initial sample size. These instances are considered later when we calculate the response rate. Often, as in the following symphony example, a number of variables are used for qualifying potential respondents, thereby decreasing the incidence rate.

Real Research

Tuning Up a Symphony Sample

A telephone survey was conducted to determine consumers' awareness of and attitudes toward the Jacksonville Symphony Orchestra (www.jaxsymphony.org). The screening qualifications for a respondent included in the survey were (1) has lived in the Jacksonville area for more than one year; (2) 25 years old or older; (3) listens to classical or pop music; and (4) attends live performances of classical or pop music. These qualifying criteria decreased the incidence rate to less than 15 percent, leading to a substantial increase in the number of contacts. Although having four qualifying factors resulted in a highly targeted or tuned sample, it also made the interviewing process inefficient, because several people who were called could not qualify. The survey indicated that parking was a problem and people wanted greater involvement with the symphony. Therefore, the Jacksonville Symphony Orchestra advertised the Conductor's Club in 2009. Annual fund donors who join can enjoy the perks of membership, including complimentary valet parking at all Jacksonville Symphony Masterworks and Pops concerts. All membership levels include complimentary admission to intermission receptions in the Davis Gallery at selected concerts (including open bar and hors d'oeuvres).[9] ■

Calculation of Response Rates

Following the Council of American Survey Research Organizations (www.casro.org), we define response rate as:

$$\text{Response Rate} = \frac{\text{Number of Completed Interviews}}{\text{Number of Eligible Units in Sample}}$$

To illustrate how the formula is used, consider the following simple example involving a single-stage telephone survey with individuals where no screening is involved. The sample consisted of 2,000 telephone numbers that were generated randomly. Three attempts were made to reach each respondent. The results are summarized as follows.

Call #	Attempts	Number of Individuals Interviewed	Cumulative	Response Rate
1	2,000	1,200	1,200	60.0%
2	800	400	1,600	80.0%
3	400	100	1,700	85.0%

In this example, the number of eligible units is 2,000, and the response rate after 3 calls is 85.0 percent.

Now consider the case of a single-stage sample where screening is required to determine the eligibility of the respondents, i.e., to ascertain whether the respondent is qualified to participate in the survey. The attempt to screen each respondent will result in one of three outcomes: (1) eligible, (2) ineligible, (3) not ascertained (NA.). The NA category will include refusals, busy signals, no answers, etc. In this case, we determine the number of eligible respondents in the NAs by distributing NAs in the ratio of (1) to (1 + 2). Suppose that we made 2,000 telephone calls that resulted in the following outcomes:

Number of completed interviews = 800

Number of eligible respondents = 900

Number of ineligible respondents = 600

Not ascertained (NA) = 500

The first step is to determine the number of eligible units in the NAs. This can be calculated as:

$$500 \times (900/(900+600)) = 300$$

Thus, the total number of eligible units in the sample = 900 + 300 = 1200.

Thus, the response rate = 800/1200 = 66.7 percent.

Although we illustrate the calculation of response rates for telephone interviews, the calculations for other survey methods are similar. For more complex calculation of response rates, visit the CASRO Web site (www.casro.org).

Response rates are affected by nonresponse. Hence, nonresponse issues deserve attention.

Nonresponse Issues in Sampling

The two major nonresponse issues in sampling are improving response rates and adjusting for nonresponse. Nonresponse error arises when some of the potential respondents included in the sample do not respond (see Chapter 3). This is one of the most significant problems in survey research. Nonrespondents differ from respondents in terms of demographic, psychographic, personality, attitudinal, motivational, and behavioral variables.[10] For a given study, if the nonrespondents differ from the respondents on the characteristics of interest, the sample estimates will be seriously biased. Higher response rates, in general, imply lower rates of nonresponse bias, yet response rate may not be an adequate indicator of nonresponse bias. Response rates themselves do not indicate whether the respondents are representative of the original sample.[11] Increasing the response rate may not reduce nonresponse bias if the additional respondents are not different from those who have already responded but differ from those who still do not respond. Because low response rates increase the probability of nonresponse bias, an attempt should always be made to improve the response rate.[12]

Improving the Response Rates

The primary causes of low response rates are refusals and not-at-homes, as shown in Figure 12.2.

FIGURE 12.2

Improving Response Rates

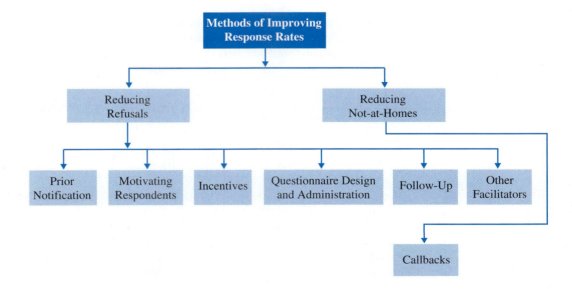

REFUSALS Refusals, which result from the unwillingness or inability of people included in the sample to participate, result in lower response rates and increased potential for nonresponse bias. Refusal rates, the percentage of contacted respondents who refuse to participate, range from 0 to 50 percent or more in telephone surveys. Refusal rates for mall-intercept interviews are even higher, and they are highest of all for mail surveys. Most refusals occur immediately after the interviewer's opening remarks or when the potential respondent first opens the mail package. In a national telephone survey, 40 percent of those contacted refused at the introduction stage, but only 6 percent refused during the interview. The following example gives further information on refusals, terminations, and completed interviews.

Real Research

Reasons for Refusal

In a study investigating the refusal problem in telephone surveys, telephone interviews were conducted with responders and nonresponders to a previous survey, using quotas of 100 for each subsample. The results are presented in the following table:

Refusals, Terminations, and Completed Interviews

Property	Total Sample	Responders	Nonresponders
Number of refusals (1)	224	31	193
Number of terminations (2)	100	33	67
Number of completed interviews (3)	203	102	101
Total number of contacts $(1 + 2 + 3)^a$	527	166	361
Refusal rate $(1/[1 + 2 + 3])^b$	42.5%	18.7%	53.5%
Termination rate $(2/[1 + 2 + 3])$	19.0%	19.9%	18.5%
Completion rate $(3/[1 + 2 + 3])^b$	38.5%	61.4%	28.0%

[a] A total of 1,388 attempts were required to make these contacts: the 166 responder contacts required 406 attempts (with one callback per respondent), and the 361 nonresponder contacts required 982 attempts (with two callbacks per respondent). The sampling frame contained 965 phone numbers—313 responders and 652 nonresponders.
[b] Responder/nonresponder differences were significant at $\alpha = 0.05$ (two-tail test).

The study found that people who are likely to participate in a telephone survey (responders) differ from those who are likely to refuse (nonresponders) in the following ways: (1) confidence in survey research, (2) confidence in the research organization, (3) demographic characteristics, and (4) beliefs and attitudes about telephone surveys.

A recent study conducted by CMOR indicated that consumers prefer Internet surveys versus the telephone method of surveys. Statistically speaking, out of 1,753 U.S. consumers, 78.9 percent of respondents chose the Internet as their first choice of survey method, whereas only 3.2 percent chose the telephone method of surveys.[13] ∎

Given the differences between responders and nonresponders that this study demonstrated, researchers should attempt to lower refusal rates. This can be done by prior notification, motivating the respondents, incentives, good questionnaire design and administration, and follow-up.

Prior notification. In prior notification, potential respondents are sent a letter notifying them of the imminent mail, telephone, personal, or Internet survey. Prior notification increases response rates for samples of the general public because it reduces surprise and uncertainty and creates a more cooperative atmosphere.[14]

Motivating the respondents. Potential respondents can be motivated to participate in the survey by increasing their interest and involvement. Two of the ways this can be done are the foot-in-the-door and door-in-the-face strategies. Both strategies attempt to obtain participation through the use of sequential requests. As explained briefly in Chapter 6, in the foot-in-the-door strategy, the interviewer starts with a relatively small request such as "Will you please take five minutes to answer five questions?" to which a large majority of people will comply. The small request is followed by a larger request, the critical request, that solicits participation in the survey or experiment. The rationale is that compliance with an initial request should increase the chances of compliance with the subsequent request. The door-in-the-face is the reverse strategy. The initial request is relatively large and a majority of people refuse to comply. The large request is followed by a smaller request, the critical request, soliciting participation in the survey. The underlying reasoning is that the concession offered by the subsequent critical request should increase the chances of compliance. Foot-in-the-door is more effective than door-in-the-face.[15]

Incentives. Response rates can be increased by offering monetary as well as nonmonetary incentives to potential respondents. Monetary incentives can be prepaid or promised. The prepaid incentive is included with the survey or questionnaire. The promised incentive is sent to only those respondents who complete the survey. The most commonly used non-monetary incentives are premiums and rewards, such as pens, pencils, books, and offers of survey results.[16]

Prepaid incentives have been shown to increase response rates to a greater extent than promised incentives. The amount of incentive can vary from 10 cents to $50 or more. The amount of incentive has a positive relationship with response rate, but the cost of large monetary incentives may outweigh the value of additional information obtained.

Questionnaire design and administration. A well-designed questionnaire can decrease the overall refusal rate as well as refusals to specific questions (see Chapter 10). Likewise, the skill used to administer the questionnaire in telephone and personal interviews can increase the response rate. Trained interviewers are skilled in refusal conversion or persuasion. They do not accept a "no" response without an additional plea. The additional plea might emphasize the brevity of the questionnaire or the importance of the respondent's opinion. Skilled interviewers can decrease refusals by about 7 percent on average. Interviewing procedures are discussed in more detail in Chapter 13.

Follow-up. Follow-up, or contacting the nonrespondents periodically after the initial contact, is particularly effective in decreasing refusals in mail surveys. The researcher might send a postcard or letter to remind nonrespondents to complete and return the questionnaire. Two or three mailings are needed, in addition to the original one. With proper follow-up, the response rate in mail surveys can be increased to 80 percent or more. Follow-ups can also be done by telephone, e-mail, or personal contacts.[17]

Other facilitators. Personalization, or sending letters addressed to specific individuals, is effective in increasing response rates.[18] The next example illustrates the procedure employed by Arbitron to increase its response rate.

Real Research

Arbitron's Response to Low Response Rates

Arbitron (www.arbitron.com) is a major marketing research supplier. For the year ending December 31, 2008, the company reported revenue of $368.82 million. Recently, Arbitron was trying to improve response rates in order to get more meaningful results from its surveys. Arbitron created a special cross-functional team of employees to work on the response rate problem. Their method was named the "breakthrough method" and the whole Arbitron system concerning the response rates was questioned and changed. The team suggested six major strategies for improving response rates:

1. Maximize the effectiveness of placement/follow-up calls.
2. Make materials more appealing and easier to complete.
3. Increase Arbitron name awareness.
4. Improve survey participant rewards.
5. Optimize the arrival of respondent materials.
6. Increase usability of returned diaries.

Eighty initiatives were launched to implement these six strategies. As a result, response rates improved significantly. However, in spite of those encouraging results, people at Arbitron remain very cautious. They know that they are not done yet and that it is an everyday fight to keep those response rates high. Arbitron's overall response rate was about 33 percent.[19] ∎

NOT-AT-HOMES The second major cause of low response rates is not-at-homes. In telephone and in-home personal interviews, low response rates can result if the potential respondents are not at home when contact is attempted. A study analyzing 182 commercial telephone surveys involving a total sample of over one million consumers revealed that a large percentage of potential respondents was never contacted. The median noncontact rate was 40 percent. In nearly 40 percent of the surveys, only a single attempt was made to contact potential respondents. The results of 259,088 first-call attempts, using the sophisticated random digit dialing M/A/R/C Telno System (www.marcgroup.com), shows that less than 10 percent of the calls resulted in completed interviews.[20]

The likelihood that potential respondents will not be at home varies with several factors. People with small children are more likely to be at home than single or divorced people. Consumers are more likely to be at home on weekends than on weekdays, and in the evening as opposed to during the afternoon. Prenotification and appointments increase the likelihood that the respondent will be at home when contact is attempted.

The percentage of not-at-homes can be substantially reduced by employing a series of callbacks, or periodic follow-up attempts to contact nonrespondents. The decision about the number of callbacks should weigh the benefits of reducing nonresponse bias against the additional costs. As callbacks are completed, the callback respondents should be compared to those who have already responded to determine the usefulness of making further callbacks. In most consumer surveys, three to four callbacks may be desirable. Whereas the first call yields the most responses, the second and third calls have a higher response per call. It is important that callbacks be made and controlled according to a prescribed plan.

Adjusting for Nonresponse

High response rates decrease the probability that nonresponse bias is substantial. Nonresponse rates should always be reported and, whenever possible, the effects of nonresponse should be estimated. This can be done by linking the nonresponse rate to estimated differences between respondents and nonrespondents. Information on differences between the two groups may be obtained from the sample itself. For example, differences found through callbacks could be extrapolated, or a concentrated follow-up could be conducted on a subsample of the nonrespondents. Alternatively, it may be possible to estimate these differences from other sources.[21] To illustrate, in a survey of owners of major appliances, demographic and other information may be obtained for respondents and nonrespondents from the warranty cards. For a mail panel, a wide variety of information is available for both groups from syndicate organizations. If the sample is supposed to be representative of the general population, then comparisons can be made with census figures. Even if it is not feasible to estimate the effects of nonresponse, some adjustments should still be made during data analysis and interpretation.[22] The strategies available to adjust for nonresponse error include subsampling of nonrespondents, replacement, substitution, subjective estimates, trend analysis, simple weighting, and imputation.

SUBSAMPLING OF NONRESPONDENTS Subsampling of nonrespondents, particularly in the case of mail surveys, can be effective in adjusting for nonresponse bias. In this technique, the researcher contacts a subsample of the nonrespondents, usually by means of telephone or personal interviews. This often results in a high response rate within that subsample. The values obtained for the subsample are then projected to all the nonrespondents, and the survey results are adjusted to account for nonresponse. This method can estimate the effect of nonresponse on the characteristic of interest.

REPLACEMENT In replacement, the nonrespondents in the current survey are replaced with nonrespondents from an earlier, similar survey. The researcher attempts to contact these nonrespondents from the earlier survey and administer the current survey questionnaire to them, possibly by offering a suitable incentive. It is important that the nature of nonresponse in the current survey be similar to that of the earlier survey. The two surveys should use similar kinds of respondents, and the time interval between them should be short. As an example, if the department store survey is being repeated one year later, the nonrespondents in the present survey may be replaced by the nonrespondents in the earlier survey.

substitution
A procedure that substitutes for nonrespondents other elements from the sampling frame that are expected to respond.

SUBSTITUTION In **substitution**, the researcher substitutes for nonrespondents other elements from the sampling frame that are expected to respond. The sampling frame is divided into subgroups that are internally homogeneous in terms of respondent characteristics, but heterogeneous in terms of response rates. These subgroups are then used to identify substitutes who are similar to particular nonrespondents but dissimilar to respondents already in the sample. Note that this approach would not reduce nonresponse bias if the substitutes are similar to respondents already in the sample.

Real Research

Exit Polling of Voters: Substituting Nonrespondents

Planning exit interviews for a presidential election begins as early as two years before the big day. Research firms such as Gallup (www.gallup.com) and Harris Interactive (www.harrisinteractive.com) systematically recruit and train workers.

The questions are short and pointed. Certain issues are well-known determinants of a voter's choice, whereas other questions deal with last-minute events such as political scandals. The questionnaires are written at the last possible moment and are designed to determine not only who people voted for but on what basis.

Uncooperative voters are a problem in exit polling. Interviewers are told to record a basic demographic profile for noncompliers. From this demographic data, a voter profile is developed to replace the uncooperative voters using the method of substitution. Age, sex, race, and residence are strong indicators of how Americans vote. For example, younger voters are more likely to be swayed by moral issues, whereas older voters are more likely to consider a candidate's personal qualities. Therefore, researchers substitute for nonrespondents other potential respondents who are similar in age, sex, race, and residence. The broad coverage of exit interviews and the substitution technique for noncompliant voters allow researchers to obtain margins of error close to 3 to 4 percent. Exit polls correctly predicted Barack Obama as the clear winner in the 2008 presidential elections.[23] ■

SUBJECTIVE ESTIMATES When it is no longer feasible to increase the response rate by subsampling, replacement, or substitution, it may be possible to arrive at subjective estimates of the nature and effect of nonresponse bias. This involves evaluating the likely effects of nonresponse based on experience and available information. For example, married adults with young children are more likely to be at home than single or divorced adults or married adults with no children. This information provides a basis for evaluating the effects of nonresponse due to not-at-homes in personal or telephone surveys.

trend analysis
A method of adjusting for nonresponse in which the researcher tries to discern a trend between early and late respondents. This trend is projected to nonrespondents to estimate their characteristic of interest.

TREND ANALYSIS **Trend analysis** is an attempt to discern a trend between early and late respondents. This trend is projected to nonrespondents to estimate where they stand on the characteristic of interest. For example, Table 12.4 presents the results of several waves of a mail survey. The characteristic of interest is average dollars spent on shopping in department stores during the last two months. The average dollar expenditures for the first three consecutive mailings can be calculated from the survey data but this value is missing for nonrespondents (Nonresponse case). The value for each successive wave of respondents becomes closer to the value for nonrespondents. For example, those responding to the second mailing spent 79 percent of the amount spent by those who responded to the first mailing. Those responding to the third mailing spent 85 percent of the amount spent by those who responded to the second mailing. Continuing this trend, one might estimate that those who did not respond spent 91 percent [85 + (85 − 79)] of the amount spent by those who responded to the third mailing, as shown in parentheses in Table 12.4. This results in an estimate of $252

TABLE 12.4
Use of Trend Analysis in Adjusting for Nonresponse

	Percentage Response	Average Dollar Expenditure	Percentage of Previous Wave's Response
First mailing	12	412	—
Second mailing	18	325	79
Third mailing	13	277	85
Nonresponse	(57)	(252)	(91)
Total	100		

(277×0.91) spent by nonrespondents, as shown in parentheses in Table 12.4, and an estimate of \$288 $(0.12 \times 412 + 0.18 \times 325 + 0.13 \times 277 + 0.57 \times 252)$ for the average amount spent in shopping at department stores during the last two months for the overall sample. Suppose we knew from mail panel records that the actual amount spent by the nonrespondents was \$230 rather than the \$252 estimated, and the actual sample average was \$275 rather than the \$288 estimated by trend analysis. Although the trend estimates are wrong, the error is smaller than the error that would have resulted from ignoring the nonrespondents. Had the nonrespondents been ignored, the average amount spent would have been estimated at \$335 $(0.12 \times 412 + 0.18 \times 325 + 0.13 \times 277)/(0.12 + 0.18 + 0.13)$ for the sample.

weighting
A statistical procedure that attempts to account for nonresponse by assigning differential weights to the data depending on the response rates.

WEIGHTING **Weighting** attempts to account for nonresponse by assigning differential weights to the data depending on the response rates.[24] For example, in a survey on personal computers, the sample was stratified according to income. The response rates were 85, 70, and 40 percent, respectively, for the high-, medium-, and low-income groups. In analyzing the data, these subgroups are assigned weights inversely proportional to their response rates. That is, the weights assigned would be (100/85), (100/70), and (100/40), respectively, for the high-, medium-, and low-income groups. Although weighting can correct for the differential effects of nonresponse, it destroys the self-weighting nature of the sampling design and can introduce complications. Weighting is further discussed in Chapter 14 on data preparation.

imputation
A method to adjust for nonresponse by assigning the characteristic of interest to the nonrespondents based on the similarity of the variables available for both nonrespondents and respondents.

IMPUTATION **Imputation** involves imputing, or assigning, the characteristic of interest to the nonrespondents based on the similarity of the variables available for both nonrespondents and respondents.[25] For example, a respondent who does not report brand usage may be imputed the usage of a respondent with similar demographic characteristics. Often there is a high correlation between the characteristic of interest and some other variables. In such cases, this correlation can be used to predict the value of the characteristic for the nonrespondents (see Chapter 17).

International Marketing Research

When conducting marketing research in foreign countries, statistical estimation of sample size may be difficult, because estimates of the population variance may be unavailable. Hence, the sample size is often determined by qualitative considerations, as discussed in Chapter 11: (1) the importance of the decision, (2) the nature of the research, (3) the number of variables, (4) the nature of the analysis, (5) sample sizes used in similar studies, (6) incidence rates, (7) completion rates, and (8) resource constraints. If statistical estimation of sample size is at all attempted, it should be realized that the estimates of the population variance may vary from country to country. For example, in measuring consumer preferences, a greater degree of heterogeneity may be encountered in countries where consumer preferences are not that well developed. Thus, it may be a mistake to assume that the population variance is the same or to use the same sample size in different countries.

Real Research

The Chinese Take to the Sky and the Sky Is the Limit

The airline industry seems to have a strong and promising market potential in China, where the airline market is growing rapidly. With billions of dollars spent, China is trying to satisfy surging demand and to catch up with the rest of the world. Strong economic growth, surging foreign trade, and a revival in tourism have helped to fuel the boom. Boeing (www.boeing.com) forecasts China will need nearly 2,300 new planes by 2023 to satisfy demand for passenger and cargo services.

Yet, for millions of Chinese, air travel is a relatively new experience, and many more millions have never flown. Hence, Chinese preferences for air travel are likely to exhibit much more variability as compared to Americans. In a survey by Delta Air Lines to compare the attitude toward air travel in China and the United States, the sample size of the Chinese survey would have to be larger than the American survey in order for the two survey estimates to have comparable precision.[26] ∎

It is important to realize that the response rates to surveys can vary widely across countries. In a 2000 business mail survey conducted in 22 countries, the response rates varied from a low of 7.1 percent in Hong Kong to a high of 42.1 percent in Denmark, with the overall response rate being 20 percent. The study also analyzed factors to help explain the differences in response rates.

Factors that were looked at included cultural and geographic distance from the Netherlands, where the survey was mailed. Other factors were foreign sales, export GNP, number of employees, power distance, and size of corporation.[27]

Ethics in Marketing Research

Although the statistical determination of sample size is usually objective, it is, nonetheless, susceptible to ethical concerns. As can be seen from the formula, the sample size is dependent on the standard deviation of the variable, and there is no way of precisely knowing the standard deviation until the data have been collected. An estimate of the standard deviation is used to calculate the sample size. This estimate is based on secondary data, judgment, or a small pilot study. By inflating the standard deviation, it is possible to increase the sample size and thus the project revenue for the research firm. Using the sample size formula, it can be seen that increasing the standard deviation by 20 percent, for example, will increase the sample size by 44 percent. It is clearly unethical to inflate the standard deviation, and thereby increase the sample size, simply to enhance the revenue of the marketing research firm.

Ethical dilemmas can arise even when the standard deviation is estimated honestly. Often, the standard deviation in the actual study is different from that estimated initially. When the standard deviation is larger than the initial estimate, the confidence interval will also be larger than desired. In such a situation, the researcher has the responsibility to discuss this with the client and jointly decide on a course of action. The ethical ramifications of miscommunicating the confidence intervals of survey estimates based on statistical samples are underscored in political polling.

Real Research | Surveys Serve Up Elections

The dissemination of some survey results has been strongly criticized as manipulative and unethical. In particular, the ethics of releasing political poll results before and during elections have been questioned. Opponents of such surveys claim that the general public is misled by these results. First, before the election, voters are influenced by whom the polls predict will win. If they see that the candidate they favor is trailing, they may decide not to vote; they assume that there is no way their candidate can win. The attempt to predict the election results while the election is in progress has come under even harsher criticism. Opponents of this practice feel that this predisposes voters to vote for the projected winner for their state, or that it may even discourage voters from voting. Even though the polls have not closed in their state, many will not vote because the media projects that there is already a winner. Furthermore, not only are the effects of these projections questionable, but frequently the accuracy of the projections is questionable as well. Although voters may be told a candidate has a certain percentage of the votes within ±1%, the confidence interval may be much larger, depending on the sample size.[28] ■

Researchers also have the ethical responsibility to investigate the possibility of nonresponse bias and make a reasonable effort to adjust for nonresponse. The methodology adopted and the extent of nonresponse bias found should be clearly communicated.

Decision Research | Procter & Gamble: Taking a Gamble on Core Brands

The Situation

A. G. Lafley, CEO of Procter & Gamble, turned around the consumer goods giant after taking the top job in 2000. He has refocused P&G on its big brands, including Tide, Pampers, and Crest. Lafley believes that there's still tremendous growth in the core brands. He has made one thing clear: P&G's stodgy corporate culture is gone for good.

In May 2001, Procter & Gamble, Inc., acquired Moist Mates, "America's first moist bath tissue on a roll." Holding the market for the past 20 years with their bath tissue Charmin, P&G found that a significant amount of consumers already try to use a wet cleaning system. "In fact, Charmin's research reveals that more than 60 percent of adult consumers have tried some alternative form of moist cleaning including sprinkling water on dry toilet paper, using baby wipes, or wetting a washcloth." With that in mind, the purchase of Moist Mates became a strategic move in the market. P&G took the product and changed the name to Charmin Fresh Mates on a roll so as to go hand-in-hand with the popular Charmin dry tissue. The biggest problem

Surveys based on appropriate sample sizes can help P&G formulate marketing strategies to increase the market share of Charmin and Charmin Fresh Mates.

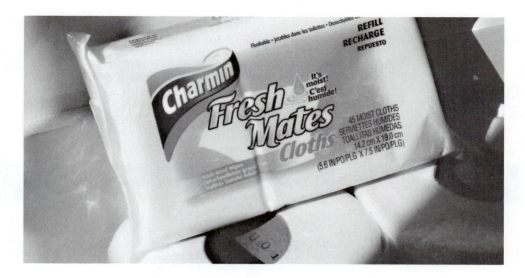

consumers felt was that their makeshift cleaning methods were inconvenient. P&G's marketing research showed that the familiarity of brand name, convenience, and easy-to-use wet tissue on a roll appealed to the consumer. "Together, these products offer consumers a convenient way to choose dry, choose moist, or choose both," says Wayne Randall, global franchise manager for Charmin. As of 2009, sales of Charmin Fresh Mates were stronger than leading wipes brands. As of 2009, Charmin and other products of Procter & Gamble were available in 180 countries around the world, and the company knows its products are "fresh."

Yet, there is some question as to whether Charmin and Charmin Fresh Mates are perceived as complementary or competing products.

The Marketing Research Decision

1. P&G would like to conduct periodic surveys to determine consumer perceptions and preferences for bath tissues, including Charmin and Charmin Fresh Mates. How should the sample size be determined?
2. Discuss the role of the sample size you recommend in enabling A. G. Lafley to determine consumer perceptions and preferences for bath tissues, including Charmin and Charmin Fresh Mates.

The Marketing Management Decision

1. What should A. G. Lafley do to further increase the market share of Charmin and Charmin Fresh Mates?
2. Discuss how the marketing management decision action that you recommend to A. G. Lafley is influenced by the sample size that you suggested earlier and by the findings of that research.[29] ■

SPSS Windows

SamplePower by SPSS can be used to calculate confidence intervals and statistically adjust the sample size. The sample size calculations are available for means as well as proportions.

Summary

The statistical approaches to determining sample size are based on confidence intervals. These approaches may involve the estimation of the mean or proportion. When estimating the mean, determination of sample size using the confidence interval approach requires the specification of precision level, confidence level, and population standard deviation. In the case of proportion, the precision level, confidence level, and an estimate of the population proportion must be specified. Figure 12.3 gives a concept map for determining the sample size for means. The sample size determined statistically represents the final or net sample size that must be achieved. In order to achieve this final sample size, a much greater number of potential respondents have to be contacted to account for reduction in response due to incidence rates and completion rates.

Nonresponse error arises when some of the potential respondents included in the sample do not respond. The primary causes of low response rates are refusals and

FIGURE 12.3

A Concept Map for Determining Sample Size for Means

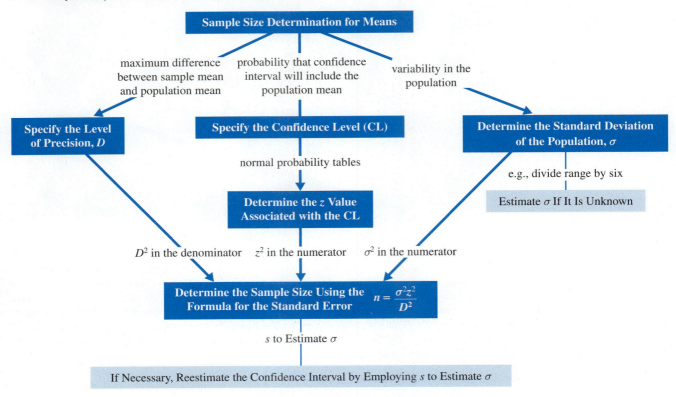

not-at-homes. Refusal rates may be reduced by prior notification, motivating the respondents, incentives, proper questionnaire design and administration, and follow-up. The percentage of not-at-homes can be substantially reduced by callbacks. Adjustments for nonresponse can be made by subsampling nonrespondents, replacement, substitution, subjective estimates, trend analysis, weighting, and imputation.

The statistical estimation of sample size is even more complicated in international marketing research, as the population variance may differ from one country to the next. The preliminary estimation of population variance for the purpose of determining the sample size also has ethical ramifications. The Internet and computers can assist in determining the sample size and adjusting it to account for expected incidence and completion rates.

Key Terms and Concepts

parameter, 372
statistic, 372
finite population correction (fpc), 372
precision level, 373
confidence interval, 373
confidence level, 373

sampling distribution, 373
statistical inference, 373
normal distribution, 373
standard error, 374
z value, 374
incidence rate, 382

completion rate, 382
substitution, 388
trend analysis, 388
weighting, 389
imputation, 389

Suggested Cases, Video Cases, and HBS Cases

Running Case with Real Data

1.1 Dell

Comprehensive Critical Thinking Cases

2.1 American Idol   2.2 Baskin-Robbins   2.3 Akron Children's Hospital

Comprehensive Cases with Real Data

4.1 JPMorgan Chase   4.2 Wendy's

Video Cases

12.1 Subaru   13.1 Intel   23.1 Marriott

Comprehensive Harvard Business School Cases

Case 5.1: The Harvard Graduate Student Housing Survey (9-505-059)
Case 5.2: BizRate.Com (9-501-024)
Case 5.3: Cola Wars Continue: Coke and Pepsi in the Twenty-First Century (9-702-442)
Case 5.4: TiVo in 2002 (9-502-062)
Case 5.5: Compaq Computer: Intel Inside? (9-599-061)
Case 5.6: The New Beetle (9-501-023)

Live Research: Conducting a Marketing Research Project

1. Discuss the qualitative and statistical considerations involved in determining the sample size.
2. Illustrate the confidence interval approach (mean or proportion) to calculate the sample size of the project, even though the sample size may have been determined based on qualitative considerations.
3. Discuss the expected incidence and completion rates and the initial sample size.

Acronym

The statistical considerations involved in determining the sample size may be summarized by the acronym

Size:

S   ampling distribution
I   nterval (confidence)
Z   value
E   stimation of population standard deviation

Exercises

Questions

1. Define the sampling distribution.
2. What is the standard error of the mean?
3. Define finite population correction.
4. Define a confidence interval.
5. What is the procedure for constructing a confidence interval around a mean?
6. Describe the difference between absolute precision and relative precision when estimating a population mean.
7. How do the degree of confidence and the degree of precision differ?
8. Describe the procedure for determining the sample size necessary to estimate a population mean, given the degree of precision and confidence and a known population variance. After the sample is selected, how is the confidence interval generated?
9. Describe the procedure for determining the sample size necessary to estimate a population mean, given the degree of precision and confidence, but when the population variance is unknown. After the sample is selected, how is the confidence interval generated?
10. How is the sample size affected when the absolute precision with which a population mean is estimated is doubled?

11. How is the sample size affected when the degree of confidence with which a population mean is estimated is increased from 95 percent to 99 percent?
12. Define what is meant by absolute precision and relative precision when estimating a population proportion.
13. Describe the procedure for determining the sample size necessary to estimate a population proportion, given the degree of precision and confidence. After the sample is selected, how is the confidence interval generated?
14. How can the researcher ensure that the generated confidence interval will be no larger than the desired interval when estimating a population proportion?
15. When several parameters are being estimated, what is the procedure for determining the sample size?
16. Define incidence rate and completion rate. How do these rates affect the determination of the final sample size?
17. What strategies are available to adjust for nonresponse?

Problems

1. Using Table 2 of the Appendix of Statistical Tables, calculate the probability that:
   a. z is less than 1.48
   b. z is greater than 1.90

c. z is between 1.48 and 1.90

d. z is between -1.48 and 1.90

2. What is the value of z if:

a. 60 percent of all values of z are larger

b. 10 percent of all values of z are larger

c. 68.26 percent of all possible z values (symmetrically distributed around the mean) are to be contained in this interval

3. The management of a local restaurant wants to determine the average monthly amount spent by households in restaurants. Some households in the target market do not spend anything at all, whereas other households spend as much as $300 per month. Management wants to be 95 percent confident of the findings and does not want the error to exceed plus or minus $5.

a. What sample size should be used to determine the average monthly household expenditure?

b. After the survey was conducted, the average expenditure was found to be $90.30 and the standard deviation was

$45. Construct a 95 percent confidence interval. What can be said about the level of precision?

4. To determine the effectiveness of the advertising campaign for a new DVD player, management would like to know what percentage of the households are aware of the new brand. The advertising agency thinks that this figure is as high as 70 percent. The management would like a 95 percent confidence interval and a margin of error no greater than plus or minus 2 percent.

a. What sample size should be used for this study?

b. Suppose that management wanted to be 99 percent confident but could tolerate an error of plus or minus 3 percent. How would the sample size change?

5. Assuming that $n = 100$ and $N = 1,000$, and $\sigma = 5$, compute the standard error of the mean with and without the finite population correction factor.

Internet and Computer Exercises

1. Using a spreadsheet (e.g., EXCEL), program the formulas for determining the sample size under the various approaches. (This is very simple to do.)

2. Solve previous problems 1 through 4 using the programs that you have developed.

3. Visit the Gallup organization Web site (www.gallup.com). Identify some of the surveys recently completed by the Gallup organization. What were the sample sizes in these surveys and how were they determined?

Activities

Role Playing

1. You work in the marketing research department of Burger King. Burger King has developed a new cooking process that makes the hamburgers taste better. However, before the new hamburger is introduced in the market, taste tests will be conducted. How should the sample size for these taste tests be determined? What approach would you recommend? Justify your recommendations to a group of students representing Burger King management.

2. A major electric utility would like to determine the average amount spent per household for cooling during the summer. The management believes that a survey should be conducted. You are appointed as a consultant. What procedure would you recommend for determining the sample size? Make a presentation about this project to three students who represent the chief

operating officer, chief financial officer, and chief marketing officer of this utility.

Fieldwork

1. Visit a local marketing research firm. Find out how the sample sizes were determined in some recent surveys or experiments. Write a report about your findings.

Group Discussion

1. "Quantitative considerations are more important than qualitative considerations in determining the sample size." Discuss as a small group.

2. Discuss the relative advantages and disadvantages of the confidence interval approach.

Appendix 12A

The Normal Distribution

In this appendix, we provide a brief overview of the normal distribution and the use of the normal distribution table. The normal distribution is used in calculating the sample size, and it serves as the basis for classical statistical inference. Many continuous phenomena follow the normal distribution or can be approximated by it. The normal distribution can, likewise, be used to approximate many discrete probability distributions.[1]

The normal distribution has some important theoretical properties. It is bell-shaped and symmetrical in appearance. Its measures of central tendency (mean, median, and mode) are all identical. Its associated random variable has an infinite range $(-\infty < x < +\infty)$.

The normal distribution is defined by the population mean μ and population standard deviation σ. Since an infinite number of combination of μ and σ exist, an infinite number of

---

[1]This material is drawn from Mark L. Berenson, Timothy Krehbiel, and David M. Levine, *Basic Business Statistics: Concepts and Applications*, 11th ed. (Upper Saddle River, NJ: Prentice Hall, 2009).

normal distributions exist and an infinite number of tables would be required. However, by standardizing the data, we need only one table, such as Table 2 given in the Appendix of Statistical Tables. Any normal random variable X can be converted to a standardized normal random variable z by the formula:

$$z = \frac{X - \mu}{\sigma}$$

Note that the random variable z is always normally distributed with a mean of 0 and a standard deviation of 1. The normal probability tables are generally used for two purposes: (1) finding probabilities corresponding to known values of X or z, and (2) finding values of X or z corresponding to known probabilities. Each of these uses is discussed.

Finding Probabilities Corresponding to Known Values

Suppose Figure 12A.1 represents the distribution of the number of engineering contracts received per year by an engineering firm. Since the data span the entire history of the firm, Figure 12A.1 represents the population. Therefore, the probabilities or proportion of area under the curve must add up to 1.0. The vice president of marketing wishes to determine the probability that the number of contracts received next year will be between 50 and 55. The answer can be determined by using Table 2 of the Appendix of Statistical Tables.

Table 2 gives the probability or area under the standardized normal curve from the mean (zero) to the standardized value of interest, z. Only positive entries of z are listed in the table. For a symmetrical distribution with zero mean, the area from the mean to $+z$ (i.e., z standard deviations above the mean) is identical to the area from the mean to $-z$ (z standard deviations below the mean).

Note that the difference between 50 and 55 corresponds to a z value of 1.00. Note that to use Table 2, all z values must be recorded to two decimal places. To read the probability or area under the curve from the mean to z = $+1.00$, scan down the z column of Table 2 until the z value of interest (in tenths) is located. In this case, stop in the row $z = 1.00$. Then read across this row until you intersect the column containing the hundredths place of the z value. Thus, in Table 2, the tabulated probability for $z = 1.00$ corresponds to the intersection of the row $z = 1.0$ with the column $z = .00$. This probability is 0.3413. As shown in Figure 12A.1, the probability is 0.3413 that the number of contracts received by the firm next year will be between 50 and 55. It can also be concluded that the probability is 0.6826 (2×0.3413) that the number of contracts received next year will be between 45 and 55.

This result could be generalized to show that for any normal distribution, the probability is 0.6826 that a randomly selected item will fall within ± 1 standard deviations above or below the mean. Also, it can be verified from Table 2 that there is a 0.9544 probability that any randomly selected normally distributed observation will fall within ± 2 standard deviations above or below the mean; and a 0.9973 probability that the observation will fall within ± 3 standard deviations above or below the mean.

Finding Values Corresponding to Known Probabilities

Suppose the vice president of marketing wishes to determine how many contracts must come in so that 5 percent of the contracts for the year have come in. If 5 percent of the contracts have come in, 95 percent of the contracts have yet to come. As shown in Figure 12A.2, this 95 percent can be broken down into two parts—contracts above the mean (i.e., 50 percent) and contracts between the mean and the desired z value (i.e., 45 percent). The desired z value can be determined from Table 2, since the area under the normal curve from the standardized mean, 0, to this z must be 0.4500. From Table 2, we search for the area or probability 0.4500. The closest value is 0.4495 or 0.4505. For 0.4495, we see that the z value corresponding to the particular z row (1.6) and z column (.04) is

FIGURE 12A.1

Finding Probability Corresponding to a Known Value

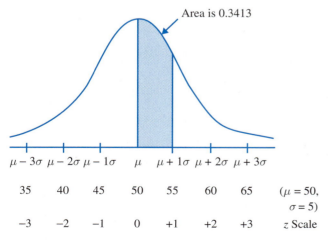

Area between μ and $\mu + 1\sigma = 0.3413$
Area between μ and $\mu + 2\sigma = 0.4772$
Area between μ and $\mu + 3\sigma = 0.4986$

FIGURE 12A.2

Finding Values Corresponding to Known Probabilities

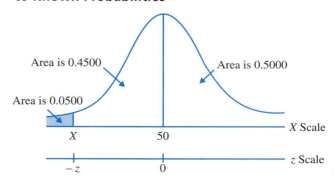

1.64. However, the z value must be recorded as negative (i.e., $z = -1.64$), since it is below the standardized mean of 0. Similarly, the z value corresponding to the area of 0.4505 is -1.65. Since 0.4500 is midway between 0.4495 and 0.4505, the appropriate z value could be midway between the two z values and estimated as -1.645. The corresponding X value can then be calculated from the standardization formula, as follows:

$$X = \mu + z\sigma$$

or

$$X = 50 + (-1.645)\,5 = 41.775$$

Suppose the vice president wanted to determine the interval in which 95 percent of the contracts for next year are expected to lie. As can be seen from Figure 12A.3, the corresponding z values are ± 1.96. This corresponds to X values of $50 \pm (1.96)\,5$, or 40.2 and 59.8. This range represents the 95 percent confidence interval.

FIGURE 12A.3

Finding Values Corresponding to Known Probabilities: Confidence Intervals

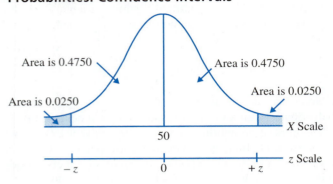

Dell Running Case

Review the Dell case, Case 1.1, and questionnaire provided toward the end of the book.

1. Search the Internet, as well as your library's online databases, to obtain information on the proportion of U.S. households that have Internet access at home.
2. In a survey of the general population on Internet usage, what should be the sample size for a 95 percent confidence level and a 5 percent precision level? Use the estimate of the population proportion that you determined in step 1.
3. As the director of marketing for Dell PCs and notebooks, what information would you need to formulate marketing strategies to increase your sales?

Video Cases

VIDEO CASE 12.1   Subaru: "Mr. Survey" Monitors Customer Satisfaction

Subaru of America (www.subaru.com) is the automobile division of Fuji Heavy Industries (FHI). Subaru has been operating in the United States since 1968, when it began selling the 360 Minicar. Headquartered in Cherry Hill, New Jersey, the company serves nearly 600 dealers nationwide. Subaru has offered many different cars over the years, but as of 2009 it sold five different brands in the United States. These brands each have a variety of different models. The five brands are the Tribeca, the Outback, the Forester, the Legacy, and the Impreza. One of the unique things about Subaru is that 100 percent of its models come with all-wheel drive.

Subaru's strategy is apparent in one of its key players, Joe Barstys. Joe has been with Subaru for more than 20 years, and he spends his time worrying about customer satisfaction. Joe and people like him are the backbone of Subaru. These people help Subaru focus on its customers and their wants and needs by conducting marketing research. Joe has incorporated the use of customer surveys into his practice, and for this he has gained the title of "Mr. Survey." Joe's goal is to develop a customer satisfaction level that will help build a certain level of loyalty in Subaru's customers. This loyalty is extremely important in the car business, because it has historically been much lower than in other industries. Marketing research has shown that although approximately 90 percent of customers are pleased with their automobile purchase, only 40 percent are loyal enough to buy the same brand again.

Surveys are a very valuable tool to Subaru in its quest for customer loyalty. The company mails a survey to each customer within 30 to 45 days of purchase to assess the customer's feelings toward the newly purchased vehicle, to obtain information on the nature of the interaction with the dealer, and to learn about other elements of the purchase process. Subsequent to the initial contact, more surveys follow throughout the "lifetime" of the customer (i.e., the duration of ownership of the car, on average 6 to 7 years). The latter surveys assess the long-term satisfaction with the vehicle and the dealership. The mail surveys have a high 50 percent response rate. As of 2009, about 500,000

surveys are mailed each year. Additional surveys are conducted over the Internet. Questions on the survey include: How was your service experience? How does Subaru compare to other service providers you have visited? What about the buying experience? How satisfied were you? What were the salespeople like? These questions help Subaru determine how customers regard their Subaru experience and what steps Subaru should take to improve this experience further.

These surveys provide important feedback, allowing Subaru to adjust its approach based on consumer demands. An example of the importance of adjustments can be found in the case of the female consumer. Through surveys, Subaru found out that it needed to adjust its marketing to include female consumers, who are becoming an increasingly large part of the market. It was important for Subaru to understand what types of things would appeal to women in order to offer a more desirable product to them.

Another benefit of marketing and survey research is that Subaru has been able to identify the types of people who are more likely to buy its automobiles. Subaru believes that the typical Subaru owner is different from the average consumer. Its average consumer is highly intelligent, highly independent, and outside the mainstream crowd. Thus, Subaru tries to market automobiles to these types of people and attempts to distinguish itself from the larger, more mainstream competitors. Results of affinity for the company are evident as customers feel motivated to send pictures of their cars to Subaru.

Joe considers his background in philosophy and theology (he has a BA in philosophy and an MA in theology) to have contributed to the role of Mr. Survey he plays at Subaru. Joe explains that his theology and philosophy background allows him to look at the human experience with a product. A customer's problem could be a dysfunction with his car, his dealer, or his own ignorance about how the car works. All of these are essentially about human experience, and hence no matter whether Joe works in the automobile industry or any other, he is, in effect, dealing with human experience. This human experience is just one aspect that he loves about his job, because he loves being with people and finding out what makes them tick. The other aspect that he is really excited about is the great responsibility and decision-making authority that he shoulders with the goal of maintaining customer loyalty, and every year he achieves success.

The company's goal is continued growth through 2015, and it hopes that with the help of marketing research it will be able to achieve this goal. It believes that listening to the customers and adapting its practices to meet their concerns will provide customers with a higher level of satisfaction and ultimately lead to a higher level of loyalty. Subaru's marketing research staff, like "Mr. Survey," will be critical to this endeavor.

Conclusion

The case presents an interesting overview of Joe Barstys's role at Subaru and the importance and utility of surveys in building customer loyalty. Surveys have helped Subaru get continuous feedback on key parameters that shape customer experience resulting in high brand loyalty. In sum, marketing research has helped Subaru understand its customers better and hence address their needs and expectations better.

Questions

1. Discuss the role that marketing research can play in helping Subaru understand why its customers are devoted to the brand.
2. In order to continue to grow, Subaru must foster and build customer loyalty. Define the management decision problem.
3. Define an appropriate marketing research problem based on the management decision problem you have identified.
4. What type of research design should be adopted to investigate the marketing research problem you have identified?
5. In what way can Subaru make use of data from the 2000 (or 2010) U.S. Census? What are the limitations of these data? How can these limitations be overcome?
6. What type of data available from syndicate marketing research firms will be useful to Subaru?
7. Discuss the role of qualitative research in understanding the devotion of consumers to a particular automobile brand. Which qualitative research technique(s) should be used and why?
8. If a survey is to be conducted to understand consumer preferences for various automobile brands, which survey method should be used and why?
9. Can Subaru make use of causal research? If yes, how?
10. Design ordinal, interval, and ratio scales for measuring consumer preferences for various automobile brands.
11. Design Likert, semantic differential, and Stapel scales for measuring consumer preferences for various automobile brands.
12. Design a questionnaire to measure consumers' evaluation of Subaru brands.
13. Develop a sampling plan for the survey of question 8.
14. How should the sample size be determined?
15. If Subaru were to conduct marketing research to determine consumer willingness to purchase automobile brands in Germany, how would the research process be different?
16. Discuss the ethical issues involved in researching consumer willingness to purchase automobile brands.

References

1. www.subaru.com, accessed February 20, 2009.
2. www.wikipedia.org, accessed February 20, 2009.
3. Donald I. Hammonds, "Subaru Adds Upscale Looks to Its Durable Image," *Knight Ridder Tribune Business News* (June 16, 2004): 1.

This part presents a practical and managerially oriented discussion of fieldwork, the fourth step in the marketing research process. We offer several guidelines for selecting, training, supervising, validating, and evaluating fieldworkers. When the fieldwork is complete, the researcher moves on to data preparation and analysis, the fifth step of the marketing research process. In this part, we emphasize the importance and discuss the process of preparing data to make them suitable for analysis. Then we describe the various data analysis techniques. We cover not only the basic techniques of frequency distribution, cross-tabulation, and hypothesis testing, but also the commonly used multivariate techniques of analysis of variance and regression. Then, we describe the more advanced techniques: discriminant, logit, factor, cluster analysis, multidimensional scaling, conjoint analysis, structural equation modeling, and path analysis. In the discussion of each statistical technique, the emphasis is on explaining the procedure, interpreting the results, and drawing managerial implications, rather than on statistical elegance. Several cases with real data sets provide ample opportunities to practice these techniques.

Communicating the research by preparing and presenting a formal report constitutes the sixth step in a marketing research project. Using a practical orientation, we provide guidelines for writing reports and preparing tables and graphs and also discuss oral presentation of the report. We focus on the international dimensions of marketing research. Although this topic has been discussed in a pervasive way in the previous chapters, this part presents additional details. We present a conceptual framework for international marketing research and illustrate, in detail, how the environment prevailing in the countries, cultural units, or international markets being researched influences the way the marketing research process should be performed.

13

"I make my living interviewing senior executives in firms. I always arrive 30 minutes early for each appointment and always write a thank-you note to anyone at the firm who helped me that day. In short, your Mom was right. Courtesy is indispensable to success."

Robert J. Berrier, Ph.D., Founder and President, Berrier Associates, Narberth, Pennsylvania

Objectives [After reading this chapter, the student should be able to:]

1. Describe the fieldwork process and explain the selection, training, and supervision of fieldworkers, the validation of fieldwork, and the evaluation of fieldworkers.

2. Discuss the training of fieldworkers in making the initial contact, asking the questions, probing, recording the answers, and terminating the interview.

3. Discuss the supervision of fieldworkers in terms of quality control and editing, sampling control, control of cheating, and central office control.

4. Describe the evaluation of fieldworkers in areas of cost and time, response rates, quality of interviewing, and the quality of data.

5. Explain the issues related to fieldwork when conducting international marketing research.

6. Discuss the ethical aspect of fieldwork.

7. Illustrate the use of the Internet and computers in fieldwork.

Fieldwork

Overview

Fieldwork is the fourth step in the marketing research process (Chapter 1). It follows problem definition, development of the approach (Chapter 2), and formulation of the research design (Chapters 3 through 12). During this phase, the fieldworkers make contact with the respondents, administer the questionnaires or observation forms, record the data, and turn in the completed forms for processing. A personal interviewer administering questionnaires door-to-door, an interviewer intercepting shoppers in a mall, a telephone interviewer calling from a central location, a worker mailing questionnaires from an office, an observer counting customers in a particular section of a store, and others involved in data collection and supervision of the process are all fieldworkers.

This chapter describes the nature of fieldwork and the general fieldwork/data-collection process. This process involves the selection, training, and supervision of fieldworkers, the validation of fieldwork, and the evaluation of fieldworkers. We briefly discuss fieldwork in the context of international marketing research, identify the relevant ethical issues, and explain the role of the Internet and computers.

Real Research

Refusing Refusals

The Council for Marketing and Opinion Research (CMOR) is a national nonprofit research industry trade group (www.cmor.org). In a CMOR survey that interviewed more than 3,700 U.S. consumers, nearly 45 percent said they had refused to participate in a survey over the past year. CMOR offers several guidelines related to fieldwork to help reduce refusal rates:

- Interviewer training programs should be routinely administered so that fieldworkers will be effective at their jobs.
- Courtesy should be exercised when deciding what hours of the day to call respondents. Calling between 9 A.M. and 9 P.M. is recommended.

Guidelines by CMOR help reduce refusal rates in surveys.

Source: www.cmor.org. Used with permission of CMOR.

- If mall respondents indicate the time is not convenient, an appointment should be made to conduct the interview later.
- The subject matter should be disclosed to the respondents if this can be done without biasing the data. The more information people are given, the less reason they have to be suspicious.
- Fieldworkers should make the interviews as pleasant and appealing as possible.[1] ■

Real Research   Create Your Own Online Survey

CreateSurvey (www.createsurvey.com) is an international online company that allows anyone to create and administer online surveys to whomever they want. It distributes the survey, monitors participation and participants, and then collects and analyzes the data, all for free. It is sponsored by Web advertising in the form of online banners that appear on the site and the questionnaires, so respondents as well as the survey creators see the advertisements. If an individual does not wish to have the advertising banners appear on the page, they can be removed, but then a fee is charged to the creator to support the service. CreateSurvey does not provide respondents. This is done by the users at their discretion. For instance, they may create a Web page and have the survey as a link from the Web page, or they may send out an e-mail with the link requesting people to participate in the survey. CreateSurvey provides a valuable service for creating and administering online surveys that have been used by many individuals, companies, universities, and even marketing research organizations. Another Web-based service that also lets you create your own surveys is (www. zoomerang.com) by MarketTools, an Internet-based, technology-enabled, full-service marketing research company (www.markettools.com). ■

The Nature of Fieldwork

Marketing research data are rarely collected by the persons who design the research. Researchers have two major options for collecting their data: They can develop their own organizations or they can contract with a fieldwork agency. In either case, data collection involves the use of some kind of field force. The field force may operate either in the field (personal in-home, mall intercept, computer-assisted personal interviewing, and observation) or from an office (telephone, mail, mail panel, e-mail, and Internet surveys). The fieldworkers who collect the data typically have little research background or training. Ethical concerns are particularly germane to fieldwork. Although there is ample opportunity for violation of ethical standards, clients need not be overly concerned when dealing with reputable fieldwork agencies. Michael Redington, senior vice president for corporate development at Marketing and Research Counselors Group (M/A/R/C Group, www.marcgroup.com), is an aggressive advocate of field quality. His evaluation of the quality of fieldwork in the marketing research industry is as follows: "I was very pleased to help shoot down the myth that data collection is characterized by a bunch of people out there attempting to bend the rules, to rip you off, and to cheat on interviews. There are a lot of people on the client side who believe just that. Quite frankly, we were out trying to find it, but we didn't. That was a revelation to us. We were afraid that there were more unethical practices in the field than there really were."[2] The quality of fieldwork is high because the fieldwork/data-collection process is streamlined and well controlled.

Fieldwork/Data-Collection Process

All fieldwork involves the selection, training, and supervision of persons who collect data.[3] The validation of fieldwork and the evaluation of fieldworkers are also parts of the process. Figure 13.1 represents a general framework for the fieldwork/data-collection process. Although we describe a general process, it should be recognized that the nature of fieldwork varies with the mode of data collection, and the relative emphasis on the different steps will be different for telephone, personal, mail, and electronic interviews.

Selection of Fieldworkers

The first step in the fieldwork process is the selection of fieldworkers. The researcher should: (1) develop job specifications for the project, taking into account the mode of data collection; (2) decide what characteristics the fieldworkers should have; and (3) recruit appropriate individuals. Interviewers' background characteristics, opinions, perceptions, expectations, and attitudes can affect the responses they elicit.[4]

FIGURE 13.1

Fieldwork/Data-Collection Process

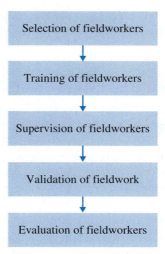

Selection of fieldworkers

↓

Training of fieldworkers

↓

Supervision of fieldworkers

↓

Validation of fieldwork

↓

Evaluation of fieldworkers

For example, the social acceptability of a fieldworker to the respondent may affect the quality of data obtained, especially in personal interviewing. Researchers generally agree that the more characteristics the interviewer and the respondent have in common, the greater the probability of a successful interview.

Real Research Searching for Common Ground

In a survey dealing with emotional well-being and mental health, older interviewers got better cooperation from respondents than younger interviewers. However, this performance appeared to be independent of years of experience. Differences in nonresponse rates also appeared between black and white interviewers. Black interviewers produced higher nonresponse rates with white respondents than did white interviewers. The more the interviewer and the respondent had in common, the greater the cooperation and the better the quality of the data.[5] ■

Thus, to the extent possible, interviewers should be selected to match respondents' characteristics. The job requirements will also vary with the nature of the problem and the type of data-collection method. However, there are some general qualifications that fieldworkers need:

- *Healthy.* Fieldwork can be strenuous and the workers must have the stamina required to do the job.
- *Outgoing.* The interviewers should be able to establish rapport with the respondents. They should be able to relate to strangers.
- *Communicative.* Effective speaking and listening skills are a great asset.
- *Pleasant appearance.* If the fieldworker's physical appearance is unpleasant or unusual, the data collected may be biased.
- *Educated.* Interviewers must have good reading and writing skills. A majority of fieldwork agencies require a high school education and many prefer some college education.
- *Experienced.* Experienced interviewers are likely to do a better job in following instructions, obtaining respondent cooperation, and conducting the interview.

Real Research Your Experience Counts

Research has found the following effects of interviewer experience on the interviewing process.

- Inexperienced interviewers are more likely to commit coding errors, to misrecord responses, and to fail to probe.
- Inexperienced interviewers have a particularly difficult time filling quotas of respondents.
- Inexperienced interviewers have larger refusal rates. They also accept more "don't know" responses and refusals to answer individual questions.[6] ■

Fieldworkers are generally paid an hourly rate or on a per-interview basis. The typical interviewer is a married woman age 35 to 54, with an above-average education and an above-average household income.

Training of Fieldworkers

Training of fieldworkers is critical to the quality of data collected. Training may be conducted in person at a central location or, if the interviewers are geographically dispersed, by mail, video-conferencing, or by using the Internet. Training ensures that all interviewers administer the questionnaire in the same manner so that the data can be collected uniformly. Training should cover making the initial contact, asking the questions, probing, recording the answers, and terminating the interview.[7]

Making the Initial Contact

The initial contact can result in cooperation or the loss of potential respondents.[8] Interviewers should be trained to make opening remarks that will convince potential respondents that their participation is important.

Project Research   Initial Contact Statement

Hello, my name is _____. I represent the Marketing Department of Georgia Tech. We are conducting a survey about household preferences for department stores. You are one of the select groups of respondents who have been scientifically chosen to participate in this survey. We highly value your opinion and would like to ask you a few questions.[9] ■

Note that the interviewer did not specifically ask the respondent's permission. Questions that directly ask permission, such as "May I have some of your valuable time?" or "Would you like to answer a few questions?" should be avoided. Interviewers should also be instructed on handling objections and refusals. For example, if the respondent says, "This is not a convenient time for me," the interviewer should respond, "What would be a more convenient time for you? I will call back then." If the foot-in-the-door or door-in-the-face techniques discussed in Chapter 12 are being employed, interviewers should be trained accordingly.

Asking the Questions

Even a slight change in the wording, sequence, or manner in which a question is asked can distort its meaning and bias the response. Asking questions is an art. Training in asking questions can yield high dividends in eliminating potential sources of bias. Changing the phrasing or order of questions during the interview can make significant differences in the response obtained. While we could be faulted for not writing as perfect a questionnaire as we possibly could, still it must be asked in the exact way it was written. It's a challenge for us to try to get the interviewers more conversational, but despite this, the field force absolutely must ask questions as they are written.[10] The following are guidelines for asking questions.[11]

1. Be thoroughly familiar with the questionnaire.
2. Ask the questions in the order in which they appear in the questionnaire.
3. Use the exact wording given in the questionnaire.
4. Read each question slowly.
5. Repeat questions that are not understood.
6. Ask every applicable question.
7. Follow instructions and skip patterns, probing carefully.

Probing

probing
A motivational technique used when asking survey questions to induce the respondents to enlarge on, clarify, or explain their answers and to help the respondents to focus on the specific content of the interview.

Probing is intended to motivate respondents to enlarge on, clarify, or explain their answers. Probing also helps respondents focus on the specific content of the interview and provide only relevant information. Probing should not introduce any bias. Some commonly used probing techniques follow:[12]

1. *Repeating the question.* Repeating the question in the same words can be effective in eliciting a response.
2. *Repeating the respondent's reply.* Respondents can be stimulated to provide further comments by repeating their replies verbatim. This can be done as the interviewer records the replies.
3. *Using a pause or silent probe.* A silent probe, or an expectant pause or look, can cue the respondent to provide a more complete response. However, the silence should not become embarrassing.
4. *Boosting or reassuring the respondent.* If the respondent hesitates, the interviewer should reassure the respondent with comments like, "There are no right or wrong answers. We are just trying to get your opinions." If the respondent needs an explanation of a word or phrase, the interviewer should not offer an interpretation. Rather, the responsibility for the interpretation should be returned to the respondent. This can be done with a comment such as, "Just whatever it means to you."
5. *Eliciting clarification.* The respondent's motivation to cooperate with the interviewer and provide complete answers can be aroused with a question like, "I don't quite understand what you mean by that—could you please tell me a little more?"
6. *Using objective/neutral questions or comments.* Some common questions or comments used as probes and the corresponding abbreviations are: Any other reason? (AO?), Anything else? (AE or Else?), What do you mean? (What mean?), and Why do you feel that way? (Why?).[13] The interviewer should record the abbreviations on the questionnaire in parentheses next to the question asked.

Recording the Answers

Although recording respondent answers seems simple, several mistakes are common.[14] All interviewers should use the same format and conventions to record the interviews and edit completed interviews. The rules for recording answers to structured questions vary with each specific questionnaire, but the general rule is to check the box that reflects the respondent's answer. The general rule for recording answers to unstructured questions is to record the responses verbatim. The *Interviewer's Manual* of the Survey Research Center provides the following specific guidelines for recording answers to unstructured questions.

1. Record responses during the interview.
2. Use the respondent's own words.
3. Do not summarize or paraphrase the respondent's answers.
4. Include everything that pertains to the question objectives.
5. Include all probes and comments.
6. Repeat the response as it is written down.

Terminating the Interview

The interview should not be closed before all the information is obtained. Any spontaneous comments the respondent offers after all the formal questions have been asked should be recorded. The interviewer should answer the respondent's questions about the project. The respondent should be left with a positive feeling about the interview. It is important to thank the respondent and express appreciation.

Real Research | ## The Centers for Disease Control Training

The Centers for Disease Control and Prevention (CDC) (www.cdc.gov) has conducted the state-based Behavioral Risk Factor Surveillance System (BRFSS), the largest continuously conducted telephone health survey in the world. This survey has collected data on risk behaviors and preventive health practices every month since 1984. Fieldworkers who are trained in their respective states administer these standardized questionnaires. The CDC receives health data on hypertension, high cholesterol, smoking, and drinking behaviors from individual states and publishes a report every year. To increase standardization in the training of fieldworkers and data collection, the CDC implemented a computer-assisted telephone interviewing (CATI) system.

The CDC understands that its field interviewers are the only link between the survey participants and the researchers conducting the survey. The CDC therefore requires states to spend a lot of time and effort training its interviewers. In training, an effort is made to ensure that the interviewer:

- Understands the nature and content of the questions
- Understands how to record responses, code questionnaires, and edit interviews
- Ensures respondents' confidentiality
- Ensures that the correct respondents are interviewed
- Records a true picture
- Executes the work clearly and accurately
- Is prepared to deal with problem situations that may arise during interviews
- Is persuasive and minimizes the number of selected households and respondents who refuse to participate
- Makes quality a priority in all aspects of interviewing
- Is courteous and friendly
- Strives for maximum efficiency without sacrificing quality

With the nature of the BRFSS, interviewers must also sign a confidentiality agreement. Respondents are sometimes concerned about confidentiality of their health information. Measures are taken to eliminate the possibility of ever identifying the specific person who has taken a survey. For instance, the last two digits of the telephone number are deleted in the final survey results. Interviewers are trained to relay this information to people who are concerned when they call them.

Other training procedures are useful in obtaining valid responses for the questionnaire and for being courteous to the participants. The table summarizes the tips for telephone interviewing that CDC uses as part of its training program. This extensive training is vital to providing the accurate information the CDC needs for its analysis of locally relevant data on risk behaviors and preventive health practices. The data are used in a variety of ways by states and health agencies for planning, implementing, and measuring the progress of their risk-reduction programs, and for developing appropriate policies and legislation.[15]

Tips for Telephone Interviewing

VOICE PERSONALITY	HANDLING DIFFICULT RESPONDENTS
Be courteous and polite.	Answer respondents.
Sound confident.	Alleviate confidentiality concerns.
Do not sound bored.	Encourage responses from reluctant respondents.
Sound interested in the responses.	Alleviate concerns about length of interview.
Put a smile in your voice.	**GENERAL KNOWLEDGE OF THE BRFSS**
PROBING AND CLARIFICATION	Recognize need for data quality.
Probe for accurate information.	Know survey objectives.
Know when to probe.	Know rationale for the questions.
Use neutral probes.	**INTERVIEWING TECHNIQUES**
ENUNCIATION OF QUESTIONNAIRE	Read questions verbatim.
Speak clearly.	Verify telephone number.
Pronounce words properly.	Follow skip patterns smoothly.
	Go from introduction to questions smoothly.
	Close interview smoothly.
	Make appointments properly.
	Provide neutral feedback. ∎

ACTIVE RESEARCH

Beyond Cosmetic Changes: Selecting and Training Field Workers

Visit www.clinique.com and conduct an Internet search using a search engine and your library's online database to obtain information on women's usage of cosmetics.

As the brand manager for Clinique, what information would you like to have to formulate marketing strategies to increase your sales?

How would you select and train fieldworkers to conduct a mall-intercept survey to determine women's usage of cosmetics in a project for Clinique?

Supervision of Fieldworkers

Supervision of fieldworkers means making sure that they are following the procedures and techniques in which they were trained. Supervision involves quality control and editing, sampling control, control of cheating, and central office control.

Quality Control and Editing

Quality control of fieldworkers requires checking to see if the field procedures are being properly implemented.[16] If any problems are detected, the supervisor should discuss them with the fieldworkers and provide additional training if necessary. To understand the interviewers' problems, the supervisors should also do some interviewing. Supervisors should collect questionnaires and other forms and edit them daily. They should examine the questionnaires to make sure all appropriate questions have been completed, unsatisfactory or incomplete answers have not been accepted, and the writing is legible.

Supervisors should also keep a record of hours worked and expenses. This will allow a determination of the cost per completed interview, whether the job is moving on schedule, and if any interviewers are having problems.

Sampling Control

sampling control

An aspect of supervision that ensures that the interviewers strictly follow the sampling plan rather than select sampling units based on convenience or accessibility.

An important aspect of supervision is **sampling control,** which attempts to ensure that the interviewers are strictly following the sampling plan rather than selecting sampling units based on convenience or accessibility. Interviewers tend to avoid dwellings or sampling units that they perceive as difficult or undesirable. If the sampling unit is not at home, the interviewers may be tempted to substitute the next available unit rather than call back. Interviewers sometimes stretch the requirements of quota samples. For example, a 58-year-old person may be placed in the 46-to-55 age category and interviewed to fulfill quota requirements.

To control these problems, supervisors should keep daily records of the number of calls made, number of not-at-homes, number of refusals, number of completed interviews for each interviewer, and the total for all interviewers under their control.

Control of Cheating

Cheating involves falsifying part of a question or the entire questionnaire. An interviewer may falsify part of an answer to make it acceptable or may fake answers. The most blatant form of cheating occurs when the interviewer falsifies the entire questionnaire, merely filling in fake answers without contacting the respondent. Cheating can be minimized through proper training, supervision, and validation of fieldwork.[17]

Central Office Control

Supervisors provide quality and cost-control information to the central office so that a total progress report can be maintained. In addition to the controls initiated in the field, other controls may be added at the central office to identify potential problems. Central office control includes tabulation of quota variables, important demographic characteristics, and answers to key variables.

Validation of Fieldwork

Validation of fieldwork means verifying that the fieldworkers are submitting authentic interviews. To validate the study, the supervisors call 10 to 25 percent of the respondents to inquire whether the fieldworkers actually conducted the interviews. The supervisors ask about the length and quality of the interview, reaction to the interviewer, and basic demographic data. The demographic information is cross-checked against the information reported by the interviewers on the questionnaires.

Evaluation of Fieldworkers

It is important to evaluate fieldworkers to provide them with feedback on their performance as well as to identify the better fieldworkers and build a better, high-quality field force. The evaluation criteria should be clearly communicated to the fieldworkers during their training.

The evaluation of fieldworkers should be based on the criteria of cost and time, response rates, quality of interviewing, and quality of data.[18]

Cost and Time

The interviewers can be compared in terms of the total cost (salary and expenses) per completed interview. If the costs differ by city size, comparisons should be made only among fieldworkers working in comparable cities. The fieldworkers should also be evaluated on how they spend their time. Time should be broken down into categories such as actual interviewing, travel, and administration.

Response Rates

It is important to monitor response rates on a timely basis so that corrective action can be taken if these rates are too low.[19] Supervisors can help interviewers with an inordinate number of refusals by listening to the introductions they use and providing immediate feedback. When all the interviews are over, different fieldworkers' percentage of refusals can be compared to identify the better ones.

Quality of Interviewing

To evaluate interviewers on the quality of interviewing, the supervisor must directly observe the interviewing process. The supervisor can do this in person, or the fieldworker can tape-record the interview. The quality of interviewing should be evaluated in terms of (1) the appropriateness of the introduction, (2) the precision with which the fieldworker asks questions, (3) the ability to probe in an unbiased manner, (4) the ability to ask sensitive questions, (5) interpersonal skills displayed during the interview, and (6) the manner in which the interview is terminated.

Quality of Data

The completed questionnaires of each interviewer should be evaluated for the quality of data. Some indicators of quality data are (1) the recorded data are legible; (2) all instructions, including skip patterns, are followed; (3) the answers to unstructured questions are recorded verbatim; (4) the answers to unstructured questions are meaningful and complete enough to be coded; and (5) item nonresponse occurs infrequently.

Real Research   Guidelines on Interviewing: The Council of American Survey
              Research Organizations

Each interviewer is to follow these techniques for good interviewing:

1. Provide his or her full name, if asked by the respondent, as well as a phone number for the research firm.
2. Read each question exactly as written. Report any problems to the supervisor as soon as possible.
3. Read the questions in the order indicated on the questionnaire, following the proper skip sequences.
4. Clarify any question by the respondent in a neutral way.
5. Do not mislead respondents as to the length of the interview.
6. Do not reveal the identity of the ultimate client unless instructed to do so.
7. Keep a tally on each terminated interview and the reason for each termination.
8. Remain neutral in interviewing. Do not indicate agreement or disagreement with the respondent.
9. Speak slowly and distinctly so that words will be understood.
10. Record all replies verbatim, not paraphrased.
11. Avoid unnecessary conversations with the respondent.
12. Probe and clarify for additional comments on all open-end questions, unless otherwise instructed. Probe and clarify in a neutral way.
13. Write neatly and legibly.
14. Check all work for thoroughness before turning in to the supervisor.
15. When terminating a respondent, do so in a neutral way such as, "Thank you," or "Our quota has already been filled in this area, but thank you anyway."

16. Keep all studies, materials, and findings confidential.
17. Do not falsify any interviews or any answers to any question.
18. Thank the respondent for participating in the study. ■

Experiential Research

Clothing Fieldwork

What's it like to shop for casual clothing? Design a questionnaire to determine students' shopping behavior for casual clothing—the kind they wear to school. Administer the survey to five different students on your campus.

1. How did you feel approaching these respondents?
2. What seemed to be the most challenging part of the survey for the respondents?
3. If other students were employed to collect the data for this survey project, how should they be trained?
4. If other students were employed to collect the data for this survey project, how should the fieldwork be supervised?
5. If other students were employed to collect the data for this survey project, how should the fieldwork be evaluated? ■

Project Research

Fieldwork

In the department store project, in-home personal interviews were conducted by interviewers who were graduate and undergraduate students enrolled in marketing research courses taught by the author. The fieldworkers' training included having each interviewer (1) act as a respondent and self-administer the questionnaire and (2) administer the questionnaire to a few other students not involved in the project (dummy respondents). Detailed guidelines for interviewing were developed and provided to each interviewer. The supervision of interviewers was carried out by graduate students who monitored the fieldwork activities on a day-to-day basis. All the respondents were called back to verify that the interviewer had actually administered the questionnaire to them and to thank them for participating in the survey. A 100 percent validation check was performed. All the fieldworkers, interviewers, and supervisors were evaluated by the author.

Project Activities

1. Discuss the training and supervision of fieldworkers in the Sears project.
2. If an Internet-based survey was administered, instead of personal in-home interviews, how would the fieldwork change? ■

International Marketing Research

The selection, training, supervision, and evaluation of fieldworkers are critical in international marketing research. Local fieldwork agencies are unavailable in many countries. Therefore, it may be necessary to recruit and train local fieldworkers or import trained foreign workers. The use of local fieldworkers is desirable, because they are familiar with the local language and culture. They can thus create an appropriate climate for the interview and be sensitive to the concerns of the respondents. Extensive training may be required and close supervision may be necessary. As observed in many countries, interviewers tend to help the respondent with the answers and select household or sampling units based on personal considerations rather than the sampling plan. Finally, interviewer cheating may be more of a problem in many foreign countries than in the United States. Validation of fieldwork is critical. Proper application of fieldwork procedures can greatly reduce these difficulties and result in consistent and useful findings.

International marketing research studies add more complexity regardless of how simple a survey may seem. Collecting data that is comparable between countries may be difficult, but it can be done using some standard methodologies with adaptations when needed. Equivalent marketing research procedures allow researchers to detect, analyze, and better understand the world's sociocultural differences. A global approach to marketing research is desired, which may require changing several methodologies for studies conducted in the United States so that U.S. data can be compared to other countries.

Real Research   Americanism Unites Europeans

An image study conducted by Research International (www.research-int.com), a U.K. market research company, showed that despite unification of the European market, European consumers still increasingly favor U.S. products. It is expected that Americanism will unite consumers in Europe. The survey was conducted in France, Germany, the United Kingdom, Italy, and the Netherlands. In each country, local interviewers and supervisors were used, because it was felt they would be able to relate to and identify better with the respondents. However, the fieldworkers were trained extensively and supervised closely in order to ensure quality results and minimize the variability in country-to-country results due to differences in interviewing procedures.

A total of 6,724 personal interviews were conducted. Some of the findings were that Europeans gave U.S products high marks for being innovative, and some countries also regarded them as fashionable and of high quality. Interestingly, France, considered to be anti-American, also emerged as pro-American. Among the 1,034 French consumers surveyed, 40 percent considered U.S. products fashionable, 38 percent believed they were innovative, and 15 percent said U.S. products were of high quality. In addition, when asked what nationality they preferred for a new company in their area, a U.S. company was the first choice. These findings were comparable and consistent across the five countries. A key to the discovery of these findings was the use of local fieldworkers and extensive training and supervision that resulted in high-quality data.

This study is very useful for marketers to drum up and overplay the American brand name in the European market. "Rather than trying to hide the fact that they are American, we think companies ought to stress or try to exploit their American heritage," says Mr. Eric Salama, director of European operations for the Henley Center, the U.K. economic forecasting consultancy. U.S. firms have, in fact, capitalized on the "made in America" equity. As a result, exports to Europe have been soaring in recent years. As of 2008, California leads the nation in being the top state in terms of exports to the European Union.[20] ∎

ACTIVE RESEARCH

GM: Extending Its Field to China

Visit www.gm.com and conduct an Internet search using a search engine and your library's online database to obtain information on Chinese consumers' preferences for cars.

As the international marketing manager for GM, what information would you like to have to formulate marketing strategies to increase your sales in China?

How would you select, train, and supervise fieldworkers conducting an in-home survey in China to determine consumers' preferences for cars?

Ethics in Marketing Research

The data, whether collected by the internal marketing research department or by an external fieldwork agency, should be obtained by following high ethical standards. The researchers and fieldworkers should make the respondents feel comfortable by addressing their apprehensions. One way in which the comfort level of the respondents can be increased is by providing them with adequate information about the research firm and the project, addressing their questions, and clearly stating the responsibilities and expectations of the fieldworkers and the respondents at the start of the interview. Moreover, the respondents should be told that they are not obligated to answer questions that make them uncomfortable, and that they can terminate the interview at any point should they experience discomfort. The researcher and fieldworkers have an ethical responsibility to respect the respondents' privacy, feelings, and dignity.[21] Moreover, the respondents should be left with a positive and pleasant experience. This will enhance goodwill and future cooperation from respondents.

The researchers and the fieldwork agencies are also responsible to the clients for following the accepted procedures for the selection, training, supervision, validation, and evaluation of fieldworkers. They must ensure the integrity of the data-collection process. The fieldwork procedures should be carefully documented and made available to the clients. Appropriate actions by researchers and fieldwork agencies can go a long way in addressing ethical concerns associated with fieldwork.

Real Research

Fielding Respondents' Ethical Concerns During Fieldwork

Information provided while responding to an 800 number, using a credit card, or purchasing a product is often used to compile lists of customers and potential customers. These lists are rarely sold to telemarketing and direct marketing organizations. The public perception is different, however, and many people feel that marketers and marketing researchers misuse the information they collect. This misperception is giving marketing research a negative image.

In an effort to fight back, many marketing researchers and fieldwork agencies are addressing this issue head-on at the start of the interview. For example, when contacting potential respondents, the Gallup Organization (www.gallup.com) provides them with information about the firm (Gallup) and the marketing research project. The respondents are assured that Gallup operates within a code of ethics. Some marketing research firms and fieldwork agencies provide potential respondents with toll-free numbers and Web site addresses to obtain more information or verify the information given by the fieldworkers. Such actions make the respondents more comfortable and informed, and result in higher quality data for the clients.[22] ■

Decision Research

Nissan: Return of the Z Sports Car

The Situation

Carlos Ghosn, president of Nissan Motor Co., was brought in to revive the financially troubled company shortly after the French automaker, Renault, acquired a controlling interest in Nissan.

Ghosn is not afraid to take different paths and knows that taking risks to meet consumer demand is what business is all about. Ghosn orchestrated a product revival at Nissan that included a return of the iconic Z sports car and entries in new segments such as the Murano crossover SUV and Titan full-size truck. At the same time under his Nissan Revival Plan, he cut costs, reduced debt, improved efficiency, and returned the company to profitability.

Nissan wants to continue its efforts to enhance the effectiveness of its marketing well into 2015. As part of that, Nissan would like to conduct mall-intercept interviews with consumers to determine the type of positioning for the Z sports car, particularly 350Z, which will appeal to the younger buyers. The questionnaire is a mix of unstructured and structured questions. Some of the questions require substantial probing of the respondents, and the supervision of the interviewers will be critical to collecting good-quality data.

The Marketing Research Decision

1. In what areas should the supervisors be trained to closely monitor the interviewers?
2. Discuss the role of the supervisor training you recommend in enabling Carlos Ghosn to identify the needs of the younger sports car buyers.

The Marketing Management Decision

1. Carlos Ghosn wants to enhance the appeal of the Z sports cars to the younger buyers. What changes should be made?
2. Discuss how the marketing management decision action that you recommend to Carlos Ghosn is influenced by the supervisor training that you suggested earlier and by the findings of mall-intercept interviews.

Given his success at Nissan, Renault's board of directors, at its meeting on April 29, 2005, appointed Carlos Ghosn president and CEO of Renault. Renault and Nissan have a strategic alliance that was signed on March 27, 1999, and was still in effect in 2009.[23] ■

Proper fieldwork can help Nissan collect high-quality data to determine the factors that will enhance the appeal of the Z sports car to younger buyers.

SPSS Windows

SPSS offers several programs to assist in fieldwork or data collection. Moreover, a number of different methods of administering the survey can be accommodated, including telephone, electronic, mail, and personal interviewing.

1. *SPSS Data Entry Station (DES):* This deployment method will put a copy of the questionnaire on a computer so that a data-entry operator or respondent can enter the answers on the screen using the keyboard and mouse (without giving them the ability to edit the form). In this way, to some extent, data entry can simulate a proper CATI system because you can prepopulate the data with the phone number and basic details of the respondent so the information appears as the operator moves through the list. However, this system completely lacks the ability to keep a call log and a callback list, which most good, true CATI systems should do.
2. *SPSS Data Entry Enterprise Server (DEES):* This deployment method will upload a copy of the questionnaire to a Web server so that data-entry operators or respondents can log on using a password and enter their results without having to install anything on their local machine. DEES can be used on both intranet and Internet settings. This software also includes technology that prevents ballot stuffing (a respondent answering the survey multiple times).
3. *Printing the form:* This can be done by using SPSS Data Entry (DE) Builder to simply print the form after it has been designed for a mail survey or personal interviewing. This is the least sophisticated method because the researcher will not be able to take advantage of space-saving pull-down menus or any of the rules that were included. The rules can be used when the follow-up data entry is done, but in many situations if there is an error, it may be too late to correct it. For a personal interview, it may be a better option for the interviewer to use a laptop with the form in DE Station, because the rules will "fire" as the questions are answered, thus allowing for quick corrections if required.

Summary

Researchers have two major options for collecting data: developing their own organizations or contracting with fieldwork agencies. In either case, data collection involves the use of a field force. Figure 13.2 gives a concept map for the fieldwork/data-collection process. Fieldworkers should be healthy, outgoing, communicative, pleasant, educated, and experienced. They should be trained in important aspects of fieldwork, including making the initial contact, asking the questions, probing, recording the answers, and terminating the interview. Supervision of fieldworkers involves quality control and editing, sampling control, control of cheating, and central office control. Validation of

FIGURE 13.2

A Concept Map for the Fieldwork/Data-Collection Process

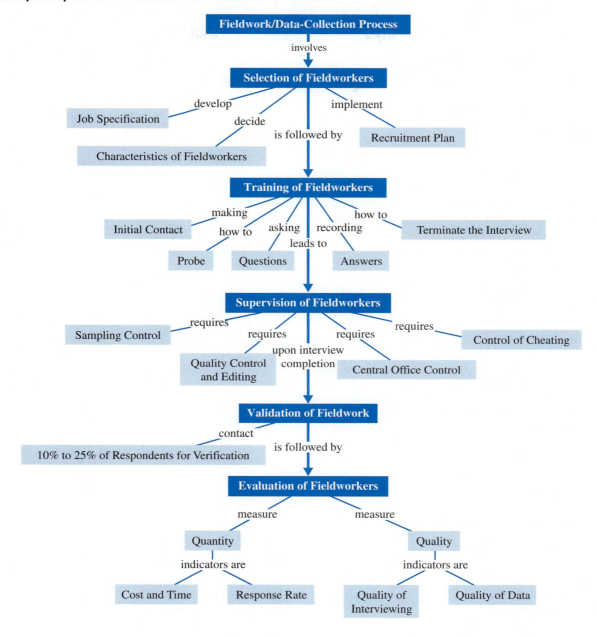

fieldwork can be accomplished by calling 10 to 25 percent of those who have been identified as interviewees and inquiring whether the interviews took place. Fieldworkers should be evaluated on the basis of cost and time, response rates, quality of interviewing, and quality of data collection.

The selection, training, supervision, and evaluation of fieldworkers is even more critical in international marketing research, as local fieldwork agencies are not available in many countries. Ethical issues include making the respondents feel comfortable in the data-collection process so that their experience is positive. Every effort must be undertaken to ensure that the data are of high quality. The Internet and computers can greatly facilitate and improve the quality of fieldwork.

Key Terms and Concepts

probing, 404
sampling control, 407

Suggested Cases, Video Cases, and HBS Cases

Running Case with Real Data

1.1 Dell

Comprehensive Critical Thinking Cases

2.1 American Idol   2.2 Baskin-Robbins   2.3 Akron Children's Hospital

Comprehensive Cases with Real Data

4.1 JPMorgan Chase   4.2 Wendy's

Video Cases

13.1 Intel   23.1 Marriott

Comprehensive Harvard Business School Cases

Case 5.1: The Harvard Graduate Student Housing Survey (9-505-059)
Case 5.2: BizRate.Com (9-501-024)
Case 5.3: Cola Wars Continue: Coke and Pepsi in the Twenty-First Century (9-702-442)
Case 5.4: TiVo in 2002 (9-502-062)
Case 5.5: Compaq Computer: Intel Inside? (9-599-061)
Case 5.6: The New Beetle (9-501-023)

Live Research: Conducting a Marketing Research Project

1. The students conducting fieldwork should be appropriately trained. Follow the guidelines in the chapter.
2. The team leaders can conduct fewer interviews but also act as supervisors. They should be trained in supervision.
3. The callback procedures should be specified (e.g., abandon a telephone number after three callback attempts).
4. If in-home interviews are to be conducted in the local area, each interviewer (student) can be assigned a specific part of a census track.

Acronyms

In the fieldwork/data-collection process, the organization in the fieldworkers:

Vests:

V alidation of fieldwork
E valuation of fieldworkers
S election of fieldworkers
T raining of fieldworkers
S upervision of fieldworkers

The areas in which fieldworkers should be trained may be summarized by the acronym

Train:

T erminating the interview
R ecording the answers
A sking the questions
I nitial contact development
N osy behavior: probing

Exercises

Questions

1. What options are available to researchers for collecting data?
2. Describe the fieldwork/data-collection process.
3. What qualifications should fieldworkers possess?
4. What are the guidelines for asking questions?
5. What is probing?
6. How should the answers to unstructured questions be recorded?
7. How should the fieldworker terminate the interview?
8. What aspects are involved in the supervision of fieldworkers?
9. How can respondent selection problems be controlled?
10. What is validation of fieldwork? How is this done?
11. Describe the criteria that should be used for evaluating fieldworkers.
12. Describe the major sources of error related to fieldwork.

Problems

1. Write some interviewer instructions for in-home personal interviews to be conducted by students.
2. Comment on the following field situations, making recommendations for corrective action.
   a. One of the interviewers has an excessive rate of refusals in in-home personal interviewing.
   b. In a CATI situation, many phone numbers are giving a busy signal during the first dialing attempt.
   c. An interviewer reports that, at the end of the interviews, many respondents asked if they had answered the questions correctly.
   d. While validating the fieldwork, a respondent reports that she cannot remember being interviewed over the telephone, but the interviewer insists that the interview was conducted.

Internet and Computer Exercises

1. Visit the Web sites of some marketing research suppliers. Make a report of all the material related to fieldwork that is posted on these sites.
2. Visit the Marketing Research Association Web site (www.mra-net.org) and examine the ethical codes relating to data collection. Write a brief report.
3. Using project management software, such as Microsoft Project, develop a fieldwork schedule for conducting a national survey of consumer preferences for fast foods involving 2,500 mall-intercept interviews in Los Angeles, Salt Lake City, Dallas, St. Louis, Milwaukee, New Orleans, Cincinnati, Orlando, Atlanta, New York City, and Boston.

Activities

Role Playing

1. You are a field supervisor. Ask a fellow student to assume the role of an interviewer and another student the role of a respondent. Train the interviewer to conduct in-home personal interviews by giving a live demonstration.
2. Exchange the roles of interviewer and supervisor in the role-playing situation described in activity 1.

Fieldwork

1. Arrange a field trip to a marketing research firm or data-collection agency. Ask the fieldwork supervisor to describe the agency's fieldwork process. How does it compare to the one described in this book?
2. Arrange a visit to a mall-intercept interviewing facility when interviews are being conducted. Observe the interviewing process. Write a report about your visit.

Group Discussion

1. Discuss the impact of women's changing lifestyles on fieldwork during the last decade.
2. Discuss the notion of interviewer cheating. Why do interviewers cheat? How can cheating be detected and prevented?

Dell Running Case

Review the Dell case, Case 1.1, and questionnaire given toward the end of the book.

What's it like to shop for notebook computers? Design a questionnaire to determine students' shopping behavior for notebook computers. Administer the survey to five different students on your campus.

1. How did you feel approaching these respondents?
2. What seemed to be the most challenging part of the survey for the respondents?
3. If other students were employed to collect the data for this survey project, how should they be trained?
4. If other students were employed to collect the data for this survey project, how should they be supervised?
5. If other students were employed to collect the data for this survey project, how should they be evaluated?

VIDEO CASE 13.1   Intel: Building Blocks Inside Out

The Intel Corporation was founded in 1968 to build semiconductor memory products. It introduced the world's first microprocessor in 1971. Microprocessors, also referred to as *central processing units (CPUs)*, often are described as the "brain" of a computer. Today, Intel supplies the building blocks for the computing and communications industries worldwide. These building blocks include chips, boards, systems, and software, and they are used in computers, servers, and networking/communications products.

Most of Intel's customers fall into two separate groups: the original equipment manufacturers (OEMs) and the PC and network communications products users. The OEMs manufacture computer systems, cellular handsets and handheld computing devices, telecommunications and networking communications equipment, and peripherals. The PC and network communications products users include individuals, large and small businesses, and service providers, who buy Intel's PC enhancements, networking products, and business communications products through reseller, retail, e-business, and OEM channels. Intel is an increasingly global company. Only 35 percent of its revenues are from North America, whereas Asia and Europe comprise 31 percent and 25 percent, respectively. Revenues for fiscal year 2008 amounted to $37.59 billion.

Intel has shown phenomenal growth as a company. Much of Intel's success can be attributed to innovation within its marketing department. This innovation was required to overcome several obstacles. The main problem Intel faced was trying to sell an ingredient brand, which is a component of a larger product. Thus, the difficulty is in reaching consumers who will never see your product and might not even know what it does or why it is there.

Intel began marketing research in the 1980s because it was having difficulty with its customers not upgrading from the 286 to the 386 microprocessor. Marketing research showed that this was due to a lack of customer awareness, and Intel set out to change that. It conducted a small but effective advertising campaign. In fact, in the process it realized that it had inadvertently created a brand in Intel. Because of the success of this small campaign, Intel began to realize the importance of marketing and

marketing research and started to focus more effort and money on these areas.

Marketing research revealed that in order to be effective in its overall marketing campaign, Intel would have to reach the consumers and convince them that what was inside the computer was as important as what was on the outside. This became the key element of the "Intel Inside" campaign conducted during the early 1990s. This slogan helped Intel put a name with its products, and it helped it encompass several of its products under one title.

Furthermore, marketing research showed that it would be most effective to cross-market with its technology partners. This would help consumers understand the products that Intel helped make up. It did this by including the "Intel Inside" logo in its partners' ads. It also helped fund these advertisements. A problem with including its slogan in other ads is that Intel did not want to intrude on the commercials. It decided to help make the small logo sink in by accompanying it with a jingle every time it was displayed. This jingle has become extremely recognizable and synonymous with Intel's slogan. All of this helped Intel realize its goal of increased consumer awareness. Longitudinal measurement of advertising effectiveness via marketing research revealed that the "Intel Inside" campaign was very effective.

Intel's next idea was to come up with a name for its microprocessor. This would help it to avoid using the numbering scheme, which was nonpatentable, and to find a name to help consumers identify their processors. After extensive marketing research, Intel chose the name Pentium, which it found generated positive reactions with its consumers. Intel has been marketing its processors under this name ever since.

Between 1990 and 1993, Intel invested $500 million in advertising to build its brand equity. By 1993, 80 percent of people in the United States recognized Intel and 75 percent had positive feelings about the brand. Most important, 50 percent of consumers looked for the brand when they were shopping. By 1994, Intel had captured 95 percent of the microprocessor market, due in large part to its marketing efforts.

Intel's market share for microprocessors slipped to about 80 percent in 2005, as a result of increased competition from its main competitor, AMD. On December 30, 2005, Intel announced a major overhaul of its corporate and product branding, a move designed to symbolize the chipmaker's transformation into a supplier for products beyond personal computers. The changes included a new version of the company's blue logo—without the lowered "e" that had long been a part of Intel's branding—along with a new tag line, "Leap ahead." As of 2006, Intel no longer used the well-known "Intel Inside" logo.

The increased competition makes Intel's marketing research efforts more important than ever as it attempts to preserve its dominant place in the market. Intel has been able to be very successful because of its focus on technology, brand image, and brand equity. Intel still faces future challenges, including increased competition, the opening of new markets, and the development of new products. Intel will continue to rely on marketing research to meet these challenges.

Conclusion

Marketing research has played a critical role in Intel's phenomenal growth. Marketing research was instrumental in developing the Intel brand, designing the "Intel Inside" campaign, and crafting the new logo with the "Leap ahead" tag line. Continued reliance on marketing research will enable Intel to enhance its image as a preeminent building block supplier inside out.

Questions

1. Discuss the role of marketing research in helping Intel devise the "Intel Inside" and "Leap ahead" campaigns.
2. Intel would like to increase the preference for Intel chips among PC users in the individual user as well as business user segments. Define the management decision problem.
3. Define an appropriate marketing research problem corresponding to the management decision problem you identified in question 2.
4. Intel would like to gain a better understanding of how businesses select PC and network communications products. What type of research design should be adopted?
5. Discuss the role of the Internet in obtaining secondary data relevant to the marketing research problem you defined in question 3.
6. Discuss the role of qualitative research in understanding how businesses select PC and network communications products. Which qualitative research techniques should be used and why?
7. If a survey is to be conducted to determine businesses' selection criteria for choosing PC and network communications products, which survey method should be used and why?
8. Design a questionnaire for determining businesses' selection criteria for choosing PC and network communications products.
9. Develop a suitable sampling plan for conducting the survey identified in question 7.
10. If Intel were to conduct mall-intercept interviews to determine consumer preferences for an ultra-light notebook that uses a newly designed chip, describe the fieldwork process that should be used.

References

1. www.intel.com, accessed January 17, 2009.
2. Don Clark, "Intel Secures Video Content for Its Viiv Multimedia Plan," *Wall Street Journal* (January 6, 2006): A14.
3. Don Clark, "Intel to Overhaul Marketing in Bid to Go Beyond PCs," *Wall Street Journal* (December 30, 2005): A3
4. Olga Kharif, "Intel Is Kicking Silicon at AMD," *BusinessWeek Online* (September 24, 2002), www.businessweek.com/technology/content/sep2002/tc20020924_6824.htm, accessed April 10, 2008.

> "No matter how often you hear 'garbage in . . . garbage out,' this must be your mantra when working with data.

Damon Jones, Office Manager, Data Acquisition and Processing,
Burke, Inc.

Objectives

[After reading this chapter, the student should be able to:]

1. Discuss the nature and scope of data preparation, and the data-preparation process.

2. Explain questionnaire checking and editing, and treatment of unsatisfactory responses by returning to the field, assigning missing values, and discarding unsatisfactory responses.

3. Describe the guidelines for coding questionnaires, including the coding of structured and unstructured questions.

4. Discuss the data-cleaning process and the methods used to treat missing responses: substitution of a neutral value, imputed response, casewise deletion, and pairwise deletion.

5. State the reasons for and methods of statistically adjusting data: weighting, variable respecification, and scale transformation.

6. Describe the procedure for selecting a data analysis strategy and the factors influencing the process.

7. Classify statistical techniques and give a detailed classification of univariate techniques as well as a classification of multivariate techniques.

8. Understand the intracultural, pancultural, and cross-cultural approaches to data analysis in international marketing research.

9. Identify the ethical issues related to data processing, particularly the discarding of unsatisfactory responses, violation of the assumptions underlying the data analysis techniques, and evaluation and interpretation of results.

10. Explain the use of the Internet and computers in data preparation and analysis.

Data Preparation

Overview

After the research problem has been defined and a suitable approach developed (Chapter 2), an appropriate research design formulated (Chapters 3 to 12), and the fieldwork conducted (Chapter 13), the researcher can move on to data preparation and analysis, the fifth step of the marketing research process. Before the raw data contained in the questionnaires can be subjected to statistical analysis, they must be converted into a form suitable for analysis. The quality of statistical results depends on the care exercised in the data-preparation phase. Paying inadequate attention to data preparation can seriously compromise statistical results, leading to biased findings and incorrect interpretation.

This chapter describes the data-collection process, which begins with checking the questionnaires for completeness. Then, we discuss the editing of data and provide guidelines for handling illegible, incomplete, inconsistent, ambiguous, or otherwise unsatisfactory responses. We also describe coding, transcribing, and data cleaning, emphasizing the treatment of missing responses and statistical adjustment of data. We discuss the selection of a data analysis strategy and classify statistical techniques. The intracultural, pancultural, and cross-cultural approaches to data analysis in international marketing research are explained. The ethical issues related to data processing are identified with emphasis on the discarding of unsatisfactory responses, violation of the assumptions underlying the data analysis techniques, and evaluation and interpretation of results.

Finally, we discuss using computers in data preparation and analysis. Help for running the SPSS and SAS Learning Edition programs used in this chapter is provided in four ways: (1) detailed step-by-step instructions are given later in the chapter, (2) you can download (from the Web site for this book) computerized demonstration movies illustrating these step-by-step instructions, (3) you can download screen captures with notes illustrating these step-by-step instructions, and (4) you can refer to the *Study Guide and Technology Manual*, a supplement that accompanies this book.

Project Research   Data Preparation

In the department store project, the data were obtained through in-home personal interviews. The supervisors edited the questionnaires as the interviewers turned them in. The questionnaires were checked for incomplete, inconsistent, and ambiguous responses. Questionnaires with unsatisfactory responses were returned to the field and the interviewers were asked to recontact the respondents to obtain the required information. Nine questionnaires were discarded because the proportion of unsatisfactory responses was large. This resulted in a final sample size of 271.

A codebook was developed for coding the questionnaires. Coding was relatively simple because there were no open-ended questions. The data were transcribed onto a computer tape via keypunching. About 25 percent of the data were verified for keypunching errors. The data were cleaned by identifying out-of-range and logically inconsistent responses. Most of the rating information was obtained using 6-point scales, so responses of 0, 7, and 8 were considered out of range and a code of 9 was assigned to missing responses.

Any missing responses were treated by casewise deletion, in which respondents with any missing values were dropped from the analysis. Casewise deletion was selected because the number of cases (respondents) with missing values was small and the sample size was sufficiently large. In statistically adjusting the data, dummy variables were created for the categorical variables. New variables that were composites of original variables were also created. For example, the familiarity ratings of the 10 department stores were summed to create a familiarity index. Finally, a data analysis strategy was developed. ■

Real Research   Data Cleaning: The Burke Way

According to Damon Jones, Office Manager, Data Acquisition and Processing, Burke, Inc. (www.burke.com), completed questionnaires from the field often have many small errors because of the inconsistent quality of interviewing. For example, qualifying responses are not circled, or skip patterns are not followed accurately.

These small errors can be costly. When responses from such questionnaires are put into a computer, Burke runs a cleaning program that checks for completeness and logic. Discrepancies are identified and checked by the tabulation supervisors. Once the errors are identified, appropriate corrective action is taken before data analysis is carried out. Burke has found that this procedure substantially increases the quality of statistical results.[1] ■

Burke places a lot of emphasis on adequately preparing the data before any analysis is conducted.

Source: www.burke.com. Used with permission of Burke.

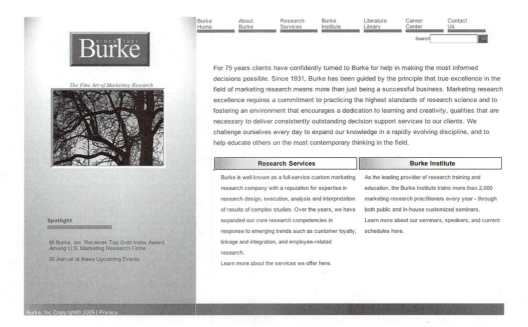

The department store example describes the various phases of the data-preparation process. Note that the process is initiated while the fieldwork is still in progress. The Burke example describes the importance of cleaning data and identifying and correcting errors before the data are analyzed. A systematic description of the data-preparation process follows.

The Data-Preparation Process

The data-preparation process is shown in Figure 14.1. The entire process is guided by the preliminary plan of data analysis that was formulated in the research design phase (Chapter 3). The first step is to check for acceptable questionnaires. This is followed by editing, coding, and transcribing the data. The data are cleaned and a treatment for missing responses prescribed. Often, statistical adjustment of the data may be necessary to make them representative of the population of interest. The researcher should then select an appropriate data analysis strategy. The final data analysis strategy differs from the preliminary plan of data analysis due to the information and insights gained since the preliminary plan was formulated. Data preparation should begin as soon as the first batch of questionnaires is received from the field, while the fieldwork is still going on. Thus if any problems are detected, the fieldwork can be modified to incorporate corrective action.

Questionnaire Checking

The initial step in questionnaire checking involves a check of all questionnaires for completeness and interviewing quality. Often these checks are made while fieldwork is still underway. If the fieldwork was contracted to a data-collection agency, the researcher should make an independent check after it is over. A questionnaire returned from the field may be unacceptable for several reasons.

FIGURE 14.1

Data-Preparation Process

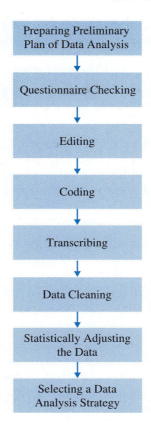

Preparing Preliminary Plan of Data Analysis

↓

Questionnaire Checking

↓

Editing

↓

Coding

↓

Transcribing

↓

Data Cleaning

↓

Statistically Adjusting the Data

↓

Selecting a Data Analysis Strategy

1. Parts of the questionnaire may be incomplete.
2. The pattern of responses may indicate that the respondent did not understand or follow the instructions. For example, skip patterns may not have been followed.
3. The responses show little variance. For example, a respondent has checked only 4s on a series of 7-point rating scales.
4. The returned questionnaire is physically incomplete: one or more pages are missing.
5. The questionnaire is received after the preestablished cutoff date.
6. The questionnaire is answered by someone who does not qualify for participation.

If quotas or cell group sizes have been imposed, the acceptable questionnaires should be classified and counted accordingly. Any problems in meeting the sampling requirements should be identified and corrective action taken, such as conducting additional interviews in the underrepresented cells, before the data are edited.

Editing

editing

A review of the questionnaires with the objective of increasing accuracy and precision of the collected data.

Editing is the review of the questionnaires with the objective of increasing accuracy and precision. It consists of screening questionnaires to identify illegible, incomplete, inconsistent, or ambiguous responses.

Responses may be illegible if they have been poorly recorded. This is particularly common in questionnaires with a large number of unstructured questions. The data must be legible if they are to be properly coded. Likewise, questionnaires may be incomplete to varying degrees. A few or many questions may be unanswered.

At this stage, the researcher makes a preliminary check for consistency. Certain obvious inconsistencies can be easily detected. For example, a respondent reports an annual income of less than $20,000, yet indicates frequent shopping at prestigious department stores such as Saks Fifth Avenue and Neiman Marcus.

Responses to unstructured questions may be ambiguous and difficult to interpret clearly. The answer may be abbreviated, or some ambiguous words may have been used. For structured questions, more than one response may be marked for a question designed to elicit a single response.

Suppose a respondent circles 2 and 3 on a 5-point rating scale. Does this mean that 2.5 was intended? To complicate matters further, the coding procedure may allow for only a single-digit response.

Treatment of Unsatisfactory Responses

Unsatisfactory responses are commonly handled by returning to the field to get better data, assigning missing values, or discarding unsatisfactory respondents.

RETURNING TO THE FIELD   The questionnaires with unsatisfactory responses may be returned to the field, where the interviewers recontact the respondents. This approach is particularly attractive for business and industrial marketing surveys, where the sample sizes are small and the respondents are easily identifiable. However, the data obtained the second time may be different from those obtained during the original survey. These differences may be attributed to changes over time or differences in the mode of questionnaire administration (e.g., telephone versus in-person interview).

ASSIGNING MISSING VALUES   If returning the questionnaires to the field is not feasible, the editor may assign missing values to unsatisfactory responses. This approach may be desirable if (1) the number of respondents with unsatisfactory responses is small, (2) the proportion of unsatisfactory responses for each of these respondents is small, or (3) the variables with unsatisfactory responses are not the key variables.

DISCARDING UNSATISFACTORY RESPONDENTS   In this approach, the respondents with unsatisfactory responses are simply discarded. This approach may have merit when (1) the proportion of unsatisfactory respondents is small (less than 10 percent), (2) the sample size is large, (3) the unsatisfactory respondents do not differ from satisfactory respondents in obvious ways (e.g., demographics, product usage characteristics), (4) the proportion of unsatisfactory responses for each of these respondents is large, or (5) responses on key variables are missing. However, unsatisfactory respondents may differ from satisfactory respondents in systematic ways, and the decision to designate a respondent as unsatisfactory may be subjective. Both these factors bias the results. If the researcher decides to discard unsatisfactory respondents, the procedure adopted to identify these respondents and their number should be reported.

Real Research   Declaring Discards

In a cross-cultural survey of marketing managers from English-speaking African countries, questionnaires were mailed to 565 firms. A total of 192 completed questionnaires were returned, of which four were discarded because respondents suggested that they were not in charge of overall marketing decisions. The decision to discard the four questionnaires was based on the consideration that the sample size was sufficiently large and the proportion of unsatisfactory respondents was small.[2] ∎

Coding

coding
The assignment of a code to represent a specific response to a specific question along with the data record and column position that code will occupy.

Coding means assigning a code, usually a number, to each possible response to each question. If the questionnaire contains only structured questions or very few unstructured questions, it is precoded. This means that codes are assigned before fieldwork is conducted. If the questionnaire contains unstructured questions, codes are assigned after the questionnaires have been returned from the field (postcoding). Although precoding was briefly discussed in Chapter 10 on questionnaire design, we provide further guidelines on coding structured and open-ended questions in the next section.[3]

Coding Questions

fixed-field codes
A code in which the number of records for each respondent is the same, and the same data appear in the same columns for all respondents.

The respondent code and the record number should appear on each record in the data. However, the record code can be dispensed if there is only one record for each respondent. The following additional codes should be included for each respondent: project code, interviewer code, date and time codes, and validation code. **Fixed-field codes**, which mean that the number of records for each respondent is the same and the same data appear in the same column(s) for all respondents, are highly desirable. If possible, standard codes should be used for missing data. For example, a code of 9 could be used for a single-column variable, 99 for a double-column variable, and so on. The missing value codes should be distinct from the codes assigned to the legitimate responses.

Coding of structured questions is relatively simple, because the response options are predetermined. The researcher assigns a code for each response to each question and specifies the appropriate record and columns in which the response codes are to appear. For example,

Do you have a currently valid passport?
1. Yes   2. No   (1/54)

For this question, a "Yes" response is coded 1 and a "No" response, 2. The numbers in parentheses indicate that the code assigned will appear on the first record for this respondent in column 54. Because only one response is allowed and there are only two possible responses (1 or 2), a single column is sufficient. In general, a single column is sufficient to code a structured question with a single response if there are fewer than nine possible responses.
In questions that permit a large number of responses, each possible response option should be assigned a separate column. Such questions include those about brand ownership or usage, magazine readership, and television viewing. For example,

Which accounts do you *now* have at this bank? ("X" as many as apply)

Regular savings account	☐	(162)
Regular checking account	☐	(163)
Mortgage	☐	(164)
Now account	☐	(165)
Club account (Christmas, etc.)	☐	(166)
Line of credit	☐	(167)
Term savings account (time deposits, etc.)	☐	(168)
Savings bank life insurance	☐	(169)
Home improvement loan	☐	(170)
Auto loan	☐	(171)
Other services	☐	(172)

In this example, suppose a respondent checked regular savings, regular checking, and term savings accounts. On record #1, a 1 will be entered in the column numbers 162, 163, and 168. All the other columns (164, 165, 166, 167, 169, 170, 171, and 172) will receive a 0. Because there is only one record per respondent, the record number has been omitted.

The coding of unstructured or open-ended questions is more complex. Respondents' verbatim responses are recorded on the questionnaire. Codes are then developed and assigned to these responses. Sometimes, based on previous projects or theoretical considerations, the researcher can develop the codes before beginning fieldwork. Usually, this must wait until the completed questionnaires are received. Then the researcher lists 50 to 100 responses to an unstructured question to identify the categories suitable for coding. Once codes are developed, the coders should be trained to assign the correct codes to the verbatim responses. The following guidelines are suggested for coding unstructured questions and questionnaires in general.[4]

Category codes should be mutually exclusive and collectively exhaustive. Categories are mutually exclusive if each response fits into one and only one category code. Categories should not overlap. Categories are collectively exhaustive if every response fits into one of the assigned category codes. This can be achieved by adding an additional category code of "other" or "none of the above." However, only a few (10 percent or less) of the responses should fall into this category. The vast majority of the responses should be classified into meaningful categories.

Category codes should be assigned for critical issues even if no one has mentioned them. It may be important to know that no one has mentioned a particular response. For example, the management of a major consumer goods company was concerned about the packaging for a new brand of toilet soap. Hence, packaging was included as a separate category in coding responses to the question, "What do you like least about this toilet soap?"

Data should be coded to retain as much detail as possible. For example, if data on the exact number of trips made on commercial airlines by business travelers have been obtained, they should be coded as such, rather than grouped into two category codes of "infrequent fliers" and "frequent fliers." Obtaining information on the exact number of trips allows the researcher to later define categories of business travelers in several different ways. If the categories were predefined, the subsequent analysis of data would be limited by those categories.

Developing a Data File

The code for a response to a question includes an indication of the column position (field) and data record it will occupy. For example, gender of respondents may be coded as 1 for females and 2 for males. A field represents a single variable value or item of data, such as the gender of a single respondent. Although numeric information is most common in marketing research, a field can also contain alphabetic or symbolic information. A record consists of related fields, i.e., variable values, such as sex, marital status, age, household size, occupation, and so forth, all pertaining to a single respondent. Thus, each record can have several columns. Generally, all the data for a respondent will be stored on a single record, although a number of records may be used for each respondent. Data files are sets of records, generally data from all the respondents in a study, that are grouped together for storage in the computer. If a single record is used for each respondent, records represent rows in a data file. In such a case, a data file may be viewed as an $n \times m$ matrix of numbers or values, where n is the number of respondents and m is the number of variables or fields. It is often helpful to prepare a **codebook** containing the coding instructions and the necessary information about the variables in the data set (see the opening Project Research example).

codebook

A book containing coding instructions and the necessary information about variables in the data set.

One can use a spreadsheet program, such as EXCEL, to enter the data, as most analysis programs can import data from a spreadsheet. In this case, the data for each respondent for each field is a cell. Typically, each row of the (EXCEL) spreadsheet contains the data of one respondent or case. The columns will contain the variables, with one column for each variable or response. The use of EXCEL can be complicated if there are more than 256 variables.

We illustrate these concepts using the data of Table 14.1. For illustrative purposes, we consider only a small number of observations. In actual practice, data analysis is performed on a much larger sample such as that in the Dell running case and other cases with real data that are

SPSS Data File

SAS Data File

TABLE 14.1						
Restaurant Preference						
Id	Preference	Quality	Quantity	Value	Service	Income
1	2	2	3	1	3	6
2	6	5	6	5	7	2
3	4	4	3	4	5	3
4	1	2	1	1	2	5
5	7	6	6	5	4	1
6	5	4	4	5	4	3
7	2	2	3	2	3	5
8	3	3	4	2	3	4
9	7	6	7	6	5	2
10	2	3	2	2	2	5
11	2	3	2	1	3	6
12	6	6	6	6	7	2
13	4	4	3	3	4	3
14	1	1	3	1	2	4
15	7	7	5	5	4	2
16	5	5	4	5	5	3
17	2	3	1	2	3	4
18	4	4	3	3	3	3
19	7	5	5	7	5	5
20	3	2	2	3	3	3

presented in this book. Table 14.1 gives the data from a pretest sample of 20 respondents on preferences for restaurants.

Each respondent was asked to rate preference to eat in a familiar restaurant (1 = Weak Preference, 7 = Strong Preference), and to rate the restaurant in terms of quality of food, quantity of portions, value, and service (1= Poor, 7 = Excellent). Annual household income was also obtained and coded as: 1 = Less than $20,000; 2 = $20,000 to 34,999; 3 = $35,000 to 49,999; 4 = $50,000 to 74,999; 5 = $75,000 to 99,999; 6 = $100,000 or more. The codebook for coding these data is given in Figure 14.2. Figure 14.3 is an example of questionnaire coding, showing the coding of demographic data typically obtained in consumer surveys. This questionnaire was precoded.

If the data of Table 14.1 are entered using either EXCEL or SPSS, the resulting data files will resemble Table 14.1. You can verify this by downloading EXCEL and SPSS files for Table 14.1 from the student Web site for this book (www.pearsonhighered.com/malhotra). Note that the SPSS data file has two views: the data view and the variable view. The data view gives a listing of the data and resembles Table 14.1. The variable view gives a listing of the variables showing the type, labels or description, values, and underlying coding for each variable, as shown in Table 14.2. Clicking on the "Values" column of the SPSS file opens a "Value Labels" dialog box. Value labels are unique labels assigned to each possible value of a variable. For example, 1 denotes weak preference and 7 denotes strong preference. If descriptors were used for the other preference values, those other preference values would also be assigned the corresponding "Value Labels." The other columns of Table 14.2 are self-explanatory.

FIGURE 14.2

A Codebook Excerpt

Column Number	Variable Number	Variable Name	Question Number	Coding Instructions
1	1	ID		1 to 20 as coded
2	2	Preference	1	**Input the number circled** 1 = Weak preference 7 = Strong preference
3	3	Quality	2	**Input the number circled** 1 = Poor 7 = Excellent
4	4	Quantity	3	**Input the number circled** 1 = Poor 7 = Excellent
5	5	Value	4	**Input the number circled** 1 = Poor 7 = Excellent
6	6	Service	5	**Input the number circled** 1 = Poor 7 = Excellent
7	7	Income	6	**Input the number circled** 1 = Less than $20,000 2 = $20,000 to $34,999 3 = $35,000 to $49,999 4 = $50,000 to $74,999 5 = $75,000 to $99,999 6 = $100,000 or more

Finally, in this part of the questionnaire we would like to ask you some background information for classification purposes.

PART D

1. This questionnaire was answered by   (229)
   1. _____ Primarily the male head of household
   2. _____ Primarily the female head of household
   3. _____ Jointly by the male and female heads of household

2. Marital Status   (230)
   1. _____ Married
   2. _____ Never married
   3. _____ Divorced/separated/widowed

3. What is the total number of family members living at home? _____   (231–232)

4. Number of children living at home:
   1. Under six years _____   (233)
   2. Over six years _____   (234)

5. Number of children not living at home _____   (235)

6. Number of years of formal education which you (and your spouse,
   if applicable) have completed. (please circle)

		College		
	High School	Undergraduate	Graduate	
1. You	8 or less 9 10 11 12	13 14 15 16	17 18 19 20 21 22 or more	(236–237)
2. Spouse	8 or less 9 10 11 12	13 14 15 16	17 18 19 20 21 22 or more	(238–239)

7. 1. Your age _____   (240–241)
   2. Age of spouse (if applicable) _____   (242–243)

8. If employed, please indicate your household's occupations by checking
   the appropriate category.

	(244) Male head	(245) Female head
1. Professional and technical	_____	_____
2. Managers and administrators	_____	_____
3. Sales workers	_____	_____
4. Clerical and kindred workers	_____	_____
5. Craftsmen/operative/laborers	_____	_____
6. Homemakers	_____	_____
7. Others (please specify)	_____	_____
8. Not applicable	_____	_____

9. Is your place of residence currently owned by household?   (246)
   1. Owned _____
   2. Rented _____

10. How many years have you been residing in the greater Atlanta area?
    _____ years.   (247–248)

11. What is the approximate combined annual income of your household
    before taxes? Please check.   (249–250)

    1. Less than $10,000 _____   8. $40,000 to 44,999 _____
    2. $10,000 to 14,999 _____   9. $45,000 to 49,999 _____
    3. $15,000 to 19,999 _____   10. $50,000 to 54,999 _____
    4. $20,000 to 24,999 _____   11. $55,000 to 59,999 _____
    5. $25,000 to 29,999 _____   12. $60,000 to 69,999 _____
    6. $30,000 to 34,999 _____   13. $70,000 to 89,999 _____
    7. $35,000 to 39,999   14. $90,000 and over _____

Note: Columns 1 through 228 contain the respondent ID, project information, and information pertaining to parts A, B, and C of the questionnaire. There is only one record per respondent.

TABLE 14.2
SPSS Variable View of the Data of Table 14.1

Name	Type	Width	Decimals	Label	Values	Missing	Columns	Align	Measure
ID	Numeric	8	0	Respondent Number	None	None	8	Right	Scale
PREFERENC	Numeric	8	0	Restaurant Preference	{1, Weak Preference} . . .	None	11	Right	Scale
QUALITY	Numeric	8	0	Quality of Food	{1, Poor} . . .	None	10	Right	Scale
QUANTITY	Numeric	8	0	Quantity of Portions	{1, Poor} . . .	None	10	Right	Scale
VALUE	Numeric	8	0	Overall Value	{1, Poor} . . .	None	10	Right	Scale
SERVICE	Numeric	8	0	Restaurant Service	{1, Poor} . . .	None	10	Right	Scale
INCOME	Numeric	8	0	Annual Household Income	{1, Less than $20,000} . . .	None	10	Right	Scale

In Table 14.1, as well as in the corresponding EXCEL and SPSS files, the columns represent the fields, and the rows represent the records or respondents, as there is one record per respondent. Notice that there are seven columns. The first column contains the respondent ID, and the second column contains the preference for the restaurant. Columns three to six contain the evaluations of the restaurant on quality of food, quantity of portions, value, and service, respectively. Finally, the seventh column contains the respondent's income, coded as specified in the codebook. Each row contains all the data of a single respondent and represents a record. There are 20 rows or records, indicating that data for 20 respondents are stored in this data file. Note that Table 14.1 is a 20 × 7 matrix, as there are 20 respondents and 7 variables (including ID). Databases consist of one or more files that are interrelated. For example, a database may contain all the customer satisfaction surveys conducted quarterly for the last 5 years.

ACTIVE RESEARCH

Are There Any Patriotic Feelings Toward the New England Patriots?

Visit www.patriots.com and conduct an Internet search using a search engine and your library's online database to obtain information on why people attend professional football games.

As the marketing director for the New England Patriots, what information would you like to have to formulate marketing strategies to increase the attendance at the Patriots home games?

A survey was administered to attendees at a Patriots home game to determine why they were attending. What principle will you follow in checking the questionnaire, editing, and coding?

Transcribing

Transcribing data involves transferring the coded data from the questionnaires or coding sheets onto disks or directly into computers by keypunching or other means. If the data have been collected via computer-assisted telephone interviewing (CATI), computer-assisted personal interviewing (CAPI), or Internet surveys, this step is unnecessary because the data are entered directly into the computer as they are collected. Besides keypunching, the data can be transferred by using optical recognition, digital technologies, bar codes, or other technologies (Figure 14.4).

Optical character recognition programs transcribe printed text into computer files. Optical scanning is a data transcribing process by which answers recorded on computer-readable forms are scanned to form a data record. This requires responses to be recorded with a special pencil in a predesignated area coded for that response. A machine can then read the data. A more flexible

FIGURE 14.4

Data Transcription

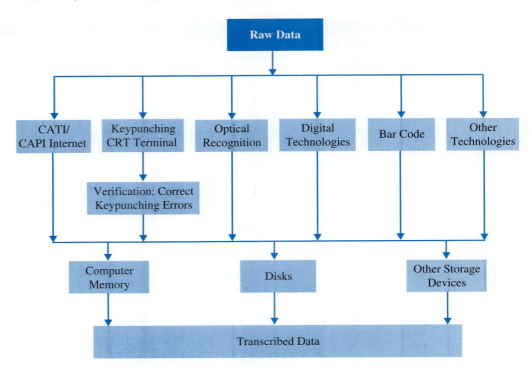

process is optical mark recognition, where a spreadsheet type of interface is used to read and process forms created by users. These marked-sensed forms are then processed by optical scanners and the data are stored in a computer file. Digital technology has resulted in computerized sensory analysis systems, which automate the data-collection process. The questions appear on a computerized grid pad, and responses are recorded directly into the computer using a sensing device. Field interviewers use notebook computers, PDAs, and other handheld devices to record responses, which are then sent via a built-in communication modem, wireless LAN, or cellular link directly to another computer in the field or a remote location. Bar codes involve direct machine reading of the codes and simultaneous transcription. A familiar example is the transcription of universal product code (UPC) data at supermarket checkout counters. Census 2000 used bar codes to identify residents. Companies like UPS and FedEx use bar codes on labels for expedited package shipments.

Several other technologies may also be used to transcribe the data. Voice recognition and voice response systems can translate recorded voice responses into data files. For example, Microsoft XP software includes advanced speech recognition functions and can be used to transcribe data by speaking into a microphone. Newer technologies are being developed. We now have the capability to integrate visual images, streaming video, audio, and data that could well be used for recording a focus group or a survey interview.

When CATI, CAPI, or electronic methods are used, data are verified as they are collected. In the case of inadmissible responses, the computer will prompt the interviewer or respondent. In case of admissible responses, the interviewer or the respondent can see the recorded response on the screen and verify it before proceeding.

The selection of a data transcription method is guided by the type of interviewing method used and the availability of equipment. If CATI, CAPI, or electronic methods are used, the data are entered directly into the computer. Keypunching into a computer is most frequently used for ordinary telephone, in-home, mall intercept, and mail interviews. However, the use of digital technology in personal interviews is growing with the increasing use of grid pads and handheld computers. Optical scanning can be used in structured and repetitive surveys, and optical mark recognition is used in special cases. Bar codes are used to collect scanner data and in a variety of other applications.[5]

Real Research

Scanning the Seas

As of 2009, Princess Cruises (www.princess.com), part of Carnival Corporation, annually carried more than a million passengers. Princess wished to know what passengers thought of the cruise experience, but wanted to determine this information in a cost-effective way. A scannable questionnaire was developed that allowed the cruise line to quickly transcribe the data from thousands of surveys, thus expediting data preparation and analysis. This questionnaire is distributed to measure customer satisfaction on all voyages.

In addition to saving time as compared to keypunching, scanning has also increased the accuracy of the survey results. The senior market researcher for Princess Cruises, Jaime Goldfarb, commented, "When we compared the data files from the two methods, we found that although the scanned system occasionally missed marks because they had not been filled in properly, the scanned data file was still more accurate than the keypunched file."

A monthly report by cruise destination and ship is produced. This report identifies any specific problems that have been noticed, and steps are taken to make sure these problems are addressed. Recently, these surveys have led to changes in the menu and the various buffets located around the ship.[5] ∎

Data Cleaning

data cleaning
Thorough and extensive checks for consistency and treatment of missing responses.

Data cleaning includes consistency checks and treatment of missing responses. Although preliminary consistency checks have been made during editing, the checks at this stage are more thorough and extensive, because they are made by computer.

Consistency Checks

consistency checks
A part of the data-cleaning process that identifies data that are out of range, logically inconsistent, or have extreme values. Data with values not defined by the coding scheme are inadmissible.

Consistency checks identify data that are out of range, logically inconsistent, or have extreme values. Out-of-range data values are inadmissible and must be corrected. For example, respondents have been asked to express their degree of agreement with a series of lifestyle statements on a 1-to-5 scale. Assuming that 9 has been designated for missing values, data values of 0, 6, 7, and 8 are out of range. Computer packages like SPSS, SAS, EXCEL, and MINITAB can be programmed to identify out-of-range values for each variable and print out the respondent code, variable code, variable name, record number, column number, and out-of-range value.[6] This makes it easy to check each variable systematically for out-of-range values. The correct responses can be determined by going back to the edited and coded questionnaire.

Responses can be logically inconsistent in various ways. For example, a respondent may indicate that she charges long-distance calls to a calling card, although she does not have one. Or a respondent reports both unfamiliarity with, and frequent usage of, the same product. The necessary information (respondent code, variable code, variable name, record number, column number, and inconsistent values) can be printed to locate these responses and take corrective action.

Finally, extreme values should be closely examined. Not all extreme values result from errors, but they may point to problems with the data. For example, an extremely low evaluation of a brand may be the result of the respondent indiscriminately circling 1s (on a 1-to-7 rating scale) on all attributes of this brand.

Treatment of Missing Responses

missing responses
Values of a variable that are unknown, because these respondents did not provide unambiguous answers to the question.

Missing responses represent values of a variable that are unknown, either because respondents provided ambiguous answers or their answers were not properly recorded. The former cause is also known as *item nonresponse* that occurs because the respondent refuses, or is unable, to answer specific questions or items because of the content, form, or the effort required. Treatment of missing responses poses problems, particularly if the proportion of missing responses is more than 10 percent. The following options are available for the treatment of missing responses.[7]

1. *Substitute a Neutral Value.* A neutral value, typically the mean response to the variable, is substituted for the missing responses. Thus, the mean of the variable remains unchanged and other statistics, such as correlations, are not affected much. Although this approach has some merit, the logic of substituting a mean value (say 4) for respondents who, if they had answered, might have used either high ratings (6 or 7) or low ratings (1 or 2) is questionable.[8]

2. *Substitute an Imputed Response.* The respondents' pattern of responses to other questions is used to impute or calculate a suitable response to the missing questions. The researcher attempts to infer from the available data the responses the individuals would have given if they had answered the questions. This can be done statistically by determining the relationship of the variable in question to other variables, based on the available data. For example, product usage could be related to household size for respondents who have provided data on both variables. The missing product usage response for a respondent could then be calculated, given that respondent's household size. However, this approach requires considerable effort and can introduce serious bias. Sophisticated statistical procedures have been developed to calculate imputed values for missing responses.

Real Research

Imputation Increases Integrity

A project was undertaken to assess the willingness of households to implement the recommendations of an energy audit (dependent variable), given the financial implications. The independent variables consisted of five financial factors that were manipulated at known levels, and their values were always known by virtue of the design adopted. However, several values of the dependent variable were missing. These missing values were replaced with imputed values. The imputed values were statistically calculated, given the corresponding values of the independent variables. The treatment of missing responses in this manner greatly increased the simplicity and validity of subsequent analysis.[9] ■

casewise deletion
A method for handling missing responses in which cases or respondents with any missing responses are discarded from the analysis.

pairwise deletion
A method of handling missing values in which all cases, or respondents, with any missing values are not automatically discarded; rather, for each calculation only the cases or respondents with complete responses are considered.

3. *Casewise Deletion.* In **casewise deletion**, cases, or respondents, with any missing responses are discarded from the analysis. Because many respondents may have some missing responses, this approach could result in a small sample. Throwing away large amounts of data is undesirable, because it is costly and time-consuming to collect data. Furthermore, respondents with missing responses could differ from respondents with complete responses in systematic ways. If so, casewise deletion could seriously bias the results.

4. *Pairwise Deletion.* In **pairwise deletion**, instead of discarding all cases with any missing values, the researcher uses only the cases or respondents with complete responses for the variable(s) involved in each calculation. As a result, different calculations in an analysis may be based on different sample sizes. This procedure may be appropriate when (1) the sample size is large, (2) there are few missing responses, and (3) the variables are not highly related. Yet this procedure can produce results that are unappealing or even infeasible.

The different procedures for the treatment of missing responses may yield different results, particularly when the responses are not missing at random and the variables are related. Hence, missing responses should be kept to a minimum. The researcher should carefully consider the implications of the various procedures before selecting a particular method for the treatment of nonresponse. It is a good practice to use more than one method of treating missing responses and examine the impact of the different methods on the results.

Statistically Adjusting the Data

Procedures for statistically adjusting the data consist of weighting, variable respecification, and scale transformations. These adjustments are not always necessary but can enhance the quality of data analysis.

Weighting

weighting
A statistical adjustment to the data in which each case or respondent in the database is assigned a weight to reflect its importance relative to other cases or respondents.

In **weighting**, each case or respondent in the database is assigned a weight to reflect its importance relative to other cases or respondents. The value 1.0 represents the unweighted case. The effect of weighting is to increase or decrease the number of cases in the sample that possess certain characteristics. (See Chapter 12, which discussed the use of weighting to adjust for nonresponse.)

Weighting is most widely used to make the sample data more representative of a target population on specific characteristics. For example, it may be used to give greater importance to cases or respondents with higher quality data. Yet another use of weighting is to adjust the sample so that greater importance is attached to respondents with certain characteristics. If a study is conducted to determine what modifications should be made to an existing product, the researcher might want to attach greater weight to the opinions of heavy users of the product. This could be accomplished by assigning weights of 3.0 to heavy users, 2.0 to medium users, and 1.0 to light users and nonusers. Weighting should be applied with caution, because it destroys the self-weighting nature of the sample design.[10]

| **Real Research** | Determining the Weight of Fast-Food Customers |

A mail survey was conducted in the Los Angeles–Long Beach area to determine consumer patronage of fast-food restaurants. The resulting sample composition differed in educational level from the area population distribution as compiled from recent census data. Therefore, the sample was weighted to make it representative in terms of educational level. The weights applied were determined by dividing the population percentage by the corresponding sample percentage. The distribution of education for the sample and population, as well as the weights applied, are given in the following table.

Use of Weighting for Representativeness

Years of Education	Sample Percentage	Population Percentage	Weight
Elementary School			
0 to 7 years	2.49	4.23	1.70
8 years	1.26	2.19	1.74
High School			
1 to 3 years	6.39	8.65	1.35
4 years	25.39	29.24	1.15
College			
1 to 3 years	22.33	29.42	1.32
4 years	15.02	12.01	0.80
5 to 6 years	14.94	7.36	0.49
7 years or more	12.18	6.90	0.57
Totals	100.00	100.00	

Categories underrepresented in the sample received higher weights, whereas overrepresented categories received lower weights. Thus, the data for a respondent with 1 to 3 years of college education should be overweighted by multiplying by (29.42/22.33 =) 1.32, whereas the data for a respondent with 7 or more years of college education should be underweighted by multiplying by (6.90/12.18 =) 0.57. ■

If used, the weighting procedure should be documented and made a part of the project report.

Variable Respecification

Variable respecification involves the transformation of data to create new variables or modify existing variables. The purpose of respecification is to create variables that are consistent with the objectives of the study. For example, suppose the original variable was product usage, with 10 response categories. These might be collapsed into four categories: heavy, medium, light, and nonuser. Or the researcher may create new variables that are composites of several other variables. For example, the researcher may create an Index of Information Search (IIS), which is the sum of information customers seek from dealers, promotional materials, the Internet, and other independent sources. Likewise, one may take the ratio of variables. If the amount of purchases at department stores (X_1) and the amount of purchases charged (X_2) have been measured, the proportion of purchases charged can be a new variable created by taking the ratio of the two (X_2/X_1). Other respecifications of variables include square root and log transformations, which are often applied to improve the fit of the model being estimated.

dummy variables
A respecification procedure using variables that take on only two values, usually 0 or 1.

An important respecification procedure involves the use of dummy variables for respecifying categorical variables. **Dummy variables** are also called *binary, dichotomous, instrumental,* or *qualitative* variables. They are variables that may take on only two values, such as 0 or 1. The general rule is that to respecify a categorical variable with K categories, $K - 1$ dummy variables are needed. The reason for having $K - 1$, rather than K, dummy variables is that only $K - 1$ categories are independent. Given the sample data, information about the Kth category can be derived from information about the other $K - 1$ categories. Consider sex, a variable having two categories. Only one dummy variable is needed. Information on the number or percentage of males in the sample can be readily derived from the number or percentage of females.

Real Research

"Frozen" Consumers Treated as Dummies

In a study of consumer preferences for frozen foods, the respondents were classified as heavy, medium, light, and nonusers and originally assigned codes of 4, 3, 2, and 1, respectively. This coding was not meaningful for several statistical analyses. In order to conduct these analyses, product usage was represented by three dummy variables, X_1, X_2, and X_3, as shown.

Product Usage Category	Original Variable Code	Dummy Variable Code X_1	X_2	X_3
Nonusers	1	1	0	0
Light users	2	0	1	0
Medium users	3	0	0	1
Heavy users	4	0	0	0

Note that $X_1 = 1$ for nonusers and 0 for all others. Likewise, $X_2 = 1$ for light users and 0 for all others, and $X_3 = 1$ for medium users and 0 for all others. In analyzing the data, X_1, X_2, and X_3 are used to represent all user/nonuser groups. ■

Scale Transformation

scale transformation
A manipulation of scale values to ensure comparability with other scales or otherwise make the data suitable for analysis.

Scale transformation involves a manipulation of scale values to ensure comparability with other scales or otherwise make the data suitable for analysis. Frequently, different scales are employed for measuring different variables. For example, image variables may be measured on a 7-point semantic differential scale, attitude variables on a continuous rating scale, and lifestyle variables on a 5-point Likert scale. Therefore, it would not be meaningful to make comparisons across the measurement scales for any respondent. To compare attitudinal scores with lifestyle or image scores, it would be necessary to transform the various scales. Even if the same scale is employed for all the variables, different respondents may use the scale differently. For example, some respondents consistently use the upper end of a rating scale, whereas others consistently use the lower end. These differences can be corrected by appropriately transforming the data.

Real Research

Health Care Services—Transforming Consumers

In a study examining preference segmentation of health care services, respondents were asked to rate the importance of 18 factors affecting preferences for hospitals on a 3-point scale (very, somewhat, or not important). Before analyzing the data, each individual's ratings were transformed. For each individual, preference responses were averaged across all 18 items. Then this mean was subtracted from each item rating and a constant was added to the difference. Thus, the transformed data, X_t, were obtained by:

$$X_t = X_i - \bar{X} + C$$

Subtraction of the mean value corrected for uneven use of the importance scale. The constant C was added to make all the transformed values positive, because negative importance ratings are not meaningful conceptually. This transformation was desirable because some respondents, especially those with low incomes, had rated almost all the preference items as very important. Others, high-income respondents in particular, had assigned the very important rating to only a few preference items. Thus, subtraction of the mean value provided a more accurate idea of the relative importance of the factors.[11] ■

standardization

The process of correcting data to reduce them to the same scale by subtracting the sample mean and dividing by the standard deviation.

In this example, the scale transformation is corrected only for the mean response. A more common transformation procedure is **standardization**. To standardize a scale X_i, we first subtract the mean, $\overline{X}$, from each score and then divide by the standard deviation, s. Thus, the standardized scale will have a mean of zero and a standard deviation of 1. This is essentially the same as the calculation of z scores (see Chapter 12). Standardization allows the researcher to compare variables that have been measured using different types of scales.[12] Mathematically, standardized scores, z_i, may be obtained as:

$$z_i = (X_i - \overline{X})/s$$

ACTIVE RESEARCH

Lexus: The Treatment of Luxury

Visit www.lexus.com and conduct an Internet search using a search engine and your library's online database to obtain information on the criteria buyers use in selecting a luxury car brand.

Demographic and psychographic data were obtained in a survey designed to explain the choice of a luxury car brand. What kind of consistency checks, treatment of missing responses, and variable respecification should be conducted?

As the marketing manager for Lexus, what information would you like to have to formulate marketing strategies to increase your market share?

Selecting a Data Analysis Strategy

The process of selecting a data analysis strategy is described in Figure 14.5. The selection of a data analysis strategy should be based on the earlier steps of the marketing research process, known characteristics of the data, properties of statistical techniques, and the background and philosophy of the researcher.

Data analysis is not an end in itself. Its purpose is to produce information that will help address the problem at hand. The selection of a data analysis strategy must begin with a consideration of the earlier steps in the process: problem definition (Step I), development of an approach (Step II), and research design (Step III). The preliminary plan of data analysis prepared as part of the research design should be used as a springboard. Changes may be necessary in light of additional information generated in subsequent stages of the research process.

The next step is to consider the known characteristics of the data. The measurement scales used exert a strong influence on the choice of statistical techniques (see Chapter 8). In addition, the research design may favor certain techniques. For example, analysis of variance (see Chapter 16) is

FIGURE 14.5

Selecting a Data Analysis Strategy

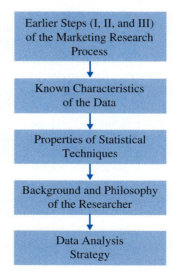

suited for analyzing experimental data from causal designs. The insights into the data obtained during data preparation can be valuable for selecting a strategy for analysis.

It is also important to take into account the properties of the statistical techniques, particularly their purpose and underlying assumptions. Some statistical techniques are appropriate for examining differences in variables, others for assessing the magnitudes of the relationships between variables, and others for making predictions. The techniques also involve different assumptions, and some techniques can withstand violations of the underlying assumptions better than others. A classification of statistical techniques is presented in the next section.

Finally, the researcher's background and philosophy affect the choice of a data analysis strategy. The experienced, statistically trained researcher will employ a range of techniques, including advanced statistical methods. Researchers differ in their willingness to make assumptions about the variables and their underlying populations. Researchers who are conservative about making assumptions will limit their choice of techniques to distribution-free methods. In general, several techniques may be appropriate for analyzing the data from a given project.

A Classification of Statistical Techniques

Statistical techniques can be classified as univariate or multivariate. **Univariate techniques** are appropriate when there is a single measurement of each element in the sample, or there are several measurements of each element but each variable is analyzed in isolation. **Multivariate techniques,** on the other hand, are suitable for analyzing data when there are two or more measurements of each element and the variables are analyzed simultaneously. Multivariate techniques are concerned with the simultaneous relationships among two or more phenomena. Multivariate techniques differ from univariate techniques in that they shift the focus away from the levels (averages) and distributions (variances) of the phenomena, concentrating instead upon the degree of relationships (correlations or covariances) among these phenomena.[13] The univariate and multivariate techniques are described in detail in subsequent chapters; here we show how the various techniques relate to each other in an overall scheme of classification.

Univariate techniques can be classified based on whether the data are metric or nonmetric. **Metric data** are measured on an interval or ratio scale. **Nonmetric data** are measured on a nominal or ordinal scale (see Chapter 8). These techniques can be further classified based on whether one, two, or more samples are involved. It should be noted that here the number of samples is determined based on how the data are treated for the purpose of analysis, not based on how the data were collected. For example, the data for males and females may well have been collected as a single sample, but if the analysis involves an examination of sex differences, two sample techniques will be used. The samples are **independent** if they are drawn randomly from different populations. For the purpose of analysis, data pertaining to different groups of respondents, for example, males and females, are generally treated as independent samples. On the other hand, the samples are **paired** when the data for the two samples relate to the same group of respondents.

For metric data, when there is only one sample, the z test and the t test can be used. When there are two or more independent samples, the z test and t test can be used for two samples, and one-way analysis of variance (one-way ANOVA) for more than two samples. In the case of two related samples, the paired t test can be used. For nonmetric data involving a single sample, frequency distribution, chi-square, Kolmogorov-Smirnov, runs, and binomial tests can be used. For two independent samples with nonmetric data, the chi-square, Mann-Whitney, Median, K-S, and Kruskal-Wallis one-way analysis of variance (K-W ANOVA) can be used. In contrast, when there are two or more related samples, the sign, Wilcoxon, McNemar, and chi-square tests should be used (see Figure 14.6).

Multivariate statistical techniques can be classified as dependence techniques or interdependence techniques (see Figure 14.7). **Dependence techniques** are appropriate when one or more variables can be identified as dependent variables and the remaining as independent variables. When there is only one dependent variable, cross-tabulation, analysis of variance and covariance, regression, two-group discriminant analysis, logit analysis, and conjoint analysis can be used. However, if there is more than one dependent variable, the appropriate techniques are multivariate analysis of variance and covariance, canonical correlation, multiple discriminant analysis,

univariate techniques
Statistical techniques appropriate for analyzing data when there is a single measurement of each element in the sample or, if there are several measurements on each element, but each variable is analyzed in isolation.

multivariate techniques
Statistical techniques suitable for analyzing data when there are two or more measurements on each element and the variables are analyzed simultaneously. Multivariate techniques are concerned with the simultaneous relationships among two or more phenomena.

metric data
Data that are interval or ratio in nature.

nonmetric data
Data derived from a nominal or ordinal scale.

independent
The samples are independent if they are drawn randomly from different populations.

paired
The samples are paired when the data for the two samples relate to the same group of respondents.

dependence techniques
Multivariate techniques appropriate when one or more of the variables can be identified as dependent variables and the remaining as independent variables.

FIGURE 14.6

A Classification of Univariate Techniques

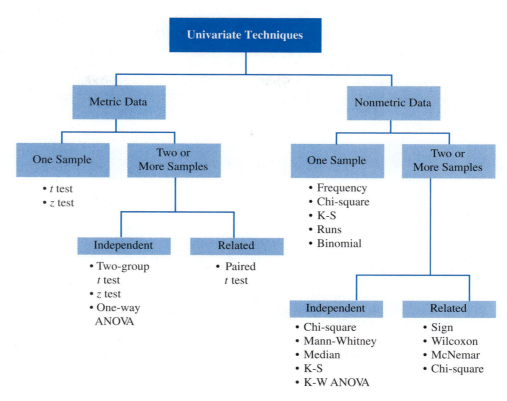

interdependence techniques
Multivariate statistical techniques that attempt to group data based on underlying similarity, and thus allow for interpretation of the data structures. No distinction is made as to which variables are dependent and which are independent.

logit analysis, structural equation modeling, and path analysis. In **interdependence techniques**, the variables are not classified as dependent or independent; rather, the whole set of interdependent relationships is examined. These techniques focus on either variable interdependence or interobject similarity. The major techniques for examining variable interdependence are factor analysis and confirmatory factor analysis. Analysis of interobject similarity can be conducted by cluster analysis and multidimensional scaling.[14]

FIGURE 14.7

A Classification of Multivariate Techniques

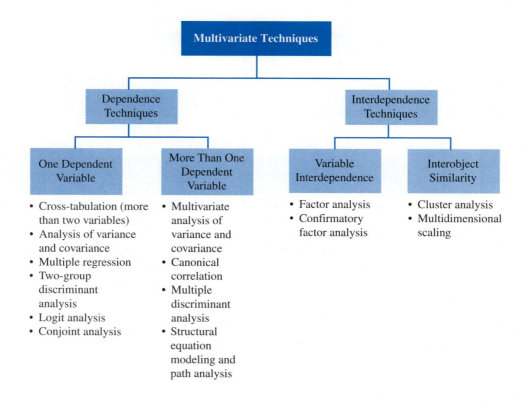

International Marketing Research

Before analyzing the data, the researcher should ensure that the units of measurement are comparable across countries or cultural units. For example, the data may have to be adjusted to establish currency equivalents or metric equivalents. Furthermore, standardization or normalization of the data may be necessary to make meaningful comparisons and achieve consistent results.

Real Research

A Worldwide Scream for Ice Cream

As of 2009, Häagen-Dazs (www.haagen-dazs.com) had become a global phenomenon, available in more than 50 countries. How did this come about? The strategy for whetting foreign appetites is simple. Marketing research conducted in several European (e.g., Britain, France, and Germany) and several Asian (e.g., Japan, Singapore, and Taiwan) countries revealed that consumers were hungry for a high-quality ice cream with a premium image and were willing to pay a premium price for it. These consistent findings emerged after the price of ice cream in each country was standardized to have a mean of zero and a standard deviation of unity. Standardization was desirable, because the prices were specified in different local currencies and a common basis was needed for comparison across countries. Also, in each country, the premium price had to be defined in relation to the prices of competing brands. Standardization accomplished both these objectives.

Based on these findings, Häagen-Dazs first introduced the brand at a few high-end retailers; then built company-owned stores in high-traffic areas; and finally rolled into convenience stores and supermarkets. Hungry for a quality product, British consumers shelled out $5 a pint—double or triple the price of some home brands. "It is easily the largest selling ice cream shop in the world under a trademark name," says John Riccitiello, senior vice president for international sales. In the United States, Häagen-Dazs remains popular although faced with intense competition and health consciousness. This added to the impetus to enter the foreign markets.[15] ∎

The data analysis could be conducted at three levels: (1) individual, (2) within country or cultural unit, and (3) across countries or cultural units. Individual-level analysis requires that the data from each respondent be analyzed separately. For example, one might compute a correlation coefficient or run a regression analysis for each respondent. This means that enough data must be obtained from each individual to allow analysis at the individual level, which is often not feasible. Yet it has been argued that in international marketing or cross-cultural research, the researcher should possess a sound knowledge of the consumer in each culture. This can best be accomplished by individual-level analysis.[16]

intracultural analysis
Within-country analysis of international data.

pancultural analysis
Across-countries analysis in which the data for all respondents from all the countries are pooled and analyzed.

cross-cultural analysis
A type of across-countries analysis in which the data could be aggregated for each country and these aggregate statistics analyzed.

In within-country or cultural-unit analysis, the data are analyzed separately for each country or cultural unit. This is also referred to as **intracultural analysis**. This level of analysis is quite similar to that conducted in domestic marketing research. The objective is to gain an understanding of the relationships and patterns existing in each country or cultural unit. In across-countries analysis, the data of all the countries are analyzed simultaneously. Two approaches to this method are possible. The data for all respondents from all the countries can be pooled and analyzed. This is referred to as **pancultural analysis**. Alternatively, the data can be aggregated for each country and these aggregate statistics analyzed. For example, one could compute means of variables for each country, and then compute correlations on these means. This is referred to as **cross-cultural analysis**. The objective of this level of analysis is to assess the comparability of findings from one country to another. The similarities as well as the differences between countries should be investigated. When examining differences, not only differences in means but also differences in variance and distribution should be assessed. All the statistical techniques that have been discussed in this book can be applied to within-country or across-country analysis and, subject to the amount of data available, to individual-level analysis as well.[17]

Ethics in Marketing Research

Ethical issues that arise during the data-preparation and analysis step of the marketing research process pertain mainly to the researcher. While checking, editing, coding, transcribing, and cleaning, researchers should try to get some idea about the quality of the data. An attempt should be made to identify respondents who have provided data of questionable quality. Consider, for example, a respondent who checks the "7" response to all the 20 items measuring attitude toward spectator sports on a 1-to-7 Likert-type scale. Apparently, this respondent did not realize that some of the statements were negative whereas the others were positive. Thus, this respondent indicates an extremely favorable attitude toward spectator sports on all the positive statements and an extremely negative attitude on the statements that were reversed. Decisions whether such respondents should be discarded, that is, not included in the analysis, can raise ethical concerns. A good rule of thumb is to make such decisions during the data-preparation phase before conducting any analysis.

In contrast, suppose the researcher conducted the analysis without first attempting to identify unsatisfactory respondents. The analysis, however, does not reveal the expected relationship, that is, the analysis does not show that attitude toward spectator sports influences attendance at spectator sports. The researcher then decides to examine the quality of data obtained. In checking the questionnaires, a few respondents with unsatisfactory data are identified. In addition to the type of unsatisfactory responses mentioned earlier, there were other questionable patterns as well. To illustrate, some respondents had checked all responses as "4," the "neither agree nor disagree" response, to all the 20 items measuring attitude toward spectator sports. When these respondents are eliminated and the reduced data set analyzed, the expected results are obtained, showing a positive influence of attitude on attendance at spectator sports. Discarding respondents after analyzing the data raises ethical concerns, particularly if the report does not state that the initial analysis was inconclusive. Moreover, the procedure used to identify unsatisfactory respondents and the number of respondents discarded should be clearly disclosed.

Real Research   ## The Ethics of Downsizing

The effects of a softened economy in 2008 forced many U.S. companies to downsize. A study was recently conducted on the differences between employee and CEO perceptions on whether downsizing is ethical or not. A total of 410 surveys were mailed to employees of U.S. corporations and 231 completed surveys were returned, but 53 were determined to be unusable. The surveys were unusable because they either contained incomplete responses to questions or were filled by unqualified respondents. This resulted in an employee sample size of 178. The survey was also mailed to 179 CEOs of companies that had been identified as going through at least one downsizing during the last five years. Out of the 179, only 36 surveys were returned, of which five CEOs indicated they had never actually been with a company during a downsizing. Therefore, only 31 CEO surveys were determined to be usable in the study. This is an example of ethical editing of the data. The criterion for unusable or unsatisfactory responses is clearly stated, the unsatisfactory respondents are identified before the analysis, and the number of respondents eliminated is disclosed.

The findings of this study were that the employees and CEOs hold different perceptions about downsizing, and different factors can influence someone's perceptions of downsizing. The employees found the downsizing to be unethical when they had been a casualty of the downsizing, when information was withheld, and when the downsizing was done around the holiday season. These perceptions may often affect an employee's work if they cause the employee to view the company in a negative manner.[18] ∎

While analyzing the data, the researcher may also have to deal with ethical issues. The assumptions underlying the statistical techniques used to analyze the data must be satisfied to obtain meaningful results. Any departure from these assumptions should be critically examined to determine the appropriateness of the technique for analyzing the data at hand. The researcher has the responsibility of justifying the statistical techniques used for analysis. When this is not done, ethical questions can be raised. Moreover, there should be no intentional or deliberate misrepresentation of research methods or results. Similarly, ethical issues can arise in interpreting the results, drawing conclusions, making recommendations, and in implementation. Although interpretations, conclusions, recommendations, and implementations necessarily involve subjective judgment, this judgment must be exercised honestly, free from personal biases or agendas of the researcher or the client.

Decision Research   Banana Republic: Going Bananas over a Makeover

The Situation

For most of its time as a leading retailer, Gap Inc. has carefully honed its image through its in-house resources, starting from the design of its clothing to the look of its ads. But that changed as soon as Jack Calhoun, Banana Republic's new chief marketing officer, took over.

Mr. Calhoun was one of the first marketing hires by former Walt Disney executive Paul Pressler, who took over as Gap Inc. president–CEO, succeeding Millard "Mickey" Drexler. One of Mr. Pressler's first acts was to hire Publicis Groupe's Leo Burnett USA, Chicago, to oversee segmentation studies of the three Gap brands, including Banana Republic and Old Navy. Mr. Calhoun reported to newly hired Banana Republic President Marka Hansen, most recently Gap's head of adult merchandising.

The Banana Republic makeover will be the second in the history of the chain, which started out as a travel catalog and opened safari-themed stores with beat-up jeeps in its storefronts. After the chain was purchased by Gap Inc., Mr. Drexler, known for his ability to spot fashion trends, remade it into an upscale version of Gap.

But in recent months, Banana Republic's buzz has quieted and sales have not recovered at a pace that's up to speed with siblings Old Navy and Gap. "The challenge for Banana is the repetition of the fashion lines and marginal quality for the price," said Burt Flickinger, managing director, Strategic Resource Group/Flickinger Consulting, New York.

Mr. Calhoun said he and Gap management are carefully building a new positioning for Banana Republic, which traditionally had advertising echoing that of the lower-priced Gap. "We want to build an architecturally sound and beautiful house," said Mr. Calhoun of the makeover. "We don't want a Cape Cod with a lot of additions."

A telephone survey was conducted to determine consumers' perceptions of the Banana Republic brand and how the brand could be positioned to offer more value to the consumers.

The Marketing Research Decision

1. The telephone survey resulted in a sample size of 1,008. As the data were being prepared for analysis, it was realized that 132 respondents had missing values. However, the variables with unsatisfactory responses were not the key variables. How should the missing values be treated?
2. Discuss how the treatment of missing values you recommend influences Jack Calhoun's decision to enhance the image of Banana Republic.

The Marketing Management Decision

1. What should Jack Calhoun do to enhance the perceived value of the Banana Republic brand?
2. Discuss how the marketing management decision action that you recommend to Jack Calhoun is influenced by the treatment of missing values that you suggested earlier and by the findings of the telephone survey.[20] ∎

Appropriate data preparation and analysis can help Banana Republic determine strategies for enhancing the perceived value of its brand.

Statistical Software

Major statistical packages such as SPSS (www.spss.com), SAS (www.sas.com), MINITAB (www.minitab.com), and EXCEL (www.microsoft.com/office/excel) have Internet sites that can be accessed for a variety of information. We discuss the use of SPSS and SAS in detail while Exhibit 14.1 describes the use of MINITAB and EXCEL to make consistency checks. These packages also contain options for handling missing responses and for statistically adjusting the data. In addition, a number of statistical packages can now be found on the Internet. Although some of these programs may not offer integrated data analysis and management, they can nevertheless be very useful for conducting specific statistical analyses.

Information useful for formulating a data analysis strategy is readily available on the Internet. A lot of information can be obtained about the appropriateness of using certain statistical techniques in specific settings. It is possible to surf the Internet for new statistical techniques that are not yet available in commonly used statistical packages. Newsgroups and special-interest groups are useful sources for a variety of statistical information.

SPSS and SAS Computerized Demonstration Movies

We have developed computerized demonstration movies that give step-by-step instructions for running all the SPSS and SAS Learning Edition programs that are discussed in this book. These demonstrations can be downloaded from the Web site for this book. The instructions for running these demonstrations are given in Exhibit 14.2.

SPSS and SAS Screen Captures with Notes

The step-by-step instructions for running the various SPSS and SAS Learning Edition programs discussed in this book are also illustrated in screen captures with appropriate notes. These screen captures can be downloaded from the Web site for this book.

SPSS Windows

Using the Base module of SPSS, out-of-range values can be selected using the SELECT IF command. These cases, with the identifying information (subject ID, record number, variable name, and variable value) can then be printed using the LIST or PRINT commands. The PRINT command will save active cases to an external file. If a formatted list is required, the SUMMARIZE command can be used.

SPSS Data Entry can facilitate data preparation. You can verify that respondents have answered completely by setting rules. These rules can be used on existing datasets to validate and check the data, whether or not the questionnaire used to collect the data was constructed in Data Entry. Data Entry allows you to control and check the entry of data through three types of rules: validation, checking, and skip and fill rules.

Although the missing values can be treated within the context of the Base module, SPSS Missing Values Analysis can assist in diagnosing missing values with estimates. TextSmart by SPSS can help in the coding and analysis of open-ended responses.

Creating a Variable Called *Overall Evaluation*

We illustrate the use of the Base module in creating new variables and recoding existing ones using the data of Table 14.1. We want to create a variable called *Overall Evaluation (Overall)* that is the sum of the ratings on quality, quantity, value, and service. Thus,

Overall = Quality + Quantity + Value + Service

EXHIBIT 14.1

MINITAB and EXCEL Programs for Data Preparation

> *Minitab*
> There are control statements that permit the control of the order of commands in a macro. The IF command allows implementation of different blocks of commands. This includes IF, ELSEIF, ELSE, and ENDIF.
>
> *Excel*
> The IF statement can be used to make logical checks and check out-of-range values. The IF statement can be accessed under INSERT>FUNCTION>ALL>IF.

EXHIBIT 14.2

Instructions for Running Computerized Demonstrations

For best results while viewing the SPSS and SAS demonstrations, ensure that the "Display" resolution of your computer is set to 1280 by 1024 pixels. To check that, click on the "Display" icon under your computer's Control Panel. Although we give instructions for running SPSS demonstrations, those for SAS are very similar.

To initiate an SPSS demonstration, pick the folder with the appropriate name. For example, to create the Overall Evaluation variable using the data of Table 14.1, use the "14-Transform_demo" folder. Each folder will have several files. It is important that you download all the files in a folder and save them in one separate folder. All the files in a folder are required to run the demonstration. For example, "14-Transform_demo" has four files. However, some folders have more files. All the files in each folder should be downloaded and saved in the same separate folder. The file that you should select to run the demonstration movie is the one that has the same name as the folder, but with the ".htm" extension appended to its name. For example, if you want to run a demonstration of creating the Overall Evaluation variable using the data of Table 14.1 using SPSS, then double-click the file "14-Transform _demo.htm" in the "14-Transform_demo" folder. Once you double-click, Internet Explorer (or your default Web browser) will be loaded, and the demonstration movie will start automatically. Note that the other three files that also need to be in the same folder are "14-Transform_demo_skin.swf," "14-Transform_demo.swf," and "standard.js."

If you want to stop the demonstration movie at any specific point in the demonstration, simply click the ▮▮ button. The demonstration stops at that point. That button now changes form and looks like ▶. To continue viewing the demonstration from that point on, simply click the ▶ button. To fast-forward the demonstration, you can click the ▶ button. Click it multiple times if you need to fast-forward through longer intervals. To rewind the demonstration, simply click the ◀ button. Click it multiple times if you need to rewind through longer intervals. At any time, if you want to replay the demonstration, right from the beginning, then simply click the ↺ button. Finally, you can also move the slide ▭ left or right to navigate through the demonstration. The slider achieves the same purpose as that of the fast-forward and rewind buttons.

These steps are as follows.

1. Select TRANSFORM.
2. Click on COMPUTE VARIABLE.
3. Type "overall" in the TARGET VARIABLE box.
4. Click on "quality" and move it to the NUMERIC EXPRESSIONS box.
5. Click on the "+" sign.
6. Click on "quantity" and move it to the NUMERIC EXPRESSIONS box.
7. Click on the "+" sign.
8. Click on "value" and move it to the NUMERIC EXPRESSIONS box.
9. Click on the "+" sign.
10. Click on "service" and move it to the NUMERIC EXPRESSIONS box.
11. Click on TYPE & LABEL under the TARGET VARIABLE box and type "Overall Evaluation." Click on CONTINUE.
12. Click OK.

Recoding to Create New Variable Called *Recoded Income*

We also want to illustrate the recoding of variables to create new variables. Income category 1 occurs only once and income category 6 occurs only twice. So we want to combine income categories 1 and 2, and categories 5 and 6, and create a new income variable "rincome" labeled "Recoded Income." Note that rincome has only four categories that are coded as 1 to 4. This can be done in SPSS Windows, as follows.

1. Select TRANSFORM.
2. Click on RECODE and select INTO DIFFERENT VARIABLES.
3. Click on income and move it to NUMERIC VARIABLE → OUTPUT VARIABLE box.
4. Type "rincome" in OUTPUT VARIABLE NAME box.
5. Type "Recode Income" in OUTPUT VARIABLE LABEL box.
6. Click OLD AND NEW VALUES box.
7. Under OLD VALUES on the left, click RANGE. Type 1 and 2 in the range boxes. Under NEW VALUES on the right, click VALUE and type 1 in the value box. Click ADD.

8. Under OLD VALUES on the left, click VALUE. Type 3 in the value box. Under NEW VALUES on the right, click VALUE and type 2 in the value box. Click ADD.
9. Under OLD VALUES on the left, click VALUE. Type 4 in the value box. Under NEW VALUES on the right, click VALUE and type 3 in the value box. Click ADD.
10. Under OLD VALUES on the left, click RANGE. Type 5 and 6 in the range boxes. Under NEW VALUES on the right, click VALUE and type 4 in the value box. Click ADD.
11. Click CONTINUE.
12. Click CHANGE.
13. Click OK.

SAS Learning Edition

The instructions given here and in all the data analysis chapters (14 to 22) will work with the SAS Learning Edition as well as with the SAS Enterprise Guide. Within BASE SAS the IF, IF-THEN, and IF-THEN ELSE can be used to select cases with missing or out-of-range values. The LIST statement is useful for printing suspicious input lines.[21]

SAS Learning Edition allows the user to identify missing or out-of-range values with the Filter Data tab within the Query and Filter Data task. The procedures MI and MIANALYZE in SAS/STAT also offer the capability of imputing missing values when a more sophisticated approach is required. We illustrate the use of the Base module in creating new variables and recoding existing ones using the data of Table 14.1.

Creating a Variable Called *Overall Evaluation*

(TIP: Before completing the following tasks, go to TOOLS Q OPTIONS Q QUERY and be sure "Automatically add columns from input tables to result set of query" is checked.)

1. Select DATA.
2. Click on FILTER AND QUERY.
3. Move all variables to SELECT DATA tab.
4. Select the COMPUTED COLUMNS button.
5. Click on NEW.
6. Select BUILD EXPRESSION.
7. Select "QUALITY" and click on ADD TO EXPRESSION.
8. Click on the "+" sign.
9. Select "QUANTITY" and click on ADD TO EXPRESSION.
10. Click on the "+" sign.
11. Select "VALUE" and click on ADD TO EXPRESSION.
12. Click on the "+" sign.
13. Select "SERVICE" and click on ADD TO EXPRESSION.
14. Click OK.
15. Select "CALCULATION1" and click on RENAME.
16. Type OVERALL.
17. Click on CLOSE.
18. Select RUN.

Recoding to Create New Variable Called *Recoded Income*

1. Select DATA.
2. Click on FILTER AND QUERY.
3. Move all variables to SELECT DATA tab.
4. Right-click on INCOME.
5. Select RECODE.
6. In NEW COLUMN NAME box, type "RINCOME".
7. Click ADD.
8. Under REPLACE VALUES enter 2.
9. Under WITH THIS VALUE enter 1.
10. Click OK.

11. Click ADD.
12. Under REPLACE VALUES enter 3.
13. Under WITH THIS VALUE enter 2.
14. Click OK.
15. Click ADD.
16. Under REPLACE VALUES enter 4.
17. Under WITH THIS VALUE enter 3.
18. Click OK.
19. Click ADD.
20. Select the REPLACE A RANGE tab.
21. Check SET A LOWER LIMIT and enter 5.
22. Check SET AN UPPER LIMIT and enter 6.
23. Under WITH THIS VALUE enter 4.
24. Click OK.
25. Click OK.
26. Click RUN.

Project Research   Data Analysis Strategy

As part of the analysis conducted in the department store project, store choice was modeled in terms of store image characteristics or the factors influencing the choice criteria. The sample was split into halves. The respondents in each half were clustered on the basis of the importance attached to the store image characteristics. Statistical tests for clusters were conducted and four segments were identified. Store preference was modeled in terms of the evaluations of the stores on the image variables. The model was estimated separately for each segment. Differences between segment preference functions were statistically tested. Finally, model validation and cross-validation were conducted for each segment. The data analysis strategy adopted is depicted in the following diagram.

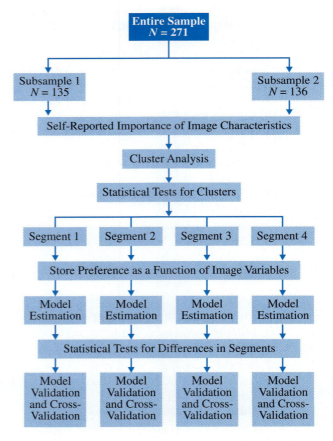

SPSS Data File

SAS Data File

Project Activities

Download the SPSS or SAS data file *Sears Data 14* from the Web site for this book. This file contains information on who in the household does most of the shopping in department stores, familiarity ratings with each of the 10 department stores, and demographic data. The measurement of these variables is described in Chapter 1. The remaining variables have not been included so that the number of variables will be less than 50 and you can use the student SPSS software.

1. Determine how many cases of familiarity with Kohl's have missing values.
2. How are missing values coded?
3. Replace the missing values of familiarity with Kohl's with the mean value.
4. Compute an overall familiarity score by summing the familiarity with each of the 10 department stores.
5. The demographic variables are described in Figure 14.3.

Recode the demographic variables as follows:

Marital status: 1 = 1; 2 or 3 = 2
Total number of family members: 1 = 1; 2 = 2; 3 = 3; 4 = 4; and 5 or more = 5
Children under six years: 0 = 1; 1 or more = 2
Children over six years: 0 = 1; 1 = 2; 2 or more = 3
Children not living at home: 0 = 1; 1 = 2; 2 = 3; 3 or more = 4
Formal education (you and spouse): 12 or less = 1; 13 to 15 = 2; 16 to 18 = 3; 19 or more = 4
Age (you and spouse): less than 30 = 1; 30 to 39 = 2; 40 to 49 = 3; 50 to 59 = 4; 60 to 69 = 5; 70 or older = 6
Occupation (Male Head): 1 or 2 = 1; 3, 4, or 5 = 2; 6, 7, or 8 = 3
Occupation (Female Head): 1 or 2 = 1; 3, 4, or 5 = 2; 6, 7, or 8 = 3
Years of residency: 5 or less = 1; 6 to 10 = 2; 11 to 20 = 3; 21 to 30 = 4; 31 to 40 = 5; 41 or more = 6
Income: 1, 2, 3, or 4 = 1; 5, 6, or 7 = 2; 8 or 9 = 3; 10 or 11 = 4; 12, 13, or 14 = 5
Number of checking accounts: 1 or less = 1; 2 = 2; 3 or more = 3
Number of savings accounts: 1 or less = 1; 2 = 2; 3 or more = 3 ■

Summary

Figure 14.8 gives a concept map for the data-preparation process. Data preparation begins with a preliminary check of all questionnaires for completeness and interviewing quality. Then more thorough editing takes place. Editing consists of screening questionnaires to identify illegible, incomplete, inconsistent, or ambiguous responses. Such responses may be handled by returning questionnaires to the field, assigning missing values, or discarding the unsatisfactory respondents.

The next step is coding. A numerical or alphanumeric code is assigned to represent a specific response to a specific question, along with the column position that code will occupy. It is often helpful to prepare a codebook containing the coding instructions and the necessary information about the variables in the data set. The coded data are transcribed onto computer memory, disks, or other storage devices. For this purpose, keypunching, optical recognition, digital technologies, bar codes, or other technologies may be used.

Cleaning the data requires consistency checks and treatment of missing responses. Options available for treating missing responses include substitution of a neutral value such as the mean, substitution of an imputed response, casewise deletion, and pairwise deletion. Statistical adjustments such as weighting, variable respecification, and scale transformations often enhance the quality of data analysis. The selection of a data analysis strategy should be based on the earlier steps of the marketing research process, known characteristics of the data, properties of statistical techniques, and the background and philosophy of the researcher. Statistical techniques may be classified as univariate or multivariate.

Before analyzing the data in international marketing research, the researcher should ensure that the units of measurement are comparable across countries or cultural units. The data analysis could be conducted at three levels: (1) individual, (2) within country or cultural unit (intracultural analysis), and (3) across countries or cultural units: pancultural or cross-cultural analysis. Several ethical issues are related to data processing, particularly the discarding of unsatisfactory responses, violation of the assumptions underlying the data analysis techniques, and evaluation and interpretation of results. The Internet and computers play a significant role in data preparation and analysis.

FIGURE 14.8

A Concept Map for the Data-Preparation Process

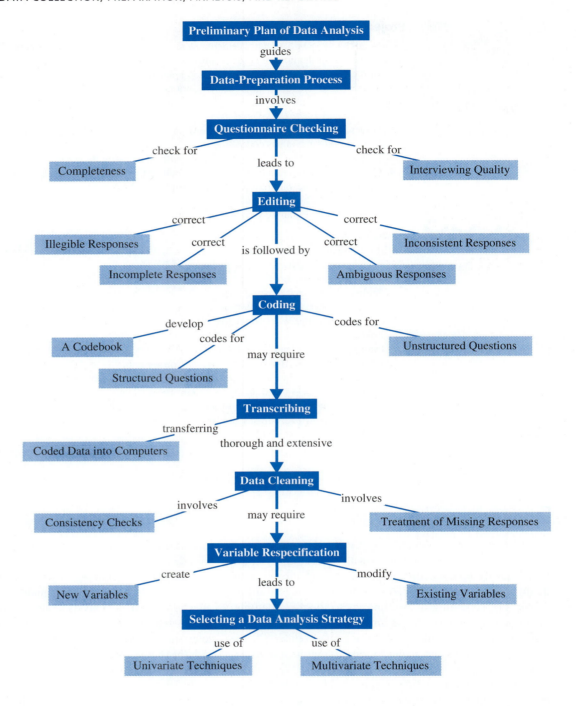

Key Terms and Concepts

Suggested Cases, Video Cases, and HBS Cases

Running Case with Real Data

1.1 Dell

Comprehensive Critical Thinking Cases

2.1 American Idol   2.2 Baskin-Robbins   2.3 Akron Children's Hospital

Data Analysis Cases with Real Data

3.1 AT&T   3.2 IBM   3.3 Kimberly-Clark

Comprehensive Cases with Real Data

4.1 JPMorgan Chase   4.2 Wendy's

Video Cases

23.1 Marriott

Live Research: Conducting a Marketing Research Project

1. The project coordinators should number the questionnaires and keep track of any quotas.
2. The team leaders should be responsible for initial editing of the questionnaires.
3. Each student should be responsible for coding his or her questionnaires and for data entry. It is recommended that the data be entered into an Excel spreadsheet using the coding scheme developed by the instructor.
4. The project coordinators should assemble all the student files into one data file, conduct the computer checks, and clean up the data.
5. The data analysis strategy should be specified by the instructor.

Acronym

The data preparation process may be summarized by the acronym

Data PREP:

D ata cleaning
A djusting the data statistically
T ranscribing
A nalysis strategy

P ost fieldwork questionnaire checking
R ecording numerical or alphanumerical values: Coding
E diting
P reliminary plan of data analysis

Exercises

Questions

1. Describe the data-preparation process.
2. What activities are involved in the preliminary checking of questionnaires that have been returned from the field?
3. What is meant by editing a questionnaire?
4. How are unsatisfactory responses discovered in editing treated?
5. What is the difference between precoding and postcoding?
6. Describe the guidelines for the coding of unstructured questions.
7. What does transcribing the data involve?
8. What kinds of consistency checks are made in cleaning the data?
9. What options are available for the treatment of missing data?
10. What kinds of statistical adjustments are sometimes made to the data?
11. Describe the weighting process. What are the reasons for weighting?
12. What are dummy variables? Why are such variables created?
13. Explain why scale transformations are made.
14. Which scale transformation procedure is most commonly used? Briefly describe this procedure.
15. What considerations are involved in selecting a data analysis strategy?

Problems

1. Develop dummy variable coding schemes for the following variables.
   - Sex
   - Marital status consisting of the following four categories: never married, now married, divorced, other (separated, widowed, etc.)

■ Frequency of international travel, measured as:
1. Do not travel abroad
2. Travel abroad 1 or 2 times a year
3. Travel abroad 3 to 5 times a year
4. Travel abroad 6 to 8 times a year
5. Travel abroad more than 8 times a year

2. Part of a questionnaire used to determine consumer preferences for digital cameras follows. Set up a coding scheme for these three questions.

9. Please rate the importance of the following features you would consider when shopping for a new camera.

	Not so Important				Very Important
Batteries	1	2	3	4	5
Automatic Mode	1	2	3	4	5
Aperture Control	1	2	3	4	5
LCD Screen	1	2	3	4	5

10. If you were to buy a new digital camera, which of the following outlets would you visit? Please check as many as apply.
a. _____ Drugstore
b. _____ Camera store
c. _____ Discount/mass merchandiser
d. _____ Electronics store
e. _____ Internet
f. _____ Other

11. Where do you get most of your photo processing done? Please check only one option.
a. _____ Drugstore
b. _____ Minilabs
c. _____ Camera stores
d. _____ Discount/mass merchandiser
e. _____ Supermarkets
f. _____ Mail order
g. _____ Internet
h. _____ Kiosk/other

Internet and Computer Exercises

1. Explain how you would make consistency checks for the questionnaire given in problem 2 using SPSS, SAS, MINITAB, or EXCEL.
2. Use an electronic questionnaire design and administration package such as Ci3 to program the camera preference questionnaire given in problem 2. Add one or two questions of your own. Administer the questionnaire to five students and prepare the data for analysis. Does computer administration of the questionnaire facilitate data preparation?

Activities

Role Playing

1. You are a project supervisor with SDR Consulting (www.sdrnet.com), a firm based in Atlanta that specializes in data analysis. You are supervising the data-preparation process for a large survey conducted for a leading manufacturer of paper towels. The data are being collected via in-home personal interviews and 1,823 questionnaires have been returned from the field. In cleaning the data, you find that 289 questionnaires have missing responses. The data analyst preparing the data (a student in your class), not knowing how to deal with these missing responses, approaches you for help and instructions. Please explain to the data analyst how the missing responses should be handled.
2. You are the marketing research manager for Whirlpool Appliances. Whirlpool (www.whirlpool.com) has developed a luxury refrigerator model that has several innovative features and will be sold for a premium price of $1,995. A national survey was conducted to determine consumer response to the proposed model. The data were obtained by conducting mall-intercept interviews in 10 major U.S. cities. Although the resulting sample of 2,639 respondents is fairly representative on all other demographic characteristics, it underrepresents the upper-income households. The marketing research analyst, who reports to you, feels that weighting is not necessary. Discuss this question with the analyst (a student in your class).

Fieldwork

1. Visit a marketing research firm or a business firm with an in-house marketing research department. Investigate the data-preparation process this firm followed in a recently completed project. How does this process compare with the one described in the book?
2. Obtain a codebook or coding instructions used by a marketing research firm for a completed project. Examine the codebook or coding instructions carefully. Can you improve on the coding scheme followed by the firm?

Group Discussion

1. As a small group, discuss the following statements. "Data preparation is a time-consuming process. In projects with severe time constraints, data preparation should be circumvented."
2. As a group, discuss the following: "The researcher should always use computer-assisted interviewing (CATI or CAPI) to collect the data, because these methods greatly facilitate data preparation."

Dell Running Case

Review the Dell case, Case 1.1, and questionnaire given toward the end of the book. Download the Dell case data file from the Web site for this book.

1. Recode the respondents based on total hours per week spent online into two groups: 5 hours or less (light users), and 6 hours or more (heavy users). Calculate a frequency distribution.

2. Recode the respondents based on total hours per week spent online into three groups: 5 hours or less (light users), 6 to 10 hours (medium users), and 11 hours or more (heavy users). Calculate a frequency distribution.

3. Form a new variable that denotes the total number of things that people have ever done online based on q2_1 to q2_7. Run a frequency distribution of the new variable and interpret the results. Note the missing values for q2_1 to q2_7 are coded as 0.

4. Recode q4 (overall satisfaction) into two groups: Very satisfied (rating of 1), and somewhat satisfied or dissatisfied (ratings of 2, 3, and 4). Calculate a frequency distribution of the new variable and interpret the results.

5. Recode q5 (would recommend) into two groups: Definitely would recommend (rating of 1), and probably would or less likely to recommend (ratings of 2, 3, 4, and 5). Calculate a frequency distribution of the new variable and interpret the results.

6. Recode q6 (likelihood of choosing Dell) into two groups: Definitely would choose (rating of 1), and probably would or less likely to choose (ratings of 2, 3, 4, and 5). Calculate a frequency distribution of the new variable and interpret the results.

7. Recode q9_5per into three groups: Definitely or probably would have purchased (ratings of 1 and 2), Might or might not have purchased (rating of 3), and Probably or definitely would not have purchased (ratings of 4, and 5). Calculate a frequency distribution of the new variable and interpret the results.

8. Recode q9_10per into three groups: Definitely or probably would have purchased and might or might not have purchased (ratings of 1, 2, and 3), Probably would not have purchased (rating of 4), and Definitely would not have purchased (rating of 5). Calculate a frequency distribution of the new variable and interpret the results.

9. Recode the demographics as follows. (a) Combine the two lowest education (q11) categories into a single category. Thus, Some high school or less and High school graduate will be combined into a single category labeled High school graduate or less. (b) Recode age (q12) into four new categories: 18 to 29, 30 to 39, 40 to 49, and 50 or older. (c) Combine the two lowest income (q13) categories into a single category labeled Under $30,000. Calculate frequency distributions of the new variables and interpret the results.

15

> "Frequency distribution and cross-tabulations are basic techniques that provide rich insights into the data and lay the foundation for more advanced analysis."
>
> *Laurie Harrington, Marketing Manager—Customer Retention,*
> *First Choice Power*

Objectives   [At the end of this chapter, the student should be able to:]

1. Describe the significance of preliminary data analysis and the insights that can be obtained from such an analysis.

2. Discuss data analysis associated with frequencies, including measures of location, measures of variability, and measures of shape.

3. Explain data analysis associated with cross-tabulations and the associated statistics: chi-square, phi coefficient, contingency coefficient, Cramer's *V*, and lambda coefficient.

4. Describe data analysis associated with parametric hypothesis testing for one sample, two independent samples, and paired samples.

5. Understand data analysis associated with nonparametric hypothesis testing for one sample, two independent samples, and paired samples.

Frequency Distribution, Cross-Tabulation, and Hypothesis Testing

Overview

Once the data have been prepared for analysis (Chapter 14), the researcher should conduct some basic analysis. This chapter describes basic data analysis, including frequency distribution, cross-tabulation, and hypothesis testing. First, we describe the frequency distribution and explain how it provides both an indication of the number of out-of-range, missing, or extreme values as well as insights into the central tendency, variability, and shape of the underlying distribution. Next, we introduce hypothesis testing by describing the general procedure. Hypothesis-testing procedures are classified as tests of associations or tests of differences. We consider the use of cross-tabulation for understanding the associations between variables taken two or three at a time. Although the nature of the association can be observed from tables, statistics are available for examining the significance and strength of the association. Then, we present tests for examining hypotheses related to differences based on one or two samples. Finally, we discuss the use of software in frequencies, cross-tabulations, and hypotheses testing. Help for running the SPSS and SAS Learning Edition programs used in this chapter is provided in four ways: (1) detailed step-by-step instructions are given later in the chapter, (2) you can download (from the Web site for this book) computerized demonstration movies illustrating these step-by-step instructions, (3) you can download screen captures with notes illustrating these step-by-step instructions, and (4) you can refer to the *Study Guide and Technology Manual*, a supplement that accompanies this book.

Many commercial marketing research projects do not go beyond basic data analysis. These findings are often displayed using tables and graphs, as discussed further in Chapter 23. Although the findings of basic analysis are valuable in their own right, they also provide guidance for conducting multivariate analysis. The insights gained from the basic analysis are also invaluable in interpreting the results obtained from more sophisticated statistical techniques. To provide the reader with a flavor of these techniques, we illustrate the use of cross-tabulation, chi-square analysis, and hypothesis testing.

Real Research

Commercial Battle of the Sexes

A comparison of television advertising in Australia, Mexico, and the United States focused on the analysis of sex roles in advertising. Results showed differences in the portrayal of the sexes in different countries. Australian advertisements revealed somewhat fewer, and Mexican advertisements slightly more, sex-role differences than U.S. advertisements. Cross-tabulation and chi-square analysis provided the following information for Mexico.

These results indicate that in Mexican commercials, women appeared in commercials for products used by women or by either sex but rarely in commercials for men's products. Men appeared in commercials for

Product Advertised Used by	Persons Appearing in the AD (%)	
	Women	Men
Females	25.0	4.0
Males	6.8	11.8
Either	68.2	84.2

$\chi^2 = 19.73, p \leq 0.001$

Cross-tabulations have been used to analyze sex roles in advertising in Australia, Mexico, and the United States.

products used by either sex. These differences were also found in the U.S. ads, although to a lesser extent, but were not found in Australian ads. Therefore, U.S. consumer products companies should not be advertising in Mexico in the same ways in which they advertise to the U.S. market. In the United States, the increasing population of Hispanic Americans has turned many advertisers' attention to Spanish-language television advertising. Sex roles in the Hispanic culture show women as traditional homemakers, conservative, and dependent upon men for support, but many Hispanic families in the United States do not fit this traditionally held view. In 2009, more than half of Hispanic women worked outside the home, which almost matched the proportion of women in the Anglo population that worked outside the home in the United States.[1] ■

Real Research

Catalogs Are Risky Business

Twelve product categories were examined to compare catalog to store shopping. The null hypothesis that there is no significant difference in the overall amount of risk perceived when buying products by catalog compared to buying the same products in a retail store was rejected. The hypothesis was tested by computing 12 (one for each product) paired-observations t tests. Mean scores for overall perceived risk for some of the products in both buying situations are presented in the following table, with higher scores indicating greater risk.

Mean Scores of Overall Perceived Risk
for Products by Purchase Mode

Product	Overall Perceived Risk	
	Catalog	Retail Store
Stereo hi-fi	48.89	41.98*
Music album	32.65	28.74*
Dress shoes	58.60	50.80*
TV	48.53	40.91*
Athletic socks	35.22	30.22*
Pocket PC/PDA	49.62	42.00*
Digital camera	48.13	39.52*
Perfume	34.85	29.79*

*Significant at 0.01 level

As can be seen, a significantly ($p < 0.01$) higher overall amount of perceived risk was attached to products purchased by catalog as compared to those purchased from a retail store. Although this study reveals risk associated with catalog purchasing, terrorist threats, time shortage, and increased convenience have increased the amount of products that are purchased from catalogs as well as online.[2] ■

SPSS Data File

SAS Data File

These two examples show how basic data analysis can be useful in its own right. The cross-tabulation and chi-square analysis in the international television advertising example, and the paired t tests in the catalog shopping example, enabled us to draw specific conclusions from the data. These and other concepts discussed in this chapter are illustrated in the context of explaining Internet usage for personal (nonprofessional) reasons. Table 15.1 contains data for 30 respondents giving the sex (1 = male, 2 = female), familiarity with the Internet (1 = very unfamiliar, 7 = very familiar), Internet usage in hours per week, attitude toward the Internet and toward technology, both measured on a 7-point scale (1 = very unfavorable, 7 = very favorable), and whether the respondents have done shopping or banking on the Internet (1 = yes, 2 = no). For illustrative purposes, we consider only a small number of observations. In actual practice, frequencies, cross-tabulations and hypotheses tests are performed on much larger samples, such as that in the Dell

TABLE 15.1
Internet Usage Data

Respondent Number	Sex	Familiarity	Internet Usage	Attitude Toward Internet	Attitude Toward Technology	Usage of Internet: Shopping	Usage of Internet: Banking
1	1.00	7.00	14.00	7.00	6.00	1.00	1.00
2	2.00	2.00	2.00	3.00	3.00	2.00	2.00
3	2.00	3.00	3.00	4.00	3.00	1.00	2.00
4	2.00	3.00	3.00	7.00	5.00	1.00	2.00
5	1.00	7.00	13.00	7.00	7.00	1.00	1.00
6	2.00	4.00	6.00	5.00	4.00	1.00	2.00
7	2.00	2.00	2.00	4.00	5.00	2.00	2.00
8	2.00	3.00	6.00	5.00	4.00	2.00	2.00
9	2.00	3.00	6.00	6.00	4.00	1.00	2.00
10	1.00	9.00	15.00	7.00	6.00	1.00	2.00
11	2.00	4.00	3.00	4.00	3.00	2.00	2.00
12	2.00	5.00	4.00	6.00	4.00	2.00	2.00
13	1.00	6.00	9.00	6.00	5.00	2.00	1.00
14	1.00	6.00	8.00	3.00	2.00	2.00	2.00
15	1.00	6.00	5.00	5.00	4.00	1.00	2.00
16	2.00	4.00	3.00	4.00	3.00	2.00	2.00
17	1.00	6.00	9.00	5.00	3.00	1.00	1.00
18	1.00	4.00	4.00	5.00	4.00	1.00	2.00
19	1.00	7.00	14.00	6.00	6.00	1.00	1.00
20	2.00	6.00	6.00	6.00	4.00	2.00	2.00
21	1.00	6.00	9.00	4.00	2.00	2.00	2.00
22	1.00	5.00	5.00	5.00	4.00	2.00	1.00
23	2.00	3.00	2.00	4.00	2.00	2.00	2.00
24	1.00	7.00	15.00	6.00	6.00	1.00	1.00
25	2.00	6.00	6.00	5.00	3.00	1.00	2.00
26	1.00	6.00	13.00	6.00	6.00	1.00	1.00
27	2.00	5.00	4.00	5.00	5.00	1.00	1.00
28	2.00	4.00	2.00	3.00	2.00	2.00	2.00
29	1.00	4.00	4.00	5.00	3.00	1.00	2.00
30	1.00	3.00	3.00	7.00	5.00	1.00	2.00

running case and other cases with real data that are presented in this book. As a first step in the analysis, it is often useful to examine the frequency distributions of the relevant variables.

Frequency Distribution

Marketing researchers often need to answer questions about a single variable. For example:

- How many users of the brand may be characterized as brand loyal?
- What percentage of the market consists of heavy users, medium users, light users, and nonusers?
- How many customers are very familiar with a new product offering? How many are familiar, somewhat familiar, and unfamiliar with the brand? What is the mean familiarity rating? Is there much variance in the extent to which customers are familiar with the new product?
- What is the income distribution of brand users? Is this distribution skewed toward low-income brackets?

frequency distribution
A mathematical distribution whose objective is to obtain a count of the number of responses associated with different values of one variable and to express these counts in percentage terms.

The answers to these kinds of questions can be determined by examining frequency distributions. In a **frequency distribution**, one variable is considered at a time. The objective is to obtain a count of the number of responses associated with different values of the variable. The relative occurrence, or frequency, of different values of the variable is then expressed in percentages. A frequency distribution for a variable produces a table of frequency counts, percentages, and cumulative percentages for all the values associated with that variable.

Table 15.2 gives the frequency distribution of familiarity with the Internet. In the table, the first column contains the labels assigned to the different categories of the variable, and the second column indicates the codes assigned to each value. Note that a code of 9 has been assigned to missing values. The third column gives the number of respondents checking each value. For example, three respondents checked value 5, indicating that they were somewhat familiar with the Internet. The fourth column displays the percentage of respondents checking each value. The next column shows percentages calculated by excluding the cases with missing values. If there were no missing values, columns 4 and 5 would be identical. The last column represents cumulative percentages after adjusting for missing cases. As can be seen, of the 30 respondents who participated in the survey, 10.0 percent checked value 5. If the one respondent with a missing value is excluded, this percentage changes to 10.3. The cumulative percentage corresponding to the value of 5 is 58.6. In other words, 58.6 percent of the respondents with valid responses indicated a familiarity value of 5 or less.

A frequency distribution helps determine the extent of item nonresponse (1 respondent out of 30 in Table 15.1). It also indicates the extent of illegitimate responses. Values of 0 and 8 would be illegitimate responses, or errors. The cases with these values could be identified and corrective action taken. The presence of outliers or cases with extreme values can also be detected. In the case of a frequency distribution of household size, a few isolated families with household sizes of 9 or more might be considered outliers. A frequency distribution also indicates the shape of the empirical distribution of the variable. The frequency data may be used to construct a histogram, or a vertical bar chart, in which the values of the variable are portrayed along the X-axis and the absolute

SPSS Output File

SAS Output File

TABLE 15.2
Frequency Distribution of Familiarity with the Internet

Value Label	Value	Frequency (n)	Percentage	Valid Percentage	Cumulative Percentage
Very unfamiliar	1	0	0.0	0.0	0.0
	2	2	6.7	6.9	6.9
	3	6	20.0	20.7	27.6
	4	6	20.0	20.7	48.3
	5	3	10.0	10.3	58.6
	6	8	26.7	27.6	86.2
Very familiar	7	4	13.3	13.8	100.0
Missing	9	1	3.3		
TOTAL		30	100.0	100.0	

FIGURE 15.1

Frequency Histogram

SPSS Output File

SAS Output File

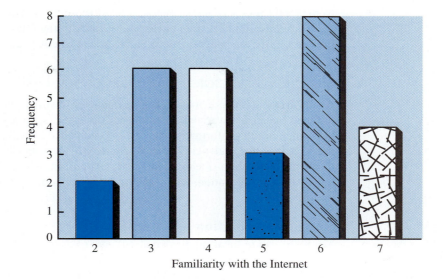

or relative frequencies of the values are placed along the Y-axis. Figure 15.1 is a histogram of the frequency data in Table 15.1. From the histogram, one could examine whether the observed distribution is consistent with an expected or assumed distribution, such as the normal distribution.

Real Research

Basic Analysis Yields Olympic Results

For the 1996 Olympic games in Atlanta, more than 2 million unique visitors came to the games and more than 11 million tickets were sold. In Sydney, at the 2000 Olympic games, as well as in Athens at the 2004 Olympic games, 5 million tickets were sold. It is obvious that this is a potential target market that cannot be ignored. Researchers at the University of Colorado at Boulder decided to find what motivated the international and domestic travelers to come to the Olympic games. A survey was developed and administered to visitors to Olympic games via personal interviews. Three hundred twenty surveys were completed correctly and were used in the data analysis.

The results (see the following table) showed that the top three factors that motivated people to attend the games were a once-in-a-lifetime opportunity, availability of housing, and availability of tickets. The results of this study helped planners for the 2008 Olympic games in Beijing find what specific characteristics the city needed to improve. For instance, from this research, Beijing put funds into projects that added hotel rooms to the city. They also constructed state-of-the-art transportation and unique venues (Olympic parks, stadiums, tourist sites) so that visitors truly felt that they were getting a once-in-a-lifetime experience. As this survey continues to evolve over the years, the data received will become very valuable to the next host city. The planning for the 2012 Olympic games in London was also guided by these findings.[3]

Motivational Factors That Influenced the Decision to Attend the Olympic Games

Motivational Factor	Frequency	Percentage
Once-in-a-lifetime opportunity	95	29.7
Availability of housing	36	11.2
Availability of tickets	27	8.4
Distance away from home	24	7.5
Business/employment	17	5.3
Availability of money—overall expenses	17	5.3
Availability of time	12	3.8
Personal relationship with participant or official	8	2.5
Other motivational factor	8	2.5
Visit Olympic city	4	1.3
Security	3	0.9
Did not respond	69	21.6
Total	320	100.0 ■

Note that the numbers and percentages in the preceding example indicate the extent to which the various motivational factors attract individuals to the Olympic games. Because numbers are involved, a frequency distribution can be used to calculate descriptive or summary statistics.

Statistics Associated with Frequency Distribution

As illustrated in the previous section, a frequency distribution is a convenient way of looking at different values of a variable. A frequency table is easy to read and provides basic information, but sometimes this information may be too detailed and the researcher must summarize it by the use of descriptive statistics. The most commonly used statistics associated with frequencies are measures of location (mean, mode, and median), measures of variability (range, interquartile range, standard deviation, and coefficient of variation), and measures of shape (skewness and kurtosis).[4]

Measures of Location

measures of location
A statistic that describes a location within a data set. Measures of central tendency describe the center of the distribution.

The **measures of location** that we discuss are measures of central tendency because they tend to describe the center of the distribution. If the entire sample is changed by adding a fixed constant to each observation, then the mean, mode, and median change by the same fixed amount.

MEAN The **mean**, or average value, is the most commonly used measure of central tendency. It is used to estimate the mean when the data have been collected using an interval or ratio scale. The data should display some central tendency, with most of the responses distributed around the mean.

mean
The average; that value obtained by summing all elements in a set and dividing by the number of elements.

The mean, $\overline{X}$, is given by

$$\overline{X} = \sum_{i=1}^{n} X_i/n$$

where

X_i = observed values of the variable X

n = number of observations (sample size)

If there are no outliers, the mean is a robust measure and does not change markedly as data values are added or deleted. For the frequencies given in Table 15.2, the mean value is calculated as follows:

$$\overline{X} = (2 \times 2 + 6 \times 3 + 6 \times 4 + 3 \times 5 + 8 \times 6 + 4 \times 7)/29$$
$$= (4 + 18 + 24 + 15 + 48 + 28)/29$$
$$= 137/29$$
$$= 4.724$$

mode
A measure of central tendency given as the value that occurs the most in a sample distribution.

MODE The **mode** is the value that occurs most frequently. It represents the highest peak of the distribution. The mode is a good measure of location when the variable is inherently categorical or has otherwise been grouped into categories. The mode in Table 15.2 is 6.000.

median
A measure of central tendency given as the value above which half of the values fall and below which half of the values fall.

MEDIAN The **median** of a sample is the middle value when the data are arranged in ascending or descending order. If the number of data points is even, the median is usually estimated as the midpoint between the two middle values—by adding the two middle values and dividing their sum by 2. The median is the 50th percentile. The median is an appropriate measure of central tendency for ordinal data. In Table 15.2, the median is 5.000.

For the data in Table 15.1, the three measures of central tendency for this distribution are different (mean = 4.724, mode = 6.000, median = 5.000). This is not surprising, because each measure defines central tendency in a different way. So which measure should be used? If the variable is measured on a nominal scale, the mode should be used. If the variable is measured on an ordinal scale, the median is appropriate. If the variable is measured on an interval or ratio scale, the mode is a poor measure of central tendency. This can be seen from Table 15.2. Although the modal value of 6.000 has the highest frequency, it represents only 27.6 percent of the sample. In general, for interval or ratio data, the median is a better measure of central tendency, although it too ignores available information about the variable. The actual values of the variable above and below the median are ignored. The mean is the most appropriate measure of central tendency for interval or ratio data. The mean makes use of all the information available because all of the values are used in computing it. However, the mean is sensitive to extremely small or extremely large values (outliers). When there are outliers in the data, the mean is not a good measure of central tendency and it is useful to consider both the mean and the median.

In Table 15.2, since there are no extreme values and the data are treated as interval, the mean value of 4.724 is a good measure of location or central tendency. Although this value is greater than 4, it is still not high (i.e., it is less than 5). If this were a large and representative sample, the interpretation would be that people, on the average, are only moderately familiar with the Internet. This would call for both managerial action on the part of Internet service providers and public policy initiatives on the part of governmental bodies to make people more familiar with the Internet and increase Internet usage.

Measures of Variability

measures of variability
A statistic that indicates the distribution's dispersion.

The **measures of variability**, which are calculated on interval or ratio data, include the range, interquartile range, variance or standard deviation, and coefficient of variation.

range
The difference between the largest and smallest values of a distribution.

RANGE   The **range** measures the spread of the data. It is simply the difference between the largest and smallest values in the sample. As such, the range is directly affected by outliers.

$$\text{Range} = X_{\text{largest}} - X_{\text{smallest}}$$

If all the values in the data are multiplied by a constant, the range is multiplied by the same constant. The range for the data in Table 15.2 is $7 - 2 = 5.000$.

interquartile range
The range of a distribution encompassing the middle 50 percent of the observations.

INTERQUARTILE RANGE   The **interquartile range** is the difference between the 75th and 25th percentile. For a set of data points arranged in order of magnitude, the pth percentile is the value that has p percent of the data points below it and $(100 - p)$ percent above it. If all the data points are multiplied by a constant, the interquartile range is multiplied by the same constant. The interquartile range for the data in Table 15.2 is $6 - 3 = 3.000$.

variance
The mean squared deviation of all the values from the mean.

standard deviation
The square root of the variance.

VARIANCE AND STANDARD DEVIATION   The difference between the mean and an observed value is called the *deviation from the mean*. The **variance** is the mean squared deviation from the mean. The variance can never be negative. When the data points are clustered around the mean, the variance is small. When the data points are scattered, the variance is large. If all the data values are multiplied by a constant, the variance is multiplied by the square of the constant. The **standard deviation** is the square root of the variance. Thus, the standard deviation is expressed in the same units as the data, rather than in squared units. The standard deviation of a sample, s, is calculated as:

$$s = \sqrt{\frac{\sum_{i=1}^{n}(X_i - \overline{X})^2}{n - 1}}$$

We divide by $n - 1$ instead of n because the sample is drawn from a population and we are trying to determine how much the responses vary from the mean of the entire population. However, the population mean is unknown; therefore the sample mean is used instead. The use of the sample mean makes the sample seem less variable than it really is. By dividing by $n - 1$, instead of n, we compensate for the smaller variability observed in the sample. For the data given in Table 15.2, the variance is calculated as follows:

$$s^2 = \frac{\{2 \times (2 - 4.724)^2 + 6 \times (3 - 4.724)^2 + 6 \times (4 - 4.724)^2 + 3 \times (5 - 4.724)^2 + 8 \times (6 - 4.724)^2 + 4 \times (7 - 4.724)^2\}}{28}$$

$$= \frac{\{14.840 + 17.833 + 3.145 + 0.229 + 13.025 + 20.721\}}{28}$$

$$= \frac{69.793}{28}$$

$$= 2.493$$

The standard deviation, therefore, is calculated as:

$$s = \sqrt{2.493}$$
$$= 1.579$$

coefficient of variation
A useful expression in sampling theory for the standard deviation as a percentage of the mean.

COEFFICIENT OF VARIATION   The **coefficient of variation** is the ratio of the standard deviation to the mean, expressed as a percentage, and it is a unitless measure of relative variability. The coefficient of variation, CV, is expressed as:

$$CV = \frac{s}{X}$$

The coefficient of variation is meaningful only if the variable is measured on a ratio scale. It remains unchanged if all the data values are multiplied by a constant. Because familiarity with the Internet is not measured on a ratio scale, it is not meaningful to calculate the coefficient of variation for the data in Table 15.2. From a managerial viewpoint, measures of variability are important because if a characteristic shows good variability, then perhaps the market could be segmented based on that characteristic.

Measures of Shape

In addition to measures of variability, measures of shape are also useful in understanding the nature of the distribution. The shape of a distribution is assessed by examining skewness and kurtosis.

skewness
A characteristic of a distribution that assesses its symmetry about the mean.

SKEWNESS   Distributions can be either symmetric or skewed. In a symmetric distribution, the values on either side of the center of the distribution are the same, and the mean, mode, and median are equal. The positive and corresponding negative deviations from the mean are also equal. In a skewed distribution, the positive and negative deviations from the mean are unequal. **Skewness** is the tendency of the deviations from the mean to be larger in one direction than in the other. It can be thought of as the tendency for one tail of the distribution to be heavier than the other (see Figure 15.2). The skewness value for the data of Table 15.2 is –0.094, indicating a slight negative skew.

kurtosis
A measure of the relative peakedness or flatness of the curve defined by the frequency distribution.

KURTOSIS   **Kurtosis** is a measure of the relative peakedness or flatness of the curve defined by the frequency distribution. The kurtosis of a normal distribution is zero. If the kurtosis is

FIGURE 15.2

Skewness of a Distribution

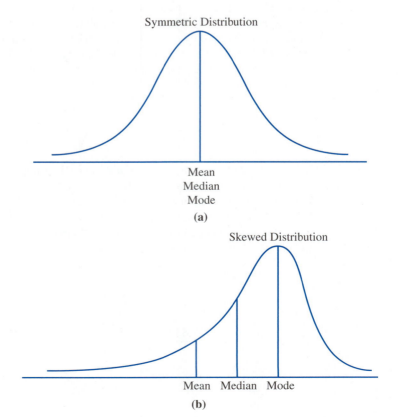

positive, then the distribution is more peaked than a normal distribution. A negative value means that the distribution is flatter than a normal distribution. The value of this statistic for Table 15.2 is -1.261, indicating that the distribution is flatter than a normal distribution. Measures of shape are important, because if a distribution is highly skewed or markedly peaked or flat, then statistical procedures that assume normality should be used with caution.

ACTIVE RESEARCH

Wendy's Customers: Who Are the Heavyweights?

Visit www.wendys.com and conduct an Internet search using a search engine and your library's online database to obtain information on the heavy users of fast-food restaurants.

As the marketing director for Wendy's, how would you target the heavy users of fast-food restaurants?

In a survey for Wendy's, information was obtained on the number of visits to Wendy's per month. How would you identify the heavy users of Wendy's and what statistics would you compute to summarize the number of visits to Wendy's per month?

Introduction to Hypothesis Testing

Basic analysis invariably involves some hypothesis testing. Examples of hypotheses generated in marketing research abound:

- The department store is being patronized by more than 10 percent of the households.
- The heavy and light users of a brand differ in terms of psychographic characteristics.
- One hotel has a more upscale image than its close competitor.
- Familiarity with a restaurant results in greater preference for that restaurant.

Chapter 12 covered the concepts of the sampling distribution, standard error of the mean or the proportion, and the confidence interval.[5] All these concepts are relevant to hypothesis testing and should be reviewed. Now we describe a general procedure for hypothesis testing that can be applied to test hypotheses about a wide range of parameters.

A General Procedure for Hypothesis Testing

The following steps are involved in hypothesis testing (Figure 15.3).

1. Formulate the null hypothesis H_0 and the alternative hypothesis H_1.
2. Select an appropriate statistical technique and the corresponding test statistic.
3. Choose the level of significance, α.
4. Determine the sample size and collect the data. Calculate the value of the test statistic.
5. Determine the probability associated with the test statistic under the null hypothesis, using the sampling distribution of the test statistic. Alternatively, determine the critical values associated with the test statistic that divide the rejection and nonrejection regions.
6. Compare the probability associated with the test statistic with the level of significance specified. Alternatively, determine whether the test statistic has fallen into the rejection or the nonrejection region.
7. Make the statistical decision to reject or not reject the null hypothesis.
8. Express the statistical decision in terms of the marketing research problem.

Step 1: Formulate the Hypotheses

null hypothesis
A statement in which no difference or effect is expected. If the null hypothesis is not rejected, no changes will be made.

alternative hypothesis
A statement that some difference or effect is expected. Accepting the alternative hypothesis will lead to changes in opinions or actions.

The first step is to formulate the null and alternative hypotheses. A **null hypothesis** is a statement of the status quo, one of no difference or no effect. If the null hypothesis is not rejected, no changes will be made. An **alternative hypothesis** is one in which some difference or effect is expected. Accepting the alternative hypothesis will lead to changes in opinions or actions. Thus, the alternative hypothesis is the opposite of the null hypothesis.

The null hypothesis is always the hypothesis that is tested. The null hypothesis refers to a specified value of the population parameter (e.g., μ, σ, π), not a sample statistic (e.g., $\overline{X}$, s, p). A null hypothesis may be rejected, but it can never be accepted based on a single test. A statistical test can have one of two outcomes. One is that the null hypothesis is rejected and the alternative

FIGURE 15.3

**A General
Procedure for
Hypothesis Testing**

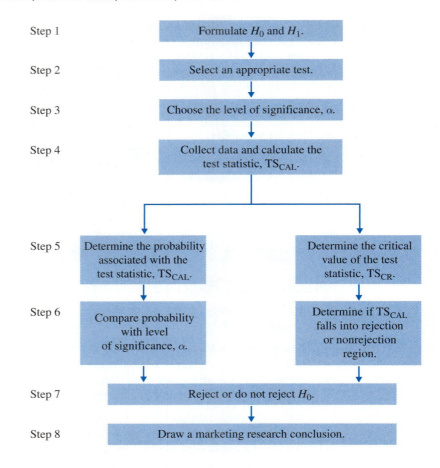

Step 1   Formulate H_0 and H_1.

Step 2   Select an appropriate test.

Step 3   Choose the level of significance, α.

Step 4   Collect data and calculate the test statistic, TS_{CAL}.

Step 5   Determine the probability associated with the test statistic, TS_{CAL}.   Determine the critical value of the test statistic, TS_{CR}.

Step 6   Compare probability with level of significance, α.   Determine if TS_{CAL} falls into rejection or nonrejection region.

Step 7   Reject or do not reject H_0.

Step 8   Draw a marketing research conclusion.

hypothesis is accepted. The other outcome is that the null hypothesis is not rejected based on the evidence. However, it would be incorrect to conclude that because the null hypothesis is not rejected, it can be accepted as valid. In classical hypothesis testing, there is no way to determine whether the null hypothesis is true.

In marketing research, the null hypothesis is formulated in such a way that its rejection leads to the acceptance of the desired conclusion. The alternative hypothesis represents the conclusion for which evidence is sought. For example, a major department store is considering the introduction of an Internet shopping service. The new service will be introduced if more than 40 percent of the Internet users shop via the Internet. The appropriate way to formulate the hypotheses is:

$$H_0: \pi \leq 0.40$$
$$H_1: \pi > 0.40$$

If the null hypothesis H_0 is rejected, then the alternative hypothesis H_1 will be accepted and the new Internet shopping service will be introduced. On the other hand, if H_0 is not rejected, then the new service should not be introduced unless additional evidence is obtained.

one-tailed test
A test of the null hypothesis where the alternative hypothesis is expressed directionally.

This test of the null hypothesis is a **one-tailed test**, because the alternative hypothesis is expressed directionally: The proportion of Internet users who use the Internet for shopping is greater than 0.40. On the other hand, suppose the researcher wanted to determine whether the proportion of Internet users who shop via the Internet is different from 40 percent. Then a **two-tailed test** would be required, and the hypotheses would be expressed as:

$$H_0: \pi = 0.40$$
$$H_1: \pi \neq 0.40$$

two-tailed test
A test of the null hypothesis where the alternative hypothesis is not expressed directionally.

In commercial marketing research, the one-tailed test is used more often than a two-tailed test. Typically, there is some preferred direction for the conclusion for which evidence is sought. For example, the higher the profits, sales, and product quality, the better. The one-tailed test is more powerful than the two-tailed test. The power of a statistical test is discussed further in step 3.

Step 2: Select an Appropriate Test

test statistic
A measure of how close the sample has come to the null hypothesis. It often follows a well-known distribution, such as the normal, *t*, or chi-square distribution.

To test the null hypothesis, it is necessary to select an appropriate statistical technique. The researcher should take into consideration how the test statistic is computed and the sampling distribution that the sample statistic (e.g., the mean) follows. The **test statistic** measures how close the sample has come to the null hypothesis. The test statistic often follows a well-known distribution, such as the normal, *t*, or chi-square distribution. Guidelines for selecting an appropriate test or statistical technique are discussed later in this chapter. In our example, the *z* statistic, which follows the standard normal distribution, would be appropriate. This statistic would be computed as follows:

$$z = \frac{p - \pi}{\sigma_p}$$

where

$$\sigma_p = \sqrt{\frac{\pi(1 - \pi)}{n}}$$

Step 3: Choose Level of Significance, α

Whenever we draw inferences about a population, there is a risk that an incorrect conclusion will be reached. Two types of errors can occur.

Type I error
Also known as *alpha error*, it occurs when the sample results lead to the rejection of a null hypothesis that is in fact true.

TYPE I ERROR   **Type I error** occurs when the sample results lead to the rejection of the null hypothesis when it is in fact true. In our example, a Type I error would occur if we concluded, based on the sample data, that the proportion of customers preferring the new service plan was greater than 0.40, when in fact it was less than or equal to 0.40. The probability of Type I error (α) is also called the **level of significance**. The Type I error is controlled by establishing the tolerable level of risk of rejecting a true null hypothesis. The selection of a particular risk level should depend on the cost of making a Type I error.

level of significance
The probability of making a Type I error.

Type II error
Also known as *beta error*, it occurs when the sample results lead to the nonrejection of a null hypothesis that is in fact false.

TYPE II ERROR   **Type II error** occurs when, based on the sample results, the null hypothesis is not rejected when it is in fact false. In our example, the Type II error would occur if we concluded, based on sample data, that the proportion of customers preferring the new service plan was less than or equal to 0.40 when, in fact, it was greater than 0.40. The probability of Type II error is denoted by β. Unlike α, which is specified by the researcher, the magnitude of β depends on the actual value of the population parameter (proportion). The probability of Type I error (α) and the probability of Type II error (β) are shown in Figure 15.4. The complement ($1 - \beta$) of the probability of a Type II error is called the *power of a statistical test*.

FIGURE 15.4

Type I Error (α) and Type II Error (β)

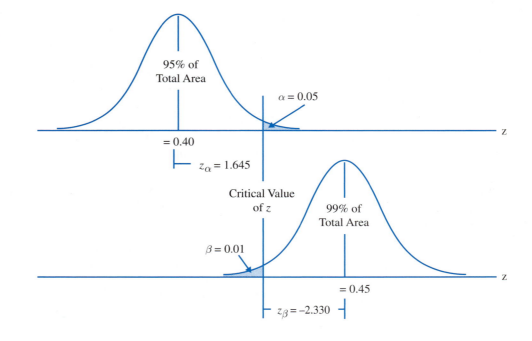

power of a test

The probability of rejecting the null hypothesis when it is in fact false and should be rejected.

POWER OF A TEST   The **power of a test** is the probability $(1 - \beta)$ of rejecting the null hypothesis when it is false and should be rejected. Although β is unknown, it is related to α. An extremely low value of α (e.g., $= 0.001$) will result in intolerably high β errors. So it is necessary to balance the two types of errors. As a compromise, α is often set at 0.05; sometimes it is 0.01; other values of α are rare. The level of α along with the sample size will determine the level of β for a particular research design. The risk of both α and β can be controlled by increasing the sample size. For a given level of α, increasing the sample size will decrease β, thereby increasing the power of the test.

Step 4: Collect Data and Calculate Test Statistic

Sample size is determined after taking into account the desired α and β errors and other qualitative considerations, such as budget constraints. Then the required data are collected and the value of the test statistic computed. In our example, 30 users were surveyed and 17 indicated that they used the Internet for shopping. Thus the value of the sample proportion is $p = 17/30 = 0.567$.

The value of σ_p can be determined as follows:

$$\sigma_p = \sqrt{\frac{\pi(1 - \pi)}{n}}$$

$$= \sqrt{\frac{(0.40)(0.60)}{30}}$$

$$= 0.089$$

The test statistic z can be calculated as follows:

$$z = \frac{p - \pi}{\sigma_p}$$

$$= \frac{0.567 - 0.40}{0.089}$$

$$= 1.88$$

Step 5: Determine the Probability (or Critical Value)

Using standard normal tables (Table 2 of the Statistical Appendix), the probability of obtaining a z value of 1.88 can be calculated (see Figure 15.5). The shaded area between $-\infty$ and 1.88 is 0.9699. Therefore, the area to the right of $z = 1.88$ is $1.0000 - 0.9699 = 0.0301$. This is also called the **p value** and is the probability of observing a value of the test statistic as extreme as, or more extreme than, the value actually observed, assuming that the null hypothesis is true.

Alternatively, the critical value of z, which will give an area to the right side of the critical value of 0.05, is between 1.64 and 1.65 and equals 1.645. Note that in determining the critical value of the test statistic, the area in the tail beyond the critical value is either α or $\alpha/2$. It is α for a one-tailed test and $\alpha/2$ for a two-tailed test.

p value

This is the probability of observing a value of the test statistic as extreme as, or more extreme than, the value actually observed, assuming that the null hypothesis is true.

Steps 6 and 7: Compare the Probability (or Critical Value) and Make the Decision

The probability associated with the calculated or observed value of the test statistic is 0.0301. This is the probability of getting a p value of 0.567 when $\pi = 0.40$. This is less than the level of

FIGURE 15.5

Probability of z with a One-Tailed Test

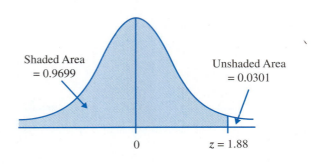

Shaded Area = 0.9699

Unshaded Area = 0.0301

0          $z = 1.88$

significance of 0.05. Hence, the null hypothesis is rejected. Alternatively, the calculated value of the test statistic $z = 1.88$ lies in the rejection region, beyond the value of 1.645. Again, the same conclusion to reject the null hypothesis is reached. Note that the two ways of testing the null hypothesis are equivalent but mathematically opposite in the direction of comparison. If the probability associated with the calculated or observed value of the test statistic (TS_{CAL}) is *less than* the level of significance (α), the null hypothesis is rejected. However, if the absolute value of the calculated value of the test statistic is *greater than* the absolute value of the critical value of the test statistic (TS_{CR}), the null hypothesis is rejected. The reason for this sign shift is that the larger the absolute value of TS_{CAL}, the smaller the probability of obtaining a more extreme value of the test statistic under the null hypothesis. This sign shift can be easily seen:

if probability of $TS_{CAL} <$ significance level (α), then reject H_0,

but

if $|TS_{CAL}| > |TS_{CR}|$, then reject H_0.

Step 8: Marketing Research Conclusion

The conclusion reached by hypothesis testing must be expressed in terms of the marketing research problem. In our example, we conclude that there is evidence that the proportion of Internet users who shop via the Internet is significantly greater than 0.40. Hence, the recommendation to the department store would be to introduce the new Internet shopping service.

As can be seen from Figure 15.6, hypotheses testing can be related to either an examination of associations or an examination of differences. In tests of associations, the null hypothesis is that there is no association between the variables (H_0: . . . is NOT related to . . .). In tests of differences, the null hypothesis is that there is no difference (H_0: . . . is NOT different from . . .). Tests of differences could relate to distributions, means, proportions, medians, or rankings. First, we discuss hypotheses related to associations in the context of cross-tabulations.

Cross-Tabulations

cross-tabulation
A statistical technique that describes two or more variables simultaneously and results in tables that reflect the joint distribution of two or more variables that have a limited number of categories or distinct values.

Although answers to questions related to a single variable are interesting, they often raise additional questions about how to link that variable to other variables. To introduce the frequency distribution, we posed several representative marketing research questions. For each of these, a researcher might pose additional questions to relate these variables to other variables. For example:

- How many brand-loyal users are males?
- Is product use (measured in terms of heavy users, medium users, light users, and nonusers) related to interest in outdoor activities (high, medium, and low)?
- Is familiarity with a new product related to age and education levels?
- Is product ownership related to income (high, medium, and low)?

The answers to such questions can be determined by examining cross-tabulations. Whereas a frequency distribution describes one variable at a time, a **cross-tabulation** describes two or

FIGURE 15.6

A Broad Classification of Hypothesis Tests

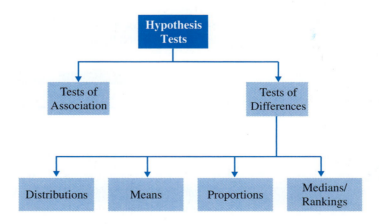

TABLE 15.3
Sex and Internet Usage

| | Sex | | |
Internet Usage	Male	Female	Row Total
Light (1)	5	10	15
Heavy (2)	10	5	15
Column totals	15	15	

more variables simultaneously. A cross-tabulation is the merging of the frequency distribution of two or more variables in a single table. It helps us to understand how one variable such as brand loyalty relates to another variable such as sex. Cross-tabulation results in tables that reflect the joint distribution of two or more variables with a limited number of categories or distinct values. The categories of one variable are cross-classified with the categories of one or more other variables. Thus, the frequency distribution of one variable is subdivided according to the values or categories of the other variables.

Suppose we are interested in determining whether Internet usage is related to sex. For the purpose of cross-tabulation, respondents are classified as light or heavy users. Those reporting 5 hours or less usage are classified as light users, and the remaining are heavy users. The cross-tabulation is shown in Table 15.3. A cross-tabulation includes a cell for every combination of the categories of the two variables. The number in each cell shows how many respondents gave that combination of responses. In Table 15.3, 10 respondents were females who reported light Internet usage. The marginal totals in this table indicate that of the 30 respondents with valid responses on both the variables, 15 reported light usage and 15 were heavy users. In terms of sex, 15 respondents were females and 15 were males. Note that this information could have been obtained from a separate frequency distribution for each variable. In general, the margins of a cross-tabulation show the same information as the frequency tables for each of the variables. Cross-tabulation tables are also called **contingency tables**. The data are considered to be qualitative or categorical data, because each variable is assumed to have only a nominal scale.[6]

contingency table
A cross-tabulation table. It contains a cell for every combination of categories of the two variables.

Cross-tabulation is widely used in commercial marketing research, because (1) cross-tabulation analysis and results can be easily interpreted and understood by managers who are not statistically oriented; (2) the clarity of interpretation provides a stronger link between research results and managerial action; (3) a series of cross-tabulations may provide greater insights into a complex phenomenon than a single multivariate analysis; (4) cross-tabulation may alleviate the problem of sparse cells, which could be serious in discrete multivariate analysis; and (5) cross-tabulation analysis is simple to conduct and appealing to less sophisticated researchers.[7]

Two Variables

Cross-tabulation with two variables is also known as *bivariate cross-tabulation*. Consider again the cross-classification of Internet usage with sex given in Table 15.3. Is usage related to sex? It appears to be from Table 15.3. We see that disproportionately more of the respondents who are males are heavy Internet users as compared to females. Computation of percentages can provide more insights.

Because two variables have been cross-classified, percentages could be computed either columnwise, based on column totals (Table 15.4), or rowwise, based on row totals (Table 15.5).

TABLE 15.4
Sex by Internet Usage

| | Sex | |
Internet Usage	Male	Female
Light	33.3%	66.7%
Heavy	66.7%	33.3%
Column totals	100.0%	100.0%

SPSS Output File

SAS Output File

TABLE 15.5			
Internet Usage by Sex			
	Internet Usage		
Sex	Light	Heavy	Total
Male	33.3%	66.7%	100.0%
Female	66.7%	33.3%	100.0%

Which of these tables is more useful? The answer depends on which variable will be considered as the independent variable and which as the dependent variable. The general rule is to compute the percentages in the direction of the independent variable, across the dependent variable. In our analysis, sex may be considered as the independent variable and Internet usage as the dependent variable, and the correct way of calculating percentages is as shown in Table 15.4. Note that whereas 66.7 percent of the males are heavy users, only 33.3 percent of females fall into this category. This seems to indicate that males are more likely to be heavy users of the Internet as compared to females.

Note that computing percentages in the direction of the dependent variable across the independent variable, as shown in Table 15.5, is not meaningful in this case. Table 15.5 implies that heavy Internet usage causes people to be males. This latter finding is implausible. It is possible, however, that the association between Internet usage and sex is mediated by a third variable, such as age or income. This kind of possibility points to the need to examine the effect of a third variable.

Three Variables

Often the introduction of a third variable clarifies the initial association (or lack of it) observed between two variables. As shown in Figure 15.7, the introduction of a third variable can result in four possibilities.

1. It can refine the association observed between the two original variables.
2. It can indicate no association between the two variables, although an association was initially observed. In other words, the third variable indicates that the initial association between the two variables was spurious.
3. It can reveal some association between the two variables, although no association was initially observed. In this case, the third variable reveals a suppressed association between the first two variables: a suppressor effect.
4. It can indicate no change in the initial association.[8]

These cases are explained with examples based on a sample of 1,000 respondents. Although these examples are contrived to illustrate specific cases, such cases are not uncommon in commercial marketing research.

FIGURE 15.7

The Introduction of a Third Variable in Cross-Tabulation

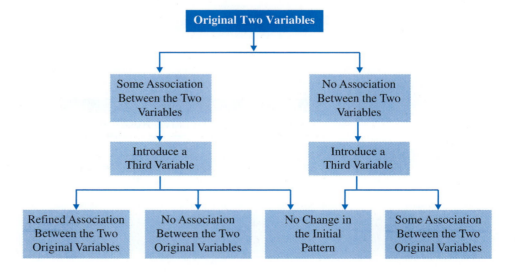

TABLE 15.6
Purchase of Fashion Clothing by Marital Status

Purchase of Fashion Clothing	Current Marital Status	
	Married	Unmarried
High	31%	52%
Low	69%	48%
Column totals	100%	100%
Number of respondents	700	300

REFINE AN INITIAL RELATIONSHIP   An examination of the relationship between the purchase of fashion clothing and marital status resulted in the data reported in Table 15.6. The respondents were classified into either high or low categories based on their purchase of fashion clothing. Marital status was also measured in terms of two categories: currently married or unmarried. As can be seen from Table 15.6, 52 percent of unmarried respondents fell in the high-purchase category, as opposed to 31 percent of the married respondents. Before concluding that unmarried respondents purchase more fashion clothing than those who are married, a third variable, the buyer's sex, was introduced into the analysis.

The buyer's sex was selected as the third variable based on past research. The relationship between purchase of fashion clothing and marital status was reexamined in light of the third variable, as shown in Table 15.7. In the case of females, 60 percent of the unmarried fall in the high-purchase category, as compared to 25 percent of those who are married. On the other hand, the percentages are much closer for males, with 40 percent of the unmarried and 35 percent of the married falling in the high-purchase category. Hence, the introduction of sex (third variable) has refined the relationship between marital status and purchase of fashion clothing (original variables). Unmarried respondents are more likely to fall in the high-purchase category than married ones, and this effect is much more pronounced for females than for males.

INITIAL RELATIONSHIP WAS SPURIOUS   A researcher working for an advertising agency promoting a line of automobiles costing more than $30,000 was attempting to explain the ownership of expensive automobiles (see Table 15.8). The table shows that 32 percent of those

TABLE 15.7
Purchase of Fashion Clothing by Marital Status and Sex

Purchase of Fashion Clothing	Sex			
	Male Marital Status		Female Marital Status	
	Married	Unmarried	Married	Unmarried
High	35%	40%	25%	60%
Low	65%	60%	75%	40%
Column totals	100%	100%	100%	100%
Number of cases	400	120	300	180

TABLE 15.8
Ownership of Expensive Automobiles by Education Level

Own Expensive Automobile	Education	
	College Degree	No College Degree
Yes	32%	21%
No	68%	79%
Column totals	100%	100%
Number of cases	250	750

TABLE 15.9

Ownership of Expensive Automobiles by Education and Income Levels

	Income			
	Low Income Education		High Income Education	
Own Expensive Automobile	College Degree	No College Degree	College Degree	No College Degree
Yes	20%	20%	40%	40%
No	80%	80%	60%	60%
Column totals	100%	100%	100%	100%
Number of respondents	100	700	150	50

with college degrees own an expensive automobile, as compared to 21 percent of those without college degrees. The researcher was tempted to conclude that education influenced ownership of expensive automobiles. Realizing that income may also be a factor, the researcher decided to reexamine the relationship between education and ownership of expensive automobiles in light of income level. This resulted in Table 15.9. Note that the percentages of those with and without college degrees who own expensive automobiles are the same for each of the income groups. When the data for the high-income and low-income groups are examined separately, the association between education and ownership of expensive automobiles disappears, indicating that the initial relationship observed between these two variables was spurious.

REVEAL SUPPRESSED ASSOCIATION   A researcher suspected desire to travel abroad may be influenced by age. However, a cross-tabulation of the two variables produced the results in Table 15.10, indicating no association. When sex was introduced as the third variable, Table 15.11 was obtained. Among men, 60 percent of those under 45 indicated a desire to travel abroad, as compared to 40 percent of those 45 or older. The pattern was reversed for women, where 35 percent of those under 45 indicated a desire to travel abroad, as opposed to 65 percent of those 45 or older. Because the association between desire to travel abroad and age runs in the opposite direction for males and females, the relationship between these two variables is masked when the data are aggregated across sex, as in Table 15.10. But when the

TABLE 15.10

Desire to Travel Abroad by Age

	Age	
Desire to Travel Abroad	Less Than 45	45 or More
Yes	50%	50%
No	50%	50%
Column totals	100%	100%
Number of respondents	500	500

TABLE 15.11

Desire to Travel Abroad by Age and Sex

	Sex			
	Male Age		Female Age	
Desire to Travel Abroad	<45	≤45	<45	≥45
Yes	60%	40%	35%	65%
No	40%	60%	65%	35%
Column totals	100%	100%	100%	100%
Number of cases	300	300	200	200

TABLE 15.12
Eating Frequently in Fast-Food Restaurants by Family Size

Eat Frequently in Fast-Food Restaurants	Family Size	
	Small	Large
Yes	65%	65%
No	35%	35%
Column totals	100%	100%
Number of cases	500	500

TABLE 15.13
Eating Frequently in Fast-Food Restaurants by Family Size and Income

Eat Frequently in Fast-Food Restaurants	Income			
	Low Income		High Income	
	Family Size		Family Size	
	Small	Large	Small	Large
Yes	65%	65%	65%	65%
No	35%	35%	35%	35%
Column totals	100%	100%	100%	100%
Number of respondents	250	250	250	250

effect of sex is controlled, as in Table 15.11, the suppressed association between desire to travel abroad and age is revealed for the separate categories of males and females.

NO CHANGE IN INITIAL RELATIONSHIP In some cases, the introduction of the third variable does not change the initial relationship observed, regardless of whether the original variables were associated. This suggests that the third variable does not influence the relationship between the first two. Consider the cross-tabulation of family size and the tendency to eat out frequently in fast-food restaurants, as shown in Table 15.12. The respondents were classified into small and large family size categories based on a median split of the distribution, with 500 respondents in each category. No association is observed. The respondents were further classified into high- or low-income groups based on a median split. When income was introduced as a third variable in the analysis, Table 15.13 was obtained. Again, no association was observed.

General Comments on Cross-Tabulation

More than three variables can be cross-tabulated, but the interpretation is quite complex. Also, because the number of cells increases multiplicatively, maintaining an adequate number of respondents or cases in each cell can be problematic. As a general rule, there should be at least five expected observations in each cell for the statistics computed to be reliable. Thus, cross-tabulation is an inefficient way of examining relationships when there are several variables. Note that cross-tabulation examines association between variables, not causation. To examine causation, the causal research design framework should be adopted (see Chapter 7).

Statistics Associated with Cross-Tabulation

We will discuss the statistics commonly used for assessing the statistical significance and strength of association of cross-tabulated variables. The statistical significance of the observed association is commonly measured by the chi-square statistic. The strength of association, or degree of association, is important from a practical or substantive perspective. Generally, the strength of association is of interest only if the association is statistically significant. The strength of the association can be measured by the phi correlation coefficient, the contingency coefficient, Cramer's V, and the lambda coefficient.

Chi-Square

chi-square statistic

The statistic used to test the statistical significance of the observed association in a cross-tabulation. It assists us in determining whether a systematic association exists between the two variables.

The **chi-square statistic** (χ^2) is used to test the statistical significance of the observed association in a cross-tabulation. It assists us in determining whether a systematic association exists between the two variables. The null hypothesis, H_0, is that there is no association between the variables. The test is conducted by computing the cell frequencies that would be expected if no association were present between the variables, given the existing row and column totals. These expected cell frequencies, denoted f_e, are then compared to the actual observed frequencies, f_o, found in the cross-tabulation to calculate the chi-square statistic. The greater the discrepancies between the expected and actual frequencies, the larger the value of the statistic. Assume that a cross-tabulation has r rows and c columns and a random sample of n observations. Then the expected frequency for each cell can be calculated by using a simple formula:

$$f_e = \frac{n_r \, n_c}{n}$$

where

$$n_r = \text{total number in the row}$$
$$n_c = \text{total number in the column}$$
$$n = \text{total sample size}$$

For the Internet usage data in Table 15.3, the expected frequencies for the cells, going from left to right and from top to bottom, are:

$$\frac{15 \times 15}{30} = 7.50 \qquad \frac{15 \times 15}{30} = 7.50$$

$$\frac{15 \times 15}{30} = 7.50 \qquad \frac{15 \times 15}{30} = 7.50$$

Then the value of χ^2 is calculated as follows:

$$\chi^2 = \sum_{\substack{\text{all} \\ \text{cells}}} \frac{(f_o - f_e)^2}{f_e}$$

For the data in Table 15.3, the value of χ^2 is calculated as:

$$\chi^2 = \frac{(5 - 7.5)^2}{7.5} + \frac{(10 - 7.5)^2}{7.5} + \frac{(10 - 7.5)^2}{7.5} + \frac{5 - 7.5)^2}{7.5}$$

$$= 0.833 + 0.833 + 0.833 + 0.833$$

$$= 3.333$$

To determine whether a systematic association exists, the probability of obtaining a value of chi-square as large as or larger than the one calculated from the cross-tabulation is estimated. An important characteristic of the chi-square statistic is the number of degrees of freedom (df) associated with it. In general, the number of degrees of freedom is equal to the number of observations less the number of constraints needed to calculate a statistical term. In the case of a chi-square statistic associated with a cross-tabulation, the number of degrees of freedom is equal to the product of number of rows (r) less one and the number of columns (c) less one. That is, df $= (r - 1) \times (c - 1)$.[9] The null hypothesis (H_0) of no association between the two variables will be rejected only when the calculated value of the test statistic is greater than the critical value of the chi-square distribution with the appropriate degrees of freedom, as shown in Figure 15.8.

chi-square distribution

A skewed distribution whose shape depends solely on the number of degrees of freedom. As the number of degrees of freedom increases, the chi-square distribution becomes more symmetrical.

The **chi-square distribution** is a skewed distribution whose shape depends solely on the number of degrees of freedom.[10] As the number of degrees of freedom increases, the chi-square

FIGURE 15.8

Chi-Square Test of Association

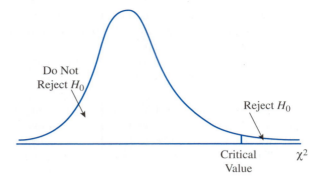

distribution becomes more symmetrical. Table 3 in the Statistical Appendix contains upper-tail areas of the chi-square distribution for different degrees of freedom. In this table, the value at the top of each column indicates the area in the upper portion (the right side, as shown in Figure 15.8) of the chi-square distribution. To illustrate, for 1 degree of freedom, the value for an upper-tail area of 0.05 is 3.841. This indicates that for 1 degree of freedom, the probability of exceeding a chi-square value of 3.841 is 0.05. In other words, at the 0.05 level of significance with 1 degree of freedom, the critical value of the chi-square statistic is 3.841.

For the cross-tabulation given in Table 15.3, there are $(2 - 1) \times (2 - 1) = 1$ degree of freedom. The calculated chi-square statistic had a value of 3.333. Because this is less than the critical value of 3.841, the null hypothesis of no association cannot be rejected, indicating that the association is not statistically significant at the 0.05 level. Note that this lack of significance is mainly due to the small sample size (30). If, instead, the sample size were 300 and each entry of Table 15.3 were multiplied by 10, it can be seen that the value of the chi-square statistic would be multiplied by 10 and would be 33.33, which is significant at the 0.05 level.

The chi-square statistic can also be used in goodness-of-fit tests to determine whether certain models fit the observed data. These tests are conducted by calculating the significance of sample deviations from assumed theoretical (expected) distributions, and can be performed on cross-tabulations as well as on frequencies (one-way tabulations). The calculation of the chi-square statistic and the determination of its significance is the same as illustrated here.

The chi-square statistic should be estimated only on counts of data. When the data are in percentage form, they should first be converted to absolute counts or numbers. In addition, an underlying assumption of the chi-square test is that the observations are drawn independently. As a general rule, chi-square analysis should not be conducted when the expected or theoretical frequencies in any of the cells is less than five. If the number of observations in any cell is less than 10, or if the table has two rows and two columns (a 2 × 2 table), a correction factor should be applied.[11] With the correction factor, the value is 2.133, which is not significant at the 0.05 level. The calculation of the correction factor is complex but can be conveniently done using appropriate software. In the case of a 2 × 2 table, the chi-square is related to the phi coefficient.

Phi Coefficient

phi coefficient
A measure of the strength of association in the special case of a table with two rows and two columns (a 2 × 2 table).

The **phi coefficient** (ϕ) is used as a measure of the strength of association in the special case of a table with two rows and two columns (a 2 × 2 table). The phi coefficient is proportional to the square root of the chi-square statistic. For a sample of size n, this statistic is calculated as:

$$\phi = \sqrt{\frac{\chi^2}{n}}$$

It takes the value of 0 when there is no association, which would be indicated by a chi-square value of 0 as well. When the variables are perfectly associated, phi assumes the value of 1 and all the observations fall just on the main or minor diagonal. (In some computer programs, phi assumes a value of −1 rather than 1 when there is perfect negative association.) In our case, because the association was not significant at the 0.05 level, we would not normally compute the phi value. However, for the purpose of illustration, we show how the values of phi and other measures of the strength of association would be computed. The value of phi is:

$$\phi = \sqrt{\frac{3.333}{30}}$$
$$= 0.333$$

Thus, the association is not very strong. In the more general case involving a table of any size, the strength of association can be assessed by using the contingency coefficient.

Contingency Coefficient

contingency coefficient (C)
A measure of the strength of association in a table of any size.

Whereas the phi coefficient is specific to a 2 × 2 table, the **contingency coefficient (C)** can be used to assess the strength of association in a table of any size. This index is also related to chi-square, as follows:

$$C = \sqrt{\frac{\chi^2}{\chi^2 + n}}$$

The contingency coefficient varies between 0 and 1. The 0 value occurs in the case of no association (i.e., the variables are statistically independent), but the maximum value of 1 is never achieved. Rather, the maximum value of the contingency coefficient depends on the size of the table (number of rows and number of columns). For this reason, it should be used only to compare tables of the same size. The value of the contingency coefficient for Table 15.3 is:

$$C = \sqrt{\frac{3.333}{3.333 + 30}}$$
$$= 0.316$$

This value of C indicates that the association is not very strong. Another statistic that can be calculated for any table is Cramer's V.

Cramer's V

Cramer's V
A measure of the strength of association used in tables larger than 2 × 2.

Cramer's V is a modified version of the phi correlation coefficient, ϕ, and is used in tables larger than 2 × 2. When phi is calculated for a table larger than 2 × 2, it has no upper limit. Cramer's V is obtained by adjusting phi for either the number of rows or the number of columns in the table, based on which of the two is smaller. The adjustment is such that V will range from 0 to 1. A large value of V merely indicates a high degree of association. It does not indicate how the variables are associated. For a table with r rows and c columns, the relationship between Cramer's V and the phi correlation coefficient is expressed as:

$$V = \sqrt{\frac{\phi^2}{\min(r - 1), (c - 1)}}$$

or

$$V = \sqrt{\frac{\chi^2/n}{\min(r - 1), (c - 1)}}$$

The value of Cramer's V for Table 15.3 is:

$$V = \sqrt{\frac{3.333/30}{1}}$$
$$= 0.333$$

asymmetric lambda
A measure of the percentage improvement in predicting the value of the dependent variable, given the value of the independent variable in contingency table analysis. Lambda also varies between 0 and 1.

Thus, the association is not very strong. As can be seen, in this case $V = \phi$. This is always the case for a 2 × 2 table. Another statistic commonly estimated is the lambda coefficient.

Lambda Coefficient

Lambda assumes that the variables are measured on a nominal scale. **Asymmetric lambda** measures the percentage improvement in predicting the value of the dependent variable, given the value of the

symmetric lambda
The symmetric lambda does not make an assumption about which variable is dependent. It measures the overall improvement when prediction is done in both directions.

independent variable. Lambda also varies between 0 and 1. A value of 0 means no improvement in prediction. A value of 1 indicates that the prediction can be made without error. This happens when each independent variable category is associated with a single category of the dependent variable.

Asymmetric lambda is computed for each of the variables (treating it as the dependent variable). In general, the two asymmetric lambdas are likely to be different because the marginal distributions are not usually the same. A **symmetric lambda** is also computed, which is a kind of average of the two asymmetric values. The symmetric lambda does not make an assumption about which variable is dependent. It measures the overall improvement when prediction is done in both directions.[12] The value of asymmetric lambda in Table 15.3, with usage as the dependent variable, is 0.333. This indicates that knowledge of sex increases our predictive ability by the proportion of 0.333, that is, a 33.3 percent improvement. The symmetric lambda is also 0.333.

Other Statistics

Note that in the calculation of the chi-square statistic, the variables are treated as being measured on only a nominal scale. Other statistics such as tau *b*, tau *c*, and gamma are available to measure association between two ordinal-level variables. All these statistics use information about the ordering of categories of variables by considering every possible pair of cases in the table. Each pair is examined to determine if its relative ordering on the first variable is the same as its relative ordering on the second variable (concordant), if the ordering is reversed (discordant), or if the pair is tied. The manner in which the ties are treated is the basic difference between these statistics. Both tau *b* and tau *c* adjust for ties. **Tau *b*** is the most appropriate with square tables, in which the number of rows and the number of columns are equal. Its value varies between +1 and −1. Thus the direction (positive or negative) as well as the strength (how close the value is to 1) of the relationship can be determined. For a rectangular table in which the number of rows is different from the number of columns, **tau *c*** should be used. **Gamma** does not make an adjustment for either ties or table size. Gamma also varies between +1 and −1 and generally has a higher numerical value than tau *b* or tau *c*. For the data in Table 15.3, as sex is a nominal variable, it is not appropriate to calculate ordinal statistics. All these statistics can be estimated by using the appropriate computer programs for cross-tabulation. Other statistics for measuring the strength of association, namely product moment correlation and nonmetric correlation, are discussed in Chapter 17.

Cross-Tabulation in Practice

When conducting cross-tabulation analysis in practice, it is useful to proceed along the following steps.

1. Test the null hypothesis that there is no association between the variables using the chi-square statistic. If you fail to reject the null hypothesis, then there is no relationship.
2. If H_0 is rejected, then determine the strength of the association using an appropriate statistic (phi coefficient, contingency coefficient, Cramer's *V*, lambda coefficient, or other statistics).
3. If H_0 is rejected, interpret the pattern of the relationship by computing the percentages in the direction of the independent variable, across the dependent variable.
4. If the variables are treated as ordinal rather than nominal, use tau *b*, tau *c*, or gamma as the test statistic. If H_0 is rejected, then determine the strength of the association using the magnitude, and the direction of the relationship using the sign of the test statistic.
5. Translate the results of hypothesis testing, strength of association, and pattern of association into managerial implications and recommendations where meaningful.

tau *b*
Test statistic that measures the association between two ordinal-level variables. It makes an adjustment for ties and is most appropriate when the table of variables is square.

tau *c*
Test statistic that measures the association between two ordinal-level variables. It makes an adjustment for ties and is most appropriate when the table of variables is not square but a rectangle.

gamma
Test statistic that measures the association between two ordinal-level variables. It does not make an adjustment for ties.

ACTIVE RESEARCH

Analyzing Usage of Cosmetics Is No Cosmetic Effort

Visit www.loreal.com and conduct an Internet search using a search engine and your library's online database to obtain information on the heavy users, light users, and nonusers of cosmetics.

How would you analyze the data to determine whether the heavy, light, and nonusers differ in terms of demographic characteristics?

As the marketing director for L'Oréal, what marketing strategies would you adopt to reach the heavy users, light users, and nonusers of cosmetics?

Hypothesis Testing Related to Differences

The previous section considered hypothesis testing related to associations. We now focus on hypothesis testing related to differences. A classification of hypothesis-testing procedures for examining differences is presented in Figure 15.9. Note that Figure 15.9 is consistent with the classification of univariate techniques presented in Figure 14.6. The major difference is that Figure 14.6 also accommodates more than two samples and thus deals with techniques such as one-way ANOVA and K-W ANOVA (Chapter 14), whereas Figure 15.9 is limited to no more than two samples. Also, one-sample techniques such as frequencies, which do not involve statistical testing, are not covered in Figure 15.9. Hypothesis-testing procedures can be broadly classified as parametric or nonparametric, based on the measurement scale of the variables involved. **Parametric tests** assume that the variables of interest are measured on at least an interval scale. **Nonparametric tests** assume that the variables are measured on a nominal or ordinal scale. These tests can be further classified based on whether one, two, or more samples are involved. As explained in Chapter 14, the number of samples is determined based on how the data are treated for the purpose of analysis, not based on how the data were collected. The samples are *independent* if they are drawn randomly from different populations. For the purpose of analysis, data pertaining to different groups of respondents, for example, males and females, are generally treated as independent samples. On the other hand, the samples are *paired* when the data for the two samples relate to the same group of respondents.

The most popular parametric test is the *t* test, conducted for examining hypotheses about means. The *t* test could be conducted on the mean of one sample or two samples of observations. In the case of two samples, the samples could be independent or paired. Nonparametric tests based on observations drawn from one sample include the Kolmogorov-Smirnov test, the chi-square test, the runs test, and the binomial test. In case of two independent samples, the Mann-Whitney *U* test, the median test, and the Kolmogorov-Smirnov two-sample test are used for examining hypotheses about location. These tests are nonparametric counterparts of the two-group *t* test. The chi-square test can also be conducted. For paired samples, nonparametric tests include the Wilcoxon matched-pairs signed-ranks test and the sign test. These are the counterparts of the paired *t* test. In addition, the McNemar and chi-square tests can also be used. Parametric as well as nonparametric tests are also available for evaluating hypotheses relating to more than two samples. These tests are considered in later chapters.

parametric tests
Hypothesis-testing procedures that assume that the variables of interest are measured on at least an interval scale.

nonparametric tests
Hypothesis-testing procedures that assume that the variables are measured on a nominal or ordinal scale.

FIGURE 15.9

Hypothesis Tests Related to Differences

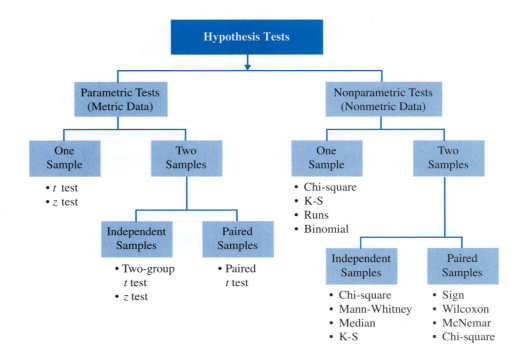

Parametric Tests

t test

A univariate hypothesis test using the *t* distribution, which is used when the standard deviation is unknown and the sample size is small.

t statistic

A statistic that assumes that the variable has a symmetric bell-shaped distribution, the mean is known (or assumed to be known), and the population variance is estimated from the sample.

t distribution

A symmetric bell-shaped distribution that is useful for small sample ($n < 30$) testing, when the mean is known and the population variance is estimated from the sample.

Parametric tests provide inferences for making statements about the means of parent populations. A *t* **test** is commonly used for this purpose. This test is based on the Student's *t* statistic. The *t* **statistic** assumes that the variable is normally distributed and the mean is known (or assumed to be known), and the population variance is estimated from the sample. Assume that the random variable X is normally distributed, with mean μ and unknown population variance σ^2, which is estimated by the sample variance s^2. Recall that the standard deviation of the sample mean, $\overline{X}$, is estimated as $s_{\overline{X}} = s/\sqrt{n}$. Then $t = (\overline{X} - \mu)/s_{\overline{X}}$ is *t* distributed with $n - 1$ degrees of freedom.

The *t* **distribution** is similar to the normal distribution in appearance. Both distributions are bell shaped and symmetric. However, as compared to the normal distribution, the *t* distribution has more area in the tails and less in the center. This is because population variance σ^2 is unknown and is estimated by the sample variance s^2. Given the uncertainty in the value of s^2, the observed values of *t* are more variable than those of *z*. Thus, we must go a larger number of standard deviations from 0 to encompass a certain percentage of values from the *t* distribution than is the case with the normal distribution. Yet, as the number of degrees of freedom increases, the *t* distribution approaches the normal distribution. In fact, for large samples of 120 or more, the *t* distribution and the normal distribution are virtually indistinguishable. Table 4 in the Statistical Appendix shows selected percentiles of the *t* distribution. Although normality is assumed, the *t* test is quite robust to departures from normality.

The procedure for hypothesis testing, for the special case when the *t* statistic is used, is as follows.

1. Formulate the null (H_0) and the alternative (H_1) hypotheses.
2. Select the appropriate formula for the *t* statistic.
3. Select a significance level, α, for testing H_0. Typically, the 0.05 level is selected.[13]
4. Take one or two samples and compute the mean and standard deviation for each sample.
5. Calculate the *t* statistic assuming H_0 is true.
6. Calculate the degrees of freedom and estimate the probability of getting a more extreme value of the statistic from Table 4. (Alternatively, calculate the critical value of the *t* statistic.)
7. If the probability computed in step 6 is smaller than the significance level selected in step 3, reject H_0. If the probability is larger, do not reject H_0. (Alternatively, if the absolute value of the calculated *t* statistic in step 5 is larger than the absolute critical value determined in step 6, reject H_0. If the absolute calculated value is smaller than the absolute critical value, do not reject H_0.) Failure to reject H_0 does not necessarily imply that H_0 is true. It only means that the true state is not significantly different from that assumed by H_0.[14]
8. Express the conclusion reached by the *t* test in terms of the marketing research problem.

One Sample

In marketing research, the researcher is often interested in making statements about a single variable against a known or given standard. Examples of such statements include: The market share for a new product will exceed 15 percent; at least 65 percent of customers will like a new package design; 80 percent of dealers will prefer the new pricing policy. These statements can be translated to null hypotheses that can be tested using a one-sample test, such as the *t* test or the *z* test. In the case of a *t* test for a single mean, the researcher is interested in testing whether the population mean conforms to a given hypothesis (H_0). For the data in Table 15.1, suppose we wanted to test the hypothesis that the mean familiarity rating exceeds 4.0, the neutral value on a 7-point scale. A significance level of $\alpha = 0.05$ is selected. The hypotheses may be formulated as:

$$H_0 : \mu \leq 4.0$$
$$H_1 : \mu > 4.0$$

$$t = \frac{(\overline{X} - \mu)}{s_{\overline{X}}}$$

$$s_{\overline{X}} = \frac{s}{\sqrt{n}}$$

$$s_{\overline{X}} = 1.579/\sqrt{29} = 1.579/5.385 = 0.293$$

$$t = (4.724 - 4.0) / 0.293 = 0.724 / 0.293 = 2.471$$

The degrees of freedom for the t statistic to test the hypothesis about one mean are $n - 1$. In this case, $n - 1 = 29 - 1$ or 28. From Table 4 in the Statistical Appendix, the probability of getting a more extreme value than 2.471 is less than 0.05. (Alternatively, the critical t value for 28 degrees of freedom and a significance level of 0.05 is 1.7011, which is less than the calculated value.) Hence, the null hypothesis is rejected. The familiarity level does exceed 4.0.

Note that if the population standard deviation was assumed to be known as 1.5, rather than estimated from the sample, a **z test** would be appropriate. In this case, the value of the z statistic would be:

$$z = (\overline{X} - \mu)/\sigma_{\overline{X}}$$

where

$$\sigma_{\overline{X}} = 1.5/\sqrt{29} = 1.5/5.385 = 0.279$$

and

$$z = (4.724 - 4.0)/0.279 = 0.724/0.279 = 2.595$$

From Table 2 in the Statistical Appendix, the probability of getting a more extreme value of z than 2.595 is less than 0.05. (Alternatively, the critical z value for a one-tailed test and a significance level of 0.05 is 1.645, which is less than the calculated value.) Therefore, the null hypothesis is rejected, reaching the same conclusion arrived at earlier by the t test.

The procedure for testing a null hypothesis with respect to a proportion for a single sample was illustrated earlier in this chapter when we introduced hypothesis testing.

Two Independent Samples

Several hypotheses in marketing relate to parameters from two different populations: for example, the users and nonusers of a brand differ in terms of their perceptions of the brand, the high-income consumers spend more on entertainment than low-income consumers, or the proportion of brand-loyal users in segment I is more than the proportion in segment II. Samples drawn randomly from different populations are termed **independent samples**. As in the case for one sample, the hypotheses could relate to means or proportions.

MEANS   In the case of means for two independent samples, the hypotheses take the following form.

$$H_0: \mu_1 = \mu_2$$
$$H_1: \mu_1 \neq \mu_2$$

The two populations are sampled and the means and variances computed based on samples of sizes n_1 and n_2. If both populations are found to have the same variance, a pooled variance estimate is computed from the two sample variances as follows:

$$s^2 = \frac{\sum_{i=1}^{n_1}(X_{i1} - \overline{X}_1)^2 + \sum_{i=1}^{n_2}(X_{i2} - \overline{X}_2)^2}{n_1 + n_2 - 2}$$

or

$$s^2 = \frac{(n_1 - 1)s_1^2 + (n_2 - 1)s_2^2}{n_1 + n_2 - 2}$$

The standard deviation of the test statistic can be estimated as:

$$s_{\overline{X}_1 - \overline{X}_2} = \sqrt{s^2\left(\frac{1}{n_1} + \frac{1}{n_2}\right)}$$

The appropriate value of t can be calculated as:

$$t = \frac{(\overline{X}_1 - \overline{X}_2) - (\mu_1 - \mu_2)}{s_{\overline{X}_1 - \overline{X}_2}}$$

The degrees of freedom in this case are $(n_1 + n_2 - 2)$.

If the two populations have unequal variances, an exact t cannot be computed for the difference in sample means. Instead, an approximation to t is computed. The number of degrees of

z test
A univariate hypothesis test using the standard normal distribution.

independent samples
Two samples that are not experimentally related. The measurement of one sample has no effect on the values of the second sample.

freedom in this case is usually not an integer, but a reasonably accurate probability can be obtained by rounding to the nearest integer.[15]

F test
A statistical test of the equality of the variances of two populations.

An **F test** of sample variance may be performed if it is not known whether the two populations have equal variance. In this case the hypotheses are:

$$H_0: \sigma_1^2 = \sigma_2^2$$
$$H_1: \sigma_1^2 \neq \sigma_2^2$$

F statistic
The F statistic is computed as the ratio of two sample variances.

The **F statistic** is computed from the sample variances as follows:

$$F_{(n_1 - 1), (n_2 - 1)} = \frac{s_1^2}{s_2^2}$$

where

$$n_1 = \text{size of sample 1}$$
$$n_2 = \text{size of sample 2}$$
$$n_1 - 1 = \text{degrees of freedom for sample 1}$$
$$n_2 - 1 = \text{degrees of freedom for sample 2}$$
$$s_1^2 = \text{sample variance for sample 1}$$
$$s_2^2 = \text{sample variance for sample 2}$$

F distribution
A frequency distribution that depends upon two sets of degrees of freedom—the degrees of freedom in the numerator and the degrees of freedom in the denominator.

As can be seen, the critical value of the **F distribution** depends upon two sets of degrees of freedom—those in the numerator and those in the denominator. The critical values of F for various degrees of freedom for the numerator and denominator are given in Table 5 of the Statistical Appendix. If the probability of F is greater than the significance level α, H_0 is not rejected, and t based on the pooled variance estimate can be used. On the other hand, if the probability of F is less than or equal to α, H_0 is rejected and t based on a separate variance estimate is used.

Using the data of Table 15.1, suppose we wanted to determine whether Internet usage was different for males as compared to females. A two-independent-samples t test was conducted. The results are presented in Table 15.14. Note that the F test of sample variances has a probability that is less than 0.05. Accordingly, H_0 is rejected, and the t test based on "equal variances not assumed" should be used. The t value is -4.492 and, with 18.014 degrees of freedom, this gives a probability of 0.000, which is less than the significance level of 0.05. Therefore, the null hypothesis of equal means is rejected. Because the mean usage for males (sex = 1) is 9.333 and that for females (sex = 2) is 3.867, we conclude that males use the Internet to a significantly greater extent than females. We also show the t test assuming equal variances because most computer programs can automatically

SPSS Output File

SAS Output File

TABLE 15.14
Two-Independent-Samples t Test

Summary Statistics			
	Number of Cases	Mean	Standard Error Mean
Male	15	9.333	1.137
Female	15	3.867	0.435

F Test for Equality of Variances	
F Value	2-Tail Probability
15.507	0.000

t Test					
Equal Variances Assumed			Equal Variances Not Assumed		
t Value	Degrees of Freedom	2-Tail Probability	t Value	Degrees of Freedom	2-Tail Probability
−4.492	28	0.000	−4.492	18.014	0.000

conduct the t test both ways. Instead of the small sample of 30, if this were a large and representative sample, there are profound implications for Internet service providers such as AOL, EarthLink, and the various telephone (e.g., Verizon) and cable (e.g., Comcast) companies. In order to target the heavy Internet users, these companies should focus on males. Thus, more advertising dollars should be spent on magazines that cater to male audiences than those that target females.

Real Research

Stores Seek to Suit Elderly to a "t"

A study based on a national sample of 789 respondents who were age 65 or older attempted to determine the effect that lack of mobility has on patronage behavior. A major research question related to the differences in the physical requirements of dependent and self-reliant elderly persons. That is, did the two groups require different things to get to the store or after they arrived at the store? A more detailed analysis of the physical requirements conducted by two-independent-sample t tests (shown in the accompanying table) indicated that dependent elderly persons are more likely to look for stores that offer home delivery and phone orders, and stores to which they have accessible transportation. They are also more likely to look for a variety of stores located close together. Retailers, now more than ever, are realizing the sales potential in the elderly market. With the baby-boomer generation nearing retirement in 2010, stores such as Wal-Mart, Coldwater Creek, and Williams-Sonoma see "the icing on the cake." The elderly shoppers are more likely to spend more money and become patrons of a store. However, to attract them, stores should offer home delivery and phone orders, and arrange accessible transportation.[16]

Differences in Physical Requirements Between Dependent and Self-Reliant Elderly

Physical Requirement Items	Mean[a]		t Test Probability
	Self-Reliant	Dependent	
Delivery to home	1.787	2.000	0.023
Phone-in order	2.030	2.335	0.003
Transportation to store	2.188	3.098	0.000
Convenient parking	4.001	4.095	0.305
Location close to home	3.177	3.325	0.137
Variety of stores close together	3.456	3.681	0.023

[a]Measured on a 5-point scale from not important (1) to very important (5). ■

In this example, we tested the difference between means. A similar test is available for testing the difference between proportions for two independent samples.

PROPORTIONS   The case involving proportions for two independent samples is also illustrated using the data of Table 15.1, which gives the number of males and females who use the Internet for shopping. Is the proportion of respondents using the Internet for shopping the same for males and females? The null and alternative hypotheses are:

$$H_0: \pi_1 = \pi_2$$
$$H_1: \pi_1 \neq \pi_2$$

A z test is used as in testing the proportion for one sample. However, in this case the test statistic is given by:

$$z = \frac{p_1 - p_2}{s_{p_1 - p_2}}$$

In the test statistic, the numerator is the difference between the proportions in the two samples, p_1 and p_2. The denominator is the standard error of the difference in the two proportions and is given by:

$$s_{p_1 - p_2} = \sqrt{p(1 - p)\left[\frac{1}{n_1} + \frac{1}{n_2}\right]}$$

where

$$p = \frac{n_1 p_1 + n_2 p_2}{n_1 + n_2}$$

A significance level of $\alpha = 0.05$ is selected. Given the data of Table 15.1, the test statistic can be calculated as:

$$p_1 - p_2 = (11/15) - (6/15)$$
$$= 0.733 - 0.400 = 0.333$$
$$p = (15 \times 0.733 + 15 \times 0.4)/(15 + 15) = 0.567$$
$$s_{p_1 - p_2} = \sqrt{0.567 \times 0.433 \left(\frac{1}{15} + \frac{1}{15}\right)} = 0.181$$
$$z = 0.333/0.181 = 1.84$$

Given a two-tail test, the area to the right of the critical value is $\alpha/2$ or 0.025. Hence, the critical value of the test statistic is 1.96. Because the calculated value is less than the critical value, the null hypothesis cannot be rejected. Thus, the proportion of users (0.733) for males and (0.400) for females is not significantly different for the two samples. Note that although the difference is substantial, it is not statistically significant due to the small sample sizes (15 in each group).

Paired Samples

paired samples
In hypothesis testing, the observations are paired so that the two sets of observations relate to the same respondents.

paired samples *t* test
A test for differences in the means of paired samples.

In many marketing research applications, the observations for the two groups are not selected from independent samples. Rather, the observations relate to **paired samples** in that the two sets of observations relate to the same respondents. A sample of respondents may rate two competing brands, indicate the relative importance of two attributes of a product, or evaluate a brand at two different times. The difference in these cases is examined by a **paired samples *t* test**. To compute *t* for paired samples, the paired difference variable, denoted by *D,* is formed and its mean and variance calculated. Then the *t* statistic is computed. The degrees of freedom are $n - 1$, where *n* is the number of pairs. The relevant formulas are:

$$H_0: \mu_D = 0$$
$$H_1: \mu_D \neq 0$$
$$t_{n-1} = \frac{\overline{D} - \mu_D}{\dfrac{s_D}{\sqrt{n}}}$$

where

$$\overline{D} = \frac{\displaystyle\sum_{i=1}^{n} D_i}{n}$$

$$s_D = \sqrt{\frac{\displaystyle\sum_{i=1}^{n}(D_i - \overline{D})^2}{n-1}}$$

$$s_{\overline{D}} = \frac{s_D}{\sqrt{n}}$$

In the Internet usage example (Table 15.1), a paired *t* test could be used to determine if the respondents differed in their attitude toward the Internet and attitude toward technology. The resulting output is shown in Table 15.15. The mean attitude toward the Internet is 5.167 and that toward technology is 4.10. The mean difference between the variables is 1.067, with a standard deviation of 0.828 and a standard error of 0.1511. This results in a *t* value of (1.067/0.1511) 7.06, with $30 - 1 = 29$ degrees of freedom and a probability of less than 0.001. Therefore, the respondents have a more favorable attitude toward the Internet as compared to technology in general. An implication, if this were a large and representative sample, would be that Internet service providers should not hesitate to market their services to consumers who do not have a very positive attitude toward technology and do not consider

SPSS Output File

SAS Output File

TABLE 15.15					
Paired Samples *t* Test					
Variable	Number of Cases	Mean		Standard Deviation	Standard Error
Internet Attitude	30	5.167		1.234	0.225
Technology Attitude	30	4.100		1.398	0.255

Difference = Internet − Technology

Difference Mean	Standard Deviation	Standard Error	Correlation	2-Tail Probability	*t* Value	Degrees of Freedom	2-Tail Probability
1.067	0.828	0.1511	0.809	0.000	7.059	29	0.000

themselves to be technologically savvy. Another application is provided in the context of determining the relative effectiveness of 15-second versus 30-second television commercials.

Real Research

Seconds Count

A survey of 83 media directors of the largest Canadian advertising agencies was conducted to determine the relative effectiveness of 15-second versus 30-second commercial advertisements. Using a 5-point rating scale (1 being excellent and 5 being poor), 15- and 30-second commercials were rated by each respondent for brand awareness, main idea recall, persuasion, and ability to tell an emotional story. The accompanying table indicates that 30-second commercials were rated more favorably on all the dimensions. Paired *t* tests indicated that these differences were significant, and the 15-second commercials were evaluated as less effective. Thus, 15-second commercials may not be the answer marketers are looking for. Actually, today, the problem may not be how effective television commercials are, but whether the consumers actually will be watching the commercials. One in five users never watched a commercial in 2008, and there is a threat that this number will increase in the future. Heavy advertisers such as General Motors will have to come up with more effective and creative ways to show their commercials.[17]

Mean Rating of 15- and 30-Second Commercials on the Four Communication Variables

Brand Awareness		Main Idea Recall		Persuasion		Ability to Tell Emotional Story	
15	*30*	*15*	*30*	*15*	*30*	*15*	*30*
2.5	1.9	2.7	2.0	3.7	2.1	4.3	1.9 ■

The difference in proportions for paired samples can be tested by using the McNemar test or the chi-square test, as explained in the following section on nonparametric tests.

ACTIVE RESEARCH

Users and Nonusers: Are Their Evaluations of Reebok Different?

Visit www.reebok.com and conduct an Internet search using a search engine and your library's online database to obtain information on the factors consumers use to evaluate competing brands of athletic shoes.

As the marketing director for Reebok, how would you improve the image and competitive positioning of your brand?

The users and nonusers of Reebok evaluated the brand on five factors using Likert-type scales. How would you analyze these data using two independent samples and paired samples *t* tests?

Nonparametric Tests

Nonparametric tests are used when the independent variables are nonmetric. Like parametric tests, nonparametric tests are available for testing variables from one sample, two independent samples, or two related samples.

One Sample

Kolmogorov-Smirnov (K-S) one-sample test
A one-sample nonparametric goodness-of-fit test that compares the cumulative distribution function for a variable with a specified distribution.

Sometimes the researcher wants to test whether the observations for a particular variable could reasonably have come from a particular distribution, such as the normal, uniform, or Poisson distribution. Knowledge of the distribution is necessary for finding probabilities corresponding to known values of the variable or variable values corresponding to known probabilities (see Appendix 12A). The **Kolmogorov-Smirnov (K-S) one-sample test** is one such goodness-of-fit test. The K-S compares the cumulative distribution function for a variable with a specified distribution. A_i denotes the cumulative relative frequency for each category of the theoretical (assumed) distribution, and O_i the comparable value of the sample frequency. The K-S test is based on the maximum value of the absolute difference between A_i and O_i. The test statistic is:

$$K = \text{Max} \,|A_i - O_i|$$

The decision to reject the null hypothesis is based on the value of K. The larger the K is, the more confidence we have that H_0 is false. For $\alpha = 0.05$, the critical value of K for large samples (over 35) is given by $1.36/\sqrt{n}$.[18] Alternatively, K can be transformed into a normally distributed z statistic and its associated probability determined.

In the context of the Internet usage example, suppose we wanted to test whether the distribution of Internet usage was normal. A K-S one-sample test is conducted, yielding the data shown in Table 15.16. The largest absolute difference between the observed and normal distribution was $K = 0.222$. Although our sample size is only 30 (less than 35), we can use the approximate formula and the critical value for K is $1.36/\sqrt{30} = 0.248$. Because the calculated value of K is smaller than the critical value, the null hypothesis cannot be rejected. Alternatively, Table 15.16 indicates that the probability of observing a K value of 0.222, as determined by the normalized z statistic, is 0.103. Because this is more than the significance level of 0.05, the null hypothesis cannot be rejected, leading to the same conclusion. Hence, the distribution of Internet usage does not deviate significantly from the normal distribution. The implication is that we are safe in using statistical tests (e.g., the z test) and procedures that assume the normality of this variable.

runs test
A test of randomness for a dichotomous variable.

binomial test
A goodness-of-fit statistical test for dichotomous variables. It tests the goodness of fit of the observed number of observations in each category to the number expected under a specified binomial distribution.

As mentioned earlier, the chi-square test can also be performed on a single variable from one sample. In this context, the chi-square serves as a goodness-of-fit test. It tests whether a significant difference exists between the observed number of cases in each category and the expected number. Other one-sample nonparametric tests include the runs test and the binomial test. The **runs test** is a test of randomness for the dichotomous variables. This test is conducted by determining whether the order or sequence in which observations are obtained is random. The **binomial test** is also a goodness-of-fit test for dichotomous variables. It tests the goodness of fit of the observed number of observations in each category to the number expected under a specified binomial distribution. For more information on these tests, refer to standard statistical literature.[19]

Two Independent Samples

Mann-Whitney U test
A statistical test for a variable measured on an ordinal scale, comparing the difference in the location of two populations based on observations from two independent samples.

When the difference in the location of two populations is to be compared based on observations from two independent samples, and the variable is measured on an ordinal scale, the **Mann-Whitney U test** can be used.[20] This test corresponds to the two-independent-sample t test for interval scale variables, when the variances of the two populations are assumed equal.

SPSS Output File

SAS Output File

TABLE 15.16				
K-S One-Sample Test for Normality for Internet Usage				
Test Distribution—Normal				
Mean:		6.600		
Standard Deviation:		4.296		
Cases:		30		
Most Extreme Differences				
Absolute	Positive	Negative	K-S z	2-tailed p
0.222	0.222	−0.142	1.217	0.103

SPSS Output File

SAS Output File

TABLE 15.17
Mann-Whitney *U* Test

Mann-Whitney *U*—Wilcoxon Rank Sum *W* Test Internet Usage by Sex		
Sex	Mean Rank	Cases
Male	20.93	15
Female	10.07	15
Total		30

U	*W*	*z*	Corrected for Ties 2-tailed *p*
31.000	151.000	−3.406	0.001

Note:
U = Mann-Whitney test statistic
W = Wilcoxon *W* statistic
z = *U* transformed into a normally distributed *z* statistic

In the Mann-Whitney *U* test, the two samples are combined and the cases are ranked in order of increasing size. The test statistic, *U*, is computed as the number of times a score from sample 1 or group 1 precedes a score from group 2. If the samples are from the same population, the distribution of scores from the two groups in the rank list should be random. An extreme value of *U* would indicate a nonrandom pattern, pointing to the inequality of the two groups. For samples of less than 30, the exact significance level for *U* is computed. For larger samples, *U* is transformed into a normally distributed *z* statistic. This *z* can be corrected for ties within ranks.

We examine again the difference in the Internet usage of males and females. This time, though, the Mann-Whitney *U* test is used. The results are given in Table 15.17. Again, a significant difference is found between the two groups, corroborating the results of the two-independent-samples *t* test reported earlier. Because the ranks are assigned from the smallest observation to the largest, the higher mean rank (20.93) of males indicates that they use the Internet to a greater extent than females (mean rank = 10.07).

Researchers often wish to test for a significant difference in proportions obtained from two independent samples. As an alternative to the parametric *z* test considered earlier, one could also use the cross-tabulation procedure to conduct a chi-square test.[21] In this case, we will have a 2 × 2 table. One variable will be used to denote the sample and will assume the value 1 for sample 1 and the value of 2 for sample 2. The other variable will be the binary variable of interest.

two-sample median test
Nonparametric test statistic that determines whether two groups are drawn from populations with the same median. This test is not as powerful as the Mann-Whitney *U*.

Two other independent-samples nonparametric tests are the median test and Kolmogorov-Smirnov test. The **two-sample median test** determines whether the two groups are drawn from populations with the same median. It is not as powerful as the Mann-Whitney *U* test because it merely uses the location of each observation relative to the median, and not the rank, of each observation. The **Kolmogorov-Smirnov two-sample test** examines whether the two distributions are the same. It takes into account any differences between the two distributions, including the median, dispersion, and skewness, as illustrated by the following example.

Kolmogorov-Smirnov two-sample test
Nonparametric test statistic that determines whether two distributions are the same. It takes into account any differences in the two distributions, including median, dispersion, and skewness.

Real Research

Directors Change Direction

How do marketing research directors and users in *Fortune* 500 manufacturing firms perceive the role of marketing research in initiating changes in marketing strategy formulation? It was found that the marketing research directors were more strongly in favor of initiating changes in strategy and less in favor of holding back than were users of marketing research. The percentage responses to one of the items, "Initiate change in the marketing strategy of the firm whenever possible," are given in the following table. Using the Kolmogorov-Smirnov (K-S) test, these differences of role definition were statistically significant at the 0.05 level, as shown in the table.

The users of marketing research became even more reluctant to initiate marketing strategy changes during the uncertain economy of 2009. In today's business climate, however, the reluctance of these marketing research users must be overcome to help gain a better understanding of the buyer's power. Thus, marketing research firms should devote considerable effort in convincing the users (generally, the marketing managers) of the value of marketing research.[22]

The Role of Marketing Research in Strategy Formulation

		Responses (%)				
Sample	N	Absolutely Must	Preferably Should	May or May Not	Preferably Should Not	Absolutely Must Not
D	77	7	26	43	19	5
U	68	2	15	32	35	16

K-S significance = 0.05
*D = directors, U = users ∎

In this example, the marketing research directors and users comprised two independent samples. However, the samples are not always independent. In the case of paired samples, a different set of tests should be used.

Paired Samples

Wilcoxon matched-pairs signed-ranks test
A nonparametric test that analyzes the differences between the paired observations, taking into account the magnitude of the differences.

An important nonparametric test for examining differences in the location of two populations based on paired observations is the **Wilcoxon matched-pairs signed-ranks test**. This test analyzes the differences between the paired observations, taking into account the magnitude of the differences. So it requires that the data are measured at an interval level of measurement. However it does not require assumptions about the form of the distribution of the measurements. It should therefore be used whenever the distributional assumptions that underlie the t test cannot be satisfied. This test computes the differences between the pairs of variables and ranks the absolute differences. The next step is to sum the positive and negative ranks. The test statistic, z, is computed from the positive and negative rank sums. Under the null hypothesis of no difference, z is a standard normal variate with mean 0 and variance 1 for large samples. This test corresponds to the paired t test considered earlier.[23]

The example considered for the paired t test, whether the respondents differed in terms of attitude toward the Internet and attitude toward technology, is considered again. Suppose we assume that both these variables are measured on ordinal rather than interval scales. Accordingly, we use the Wilcoxon test. The results are shown in Table 15.18. Again, a significant difference is found in the variables, and the results are in accordance with the conclusion reached by the paired t test. There are 23 negative differences (attitude toward technology is less favorable than attitude toward Internet). The mean rank of these negative differences is 12.72. On the other hand, there is only one positive difference (attitude toward technology is more favorable than attitude toward Internet). The mean rank of this difference is 7.50. There are six ties, or observations with the same value for both variables. These numbers indicate that the attitude toward the Internet is more favorable than toward technology. Furthermore, the probability associated with the z statistic is less than 0.05, indicating that the difference is indeed significant.

SPSS Output File

SAS Output File

TABLE 15.18
Wilcoxon Matched-Pairs Signed-Rank Test

Internet with Technology		
(Technology—Internet)	Cases	Mean Rank
− Ranks	23	12.72
+ Ranks	1	7.50
Ties	6	
Total	30	
$z = -4.207$		2-tailed $p = 0.0000$

Decision Research General Mills' Curves Cereal: Helping Women Achieve Their Curves

The Situation

Stephen W. Sanger, CEO of General Mills (www.generalmills.com), is constantly faced with the challenge of how to keep up with consumers' changing tastes and preferences. General Mills recently conducted thorough focus-group research on the most important consumers in grocery stores today: women. It is a known fact that three out of every four grocery shoppers in the United States are women, and many of these women are focusing more on their health and the nutritious value of foods. Although there are many cereals on the market with the same amount of valuable vitamins and minerals, such as Total or Kellogg's Smart Start, General Mills decided to design a product specifically for women.

Dietician Roberta Duyff claims that women do not get enough nutrients such as calcium or folic acid from day to day. According to Duyff, "It is great that a woman can now increase her intake of these important nutrients with a simple bowl of cereal for breakfast, and if you add milk, the vitamin D in milk makes the calcium in both the fortified cereal and milk itself more absorbable." This is one way in which General Mills saw an advantage—convenience for the woman. She can grab a bowl in the morning and start off her day with the nutrients she needs. Not only is the convenience of the product an incentive to market it, but focus group findings also indicated that women like to have a product of their own. In fact, according to Megan Nightingale, assistant marketing manager at General Mills, "Our research has shown that women are looking for something that's nutritious, fast, convenient, and has a good taste."

In 2007, General Mills, in partnership with Curves International, launched the Curves Cereal. This new cereal of lightly sweetened toasted flakes of whole grain rice and wheat is available in two delicious flavors, Whole Grain Crunch and Honey Crunch. Both have fewer than 200 calories per serving and contain at least 33 percent of the recommended amounts of whole grains and 2 grams of fiber. They also are an excellent source of several important vitamins and minerals.

A telephone survey was conducted to determine the preference for and consumption of Curves and the relative importance that women attached to a cereal being nutritious, fast, convenient, and good tasting.

The Marketing Research Decision

1. What is the relative importance of the four variables (nutritious, fast, convenient, and good taste) in influencing women to buy Curves Cereal? What type of analysis should be conducted?
    a. Frequency distribution of the importance attached to the four factors
    b. Mean levels of importance of the four variables
    c. Cross-tabulation of Curves Cereal purchases with the importance of the four variables: chi-square analysis
    d. Cross-tabulation of Curves Cereal purchases with the importance of the four variables: Cramer's V
    e. All of the above
2. Discuss the role of the type of data analysis you recommend in enabling Stephen W. Sanger to understand women's preference for and consumption of Curves Cereal.

The Marketing Management Decision

1. Advertising for Curves Cereal should stress which of the four factors?
    a. Nutrition
    b. Quick consumption
    c. Convenience
    d. Good taste
    e. All of the above
2. Discuss how the management decision action that you recommend to Stephen W. Sanger is influenced by the type of data analysis you suggested earlier and by the findings of that analysis.[24] ■

sign test

A nonparametric test for examining differences in the location of two populations, based on paired observations, that compares only the signs of the differences between pairs of variables without taking into account the ranks.

Another paired sample nonparametric test is the **sign test**.[25] This test is not as powerful as the Wilcoxon matched-pairs signed-ranks test, as it compares only the signs of the differences between pairs of variables without taking into account the ranks. In the special case of a binary variable where the researcher wishes to test differences in proportions, the McNemar test can be used. Alternatively, the chi-square test can also be used for binary variables. The various parametric and nonparametric tests for differences are summarized in Table 15.19. The tests in Table 15.19 can be easily related to those in Figure 15.9. Table 15.19 classifies the tests in more detail because parametric tests (based on metric data) are classified separately for means and proportions. Likewise, nonparametric tests

Frequency distribution, cross-tabulation, and hypothesis testing can help General Mills understand women's cereal preferences and develop appropriate advertising.

TABLE 15.19

A Summary of Hypothesis Tests Related to Differences

Sample	Application	Level of Scaling	Test/Comments
One Sample			
One sample	Distributions	Nonmetric	K-S and chi-square for goodness of fit
			Runs test for randomness
			Binomial test for goodness of fit for dichotomous variables
One sample	Means	Metric	t test, if variance is unknown
			z test, if variance is known
One Sample	Proportions	Metric	z test
Two Independent Samples			
Two independent samples	Distributions	Nonmetric	K-S two-sample test for examining the equivalence of two distributions
Two independent samples	Means	Metric	Two-group t test
			F test for equality of variances
Two independent samples	Proportions	Metric	z test
		Nonmetric	Chi-square test
Two independent samples	Rankings/Medians	Nonmetric	Mann-Whitney U test is more powerful than the median test
Paired Samples			
Paired samples	Means	Metric	Paired t test
Paired samples	Proportions	Nonmetric	McNemar test for binary variables
			Chi-square test
Paired samples	Rankings/Medians	Nonmetric	Wilcoxon matched-pairs ranked-signs test is more powerful than the sign test

(based on nonmetric data) are classified separately for distributions and rankings/medians. The next example illustrates the use of hypothesis testing in international branding strategy, and the example after that cites the use of descriptive statistics in research on ethics.

Real Research   International Brand Equity—The Name of the Game

In the 2000s, the trend is toward global marketing. How can marketers market a brand abroad where there exist diverse historical and cultural differences? In general, a firm's international brand structure includes firm-based characteristics, product market characteristics, and market dynamics. More specifically, according to Bob Kroll, the former president of Del Monte International, uniform packaging may be an asset to marketing internationally, yet catering to individual countries' culinary taste preferences is more important. One recent survey on international product marketing makes this clear. Marketing executives now believe it is best to think globally but act locally. Respondents included 100 brand and product managers and marketing people from some of the nation's largest food, pharmaceutical, and personal product companies. Thirty-nine percent said that it would not be a good idea to use uniform packaging in foreign markets, whereas 38 percent were in favor of it. Those in favor of regionally targeted packaging, however, mentioned the desirability of maintaining as much brand equity and package consistency as possible from market to market. But they also believed it was necessary to tailor the package to fit the linguistic and regulatory needs of different markets. Based on this finding, a suitable research question can be: Do consumers in different countries prefer to buy global name brands with different packaging customized to suit their local needs? Based on this research question, one can frame a hypothesis that, other things being constant, standardized branding with customized packaging for a well-established name brand will result in greater market share. The hypotheses may be formulated as follows:

H_0: Standardized branding with customized packaging for a well-established name brand will not lead to greater market share in the international market.

H_1: Other factors remaining equal, standardized branding with customized packaging for a well-established name brand will lead to greater market share in the international market.

To test the null hypothesis, a well-established brand such as Colgate toothpaste, which has followed a mixed strategy, can be selected. The market share in countries with standardized branding and standardized packaging can be compared with market share in countries with standardized branding and customized packaging, after controlling for the effect of other factors. A two-independent-samples t test can be used.[26] ■

Real Research

Statistics Describe Distrust

Descriptive statistics indicate that the public perception of ethics in business, and thus ethics in marketing, is poor. In a poll conducted by *Business Week*, 46 percent of those surveyed said that the ethical standards of business executives are only fair. A *Time* magazine survey revealed that 76 percent of Americans felt that business managers (and thus researchers) lacked ethics and that this lack contributes to the decline of moral standards in the United States. However, the general public is not alone in its disparagement of business ethics. In a Touche Ross survey of businesspeople, results showed that the general feeling was that ethics were a serious concern and media portrayal of the lack of ethics in business has not been exaggerated. However, a recent research study conducted by the Ethics Resource Center of Washington, D.C., found that 90 percent of American businesspeople expected their organization to do what is right, not just what is profitable. Twelve percent of those polled said they felt pressure to compromise their organization's ethical standards. Twenty-six percent of those polled cited the most common ethical slip in the workplace to be lying to customers, other employees, vendors, or the public, whereas 25 percent cited withholding needed information from those parties. A mere 5 percent of those polled have seen people giving or taking bribes or inappropriate gifts. Despite the fact that American businesspeople expect their organization to conduct business in an ethical manner, these studies reveal that unethical behavior remains a common practice in the workplace.[27] ■

Statistical Software

We discuss the use of SPSS and SAS in detail in the subsequent sections. Here, we briefly describe the use of MINITAB and EXCEL. In MINITAB, the main function for frequencies is Stats>Descriptive Statistics. The output values include the mean, median, standard deviation, minimum, maximum, and quartiles. Histograms in a bar chart or graph can be produced from the Graph>Histogram selection. Several of the spreadsheets can also be used to obtain frequencies and descriptive statistics. In Excel, the Data>Data Analysis function computes the descriptive statistics. The output produces the mean, standard error, median, mode, standard deviation, variance, kurtosis, skewness, range, minimum, maximum, sum, count, and confidence level. Frequencies can be selected under the Histogram function. A histogram can be produced in bar format.

In MINITAB, cross-tabulations (cross-tabs) and chi-square are under the Stats>Tables function. Each of these features must be selected separately under the Tables function. The Data>Pivot Table function performs cross-tabs in EXCEL. To do additional analysis or customize data, select a different summary function such as max, min, average, or standard deviation. In addition, a custom calculation can be selected to perform values based on other cells in the data plane. ChiTest can be accessed under the Insert>Function>Statistical>ChiTest function.

Parametric tests available in MINITAB in descriptive stat function are z test mean, t test of the mean, and two-sample t test. The nonparametric tests can be accessed under the Stat>Time Series function. The output includes the one-sample sign, one-sample Wilcoxon, Mann-Whitney, Kruskal-Wallis, Mood's Median test, Friedman, runs test, pairwise average, pairwise differences, and pairwise slopes. The available parametric tests in EXCEL and other spreadsheets include the t test: paired two sample for means; t test: two independent samples assuming equal variances; t test: two independent samples assuming unequal variances; z test: two samples for means; and F test: two samples for variances. Nonparametric tests are not available.

SPSS and SAS Computerized Demonstration Movies

We have developed computerized demonstration movies that give step-by-step instructions for running all the SPSS and SAS Learning Edition programs that are discussed in this chapter. These demonstrations can be downloaded from the Web site for this book. The instructions for running these demonstrations are given in Exhibit 14.2.

SPSS and SAS Screen Captures with Notes

The step-by-step instructions for running the various SPSS and SAS Learning Edition programs discussed in this chapter are also illustrated in screen captures with appropriate notes. These screen captures can be downloaded from the Web site for this book.

SPSS Windows

The main program in SPSS is FREQUENCIES. It produces a table of frequency counts, percentages, and cumulative percentages for the values of each variable. It gives all of the associated statistics. If the data are interval scaled and only the summary statistics are desired, the DESCRIPTIVES procedure can be used. All of the statistics computed by DESCRIPTIVES are available in FREQUENCIES. However, DESCRIPTIVES is more efficient because it does not sort values into a frequency table. Moreover, the DESCRIPTIVES procedure displays summary statistics for several variables in a single table and can also calculate standardized values (z scores). The EXPLORE procedure produces summary statistics and graphical displays, either for all the cases or separately for groups of cases. Mean, median, variance, standard deviation, minimum, maximum, and range are some of the statistics that can be calculated.

To select these procedures, click:

Analyze>Descriptive Statistics>Frequencies

Analyze>Descriptive Statistics>Descriptives

Analyze>Descriptive Statistics>Explore

We give detailed steps for running frequencies on Familiarity with the Internet (Table 15.1) and plotting the histogram (Figure 15.1).

1. Select ANALYZE on the SPSS menu bar.
2. Click DESCRIPTIVE STATISTICS and select FREQUENCIES.
3. Move the variable "Familiarity [familiar]" to the VARIABLE(s) box.
4. Click STATISTICS.
5. Select MEAN, MEDIAN, MODE, STD. DEVIATION, VARIANCE, and RANGE.
6. Click CONTINUE.
7. Click CHARTS.
8. Click HISTOGRAMS, then click CONTINUE.
9. Click OK.

The major cross-tabulation program is CROSSTABS. This program will display the cross-classification tables and provide cell counts, row and column percentages, the chi-square test for significance, and all the measures of the strength of the association that have been discussed.

To select these procedures, click:

Analyze>Descriptive Statistics>Crosstabs

We give detailed steps for running the cross-tabulation of sex and usage of the Internet given in Table 15.3 and calculating the chi-square, contingency coefficient, and Cramer's *V*.

1. Select ANALYZE on the SPSS menu bar.
2. Click on DESCRIPTIVE STATISTICS and select CROSSTABS.
3. Move the variable "Internet Usage Group [iusagegr]" to the ROW(S) box.
4. Move the variable "Sex[sex]" to the COLUMN(S) box.
5. Click on CELLS.
6. Select OBSERVED under COUNTS and COLUMN under PERCENTAGES.
7. Click CONTINUE.
8. Click STATISTICS.
9. Click on CHI-SQUARE, PHI, and CRAMER'S *V*.
10. Click CONTINUE.
11. Click OK.

The major program for conducting parametric tests in SPSS is COMPARE MEANS. This program can be used to conduct *t* tests on one sample or independent or paired samples. To select these procedures using SPSS for Windows, click:

Analyze>Compare Means>Means . . .

Analyze>Compare Means>One-Sample T Test . . .

Analyze>Compare Means>Independent-Samples T Test . . .

Analyze>Compare Means>Paired-Samples T Test . . .

We give the detailed steps for running a one-sample test on the data of Table 15.1. We wanted to test the hypothesis that the mean familiarity rating exceeds 4.0. The null hypothesis is that the mean familiarity rating is less than or equal to 4.0.

1. Select ANALYZE from the SPSS menu bar.
2. Click COMPARE MEANS and then ONE SAMPLE T TEST.
3. Move "Familiarity [familiar]" into the TEST VARIABLE(S) box.
4. Type "4" in the TEST VALUE box.
5. Click OK.

We give the detailed steps for running a two-independent-samples *t* test on the data of Table 15.1. The null hypothesis is that the Internet usage for males and females is the same.

1. Select ANALYZE from the SPSS menu bar.
2. Click COMPARE MEANS and then INDEPENDENT SAMPLES T TEST.
3. Move "Internet Usage Hrs/Week [iusage]" into the TEST VARIABLE(S) box.
4. Move "Sex[sex]" to the GROUPING VARIABLE box.
5. Click DEFINE GROUPS.
6. Type "1" in box GROUP 1 and "2" in box GROUP 2.
7. Click CONTINUE.
8. Click OK.

We give the detailed steps for running a paired samples *t* test on the data of Table 15.1. The null hypothesis is that there is no difference in the attitude toward the Internet and attitude toward technology.

1. Select ANALYZE from the SPSS menu bar.
2. Click COMPARE MEANS and then PAIRED SAMPLES T TEST.
3. Select "Attitude toward Internet [iattitude]" and then select "Attitude toward technology [tattitude]". Move these variables into the PAIRED VARIABLE(S) box.
4. Click OK.

The nonparametric tests discussed in this chapter can be conducted using NONPARAMETRIC TESTS. To select these procedures using SPSS for Windows, click:

Analyze>Nonparametric Tests>Chi-Square . . .

Analyze>Nonparametric Tests>Binomial . . .

Analyze>Nonparametric Tests>Runs . . .

Analyze>Nonparametric Tests>1-Sample K-S . . .

Analyze>Nonparametric Tests>2 Independent Samples . . .

Analyze>Nonparametric Tests>2 Related Samples . . .

The detailed steps for the nonparametric tests are similar to those for parametric tests and are not shown due to space constraints.

SAS Learning Edition

The instructions given here and in all the data analysis chapters (14 to 22) will work with the SAS Learning Edition as well as with the SAS Enterprise Guide. The Summary Statistics task provides summary statistics including basic summary statistics, percentile summary statistics, and more advanced summary statistics including confidence intervals, t statistics, coefficient of variation, and sums of squares. It also provides graphical displays including histograms and box-and-whisker plots. The One-Way Frequencies task can be used to generate frequency tables as well as binomial and chi-square tests.

To select these tasks, click:

Describe>Summary Statistics

Describe>One-Way Frequencies

We give detailed steps for running frequencies on Familiarity with the Internet and plotting the histogram.

1. Select DESCRIBE on the SAS Learning Edition menu bar.
2. Click SUMMARY STATISTICS.
3. Move the variable "FAMILIARITY" to the Analysis variables role.
4. Click BASIC.
5. Select MEAN, STANDARD DEVIATION, VARIANCE, and RANGE.
6. Click PLOTS.
7. Click HISTOGRAM.
8. Click RUN.

The major cross-tabulation task is called TABLE ANALYSIS. This task will display the cross-classification table and provide cell counts, row and column percentages, the chi-square test for significance, and all the measures of strength of the association that have been discussed.

To select this task, click:

Describe>Table Analysis

We give detailed steps for running the cross-tabulation of sex and usage of the Internet given in Table 15.3 and calculating the chi-square, contingency coefficient, and Cramer's *V*.

1. Select DESCRIBE from the SAS Learning Edition menu bar.
2. Click TABLE ANALYSIS.
3. Move the variables "IUSAGEGROUP" and "SEX" to the Table variables role.
4. Click TABLES.
5. Move "SEX" and then "IUSAGEGROUP".
6. Click CELL STATISTICS.
7. Select COLUMN PERCENTAGES and CELL FREQUENCIES.
8. Click ASSOCIATION under TABLE STATISTICS.
9. Click CHI_SQUARE TESTS under TESTS OF ASSOCIATION.
10. Click RUN.

The major task for conducting parametric tests in SAS Learning Edition is T TEST. This task can be used to conduct t tests on one sample or independent or paired samples. To select this task using SAS Learning Edition, click:

Analyze>ANOVA>t Test

We give the detailed steps for running a one-sample test on the data of Table 15.1. We wanted to test the hypothesis that the mean familiarity ratings exceed 4.0. The null hypothesis is that the mean familiarity rating is less than or equal to 4.0.

1. Select ANALYZE from the SAS Learning Edition menu bar.
2. Click ANOVA and then T TEST.
3. Click ONE SAMPLE.
4. Click TASK ROLES.
5. Move FAMILIARITY to the Analysis variables role.
6. Click ANALYSIS.
7. Enter "4" into the Null Hypothesis field.
8. Click RUN.

We give the detailed steps for running a two-independent-samples *t* test on the data of Table 15.1. The null hypothesis is that the Internet usage for males and females is the same.

1. Select ANALYZE from the SAS Learning Edition menu bar.
2. Click ANOVA and then T TEST.
3. Click TWO SAMPLE.
4. Click TASK ROLES.
5. Move "IUSAGE" to the Analysis variables role.
6. Move "SEX" to the Group by role.
7. Click RUN.

We give the detailed steps for running a paired samples *t* test on the data of Table 15.1. The null hypothesis is that there is no difference in the attitude toward the Internet and attitude toward technology.

1. Select ANALYZE from the SAS Learning Edition menu bar.
2. Click ANOVA and then T TEST.
3. Click PAIRED.
4. Click TASK ROLES.
5. Move "IATTITUDE" and "TATTITUDE" to the Paired variables role.
6. Click RUN.

The nonparametric tests discussed in this chapter can be conducted as follows.

Nonparametric one sample test (Kolmogorov-Smirnov one sample test)

1. Select DESCRIBE from the SAS Learning Edition menu bar.
2. Click DISTRIBUTION ANALYSIS.
3. Click TASK ROLES.
4. Move "IUSAGE" to the ANALYSIS variable role.
5. Click TABLES.
6. Check on TESTS FOR NORMALITY.
7. Click RUN.

Note that you check TEST FOR NORMALITY if you want a one-way test of distribution. If you want a nonparametric test for location, perform the same steps above except select TEST FOR LOCATION in Step 6. In addition to the (parametric) *t*-test, you will get the Sign Test and the Wilcoxon Signed Rank Test (also known as the Mann Whitney test).

Nonparametric two independent samples (Wilcoxon test which is also known as the Mann-Whitney test)

1. Select ANALYZE from the SAS Learning Edition menu bar.
2. Click ANOVA and then NONPARAMETRIC ONE-WAY ANOVA.
3. Click TASK ROLES.
4. Move "IUSAGE" to the Dependent variable role.
5. Move "SEX" to the Independent variable role.
6. Click ANALYSIS.
7. Click WILCOXON.
8. Click RUN.

Nonparametric two paired samples (Wilcoxon matched-pairs signed-ranks test)

Create a "difference score" that is calculated as DIFF=IATTITUDE-TATTITUDE and then use one sample method to analyze DIFF:

1. Select DESCRIBE from the SAS Learning Edition menu bar.
2. Click DISTRIBUTION ANALYSIS.
3. Click TASK ROLES.
4. Move "DIFF" to the ANALYSIS variable role.
5. Click TABLES.
6. Check on TESTS FOR NORMALITY
7. Click RUN.

Project Research   Basic Data Analysis
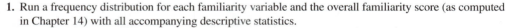

In the department store project, basic data analysis formed the foundation for conducting subsequent multivariate analysis. Data analysis began by obtaining a frequency distribution and descriptive statistics for each variable. In addition to identifying possible problems with the data (see Chapter 14), this information provided a good feel for the data and insights into how specific variables should be treated in subsequent analyses. For example, should some variables be treated as categorical, and, if so, how many categories should there be? Several two- and three-variable cross-tabulations were also conducted to identify associations in the data. The effects of variables with two categories on the metric dependent variables of interest were examined by means of *t* tests and other hypothesis-testing procedures.

Project Activities

SPSS Data File

SAS Data File

Download the SPSS or SAS data file *Sears Data 14* from the Web site for this book. See Chapter 14 for a description of this file.

1. Run a frequency distribution for each familiarity variable and the overall familiarity score (as computed in Chapter 14) with all accompanying descriptive statistics.
2. Recode the overall familiarity score as follows: 32 or less = 1; 33 to 37 = 2; 38 to 43 = 3; 44 to 60 = 4. Run cross-tabs of the recoded overall familiarity score with demographic variables as recoded in Chapter 14. Interpret the results.
3. Test the null hypothesis that the average overall familiarity score is less than or equal to 30.
4. Do a parametric and a corresponding nonparametric test to determine whether the married and not married (recoded marital status) differ in their overall familiarity score.
5. Do a parametric and a corresponding nonparametric test to determine whether the respondents differ in their familiarity with Neiman Marcus and JCPenney. ■

Summary

Basic data analysis provides valuable insights and guides the rest of the data analysis as well as the interpretation of the results. A frequency distribution should be obtained for each variable in the data. This analysis produces a table of frequency counts, percentages, and cumulative percentages for all the values associated with that variable. It indicates the extent of out-of-range, missing, or extreme values. The mean, mode, and median of a frequency distribution are measures of central tendency. The variability of the distribution is described by the range, the variance or standard deviation, coefficient of variation, and interquartile range. Skewness and kurtosis provide an idea of the shape of the distribution. Figure 15.10 gives a concept map for frequency distribution.

The general procedure for hypothesis testing involves eight steps. Formulate the null and the alternative hypotheses, select an appropriate test statistic, choose the level of significance (α), calculate the value of the test statistic, and determine the probability associated with the test statistic calculated from the sample data under the null hypothesis. Alternatively, determine the critical value associated with the test statistic. Compare the probability associated with the test statistic with the level of significance specified or, alternatively, determine whether the calculated value of the test statistic falls into the rejection or the nonrejection region. Accordingly, make the decision to reject or not reject the null hypothesis, and arrive at a conclusion.

Cross-tabulations are tables that reflect the joint distribution of two or more variables. In cross-tabulation, the percentages can be computed either columnwise, based on column totals, or rowwise, based on row totals. The

FIGURE 15.10

A Concept Map for Frequency Analysis

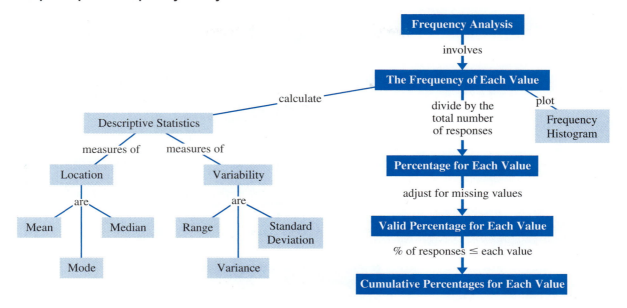

general rule is to compute the percentages in the direction of the independent variable, across the dependent variable. Often the introduction of a third variable can provide additional insights. The chi-square statistic provides a test of the statistical significance of the observed association in a cross-tabulation. The phi coefficient, contingency coefficient, Cramer's *V,* and the lambda coefficient provide measures of the strength of association between the variables. Figure 15.11 presents a concept map for cross-tabulation.

Parametric and nonparametric tests are available for testing hypotheses related to differences. In the parametric case, the *t* test is used to examine hypotheses related to the population mean. Different forms of the *t* test are suitable for testing hypotheses based on one sample, two independent samples, or paired samples. Figure 15.12 shows a concept

FIGURE 15.11

A Concept Map for Cross-Tabulation

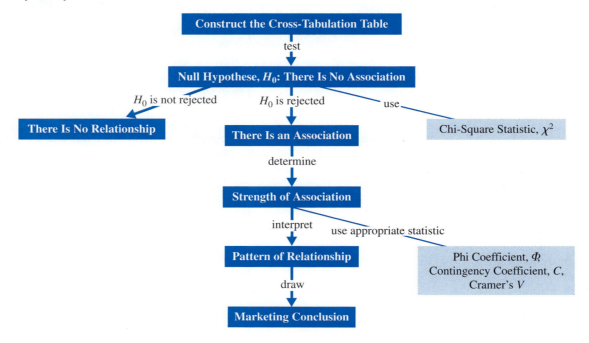

FIGURE 15.12

A Concept Map for Conducting *t* Tests

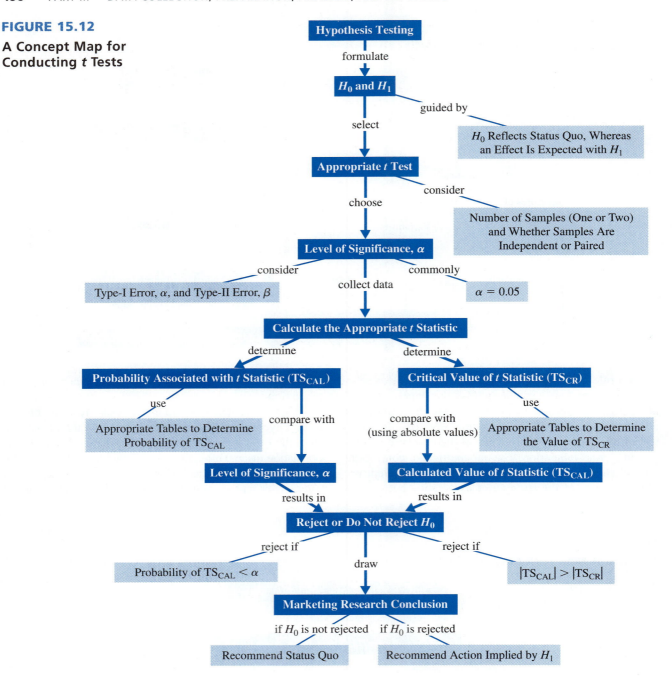

map for conducting *t* tests. In the nonparametric case, popular one-sample tests include the Kolmogorov-Smirnov, chi-square, runs test, and the binomial test. For two independent nonparametric samples, the Mann-Whitney *U* test, median test, and the Kolmogorov-Smirnov test can be used. For paired samples, the Wilcoxon matched-pairs signed-ranks test and the sign test are useful for examining hypotheses related to measures of location.

Key Terms and Concepts

standard deviation, 455
coefficient of variation, 456
skewness, 456
kurtosis, 456
null hypothesis, 457
alternative hypothesis, 457
one-tailed test, 458
two-tailed test, 458
test statistic, 459
Type I error, 459
level of significance, 459
Type II error, 459
power of a test, 460
p value, 460
cross-tabulation, 461
contingency table, 462
chi-square statistic, 467

chi-square distribution, 467
phi coefficient, 468
contingency coefficient (C), 469
Cramer's V, 469
asymmetric lambda, 469
symmetric lambda, 470
tau b, 470
tau c, 470
gamma, 470
parametric tests, 471
nonparametric tests, 471
t test, 472
t statistic, 472
t distribution, 472
z test, 473
independent samples, 473

F test, 474
F statistic, 474
F distribution, 474
paired samples, 476
paired samples t test, 476
Kolmogorov-Smirnov (K-S)
  one-sample test, 478
runs test, 478
binomial test, 478
Mann-Whitney U test, 478
two-sample median test, 479
Kolmogorov-Smirnov two-sample
  test, 479
Wilcoxon matched-pairs signed-ranks
  test, 480
sign test, 481

Suggested Cases, Video Cases, and HBS Cases

Running Case with Real Data
1.1 Dell

Comprehensive Critical Thinking Cases
2.1 American Idol   2.2 Baskin-Robbins   2.3 Akron Children's Hospital

Data Analysis Cases with Real Data
3.1 AT&T   3.2 IBM   3.3 Kimberly-Clark

Comprehensive Cases with Real Data
4.1 JPMorgan Chase   4.2 Wendy's

Video Case
23.1 Marriott

Live Research: Conducting a Marketing Research Project

1. Each team can conduct the entire analysis, or the data analysis can be split between teams with each team conducting a different type of analysis.
2. It is helpful to run a frequency count for every variable. This gives a good feel for the data.
3. Calculate the measures of location (mean, median, mode), measures of variability (range and standard deviation), as well as the measures of shape (skewness and kurtosis) for each variable.
4. Relevant associations can be examined by conducting cross-tabulations. Procedures should be specified for categorizing interval- or ratio-scaled variables.

5. Differences between groups are of interest in most projects. In case of two groups, these can be examined by using independent samples t tests.
6. Often each respondent evaluates many stimuli. For example, each respondent may evaluate different brands or provide importance ratings for different attributes. In such cases, differences between pairs of stimuli may be examined using the paired samples t test.

Acronyms

The statistics associated with frequencies may be summarized by the acronym

Frequencies:

F   latness or peakedness: kurtosis
R   ange
E   stimate of location: mean
Q   uotients: percentages
U   ndulation: variance
E   stimate of location: mode
N   umbers or counts
C   oefficient of variation
I   nterquartile range
E   stimate of location: median
S   kewness

The salient characteristics of cross-tabulations may be summarized by the acronym

C Tabulations:

C   ube: chi-square, contingency coefficient, and Cramer's *V*
T   wo-by-two table statistic: phi coefficient
A   dditional insights or refinements provided by third variable
B   ased on expected cell count of at least five
U   nchanged association with third variable introduction
L   ambda coefficient
A   ssociation and not causation is measured
T   wo- and three-variable cases
I   nitial relationship may be spurious
O   ver three variables pose problems
N   umbers and percentages
S   uppressed association may be revealed

Exercises

Questions

1. Describe the procedure for computing frequencies.
2. What measures of location are commonly computed?
3. Define the interquartile range. What does it measure?
4. What is meant by the coefficient of variation?
5. How is the relative flatness or peakedness of a distribution measured?
6. What is a skewed distribution? What does it mean?
7. What is the major difference between cross-tabulation and frequency distribution?
8. What is the general rule for computing percentages in cross-tabulation?
9. Define a spurious correlation.
10. What is meant by a suppressed association? How is it revealed?
11. Discuss the reasons for the frequent use of cross-tabulations. What are some of its limitations?
12. Present a classification of hypothesis-testing procedures.
13. Describe the general procedure for conducting a *t* test.
14. What is the major difference between parametric and nonparametric tests?
15. Which nonparametric tests are the counterparts of the two-independent-samples *t* test for parametric data?
16. Which nonparametric tests are the counterparts of the paired samples *t* test for parametric data?

Problems

1. In each of the following situations, indicate the statistical analysis you would conduct and the appropriate test or test statistic that should be used.
   a. Consumer preferences for Camay bathing soap were obtained on an 11-point Likert scale. The same consumers were then shown a commercial about Camay. After the commercial, preferences for Camay were again measured. Has the commercial been successful in inducing a change in preferences?
   b. Does the preference for Camay soap follow a normal distribution?
   c. Respondents in a survey of 1,000 households were classified as heavy, medium, light, or nonusers of ice cream. They were also classified as being in high-, medium-, or low-income categories. Is the consumption of ice cream related to income level?
   d. In a survey using a representative sample of 2,000 households from the Greenfield Online consumer Internet panel, the respondents were asked to rank 10 department stores, including Sears, in order of preference. The sample was divided into small and large households based on a median split of the household size. Does preference for shopping in Sears vary by household size?
2. The current advertising campaign for a major soft drink brand would be changed if less than 30 percent of the consumers like it.
   a. Formulate the null and alternative hypotheses.
   b. Discuss the Type I and Type II errors that could occur in hypothesis testing.
   c. Which statistical test would you use? Why?
   d. A random sample of 300 consumers was surveyed, and 84 respondents indicated that they liked the campaign. Should the campaign be changed? Why?
3. A major department store chain is having an end-of-season sale on refrigerators. The number of refrigerators sold during this sale at a sample of 10 stores was:

   80   110   0   40   70   80   100   50   80   30

   a. Is there evidence that an average of more than 50 refrigerators per store were sold during this sale? Use $\alpha = 0.05$.
   b. What assumption is necessary to perform this test?

Internet and Computer Exercises

SPSS Data File   SAS Data File

1. In a pretest, data on Nike were obtained from 45 respondents. These data are given in the following table, which gives the usage, sex, awareness, attitude, preference, intention, and loyalty toward Nike of a sample of Nike users. Usage has been coded as 1, 2, or 3, representing light, medium, or heavy users. The sex has been coded as 1 for females and 2 for males. Awareness, attitude, preference, intention, and loyalty are measured on 7-point Likert-type scales (1 = very unfavorable, 7 = very favorable). Note that five respondents have missing values that are denoted by 9.

Number	Usage	Sex	Awareness	Attitude	Preference	Intention	Loyalty
1	3	2	7	6	5	5	6
2	1	1	2	2	4	6	5
3	1	1	3	3	6	7	6
4	3	2	6	5	5	3	2
5	3	2	5	4	7	4	3
6	2	2	4	3	5	2	3
7	2	1	5	4	4	3	2
8	1	1	2	1	3	4	5
9	2	2	4	4	3	6	5
10	1	1	3	1	2	4	5
11	3	2	6	7	6	4	5
12	3	2	6	5	6	4	4
13	1	1	4	3	3	1	1
14	3	2	6	4	5	3	2
15	1	2	4	3	4	5	6
16	1	2	3	4	2	4	2
17	3	1	7	6	4	5	3
18	2	1	6	5	4	3	2
19	1	1	1	1	3	4	5
20	3	1	5	7	4	1	2
21	3	2	6	6	7	7	5
22	2	2	2	3	1	4	2
23	1	1	1	1	3	2	2
24	3	1	6	7	6	7	6
25	1	2	3	2	2	1	1
26	2	2	5	3	4	4	5
27	3	2	7	6	6	5	7
28	2	1	6	4	2	5	6
29	1	1	9	2	3	1	3
30	2	2	5	9	4	6	5
31	1	2	1	2	9	3	2
32	1	2	4	6	5	9	3
33	2	1	3	4	3	2	9
34	2	1	4	6	5	7	6
35	3	1	5	7	7	3	3
36	3	1	6	5	7	3	4
37	3	2	6	7	5	3	4
38	3	2	5	6	4	3	2
39	3	2	7	7	6	3	4
40	1	1	4	3	4	6	5
41	1	1	2	3	4	5	6
42	1	1	1	3	2	3	4
43	1	1	2	4	3	6	7
44	1	1	3	3	4	6	5
45	1	1	1	1	4	5	3

Analyze the Nike data to answer the following questions. In each case, formulate the null and the alternative hypotheses and conduct the appropriate statistical test(s).

a. Obtain a frequency distribution for each of the following variables and calculate the relevant statistics: awareness, attitude, preference, intention, and loyalty toward Nike.

b. Conduct a cross-tabulation of the usage with sex. Interpret the results.

c. Does the awareness for Nike exceed 3.0?

d. Do the males and females differ in their awareness for Nike? Their attitude toward Nike? Their loyalty for Nike?

e. Do the respondents in the pretest have a higher level of awareness than loyalty?

f. Does awareness of Nike follow a normal distribution?

g. Is the distribution of preference for Nike normal?

h. Assume that awareness toward Nike was measured on an ordinal scale rather than an interval scale. Do males and females differ in their awareness toward Nike?

i. Assume that loyalty toward Nike was measured on an ordinal scale rather than an interval scale. Do males and females differ in their loyalty toward Nike?

j. Assume that attitude and loyalty toward Nike were measured on an ordinal scale rather than an interval scale. Do the respondents have greater awareness of Nike than loyalty for Nike?

2. In a pretest, respondents were asked to express their preference for an outdoor lifestyle using a 7-point scale: 1 = not at all preferred, to 7 = greatly preferred (V1). They were also asked to indicate the importance of the following variables on a 7-point scale: 1 = not at all important, to 7 = very important.

    V2 = enjoying nature
    V3 = relating to the weather
    V4 = living in harmony with the environment
    V5 = exercising regularly
    V6 = meeting other people

The sex of the respondent (V7) was coded as 1 for females and 2 for males. The location of residence (V8) was coded as: 1 = midtown/downtown, 2 = suburbs, and 3 = countryside. The data obtained are given in the following table:

V1	V2	V3	V4	V5	V6	V7	V8
7.00	3.00	6.00	4.00	5.00	2.00	1.00	1.00
1.00	1.00	1.00	2.00	1.00	2.00	1.00	1.00
6.00	2.00	5.00	4.00	4.00	5.00	1.00	1.00
4.00	3.00	4.00	6.00	3.00	2.00	1.00	1.00
1.00	2.00	2.00	3.00	1.00	2.00	1.00	1.00
6.00	3.00	5.00	4.00	6.00	2.00	1.00	1.00
5.00	3.00	4.00	3.00	4.00	5.00	1.00	1.00
6.00	4.00	5.00	4.00	5.00	1.00	1.00	1.00
3.00	3.00	2.00	2.00	2.00	2.00	1.00	1.00
2.00	4.00	2.00	6.00	2.00	2.00	1.00	1.00
6.00	4.00	5.00	3.00	5.00	5.00	1.00	2.00
2.00	3.00	1.00	4.00	2.00	2.00	1.00	2.00

7.00	2.00	6.00	4.00	5.00	6.00	1.00	2.00
4.00	6.00	4.00	5.00	3.00	3.00	1.00	2.00
1.00	3.00	1.00	2.00	1.00	4.00	1.00	2.00
6.00	6.00	6.00	3.00	4.00	5.00	2.00	2.00
5.00	5.00	6.00	4.00	4.00	6.00	2.00	2.00
7.00	7.00	4.00	4.00	7.00	7.00	2.00	2.00
2.00	6.00	3.00	7.00	4.00	3.00	2.00	2.00
3.00	7.00	3.00	6.00	4.00	4.00	2.00	2.00
1.00	5.00	2.00	6.00	3.00	3.00	2.00	3.00
5.00	6.00	4.00	7.00	5.00	6.00	2.00	3.00
2.00	4.00	1.00	5.00	4.00	4.00	2.00	3.00
4.00	7.00	4.00	7.00	4.00	6.00	2.00	3.00
6.00	7.00	4.00	2.00	1.00	7.00	2.00	3.00
3.00	6.00	4.00	6.00	4.00	4.00	2.00	3.00
4.00	7.00	7.00	4.00	2.00	5.00	2.00	3.00
3.00	7.00	2.00	6.00	4.00	3.00	2.00	3.00
4.00	6.00	3.00	7.00	2.00	7.00	2.00	3.00
5.00	6.00	2.00	6.00	7.00	2.00	2.00	3.00

Using a statistical package of your choice, please answer the following questions. In each case, formulate the null and the alternative hypotheses and conduct the appropriate statistical test(s).

a. Does the mean preference for an outdoor lifestyle exceed 3.0?
b. Does the mean importance of enjoying nature exceed 3.5?
c. Does the mean preference for an outdoor lifestyle differ for males and females?
d. Does the importance attached to V2 to V6 differ for males and females?

e. Do the respondents attach more importance to enjoying nature than they do to relating to the weather?
f. Do the respondents attach more importance to relating to the weather than they do to meeting other people?
g. Do the respondents attach more importance to living in harmony with the environment than they do to exercising regularly?
h. Does the importance attached to V2 to V6 differ for males and females if these variables are treated as ordinal rather than interval scaled?
i. Do the respondents attach more importance to relating to the weather than they do to meeting other people if these variables are treated as ordinal rather than interval?

3. Use one of the mainframe statistical packages (SPSS, SAS, MINITAB, or EXCEL) to conduct the following analysis for the soft drink data that you have collected as part of your fieldwork (described later).
a. Obtain a frequency distribution of the weekly soft drink consumption.
b. Obtain the summary statistics related to the weekly amount spent on soft drinks.
c. Conduct a cross-tabulation of the weekly consumption of soft drinks with sex of the respondent. Does your data show any association?
d. Do a two-independent-sample t test to determine whether the weekly amount spent on soft drinks is different for males and females.
e. Conduct a test to determine whether there is any difference between the weekly amount spent on soft drinks and that spent on other nonalcoholic beverages. What is your conclusion?

Activities

Role Playing

1. You have been hired as a marketing research analyst by a major industrial marketing company in the country. Your boss, the market research manager, is a high-powered statistician who does not believe in using rudimentary techniques such as frequency distributions, cross-tabulations, and simple t tests. Convince your boss (a student in your class) of the merits of conducting these analyses.

Fieldwork

1. Develop a questionnaire to obtain the following information from students on your campus.

a. Average amount per week spent on the consumption of soft drinks
b. Average amount per week spent on the consumption of other nonalcoholic beverages (milk, coffee, tea, fruit juices, etc.)

c. Frequency of weekly soft drink consumption. Measure this as a categorical variable with the following question: "How often do you consume soft drinks? (1) once a week or less often, (2) two or three times a week, (3) four to six times a week, and (4) more than six times a week."
d. Sex of the respondent

Administer this questionnaire to 40 students. Code the data and transcribe them for computer analysis. As compared to males, do females: (i) spend more on soft drinks, (ii) spend more on other nonalcoholic beverages, (iii) consume more soft drinks?

Group Discussion

1. "Because cross-tabulation has certain basic limitations, this technique should not be used extensively in commercial marketing research." Discuss as a small group.
2. "Why waste time doing basic data analysis? Why not just conduct sophisticated multivariate data analysis?" Discuss.

Dell Running Case

Review the Dell case, Case 1.1, and questionnaire given toward the end of the book. Download the Dell case data file from the Web site for this book.

1. Calculate the frequency distribution for each variable in the data file. Examine the distribution to get a feel for the data.
2. Cross-tabulate the recoded questions q4 (Overall satisfaction with Dell), q5 (Would recommend Dell), and q6 (Likelihood of choosing Dell) with the recoded demographic characteristics. Interpret the results.
3. Cross-tabulate the recoded questions on price sensitivity (q9_5per and q9_10per) with the recoded demographic characteristics. Interpret the results.
4. The mean response on which of the evaluations of Dell (q8_1 to q8_13) exceeds 5 (the midpoint of the scale)?
5. The response on which of the evaluations of Dell (q8_1 to q8_13) is normally distributed? What are the implications of your results for data analysis?
6. Are the two overall satisfaction groups derived based on the recoding of q4 as specified in Chapter 14 different in terms of each of the evaluations of Dell (q8_1 to q8_13)? How would your analysis change if the evaluations of Dell (q8_1 to q8_13) are to be treated as ordinal rather than interval scaled?
7. Are the two Likely to recommend groups derived based on the recoding of q5 as specified in Chapter 14 different in terms of

each of the evaluations of Dell (q8_1 to q8_13)? How would your analysis change if the evaluations of Dell (q8_1 to q8_13) are to be treated as ordinal rather than interval scaled?

8. Are the two Likelihood of choosing Dell groups derived based on the recoding of q6 as specified in Chapter 14 different in terms of each of the evaluations of Dell (q8_1 to q8_13)? How would your analysis change if the evaluations of Dell (q8_1 to q8_13) are to be treated as ordinal rather than interval scaled?
9. Is the mean of responses to q8b_1 (Make ordering a computer system easy) and q8b_2 (Let customers order computer systems customized to their specifications) different? How would your analysis change if the evaluations of Dell (q8_1 and q8_2) are to be treated as ordinal rather than interval scaled?
10. Is the mean of responses to q8b_9 ("Bundle" its computers with appropriate software) and q8b_10 ("Bundle" its computers with Internet access) different? How would your analysis change if the evaluations of Dell (q8_9 and q8_10) are to be treated as ordinal rather than interval scaled?
11. Is the mean of responses to q8b_6 (Have computers that run programs quickly) and q8b_7 (Have high-quality computers with no technical problems) different? How would your analysis change if the evaluations of Dell (q8_6 and q8_7) are to be treated as ordinal rather than interval scaled?

Chapter 6

> " Analysis of variance is a straightforward way to look at differences among more than two groups of responses measured on interval or ratio scales. "

Terry Grapentine, Grapentine Company, Inc.

Objectives   [After reading this chapter, the student should be able to:]

1. Discuss the scope of the analysis of variance (ANOVA) technique and its relationship to the *t* test and regression.

2. Describe one-way analysis of variance, including decomposition of the total variation, measurement of effects, significance testing, and interpretation of results.

3. Describe *n*-way analysis of variance and the testing of the significance of the overall effect, the interaction effect, and the main effect of each factor.

4. Describe analysis of covariance and show how it accounts for the influence of uncontrolled independent variables.

5. Explain key factors pertaining to the interpretation of results with emphasis on interactions, relative importance of factors, and multiple comparisons.

6. Discuss specialized ANOVA techniques applicable to marketing such as repeated measures ANOVA, nonmetric analysis of variance, and multivariate analysis of variance (MANOVA).

Analysis of Variance and Covariance

Overview

In Chapter 15, we examined tests of differences between two means or two medians. In this chapter, we discuss procedures for examining differences between more than two means or medians. These procedures are called *analysis of variance* and *analysis of covariance*. Although these procedures have traditionally been used for analyzing experimental data, they are also used for analyzing survey or observational data.

We describe the analysis of variance and covariance procedures and discuss their relationship to other techniques. Then we describe one-way analysis of variance, the simplest of these procedures, followed by *n*-way analysis of variance and analysis of covariance. Special attention is given to issues in interpretation of results as they relate to interactions, relative importance of factors, and multiple comparisons. Some specialized topics, such as repeated measures analysis of variance, nonmetric analysis of variance, and multivariate analysis of variance, are briefly discussed.

Finally, we discuss the use of software in analysis of variance and covariance. Help for running the SPSS and SAS Learning Edition programs used in this chapter is provided in four ways: (1) detailed step-by-step instructions are given later in the chapter, (2) you can download (from the Web site for this book) computerized demonstration movies illustrating these step-by-step instructions, (3) you can download screen captures with notes illustrating these step-by-step instructions, and (4) you can refer to the *Study Guide and Technology Manual*, a supplement that accompanies this book.

Real Research

Analysis of Tourism Destinations

A marketing research survey conducted by EgeBank in Istanbul, Turkey, focused on the importance of U.S. tour operators' and travel agents' perceptions of selected Mediterranean tourist destinations (Egypt, Greece, Italy, and Turkey). This study was conducted with the help of the Department of Tourism and Convention Administration at the University of Nevada–Las Vegas (www.unlv.edu).

Operators/travel agents were mailed surveys based on the locations of tours, broken down as follows: Egypt (53), Greece (130), Italy (150), and Turkey (65). The survey consisted of questions on affective and perceptual/cognitive evaluations of the four destinations. The four affective questions were asked on a 7-point semantic differential scale, whereas the 14 perceptual/cognitive evaluations were measured on a 5-point Likert scale (1 = offers very little, 2 = offers somewhat little, 3 = offers neither little nor much, 4 = offers somewhat much, and 5 = offers very much). The differences in the evaluations of the four locations were examined using one-way analysis of variance (ANOVA), as seen in the following table.

The ANOVA table shows that "unpleasant–pleasant" and "distressing–relaxing" affective factors have significant differences among the four destinations. For instance, Greece and Italy were perceived as being significantly more relaxing than Egypt. As for the perceptual factors, eight of the 14 factors were significant. Turkey was perceived as a significantly better value for the money than Greece and Italy. Turkey's main strength appears to be "good value," and the country's tourism agencies should

Image Variations of Destinations Promoted to Tour Operators and Travel Agencies

Image Items	Turkey (n = 36)	Egypt (n = 29)	Greece (n = 37)	Italy (n = 34)	Significance
Affective (Scale 1–7)					
Unpleasant–pleasant	6.14	5.62	6.43	6.50	0.047[a]
Sleepy–arousing	6.24	5.61	6.14	6.56	0.053
Distressing–relaxing	5.60	4.86	6.05	6.09	0.003[a]
Gloomy–exciting	6.20	5.83	6.32	6.71	0.061
Perceptual (Scale 1–5)					
Good value for money	4.62	4.32	3.89	3.27	0.000[a]
Beautiful scenery and natural attractions	4.50	4.04	4.53	4.70	0.011[a]
Good climate	4.29	4.00	4.41	4.35	0.133
Interesting cultural attractions	4.76	4.79	4.67	4.79	0.781
Suitable accommodations	4.17	4.28	4.35	4.62	0.125
Appealing local food (cuisine)	4.44	3.57	4.19	4.85	0.000[a]
Great beaches and water sports	3.91	3.18	4.27	3.65	0.001[a]
Quality of infrastructure	3.49	2.97	3.68	4.09	0.000[a]
Personal safety	3.83	3.28	4.19	4.15	0.000[a]
Interesting historical attractions	4.71	4.86	4.81	4.82	0.650
Unpolluted and unspoiled environment	3.54	3.34	3.43	3.59	0.784
Good nightlife and entertainment	3.44	3.15	4.06	4.27	0.000[a]
Standard hygiene and cleanliness	3.29	2.79	3.76	4.29	0.000[a]
Interesting and friendly people	4.34	4.24	4.35	4.32	0.956

[a]Significant at 0.05 level

promote this in their marketing strategies. On the other hand, Turkey needs to improve the perception of its infrastructure, cleanliness, and entertainment to encourage more tour operators and travel agencies in the United States to offer travel packages to Turkey. In 2007, 23 million tourists visited Turkey and tourism revenues amounted to U.S. $18 billion.[1] ■

Analysis of variance techniques can help identify affective and perceptual factors that differentiate alternative tourist destinations.

Real Research

Electronic Shopping Risks

Analysis of variance was used to test differences in preferences for electronic shopping for products with different economic and social risks. In a 2×2 design, economic risk and social risk were varied at two levels each (high, low). Preference for electronic shopping served as the dependent variable. The results indicated a significant interaction of social risk with economic risk. Electronic shopping was not perceived favorably for high-social-risk products, regardless of the level of economic product risk, but it was preferred for low-economic-risk products over high-economic-risk products when the level of social risk was low.

Despite the results of this study, the number of online shoppers continues to grow. As of 2008, more than 875 million consumers had shopped online, representing more than 80 percent of the world's online population. The increase in shoppers can be attributed to bargain-seeking consumers, convenience of using the Internet, and, surprisingly, an added sense of safety associated with purchasing online. Improved Web sites, streamlined order taking and delivery, and assurances of more secure payment systems have increased the flow of new shoppers to the Internet while decreasing the traditional risk associated with online transaction purchases.[2] ∎

analysis of variance (ANOVA)
A statistical technique for examining the differences among means for two or more populations.

factors
Categorical independent variables. The independent variables must be all categorical (nonmetric) to use ANOVA.

treatment
In ANOVA, a particular combination of factor levels or categories.

one-way analysis of variance
An ANOVA technique in which there is only one factor.

n-way analysis of variance
An ANOVA model where two or more factors are involved.

analysis of covariance (ANCOVA)
An advanced analysis of variance procedure in which the effects of one or more metric-scaled extraneous variables are removed from the dependent variable before conducting the ANOVA.

covariate
A metric independent variable used in ANCOVA.

The tourist destination example presented a situation with four categories. The *t* test was not appropriate for examining the overall difference in category means, so analysis of variance was used instead. The electronic shopping study involved a comparison of means when there were two factors (independent variables), each of which was varied at two levels. In this example, *t* tests were not appropriate, because the effect of each factor was not independent of the effect of the other factor (in other words, interactions were significant). Analysis of variance provided meaningful conclusions in these studies. The relationship of analysis of variance to the *t* test and other techniques is considered in the next section.

Relationship Among Techniques

Analysis of variance and analysis of covariance are used for examining the differences in the mean values of the dependent variable associated with the effect of the controlled independent variables, after taking into account the influence of the uncontrolled independent variables. Essentially, **analysis of variance (ANOVA)** is used as a test of means for two or more populations. The null hypothesis, typically, is that all means are equal. For example, suppose the researcher were interested in examining whether heavy, medium, light, and nonusers of cereals differed in their preference for Total cereal, measured on a 9-point Likert scale. The null hypothesis that the four groups were not different in preference for Total could be tested using analysis of variance.

In its simplest form, analysis of variance must have a dependent variable (preference for Total cereal) that is metric (measured using an interval or ratio scale). There must also be one or more independent variables (product use: heavy, medium, light, and nonusers). The independent variables must be all categorical (nonmetric). Categorical independent variables are also called **factors**. A particular combination of factor levels, or categories, is called a **treatment**. **One-way analysis of variance** involves only one categorical variable, or a single factor. The differences in preference of heavy, medium, light, and nonusers would be examined by one-way ANOVA. In one-way analysis of variance, a treatment is the same as a factor level (medium users constitute a treatment). If two or more factors are involved, the analysis is termed **n-way analysis of variance**. If, in addition to product use, the researcher also wanted to examine the preference for Total cereal of customers who are loyal and those who are not, an *n*-way analysis of variance would be conducted.

If the set of independent variables consists of both categorical and metric variables, the technique is called **analysis of covariance (ANCOVA)**. For example, analysis of covariance would be required if the researcher wanted to examine the preference of product use groups and loyalty groups, taking into account the respondents' attitudes toward nutrition and the importance they attached to breakfast as a meal. The latter two variables would be measured on 9-point Likert scales. In this case, the categorical independent variables (product use and brand loyalty) are still referred to as factors, whereas the metric-independent variables (attitude toward nutrition and importance attached to breakfast) are referred to as **covariates**.

FIGURE 16.1

Relationship
Between *t* Test,
Analysis of
Variance, Analysis
of Covariance, and
Regression

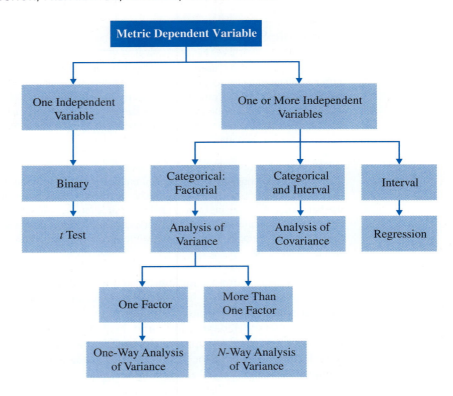

The relationship of analysis of variance to *t* tests and other techniques, such as regression (see Chapter 17), is shown in Figure 16.1. All of these techniques involve a metric dependent variable. ANOVA and ANCOVA can include more than one independent variable (product use, brand loyalty, attitude, and importance). Furthermore, at least one of the independent variables must be categorical, and the categorical variables may have more than two categories (in our example, product use has four categories). A *t* test, on the other hand, involves a single, binary independent variable. For example, the difference in the preferences of loyal and nonloyal respondents could be tested by conducting a *t* test. Regression analysis, like ANOVA and ANCOVA, can also involve more than one independent variable. However, all the independent variables are generally interval scaled, although binary or categorical variables can be accommodated using dummy variables. For example, the relationship between preference for Total cereal, attitude toward nutrition, and importance attached to breakfast could be examined via regression analysis, with preference for Total serving as the dependent variable and attitude and importance as independent variables.

One-Way Analysis of Variance

Marketing researchers are often interested in examining the differences in the mean values of the dependent variable for several categories of a single independent variable or factor. For example:

- Do the various segments differ in terms of their volume of product consumption?
- Do the brand evaluations of groups exposed to different commercials vary?
- Do retailers, wholesalers, and agents differ in their attitudes toward the firm's distribution policies?
- How do consumers' intentions to buy the brand vary with different price levels?
- What is the effect of consumers' familiarity with the store (measured as high, medium, and low) on preference for the store?

The answers to these and similar questions can be determined by conducting one-way analysis of variance. Before describing the procedure, we define the important statistics associated with one-way analysis of variance.[3]

Statistics Associated with One-Way Analysis of Variance

eta² (η^2). The strength of the effects of X (independent variable or factor) on Y (dependent variable) is measured by *eta²* (η^2). The value of (η^2) varies between 0 and 1.

F **statistic**. The null hypothesis that the category means are equal in the population is tested by an F statistic based on the ratio of mean square related to X and mean square related to error.

Mean square. The mean square is the sum of squares divided by the appropriate degrees of freedom.

$SS_{between}$. Also denoted as SS_x, this is the variation in Y related to the variation in the means of the categories of X. This represents variation between the categories of X, or the portion of the sum of squares in Y related to X.

SS_{within}. Also referred to as SS_{error}, this is the variation in Y due to the variation within each of the categories of X. This variation is not accounted for by X.

SS_y. The total variation in Y is SS_y.

Conducting One-Way Analysis of Variance

The procedure for conducting one-way analysis of variance is described in Figure 16.2. It involves identifying the dependent and independent variables, decomposing the total variation, measuring effects, testing significance, and interpreting results. We consider these steps in detail and illustrate them with some applications.

Identify the Dependent and Independent Variables

The dependent variable is denoted by Y and the independent variable by X. X is a categorical variable having c categories. There are n observations on Y for each category of X, as shown in Table 16.1. As can be seen, the sample size in each category of X is n, and the total sample size $N = n \times c$. Although the sample sizes in the categories of X (the group sizes) are assumed to be equal for the sake of simplicity, this is not a requirement.

Decompose the Total Variation

decomposition of the total variation
In one-way ANOVA, separation of the variation observed in the dependent variable into the variation due to the independent variables plus the variation due to error.

In examining the differences among means, one-way analysis of variance involves the **decomposition of the total variation** observed in the dependent variable. This variation is measured by the sums of squares corrected for the mean (SS). Analysis of variance is so named because it examines the variability or variation in the sample (dependent variable) and, based on the variability, determines whether there is reason to believe that the population means differ.

The total variation in Y, denoted by SS_y, can be decomposed into two components:

$$SS_y = SS_{between} + SS_{within}$$

FIGURE 16.2

Conducting One-Way ANOVA

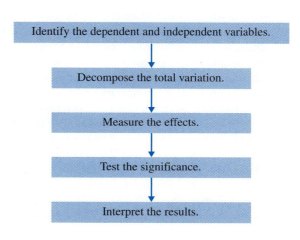

TABLE 16.1

Decomposition of the Total Variation: One-Way ANOVA

	Independent Variable				X		
			Categories			Total Sample	

where the subscripts *between* and *within* refer to the categories of X. $SS_{between}$ is the variation in Y related to the variation in the means of the categories of X. It represents variation between the categories of X. In other words, $SS_{between}$ is the portion of the sum of squares in Y related to the independent variable or factor X. For this reason, $SS_{between}$ is also denoted as SS_x. SS_{within} is the variation in Y related to the variation within each category of X. SS_{within} is not accounted for by X. Therefore it is referred to as SS_{error}. The total variation in Y may be decomposed as:

$$SS_y = SS_x + SS_{error}$$

where

$$SS_y = \sum_{i=1}^{N}(Y_i - \bar{Y})^2$$

$$SS_x = \sum_{j=1}^{c} n(\bar{Y}_j - \bar{Y})^2$$

$$SS_{error} = \sum_{j=1}^{c}\sum_{i=1}^{n}(Y_{ij} - \bar{Y}_j)^2$$

Y_i = individual observation

$\bar{Y}_j$ = mean for category j

$\bar{Y}$ = mean over the whole sample, or grand mean

Y_{ij} = ith observation in the jth category

The logic of decomposing the total variation in Y, SS_y, into $SS_{between}$ and SS_{within} in order to examine differences in group means can be intuitively understood. Recall from Chapter 15 that if the variation of the variable in the population was known or estimated, one could estimate how much the sample mean should vary because of random variation alone. In analysis of variance, there are several different groups (e.g., heavy, medium, light, and nonusers). If the null hypothesis is true and all the groups have the same mean in the population, one can estimate how much the sample means should vary because of sampling (random) variations alone. If the observed variation in the sample means is more than what would be expected by sampling variation, it is reasonable to conclude that this extra variability is related to differences in group means in the population.

In analysis of variance, we estimate two measures of variation: within groups (SS_{within}) and between groups ($SS_{between}$). Within-group variation is a measure of how much the observations, Y values, within a group vary. This is used to estimate the variance within a group in the population. It is assumed that all the groups have the same variation in the population. However, because it is not known that all the groups have the same mean, we cannot calculate the variance of all the observations together. The variance for each of the groups must be calculated individually, and these are combined into an "average" or "overall" variance. Likewise, another estimate of the variance of the

Y values may be obtained by examining the variation between the means. (This process is the reverse of determining the variation in the means, given the population variances.) If the population mean is the same in all the groups, then the variation in the sample means and the sizes of the sample groups can be used to estimate the variance of Y. The reasonableness of this estimate of the Y variance depends on whether the null hypothesis is true. If the null hypothesis is true and the population means are equal, the variance estimate based on between-group variation is correct. On the other hand, if the groups have different means in the population, the variance estimate based on between-group variation will be too large. Thus, by comparing the Y variance estimates based on between-group and within-group variation, we can test the null hypothesis. Decomposition of the total variation in this manner also enables us to measure the effects of X on Y.

Measure the Effects

The effects of X on Y are measured by SS_x. Because SS_x is related to the variation in the means of the categories of X, the relative magnitude of SS_x increases as the differences among the means of Y in the categories of X increase. The relative magnitude of SS_x also increases as the variations in Y within the categories of X decrease. The strength of the effects of X on Y are measured as follows:

$$\eta^2 = \frac{SS_x}{SS_y} = \frac{(SS_y - SS_{error})}{SS_y}$$

The value of η^2 varies between 0 and 1. It assumes a value of 0 when all the category means are equal, indicating that X has no effect on Y. The value of η^2 will be 1 when there is no variability within each category of X but there is some variability between categories. Thus, η^2 is a measure of the variation in Y that is explained by the independent variable X. Not only can we measure the effects of X on Y, but we can also test for their significance.

Test the Significance

In one-way analysis of variance, the interest lies in testing the null hypothesis that the category means are equal in the population.[4] In other words,

$$H_0: \mu_1 = \mu_2 = \mu_3 = \ldots = \mu_c$$

Under the null hypothesis, SS_x and SS_{error} come from the same source of variation. In such a case, the estimate of the population variance of Y can be based on either between-category variation or within-category variation. In other words, the estimate of the population variance of Y,

$$S_y^2 = \frac{SS_x}{(c - 1)}$$
$$= \text{mean square due to } X$$
$$= MS_x$$

or

$$S_y^2 = \frac{SS_{error}}{(N - c)}$$
$$= \text{mean square due to error}$$
$$= MS_{error}$$

The null hypothesis may be tested by the F statistic based on the ratio between these two estimates:

$$F = \frac{SS_x / (c - 1)}{SS_{error} / (N - c)} = \frac{MS_x}{MS_{error}}$$

This statistic follows the F distribution, with $(c - 1)$ and $(N - c)$ degrees of freedom (df). A table of the F distribution is given as Table 5 in the Statistical Appendix at the end of the book.

As mentioned in Chapter 15, the F distribution is a probability distribution of the ratios of sample variances. It is characterized by degrees of freedom for the numerator and degrees of freedom for the denominator.[5]

Interpret the Results

If the null hypothesis of equal category means is not rejected, then the independent variable does not have a significant effect on the dependent variable. On the other hand, if the null hypothesis is rejected, then the effect of the independent variable is significant. In other words, the mean value of the dependent variable will be different for different categories of the independent variable. A comparison of the category mean values will indicate the nature of the effect of the independent variable. Other salient issues in the interpretation of results, such as examination of differences among specific means, are discussed later.

Illustrative Data

We illustrate the concepts discussed in this chapter using the data presented in Table 16.2. For illustrative purposes, we consider only a small number of observations. In actual practice,

SPSS Data File

SAS Data File

TABLE 16.2				
Coupon Level, In-Store Promotion, Sales, and Clientele Rating				
Store Number	Coupon Level	In-Store Promotion	Sales	Clientele Rating
1	1	1	10	9
2	1	1	9	10
3	1	1	10	8
4	1	1	8	4
5	1	1	9	6
6	1	2	8	8
7	1	2	8	4
8	1	2	7	10
9	1	2	9	6
10	1	2	6	9
11	1	3	5	8
12	1	3	7	9
13	1	3	6	6
14	1	3	4	10
15	1	3	5	4
16	2	1	8	10
17	2	1	9	6
18	2	1	7	8
19	2	1	7	4
20	2	1	6	9
21	2	2	4	6
22	2	2	5	8
23	2	2	5	10
24	2	2	6	4
25	2	2	4	9
26	2	3	2	4
27	2	3	3	6
28	2	3	2	10
29	2	3	1	9
30	2	3	2	8

analysis of variance is performed on a much larger sample such as that in the Dell running case and other cases with real data that are presented in this book. These data were generated by an experiment in which a major department store chain wanted to examine the effect of the level of in-store promotion and a storewide coupon on sales. In-store promotion was varied at three levels: high (1), medium (2), and low (3). Couponing was manipulated at two levels. Either a $20 storewide coupon was distributed to potential shoppers (denoted by 1) or it was not (denoted by 2 in Table 16.2). In-store promotion and couponing were crossed, resulting in a 3×2 design with six cells. Thirty stores were randomly selected, and five stores were randomly assigned to each treatment condition, as shown in Table 16.2. The experiment was run for two months. Sales in each store were measured, normalized to account for extraneous factors (store size, traffic, etc.), and converted to a 1-to-10 scale. In addition, a qualitative assessment was made of the relative affluence of the clientele of each store, again using a 1-to-10 scale. In these scales, higher numbers denote higher sales or more affluent clientele.

Illustrative Applications of One-Way Analysis of Variance

We illustrate one-way ANOVA first with an example showing calculations done by hand and then using computer analysis. Suppose that only one factor, namely in-store promotion, was manipulated, that is, let us ignore couponing for the purpose of this illustration. The department store is attempting to determine the effect of in-store promotion (X) on sales (Y). For the purpose of illustrating hand calculations, the data of Table 16.2 are transformed in Table 16.3 to show the store (Y_{ij}) for each level of promotion.

The null hypothesis is that the category means are equal:

$$H_0: \mu_1 = \mu_2 = \mu_3$$

To test the null hypothesis, the various sums of squares are computed as follows:

$$
\begin{aligned}
SS_y = {} & (10 - 6.067)^2 + (9 - 6.067)^2 + (10 - 6.067)^2 + (8 - 6.067)^2 + (9 - 6.067)^2 \\
& + (8 - 6.067)^2 + (9 - 6.067)^2 + (7 - 6.067)^2 + (7 - 6.067)^2 + (6 - 6.067)^2 \\
& + (8 - 6.067)^2 + (8 - 6.067)^2 + (7 - 6.067)^2 + (9 - 6.067)^2 + (6 - 6.067)^2
\end{aligned}
$$

TABLE 16.3

Effect of In-Store Promotion on Sales

	Level of In-Store Promotion		
Store No.	High	Medium	Low
		Normalized Sales	
1	10	8	5
2	9	8	7
3	10	7	6
4	8	9	4
5	9	6	5
6	8	4	2
7	9	5	3
8	7	5	2
9	7	6	1
10	6	4	2
Column Totals	83	62	37
Category means: $\bar{Y}_j$	$\dfrac{83}{10}$	$\dfrac{62}{10}$	$\dfrac{37}{10}$
	$= 8.3$	$= 6.2$	$= 3.7$
Grand mean, $\bar{Y}$		$= \dfrac{(83 + 62 + 37)}{30} = 6.067$	

$$+ (4 - 6.067)^2 + (5 - 6.067)^2 + (5 - 6.067)^2 + (6 - 6.067)^2 + (4 - 6.067)^2$$
$$+ (5 - 6.067)^2 + (7 - 6.067)^2 + (6 - 6.067)^2 + (4 - 6.067)^2 + (5 - 6.067)^2$$
$$+ (2 - 6.067)^2 + (3 - 6.067)^2 + (2 - 6.067)^2 + (1 - 6.067)^2 + (2 - 6.067)^2$$

$$= (3.933)^2 + (2.933)^2 + (3.933)^2 + (1.933)^2 + (2.933)^2$$
$$+ (1.933)^2 + (2.933)^2 + (0.933)^2 + (0.933)^2 + (-0.067)^2$$
$$+ (1.933)^2 + (1.933)^2 + (0.933)^2 + (2.933)^2 + (-0.067)^2$$
$$+ (-2.067)^2 + (-1.067)^2 + (-1.067)^2 + (-0.067)^2 + (-2.067)^2$$
$$+ (-1.067)^2 + (0.933)^2 + (-0.067)^2 + (-2.067)^2 + (-1.067)^2$$
$$+ (-4.067)^2 + (-3.067)^2 + (-4.067)^2 + (-5.067)^2 + (-4.067)^2$$

$$= 185.867$$

$$
\begin{aligned}
SS_x &= 10(8.3 - 6.067)^2 + 10(6.2 - 6.067)^2 + 10(3.7 - 6.067)^2 \\
&= 10(2.233)^2 + 10(0.133)^2 + 10(-2.367)^2 \\
&= 106.067
\end{aligned}
$$

$$
\begin{aligned}
SS_{error} &= (10 - 8.3)^2 + (9 - 8.3)^2 + (10 - 8.3)^2 + (8 - 8.3)^2 + (9 - 8.3)^2 \\
&+ (8 - 8.3)^2 + (9 - 8.3)^2 + (7 - 8.3)^2 + (7 - 8.3)^2 + (6 - 8.3)^2 \\
&+ (8 - 6.2)^2 + (8 - 6.2)^2 + (7 - 6.2)^2 + (9 - 6.2)^2 + (6 - 6.2)^2 \\
&+ (4 - 6.2)^2 + (5 - 6.2)^2 + (5 - 6.2)^2 + (6 - 6.2)^2 + (4 - 6.2)^2 \\
&+ (5 - 3.7)^2 + (7 - 3.7)^2 + (6 - 3.7)^2 + (4 - 3.7)^2 + (5 - 3.7)^2 \\
&+ (2 - 3.7)^2 + (3 - 3.7)^2 + (2 - 3.7)^2 + (1 - 3.7)^2 + (2 - 3.7)^2
\end{aligned}
$$

$$
\begin{aligned}
&= (1.7)^2 + (0.7)^2 + (1.7)^2 + (-0.3)^2 + (0.7)^2 \\
&+ (-0.3)^2 + (0.7)^2 + (-1.3)^2 + (-1.3)^2 + (-2.3)^2 \\
&+ (1.8)^2 + (1.8)^2 + (0.8)^2 + (2.8)^2 + (-0.2)^2 \\
&+ (-2.2)^2 + (-1.2)^2 + (-1.2)^2 + (-0.2)^2 + (-2.2)^2 \\
&+ (1.3)^2 + (3.3)^2 + (2.3)^2 + (0.3)^2 + (1.3)^2 \\
&+ (-1.7)^2 + (-0.7)^2 + (-1.7)^2 + (-2.7)^2 + (-1.7)^2
\end{aligned}
$$

$$= 79.80$$

It can be verified that

$$SS_y = SS_x + SS_{error}$$

as follows:

$$185.867 = 106.067 + 79.80$$

The strength of the effects of X on Y are measured as follows:

$$
\begin{aligned}
\eta^2 &= \frac{SS_x}{SS_y} \\
&= \frac{106.067}{185.867} \\
&= 0.571
\end{aligned}
$$

In other words, 57.1 percent of the variation in sales (Y) is accounted for by in-store promotion (X), indicating a modest effect. The null hypothesis may now be tested.

$$F = \frac{SS_x /(c - 1)}{SS_{error}/(N - c)} = \frac{MS_x}{MS_{error}}$$

$$F = \frac{106.067/(3 - 1)}{79.800/(30 - 3)}$$

$$= 17.944$$

From Table 5 in the Statistical Appendix, we see that for 2 and 27 degrees of freedom, the critical value of F is 3.35 for $\alpha = 0.05$. Because the calculated value of F is greater than the critical value, we reject the null hypothesis. We conclude that the population means for the three levels of in-store promotion are indeed different. The relative magnitudes of the means for the three categories indicate that a high level of in-store promotion leads to significantly higher sales.

We now illustrate the analysis-of-variance procedure using a computer program. The results of conducting the same analysis by computer are presented in Table 16.4. The value of SS_x denoted by between groups is 106.067 with 2 df; that of SS_{error} denoted by within groups is 79.80 with 27 df. Therefore, $MS_x = 106.067/2 = 53.033$, and $MS_{error} = 79.80/27 = 2.956$. The value of $F = 53.033/2.956 = 17.944$ with 2 and 27 degrees of freedom, resulting in a probability of 0.000. Because the associated probability is less than the significance level of 0.05, the null hypothesis of equal population means is rejected. Alternatively, it can be seen from Table 5 in the Statistical Appendix that the critical value of F for 2 and 27 degrees of freedom is 3.35. Because the calculated value of F (17.944) is larger than the critical value, the null hypothesis is rejected. As can be seen from Table 16.4, the sample means, with values of 8.3, 6.2, and 3.7, are quite different. Stores with a high level of in-store promotion have the highest average sales (8.3) and stores with a low level of in-store promotion have the lowest average sales (3.7). Stores with a medium level of in-store promotion have an intermediate level of average sales (6.2). These findings seem plausible. Instead of 30 stores, if this were a large and representative sample, the implications would be that management seeking to increase sales should emphasize in-store promotion.

The procedure for conducting one-way analysis of variance and the illustrative application help us understand the assumptions involved.

ACTIVE RESEARCH

Experts, Novices, and Nonusers of Home Computers: Are Their Psychographics Different?

Visit www.hp.com and conduct an Internet search using a search engine and your library's online database to obtain information on computer usage in U.S. households.

As the marketing director for Hewlett-Packard, how would you segment the home computer market?

As a marketing research analyst working for HP, how would you determine whether the three home computer usage segments (experts, novices, and nonusers) differ in terms of each of 10 psychographic characteristics, each measured on a 7-point scale?

SPSS Output File

SAS Output File

TABLE 16.4
One-Way ANOVA: Effect of In-Store Promotion on Store Sales

Source of Variation	Sum of Squares	df	Mean Square	F Ratio	F Prob.
Between groups (In-store promotion)	106.067	2	53.033	17.944	0.000
Within groups (Error)	79.800	27	2.956		
TOTAL	185.867	29	6.409		

Cell Means Level of In-store Promotion	Count	Mean
High (1)	10	8.300
Medium (2)	10	6.200
Low (3)	10	3.700
TOTAL	30	6.067

Assumptions in Analysis of Variance

The salient assumptions in analysis of variance can be summarized as follows.

1. Ordinarily, the categories of the independent variable are assumed to be fixed. Inferences are made only to the specific categories considered. This is referred to as the *fixed-effects model*. Other models are also available. In the *random-effects model,* the categories or treatments are considered to be random samples from a universe of treatments. Inferences are made to other categories not examined in the analysis. A *mixed-effects model* results if some treatments are considered fixed and others random.[6]
2. The error term is normally distributed, with a zero mean and a constant variance. The error is not related to any of the categories of *X*. Modest departures from these assumptions do not seriously affect the validity of the analysis. Furthermore, the data can be transformed to satisfy the assumption of normality or equal variances.
3. The error terms are uncorrelated. If the error terms are correlated (i.e., the observations are not independent), the *F* ratio can be seriously distorted.

In many data analysis situations, these assumptions are reasonably met. Analysis of variance is therefore a common procedure, as illustrated by the following example.

Real Research

Viewing Ethical Perceptions from Different Lenses

A survey was conducted to examine differences in perceptions of ethical issues. The data were obtained from 31 managers, 21 faculty, 97 undergraduate business students, and 48 MBA students. As part of the survey, respondents were required to rate five ethical items on a scale of 1 = strongly agree and 5 = strongly disagree with 3 representing a neutral response. The means for each group are shown. One-way analysis of variance was conducted to examine the significance of differences between groups for each survey item, and the *F* and *p* values obtained are also shown.

Item No.	Survey Item	Managers	Faculty	Graduate Students	Undergraduate Students	F Value	p Value
1	Students caught cheating should receive an F.	3.7	3.8	3.8	4.0	0.94	0.42
2	Plagiarism should be reported.	4.1	3.4	3.8	3.5	2.2	0.09
3	Student grades should be raised to get employer pay for course.	1.6	1.7	2.7	2.8	18.3	0.00
4	Use of school printers for personal printing should be stopped.	4.5	3.4	3.5	3.2	11.0	0.00
5	Course work should be simplified to accommodate weaker students.	1.7	1.8	2.4	2.8	13.4	0.00

The findings indicating significant differences on three of the five ethics items point to the need for more communication among the four groups so as to better align perceptions of ethical issues in management education.[7] ■

N-Way Analysis of Variance

In marketing research, one is often concerned with the effect of more than one factor simultaneously.[8] For example:

- How do the consumers' intentions to buy a brand vary with different levels of price and different levels of distribution?
- How do advertising levels (high, medium, and low) interact with price levels (high, medium, and low) to influence a brand's sales?

- Do educational levels (less than high school, high school graduate, some college, and college graduate) and age (less than 35, 35–55, more than 55) affect consumption of a brand?
- What is the effect of consumers' familiarity with a department store (high, medium, and low) and store image (positive, neutral, and negative) on preference for the store?

interaction

When assessing the relationship between two variables, an interaction occurs if the effect of X_1 depends on the level of X_2, and vice versa.

In determining such effects, *n*-way analysis of variance can be used. A major advantage of this technique is that it enables the researcher to examine interactions between the factors. **Interactions** occur when the effects of one factor on the dependent variable depend on the level (category) of the other factors. The procedure for conducting *n*-way analysis of variance is similar to that for one-way analysis of variance. The statistics associated with *n*-way analysis of variance are also defined similarly. Consider the simple case of two factors, X_1 and X_2, having categories c_1 and c_2. The total variation in this case is partitioned as follows:

$$SS_{total} = SS \text{ due to } X_1 + SS \text{ due to } X_2 + SS \text{ due to interaction of } X_1 \text{ and } X_2 + SS_{within}$$

or

$$SS_y = SS_{x_1} + SS_{x_2} + SS_{x_1 x_2} + SS_{error}$$

A larger effect of X_1 will be reflected in a greater mean difference in the levels of X_1 and a larger SS_{x_1}. The same is true for the effect of X_2. The larger the interaction between X_1 and X_2, the larger $SS_{x_1 x_2}$ will be. On the other hand, if X_1 and X_2 are independent, the value of $SS_{x_1 x_2}$ will be close to zero.[9]

multiple η^2

The strength of the joint effect of two (or more) factors, or the overall effect.

The strength of the joint effect of two factors, called the overall effect, or **multiple η^2**, is measured as follows:

$$\text{multiple } \eta^2 = \frac{(SS_{x_1} + SS_{x_2} + SS_{x_1 x_2})}{SS_y}$$

significance of the overall effect

A test that some differences exist between some of the treatment groups.

The **significance of the overall effect** may be tested by an F test, as follows:

$$F = \frac{(SS_{x_1} + SS_{x_2} + SS_{x_1 x_2})/df_n}{SS_{error}/df_d}$$

$$= \frac{SS_{x_1, x_2, x_1 x_2}/df_n}{SS_{error}/df_d}$$

$$= \frac{MS_{x_1, x_2, x_1 x_2}}{MS_{error}}$$

where

$$df_n = \text{degrees of freedom for the numerator}$$
$$= (c_1 - 1) + (c_2 - 1) + (c_1 - 1)(c_2 - 1)$$
$$= c_1 c_2 - 1$$
$$df_d = \text{degrees of freedom for the denominator}$$
$$= N - c_1 c_2$$
$$MS = \text{mean square}$$

significance of the interaction effect

A test of the significance of the interaction between two or more independent variables.

If the overall effect is significant, the next step is to examine the **significance of the interaction effect**. Under the null hypothesis of no interaction, the appropriate F test is:

$$F = \frac{SS_{x_1 x_2}/df_n}{SS_{error}/df_d}$$

$$= \frac{MS_{x_1 x_2}}{MS_{error}}$$

where

$$df_n = (c_1 - 1)(c_2 - 1)$$
$$df_d = N - c_1 c_2$$

If the interaction effect is found to be significant, then the effect of X_1 depends on the level of X_2, and vice versa. Because the effect of one factor is not uniform, but varies with the level of the other factor, it is not generally meaningful to test the significance of the main effects. However, it is meaningful to test the significance of each main effect of each factor if the interaction effect is not significant.[10]

significance of the main effect

A test of the significance of the main effect for each individual factor.

The **significance of the main effect** of each factor may be tested as follows for X_1:

$$F = \frac{SS_{x_1}/df_n}{SS_{error}/df_d}$$
$$= \frac{MS_{x_1}}{MS_{error}}$$

where

$$df_n = c_1 - 1$$
$$df_d = N - c_1 c_2$$

The foregoing analysis assumes that the design was orthogonal, or balanced (the number of cases in each cell was the same). If the cell size varies, the analysis becomes more complex.

Illustrative Application of N-Way Analysis of Variance

Returning to the data of Table 16.2, let us now examine the effect of the level of in-store promotion and couponing on store sales. The results of running a 3 × 2 ANOVA on the computer are presented in Table 16.5. For the main effect of level of promotion, the sum of squares SS_{xp}, degrees of freedom, and mean square MS_{xp} are the same as earlier determined in Table 16.4. The sum of squares for couponing $SS_{xc} = 53.333$ with 1 df, resulting in an identical value for the mean square MS_{xc}. The combined main effect is determined by adding the sum of squares due to the two main effects ($SS_{xp} + SS_{xc} = 106.067 + 53.333 = 159.400$) as well as adding the degrees of freedom (2 + 1 = 3). For the promotion and coupon interaction effect, the sum of squares $SS_{xpxc} = 3.267$ with (3 − 1) (2 − 1) = 2 degrees of freedom, resulting in $MS_{xpxc} = 3.267/2 = 1.633$. For the overall (model) effect, the sum of squares is the addition of the sum of squares for promotion main effect, coupon main effect, and interaction effect = 106.067 + 53.333 + 3.267 = 162.667 with 2 + 1 + 2 = 5 degrees of freedom, resulting in a mean square of 162.667/5 = 32.533. Note, however, the error statistics are now different than in Table 16.4. This is due to the fact that we now have two factors instead of one. $SS_{error} = 23.2$ with (30 − 3 × 2) or 24 degrees of freedom resulting in $MS_{error} = 23.2/24 = 0.967$.

The test statistic for the significance of the overall effect is

$$F = (32.533/0.967)$$
$$= 33.655$$

with 5 and 24 degrees of freedom, which is significant at the 0.05 level.

The test statistic for the significance of the interaction effect is

$$F = (1.633/0.967)$$
$$= 1.690$$

with 2 and 24 degrees of freedom, which is not significant at the 0.05 level.

Because the interaction effect is not significant, the significance of the main effects can be evaluated. The test statistic for the significance of the main effect of promotion is

$$F = (53.033/0.967)$$
$$= 54.862$$

with 2 and 24 degrees of freedom, which is significant at the 0.05 level.

SPSS Output File

SAS Output File

TABLE 16.5
Two-Way Analysis of Variance

Source of Variation	Sum of Squares	df	Mean Square	F	Sig. of F	ω^2
Main Effects						
In-store promotion	106.067	2	53.033	54.862	0.000	0.557
Coupon	53.333	1	53.333	55.172	0.000	0.280
Combined	159.400	3	53.133	54.966	0.000	
Two-way interaction	3.267	2	1.633	1.690	0.206	
Model	162.667	5	32.533	33.655	0.000	
Residual (Error)	23.200	24	0.967			
TOTAL	185.867	29	6.409			

Cell Means In-store Promotion	Coupon	Count	Mean
High	Yes	5	9.200
High	No	5	7.400
Medium	Yes	5	7.600
Medium	No	5	4.800
Low	Yes	5	5.400
Low	No	5	2.000

Factor Level Means Promotion	Coupon	Count	Mean
High		10	8.300
Medium		10	6.200
Low		10	3.700
	Yes	15	7.400
	No	15	4.733
Grand Mean		30	6.067

The test statistic for the significance of the main effect of coupon is

$$F = (53.333/0.967)$$
$$= 55.172$$

with 1 and 24 degrees of freedom, which is significant at the 0.05 level. Thus, a higher level of promotion results in higher sales. The distribution of a storewide coupon results in higher sales. The effect of each is independent of the other. If this were a large and representative sample, the implications are that management can increase sales by increasing in-store promotion and the use of coupons, independently of the other.

Real Research

Country Affiliation Affects TV Reception

A study examined the impact of country affiliation on the credibility of product-attribute claims for TVs. The dependent variables were the following product-attribute claims: good sound, reliability, crisp-clear picture, and stylish design. The independent variables that were manipulated consisted of price, country affiliation, and store distribution. A $2 \times 2 \times 2$ between-subjects design was used. Two levels of price, $949.95 (low) and $1,249.95 (high), two levels of country affiliation, Korea and the United States, and two levels of store distribution, Best Buy and without Best Buy, were specified.

Data were collected from two suburban malls in a large U.S. city. Thirty respondents were randomly assigned to each of the eight treatment cells for a total of 240 subjects. Table 1 presents the results for manipulations that had significant effects on each of the dependent variables.

Table 1 Analyses for Significant Manipulations

Effect	Dependent Variable	Univariate F	df	p
Country × price	Good sound	7.57	1,232	0.006
Country × price	Reliability	6.57	1,232	0.011
Country × distribution	Crisp-clear picture	6.17	1,232	0.014
Country × distribution	Reliability	6.57	1,232	0.011
Country × distribution	Stylish design	10.31	1,232	0.002

The directions of country-by-distribution interaction effects for the three dependent variables are shown in Table 2. Whereas the credibility ratings for the crisp-clear picture, reliability, and stylish design claims are improved by distributing the Korean-made TV set through Best Buy, rather than some other distributor, the same is not true of a U.S.-made set. Similarly, the directions of country-by-price interaction effects for the two dependent variables are shown in Table 3. At $1,249.95, the credibility ratings for the "good sound" and "reliability" claims are higher for the U.S.-made TV set than for its Korean counterpart, but there is little difference related to country affiliation when the product is priced at $949.95.

Table 2 Country-by-Distribution Interaction Means

Country × Distribution	Crisp-Clear Picture	Reliability	Stylish Design
Korea			
Best Buy	3.67	3.42	3.82
Without Best Buy	3.18	2.88	3.15
United States			
Best Buy	3.60	3.47	3.53
Without Best Buy	3.77	3.65	3.75

Table 3 Country-by-Price Interaction Means

Country × Price	Good Sound	Reliability
$949.95		
Korea	3.75	3.40
United States	3.53	3.45
$1,249.95		
Korea	3.15	2.90
United States	3.73	3.67

This study demonstrates that credibility of attribute claims, for products traditionally exported to the United States by a company in a newly industrialized country, can be significantly improved if the same company distributes the product through a well-known U.S. retailer and considers making manufacturing investments in the United States. Specifically, three product attribute claims (crisp-clear picture, reliability, and stylish design) are perceived as more credible when the TVs are made in Korea if they are also distributed through a well-known U.S. retailer. Also, the "good sound" and "reliability" claims for TVs are perceived to be more credible for a U.S-made set sold at a higher price, possibly offsetting the potential disadvantage of higher manufacturing costs in the United States. Thus, Thomson, the manufacturer of RCA products (www.rca.com), may be better off manufacturing its TV sets in the United States and selling them at a higher price.[11] ■

ACTIVE RESEARCH

The Effect of Price and Quality on Preferences for Jeans

Visit www.levis.com and search the Internet using a search engine as well as your library's online database to find information on consumer preferences for jeans.

Levi's would like to conduct marketing research to increase its share of the jeans market. Past studies suggest that the two most important factors determining the preferences for jeans are price (high, medium, and low) and quality (high, medium, and low). What design would you adopt and what analysis would you conduct to determine the effects of these factors on preference for jeans?

As Levi's marketing chief, what information would you need to formulate strategies aimed at increasing market share?

Analysis of Covariance

When examining the differences in the mean values of the dependent variable related to the effect of the controlled independent variables, it is often necessary to take into account the influence of uncontrolled independent variables. For example:

- In determining how consumers' intentions to buy a brand vary with different levels of price, attitude toward the brand may have to be taken into consideration.
- In determining how different groups exposed to different commercials evaluate a brand, it may be necessary to control for prior knowledge.
- In determining how different price levels will affect a household's cereal consumption, it may be essential to take household size into account.

In such cases, analysis of covariance should be used. Analysis of covariance includes at least one categorical independent variable and at least one interval or metric independent variable. The categorical independent variable is called a *factor*, whereas the metric independent variable is called a *covariate*. The most common use of the covariate is to remove extraneous variation from the dependent variable, because the effects of the factors are of major concern. The variation in the dependent variable due to the covariates is removed by an adjustment of the dependent variable's mean value within each treatment condition. An analysis of variance is then performed on the adjusted scores.[12] The significance of the combined effect of the covariates, as well as the effect of each covariate, is tested by using the appropriate F tests. The coefficients for the covariates provide insights into the effect that the covariates exert on the dependent variable. Analysis of covariance is most useful when the covariate is linearly related to the dependent variable and is not related to the factors.[13]

We again use the data of Table 16.2 to illustrate analysis of covariance. Suppose that we wanted to determine the effect of in-store promotion and couponing on sales while controlling for the effect of clientele. It is felt that the affluence of the clientele may also have an effect on sales of the department store. The dependent variable consists of store sales. As before, promotion has three levels and couponing has two. Clientele measured on an interval scale serves as the covariate. The results are shown in Table 16.6. As can be seen, the sum of squares attributable to the covariate is very small (0.838) with 1 df resulting in an identical value for the mean square. The associated F value is 0.838/0.972 = 0.862, with 1 and 23 degrees of freedom, which is not significant at the 0.05 level. Thus, the conclusion is that the affluence of the clientele does not have an effect on the sales of the department store. If the effect of the covariate is significant, the sign of the raw coefficient can be used to interpret the direction of the effect on the dependent variable.

Issues in Interpretation

Important issues involved in the interpretation of ANOVA results include interactions, relative importance of factors, and multiple comparisons.

Interactions

The different interactions that can arise when conducting ANOVA on two or more factors are shown in Figure 16.3. One outcome is that ANOVA may indicate that there are no interactions (the interaction effects are not found to be significant). The other possibility is that the interaction

SPSS Output File

SAS Output File

TABLE 16.6
Analysis of Covariance

Source of Variation	Sum of Squares	df	Mean Square	F	Sig. of F
Covariates					
Clientele	0.838	1	0.838	0.862	0.363
Main effects					
Promotion	106.067	2	53.033	54.546	0.000
Coupon	53.333	1	53.333	54.855	0.000
Combined	159.400	3	53.133	54.649	0.000
2-way interaction					
Promotion × Coupon	3.267	2	1.633	1.680	0.208
Model	163.505	6	27.251	28.028	0.000
Residual (Error)	22.362	23	0.972		
TOTAL	185.867	29	6.409		
Covariate	Raw coefficient				
Clientele	−0.078				

ordinal interaction
An interaction where the rank order of the effects attributable to one factor does not change across the levels of the second factor.

disordinal interaction
The change in the rank order of the effects of one factor across the levels of another.

is significant. An *interaction effect* occurs when the effect of an independent variable on a dependent variable is different for different categories or levels of another independent variable. The interaction may be ordinal or disordinal. In **ordinal interaction**, the rank order of the effects related to one factor does not change across the levels of the second factor. **Disordinal interaction**, on the other hand, involves a change in the rank order of the effects of one factor across the levels of another. If the interaction is disordinal, it could be of a noncrossover or crossover type.[14]

These interaction cases are displayed in Figure 16.4, which assumes that there are two factors, X_1 with three levels (X_{11}, X_{12}, and X_{13}), and X_2 with two levels (X_{21} and X_{22}). Case 1 depicts no interaction. The effects of X_1 on Y are parallel over the two levels of X_2. Although there is some departure from parallelism, this is not beyond what might be expected from chance. Parallelism implies that the net effect of X_{22} over X_{21} is the same across the three levels of X_1. In the absence of interaction, the joint effect of X_1 and X_2 is simply the sum of their individual main effects.

Case 2 depicts an ordinal interaction. The line segments depicting the effects of X_1 and X_2 are not parallel. The difference between X_{22} and X_{21} increases as we move from X_{11} to X_{12} and from X_{12} to X_{13}, but the rank order of the effects of X_1 is the same over the two levels of X_2. This rank order, in ascending order, is X_{11}, X_{12}, X_{13}, and it remains the same for X_{21} and X_{22}.

FIGURE 16.3

A Classification of Interaction Effects

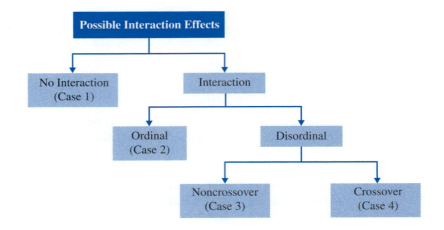

FIGURE 16.4

Patterns of Interaction

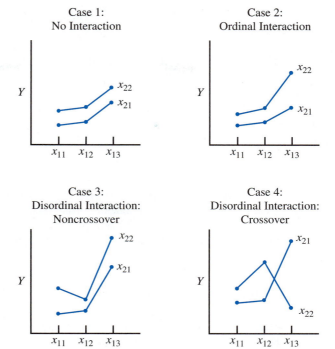

Disordinal interaction of a noncrossover type is displayed by case 3. The lowest effect of X_1 at level X_{21} occurs at X_{11}, and the rank order of effects is X_{11}, X_{12}, and X_{13}. However, at level X_{22}, the lowest effect of X_1 occurs at X_{12}, and the rank order is changed to X_{12}, X_{11}, and X_{13}. Because it involves a change in rank order, disordinal interaction is stronger than ordinal interaction.

In disordinal interactions of a crossover type, the line segments cross each other, as shown by case 4 in Figure 16.4. In this case, the relative effect of the levels of one factor changes with the levels of the other. Note that X_{22} has a greater effect than X_{21} when the levels of X_1 are X_{11} and X_{12}. When the level of X_1 is X_{13}, the situation is reversed, and X_{21} has a greater effect than X_{22}. (Note that in cases 1, 2, and 3, X_{22} had a greater impact than X_{21} across all three levels of X_1.) Hence, disordinal interactions of a crossover type represent the strongest interactions.[15]

Relative Importance of Factors

Experimental designs are usually balanced, in that each cell contains the same number of respondents. This results in an orthogonal design in which the factors are uncorrelated. Hence, it is possible to determine unambiguously the relative importance of each factor in explaining the variation in the dependent variable. The most commonly used measure in ANOVA is **omega squared, ω^2**. This measure indicates what proportion of the variation in the dependent variable is related to a particular independent variable or factor. The relative contribution of a factor X is calculated as follows:[16]

omega squared (ω^2)
A measure indicating the proportion of the variation in the dependent variable explained by a particular independent variable or factor.

$$\omega_x^2 = \frac{SS_x - (df_x \times MS_{error})}{SS_{total} + MS_{error}}$$

Normally, ω^2 is interpreted only for statistically significant effects.[17] In Table 16.5, ω^2 associated with the level of in-store promotion is calculated as follows:

$$\omega_p^2 = \frac{106.067 - (2 \times 0.967)}{185.867 + 0.967}$$

$$= \frac{104.133}{186.834}$$

$$= 0.557$$

Note, in Table 16.5, that

$$SS_{total} = 106.067 + 53.333 + 3.267 + 23.2$$
$$= 185.867$$

Likewise, the ω^2 associated with couponing is

$$\omega_c^2 = \frac{53.333 - (1 \times 0.967)}{185.867 + 0.967}$$

$$= \frac{52.366}{186.834}$$

$$= 0.280$$

As a guide to interpreting ω^2, a large experimental effect produces an ω^2 of 0.15 or greater, a medium effect produces an index of around 0.06, and a small effect produces an index of 0.01.[18] In Table 16.5, although the effect of promotion and couponing are both large, the effect of promotion is much larger. Therefore, in-store promotion will be more effective in increasing sales than couponing.

Multiple Comparisons

contrasts
In ANOVA, a method of examining differences among two or more means of the treatment groups.

a priori contrasts
Contrasts that are determined before conducting the analysis, based on the researcher's theoretical framework.

a posteriori contrasts
Contrasts made after the analysis. These are generally multiple comparison tests.

multiple comparison test
A posteriori contrasts that enable the researcher to construct generalized confidence intervals that can be used to make pairwise comparisons of all treatment means.

repeated measures analysis of variance
An ANOVA technique used when respondents are exposed to more than one treatment condition and repeated measurements are obtained.

The ANOVA F test examines only the overall difference in means. If the null hypothesis of equal means is rejected, we can conclude only that not all of the group means are equal. However, only some of the means may be statistically different and we may wish to examine differences among specific means. This can be done by specifying appropriate **contrasts**, or comparisons used to determine which of the means are statistically different. Contrasts may be a priori or a posteriori. **A priori contrasts** are determined before conducting the analysis, based on the researcher's theoretical framework. Generally, a priori contrasts are used in lieu of the ANOVA F test. The contrasts selected are orthogonal (they are independent in a statistical sense).

A posteriori contrasts are made after the analysis. These are generally **multiple comparison tests**. They enable the researcher to construct generalized confidence intervals that can be used to make pairwise comparisons of all treatment means. These tests, listed in order of decreasing power, include least significant difference, Duncan's multiple range test, Student-Newman-Keuls, Tukey's alternate procedure, honestly significant difference, modified least significant difference, and Scheffe's test. Of these tests, least significant difference is the most powerful; Scheffe's, the most conservative. For further discussion on a priori and a posteriori contrasts, refer to the literature.[19]

Our discussion so far has assumed that each subject is exposed to only one treatment or experimental condition. Sometimes subjects are exposed to more than one experimental condition, in which case repeated measures ANOVA should be used.

Repeated Measures ANOVA

In marketing research there are often large differences in the background and individual characteristics of respondents. If this source of variability can be separated from treatment effects (effects of the independent variable) and experimental error, then the sensitivity of the experiment can be enhanced. One way of controlling the differences between subjects is by observing each subject under each experimental condition (see Table 16.7). In this sense, each subject serves as its own control. For example, in a survey attempting to determine differences in evaluations of various airlines, each respondent evaluates all the major competing airlines. Because repeated measurements are obtained from each respondent, this design is referred to as within-subjects design or **repeated measures analysis of variance**. This differs from the assumption we made in our earlier discussion that each respondent is exposed to only one treatment condition, also referred to as *between-subjects design*.[20] Repeated measures analysis of variance may be thought of as an extension of the paired-samples t test to the case of more than two related samples.

TABLE 16.7

Decomposition of the Total Variation: Repeated Measures ANOVA

	Independent Variable				X		
	Subject No.			Categories		Total Sample	
	1	X_1	X_2	X_3	$\cdots$	X_c	
	2	Y_{11}	Y_{12}	Y_{13}		Y_{1c}	Y_1
Between-People Variation $= SS_{between\ people}$		Y_{22}	Y_{22}	Y_{23}		Y_{2c}	Y_2
		•					•
		•					•
		•					•
	n	Y_{n1}	Y_{n2}	Y_{n3}		Y_{nc}	Y_N
Category Mean		$\bar{Y}_1$	$\bar{Y}_2$	$\bar{Y}_3$		$\bar{Y}_c$	$\bar{Y}$

Total variation $= SS_y$

Within-People Variation $= SS_{within\ people}$

In the case of a single factor with repeated measures, the total variation, with $nc - 1$ degrees of freedom, may be split into between-people variation and within-people variation.

$$SS_{total} = SS_{between\ people} + SS_{within\ people}$$

The between-people variation, which is related to the differences between the means of people, has $n - 1$ degrees of freedom. The within-people variation has $n(c - 1)$ degrees of freedom. The within-people variation may, in turn, be divided into two different sources of variation. One source is related to the differences between treatment means, and the second consists of residual or error variation. The degrees of freedom corresponding to the treatment variation are $c - 1$, and those corresponding to residual variation are $(n - 1)(c - 1)$. Thus,

$$SS_{within\ people} = SS_x + SS_{error}$$

A test of the null hypothesis of equal means may now be constructed in the usual way:

$$F = \frac{SS_x/(c - 1)}{SS_{error}/(n - 1)(c - 1)} = \frac{MS_x}{MS_{error}}$$

So far we have assumed that the dependent variable is measured on an interval or ratio scale. If the dependent variable is nonmetric, however, a different procedure should be used.

Decision Research Marriott: Luring Business Travelers

The Situation

Marriott International, Inc., is a leading worldwide hospitality company. Its heritage can be traced to a small root beer stand opened in Washington, D.C., in 1927 by J. Willard and Alice S. Marriott. As of 2009, the company operated or franchised about 3,000 lodging properties located in the United States and 67 other countries and territories. Among Marriott's most frequent visitors are its business traveler customers. For many years, business travelers have faced a fundamental problem—figuring out a comfortable and convenient way to get their jobs accomplished in hotel rooms without a functional workspace. Though many were not very productive, they did hone important skills such as writing legibly on top of a comforter, stretching arms beyond maximum length to reach hidden outlets behind or underneath furniture, and squinting tightly to make documents readable.

Analysis of variance techniques can help Marriott determine what features of a hotel room are most important to business travelers.

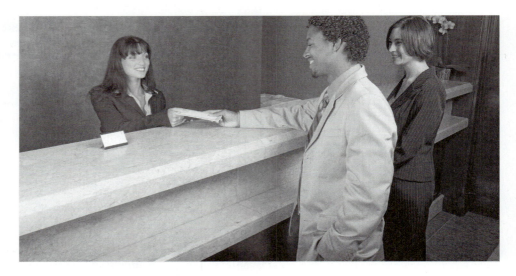

Marriott recognized these needs of its business travelers and wanted to do something about it. Susan Hodapp, brand director for Marriott Hotels, Resorts, and Suites, commissioned a survey to determine business travelers' preferences for hotels and the factors that are important in their hotel selection process. Part of the questionnaire focused attention on the features of the hotel room. Each respondent rated the relative importance of the following factors on a 7-point scale (1 = not at all important, 7 = extremely important): room décor, room lighting, room furniture, voice and data access in the room, and price of the room per night.

The Marketing Research Decision

1. Marriott would like to determine what features of a hotel room are most important in business travelers' choice of a hotel. Each feature could be offered at several levels, for example, room lighting could be bright, medium, or dim. What analysis should be conducted?
2. Discuss the role of the type of data analysis you recommend in enabling Susan Hodapp to understand business travelers' preferences for hotel rooms.

The Marketing Management Decision

1. What should Marriott do in order to lure the business travelers? What features should it stress?
2. Discuss how the marketing management decision action that you recommend to Susan Hodapp is influenced by the type of data analysis that you suggested earlier and by the findings of that analysis.[21] ■

Nonmetric Analysis of Variance

nonmetric analysis of variance
An ANOVA technique for examining the difference in the central tendencies of more than two groups when the dependent variable is measured on an ordinal scale.

k-sample median test
Nonparametric test that is used to examine differences among groups when the dependent variable is measured on an ordinal scale.

Kruskal-Wallis one-way analysis of variance
A nonmetric ANOVA test that uses the rank value of each case, not merely its location relative to the median.

Nonmetric analysis of variance examines the difference in the central tendencies of more than two groups when the dependent variable is measured on an ordinal scale. One such procedure is the **k-sample median test**. As its name implies, this is an extension of the median test for two groups, which was considered in Chapter 15. The null hypothesis is that the medians of the k populations are equal. The test involves the computation of a common median over the k samples. Then a $2 \times k$ table of cell counts based on cases above or below the common median is generated. A chi-square statistic is computed. The significance of the chi-square implies a rejection of the null hypothesis.

A more powerful test is the **Kruskal-Wallis one-way analysis of variance**. This is an extension of the Mann-Whitney test (Chapter 15). This test also examines the difference in medians. The null hypothesis is the same as in the k-sample median test, but the testing procedure is different. All cases from the k groups are ordered in a single ranking. If the k populations are the same, the groups should be similar in terms of ranks within each group. The rank sum is calculated for each group. From these, the Kruskal-Wallis H statistic, which has a chi-square distribution, is computed.

The Kruskal-Wallis test is more powerful than the k-sample median test because it uses the rank value of each case, not merely its location relative to the median. However, if there are a large number of tied rankings in the data, the k-sample median test may be a better choice.

Nonmetric analysis of variance is not popular in commercial marketing research. Another procedure, which is also only rarely used, is multivariate analysis of variance.

Multivariate Analysis of Variance

multivariate analysis of variance (MANOVA)
An ANOVA technique using two or more metric dependent variables.

Multivariate analysis of variance (MANOVA) is similar to analysis of variance (ANOVA), except that instead of one metric dependent variable, we have two or more. The objective is the same; MANOVA is also concerned with examining differences between groups. Whereas ANOVA examines group differences on a single dependent variable, MANOVA examines group differences across multiple dependent variables simultaneously. In ANOVA, the null hypothesis is that the means of the dependent variable are equal across the groups. In MANOVA, the null hypothesis is that the vectors of means on multiple dependent variables are equal across groups. Multivariate analysis of variance is appropriate when there are two or more dependent variables that are correlated. If there are multiple dependent variables that are uncorrelated or orthogonal, ANOVA on each of the dependent variables is more appropriate than MANOVA.[22]

As an example, suppose that four groups, each consisting of 100 randomly selected individuals, were exposed to four different commercials about Tide detergent. After seeing the commercial, each individual provided ratings on preference for Tide, preference for Procter & Gamble (the company marketing Tide), and preference for the commercial itself. Because these three preference variables are correlated, multivariate analysis of variance should be conducted to determine which commercial is the most effective (produced the highest preference across the three preference variables). The next example illustrates the application of ANOVA and MANOVA in international marketing research, and the example after that shows an application of these techniques in examining ethics in marketing research.

Real Research   The Commonality of Unethical Research Practices Worldwide

As of 2009, mass media is continuing to focus more attention on the highly visible practices of unethical marketing research, and this poses a serious threat to marketing research practitioners. A study examined marketing professionals' perceptions of the commonality of unethical marketing research practices on a cross-national basis. The sample of marketing professionals was drawn from Australia, Canada, Great Britain, and the United States.

Respondents' evaluations were analyzed using computer programs for MANOVA and ANOVA. Country of respondent comprised the predictor variable in the analysis, and 15 commonality evaluations served as the criterion variables. The F values from the ANOVA analyses indicated that only two of the 15 commonality evaluations achieved significance ($p < 0.05$). Further, the MANOVA F value was not statistically significant, implying the lack of overall differences in commonality evaluations across respondents of the four countries. Therefore, it was concluded that marketing professionals in the four countries evince similar perceptions of the commonality of unethical research practices. This finding is not surprising, given research evidence that organizations in the four countries reflect similar corporate cultures. Thus, the marketing research industry in these four countries should adopt a common platform in fighting unethical practices.[23] ■

Real Research

"MAN"OVA Demonstrates That Man Is Different from Woman

In order to investigate differences between research ethics judgments in men and women, the statistical techniques of MANOVA and ANOVA were used. Respondents were asked to indicate their degree of approval with regard to a series of scenarios involving decisions of an ethical nature. These evaluations served as the dependent variable in the analysis, and sex of the respondent served as the independent variable. MANOVA was used for multivariate analysis and its resultant F value was significant at the $p < 0.001$ level—indicating that there was an "overall" difference between males and females in research ethics judgments. Univariate analysis was conducted via ANOVA, and F values indicated that three items were the greatest contributors to the overall gender difference in ethical evaluations: the use of ultraviolet ink to precode a mail questionnaire, the use of an ad that encourages consumer misuse of a product, and unwillingness by a researcher to offer data help to an inner-city advisory group. Another recent study examined how ethical beliefs are related to age and gender of business professionals. The results of this particular study indicated that overall, younger business professionals exhibited a lower standard of ethical beliefs. In the younger age group, females demonstrated a higher level of ethical beliefs compared to males. However, in the older age group, results showed that males had a slightly higher level of ethical beliefs. Thus, companies should emphasize ethical values and training to the younger professionals, especially men.[24] ∎

Statistical Software

The major computer packages (SPSS and SAS) have programs for conducting analysis of variance and covariance available in the microcomputer and mainframe versions. In addition to the basic analysis that we have considered, these programs can also perform more complex analysis. MINITAB and EXCEL also offer some programs. Exhibit 16.1 contains a description of the relevant programs for MINITAB and EXCEL. Refer to the user manuals for these packages for more information. We discuss the use of SPSS and SAS in detail.

SPSS and SAS Computerized Demonstration Movies

We have developed computerized demonstration movies that give step-by-step instructions for running all the SPSS and SAS Learning Edition programs that are discussed in this chapter. These demonstrations can be downloaded from the Web site for this book. The instructions for running these demonstrations are given in Exhibit 14.2.

SPSS and SAS Screen Captures with Notes

The step-by-step instructions for running the various SPSS and SAS Learning Edition programs discussed in this chapter are also illustrated in screen captures with appropriate notes. These screen captures can be downloaded from the Web site for this book.

EXHIBIT 16.1

MINITAB and EXCEL Programs for ANOVA and ANCOVA

Minitab

Analysis of variance and covariance can be accessed from the Stats>ANOVA function. This function performs one-way ANOVA, two-way ANOVA, analysis of means, balanced ANOVA, analysis of covariance, general linear model, main effects plot, interactions plot, and residual plots. In order to compute the mean and standard deviation, the CROSSTAB function must be used. To obtain F and p values, use the balanced ANOVA.

Excel

Both a one-way ANOVA and two-way ANOVA can be performed under the DATA>DATA ANALYSIS function. The two-way ANOVA has the features of a two-factor with replication and a two-factor without replication. The two-factor with replication includes more than one sample for each group of data. The two-factor without replication does not include more than one sampling per group.

SPSS Windows

One-way ANOVA can be efficiently performed using the program COMPARE MEANS and then ONE-WAY ANOVA. To select this procedure using SPSS for Windows, click:

Analyze>Compare Means>One-Way ANOVA . . .

The following are the detailed steps for running a one-way ANOVA on the data of Table 16.2. The null hypothesis is that there is no difference in mean normalized sales for the three levels of in-store promotion.

1. Select ANALYZE from the SPSS menu bar.
2. Click COMPARE MEANS and then ONE-WAY ANOVA.
3. Move "Sales [sales]" into the DEPENDENT LIST box.
4. Move "In-Store Promotion [promotion]" to the FACTOR box.
5. Click OPTIONS.
6. Click Descriptive.
7. Click CONTINUE.
8. Click OK.

N-way analysis of variance, analysis of covariance, MANOVA, and repeated measures ANOVA can be performed using GENERAL LINEAR MODEL. To select this procedure using SPSS for Windows, click:

Analyze>General Linear Model>Univariate . . .

Analyze>General Linear Model>Multivariate . . .

Analyze>General Linear Model>Repeated Measures . . .

We show the detailed steps for performing the analysis of covariance given in Table 16.6.

1. Select ANALYZE from the SPSS menu bar.
2. Click GENERAL LINEAR MODEL and then UNIVARIATE.
3. Move "Sales [sales]" into the DEPENDENT VARIABLE box.
4. Move "In-Store Promotion [promotion]" to the FIXED FACTOR(S) box. Then move "Coupon [coupon]" to the FIXED FACTOR(S) box.
5. Move "Clientel [clientel]" to the COVARIATE(S) box.
6. Click OK.

For nonmetric analysis of variance, including the *k*-sample median test and Kruskal-Wallis one-way analysis of variance, the program Nonparametric Tests should be used.

Analyze>Nonparametric Tests>K Independent Samples . . .

Analyze>Nonparametric Tests>K Related Samples . . .

The detailed steps for the other procedures are similar to those shown and are not given here due to space constraints.

SAS Learning Edition

The instructions given here and in all the data analysis chapters (14 to 22) will work with the SAS Learning Edition as well as with the SAS Enterprise Guide. for a point-and-click approach for performing analysis of variance, use Analyze within SAS Learning Edition. The ANOVA task offers one-way analysis of variance, nonparametric one-way analysis of variance, and mixed and linear models.

One-way ANOVA can be efficiently performed using One-Way ANOVA within the ANOVA task. To select this task click:

Analyze>ANOVA>One-Way ANOVA

The following are the detailed steps for running a one-way ANOVA on the data of Table 16.2. The null hypothesis is that there is no difference in mean normalized sales for the three levels of in-store promotion.

1. Select ANALYZE from the SAS Learning Edition menu bar.
2. Click ANOVA and then One-Way ANOVA.
3. Move SALES to the dependent variable task role.
4. Move PROMOTION to the independent variable task role.
5. Click RUN.

N-way analysis of variance, analysis of covariance, MANOVA, and repeated measures ANOVA can be performed using the Linear Models task:

Analyze>ANOVA>Linear Models

We show the detailed steps for performing the analysis of covariance given in Table 16.6.

1. Select ANALYZE from the SAS Learning Edition menu bar.
2. Click ANOVA and then Linear Models.
3. Move SALES to the dependent variable task role.
4. Move PROMOTION and COUPON to the quantitative variables task role.
5. Move CLIENTEL to the classification variable task role.
6. Click Model.
7. Select PROMOTION and COUPON and then click Main.
8. Select PROMOTION and COUPON and then click Cross.
9. Click RUN.

For nonmetric analysis of variance, including the *k*-sample median test and Kruskal-Wallis one-way analysis of variance, the Nonparametric One-Way ANOVA task should be used.

Analyze>ANOVA>Nonparametric One-Way ANOVA

Project Research   Department Store Project

Analysis of Variance

In the department store project, several independent variables were examined as categorical variables having more than two categories. For example, familiarity with the department stores considered was respecified as high, medium, or low. The effects of these independent variables on metric dependent variables were examined using analysis of variance procedures. Several useful insights were obtained that guided subsequent data analysis and interpretation. For example, a three-category respecification of familiarity produced results that were not significant, whereas treating familiarity as a binary variable (high or low) produced significant results. This, along with the frequency distribution, indicated that treating familiarity as having only two categories was most appropriate.

Project Activities

Download the SPSS or SAS data file *Sears Data 14* from the Web site for this book. See Chapter 14 for a description of this file.

1. Run separate one-way ANOVAs to determine which recoded demographic variables explain the overall familiarity score. ■

SPSS Data File

SAS Data File

Summary

In ANOVA and ANCOVA, the dependent variable is metric and the independent variables are all categorical, or combinations of categorical and metric variables. Figure 16.5 gives a concept map for conducting one-way ANOVA. One-way ANOVA involves a single independent categorical variable. Interest lies in testing the null hypothesis that the category means are equal in the population. The total variation in the dependent variable is decomposed into two components: variation related to the independent variable and variation related to error. The variation is measured in terms of the sum of squares corrected for the mean (SS). The mean square is obtained by dividing the SS by the corresponding degrees of freedom (df). The null hypothesis of equal means is tested by an F statistic, which is the ratio of the mean square related to the independent variable to the mean square related to error.

N-way analysis of variance involves the simultaneous examination of two or more categorical independent variables. A major advantage is that the interactions between the independent variables can be examined. The significance of the overall effect, interaction terms, and main effects of individual factors are examined by appropriate F tests. It is meaningful to test the significance of main effects only if the corresponding interaction terms are not significant.

ANCOVA includes at least one categorical independent variable and at least one interval or metric independent variable. The metric independent variable, or covariate, is commonly used to remove extraneous variation from the dependent variable.

When analysis of variance is conducted on two or more factors, interactions can arise. An interaction occurs when the effect of an independent variable on a dependent variable is different for different categories or levels of another independent variable. If the interaction is significant, it may be ordinal or disordinal. Disordinal interaction may be of a noncrossover or crossover type. In balanced designs, the relative importance of factors in explaining the variation in the dependent variable is measured by omega squared (ω^2). Multiple comparisons in the form of a priori or a posteriori contrasts can be used for examining differences among specific means.

In repeated measures analysis of variance, observations on each subject are obtained under each treatment condition. This design is useful for controlling for the differences in subjects that exist prior to the experiment. Nonmetric analysis of variance involves examining the differences in the central tendencies of two or more groups when the dependent variable is measured on an ordinal scale. Multivariate analysis of variance (MANOVA) involves two or more metric dependent variables.

FIGURE 16.5

A Concept Map for One-Way ANOVA

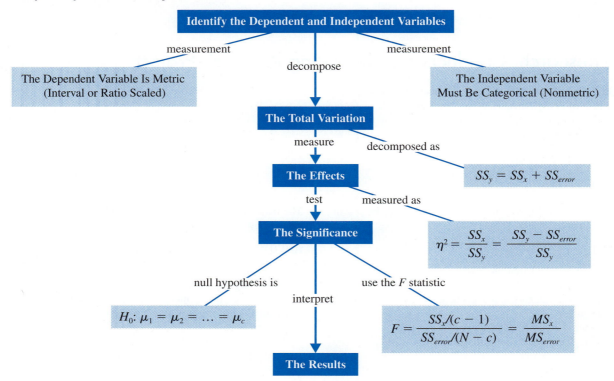

Key Terms and Concepts

Suggested Cases, Video Cases, and HBS Cases

Running Case with Real Data

1.1 Dell

Comprehensive Critical Thinking Cases

2.1 American Idol   2.2 Baskin-Robbins   2.3 Akron Children's Hospital

Data Analysis Cases with Real Data

3.1 AT&T   3.2 IBM   3.3 Kimberly-Clark

Comprehensive Cases with Real Data

4.1 JPMorgan Chase   4.2 Wendy's

Video Case

23.1 Marriott

Live Research: Conducting a Marketing Research Project

1. Differences between groups are of interest in most projects. In case of two groups, these can be examined by using independent samples t tests for two groups or one-way ANOVA for more than two groups.

Acronyms

The major characteristics of analysis of variance may be described by the acronym

ANOVA:

A nalysis of total variation
N ormally distributed errors that are uncorrelated
O ne or more categorical independent variables with fixed categories
V ariance is assumed to be constant
A single dependent variable that is metric

The major characteristics of analysis of covariance may be summarized by the acronym

ANCOVA:

A nalysis of total variation
N ormally distributed errors that are uncorrelated
C ovariates: one or more metric independent variables
O ne or more categorical independent variables with fixed categories
V ariance is assumed to be constant
A single dependent variable that is metric

Exercises

Questions

1. Discuss the similarities and differences between analysis of variance and analysis of covariance.
2. What is the relationship between analysis of variance and the *t* test?
3. What is total variation? How is it decomposed in a one-way analysis of variance?
4. What is the null hypothesis in one-way ANOVA? What basic statistic is used to test the null hypothesis in one-way ANOVA? How is this statistic computed?
5. How does *n*-way analysis of variance differ from the one-way procedure?
6. How is the total variation decomposed in *n*-way analysis of variance?
7. What is the most common use of the covariate in ANCOVA?
8. Define an interaction.
9. What is the difference between ordinal and disordinal interaction?
10. How is the relative importance of factors measured in a balanced design?
11. What is an a priori contrast?
12. What is the most powerful test for making a posteriori contrasts? Which test is the most conservative?
13. What is meant by repeated measures ANOVA? Describe the decomposition of variation in repeated measures ANOVA.
14. What are the differences between metric and nonmetric analyses of variance?
15. Describe two tests used for examining differences in central tendencies in nonmetric ANOVA.
16. What is multivariate analysis of variance? When is it appropriate?

Problems

1. After receiving some complaints from the readers, your campus newspaper decides to redesign its front page. Two new formats, B and C, were developed and tested against the current format, A. A total of 75 students were randomly selected and 25 students were randomly assigned to each of three format conditions. The students were asked to evaluate the effectiveness of the format on an 11-point scale (1 = poor, 11 = excellent).
   a. State the null hypothesis.
   b. What statistical test should you use?
   c. What are the degrees of freedom associated with the test statistic?
2. A marketing researcher wants to test the hypothesis that, in the population, there is no difference in the importance attached to shopping by consumers living in the northern, southern, eastern, and western United States. A study is conducted and analysis of variance is used to analyze the data. The results obtained are presented in the following table.
   a. Is there sufficient evidence to reject the null hypothesis?
   b. What conclusion can be drawn from the table?
   c. If the average importance were computed for each group, would you expect the sample means to be similar or different?
   d. What was the total sample size in this study?

Source	df	Sum of Squares	Mean Squares	F Ratio	F Probability
Between groups	3	70.212	23.404	1.12	0.3
Within groups	996	2082.416	20.896		

3. In a pilot study examining the effectiveness of three commercials (A, B, and C), 10 consumers were assigned to view each commercial and rate it on a 9-point Likert scale. The data obtained from the 30 respondents are shown in the table.

	Commercial			Commercial	
A	B	C	A	B	C
4	7	8	4	6	7
5	4	7	4	5	8
3	6	7	3	5	8
4	5	6	5	4	5
3	4	8	5	4	6

   a. Calculate the category means and the grand mean.
   b. Calculate SS_y, SS_x, and SS_{error}.
   c. Calculate η^2.
   d. Calculate the value of *F*.
   e. Are the three commercials equally effective?
4. An experiment tested the effects of package design and shelf display on the likelihood of purchase of Product 19 cereal. Package design and shelf display were varied at two levels each, resulting in a 2×2 design. Purchase likelihood was measured on a 7-point scale. The results are partially described in the following table.

Source of Variation	Sum of Squares	df	Mean Square	F	Significance of F	ω^2
Package design	68.76	1				
Shelf display	320.19	1				
Two-way interaction	55.05	1				
Residual error	176.00	40				

   a. Complete the table by calculating the mean square, *F*, significance of *F*, and ω^2 values.
   b. How should the main effects be interpreted?

Internet and Computer Exercises

1. Analyze the Nike data given in Internet and Computer Exercises 1 of Chapter 15. Do the three usage groups differ in terms of awareness, attitude, preference, intention, and loyalty toward Nike when these variables are considered individually, i.e., one at a time?
2. Conduct the following analyses for the outdoor lifestyle data given in Internet and Computer Exercises 2 of Chapter 15.
   a. Do the three groups based on location of residence differ in their preference for an outdoor lifestyle?
   b. Do the three groups based on location of residence differ in terms of the importance attached to enjoying nature?
   c. Do the three groups based on location of residence differ in terms of the importance attached to living in harmony with the environment?
   d. Do the three groups based on location of residence differ in terms of the importance attached to exercising regularly?
3. In an experiment designed to measure the effect of sex and frequency of travel on preference for foreign travel a 2 (sex) × 3 (frequency of travel) between-subjects design was adopted. Five respondents were assigned to each cell for a total sample size of 30. Preference for foreign travel was measured on a 9-point scale (1 = no preference, 9 = strong preference). Sex was coded as male = 1 and female = 2. Frequency of travel was coded as light = 1, medium = 2, and heavy = 3. The data obtained are shown here.

Number	Sex	Travel Group	Preference
1	1	1	2
2	1	1	3
3	1	1	4
4	1	1	4
5	1	1	2
6	1	2	4
7	1	2	5
8	1	2	5
9	1	2	3
10	1	2	3
11	1	3	8
12	1	3	9
13	1	3	8
14	1	3	7
15	1	3	7
16	2	1	6
17	2	1	7
18	2	1	6
19	2	1	5
20	2	1	7
21	2	2	3
22	2	2	4
23	2	2	5
24	2	2	4
25	2	2	5
26	2	3	6
27	2	3	6
28	2	3	6
29	2	3	7
30	2	3	8

Using software of your choice, perform the following analysis.
   a. Do the males and the females differ in their preference for foreign travel?
   b. Do the light, medium, and heavy travelers differ in their preference for foreign travel?
   c. Conduct a 2 × 3 analysis of variance with preference for foreign travel as the dependent variable and sex and travel frequency as the independent variables or factors. Interpret the results.
4. Using the appropriate microcomputer and mainframe programs in the package of your choice (SPSS, SAS, Minitab, or Excel), analyze the data collected in Fieldwork assignment 1. Should the campus newspaper change the format of the cover page? What is your conclusion?

Activities

Role Playing

1. You have been hired as a marketing research analyst by a major consumer marketing company in the country. Your boss, the project director, is not well trained in statistical methods and wonders why it is necessary to do one-way ANOVA when a series of *t*-tests will do the job. Convince your boss (a student in your class) of the merits of conducting one-way ANOVA.

Fieldwork

1. Contact your campus newspaper. Collect data for the experiment described in problem 1. Because this may be too much work for one student, this project may be handled in teams of three.

Group Discussion

1. Which procedure is more useful in marketing research—analysis of variance or analysis of covariance? Discuss as a small group.

Dell Running Case

Review the Dell case, Case 1.1, and questionnaire given toward the end of the book. Download the Dell case data file from the Web site for this book.

1. Are the three price-sensitive groups based on q9_5per as derived in Chapter 14 different in terms of each of the evaluations of Dell (q8_1 to q8_13)? Interpret the results.
2. Are the three price-sensitive groups based on q9_10per as derived in Chapter 14 different in terms of each of the evaluations of Dell (q8_1 to q8_13)? Interpret the results.
3. Do the demographic groups as recoded in Chapter 14 (recoded q11, q12, q13) and q14 differ in terms of overall satisfaction with Dell computers (q4)? Interpret the results.
4. Do the demographic groups as recoded in Chapter 14 (recoded q11, q12, q13) and q14 differ in terms of likelihood of recommending Dell computers (q5)? Interpret the results.
5. Do the demographic groups as recoded in Chapter 14 (recoded q11, q12, q13) and q14 differ in terms of likelihood of choosing Dell computers (q6)? Interpret the results.

"Correlation is a simple but powerful way to look at the linear relationship between two metric variables. Multiple regression extends this concept, enabling the researcher to examine the relationship between one variable and several others."

Jim McGee, Mission Research Specialist, Global Mapping International

Objectives [After reading this chapter, the student should be able to:]

1. Discuss the concepts of product moment correlation, partial correlation, and part correlation and show how they provide a foundation for regression analysis.

2. Explain the nature and methods of bivariate regression analysis and describe the general model, estimation of parameters, standardized regression coefficient, significance testing, prediction accuracy, residual analysis, and model cross-validation.

3. Explain the nature and methods of multiple regression analysis and the meaning of partial regression coefficients.

4. Describe specialized techniques used in multiple regression analysis, particularly stepwise regression, regression with dummy variables, and analysis of variance and covariance with regression.

5. Discuss nonmetric correlation and measures such as Spearman's rho and Kendall's tau.

Correlation and Regression

Overview

Chapter 16 examined the relationship among the *t* test, analysis of variance and covariance, and regression. This chapter describes regression analysis, which is widely used for explaining variation in market share, sales, brand preference, and other marketing results in terms of marketing management variables such as advertising, price, distribution, and product quality. However, before discussing regression, we describe the concepts of product moment correlation and partial correlation coefficient, which lay the conceptual foundation for regression analysis.

In introducing regression analysis, we discuss the simple bivariate case first. We describe estimation, standardization of the regression coefficients, testing and examination of the strength and significance of association between variables, prediction accuracy, and the assumptions underlying the regression model. Next, we discuss the multiple regression model, emphasizing the interpretation of parameters, strength of association, significance tests, and examination of residuals.

Then we cover topics of special interest in regression analysis, such as stepwise regression, multicollinearity, relative importance of predictor variables, and cross-validation. We describe regression with dummy variables and the use of this procedure to conduct analysis of variance and covariance.

Finally, we discuss the use of software in correlation and regression analysis. Help for running the SPSS and SAS Learning Edition programs used in this chapter is provided in four ways: (1) detailed step-by-step instructions are given later in the chapter, (2) you can download (from the Web site for this book) computerized demonstration movies illustrating these step-by-step instructions, (3) you can download screen captures with notes illustrating these step-by-step instructions, and (4) you can refer to the *Study Guide and Technology Manual*, a supplement that accompanies this book.

Real Research

Regression Rings the Right Bell for Avon

Avon Products, Inc. (www.avon.com), was having significant problems with the sales staff. The company's business, dependent on sales representatives, was facing a shortage of sales reps without much hope of getting new ones. Regression models were developed to reveal the possible variables that were fueling this situation. The models revealed that the most significant variable was the level of the appointment fee that reps pay for materials and second was the employee benefits. With data to back up its actions, the company lowered the fee. The company also hired senior manager Michele Schneider to improve the way Avon informed new hires of their employee benefits program. Schneider revamped Avon's benefits program information packet, which yielded an informative and easy way to navigate "Guide to Your Personal Benefits." These changes resulted in an improvement in the recruitment and retention of sales reps. As of 2009, Avon was the world's largest direct seller of beauty and related products, selling products in more than 100 countries.[1] ∎

Real Research

Retailing Revolution

Many retailing experts suggest that electronic shopping will be the next revolution in retailing. Whereas many traditional retailers experienced sluggish, single-digit sales growth in the 2000s, online sales records were off the charts. Although e-tailing continues to make up a very small portion of overall retail sales (less than 5 percent in 2009), the trend looks very promising for the future. A research project investigating this trend looked for correlates of consumers' preferences for electronic shopping services. The explanation of consumers' preferences was sought in psychographic, demographic, and communication variables suggested in the literature.

Good products, well-trained sales reps, and sophisticated regression models have opened the doors for Avon, enabling it to penetrate the cosmetics market and become the world's largest direct seller of beauty products.

Multiple regression was used to analyze the data. The overall multiple regression model was significant at the 0.05 level. Univariate t tests indicated that the following variables in the model were significant at the 0.05 level or better: price orientation, sex, age, occupation, ethnicity, and education. None of the three communication variables (mass media, word of mouth, and publicity) was significantly related to consumer preference, the dependent variable.

The results suggest that electronic shopping is preferred by white females who are older, better educated, working in supervisory or higher level occupations, and price-oriented shoppers. Information of this type is valuable in targeting marketing efforts to electronic shoppers.[2] ■

These examples illustrate some of the uses of regression analysis in determining which independent variables explain a significant variation in the dependent variable of interest, the structure and form of the relationship, the strength of the relationship, and predicted values of the dependent variable. Fundamental to regression analysis is an understanding of the product moment correlation.

Product Moment Correlation

In marketing research, we are often interested in summarizing the strength of association between two metric variables, as in the following situations:

- How strongly are sales related to advertising expenditures?
- Is there an association between market share and size of the sales force?
- Are consumers' perceptions of quality related to their perceptions of prices?

product moment correlation (r)
A statistic summarizing the strength of association between two metric variables.

In situations like these, the **product moment correlation, r**, is the most widely used statistic, summarizing the strength of association between two metric (interval or ratio scaled) variables, say X and Y. It is an index used to determine whether a linear, or straight-line, relationship exists between X and Y. It indicates the degree to which the variation in one variable, X, is related to the variation in another variable, Y. Because it was originally proposed by Karl Pearson, it is also known as the *Pearson correlation coefficient*. It is also referred to as *simple correlation*, *bivariate correlation*, or merely the *correlation coefficient*. From a sample of n observations, X and Y, the product moment correlation, r, can be calculated as:

$$r = \frac{\sum_{i=1}^{n}(X_i - \overline{X})(Y_i - \overline{Y})}{\sqrt{\sum_{i=1}^{n}(X_i - \overline{X})^2 \sum_{i=1}^{n}(Y_i - \overline{Y})^2}}$$

Division of the numerator and denominator by $n - 1$ gives

$$r = \frac{\displaystyle\sum_{i=1}^{n} \frac{(X_i - \overline{X})(Y_i - \overline{Y})}{n - 1}}{\sqrt{\displaystyle\sum_{i=1}^{n} \frac{(X_i - \overline{X})^2}{n - 1} \sum_{i=1}^{n} \frac{(Y_i - \overline{Y})^2}{n - 1}}}$$

$$= \frac{COV_{xy}}{s_x\, s_y}$$

covariance

A systematic relationship between two variables in which a change in one implies a corresponding change in the other (COV_{xy}).

In these equations, $\overline{X}$ and $\overline{Y}$ denote the sample means, and s_x and s_y the standard deviations. COV_{xy}, the **covariance** between X and Y, measures the extent to which X and Y are related. The covariance may be either positive or negative. Division by $s_x s_y$ achieves standardization, so that r varies between -1.0 and 1.0. Thus, correlation is a special case of covariance, and is obtained when the data are standardized. Note that the correlation coefficient is an absolute number and is not expressed in any unit of measurement. The correlation coefficient between two variables will be the same regardless of their underlying units of measurement.

As an example, suppose a researcher wants to explain attitudes toward a respondent's city of residence in terms of duration of residence in the city. The attitude is measured on an 11-point scale ($1 =$ do not like the city, $11 =$ very much like the city), and the duration of residence is measured in terms of the number of years the respondent has lived in the city. In addition, importance attached to the weather is also measured on an 11-point scale ($1 =$ not important, $11 =$ very important). In a pretest of 12 respondents, the data shown in Table 17.1 are obtained. For illustrative purposes, we consider only a small number of observations so that we can show the calculations by hand. In actual practice, correlation and regression analyses are performed on a much larger sample such as that in the Dell running case and other cases with real data that are presented in this book.

The correlation coefficient may be calculated as follows:

$$\overline{X} = \frac{(10 + 12 + 12 + 4 + 12 + 6 + 8 + 2 + 18 + 9 + 17 + 2)}{12}$$

$$= 9.333$$

$$\overline{Y} = \frac{(6 + 9 + 8 + 3 + 10 + 4 + 5 + 2 + 11 + 9 + 10 + 2)}{12}$$

$$= 6.583$$

SPSS Output File

SAS Output File

TABLE 17.1			
Explaining Attitude Toward the City of Residence			
Respondent No.	Attitude Toward the City	Duration of Residence	Importance Attached to Weather
1	6	10	3
2	9	12	11
3	8	12	4
4	3	4	1
5	10	12	11
6	4	6	1
7	5	8	7
8	2	2	4
9	11	18	8
10	9	9	10
11	10	17	8
12	2	2	5

$$\sum_{i=1}^{n} (X_i - \overline{X})(Y_i - \overline{Y}) = (10 - 9.33)(6 - 6.58) + (12 - 9.33)(9 - 6.58)$$
$$+ (12 - 9.33)(8 - 6.58) + (4 - 9.33)(3 - 6.58)$$
$$+ (12 - 9.33)(10 - 6.58) + (6 - 9.33)(4 - 6.58)$$
$$+ (8 - 9.33)(5 - 6.58) + (2 - 9.33)(2 - 6.58)$$
$$+ (18 - 9.33)(11 - 6.58) + (9 - 9.33)(9 - 6.58)$$
$$+ (17 - 9.33)(10 - 6.58) + (2 - 9.33)(2 - 6.58)$$
$$= -0.3886 + 6.4614 + 3.7914 + 19.0814$$
$$+ 9.1314 + 8.5914 + 2.1014 + 33.5714$$
$$+ 38.3214 - 0.7986 + 26.2314 + 33.5714$$
$$= 179.6668$$

$$\sum_{i=1}^{n} (X_i - \overline{X})^2 = (10 - 9.33)^2 + (12 - 9.33)^2 + (12 - 9.33)^2 + (4 - 9.33)^2$$
$$+ (12 - 9.33)^2 + (6 - 9.33)^2 + (8 - 9.33)^2 + (2 - 9.33)^2$$
$$+ (18 - 9.33)^2 + (9 - 9.33)^2 + (17 - 9.33)^2 + (2 - 9.33)^2$$
$$= 0.4489 + 7.1289 + 7.1289 + 28.4089$$
$$+ 7.1289 + 11.0889 + 1.7689 + 53.7289$$
$$+ 75.1689 + 0.1089 + 58.8289 + 53.7289$$
$$= 304.6668$$

$$\sum_{i=1}^{n} (Y_i - \overline{Y})^2 = (6 - 6.58)^2 + (9 - 6.58)^2 + (8 - 6.58)^2 + (3 - 6.58)^2$$
$$+ (10 - 6.58)^2 + (4 - 6.58)^2 + (5 - 6.58)^2 + (2 - 6.58)^2$$
$$+ (11 - 6.58)^2 + (9 - 6.58)^2 + (10 - 6.58)^2 + (2 - 6.58)^2$$
$$= 0.3364 + 5.8564 + 2.0164 + 12.8164$$
$$+ 11.6964 + 6.6564 + 2.4964 + 20.9764$$
$$+ 19.5364 + 5.8564 + 11.6964 + 20.9764$$
$$= 120.9168$$

Thus,

$$r = \frac{179.6668}{\sqrt{(304.6668)(120.9168)}}$$
$$= 0.9361$$

In this example, $r = 0.9361$, a value close to 1.0. This means that respondents' duration of residence in the city is strongly associated with their attitude toward the city. Furthermore, the positive sign of r implies a positive relationship; the longer the duration of residence, the more favorable the attitude and vice versa.

Because r indicates the degree to which variation in one variable is related to variation in another, it can also be expressed in terms of the decomposition of the total variation (see Chapter 16). In other words,

$$r^2 = \frac{\text{Explained variation}}{\text{Total variation}}$$
$$= \frac{SS_x}{SS_y}$$
$$= \frac{\text{Total variation} - \text{Error variation}}{\text{Total variation}}$$
$$= \frac{SS_y - SS_{error}}{SS_y}$$

Hence, r^2 measures the proportion of variation in one variable that is explained by the other. Both r and r^2 are symmetric measures of association. In other words, the correlation of X with Y is the same as the correlation of Y with X. It does not matter which variable is considered to be the dependent variable and which the independent. The product moment coefficient measures the strength of the linear relationship and is not designed to measure nonlinear relationships. Thus, $r = 0$ merely indicates that there is no linear relationship between X and Y. It does not mean that X and Y are unrelated. There could well be a nonlinear relationship between them, which would not be captured by r (see Figure 17.1).

When it is computed for a population rather than a sample, the product moment correlation is denoted by ρ, the Greek letter rho. The coefficient r is an estimator of ρ. Note that the calculation of r assumes that X and Y are metric variables whose distributions have the same shape. If these assumptions are not met, r is deflated and underestimates ρ. In marketing research, data obtained by using rating scales with a small number of categories may not be strictly interval. This tends to deflate r, resulting in an underestimation of ρ.[3]

The statistical significance of the relationship between two variables measured by using r can be conveniently tested. The hypotheses are:

$$H_0: \rho = 0$$
$$H_1: \rho \neq 0$$

The test statistic is:

$$t = r\left[\frac{n-2}{1-r^2}\right]^{1/2}$$

which has a t distribution with $n - 2$ degrees of freedom.[4] For the correlation coefficient calculated based on the data given in Table 17.1,

$$t = 0.9361\left[\frac{12-2}{1-(0.9361)^2}\right]^{1/2}$$
$$= 8.414$$

and the degrees of freedom $= 12 - 2 = 10$. From the t distribution table (Table 4 in the Statistical Appendix), the critical value of t for a two-tailed test and $\alpha = 0.05$ is 2.228. Hence, the null hypothesis of no relationship between X and Y is rejected. This, along with the positive sign of r, indicates that attitude toward the city is positively related to the duration of residence in the city. Moreover, the high value of r indicates that this relationship is strong. If this were a large and representative sample, the implication would be that managers, city officials, and politicians wishing to reach people with a favorable attitude toward the city should target long-time residents of that city.

In conducting multivariate data analysis, it is often useful to examine the simple correlation between each pair of variables. These results are presented in the form of a correlation matrix, which indicates the coefficient of correlation between each pair of variables. Usually, only the lower triangular portion of the matrix is considered. The diagonal elements all equal 1.00, because a variable correlates perfectly with itself. The upper triangular portion of the matrix is a mirror image of the lower triangular portion, because r is a symmetric measure of association. The form of a correlation matrix for five variables, V_1 through V_5, is as follows.

FIGURE 17.1

A Nonlinear Relationship for Which $r = 0$

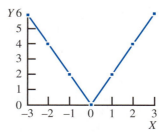

	V_1	V_2	V_3	V_4	V_5
V_1					
V_2	0.5				
V_3	0.3	0.4			
V_4	0.1	0.3	0.6		
V_5	0.2	0.5	0.3	0.7	

Although a matrix of simple correlations provides insights into pairwise associations, sometimes researchers want to examine the association between two variables after controlling for one or more other variables. In the latter case, partial correlation should be estimated.

Partial Correlation

partial correlation coefficient

A measure of the association between two variables after controlling or adjusting for the effects of one or more additional variables.

Whereas the product moment or simple correlation is a measure of association describing the linear association between two variables, a **partial correlation coefficient** measures the association between two variables after controlling for or adjusting for the effects of one or more additional variables. This statistic is used to answer the following questions:

- How strongly are sales related to advertising expenditures when the effect of price is controlled?
- Is there an association between market share and size of the sales force after adjusting for the effect of sales promotion?
- Are consumers' perceptions of quality related to their perceptions of prices when the effect of brand image is controlled?

As in these situations, suppose one wanted to calculate the association between X and Y after controlling for a third variable, Z. Conceptually, one would first remove the effect of Z from X. To do this, one would predict the values of X based on a knowledge of Z by using the product moment correlation between X and Z, r_{xz}. The predicted value of X is then subtracted from the actual value of X to construct an adjusted value of X. In a similar manner, the values of Y are adjusted to remove the effects of Z. The product moment correlation between the adjusted values of X and the adjusted values of Y is the partial correlation coefficient between X and Y, after controlling for the effect of Z, and is denoted by $r_{xy.z}$. Statistically, because the simple correlation between two variables completely describes the linear relationship between them, the partial correlation coefficient can be calculated by a knowledge of the simple correlations alone, without using individual observations.

$$r_{xy.z} = \frac{r_{xy} - (r_{xz})(r_{yz})}{\sqrt{1 - r_{xz}^2}\sqrt{1 - r_{yz}^2}}$$

To continue our example, suppose the researcher wanted to calculate the association between attitude toward the city, Y, and duration of residence, X_1, after controlling for a third variable, importance attached to weather, X_2. These data are presented in Table 17.1. The simple correlations between the variables are:

$$r_{yx_1} = 0.9361 \quad r_{yx_2} = 0.7334 \quad r_{x_1 x_2} = 0.5495$$

The required partial correlation is calculated as follows:

$$r_{yx_1.x_2} = \frac{0.9361 - (0.5495)(0.7334)}{\sqrt{1 - (0.5495)^2}\sqrt{1 - (0.7334)^2}}$$

$$= 0.9386$$

As can be seen, controlling for the effect of importance attached to weather has little effect on the association between attitude toward the city and duration of residence. Thus, regardless of the importance they attach to weather, those who have stayed in a city longer have more favorable attitudes toward the city and vice versa.

Partial correlations have an *order* associated with them. The order indicates how many variables are being adjusted or controlled. The simple correlation coefficient, r, has a zero-order, as it does not control for any additional variables when measuring the association between two variables. The coefficient $r_{xy.z}$ is a first-order partial correlation coefficient, as it controls for the effect of one additional variable, Z. A second-order partial correlation coefficient controls for the effects of two variables, a third-order for the effects of three variables, and so on. The higher-order partial correlations are calculated similarly. The $(n + 1)$th-order partial coefficient may be calculated by replacing the simple correlation coefficients on the right side of the preceding equation with the nth-order partial coefficients.

Partial correlations can be helpful for detecting spurious relationships (see Chapter 15). The relationship between X and Y is spurious if it is solely due to the fact that X is associated with Z, which is indeed the true predictor of Y. In this case, the correlation between X and Y disappears when the effect of Z is controlled. Consider a case in which consumption of a cereal brand (C) is positively associated with income (I), with $r_{ci} = 0.28$. Because this brand was popularly priced, income was not expected to be a significant factor. Therefore, the researcher suspected that this relationship was spurious. The sample results also indicated that income is positively associated with household size (H), $r_{hi} = 0.48$, and that household size is associated with cereal consumption, $r_{ch} = 0.56$. These figures seem to indicate that the real predictor of cereal consumption is not income but household size. To test this assertion, the first-order partial correlation between cereal consumption and income is calculated, controlling for the effect of household size. The reader can verify that this partial correlation, $r_{ci.h}$, is 0.02, and the initial correlation between cereal consumption and income vanishes when the household size is controlled. Therefore, the correlation between income and cereal consumption is spurious. The special case when a partial correlation is larger than its respective zero-order correlation involves a suppressor effect (see Chapter 15).[5]

part correlation coefficient

A measure of the correlation between Y and X when the linear effects of the other independent variables have been removed from X but not from Y.

Another correlation coefficient of interest is the **part correlation coefficient**. This coefficient represents the correlation between Y and X when the linear effects of the other independent variables have been removed from X but not from Y. The part correlation coefficient, $r_{y(x.z)}$, is calculated as follows:

$$r_{y(x.z)} = \frac{r_{xy} - r_{xz}r_{yz}}{\sqrt{1 - r_{xz}^2}}$$

The part correlation between attitude toward the city and the duration of residence, when the linear effects of the importance attached to weather have been removed from the duration of residence, can be calculated as:

$$r_{y(x_1.x_2)} = \frac{0.9361 - (0.5495)(0.7334)}{\sqrt{1 - (0.5495)^2}}$$

$$= 0.63806$$

Real Research

Selling Ads to Home Shoppers

Advertisements play a very important role in forming attitudes/preferences for brands. Often advertisers use celebrity spokespersons as a credible source to influence consumers' attitudes and purchase intentions. Another type of source credibility is corporate credibility, which can also influence consumer reactions to advertisements and shape brand attitudes. In general, it has been found that for low-involvement products, attitude toward the advertisement mediates brand cognition (beliefs about the brand) and attitude toward the brand. What would happen to the effect of this mediating variable when products are purchased through a home shopping network? Home Shopping Budapest in Hungary conducted research to assess the impact of advertisements toward purchase. A survey was conducted where several measures were taken, such as attitude toward the product, attitude toward the brand, attitude toward the ad characteristics, brand cognitions, and so on. It was hypothesized that in a home shopping network, advertisements largely determined attitude toward the brand. In order to find the degree of association of attitude toward the ad with both attitude toward the brand and brand cognition, a partial correlation coefficient could be computed. The partial correlation would be calculated between attitude toward the brand and brand cognition after controlling for the effects of attitude toward the ad on the two variables. If attitude toward the ad is significantly high, then the partial correlation coefficient should be significantly less than the product moment correlation between brand cognition and attitude toward the brand. Research was conducted that supported this hypothesis. Then, Saatchi & Saatchi (www.saatchi.com) designed the ads aired on Home Shopping Budapest to generate positive attitude toward the advertising, and this turned out to be a major competitive weapon for the network.[6] ■

The partial correlation coefficient is generally viewed as more important than the part correlation coefficient because it can be used to determine spurious and suppressor effects. The product moment correlation, partial correlation, and the part correlation coefficients all assume that the data are interval or ratio scaled. If the data do not meet these requirements, the researcher should consider the use of nonmetric correlation.

Nonmetric Correlation

nonmetric correlation
A correlation measure for two nonmetric variables that relies on rankings to compute the correlation.

At times, the researcher may have to compute the correlation coefficient between two variables that are nonmetric. It may be recalled that nonmetric variables do not have interval or ratio scale properties and do not assume a normal distribution. If the nonmetric variables are ordinal and numeric, Spearman's rho, ρ_s, and Kendall's tau, τ, are two measures of **nonmetric correlation** that can be used to examine the correlation between them. Both these measures use rankings rather than the absolute values of the variables and the basic concepts underlying them are quite similar. Both vary from -1.0 to 1.0 (see Chapter 15).

In the absence of ties, Spearman's ρ_s yields a closer approximation to the Pearson product moment correlation coefficient, ρ, than Kendall's τ. In these cases, the absolute magnitude of τ tends to be smaller than Pearson's ρ. On the other hand, when the data contain a large number of tied ranks, Kendall's τ seems more appropriate. As a rule of thumb, Kendall's τ is to be preferred when a large number of cases fall into a relatively small number of categories (thereby leading to a large number of ties). Conversely, the use of Spearman's ρ_s is preferable when we have a relatively larger number of categories (thereby having fewer ties).[7]

The product moment as well as the partial and part correlation coefficients provide a conceptual foundation for bivariate as well as multiple regression analysis.

Regression Analysis

regression analysis
A statistical procedure for analyzing associative relationships between a metric dependent variable and one or more independent variables.

Regression analysis is a powerful and flexible procedure for analyzing associative relationships between a metric dependent variable and one or more independent variables. It can be used in the following ways:

1. Determine whether the independent variables explain a significant variation in the dependent variable: whether a relationship exists
2. Determine how much of the variation in the dependent variable can be explained by the independent variables: strength of the relationship
3. Determine the structure or form of the relationship: the mathematical equation relating the independent and dependent variables
4. Predict the values of the dependent variable
5. Control for other independent variables when evaluating the contributions of a specific variable or set of variables

Although the independent variables may explain the variation in the dependent variable, this does not necessarily imply causation. The use of the terms *dependent* or *criterion* variables, and *independent* or *predictor* variables, in regression analysis arises from the mathematical relationship between the variables. These terms do not imply that the criterion variable is dependent on the independent variables in a causal sense. Regression analysis is concerned with the nature and degree of association between variables and does not imply or assume any causality.

Bivariate Regression

bivariate regression
A procedure for deriving a mathematical relationship, in the form of an equation, between a single metric dependent variable and a single metric independent variable.

Bivariate regression is a procedure for deriving a mathematical relationship, in the form of an equation, between a single metric dependent or criterion variable and a single metric independent or predictor variable. The analysis is similar in many ways to determining the simple correlation between two variables. However, because an equation has to be derived, one variable must be identified as the dependent and the other as the independent variable. The examples given earlier in the context of simple correlation can be translated into the regression context.

- Can variation in sales be explained in terms of variation in advertising expenditures? What is the structure and form of this relationship, and can it be modeled mathematically by an equation describing a straight line?
- Can the variation in market share be accounted for by the size of the sales force?
- Are consumers' perceptions of quality determined by their perceptions of price?

Before discussing the procedure for conducting bivariate regression, we define some important statistics.

Statistics Associated with Bivariate Regression Analysis

The following statistics and statistical terms are associated with bivariate regression analysis.

Bivariate regression model. The basic regression equation is $Y_i = \beta_0 + \beta_1 X_i + e_i$, where Y = dependent or criterion variable, X = independent or predictor variable, β_0 = intercept of the line, β_1 = slope of the line, and e_i is the error term associated with the ith observation.

Coefficient of determination. The strength of association is measured by the coefficient of determination, r^2. It varies between 0 and 1 and signifies the proportion of the total variation in Y that is accounted for by the variation in X.

Estimated or predicted value. The estimated or predicted value of Y_i is $\hat{Y}_i = a + bx$, where $\hat{Y}_i$ is the predicted value of Y_i, and a and b are estimators of β_0 and β_1, respectively.

Regression coefficient. The estimated parameter b is usually referred to as the nonstandardized regression coefficient.

Scattergram. A scatter diagram, or scattergram, is a plot of the values of two variables for all the cases or observations.

Standard error of estimate. This statistic, *SEE,* is the standard deviation of the actual Y values from the predicted $\hat{Y}$ values.

Standard error. The standard deviation of b, SE_b, is called the standard error.

Standardized regression coefficient. Also termed the *beta coefficient* or *beta weight*, this is the slope obtained by the regression of Y on X when the data are standardized.

Sum of squared errors. The distances of all the points from the regression line are squared and added together to arrive at the sum of squared errors, which is a measure of total error, Σe_j^2.

t *statistic*. A t statistic with $n-2$ degrees of freedom can be used to test the null hypothesis that no linear relationship exists between X and Y, or

$$H_0: \beta_1 = 0, \text{ where } t = \frac{b}{SE_b}.$$

Conducting Bivariate Regression Analysis

The steps involved in conducting bivariate regression analysis are described in Figure 17.2. Suppose the researcher wants to explain attitudes toward the city of residence in terms of the duration of residence (see Table 17.1). In deriving such relationships, it is often useful to first examine a scatter diagram.

Plot the Scatter Diagram

A scatter diagram, or scattergram, is a plot of the values of two variables for all the cases or observations. It is customary to plot the dependent variable on the vertical axis and the independent variable on the horizontal axis. A scatter diagram is useful for determining the form of the relationship between the variables. A plot can alert the researcher to patterns in the data, or to possible problems. Any unusual combinations of the two variables can be easily identified.

FIGURE 17.2

Conducting Bivariate Regression Analysis

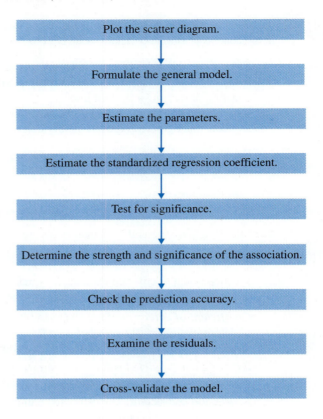

Plot the scatter diagram.

Formulate the general model.

Estimate the parameters.

Estimate the standardized regression coefficient.

Test for significance.

Determine the strength and significance of the association.

Check the prediction accuracy.

Examine the residuals.

Cross-validate the model.

A plot of Y (attitude toward the city) against X (duration of residence) is given in Figure 17.3. The points seem to be arranged in a band running from the bottom left to the top right. One can see the pattern: As one variable increases, so does the other. It appears from this scattergram that the relationship between X and Y is linear and could be well described by a straight line. However, as seen in Figure 17.4, several straight lines can be drawn through the data. How should the straight line be fitted to best describe the data?

least-squares procedure
A technique for fitting a straight line to a scattergram by minimizing the square of the vertical distances of all the points from the line and the procedure is called ordinary least squares (OLS) regression.

The most commonly used technique for fitting a straight line to a scattergram is the **least-squares procedure**. This technique determines the best-fitting line by minimizing the square of the vertical distances of all the points from the line and the procedure is called ordinary least squares (OLS) regression. The best-fitting line is called the *regression line*. Any point that does not fall on the regression line is not fully accounted for. The vertical distance from the point to the line is the error, e_j (see Figure 17.5). The distances of all the points from the line are squared and added together to arrive at the sum of squared errors, which is a measure of total error, Σe_j^2. In fitting the line, the least-squares procedure minimizes the sum of

FIGURE 17.3

Plot of Attitude with Duration

SPSS Output File

SAS Output File

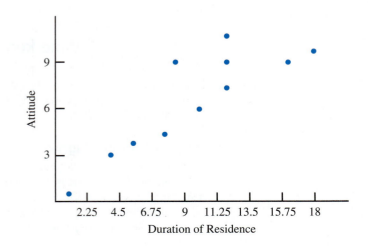

FIGURE 17.4

Which Straight Line Is Best?

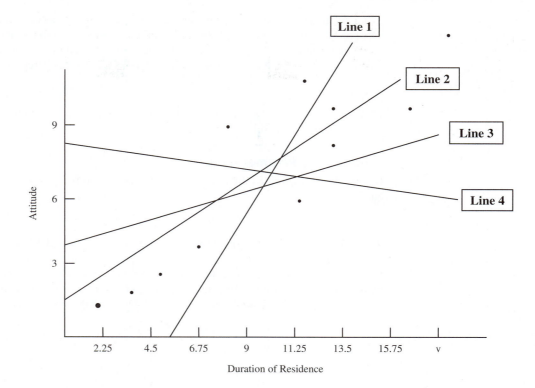

squared errors. If Y is plotted on the vertical axis and X on the horizontal axis, as in Figure 17.5, the best-fitting line is called the regression of Y on X, because the vertical distances are minimized. The scatter diagram indicates whether the relationship between Y and X can be modeled as a straight line and, consequently, whether the bivariate regression model is appropriate.

Formulate the Bivariate Regression Model

In the bivariate regression model, the general form of a straight line is:

$$Y = \beta_0 + \beta_1 X$$

where

Y = dependent or criterion variable
X = independent or predictor variable
β_0 = intercept of the line
β_1 = slope of the line

FIGURE 17.5

Bivariate Regression

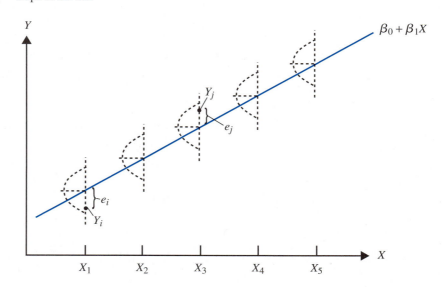

This model implies a deterministic relationship, in that Y is completely determined by X. The value of Y can be perfectly predicted if β_0 and β_1 are known. In marketing research, however, very few relationships are deterministic. So the regression procedure adds an error term to account for the probabilistic or stochastic nature of the relationship. The basic regression equation becomes:

$$Y_i = \beta_0 + \beta_1 X_i + e_i$$

where e_i is the error term associated with the ith observation.[8] Estimation of the regression parameters, β_0 and β_1, is relatively simple.

Estimate the Parameters

In most cases, β_0 and β_1 are unknown and are estimated from the sample observations using the equation

$$\hat{Y}_i = a + bx_i$$

where $\hat{Y}_i$ is the estimated or predicted value of Y_i, and a and b are estimators of β_0 and β_1, respectively. The constant b is usually referred to as the nonstandardized regression coefficient. It is the slope of the regression line and it indicates the expected change in Y when X is changed by one unit. The formulas for calculating a and b are simple.[9] The slope, b, may be computed in terms of the covariance between X and Y, (COV_{xy}), and the variance of X as:

$$b = \frac{COV_{xy}}{s_x^2}$$

$$= \frac{\sum_{i=1}^{n}(X_i - \bar{X})(Y_i - \bar{Y})}{\sum_{i=1}^{n}(X_i - \bar{X})^2}$$

$$= \frac{\sum_{i=1}^{n} X_i Y_i - n\bar{X}\bar{Y}}{\sum_{i=1}^{n} X_i^2 - n\bar{X}^2}$$

The intercept, a, may then be calculated using:

$$a = \bar{Y} - b\bar{X}$$

For the data in Table 17.1, the estimation of parameters may be illustrated as follows:

$$\sum_{i=1}^{12} X_i Y_i = (10)(6) + (12)(9) + (12)(8) + (4)(3) + (12)(10) + (6)(4)$$
$$+ (8)(5) + (2)(2) + (18)(11) + (9)(9) + (17)(10) + (2)(2)$$
$$= 917$$

$$\sum_{i=1}^{12} X_i^2 = 10^2 + 12^2 + 12^2 + 4^2 + 12^2 + 6^2$$
$$+ 8^2 + 2^2 + 18^2 + 9^2 + 17^2 + 2^2$$
$$= 1,350$$

It may be recalled from earlier calculations of the simple correlation that

$$\bar{X} = 9.333$$
$$\bar{Y} = 6.583$$

Given $n = 12$, b can be calculated as:

$$b = \frac{917 - (12)(9.333)(6.583)}{1350 - (12)(9.333)^2}$$
$$= 0.5897$$

$$a = \overline{Y} - b\overline{X}$$
$$= 6.583 - (0.5897)(9.333)$$
$$= 1.0793$$

Note that these coefficients have been estimated on the raw (untransformed) data. Should standardization of the data be considered desirable, the calculation of the standardized coefficients is also straightforward.

Estimate Standardized Regression Coefficient

Standardization is the process by which the raw data are transformed into new variables that have a mean of 0 and a variance of 1 (Chapter 14). When the data are standardized, the intercept assumes a value of 0. The term *beta coefficient* or *beta weight* is used to denote the standardized regression coefficient. In this case, the slope obtained by the regression of Y on X, B_{yx}, is the same as the slope obtained by the regression of X on Y, B_{xy}. Moreover, each of these regression coefficients is equal to the simple correlation between X and Y.

$$B_{yx} = B_{xy} = r_{xy}$$

There is a simple relationship between the standardized and nonstandardized regression coefficients:

$$B_{yx} = b_{yx}(s_x/s_y)$$

For the regression results given in Table 17.2, the value of the beta coefficient is estimated as 0.9361. Note that this is also the value of r calculated earlier in this chapter.

Once the parameters have been estimated, they can be tested for significance.

Test for Significance

The statistical significance of the linear relationship between X and Y may be tested by examining the hypotheses:

$$H_0: \beta_1 = 0$$
$$H_1: \beta_1 \neq 0$$

The null hypothesis implies that there is no linear relationship between X and Y. The alternative hypothesis is that there is a relationship, positive or negative, between X and Y. Typically, a two-tailed test is done. A t statistic with $n - 2$ degrees of freedom can be used, where

$$t = \frac{b}{SE_b}$$

SPSS Output File

SAS Output File

TABLE 17.2
Bivariate Regression

Multiple R	0.93608
R^2	0.87624
Adjusted R^2	0.86387
Standard error	1.22329

	df	Analysis of Variance Sum of Squares	Mean Square
Regression	1	105.95222	105.95222
Residual	10	14.96444	1.49644

$F = 70.80266$ Significance of $F = 0.0000$

			Variables in the Equation		
Variable	b	SE_B	Beta (B)	t	Significance of t
DURATION	0.58972	0.07008	0.93608	8.414	0.0000
(Constant)	1.07932	0.74335		1.452	0.1772

SE_b denotes the standard deviation of b and is called the *standard error*.[10] The t distribution was discussed in Chapter 15.

Using a computer program, the regression of attitude on duration of residence, using the data shown in Table 17.1, yielded the results shown in Table 17.2. The intercept, a, equals 1.0793, and the slope, b, equals 0.5897. Therefore, the estimated equation is:

$$\text{Attitude } (\hat{Y}) = 1.0793 + 0.5897 \text{ (Duration of residence)}$$

The standard error or standard deviation of b is estimated as 0.07008, and the value of the t statistic, $t = 0.5897/0.07008 = 8.414$, with $n - 2 = 10$ degrees of freedom. From Table 4 in the Statistical Appendix, we see that the critical value of t with 10 degrees of freedom and $\alpha = 0.05$ is 2.228 for a two-tailed test. Because the calculated value of t is larger than the critical value, the null hypothesis is rejected. Hence, there is a significant linear relationship between attitude toward the city and duration of residence in the city. The positive sign of the slope coefficient indicates that this relationship is positive. In other words, those who have resided in the city for a longer time have more positive attitudes toward the city. The implication for managers, city officials, and politicians is the same as that discussed for simple correlation, subject to the representativeness of the sample.

Determine the Strength and Significance of Association

A related inference involves determining the strength and significance of the association between Y and X. The strength of association is measured by the coefficient of determination, r^2. In bivariate regression, r^2 is the square of the simple correlation coefficient obtained by correlating the two variables. The coefficient r^2 varies between 0 and 1. It signifies the proportion of the total variation in Y that is accounted for by the variation in X. The decomposition of the total variation in Y is similar to that for analysis of variance (Chapter 16). As shown in Figure 17.6, the total variation, SS_y, may be decomposed into the variation accounted for by the regression line, SS_{reg}, and the error or residual variation, SS_{error} or SS_{res}, as follows:

$$SS_y = SS_{reg} + SS_{res}$$

where

$$SS_y = \sum_{i=1}^{n} (Y_i - \overline{Y})^2$$

$$SS_{reg} = \sum_{i=1}^{n} (\hat{Y}_i - \overline{Y})^2$$

$$SS_{res} = \sum_{i=1}^{n} (Y_i - \hat{Y}_i)^2$$

The strength of association may then be calculated as follows:

$$r^2 = \frac{SS_{reg}}{SS_y}$$

$$= \frac{SS_y - SS_{res}}{SS_y}$$

FIGURE 17.6

Decomposition of the Total Variation in Bivariate Regression

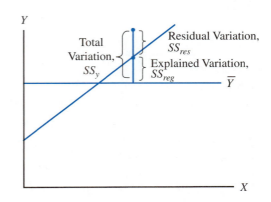

To illustrate the calculations of r^2, let us consider again the regression of attitude toward the city on the duration of residence. It may be recalled from earlier calculations of the simple correlation coefficient that:

$$SS_y = \sum_{i=1}^{n} (Y_i - \overline{Y})^2$$
$$= 120.9168$$

The predicted values $(\hat{Y})$ can be calculated using the regression equation:

$$\text{Attitude } (\hat{Y}) = 1.0793 + 0.5897 \text{ (Duration of residence)}$$

For the first observation in Table 17.1, this value is:

$$(\hat{Y}) = 1.0793 + 0.5897 \times 10 = 6.9763$$

For each successive observation, the predicted values are, in order, 8.1557, 8.1557, 3.4381, 8.1557, 4.6175, 5.7969, 2.2587, 11.6939, 6.3866, 11.1042, and 2.2587. Therefore,

$$
\begin{aligned}
SS_{reg} = \sum_{i=1}^{n} (\hat{Y}_i - \overline{Y})^2 &= (6.9763 - 6.5833)^2 + (8.1557 - 6.5833)^2 \\
&\quad + (8.1557 - 6.5833)^2 + (3.4381 - 6.5833)^2 \\
&\quad + (8.1557 - 6.5833)^2 + (4.6175 - 6.5833)^2 \\
&\quad + (5.7969 - 6.5833)^2 + (2.2587 - 6.5833)^2 \\
&\quad + (11.6939 - 6.5833)^2 + (6.3866 - 6.5833)^2 \\
&\quad + (11.1042 - 6.5833)^2 + (2.2587 - 6.5833)^2 \\
&= 0.1544 + 2.4724 + 2.4724 + 9.8922 + 2.4724 \\
&\quad + 3.8643 + 0.6184 + 18.7021 + 26.1182 \\
&\quad + 0.0387 + 20.4385 + 18.7021 \\
&= 105.9524
\end{aligned}
$$

$$
\begin{aligned}
SS_{res} = \sum_{i=1}^{n} (Y_i - \hat{Y}_i)^2 &= (6 - 6.9763)^2 + (9 - 8.1557)^2 + (8 - 8.1557)^2 \\
&\quad + (3 - 3.4381)^2 + (10 - 8.1557)^2 + (4 - 4.6175)^2 \\
&\quad + (5 - 5.7969)^2 + (2 - 2.2587)^2 + (11 - 11.6939)^2 \\
&\quad + (9 - 6.3866)^2 + (10 - 11.1042)^2 + (2 - 2.2587)^2 \\
&= 14.9644
\end{aligned}
$$

It can be seen that $SS_y = SS_{reg} + SS_{res}$. Furthermore,

$$
\begin{aligned}
r^2 &= \frac{SS_{reg}}{SS_y} \\
&= \frac{105.9524}{120.9168} \\
&= 0.8762
\end{aligned}
$$

Another equivalent test for examining the significance of the linear relationship between X and Y (significance of b) is the test for the significance of the coefficient of determination. The hypotheses in this case are:

$$H_0: R^2_{pop} = 0$$
$$H_1: R^2_{pop} > 0$$

The appropriate test statistic is the F statistic:

$$F = \frac{SS_{reg}}{SS_{res}/(n - 2)}$$

which has an F distribution with 1 and $n - 2$ degrees of freedom. The F test is a generalized form of the t test (see Chapter 15). If a random variable t is distributed with n degrees of freedom, then t^2 is F distributed with 1 and n degrees of freedom. Hence, the F test for testing the significance of the coefficient of determination is equivalent to testing the following hypotheses:

$$H_0: \beta_1 = 0$$
$$H_1: \beta_1 \neq 0$$

or

$$H_0: \rho = 0$$
$$H_1: \rho \neq 0$$

From Table 17.2, it can be seen that:

$$r^2 = \frac{105.9524}{(105.9524 + 14.9644)}$$
$$= 0.8762$$

which is the same as the value calculated earlier. The value of the F statistic is:

$$F = \frac{105.9524}{(14.9644/10)}$$
$$= 70.8027$$

with 1 and 10 degrees of freedom. The calculated F statistic exceeds the critical value of 4.96 determined from Table 5 in the Statistical Appendix. Therefore, the relationship is significant at $\alpha = 0.05$, corroborating the results of the t test. If the relationship between X and Y is significant, it is meaningful to predict the values of Y based on the values of X and to estimate prediction accuracy.

Check Prediction Accuracy

To estimate the accuracy of predicted values, $\hat{Y}$, it is useful to calculate the standard error of estimate, *SEE*. This statistic is the standard deviation of the actual Y values from the predicted $\hat{Y}$ values.

$$SEE = \sqrt{\frac{\sum_{i=1}^{n}(Y_i - \hat{Y})^2}{n - 2}}$$

or

$$SEE = \sqrt{\frac{SS_{res}}{n - 2}}$$

or more generally, if there are k independent variables,

$$SEE = \sqrt{\frac{SS_{res}}{n - k - 1}}$$

SEE may be interpreted as a kind of average residual or average error in predicting Y from the regression equation.[11]

Two cases of prediction may arise. The researcher may want to predict the mean value of Y for all the cases with a given value of X, say X_0, or predict the value of Y for a single case. In both situations, the predicted value is the same and is given by $\hat{Y}$, where

$$\hat{Y} = a + bX_0$$

However, the standard error is different in the two situations, although in both situations it is a function of *SEE*. For large samples, the standard error for predicting mean value of Y is $SEE/\sqrt{n}$, and for predicting individual Y values it is *SEE*. Hence, the construction of confidence intervals (see Chapter 12) for the predicted value varies, depending upon whether the mean value or the value for a single observation is being predicted.

For the data given in Table 17.2, the *SEE* is estimated as follows:

$$SEE = \sqrt{\frac{14.9644}{(12 - 2)}}$$

$$= 1.22329$$

The final two steps in conducting bivariate regression, namely examination of residuals and model cross-validation, are considered later, but we now focus on the assumptions.

Assumptions

The regression model makes a number of assumptions in estimating the parameters and in significance testing (see Figure 17.5):

1. The error term is normally distributed. For each fixed value of X, the distribution of Y is normal.[12]
2. The means of all these normal distributions of Y, given X, lie on a straight line with slope b.
3. The mean of the error term is 0.
4. The variance of the error term is constant. This variance does not depend on the values assumed by X.
5. The error terms are uncorrelated. In other words, the observations have been drawn independently.

Insights into the extent to which these assumptions have been met can be gained by an examination of residuals, which is covered in the next section on multiple regression.[13]

ACTIVE RESEARCH

Associating Ford Advertising and Sales

Visit www.ford.com and conduct an Internet search using a search engine and your library's online database to obtain information on the relationship between advertising and sales for automobile manufacturers.

Formulate a bivariate regression model explaining the relationship between advertising and sales in the automobile industry.

As the marketing director for Ford Motor Company, how would you determine your advertising expenditures?

Multiple Regression

multiple regression
A statistical technique that simultaneously develops a mathematical relationship between two or more independent variables and an interval-scaled dependent variable.

Multiple regression involves a single dependent variable and two or more independent variables. The questions raised in the context of bivariate regression can also be answered via multiple regression by considering additional independent variables.

- Can variation in sales be explained in terms of variation in advertising expenditures, prices, and level of distribution?
- Can variation in market shares be accounted for by the size of the sales force, advertising expenditures, and sales promotion budgets?
- Are consumers' perceptions of quality determined by their perceptions of prices, brand image, and brand attributes?

Additional questions can also be answered by multiple regression.

- How much of the variation in sales can be explained by advertising expenditures, prices, and level of distribution?
- What is the contribution of advertising expenditures in explaining the variation in sales when the levels of prices and distribution are controlled?
- What levels of sales may be expected, given the levels of advertising expenditures, prices, and level of distribution?

Real Research

Global Brands—Local Ads

Europeans welcome brands from other countries, but when it comes to advertising, they prefer the homegrown variety. A survey done by Yankelovich and Partners (www.yankelovich.com) and its affiliates finds that most European consumers' favorite commercials are for local brands even though they are more than likely to buy foreign brands. Respondents in France, Germany, and the United Kingdom named Coca-Cola as the most often purchased soft drink. However, the French selected the famous award-winning spot for France's Perrier bottled water as their favorite commercial. Similarly, in Germany, the favorite advertising was for a German brand of nonalcoholic beer—Clausthaler. However, in the United Kingdom, Coca-Cola was the favorite soft drink and also the favorite advertising. In light of such findings, the important question is—does advertising help? Does it help increase the purchase probability of the brand or does it merely maintain a high brand recognition rate? One way of finding out is by running multiple regressions where the dependent variable is the likelihood of brand purchase and the independent variables are brand attribute evaluations and advertising evaluations. Separate models with and without advertising can be run to assess any significant difference in the contribution. Individual t tests could also be examined to find out the significant contribution of both the brand attributes and advertising. The results will indicate the degree to which advertising plays an important part in brand purchase decisions. In conjunction with these results, a recent study revealed that attempting to build brand loyalty purchases by means of a sales promotion is not a desirable way to achieve such an objective. According to the study, sales promotions only encourage momentary brand switching and merely enhance short-term performance for companies. Furthermore, over the long run, a sales promotion may imply a low quality or unstable brand image to consumers or it may confuse consumers, which could also lead to a decline in brand loyalty. The results of this study show that sacrificing advertising and relying on sales promotions reduces brand associations, which ultimately leads to a decrease in brand loyalty purchases.[14] ■

multiple regression model

An equation used to explain the results of multiple regression analysis.

The general form of the **multiple regression model** is as follows:

$$Y = \beta_0 + \beta_1 X_1 + \beta_2 X_2 + \beta_3 X_3 + \ldots + \beta_k X_k + e$$

which is estimated by the following equation:

$$\hat{Y} = a + b_1 X_1 + b_2 X_2 + b_3 X_3 + \ldots + b_k X_k$$

As before, the coefficient a represents the intercept, but the bs are now the partial regression coefficients. The least-squares criterion estimates the parameters in such a way as to minimize the total error, SS_{res}. This process also maximizes the correlation between the actual values of Y and the predicted values, $\hat{Y}$. All the assumptions made in bivariate regression also apply in multiple regression. We define some associated statistics and then describe the procedure for multiple regression analysis.[15]

Statistics Associated with Multiple Regression

Most of the statistics and statistical terms described under bivariate regression also apply to multiple regression. In addition, the following statistics are used:

Adjusted R^2. R^2, coefficient of multiple determination, is adjusted for the number of independent variables and the sample size to account for diminishing returns. After the first few variables, the additional independent variables do not make much contribution.

Coefficient of multiple determination. The strength of association in multiple regression is measured by the square of the multiple correlation coefficient, R^2, which is also called the *coefficient of multiple determination*.

F *test*. The F test is used to test the null hypothesis that the coefficient of multiple determination in the population, R^2_{pop}, is zero. This is equivalent to testing the null hypothesis H_0: $\beta_1 = \beta_2 = \beta_3 = \ldots = \beta_k = 0$. The test statistic has an F distribution with k and $(n - k - 1)$ degrees of freedom.

Partial **F** *test*. The significance of a partial regression coefficient, β_i, of X_i may be tested using an incremental F statistic. The incremental F statistic is based on the increment in the explained sum of squares resulting from the addition of the independent variable X_i to the regression equation after all the other independent variables have been included.

Partial regression coefficient. The partial regression coefficient, b_1, denotes the change in the predicted value, $\hat{Y}$, per unit change in X_1 when the other independent variables, X_2 to X_k, are held constant.

Conducting Multiple Regression Analysis

The steps involved in conducting multiple regression analysis are similar to those for bivariate regression analysis. The discussion focuses on partial regression coefficients, strength of association, significance testing, and examination of residuals.

Partial Regression Coefficients

To understand the meaning of a partial regression coefficient, let us consider a case in which there are two independent variables, so that:

$$\hat{Y} = a + b_1X_1 + b_2X_2$$

First, note that the relative magnitude of the partial regression coefficient of an independent variable is, in general, different from that of its bivariate regression coefficient. In other words, the partial regression coefficient, b_1, will be different from the regression coefficient, b, obtained by regressing Y on only X_1. This happens because X_1 and X_2 are usually correlated. In bivariate regression, X_2 was not considered, and any variation in Y that was shared by X_1 and X_2 was attributed to X_1. However, in the case of multiple independent variables, this is no longer true.

The interpretation of the partial regression coefficient, b_1, is that it represents the expected change in Y when X_1 is changed by one unit but X_2 is held constant or otherwise controlled. Likewise, b_2 represents the expected change in Y for a unit change in X_2, when X_1 is held constant. Thus, calling b_1 and b_2 partial regression coefficients is appropriate. It can also be seen that the combined effects of X_1 and X_2 on Y are additive. In other words, if X_1 and X_2 are each changed by one unit, the expected change in Y would be $(b_1 + b_2)$.

Conceptually, the relationship between the bivariate regression coefficient and the partial regression coefficient can be illustrated as follows. Suppose one were to remove the effect of X_2 from X_1. This could be done by running a regression of X_1 on X_2. In other words, one would estimate the equation $\hat{X}_1 = a + bX_2$ and calculate the residual $X_r = (X_1 - \hat{X}_1)$. The partial regression coefficient, b_1, is then equal to the bivariate regression coefficient, b_r, obtained from the equation $\hat{Y} = a + b_r X_r$. In other words, the partial regression coefficient, b_1, is equal to the regression coefficient, b_r, between Y and the residuals of X_1 from which the effect of X_2 has been removed. The partial coefficient, b_2, can also be interpreted along similar lines.

Extension to the case of k variables is straightforward. The partial regression coefficient, b_1, represents the expected change in Y when X_1 is changed by one unit and X_2 through X_k are held constant. It can also be interpreted as the bivariate regression coefficient, b, for the regression of Y on the residuals of X_1, when the effect of X_2 through X_k has been removed from X_1.

The beta coefficients are the partial regression coefficients obtained when all the variables $(Y, X_1, X_2, \ldots X_k)$ have been standardized to a mean of 0 and a variance of 1 before estimating the regression equation. The relationship of the standardized to the nonstandardized coefficients remains the same as before:

$$B_1 = b_1\left(\frac{s_{x_1}}{s_y}\right)$$

$$.$$
$$.$$
$$.$$

$$B_k = b_k\left(\frac{s_{x_k}}{s_y}\right)$$

The intercept and the partial regression coefficients are estimated by solving a system of simultaneous equations derived by differentiating and equating the partial derivatives to 0. Because these coefficients are automatically estimated by the various computer programs, we will not present the details. Yet it is worth noting that the equations cannot be solved if (1) the

SPSS Output File

SAS Output File

TABLE 17.3
Multiple Regression

Multiple R	0.97210
R^2	0.94498
Adjusted R^2	0.93276
Standard error	0.85974

	df	Analysis of Variance Sum of Squares	Mean Square
Regression	2	114.26425	57.13213
Residual	9	6.65241	0.73916

$F = 77.29364$ Significance of $F = 0.0000$

Variables in the Equation

Variable	b	SE_B	Beta (B)	t	Significance of t
IMPORTANCE	0.28865	0.08608	0.31382	3.353	0.0085
DURATION	0.48108	0.05895	0.76363	8.160	0.0000
(Constant)	0.33732	0.56736		0.595	0.5668

sample size, n, is smaller than or equal to the number of independent variables, k; or (2) one independent variable is perfectly correlated with another.

Suppose that, in explaining the attitude toward the city, we now introduce a second variable, importance attached to the weather. The data for the 12 pretest respondents on attitude toward the city, duration of residence, and importance attached to the weather are given in Table 17.1. The results of multiple regression analysis are depicted in Table 17.3. The partial regression coefficient for duration (X_1) is now 0.48108, different from what it was in the bivariate case. The corresponding beta coefficient is 0.7636. The partial regression coefficient for importance attached to weather (X_2) is 0.28865, with a beta coefficient of 0.3138. The estimated regression equation is:

$$(\hat{Y}) = 0.33732 + 0.48108X_1 + 0.28865X_2$$

or

$$\text{Attitude} = 0.33732 + 0.48108 \, (\text{Duration}) + 0.28865 \, (\text{Importance})$$

This equation can be used for a variety of purposes, including predicting attitudes toward the city, given a knowledge of the respondents' duration of residence in the city and the importance they attach to weather. Note that both duration and importance are significant and useful in this prediction.

Strength of Association

The strength of the relationship stipulated by the regression equation can be determined by using appropriate measures of association. The total variation is decomposed as in the bivariate case:

$$SS_y = SS_{reg} + SS_{res}$$

where

$$SS_y = \sum_{i=1}^{n}(Y_i - \bar{Y})^2$$

$$SS_{reg} = \sum_{i=1}^{n}(\hat{Y}_i - \bar{Y})^2$$

$$SS_{res} = \sum_{i=1}^{n}(Y_i - \hat{Y}_i)^2$$

The strength of association is measured by the square of the multiple correlation coefficient, R^2, which is also called the *coefficient of multiple determination*.

$$R^2 = \frac{SS_{reg}}{SS_y}$$

The multiple correlation coefficient, R, can also be viewed as the simple correlation coefficient, r, between Y and $\hat{Y}$. Several points about the characteristics of R^2 are worth noting. The coefficient of multiple determination, R^2, cannot be less than the highest bivariate, r^2, of any individual independent variable with the dependent variable. R^2 will be larger when the correlations between the independent variables are low. If the independent variables are statistically independent (uncorrelated), then R^2 will be the sum of bivariate r^2 of each independent variable with the dependent variable. R^2 cannot decrease as more independent variables are added to the regression equation. Yet diminishing returns set in, so that after the first few variables, the additional independent variables do not make much of a contribution.[16] For this reason, R^2 is adjusted for the number of independent variables and the sample size by using the following formula:

$$\text{Adjusted } R^2 = R^2 - \frac{k(1 - R^2)}{n - k - 1}$$

For the regression results given in Table 17.3, the value of R^2 is:

$$R^2 = \frac{114.2643}{(114.2643 + 6.6524)}$$
$$= 0.9450$$

This is higher than the r^2 value of 0.8762 obtained in the bivariate case. The r^2 in the bivariate case is the square of the simple (product moment) correlation between attitude toward the city and duration of residence. The R^2 obtained in multiple regression is also higher than the square of the simple correlation between attitude and importance attached to weather (which can be estimated as 0.5379). The adjusted R^2 is estimated as:

$$\text{Adjusted } R^2 = 0.9450 - \frac{2(1.0 - 0.9450)}{(12 - 2 - 1)}$$
$$= 0.9328$$

Note that the value of adjusted R^2 is close to R^2 and both are higher than r^2 for the bivariate case. This suggests that the addition of the second independent variable, importance attached to weather, makes a contribution in explaining the variation in attitude toward the city.

Significance Testing

Significance testing involves testing the significance of the overall regression equation as well as specific partial regression coefficients. The null hypothesis for the overall test is that the coefficient of multiple determination in the population, R^2_{pop}, is zero.

$$H_0: R^2_{pop} = 0$$

This is equivalent to the following null hypothesis:

$$H_0: \beta_1 = \beta_2 = \beta_3 = \ldots = \beta_\kappa = 0$$

The overall test can be conducted by using an F statistic:

$$F = \frac{SS_{reg}/k}{SS_{res}/(n - k - 1)}$$
$$= \frac{R^2/k}{(1 - R^2)/(n - k - 1)}$$

which has an F distribution with k and $(n - k - 1)$ degrees of freedom.[17] For the multiple regression results given in Table 17.3,

$$F = \frac{114.2643/2}{6.6524/9} = 77.2936$$

which is significant at $\alpha = 0.05$.

If the overall null hypothesis is rejected, one or more population partial regression coefficients have a value different from 0. To determine which specific coefficients (β_is) are nonzero, additional tests are necessary. Testing for the significance of the (β_is) can be done in a manner similar to that in the bivariate case by using t tests. The significance of the partial coefficient for importance attached to weather may be tested by the following equation:

$$t = \frac{b}{SE_b}$$

$$= \frac{0.2887}{0.08608}$$

$$= 3.353$$

which has a t distribution with $n - k - 1$ degrees of freedom. This coefficient is significant at $\alpha = 0.05$. The significance of the coefficient for duration of residence is tested in a similar way and found to be significant. Therefore, both the duration of residence and importance attached to weather are important in explaining attitude toward the city.

Some computer programs provide an equivalent F test, often called the *partial F test*. This involves a decomposition of the total regression sum of squares, SS_{reg}, into components related to each independent variable. In the standard approach, this is done by assuming that each independent variable has been added to the regression equation after all the other independent variables have been included. The increment in the explained sum of squares, resulting from the addition of an independent variable, X_i, is the component of the variation attributed to that variable and is denoted by SS_{x_i}.[18] The significance of the partial regression coefficient for this variable, b_i, is tested using an incremental F statistic:

$$F = \frac{SS_{x_i}/1}{SS_{res}/(n - k - 1)}$$

which has an F distribution with 1 and $(n - k - 1)$ degrees of freedom.

Although high R^2 and significant partial regression coefficients are comforting, the efficacy of the regression model should be evaluated further by an examination of the residuals.

Examination of Residuals

residual

The difference between the observed value of Y_i and the value predicted by the regression equation, $\hat{Y}_i$.

A **residual** is the difference between the observed value of Y_i and the value predicted by the regression equation, $\hat{Y}_i$. Residuals are used in the calculation of several statistics associated with regression. In addition, scattergrams of the residuals, in which the residuals are plotted against the predicted values, $\hat{Y}_i$, time, or predictor variables, provide useful insights in examining the appropriateness of the underlying assumptions and regression model fitted.[19]

The assumption of a normally distributed error term can be examined by constructing a histogram of the standardized residuals. A visual check reveals whether the distribution is normal. It is also useful to examine the normal probability plot of standardized residuals. The normal probability plot shows the observed standardized residuals compared to expected standardized residuals from a normal distribution. If the observed residuals are normally distributed, they will fall on the 45-degree line. Also, look at the table of residual statistics and identify any standardized predicted values or standardized residuals that are more than plus or minus one and two standard deviations. These percentages can be compared with what would be expected under the normal distribution (68 percent and 95 percent, respectively). More formal assessment can be made by running the K-S one-sample test.

The assumption of constant variance of the error term can be examined by plotting the standardized residuals against the standardized predicted values of the dependent variable, $\hat{Y}_i$. If the pattern is not random, the variance of the error term is not constant. Figure 17.7 shows a pattern whose variance is dependent upon the $\hat{Y}_i$ values.

A plot of residuals against time, or the sequence of observations, will throw some light on the assumption that the error terms are uncorrelated. A random pattern should be seen if this assumption is true. A plot like the one in Figure 17.8 indicates a linear relationship

FIGURE 17.7

Residual Plot Indicating That Variance Is Not Constant

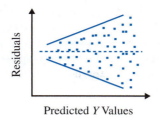

Predicted *Y* Values

FIGURE 17.8

Plot Indicating a Linear Relationship Between Residuals and Time

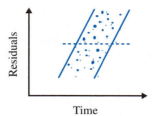

Time

between residuals and time. A more formal procedure for examining the correlations between the error terms is the Durbin-Watson test.[20]

Plotting the residuals against the independent variables provides evidence of the appropriateness or inappropriateness of using a linear model. Again, the plot should result in a random pattern. The residuals should fall randomly, with relatively equal distribution dispersion about 0. They should not display any tendency to be either positive or negative.

To examine whether any additional variables should be included in the regression equation, one could run a regression of the residuals on the proposed variables. If any variable explains a significant proportion of the residual variation, it should be considered for inclusion. Inclusion of variables in the regression equation should be strongly guided by the researcher's theory. Thus, an examination of the residuals provides valuable insights into the appropriateness of the underlying assumptions and the model that is fitted. Figure 17.9 shows a plot that indicates that the underlying assumptions are met and that the linear model is appropriate. If an examination of the residuals indicates that the assumptions underlying linear regression are not met, the researcher can transform the variables in an attempt to satisfy the assumptions. Transformations, such as taking logs, square roots, or reciprocals, can stabilize the variance, make the distribution normal, or make the relationship linear.

The plots and the residual table can be requested when the regression is run, for example, when using SPSS. You should conduct these analyses for multiple regression on the data of Table 17.1. From the histogram, it can be seen that five residuals are positive, whereas seven residuals are negative. By comparing the frequency distribution with the normal distribution that is plotted in the same output, you can see that the assumption of normality is probably not met but that the departure from normality might not be severe. Of course, one can do a more formal statistical test for normality if that is warranted. All the standardized residuals are within plus or minus two standard deviations. Furthermore, many of the residuals are relatively small, which means that most of the model predictions are quite good.

The normal probability plot shows that the residuals are quite close to the 45-degree line shown in the graph. When you look at the plot of the standardized residuals against the standardized predicted values, no systematic pattern can be discerned in the spread of the residuals. Finally, the

FIGURE 17.9

Plot of Residuals Indicating That a Fitted Model Is Appropriate

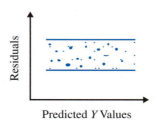

Predicted *Y* Values

table of residual statistics indicates that all the standardized predicted values and all the standardized residuals are within plus or minus two standard deviations. Hence, we can conclude that multiple regression on the data of Table 17.1 does not appear to result in gross violations of the assumptions. This suggests that the relationship we are trying to predict is linear and that the error terms are more or less normally distributed.

Real Research

What Influences Sports Ticket Prices? A New Stadium!

A major source of revenue for any professional sports team is through ticket sales, especially sales to season ticket subscribers. A study performed a regression analysis to determine what factors caused ticket prices to vary among teams in the same league within a given year. The regression equation was:

$$LTIX = a_0 + a_1 HWIN + a_2 INCOME + a_3 PAY + a_4 POPL + a_5 TREND + a_6 CAP + a_7 STAD$$

where

LTIX =	natural log of average ticket price
TIX =	average ticket price
HWIN =	average number of wins by the team in the previous three seasons
INCOME =	average income level of city population
PAY =	team payroll
POPL =	population size of city
TREND =	trends in the industry
CAP =	attendance as a percentage of capacity
STAD =	if the team is playing in a new stadium

The research gathered data covering a span of seven years (1996–2002). The financial data were gathered through Team Marketing Reports and the rest of the data were collected using publicly available sources such as sports reports. The results of the regression analyses can be seen in the accompanying table.

The results suggest that several factors influenced ticket prices, and the largest factor was that the team was playing in a new stadium.[21] ∎

Regression Results

Variable	MLB Coefficient	MLB t-Statistic	MLB p-Value	NBA Coefficient	NBA t-Statistic	NBA p-Value	NFL Coefficient	NFL t-Statistic	NFL p-Value	NHL Coefficient	NHL t-Statistic	NHL p-Value
Constant	1.521	12.012	0.000	2.965	20.749	0.000	2.886	18.890	0.000	3.172	16.410	0.000
POPL	0.000	5.404	0.000	0.000	5.036	0.000	0.000	−2.287	0.023	0.000	2.246	0.026
INCOME	0.000	3.991	0.000	0.000	0.208	0.836	0.000	3.645	0.000	0.000	0.669	0.504
STAD	0.337	5.356	0.000	0.108	3.180	0.002	0.226	3.357	0.001	0.321	4.087	0.000
HWIN	0.000	0.091	0.927	0.004	3.459	0.001	0.013	2.190	0.030	0.001	0.369	0.713
CAP	0.006	8.210	0.000	0.000	2.968	0.003	0.002	1.325	0.187	0.005	3.951	0.000
PAY	0.004	4.192	0.000	0.008	5.341	0.000	0.001	0.607	0.545	0.002	1.099	0.273
TREND	0.047	6.803	0.000	0.016	1.616	0.100	0.058	6.735	0.000	0.009	0.718	0.474
CAN (Canada)										−0.146	−3.167	0.002
Adjusted R-squared		0.778			0.488			0.443				0.292
F Statistic		98.366			28.227			24.763				9.545
F Significance		0.000			0.000			0.000				

As in the preceding example, some independent variables considered in a study often turn out not to be significant. When there are a large number of independent variables and the researcher suspects that not all of them are significant, stepwise regression should be used.

Stepwise Regression

stepwise regression
A regression procedure in which the predictor variables enter or leave the regression equation one at a time.

The purpose of **stepwise regression** is to select, from a large number of predictor variables, a small subset of variables that account for most of the variation in the dependent or criterion variable. In this procedure, the predictor variables enter or are removed from the regression equation one at a time.[22] There are several approaches to stepwise regression.

1. *Forward inclusion*. Initially, there are no predictor variables in the regression equation. Predictor variables are entered one at a time, only if they meet certain criteria specified in terms of the *F* ratio. The order in which the variables are included is based on the contribution to the explained variance.
2. *Backward elimination*. Initially, all the predictor variables are included in the regression equation. Predictors are then removed one at a time based on the *F* ratio.
3. *Stepwise solution*. Forward inclusion is combined with the removal of predictors that no longer meet the specified criterion at each step.

Stepwise procedures do not result in regression equations that are optimal, in the sense of producing the largest R^2, for a given number of predictors. Because of the correlations between predictors, an important variable may never be included, or less important variables may enter the equation. To identify an optimal regression equation, one would have to compute combinatorial solutions in which all possible combinations are examined. Nevertheless, stepwise regression can be useful when the sample size is large in relation to the number of predictors, as shown in the following example.

Real Research

Stepping Out . . . to the Mall

Even in the twenty-first century, browsing is a fundamental part of shopping—whether it is online or in the mall. Customers like to consider their purchase decisions before actually carrying them out. Many consider store-based retailers to have an advantage over Web-based retailers when it comes to browsing because store-based retailers are larger in size and product offerings. Although the Web appeals to younger shoppers, the mall will remain ahead of the game, especially with so many entertainment factors now being built inside malls. A profile of browsers in regional shopping malls was constructed using three sets of independent variables: demographics, shopping behavior, and psychological and attitudinal variables. The dependent variable consisted of a browsing index. In a stepwise regression including all three sets of variables, demographics were found to be the most powerful predictors of browsing behavior. The final regression equation, which contained 20 of the possible 36 variables, included all of the demographics. The accompanying table presents the regression coefficients, standard errors of the coefficients, and their significance levels.

In interpreting the coefficients, it should be recalled that the smaller the browsing index (the dependent variable), the greater the tendency to exhibit behaviors associated with browsing. The two predictors with the largest coefficients are sex and employment status. Browsers are more likely to be employed females. They

Regression of Browsing Index on Descriptive and Attitudinal Variables by Order of Entry into Stepwise Regression

Variable Description	Coefficient	SE	Significance
Sex (0 = Male, 1 = Female)	−0.485	0.164	0.001
Employment status (0 = Employed)	0.391	0.182	0.003
Self-confidence	−0.152	0.128	0.234
Education	0.079	0.072	0.271
Brand intention	−0.063	0.028	0.024
Watch daytime TV? (0 = Yes)	0.232	0.144	0.107
Tension	−0.182	0.069	0.008
Income	0.089	0.061	0.144
Frequency of mall visits	−0.130	0.059	0.028

(continued)

Fewer friends than most	0.162	0.084	0.054
Good shopper	−0.122	0.090	0.174
Others' opinions important	−0.147	0.065	0.024
Control over life	−0.069	0.069	0.317
Family size	−0.086	0.062	0.165
Enthusiastic person	−0.143	0.099	0.150
Age	0.036	0.069	0.603
Number of purchases made	−0.068	0.043	0.150
Purchases per store	0.209	0.152	0.167
Shop on tight budget	−0.055	0.067	0.412
Excellent judge of quality	−0.070	0.089	0.435
CONSTANT	3.250		

Overall $R^2 = 0.477$

also tend to be somewhat downscale, compared to other mall patrons, exhibiting lower levels of education and income, after accounting for the effects of sex and employment status. Although browsers tend to be somewhat younger than nonbrowsers, they are not necessarily single; those who reported larger family sizes tended to be associated with smaller values of the browsing index.

The downscale profile of browsers relative to other mall patrons indicates that specialty stores in malls should emphasize moderately priced products. This may explain the historically low rate of failure in malls among such stores and the tendency of high-priced specialty shops to be located in only the prestigious malls or upscale nonenclosed shopping centers.[23] ■

Multicollinearity

multicollinearity
A state of very high intercorrelations among independent variables.

Stepwise regression and multiple regression are complicated by the presence of multicollinearity. Virtually all multiple regression analyses done in marketing research involve predictors or independent variables that are related. However, **multicollinearity** arises when intercorrelations among the predictors are very high. Multicollinearity can result in several problems, including:

1. The partial regression coefficients may not be estimated precisely. The standard errors are likely to be high.
2. The magnitudes as well as the signs of the partial regression coefficients may change from sample to sample.
3. It becomes difficult to assess the relative importance of the independent variables in explaining the variation in the dependent variable.
4. Predictor variables may be incorrectly included or removed in stepwise regression.

What constitutes serious multicollinearity is not always clear, although several rules of thumb and procedures have been suggested in the literature. Procedures of varying complexity have also been suggested to cope with multicollinearity.[24] A simple procedure consists of using only one of the variables in a highly correlated set of variables. Alternatively, the set of independent variables can be transformed into a new set of predictors that are mutually independent by using techniques such as principal components analysis (see Chapter 19). More specialized techniques, such as ridge regression and latent root regression, can also be used.[25]

ACTIVE RESEARCH

Brand Evaluation and Preference for Lenovo Laptops

Visit www.lenovo.com and conduct an Internet search using a search engine and your library's online database to obtain information on the factors consumers use to evaluate competing brands of laptop computers.

As the marketing director for Lenovo computers, how would you improve the image and competitive positioning of your brand?

Formulate a multiple regression model explaining consumer preferences for laptop computer brands as a function of the brand evaluations on the consumer choice criteria factors used to evaluate competing brands.

Relative Importance of Predictors

When multicollinearity is present, special care is required in assessing the relative importance of independent variables. In applied marketing research, it is valuable to determine the *relative importance of the predictors*. In other words, how important are the independent variables in accounting for the variation in the criterion or dependent variable?[26] Unfortunately, because the predictors are correlated, there is no unambiguous measure of relative importance of the predictors in regression analysis.[27] However, several approaches are commonly used to assess the relative importance of predictor variables.

1. *Statistical significance.* If the partial regression coefficient of a variable is not significant, as determined by an incremental F test, that variable is judged to be unimportant. An exception to this rule is made if there are strong theoretical reasons for believing that the variable is important.
2. *Square of the simple correlation coefficient.* This measure, r^2, represents the proportion of the variation in the dependent variable explained by the independent variable in a bivariate relationship.
3. *Square of the partial correlation coefficient.* This measure, $R^2_{yx_i.x_j x_k}$, is the coefficient of determination between the dependent variable and the independent variable, controlling for the effects of the other independent variables.
4. *Square of the part correlation coefficient.* This coefficient represents an increase in R^2 when a variable is entered into a regression equation that already contains the other independent variables.
5. *Measures based on standardized coefficients or beta weights.* The most commonly used measures are the absolute values of the beta weights, $|B_i|$, or the squared values, B_i^2. Because they are partial coefficients, beta weights take into account the effect of the other independent variables. These measures become increasingly unreliable as the correlations among the predictor variables increase (multicollinearity increases).
6. *Stepwise regression.* The order in which the predictors enter or are removed from the regression equation is used to infer their relative importance.

Given that the predictors are correlated, at least to some extent, in virtually all regression situations, none of these measures is satisfactory. It is also possible that the different measures may indicate a different order of importance of the predictors.[28] Yet, if all the measures are examined collectively, useful insights may be obtained into the relative importance of the predictors.

Decision Research The West Michigan Whitecaps: Fanning Fan Loyalty

The Situation

The West Michigan Whitecaps (www.whitecaps-baseball.com), a minor league baseball team in Grand Rapids, wondered what they should do to develop fan loyalty. How could they best keep it, make it grow, and take advantage of it? General Manager Scott Lane got Message Factors (www.messagefactors.com), a Memphis, Tennessee–based research firm, to help them determine how to effectively maintain fan loyalty on a limited budget. Message Factors developed a study that used a proprietary value analysis technique that would examine the relationship between the overall perceived value and specific satisfaction attributes in order to determine loyalty drivers. It helps determine the four things your customers want to tell you, which are the basics—what customers expect of the company; value issues—what customers value about the company; irritations—what customers do not like about the company; and unimportants—what customers do not care about.

Qualitative research was conducted to identify a set of 71 attributes that influenced fan loyalty. Next, a questionnaire designed to incorporate the 71 attributes was administered to fans at Whitecaps games. The questionnaire was administered to 1,010 respondents. From this, the marketing research company was able to determine the information they were looking for. The basics were determined to be values such as stadium safety, restroom cleanliness, and variety in the food items available. The Whitecaps not only want to meet these basic expectations, but also to surpass them to guarantee that

Regression analysis can help the West Michigan Whitecaps determine the value drivers and enhance the value of Whitecaps games to the fans.

fans will return and be loyal. The value issues are the ones that can really help the team build loyalty. These included things like helpful box office personnel, convenience of purchasing tickets, convenience of parking, and providing the opportunity for autographs. Irritations were determined to involve souvenir price, quality, and lack of variety. However, the research also showed that fans don't really expect to be pleased with this area of sports attendance. It was also determined that there were no unimportant aspects in this survey.

The Marketing Research Decision

1. In order to determine the relative importance of value drivers, what type of data analysis should Message Factors conduct?
2. Discuss the role of the type of data analysis you recommend in enabling Scott Lane to determine the relative importance of the four value drivers.

The Marketing Management Decision

1. In order to enhance the value of Whitecaps games to the fans, what should Scott Lane do?
2. Discuss how the marketing management decision action that you recommend to Scott Lane is influenced by the type of data analysis that you suggested earlier and by the findings of that analysis.[29] ■

Cross-Validation

Before assessing the relative importance of the predictors or drawing any other inferences, it is necessary to cross-validate the regression model. Regression and other multivariate procedures tend to capitalize on chance variations in the data. This could result in a regression model or equation that is unduly sensitive to the specific data used to estimate the model. One approach for evaluating the model for this, and other problems associated with regression, is cross-validation. **Cross-validation** examines whether the regression model continues to hold on comparable data not used in the estimation. The typical cross-validation procedure used in marketing research is as follows:

cross-validation
A test of validity that examines whether a model holds on comparable data not used in the original estimation.

1. The regression model is estimated using the entire data set.
2. The available data are split into two parts, the *estimation sample* and the *validation sample*. The estimation sample generally contains 50 to 90 percent of the total sample.
3. The regression model is estimated using the data from the estimation sample only. This model is compared to the model estimated on the entire sample to determine the agreement in terms of the signs and magnitudes of the partial regression coefficients.

4. The estimated model is applied to the data in the validation sample to predict the values of the dependent variable, $\hat{Y}_i$, for the observations in the validation sample.
5. The observed values, Y_i, and the predicted values, $\hat{Y}_i$, in the validation sample are correlated to determine the simple r^2. This measure, r^2, is compared to R^2 for the total sample and to R^2 for the estimation sample to assess the degree of shrinkage.

double cross-validation
A special form of validation in which the sample is split into halves. One half serves as the estimation sample and the other as a validation sample. The roles of the estimation and validation halves are then reversed and the cross-validation process is repeated.

A special form of validation is called double cross-validation. In **double cross-validation**, the sample is split into halves. One half serves as the estimation sample, and the other is used as a validation sample in conducting cross-validation. The roles of the estimation and validation halves are then reversed, and the cross-validation is repeated.

Regression with Dummy Variables

Cross-validation is a general procedure that can be applied even in some special applications of regression, such as regression with dummy variables. Nominal or categorical variables may be used as predictors or independent variables by coding them as dummy variables. The concept of dummy variables was introduced in Chapter 14. In that chapter, we explained how a categorical variable with four categories (heavy, medium, light, and nonusers) can be coded in terms of three dummy variables, D_1, D_2, and D_3, as shown.

Product Usage Category	Original Variable Code	Dummy Variable Code		
		D_1	D_2	D_3
Nonusers	1	1	0	0
Light users	2	0	1	0
Medium users	3	0	0	1
Heavy users	4	0	0	0

Suppose the researcher was interested in running a regression analysis of the effect of attitude toward the brand on product use. The dummy variables D_1, D_2, and D_3 would be used as predictors. *Regression with dummy variables* would be modeled as:

$$\hat{Y}_i = a + b_1 D_1 + b_2 D_2 + b_3 D_3$$

In this case, "heavy users" has been selected as a reference category and has not been directly included in the regression equation. Note that for heavy users, D_1, D_2, and D_3 assume a value of 0, and the regression equation becomes:

$$\hat{Y}_i = a$$

For nonusers, $D_1 = 1$, and $D_2 = D_3 = 0$, and the regression equation becomes:

$$\hat{Y}_i = a + b_1$$

Thus the coefficient b_1 is the difference in predicted $\hat{Y}_i$ for nonusers, as compared to heavy users. The coefficients b_2 and b_3 have similar interpretations. Although "heavy users" was selected as a reference category, any of the other three categories could have been selected for this purpose.[30]

Analysis of Variance and Covariance with Regression

Regression with dummy variables provides a framework for understanding analysis of variance and covariance. Although multiple regression with dummy variables provides a general procedure for the analysis of variance and covariance, we show only the equivalence of regression with dummy variables to one-way analysis of variance. In regression with dummy variables, the predicted $\hat{Y}$ for each category is the mean of Y for each category. To illustrate using the dummy variable coding of product use we just considered, the predicted $\hat{Y}$ and mean values for each category are as follows:

Product Usage Category	Predicted Value $\hat{Y}$	Mean Value $\overline{Y}$
Nonusers	$a + b_1$	$a + b_1$
Light users	$a + b_2$	$a + b_2$
Medium users	$a + b_3$	$a + b_3$
Heavy users	a	a

Given this equivalence, it is easy to see further relationships between dummy variable regression and one-way ANOVA.[31]

Dummy Variable Regression	One-Way ANOVA
$SS_{res} = \sum_{i=1}^{n}(Y_i - \hat{Y}_i)^2$	$= SS_{within} = SS_{error}$
$SS_{reg} = \sum_{i=1}^{n}(\hat{Y}_i - \overline{Y})^2$	$= SS_{between} = SS_x$
R^2	$= \eta^2$
Overall F test	$= F$ test

Thus, we see that regression in which the single independent variable with c categories has been recoded into $c - 1$ dummy variables is equivalent to one-way analysis of variance. Using similar correspondences, one can also illustrate how n-way analysis of variance and analysis of covariance can be performed using regression with dummy variables.

Regression analysis, in its various forms, is a widely used technique. The next example illustrates an application in the context of international marketing research, and the example after that shows how regression can be used in investigating ethics in marketing research.

Real Research

Frequent Fliers—Fly from the Clouds to the Clear

Airline companies in Asia had been facing uncertainty and tough competition from U.S. carriers for a long time. Asian airlines, hit by high fuel costs, global recession, and preemptive competitive deals, realized they could band together to increase air patronage. Secondary data revealed that among the important factors leading to airline selection by consumers were price, on-time schedules, destinations, deals available, kitchen and food service, on-flight service, and so on. Asian airlines offered these services at par if not better. In fact, research showed that in-flight and kitchen services might have been even better. So why were they feeling the competitive pressure? Qualitative research in the form of focus groups revealed that the frequent flier program was a critical factor for a broad segment in general and the business segment in particular. A survey of international passengers was conducted and a series of multiple regression analyses were used to analyze the data. The likelihood of flying and other choice measures served as the dependent variable and the set of service factors, including the frequent flier program, were the independent variables. The results indicated that frequent flier program indeed had a significant effect on the choice of an airline. Based on these findings, Cathay Pacific, Singapore International Airlines, Thai Airways International, and Malaysian Airlines introduced a cooperative frequent flier program called Asia Plus, available to all travelers. The program was the first time the Asian carriers had offered free travel in return for regular patronage. A multimillion-dollar marketing and advertising campaign was started to promote Asia Plus. Frequent fliers, thus, flew from the clouds to the clear and the Asian airlines experienced increased passenger traffic. Although Asia Plus and other frequent flier programs proved successful for Asian airlines, the uncertain economy of 2009 pushed them into a huge crisis. The Association of Asia Pacific Airlines (AAPA) said at its annual assembly that the current state of the industry was not encouraging. Despite the challenges ahead for Asian airlines in 2010 to 2015, many believe that it will be possible to renew growth and restore profitability in the future. The director of the AAPA, General Richard Stirland, said, "The industry should seize the opportunity, think the unthinkable, and set a new course to establish a less fragmented and healthier industry."[32] ∎

Real Research

Reasons for Researchers Regressing to Unethical Behavior

As of 2009, the Internet is being used more and more to conduct marketing research studies. Therefore, it is crucial that the research community create an ethical code of standards to follow when researching in an online environment. Many online researchers are distressed at the way other researchers are abusing the Internet as a means of collecting data. Those who conduct online research in an ethical manner feel that an accepted code of ethics of online research and online marketing behavior must be established. Without such a code, dishonest marketing tactics will prevail and ultimately make online research an impractical means of collecting important consumer data. Not only does online marketing research raise ethical problems and concerns, but also traditional marketing research has been targeted as a major source of ethical problems within the discipline of marketing. In particular, marketing research has been charged with engaging in deception, conflict of interest, violation of anonymity, invasion of privacy, data falsifications, dissemination of faulty research findings, and the use of research as a guise to sell merchandise. It has been posited that when a researcher chooses to participate in unethical activities, that decision may be influenced by organizational factors. Therefore, a study using multiple regression analysis was designed to examine organizational factors as determinants of the incidence of unethical research practices. Six organizational variables were used as the independent variables, namely: extent of ethical problems within the organization, top management actions on ethics, code of ethics, organizational rank, industry category, and organizational role. The respondent's evaluation of the incidence of unethical marketing research practices served as the dependent variable. Regression analysis of the data suggested that four of the six organization variables influenced the extent of unethical research practice: extent of ethical problems within the organization, top management actions on ethics, organizational role, and industry category. Thus, to reduce the incidence of unethical research practice, top management should take stern actions, clarify organizational roles and responsibilities for ethical violations, and address the extent of general ethical problems within the organization.[33] ■

Statistical Software

The major computer packages (SPSS and SAS) have programs for conducting correlation and regression analysis. MINITAB and EXCEL also offer some programs. Exhibit 17.1 contains a description of the relevant programs for MINITAB and EXCEL. Refer to the user manuals for these packages for more information. We discuss the use of SPSS and SAS in detail.

EXHIBIT 17.1

MINITAB and EXCEL Programs for Correlation and Regression

MINITAB

Correlations can be computed using the STAT>BASIC STATISTICS>CORRELATION function. It calculates Pearson's product moment using all the columns. Spearman's ranks the columns first and then performs the correlation on the ranked columns.

To compute partial correlation, use the menu commands STAT>BASIC STATISTICS>CORRELATION and STAT>REGRESSION>REGRESSION. Partial correlations can also be calculated by using session commands.

Regression analysis under the STAT>REGRESSION function can perform simple, polynomial, and multiple analysis. The output includes a linear regression equation, table of coefficients, R square, R squared adjusted, analysis of variance table, a table of fits, and residuals that provide unusual observations. Other available features include stepwise, best subsets, fitted line plot, and residual plots.

EXCEL

Correlations can be determined in EXCEL by using the DATA>DATA ANALYSIS>CORRELATION function. Utilize the Correlation Worksheet function when a correlation coefficient for two cell ranges is needed. There is no separate function for partial correlations.

Regression can be accessed from the DATA>DATA ANALYSIS menu. Depending on the features selected, the output can consist of a summary output table, including an ANOVA table, a standard error of y estimate, coefficients, standard error of coefficients, R^2 values, and the number of observations. In addition, the function computes a residual output table, a residual plot, a line fit plot, normal probability plot, and a two-column probability data output table.

SPSS and SAS Computerized Demonstration Movies

We have developed computerized demonstration movies that give step-by-step instructions for running all the SPSS and SAS Learning Edition programs that are discussed in this chapter. These demonstrations can be downloaded from the Web site for this book. The instructions for running these demonstrations are given in Exhibit 14.2.

SPSS and SAS Screen Captures with Notes

The step-by-step instructions for running the various SPSS and SAS Learning Edition programs discussed in this chapter are also illustrated in screen captures with appropriate notes. These screen captures can be downloaded from the Web site for this book.

SPSS Windows

The CORRELATE program computes Pearson product moment correlations and partial correlations with significance levels. Univariate statistics, covariance, and cross-product deviations may also be requested. Significance levels are included in the output. To select this procedure using SPSS for Windows, click:

Analyze>Correlate>Bivariate . . .

Analyze>Correlate>Partial . . .

Scatterplots can be obtained by clicking:

Graphs>Scatter . . . >Simple>Define

The following are the detailed steps for running a correlation between attitude toward the city and duration of residence given in Table 17.1. A positive correlation is to be expected.

1. Select ANALYZE from the SPSS menu bar.
2. Click CORRELATE and then BIVARIATE.
3. Move "Attitude[attitude]" into the VARIABLES box. Then move "Duration[duration]" into the VARIABLES box.
4. Check PEARSON under CORRELATION COEFFICIENTS.
5. Check ONE_TAILED under TEST OF SIGNIFICANCE.
6. Check FLAG SIGNIFICANT CORRELATIONS.
7. Click OK.

REGRESSION calculates bivariate and multiple regression equations, associated statistics, and plots. It allows for an easy examination of residuals. This procedure can be run by clicking:

Analyze>Regression>Linear . . .

The following are the detailed steps for running a bivariate regression with attitude toward the city as the dependent variable and duration of residence as the independent variable using the data of Table 17.1.

1. Select ANALYZE from the SPSS menu bar.
2. Click REGRESSION and then LINEAR.
3. Move "Attitude[attitude]" into the DEPENDENT box.
4. Move "Duration[duration]" into the INDEPENDENT(S) box.
5. Select ENTER in the METHOD box.
6. Click on STATISTICS and check ESTIMATES under REGRESSION COEFFICIENTS.
7. Check MODEL FIT.
8. Click CONTINUE.
9. Click PLOTS.
10. In the LINEAR REGRESSION:PLOTS box, move *ZRESID into the Y: box and *ZPRED into the X: box.
11. Check HISTOGRAM and NORMAL PROBABILITY PLOT in the STANDARDIZED RESIDUALS PLOTS.
12. Click CONTINUE.
13. Click OK.

The steps for running multiple regression are similar except for step 4. In step 4, move "Duration[duration]" and "Importance[importance]" into the INDEPENDENT(S) box.

SAS Learning Edition

The instructions given here and in all the data analysis chapters (14 to 22) will work with the SAS Learning Edition as well as with the SAS Enterprise Guide. For a point-and-click approach for performing metric and nonmetric correlations, use the Analyze task within SAS Learning Edition. The Multivariate>Correlations task offers these correlation types: Pearson product-moment correlations, Kendall tau-b, and Spearman rank-order correlations. The task also offers Pearson, Spearman, and Kendall partial correlations. To select this task click:

Analyze>Multivariate>Correlations

(You can do correlations, partial correlations, and scatterplots within this task.)

The following are the detailed steps for running a correlation between attitude toward the city and duration of residence given in Table 17.1. A positive correlation is to be expected.

1. Select ANALYZE from the SAS Learning Edition menu bar.
2. Click MULTIVARIATE and then CORRELATIONS.
3. Move CITY and DURATION to the analysis variable task role.
4. Click OPTIONS.
5. Click PEARSON under correlation types.
6. Click RUN.

For a point-and-click approach for performing regression analysis, use the Analyze task within SAS Learning Edition. The Regression task calculates bivariate and multiple regression equations, associated statistics, and plots. It allows for an easy examination of residuals. The Regression task offers not only Linear, but also Nonlinear and Logistic Regression as well as Generalized Linear Models. This procedure can be run by clicking:

Analyze>Regression>Linear

The following are the detailed steps for running a bivariate regression with attitude toward the city as the dependent variable and duration of residence as the independent variable using the data of Table 17.1.

1. Select ANALYZE from the SAS Learning Edition menu bar.
2. Click REGRESSION and then LINEAR.
3. Move CITY to the dependent variable task role.
4. Move DURATION to the explanatory variables task role.
5. Click MODEL.
6. Select Full model fitted (no selection) under Model selection method.
7. Click RUN. *(The model fit stats and the estimates are part of the automatic output.)*

The steps for running multiple regression are similar except for step 4. In step 4, move DURATION and WEATHER to the explanatory variables task role.

Project Research   Multiple Regression

In the department store project, multiple regression analysis was used to develop a model that explained store preference in terms of respondents' evaluations of the store on the eight choice criteria. The dependent variable was preference for each store. The independent variables were the evaluations of each store on quality of merchandise, variety and assortment of merchandise, returns and adjustment policy, service of store personnel, prices, convenience of location, layout of store, and credit and billing policies. The results indicated that all the factors of the choice criteria, except service of store personnel, were significant in explaining store preference. The coefficients of all the variables were positive, indicating that higher evaluations on each of the significant factors led to higher preference for that store. The model had a good fit and good ability to predict store preference.

SPSS Data File

SAS Data File

Project Activities

Download the SPSS or SAS data file *Sears Data 17* from the Web site for this book. This file contains the evaluation of Sears on the eight factors of the choice criteria (quality, variety and assortment, return policy, service of store personnel, fair prices, convenience of location, store layout, and credit and billing policies), the preference for Sears, importance attached to eight factors of the choice criteria, and agreement with the 21 lifestyle statements. The measurement of these variables is described in Chapter 1. The remaining variables have not been included to keep the number of variables below 50 so that you can use the student SPSS software.

1. Run product moment correlations between the evaluation of Sears on the eight factors of the choice criteria and the preference for Sears.
2. Run multiple regressions, with preference for Sears as the dependent variable and evaluations of Sears on the eight factors of the choice criteria as the independent variables. Interpret the results. ■

Summary

The product moment correlation coefficient, r, measures the linear association between two metric (interval or ratio scaled) variables. Its square, r^2, measures the proportion of variation in one variable explained by the other. Figure 17.10 gives a concept map for product moment correlation. The partial correlation coefficient measures the association between two variables after controlling, or adjusting for, the effects of one or more additional variables. The order of a partial correlation indicates how many variables are being adjusted or controlled. Partial correlations can be very helpful for detecting spurious relationships.

FIGURE 17.10

A Concept Map for Product Moment Correlation

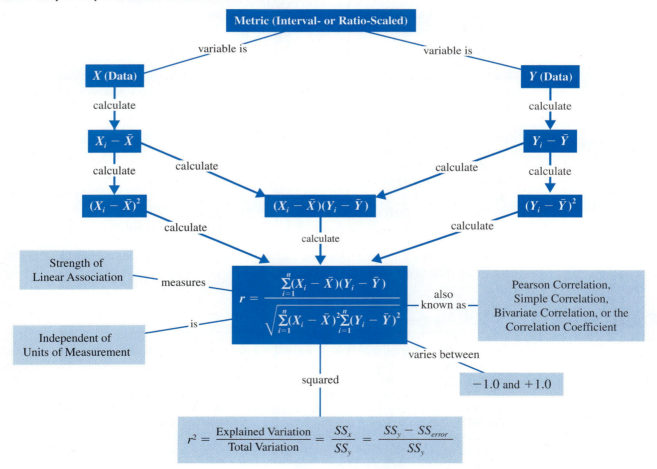

Bivariate regression derives a mathematical equation between a single metric criterion variable and a single metric predictor variable. The equation is derived in the form of a straight line by using the least-squares procedure. When the regression is run on standardized data, the intercept assumes a value of 0, and the regression coefficients are called *beta weights*. The strength of association is measured by the coefficient of determination, r^2, which is obtained by computing a ratio of SS_{reg} to SS_y. The standard error of estimate is used to assess the accuracy of prediction and may be interpreted

FIGURE 17.11

A Concept Map for Conducting Bivariate Regression

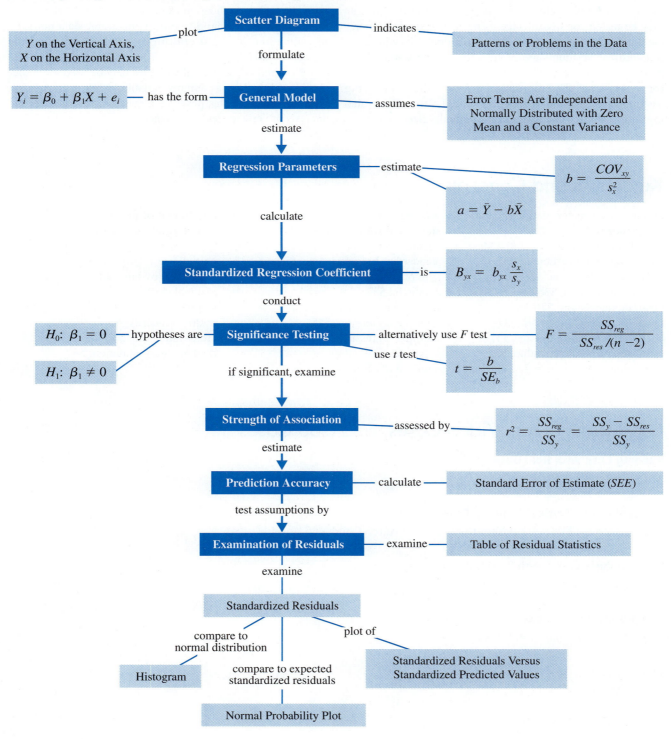

as a kind of average error made in predicting Y from the regression equation. Figure 17.11 presents a concept map for conducting bivariate regression.

Multiple regression involves a single dependent variable and two or more independent variables. The partial regression coefficient, b_1, represents the expected change in Y when X_1 is changed by one unit and X_2 through X_k are held constant. The strength of association is measured by the coefficient of multiple determination, R^2. The significance of the overall regression equation may be tested by the overall F test. Individual partial regression coefficients may be tested for significance using the t test or the incremental F test. Scattergrams of the residuals, in which the standardized residuals are plotted against the standardized predicted values, $\hat{Y}$ time, or predictor variables, are useful for examining the appropriateness of the underlying assumptions and the regression model fitted. It is also useful to examine the histogram of standardized residuals, normal probability plot of standardized residuals, and the table of residual statistics.

In stepwise regression, the predictor variables are entered or removed from the regression equation one at a time for the purpose of selecting a smaller subset of predictors that account for most of the variation in the criterion variable. Multicollinearity, or very high intercorrelations among the predictor variables, can result in several problems. Because the predictors are correlated, regression analysis provides no unambiguous measure of relative importance of the predictors. Cross-validation examines whether the regression model continues to hold true for comparable data not used in estimation. It is a useful procedure for evaluating the regression model.

Nominal or categorical variables may be used as predictors by coding them as dummy variables. Multiple regression with dummy variables provides a general procedure for the analysis of variance and covariance.

Key Terms and Concepts

product moment correlation (r), 530
covariance (COV_{xy}), 531
partial correlation coefficient, 534
part correlation coefficient, 535
nonmetric correlation, 536
regression analysis, 536
bivariate regression, 536
bivariate regression model, 537
coefficient of determination, 537
estimated or predicted value, 537
regression coefficient, 537

scattergram, 537
standard error of estimate, 537
standard error, 537
standardized regression coefficient, 537
sum of squared errors, 537
t statistic, 537
least-squares procedure, 538
multiple regression, 545
multiple regression
   model, 546
adjusted R^2, 546

coefficient of multiple
   determination, 546
F test, 546
partial F test, 546
partial regression coefficient, 547
residual, 550
stepwise regression, 553
multicollinearity, 554
cross-validation, 556
double cross-validation, 557

Suggested Cases, Video Cases, and HBS Cases

Running Case with Real Data

   1.1 Dell

Comprehensive Critical Thinking Cases

   2.1 American Idol   2.2 Baskin-Robbins   2.3 Akron Children's Hospital

Data Analysis Cases with Real Data

   3.1 AT&T   3.2 IBM   3.3 Kimberly-Clark

Comprehensive Cases with Real Data

   4.1 JPMorgan Chase   4.2 Wendy's

Video Case

   23.1 Marriott

Live Research: Conducting a Marketing Research Project

1. It is desirable to calculate product moment correlations between all interval scaled variables. This gives an idea of the correlations between variables.
2. Run several bivariate regressions and compare these results with the corresponding product moment correlations.
3. Multiple regressions should be run when examining the association between a single dependent variable and several independent variables.

Acronym

The main features of regression analysis may be summarized by the acronym

Regression:

R esidual analysis is useful
E stimation of parameters: solution of simultaneous equations
G eneral model is linear
R^2 strength of association
E rror terms are independent and $N(0, \sigma^2)$
S tandardized regression coefficients
S tandard error of estimate: prediction accuracy
I ndividual coefficients and overall F tests
O ptimal: minimizes total error
N onstandardized regression coefficients

Exercises

Questions

1. What is the product moment correlation coefficient? Does a product moment correlation of 0 between two variables imply that the variables are not related to each other?
2. What is a partial correlation coefficient?
3. What are the main uses of regression analysis?
4. What is the least-squares procedure?
5. Explain the meaning of standardized regression coefficients.
6. How is the strength of association measured in bivariate regression? In multiple regression?
7. What is meant by prediction accuracy?
8. What is the standard error of estimate?
9. What assumptions underlie bivariate regression?
10. What is multiple regression? How is it different from bivariate regression?
11. Explain the meaning of a partial regression coefficient. Why is it so called?
12. State the null hypothesis in testing the significance of the overall multiple regression equation. How is this null hypothesis tested?
13. What is gained by an examination of residuals?
14. Explain the stepwise regression approach. What is its purpose?
15. What is multicollinearity? What problems can arise because of multicollinearity?
16. What are some of the measures used to assess the relative importance of predictors in multiple regression?
17. Describe the cross-validation procedure. Describe the double cross-validation procedure.
18. Demonstrate the equivalence of regression with dummy variables to one-way ANOVA.

Problems

1. A major supermarket chain wants to determine the effect of promotion on relative competitiveness. Data were obtained from 15 states on the promotional expenses relative to a major competitor (competitor expenses = 100) and on sales relative to this competitor (competitor sales = 100).

State No.	Relative Promotional Expense	Relative Sales
1	95	98
2	92	94
3	103	110
4	115	125
5	77	82
6	79	84
7	105	112
8	94	99
9	85	93
10	101	107
11	106	114
12	120	132
13	118	129
14	75	79
15	99	105

You are assigned the task of telling the manager whether there is any relationship between relative promotional expense and relative sales.

a. Plot the relative sales (Y-axis) against the relative promotional expense (X-axis), and interpret this diagram.

b. Which measure would you use to determine whether there is a relationship between the two variables? Why?

c. Run a bivariate regression analysis of relative sales on relative promotional expense.

d. Interpret the regression coefficients.

e. Is the regression relationship significant?

f. If the company matched the competitor in terms of promotional expense (if the relative promotional expense was 100), what would the company's relative sales be?

g. Interpret the resulting r^2.

2. To understand the role of quality and price in influencing the patronage of drugstores, 14 major stores in a large metropolitan area were rated in terms of preference to shop, quality of merchandise, and fair pricing. All the ratings were obtained on an 11-point scale, with higher numbers indicating more positive ratings.

SPSS Data File

SAS Data File

Store No.	Preference	Quality	Price
1	6	5	3
2	9	6	11
3	8	6	4
4	3	2	1
5	10	6	11
6	4	3	1
7	5	4	7
8	2	1	4
9	11	9	8
10	9	5	10
11	10	8	8
12	2	1	5
13	9	8	5
14	5	3	2

a. Run a multiple regression analysis explaining store preference in terms of quality of merchandise and price.

b. Interpret the partial regression coefficients.

c. Determine the significance of the overall regression.

d. Determine the significance of the partial regression coefficients.

e. Do you think that multicollinearity is a problem in this case? Why or why not?

3. You come across a magazine article reporting the following relationship between annual expenditure on prepared dinners (PD) and annual income (INC):

$$PD = 23.4 + 0.003\ INC$$

The coefficient of the INC variable is reported as significant.

a. Does this relationship seem plausible? Is it possible to have a coefficient that is small in magnitude and yet significant?

b. From the information given, can you tell how good the estimated model is?

c. What are the expected expenditures on prepared dinners of a family earning $30,000?

d. If a family earning $40,000 spent $130 annually on prepared dinners, what is the residual?

e. What is the meaning of a negative residual?

Internet and Computer Exercises

1. Conduct the following analyses for the Nike data given in Internet and Computer Exercises 1 of Chapter 15.

a. Calculate the simple correlations between awareness, attitude, preference, intention, and loyalty toward Nike and interpret the results.

b. Run a bivariate regression with loyalty as the dependent variable and intention as the independent variable. Interpret the results.

c. Run a multiple regression with loyalty as the dependent variable and awareness, attitude, preference, and intention as the independent variables. Interpret the results. Compare the coefficients for intention obtained in bivariate and multiple regressions.

2. Conduct the following analyses for the outdoor lifestyle data given in Internet and Computer Exercises 2 of Chapter 15.

a. Calculate the simple correlations between V_1 to V_6 and interpret the results.

b. Run a bivariate regression with preference for an outdoor lifestyle (V_1) as the dependent variable and meeting people (V_6) as the independent variable. Interpret the results.

c. Run a multiple regression with preference for an outdoor lifestyle as the dependent variable and V_2 to V_6 as the independent variables. Interpret the results. Compare the coefficients for V_6 obtained in the bivariate and the multiple regressions.

3. In a pretest, data were obtained from 20 respondents on preferences for sneakers on a 7-point scale, 1 = not preferred, 7 = greatly preferred (V_1). The respondents also provided their evaluations of the sneakers on comfort (V_2), style (V_3), and durability (V_4), also on 7-point scales, 1 = poor and 7 = excellent. The resulting data are given in the following table.

V_1	V_2	V_3	V_4
6.00	6.00	3.00	5.00
2.00	3.00	2.00	4.00
7.00	5.00	6.00	7.00
4.00	6.00	4.00	5.00
1.00	3.00	2.00	2.00
6.00	5.00	6.00	7.00
5.00	6.00	7.00	5.00
7.00	3.00	5.00	4.00
2.00	4.00	6.00	3.00
3.00	5.00	3.00	6.00

SPSS Data File

SAS Data File

1.00	3.00	2.00	3.00
5.00	4.00	5.00	4.00
2.00	2.00	1.00	5.00
4.00	5.00	4.00	6.00
6.00	5.00	4.00	7.00
3.00	3.00	4.00	2.00
4.00	4.00	3.00	2.00
3.00	4.00	3.00	2.00
4.00	4.00	3.00	2.00
2.00	3.00	2.00	4.00

a. Calculate the simple correlations between V_1 to V_4 and interpret the results.
b. Run a bivariate regression with preference for sneakers (V_1) as the dependent variable and evaluation on comfort (V_2) as the independent variable. Interpret the results.

c. Run a bivariate regression with preference for sneakers (V_1) as the dependent variable and evaluation on style (V_3) as the independent variable. Interpret the results.
d. Run a bivariate regression with preference for sneakers (V_1) as the dependent variable and evaluation on durability (V_4) as the independent variable. Interpret the results.
e. Run a multiple regression with preference for sneakers (V_1) as the dependent variable and V_2 to V_4 as the independent variables. Interpret the results. Compare the coefficients for V_2, V_3, and V_4 obtained in the bivariate and the multiple regressions.

4. Use an appropriate computer program (SPSS, SAS, MINITAB, or EXCEL) to analyze the data for:
a. Problem 1
b. Problem 2
c. Fieldwork exercise

Activities

Role Playing

1. You have been hired as a marketing research analyst by Burger King. Your boss, the marketing manager, is wondering what statistical analysis should be conducted to explain the patronage of Burger King in terms of the consumers' evaluations of Burger King on the factors of consumers' choice criteria. Explain to your boss (a student in your class) the analysis that you would conduct.

Fieldwork

1. Visit 10 different drugstores in your area. Evaluate each store in terms of its overall image and quality of in-store service using 11-point rating scales (1 = poor, 11 = excellent). Then analyze the data you have collected as follows:
a. Plot the overall image (Y-axis) against relative in-store service (X-axis) and interpret this diagram.
b. Which measure would you use to determine whether there is a relationship between the two variables? Why?

c. Run a bivariate regression analysis of overall image on in-store service.
d. Interpret the regression coefficients.
e. Is the regression relationship significant?
f. Interpret the resulting r^2.

Group Discussion

1. As a small group, discuss the following statement: "Regression is such a basic technique that it should always be used in analyzing data."
2. As a small group, discuss the relationship among bivariate correlation, bivariate regression, multiple regression, and analysis of variance.

Dell Running Case

Review the Dell case, Case 1.1, and questionnaire given toward the end of the book. Go to the Web site for this book and download the Dell data file.

1. Can the overall satisfaction (q4) be explained in terms of all 13 evaluations of Dell (q8_1 to q8_13) when the independent variables are considered simultaneously? Interpret the results.
2. Can the likelihood of choosing Dell (q6) be explained in terms of all 13 evaluations of Dell (q8_1 to q8_13) when the independent variables are considered simultaneously? Interpret the results.

3. Can price sensitivity ratings of q9_5per be explained in terms of all 13 evaluations of Dell (q8_1 to q8_13) when the independent variables are considered simultaneously? Interpret the results.
4. Can price sensitivity ratings of q9_10per be explained in terms of all 13 evaluations of Dell (q8_1 to q8_13) when the independent variables are considered simultaneously? Interpret the results.

Chapter 8

> "Often you have measured different groups of respondents on many metric variables. Discriminant analysis is a useful way to answer the questions . . . are the groups different? . . . On what variables are they most different? . . . Can I predict which group a person belongs to using these variables?"

Jamie Baker-Prewitt, Senior Vice President/Director,
Decision Sciences, Burke, Inc.

Objectives   [After reading this chapter, the student should be able to:]

1. Describe the concept of discriminant analysis, its objectives, and its applications in marketing research.

2. Outline the procedures for conducting discriminant analysis, including the formulation of the problem, estimation of the discriminant function coefficients, determination of significance, interpretation, and validation.

3. Discuss multiple discriminant analysis and the distinction between two-group and multiple discriminant analysis.

4. Explain stepwise discriminant analysis and describe the Mahalanobis procedure.

5. Describe the binary logit model and its advantages over discriminant and regression analysis.

Discriminant and Logit Analysis

Overview

This chapter discusses the techniques of discriminant analysis and logit analysis. We begin by examining the relationship of discriminant and logit analysis to analysis of variance (Chapter 16) and regression analysis (Chapter 17). We present a model and describe the general procedure for conducting discriminant analysis, with emphasis on formulation, estimation, determination of significance, interpretation, and validation of the results. The procedure is illustrated with an example of two-group discriminant analysis, followed by an example of multiple (three-group) discriminant analysis. The stepwise discriminant analysis procedure is also covered. When the dependent variable is binary, the logit model can also be used instead of two-group discriminant analysis. We explain the logit model and discuss its relative merits versus discriminant and regression analysis.

Finally, we discuss the use of software in discriminant and logit analysis. Help for running the SPSS and SAS Learning Edition programs used in this chapter is provided in four ways: (1) detailed step-by-step instructions are given later in the chapter, (2) you can download (from the Web site for this book) computerized demonstration movies illustrating these step-by-step instructions, (3) you can download screen captures with notes illustrating these step-by-step instructions, and (4) you can refer to the *Study Guide and Technology Manual*, a supplement that accompanies this book.

Real Research

Rebate Redeemers

A study of 294 consumers was undertaken to determine the correlates of rebate proneness, or the characteristics of consumers who respond favorably to rebate promotions. The predictor variables were four factors related to household shopping attitudes and behaviors, and selected demographic characteristics

Multiple discriminant analysis can help identify the factors that differentiate frequent users, light users, and nonusers of rebates.

(sex, age, and income). The dependent variable was the respondent's degree of rebate proneness, of which three levels were identified. Respondents who reported no rebate-triggered purchases during the past 12 months were classified as nonusers; those who reported one or two such purchases as light users; and those with more than two purchases, frequent users of rebates. Multiple discriminant analysis was used to analyze the data.

Two primary findings emerged. First, consumers' perception of the effort/value relationship was the most effective variable in discriminating among frequent, light, and nonusers of rebate offers. Clearly, rebate-sensitive consumers associate less effort with fulfilling the requirements of the rebate purchase, and they are willing to accept a relatively smaller refund than other customers. Second, consumers who are aware of the regular prices of products, so that they recognize bargains, are more likely than others to respond to rebate offers.

These findings were utilized by Dell (www.dell.com) when it offered up to $150 cash rebates on its notebook computers during April 2009. The company felt that this would encourage the rebate-sensitive customers to choose Dell notebooks.[1] ■

The rebate proneness example examined three groups (nonusers, light users, and frequent users of rebates). Significant intergroup differences were found using multiple predictor variables. An examination of differences across groups lies at the heart of the basic concept of discriminant analysis.

Basic Concept of Discriminant Analysis

discriminant analysis
A technique for analyzing marketing research data when the criterion or dependent variable is categorical and the predictor or independent variables are interval in nature.

Discriminant analysis is a technique for analyzing data when the criterion or dependent variable is categorical and the predictor or independent variables are metric, i.e., measured on at least interval scales.[2] For example, the dependent variable may be the choice of a brand of personal computer (brand A, B, or C) and the independent variables may be ratings of attributes of PCs on a 7-point Likert scale. The objectives of discriminant analysis are as follows:

1. Development of **discriminant functions**, or linear combinations of the predictor or independent variables, which will best discriminate between the categories of the criterion or dependent variable (groups)
2. Examination of whether significant differences exist among the groups, in terms of the predictor variables
3. Determination of which predictor variables contribute to most of the intergroup differences
4. Classification of cases to one of the groups based on the values of the predictor variables
5. Evaluation of the accuracy of classification

discriminant functions
The linear combination of independent variables developed by discriminant analysis that will best discriminate between the categories of the dependent variable.

Discriminant analysis techniques are described by the number of categories possessed by the criterion variable. When the criterion variable has two categories, the technique is known as **two-group discriminant analysis**. When three or more categories are involved, the technique is referred to as **multiple discriminant analysis**. The main distinction is that, in the two-group case, it is possible to derive only one discriminant function. In multiple discriminant analysis, more than one function may be computed.[3]

two-group discriminant analysis
Discriminant analysis technique where the criterion variable has two categories.

Examples of discriminant analysis abound in marketing research. This technique can be used to answer questions such as:

multiple discriminant analysis
Discriminant analysis technique where the criterion variable involves three or more categories.

- In terms of demographic characteristics, how do customers who exhibit store loyalty differ from those who do not?
- Do heavy, medium, and light users of soft drinks differ in terms of their consumption of frozen foods?
- What psychographic characteristics help differentiate between price-sensitive and non-price-sensitive buyers of groceries?
- Do the various market segments differ in their media consumption habits?
- In terms of lifestyles, what are the differences between heavy patrons of regional department store chains and patrons of national chains?
- What are the distinguishing characteristics of consumers who respond to direct mail solicitations?

Relationship of Discriminant and Logit Analysis to ANOVA and Regression

The relationship among discriminant analysis, analysis of variance (ANOVA), and regression analysis is shown in Table 18.1. We explain this relationship with an example in which the researcher is attempting to explain the amount of life insurance purchased in terms of age and income. All three procedures involve a single criterion or dependent variable and multiple predictor or independent variables. However, the nature of these variables differs. In analysis of variance and regression analysis, the dependent variable is metric or interval scaled (amount of life insurance purchased in dollars), whereas in discriminant analysis it is categorical (amount of life insurance purchased classified as high, medium, or low). The independent variables are categorical in the case of analysis of variance (age and income are each classified as high, medium, or low) but metric in the case of regression and discriminant analysis (age in years and income in dollars, i.e., both measured on a ratio scale).

Two-group discriminant analysis, in which the dependent variable has only two categories, is closely related to multiple regression analysis. In this case, multiple regression, in which the dependent variable is coded as a 0 or 1 dummy variable, results in partial regression coefficients that are proportional to discriminant function coefficients (see the following section on the discriminant analysis model). The nature of dependent and independent variables in the binary logit model is similar to that in two-group discriminant analysis.

Discriminant Analysis Model

discriminant analysis model
The statistical model on which discriminant analysis is based.

The **discriminant analysis model** involves linear combinations of the following form:

$$D = b_0 + b_1 X_1 + b_2 X_2 + b_3 X_3 + \cdots + b_k X_k$$

where

D = discriminant score

b's = discriminant coefficient or weight

X's = predictor or independent variable

The coefficients, or weights (b), are estimated so that the groups differ as much as possible on the values of the discriminant function. This occurs when the ratio of between-group sum of squares to within-group sum of squares for the discriminant scores is at a maximum. Any other linear combination of the predictors will result in a smaller ratio.

We give a brief geometrical exposition of two-group discriminant analysis. Suppose we had two groups, G1 and G2, and each member of these groups was measured on two variables X_1 and X_2. A scatter diagram of the two groups is shown in Figure 18.1, where X_1 and X_2 are the two axes. Members of G1 are denoted by 1 and members of G2 by 2. The resultant ellipses encompass some specified percentage of the points (members), say 93 percent in each group. A straight line is drawn through the two points where the ellipses intersect and then projected to a new axis, D. The

TABLE 18.1
Similarities and Differences Among ANOVA, Regression, and Discriminant/Logit Analysis

	ANOVA	Regression	Discriminant/ Logit Analysis
Similarities			
Number of dependent variables	One	One	One
Number of independent variables	Multiple	Multiple	Multiple
Differences			
Nature of the dependent variables	Metric	Metric	Categorical/Binary
Nature of the independent variables	Categorical	Metric	Metric

FIGURE 18.1

A Geometric Interpretation of Two-Group Discriminant Analysis

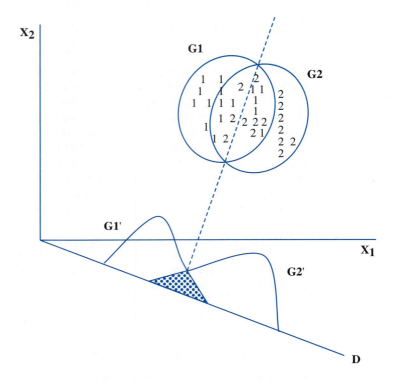

overlap between the univariate distributions G1' and G2', represented by the shaded area in Figure 18.1, is smaller than would be obtained by any other line drawn through the ellipses representing the scatter plots. Thus, the groups differ as much as possible on the D axis. Several statistics are associated with discriminant analysis.

Statistics Associated with Discriminant Analysis

The important statistics associated with discriminant analysis include the following.

Canonical correlation. Canonical correlation measures the extent of association between the discriminant scores and the groups. It is a measure of association between the single discriminant function and the set of dummy variables that define the group membership.

Centroid. The centroid is the mean values for the discriminant scores for a particular group. There are as many centroids as there are groups, because there is one for each group. The means for a group on all the functions are the *group centroids*.

Classification matrix. Sometimes also called *confusion* or *prediction matrix,* the classification matrix contains the number of correctly classified and misclassified cases. The correctly classified cases appear on the diagonal, because the predicted and actual groups are the same. The off-diagonal elements represent cases that have been incorrectly classified. The sum of the diagonal elements divided by the total number of cases represents the *hit ratio.*

Discriminant function coefficients. The discriminant function coefficients (unstandardized) are the multipliers of variables, when the variables are in the original units of measurement.

Discriminant scores. The unstandardized coefficients are multiplied by the values of the variables. These products are summed and added to the constant term to obtain the discriminant scores.

Eigenvalue. For each discriminant function, the eigenvalue is the ratio of between-group to within-group sums of squares. Large eigenvalues imply superior functions.

F *values and their significance*. These are calculated from a one-way ANOVA, with the grouping variable serving as the categorical independent variable. Each predictor, in turn, serves as the metric dependent variable in the ANOVA.

Group means and group standard deviations. These are computed for each predictor for each group.

Pooled within-group correlation matrix. The pooled within-group correlation matrix is computed by averaging the separate covariance matrices for all the groups.

Standardized discriminant function coefficients. The standardized discriminant function coefficients are the discriminant function coefficients and are used as the multipliers when the variables been standardized to a mean of 0 and a variance of 1.

Structure correlations. Also referred to as *discriminant loadings,* the structure correlations represent the simple correlations between the predictors and the discriminant function.

Total correlation matrix. If the cases are treated as if they were from a single sample and the correlations computed, a total correlation matrix is obtained.

Wilks' λ. Sometimes also called the *U* statistic, Wilks' λ for each predictor is the ratio of the within-group sum of squares to the total sum of squares. Its value varies between 0 and 1. Large values of λ (near 1) indicate that group means do not seem to be different. Small values of λ (near 0) indicate that the group means seem to be different.

The assumptions in discriminant analysis are that each of the groups is a sample from a multivariate normal population and all of the populations have the same covariance matrix. The role of these assumptions and the statistics just described can be better understood by examining the procedure for conducting discriminant analysis.

Conducting Discriminant Analysis

The steps involved in conducting discriminant analysis consist of formulation, estimation, determination of significance, interpretation, and validation (see Figure 18.2). These steps are discussed and illustrated within the context of two-group discriminant analysis. Discriminant analysis with more than two groups is discussed later in this chapter.

Formulate the Problem

The first step in discriminant analysis is to formulate the problem by identifying the objectives, the criterion variable, and the independent variables. The criterion variable must consist of two or more mutually exclusive and collectively exhaustive categories. When the dependent variable is interval or ratio scaled, it must first be converted into categories. For example, attitude toward the brand, measured on a 7-point scale, could be categorized as unfavorable (1, 2, 3), neutral (4), or favorable (5, 6, 7). Alternatively, one could plot the distribution of the dependent variable and form groups of equal size by determining the appropriate cutoff points for each category. The predictor variables should be selected based on a theoretical model or previous research, or, in the case of exploratory research, the experience of the researcher should guide their selection.

The next step is to divide the sample into two parts. One part of the sample, called the estimation or **analysis sample**, is used for estimation of the discriminant function. The other part, called the *holdout* or **validation sample**, is reserved for validating the discriminant function. When the sample is large enough, it can be split in half. One half serves as the analysis

analysis sample
Part of the total sample that is used for estimation of the discriminant function.

validation sample
That part of the total sample used to check the results of the estimation sample.

FIGURE 18.2

Conducting Discriminant Analysis

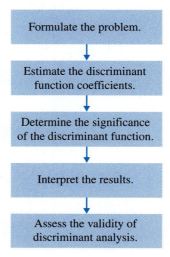

sample and the other is used for validation. The role of the halves is then interchanged and the analysis is repeated. This is called *double cross-validation* and is similar to the procedure discussed in regression analysis (Chapter 17).

Often the distribution of the number of cases in the analysis and validation samples follows the distribution in the total sample. For instance, if the total sample contained 50 percent loyal and 50 percent nonloyal consumers, then the analysis and validation samples would each contain 50 percent loyal and 50 percent nonloyal consumers. On the other hand, if the sample contained 25 percent loyal and 75 percent nonloyal consumers, the analysis and validation samples would be selected to reflect the same distribution (25 percent versus 75 percent).

Finally, it has been suggested that the validation of the discriminant function should be conducted repeatedly. Each time, the sample should be split into different analysis and validation parts. The discriminant function should be estimated and the validation analysis carried out. Thus, the validation assessment is based on a number of trials. More rigorous methods have also been suggested.[4]

To better illustrate two-group discriminant analysis, let us look at an example. Suppose we want to determine the salient characteristics of families that have visited a vacation resort during the last two years. Data were obtained from a pretest sample of 42 households. Of these, 30 households shown in Table 18.2 were included in the analysis sample and the remaining 12

SPSS Data File

SAS Data File

TABLE 18.2

Information on Resort Visits: Analysis Sample

No.	Resort Visit	Annual Family Income ($000)	Attitude Toward Travel	Importance Attached to Family Vacation	Household Size	Age of Head of Household	Amount Spent on Family Vacation
1	1	50.2	5	8	3	43	M (2)
2	1	70.3	6	7	4	61	H (3)
3	1	62.9	7	5	6	52	H (3)
4	1	48.5	7	5	5	36	L (1)
5	1	52.7	6	6	4	55	H (3)
6	1	75.0	8	7	5	68	H (3)
7	1	46.2	5	3	3	62	M (2)
8	1	57.0	2	4	6	51	M (2)
9	1	64.1	7	5	4	57	H (3)
10	1	68.1	7	6	5	45	H (3)
11	1	73.4	6	7	5	44	H (3)
12	1	71.9	5	8	4	64	H (3)
13	1	56.2	1	8	6	54	M (2)
14	1	49.3	4	2	3	56	H (3)
15	1	62.0	5	6	2	58	H (3)
16	2	32.1	5	4	3	58	L (1)
17	2	36.2	4	3	2	55	L (1)
18	2	43.2	2	5	2	57	M (2)
19	2	50.4	5	2	4	37	M (2)
20	2	44.1	6	6	3	42	M (2)
21	2	38.3	6	6	2	45	L (1)
22	2	55.0	1	2	2	57	M (2)
23	2	46.1	3	5	3	51	L (1)
24	2	35.0	6	4	5	64	L (1)
25	2	37.3	2	7	4	54	L (1)
26	2	41.8	5	1	3	56	M (2)
27	2	57.0	8	3	2	36	M (2)
28	2	33.4	6	8	2	50	L (1)
29	2	37.5	3	2	3	48	L (1)
30	2	41.3	3	3	2	42	L (1)

TABLE 18.3
Information on Resort Visits: Holdout Sample

No.	Resort Visit	Annual Family Income ($000)	Attitude Toward Travel	Importance Attached to Family Vacation	Household Size	Age of Head of Household	Amount Spent on Family Vacation
1	1	50.8	4	7	3	45	M (2)
2	1	63.6	7	4	7	55	H (3)
3	1	54.0	6	7	4	58	M (2)
4	1	45.0	5	4	3	60	M (2)
5	1	68.0	6	6	6	46	H (3)
6	1	62.1	5	6	3	56	H (3)
7	2	35.0	4	3	4	54	L (1)
8	2	49.6	5	3	5	39	L (1)
9	2	39.4	6	5	3	44	H (3)
10	2	37.0	2	6	5	51	L (1)
11	2	54.5	7	3	3	37	M (2)
12	2	38.2	2	2	3	49	L (1)

SPSS Data File

SAS Data File

direct method
An approach to discriminant analysis that involves estimating the discriminant function so that all the predictors are included simultaneously.

stepwise discriminant analysis
Discriminant analysis in which the predictors are entered sequentially based on their ability to discriminate between the groups.

shown in Table 18.3 were part of the validation sample. For illustrative purposes, we consider only a small number of observations. In actual practice, discriminant analysis is performed on a much larger sample such as that in the Dell running case and other cases with real data that are presented in this book. The households that visited a resort during the last two years are coded as 1; those that did not, as 2 (VISIT). Both the analysis and validation samples were balanced in terms of VISIT. As can be seen, the analysis sample contains 15 households in each category, whereas the validation sample has six in each category. Data were also obtained on annual family income (INCOME), attitude toward travel (TRAVEL, measured on a 9-point scale), importance attached to family vacation (VACATION, measured on a 9-point scale), household size (HSIZE), and age of the head of the household (AGE).

Estimate the Discriminant Function Coefficients

Once the analysis sample has been identified, as in Table 18.2, we can estimate the discriminant function coefficients. Two broad approaches are available. The **direct method** involves estimating the discriminant function so that all the predictors are included simultaneously. In this case, each independent variable is included, regardless of its discriminating power. This method is appropriate when, based on previous research or a theoretical model, the researcher wants the discrimination to be based on all the predictors. An alternative approach is the stepwise method. In **stepwise discriminant analysis**, the predictor variables are entered sequentially, based on their ability to discriminate among groups. This method, described in more detail later, is appropriate when the researcher wants to select a subset of the predictors for inclusion in the discriminant function.

The results of running two-group discriminant analysis on the data of Table 18.2 using a popular computer program are presented in Table 18.4. Some intuitive feel for the results may be obtained by examining the group means and standard deviations. It appears that the two groups are more widely separated in terms of income than other variables. There appears to be more of a separation on the importance attached to family vacation than on attitude toward travel. The difference between the two groups on age of the head of the household is small, and the standard deviation of this variable is large.

The pooled within-groups correlation matrix indicates low correlations between the predictors. Multicollinearity is unlikely to be a problem. The significance of the univariate F ratios indicates that when the predictors are considered individually, only income, importance of vacation, and household size significantly differentiate between those who visited a resort and those who did not.

Because there are two groups, only one discriminant function is estimated. The eigenvalue associated with this function is 1.7862 and it accounts for 100 percent of the explained variance. The canonical correlation associated with this function is 0.8007. The square of this correlation,

TABLE 18.4
Results of Two-Group Discriminant Analysis

Group Means

Visit	Income	Travel	Vacation	Hsize	Age
1	60.52000	5.40000	5.80000	4.33333	53.73333
2	41.91333	4.33333	4.06667	2.80000	50.13333
Total	51.21667	4.86667	4.93333	3.56667	51.93333

Group Standard Deviations

1	9.83065	1.91982	1.82052	1.23443	8.77062
2	7.55115	1.95180	2.05171	0.94112	8.27101
Total	12.79523	1.97804	2.09981	1.33089	8.57395

Pooled Within-Groups Correlation Matrix

	Income	Travel	Vacation	Hsize	Age
INCOME	1.00000				
TRAVEL	0.19745	1.00000			
VACATION	0.09148	0.08434	1.00000		
HSIZE	0.08887	−0.01681	0.07046	1.00000	
AGE	−0.01431	−0.19709	0.01742	−0.04301	1.00000

Wilks' λ (*U*-statistic) and univariate F ratio with 1 and 28 degrees of freedom

Variable	Wilks' λ	F	Significance
INCOME	0.45310	33.80	0.0000
TRAVEL	0.92479	2.277	0.1425
VACATION	0.82377	5.990	0.0209
HSIZE	0.65672	14.64	0.0007
AGE	0.95441	1.338	0.2572

Canonical Discriminant Functions

Function	Eigenvalue	Percent of Variance	Cumulative Percent	Canonical Correlation		After Function	Wilks' λ	Chi-Square	df	Sig.
					:	0	0.3589	26.130	5	0.0001
1*	1.7862	100.00	100.00	0.8007	:					

*Marks the 1 canonical discriminant functions remaining in the analysis.

Standard Canonical Discriminant Function Coefficients

	Func 1
INCOME	0.74301
TRAVEL	0.09611
VACATION	0.23329
HSIZE	0.46911
AGE	0.20922

Structure Matrix

Pooled within-groups correlations between discriminating variables and canonical discriminant functions (variables ordered by size of correlation within function).

	Func 1
INCOME	0.82202
HSIZE	0.54096
VACATION	0.34607

(continued)

TABLE 18.4

Results of Two-Group Discriminant Analysis (*continued*)

TRAVEL	0.21337
AGE	0.16354

Unstandardized Canonical Discriminant Function Coefficients

	Func 1
INCOME	0.8476710E-01
TRAVEL	0.4964455E-01
VACATION	0.1202813
HSIZE	0.4273893
AGE	0.2454380E-01
(constant)	−7.975476

Canonical Discriminant Functions Evaluated at Group Means (Group Centroids)

Group	Func 1
1	1.29118
2	−1.29118

Classification Results

			Predicted Group Membership		
		Visit	1	2	Total
Original	Count	1	12	3	15
		2	0	15	15
	%	1	80.0	20.0	100.0
		2	0.0	100.0	100.0
Cross-validated	Count	1	11	4	15
		2	2	13	15
	%	1	73.3	26.7	100.0
		2	13.3	86.7	100.0

[a] Cross-validation is done only for those cases in the analysis. In cross-validation, each case is classified by the functions derived from all cases other than that case.
[b] 90.0% of original grouped cases correctly classified.
[c] 80.0% of cross-validated grouped cases correctly classified.

Classification Results for Cases Not Selected for Use in the Analysis (Holdout Sample)

			Predicted Group Membership	
	Actual Group	No. of Cases	1	2
Group	1	6	4	2
			66.7%	33.3%
Group	2	6	0	6
			0.0%	100.0%

Percent of grouped cases correctly classified: 83.33%.

$(0.8007)^2 = 0.64$, indicates that 64 percent of the variance in the dependent variable (VISIT) is explained or accounted for by this model.

Determine the Significance of the Discriminant Function

It would not be meaningful to interpret the analysis if the discriminant functions estimated were not statistically significant. The null hypothesis that, in the population, the means of all discriminant functions in all groups are equal can be statistically tested. In SPSS, this test is based on Wilks' λ. If several functions are tested simultaneously (as in the case of multiple discriminant analysis), the Wilks' λ statistic is the product of the univariate λ for each function. The significance level is estimated based on a chi-square transformation of the statistic. In testing for significance in the vacation resort example (see Table 18.4), it may be noted that the Wilks' λ associated with the function is 0.3589, which transforms to a chi-square of 26.13 with 5 degrees of freedom. This is significant beyond the 0.05 level. In SAS, an approximate F statistic, based on an approximation to the distribution of the likelihood ratio, is calculated. A test of significance is not available in MINITAB. If the null hypothesis is rejected, indicating significant discrimination, one can proceed to interpret the results.[5]

Interpret the Results

The interpretation of the discriminant weights, or coefficients, is similar to that in multiple regression analysis. The value of the coefficient for a particular predictor depends on the other predictors included in the discriminant function. The signs of the coefficients are arbitrary, but they indicate which variable values result in large and small function values and associate them with particular groups.

Given the multicollinearity in the predictor variables, there is no unambiguous measure of the relative importance of the predictors in discriminating between the groups.[6] With this caveat in mind, we can obtain some idea of the relative importance of the variables by examining the absolute magnitude of the standardized discriminant function coefficients. Generally, predictors with relatively large standardized coefficients contribute more to the discriminating power of the function, as compared with predictors with smaller coefficients, and are, therefore, more important.

Some idea of the relative importance of the predictors can also be obtained by examining the structure correlations, also called *canonical loadings* or *discriminant loadings*. These simple correlations between each predictor and the discriminant function represent the variance that the predictor shares with the function. The greater the magnitude of a structure correlation, the more important the corresponding predictor. Like the standardized coefficients, these correlations must also be interpreted with caution.

An examination of the standardized discriminant function coefficients for the vacation resort example is instructive. Given the low intercorrelations between the predictors, one might cautiously use the magnitudes of the standardized coefficients to suggest that income is the most important predictor in discriminating between the groups, followed by household size and importance attached to family vacation. The same observation is obtained from examination of the structure correlations. These simple correlations between the predictors and the discriminant function are listed in order of magnitude.

The unstandardized discriminant function coefficients are also given. These can be applied to the raw values of the variables in the holdout set for classification purposes. The group centroids, giving the value of the discriminant function evaluated at the group means, are also shown. Group 1, those who have visited a resort, has a positive value (1.29118), whereas group 2 has an equal negative value. The signs of the coefficients associated with all the predictors are positive. This suggests that higher family income, larger household size, more importance attached to family vacation, more favorable attitude toward travel, and older heads of households are more likely to result in the family visiting the resort. It would be reasonable to develop a profile of the two groups in terms of the three predictors that seem to be the most important: income, household size, and importance of vacation. The values of these three variables for the two groups are given at the beginning of Table 18.4.

The determination of relative importance of the predictors is further illustrated by the following example.

Real Research   Satisfied Salespeople Stay

A recent survey asked businesspeople about the concern of hiring and maintaining employees during the current harsh economic climate. It was reported that 85 percent of respondents were concerned about recruiting employees and 81 percent said they were concerned about retaining employees. When the economy is uncertain, as in 2008–2009, turnover is rapid. Generally speaking, if an organization wants to retain its employees, it must learn why people leave their jobs and why others stay and are satisfied with their jobs. Discriminant analysis was used to determine what factors explained the differences between salespeople who left a large computer manufacturing company and those who stayed. The independent variables were company rating, job security, seven job-satisfaction dimensions, four role-conflict dimensions, four role-ambiguity dimensions, and nine measures of sales performance. The dependent variable was the dichotomy between those who stayed and those who left. The canonical correlation, an index of discrimination ($R = 0.4572$), was significant (Wilks' $\lambda = 0.7909$, $F_{26,173} = 1.7588$, $p = 0.0180$). This result indicated that the variables discriminated between those who left and those who stayed.

The results from simultaneously entering all variables in discriminant analysis are presented in the accompanying table. The rank order of importance, as determined by the relative magnitude of the structure correlations, is presented in the first column. Satisfaction with the job and promotional opportunities were the two most important discriminators, followed by job security. Those who stayed in the company found the job to be more exciting, satisfying, challenging, and interesting than those who left.[7]

Discriminant Analysis Results

Variable	Coefficients	Standardized Coefficients	Structure Correlations
1. Work[a]	0.0903	0.3910	0.5446
2. Promotion[a]	0.0288	0.1515	0.5044
3. Job security	0.1567	0.1384	0.4958
4. Customer relations[b]	0.0086	0.1751	0.4906
5. Company rating	0.4059	0.3240	0.4824
6. Working with others[b]	0.0018	0.0365	0.4651
7. Overall performance[b]	−0.0148	−0.3252	0.4518
8. Time–territory management[b]	0.0126	0.2899	0.4496
9. Sales produced[b]	0.0059	0.1404	0.4484
10. Presentation skill[b]	0.0118	0.2526	0.4387
11. Technical information[b]	0.0003	0.0065	0.4173
12. Pay–benefits[a]	0.0600	0.1843	0.3788
13. Quota achieved[b]	0.0035	0.2915	0.3780
14. Management[a]	0.0014	0.0138	0.3571
15. Information collection[b]	−0.0146	−0.3327	0.3326
16. Family[c]	−0.0684	−0.3408	−0.3221
17. Sales manager[a]	−0.0121	−0.1102	0.2909
18. Coworker[a]	0.0225	0.0893	0.2671
19. Customer[c]	−0.0625	−0.2797	−0.2602
20. Family[d]	0.0473	0.1970	0.2180
21. Job[d]	0.1378	0.5312	0.2119
22. Job[c]	0.0410	0.5475	−0.1029
23. Customer[d]	−0.0060	−0.0255	0.1004
24. Sales manager[c]	−0.0365	−0.2406	−0.0499
25. Sales manager[d]	−0.0606	−0.3333	0.0467
26. Customer[a]	−0.0338	−0.1488	0.0192

Note: Rank order of importance is based on the absolute magnitude of the structure correlations.
[a] Satisfaction
[b] Performance
[c] Ambiguity
[d] Conflict ■

Note that in this example, promotion was identified as the second most important variable based on the structure correlations. However, it is not the second most important variable based on the absolute magnitude of the standardized discriminant function coefficients. This anomaly results from multicollinearity.

characteristic profile
An aid to interpreting discriminant analysis results by describing each group in terms of the group means for the predictor variables.

Another aid to interpreting discriminant analysis results is to develop a **characteristic profile** for each group by describing each group in terms of the group means for the predictor variables. If the important predictors have been identified, then a comparison of the group means on these variables can assist in understanding the intergroup differences. However, before any findings can be interpreted with confidence, it is necessary to validate the results.

Assess Validity of Discriminant Analysis

Many computer programs, such as SPSS, offer a leave-one-out cross-validation option. In this option, the discriminant model is reestimated as many times as there are respondents in the sample. Each reestimated model leaves out one respondent and the model is used to predict for that respondent. When a large holdout sample is not possible, this gives a sense of the robustness of the estimate using each respondent, in turn, as a holdout.

As explained earlier, where possible, the data should be randomly divided into two subsamples: analysis and validation. The analysis sample is used for estimating the discriminant function; the validation sample is used for developing the classification matrix. The discriminant weights, estimated by using the analysis sample, are multiplied by the values of the predictor variables in the holdout sample to generate discriminant scores for the cases in the holdout sample. The cases are then assigned to groups based on their discriminant scores and an appropriate decision rule. For example, in two-group discriminant analysis, a case will be assigned to the group whose centroid is the closest. The **hit ratio**, or the percentage of cases correctly classified, can then be determined by summing the diagonal elements and dividing by the total number of cases.[8]

> **hit ratio**
> The percentage of cases correctly classified by discriminant analysis.

It is helpful to compare the percentage of cases correctly classified by discriminant analysis to the percentage that would be obtained by chance. When the groups are equal in size, the percentage of chance classification is 1 divided by the number of groups. How much improvement should be expected over chance? No general guidelines are available, although some authors have suggested that classification accuracy achieved by discriminant analysis should be at least 25 percent greater than that obtained by chance.[9]

Most discriminant analysis programs also estimate a classification matrix based on the analysis sample. Because they capitalize on chance variation in the data, such results are invariably better than leave-one-out classification or the classification obtained on the holdout sample.

Table 18.4 of the vacation resort example also shows the classification results based on the analysis sample. The hit ratio, or the percentage of cases correctly classified, is $(12 + 15)/30 = 0.90$, or 90 percent. One might suspect that this hit ratio is artificially inflated, as the data used for estimation was also used for validation. Leave-one-out cross-validation correctly classifies only $(11 + 13)/30 = 0.80$ or 80 percent of the cases. Conducting classification analysis on an independent holdout set of data results in the classification matrix with a hit ratio of $(4 + 6)/12 = 0.833$, or 83.3 percent (see Table 18.4). Given two groups of equal size, by chance one would expect a hit ratio of $1/2 = 0.50$, or 50 percent. Hence, the improvement over chance is more than 25 percent, and the validity of the discriminant analysis is judged as satisfactory.

Real Research

Home Bodies and Couch Potatoes

Two-group discriminant analysis was used to assess the strength of each of five dimensions used in classifying individuals as TV users or nonusers. The procedure was appropriate for this use because of the nature of the predefined categorical groups (users and nonusers) and the interval scales used to generate individual factor scores.

Two equal groups of 185 elderly consumers, users and nonusers (total $n = 370$), were created. The discriminant equation for the analysis was estimated by using a subsample of 142 respondents from the sample of 370. Of the remaining respondents, 198 were used as a validation subsample in a cross-validation of the equation. Thirty respondents were excluded from the analysis because of missing values.

The canonical correlation for the discriminant function was 0.4291, significant at the $p < 0.0001$ level. The eigenvalue was 0.2257. The accompanying table summarizes the standardized canonical discriminant coefficients. A substantial portion of the variance is explained by the discriminant function. In addition, as the table shows, the home orientation dimension made a fairly strong contribution to classifying individuals as users or nonusers of television. Morale, security and health, and respect also contributed significantly. The social factor appeared to make little contribution.

The cross-validation procedure using the discriminant function from the analysis sample gave support to the contention that the dimensions aided researchers in discriminating between users and nonusers of television. As the table shows, the discriminant function was successful in classifying 75.76 percent of the cases. This suggests that consideration of the identified dimensions will help marketers understand the elderly market. Although it is very important for marketers to know and understand the elderly market, the Generation Xers (those born between 1961 and 1981) are also a group that should not be overlooked by marketers. Due to technological advances with the Internet and television, a revolutionary form of interactive TV (ITV) has been created. As of 2009, ITV services were fully deployed and operational and combined Internet and broadcasting with software programs and hardware components to give consumers Internet access, online shopping, music downloads, and an interactive broadcast program, all through their television. With a prosperous-looking forecast for ITV, who better to target this revolutionary form of television than Generation Xers? Discriminant analysis can again be used to determine who among Generation Xers are users or nonusers of ITV and to market ITV services successfully.[10]

Summary of Discriminant Analysis

Standard Canonical Discriminant Function Coefficients

Morale	0.27798
Security and health	0.39850
Home orientation	0.77496
Respect	0.32069
Social	−0.01996

Classification Results for Cases Selected for Use in the Analysis

Actual Group	Number of Cases	Predicted Group Membership	
		Nonusers	Users
TV nonusers	77	56	21
		72.7%	27.3%
TV users	65	24	41
		36.9%	63.1%

Percent of grouped cases correctly classified: 68.31%

Classification Results for Cases Used for Cross-Validation

Actual Group	Number of Cases	Predicted Group Membership	
		Nonusers	Users
TV nonusers	108	85	23
		78.7%	21.3%
TV users	90	25	65
		27.8%	72.2%

Percent of grouped cases correctly classified: 75.76% ∎

ACTIVE RESEARCH

Timberland: Differentiating Users and Nonusers of Outdoor Shoes

Visit www.timberland.com and conduct an Internet search using a search engine and your library's online database to obtain information on Timberland's marketing program for outdoor shoes.

As the marketing manager for Timberland, how would your understanding of the consumers' decision-making process affect your decision to sell outdoor shoes on the Internet?

What type of data would you collect and what analysis would you conduct to determine the differentiating characteristics of users and nonusers of rugged outdoor shoes?

The extension from two-group discriminant analysis to multiple discriminant analysis involves similar steps.

Multiple Discriminant Analysis

Formulate the Problem

The data presented in Tables 18.2 and 18.3 can also be used to illustrate three-group discriminant analysis. In the last column of these tables, the households are classified into three categories, based on the amount spent on family vacation (high, medium, or low). Ten households fall in each category. The question of interest is whether the households that spend high, medium, or low amounts on their vacations (AMOUNT) can be differentiated in terms of annual family income (INCOME), attitude toward travel (TRAVEL), importance attached to family vacation (VACATION), household size (HSIZE), and age of the head of household (AGE).[11]

Estimate the Discriminant Function Coefficients

Table 18.5 presents the results of estimating three-group discriminant analysis. An examination of group means indicates that income appears to separate the groups more widely than any other variable. There is some separation on travel and vacation. Groups 1 and 2 are very close in terms of household size and age. Age has a large standard deviation relative to the separation between the groups. The pooled within-groups correlation matrix indicates some correlation of vacation and household size with income. Age has some negative correlation with travel. Yet these correlations are on the lower side, indicating that although multicollinearity may be of some concern, it is not likely to be a serious problem. The significance attached to the univariate F ratios indicates that when the predictors are considered individually, only income and travel are significant in differentiating between the two groups.

In multiple discriminant analysis, if there are G groups, $G-1$ discriminant functions can be estimated if the number of predictors is larger than this quantity. In general, with G groups and k predictors, it is possible to estimate up to the smaller of $G-1$ or k discriminant functions. The first function has the highest ratio of between-groups to within-groups sum of squares. The second function, uncorrelated with the first, has the second highest ratio, and so on. However, not all the functions may be statistically significant.

Because there are three groups, a maximum of two functions can be extracted. The eigenvalue associated with the first function is 3.8190, and this function accounts for 93.93 percent of the explained variance. Because the eigenvalue is large, the first function is likely to be superior. The second function has a small eigenvalue of 0.2469 and accounts for only 6.07 percent of the explained variance.

Determine the Significance of the Discriminant Function

To test the null hypothesis of equal group centroids, both the functions must be considered simultaneously. It is possible to test the means of the functions successively by first testing all means simultaneously. Then one function is excluded at a time, and the means of the remaining functions are tested at each step. In Table 18.5, the 0 below "After Fcn (after functions removed)" indicates that no functions have been removed. The value of Wilks' λ is 0.1664. This transforms to a chi-square of 44.831, with 10 degrees of freedom, which is significant beyond the 0.05 level. Thus, the two functions together significantly discriminate among the three groups. However, when the first function is removed, the Wilks' λ associated with the second function is 0.8020, which is not significant at the 0.05 level. Therefore, the second function does not contribute significantly to group differences.

Interpret the Results

The interpretation of the results is aided by an examination of the standardized discriminant function coefficients, the structure correlations, and certain plots. The standardized coefficients indicate a large coefficient for income on function 1, whereas function 2 has relatively larger coefficients for travel, vacation, and age. A similar conclusion is reached by an examination of the structure matrix (see Table 18.5). To help interpret the functions, variables with large coefficients for a particular function are grouped together. These groupings are shown with asterisks. Thus, income and household size have asterisks for function 1 because these variables have coefficients that are larger for function 1 than for function 2. These variables are associated primarily with function 1. On the other hand, travel, vacation, and age are predominantly associated with function 2, as indicated by the asterisks.

Figure 18.3 is a scattergram plot of all the groups on function 1 and function 2. It can be seen that group 3 has the highest value on function 1, and group 1 the lowest. Because function 1 is primarily associated with income and household size, one would expect the three groups to be ordered on these two variables. Those with higher incomes and higher household size are likely to spend large amounts of money on vacations. Conversely, those with low incomes and smaller household size are likely to spend small amounts on vacations. This interpretation is further strengthened by an examination of group means on income and household size.

TABLE 18.5
Results of Three-Group Discriminant Analysis

Group Means

Amount	Income	Travel	Vacation	Hsize	Age
1	38.57000	4.50000	4.70000	3.10000	50.30000
2	50.11000	4.00000	4.20000	3.40000	49.50000
3	64.97000	6.10000	5.90000	4.20000	56.00000
Total	51.21667	4.86667	4.93333	3.56667	51.93333

Group Standard Deviations

1	5.29718	1.71594	1.88856	1.19722	8.09732
2	6.00231	2.35702	2.48551	1.50555	9.25263
3	8.61434	1.19722	1.66333	1.13529	7.60117
Total	12.79523	1.97804	2.09981	1.33089	8.57395

Pooled Within-Groups Correlation Matrix

	Income	Travel	Vacation	Hsize	Age
INCOME	1.00000				
TRAVEL	0.05120	1.00000			
VACATION	0.30681	0.03588	1.00000		
HSIZE	0.38050	0.00474	0.22080	1.00000	
AGE	−0.20939	−0.34022	−0.01326	−0.02512	1.00000

Wilks' λ (U-statistic) and univariate F ratio with 2 and 27 degrees of freedom.

Variable	Wilks' λ	F	Significance
INCOME	0.26215	38.000	0.0000
TRAVEL	0.78790	3.634	0.0400
VACATION	0.88060	1.830	0.1797
HSIZE	0.87411	1.944	0.1626
AGE	0.88214	1.804	0.1840

Canonical Discriminant Functions

Fcn	Eigenvalue	% of Variance	CUM Pct	Canonical Corr		After Fcn	Wilks' λ	Chi-square	df	Sig.
					:	0	0.1664	44.831	10	0.00
1*	3.8190	93.93	93.93	0.8902	:	1	0.8020	5.517	4	0.24
2*	0.2469	6.07	100.00	0.4450						

*Marks the two canonical discriminant functions remaining in the analysis.

Standardized Canonical Discriminant Function Coefficients

	Func 1	Func 2
INCOME	1.04740	−0.42076
TRAVEL	0.33991	0.76851
VACATION	−0.14198	0.53354
HSIZE	−0.16317	0.12932
AGE	0.49474	0.52447

Structure Matrix

Pooled within-groups correlations between discriminating variables and canonical discriminant functions (variables ordered by size of correlation within function).

(continued)

TABLE 18.5

Results of Three-Group Discriminant Analysis (*continued*)

	Func 1	Func 2
INCOME	0.85556*	−0.27833
HSIZE	0.19319*	0.07749
VACATION	0.21935	0.58829*
TRAVEL	0.14899	0.45362*
AGE	0.16576	0.34079*

Unstandardized Canonical Discriminant Function Coefficients

	Func 1	Func 2
INCOME	0.1542658	−0.6197148E-01
TRAVEL	0.1867977	0.4223430
VACATION	−0.6952264E-01	0.2612652
HSIZE	−0.1265334	0.1002796
AGE	0.5928055E-01	0.6284206E-01
(constant)	−11.09442	−3.791600

Canonical Discriminant Functions Evaluated at Group Means (Group Centroids)

Group	Func 1	Func 2
1	−2.04100	0.41847
2	−0.40479	−0.65867
3	2.44578	0.24020

Classification Results

			Predicted Group Membership			
		Amount	1	2	3	Total
Original	Count	1	9	1	0	10
		2	1	9	0	10
		3	0	2	8	10
	%	1	90.0	10.0	0.0	100.0
		2	10.0	90.0	0.0	100.0
		3	0.0	20.0	80.0	100.0
Cross-validated	Count	1	7	3	0	10
		2	4	5	1	10
		3	0	2	8	10
	%	1	70.0	30.0	0.0	100.0
		2	40.0	50.0	10.0	100.0
		3	0.0	20.0	80.0	100.0

[a] Cross-validation is done only for those cases in the analysis. In cross-validation, each case is classified by the functions derived from all cases other than that case.
[b] 86.7% of original grouped cases correctly classified.
[c] 66.7% of cross-validated grouped cases correctly classified.

Classification Results for Cases Not Selected for Use in the Analysis

	Actual Group	No. of Cases	Predicted Group Membership		
			1	2	3
Group	1	4	3	1	0
			75.0%	25.0%	0.0%
Group	2	4	0	3	1
			0.0%	75.0%	25.0%
Group	3	4	1	0	3
			25.0%	0.0%	75.0%

Percent of grouped cases correctly classified: 75.0%

FIGURE 18.3

All-Groups Scattergram

SPSS Output File

SAS Output File

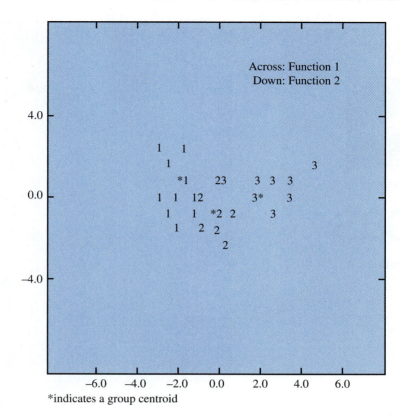

*indicates a group centroid

Figure 18.3 further indicates that function 2 tends to separate group 1 (highest value) and group 2 (lowest value). This function is primarily associated with travel, vacation, and age. Given the positive correlations of these variables with function 2 in the structure matrix, we expect to find group 1 to be higher than group 2 in terms of travel, vacation, and age. This is indeed true for travel and vacation, as indicated by the group means of these variables. If families in group 1 have more favorable attitudes toward travel and attach more importance to family vacation than group 2, why do they spend less? Perhaps they would like to spend more on vacations but cannot afford it because they have low incomes.

A similar interpretation is obtained by examining a **territorial map**, as shown in Figure 18.4. In a territorial map, each group centroid is indicated by an asterisk. The group boundaries are shown by numbers corresponding to the groups. Thus, group 1 centroid is bounded by 1s, group 2 centroid by 2s, and group 3 centroid by 3s.

territorial map
A tool for assessing discriminant analysis results that plots the group membership of each case on a graph.

Assess Validity of Discriminant Analysis

The classification results based on the analysis sample indicate that $(9 + 9 + 8)/30 = 86.7$ percent of the cases are correctly classified. Leave-one-out cross-validation correctly classifies only $(7 + 5 + 8)/30 = 0.667$ or 66.7 percent of the cases. When the classification analysis is conducted on the independent holdout sample of Table 18.3, a hit ratio of $(3 + 3 + 3)/12 = 75$ percent is obtained. Given three groups of equal size, by chance alone one would expect a hit ratio of $1/3 = 0.333$ or 33.3 percent. Thus, the improvement over chance is greater than 25 percent, indicating at least satisfactory validity.

Real Research

The Home Is Where the Patient's Heart Is

As of 2009, the largest industry sector in the U.S. economy was the health services industry. Through 2015, it is expected that spending on health care services will grow significantly faster than the economy. Contributing to the positive outlook for this industry are the current demographics, especially with demand for long-term care increasing as the population ages. It is expected that the number of Americans who are 85 and older will increase greatly by 2020, and with such a large increase, it is crucial that the health care system be portrayed positively to this segment of the population. Consumers were surveyed to determine

FIGURE 18.4

Territorial Map

SPSS Output File

SAS Output File

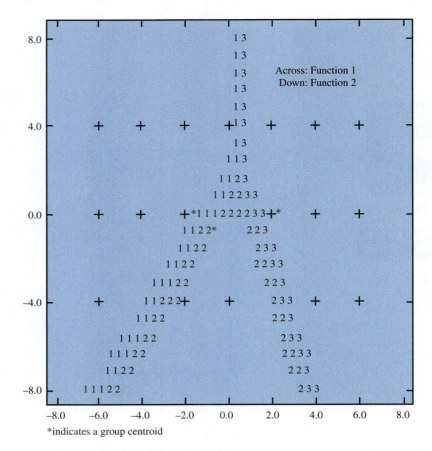

*indicates a group centroid

their attitudes toward four systems of health care delivery (home health care, hospitals, nursing homes, and outpatient clinics) along 10 attributes. A total of 102 responses were obtained, and the results were analyzed using multiple discriminant analysis (Table 1). Three discriminant functions were identified. Chi-square tests performed on the results indicated that all three discriminant functions were significant at the 0.01 level. The first function accounted for 63 percent of the total discriminative power, and the remaining two functions contributed 29.4 percent and 7.6 percent, respectively.

Table 1   Standardized Discriminant Function Coefficients

	Discriminant Function		
Variable	1	2	3
Safe	−0.20	−0.04	0.15
Convenient	0.08	0.08	0.07
Chance of medical complications[a]	−0.27	0.10	0.16
Expensive[a]	0.30	−0.28	0.52
Comfortable	0.53	0.27	−0.19
Sanitary	−0.27	−0.14	−0.70
Best medical care	−0.25	0.67	−0.10
Privacy	0.40	0.08	0.49
Faster recovery	0.30	0.32	−0.15
Staffed with best medical personnel	−0.17	−0.03	0.18
Percentage of explained variance	63.0	29.4	7.6
Chi-square	663.3[b]	289.2[b]	70.1[b]

[a] These two items were worded negatively on the questionnaire. They were reverse coded for purposes of data analysis.
[b] $p < 0.01$.

Table 2   Centroids of Health Care Systems in Discriminant Space

System	Discriminant Function		
	1	2	3
Hospital	−1.66	0.97	−0.08
Nursing home	−0.60	−1.36	−0.27
Outpatient clinic	0.54	−0.13	0.77
Home health care	1.77	0.50	−0.39

Table 3   Classification Table

System	Classification (%)			
	Hospital	Nursing Home	Outpatient Clinic	Home Health Care
Hospital	86	6	6	2
Nursing home	9	78	10	3
Outpatient clinic	9	13	68	10
Home health care	5	4	13	78

Table 1 gives the standardized discriminant function coefficients of the 10 variables in the discriminant equations. Coefficients ranged in value from −1 to 1. In determining the ability of each attribute to classify the delivery system, absolute values were used. In the first discriminant function, the two variables with the largest coefficients were comfort (0.53) and privacy (0.40). Because both related to personal attention and care, the first dimension was labeled "personalized care." In the second function, the two variables with the largest coefficients were quality of medical care (0.67) and likelihood of faster recovery (0.32). Hence, this dimension was labeled "quality of medical care." In the third discriminant function, the most significant attributes were sanitation (−0.70) and expense (0.52). Because these two attributes represent value and price, the third discriminant function was labeled "value."

The four group centroids are shown in Table 2. This table shows that home health care was evaluated most favorably along the dimension of personalized care, and hospitals least favorably. Along the dimension of quality of medical care, there was a substantial separation between nursing homes and the other three systems. Also, home health care received higher evaluations on the quality of medical care than did outpatient clinics. Outpatient clinics, on the other hand, were judged to offer the best value.

Classification analysis of the 102 responses, reported in Table 3, showed correct classifications ranging from 86 percent for hospitals to 68 percent for outpatient clinics. The misclassifications for hospitals were 6 percent each to nursing homes and outpatient clinics, and 2 percent to home health care. Nursing homes showed misclassifications of 9 percent to hospitals, 10 percent to outpatient clinics, and 3 percent to home health care. For outpatient clinics, 9 percent misclassifications were made to hospitals, 13 percent to nursing homes, and 10 percent to home health care. For home health care, the misclassifications were 5 percent to hospitals, 4 percent to nursing homes, and 13 percent to outpatient clinics. The results demonstrated that the discriminant functions were fairly accurate in predicting group membership.[12] ■

ACTIVE RESEARCH

Who Are the Tennis Players and What Do They Want in *Tennis*?

Visit www.tennis.com and write a report about the current editorial content and features of *Tennis* magazine.

Tennis magazine would like to determine what editorial content and feature preferences differentiate its readers, who vary in their tennis activity level, characterized as high, medium, or low. What data should be obtained and what analysis should be conducted to arrive at an answer?

As the editor of *Tennis* magazine, how would you change the editorial content of the magazine if the formulated hypotheses were supported by data collected in a survey of readers?

Stepwise Discriminant Analysis

Stepwise discriminant analysis is analogous to stepwise multiple regression (see Chapter 17) in that the predictors are entered sequentially based on their ability to discriminate between the groups. An F ratio is calculated for each predictor by conducting a univariate analysis of variance in which the groups are treated as the categorical variable and the predictor as the criterion variable. The predictor with the highest F ratio is the first to be selected for inclusion in the discriminant function, if it meets certain significance and tolerance criteria. A second predictor is added based on the highest adjusted or partial F ratio, taking into account the predictor already selected.

Each predictor selected is tested for retention based on its association with the other predictors selected. The process of selection and retention is continued until all predictors meeting the significance criteria for inclusion and retention have been entered in the discriminant function. Several statistics are computed at each stage. In addition, at the conclusion, a summary of the predictors entered or removed is provided. The standard output associated with the direct method is also available from the stepwise procedure.

The selection of the stepwise procedure is based on the optimizing criterion adopted. The **Mahalanobis procedure** is based on maximizing a generalized measure of the distance between the two closest groups. This procedure allows marketing researchers to make maximal use of the available information.[13]

The Mahalanobis method was used to conduct a two-group stepwise discriminant analysis on the data pertaining to the visit variable in Tables 18.2 and 18.3. The first predictor variable to be selected was income, followed by household size and then vacation. The order in which the variables were selected also indicates their importance in discriminating between the groups. This was further corroborated by an examination of the standardized discriminant function coefficients and the structure correlation coefficients. Note that the findings of the stepwise analysis agree with the conclusions reported earlier by the direct method.

> **Mahalanobis procedure**
> A stepwise procedure used in discriminant analysis to maximize a generalized measure of the distance between the two closest groups.

The Logit Model

When the dependent variable is binary and there are several independent variables that are metric, in addition to two-group discriminant analysis one can also use ordinary least squares (OLS) regression, the logit, and the probit models for estimation. The data preparation for running OLS regression, logit, and probit models is similar in that the dependent variable is coded as 0 or 1. OLS regression was discussed in Chapter 17. The probit model is less commonly used and will not be discussed, but we give an explanation of the binary logit model.

Conducting Binary Logit Analysis

The steps involved in conducting binary logit analysis are given in Figure 18.5.[14]

FIGURE 18.5

Conducting Binary Logit Analysis

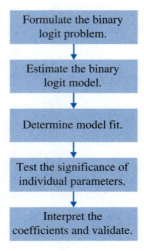

Formulate the binary logit problem.

Estimate the binary logit model.

Determine model fit.

Test the significance of individual parameters.

Interpret the coefficients and validate.

Formulate the Problem

As discussed earlier under the basic concept of discriminant analysis, there are several instances in marketing where we want to explain a binary dependent variable in terms of metric independent variables. (Note that logit analysis can also handle categorical independent variables when these are recoded using dummy variables, as discussed in Chapters 14 and 17.) Discriminant analysis deals with the issue of which group an observation is likely to belong to. On the other hand, the **binary logit model** commonly deals with the issue of how likely an observation is to belong to each group. It estimates the probability of an observation belonging to a particular group. Thus, the logit model falls somewhere between regression and discriminant analysis in application. We can estimate the probability of a binary event taking place using the binary logit model, also called *logistic regression*. Consider an event that has two outcomes: success and failure. The probability of success may be modeled using the logit model as:

binary logit model
The binary logit model commonly deals with the issue of how likely an observation is to belong to each group. It estimates the probability of an observation belonging to a particular group.

$$\log_e\left(\frac{p}{1-p}\right) = a_0 + a_1 X_1 + a_2 X_2 + \cdots + a_k X_k$$

or

$$\log_e\left(\frac{p}{1-p}\right) = \sum_{i=0}^{k} a_i X_i$$

or

$$p = \frac{\exp\left(\sum_{i=0}^{k} a_i X_i\right)}{1 + \exp\left(\sum_{i=0}^{k} a_i X_i\right)}$$

where

    p = probability of success

    X_i = independent variable i

    a_i = parameter to be estimated

It can be seen from the third equation that although X_i may vary from $-\infty$ to $+\infty$, p is constrained to lie between 0 and 1. When X_i approaches $-\infty$, p approaches 0, and when X_i approaches $+\infty$, p approaches 1. This is desirable because p is a probability and must lie between 0 and 1. On the other hand, when OLS regression is used the estimation model is

$$p = \sum_{i=0}^{n} a_i X_i$$

Thus, when OLS regression is used, p is not constrained to lie between 0 and 1; it is possible to obtain estimated values of p that are less than 0 or greater than 1. These values are, of course, conceptually and intuitively unappealing. We demonstrate this phenomenon in our illustrative application. As in the case of discriminant analysis, the researcher should specify the objectives and clearly identify the binary criterion variables and the independent variables that will be considered in the analysis. Moreover, the sample may have to be divided into the analysis and validation subsamples.

Estimating the Binary Logit Model

As discussed in Chapter 17, the linear regression model is fit by the ordinary least squares (OLS) procedure. In OLS regression, the parameters are estimated so as to minimize the sum of squared errors of prediction. The error terms in regression can take on any values and are assumed to follow a normal distribution when conducting statistical tests. In contrast, in the binary logit model, each error can assume only two values. If $Y = 0$, the error is p, and if $Y = 1$, the error is $1 - p$. Therefore, we would like to estimate the parameters in such a way that the estimated values of p would be close to 0 when $Y = 0$ and close to 1 when $Y = 1$. The procedure that is used to achieve this and estimate the parameters of the binary logit model is called the *maximum likelihood method*. This method is so called because it estimates the parameters so as to maximize the likelihood or probability of observing the actual data.

Model Fit

In multiple regression the model fit is measured by the square of the multiple correlation coefficient, R^2, which is also called the *coefficient of multiple determination* (see Chapter 17). In logistic regression (binary logit), commonly used measures of model fit are based on the likelihood function and are Cox & Snell R square and Nagelkerke R square. Both these measures are similar to R^2 in multiple regression. The Cox & Snell R square is constrained in such a way that it cannot equal 1.0, even if the model perfectly fits the data. This limitation is overcome by the Nagelkerke R square.

As discussed earlier in this chapter, in discriminant analysis, the model fit is assessed by determining the proportion of correct prediction. A similar procedure can also be used for the binary logit model. If the estimated probability is greater than 0.5, then the predicted value of Y is set to 1. On the other hand, if the estimated probability is less than 0.5, then the predicted value of Y is set to 0. The predicted values of Y can then be compared to the corresponding actual values to determine the percentage of correct predictions.

Significance Testing

The testing of individual estimated parameters or coefficients for significance is similar to that in multiple regression. In this case, the significance of the estimated coefficients is based on Wald's statistic. This statistic is a test of significance of the logistic regression coefficient based on the asymptotic normality property of maximum likelihood estimates and is estimated as:

$$\text{Wald} = (a_i / \text{SE}_{a_i})^2$$

where

$$a_i = \text{logistical coefficient for that predictor variable}$$
$$\text{SE}_{a_i} = \text{standard error of the logistical coefficient}$$

The Wald statistic is chi-square distributed with 1 degree of freedom if the variable is metric and the number of categories minus 1 if the variable is nonmetric.

The associated significance has the usual interpretation. For practical purposes, the significance of the null hypothesis that $a_{i=0}$ can also be tested using a t test where the degrees of freedom equal the number of observations minus the number of estimated parameters. The ratio of the coefficient to its standard error is compared to the critical t value. For a large number of observations, the z test can be used.

Interpretation of the Coefficients and Validation

The interpretation of the coefficients or estimated parameters is similar to that in multiple regression, of course taking into account that the nature of the dependent variable is different. In logistic regression, the log odds, that is, $\log_e\left(\frac{p}{1-p}\right)$, is a linear function of the estimated parameters. Thus, if X_i is increased by one unit, the log odds will increase by a_i units, when the effect of other independent variables is held constant. Thus a_i is the size of the increase in the log odds of the dependent variable event when the corresponding independent variable X_i is increased by one unit and the effect of the other independent variables is held constant. The sign of a_i will determine whether the probability increases (if the sign is positive) or decreases (if the sign is negative).

The validation process is very similar to that discussed for discriminant analysis. The analysis sample is used for estimating the model coefficients; the validation sample is used for developing the classification matrix. As before, the hit ratio is the percentage of cases correctly classified.

An Illustrative Application of Logistic Regression

We illustrate the logit model by analyzing the data of Table 18.6. This table gives the data for 30 respondents, 15 of whom are brand loyal (indicated by 1) and 15 of whom are not (indicated by 0). We also measure attitude toward the brand (Brand), attitude toward the product category (Product), and attitude toward shopping (Shopping), all on a 1 (unfavorable) to 7 (favorable) scale. The objective is to estimate the probability of a consumer being brand loyal as a function of attitude toward the brand, the product category, and shopping.

First we run an OLS regression on the data of Table 18.6 to illustrate the limitations of this procedure for analyzing binary data. The estimated equation is given by

$$p = -0.684 + 0.183 \text{ Brand} + 0.020 \text{ Product} + 0.074 \text{ Shopping}$$

where

p = probability of a consumer being brand loyal

Only the constant term and Brand are significant at the 0.05 level. It can be seen from the estimated regression equation that the estimated values of p are negative for low values of the

SPSS Data File

SAS Data File

TABLE 18.6				
Explaining Brand Loyalty				
No.	Loyalty	Brand	Product	Shopping
1	1	4	3	5
2	1	6	4	4
3	1	5	2	4
4	1	7	5	5
5	1	6	3	4
6	1	3	4	5
7	1	5	5	5
8	1	5	4	2
9	1	7	5	4
10	1	7	6	4
11	1	6	7	2
12	1	5	6	4
13	1	7	3	3
14	1	5	1	4
15	1	7	5	5
16	0	3	1	3
17	0	4	6	2
18	0	2	5	2
19	0	5	2	4
20	0	4	1	3
21	0	3	3	4
22	0	3	4	5
23	0	3	6	3
24	0	4	4	2
25	0	6	3	6
26	0	3	6	3
27	0	4	3	2
28	0	3	5	2
29	0	5	5	3
30	0	1	3	2

independent variables (e.g., when Brand = 1, Product = 1, and Shopping = 1, and for many other values of Brand = 1, 2, or 3). Likewise, the estimated values of p are greater than 1 for high values of the independent variables (e.g., when Brand = 7, Product = 7, and Shopping = 7). This is intuitively and conceptually unappealing because p is a probability and must lie between 0 and 1.

This limitation of OLS regression is overcome by logistic regression. The output for logistic regression when analyzing the data for Table 18.6 is shown in Table 18.7. The Cox & Snell R square and Nagelkerke R square measures indicate a reasonable fit of the model to the data. This is further verified by the classification table that reveals that 24 of the 30, that is, 80 percent of the cases, are correctly classified. The significance of the estimated coefficients is based on Wald's statistic. We note that only attitude toward the brand is significant in explaining brand loyalty. Unlike discriminant analysis, logistic regression results in standard error estimates for the estimated coefficients and hence their significance can be assessed. The positive sign for the coefficient indicates that positive attitude toward the brand results in higher loyalty toward the brand. Attitude toward the product category and attitude toward shopping do not influence brand loyalty. Thus, a manager seeking to increase brand loyalty should focus on fostering more positive attitude toward the brand and not worry about attitude toward the product category or attitude toward shopping.

The logit model can also be used when the dependent variable has more than two categories. In this case, the model is termed the *multinomial logit*. This procedure is discussed elsewhere by the author.[15]

SPSS Output File

SAS Output File

TABLE 18.7
Results of Binary Logit Model or Logistic Regression

Dependent Variable Encoding

Original Value	Internal Value
Not Loyal	0
Loyal	1

Model Summary

Step	−2 Log Likelihood	Cox & Snell R Square	Nagelkerke R Square
1	23.471[a]	.453	.604

[a]Estimation terminated at iteration number 6 because parameter estimates changed by less than .001.

Classification Table[a]

	Observed		Predicted		
			Loyalty to the Brand		Percentage Correct
			Not Loyal	Loyal	
Step 1	Loyalty to the brand	Not Loyal	12	3	80.0
		Loyal	3	12	80.0
	Overall Percentage				80.0

[a]The cut Value is .500

Variables in the Equation

		B	S.E.	Wald	df	Sig.	Exp (B)
Step 1[a]	Brand	1.274	.479	7.075	1	.008	3.575
	Product	.186	.322	.335	1	.563	1.205
	Shopping	.590	.491	1.442	1	.230	1.804
	Constant	−8.642	3.346	6.672	1	.010	.000

[a]Variable(s) entered on step 1: Brand, Product, Shopping.

Decision Research   Boston Market: Sizing the Market

The Situation

Richard Arras, president and CEO of Boston Market, is well aware of the fact that according to syndicated data, home meal replacement (HMR) will be the family dining business of this century. HMR is portable, high-quality food that's meant for takeout, and it is the fastest-growing and most significant opportunity in the food industry today. According to Nielsen's consumer panel data (www.nielsen.com), 55 percent of respondents purchased a meal for at-home consumption several times a month. Convenience and type of food were the two most influential factors when purchasing HMR. Also, 77 percent of the respondents preferred their meals ready to eat.

Another recent study by the NPD Group (www.npd.com) projected that between 2009 and 2010, virtually all growth in food sales will come from food service, defined as food prepared at least partially away from home. Estimates of total HMR market size, as well as future potential, vary widely. Sara Lee's research shows HMR accounting for as much as 80 percent of food industry growth in 2010. Findings by McKinsey & Co. support that premise from two perspectives: first, the fact that virtually all food sales growth by the year 2010 will come from food service; second, that by 2010 many Americans will never have cooked a meal from scratch. It is the most important trend to hit the food industry since the advent of frozen food.

Boston Market is now the HMR leader. As of 2009, Boston Market had more than 600 restaurants and operated in 28 states. Richard Arras wants to capitalize upon this HMR trend, and to do so would like to determine who the heavy users of HMR are and how they differ from the light users and nonusers of HMR.

The Marketing Research Decision

1. What data analysis should be conducted to determine a profile of the heavy users of HMR and to identify the differences between the heavy users, the light users, and the nonusers of HMR?
2. Discuss the role of the type of research you recommend in enabling Richard Arras to size the HMR market and determine what new products and services Boston Market should introduce.

The Marketing Management Decision

1. What new products and services should Richard Arras introduce to target the heavy users of HMR?
2. Discuss how the marketing management decision action that you recommend to Richard Arras is influenced by the syndicated sources of data that you suggested earlier and by the content of information they provide. ∎

The next example gives an application of discriminant analysis in international marketing research; the example after that presents an application in ethics.

Discriminant analysis can help Boston Market identify the differences between the heavy users, light users, and the nonusers of home meal replacement.

Real Research   Satisfactory Results of Satisfaction Programs in Europe

These days, more and more computer companies are emphasizing customer service programs rather than their erstwhile emphasis on computer features and capabilities. Hewlett-Packard (www.hp.com) learned this lesson while doing business in Europe. Research conducted on the European market revealed that there was a difference in emphasis on service requirements across age segments. Focus groups revealed that customers above 40 years of age had a hard time with the technical aspects of the computer and greatly required the customer service programs. On the other hand, younger customers appreciated the technical aspects of the product, which added to their satisfaction. Further research in the form of a large single cross-sectional survey was done to uncover the factors leading to differences in the two segments. A two-group discriminant analysis was conducted with satisfied and dissatisfied customers as the two groups and several independent variables such as technical information, ease of operation, variety and scope of customer service programs, and so on. Results confirmed the fact that the variety and scope of customer satisfaction programs was indeed a strong differentiating factor. This was a crucial finding because HP could better handle dissatisfied customers by focusing more on customer services than technical details. Consequently, HP successfully started three programs on customer satisfaction—customer feedback, customer satisfaction surveys, and total quality control. This effort resulted in increased customer satisfaction. After seeing the successful results of these programs in Europe, HP developed a goal to earn and keep customers' satisfaction, trust, and loyalty and to enable them to successfully apply technology to meet their business and personal needs. To achieve this goal, HP established and implemented a total customer experience and quality (TCE&Q) leadership framework in 2005. The details of this framework were documented in HP's 2005 Global Citizenship report. This framework was still in operation in 2009.[16] ∎

Real Research   Discriminant Analysis Discriminates Ethical and Unethical Firms

In order to identify the important variables that predict ethical and unethical behavior, discriminant analysis was used. Prior research suggested that the variables that affect ethical decisions are attitudes, leadership, the presence or absence of ethical codes of conduct, and the organization's size.

To determine which of these variables are the best predictors of ethical behavior, 149 firms were surveyed and asked to indicate how their firm operates in 18 different ethical situations. Of these 18 situations, nine related to marketing activities. These activities included using misleading sales presentations, accepting gifts for preferential treatment, pricing below out-of-pocket expenses, and so forth. Based on these nine issues, the respondent firms were classified into two groups: "never practice" and "practice."

An examination of the variables that influenced classification via two-group discriminant analysis indicated that attitudes and a company's size were the best predictors of ethical behavior. Evidently, smaller firms tend to demonstrate more ethical behavior on marketing issues. One particular company aimed at conducting ethical business practices is the Smile Internet Bank in the United Kingdom (www.smile.co.uk). In early 2002, Smile's marketing group launched six cartoon characters that focused on the bank's ethical position. Each cartoon character symbolized one of six bad banking traits, and ultimately positioned Smile as offering the opposite of these traits. In 2008, Smile was marketing a series of ethical mutual funds that invested in ethically sound companies. This marketing strategy has been successful.[17] ∎

Statistical Software

We discuss the use of SPSS and SAS in detail in the subsequent sections. Here, we briefly describe the use of MINITAB. In MINITAB, discriminant analysis can be conducted using the Stat>Multivariate>Discriminant Analysis function. It computes both linear and quadratic discriminant analysis in the classification of observations into two or more groups. Discriminant analysis is not available in EXCEL.

SPSS and SAS Computerized Demonstration Movies

We have developed computerized demonstration movies that give step-by-step instructions for running all the SPSS and SAS Learning Edition programs that are discussed in this chapter. These demonstrations can be downloaded from the Web site for this book. The instructions for running these demonstrations are given in Exhibit 14.2.

SPSS and SAS Screen Captures with Notes

The step-by-step instructions for running the various SPSS and SAS Learning Edition programs discussed in this chapter are also illustrated in screen captures with appropriate notes. These screen captures can be downloaded from the Web site for this book.

SPSS Windows

The DISCRIMINANT program performs both two-group and multiple discriminant analysis. To select this procedure using SPSS for Windows, click:

> Analyze>Classify>Discriminant . . .

The following are the detailed steps for running a two-group discriminant analysis with Resort Visit (visit) as the dependent variable and annual family income (income), attitude toward travel (attitude), importance attached to family vacation (vacation), household size (hsize), and age of the household (age) as the independent variables, using the data of Table 18.2.

1. Select ANALYZE from the SPSS menu bar.
2. Click CLASSIFY and then DISCRIMINANT.
3. Move "visit" into the GROUPING VARIABLE box.
4. Click DEFINE RANGE. Enter 1 for MINIMUM and 2 for MAXIMUM. Click CONTINUE.
5. Move "income," "travel," "vacation," "hsize," and "age" into the INDEPENDENTS box.
6. Select ENTER INDEPENDENTS TOGETHER (default option).
7. Click on STATISTICS. In the pop-up window, in the DESCRIPTIVES box check MEANS and UNIVARIATE ANOVAS. In the MATRICES box check WITHIN-GROUP CORRE-LATIONS. Click CONTINUE.
8. Click CLASSIFY. . . . In the pop-up window in the PRIOR PROBABILITIES box check ALL GROUPS EQUAL (default). In the DISPLAY box check SUMMARY TABLE and LEAVE-ONE-OUT CLASSIFICATION. In the USE COVARIANCE MATRIX box check WITHIN-GROUPS. Click CONTINUE.
9. Click OK.

The steps for running three-group discriminant analysis are similar. Select the appropriate dependent and independent variables. In step 4, click DEFINE RANGE. Enter 1 for MINIMUM and 3 for MAXIMUM. Click CONTINUE. For running stepwise discriminant analysis, in step 6 select USE STEPWISE METHOD.

To run logit analysis or logistic regression using SPSS for Windows, click:

> Analyze>Regression>Binary Logistic . . .

The following are the detailed steps for running logit analysis with brand loyalty as the dependent variable and attitude toward the brand (brand), attitude toward the product category (product), and attitude toward shopping (shopping) as the independent variables using the data of Table 18.6.

1. Select ANALYZE from the SPSS menu bar.
2. Click REGRESSION and then BINARY LOGISTIC.
3. Move "Loyalty to the Brand [Loyalty]" into the DEPENDENT VARIABLE box.
4. Move "Attitude toward the Brand [Brand]," "Attitude toward the Product category [Product]," and "Attitude toward Shopping [Shopping]" into the COVARIATES (S box).
5. Select ENTER for METHOD (default option).
6. Click OK.

SAS Learning Edition

The instructions given here and in all the data analysis chapters (14 to 22) will work with the SAS Learning Edition as well as with the SAS Enterprise Guide. For a point-and-click approach for performing discriminant analysis, use the Analyze task within the SAS Learning

Edition. The Multivariate>Discriminant Analysis task offers both two-group and multiple discriminant analysis.

Both two-group and multiple discriminant analysis can be performed using the Discriminant Analysis task within the SAS Learning Edition. To select this task click:

Analyze>Multivariate>Discriminant Analysis . . .

The following are the detailed steps for running a two-group discriminant analysis with Resort Visit (VISIT) as the dependent variable and annual family income (INCOME), attitude toward travel (TRAVEL), importance attached to family vacation (VACATION), household size (HSIZE), and the age of the household (AGE) as the independent variables, using the data of Table 18.2.

1. Select ANALYZE from the SAS Learning Edition menu bar.
2. Click MULTIVARIATE and then DISCRIMINANT ANALYSIS.
3. Move VISIT to the classification variable task role.
4. Move INCOME, TRAVEL, VACATION, HSIZE, and AGE to the analysis variables task role.
5. Click OPTIONS.
6. Select UNIVARIATE test for equality of class means and SUMMARY results of cross-validation classification. (If means are desired, then use the Summary Statistics task).
7. Click the PREVIEW CODE button.
8. Click the Insert Code . . . button.
9. Double-click to insert code before the CROSSVALIDATE option.
10. Add the CAN and PCORE options in the pop-up box and then click OK.
11. Click OK and then close the PREVIEW CODE window.
12. Click RUN.

The steps for running three-group discriminant analysis are similar to these steps.

To run logit analysis or logistic regression using the SAS Learning Edition, click:

Analyze>Regression>Logistic . . .

The following are the detailed steps for running logit analysis with brand loyalty as the dependent variable and attitude toward the brand, attitude toward the product category, and attitude toward shopping as the independent variables using the data of Table 18.6.

1. Select ANALYZE from the SAS Learning Edition menu bar.
2. Click REGRESSION and then LOGISTIC.
3. Move LOYALTY to the Dependent variable task role.
4. Move BRAND, PRODUCT, and SHOPPING to the Quantitative variables task role.
5. Select MODEL EFFECTS.
6. Choose BRAND, PRODUCT, and SHOPPING as Main Effects.
7. Select MODEL OPTIONS.
8. Check SHOW CLASSIFICATION TABLE and enter 0.5 as the critical probability value.
9. Click RUN.

Project Research   Two-Group Discriminant Analysis

In the department store project, two-group discriminant analysis was used to examine whether those respondents who were familiar with the stores, versus those who were unfamiliar, attached different relative importance to the eight factors of the choice criteria. The dependent variable was the two familiarity groups, and the independent variables were the importance attached to the eight factors of the choice criteria. The overall discriminant function was significant, indicating significant differences between the two groups. The results

SPSS Data File

SAS Data File

indicated that, as compared to the unfamiliar respondents, the familiar respondents attached greater relative importance to quality of merchandise, return and adjustment policy, service of store personnel, and credit and billing policies.

Project Activities

Download the SPSS or SAS data file *Sears Data 17* from the Web site for this book. See Chapter 17 for a description of this file.

1. Recode preference for Sears into two groups: 1 to 4 = 1; 5 to 6 = 2. Can these two groups be explained in terms of the evaluations of Sears on the eight factors of the choice criteria? Compare these results to the regression results in Chapter 17.
2. Recode preference for Sears into three groups: 1 to 3 =1; 4 = 2; 5 to 6 =3. Can these three groups be explained in terms of the evaluations of Sears on the eight factors of the choice criteria? Compare these results to the regression results in Chapter 17. ■

Summary

Discriminant analysis is useful for analyzing data when the criterion or dependent variable is categorical and the predictor or independent variables are interval scaled. When the criterion variable has two categories, the technique is known as two-group discriminant analysis. Multiple discriminant analysis refers to the case when three or more categories are involved.

Conducting discriminant analysis is a five-step procedure, as specified in the concept map of Figure 18.6. First, formulating the discriminant problem requires identification of the objectives and the criterion and predictor variables. The sample is divided into two parts. One part, the analysis sample, is used to estimate the discriminant function. The other part, the holdout sample, is reserved for validation. Estimation, the

second step, involves developing a linear combination of the predictors, called discriminant functions, so that the groups differ as much as possible on the predictor values.

Determination of statistical significance is the third step. It involves testing the null hypothesis that, in the population, the means of all discriminant functions in all groups are equal. If the null hypothesis is rejected, it is meaningful to interpret the results.

The fourth step, the interpretation of discriminant weights or coefficients, is similar to that in multiple regression analysis. Given the multicollinearity in the predictor variables, there is no unambiguous measure of the relative importance of the predictors in discriminating between the

FIGURE 18.6

A Concept Map for Conducting Discriminant Analysis

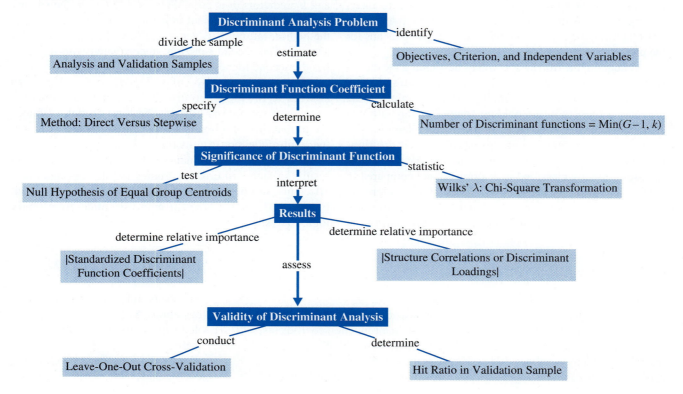

FIGURE 18.7

A Concept Map for Binary Logit Analysis

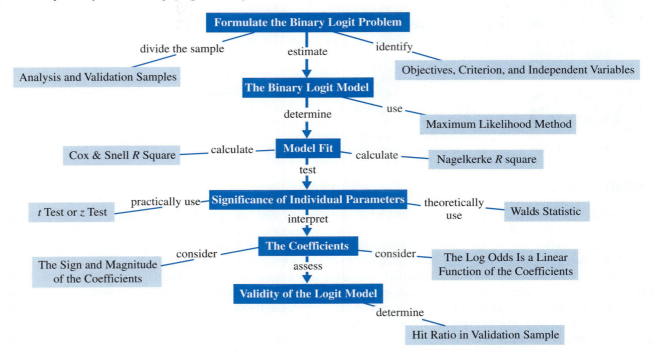

groups. However, some idea of the relative importance of the variables may be obtained by examining the absolute magnitude of the standardized discriminant function coefficients and by examining the structure correlations or discriminant loadings. These simple correlations between each predictor and the discriminant function represent the variance that the predictor shares with the function. Another aid to interpreting discriminant analysis results is to develop a characteristic profile for each group, based on the group means for the predictor variables.

Validation, the fifth step, involves developing the classification matrix. The discriminant weights estimated by using the analysis sample are multiplied by the values of the predictor variables in the holdout sample to generate discriminant scores for the cases in the holdout sample. The cases are then assigned to groups based on their discriminant scores and an appropriate decision rule. The percentage of cases correctly classified is determined and compared to the rate that would be expected by chance classification.

Two broad approaches are available for estimating the coefficients. The direct method involves estimating the discriminant function so that all the predictors are included simultaneously. An alternative is the stepwise method, in which the predictor variables are entered sequentially, based on their ability to discriminate among groups.

In multiple discriminant analysis, if there are G groups and k predictors, it is possible to estimate up to the smaller of $G - 1$ or k discriminant functions. The first function has the highest ratio of between-group to within-group sums of squares. The second function, uncorrelated with the first, has the second highest ratio, and so on.

Logit analysis, also called *logistic regression*, is an alternative to two-group discriminant analysis when the dependent variable is binary. The logit model estimates the probability of a binary event. Unlike OLS regression, the logit model constraints the probability to lie between 0 and 1. Unlike discriminant analysis, logistic regression results in standard error estimates for the estimated coefficients and hence their significance can be assessed. Figure 18.7 gives a concept map for conducting binary logit analysis.

Key Terms and Concepts

Suggested Cases, Video Cases, and HBS Cases

Running Case with Real Data

1.1 Dell

Comprehensive Critical Thinking Cases

2.1 American Idol   2.2 Baskin-Robbins   2.3 Akron Children's Hospital

Data Analysis Cases with Real Data

3.1 AT&T   3.2 IBM   3.3 Kimberly-Clark

Comprehensive Cases with Real Data

4.1 JPMorgan Chase   4.2 Wendy's

Video Case

23.1 Marriott

Live Research: Conducting a Marketing Research Project

1. Differences between groups (e.g., loyalty groups, usage groups, lifestyle groups, etc.) are of interest in most projects. These differences in terms of multiple variables can be examined using discriminant analysis.

2. If market segmentation has been conducted, then differences between segments can be examined using discriminant analysis.

Acronym

The steps involved and some key concepts in discriminant analysis may be summarized by the acronym

Discriminant:

D ependent variable: categorical
I ndpendent variable: metric
S tructure correlations or discriminant loadings
C alculation of the discriminant function
R elative importance of predictors: ambiguous
I nterpretation: scattergram and territorial map
M eans and standard deviations for groups
I nference: determination of significance
N umber of functions possible: Minimum $(G-1, k)$
A ssociation: canonical correlation
N umber 1 function has highest eigenvalue
T esting for validity: classification analysis

Exercises

Questions

1. What are the objectives of discriminant analysis?
2. What is the main distinction between two-group and multiple discriminant analysis?
3. Describe the relationship of discriminant analysis to regression and ANOVA.
4. What are the steps involved in conducting discriminant analysis?
5. How should the total sample be split for estimation and validation purposes?
6. What is Wilks' λ? For what purpose is it used?
7. Define discriminant scores.

8. Explain what is meant by an eigenvalue.
9. What is a classification matrix?
10. Explain the concept of structure correlations.
11. How is the statistical significance of discriminant analysis determined?
12. Describe a common procedure for determining the validity of discriminant analysis.
13. When the groups are of equal size, how is the accuracy of chance classification determined?
14. How does the stepwise discriminant procedure differ from the direct method?

Problems

1. In investigating the differences between heavy and light or nonusers of frozen foods, it was found that the two largest standardized discriminant function coefficients were 0.97 for convenience orientation and 0.61 for income. Is it correct to conclude that convenience orientation is more important than income when each variable is considered by itself?

2. Given the following information, calculate the discriminant score for each respondent. The value of the constant is 2.04.

Unstandardized Discriminant Function Coefficients

Age	0.38
Income	0.44
Risk taking	−0.39
Optimistic	1.26

Respondent ID	Age	Income	Risk Taking	Optimistic
0246	36	43.7	21	65
1337	44	62.5	28	56
2375	57	33.5	25	40
2454	63	38.7	16	36

Internet and Computer Exercises

1. Conduct a two-group discriminant analysis on the data given in Tables 18.2 and 18.3 using the SPSS, SAS, and MINITAB packages. Compare the output from all the packages. Discuss the similarities and differences.
2. Conduct a three-group stepwise discriminant analysis on the data given in Tables 18.2 and 18.3 using the SPSS, SAS, or MINITAB package. Compare the results to those given in Table 18.5 for three-group discriminant analysis.
3. Analyze the Nike data given in Internet and Computer Exercises 1 of Chapter 15. Do the three usage groups differ in terms of awareness, attitude, preference, intention, and loyalty toward Nike when these variables are considered simultaneously?

4. Analyze the outdoor lifestyle data given in Internet and Computer Exercises 2 of Chapter 15. Do the three groups based on location of residence differ on the importance attached to enjoying nature, relating to the weather, living in harmony with the environment, exercising regularly, and meeting other people (V_2 to V_6) when these variables are considered simultaneously?
5. Conduct a two-group discriminant analysis on the data you obtained in Fieldwork Activity 1, using the SPSS, SAS, or MINITAB package. Is it possible to differentiate between graduate and undergraduate students using the four attitudinal measures?

Activities

Role Playing

1. You have been hired as a marketing research analyst by American Airlines. Your boss, the marketing manager, is wondering what statistical analysis should be conducted to determine the differences between the frequent fliers and occasional fliers in terms of five statements measuring attitude toward American Airlines on a Likert scale. Explain to your boss (a student in your class) the analysis that you would conduct.

Fieldwork

1. Interview 15 graduate and 15 undergraduate students. Measure their attitudes toward college education (It is worthwhile getting a college degree), enjoyment in life (It is important to have fun in life), your university (I am not very happy that I chose to go to school here), and work ethic (In general, there is a lack of work ethic on the college campus). For each attitude, measure the degree of disagreement/agreement using a 7-point rating scale (1 = disagree, 7 = agree).

Group Discussion

1. Is it meaningful to determine the relative importance of predictors in discriminating between the groups? Why or why not? Discuss as a small group.

Dell Running Case

Review the Dell case, Case 1.1, and questionnaire given toward the end of the book. Go to the Web site for this book and download the Dell data file.

1. Do a two-group discriminant analysis with the two overall satisfaction groups derived based on the recoding of q4 (as specified in Chapter 14) as the dependent variables and all the 13 evaluations of Dell (q8_1 to q8_13) as the independent variables. Interpret the results. Do a similar analysis using the logit model and compare the results with those obtained by two-group discriminant analysis.

2. Do a two-group discriminant analysis with the likelihood of choosing Dell groups derived based on the recoding of q6 (as specified in Chapter 14) as the dependent variables and all the 13 evaluations of Dell (q8_1 to q8_13) as the independent variables. Interpret the results. Do a similar analysis using the logit model and compare the results with those obtained by two-group discriminant analysis.

3. Do a three-group discriminant analysis with the three price sensitivity groups derived based on the recoding of q9_5per (as specified in Chapter 14) as the dependent variables and all the 13 evaluations of Dell (q8_1 to q8_13) as the independent variables. Interpret the results

4. Do a three-group discriminant analysis with the three price sensitivity groups derived based on the recoding of q9_10per (as specified in Chapter 14) as the dependent variables and all the 13 evaluations of Dell (q8_1 to q8_13) as the independent variables. Interpret the results.

" Factor analysis allows us to look at groups of variables that tend to be correlated to each other and identify underlying dimensions that explain these correlations. "

William D. Neal, Senior Partner, SDR Consulting

Objectives [After reading this chapter, the student should be able to:]

1. Describe the concept of factor analysis and explain how it is different from analysis of variance, multiple regression, and discriminant analysis.

2. Discuss the procedure for conducting factor analysis, including problem formulation, construction of the correlation matrix, selection of an appropriate method, determination of the number of factors, rotation, and interpretation of factors.

3. Understand the distinction between principal component factor analysis and common factor analysis methods.

4. Explain the selection of surrogate variables and their application, with emphasis on their use in subsequent analysis.

5. Describe the procedure for determining the fit of a factor analysis model using the observed and the reproduced correlations.

Factor Analysis

Overview

In analysis of variance (Chapter 16), regression (Chapter 17), and discriminant analysis (Chapter 18), one of the variables is clearly identified as the dependent variable. We now turn to a procedure, factor analysis, in which variables are not classified as independent or dependent. Instead, the whole set of interdependent relationships among variables is examined. This chapter discusses the basic concept of factor analysis and gives an exposition of the factor model. We describe the steps in factor analysis and illustrate them in the context of principal components analysis. Next, we present an application of common factor analysis.

Finally, we discuss the use of software in factor analysis. Help for running the SPSS and SAS Learning Edition programs used in this chapter is provided in four ways: (1) detailed step-by-step instructions are given later in the chapter, (2) you can download (from the Web site for this book) computerized demonstration movies illustrating these step-by-step instructions, (3) you can download screen captures with notes illustrating these step-by-step instructions, and (4) you can refer to the *Study Guide and Technology Manual*, a supplement that accompanies this book.

To begin, we provide some examples to illustrate the usefulness of factor analysis.

Real Research

Factor Analysis Earns Interest at Banks

How do consumers evaluate banks? Respondents in a survey were asked to rate the importance of 15 bank attributes. A 5-point scale ranging from not important to very important was employed. These data were analyzed via principal components analysis.

A four-factor solution resulted, with the factors being labeled as traditional services, convenience, visibility, and competence. Traditional services included interest rates on loans, reputation in the community, low rates for checking, friendly and personalized service, easy-to-read monthly statements, and obtainability of loans. Convenience was comprised of convenient branch location, convenient ATM locations, speed of service, and convenient banking hours. The visibility factor included recommendations from friends and

Factor analysis helped JPMorgan Chase & Co. to identify the dimensions consumers use to evaluate banks and to develop appropriate marketing strategies enabling it to become one of the largest U.S. banks.

relatives, attractiveness of the physical structure, community involvement, and obtainability of loans. Competence consisted of employee competence and availability of auxiliary banking services. It was concluded that consumers evaluated banks using the four basic factors of traditional services, convenience, visibility, and competence, and banks must excel on these factors to project a good image. By emphasizing these factors, JPMorgan Chase & Co. became one of the largest U.S. banks and bought the banking operations of bankrupt rival Washington Mutual in September 2008.[1] ■

Basic Concept

factor analysis
A class of procedures primarily used for data reduction and summarization.

Factor analysis is a general name denoting a class of procedures primarily used for data reduction and summarization. In marketing research, there may be a large number of variables, most of which are correlated and which must be reduced to a manageable level. Relationships among sets of many interrelated variables are examined and represented in terms of a few underlying factors. For example, store image may be measured by asking respondents to evaluate stores on a series of items on a semantic differential scale. These item evaluations may then be analyzed to determine the factors underlying store image.

In analysis of variance, multiple regression, and discriminant analysis, one variable is considered as the dependent or criterion variable, and the others as independent or predictor variables. However, no such distinction is made in factor analysis. Rather, factor analysis is an **interdependence technique** in that an entire set of interdependent relationships is examined.[2]

interdependence technique
Multivariate statistical techniques in which the whole set of interdependent relationships is examined.

Factor analysis is used in the following circumstances:

1. To identify underlying dimensions, or **factors**, that explain the correlations among a set of variables. For example, a set of lifestyle statements may be used to measure the psychographic profiles of consumers. These statements may then be factor analyzed to identify the underlying psychographic factors, as illustrated in the department store example. This is also illustrated in Figure 19.1 derived based on empirical analysis, where the seven psychographic variables can be represented by two factors. In this figure, factor 1 can be interpreted as homebody versus socialite, and factor 2 can be interpreted as sports versus movies/plays.

factors
An underlying dimension that explains the correlations among a set of variables.

2. To identify a new, smaller set of uncorrelated variables to replace the original set of correlated variables in subsequent multivariate analysis (regression or discriminant analysis). For example, the psychographic factors identified may be used as independent variables in explaining the differences between loyal and nonloyal consumers. Thus, instead of the seven correlated psychographic variables of Figure 19.1, we can use the two uncorrelated factors, i.e., homebody versus socialite, and sports versus movies/plays, in subsequent analysis.

3. To identify a smaller set of salient variables from a larger set for use in subsequent multivariate analysis. For example, a few of the original lifestyle statements that correlate highly with the identified factors may be used as independent variables to explain the differences between the loyal and nonloyal users. Specifically, based on theory and empirical results

FIGURE 19.1

Factors Underlying Selected Psychographics and Lifestyles

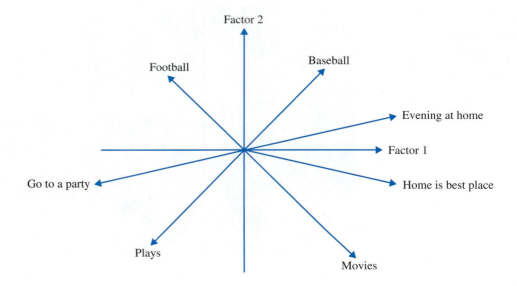

(Figure 19.1), we can select home is best place and football as independent variables, and drop the other five variables to avoid problems due to multicollinearity (see Chapter 17).

All these uses are exploratory in nature and, therefore, factor analysis is also called exploratory factor analysis (EFA). The technique has numerous applications in marketing research. For example:

- It can be used in market segmentation for identifying the underlying variables on which to group the customers. New car buyers might be grouped based on the relative emphasis they place on economy, convenience, performance, comfort, and luxury. This might result in five segments: economy seekers, convenience seekers, performance seekers, comfort seekers, and luxury seekers.
- In product research, factor analysis can be employed to determine the brand attributes that influence consumer choice. Toothpaste brands might be evaluated in terms of protection against cavities, whiteness of teeth, taste, fresh breath, and price.
- In advertising studies, factor analysis can be used to understand the media consumption habits of the target market. The users of frozen foods may be heavy viewers of cable TV, see a lot of movies, and listen to country music.
- In pricing studies, it can be used to identify the characteristics of price-sensitive consumers. For example, these consumers might be methodical, economy minded, and home centered.

Factor Analysis Model

Mathematically, factor analysis is somewhat similar to multiple regression analysis, in that each variable is expressed as a linear combination of underlying factors. The amount of variance a variable shares with all other variables included in the analysis is referred to as *communality*. The covariation among the variables is described in terms of a small number of common factors plus a unique factor for each variable. These factors are not overtly observed. If the variables are standardized, the factor model may be represented as:

$$X_i = A_{i1}F_1 + A_{i2}F_2 + A_{i3}F_3 + \cdots + A_{im}F_m + V_i U_i$$

where

X_i = *i*th standardized variable

A_{ij} = standardized multiple regression coefficient of variable *i* on common factor *j*

F = common factor

V_i = standardized regression coefficient of variable *i* on unique factor *i*

U_i = the unique factor for variable *i*

m = number of common factors

The unique factors are uncorrelated with each other and with the common factors.[3] The common factors themselves can be expressed as linear combinations of the observed variables.

$$F_i = W_{i1}X_1 + W_{i2}X_2 + W_{i3}X_3 + \cdots + W_{ik}X_k$$

where

F_i = estimate of *i*th factor

W_i = weight or factor score coefficient

k = number of variables

It is possible to select weights or factor score coefficients so that the first factor explains the largest portion of the total variance. Then a second set of weights can be selected, so that the second factor accounts for most of the residual variance, subject to being uncorrelated with the first factor. This same principle could be applied to selecting additional weights for the additional factors. Thus, the factors can be estimated so that their factor scores, unlike the values of the original variables, are not correlated. Furthermore, the first factor accounts for the highest variance in the data, the second factor the second highest, and so on. A simplified graphical illustration of factor analysis in the case of two variables is presented in Figure 19.2. Several statistics are associated with factor analysis.

FIGURE 19.2

Graphical
Illustration
of Factor
Analysis

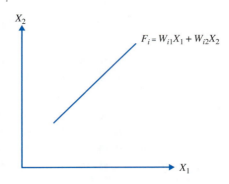

Statistics Associated with Factor Analysis

The key statistics associated with factor analysis are as follows:

Bartlett's test of sphericity. Bartlett's test of sphericity is a test statistic used to examine the hypothesis that the variables are uncorrelated in the population. In other words, the population correlation matrix is an identity matrix; each variable correlates perfectly with itself ($r = 1$) but has no correlation with the other variables ($r = 0$).

Correlation matrix. A correlation matrix is a lower triangle matrix showing the simple correlations, r, between all possible pairs of variables included in the analysis. The diagonal elements, which are all 1, are usually omitted.

Communality. Communality is the amount of variance a variable shares with all the other variables being considered. This is also the proportion of variance explained by the common factors.

Eigenvalue. The eigenvalue represents the total variance explained by each factor.

Factor loadings. Factor loadings are simple correlations between the variables and the factors.

Factor loading plot. A factor loading plot is a plot of the original variables using the factor loadings as coordinates.

Factor matrix. A factor matrix contains the factor loadings of all the variables on all the factors extracted.

Factor scores. Factor scores are composite scores estimated for each respondent on the derived factors.

Factor scores coefficient matrix. This matrix contains the weights, or factor score coefficients, used to combine the standardized variables to obtain factor scores.

Kaiser-Meyer-Olkin (KMO) measure of sampling adequacy. The Kaiser-Meyer-Olkin (KMO) measure of sampling adequacy is an index used to examine the appropriateness of factor analysis. High values (between 0.5 and 1.0) indicate factor analysis is appropriate. Values below 0.5 imply that factor analysis may not be appropriate.

Percentage of variance. This is the percentage of the total variance attributed to each factor.

Residuals. Residuals are the differences between the observed correlations, as given in the input correlation matrix, and the reproduced correlations, as estimated from the factor matrix.

Scree plot. A scree plot is a plot of the eigenvalues against the number of factors in order of extraction.

In the next section, we describe the uses of these statistics in the context of the procedure for conducting factor analysis.

Conducting Factor Analysis

The steps involved in conducting factor analysis are illustrated in Figure 19.3. The first step is to define the factor analysis problem and identify the variables to be factor analyzed. Then a correlation matrix of these variables is constructed and a method of factor analysis selected.

FIGURE 19.3

Conducting Factor Analysis

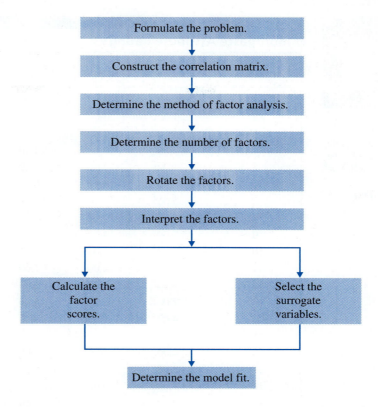

The researcher decides on the number of factors to be extracted and the method of rotation. Next, the rotated factors should be interpreted. Depending upon the objectives, the factor scores may be calculated, or surrogate variables selected, to represent the factors in subsequent multivariate analysis. Finally, the fit of the factor analysis model is determined. We discuss these steps in more detail in the following sections.[4]

Formulate the Problem

Problem formulation includes several tasks. First, the objectives of factor analysis should be identified. The variables to be included in the factor analysis should be specified based on past research, theory, and judgment of the researcher. It is important that the variables be appropriately measured on an interval or ratio scale. An appropriate sample size should be used. As a rough guideline, there should be at least four or five times as many observations (sample size) as there are variables.[5] In many marketing research situations, the sample size is small and this ratio is considerably lower. In these cases, the results should be interpreted cautiously.

To illustrate factor analysis, suppose the researcher wants to determine the underlying benefits consumers seek from the purchase of a toothpaste. A sample of 30 respondents was interviewed using mall-intercept interviewing. The respondents were asked to indicate their degree of agreement with the following statements using a 7-point scale (1 = strongly disagree, 7 = strongly agree):

V_1: It is important to buy a toothpaste that prevents cavities.

V_2: I like a toothpaste that gives shiny teeth.

V_3: A toothpaste should strengthen your gums.

V_4: I prefer a toothpaste that freshens breath.

V_5: Prevention of tooth decay is not an important benefit offered by a toothpaste.

V_6: The most important consideration in buying a toothpaste is attractive teeth.

The data obtained are given in Table 19.1. For illustrative purposes, we consider only a small number of observations. In actual practice, factor analysis is performed on a much larger sample such as that in the Dell running case and other cases with real data that are presented in this book. A correlation matrix was constructed based on these ratings data.

SPSS Data File

SAS Data File

TABLE 19.1
Toothpaste Attribute Ratings

Respondent Number	V_1	V_2	V_3	V_4	V_5	V_6
1	7.00	3.00	6.00	4.00	2.00	4.00
2	1.00	3.00	2.00	4.00	5.00	4.00
3	6.00	2.00	7.00	4.00	1.00	3.00
4	4.00	5.00	4.00	6.00	2.00	5.00
5	1.00	2.00	2.00	3.00	6.00	2.00
6	6.00	3.00	6.00	4.00	2.00	4.00
7	5.00	3.00	6.00	3.00	4.00	3.00
8	6.00	4.00	7.00	4.00	1.00	4.00
9	3.00	4.00	2.00	3.00	6.00	3.00
10	2.00	6.00	2.00	6.00	7.00	6.00
11	6.00	4.00	7.00	3.00	2.00	3.00
12	2.00	3.00	1.00	4.00	5.00	4.00
13	7.00	2.00	6.00	4.00	1.00	3.00
14	4.00	6.00	4.00	5.00	3.00	6.00
15	1.00	3.00	2.00	2.00	6.00	4.00
16	6.00	4.00	6.00	3.00	3.00	4.00
17	5.00	3.00	6.00	3.00	3.00	4.00
18	7.00	3.00	7.00	4.00	1.00	4.00
19	2.00	4.00	3.00	3.00	6.00	3.00
20	3.00	5.00	3.00	6.00	4.00	6.00
21	1.00	3.00	2.00	3.00	5.00	3.00
22	5.00	4.00	5.00	4.00	2.00	4.00
23	2.00	2.00	1.00	5.00	4.00	4.00
24	4.00	6.00	4.00	6.00	4.00	7.00
25	6.00	5.00	4.00	2.00	1.00	4.00
26	3.00	5.00	4.00	6.00	4.00	7.00
27	4.00	4.00	7.00	2.00	2.00	5.00
28	3.00	7.00	2.00	6.00	4.00	3.00
29	4.00	6.00	3.00	7.00	2.00	7.00
30	2.00	3.00	2.00	4.00	7.00	2.00

Construct the Correlation Matrix

The analytical process is based on a matrix of correlations between the variables. Valuable insights can be gained from an examination of this matrix. For the factor analysis to be appropriate, the variables must be correlated. In practice, this is usually the case. If the correlations between all the variables are small, factor analysis may not be appropriate. We would also expect that variables that are highly correlated with each other would also highly correlate with the same factor or factors.

Formal statistics are available for testing the appropriateness of the factor model. Bartlett's test of sphericity can be used to test the null hypothesis that the variables are uncorrelated in the population; in other words, the population correlation matrix is an identity matrix. In an identity matrix, all the diagonal terms are 1, and all off-diagonal terms are 0. The test statistic for sphericity is based on a chi-square transformation of the determinant of the correlation matrix. A large value of the test statistic will favor the rejection of the null hypothesis. If this hypothesis cannot be rejected, then the appropriateness of factor analysis should be questioned. Another useful statistic is the Kaiser-Meyer-Olkin (KMO) measure of sampling adequacy. This index compares the magnitudes of the observed correlation coefficients to the magnitudes of the partial correlation

SPSS Output File

SAS Output File

TABLE 19.2
Correlation Matrix

Variables	V_1	V_2	V_3	V_4	V_5	V_6
V_1	1.00					
V_2	−0.053	1.00				
V_3	0.873	−0.155	1.00			
V_4	−0.086	0.572	−0.248	1.00		
V_5	−0.858	0.020	−0.778	−0.007	1.00	
V_6	0.004	0.640	−0.018	0.640	−0.136	1.00

coefficients. Small values of the KMO statistic indicate that the correlations between pairs of variables cannot be explained by other variables and that factor analysis may not be appropriate. Generally, a value greater than 0.5 is desirable.

The correlation matrix, constructed from the data obtained to understand toothpaste benefits (Table 19.1), is shown in Table 19.2. There are relatively high correlations among V_1 (prevention of cavities), V_3 (strong gums), and V_5 (prevention of tooth decay). We would expect these variables to correlate with the same set of factors. Likewise, there are relatively high correlations among V_2 (shiny teeth), V_4 (fresh breath), and V_6 (attractive teeth). These variables may also be expected to correlate with the same factors.[6]

The results of principal components analysis are given in Table 19.3. The null hypothesis, that the population correlation matrix is an identity matrix, is rejected by Bartlett's test of sphericity. The approximate chi-square statistic is 111.314 with 15 degrees of freedom, which is significant at the 0.05 level. The value of the KMO statistic (0.660) is also large (> 0.5). Thus, factor analysis may be considered an appropriate technique for analyzing the correlation matrix of Table 19.2.

SPSS Output File

SAS Output File

TABLE 19.3
Results of Principal Components Analysis

Bartlett test of sphericity
Approx. chi-square = 111.314, df = 15, significance = 0.00000
Kaiser-Meyer-Olkin measure of sampling adequacy = 0.660

Communalities

Variable	Initial	Extraction
V_1	1.000	0.926
V_2	1.000	0.723
V_3	1.000	0.894
V_4	1.000	0.739
V_5	1.000	0.878
V_6	1.000	0.790

Initial Eigenvalues

Factor	Eigenvalue	% of Variance	Cumulative %
1	2.731	45.520	45.520
2	2.218	36.969	82.488
3	0.442	7.360	89.848
4	0.341	5.688	95.536
5	0.183	3.044	98.580
6	0.085	1.420	100.000

(continued)

TABLE 19.3

Results of Principal Components Analysis (*continued*)

Extraction Sums of Squared Loadings

Factor	Eigenvalue	% of Variance	Cumulative %
1	2.731	45.520	45.520
2	2.218	36.969	82.488

Factor Matrix	Factor 1	Factor 2
V_1	0.928	0.253
V_2	−0.301	0.795
V_3	0.936	0.131
V_4	−0.342	0.789
V_5	−0.869	−0.351
V_6	−0.177	0.871

Rotation Sums of Squared Loadings

Factor	Eigenvalue	% of Variance	Cumulative %
1	2.688	44.802	44.802
2	2.261	37.687	82.488

Rotated Factor Matrix

	Factor 1	Factor 2
V_1	0.962	−0.027
V_2	−0.057	0.848
V_3	0.934	−0.146
V_4	−0.098	0.854
V_5	−0.933	−0.084
V_6	0.083	0.885

Factor Score Coefficient Matrix

	Factor 1	Factor 2
V_1	0.358	0.011
V_2	−0.001	0.375
V_3	0.345	−0.043
V_4	−0.017	0.377
V_5	−0.350	−0.059
V_6	0.052	0.395

Reproduced Correlation Matrix

	V_1	V_2	V_3	V_4	V_5	V_6
V_1	0.926*	0.024	−0.029	0.031	0.038	−0.053
V_2	−0.078	0.723*	0.022	−0.158	0.038	−0.105
V_3	0.902	−0.177	0.894*	−0.031	0.081	0.033
V_4	−0.117	0.730	−0.217	0.739*	−0.027	−0.107
V_5	−0.895	−0.018	−0.859	0.020	0.878*	0.016
V_6	0.057	0.746	−0.051	0.748	−0.152	0.790*

*The lower left triangle contains the reproduced correlation matrix; the diagonal, the communalities; the upper right triangle, the residuals between the observed correlations and the reproduced correlations.

Determine the Method of Factor Analysis

principal components analysis
An approach to factor analysis that considers the total variance in the data.

Once it has been determined that factor analysis is suitable for analyzing the data, an appropriate method must be selected. The approach used to derive the weights or factor score coefficients differentiates the various methods of factor analysis. The two basic approaches are principal components analysis and common factor analysis. In **principal components analysis**, the total variance in the data is considered. The diagonal of the correlation matrix consists of unities, and full variance is brought into the factor matrix. Principal components analysis is recommended when the primary concern is to determine the minimum number of factors that will account for maximum variance in the data for use in subsequent multivariate analysis. The factors are called *principal components*.

common factor analysis
An approach to factor analysis that estimates the factors based only on the common variance.

In **common factor analysis**, the factors are estimated based only on the common variance. Communalities are inserted in the diagonal of the correlation matrix. This method is appropriate when the primary concern is to identify the underlying dimensions and the common variance is of interest. This method is also known as *principal axis factoring*.

Other approaches for estimating the common factors are also available. These include the methods of unweighted least squares, generalized least squares, maximum likelihood, alpha method, and image factoring. These methods are complex and are not recommended for inexperienced users.[7]

Table 19.3 shows the application of principal components analysis to the toothpaste example. Under "Communalities," "Initial" column, it can be seen that the communality for each variable, V_1 to V_6, is 1.0 as unities were inserted in the diagonal of the correlation matrix. The table labeled "Initial Eigenvalues" gives the eigenvalues. The eigenvalues for the factors are, as expected, in decreasing order of magnitude as we go from factor 1 to factor 6. The eigenvalue for a factor indicates the total variance attributed to that factor. The total variance accounted for by all six factors is 6.00, which is equal to the number of variables. Factor 1 accounts for a variance of 2.731, which is (2.731/6) or 45.52 percent of the total variance. Likewise, the second factor accounts for (2.218/6) or 36.97 percent of the total variance, and the first two factors combined account for 82.49 percent of the total variance. Several considerations are involved in determining the number of factors that should be used in the analysis.

Determine the Number of Factors

It is possible to compute as many principal components as there are variables, but in doing so, no parsimony is gained. In order to summarize the information contained in the original variables, a smaller number of factors should be extracted. The question is, how many? Several procedures have been suggested for determining the number of factors. These include *a priori* determination and approaches based on eigenvalues, scree plot, percentage of variance accounted for, split-half reliability, and significance tests.

A PRIORI DETERMINATION Sometimes, because of prior knowledge, the researcher knows how many factors to expect and thus can specify the number of factors to be extracted beforehand. The extraction of factors ceases when the desired number of factors have been extracted. Most computer programs allow the user to specify the number of factors, allowing for an easy implementation of this approach.

DETERMINATION BASED ON EIGENVALUES In this approach, only factors with eigenvalues greater than 1.0 are retained; the other factors are not included in the model. An eigenvalue represents the amount of variance associated with the factor. Hence, only factors with a variance greater than 1.0 are included. Factors with variance less than 1.0 are no better than a single variable, because, due to standardization, each individual variable has a variance of 1.0. If the number of variables is less than 20, this approach will result in a conservative number of factors.

DETERMINATION BASED ON SCREE PLOT A scree plot is a plot of the eigenvalues against the number of factors in order of extraction. The shape of the plot is used to determine the number of factors. Typically, the plot has a distinct break between the steep slope of factors, with large eigenvalues and a gradual trailing off associated with the rest of the factors. This gradual trailing off is referred to as the *scree*. Experimental evidence indicates that the point at which the scree begins denotes the true number of factors. Generally, the number of factors determined by a scree plot will be one or a few more than that determined by the eigenvalue criterion.

DETERMINATION BASED ON PERCENTAGE OF VARIANCE In this approach, the number of factors extracted is determined so that the cumulative percentage of variance extracted by the factors reaches a satisfactory level. What level of variance is satisfactory depends upon the problem. However, it is recommended that the factors extracted should account for at least 60 percent of the variance.

DETERMINATION BASED ON SPLIT-HALF RELIABILITY The sample is split in half and factor analysis is performed on each half. Only factors with high correspondence of factor loadings across the two subsamples are retained.

DETERMINATION BASED ON SIGNIFICANCE TESTS It is possible to determine the statistical significance of the separate eigenvalues and retain only those factors that are statistically significant. A drawback is that with large samples (size greater than 200), many factors are likely to be statistically significant, although from a practical viewpoint many of these account for only a small proportion of the total variance.

In Table 19.3, we see that the eigenvalue greater than 1.0 (default option) results in two factors being extracted. Our *a priori* knowledge tells us that toothpaste is bought for two major reasons. The scree plot associated with this analysis is given in Figure 19.4. From the scree plot, a distinct break occurs at three factors. Finally, from the cumulative percentage of variance accounted for, we see that the first two factors account for 82.49 percent of the variance, and that the gain achieved in going to three factors is marginal. Furthermore, split-half reliability also indicates that two factors are appropriate. Thus, two factors appear to be reasonable in this situation.

The second column under "Communalities" in Table 19.3 gives relevant information after the desired number of factors has been extracted. The communalities for the variables under "Extraction" are different than under "Initial" because all of the variances associated with the variables are not explained unless all the factors are retained. The "Extraction Sums of Squared Loadings" give the variances associated with the factors that are retained. Note that these are the same as under "Initial Eigenvalues." This is always the case in principal components analysis. The percentage variance accounted for by a factor is determined by dividing the associated eigenvalue with the total number of factors (or variables) and multiplying by 100. Thus, the first factor accounts for (2.731/6) × 100 or 45.52 percent of the variance of the six variables. Likewise, the second factor accounts for (2.218/6) × 100 or 36.969 percent of the variance. Interpretation of the solution is often enhanced by a rotation of the factors.

Rotate Factors

An important output from factor analysis is the factor matrix, also called the *factor pattern matrix*. The factor matrix contains the coefficients used to express the standardized variables in terms of the factors. These coefficients, the factor loadings, represent the correlations between the factors and

FIGURE 19.4
Scree Plot

SPSS Output File

SAS Output File

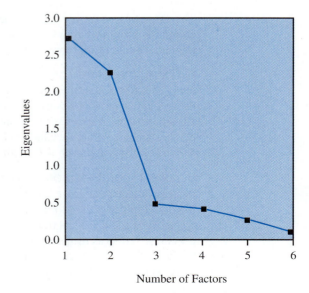

the variables. A coefficient with a large absolute value indicates that the factor and the variable are closely related. The coefficients of the factor matrix can be used to interpret the factors.

Although the initial or unrotated factor matrix indicates the relationship between the factors and individual variables, it seldom results in factors that can be interpreted, because the factors are correlated with many variables. For example, in Table 19.3, under "Factor Matrix", factor 1 is at least somewhat correlated with five of the six variables (an absolute value of factor loading greater than 0.3). Likewise, factor 2 is at least somewhat correlated with four of the six variables. Moreover, variables 2 and 5 load at least somewhat on both the factors. This is illustrated in Figure 19.5(a). How should these factors be interpreted? In such a complex matrix it is difficult to interpret the factors. Therefore, through rotation, the factor matrix is transformed into a simpler one that is easier to interpret.

In rotating the factors, we would like each factor to have nonzero, or significant, loadings or coefficients for only some of the variables. Likewise, we would like each variable to have nonzero or significant loadings with only a few factors, if possible with only one. If several factors have high loadings with the same variable, it is difficult to interpret them. Rotation does not affect the communalities and the percentage of total variance explained. However, the percentage of variance accounted for by each factor does change. This is seen in Table 19.3 by comparing "Extraction Sums of Squared Loadings" with "Rotation Sums of Squared Loadings." The variance explained by the individual factors is redistributed by rotation. Hence, different methods of rotation may result in the identification of different factors.

The rotation is called **orthogonal rotation** if the axes are maintained at right angles. The most commonly used method for rotation is the **varimax procedure**. This is an orthogonal method of rotation that minimizes the number of variables with high loadings on a factor, thereby enhancing the interpretability of the factors.[8] Orthogonal rotation results in factors that are uncorrelated. The rotation is called **oblique rotation** when the axes are not maintained at right angles, and the factors are correlated. Sometimes, allowing for correlations among factors can simplify the factor pattern matrix. Oblique rotation should be used when factors in the population are likely to be strongly correlated.

In Table 19.3, by comparing the varimax rotated factor matrix with the unrotated matrix (titled "Factor Matrix"), we can see how rotation achieves simplicity and enhances interpretability. Whereas five variables correlated with factor 1 in the unrotated matrix, only variables V_1, V_3, and V_5 correlate with factor 1 after rotation. The remaining variables, V_2, V_4, and V_6, correlate highly with factor 2. Furthermore, no variable correlates highly with both the factors. This can be seen clearly in Figure 19.5(b). The rotated factor matrix forms the basis for interpretation of the factors.

Interpret Factors

Interpretation is facilitated by identifying the variables that have large loadings on the same factor. That factor can then be interpreted in terms of the variables that load high on it. Another useful aid in interpretation is to plot the variables using the factor loadings as coordinates. Variables at the end of an axis are those that have high loadings on only that factor, and hence describe the factor. Variables near the origin have small loadings on both the factors. Variables that are not near any of the axes are related to both the factors. If a factor cannot be clearly defined in terms of the original variables, it should be labeled as an undefined or a general factor.

In the rotated factor matrix of Table 19.3, factor 1 has high coefficients for variables V_1 (prevention of cavities) and V_3 (strong gums), and a negative coefficient for V_5 (prevention of tooth decay is not important). Therefore, this factor may be labeled a health benefit factor.

orthogonal rotation
Rotation of factors in which the axes are maintained at right angles.

varimax procedure
An orthogonal method of factor rotation that minimizes the number of variables with high loadings on a factor, thereby enhancing the interpretability of the factors.

oblique rotation
Rotation of factors when the axes are not maintained at right angles.

FIGURE 19.5

Factor Matrix Before and After Rotation

Variables	Factors 1	Factors 2
1	X	
2	X	X
3	X	
4	X	X
5	X	X
6		X

(a)
High Loadings Before Rotation

Variables	Factors 1	Factors 2
1	X	
2		X
3	X	
4		X
5	X	
6		X

(b)
High Loadings After Rotation

FIGURE 19.6

Factor Loading Plot

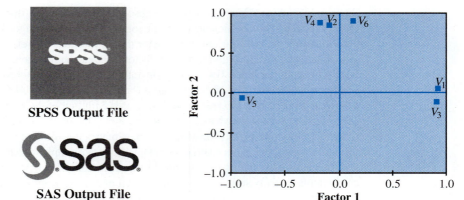

SPSS Output File

SAS Output File

Note that a negative coefficient for a negative variable (V_5) leads to a positive interpretation that prevention of tooth decay is important. Factor 2 is highly related with variables V_2 (shiny teeth), V_4 (fresh breath), and V_6 (attractive teeth). Thus, factor 2 may be labeled a social benefit factor. A plot of the factor loadings, given in Figure 19.6, confirms this interpretation. Variables V_1, V_3, and V_5 are at the ends of the horizontal axis (factor 1), with V_5 at the end opposite to V_1 and V_3, whereas variables V_2, V_4, and V_6 are at the end of the vertical axis (factor 2). One could summarize the data by stating that consumers appear to seek two major kinds of benefits from a toothpaste: health benefits and social benefits.

Calculate Factor Scores

Following interpretation, factor scores can be calculated, if necessary. Factor analysis has its own stand-alone value. However, if the goal of factor analysis is to reduce the original set of variables to a smaller set of composite variables (factors) for use in subsequent multivariate analysis, it is useful to compute factor scores for each respondent. A factor is simply a linear combination of the original variables. The **factor scores** for the ith factor may be estimated as follows:

factor scores
Composite scores estimated for each respondent on the derived factors.

$$F_i = W_{i1}X_1 + W_{i2}X_2 + W_{i3}X_3 + \cdots + W_{ik}X_k$$

These symbols were defined earlier in the chapter.

The weights, or factor score coefficients, used to combine the standardized variables are obtained from the factor score coefficient matrix. Most computer programs allow you to request factor scores. Only in the case of principal components analysis is it possible to compute exact factor scores. Moreover, in principal component analysis, these scores are uncorrelated. In common factor analysis, estimates of these scores are obtained, and there is no guarantee that the factors will be uncorrelated with each other. The factor scores can be used instead of the original variables in subsequent multivariate analysis. For example, using the "Factor Score Coefficient Matrix" in Table 19.3, one could compute two factor scores for each respondent. The standardized variable values would be multiplied by the corresponding factor score coefficients to obtain the factor scores.

Select Surrogate Variables

Sometimes, instead of computing factor scores, the researcher wishes to select surrogate variables. Selection of substitute or *surrogate variables* involves singling out some of the original variables for use in subsequent analysis. This allows the researcher to conduct subsequent analysis and interpret the results in terms of original variables rather than factor scores. By examining the factor matrix, one could select for each factor the variable with the highest loading on that factor. That variable could then be used as a surrogate variable for the associated factor. This process works well if one factor loading for a variable is clearly higher than all other factor loadings. However, the choice is not as easy if two or more variables have similarly high loadings. In such a case, the choice between these variables should be based on theoretical and measurement considerations. For example, theory may suggest that a variable with a slightly lower loading is more important than one with a slightly higher loading. Likewise, if a variable has a slightly lower loading but has been measured more precisely, it should be selected as the surrogate variable. In Table 19.3, the variables V_1, V_3, and V_5 all have high loadings on factor 1, and all are fairly close in magnitude, although V_1 has relatively the highest loading and would therefore be a likely candidate. However, if prior knowledge suggests that prevention of tooth decay is a very important benefit, V_5 would be selected as the surrogate for factor 1. Also, the choice of a surrogate for factor 2 is not straight forward. Variables V_2, V_4, and V_6 all have comparable high loadings on this factor. If prior knowledge suggests that attractive teeth is the most important social benefit sought from a toothpaste, the researcher would select V_6.

Determine the Model Fit

The final step in factor analysis involves the determination of model fit. A basic assumption underlying factor analysis is that the observed correlation between variables can be attributed to common factors. Hence, the correlations between the variables can be deduced or reproduced from the estimated correlations between the variables and the factors. The differences between the observed correlations (as given in the input correlation matrix) and the reproduced correlations (as estimated from the factor matrix) can be examined to determine model fit. These differences are called *residuals*. If there are many large residuals, the factor model does not provide a good fit to the data and the model should be reconsidered. In the upper right triangle of the "Reproduced Correlation Matrix" of Table 19.3, we see that only five residuals are larger than 0.05, indicating an acceptable model fit.

ACTIVE RESEARCH

Nokia: Factoring Preferences for Cellular Handsets

Visit www.nokia.com and search the Internet using a search engine as well as your library's online database to obtain information on consumers' preferences for cellular handsets.

Nokia would like to determine the factors that underlie the cellular handset preferences of 15- to 24-year-olds, the heavy users of cellular handsets. What data would you collect and how would you analyze that data?

As the marketing manager for Nokia, what strategies would you formulate to target the 15- to 24-year-olds, the heavy users of cellular handsets?

Real Research   ## Manufacturing Promotion Components

The objective of this study was to develop a rather comprehensive inventory of manufacturer-controlled trade promotion variables and to demonstrate that an association exists between these variables and the retailer's promotion support decision. Retailer or trade support was defined operationally as the trade buyer's attitude toward the promotion.

Factor analysis was performed on the explanatory variables with the primary goal of data reduction. The principal components method, using varimax rotation, reduced the 30 explanatory variables to eight factors having eigenvalues greater than 1.0. For the purpose of interpretation, each factor was composed of variables that loaded 0.40 or higher on that factor. In two instances, where variables loaded 0.40 or above on two factors, each variable was assigned to the factor where it had the highest loading. Only one variable, "ease of handling/stocking at retail," did not load at least 0.40 on any factor. In all, the eight factors explained 62 percent of the total variance. Interpretation of the factor loading matrix was straightforward. Table 1 lists the factors in the order in which they were extracted.

Stepwise discriminant analysis was conducted to determine which, if any, of the eight factors predicted trade support to a statistically significant degree. The factor scores for the eight factors were the explanatory variables. The dependent variable consisted of the retail buyer's overall rating of the deal (Rating), which was collapsed into a three-group (low, medium, and high) measure of trade support. The results of the discriminant analyses are shown in Table 2. All eight entered the discriminant functions. Goodness-of-fit measures indicated that, as a group, the eight factors discriminated between high, medium, and low levels of trade support. Multivariate F ratios, indicating the degree of discrimination between each pair of groups,

Table 1 Factors Influencing Trade Promotional Support

Factor	Factor Interpretation (% variance explained)	Loading	Variables Included in the Factor
F_1	Item importance (16.3%)	0.77	Item is significant enough to warrant promotion
		0.75	Category responds well to promotion
		0.66	Closest trade competitor is likely to promote item
		0.64	Importance of promoted product category
		0.59	Item regular (nondeal) sales volume
		0.57	Deal meshes with trade promotional requirements
F_2	Promotion elasticity (9.3%)		Buyer's estimate of sales increase on the basis of:
		0.86	Price reduction and display
		0.82	Display only
		0.80	Price reduction only
		0.70	Price reduction, display, and advertising
F_3	Manufacturer brand support (8.2%)		Manufacturer's brand support in form of:
		0.85	Coupons
		0.81	Radio and television advertising
		0.80	Newspaper advertising
		0.75	Point-of-purchase promotion (e.g., display)
F_4	Manufacturer reputation (7.3%)	0.72	Manufacturer's overall reputation
		0.72	Manufacturer cooperates in meeting trade's promotional needs
		0.64	Manufacturer cooperates on emergency orders
		0.55	Quality of sales presentation
		0.51	Manufacturer's overall product quality
F_5	Promotion wearout (6.4%)	0.93	Product category is overpromoted
		0.93	Item is overpromoted
F_6	Sales velocity (5.4%)	−0.81	Brand market share rank[a]
		0.69	Item regular sales volume[a]
		0.46	Item regular sales volume
F_7	Item profitability (4.5%)	0.79	Item regular gross margin
		0.72	Item regular gross margin[a]
		0.49	Reasonableness of deal performance requirements
F_8	Incentive amount (4.2%)	0.83	Absolute amount of deal allowances
		0.81	Deal allowances as percent of regular trade cost[a]
		0.49	Absolute amount of deal allowances[a]

[a]Denotes objective (archival) measure

Table 2 Discriminant Analysis Results: Analysis of Rating ($N = 564$)

Factor		Standardized Discriminant Coefficients Analysis of Rating	
		Function 1	Function 2
F_1	Item importance	0.861	−0.253
F_2	Promotion elasticity	0.081	0.398
F_3	Manufacturer brand support	0.127	−0.036
F_4	Manufacturer reputation	0.394	0.014
F_5	Promotion wearout	−0.207	0.380
F_6	Sales velocity	0.033	−0.665
F_7	Item profitability	0.614	0.357
F_8	Incentive amount	0.461	0.254
	Wilks' λ (for each factor)	All significant at $p < 0.001$	
	Multivariate F ratios	All significant at $p < 0.001$	
	% Cases correctly classified	65% correct	

Table 3 Relative Importance of Trade Support Influencers (as Indicated by Order of Entry into the Discriminant Analysis)

Analysis of Rating	
Order of Entry	Factor Name
1	Item importance
2	Item profitability
3	Incentive amount
4	Manufacturer reputation
5	Promotion wearout
6	Sales velocity
7	Promotion elasticity
8	Manufacturer brand support

were significant at $p < 0.001$. Correct classification into high, medium, and low categories was achieved for 65 percent of the cases. The order of entry into discriminant analysis was used to determine the relative importance of factors as trade support influencers, as shown in Table 3.[9]

In keeping with the results of this study, P&G decided to emphasize item importance, item profitability, incentive amount, and its reputation in order to garner retailers' promotion support. Partially as a result of these efforts, P&G brands touched the lives of people around the world three billion times a day in 2009. ∎

Applications of Common Factor Analysis

The data of Table 19.1 were analyzed using the common factor analysis model. Instead of using unities in the diagonal, the communalities were inserted. The output, shown in Table 19.4, is similar to the output from principal components analysis presented in Table 19.3. Under "Communalities" under the "Initial" column, the communalities for the variables are no longer 1.0. Based on the eigenvalue criterion, again two factors are extracted. The variances, after extracting the factors, are different from the initial eigenvalues. The first factor accounts for 42.84 percent of the variance, whereas the second accounts for 31.13 percent, in each case a little less than what was observed in principal components analysis.

The values in the unrotated "Factor Matrix" of Table 19.4 are a little different from those in Table 19.3, although the pattern of the coefficients is similar. Sometimes, however, the pattern of loadings for common factor analysis is different from that for principal components analysis, with some variables loading on different factors. The rotated factor matrix has the same pattern as that in Table 19.3, leading to a similar interpretation of the factors. Another application is provided in the context of "common" rebate perceptions.

ACTIVE RESEARCH

Wendy's: How Old Fashioned Is Consumer's Choice Criteria for Fast Foods

Visit www.wendys.com and search the Internet using a search engine as well as your library's online database to determine the choice criteria of consumers in selecting a fast-food restaurant.

As the marketing director for Wendy's, what marketing strategies would you formulate to increase your patronage?

Describe the data you would collect and the analysis you would conduct to determine the choice criteria of consumers in selecting a fast-food restaurant.

SPSS Output File

SAS Output File

TABLE 19.4
Results of Common Factor Analysis

Bartlett test of sphericity
Approx. chi-square = 111.314, df = 15, significance = 0.00000
Kaiser-Meyer-Olkin measure of sampling adequacy = 0.660

Communalities

Variable	Initial	Extraction
V_1	0.859	0.928
V_2	0.480	0.562
V_3	0.814	0.836
V_4	0.543	0.600
V_5	0.763	0.789
V_6	0.587	0.723

Initial Eigenvalues

Factor	Eigenvalue	% of Variance	Cumulative %
1	2.731	45.520	45.520
2	2.218	36.969	82.488
3	0.442	7.360	89.848
4	0.341	5.688	95.536
5	0.183	3.044	98.580
6	0.085	1.420	100.000

Extraction Sums of Squared Loadings

Factor	Eigenvalue	% of Variance	Cumulative %
1	2.570	42.837	42.837
2	1.868	31.126	73.964

Factor Matrix

	Factor 1	Factor 2
V_1	0.949	0.168
V_2	−0.206	0.720
V_3	0.914	0.038
V_4	−0.246	0.734
V_5	−0.850	−0.259
V_6	−0.101	0.844

Rotation Sums of Squared Loadings

Factor	Eigenvalue	% of Variance	Cumulative %
1	2.541	42.343	42.343
2	1.897	31.621	73.964

Rotated Factor Matrix

	Factor 1	Factor 2
V_1	0.963	−0.030
V_2	−0.054	0.747
V_3	0.902	−0.150
V_4	−0.090	0.769
V_5	−0.885	−0.079
V_6	0.075	0.847

(continued)

TABLE 19.4
Results of Common Factor Analysis (*continued*)

Factor Score Coefficient Matrix

	Factor 1	Factor 2
V_1	0.628	0.101
V_2	−0.024	0.253
V_3	0.217	−0.169
V_4	−0.023	0.271
V_5	−0.166	−0.059
V_6	0.083	0.500

Reproduced Correlation Matrix

	V_1	V_2	V_3	V_4	V_5	V_6
V_1	0.928*	0.022	−0.000	0.024	−0.008	−0.042
V_2	−0.075	0.562*	0.006	−0.008	0.031	0.012
V_3	0.873	−0.161	0.836*	−0.051	0.008	0.042
V_4	−0.110	0.580	−0.197	0.600*	−0.025	−0.004
V_5	−0.850	−0.012	−0.786	0.019	0.789*	−0.003
V_6	0.046	0.629	−0.060	0.645	−0.133	0.723*

*The lower left triangle contains the reproduced correlation matrix; the diagonal, the communalities; the upper right triangle, the residuals between the observed correlations and the reproduced correlations.

Real Research

"Common" Rebate Perceptions

Rebates are effective in obtaining new users, brand-switching, and repeat purchases among current users. In March 2009, AT&T deployed a rebate program as a means to draw new users to their Internet services. AT&T's intent behind this rebate plan was to acquire new users from rivals such as Verizon. What makes rebates effective?

A study was undertaken to determine the factors underlying consumer perception of rebates. A set of 24 items measuring consumer perceptions of rebates was constructed. Respondents were asked to express their degree of agreement with these items on 5-point Likert scales. The data were collected by a one-stage area telephone survey conducted in the Memphis metropolitan area. A total of 303 usable questionnaires were obtained.

The 24 items measuring perceptions of rebates were analyzed using common factor analysis. The initial factor solution did not reveal a simple structure of underlying rebate perceptions. Therefore, items that had low loadings were deleted from the scale, and the factor analysis was performed on the remaining items. This second solution yielded three interpretable factors. The factor loadings are presented in the accompanying table, where large loadings have been underscored. The three factors contained four, four, and three items,

Factor Analysis of Perceptions of Rebates

	Factor Loading		
Scale Items[a]	Factor 1	Factor 2	Factor 3
Manufacturers make the rebate process too complicated.	0.194	0.671	−0.127
Mail-in rebates are not worth the trouble involved.	−0.031	0.612	0.352
It takes too long to receive the rebate check from the manufacturer.	0.013	0.718	0.051
Manufacturers could do more to make rebates easier to use.	0.205	0.616	0.173
Manufacturers offer rebates because consumers want them.[b]	0.660	0.172	0.101
Today's manufacturers take a real interest in consumer welfare.[b]	0.569	0.203	0.334
Consumer benefit is usually the primary consideration in rebate offers.[b]	0.660	0.002	0.318

(continued)

Factor Analysis of Perceptions of Rebates   (*continued*)

Scale Items[a]	Factor Loading		
	Factor 1	Factor 2	Factor 3
In general, manufacturers are sincere in their rebate offers to consumers.[b]	0.716	0.047	−0.033
Manufacturers offer rebates to get consumers to buy something they don't really need.	0.099	0.156	0.744
Manufacturers use rebate offers to induce consumers to buy slow-moving items.	0.090	0.027	0.702
Rebate offers require you to buy more of a product than you need.	0.230	0.066	0.527
Eigenvalues	2.030	1.344	1.062
Percentage of explained variance	27.500	12.200	9.700

[a]The response categories for all items were: strongly agree (1), agree (2), neither agree nor disagree (3), disagree (4), strongly disagree (5), and don't know (6). "Don't know" responses were excluded from data analysis.
[b]The scores of these items were reversed.

respectively. Factor 1 was defined as a representation of consumers' faith in the rebate system (Faith). Factor 2 seemed to capture the consumers' perceptions of the efforts and difficulties associated with rebateredemption (Efforts). Factor 3 represented consumers' perceptions of the manufacturers' motives for offering rebates (Motives). The loadings of items on their respective factor ranged from 0.527 to 0.744.

Therefore, companies such as AT&T that employ rebates should ensure that the effort and difficulties of consumers in taking advantage of the rebates are minimized. They should also try to build consumers' faith in the rebate system and portray honest motives for offering rebates.[10] ■

Note that in this example, when the initial factor solution was not interpretable, items that had low loadings were deleted and the factor analysis was performed on the remaining items. If the number of variables is large (greater than 15), principal components analysis and common factor analysis result in similar solutions. However, principal components analysis is less prone to misinterpretation and is recommended for the nonexpert user. The next example illustrates an application of principal components analysis in international marketing research, and the example after that presents an application in the area of ethics.

Real Research   ## Driving Nuts for Beetles

Generally, with time, consumer needs and tastes change. Consumer preferences for automobiles need to be continually tracked to identify changing demands and specifications. However, there is one car that is quite an exception—the Volkswagen Beetle. More than 22 million have been built since it was introduced in 1938. Surveys have been conducted in different countries to determine the reasons why people purchase Beetles. Principal components analyses of the variables measuring the reasons for owning Beetles have consistently revealed one dominant factor—fanatical loyalty. The company has long wished for the car's natural death but without any effect. This noisy and cramped "bug" has inspired devotion in drivers. Now old bugs are being sought everywhere. "The Japanese are going absolutely nuts for Beetles," says Jack Finn, a recycler of old Beetles in West Palm Beach, Florida. Because of faithful loyalty to the "bug," VW reintroduced it in 1998 as the New Beetle. The New Beetle has proven itself as much more than a sequel to its legendary namesake. It has won several distinguished automotive awards. The 2009 Beetle was offered in coupe and convertible versions and the base model had a starting MSRP of $17,990.[11] ■

Real Research   ## Factors Predicting Unethical Marketing Research Practices

Unethical employee behavior was identified as a root cause for the global banking and financial mess of 2008–2009. If companies want ethical employees, then they themselves must conform to high ethical standards. This also applies to the marketing research industry. In order to identify organizational variables that are determinants of the incidence of unethical marketing research practices, a sample of 420 marketing professionals was surveyed. These marketing professionals were asked to provide responses on several scales, and to provide evaluations of incidence of 15 research practices that have been found to pose research ethics problems.

Factor Analysis of Ethical Problems and Top Management Action Scales

	Extent of Ethical Problems Within the Organization (Factor 1)	Top Management Actions on Ethics (Factor 2)
1. Successful executives in my company make rivals look bad in the eyes of important people in my company.	0.66	
2. Peer executives in my company often engage in behaviors that I consider to be unethical.	0.68	
3. There are many opportunities for peer executives in my company to engage in unethical behaviors.	0.43	
4. Successful executives in my company take credit for the ideas and accomplishment of others.	0.81	
5. In order to succeed in my company, it is often necessary to compromise one's ethics.	0.66	
6. Successful executives in my company are generally more unethical than unsuccessful executives.	0.64	
7. Successful executives in my company look for a "scapegoat" when they feel they may be associated with failure.	0.78	
8. Successful executives in my company withhold information that is detrimental to their self-interest.	0.68	
9. Top management in my company has let it be known in no uncertain terms that unethical behaviors will not be tolerated.		0.73
10. If an executive in my company is discovered to have engaged in unethical behavior that results primarily in personal gain (rather than corporate gain), he/she will be promptly reprimanded.		0.80
11. If an executive in my company is discovered to have engaged in an unethical behavior that results primarily in corporate gain (rather than personal gain), he/she will be promptly reprimanded.		0.78
Eigenvalue	5.06	1.17
% of Variance Explained	46%	11%
Coefficient Alpha	0.87	0.75

To simplify the table, only varimax rotated loadings of 0.40 or greater are reported. Each was rated on a 5-point scale with 1 = "strongly agree" and 5 = "strongly disagree."

One of these scales included 11 items pertaining to the extent that ethical problems plagued the organization, and what top management's actions were toward ethical situations. A principal components analysis with varimax rotation indicated that the data could be represented by two factors.

These two factors were then used in a multiple regression along with four other predictor variables. They were found to be the two best predictors of unethical marketing research practices.[12] ■

Decision Research   Tiffany: Focusing on the Core

The Situation

Tiffany & Co. (www.tiffany.com) is the internationally renowned retailer, designer, manufacturer, and distributor of fine jewelry, timepieces, sterling silverware, china, crystal, stationery, fragrances, and accessories. Founded in 1837 by Charles Lewis Tiffany, there were 184 Tiffany & Co. stores and boutiques that served customers in the United States and international markets in 2009. Tiffany's main growth strategies consist of expanding its channels of distribution in important markets around the world, complementing its existing product offerings with an active product development program, enhancing customer awareness of its product designs, quality, and value, and providing levels of customer service that guarantee a great shopping experience. Tiffany & Company's revenues exceeded $2.94 billion in 2008.

Tiffany is slowly and subtly embracing the middle class, a potential danger for one of retail's most exclusive names. Over the past decade, the luxury jewelry retailer has nearly tripled its stores in the United States and changed its promotions to highlight more lower-price wares. It currently has 70 U.S. locations and another 114 overseas. Tiffany's new 5,000-square-foot format will allow it to also expand into smaller markets and double up in bigger towns. In the process of reaching out to embrace more markets, Tiffany

Factor analysis can help
Tiffany identify the
psychographic profile
of its core customers.

may be driving away some of its core customers. Although Tiffany has a long way to go before it is fully accessible, the Tiffany Heart Tag silver bracelet has become quite a popular item among many, including Reese Witherspoon and her entourage in *Legally Blonde*. Mr. James E. Quinn, president, is wondering what the psychographic profile of Tiffany's core customers is and what the company should do to maintain and build upon the loyalty of its core customers. This is critical to success in the future.

The Marketing Research Decision

1. What data should be collected and how should they be analyzed to determine the psychographic profile of Tiffany's core customers?
2. Discuss the role of the type of research you recommend in enabling James E. Quinn to maintain and build upon the loyalty of Tiffany's core customers.

The Marketing Management Decision

1. What new strategies should James E. Quinn formulate to target the core customers?
2. Discuss how the marketing management decision action that you recommend to James E. Quinn is influenced by the data analysis that you suggested earlier and by the likely findings.[13] ■

Statistical Software

Computer programs are available to implement both of the approaches: principal components analysis and common factor analysis. We discuss the use of SPSS and SAS in detail in the subsequent sections. Here, we briefly describe the use of MINITAB. In MINITAB, factor analysis can be assessed using Multivariate>Factor analysis. Principal components or maximum likelihood can be used to determine the initial factor extraction. If maximum likelihood is used, specify the number of factors to extract. If a number is not specified with a principal component extraction, the program will set it equal to a number of variables in the data set. Factor analysis is not available in EXCEL.

SPSS and SAS Computerized Demonstration Movies

We have developed computerized demonstration movies that give step-by-step instructions for running all the SPSS and SAS Learning Edition programs that are discussed in this chapter. These demonstrations can be downloaded from the Web site for this book. The instructions for running these demonstrations are given in Exhibit 14.2.

SPSS and SAS Screen Captures with Notes

The step-by-step instructions for running the various SPSS and SAS Learning Edition programs discussed in this chapter are also illustrated in screen captures with appropriate notes. These screen captures can be downloaded from the Web site for this book.

SPSS Windows

To select this procedure using SPSS for Windows, click:

Analyze>Data Reduction>Factor . . .

The following are the detailed steps for running principal components analysis on the toothpaste attribute ratings (V_1 to V_6) using the data of Table 19.1.

1. Select ANALYZE from the SPSS menu bar.
2. Click DIMENSION REDUCTION and then FACTOR.
3. Move "Prevents Cavities [v1]," "Shiny Teeth [v2]," "Strengthen Gums [v3]," "Freshens Breath [v4]," "Tooth Decay Unimportant [v5]," and "Attractive Teeth [v6]." into the VARIABLES box.
4. Click on DESCRIPTIVES. In the pop-up window, in the STATISTICS box check INITIAL SOLUTION. In the CORRELATION MATRIX box check KMO AND BARTLETT'S TEST OF SPHERICITY and also check REPRODUCED. Click CONTINUE.
5. Click on EXTRACTION. In the pop-up window, for METHOD select PRINCIPAL COMPONENTS (default). In the ANALYZE box, check CORRELATION MATRIX. In the EXTRACT box, select BASED ON EIGENVALUE and enter 1 for EIGENVALUES GREATER THAN box. In the DISPLAY box check UNROTATED FACTOR SOLUTION. Click CONTINUE.
6. Click on ROTATION. In the METHOD box check VARIMAX. In the DISPLAY box check ROTATED SOLUTION. Click CONTINUE.
7. Click on SCORES. In the pop-up window, check DISPLAY FACTOR SCORE COEFFICIENT MATRIX. Click CONTINUE.
8. Click OK.

The procedure for running common factor analysis is similar, except that in step 5, for METHOD select PRINCIPAL AXIS FACTORING.

SAS Learning Edition

The instructions given here and in all the data analysis chapters (14 to 22) will work with the SAS Learning Edition as well as with the SAS Enterprise Guide. For a point-and-click approach for performing principal components analysis and factor analysis, use the Analyze task within the SAS Learning Edition. The Multivariate>Factor Analysis tasks performs both Principal Components Analysis and Factor Analysis. The Multivariate>Principal Components tasks also performs Principal Components Analysis.

To perform principal components analysis, click:

Analyze>Multivariate>Factor Analysis

The following are the detailed steps for running principal components analysis on the toothpaste attribute ratings (V_1 to V_6) using the data of Table 19.1.

1. Select ANALYZE from the SAS Learning Edition menu bar.
2. Click MULTIVARIATE and then FACTOR ANALYSIS.
3. Move V1-V6 to the ANALYSIS variables task role.
4. Click FACTORING METHOD and change the SMALLEST EIGENVALUE to 1.
5. Click on ROTATION AND PLOTS and select ORTHOGONAL VARIMAX as the Rotation method and the SCREE PLOT under the PLOTS TO SHOW.
6. Click on RESULTS and select EIGENVECTORS, FACTOR SCORING COEFFICIENTS under FACTOR RESULTS, and MEANS AND STANDARD DEVIATIONS of input columns, CORRELATION MATRIX of input columns and KAISER'S MEASURE OF SAMPLING ADEQUACY under RELATED STATISTICS.
7. Click RUN.

The procedure for running common factor analysis is similar, except that in step 5, select PRINCIPAL AXIS FACTORING as the ROTATION METHOD.

Project Research Factor Analysis

SPSS Data File

SAS Data File

In the department store project, the respondents' ratings of 21 lifestyle statements were factor analyzed to determine the underlying lifestyle factors. Seven factors emerged: bank card versus store card preference, credit proneness, credit avoidance, leisure time orientation, credit card favorableness, credit convenience, and credit card cost consciousness. These factors, along with the demographic characteristics, were used to profile the segments formed as a result of clustering.

Project Activities

Download the SPSS or SAS data file *Sears Data 17* from the Web site for this book. See Chapter 17 for a description of this file.

1. Can the 21 lifestyle statements be represented by a reduced set of factors? If so, what would be the interpretation of these factors? Conduct a principal components analysis and save the factor scores.
2. Can the importance attached to the eight factors of the choice criteria be represented by a reduced set of factors? If so, what would be the interpretation of these factors? Conduct a principal components analysis. ∎

Summary

Factor analysis, also called exploratory factor analysis (EFA), is a class of procedures used for reducing and summarizing data. Each variable is expressed as a linear combination of the underlying factors. Likewise, the factors themselves can be expressed as linear combinations of the observed variables. The factors are extracted in such a way that the first factor accounts for the highest variance in the data, the second the next highest, and so on. Additionally, it is possible to extract the factors so that the factors are uncorrelated, as in principal components analysis. Figure 19.7 gives a concept map for factor analysis.

FIGURE 19.7

A Concept Map for Factor Analysis

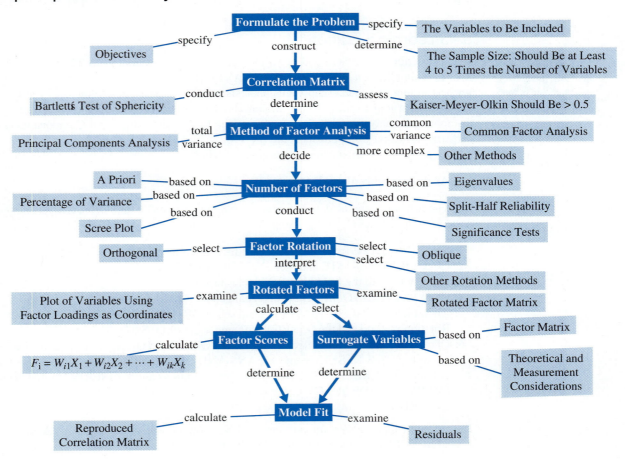

In formulating the factor analysis problem, the variables to be included in the analysis should be specified based on past research, theory, and the judgment of the researcher. These variables should be measured on an interval or ratio scale. Factor analysis is based on a matrix of correlation between the variables. The appropriateness of the correlation matrix for factor analysis can be statistically tested.

The two basic approaches to factor analysis are principal components analysis and common factor analysis. In principal components analysis, the total variance in the data is considered. Principal components analysis is recommended when the researcher's primary concern is to determine the minimum number of factors that will account for maximum variance in the data for use in subsequent multivariate analysis. In common factor analysis, the factors are estimated based only on the common variance. This method is appropriate when the primary concern is to identify the underlying dimensions, and when the common variance is of interest. This method is also known as principal axis factoring.

The number of factors that should be extracted can be determined *a priori* or based on eigenvalues, scree plots, percentage of variance, split-half reliability, or significance tests. Although the initial or unrotated factor matrix indicates the relationship between the factors and individual variables, it seldom results in factors that can be interpreted, because the factors are correlated with many variables. Therefore, rotation is used to transform the factor matrix into a simpler one that is easier to interpret. The most commonly used method of rotation is the varimax procedure, which results in orthogonal factors. If the factors are highly correlated in the population, oblique rotation can be utilized. The rotated factor matrix forms the basis for interpreting the factors.

Factor scores can be computed for each respondent. Alternatively, surrogate variables may be selected by examining the factor matrix and selecting for each factor a variable with the highest or near highest loading. The differences between the observed correlations and the reproduced correlations, as estimated from the factor matrix, can be examined to determine model fit.

Key Terms and Concepts

factor analysis, 604
interdependence technique, 604
factors, 604
Bartlett's test of sphericity, 606
correlation matrix, 606
communality, 606
eigenvalue, 606
factor loadings, 606

factor loading plot, 606
factor matrix, 606
factor scores coefficient matrix, 606
Kaiser-Meyer-Olkin (KMO) measure
  of sampling adequacy, 606
percentage of variance, 606
residuals, 606
scree plot, 606

principal components analysis, 611
common factor analysis, 611
orthogonal rotation, 613
varimax procedure, 613
oblique rotation, 613
factor scores, 614

Suggested Cases, Video Cases, and HBS Cases

Running Case with Real Data

1.1 Dell

Comprehensive Critical Thinking Cases

2.1 American Idol   2.2 Baskin-Robbins   2.3 Akron Children's Hospital

Data Analysis Cases with Real Data

3.1 AT&T   3.2 IBM   3.3 Kimberly-Clark

Comprehensive Cases with Real Data

4.1 JPMorgan Chase   4.2 Wendy's

Video Case

23.1 Marriott

Live Research: Conducting a Marketing Research Project

1. The objectives of factor analysis should be clearly specified.
2. If multicollinearity is a problem, factor analysis can be used to generate uncorrelated factor scores or to identify a smaller set of the original variables, which can be used in subsequent multivariate analysis.
3. It is instructive to use different guidelines for determining the number of factors and different methods of rotation and to examine the effect on the factor solutions.

Acronym

The steps involved in conducting factor analysis may be summarized by the acronym

Factor Step:

F   ormulate the problem
A   *priori* or otherwise determine the number of factors
C   orrelation matrix
T   est for the appropriateness of factor analysis
O   bserve the rotated factor matrix: interpretation of factors
R   otation

S   urrogate variable
T   esting for model fit
E   stimate the factor scores
P   rincipal components or common factor analysis

Exercises

Questions

1. How is factor analysis different from multiple regression and discriminant analysis?
2. What are the major uses of factor analysis?
3. Describe the factor analysis model.
4. What hypothesis is examined by Bartlett's test of sphericity? For what purpose is this test used?
5. What is meant by the term "communality of a variable"?
6. Briefly define the following: eigenvalue, factor loadings, factor matrix, factor scores.
7. For what purpose is the Kaiser-Meyer-Olkin measure of sampling adequacy used?
8. What is the major difference between principal components analysis and common factor analysis?
9. Explain how eigenvalues are used to determine the number of factors.
10. What is a scree plot? For what purpose is it used?
11. Why is it useful to rotate the factors? Which is the most common method of rotation?
12. What guidelines are available for interpreting the factors?
13. When is it useful to calculate factor scores?
14. What are surrogate variables? How are they determined?
15. How is the fit of the factor analysis model examined?

Problems

1. Complete the following portion of an output from principal component analysis:

Variable	Communality	Factor	Eigenvalue	% of Variance
V_1	1.0	1	3.25	
V_2	1.0	2	1.78	
V_3	1.0	3	1.23	
V_4	1.0	4	0.78	
V_5	1.0	5	0.35	
V_6	1.0	6	0.30	
V_7	1.0	7	0.19	
V_8	1.0	8	0.12	

2. Draw a scree plot based on the data given in problem 1.
3. How many factors should be extracted in problem 1? Explain your reasoning.

Internet and Computer Exercises

1. In a study of the relationship between household behavior and shopping behavior, data on the following lifestyle statements were obtained on a 7-point scale (1 = disagree, 7 = agree):

   V_1 I would rather spend a quiet evening at home than go out to a party.
   V_2 I always check prices, even on small items.
   V_3 Magazines are more interesting than movies.
   V_4 I would not buy products advertised on billboards.
   V_5 I am a homebody.
   V_6 I save and cash coupons.
   V_7 Companies waste a lot of money advertising.

   The data obtained from a pretest sample of 25 respondents are given in the following table:
   a. Analyze this data using principal components analysis, using the varimax rotation procedure.
   b. Interpret the factors extracted.
   c. Calculate factor scores for each respondent.

SPSS SPSS Data File   **Ssas** SAS Data File

No.	V_1	V_2	V_3	V_4	V_5	V_6	V_7
1	6	2	7	6	5	3	5
2	5	7	5	6	6	6	4
3	5	3	4	5	6	6	7
4	3	2	2	5	1	3	2
5	4	2	3	2	2	1	3
6	2	6	2	4	3	7	5
7	1	3	3	6	2	5	7
8	3	5	1	4	2	5	6
9	7	3	6	3	5	2	4
10	6	3	3	4	4	6	5
11	6	6	2	6	4	4	7
12	3	2	2	7	6	1	6
13	5	7	6	2	2	6	1
14	6	3	5	5	7	2	3
15	3	2	4	3	2	6	5

16	2	7	5	1	4	5	2
17	3	2	2	7	2	4	6
18	6	4	5	4	7	3	3
19	7	2	6	2	5	2	1
20	5	6	6	3	4	5	3
21	2	3	3	2	1	2	6
22	3	4	2	1	4	3	6
23	2	6	3	2	1	5	3
24	6	5	7	4	5	7	2
25	7	6	5	4	6	5	3

d. If surrogate variables were to be selected, which ones would you select?

e. Examine the model fit.

f. Analyze the data using common factor analysis, and answer questions b through e again.

2. Conduct the following analysis on the Nike data given in Internet and Computer Exercises 1 of Chapter 15. Consider only the following variables: awareness, attitude, preference, intention, and loyalty toward Nike.

   a. Analyze this data using principal components analysis, using the varimax rotation procedure.

   b. Interpret the factors extracted.

   c. Calculate factor scores for each respondent.

   d. If surrogate variables were to be selected, which ones would you select?

   e. Examine the model fit.

   f. Analyze the data using common factor analysis, and answer questions b through e again.

3. Conduct the following analysis on the outdoor lifestyle data given in Internet and Computer Exercises 2 of Chapter 15. Consider only the following variables: the importance attached

to enjoying nature, relating to the weather, living in harmony with the environment, exercising regularly, and meeting other people (V_2 to V_6).

   a. Analyze this data using principal components analysis, using the varimax rotation procedure.

   b. Interpret the factors extracted.

   c. Calculate factor scores for each respondent.

   d. If surrogate variables were to be selected, which ones would you select?

   e. Examine the model fit.

   f. Analyze the data using common factor analysis, and answer questions b through e again.

4. Conduct the following analysis on the sneakers data given in Internet and Computer Exercises 3 of Chapter 17. Consider only the following variables: evaluations of the sneakers on comfort (V_2), style (V_3), and durability (V_4).

   a. Analyze this data using principal components analysis, using the varimax rotation procedure.

   b. Interpret the factors extracted.

   c. Calculate factor scores for each respondent.

   d. If surrogate variables were to be selected, which ones would you select?

   e. Examine the model fit.

   f. Analyze the data using common factor analysis, and answer questions b through e again.

5. Factor analyze the clothing psychographic and lifestyle data collected in Fieldwork Activity 1, using principal components analysis. Use an appropriate program from SPSS, SAS, or MINITAB.

6. Factor analyze the leisure time data collected in Fieldwork Activity 2, using common factor analysis. Use SPSS, SAS, or MINITAB.

Activities

Role Playing

1. You have been hired as a marketing research analyst by Kroger, a major supermarket. Your boss, the marketing manager, is wondering whether the ratings of Kroger's customers on 15 lifestyle factors can be represented more succinctly. Explain to your boss (a student in your class) the analysis that you would conduct.

Fieldwork

1. You are a marketing research analyst for a manufacturer of casual clothing. You have been asked to develop a set of 10 statements for measuring student psychographic characteristics and lifestyles, because they may relate to the use of casual clothing. The respondents will be asked to indicate their degree of agreement with the statements using a 7-point scale

($1 =$ completely disagree, $7 =$ completely agree). Obtain data from 40 students on your campus.

2. You have been commissioned by a manufacturer of sporting goods to determine student attitudes toward leisure behavior. Construct an 8-item scale for this purpose. Administer this scale to 35 students on the campus.

Group Discussion

1. As a small group, identify the uses of factor analysis in each of the following major decision areas in marketing:

   a. Market segmentation

   b. Product decisions

   c. Promotion decisions

   d. Pricing decisions

   e. Distribution decisions

Dell Running Case

Review the Dell case, Case 1.1, and questionnaire given toward the end of the book. Go to the Web site for this book and download the Dell data file.

1. Can evaluations of Dell (variables q8_1 through Q8_13) be represented by a reduced set of factors? If so, what would be the interpretation of these factors? (*Hint:* Do a principal components analysis with varimax rotation.)

2. Can the Market Maven, Innovativeness, and Opinion Leadership items (variables q10_1 through Q10_13) be represented by a reduced set of factors? If so, what would be the interpretation of these factors? (*Hint:* Do a principal components analysis with varimax rotation.)

20

Cluster analysis helps us identify groups or

segments that are more like each other

than they are like members of other

groups or segments."

Tom Myers, Senior Vice President,
Client Services Manager, Burke, Inc.

Objectives   [After reading this chapter, the student should be able to:]

1. Describe the basic concept and scope of cluster analysis and its importance in marketing research.

2. Discuss the statistics associated with cluster analysis.

3. Explain the procedure for conducting cluster analysis, including formulating the problem, selecting a distance measure, selecting a clustering procedure, deciding on the number of clusters, and interpreting and profiling clusters.

4. Describe the purpose and methods for evaluating the quality of clustering results and assessing reliability and validity.

5. Discuss the applications of nonhierarchical clustering and clustering of variables.

Cluster Analysis

Overview

Like factor analysis (Chapter 19), cluster analysis examines an entire set of interdependent relationships. Cluster analysis makes no distinction between dependent and independent variables. Rather, interdependent relationships between the whole set of variables are examined. The primary objective of cluster analysis is to classify objects into relatively homogeneous groups based on the set of variables considered. Objects in a group are relatively similar in terms of these variables and different from objects in other groups. When used in this manner, cluster analysis is the obverse of factor analysis, in that it reduces the number of objects, not the number of variables, by grouping them into a much smaller number of clusters.

This chapter describes the basic concept of cluster analysis. The steps involved in conducting cluster analysis are discussed and illustrated in the context of hierarchical clustering by using a popular computer program. Then an application of nonhierarchical clustering is presented, followed by the TwoStep procedure and a discussion of clustering of variables.

Finally, we discuss the use of software in cluster analysis. Help for running the SPSS and SAS Learning Edition programs used in this chapter is provided in four ways: (1) detailed step-by-step instructions are given later in the chapter, (2) you can download (from the Web site for this book) computerized demonstration movies illustrating these step-by-step instructions, (3) you can download screen captures with notes illustrating these step-by-step instructions, and (4) you can refer to the *Study Guide and Technology Manual*, a supplement that accompanies this book.

To begin, we provide some examples to illustrate the usefulness of cluster analysis.

Real Research

Ice Cream Shops for "Hot" Regions

Häagen-Dazs Shoppe Co. (www.haagen-dazs.com), with more than 850 retail ice cream shops in over 50 countries in 2009, was interested in expanding its customer base. The objective was to identify potential consumer segments that could generate additional sales. Geodemography, a method of clustering

Häagen-Dazs increased its penetration by identifying geodemographic clusters offering potential for increased ice cream sales.

consumers based on geographic, demographic, and lifestyle characteristics, was employed for this purpose. Primary research was conducted to develop demographic and psychographic profiles of Häagen-Dazs Shoppe users, including frequency of purchase, time of the day they came in, day of the week, and other product use variables. The addresses and zip codes of the respondents were also obtained. The respondents were then assigned to 40 geodemographic clusters based on the clustering procedure developed by Nielsen Claritas (www.claritas.com). For each geodemographic cluster, the profile of Häagen-Dazs customers was compared to the cluster profile to determine the degree of penetration. Using this information, Häagen-Dazs was also able to identify several potential customer groups from which to attract traffic. In addition to expanding Häagen-Dazs' customer base, product advertising was established to target new customers accordingly. New products were introduced. As of 2009, the Häagen-Dazs brand was owned by General Mills. However, in the United States and Canada, Häagen-Dazs products were produced by Nestlé under a preexisting license.[1] ■

The Häagen-Dazs example illustrates the use of clustering to arrive at homogeneous segments for the purpose of formulating specific marketing strategies.

Basic Concept

Cluster analysis is a class of techniques used to classify objects or cases into relatively homogeneous groups called *clusters*. Objects in each cluster tend to be similar to each other and dissimilar to objects in the other clusters. Cluster analysis is also called *classification analysis,* or *numerical taxonomy.*[2] We will be concerned with clustering procedures that assign each object to one and only one cluster.[3] Figure 20.1 shows an ideal clustering situation, in which the clusters are distinctly separated on two variables: quality consciousness (variable 1) and price sensitivity (variable 2). Note that each consumer falls into one cluster and there are no overlapping areas. Figure 20.2, on the other hand, presents a clustering situation that is more likely to be encountered in practice. In Figure 20.2, the boundaries for some of the clusters are not clear-cut, and the classification of some consumers is not obvious, because many of them could be grouped into one cluster or another.

FIGURE 20.1

An Ideal Clustering Situation

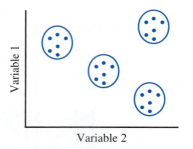

FIGURE 20.2

A Practical Clustering Situation

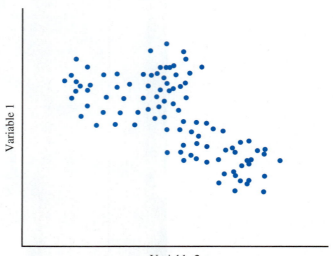

Both cluster analysis and discriminant analysis are concerned with classification. However, discriminant analysis requires prior knowledge of the cluster or group membership for each object or case included to develop the classification rule. In contrast, in cluster analysis there is no *a priori* information about the group or cluster membership for any of the objects. Groups or clusters are suggested by the data, not defined *a priori*.[4]

Cluster analysis has been used in marketing for a variety of purposes, including the following:[5]

- *Segmenting the market*: For example, consumers may be clustered on the basis of benefits sought from the purchase of a product. Each cluster would consist of consumers who are relatively homogeneous in terms of the benefits they seek.[6] This approach is called *benefit segmentation*.

Real Research

The Vacationing Demanders, Educationalists, and Escapists

In a study examining decision-making patterns among international vacationers, 260 respondents provided information on six psychographic orientations: psychological, educational, social, relaxational, physiological, and aesthetic. Cluster analysis was used to group respondents into psychographic segments. The results suggested that there were three meaningful segments based upon these lifestyles. The first segment (53 percent) consisted of individuals who were high on nearly all lifestyle scales. This group was called the "demanders." The second group (20 percent) was high on the educational scale and was named the "educationalists." The last group (26 percent) was high on relaxation and low on social scales and was named the "escapists." Specific marketing strategies were formulated to attract vacationers in each segment. In order to recover from the aftermath of the economic downturn in 2008–2009, Thailand made a special effort to reach the "escapists" segment in 2010, because the country would appeal the most to these vacationers, given its many relaxation opportunities rich in natural beauty.[7] ■

- *Understanding buyer behaviors*: Cluster analysis can be used to identify homogeneous groups of buyers. Then the buying behavior of each group may be examined separately, as in the department store project, where respondents were clustered on the basis of self-reported importance attached to each factor of the choice criteria utilized in selecting a department store. Cluster analysis has also been used to identify the kinds of strategies automobile purchasers use to obtain external information.
- *Identifying new product opportunities*: By clustering brands and products, competitive sets within the market can be determined. Brands in the same cluster compete more fiercely with each other than with brands in other clusters. A firm can examine its current offerings compared to those of its competitors to identify potential new product opportunities.
- *Selecting test markets*: By grouping cities into homogeneous clusters, it is possible to select comparable cities to test various marketing strategies.
- *Reducing data*: Cluster analysis can be used as a general data reduction tool to develop clusters or subgroups of data that are more manageable than individual observations. Subsequent multivariate analysis is conducted on the clusters rather than on the individual observations. For example, to describe differences in consumers' product usage behavior, the consumers may first be clustered into groups. The differences among the groups may then be examined using multiple discriminant analysis.

Statistics Associated with Cluster Analysis

Before discussing the statistics associated with cluster analysis, it should be mentioned that most clustering methods are relatively simple procedures that are not supported by an extensive body of statistical reasoning. Rather, most clustering methods are heuristics, which are based on algorithms. Thus, cluster analysis contrasts sharply with analysis of variance, regression, discriminant analysis, and factor analysis, which are based upon an extensive body of statistical reasoning. Although many clustering methods have important statistical properties, the fundamental simplicity of these methods needs to be recognized.[8] The following statistics and concepts are associated with cluster analysis.

Agglomeration schedule. An agglomeration schedule gives information on the objects or cases being combined at each stage of a hierarchical clustering process.

Cluster centroid. The cluster centroid is the mean values of the variables for all the cases or objects in a particular cluster.

Cluster centers. The cluster centers are the initial starting points in nonhierarchical clustering. Clusters are built around these centers or *seeds.*

Cluster membership. Cluster membership indicates the cluster to which each object or case belongs.

Dendrogram. A dendrogram, or *tree graph,* is a graphical device for displaying clustering results. Vertical lines represent clusters that are joined together. The position of the line on the scale indicates the distances at which clusters were joined. The dendrogram is read from left to right. Figure 20.8 is a dendrogram.

Distances between cluster centers. These distances indicate how separated the individual pairs of clusters are. Clusters that are widely separated are distinct, and therefore desirable.

Icicle plot. An icicle plot is a graphical display of clustering results, so called because it resembles a row of icicles hanging from the eaves of a house. The columns correspond to the objects being clustered, and the rows correspond to the number of clusters. An icicle plot is read from bottom to top. Figure 20.7 is an icicle plot.

Similarity/distance coefficient matrix. A similarity/distance coefficient matrix is a lower-triangle matrix containing pairwise distances between objects or cases.

Conducting Cluster Analysis

The steps involved in conducting cluster analysis are listed in Figure 20.3. The first step is to formulate the clustering problem by defining the variables on which the clustering will be based. Then an appropriate distance measure must be selected. The distance measure determines how similar or dissimilar the objects being clustered are. Several clustering procedures have been developed and the researcher should select one that is appropriate for the problem at hand. Deciding on the number of clusters requires judgment on the part of the researcher. The derived clusters should be interpreted in terms of the variables used to cluster them and profiled in terms of additional salient variables. Finally, the researcher must assess the validity of the clustering process.

Formulate the Problem

Perhaps the most important part of formulating the clustering problem is selecting the variables on which the clustering is based. Inclusion of even one or two irrelevant variables may distort an otherwise useful clustering solution. Basically, the set of variables selected should describe the similarity between objects in terms that are relevant to the marketing research problem. The variables should be selected based on past research, theory, or a consideration of the hypotheses being tested. In exploratory research, the researcher should exercise judgment and intuition.

FIGURE 20.3

Conducting Cluster Analysis

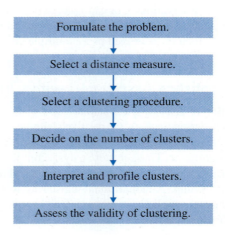

To illustrate, we consider a clustering of consumers based on attitudes toward shopping. Based on past research, six attitudinal variables were identified. Consumers were asked to express their degree of agreement with the following statements on a 7-point scale (1 = disagree, 7 = agree):

V_1: Shopping is fun.

V_2: Shopping is bad for your budget.

V_3: I combine shopping with eating out.

V_4: I try to get the best buys when shopping.

V_5: I don't care about shopping.

V_6: You can save a lot of money by comparing prices.

Data obtained from a pretest sample of 20 respondents are shown in Table 20.1. A small sample size has been used to illustrate the clustering process. In actual practice, cluster analysis is performed on a much larger sample such as that in the Dell running case and other cases with real data that are presented in this book.

Select a Distance or Similarity Measure

Because the objective of clustering is to group similar objects together, some measure is needed to assess how similar or different the objects are. The most common approach is to measure similarity in terms of distance between pairs of objects. Objects with smaller distances between them are more similar to each other than are those at larger distances. There are several ways to compute the distance between two objects.[9]

euclidean distance
The square root of the sum of the squared differences in values for each variable.

The most commonly used measure of similarity is the euclidean distance or its square. The **euclidean distance** is the square root of the sum of the squared differences in values for each variable. Other distance measures are also available. The *city-block* or *Manhattan distance* between two objects is the sum of the absolute differences in values for each variable. The

SPSS Data File

SAS Data File

TABLE 20.1
Attitudinal Data for Clustering

Case No.	V_1	V_2	V_3	V_4	V_5	V_6
1	6	4	7	3	2	3
2	2	3	1	4	5	4
3	7	2	6	4	1	3
4	4	6	4	5	3	6
5	1	3	2	2	6	4
6	6	4	6	3	3	4
7	5	3	6	3	3	4
8	7	3	7	4	1	4
9	2	4	3	3	6	3
10	3	5	3	6	4	6
11	1	3	2	3	5	3
12	5	4	5	4	2	4
13	2	2	1	5	4	4
14	4	6	4	6	4	7
15	6	5	4	2	1	4
16	3	5	4	6	4	7
17	4	4	7	2	2	5
18	3	7	2	6	4	3
19	4	6	3	7	2	7
20	2	3	2	4	7	2

hierarchical clustering
A clustering procedure characterized by the development of a hierarchy or tree-like structure.

agglomerative clustering
Hierarchical clustering procedure where each object starts out in a separate cluster. Clusters are formed by grouping objects into bigger and bigger clusters.

divisive clustering
Hierarchical clustering procedure where all objects start out in one giant cluster. Clusters are formed by dividing this cluster into smaller and smaller clusters.

linkage methods
Agglomerative methods of hierarchical clustering that cluster objects based on a computation of the distance between them.

Chebychev distance between two objects is the maximum absolute difference in values for any variable. For our example, we will use the squared euclidean distance.

If the variables are measured in vastly different units, the clustering solution will be influenced by the units of measurement. In a supermarket shopping study, attitudinal variables may be measured on a 9-point Likert-type scale; patronage, in terms of frequency of visits per month and the dollar amount spent; and brand loyalty, in terms of percentage of grocery shopping expenditure allocated to the favorite supermarket. In these cases, before clustering respondents, we must standardize the data by rescaling each variable to have a mean of zero and a standard deviation of unity. Although standardization can remove the influence of the unit of measurement, it can also reduce the differences between groups on variables that may best discriminate groups or clusters. It is also desirable to eliminate outliers (cases with atypical values).[10]

Use of different distance measures may lead to different clustering results. Hence, it is advisable to use different measures and compare the results. Having selected a distance or similarity measure, we can next select a clustering procedure.

Select a Clustering Procedure

Figure 20.4 is a classification of clustering procedures. Clustering procedures can be hierarchical, nonhierarchical, or other procedures. **Hierarchical clustering** is characterized by the development of a hierarchy or tree-like structure. Hierarchical methods can be agglomerative or divisive. **Agglomerative clustering** starts with each object in a separate cluster. Clusters are formed by grouping objects into bigger and bigger clusters. This process is continued until all objects are members of a single cluster. **Divisive clustering** starts with all the objects grouped in a single cluster. Clusters are divided or split until each object is in a separate cluster.

Agglomerative methods are commonly used in marketing research. They consist of linkage methods, error sums of squares or variance methods, and centroid methods. **Linkage methods** include single linkage, complete linkage, and average linkage. The **single linkage** method is

FIGURE 20.4
A Classification of Clustering Procedures

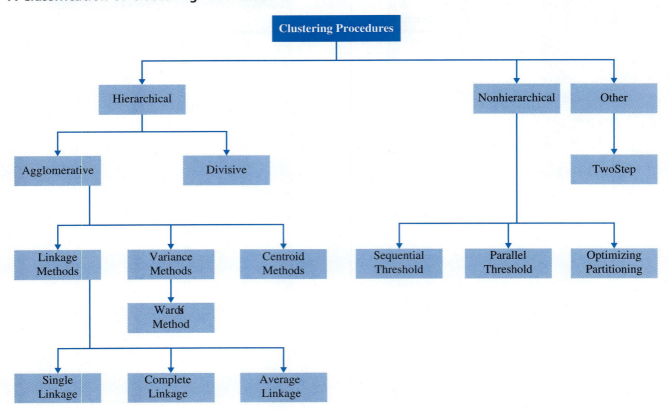

single linkage
Linkage method that is based on minimum distance or the nearest neighbor rule.

complete linkage
Linkage method that is based on maximum distance or the furthest neighbor approach.

average linkage
A linkage method based on the average distance between all pairs of objects, where one member of the pair is from each of the clusters.

variance methods
An agglomerative method of hierarchical clustering in which clusters are generated to minimize the within-cluster variance.

Ward's procedure
Variance method in which the squared euclidean distance to the cluster means is minimized.

centroid methods
A method of hierarchical clustering in which clusters are generated so as to maximize the distances between the centers or centroids of clusters.

based on minimum distance or the nearest neighbor rule. The first two objects clustered are those that have the smallest distance between them. The next shortest distance is identified, and either the third object is clustered with the first two, or a new two-object cluster is formed. At every stage, the distance between two clusters is the distance between their two closest points (see Figure 20.5). Two clusters are merged at any stage by the single shortest link between them. This process is continued until all objects are in one cluster. The single linkage method does not work well when the clusters are poorly defined. The **complete linkage** method is similar to single linkage, except that it is based on the maximum distance or the furthest neighbor approach. In complete linkage, the distance between two clusters is calculated as the distance between their two furthest points. The **average linkage** method works similarly. However, in this method, the distance between two clusters is defined as the average of the distances between all pairs of objects, where one member of the pair is from each of the clusters (Figure 20.5). As can be seen, the average linkage method uses information on all pairs of distances, not merely the minimum or maximum distances. For this reason, it is usually preferred to the single and complete linkage methods.

The **variance methods** attempt to generate clusters to minimize the within-cluster variance. A commonly used variance method is **Ward's procedure**. For each cluster, the means for all the variables are computed. Then, for each object, the squared euclidean distance to the cluster means is calculated (Figure 20.6). These distances are summed for all the objects. At each stage, the two clusters with the smallest increase in the overall sum of squares within cluster distances are combined. In the **centroid methods**, the distance between two clusters is the distance between their centroids (means for all the variables), as shown in Figure 20.6. Clusters are generated so as to maximize the distances between the centers or centroids of clusters. Every time objects are grouped, a new centroid is computed. Of the hierarchical methods, average linkage and Ward's methods have been shown to perform better than the other procedures.[11]

The second type of clustering procedures, the **nonhierarchical clustering** method, is frequently referred to as *k*-means clustering. These methods include sequential threshold, parallel threshold, and optimizing partitioning. In the **sequential threshold method**, a cluster center is selected and all objects within a prespecified threshold value from the center are grouped together. Then a new cluster center or seed is selected, and the process is repeated for the unclustered points. Once an object is clustered with a seed, it is no longer considered for

FIGURE 20.5

**Linkage Methods
of Clustering**

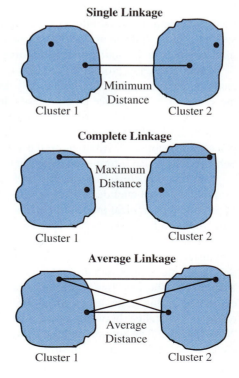

Single Linkage

Minimum Distance

Cluster 1   Cluster 2

Complete Linkage

Maximum Distance

Cluster 1   Cluster 2

Average Linkage

Average Distance

Cluster 1   Cluster 2

FIGURE 20.6

**Other
Agglomerative
Clustering
Methods**

Ward's Method

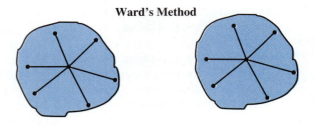

Centroid Method

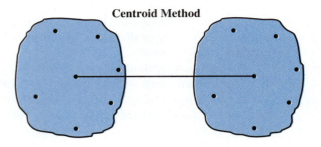

**nonhierarchical
clustering**

A procedure that first assigns
or determines one or more
cluster centers and then
groups all objects within a
prespecified threshold value
from the center(s).

**sequential threshold
method**

A nonhierarchical clustering
method in which a cluster
center is selected and all
objects within a
prespecified threshold value
from the center are
grouped together.

**parallel threshold
method**

Nonhierarchical clustering
method that specifies
several cluster centers at
once. All objects that are
within a prespecified
threshold value from the
center are grouped
together.

**optimizing
partitioning method**

Nonhierarchical clustering
method that allows for later
reassignment of objects to
clusters to optimize an
overall criterion.

clustering with subsequent seeds. The **parallel threshold method** operates similarly, except that several cluster centers are selected simultaneously, and objects within the threshold level are grouped with the nearest center. The **optimizing partitioning method** differs from the two threshold procedures in that objects can later be reassigned to clusters to optimize an overall criterion, such as average within-cluster distance for a given number of clusters.

Two major disadvantages of the nonhierarchical procedures are that the number of clusters must be prespecified and the selection of cluster centers is arbitrary. Furthermore, the clustering results may depend on how the centers are selected. Many nonhierarchical programs select the first k (k = number of clusters) cases without missing values as initial cluster centers. Thus, the clustering results may depend on the order of observations in the data. Yet nonhierarchical clustering is faster than hierarchical methods and has merit when the number of objects or observations is large. It has been suggested that the hierarchical and nonhierarchical methods be used in tandem. First, an initial clustering solution is obtained using a hierarchical procedure, such as average linkage or Ward's. The number of clusters and cluster centroids so obtained are used as inputs to the optimizing partitioning method.[12]

Other clustering procedures are also available; one of particular interest is TwoStep cluster analysis. This procedure can automatically determine the optimal number of clusters by comparing the values of model-choice criteria across different clustering solutions. It also has the ability to create cluster models based on categorical and continuous variables. In addition to euclidean distance, the TwoStep procedure also uses the log-likelihood measure. The log-likelihood measure places a probability distribution on the variables. It also accommodates two clustering criteria: Schwarz's Bayesian Information Criterion (BIC) or the Akaike Information Criterion (AIC).

Choice of a clustering method and choice of a distance measure are interrelated. For example, squared euclidean distances should be used with the Ward's and centroid methods. Several nonhierarchical procedures also use squared euclidean distances. In the TwoStep procedure, the euclidean measure can be used only when all of the variables are continuous.

We will use the Ward's procedure to illustrate hierarchical clustering. The output obtained by clustering the data of Table 20.1 is given in Table 20.2. Useful information is contained in the "Agglomeration Schedule", which shows the number of cases or clusters being combined at each stage. The first line represents stage 1, with 19 clusters. Respondents 14 and 16 are combined at this stage, as shown in the columns labeled "Clusters Combined." The squared euclidean distance between these two respondents is given under the column labeled "Coefficients." The column entitled "Stage Cluster First Appears" indicates the stage at which a cluster is first formed. To illustrate, an entry of 1 at stage 6 indicates that respondent 14 was

SPSS Output File

SAS Output File

TABLE 20.2
Results of Hierarchical Clustering

Case Processing Summary[a,b]

Valid		Cases Missing		Total	
N	Percent	N	Percent	N	Percent
20	100.0	0	0.0	20	100.0

[a] Squared Euclidean Distance used
[b] Ward Linkage

Ward Linkage

Agglomeration Schedule

	Cluster Combined			Stage Cluster First Appears		
Stage	Cluster 1	Cluster 2	Coefficients	Cluster 1	Cluster 2	Next Stage
1	14	16	1.000	0	0	6
2	6	7	2.000	0	0	7
3	2	13	3.500	0	0	15
4	5	11	5.000	0	0	11
5	3	8	6.500	0	0	16
6	10	14	8.167	0	1	9
7	6	12	10.500	2	0	10
8	9	20	13.000	0	0	11
9	4	10	15.583	0	6	12
10	1	6	18.500	0	7	13
11	5	9	23.000	4	8	15
12	4	19	27.750	9	0	17
13	1	17	33.100	10	0	14
14	1	15	41.333	13	0	16
15	2	5	51.833	3	11	18
16	1	3	64.500	14	5	19
17	4	18	79.667	12	0	18
18	2	4	172.667	15	17	19
19	1	2	328.600	16	18	0

Cluster Membership

Case	4 Clusters	3 Clusters	2 Clusters
1	1	1	1
2	2	2	2
3	1	1	1
4	3	3	2
5	2	2	2
6	1	1	1
7	1	1	1
8	1	1	1
9	2	2	2
10	3	3	2
11	2	2	2
12	1	1	1
13	2	2	2
14	3	3	2

(continued)

TABLE 20.2
Results of Hierarchical Clustering (*continued*)

15	1	1	1
16	3	3	2
17	1	1	1
18	4	3	2
19	3	3	2
20	2	2	2

first grouped at stage 1. The last column, "Next Stage," indicates the stage at which another case (respondent) or cluster is combined with this one. Because the number in the first line of the last column is 6, we see that at stage 6, respondent 10 is combined with 14 and 16 to form a single cluster. Similarly, the second line represents stage 2 with 18 clusters. In stage 2, respondents 6 and 7 are grouped together.

Another important part of the output is contained in the icicle plot given in Figure 20.7. The columns correspond to the objects being clustered, in this case respondents labeled 1 through 20. The rows correspond to the number of clusters. This figure is read from bottom to top. At first, all cases are considered as individual clusters. Because there are 20 respondents, there are 20 initial clusters. At the first step, the two closest objects are combined, resulting in 19 clusters. The last row of Figure 20.7 shows these 19 clusters. The two cases, respondents 14 and 16, which have been combined at this stage, have in the column between them, all Xs in rows 1 through 19. Row number 18 corresponds to the next stage, with 18 clusters. At this stage, respondents 6 and 7 are grouped together. The column of Xs between respondents 6 and 7 has a blank in row 19. Thus, at this stage there are 18 clusters; 16 of them consist of individual respondents, and two contain two respondents each. Each subsequent step leads to the formation of a new cluster in one of three ways: (1) two individual cases are grouped together, (2) a case is joined to an already existing cluster, or (3) two clusters are grouped together.

Another graphic device that is useful in displaying clustering results is the dendrogram (see Figure 20.8). The dendrogram is read from left to right. Vertical lines represent clusters that are joined together. The position of the line on the scale indicates the distances at which clusters were joined. Because many of the distances in the early stages are of similar magnitude, it is difficult to tell the sequence in which some of the early clusters are formed. However, it is clear that in the last two stages, the distances at which the clusters are being combined are large. This information is useful in deciding on the number of clusters.

It is also possible to obtain information on cluster membership of cases if the number of clusters is specified. Although this information can be discerned from the icicle plot, a tabular display is helpful. Table 20.2 contains the "Cluster Membership" for the cases, depending on whether the final solution contains two, three, or four clusters. Information of this type can be obtained for any number of clusters and is useful for deciding on the number of clusters.

Decide on the Number of Clusters

A major issue in cluster analysis is deciding on the number of clusters. Although there are no hard and fast rules, some guidelines are available:

1. Theoretical, conceptual, or practical considerations may suggest a certain number of clusters. For example, if the purpose of clustering is to identify market segments, management may want a particular number of clusters.
2. In hierarchical clustering, the distances at which clusters are combined can be used as criteria. This information can be obtained from the agglomeration schedule or from the dendrogram. In our case, we see from the "Agglomeration Schedule" in Table 20.2 that the value in the "Coefficients" column suddenly more than doubles between stages 17 (three clusters) and 18 (two clusters). Likewise, at the last two stages of the dendrogram in Figure 20.8, the clusters are being combined at large distances. Therefore, it appears that a three-cluster solution is appropriate.

CASE
NUMBER OF CLUSTERS   18 19 16 14 10 4 20 9 11 5 13 2 8 3 15 17 12 7 6 1

FIGURE 20.7

Vertical Icicle Plot Using Ward's Procedure

SPSS Output File

SAS Output File

FIGURE 20.8

Dendrogram Using Ward's Procedure

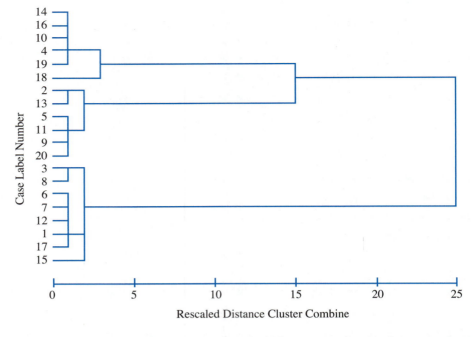

3. In nonhierarchical clustering, the ratio of total within-group variance to between-group variance can be plotted against the number of clusters. The point at which an elbow or a sharp bend occurs indicates an appropriate number of clusters. Increasing the number of clusters beyond this point is usually not worthwhile.

4. The relative sizes of the clusters should be meaningful. In Table 20.2, by making a simple frequency count of cluster membership, we see that a three-cluster solution results in clusters with eight, six, and six elements. However, if we go to a four-cluster solution, the sizes of the clusters are eight, six, five, and one. It is not meaningful to have a cluster with only one case, so a three-cluster solution is preferable in this situation.

Interpret and Profile the Clusters

Interpreting and profiling clusters involves examining the cluster centroids. The centroids represent the mean values of the objects contained in the cluster on each of the variables. The centroids enable us to describe each cluster by assigning it a name or label. If the clustering program does not print this information, it may be obtained through discriminant analysis. Table 20.3 gives the centroids or mean values for each cluster in our example. Cluster 1 has relatively high values on variables V_1 (shopping is fun) and V_3 (I combine shopping with eating out). It also has a low value on V_5 (I don't care about shopping). Hence, cluster 1 could be labeled "fun-loving and concerned shoppers." This cluster consists of cases 1, 3, 6, 7, 8, 12, 15, and 17. Cluster 2 is just the opposite, with low values on V_1 and V_3 and a high value on V_5, and this cluster could be labeled "apathetic shoppers." Members of cluster 2 are cases 2, 5, 9, 11, 13, and 20. Cluster 3 has high values on V_2 (shopping upsets my budget), V_4 (I try to get the best buys when shopping), and V_6 (you can save a lot of money by comparing prices). Thus, this cluster could be labeled "economical shoppers." Cluster 3 comprises cases 4, 10, 14, 16, 18, and 19.

TABLE 20.3

Cluster Centroids

Cluster No.	V_1	V_2	V_3	V_4	V_5	V_6
			Means of Variables			
1	5.750	3.625	6.000	3.125	1.750	3.875
2	1.667	3.000	1.833	3.500	5.500	3.333
3	3.500	5.833	3.333	6.000	3.500	6.000

Often it is helpful to profile the clusters in terms of variables that were not used for clustering. These may include demographic, psychographic, product usage, media usage, or other variables. For example, the clusters may have been derived based on benefits sought. Further profiling may be done in terms of demographic and psychographic variables to target marketing efforts for each cluster. The variables that significantly differentiate between clusters can be identified via discriminant analysis and one-way analysis of variance.

Assess Reliability and Validity

Given the several judgments entailed in cluster analysis, no clustering solution should be accepted without some assessment of its reliability and validity. Formal procedures for assessing the reliability and validity of clustering solutions are complex and not fully defensible.[13] Hence, we omit them here. However, the following procedures provide adequate checks on the quality of clustering results.

1. Perform cluster analysis on the same data using different distance measures. Compare the results across measures to determine the stability of the solutions.
2. Use different methods of clustering and compare the results.
3. Split the data randomly into halves. Perform clustering separately on each half. Compare cluster centroids across the two subsamples.
4. Delete variables randomly. Perform clustering based on the reduced set of variables. Compare the results with those obtained by clustering based on the entire set of variables.
5. In nonhierarchical clustering, the solution may depend on the order of cases in the data set. Make multiple runs using a different order of cases until the solution stabilizes.

We further illustrate hierarchical clustering with a study of differences in marketing strategy among American, Japanese, and British firms.

Real Research   It Is a Small World

Data for a study of U.S., Japanese, and British competitors were obtained from detailed personal interviews with chief executives and top marketing decision makers for defined product groups in 90 companies. To control for market differences, the methodology was based upon matching 30 British companies with their major American and Japanese competitors in the U.K. market. The study involved 30 triads of companies, each composed of a British, American, and Japanese business that competed directly with one another.

Most of the data on the characteristics of the companies' performance, strategy, and organization were collected on 5-point semantic differential scales. The first stage of the analysis involved factor analysis of variables describing the firms' strategies and marketing activities. The factor scores were used to identify groups of similar companies using Ward's hierarchical clustering routine. A six-cluster solution was developed.

Strategic Clusters

Cluster	I	II	III	IV	V	VI
Name	Innovators	Quality Marketeers	Price Promoters	Product Marketeers	Mature Marketeers	Aggressive Pushers
Size	22	11	14	13	13	17
Successful (%)	55	100	36	38	77	41
Nationality (%):						
Japanese	59	46	22	31	15	18
American	18	36	14	31	54	53
British	23	18	64	38	31	29

Membership in the six clusters was then interpreted against the original performance, strategy, and organizational variables. All the clusters contained some successful companies, although some contained significantly more than others. The clusters lent support to the hypothesis that successful companies were similar irrespective of nationality, because American, British, and Japanese companies were found in all the clusters. There was, however, a preponderance of Japanese companies in the more successful clusters and a predominance of British companies in the two least successful clusters. Apparently, Japanese companies do not deploy strategies that are unique to them; rather, more of them pursue strategies that work effectively in the British market.

The findings indicate that there are generic strategies that describe successful companies irrespective of their industry. Three successful strategies can be identified. The first is the Quality Marketeers strategy. These companies have strengths in marketing and research and development. They concentrate their technical developments on achieving high quality rather than pure innovation. These companies are characterized by entrepreneurial organizations, long-range planning, and a well-communicated sense of mission. The second generic strategy is that of the Innovators, who are weaker on advanced R&D but are entrepreneurial and driven by a quest for innovation. The last successful group is the Mature Marketeers, who are highly profit oriented and have in-depth marketing skills. All three appear to consist of highly marketing-oriented businesses. Foreign investment in the United Kingdom continued to be robust. In 2009, the United Kingdom was leading other European countries in terms of foreign direct investments. The United States and Japan continued to be major investors.[14] ■

Applications of Nonhierarchical Clustering

We illustrate the nonhierarchical procedure using the data in Table 20.1 and an optimizing partitioning method. Based on the results of hierarchical clustering, a three-cluster solution was prespecified. The results are presented in Table 20.4. The "Initial Cluster Centers" are the values of three randomly selected cases. In some programs, the first three cases are selected. The classification cluster centers are interim centers used for the assignment of cases. Each case is assigned to the nearest classification cluster center. The classification centers are updated until the stopping criteria are reached. The "Final Cluster Centers" represent the variable means for the cases in the final clusters. In SPSS Windows, these are rounded to the nearest integer.

SPSS Output File

SAS Output File

TABLE 20.4
Results of Nonhierarchical Clustering

Initial Cluster Centers

	Cluster		
	1	2	3
V_1	4	2	7
V_2	6	3	2
V_3	3	2	6
V_4	7	4	4
V_5	2	7	1
V_6	7	2	3

Iteration History[a]

	Change In Cluster Centers		
Iteration	1	2	3
1	2.154	2.102	2.550
2	0.000	0.000	0.000

[a]Convergence achieved due to no or small distance change. The maximum distance by which any center has changed is 0.000. The current iteration is 2. The minimum distance between initial centers is 7.746.

Cluster Membership

Case Number	Cluster	Distance
1	3	1.414
2	2	1.323
3	3	2.550
4	1	1.404
5	2	1.848
6	3	1.225

(continued)

TABLE 20.4
Results of Nonhierarchical Clustering (*continued*)

7	3	1.500
8	3	2.121
9	2	1.756
10	1	1.143
11	2	1.041
12	3	1.581
13	2	2.598
14	1	1.404
15	3	2.828
16	1	1.624
17	3	2.598
18	1	3.555
19	1	2.154
20	2	2.102

Final Cluster Centers

	Cluster		
	1	2	3
V_1	4	2	6
V_2	6	3	4
V_3	3	2	6
V_4	6	4	3
V_5	4	6	2
V_6	6	3	4

Distances Between Final Cluster Centers

Cluster	1	2	3
1		5.568	5.698
2	5.568		6.928
3	5.698	6.928	

ANOVA

	Cluster		Error			
	Mean Square	df	Mean Square	df	F	Sig.
V_1	29.108	2	0.608	17	47.888	0.000
V_2	13.546	2	0.630	17	21.505	0.000
V_3	31.392	2	0.833	17	37.670	0.000
V_4	15.713	2	0.728	17	21.585	0.000
V_5	22.537	2	0.816	17	27.614	0.000
V_6	12.171	2	1.071	17	11.363	0.001

The *F* tests should be used only for descriptive purposes because the clusters have been chosen to maximize the differences among cases in different clusters. The observed significance levels are not corrected for this and thus cannot be interpreted as tests of the hypothesis that the cluster means are equal.

Number of Cases in Each Cluster

Cluster 1	6.000
2	6.000
3	8.000
Valid	20.000
Missing	0.000

Table 20.4 also displays "Cluster Membership" and the distance between each case and its classification center. Note that the cluster memberships given in Table 20.2 (hierarchical clustering) and Table 20.4 (nonhierarchical clustering) are identical. (Cluster 1 of Table 20.2 is labeled cluster 3 in Table 20.4, and cluster 3 of Table 20.2 is labeled cluster 1 in Table 20.4.) The "Distances Between the Final Cluster Centers" indicate that the pairs of clusters are well separated. The univariate F test for each clustering variable is presented. These F tests are only descriptive. Because the cases or objects are systematically assigned to clusters to maximize differences on the clustering variables, the resulting probabilities should not be interpreted as testing the null hypothesis of no differences among clusters.

The following example of hospital choice further illustrates nonhierarchical clustering.

Real Research   Segmentation with Surgical Precision

Cluster analysis was used to classify respondents who preferred hospitals for inpatient care to identify hospital preference segments. The clustering was based on the reasons respondents gave for preferring a hospital. The demographic profiles of the grouped respondents were compared to learn whether the segments could be identified efficiently.

The k-Means clustering method (SPSS) was used for grouping the respondents based on their answers to the hospital preference items. The squared euclidean distances between all clustering variables were minimized. Because different individuals perceive scales of importance differently, each individual's ratings were normalized before clustering. The results indicated that the respondents could best be classified into four clusters. The cross-validation procedure for cluster analysis was run twice, on halves of the total sample.

As expected, the four groups differed substantially by their distributions and average responses to the reasons for their hospital preferences. The names assigned to the four groups reflected the demographic characteristics and reasons for hospital preferences: Old-Fashioned, Affluent, Value Conscious, and Professional Want-It-Alls.[15] ∎

Applications of TwoStep Clustering

The data of Table 20.1 were also analyzed using the TwoStep procedure in SPSS. Since all of the variables were continuous, we used the euclidean distance measure. The clustering criterion was the Akaike Information Criterion (AIC). The number of clusters was determined automatically. The results are shown in Table 20.5. As can be seen, a three-cluster solution was obtained, similar to that in hierarchical and nonhierarchical clustering. Note that the AIC is at a minimum (97.594) for a three-cluster solution. A comparison of cluster centroids in Table 20.5 with those in Table 20.3 show that Cluster 1 of Table 20.5 corresponds to Cluster 2 of Table 20.3 (hierarchical clustering), Cluster 2 of Table 20.5 corresponds to Cluster 3 of Table 20.3 and Cluster 3 of TwoStep corresponds to Cluster 1. The interpretation and implications are similar to those discussed earlier. In this case all three methods (hierarchical, nonhierarchical, and TwoStep) gave similar results. In other cases, different methods may yield different results. It is a good idea to analyze a given data set using different methods to examine the stability of clustering solutions.

Decision Research   Sony: Attacking the Market Segment by Segment

The Situation

Headquartered in Tokyo, Sony Corporation (www.sony.com) is a leading manufacturer of audio, video, communications, and information technology products for consumers and professional markets. Sony's main U.S. businesses include Sony Electronics, Inc., Sony Pictures Entertainment, Sony BMG Music Entertainment, Inc., and Sony Computer Entertainment America, Inc. Sony recorded consolidated annual sales of $88.7 billion for the fiscal year ended March 31, 2008. Sony's consolidated sales in the United States for the fiscal year ended March 31, 2008, were $29 billion. According to the Harris Poll (www.harrisinteractive.com), Sony has been chosen as the number one brand for the third year in a row, and for the fifth time in the last eight years.

TABLE 20.5
Results of TwoStep Clustering

Auto-Clustering

Number of Clusters	Akaike's Information Criterion (AIC)	AIC Change[a]	Ratio of AIC Changes[b]	Ratio of Distance Measures[c]
1	104.140			
2	101.171	−2.969	1.000	.847
3	97.594	−3.577	1.205	1.583
4	116.896	19.302	−6.502	2.115
5	138.230	21.335	−7.187	1.222
6	158.586	20.355	−6.857	1.021
7	179.340	20.755	−6.991	1.224
8	201.628	22.288	−7.508	1.006
9	224.055	22.426	−7.555	1.111
10	246.522	22.467	−7.568	1.588
11	269.570	23.048	−7.764	1.001
12	292.718	23.148	−7.798	1.055
13	316.120	23.402	−7.883	1.002
14	339.223	23.103	−7.782	1.044
15	362.650	23.427	−7.892	1.004

[a] The changes are from the previous number of clusters in the table.
[b] The ratios of changes are relative to the change for the two cluster solution.
[c] The ratios of distance measures are based on the current number of clusters against the previous number of clusters.

Cluster Distribution

	N	% of Combined	% of Total
Cluster 1	6	30.0%	30.0%
2	6	30.0%	30.0%
3	8	40.0%	40.0%
Combined	20	100.0%	100.0%
Total	20		100.0%

Centroids

	Fun Mean	Fun Std. Deviation	Bad for Budget Mean	Bad for Budget Std. Deviation
Cluster 1	1.67	.516	3.00	.632
2	3.50	.548	5.83	.753
3	5.75	1.035	3.63	.916
Combined	3.85	1.899	4.10	1.410

Centroids

	Eating Out Mean	Eating Out Std. Deviation	Best Buys Mean	Best Buys Std. Deviation
Cluster 1	1.83	.753	3.50	1.049
2	3.33	.816	6.00	.632
3	6.00	1.089	3.13	.835
Combined	3.95	2.012	4.10	1.518

Centroids

	Don't Care Mean	Don't Care Std. Deviation	Compare Prices Mean	Compare Prices Std. Deviation
Cluster 1	5.50	1.049	3.33	.816
2	3.50	.837	6.00	1.549
3	1.80	.835	3.88	.641
Combined	3.45	1.761	4.35	1.496

Cluster analysis can help Sony segment the U.S. electronics market based on psychographics and lifestyles.

The main focus of Sony's marketing strategy is to get closer to the consumer. Ryoji Chubachi, Sony Electronics CEO, says, "It is hard to differentiate products today. . . . Differentiation is our mission. We must see the customer first, sell as much products to those specific consumers as possible through the right retail channels." In order to implement this idea, Sony has divided its target market into the following segments: Affluent Alphas (early adopters), Zoomers (55+), Small Office/Home Office, Young Professionals (25–34), Families, and Generation Y (under 30).

These six demographic segments make up the Diamond Plan. Instead of individual products being marketed by product managers, Sony plans to assign executives to these demographic segments. This new approach to marketing will affect product development and design, retail merchandising, advertising, and consumer loyalty programs. Media dollars will also be adjusted to effectively target the new segments. However, before a full-scale implementation of the Diamond Plan, Ryoji Chubachi would like to determine if there is a better way to segment the U.S. electronics market, such as by psychographics and lifestyles, that will lead to increased sales and market share.[16]

The Marketing Research Decision

1. What data should be collected and how should they be analyzed to segment the U.S. electronics market based on psychographics and lifestyles?
2. Discuss the role of the type of research you recommend in enabling Ryoji Chubachi to increase sales and market share.

The Marketing Management Decision

1. What new strategies should Ryoji Chubachi formulate to increase sales and market share?
2. Discuss how the marketing management decision action that you recommend to Ryoji Chubachi is influenced by the data analysis that you suggested earlier and by the likely findings. ■

ACTIVE RESEARCH

Segmenting the Market for Nordstrom

Conduct an Internet search using a search engine and your library's online database to obtain information on the type of consumers who shop at high-end department stores such as Nordstrom.

Describe what data should be collected and how they should be analyzed to segment the market for a high-end department store such as Nordstrom.

As the CEO of Nordstrom, how would you segment your market?

Clustering Variables

Sometimes cluster analysis is also used for clustering variables to identify homogeneous groups. In this instance, the units used for analysis are the variables, and the distance measures are computed for all pairs of variables. For example, the correlation coefficient, either the absolute value or with the sign, can be used as a measure of similarity (the opposite of distance) between variables.

Hierarchical clustering of variables can aid in the identification of unique variables, or variables that make a unique contribution to the data. Clustering can also be used to reduce the number of variables. Associated with each cluster is a linear combination of the variables in the cluster, called the *cluster component.* A large set of variables can often be replaced by the set of cluster components with little loss of information. However, a given number of cluster components do not generally explain as much variance as the same number of principal components. Why, then, should the clustering of variables be used? Cluster components are usually easier to interpret than the principal components, even if the latter are rotated.[17] We illustrate the clustering of variables with an example from advertising research.

Real Research   ## Feelings—Nothing More Than Feelings

As it faced stiff competition in digital cameras, Nikon (www.nikon.com) was marketing its Coolpix line in 2009 with the tag lines such as, **"passion made powerful," "brilliance made beautiful,"** and **"memories made easy."** The campaign was designed to evoke emotional feelings in consumers.

Nikon based this campaign on a study conducted to identify feelings that are precipitated by advertising. A total of 655 feelings were reduced to a set of 180 that were judged by respondents to be most likely to be stimulated by advertising. This group was clustered on the basis of judgments of similarity between feelings, resulting in 31 feeling clusters. These were divided into 16 positive and 15 negative clusters.[18]

Positive Feelings	Negative Feelings
1. Playful/childish	1. Fear
2. Friendly	2. Bad/sick
3. Humorous	3. Confused
4. Delighted	4. Indifferent
5. Interested	5. Bored
6. Strong/confident	6. Sad
7. Warm/tender	7. Anxious
8. Relaxed	8. Helpless/timid
9. Energetic/impulsive	9. Ugly/stupid
10. Eager/excited	10. Pity/deceived
11. Contemplative	11. Mad
12. Proud	12. Disagreeable
13. Persuaded/expectant	13. Disgusted
14. Vigorous/challenged	14. Irritated
15. Amazed	15. Moody/frustrated
16. Set/informed	

Thus, 655 feeling responses to advertising were reduced to a core set of 31 feelings. As such, advertisers now have a manageable set of feelings for understanding and measuring emotional responses to advertising. When measured, these feelings can provide information on a commercial's ability to persuade the target consumers, as in the case of Nikon cameras. ■

Cluster analysis, particularly clustering of objects, is also frequently used in international marketing research (as in the next example) and could also be useful in researching ethical evaluations (as in the example after that).

Real Research   Perceived Product Parity—Once Rarity—Now Reality

How do consumers in different countries perceive brands in different product categories? Surprisingly, the answer is that the product perception parity rate is quite high. Perceived product parity means that consumers perceive all/most of the brands in a product category as similar to each other, or at par. A new study by BBDO Worldwide (www.bbdo.com) shows that two-thirds of consumers surveyed in 28 countries considered brands in 13 product categories to be at parity. The product categories ranged from airlines to credit cards to coffee. Perceived parity averaged 63 percent for all categories in all countries. The Japanese have the highest perception of parity across all product categories at 99 percent, and Colombians the lowest at 28 percent. Viewed by product category, credit cards have the highest parity perception at 76 percent, and cigarettes the lowest at 52 percent.

BBDO clustered the countries based on product parity perceptions to arrive at clusters that exhibited similar levels and patterns of parity perceptions. The highest perception parity figure came from the Asia/Pacific region (83 percent) that included countries of Australia, Japan, Malaysia, and South Korea, and also France. It is no surprise that France was in this list because, for most products, they use highly emotional, visual advertising that is feelings oriented. The next cluster was U.S.-influenced markets (65 percent), which included Argentina, Canada, Hong Kong, Kuwait, Mexico, Singapore, and United States. The third cluster, primarily European countries (60 percent), included Austria, Belgium, Denmark, Italy, Netherlands, South Africa, Spain, United Kingdom, and Germany.

What all this means is that in order to differentiate the product/brand, advertising cannot focus just on product performance, but also must relate the product to the person's life in an important way. Also, much greater marketing effort will be required in the Asia/Pacific region and in France in order to differentiate the brand from competition and establish a unique image. A big factor in this growing parity is, of course, the emergence of the global market. A recent study explored the issues underlying the factual informational content of advertising under the conditions of product parity and product type. The data for this study were derived from content analysis from more than 17,000 newspaper advertisements and 9,800 television advertisements. Analysis showed that advertisements for low-parity products contain more factual information than their counterparts. When the two conditions were seen together, parity influences factual informational content but not to the same degree as product type. The study revealed that overall, when it comes to including factual information in advertisements, advertisers respond more to product type than product parity.[19] ■

ACTIVE RESEARCH

Going Global Is American!

Visit www.americanairlines.com and search the Internet using a search engine as well as your library's online database to obtain information on consumers' airline preferences for global travel.

As the CEO of American Airlines (www.aa.com), how would you segment the global market for travel by air?

What data should be obtained and how they should be analyzed to segment the market for global air travel?

Real Research   Clustering Marketing Professionals Based on Ethical Evaluations

Cluster analysis can be used to explain differences in ethical perceptions by using a large multi-item, multidimensional scale developed to measure how ethical different situations are. One such scale was developed by Reidenbach and Robin. This scale has 29 items that compose five dimensions that measure how a respondent judges a certain action. For illustration, a given respondent will read about a marketing researcher that has provided proprietary information of one of his clients to a second client. The respondent is then asked to complete the 29-item ethics scale. For example, the respondent marks the scale to indicate if this action is:

Just: ___:___:___:___:___:___:___ : Unjust

Traditionally acceptable: ___:___:___:___:___:___:___: Unacceptable

Violates: ___:___:___:___:___:___:___: Does not violate an unwritten
contract

This scale could be administered to a sample of marketing professionals. By clustering respondents based on these 29 items, two important questions should be investigated. First, how do the clusters differ with respect to the five ethical dimensions—in this case, Justice, Relativist, Egoism, Utilitarianism, and Deontology? Second, what types of firms compose each cluster? The clusters could be described in terms of North American Industry Classification System (NAICS) industrial category, firm size, and firm profitability. Answers to these two questions should provide insight into what types of firms use what dimensions to evaluate ethical situations. For instance, do large firms fall into a different cluster than small firms? Do more profitable firms perceive questionable situations more acceptable than less profitable firms? An empirical study conducted recently compared Taiwanese and U.S. perceptions of corporate ethics. A self-administered questionnaire was used that consisted of five measures. One of the measures, individual moral values, was measured using the Reidenbach and Robin scale. Results showed that in both national cultures, individual perceptions of corporate ethics appear to determine organizational commitment more than individual moral values.[20] ■

Statistical Software

We discuss the use of SPSS and SAS in detail in the subsequent sections. Here, we briefly describe the use of MINITAB. In MINITAB, cluster analysis can be accessed in the Stat>Multivariate>Cluster Observation function. Also available are Clustering of Variables and Cluster K-Means. Cluster analysis is not available in EXCEL.

SPSS and SAS Computerized Demonstration Movies

We have developed computerized demonstration movies that give step-by-step instructions for running all the SPSS and SAS Learning Edition programs that are discussed in this chapter. These demonstrations can be downloaded from the Web site for this book. The instructions for running these demonstrations are given in Exhibit 14.2.

SPSS and SAS Screen Captures with Notes

The step-by-step instructions for running the various SPSS and SAS Learning Edition programs discussed in this chapter are also illustrated in screen captures with appropriate notes. These screen captures can be downloaded from the Web site for this book.

SPSS Windows

In SPSS, the main program for hierarchical clustering of objects or cases is HIERARCHICAL CLUSTER. Different distance measures can be computed, and all the hierarchical clustering procedures discussed here are available. For nonhierarchical clustering, the K-MEANS CLUSTER program can be used. This program is particularly helpful for clustering a large number of cases. The TWOSTEP CLUSTER procedure is also available.

To select these procedures using SPSS for Windows, click:

Analyze>Classify>Hierarchical Cluster . . .

Analyze>Classify>K-Means Cluster . . .

Analyze>Classify>TwoStep Cluster . . .

The following are the detailed steps for running hierarchical cluster analysis on attitudinal data (V_1 to V_6) of Table 20.1.

1. Select ANALYZE from the SPSS menu bar.
2. Click CLASSIFY and then HIERARCHICAL CLUSTER.
3. Move "Fun [v1]," "Bad for Budget [v2]," "Eating Out [v3]," "Best Buys [v4]," "Don't Care [v5]," and "Compare Prices [v6]" into the VARIABLES box.
4. In the CLUSTER box check CASES (default option). In the DISPLAY box check STATISTICS and PLOTS (default options).
5. Click on STATISTICS. In the pop-up window, check AGGLOMERATION SCHEDULE. In the CLUSTER MEMBERSHIP box check RANGE OF SOLUTIONS. Then, for MINIMUM

NUMBER OF CLUSTERS enter 2, and for MAXIMUM NUMBER OF CLUSTERS enter 4. Click CONTINUE.

6. Click on PLOTS. In the pop-up window, check DENDROGRAM. In the ICICLE box check ALL CLUSTERS (default). In the ORIENTATION box, check VERTICAL. Click CONTINUE.

7. Click on METHOD. For CLUSTER METHOD select WARD'S METHOD. In the MEASURE box check INTERVAL and select SQUARED EUCLIDEAN DISTANCE. Click CONTINUE.

8. Click OK.

The procedure for clustering of variables is the same as that for hierarchical clustering except that in step 4 in the CLUSTER box check VARIABLES.

The following are the detailed steps for running nonhierarchical (K-Means) cluster analysis on attitudinal data (V_1 to V_6) of Table 20.1.

1. Select ANALYZE from the SPSS menu bar.
2. Click CLASSIFY and then K-MEANS CLUSTER.
3. Move "Fun [v1]," "Bad for Budget [v2]," "Eating Out [v3]," "Best Buys [v4]," "Don't Care [v5]," and "Compare Prices [v6]" into the VARIABLES box.
4. For NUMBER OF CLUSTERS select 3.
5. Click on OPTIONS. In the pop-up window, in the STATISTICS box, check INITIAL CLUSTER CENTERS and CLUSTER INFORMATION FOR EACH CASE. Click CONTINUE.
6. Click OK.

The following are the detailed steps for running TwoStep cluster analysis on attitudinal data (V_1 to V_6) of Table 20.1.

1. Select ANALYZE from the SPSS menu bar.
2. Click CLASSIFY and then TWOSTEP CLUSTER.
3. Move "Fun [v1]," "Bad for Budget [v2]," "Eating Out [v3]," "Best Buys [v4]," "Don't Care [v5]," and "Compare Prices [v6]" into the CONTINUOUS VARIABLES box.
4. For DISTANCE MEASURE select EUCLIDEAN.
5. For NUMBER OF CLUSTERS select DETERMINE AUTOMATICALLY.
6. For CLUSTERING CRITERION select AKAIKE'S INFORMATION CRITERION (AIC).
7. Click OK.

SAS Learning Edition

The instructions given here and in all the data analysis chapters (14 to 22) will work with the SAS Learning Edition as well as with the SAS Enterprise Guide. For a point-and-click approach for performing cluster analysis, use the Analyze task within the SAS Learning Edition. The Multivariate>Cluster Analysis task creates hierarchical clusters from data that contains either coordinate or distance data. If the data set contains coordinate data, the task computes Euclidean distances before applying the clustering methods. Alternatively, the task can create nonhierarchical clusters of coordinate data by using the k-means method. The task also produces dendrograms.

To select this procedure using SAS Learning Edition, click:

Analyze>Multivariate>Cluster Analysis

The following are the detailed steps for running hierarchical cluster analysis on attitudinal data (V_1 to V_6) of Table 20.1.

1. Select ANALYZE from the SAS Learning Edition menu bar.
2. Select MULTIVARIATE>CLUSTER ANALYSIS.

3. Move V1-V6 to the ANALYSIS VARIABLES task role.
4. Click CLUSTER and select WARD'S MINIMUM VARIANCE METHOD under CLUSTER METHOD.
5. Click RESULTS and select SIMPLE SUMMARY STATISTICS.
6. Click RUN.

The following are the detailed steps for running nonhierarchical (*k*-Means) cluster analysis on the attitudinal data of Table 20.1.

1. Select ANALYZE from the SAS Learning Edition menu bar.
2. Select MULTIVARIATE>CLUSTER ANALYSIS.
3. Move V1-V6 to the ANALYSIS VARIABLES task role.
4. Click CLUSTER and select K-MEANS ALGORITHM as the CLUSTER METHOD and 3 for the MAXIMUM NUMBER OF CLUSTERS.
5. Click RUN.

SAS does not provide TwoStep cluster analysis.

Project Research Cluster Analysis

In the department store project, respondents were clustered on the basis of self-reported importance attached to each factor of the choice criteria utilized in selecting a department store. The results indicated that respondents could be clustered into four segments. Differences among the segments were statistically tested. Thus, each segment contained respondents who were relatively homogeneous with respect to their choice criteria. The store choice model was then estimated separately for each segment. This procedure resulted in choice models that better represented the underlying choice process of respondents in specific segments.

SPSS Data File

SAS Data File

Project Activities

Download the SPSS or SAS data file *Sears Data 17* from the Web site for this book. See Chapter 17 for a description of this file.

1. Can the respondents be segmented based on the factor scores (that you generated in Chapter 19) for the 21 lifestyle statements? Use Ward's procedure to determine the number of clusters. Then conduct cluster analysis (use the *k*-means procedure) by selecting all the factor scores.
2. Can the respondents be segmented based on the importance attached to the eight factors of the choice criteria? Use Ward's procedure to determine the number of clusters. Then conduct cluster analysis (use the *k*-means procedure) by selecting all the factors. Interpret the resulting benefit segments. ■

Summary

Cluster analysis is used for classifying objects or cases, and sometimes variables, into relatively homogeneous groups. The groups or clusters are suggested by the data and are not defined *a priori*. Figure 20.9 gives a concept map for cluster analysis.

The variables on which the clustering is done should be selected based on past research, theory, the hypotheses being tested, or the judgment of the researcher. An appropriate measure of distance or similarity should be selected. The most commonly used measure is the euclidean distance or its square.

Clustering procedures may be hierarchical or nonhierarchical. Hierarchical clustering is characterized by the development of a hierarchy or tree-like structure. Hierarchical methods can be agglomerative or divisive. Agglomerative methods consist of linkage methods, variance methods, and centroid methods. Linkage methods are comprised of single linkage, complete linkage, and average linkage. A commonly used variance method is Ward's procedure. The nonhierarchical methods are frequently referred to as *k*-means clustering. These methods can be classified as sequential threshold, parallel threshold, and optimizing partitioning. Hierarchical

FIGURE 20.9

A Concept Map for Cluster Analysis

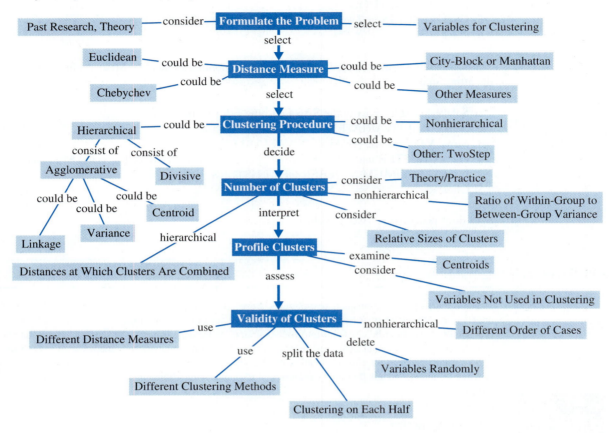

and nonhierarchical methods can be used in tandem. The TwoStep procedure can automatically determine the optimal number of clusters by comparing the values of a model-choice criteria across different clustering solutions. The choice of a clustering procedure and the choice of a distance measure are interrelated.

The number of clusters may be based on theoretical, conceptual, or practical considerations. In hierarchical clustering, the distances at which the clusters are being combined is an important criterion. The relative sizes of the clusters should be meaningful. The clusters should be interpreted in terms of cluster centroids. Often it is helpful to profile the clusters in terms of variables that were not used for clustering. The reliability and validity of the clustering solutions may be assessed in different ways.

Key Terms and Concepts

agglomeration schedule, 632
cluster centroid, 632
cluster centers, 632
cluster membership, 632
dendrogram, 632
distances between cluster centers, 632
icicle plot, 632
similarity/distance coefficient
    matrix, 632

euclidean distance, 633
hierarchical clustering, 634
agglomerative clustering, 634
divisive clustering, 634
linkage methods, 634
single linkage, 635
complete linkage, 635
average linkage, 635
variance methods, 635

Ward's procedure, 635
centroid methods, 635
nonhierarchical clustering, 635
sequential threshold
    method, 635
parallel threshold
    method, 636
optimizing partitioning
    method, 636

Suggested Cases, Video Cases, and HBS Cases

Running Case with Real Data

1.1 Dell

Comprehensive Critical Thinking Cases

2.1 American Idol   2.2 Baskin-Robbins   2.3 Akron Children's Hospital

Data Analysis Cases with Real Data

3.1 AT&T   3.2 IBM   3.3 Kimberly-Clark

Comprehensive Cases with Real Data

4.1 JPMorgan Chase   4.2 Wendy's

Video Case

23.1 Marriott

Live Research: Conducting a Marketing Research Project

1. The hierarchical and nonhierarchical methods should be used in tandem. First, obtain an initial clustering solution using a hierarchical procedure, such as average linkage or Ward's. Use the number of clusters and cluster centroids so obtained as inputs to a nonhierarchical method.

2. Choose different clustering methods and different distance measures and examine the effects on the cluster solutions.

Acronym

The steps involved and the salient concepts in clustering may be summarized by the acronym

Clustering:

C entroid methods
L inkage methods
U nderlying problem: selection of clustering variables
S imilarity or distance measures
T ype of clustering method: hierarchical vs. nonhierarchical, other
E rror sums of squares or variance methods
R eliability and validity assessment
I nterpreting and profiling clusters
N umber of clusters
G raphical aids: dendrogram and icicle plot

Exercises

Questions

1. Discuss the similarity and difference between cluster analysis and discriminant analysis.
2. What are some of the uses of cluster analysis in marketing?
3. Briefly define the following terms: dendrogram, icicle plot, agglomeration schedule, and cluster membership.
4. What is the most commonly used measure of similarity in cluster analysis?
5. Present a classification of clustering procedures.
6. Why is the average linkage method usually preferred to single linkage and complete linkage?
7. What are the two major disadvantages of nonhierarchical clustering procedures?
8. What guidelines are available for deciding on the number of clusters?
9. What is involved in the interpretation of clusters?
10. What are some of the additional variables used for profiling the clusters?
11. Describe some procedures available for assessing the quality of clustering solutions.
12. How is cluster analysis used to group variables?

Problems

1. Are the following statements true or false?
   a. Hierarchical and nonhierarchical clustering methods always produce different results.
   b. One should always standardize data before performing cluster analysis.
   c. Small distance coefficients in the agglomeration schedule imply that dissimilar cases are being merged.
   d. It does not matter which distance measure you use; the clustering solutions are essentially similar.
   e. It is advisable to analyze the same data set using different clustering procedures.

Internet and Computer Exercises

1. Analyze the data in Table 20.1 using the following hierarchical methods: (a) single linkage (nearest neighbor), (b) complete linkage (furthest neighbor), and (c) method of centroid. Use SPSS, SAS, or MINITAB. Compare your results with those given in Table 20.2.

2. Conduct the following analysis on the Nike data given in Internet and Computer Exercises 1 of Chapter 15. Consider only the following variables: awareness, attitude, preference, intention, and loyalty toward Nike.
   a. Cluster the respondents based on the identified variables using hierarchical clustering. Use Ward's method and squared euclidean distances. How many clusters do you recommend and why?
   b. Cluster the respondents based on the identified variables using k-means clustering and the number of clusters identified in a. Compare the results to those obtained in a.

3. Conduct the following analysis on the outdoor lifestyle data given in Internet and Computer Exercises 2 of Chapter 15. Consider only the following variables: the importance attached to enjoying nature, relating to the weather, living in harmony with the environment, exercising regularly, and meeting other people (V_2 to V_6).
   a. Cluster the respondents based on the identified variables using hierarchical clustering. Use Ward's method and squared euclidean distances. How many clusters do you recommend and why?

   b. Cluster the respondents based on the identified variables using the following hierarchical methods: (a) single linkage (nearest neighbor), (b) complete linkage (farthest neighbor), and (c) method of centroid.
   c. Cluster the respondents based on the identified variables using k-means clustering and the number of clusters identified in (a). Compare the results to those obtained in (a).

4. Conduct the following analysis on the sneakers data given in Internet and Computer Exercises 3 of Chapter 17. Consider only the following variables: evaluations of the sneakers on comfort (V_2), style (V_3), and durability (V_4).
   a. Cluster the respondents based on the identified variables using hierarchical clustering. Use Ward's method and squared euclidean distances. How many clusters do you recommend and why?
   b. Cluster the respondents based on the identified variables using k-means clustering and the number of clusters identified in a. Compare the results to those obtained in a.

5. Analyze the data collected in the Fieldwork Activity to cluster the respondents, using the hierarchical and nonhierarchical methods. Use one of the software packages discussed in this chapter.

6. Analyze the data collected in the Fieldwork Activity to cluster the 15 variables measuring consumer attitude toward airlines and flying. Use one of the programs described in this chapter.

Activities

Role Playing

1. You have been hired as a marketing research analyst by P&G. Your boss, the marketing manager, is wondering whether the market for toothpaste can be segmented based on the benefits consumers seek while buying toothpaste. Explain to your boss (a student in your class) the analysis that you would conduct.

Fieldwork

1. As a marketing research consultant to a major airline, you must determine consumers' attitudes toward airlines and flying. Construct a 15-item scale for this purpose. In a group of five students, obtain data on this scale and standard demographic characteristics from 50 male or female heads of households in your community. Each student should conduct 10 interviews. This data will be used to cluster respondents and to cluster the 15 variables measuring consumer attitudes toward airlines and flying.

Group Discussion

1. As a small group, discuss the role of cluster analysis in analyzing marketing research data. Emphasize the ways in which cluster analysis can be used in conjunction with other data analysis procedures.

Dell Running Case

Review the Dell case, Case 1.1, and questionnaire given toward the end of the book. Go to the Web site for this book and download the Dell data file.

1. How would you cluster the respondents based on evaluations of Dell (variables q8_1 through Q8_13)? Interpret the resulting clusters.

2. How would you cluster the respondents based on the Market Maven, Innovativeness, and Opinion Leadership items (variables q10_1 through Q10_13)? Interpret the resulting clusters.

"Often, relationships are easier to see if you can draw a picture or create a chart that illustrates the relationships . . . and that is the goal of multidimensional scaling. Conjoint analysis, on the other hand, helps us profile which attributes contribute most heavily to a person's choice among a variety of offerings made up of different combinations of these attributes."

Kunal Gupta, Vice President/Senior Consultant, Decision Sciences, Burke, Inc.

Objectives

[After reading this chapter, the student should be able to:]

1. Discuss the basic concept and scope of multidimensional scaling (MDS) in marketing research and describe its various applications.

2. Describe the steps involved in multidimensional scaling of perception data, including formulating the problem, obtaining input data, selecting an MDS procedure, deciding on the number of dimensions, labeling the dimensions and interpreting the configuration, and assessing reliability and validity.

3. Explain the multidimensional scaling of preference data and distinguish between internal and external analysis of preferences.

4. Explain correspondence analysis and discuss its advantages and disadvantages.

5. Understand the relationship among MDS, discriminant analysis, and factor analysis.

Multidimensional Scaling and Conjoint Analysis

6. Discuss the basic concepts of conjoint analysis, contrast it with MDS, and discuss its various applications.

7. Describe the procedure for conducting conjoint analysis, including formulating the problem, constructing the stimuli, deciding the form of input data, selecting a conjoint analysis procedure, interpreting the results, and assessing reliability and validity.

8. Define the concept of hybrid conjoint analysis and explain how it simplifies the data-collection task.

Overview

This chapter on data analysis presents two related techniques for analyzing consumer perceptions and preferences: multidimensional scaling (MDS) and conjoint analysis. We outline and illustrate the steps involved in conducting MDS and discuss the relationships among MDS, factor analysis, and discriminant analysis. Then we describe conjoint analysis and present a step-by-step procedure for conducting it. We also provide brief coverage of hybrid conjoint models. Finally, we discuss the use of software in MDS and conjoint analysis. Help for running the SPSS and SAS programs used in this chapter is provided in four ways: (1) detailed step-by-step instructions are given later in the chapter, (2) you can download (from the Web site for this book) computerized demonstration movies illustrating these step-by-step instructions, (3) you can download screen captures with notes illustrating these step-by-step instructions, and (4) you can refer to the *Study Guide and Technology Manual*, a supplement that accompanies this book.

Real Research

Colas Collide

In a survey, respondents were asked to rank-order all the possible pairs of 10 brands of soft drinks in terms of their similarity. These data were analyzed via multidimensional scaling and resulted in the following spatial representation of soft drinks.

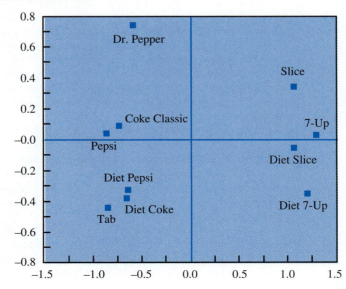

MDS has been used to understand consumer' perceptions of soft drinks and the competitive structure of the soft drink market.

From other information obtained in the questionnaire, the horizontal axis was labeled as "Cola Flavor." Tab was perceived to be the most cola flavored and 7-Up the least cola flavored. The vertical axis was labeled as "Dietness," with Tab being perceived to be the most dietetic and Dr. Pepper the most nondietetic. Note that Pepsi and Coke Classic were perceived to be very similar, as indicated by their closeness in the perceptual map. Close similarity was also perceived between 7-Up and Slice, Diet 7-Up and Diet Slice, and Tab, Diet Coke, and Diet Pepsi. Note that Dr. Pepper is perceived to be relatively dissimilar to the other brands. Such MDS maps are very useful in understanding the competitive structure of the soft drink market. The Coca-Cola Company has utilized techniques such as MDS to understand how consumers perceive their products as well as those of competitors and, as a result, reaped rich rewards by maintaining an iron grip on the U.S. carbonated soft drink market that was estimated to be about $70 billion in 2009.[1] ■

Real Research

What Do Customers Look For in a Computer Printer?

Printronix (www.printronix.com), a manufacturer of computer printers in Irvine, California, recently sponsored a nationwide conjoint analysis project using interactive software provided by Trade-Off Research Services. The objective of this direct-mail project was to identify the buying habits of present and future customers as well as those of purchasers of competitive products.

"We are in a market-driven, competitive printer industry where the customer has many choices and options," says Jack Andersen, vice president of domestic marketing for Printronix. "It is critical for the growth of this company that we know why customers buy or reject some printers over others."

Printronix mailed 1,600 diskette surveys to a prequalified list of decision makers. The surveys were divided according to the price range of the printers with only slight differences in the survey questions in both groups. Prequalifying also determined whether or not decision makers were planning on purchasing new equipment and when, and the willingness of the decision makers to participate in the survey.

Results received by Printronix management will help the company better understand the computer printer marketplace. The company will be able to identify its customer base, what the "hot" buttons are, and what type of products customers want now and in the future. Furthermore, the results tabulated will be able to provide insight into current and future product needs.

Particular marketing strategies can also be developed, for example, on how to engineer the product, how to advertise the product, and how best to sell it. "It's critical to focus your product marketing message to the needs of the buyer," says Andersen. "If we have designed certain elements into our products and then fail to promote them, we lose market share. That's the bottom line, so it's important to know as much as possible about the buyer."

Upon completion of the project and in characterizing the marketplace, Printronix will be able to cross-reference various respondents (e.g., MIS managers only; companies under $10 million; IBM-PC users only) to help identify and define vertical market potentials. Additionally, "what-if" analysis can be generated from the results. For example, if the speed of a printer were increased, with everything else remaining constant as it relates to quality and performance, how would this new input affect the current marketplace share? Such surveys and other sophisticated marketing have helped Printronix to understand the market needs and customer preferences better. The company has also developed cutting-edge products including RFID printers and thermal bar-code printers to cater to the evolving needs of these markets.[2] ∎

The first example illustrates the derivation and use of perceptual maps, which lie at the heart of MDS. The second example involves trade-offs respondents make when evaluating alternatives. The conjoint analysis procedure is based on these trade-offs.

Basic Concepts in Multidimensional Scaling (MDS)

multidimensional scaling (MDS)
A class of procedures for representing perceptions and preferences of respondents spatially by means of a visual display.

Multidimensional scaling (MDS) is a class of procedures for representing perceptions and preferences of respondents spatially by means of a visual display. Perceived or psychological relationships among stimuli are represented as geometric relationships among points in a multidimensional space. These geometric representations are often called *spatial maps*. The axes of the spatial map are assumed to denote the psychological bases or underlying dimensions respondents use to form perceptions and preferences for stimuli.[3] MDS has been used in marketing to identify:

1. The number and nature of dimensions consumers use to perceive different brands in the marketplace
2. The positioning of current brands on these dimensions
3. The positioning of consumers' ideal brand on these dimensions

Information provided by MDS has been used for a variety of marketing applications, including:

- *Image measurement.* Compare the customers' and noncustomers' perceptions of the firm with the firm's perceptions of itself and thus identify perceptual gaps.
- *Market segmentation.* Position brands and consumers in the same space and thus identify groups of consumers with relatively homogeneous perceptions.
- *New product development.* To look for gaps in the spatial map, which indicate potential opportunities for positioning new products. Also, to evaluate new product concepts and existing brands on a test basis to determine how consumers perceive the new concepts. The proportion of preferences for each new product is one indicator of its success.
- *Assessing advertising effectiveness.* Spatial maps can be used to determine whether advertising has been successful in achieving the desired brand positioning.
- *Pricing analysis.* Spatial maps developed with and without pricing information can be compared to determine the impact of pricing.
- *Channel decisions.* Judgments on compatibility of brands with different retail outlets could lead to spatial maps useful for making channel decisions.
- *Attitude scale construction.* MDS techniques can be used to develop the appropriate dimensionality and configuration of the attitude space.

Statistics and Terms Associated with MDS

The important statistics and terms associated with MDS include the following:

Similarity judgments. Similarity judgments are ratings on all possible pairs of brands or other stimuli in terms of their similarity using a Likert-type scale.

Preference rankings. Preference rankings are rank orderings of the brands or other stimuli from the most preferred to the least preferred. They are normally obtained from the respondents.

Stress. This is a lack-of-fit measure; higher values of stress indicate poorer fits.

R-square. R-square is a squared correlation index that indicates the proportion of variance of the optimally scaled data that can be accounted for by the MDS procedure. This is a goodness-of-fit measure.

Spatial map. Perceived relationships among brands or other stimuli are represented as geometric relationships among points in a multidimensional space called a *spatial map*.

FIGURE 21.1

Conducting Multidimensional Scaling

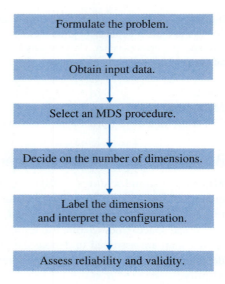

Coordinates. Coordinates indicate the positioning of a brand or a stimulus in a spatial map.

Unfolding. The representation of both brands and respondents as points in the same space is referred to as unfolding.

Conducting Multidimensional Scaling

Figure 21.1 shows the steps in MDS. The researcher must formulate the MDS problem carefully because a variety of data may be used as input into MDS. The researcher must also determine an appropriate form in which data should be obtained and select an MDS procedure for analyzing the data. An important aspect of the solution involves determining the number of dimensions for the spatial map. Also, the axes of the map should be labeled and the derived configuration interpreted. Finally, the researcher must assess the quality of the results obtained.[4] We describe each of these steps, beginning with problem formulation.

Formulate the Problem

Formulating the problem requires that the researcher specify the purpose for which the MDS results would be used and select the brands or other stimuli to be included in the analysis. The number of brands or stimuli selected and the specific brands included determine the nature of the resulting dimensions and configurations. At a minimum, eight brands or stimuli should be included so as to obtain a well-defined spatial map. Including more than 25 brands is likely to be cumbersome and may result in respondent fatigue.

The decision regarding which specific brands or stimuli to include should be made carefully. Suppose a researcher is interested in obtaining consumer perceptions of automobiles. If luxury automobiles are not included in the stimulus set, this dimension may not emerge in the results. The choice of the number and specific brands or stimuli to be included should be based on the statement of the marketing research problem, theory, and the judgment of the researcher.

Multidimensional scaling will be illustrated in the context of obtaining a spatial map for 10 toothpaste brands. These brands are Aqua-Fresh, Crest, Colgate, Aim, Gleem, Plus White, Ultra Brite, Close-Up, Pepsodent, and Sensodyne. Given the list of brands, the next question, then, is: How should we obtain data on these 10 brands?

Obtain Input Data

As shown in Figure 21.2, input data obtained from the respondents may be related to perceptions or preferences. Perception data, which may be direct or derived, is discussed first.

PERCEPTION DATA: DIRECT APPROACHES   In direct approaches to gathering perception data, the respondents are asked to judge how similar or dissimilar the various brands or stimuli are, using their

FIGURE 21.2

Input Data for Multidimensional Scaling

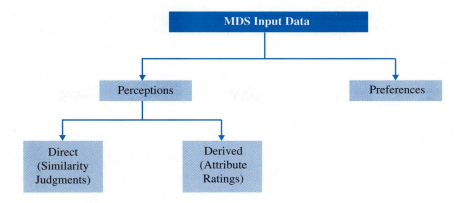

own criteria. Respondents are often required to rate all possible pairs of brands or stimuli in terms of similarity on a Likert scale. These data are referred to as *similarity judgments*. For example, similarity judgments on all the possible pairs of toothpaste brands may be obtained in the following manner:

	Very Dissimilar						Very Similar
Crest vs. Colgate	1	2	3	4	5	6	7
Aqua-Fresh vs. Crest	1	2	3	4	5	6	7
Crest vs. Aim	1	2	3	4	5	6	7
.							
.							
.							
Colgate vs. Aqua-Fresh	1	2	3	4	5	6	7

The number of pairs to be evaluated is $n(n - 1)/2$, where n is the number of stimuli. Other procedures are also available. Respondents could be asked to rank-order all the possible pairs from the most similar to the least similar. In another method, the respondent rank-orders the brands in terms of their similarity to an anchor brand. Each brand, in turn, serves as the anchor.

In our example, the direct approach was adopted. Subjects were asked to provide similarity judgments for all 45, (10 × 9/2), pairs of toothpaste brands, using a 7-point scale. The data obtained from one respondent are given in Table 21.1.[5]

PERCEPTION DATA: DERIVED APPROACHES Derived approaches to collecting perception data are attribute-based approaches requiring the respondents to rate the brands or stimuli on the

derived approaches
In MDS, attribute-based approaches to collecting perception data requiring the respondents to rate the stimuli on the identified attributes using semantic differential or Likert scales.

SPSS Data File

SAS Data File

TABLE 21.1

Similarity Ratings of Toothpaste Brands

	Aqua-Fresh	Crest	Colgate	Aim	Gleem	Plus White	Ultra Brite	Close-Up	Pepsodent	Sensodyne
Aqua-Fresh										
Crest	5									
Colgate	6	7								
Aim	4	6	6							
Gleem	2	3	4	5						
Plus White	3	3	4	4	5					
Ultra Brite	2	2	2	3	5	5				
Close-Up	2	2	2	2	6	5	6			
Pepsodent	2	2	2	2	6	6	7	6		
Sensodyne	1	2	4	2	4	3	3	4	3	

identified attributes using semantic differential or Likert scales. For example, the different brands of toothpaste may be rated on attributes such as these:

Whitens teeth	__ __ __ __ __ __ __ __ __ __	Does not whiten teeth
Prevents tooth decay	__ __ __ __ __ __ __ __ __ __	Does not prevent tooth decay
. . .		
Pleasant tasting	__ __ __ __ __ __ __ __ __ __	Unpleasant tasting

Sometimes an ideal brand is also included in the stimulus set. The respondents are asked to evaluate their hypothetical ideal brand on the same set of attributes. If attribute ratings are obtained, a similarity measure (such as euclidean distance) is derived for each pair of brands.

DIRECT VERSUS DERIVED APPROACHES Direct approaches have the advantage that the researcher does not have to identify a set of salient attributes. Respondents make similarity judgments using their own criteria, as they would under normal circumstances. The disadvantages are that the criteria are influenced by the brands or stimuli being evaluated. If the various brands of automobiles being evaluated are in the same price range, then price will not emerge as an important factor. It may be difficult to determine before analysis if and how the individual respondents' judgments should be combined. Furthermore, it may be difficult to label the dimensions of the spatial map.

The advantage of the attribute-based approach is that it is easy to identify respondents with homogeneous perceptions. The respondents can be clustered based on the attribute ratings. It is also easier to label the dimensions. A disadvantage is that the researcher must identify all the salient attributes, a difficult task. The spatial map obtained depends upon the attributes identified.

The direct approaches are more frequently used than the attribute-based approaches. However, it may be best to use both these approaches in a complementary way. Direct similarity judgments may be used for obtaining the spatial map, and attribute ratings may be used as an aid to interpreting the dimensions of the perceptual map. Similar procedures are used for preference data.

PREFERENCE DATA Preference data order the brands or stimuli in terms of respondents' preference for some property. A common way in which such data are obtained is preference rankings. Respondents are required to rank the brands from the most preferred to the least preferred. Alternatively, respondents may be required to make paired comparisons and indicate which brand in a pair they prefer. Another method is to obtain preference ratings for the various brands. (The rank order, paired comparison, and rating scales were discussed in Chapters 8 and 9 on scaling techniques.) When spatial maps are based on preference data, distance implies differences in preference. The configuration derived from preference data may differ greatly from that obtained from similarity data. Two brands may be perceived as different in a similarity map yet similar in a preference map, and vice versa. For example, Crest and Pepsodent may be perceived by a group of respondents as very different brands and thus appear far apart on a perception map. However, these two brands may be about equally preferred and appear close together on a preference map. We will continue using the perception data obtained in the toothpaste example to illustrate the MDS procedure and then consider the scaling of preference data.

Select an MDS Procedure

nonmetric MDS
A type of multidimensional scaling method that assumes that the input data are ordinal.

Selection of a specific MDS procedure depends upon whether perception or preference data are being scaled, or whether the analysis requires both kinds of data. The nature of the input data is also a determining factor. **Nonmetric MDS** procedures assume that the input data are ordinal, but they result in metric output. The distances in the resulting spatial map may be assumed to be interval scaled. These procedures find, in a given dimensionality, a spatial map whose rank

metric MDS
A multidimensional scaling method that assumes that the input data are metric.

orders of estimated distances between brands or stimuli best preserve or reproduce the input rank orders. In contrast, **metric MDS** methods assume that input data are metric. Because the output is also metric, a stronger relationship between the output and input data is maintained, and the metric (interval or ratio) qualities of the input data are preserved. The metric and nonmetric methods produce similar results.[6]

Another factor influencing the selection of a procedure is whether the MDS analysis will be conducted at the individual respondent level or at an aggregate level. In individual-level analysis, the data are analyzed separately for each respondent, resulting in a spatial map for each respondent. Although individual-level analysis is useful from a research perspective, it is not appealing from a managerial standpoint. Marketing strategies are typically formulated at the segment or aggregate level, rather than at the individual level. If aggregate-level analysis is conducted, some assumptions must be made in aggregating individual data. Typically, it is assumed that all respondents use the same dimensions to evaluate the brands or stimuli, but that different respondents weight these common dimensions differentially.

The data of Table 21.1 were treated as rank ordered and scaled using a nonmetric procedure. Because one respondent provided these data, an individual-level analysis was conducted. Spatial maps were obtained in one to four dimensions and then a decision on an appropriate number of dimensions was made. This decision is central to all MDS analyses; therefore, it is explored in greater detail in the following section.

Decide on the Number of Dimensions

The objective in MDS is to obtain a spatial map that best fits the input data in the smallest number of dimensions. However, spatial maps are computed in such a way that the fit improves as the number of dimensions increases. Therefore, a compromise has to be made. The fit of an MDS solution is commonly assessed by the stress measure. Stress is a lack-of-fit measure; higher values of stress indicate poorer fits. The following guidelines are suggested for determining the number of dimensions.

elbow criterion
A plot of stress versus dimensionality used in MDS. The point at which an elbow or a sharp bend occurs indicates an appropriate dimensionality.

1. *A priori knowledge*. Theory or past research may suggest a particular number of dimensions.
2. *Interpretability of the spatial map*. Generally, it is difficult to interpret configurations or maps derived in more than three dimensions.
3. *Elbow criterion*. A plot of stress versus dimensionality should be examined. The points in this plot usually form a convex pattern, as shown in Figure 21.3. The point at which

FIGURE 21.3
Plot of Stress Versus Dimensionality

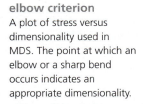
SPSS Output File

SAS Output File

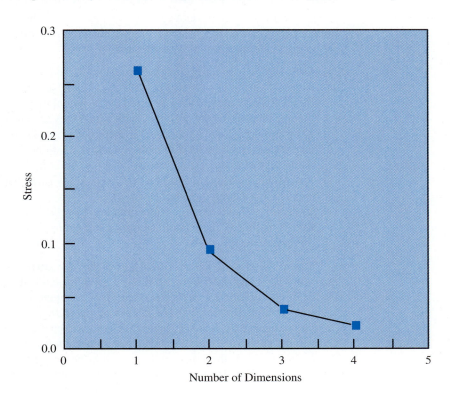

FIGURE 21.4

A Spatial Map of Toothpaste Brands

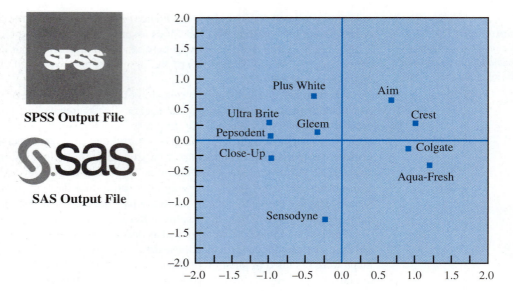

FIGURE 21.4

A Spatial Map of Toothpaste Brands

an elbow or a sharp bend occurs indicates an appropriate number of dimensions. Increasing the number of dimensions beyond this point is usually not worth the improvement in fit.

4. *Ease of use.* It is generally easier to work with two-dimensional maps or configurations than with those involving more dimensions.

5. *Statistical approaches.* For the sophisticated user, statistical approaches are also available for determining the dimensionality.[7]

Based on the plot of stress versus dimensionality (Figure 21.3), interpretability of the spatial map, and ease-of-use criteria, it was decided to retain a two-dimensional solution. This is shown in Figure 21.4.

Label the Dimensions and Interpret the Configuration

Once a spatial map is developed, the dimensions must be labeled and the configuration interpreted. Labeling the dimensions requires subjective judgment on the part of the researcher. The following guidelines can assist in this task:

1. Even if direct similarity judgments are obtained, ratings of the brands on researcher-supplied attributes may still be collected. Using statistical methods such as regression, these attribute vectors may be fitted in the spatial map (see Figure 21.5). The axes may then be labeled for the attributes with which they are most closely aligned.

2. After providing direct similarity or preference data, the respondents may be asked to indicate the criteria they used in making their evaluations. These criteria may then be subjectively related to the spatial map to label the dimensions.

3. If possible, the respondents can be shown their spatial maps and asked to label the dimensions by inspecting the configurations.

4. If objective characteristics of the brands are available (e.g., horsepower or miles per gallon for automobiles), these could be used as an aid in interpreting the subjective dimensions of the spatial maps.

Often, the dimensions represent more than one attribute. The configuration or the spatial map may be interpreted by examining the coordinates and relative positions of the brands. For example, brands located near each other compete more fiercely. An isolated brand has a unique image. Brands that are farther along in the direction of a descriptor are stronger on that characteristic. Thus, the strengths and weaknesses of each product can be understood. Gaps in the spatial map may indicate potential opportunities for introducing new products.

In Figure 21.5, the horizontal axis might be labeled as cavity-fighting protection versus whiteness of teeth. Brands with high positive values on this axis include Aqua-Fresh, Crest,

FIGURE 21.5

Using Attribute Vectors to Label Dimensions

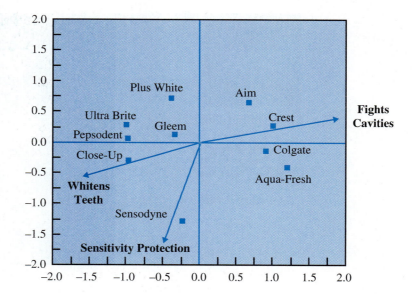

Colgate, and Aim (high cavity-fighting protection). Brands with large negative values on this dimension include Ultra Brite, Close-Up, and Pepsodent (high whiteness of teeth). The vertical axis may be interpreted as poor sensitivity protection versus good sensitivity protection. Note that Sensodyne, known for its sensitivity protection, loads negatively on the vertical axis. The gaps in the spatial map indicate potential opportunities for a brand that offers high cavity protection as well as high sensitivity protection.

Assess Reliability and Validity

The input data, and consequently the MDS solutions, are invariably subject to substantial random variability. Hence, it is necessary that some assessment be made of the reliability and validity of MDS solutions. The following guidelines are suggested.

1. The index of fit, or R-square, should be examined. This is a squared correlation index that indicates the proportion of variance of the optimally scaled data that can be accounted for by the MDS procedure. Thus, it indicates how well the MDS model fits the input data. Although higher values of R-square are desirable, values of 0.60 or better are considered acceptable.

2. Stress values are also indicative of the quality of MDS solutions. Whereas R-square is a measure of goodness of fit, stress measures badness of fit, or the proportion of variance of the optimally scaled data that is not accounted for by the MDS model. Stress values vary with the type of MDS procedure and the data being analyzed. For Kruskal's stress formula 1, the recommendations for evaluating stress values are as follows.[8]

Stress (%)	Goodness of Fit
20	poor
10	fair
5	good
2.5	excellent
0	perfect

3. If an aggregate-level analysis has been done, the original data should be split into two or more parts. MDS analysis should be conducted separately on each part and the results compared.

4. Stimuli can be selectively eliminated from the input data and the solutions determined for the remaining stimuli.

5. A random error term could be added to the input data. The resulting data are subjected to MDS analysis and the solutions compared.

6. The input data could be collected at two different points in time and the test-retest reliability determined.

FIGURE 21.6

Assessment of Stability by Deleting One Brand

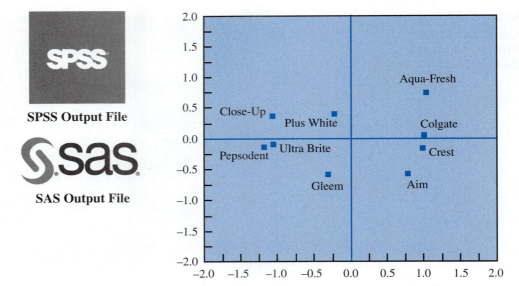

SPSS Output File

SAS Output File

Formal procedures are available for assessing the validity of MDS. In the case of our illustrative example, the stress value of 0.095 indicates a fair fit. One brand, namely Sensodyne, is different from the others. Would the elimination of Sensodyne from the stimulus set appreciably alter the relative configuration of the other brands? The spatial map obtained by deleting Sensodyne is shown in Figure 21.6. In comparing the results with Figure 21.5, note that the vertical axis is flipped in Figure 21.6. There is some change in the relative positions of the brands, particularly Gleem and Plus White. Yet the changes are modest, indicating fair stability.[9]

ACTIVE RESEARCH

Coca-Cola: Brand Positioning to Improve Competitiveness

Visit the Web site of Coca-Cola at www.cocacola.com and search the Internet using a search engine to obtain information on the positioning of Coca-Cola.

How would you obtain a competitive positioning map of the various soft drink brands?

As the brand manager for Coke, how would you alter the positioning of the various Coca-Cola brands to improve their competitiveness?

Assumptions and Limitations of MDS

It is worthwhile to point out some assumptions and limitations of MDS. It is assumed that the similarity of stimulus A to B is the same as the similarity of stimulus B to A. There are some instances where this assumption may be violated. For example, Mexico is perceived as more similar to the United States than the United States is to Mexico. MDS assumes that the distance (similarity) between two stimuli is some function of their partial similarities on each of several perceptual dimensions. Not much research has been done to test this assumption. When a spatial map is obtained, it is assumed that interpoint distances are ratio scaled and that the axes of the map are multidimensionally interval scaled. A limitation of MDS is that dimension interpretation relating physical changes in brands or stimuli to changes in the perceptual map is difficult at best. These limitations also apply to the scaling of preference data.

internal analysis of preferences
A method of configuring a spatial map such that the spatial map represents both brands or stimuli and respondent points or vectors and is derived solely from the preference data.

Scaling Preference Data

Analysis of preference data can be internal or external. In **internal analysis of preferences**, a spatial map representing both brands or stimuli and respondent points or vectors is derived solely from the preference data. Thus, by collecting preference data, both brands and respondents can

FIGURE 21.7

External Analysis of Preference Data

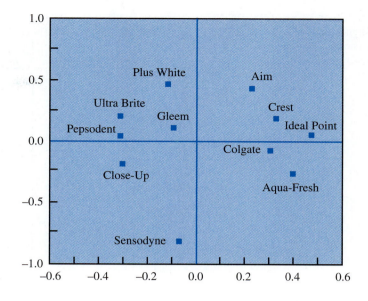

external analysis of preferences

A method of configuring a spatial map such that the ideal points or vectors based on preference data are fitted in a spatial map derived from perception data.

be represented in the same spatial map. In **external analysis of preferences**, the ideal points or vectors based on preference data are fitted in a spatial map derived from perception (e.g., similarities) data. In order to perform external analysis, both preference and perception data must be obtained. The representation of both brands and respondents as points in the same space, by using internal or external analysis, is referred to as *unfolding*.

External analysis is preferred in most situations. In internal analysis, the differences in perceptions are confounded with differences in preferences. It is possible that the nature and relative importance of dimensions may vary between the perceptual space and the preference space. Two brands may be perceived to be similar (located close to each other in the perceptual space), yet one brand may be distinctly preferred over the other (i.e., the brands may be located apart in the preference space). These situations cannot be accounted for in internal analysis. In addition, internal analysis procedures are beset with computational difficulties.[10]

We illustrate external analysis by scaling the preferences of our respondent into his spatial map. The respondent ranked the brands in the following order of preference (most preferred first): Colgate, Crest, Aim, Aqua-Fresh, Gleem, Pepsodent, Ultra Brite, Plus White, Close-Up, and Sensodyne. These preference rankings, along with the coordinates of the spatial map (Figure 21.5), were used as input into a preference scaling program to derive Figure 21.7. Notice the location of the ideal point. It is close to Colgate, Crest, Aim, and Aqua-Fresh, the four most preferred brands, and far from Close-Up and Sensodyne, the two least preferred brands. If a new brand were to be located in this space, its distance from the ideal point, relative to the distances of other brands from the ideal point, would determine the degree of preference for this brand. Another application is provided by the following example.

Real Research

Respondents Park in Different Spaces

A study conducted in 2008 examined consumer perceptions of automobiles by using multidimensional scales. Subjects rated several automobile attributes and the effect those attributes had on final product choice. Ratings were conducted using a 5-point scale, and each subject's responses were summed across each dimension. The five highest scoring attributes overall were price, fuel economy, net horsepower, braking, and acceleration. The use of multidimensional scaling can help automakers better understand what attributes are most important to consumers, and they can use that knowledge to leverage their positioning in the industry. An illustrative MDS map of selected automobile brands derived from similarity data is shown. In this spatial representation, each brand is identified by its distance from the other brands. The closer two brands are (e.g., Volkswagen and Chrysler), the more similar they are perceived to be. The farther apart two brands are (e.g., Volkswagen and Mercedes), the less similar they are perceived to be. Small distance (i.e., similarity) may also indicate competition. To illustrate, Honda competes closely with Toyota but not with Continental or Porsche. The dimensions can be interpreted as economy/prestige and sportiness/nonsportiness. The position of each car on these dimensions can be easily determined.

Joint Space Configuration
of Automobile Brands and
Consumer Preferences
(Illustrative Output)

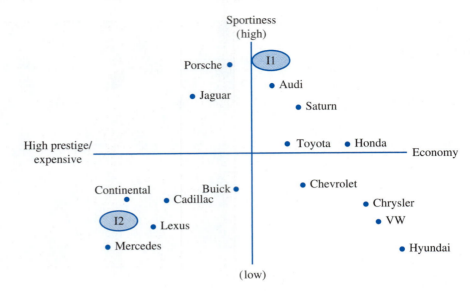

The preference data consisted of a simple rank order of the brands according to consumers' preferences. Respondents' ideal points are also located in the same spatial representation. Each ideal point represents the locus of preference of a particular respondent. Thus, respondent 1 (denoted by I1) prefers the sporty cars: Porsche, Jaguar, and Audi. Respondent 2 (denoted by I2) on the other hand, prefers luxury cars: Continental, Mercedes, Lexus, and Cadillac.

Such analysis can be done at the individual-respondent level, enabling the researcher to segment the market according to similarities in the respondents' ideal points. Alternatively, the respondents can be clustered based on their similarity with respect to the original preference ranking and ideal points established for each segment.[11] ■

Whereas, so far, we have considered only quantitative data, qualitative data can also be mapped using procedures such as correspondence analysis.

Correspondence Analysis

correspondence analysis
An MDS technique for scaling qualitative data that scales the rows and columns of the input contingency table in corresponding units so that each can be displayed in the same low-dimensional space.

Correspondence analysis is an MDS technique for scaling qualitative data in marketing research. The input data are in the form of a contingency table indicating a qualitative association between the rows and columns. Correspondence analysis scales the rows and columns in corresponding units, so that each can be displayed graphically in the same low-dimensional space. These spatial maps provide insights into (1) similarities and differences within the rows with respect to a given column category; (2) similarities and differences within the column categories with respect to a given row category; and (3) relationship among the rows and columns.[12]

The interpretation of results in correspondence analysis is similar to that in principal components analysis (Chapter 19), given the similarity of the algorithms. Correspondence analysis results in the grouping of categories (activities, brands, or other stimuli) found within the contingency table, just as principal components analysis involves the grouping of the variables. The results are interpreted in terms of proximities among the rows and columns of the contingency table. Categories that are closer together are more similar in underlying structure.

The advantage of correspondence analysis, as compared to other multidimensional scaling techniques, is that it reduces the data-collection demands imposed on the respondents, because only binary or categorical data are obtained. The respondents are merely asked to check which attributes apply to each of several brands. The input data are the number of "yes" responses for each brand on each attribute. The brands and the attributes are then displayed in the same multidimensional space. The disadvantage is that between-set (i.e., between column and row) distances cannot be meaningfully interpreted. Correspondence analysis is an exploratory data analysis technique that is not suitable for hypothesis testing.[13]

MDS, including correspondence analysis, is not the only procedure available for obtaining perceptual maps. Two other techniques that we have discussed before, discriminant analysis (Chapter 18) and factor analysis (Chapter 19), can also be used for this purpose.

Relationship Among MDS, Factor Analysis, and Discriminant Analysis

If the attribute-based approach is used to obtain input data, spatial maps can also be obtained by using factor or discriminant analysis. In this approach, each respondent rates n brands on m attributes. By factor analyzing the data, one could derive, for each respondent, n factor scores for each factor, one for each brand (see Chapter 19). By plotting brand scores on the factors, a spatial map could be obtained for each respondent. If an aggregate map is desired, the factor score for each brand for each factor can be averaged across respondents. The dimensions would be labeled by examining the factor loadings, which are estimates of the correlations between attribute ratings and underlying factors.

The goal of discriminant analysis is to select the linear combinations of attributes that best discriminate between the brands or stimuli (Chapter 18). To develop spatial maps by means of discriminant analysis, the dependent variable is the brand rated and the independent or predictor variables are the attribute ratings. A spatial map can be obtained by plotting the discriminant scores for the brands. The discriminant scores are the ratings on the perceptual dimensions, based on the attributes that best distinguish the brands. The dimensions can be labeled by examining the discriminant weights, or the weightings of attributes that make up a discriminant function or dimension.[14]

Basic Concepts in Conjoint Analysis

conjoint analysis
A technique that attempts to determine the relative importance consumers attach to salient attributes and the utilities they attach to the levels of attributes.

Conjoint analysis attempts to determine the relative importance consumers attach to salient attributes and the utilities they attach to the levels of attributes. This information is derived from consumers' evaluations of brands, or brand profiles composed of these attributes and their levels. The respondents are presented with stimuli that consist of combinations of attribute levels. They are asked to evaluate these stimuli in terms of their desirability. Conjoint procedures attempt to assign values to the levels of each attribute, so that the resulting values or utilities attached to the stimuli match, as closely as possible, the input evaluations provided by the respondents. The underlying assumption is that any set of stimuli, such as products, brands, or stores, is evaluated as a bundle of attributes.[15]

Like multidimensional scaling, conjoint analysis relies on respondents' subjective evaluations. However, in MDS, the stimuli are products or brands. In conjoint analysis, the stimuli are combinations of attribute levels determined by the researcher. The goal in MDS is to develop a spatial map depicting the stimuli in a multidimensional perceptual or preference space. Conjoint analysis, on the other hand, seeks to develop the part-worth or utility functions describing the utility consumers attach to the levels of each attribute. The two techniques are complementary.

Conjoint analysis has been used in marketing for a variety of purposes, including:

- Determining the relative importance of attributes in the consumer choice process. A standard output from conjoint analysis consists of derived relative importance weights for all the attributes used to construct the stimuli used in the evaluation task. The relative importance weights indicate which attributes are important in influencing consumer choice.
- Estimating market share of brands that differ in attribute levels. The utilities derived from conjoint analysis can be used as input into a choice simulator to determine the share of choices, and hence the market share, of different brands.
- Determining the composition of the most preferred brand. The brand features can be varied in terms of attribute levels and the corresponding utilities determined. The brand features that yield the highest utility indicate the composition of the most preferred brand.
- Segmenting the market based on similarity of preferences for attribute levels. The part-worth functions derived for the attributes may be used as a basis for clustering respondents to arrive at homogeneous preference segments.[16]

Applications of conjoint analysis have been made in consumer goods, industrial goods, financial, and other services. Moreover, these applications have spanned all areas of marketing. A survey of conjoint analysis reported applications in the areas of new product/concept identification, competitive analysis, pricing, market segmentation, advertising, and distribution.[17]

Statistics and Terms Associated with Conjoint Analysis

The important statistics and terms associated with conjoint analysis include:

Part-worth functions. The part-worth functions or *utility functions* describe the utility consumers attach to the levels of each attribute.

Relative importance weights. The relative importance weights are estimated and indicate which attributes are important in influencing consumer choice.

Attribute levels. The attribute levels denote the values assumed by the attributes.

Full profiles. Full profiles or complete profiles of brands are constructed in terms of all the attributes by using the attribute levels specified by the design.

Pairwise tables. In pairwise tables, the respondents evaluate two attributes at a time until all the required pairs of attributes have been evaluated.

Cyclical designs. Cyclical designs are designs employed to reduce the number of paired comparisons.

Fractional factorial designs. Fractional factorial designs are designs employed to reduce the number of stimulus profiles to be evaluated in the full profile approach.

Orthogonal arrays. Orthogonal arrays are a special class of fractional designs that enable the efficient estimation of all main effects.

Internal validity. This involves correlations of the predicted evaluations for the holdout or validation stimuli with those obtained from the respondents.

Conducting Conjoint Analysis

Figure 21.8 lists the steps in conjoint analysis. Formulating the problem involves identifying the salient attributes and their levels. These attributes and levels are used for constructing the stimuli to be used in a conjoint evaluation task. The respondents rate or rank the stimuli using a suitable scale and the data obtained are analyzed. The results are interpreted and their reliability and validity assessed.

Formulate the Problem

In formulating the conjoint analysis problem, the researcher must identify the attributes and attribute levels to be used in constructing the stimuli. Attribute levels denote the values assumed by the attributes. From a theoretical standpoint, the attributes selected should be salient in influencing consumer preference and choice. For example, in the choice of an automobile brand, price, gas mileage, interior space, and so forth should be included. From a managerial perspective, the attributes and their levels should be actionable. To tell a manager that consumers prefer

FIGURE 21.8

Conducting Conjoint Analysis

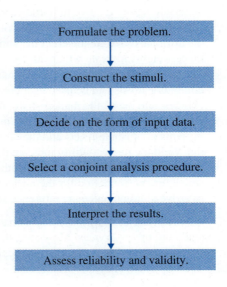

Formulate the problem.

Construct the stimuli.

Decide on the form of input data.

Select a conjoint analysis procedure.

Interpret the results.

Assess reliability and validity.

a sporty car to one that is conservative looking is not helpful, unless sportiness and conservativeness are defined in terms of attributes over which a manager has control. The attributes can be identified through discussions with management and industry experts, analysis of secondary data, qualitative research, and pilot surveys. A typical conjoint analysis study involves six or seven attributes.

Once the salient attributes have been identified, their appropriate levels should be selected. The number of attribute levels determines the number of parameters that will be estimated and also influences the number of stimuli that will be evaluated by the respondents. To minimize the respondent evaluation task, and yet estimate the parameters with reasonable accuracy, it is desirable to restrict the number of attribute levels. The utility or part-worth function for the levels of an attribute may be nonlinear. For example, a consumer may prefer a medium-sized car to either a small or large one. Likewise, the utility for price may be nonlinear. The loss of utility in going from a low to a medium price may be much smaller than the loss in utility in going from a medium to a high price. In these cases, at least three levels should be used. Some attributes, though, may naturally occur in binary form (two levels): a car does or does not have a sunroof.

The attribute levels selected will affect the consumer evaluations. If the price of an automobile brand is varied at $10,000, $12,000, and $14,000, price will be relatively unimportant. On the other hand, if the price is varied at $10,000, $20,000, and $30,000, it will be an important factor. Hence, the researcher should take into account the attribute levels prevalent in the marketplace and the objectives of the study. Using attribute levels that are beyond the range reflected in the marketplace will decrease the believability of the evaluation task, but it will increase the accuracy with which the parameters are estimated. The general guideline is to select attribute levels so that the ranges are somewhat greater than that prevalent in the marketplace but not so large as to adversely impact the believability of the evaluation task.

We illustrate the conjoint methodology by considering the problem of how students evaluate sneakers. Qualitative research identified three attributes as salient: the sole, the upper, and the price.[18] Each was defined in terms of three levels, as shown in Table 21.2. These attributes and their levels were used for constructing the conjoint analysis stimuli. Note that to keep the illustration simple, we are using only a limited number of attributes, that is, only three. It has been argued that pictorial stimuli should be used when consumers' marketplace choices are strongly guided by the product's styling, such that the choices are heavily based on an inspection of actual products or pictures of products.[19]

Construct the Stimuli

Two broad approaches are available for constructing conjoint analysis stimuli: the pairwise approach and the full-profile procedure. In the pairwise approach, also called *two-factor evaluations,* the respondents evaluate two attributes at a time until all the possible pairs of attributes have been evaluated. This approach is illustrated in the context of the sneaker example in Figure 21.9. For each pair, respondents evaluate all the combinations of levels of both the attributes, which are presented in a matrix. In the full-profile approach, also called *multiple-factor evaluations,* full or complete profiles

TABLE 21.2		
Sneaker Attributes and Levels		
Attribute	Level No.	Description
Sole	3	Rubber
	2	Polyurethane
	1	Plastic
Upper	3	Leather
	2	Canvas
	1	Nylon
Price	3	$30.00
	2	$60.00
	1	$90.00

FIGURE 21.9

Pairwise Approach to Collecting Conjoint Data

Upper \ Sole	Rubber	Polyurethane	Plastic
Leather			
Canvas			
Nylon			

Price \ Sole	Rubber	Polyurethane	Plastic
$30.00			
$60.00			
$90.00			

Upper \ Price	$30.00	$60.00	$90.00
Leather			
Canvas			
Nylon			

of brands are constructed for all the attributes. Typically, each profile is described on a separate index card. This approach is illustrated in the context of the sneaker example in Table 21.3.

It is not necessary to evaluate all the possible combinations, nor is it feasible in all cases. In the pairwise approach, it is possible to reduce the number of paired comparisons by using cyclical designs. Likewise, in the full-profile approach, the number of stimulus profiles can be greatly reduced by means of fractional factorial designs. A special class of fractional designs, called *orthogonal arrays*, allows for the efficient estimation of all main effects. Orthogonal arrays permit the measurement of all main effects of interest on an uncorrelated basis. These designs assume that all interactions are negligible.[20] Generally, two sets of data are obtained. One, the *estimation set,* is used to calculate the part-worth functions for the attribute levels. The other, the *holdout set*, is used to assess reliability and validity.

The advantage of the pairwise approach is that it is easier for the respondents to provide these judgments. However, its relative disadvantage is that it requires more evaluations than the full-profile approach. Also, the evaluation task may be unrealistic when only two attributes are being evaluated simultaneously. Studies comparing the two approaches indicate that both methods yield comparable utilities, yet the full-profile approach is more commonly used.

The sneaker example follows the full-profile approach. Given three attributes, defined at three levels each, a total of $3 \times 3 \times 3 = 27$ profiles can be constructed. To reduce the respondent evaluation task, a fractional factorial design was employed and a set of nine profiles was constructed to constitute the estimation stimuli set (see Table 21.4). Another set of nine stimuli was constructed for

TABLE 21.3

Full-Profile Approach to Collecting Conjoint Data

Example of a Sneaker Product Profile	
Sole	Made of rubber
Upper	Made of nylon
Price	$30.00

TABLE 21.4
Sneaker Profiles and Their Ratings

Profile No.	Attribute Levels[a]			Preference Rating
	Sole	Upper	Price	
1	1	1	1	9
2	1	2	2	7
3	1	3	3	5
4	2	1	2	6
5	2	2	3	5
6	2	3	1	6
7	3	1	3	5
8	3	2	1	7
9	3	3	2	6

[a]The attribute levels correspond to those in Table 21.2.

validation purposes. Input data were obtained for both the estimation and validation stimuli. However, before the data could be obtained, it was necessary to decide on the form of the input data.

Decide on the Form of Input Data

As in the case of MDS, conjoint analysis input data can be either nonmetric or metric. For nonmetric data, the respondents are typically required to provide rank order evaluations. For the pairwise approach, respondents rank all the cells of each matrix in terms of their desirability. For the full-profile approach, they rank all the stimulus profiles. Rankings involve relative evaluations of the attribute levels. Proponents of ranking data believe that such data accurately reflect the behavior of consumers in the marketplace.

In the metric form, the respondents provide ratings, rather than rankings. In this case, the judgments are typically made independently. Advocates of rating data believe that they are more convenient for the respondents and easier to analyze than rankings. In recent years, the use of ratings has become increasingly common.

In conjoint analysis, the dependent variable is usually preference or intention to buy. In other words, respondents provide ratings or rankings in terms of their preference or intentions to buy. However, the conjoint methodology is flexible and can accommodate a range of other dependent variables, including actual purchase or choice.

In evaluating sneaker profiles, respondents were required to provide preference ratings for the sneakers described by the nine profiles in the estimation set. These ratings were obtained using a 9-point Likert scale (1 = not preferred, 9 = greatly preferred). Ratings obtained from one respondent are shown in Table 21.4.

Select a Conjoint Analysis Procedure

conjoint analysis model
The mathematical model expressing the fundamental relationship between attributes and utility in conjoint analysis.

The basic **conjoint analysis model** may be represented by the following formula:[21]

$$U(X) = \sum_{i=1}^{m} \sum_{j=1}^{k_i} \alpha_{ij} x_{ij}$$

where

$U(X)$ = overall utility of an alternative

α_{ij} = the part-worth contribution or utility associated with the jth level ($j = 1, 2, \ldots k_i$) of the ith attribute ($i = 1, 2, \ldots m$)

k_i = number of levels of attribute i

m = number of attributes

x_{ij} = 1 if the jth level of the ith attribute is present

= 0 otherwise

The importance of an attribute, I_i, is defined in terms of the range of the part-worths, α_{ij}, across the levels of that attribute:

$$I_j = \{\max(\alpha_{ij}) - \min(\alpha_{ij})\}, \text{ for each } i$$

The attribute's importance is normalized to ascertain its importance relative to other attributes, W_i:

$$W_i = \frac{I_i}{\displaystyle\sum_{i=1}^{m} I_i}$$

so that

$$\sum_{i=1}^{m} W_i = 1$$

Several different procedures are available for estimating the basic model. The simplest, and one that is gaining in popularity, is dummy variable regression (see Chapter 17). In this case, the predictor variables consist of dummy variables for the attribute levels. If an attribute has k_i levels, it is coded in terms of $k_i - 1$ dummy variables (see Chapter 14). If metric data are obtained, the ratings, assumed to be interval scaled, form the dependent variable. If the data are nonmetric, the rankings may be converted to 0 or 1 by making paired comparisons between brands. In this case, the predictor variables represent the differences in the attribute levels of the brands being compared. Other procedures that are appropriate for nonmetric data include LINMAP, MONANOVA, and the LOGIT model (see Chapter 18).[22]

The researcher must also decide whether the data will be analyzed at the individual-respondent or the aggregate level. At the individual level, the data of each respondent are analyzed separately. If an aggregate-level analysis is to be conducted, some procedure for grouping the respondents must be devised. One common approach is first to estimate individual-level part-worth or utility functions. The respondents are then clustered on the basis of the similarity of their part-worths. Aggregate analysis is then conducted for each cluster. An appropriate model for estimating the parameters should be specified.[23]

The data reported in Table 21.4 were analyzed using ordinary least-squares (OLS) regression with dummy variables. The dependent variable was the preference ratings. The independent variables or predictors were six dummy variables, two for each variable. The transformed data are shown in Table 21.5. Because the data pertain to a single respondent, an individual-level analysis was conducted. The part-worth or utility functions estimated for each attribute, as well the relative importance of the attributes, are given in Table 21.6.[24]

SPSS Data File

SAS Data File

TABLE 21.5

Sneaker Data Coded for Dummy Variable Regression

Preference Ratings	Sole		Attributes Upper		Price	
Y	X_1	X_2	X_3	X_4	X_5	X_6
9	1	0	1	0	1	0
7	1	0	0	1	0	1
5	1	0	0	0	0	0
6	0	1	1	0	0	1
5	0	1	0	1	0	0
6	0	1	0	0	1	0
5	0	0	1	0	0	0
7	0	0	0	1	1	0
6	0	0	0	0	0	1

TABLE 21.6
Results of Conjoint Analysis

Attribute	No.	Level Description	Utility	Importance
Sole	3	Rubber	0.778	
	2	Polyurethane	−0.556	
	1	Plastic	−0.222	0.286
Upper	3	Leather	0.445	
	2	Canvas	0.111	
	1	Nylon	−0.556	0.214
Price	3	$30.00	1.111	
	2	$60.00	0.111	
	1	$90.00	−1.222	0.500

The model estimated may be represented as:

$$U = b_0 + b_1X_1 + b_2X_2 + b_3X_3 + b_4X_4 + b_5X_5 + b_6X_6$$

where

X_1, X_2 = dummy variables representing Sole
X_3, X_4 = dummy variables representing Upper
X_5, X_6 = dummy variables representing Price

For Sole, the attribute levels were coded as follows:

	X_1	X_2
Level 1	1	0
Level 2	0	1
Level 3	0	0

The levels of the other attributes were coded similarly. The parameters were estimated as follows:

$$b_0 = 4.222$$
$$b_1 = 1.000$$
$$b_2 = -0.333$$
$$b_3 = 1.000$$
$$b_4 = 0.667$$
$$b_5 = 2.333$$
$$b_6 = 1.333$$

Given the dummy variable coding, in which level 3 is the base level, the coefficients may be related to the part-worths. As explained in Chapter 17, each dummy variable coefficient represents the difference in the part-worth for that level minus the part-worth for the base level. For Sole we have the following:

$$\alpha_{11} - \alpha_{13} = b_1$$
$$\alpha_{12} - \alpha_{13} = b_2$$

To solve for the part-worths, an additional constraint is necessary. The part-worths are estimated on an interval scale, so the origin is arbitrary. Therefore, the additional constraint that is imposed is of the form:

$$\alpha_{11} + \alpha_{12} + \alpha_{13} = 0$$

These equations for the first attribute, Sole, are:

$$\alpha_{11} - \alpha_{13} = 1.000$$
$$\alpha_{12} - \alpha_{13} = -0.333$$
$$\alpha_{11} + \alpha_{12} + \alpha_{13} = 0$$

Solving these equations, we get,

$$\alpha_{11} = 0.778$$
$$\alpha_{12} = -0.556$$
$$\alpha_{13} = -0.222$$

The part-worths for other attributes reported in Table 21.6 can be estimated similarly. For Upper we have:

$$\alpha_{21} - \alpha_{23} = b_3$$
$$\alpha_{22} - \alpha_{23} = b_4$$
$$\alpha_{21} + \alpha_{22} + \alpha_{23} = 0$$

For the third attribute, Price, we have:

$$\alpha_{31} - \alpha_{33} = b_5$$
$$\alpha_{32} - \alpha_{33} = b_6$$
$$\alpha_{31} + \alpha_{32} + \alpha_{33} = 0$$

The relative importance weights were calculated based on ranges of part-worths, as follows:

$$\text{Sum of ranges} = (0.778 - (-0.556)) + (0.445 - (-0.556))$$
$$\text{of part-worths} \quad + (1.111 - (-1.222))$$
$$= 4.668$$

$$\text{relative importance of Sole} = \frac{[0.778 - (-0.556)]}{4.668} = \frac{1.334}{4.668} = 0.286$$

$$\text{relative importance of Upper} = \frac{[0.445 - (-0.556)]}{4.668} = \frac{1.001}{4.668} = 0.214$$

$$\text{relative importance of Price} = \frac{[1.111 - (-1.222)]}{4.668} = \frac{2.333}{4.668} = 0.500$$

The estimation of the part-worths and the relative importance weights provides the basis for interpreting the results.

Interpret the Results

For interpreting the results, it is helpful to plot the part-worth functions. The part-worth function values for each attribute given in Table 21.6 are graphed in Figure 21.10. As can be seen from Table 21.6 and Figure 21.10, this respondent has the greatest preference for a rubber sole when evaluating sneakers. Second preference is for a plastic sole, and a polyurethane sole is least preferred. A leather upper is most preferred, followed by canvas and nylon. As expected, a price of $30.00 has the highest utility and a price of $90.00 the lowest. The utility values reported in Table 21.6 have only interval-scale properties, and their origin is arbitrary. In terms of relative importance of the attributes, we see that Price is number one. Second most important is Sole, followed closely by Upper. Because price is by far the most important attribute for this respondent, this person could be labeled as price sensitive.

Assessing Reliability and Validity

Several procedures are available for assessing the reliability and validity of conjoint analysis results.[25]

1. The goodness of fit of the estimated model should be evaluated. For example, if dummy variable regression is used, the value of R^2 will indicate the extent to which the model fits the data. Models with poor fit are suspect.
2. Test-retest reliability can be assessed by obtaining a few replicated judgments later in data collection. In other words, at a later stage in the interview, the respondents are asked to

FIGURE 21.10

Part-Worth Functions

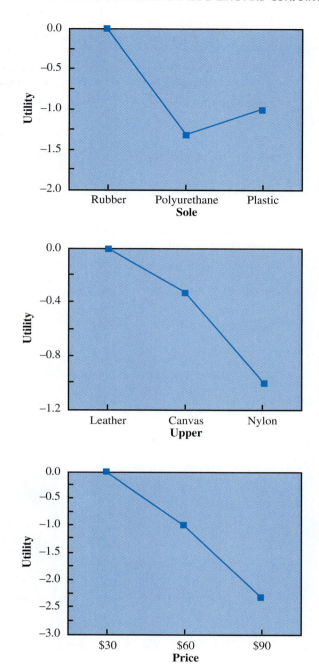

evaluate certain selected stimuli again. The two values of these stimuli are then correlated to assess test-retest reliability.

3. The evaluations for the holdout or validation stimuli can be predicted by the estimated part-worth functions. The predicted evaluations can then be correlated with those obtained from the respondents to determine internal validity.

4. If an aggregate-level analysis has been conducted, the estimation sample can be split in several ways and conjoint analysis conducted on each subsample. The results can be compared across subsamples to assess the stability of conjoint analysis solutions.

In running a regression analysis on the data of Table 21.5, an R^2 of 0.934 was obtained, indicating a good fit. The preference ratings for the nine validation profiles were predicted from the utilities reported in Table 21.6. These were correlated with the input ratings for these profiles obtained from the respondent. The correlation coefficient was 0.95, indicating good predictive ability. This correlation coefficient is significant at $\alpha = 0.05$.

Real Research   Examining Microcomputer Trade-Offs Microscopically

Conjoint analysis was used to determine how consumers make trade-offs between various attributes when selecting microcomputers. Four attributes were chosen as salient. These attributes and their levels are:

Extended Warranty
- No
- 4 Years

Monitor Maximum Resolution
- 1280 × 1024
- 1680 × 1050

Screen Size
- 17 inch
- 24 inch

Price Level
- $1,000
- $1,500
- $2,000

All possible combinations of these attribute levels result in 24 (2 × 2 × 2 × 3) profiles of microcomputers. One such profile is as follows:

Extended Warranty:	4 Years
Monitor Max. Resolution:	1680 × 1050
Screen size:	17 inches
Price level:	$1,500

Respondents rank-ordered these profiles in terms of preferences. The data for each respondent can be utilized to develop preference functions. The preference functions for one individual are illustrated.

Consumer Preferences

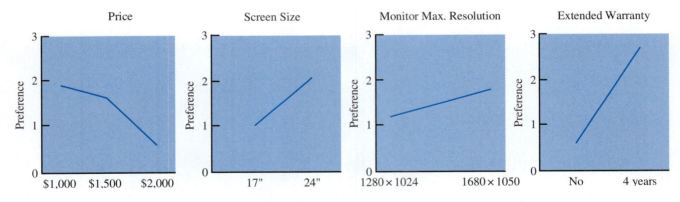

Based on the derived part-worth or preference functions, the relative importance of the various attributes in determining these consumer preferences can be estimated by comparing part-worths as follows:

Relative Importance

Evaluative Criteria	Importance
Extended Warranty	35%
Monitor Maximum Resolution	15%
Screen Size	25%
Price Level	25%

For this consumer, extended warranty is the most important feature and the 4-year warranty is the preferred option. Although price and screen size are also important, price becomes a factor only between $1,500 and $2,000. As expected, a screen size of 24" is preferred. Whether the monitor maximum resolution is 1280 × 1024 or 1680 × 1050 does not matter as much as the other factors. Information provided by the part-worth functions and relative importance weights can be used to cluster respondents to determine benefit segments for microcomputers.

Desktop and notebook computer makers such as Dell (www.dell.com) can make use of conjoint analysis to find out whether consumers place more value on features such as speed, screen size, or disk space, or if consumers place more value on cost or weight. Any way you look at it, conjoint analysis is continually being used by computer manufacturers and many other industries to deliver preferred products to consumers.[26] ■

Assumptions and Limitations of Conjoint Analysis

Although conjoint analysis is a popular technique, like MDS, it involves a number of assumptions and limitations. Conjoint analysis assumes that the important attributes of a product can be identified. Furthermore, it assumes that consumers evaluate the choice alternatives in terms of these attributes and make trade-offs. However, in situations where image or brand name is important, consumers may not evaluate the brands or alternatives in terms of attributes. Even if consumers consider product attributes, the trade-off model may not be a good representation of the choice process. Another limitation is that data collection may be complex, particularly if a large number of attributes are involved and the model must be estimated at the individual level. This problem has been mitigated to some extent by procedures such as interactive or adaptive conjoint analysis and hybrid conjoint analysis. It should also be noted that the part-worth functions are not unique.

Hybrid Conjoint Analysis

hybrid conjoint analysis
A form of conjoint analysis that can simplify the data-collection task and estimate selected interactions as well as all main effects.

Hybrid conjoint analysis is an attempt to simplify the burdensome data-collection task required in traditional conjoint analysis. In the traditional method, each respondent evaluates a large number of profiles, yet usually only simple part-worths, without any interaction effects, are estimated. In the simple part-worths or main effects model, the value of a combination is simply the sum of the separate main effects (simple part-worths). In actual practice, two attributes may interact, in the sense that the respondent may value the combination more than the average contribution of the separate parts. Hybrid models have been developed to serve two main purposes: (1) simplify the data-collection task by imposing less of a burden on each respondent, and (2) permit the estimation of selected interactions (at the subgroup level) as well as all main (or simple) effects at the individual level.

In the hybrid approach, the respondents evaluate a limited number, generally no more than nine, of conjoint stimuli, such as full profiles. These profiles are drawn from a large master design, and different respondents evaluate different sets of profiles, so that over a group of respondents, all the profiles of interest are evaluated. In addition, respondents directly evaluate the relative importance of each attribute and desirability of the levels of each attribute. By combining the direct evaluations with those derived from the evaluations of the conjoint stimuli, it is possible to estimate a model at the aggregate level and still retain some individual differences.[27]

MDS and conjoint analysis are complementary techniques and may be used in combination, as the following example shows.

Real Research | Weeding Out the Competition

In 2008, ICI (www.ici.com) became part of AkzoNobel, the world's biggest coatings manufacturer, the number one in decorative paints and performance coatings, and a leading supplier of specialty chemicals. ICI Americas Agricultural Products did not know whether it should lower the price of Fusilade, its herbicide. It knew it had developed a potent herbicide, but it was not sure the weed killer would survive in a price-conscious market. So a survey was designed to assess the relative importance of different attributes in selecting herbicides and measure and map perceptions of major herbicides on the same attributes. Personal interviews were conducted with 601 soybean and cotton farmers who had at least 200 acres dedicated to growing these crops and who had used herbicides during the past growing season. First, conjoint analysis was used to determine the relative importance of attributes farmers use when selecting herbicides. Then multidimensional scaling was used to map farmers' perceptions of herbicides. The conjoint study showed that price greatly influenced herbicide selections, and respondents were particularly sensitive when costs were more than $18 an acre. But price was not the only determinant. Farmers also considered how much weed control the herbicide provided. They were willing to pay higher prices to keep the pests off their land. The study showed that herbicides that failed to control even one of the four most common weeds would have to be very inexpensive to attain a reasonable market share. Fusilade promised good weed control. Furthermore, multidimensional scaling indicated that one of Fusilade's competitors was considered to be expensive. Hence, ICI kept its original pricing plan and did not lower the price of Fusilade.

As of 2009, however, the agriculture industry has changed. One factor that has changed the industry is a shift in technology, especially biotechnology. Roundup Ready soybeans had a huge effect on the herbicide market by making farmers switch from using traditional soybean herbicides to a new combined technology of Roundup and transgenic seed. The new technology cut the cost of per-acre herbicides in half and, as a result, competing chemical companies were forced to meet the price of the new technology. It is very important for companies to research consumer acceptance of technological innovations using techniques such as MDS and conjoint analysis to avoid being left by the wayside.[28] ■

ACTIVE RESEARCH

Fossil: Superfunctional and Fashionable Watches

Visit www.fossil.com and search the Internet using a search engine as well as your library's online database to obtain information on consumers' preferences for wristwatches.

As the marketing chief for Fossil, you are considering the introduction of a superfunctional, fashionable wristwatch for men and women priced at $99. What kind of information do you need to help you make this decision?

How would you determine consumer preferences for wristwatches that vary in terms of price ($99, $299, $499), precision (very high, high, and OK), and style (contemporary, old fashioned, futuristic)?

Both MDS and conjoint analysis are useful in conducting international marketing research, as illustrated by the next two examples. The example after that presents an application of MDS in researching ethical perceptions.

Real Research   ## Herit-Age or Merit-Age in Europe?

European car manufacturers are increasingly focusing on an attribute that competitors will not be able to buy or build—it is heritage. For BMW, it is superior engineering. A. B. Volvo of Sweden has a reputation for safe cars. Italian Alfa Romeo rides on the laurels of engines that have won numerous races. The French Renault has savoir-faire. On the other hand, Japanese cars are advanced technologically but they do not have class or heritage. For example, Lexus and Infiniti are high-performance cars, but they lack class. Philip Gamba, VP-marketing at Renault, believes Japanese brands lack the "French touch" of that automaker's design and credibility. These days, Renault is building a car with a focus on comfort. BMW is trying to emphasize not the prestige of owning a luxury automobile but the "inner value" of its cars. Communicating value in cars is of growing importance. BMW has the edge of German heritage.

Because performance and heritage are important attributes or dimensions in automobile preferences of Europeans, the positioning of different European cars on these two dimensions is shown. Note that BMW has attained the best positioning on both these dimensions. Typical of most American and Japanese cars in the 2000s has been the emphasis on quality, reliability, and efficiency. However, to compete with European cars in the twenty-first century, Americans and the Japanese are faced with the challenge of an added dimension—heritage. This calls for new marketing strategies by American and Japanese automakers. For example, GM announced in 2008 that everyone in America would get the employee discount. Under this scheme, customers paid what GM employees paid, not a cent more. This scheme helped GM to compete more effectively with European and Japanese brands.[29] ■

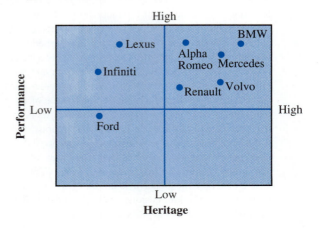

Real Research   ## Fabs' Fabulous Foamy Fight

Competition in the detergent market was brewing in Thailand. Superconcentrate detergent was fast becoming the prototype as of 2008. Market potential research in Thailand indicated that superconcentrates would continue to grow at a healthy rate, although the detergent market had slowed. In addition, this category had already dominated other Asian markets such as Taiwan, Hong Kong, and Singapore. Consequently, Colgate entered this new line of competition with Fab Power Plus with the objective of capturing 4 percent market share. The main players in the market were Kao Corp.'s Attack, Lever Brothers' Breeze Ultra and Omo, and Lion Corp.'s Pao Hand Force and Pao M. Wash. Based on qualitative research and secondary data, Colgate assessed the critical factors for the success of superconcentrates. Some of these factors were environmental appeal, hand washing and machine washing convenience, superior cleaning abilities, optimum level of suds for hand washing, and brand name. Market research also revealed that no brand had both hand and machine wash capabilities. Pao Hand Force was formulated as the hand washing brand. Pao M. Wash was the machine wash version. Lever's Breeze Ultra was targeted for machine use. Therefore, a formula that had both hand and machine wash capability was desirable. A conjoint study was designed and these factors varied at either two or three levels. Preference ratings were gathered from respondents and part-worths for the factors estimated both at the individual and the group level. Results showed that the factor of hand-machine capability had a substantial contribution, supporting earlier claims. Based on these findings, Fab Power Plus was successfully introduced as a brand with both hand and machine wash capabilities.[30] ■

Real Research   ## Ethical Perceptions of Marketing Research Firms

In a refined scale to measure the degree to which a certain situation is ethical or unethical, three factors have been found to have acceptable validity and parsimony. Two of these dimensions are particularly interesting. These are a broad-based moral equity dimension (factor 1) and a relativistic dimension (factor 2). Using multidimensional scaling, one can plot the perceived ethics of marketing research firms using these dimensions. For example, an MDS plot might look like this.

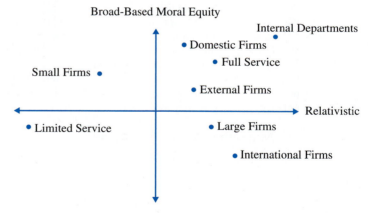

In this example, internal marketing research departments are perceived to be the most ethical on both dimensions. Large marketing research firms are perceived to be more ethical on the relativistic dimension, whereas small firms are more ethical on the moral equity factor. International marketing research firms are more ethical on relativistic terms, whereas the domestic firms are higher on the moral equity dimension. Finally, full-service firms are perceived to be more ethical on both the dimensions as compared to the limited-service firms.

As of 2009, the marketing research industry was trying hard to portray that it maintained high ethical standards. These findings imply that marketing research firms (external firms) must convince the business world that their ethical standards are as high as those of internal marketing research departments of business firms. Also, if limited-service suppliers are to compete, then they must maintain and project the same ethical standards maintained by the full-service marketing research firms.[31] ■

Decision Research   ## Wendy's: Positioning the Brand

Wendy's International, Inc. (www.wendys.com) completed its merger with the Triarc Companies, Inc., on September 29, 2008, and the combined company was named Wendy's/Arby's Group, Inc. (www. wendysarbys.com). Founded by Dave Thomas in 1969, in Columbus, Ohio, Wendy's serves one of the best

MDS and conjoint analysis can enable Wendy's to strengthen its positioning in the marketplace.

hamburgers in the business, made with fresh beef hot-off-the-grill and a choice of toppings. Frostys, soft drinks, and a variety of fresh, healthy foods such as salads and grilled chicken sandwiches, baked potatoes, and chili are also part of its menu. Quality is a vital component of Wendy's products and is reflected in Dave Thomas's slogan: "Quality is our recipe."

Wendy's International, Inc., has integrated its advertising group with its research analysis and new product marketing departments. Featuring the founder Dave Thomas, the down-to-earth commercials have elevated Wendy's advertising to its highest levels of recognition with consumers. Thomas appeared in more than 800 commercials and advertisements, often wearing a white short-sleeved shirt and red tie and never failing to smile. Industry analysts and company officials said the ads helped the company rebound from a difficult period in the mid-1980s when earnings sank. Although Wendy's founder passed away at the age of 69, he set a firm foundation for his company to continue to excel at new heights.

Advertising and promotions are a critical part of Wendy's ongoing marketing strategy. It enables Wendy's to develop a strong position for its brand in an increasingly competitive marketplace. Advertising and promotions drive the business with sales promotions at key periods throughout the year. It also maintains an ongoing presence in front of consumers through extensive television coverage. J. David Karam, president of Wendy's, would like to further strengthen the positioning of the company because he sees that as being critical to continued success.

The Marketing Research Decision

1. What data should be collected and how should they be analyzed to implement MDS and conjoint analysis to strengthen the positioning of Wendy's?
2. Discuss the role of MDS and conjoint analysis in enabling J. David Karam to strengthen the positioning of Wendy's.

The Marketing Management Decision

1. What new strategies should J. David Karam formulate to strengthen the positioning of Wendy's?
2. Discuss how the marketing management decision action that you recommend to J. David Karam is influenced by the data analysis that you suggested earlier and by the likely findings. ■

Statistical Software

Over the years, several computer programs have been developed for conducting MDS analysis using microcomputers and mainframes. The ALSCAL program, available in the mainframe versions of both SPSS and SAS, incorporates several different MDS models and can be used for conducting individual or aggregate-level analysis. Other MDS programs are easily available and widely used. Most are available in both microcomputer and mainframe versions.

- MDSCAL derives a spatial map of brands in a specified number of dimensions. Similarity data are used. A variety of input data formats and distance measures can be accommodated.
- KYST performs metric and nonmetric scaling and unfolding using similarity data.

- INDSCAL, denoting individual differences scaling, is useful for conducting MDS at the aggregate level. Similarity data are used as input.
- MDPREF performs internal analysis of preference data. The program develops vector directions for preferences and the configuration of brands or stimuli in a common space.
- PREFMAP performs external analysis of preference data. This program uses a known spatial map of brands or stimuli to portray an individual's preference data. PREFMAP2 performs both internal and external analysis.
- PC-MDS contains a variety of multidimensional scaling algorithms, including factor analysis, discriminant analysis, and some other multivariate procedures.
- APM (Adaptive Perceptual Mapping) is an adaptive scaling program, available for the microcomputer, which can handle up to 30 brands and 50 attributes. There is no limit on the number of respondents per study or the number of computers that can be used to collect the data.
- CORRESPONDENCE ANALYSIS by the Beaumont Organization Ltd. conducts correspondence analysis, what-if simulations, and ideal product analysis. Another program for correspondence analysis is SIMCA by Greenacre.

If OLS regression is used as the estimation procedure in conjoint analysis, these programs are universally available. In particular, the microcomputer and mainframe versions of SAS, SPSS, MINITAB, and EXCEL have several regression programs. These were discussed in Chapter 17. Several specialized programs are also available for conjoint analysis. MONANOVA (Monotone Analysis of Variance) is a nonmetric procedure that uses full-profile data. For pairwise data, the TRADEOFF procedure can be used. TRADEOFF is also a nonmetric procedure that uses the rank ordering of preferences for attribute-level pairs. Both MONANOVA and TRADEOFF are available for the mainframe and microcomputers. Other popular programs include LINMAP. Sawtooth Software (www.sawtoothsoftware.com) has developed a number of programs including Choice-Based Conjoint (CBC) and Adaptive Conjoint Analysis (ACA). Adaptive Choice-Based Conjoint (ACBC) is a new approach to preference modeling that leverages the best aspects of CBC (Choice-Based Conjoint) and ACA (Adaptive Conjoint Analysis). Sawtooth also offers CBC Hierarchical Bayes Module (CBC/HB).

SPSS and SAS Computerized Demonstration Movies

We have developed computerized demonstration movies that give step-by-step instructions for running all the SPSS and SAS Learning Edition programs that are discussed in this chapter. These demonstrations can be downloaded from the Web site for this book. The instructions for running these demonstrations are given in Exhibit 14.2.

SPSS and SAS Screen Captures with Notes

The step-by-step instructions for running the various SPSS and SAS Learning Edition programs discussed in this chapter are also illustrated in screen captures with appropriate notes. These screen captures can be downloaded from the Web site for this book.

SPSS Windows

The multidimensional scaling program allows individual differences as well as aggregate analysis using ALSCAL. The level of measurement can be ordinal, interval, or ratio. Both the direct and the derived approaches can be accommodated. To select multidimensional scaling procedures using SPSS for Windows, click:

Analyze>Scale>Multidimensional Scaling . . .

Following are the detailed steps for running multidimensional scaling on the similarity ratings of toothpaste brands data of Table 21.1. First convert similarity ratings to distances by subtracting each value of Table 21.1 from 8. The form of the data matrix has to be square symmetric (diagonal elements zero and distances above and below the diagonal. See SPSS file Table 21.1 Input). Note that SPSS gives solutions that are different from those presented in this chapter using different software.

1. Select ANALYZE from the SPSS menu bar.
2. Click SCALE and then MULTIDIMENSIONAL SCALING (ALSCAL).
3. Move "Aqua-Fresh [var00001]," "Crest [var00002]," "Colgate [var00003]," "Aim [var00004]," "Gleem [var00005]," "Plus White [var00006]," "Ultra-Brite [var00007]," "Close-Up [var00008]," "Pepsodent [var00009]," and "Sensodyne [var00010]" into the VARIABLES box.
4. In the DISTANCES box check DATA ARE DISTANCES. SHAPE should be SQUARE SYMMETRIC (default).
5. Click on MODEL. In the pop-up window, in the LEVEL OF MEASUREMENT box, check INTERVAL. In the SCALING MODEL box, check EUCLIDEAN DISTANCE. In the CONDITIONALITY box, check MATRIX. Click CONTINUE.
6. Click on OPTIONS. In the pop-up window, in the DISPLAY box, check GROUP PLOTS, DATA MATRIX, and MODEL AND OPTIONS SUMMARY. Click CONTINUE.
7. Click OK.

The conjoint analysis approach can be implemented using regression if the dependent variable is metric (interval or ratio). This procedure can be run by clicking:

$$\text{Analyze} > \text{Regression} > \text{Linear} \ldots$$

Detailed steps for running a regression are given in Chapter 17. SPSS Conjoint is a specialized program that is available as a separate module.

SAS Learning Edition

The instructions given here and in all the data analysis chapters (14 to 22) will work with the SAS Learning Edition as well as with the SAS Enterprise Guide. In SAS, the MDS procedure is available and shares many of the features of the ALSCAL. Within SAS, the MDS procedure generally produces results similar to those from the ALSCAL procedure if you use the following options in PROC MDS:

- FIT=SQUARED
- FORMULA=1 except for unfolding data, which require FORMULA=2
- PFINAL to get output similar to that from ALSCAL

The MDS and ALSCAL procedures may sometimes produce different results for the following reasons:

- With the LEVEL=INTERVAL option, PROC MDS fits a regression model while PROC ALSCAL fits a measurement model. These models are not equivalent if there is more than one partition, although the differences in the parameter estimates are usually minor.
- PROC MDS and PROC ALSCAL use different algorithms for initialization and optimization. Hence, different local optima may be found by PROC MDS and PROC ALSCAL for some data sets with poor fit. Using the INAV=SSCP option causes the initial estimates from PROC MDS to be more like those from PROC ALSCAL.
- The default convergence criteria in PROC MDS are stricter than those in PROC ALSCAL. The convergence measure in PROC ALSCAL may cause PROC ALSCAL to stop iterating because progress is slow rather than because a local optimum has been reached. Even if you run PROC ALSCAL with a very small convergence criterion and a very large iteration limit, PROC ALSCAL may never achieve the same degree of precision as PROC MDS. For most applications, this problem is of no practical consequence since two- or three-digit precision is sufficient. If the model does not fit well, obtaining higher precision may require hundreds of iterations.

Also, PROC MDS produces no plots so you must use output data sets to produce the plots.

Following are the detailed steps for running multidimensional scaling on the similarity ratings of toothpaste brands of Table 21.1:

1. Select File>New>Code. (Note that multidimensional scaling is not available as an SAS Learning Edition task and that SAS code needs to be submitted in order to run this analysis.)

2. Type the following SAS statements into the Code window and enter the physical location of Table 21.1 in the libname statement.

```
libname mdsdata 'Location of MDS Data';
proc mds data=mdsdata.table_21_1
    fit=squared
    formula=1
    pfinal
        out=out
;
run;
%plotit(data=out(where=(_type_='CONFIG')), datatype=mds,
    labelvar=_name_, vtoh=1.75);
```

3. Select Code>Run Code on Local.

The conjoint analysis approach can be implemented using regression if the dependent variable is metric (interval or ratio). This procedure can be run within SAS Learning Edition by clicking:

Analyze>Regression>Linear . . .

Note that the Learning Edition of SAS does not have a specific function for MDS or conjoint, so SAS code has to be inserted. The screen captures, which can be downloaded from the Web site for this book, show how to do that.

Project Research   ## Multidimensional Scaling

SPSS Data File

SAS Data File

In the department store project, respondents' evaluations of the 10 stores on each of the eight factors of the choice criteria were used to derive similarity measures between the stores. Euclidean distances were calculated between each pair of stores. These data were analyzed using multidimensional scaling to obtain spatial maps that represented the respondents' perceptions of the 10 stores. In one such map, the dimensions were identified as prestigious versus discount stores, and regional versus national store chains. Stores that competed directly with each other (e.g., JCPenney and Macy's) were located close together in the perceptual space. These perceptual maps were used to gain insights into the competitive positioning of the 10 department stores.

Project Activities

Download the SPSS or SAS data file *Sears Data 21* from the Web site for this book. This file contains the dissimilarity data for the 10 department stores for one respondent. Thus, the data represent distances.

1. Use the ALSCAL procedure to obtain a perceptual map for the 10 stores. Interpret the resulting plot. ■

Summary

Multidimensional scaling (MDS) is used for obtaining spatial representations of respondents' perceptions and preferences. Perceived or psychological relationships among stimuli are represented as geometric relationships among points in a multidimensional space. Figure 21.11 gives a concept map for MDS. Formulating the MDS problem requires a specification of the brands or stimuli to be included. The number and nature of brands selected influences the resulting solution. Input data obtained from the respondents can be related to perceptions or preferences.

Perception data can be direct or derived. The direct approaches are more common in marketing research.

The selection of an MDS procedure depends on the nature (metric or nonmetric) of the input data and whether perceptions or preferences are being scaled. Another determining factor is whether the analysis will be conducted at the individual or aggregate level. The decision about the number of dimensions in which to obtain a solution should be based on theory, interpretability, elbow criterion, and ease-of-use considerations. Labeling of the dimensions is a

FIGURE 21.11

A Concept Map for Multidimensional Scaling

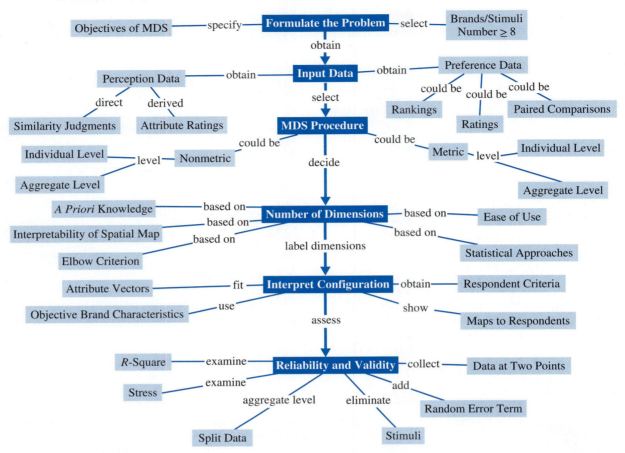

difficult task that requires subjective judgment. Several guidelines are available for assessing the reliability and validity of MDS solutions. Preference data can be subjected to either internal or external analysis. If the input data are of a qualitative nature, they can be analyzed via correspondence analysis. If the attribute-based approaches are used to obtain input data, spatial maps can also be obtained by means of factor or discriminant analysis.

Conjoint analysis is based on the notion that the relative importance that consumers attach to salient attributes, and the utilities they attach to the levels of attributes, can be determined when consumers evaluate brand profiles that are constructed using these attributes and their levels. Figure 21.12 gives a concept map for conjoint analysis. Formulating the

problem requires an identification of the salient attributes and their levels. The pairwise and the full-profile approaches are commonly employed for constructing the stimuli. Statistical designs are available for reducing the number of stimuli in the evaluation task. The input data can be either nonmetric (rankings) or metric (ratings). Typically, the dependent variable is preference or intention to buy.

Although other procedures are available for analyzing conjoint analysis data, regression using dummy variables is becoming increasingly important. Interpretation of the results requires an examination of the part-worth functions and relative importance weights. Several procedures are available for assessing the reliability and validity of conjoint analysis results.

Key Terms and Concepts

FIGURE 21.12

A Concept Map for Conjoint Analysis

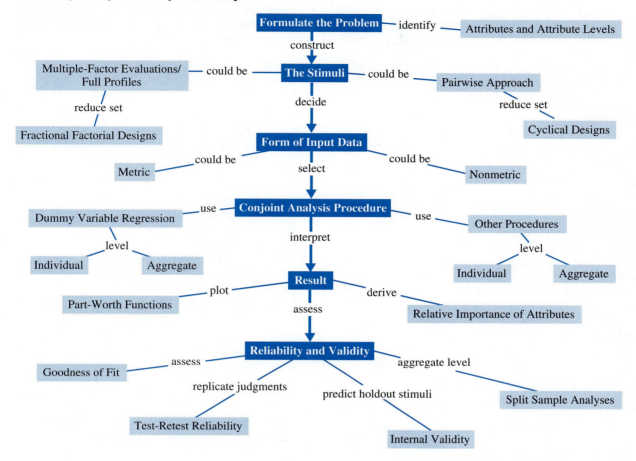

Suggested Cases, Video Cases, and HBS Cases

Running Case with Real Data

1.1 Dell

Comprehensive Critical Thinking Cases

2.1 American Idol   2.2 Baskin-Robbins   2.3 Akron Children's Hospital

Data Analysis Cases with Real Data

3.1 AT&T   3.2 IBM   3.3 Kimberly-Clark

Comprehensive Cases with Real Data

4.1 JPMorgan Chase   4.2 Wendy's

Video Case

23.1 Marriott

Live Research: Conducting a Marketing Research Project

1. MDS and conjoint analysis may not be always appropriate or feasible if the relevant data have not been obtained.
2. MDS plots can also be obtained using discriminant analysis and factor analysis. If the relevant data are available, construct spatial plots using MDS, discriminant analysis, and factor analysis and compare the results.
3. If conjoint analysis is to be conducted, the regression-based approach illustrated in this chapter is the simplest and is, therefore, recommended.

Acronyms

The steps involved in conducting multidimensional scaling may be represented by the acronym

Scaling:

S timuli selection: problem formulation
C hoice of an MDS procedure
A ssessing reliability and validity
L abeling dimensions
I nput data: metric or nonmetric
N umber of dimensions
G eometric representation and interpretation

The steps involved in conducting conjoint analysis may be represented by the acronym

Analysis:

A ssessing reliability and validity
N umber and levels of attributes: problem formulation
A ttribute importance determination
L evel of analysis: individual vs. aggregate
Y axis: utility values for attribute levels
S timuli construction: full-profile vs. pairwise
I nput data: metric or nonmetric
S election of a conjoint procedure

Exercises

Questions

1. For what purposes are MDS procedures used?
2. What is meant by a spatial map?
3. Describe the steps involved in conducting MDS.
4. Describe the direct and derived approaches to obtaining MDS input data.
5. What factors influence the choice of an MDS procedure?
6. What guidelines are used for deciding on the number of dimensions in which to obtain an MDS solution?
7. Describe the ways in which the reliability and validity of MDS solutions can be assessed.
8. What is the difference between internal and external analysis of preference data?
9. Briefly describe correspondence analysis.
10. What is involved in formulating a conjoint analysis problem?
11. Describe the full-profile approach to constructing stimuli in conjoint analysis.

12. Describe the pairwise approach to constructing stimuli in conjoint analysis.
13. How can regression analysis be used for analyzing conjoint data?
14. Graphically illustrate what is meant by part-worth functions.
15. What procedures are available for assessing the reliability and validity of conjoint analysis results?
16. Briefly describe hybrid conjoint analysis.

Problems

1. Identify two marketing research problems where MDS could be applied. Explain how you would apply MDS in these situations.
2. Identify two marketing research problems where conjoint analysis could be applied. Explain how you would apply conjoint analysis in these situations.

Internet and Computer Exercises

1. A respondent's ratings of nine luxury car brands on four dimensions are shown on the next page. Each brand was evaluated on each dimension (prestige, performance, luxury, and value) on a 7-point scale with 1 = poor and 7 = excellent. Using SPSS Windows, SAS, or alternative software, develop an MDS plot in two dimensions. Interpret the dimensions. Explain the plot.
2. Analyze the data of Table 21.1 using an appropriate MDS procedure. Compare your results to those given in the text.

SPSS Data File   SAS Data File

Brand	Prestige	Performance	Luxury	Value
Lexus	5.00	7.00	5.00	7.00
Infiniti	5.00	6.00	5.00	7.00
BMW	5.00	7.00	6.00	5.00
Mercedes	6.00	6.00	6.00	6.00
Cadillac	5.00	5.00	6.00	5.00
Lincoln	6.00	6.00	5.00	5.00
Porsche	5.00	6.00	5.00	4.00
Bentley	7.00	4.00	7.00	3.00
Rolls	7.00	5.00	7.00	1.00

3. Analyze the similarity judgments that you provided for the 12 bath soap brands in Fieldwork Activity 1. Use an appropriate MDS procedure, such as ALSCAL. Label the dimensions and interpret your own spatial map.

4. Use OLS regression to develop part-worth functions for the three sneaker attributes using the data you provided in Fieldwork Activity 2. How do your results compare with those reported in the text?

Activities

Role Playing

1. You are the director of marketing research for Macy's. Develop an MDS map showing the positioning of the 10 department stores considered in this book. See Table 8.2 in Chapter 8 for the names of these stores. Explain this map and its implications for competitive positioning of Macy's to your boss who is the vice president of marketing (role played by another student).

2. As the senior marketing research manager for Nike, explain the role that conjoint analysis can play in designing superior athletic shoes to top management (represented by a group of fellow students).

Fieldwork

1. Consider the following 12 brands of bath soap: Jergens, Dove, Zest, Dial, Camay, Ivory, Palmolive, Irish Spring, Lux, Safeguard, Tone, and Monchel. Form all the possible 66 pairs of these brands. Rate these pairs of brands in terms of similarity, using a 7-point scale.

2. Construct the nine sneaker profiles given in Table 21.4. Rate these nine profiles in terms of your preference, using a 9-point rating scale.

Group Discussion

1. In small groups, discuss the similarities and differences between MDS and conjoint analysis.

2. Discuss, in a small group, the similarities and differences among MDS, factor analysis, and discriminant analysis.

Dell Running Case

Review the Dell case, Case 1.1, and questionnaire given toward the end of the book.

1. Provide similarity ratings on a 1 to 7 scale for all possible pairs of the following brands of PCs: Dell, HP, Gateway, Sony, Toshiba, Acer, Lenovo, Apple, and Panasonic. Develop a two-dimensional MDS map. Interpret the dimensions and the map.

2. Construct 24 full profiles of PCs using the attributes and the levels given in the real research example in the book. Thus the attributes and their levels will be: price ($1,000, $1,500, $2,000), screen size (17″, 24″), monitor maximum resolution (1280 × 1024, 1689 × 1050), and extended warranty (no, 4 years). Rate the 24 profiles in terms of your preference, using a 7-point scale (1 = not at all preferred, 7 = greatly preferred). Calculate the part-worth functions and the relative importance of the attributes.

Chapter 22

Structural equation modeling is fast becoming a popular technique for testing measurement theory and structural theory.

Charles Eden, Vice President, Burke, Inc.

Objectives

[After reading this chapter, the student should be able to:]

1. Define the nature and unique characteristics of structural equation modeling (SEM).

2. Explain the basic concepts in SEM such as theory, model, path diagram, exogenous versus endogenous constructs, dependence and correlational relationships, model fit, and model identification.

3. Discuss the basic statistics associated with SEM.

4. Describe the process of conducting SEM and explain the various steps involved.

5. Know how to specify a measurement model and assess its validity.

6. Explain the concept of model fit and the differences between absolute, incremental, and parsimony fit indices.

7. Describe how to specify a structural model and assess its validity.

8. Discuss the relationship of SEM to other multivariate techniques.

9. Explain path analysis and discuss its relationship to SEM.

Structural Equation Modeling and Path Analysis

Overview

structural equation modeling (SEM)
Structural equation modeling (SEM) is a procedure for estimating a series of dependence relationships among a set of concepts or constructs represented by multiple measured variables and incorporated into an integrated model.

This chapter provides an overview of **structural equation modeling (SEM)**, a procedure for estimating a series of dependence relationships among a set of concepts or constructs represented by multiple measured variables and incorporated into an integrated model (see Chapter 2). The principles of regression (Chapter 17) and factor analysis (Chapter 19) provide a foundation for understanding SEM. First, we discuss the basic concepts of SEM, followed by an explanation of the key statistics and terms associated with this procedure. Then we describe the procedure for conducting SEM. We also cover second-order confirmatory factor analysis (CFA) and present illustrative applications of SEM. Then, we describe the related technique of path analysis.

Finally, we discuss the use of software in SEM. Help for running the SPSS and SAS programs used in this chapter is provided in four ways: (1) detailed step-by-step instructions are given later in the chapter, (2) you can download (from the Web site for this book) computerized demonstration movies illustrating these step-by-step instructions, (3) you can download screen captures with notes illustrating these step-by-step instructions, and (4) you can refer to the *Study Guide and Technology Manual*, a supplement that accompanies this book.

We begin by providing an illustrative example.[1]

Real Research

Concern for Internet Users' Information Privacy Concerns

Despite its tremendous potential, the share of electronic (e-)commerce as a percentage of total commerce remains small, less than 5 percent as of 2009. Information privacy concerns related to doing business on the Internet have been identified as a major factor hindering the growth of e-commerce. Therefore, the author

Information privacy concerns have been a major stumbling block hindering greater use of the Internet by consumers for e-commerce and other purposes.

and his colleagues developed and published a scale to measure Internet users' information privacy concerns (IUIPC). Based on social contract theory, IUIPC was conceptualized to have three dimensions: collection, control, and awareness. Based on exploratory factor analysis, collection was measured by four items or variables, and control and awareness were each represented by three measured variables. Then, another empirical study was designed, and SEM was used to evaluate the properties of the scale (see Chapter 9). First, a measurement model was estimated using CFA. This model was used to establish the composite reliability, and convergent and discriminant validity of the scale. Then, a structural model was estimated and the nomological validity of the scale was established by demonstrating that the theoretical relationships of IUIPC with constructs such as trust, risk, and behavioral intention were supported by the data.[2] ■

Basic Concept

In many instances, marketing researchers must answer a set of interrelated questions. For example, a firm providing services may be interested in the following questions: What variables determine service quality? How does service quality influence service attitude and service satisfaction? How does satisfaction with the service result in patronage intention? How does attitude toward the service combine with other variables to affect intention to patronize the service? Such interrelated questions cannot be examined in a unified analysis by any single statistical technique we have discussed so far in Chapters 14 to 21. To answer such questions in a unified and integrated manner, the researcher must make use of structural equation modeling (SEM). SEM can help us assess the measurement properties and test the proposed theoretical relationships by using a single technique.[3] For example, based on theory and previous research, we could postulate that service quality has five dimensions or factors such as tangibility, reliability, responsiveness, assurance, and empathy. Service quality could be depicted as a latent construct that is not directly observed or measured. Rather, service quality is represented by the five dimensions that are observed or measured. SEM can determine the contribution of each dimension in representing service quality, and evaluate how well a set of observed variables measuring these dimensions represents service quality, i.e., how reliable is the construct. We can then incorporate this information into the estimation of the relationships between service quality and other constructs. Service quality has a direct and positive influence on both attitude and satisfaction toward the service. Service attitude and satisfaction, in turn, determine intention to patronize the service. Thus, service attitude and service satisfaction are both dependent and independent variables in our theory. A hypothesized dependent variable (service attitude/satisfaction) can become an independent variable in a subsequent dependence relationship (explaining patronage intention). Later in the chapter, we give an empirical application of service quality in the context of banking.

SEM examines the structure of these interrelationships, which are expressed in a series of structural equations. This concept is similar to estimating a series of multiple regression equations (see Chapter 17). These equations model all the relationships among constructs, dependent as well as independent. In SEM, the **constructs** are unobservable or latent factors that are represented by multiple variables. This is similar to the concept of variables representing a factor in factor analysis (see Chapter 19), but SEM explicitly takes into account the measurement error. **Measurement error** is the degree to which the observed variables do not describe the latent constructs of interest in SEM. SEM is distinguished from other multivariate techniques we have discussed in Chapters 14 to 21 by the following characteristics.[4]

1. Representation of constructs as unobservable or latent factors in dependence relationships.
2. Estimation of multiple and interrelated dependence relationships incorporated in an integrated model.
3. Incorporation of measurement error in an explicit manner. SEM can explicitly account for less than perfect reliability of the observed variables, providing analyses of attenuation and estimation bias due to measurement error.
4. Explanation of the covariance among the observed variables. SEM seeks to represent hypotheses about the means, variances, and covariances of observed data in terms of a smaller number of structural parameters defined by a hypothesized underlying model.

SEM is also known by other names such as *covariance structure analysis*, *latent variable analysis*, and *causal modeling*. However, it should be noted that SEM by itself cannot establish causality, although it can assist in that process. To make causal inferences, all of the three conditions of causality discussed in Chapter 7 must be satisfied. This is seldom the case in SEM as

construct
In SEM, a construct is a latent or unobservable concept that can be defined conceptually but cannot be measured directly or without error. Also called a *factor*, a construct is measured by multiple indicators or observed variables.

measurement error
The degree to which the observed variables do not describe the latent constructs of interest in SEM.

such models are generally estimated on single cross-sectional data (Chapter 3) collected by surveys at a single point in time. However, SEM can provide evidence of systematic covariation.[5]

SEM is mainly used as a confirmatory, rather than exploratory, technique. Generally, we use SEM to determine whether a certain model is valid, rather than using SEM to "find" a suitable model. However, SEM analyses often involve an exploratory aspect.

Statistics Associated with SEM

Absolute fit indices. These indices measure the overall goodness of fit or badness of fit for both the measurement and structural models. Larger values of goodness of fit and smaller values of badness of fit represent better fits.

Average variance extracted (AVE). A measure used to assess convergent and discriminant validity, which is defined as the variance in the indicators or observed variables that is explained by the latent construct.

Chi-square difference statistic ($\Delta \chi^2$). A statistic used to compare two competing, nested SEM models. It is calculated as the difference between the models' chi-square values. Its degrees of freedom equal the difference in the models' degrees of freedom.

Composite reliability (CR). It is defined as the total amount of true score variance in relation to the total score variance. Thus, composite reliability corresponds to the conventional notion of reliability in classical test theory.

Confirmatory factor analysis (CFA). A technique used to estimate the measurement model. It seeks to confirm if the number of factors (or constructs) and the loadings of observed (indicator) variables on them conform to what is expected on the basis of theory. Indicator variables are selected on the basis of theory, and CFA is used to see if they load as predicted on the expected number of factors.

Endogenous construct. An endogenous construct is the latent, multi-item equivalent of a dependent variable. It is determined by constructs or variables within the model and thus it is dependent on other constructs.

Estimated covariance matrix. Denoted by Σ_k, it consists of the predicted covariances between all observed variables based on equations estimated in SEM.

Exogenous construct. An exogenous construct is the latent, multi-item equivalent of an independent variable in traditional multivariate analysis. An exogenous construct is determined by factors outside of the model and it cannot be explained by any other construct or variable in the model.

First-order factor model. Covariances between observed variables are explained with a single latent factor or construct layer.

Incremental fit indices. These measures assess how well a model specified by the researcher fits relative to some alternative baseline model. Typically, the baseline model is a null model in which all observed variables are unrelated to each other.

Measurement model. The first of two models estimated in SEM. It represents the theory that specifies the observed variables for each construct and permits the assessment of construct validity.

Modification index. An index calculated for each possible relationship that is not freely estimated but is fixed. The index shows the improvement in the overall model χ^2 if that path was freely estimated.

Nested model. A model is nested within another model if it has the same number of constructs and variables and can be derived from the other model by altering relationships, as by adding or deleting relationships.

Nonrecursive model. A structural model that contains feedback loops or dual dependencies.

Parsimony fit indices. The parsimony fit indices are designed to assess fit in relation to model complexity and are useful in evaluating competing models. These are goodness-of-fit measures and can be improved by a better fit or by a simpler, less complex model that estimates fewer parameters.

Parsimony ratio. The parsimony ratio is calculated as the ratio of degrees of freedom used by the model to the total degrees of freedom available.

Path analysis (PA). A special case of SEM with only single indicators for each of the variables in the causal model. In other words, path analysis is SEM with a structural model, but no measurement model.

Path diagram. A graphical representation of a model showing the complete set of relationships among the constructs. Dependence relationships are portrayed by straight arrows and correlational relationships by curved arrows.

Recursive model. A structural model that does not contain any feedback loops or dual dependencies.

Sample covariance matrix. Denoted by S, it consists of the variances and covariances for the observed variables.

Second-order factor model. There are two levels or layers. A second-order latent construct causes multiple first-order latent constructs, which in turn cause the observed variables. Thus, the first-order constructs now act as indicators or observed variables for the second order factor.

Squared multiple correlations. Similar to communality, these values denote the extent to which an observed variable's variance is explained by a latent construct or factor.

Structural error. Structural error is similar to an error term in regression analysis. In the case of completely standardized estimates, squared multiple correlation is equal to 1 – the structural error.

Structural model. The second of two models estimated in SEM. It represents the theory that specifies how the constructs are related to each other, often with multiple dependence relationships.

Structural relationship. Dependence relationship between an endogenous construct and another exogenous or endogenous construct.

Unidimensionality. A notion that a set of observed variables represent only one underlying construct. All cross-loadings are zero.

Foundations of SEM

Foundational to the understanding of SEM are the concepts of theory, model, path diagram, exogenous versus endogenous constructs, dependence and correlational relationships, model fit, and model identification. These fundamental concepts are discussed next.

Theory, Model, and Path Diagram

The role of theory and models in developing an approach to the problem was discussed in Chapter 2. There we defined a theory as a conceptual scheme based on foundational statements, or axioms, that are assumed to be true. A theory serves as a conceptual foundation for developing a model. It is very important that an SEM model be based on a theory because all relationships must be specified before the SEM model can be estimated. In SEM, models are often constructed to test certain hypotheses derived from the theory. An SEM model consists of two models: the measurement model and the structural model.[6] The measurement model depicts how the observed (measured) variables represent constructs. It represents the theory that specifies the observed variables for each construct and permits the assessment of construct validity (Chapter 9). The observed variables are measured by the researcher and are also referred to as *measured variables*, *manifest variables*, *indicators*, or *items* of the construct. Typically, observed variables are assumed to be dependent upon constructs.[7] Thus, straight arrows are drawn from a construct to the observed variables that are indicators of the construct (Figure 22.1). No single indicator can completely represent a construct but is used as an indication of that construct. The measurement model uses the technique of confirmatory factor analysis (CFA) in which the researcher specifies which variables define each construct (or factor). It seeks to confirm if the number of factors (or constructs) and the loadings of observed (indicator) variables on them conform to what is expected on the basis of theory. Thus, CFA is used to verify the factor structure of a set of observed variables. CFA allows the researcher to test the hypothesis

FIGURE 22.1

Dependence and Correlational Relationships in a Simple SEM Model

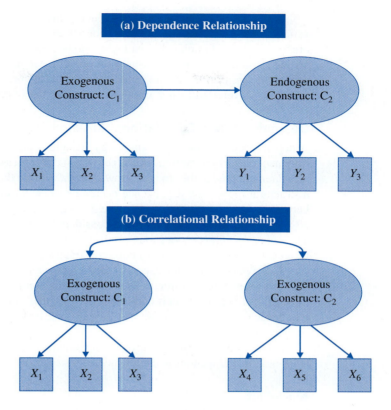

that a relationship between observed variables and their underlying latent constructs exists. The researcher uses knowledge of the theory, empirical research, or both; postulates the relationship pattern *a priori;* and then tests the hypothesis statistically. Indicator variables are selected on the basis of theory, and CFA is used to see if they load as predicted on the expected number of factors. The terms *construct* and *factor* are used interchangeably. In other words, in testing for the measurement model, the researcher has complete control over which indicators describe each construct. On the other hand, a structural model shows how the constructs are interrelated to each other, often with multiple dependence relationships. It specifies whether a relationship exists or does not exist. If a relationship is hypothesized by the theory, then an arrow is drawn. If a relationship is not hypothesized, then no arrow is drawn.

A model is portrayed in a graphical form (see Chapter 2) known as a path diagram. The following norms are followed in constructing a path diagram for a measurement model. Constructs are represented by ovals or circles while measured variables are represented by squares. Straight arrows are drawn from the constructs to the measured variables, as in Figure 22.1(a). Dependence relationships are portrayed by straight arrows (Figure 22.1(a)) and correlational relationships by curved arrows (Figure 22.1(b)).

Exogenous Versus Endogenous Constructs

As stated earlier, in SEM, a construct is an unobservable or latent variable that can be defined in conceptual terms but cannot be measured directly, for example, by asking questions in a questionnaire. Also, a construct cannot be measured without error. Rather, a construct is measured approximately and indirectly by examining the consistency among multiple observed or measured variables.

An exogenous construct is the latent, multi-item equivalent of an independent variable in traditional multivariate analysis. Multiple observed variables or items are used to represent an exogenous construct that acts as an independent variable in the model. An exogenous construct is determined by factors outside of the model, and it cannot be explained by any other construct or variable in the model. Graphically, an exogenous construct does not have any paths (single-headed arrows) coming into it from any other construct or variable in the model; it will only have paths (single-headed arrows) going out of it. In a measurement model, the indicators or measured variables for an exogenous construct are referred to as X variables. Thus, the construct C_1 in Figure 22.1(a) is an exogenous construct.

In contrast, an endogenous construct is the latent, multi-item equivalent of a dependent variable. It is determined by constructs or variables within the model and thus it is dependent on other constructs. Graphically, an endogenous construct has one or more paths (single-headed arrows) coming into it from one or more exogenous constructs or from other endogenous constructs. In a measurement model, the indicators or measured variables for an endogenous construct are referred to as Y variables, as in the case of construct C_2 in Figure 22.1(a).

Dependence and Correlational Relationships

A dependence relationship is shown by straight arrows. The arrows flow from the antecedent (independent) to the subsequent effect (dependent) measured variable or latent construct. In a measurement model, the straight arrows are drawn from the construct to its measured variables. In a structural model, the dependence occurs between constructs and so straight arrows are drawn between constructs, as shown in Figure 22.1(a). The specification of dependence relationships is also related to whether a construct is considered exogenous or endogenous, as explained earlier. Thus, construct C_2 is endogenous in this case. It should be noted that an endogenous construct can be an antecedent of other endogenous constructs.

A correlational relationship, also called *covariance relationship*, specifies a simple correlation between exogenous constructs. The theory posits that these constructs are correlated but it is not assumed that one construct is dependent upon another. A correlational relationship is depicted by a two-headed curved arrow, as shown in Figure 22.1(b). Note that both constructs, C_1 and C_2, are exogenous in this case.

A path diagram typically involves a combination of dependence and correlational relationships among endogenous and exogenous constructs, as stipulated by theory.

Model Fit

SEM tests a set of multiple relationships that are represented by multiple equations. Therefore, the fit or predictive accuracy has to be determined for the model as a whole; not for any single relationship. Other multivariate techniques decompose variance, as explained in Chapter 16 for analysis of variance and covariance, and in Chapter 17 for multiple regression. In contrast, SEM analyzes correlation or covariance. SEM determines how well the proposed theory explains the observed correlation or covariance matrix among measured variables. The data analysis is primarily based on a correlation or covariance matrix at the item level. Thus, one of the preparatory steps for SEM is to produce correlations or covariances among the items (measured or observed variables). Most contemporary SEM programs automatically generate correlations or covariances for subsequent analysis, and, thus, this step may not be apparent to most users of such software. Yet, it is important to note that SEM analysis is based on a correlation or covariance matrix, rather than raw data. As compared to correlations, we advocate the estimation of SEM based on covariances. A correlation matrix is a special case of the covariance matrix when the data are standardized (see Chapter 17). As compared to correlations, covariances contain greater information and provide more flexibility.

model fit
Model fit is determined by comparing how closely the estimated covariance matrix Σ_k matches the observed (sample) covariance matrix S, i.e., the fit statistics are based on $|S - \Sigma_k|$.

Based on the proposed measurement and structural models, it is possible to estimate the covariance matrix between the observed variables, Σ_k. **Model fit** is then determined by comparing how closely the estimated covariance matrix Σ_k matches the observed (sample) covariance matrix S, i.e., the fit statistics are based on $|S - \Sigma_k|$. A **residual** in SEM is the difference between the observed value and the estimated value of a covariance. Specific fit indices used in SEM are discussed later in the chapter.[8]

residuals
In SEM, the residuals are the differences between the observed and estimated covariance matrices.

Model Identification

model identification
Model identification concerns whether there is enough information in the covariance matrix to enable us to estimate a set of structural equations.

Model identification concerns whether there is enough information in the covariance matrix to enable us to estimate a set of structural equations. We can estimate one model parameter for each unique variance or covariance among the observed variables. If there are p observed variables, then up to a maximum of $(p(p + 1))/2$ parameters can be estimated. Note that this number is the sum of all the unique covariances ($p(p - 1)/2$) and all the variances, p. Thus,

$$(p(p + 1))/2 = p(p - 1)/2 + p$$

If the actual number of estimated parameters, k, is less than $(p(p + 1))/2$, the model is overidentified. In that case, we have positive degrees of freedom. Conversely, if k is greater than $(p(p + 1))/2$, the model is underidentified and a unique solution cannot be found. As a general guideline, having at least three observed variables for each latent construct helps in model identification, i.e., results in an overidentified model. This practice is, therefore, recommended.

Conducting SEM

The process of conducting SEM is described in Figure 22.2. The steps involved in conducting SEM are (1) define the individual constructs, (2) specify the measurement model, (3) assess measurement model reliability and validity, (4) specify the structural model if the measurement model is valid, (5) assess structural model validity, and (6) draw conclusions and make recommendations if the structural model is valid. We will describe each of these steps and discuss the relevant issues involved.

Define the Individual Constructs

As already mentioned, it is very important that SEM analysis be grounded in theory. The specific constructs, how each construct will be defined and measured, and the interrelationships among constructs must all be specified based on theory. Generally, the interest in SEM is to test both the measurement theory and the structural theory. Measurement theory specifies how the constructs are represented; structural theory posits how the constructs are interrelated. Structural relationships posited by theory are converted to hypotheses (see Chapter 2) that are then tested using SEM. The test of these hypotheses will be valid only if the underlying measurement model specifying how these constructs are represented is valid. Hence, great care should be taken in operationalizing, measuring, and scaling the relevant variables as identified and defined by theory. The measurement and scaling considerations involved, including the development of multi-items scales, were discussed in Chapters 8 and 9. This process results in scales used to measure the observed variables or indicators.

Specify the Measurement Model

Once the constructs have been defined and their observed or indicator variables measured, we are in a position to specify the measurement model. This involves the assignment of the relevant measured variables to each latent construct. The measurement model is usually represented by a

FIGURE 22.2

The Process for Structural Equation Modeling

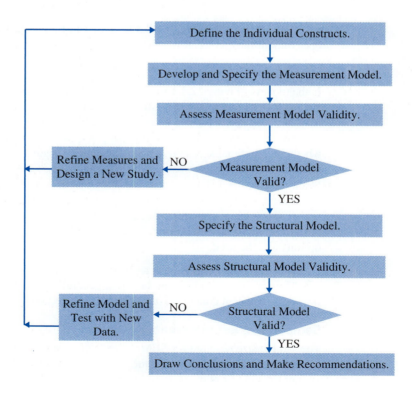

FIGURE 22.3

Path Diagram of a Simple Measurement Model

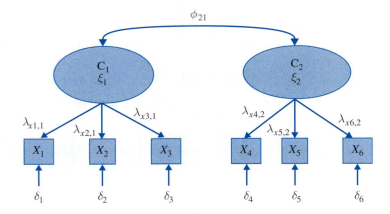

diagram, as indicated in Figure 22.3. Figure 22.3 represents a simple measurement model having two correlated constructs with each construct being represented by three indicator or measured variables. The assignment of measured variables to each latent construct is graphically equivalent to drawing arrows from each construct to the measured variables that represent that construct. The degree to which each measured variable is related to its construct is represented by that variable's loading, also shown in Figure 22.3. Only the loadings linking each measured variable to its latent construct as specified by the arrows are estimated; all other loadings are set to zero. Also, since a latent factor does not explain a measured variable perfectly, an error term is added. In a measurement model, we do not distinguish between exogenous and endogenous constructs; they are all treated as being of the same type, similar to that in factor analysis (Chapter 19).

In a measurement model, it is common to represent constructs by Greek characters and measured variables by alphabets. The common notations used are:

$$\xi = \text{latent factors}$$
$$X = \text{measured variables}$$
$$\lambda_x = \text{factor loadings}$$
$$\delta = \text{errors}$$
$$\phi = \text{correlation between constructs}$$

It can be seen that Figure 22.3 is similar to Figure 22.1(b) except that all the notations have been added. In equation form, the measurement model may be represented as:

$$X_1 = \lambda_{x1,1}\xi_1 + \delta_1$$

In the model of Figure 22.3, a total of 13 parameters need to be estimated. The parameters consist of six loading estimates, six error estimates, and one between-construct correlation. All the other paths have not been specified, i.e., no arrows have been shown. These paths will be set to zero, i.e., they will not be estimated. For each possible parameter in the model, the researcher should specify whether it is estimated or not. A free parameter is one that is estimated in the analysis. A fixed parameter is one which is not estimated by SEM but whose value is set by the researcher. Often, the value of a fixed parameter is set at zero, indicating that the specific relationship is not estimated.

Specifying the observed variables or indicators for each latent construct requires "setting the scale" of the latent construct. Because a latent construct is not observed, it has no metric scale, i.e., no range of values. Therefore, this must be provided and either one of the following two options may be used.

1. One of the factor loadings can be fixed, generally to a value of one.
2. The construct variance can be fixed, generally to a value of one. In this case, the relationships between constructs are represented by a correlation matrix.

Sample Size Requirements

The sample size required for SEM depends upon several considerations, including the complexity of the model, estimation technique, amount of missing data, amount of average error variance among the indicators or measured variables, and multivariate distribution of the data. In terms of complexity, models with more constructs or more measured variables require larger samples. Larger samples are also needed if there are less than three measured variables for each construct. Regarding estimation technique, if maximum likelihood estimation (MLE) (see Chapter 18) is used, the sample size should be generally in the range of 200 to 400, subject to other considerations.[9] If the extent of missing data is higher than 10 percent, then problems may be encountered and larger samples are required. The impact of the average error variance of indicators can be understood in terms of **communality**. Similar to the notion in factor analysis (see Chapter 19), communality is the variance of a measured variable that is explained by the construct on which it loads. Research shows that as communalities become smaller, larger samples are required. In particular, when the communalities are less than 0.5, larger samples would be required. The problem is magnified when the constructs have been measured with fewer than three indicators. Finally, as the data deviate more and more from the assumption of multivariate normality, larger samples are needed. To minimize problems with deviations from normality, it has been suggested that there should be at least 15 respondents for each parameter estimated in the model.[10]

We offer the following simplified guidelines. SEM models with five or fewer constructs, each with more than three measured variables, and communalities of at least 0.5 should be estimated with sample sizes of at least 200. For five or fewer constructs, when even some of the constructs are measured with fewer than three indicators, or the communalities are less than 0.5, the sample size should be at least 300. When there are more than five constructs, with several constructs being measured with fewer than three indicators, and there are multiple low (less than 0.5) communalities, the sample size should be at least 400. In general, larger samples produce more stable solutions, and the researcher should ensure that the SEM model is being estimated on an adequate sample size.[11]

Assess Measurement Model Reliability and Validity

The validity of the measurement model depends on the goodness-of-fit results, reliability, and evidence of construct validity, especially convergent and discriminant validity.

Assess Measurement Model Fit

As stated earlier, goodness of fit means how well the specified model reproduces the covariance matrix among the indicator items. That is, how similar is the estimated covariance of the indicator variables (Σ_k) to the observed covariance in the sample data (S). The closer the values of the two matrices are to each other, the better the model is said to fit. As shown in Figure 22.4, the various measures designed to assess fit consist of absolute fit, incremental fit, and parsimony fit indices. In absolute fit indices, each model is evaluated independently of other possible models. These indices directly measure how well the specified model reproduces the observed or sample data. Absolute fit indices may measure either goodness of fit or badness of fit. Goodness-of-fit indices indicate how well the specified model fits the observed or sample data, and so higher values of these measures are desirable. Measures that are commonly used are the goodness-of-fit index (GFI) and the adjusted goodness-of-fit index (AGFI). On the other hand, badness-of-fit indices measure error or deviation in some form and so lower values on these indices are desirable. The commonly used

communality
Communality is the variance of a measured variable that is explained by the construct on which it loads.

FIGURE 22.4

A Classification of Fit Measures

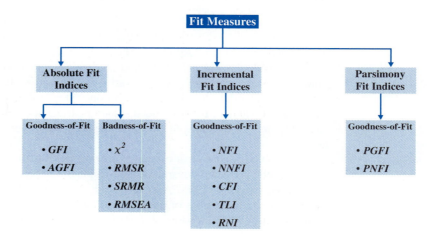

badness-of-fit measures are the chi-square (χ^2), root mean square residual (RMSR), standardized root mean square residual (SRMR), and the root mean square error of approximation (RMSEA).

In contrast to the absolute fit indices, the incremental fit indices evaluate how well the specified model fits the sample data relative to some alternative model that is treated as a baseline model. The baseline model that is commonly used is the null model that is based on the assumption that the observed variables are uncorrelated. These are goodness-of-fit measures, and the commonly used incremental fit indices include the normed fit index (NFI), non-normed fit index (NNFI), comparative fit index (CFI), the Tucker Lewis Index (TLI), and the relative noncentrality index (RNI).

The parsimony fit indices are designed to assess fit in relation to model complexity and are useful in evaluating competing models. These are goodness-of-fit measures and can be improved by a better fit or by a simpler, less complex model that estimates fewer parameters. These indices are based on the parsimony ratio that is calculated as the ratio of degrees of freedom used by the model to the total degrees of freedom available. The commonly used parsimony fit indices are the parsimony goodness-of-fit index (PGFI) and the parsimony normed fit Index (PNFI). We discuss these indices briefly and provide guidelines for their use. Given its foundational nature, chi-square (χ^2) is discussed first, followed by other indices.[12]

CHI-SQUARE (χ^2) A chi-square test provides a statistical test of the difference in the covariance matrices such that $\chi^2 = (n - 1)$ (observed sample covariance matrix—estimated covariance matrix) where n is the sample size, or

$$\chi^2 = (n - 1)(S - \Sigma_k)$$

At specified degrees of freedom, since the critical value of the χ^2 distribution is known, the probability that the observed covariance is actually equal to the estimated covariance in a given population can be found. Smaller the probability ($p < 0.05$), the greater will be the chance that the two covariance matrices are not equal, similar to the χ^2 test discussed in Chapter 15. For SEM, the degrees of freedom (df) is determined by the following formula:

$$df = 1/2[(p)(p + 1)] - k$$

where p is the total number of observed variables and k is the number of estimated parameters. Although the chi-square is the only statistically based fit measure, its limitation is that it increases with sample size and the number of observed variables, introducing a bias in the model fit. Hence, we should examine alternative model fit indexes.

OTHER ABSOLUTE FIT INDICES: GOODNESS OF FIT The goodness-of-fit (GFI) index is a measure of absolute fit whereas the adjusted goodness-of-fit index (AGFI) accounts for the degrees of freedom in the model. If F_k is the minimum fit function of the estimated model and F_0 is the fit function of the baseline model with no free parameters, then GFI $= 1 - F_k/F_0$. As the model fit improves, F_k/F_0 decreases and as a result GFI increases. AGFI adjusts for degrees of freedom and is useful for comparing across models with different complexities. AGFI $= [1 - (p(p + 1)/2df)(1 - GFI)]$ where p is the total number of observed variables and df is the degrees of freedom of the model. Higher values in the 0.90 range are considered acceptable for GFI and AGFI. GFI and AGFI are affected by sample size and can be large for models that are poorly specified and as such their use as fit indices is rather limited.

OTHER ABSOLUTE FIT INDICES: BADNESS OF FIT The notion of a residual was discussed earlier. The root mean square residual (RMSR) is the square root of the mean of these squared residuals. Thus, RMSR is an average residual covariance that is a function of the units used to measure the observed variables. Therefore, it is problematic to compare RMSR across models unless standardization is done. Standardized root mean residual (SRMR) is the standardized value of the root mean square residual and helps in comparing fit across models. Like RMSR, lower values of SRMR indicate better model fit, and values of 0.08 or less are desirable.

Root mean square error of approximation (RMSEA) examines the difference between the actual and the predicted covariance, i.e., residual or, specifically, the square root of the mean of the squared residuals. RMSEA $= \sqrt{[(\chi^2/df - 1)/(n - 1)]}$, which adjusts the chi-square value by factoring in the degrees of freedom and the sample size. Lower RMSEA values indicate better model fit. A RMSEA value of ≤ 0.08 is considered conservative.

INCREMENTAL FIT INDICES   Normed fit index (NFI) and comparative fit index (CFI) are also widely used model fit measures, and these represent incremental fit indices in that the specified model is compared to the null model in which the variables are assumed to be uncorrelated (i.e., the independence model). NFI is a ratio of the difference in the χ^2 value for the proposed model (χ^2_{prop}) and the null model (χ^2_{null}) divided by the χ^2 value for the null model (χ^2_{null}), i.e., NFI = ($\chi^2_{null} - \chi^2_{prop}$)/$\chi^2_{null}$. As the χ^2 value for the proposed model approaches zero, NFI tends to be a perfect fit of 1. NFI does not reflect parsimony; the more parameters in the model, the larger the NFI, which is why NNFI is now preferred. NNFI = (χ^2_{null}/df$_{null}$ − χ^2_{prop}/df$_{prop}$)/[(χ^2_{null}/df$_{null}$) − 1] where df$_{prop}$ and df$_{null}$ are degrees of freedom for the proposed and null models respectively. For both NFI and NNFI, values of ≥0.90 are considered acceptable.

The CFI is related to NFI and factors in degrees of freedom for model complexity and is determined by the following formula: CFI = 1 − (χ^2_{prop} − df$_{prop}$)/(χ^2_{null} − df$_{null}$) where χ^2_{prop} and df$_{prop}$ are chi-square value and degrees of freedom for the theoretically based proposed model and χ^2_{null} and df$_{null}$ are the same for the null model. CFI varies from 0 to 1, and values of 0.90 or greater are usually associated with good model fit. CFI is similar in meaning to NFI but penalizes for sample size.

The Tucker Lewis Index (TLI) is conceptually similar to CFI, but is not normed and so the values can fall outside of the 0 to 1 range. Models with good fit have a TLI value that is close to 1. The relative noncentrality index (RNI) is another incremental fit index, and its values generally range between 0 to 1 with values that are 0.90 or larger indicating a good fit.

PARSIMONY FIT INDICES   It should be emphasized that parsimony fit indices are not appropriate for evaluating the fit of a single model but are useful in comparing models of different complexities. The parsimony goodness-of-fit index (PGFI) adjusts the goodness-of-fit index by using the parsimony ratio that was defined earlier. The values of PGFI range between 0 and 1. A model with a higher PGFI is preferred based on fit and complexity. The parsimony normed fit index (PNFI) adjusts the normed fit index (NFI) by multiplication with the parsimony ratio. Like PGFI, higher values of PNFI also indicate better models in terms of fit and parsimony. Both PGFI and PNFI should be used only in a relative sense, i.e., in comparing models. PNFI is used to a greater extent as compared to PGFI.

Of the measures we have considered, CFI and RMSEA are among the measures least affected by sample size and quite popular in use. It is highly desirable that we use multiple (at least three) indices of different types. It is a good practice to always report the χ^2 value with the associated degrees of freedom. In addition, use at least one absolute goodness-of-fit, one absolute badness-of-fit, and one incremental fit measure. If models of different complexities are being compared, one parsimony fit index should also be considered.

Assess Measurement Model Reliability and Validity

The measurement accuracy, reliability, validity, and generalizaibilty considerations discussed for multi-item scales in Chapter 9 also apply to SEM. You are advised to review those concepts. Here we discuss the approaches to reliability, convergent validity, and discriminant validity that are unique to SEM.

RELIABILITY   Recall from Chapter 9 that an unreliable construct cannot be valid. So first we should assess the reliability of the constructs in the measurement model. As in Chapter 9, the coefficient alpha can be used to assess reliability. In addition, we compute composite reliability (CR), which is defined as the total amount of true score variance in relation to the total score variance. CR is computed as

$$CR = \frac{(\sum_{i=1}^{p} \lambda_i)^2}{(\sum_{i=1}^{p} \lambda_i)^2 + (\sum_{i=1}^{p} \delta_i)}$$

where

CR = composite reliability
λ = completely standardized factor loading
δ = error variance
p = number of indicators or observed variables

Thus, composite reliability corresponds to the conventional notion of reliability in classical test theory (see Chapter 9). As general guidelines, composite reliabilities of 0.7 or higher are considered good. Estimates between 0.6 and 0.7 may be considered acceptable if the estimates of the model validity are good.

CONVERGENT VALIDITY Recall from Chapter 9 that convergent validity measures the extent to which the scale correlates positively with other measures of the same construct. Hence, the size of the factor loadings provides evidence of convergent validity. High factor loadings indicate that the observed variables converge on the same construct. At a minimum, all factor loadings should be statistically significant and higher than 0.5, ideally higher than 0.7. A loading of 0.7 or higher indicates that the construct is explaining 50 percent or more of the variation in the observed variable since, $((0.71)^2 = 0.5)$. Sometimes, a cutoff level of 0.6 is used.[13]

Another measure that is used to assess convergent validity is the average variance extracted (AVE), which is defined as the variance in the indicators or observed variables that is explained by the latent construct.[14] AVE is calculated in terms of the (completely) standardized loadings as

$$AVE = \frac{\sum_{i=1}^{p} \lambda_i^2}{\sum_{i=1}^{p} \lambda_i^2 + \sum_{i=1}^{p} \delta_i}$$

where

AVE = average variance extracted
λ = completely standardized factor loading
δ = error variance
p = number of indicators or observed variables

AVE varies from 0 to 1, and it represents the ratio of the total variance that is due to the latent variable. Using the logic presented earlier, an AVE of 0.5 or more indicates satisfactory convergent validity, as it means that the latent construct accounts for 50 percent or more of the variance in the observed variables, on the average. If AVE is less than 0.5, the variance due to measurement error is larger than the variance captured by the construct, and the validity of the individual indicators, as well as the construct, is questionable. Note that AVE is a more conservative measure than CR. On the basis of CR alone, the researcher may conclude that the convergent validity of the construct is adequate, even though more than 50 percent of the variance is due to error. One should also interpret the standardized parameter estimates to ensure that they are meaningful and in accordance with theory.

DISCRIMINANT VALIDITY In order to establish discriminant validity, we must show that the construct is distinct from other constructs and thus makes a unique contribution. First, individual observed variables should load on only one latent construct. Cross-loadings indicate lack of distinctiveness and present potential problems in establishing discriminant validity. In SEM, we typically assume that a set of observed variables represents only one underlying construct, and this concept is called unidimensionality. All cross-loadings are specified (i.e., fixed) to be zero.

One formal way to show distinctiveness is to set the correlation between any two constructs as equal to one, i.e., we are specifying that observed variables measuring the two constructs might as well be represented by only one construct. Evidence of discriminant validity is obtained if the fit of the two-construct model is significantly better than the fit of the one-construct model. However, this actually turns out to be a weak test as significant fit differences may be obtained even when the correlations between the two constructs are very high.

An alternative test of discriminant validity is based on the logic that a construct should explain its observed variables better than it explains any other construct. This test is conducted by showing that the average variance extracted is greater than the square of the correlations. Equivalently, discriminant validity is achieved if the square root of the average variance extracted is larger than the correlation coefficients.

Lack of Validity: Diagnosing Problems

If the validity of the proposed measurement model is not satisfactory, then you can make use of the diagnostic information provided by CFA to make appropriate modifications. The diagnostic cues that can be used to make appropriate modifications include (1) the path estimates or loadings, (2) standardized residual, (3) modification indices, and (4) specification search.

The path estimates, or loadings, link each construct to its indicators or observed variables. You should examine the completely standardized loadings because standardization removes the effect due to the scales of measurement. Different indicators may be measured using different scales, and this is taken into account via standardization. Completely standardized loadings that are not in the –1.0 to 1.0 rage are infeasible and suggest problems that should be identified and investigated. A loading should be statistically significant. A nonsignificant loading suggests that the corresponding indicator should be dropped, unless there are strong theoretical reasons for retaining it. Furthermore, the loadings should be preferably above 0.7 or, at least, minimally greater than 0.5 when absolute values are compared. These guidelines were provided earlier. Significant but low loadings (less than 0.5) suggest that the corresponding indicators may still be candidates for deletion. The signs of the loadings should be in the direction hypothesized by theory, and the loadings should be meaningful from a theoretical viewpoint. It is also useful to evaluate the squared multiple correlations. A *squared multiple correlation* represents the extent to which the variance of an observed variable is explained by the associated latent construct.

standardized residuals
Used as a diagnostic measure of model fit, these are residuals, each divided by its standard error.

As noted earlier, residuals refer to the differences between the observed covariances (i.e., the sample data) and the estimated covariance terms. A **standardized residual** is the residual divided by its standard error. The following guidelines are observed with respect to the absolute values of the standardized residuals. Absolute values of standardized residuals exceeding 4.0 are problematic, while those between 2.5 and 4.0 should also be examined carefully but may not suggest any changes to the model if no other problems are associated with the corresponding indicators or observed variables.

SEM programs also calculate a *modification index* for each possible relationship that is not freely estimated but is fixed. The index shows the improvement in the overall model X^2 if that path was freely estimated. As a general guideline, the value of the index should be less than 4.0, and values of 4.0 or more indicate that the fit could be improved by freely estimating that relationship or path.

specification search
Specification search is an empirical approach that uses the model diagnostics and trial and error to find a better-fitting model.

A **specification search** is an empirical approach that uses the model diagnostics and trial and error to find a better-fitting model. It can be easily implemented using SEM software. In spite of this, the approach should not be used without caution because there are problems associated with determining a better-fitting model simply based on empirical data. We do not recommend this approach for the nonexpert user.

It should be noted that all such adjustments, whether based on path estimates, standardized residuals, modification indices, or specification searches, are against the intrinsic nature of CFA, which is a confirmatory technique. In fact, such adjustments are more in keeping with exploratory factor analysis (EFA). However, if the modifications are minor (e.g., deleting less than 10 percent of the observed variables), you may be able to proceed with the prescribed model and data after making the suggested changes. However, if the modifications are substantial then you must modify the measurement theory, specify a new measurement model, and collect new data to test the new model.[15]

Specify the Structural Model

Once the validity of the measurement model has been established, you can proceed with the specification of the structural model. In moving from the measurement model to the structural model, the emphasis shifts from the relationships between latent constructs and the observed variables to the nature and magnitude of the relationships between constructs. Thus, the measurement model is altered based on the relationships among the latent constructs. Because the measurement model is changed, the estimated covariance matrix based on the set of relationships examined will also change. However, the observed covariance matrix, based on the sample data, does not change as the same data are used to estimate the structural model. Thus, in general, the fits statistics will also change, indicating that the fit of the structural model is different from the fit of the measurement model.

FIGURE 22.5

**Path Diagram of a
Simple Structural
Model**

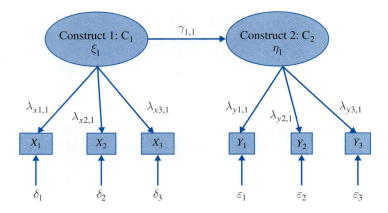

Figure 22.5 shows the structural model that is based on the measurement model of Figure 22.3. While the constructs C_1 and C_2 were correlated in Figure 22.3, there is now a dependence relationship, with C_2 being dependent on C_1. Note that the two-headed curved arrow in Figure 22.3 is now replaced with a one-headed straight arrow representing the path from C_1 to C_2. There are also some changes in the notations and symbols. The construct C_2 is now represented by η_1. This change helps us to distinguish an endogenous construct (C_2) from an exogenous construct (C_1). Also note that only the observed variables for the exogenous construct C_1 are represented by X (X_1 to X_3). On the other hand, the observed variables for the endogenous construct (C_2) are represented by Y (Y_1 to Y_3). The error variance terms for the Y variables are denoted by ε, rather than by δ. The loadings also reflect the endogenous and exogenous distinction. Loadings for the exogenous construct, as before, are still represented by λ_x. However, the loadings for the endogenous construct are represented by λ_y. The graphical representation of a structural model, such as in Figure 22.5, is called a *path diagram*. The relationships among the latent constructs, shown with one-headed straight arrows in a path diagram, are examined by estimating the structural parameters, such as in Figure 22.5. Note that only the free parameters are shown with one-headed straight arrows in the path diagram; fixed parameters, typically set at zero, are not shown. The structural parameters fall into two groups. Parameters representing relationships from exogenous constructs (ξ) to endogenous constructs (η) are denoted by the symbol γ (gamma), as shown in Figure 22.5. Parameters representing relationships from endogenous constructs to endogenous constructs are denoted by the symbol β (beta).

If the measurement model is identified, then the structural model is too, provided that it is recursive in that there are no feedback loops or dual dependencies and, in addition, there are no interaction terms. In such cases, generally the structural model is nested within the measurement model and contains fewer estimated parameters. A model is nested within another model if it has the same number of constructs and variables and can be derived from the other model by altering relationships, as by adding or deleting relationships. Dual dependencies exist when C_1 and C_2 are mutually dependent on each other, and models containing such relationships are referred to as nonrecursive.

In specifying the structural model, it is desirable to also estimate the factor loadings and the error variances along with the structural parameters. These standardized estimates from the structural model can then be compared with the corresponding estimates from the measurement model to identify any inconsistencies (differences larger than 0.05). This approach also allows us to use the measurement model fit as a basis of evaluating the fit of the structural model. An alternative approach that uses the estimates of factor loadings and error variances obtained in the measurement model as fixed parameters in the structural model is not recommended. The reason is that the change in fit between the measurement model and the structural model may be due to problems with the measurement theory instead of problems with the structural theory.

Assess Structural Model Validity

Assessing the validity of the structural model involves (1) examining the fit, (2) comparing the proposed structural model with competing models, and (3) testing structural relationships and hypotheses.

Assessing Fit

The fit of a structural model is examined along the same lines as that for the measurement model discussed earlier. As explained earlier, generally a recursive structural model has less relationships than a measurement model from which it is derived. At most, the number of relationships in a structural model can equal those in a measurement model. This means that comparatively less parameters are estimated in the structural model. Therefore, the value of χ^2 in a recursive structural model cannot be lower than that in the corresponding measurement model. In other words, a recursive structural model cannot have a better fit. Thus, the fit of the measurement model provides an upper bound to the goodness of fit of a structural model. The closer the fit of a structural model is to the fit of a measurement model, the better. The other statistics and guidelines for assessing the fit of a structural model are similar to those discussed earlier for the measurement model and the same fit indices are used.

Comparison with Competing Models

In addition to having a structural model with a good fit, it is a good practice to show that the proposed model has a better fit than competing models that might be considered as alternatives. A good fit does not prove the proposed theory or structural model best explains the sample data (covariance matrix). An alternative model may produce the same or even a better fit. Thus, a good fit does not prove that the proposed structural model is the only true explanation. Our confidence in the proposed model can be enhanced by comparing it to competing models. The proposed model (M1) and a competing model (M2) can be compared in terms of differences in χ^2, incremental or parsimony fit indices (see Figure 22.4).

When the models are nested, the comparison can be done by assessing the chi-square difference statistic ($\Delta\chi^2$). From the value of χ^2 for the proposed model, M1, χ^2 value for a lesser constrained model, M2, is subtracted. For example, M2 can have additional paths compared to M1. The degrees of freedom for the χ^2 difference is also determined as the difference in the degrees of freedom for M1 and M2.[16] The equations involved may be represented as:

$$\Delta\chi^2_{\Delta df} = \chi^2_{df(M1)} - \chi^2_{df(M2)}$$

and

$$\Delta df = df(M1) - df(M2)$$

The difference of two chi-square distributed values also has a chi-square distribution. Therefore, we can test whether the difference $\Delta\chi^2$ with Δdf degrees of freedom is statistically significant. This procedure can also be used to test the significance of the difference in the fits of the structural and measurement models. The structural model is more constrained than the measurement model and is nested within it. If the fit of the structural model is significantly and substantially worse than the fit of the measurement model, then the validity of the structural theory is questionable. On the other hand, if the fit of the structural model is not significantly worse than the fit of the measurement model, then there is evidence for the validity of the structural theory.

Testing Hypothesized Relationships

In SEM, theoretical relationships are generally transformed into hypotheses that can be empirically tested. The structural theory is considered to be valid to the extent that these hypotheses are supported in the SEM analysis. The estimated parameter for a hypothesized relationship should be statistically significant and have the correct sign. You should also examine the variance explained estimates for the endogenous constructs, an analysis that is similar to η^2 in analysis of variance (Chapter 16) or R^2 in multiple regression (Chapter 17). If SEM is being used to examine the nomological validity of a newly developed scale, then the hypotheses are replaced by known relationships that are empirically investigated to provide support for nomological validity.

Structural Model Diagnostics

The model diagnostics for the structural model are the same as for the measurement model. Thus, this examination is similar to that of the measurement model. Based on the model diagnostics, additional analysis may be conducted. For example, one or more additional paths may be specified that were not hypothesized by the original theory. However, it should be emphasized that any relationships that result based on the modifications do not have theoretical support and should not be treated in the same way as the original relationships based on structural theory. The relationships based on modifications should be theoretically meaningful and should be validated by testing the modified model on new data.

Draw Conclusions and Make Recommendations

If the assessment of the measurement model and the structural model indicate satisfactory validity, then we can arrive at conclusions and, if appropriate, make recommendations to management. The conclusions can be reached regarding the measurement of key constructs based on the CFA analysis. For example, it may be concluded that a newly developed scale has satisfactory reliability and validity and should be used in further research. Conclusions can be arrived at based on tests of hypotheses in the structural model. It may be concluded that relationships with significant and meaningful estimated structural parameters are supported. The theoretical, managerial, and/or public policy implications of these relationships can be discussed. Appropriate recommendations to the management may be made based on the managerial implications.[17]

Higher-Order Confirmatory Factor Analysis

The measurement model presented in Figure 22.3 is a first-order factor model. A first-order factor model is one in which the covariances between the observed variables (X) are explained by a single level or layer of latent constructs. In contrast, a higher-order factor model contains two or more levels or layers of latent constructs. The most common higher-order model is a second-order factor model in which there are two levels or layers. In such models, a second-order latent construct causes multiple first-order latent constructs, which in turn cause the observed variables. Thus, the first-order constructs now act as indicators or observed variables for the second-order factor. The differences between a first-order and a second-order measurement model are illustrated in Figure 22.6 and Figure 22.7. These figures describe the representation of a scale to measure Internet users' information privacy concerns (IUIPC). IUIPC has three dimensions, namely, collection (COL), control (CON), and awareness (AWA), measured by 4, 3, and three observed variables, respectively. Note that the covariances between the three latent constructs, COL, CON and AWA, are freely estimated in the first-order model, as shown by two-headed curved arrows. On the other hand, the second-order model accounts for these covariances by specifying another higher-order construct (IUIPC) that causes the first-order constructs (COL, CON, and AWA).

When we move from the measurement model to the structural model, a structural relationship between information privacy concerns and another latent construct such as trust (TRU) will be represented by multiple paths in a first-order model (COL→TRU, CON→TRU, and AWA→TRU). However, in the second-order model, it will be represented by a single path (IUIPC→TRU). Thus, a second-order model assumes that all the first-order dimensions (COL, CON, and AWA) will affect the other theoretically related latent constructs (e.g., TRU) in the same way. If this assumption is not reasonable, then the first-order factor model is preferred.

If there are four or more first-order constructs, a second-order model is more parsimonious as it uses fewer paths than a first-order model. However, it not necessarily simpler because it involves a higher level of abstraction. We emphasize that the choice between a first-order and a second-order factor model should be made based on theory.

FIGURE 22.6

First-Order Model of IUIPC

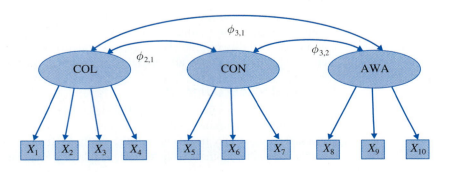

FIGURE 22.7

Second-Order Model of IUIPC

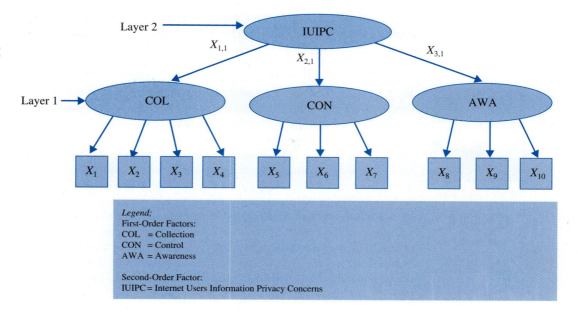

Legend;
First-Order Factors:
COL = Collection
CON = Control
AWA = Awareness

Second-Order Factor:
IUIPC = Internet Users Information Privacy Concerns

ACTIVE RESEARCH

Increasing Attendance at NHL Games

As a marketing research consultant to the National Hockey League (NHL), you are to develop a model that explains consumers' attendance of professional sports (MLB, NFL, and NHL). Visit www.mlb.com, www.nfl.com, and www.nhl.com and search the Internet to identify the factors that influence attendance of professional sports. Formulate a structural model and draw a path diagram.

As the director of marketing for the NHL, how would you use the structural model in formulating marketing strategies to increase the attendance of NHL games.

Relationship of SEM to Other Multivariate Techniques

SEM is a multivariate technique because there are multiple variables that are analyzed simultaneously (see Chapter 14). Exogenous constructs are used to predict endogenous constructs. In this vein, SEM is a dependence technique (Chapter 14) that is similar to other multivariate dependence techniques such as multiple regression (Chapter 17). The equation for each endogenous construct can be written in a form similar to a multiple regression equation. The endogenous construct is the dependent variable and the constructs with arrows pointing to the endogenous construct are the independent variables. However, there are two major differences. One is that the dependent construct in one relationship may become the independent construct in another relationship. The other is that all of the equations are estimated simultaneously. Using the same reasoning, when categorical variables are used in SEM, one can see its similarity to MANOVA (Chapter 16). (See also Chapter 17 on the similarity of analysis of variance and covariance to regression.)

The measurement model in SEM is similar to factor analysis (Chapter 19) in that both techniques have variables with loadings on factors. Concepts such as correlations and covariances are also common to both the techniques. However, there is also a major difference. In SEM, we have to specify, based on theory, which variables are associated with each construct. Thus, SEM requires the specification of the measurement model. The loadings are estimated only for these specified relationships; all other loadings are assumed to be zero. The estimation then serves as a test of the measurement theory. In this sense then, SEM is a confirmatory technique. As noted earlier, the technique to estimate the measurement model is called confirmatory factor analysis (CFA). In contrast, factor analysis as discussed in Chapter 19 is an exploratory technique, often called *exploratory factor analysis (EFA)*. EFA identifies underlying dimensions or factors that explain the correlations among a set of variables. Every variable has a loading on every factor extracted, and these loadings are contained in the factor matrix (see Chapter 19). Thus, EFA does not require any specification; rather the underlying structure is revealed by the data. EFA results can be useful in developing theory that leads to a proposed measurement model that can then be tested using CFA.[18]

When SEM is used to test a structural theory, the analysis is analogous to performing factor analysis and a series of multiple regression analyses in one step.

Application of SEM: First-Order Factor Model

SPSS Data File

SAS Data File

We give an illustrative application of SEM in the context of the technology acceptance model (TAM). TAM is a well-established model that has been used to predict individuals' reactions to an information technology application.[19] In essence, this model holds that one's intention to use a technology application (INT) is determined by two factors, namely, perceived usefulness (PU) and perceived ease-of-use (PE). Perceived usefulness refers to the degree to which the person finds it useful to use the technology application, whereas perceived ease-of-use is defined as the degree to which the person finds it easy to use the technology application. This theoretical framework was applied to explain college students' use of an educational portal in a certain university. To collect data, a Web-based survey questionnaire was administered to a sample of college students at a large university in the United States. In the survey, respondents were asked to answer the questions related to the use of a Web portal on the campus. A total of 253 completed responses were collected from the survey. The data set used in this analysis can be downloaded from the Web site for this book. In the following, we illustrate how the various steps involved in structural equation modeling presented in Figure 22.2 were carried out.

Define the Individual Constructs

In an attempt to assess measurement errors, each research latent construct was measured by multiple observed variables or items. The items were measured on 7-point scales anchored with "strongly disagree" (1) and "strongly agree" (7). Perceived usefulness was measured by three items. The items were "Using (this Web Site) increases my performance" (PU1), "Using (this Web Site) improves my productivity" (PU2), and "Using (this Web Site) enhances my effectiveness" (PU3). Perceived ease-of-use consisted of three items. The items were "(this Web Site) is easy to use" (PE1), "It is easy to become skillful at using (this Web Site)" (PE2), and "Learning to operate (this Web Site) is easy" (PE3). Intention to use was measured by the following three items: "I plan to use (this Web Site) in the next 3 months" (INT1), "I predict that I would use (this Web Site) in the next 3 months" (INT2) and "I intend to use (this Web Site) in the next 3 months" (INT3). Table 22.1 shows the means, standard deviations, and correlations of the nine variables based on the collected data.

Specify the Measurement Model

The estimates of structural relationships are likely to be biased unless the measurement instrument is reliable and valid. In this case, the measurement model is specified in a way that the three factors

TABLE 22.1
TAM Model: Means, Standard Deviations, and Correlations

| | ME | SD | Correlations Matrix | | | | | | | | |
			1	2	3	4	5	6	7	8	9
1. PU1	3.58	1.37	1								
2. PU2	3.58	1.37	.900*	1							
3. PU3	3.58	1.36	.886*	.941*	1						
4. PE1	4.70	1.35	.357*	.403*	.392*	1					
5. PE2	4.76	1.34	.350*	.374*	.393*	.845*	1				
6. PE3	4.79	1.32	.340*	.356*	.348*	.846*	.926*	1			
7. INT1	3.72	2.10	.520*	.545*	.532*	.442*	.419*	.425*	1		
8. INT2	3.84	2.12	.513*	.537*	.540*	.456*	.433*	.432*	.958*	1	
9. INT3	3.68	2.08	.534*	.557*	.559*	.461*	.448*	.437*	.959*	.950*	1

Notes:
- ME = means; SD = standard deviations
- $*p < 0.05$

FIGURE 22.8

Measurement Model for TAM

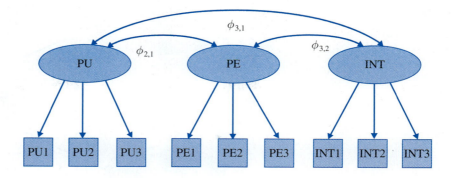

are allowed to correlate with each other, and each of the three factors is associated with the designated three items but not with the other items. Figure 22.8 the depicts the resulting measurement model. The result of data analysis produces model fit as well as various parameter estimates such as item loadings, item measurement errors, and factor correlations.

Assess Measurement Model Reliability and Validity

A three-factor measurement model was set up to validate the scales, and a confirmatory factor analysis (CFA) was conducted to test the measurement model. The fit of the model was evaluated based on three different fit indices: comparative fit index (CFI), goodness-of-fit index (GFI), and root mean square error of approximation (RMSEA). The results of CFA indicated that the model fit the data quite well [$\chi^2 = 43.32, p < 0.01$ given that df = 24]; specifically, CFI was found to be 0.99, and GFI was 0.96, and RMSEA was 0.057.

In addition to model-data fit, other psychometric properties of the scales such as composite reliability and validity were examined. As shown in Table 22.2, in terms of composite reliability (CR), the scales exceed the recommended cutoff value of 0.70; thus, it is reasonable to conclude that the scales are reliable. In terms of AVE, all the values were greater than 0.50. Furthermore, Table 22.2 shows that each of the item loadings is greater than 0.80, which provides empirical support for the convergent validity of the scales.

The estimates of correlations and their standard deviations indicated that the scales are empirically distinct from each other. Formally, the square root of the average variance extracted is larger than the correlation coefficients, indicating discriminant validity of the scales. Overall, the measurement model was believed to be appropriate given the evidence of good model fit, reliability, convergent validity, and discriminant validity.

TABLE 22.2

TAM Model: Results of Measurement Model

Constructs	Items	Item Loadings	Item Errors	CR	AVE
PU				0.97	0.91
	PU1	0.92***	0.15***		
	PU2	0.98***	0.05***		
	PU3	0.96***	0.07***		
PE				0.95	0.87
	PE1	0.88***	0.23***		
	PE2	0.96***	0.07***		
	PE3	0.96***	0.08***		
INT				0.98	0.95
	INT2	0.98***	0.03***		
	INT2	0.97***	0.05***		
	INT3	0.98***	0.05***		

Notes:
- CR = composite reliability; AVE = average variance extracted
- ***$p < 0.001$ (two-tailed)

FIGURE 22.9

Structural Model for TAM

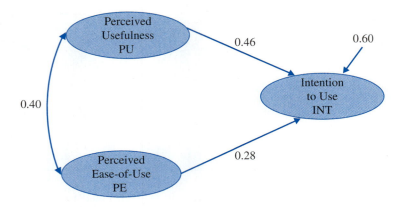

Specify the Structural Model

The structural model was specified based on TAM theory, as shown in Figure 22.9.

Assess Structural Model Validity

The results of data analysis are also shown in Figure 22.9. First, as with the case of the measurement model, the proposed model was found to fit the data satisfactorily as the fit values were well within acceptable ranges [$\chi^2(24) = 43.32$, $p < 0.01$, CFI $= 0.99$, GFI $= 0.96$, and RMSEA $= 0.057$]. According to TAM, perceived usefulness and perceived ease-of-use are the significant predictors of intention to use. As shown in Figure 22.9, perceived usefulness is significant in determining intention to use (path estimate $= 0.46$, $p < 0.001$). Similarly, perceived ease-of-use is found to have a significant effect on intention to use (path estimate $= 0.28$, $p < 0.001$). The squared multiple correlation (SMC) coefficient for intention to use is 0.40, which indicates that the two predictors, i.e., perceived usefulness and perceived ease-of-use, together explained 40 percent of the variance in intention to use.

Conclusions and Recommendations

Overall, the results of SEM indicate that TAM is a reasonable representation of individuals' reactions to a Web portal in an educational setting. Thus, in order to increase the use of the portal by the students, this university should enhance the perceived usefulness and perceived ease-of-use of the Web site. Perceived usefulness could be increased by adding features such as checking e-mail, weather, current events on the campus, schedule of classes, etc., that the students find useful and check frequently. Perceived ease-of-use could be enhanced by making the Web site easy to navigate.

Application of SEM: Second-Order Factor Model

SPSS Data File

SAS Data File

We give an illustrative application of SEM in the context of banking services. The data were collected through personal interviews, and the sample size selected for this analysis was comprised of 250 respondents. The data set used in this analysis can be downloaded from the Web site for this book. In the following, we illustrate how the various steps involved in structural equation modeling presented in Figure 22.2 were carried out.

Define the Individual Constructs

The purpose of this study was to predict bank patronage intent based on service quality. The theory developed was based on past research. Service quality was conceptualized as having five dimensions.[20] The theory postulated that service quality would influence service attitude and service satisfaction, and the latter two constructs would then influence patronage intent. Thus, in our data set, we have 8 constructs and 30 indicators, each construct having multiple indicator variables. These are the five service quality dimensions, namely, Tangibility (4 indicators), Reliability (4 indicators), Responsiveness (3 indicators), Assurance (4 indicators) and Empathy (4 indicators) and the three outcome constructs of Attitude (4 indicators), Satisfaction (4 indicators), and Patronage Intention (3 indicators). These indicators are contained in Table 22.3. Each indicator of the dimensions was measured using a 9-point scale. For example, indicator one was "When it comes to modern equipment (tangibles), my perception of my bank's service performance is Low

SEM can used to test the impact of service quality on attitude, satisfaction, and the patronage of banks.

1—2—3—4—5—6—7—8—9 High. To measure global attitude, we used four indicators on a 7-point scale: favorable–unfavorable, good–bad, positive–negative, and pleasant–unpleasant. All attitude indicators were reverse coded for analysis. To measure overall satisfaction, we used the following four indicators using a 9-point scale: I believe I am satisfied with my bank's services (strongly disagree–strongly agree), overall, I am pleased with my bank's services (strongly disagree–strongly agree), using services from my bank is usually a satisfying experience (strongly disagree–strongly agree), and my feelings toward my bank's services can best be characterized as (very dissatisfied–very satisfied). We used three indicators to measure patronage intention using a 9-point scale: The next time my friend needs the services of a bank I will recommend my bank (strongly disagree–strongly agree), I have no regrets for having patronized my bank in the past (strongly disagree–strongly agree), and I will continue to patronize the services of my bank in the future (strongly disagree–strongly agree).

Specify the Measurement Model

We first test the measurement model in order to validate the psychometric properties of our measures. In our example, because prior research has already established the reliability and validity of the five-component service quality construct, we test for the measurement properties in our sample using a confirmatory mode. In testing for the measurement model, we freely correlate the eight constructs and fix the factor loading of one indicator per construct to a value of unity. All measured indicators are allowed to load on only one construct each, and the error terms are not allowed to correlate with each other. The measurement model is described in Figure 22.10.

Assess Measurement Model Reliability and Validity

Our measurement model ($n = 250$) yields the following model fit results: $\chi^2(df = 377) = 767.77$; RMSEA = 0.064; SRMR = 0.041; NNFI = 0.94; and CFI = 0.95 (see Table 22.4). Notice that the program computes the degrees of freedom (df = 377) by using the formula df = $1/2[(p)(p + 1)] - k$, where p is the total number of observed variables and k is the number of estimated parameters. Since $p = 30$ and $k = 88$ (i.e., number of loadings (=22), measurement errors (=30), and factor covariances (=28) and variances (=8) estimated by the program), df = $1/2[(30)(30 + 1)] - 88$, which equals 377. NNFI is computed using the formula NNFI = $(\chi^2_{null}/df_{null} - \chi^2_{prop}/df_{prop})/[(\chi^2_{null}/df_{null}) - 1]$, where df_{prop} and df_{null} are degrees of freedom for the proposed and null models respectively. The null model (χ^2_{null}) equals 7780.15 with df = 435 and the proposed model (χ^2_{prop}) equals 767.77 with df = 377. NNFI = (7780.15/435 − 767.77/377) / [(7780.15/435) − 1], which equals 0.939 or approximately 0.94. CFI = $1 - (\chi^2_{prop} - df_{prop})/(\chi^2_{null} - df_{null})$ computes to $1 - (767.77 - 377)/(7780.15 - 435)$, which equals 0.947 or approximately 0.95. Similarly,

TABLE 22.3	
Service Quality Model: Psychometric Properties of Measurement Model	
When it comes to. . .	Loadings
TANG1: Modern equipment	0.71
TANG2: Visual appeal of physical facilities	0.80
TANG3: Neat, professional appearance of employees	0.76
TANG4: Visual appeal of materials associated with the service	0.72
REL1: Keeping a promise by a certain time	0.79
REL2: Performing service right the first time	0.83
REL3: Providing service at the promised time	0.91
REL4: Telling customers the exact time the service will be performed	0.81
RESP1: Giving prompt service to customers	0.73
RESP2: Willingness to always help customers	0.89
RESP3: Responding to customer requests despite being busy	0.81
ASSU1: Employees instilling confidence in customers	0.81
ASSU2: Customers' safety feelings in transactions (e.g., physical, financial, emotional, etc.)	0.71
ASSU3: Consistent courtesy to customers	0.80
ASSU4: Employees' knowledge to answer customer questions	0.86
EMP1: Giving customers individual attention	0.80
EMP2: Dealing with customers with care	0.84
EMP3: Having customer's best interests at heart	0.87
EMP4: Understanding specific needs of customers	0.87
Overall attitude toward your bank (items reverse coded):	
ATT1: Favorable 1—2—3—4—5—6—7 Unfavorable	0.95
ATT2: Good 1—2—3—4—5—6—7 Bad	0.95
ATT3: Positive 1—2—3—4—5—6—7 Negative	0.95
ATT4: Pleasant 1—2—3—4—5—6—7 Unpleasant	0.95
SAT1: I believe I am satisfied with my bank's services	0.93
SAT2: Overall, I am pleased with my bank's services	0.93
SAT3: Using services from my bank is usually a satisfying experience	0.88
SAT4: My feelings toward my bank's services can best be characterized as	0.92
PAT1: The next time my friend needs the services of a bank I will recommend my bank	0.88
PAT2: I have no regrets of having patronized my bank in the past	0.89
PAT3: I will continue to patronize the services of my bank in the future	0.88

for RMSEA, $\sqrt{[(\chi^2/df - 1)/(n - 1)]}$ can be computed as $\sqrt{[(767.77/377 - 1)/(250 - 1)]}$, which equals 0.064. Based on our previous discussion of model fit criteria, these fit indices collectively indicate that overall fit of the measurement model is acceptable and that the researcher needs to now test for reliability and validity.

RELIABILITY AND VALIDITY TESTS The main purpose of the measurement model is to assess and verify that the indicators or scale items used for each construct are both reliable and valid. We first conduct a test of reliability by examining the composite reliability. The factor loadings and the measurement error for all indicator variables are reported in Table 22.3. For example, the composite reliability for tangibility is: $[(0.71 + 0.80 + 0.76 + 0.72)^2]/[(0.71 + 0.80 + 0.76 + 0.72)^2 + (0.49 + 0.36 + 0.42 + 0.48)]$, which equals 8.94/10.69 = 0.84. Average variance extracted (AVE) reflects the overall variance in the indicators accounted for by the latent construct. For the tangibility dimension, AVE is: $[(0.71^2 + 0.80^2 + 0.76^2 + 0.72^2)]/[(0.71^2 + 0.80^2 + 0.76^2 + 0.72^2) + (0.49 + 0.36 + 0.42 + 0.48)]$, which equals 2.24/3.99 = 0.56. Values of composite reliability and AVE for each measurement are shown in Table 22.5. All constructs exceed the critical levels of 0.70 and 0.50 for composite reliability and AVE respectively. This establishes the reliability and convergent validity of the measurement scales in our study.

FIGURE 22.10

Measurement Model for Banking Application

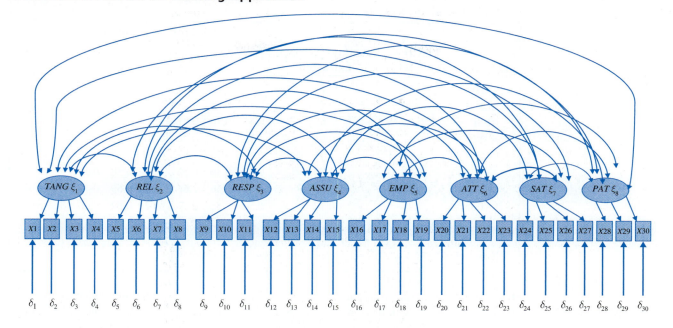

Convergent validity is further established if all item loadings are equal to or above the recommended cutoff level of 0.70. In our sample, of a total of 30 items in the measurement model, 8 items had loadings ≥ 0.90, 16 items with loadings in the range ≥ 0.80 to < 0.90, and 6 items with loadings in the range ≥ 0.70 to < 0.80 (see Table 22.3). All of the factor loadings were statistically significant at the $p < 0.05$ level. Thus, the data in our study supports convergent validity of the model. Discriminant validity is achieved if the square root of the average variance extracted is larger than correlation coefficients. In our study, we found all of the correlation estimates met the criterion except in 4 out of the 28 cases. Given that the five dimensions measure different aspects of service quality, some degree of intercorrelation is expected. However, given the size of the correlation matrix (i.e., 28 estimates), some violations can occur through chance. Test for discriminant validity is shown in Table 22.5. Values on the diagonal of the correlation matrix represent the square root of the AVE. For example, to test for discriminant validity between tangibility and responsiveness, we compare the correlation between tangibility and responsiveness with their respective square root of the average variance extracted. So, the square root of the average variance extracted for tangible and responsiveness dimensions are 0.75 and 0.81, and both are greater than their correlation of 0.65. In summary, overall the scale items were both reliable and valid for testing the structural model.

Specify the Structural Model

Based on theoretical considerations, we hypothesized perceived service quality as a higher-order construct consisting of the five dimensions of tangibility (TANG), reliability (REL), responsiveness

---

TABLE 22.4
Goodness-of-Fit Statistics (Measurement Model)
Degrees of Freedom = 377
Minimum Fit Function Chi-Square = 767.77 ($P = 0.0$)
Chi-Square for Independence Model with 435 Degrees of Freedom = 7780.15
Root Mean Square Error of Approximation (RMSEA) = 0.064
Standardized RMR = 0.041
Normed Fit Index (NFI) = 0.90
Non-Normed Fit Index (NNFI) = 0.94
Comparative Fit Index (CFI) = 0.95

TABLE 22.5

Measurement Model: Construct Reliability, Average Variance Extracted, and Correlation Matrix

Construct	Construct Reliability	Average Variance Extracted	Correlation Matrix							
			1	2	3	4	5	6	7	8
1. TANG	0.84	0.56	0.75							
2. REL	0.90	0.70	0.77	0.84						
3. RESP	0.85	0.66	0.65	0.76	0.81					
4. ASSU	0.87	0.63	0.73	0.80	0.92	0.80				
5. EMP	0.91	0.71	0.69	0.75	0.85	0.90	0.85			
6. ATT	0.97	0.90	0.42	0.46	0.52	0.54	0.58	0.95		
7. SAT	0.85	0.83	0.53	0.56	0.66	0.67	0.69	0.72	0.91	
8. PAT	0.92	0.78	0.50	0.55	0.57	0.62	0.62	0.66	0.89	0.89

- TANG = tangibility; REL = reliability; RESP = responsiveness; ASSU = assurance; EMP = empathy; ATT = attitude; SAT = satisfaction; PAT = patronage
- Value on the diagonal of the correlation matrix is the square root of AVE.

(RESP), assurance (ASSU), and empathy (EMP). Specifically, we model service quality as a second-order model with first-order dimensions of TANG, REL, RESP, ASSU, and EMP. In other words, these five dimensions are indicators of service quality and therefore the arrows flow out from service quality to the five dimensions (see Figure 22.11). On the right-hand side of the Figure 22.11, we link second-order service quality with attitude toward service (ATT) and satisfaction with service (SAT). The latter two constructs are linked to patronage intention (PAT). The entire structural model (i.e., 8 constructs) is tested simultaneously, as shown in Figure 22.11. In testing for the structural model, we free the structural linkages and fix the factor loading of one indicator per construct to a value of unity. All measured items are allowed to load on only one construct each, and the error terms are not allowed to correlate with each other. We also fix the second-order loading of one dimension (i.e., tangibility) to unity for scaling purpose. While the measurement model tests for reliability and validity of the measures, the structural model tests for the structural relations in the model.

Assess Structural Model Validity

We estimated the structural model with the same sample ($n = 250$) yielding the following model fit results: $\chi^2(\text{df} = 396) = 817.16$; RMSEA = 0.065; SRMR = 0.096; NNFI = 0.94; and CFI = 0.94 (see Table 22.6). These fit indices were computed using the formulas given earlier. For example, $CFI = 1 - (\chi^2_{prop} - \text{df}_{prop})/(\chi^2_{null} - \text{df}_{null})$ computes to $1 - (817.16 - 396)/(7780.15 - 435)$ which equals 0.943 or approximately 0.94. Similarly, $RMSEA = \sqrt{[(\chi^2/\text{df} - 1)/(n - 1)]}$ can be computed as $\sqrt{[(817.16/396 - 1)/(250 - 1)]}$ which equals 0.065. Both CFI and

FIGURE 22.11

Structure Model for Banking Application

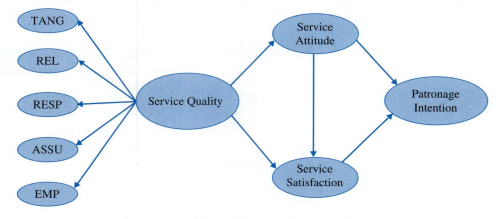

Legend TANG = tangibility; REL = reliability; RESP = responsiveness; ASSU = assurance; EMP = empathy

---

TABLE 22.6

Goodness-of-Fit Statistics (Structural Model)

Degrees of Freedom = 396

Minimum Fit Function Chi-Square = 817.16 (P = 0.0)

Chi-Square for Independence Model with 435 Degrees of Freedom = 7780.15

Root Mean Square Error of Approximation (RMSEA) = 0.065

Standardized RMR = 0.096

Normed Fit Index (NFI) = 0.89

Non-Normed Fit Index (NNFI) = 0.94

Comparative Fit Index (CFI) = 0.94

NNFI are ≥ 0.90 and RMSEA and SRMR are ≤ 0.08. Collectively, these fit indices indicate that the structural model is acceptable. That is, the second-order perceived service quality model is robust and theoretically explains the constructs of attitude, satisfaction, and patronage intention. The structural coefficients linking the five dimensions with second-order service quality (i.e., the second-order loadings) are all significant and in the expected direction. Table 22.7 contains the structural coefficients with corresponding t values. For example, the loading for tangibility is 0.82, which indicates that service quality explains 67 ($=(0.82)^2$) percent of the variance in tangibility. Similarly, the loading for reliability is 0.85, which indicates that service quality explains 72 ($=(0.85)^2$) percent of the variance in reliability. On the right-hand side of the figure, the coefficients for SQ→ATT is 0.60, for SQ→SAT is 0.45, for ATT→SAT is 0.47, for ATT→PAT is 0.03, and SAT→PAT is 0.88. All these links are significant at $p < 0.005$.except for the ATT→PAT.

Draw Conclusions and Make Recommendations

The magnitude and significance of the loading estimates indicate that all of the five dimensions of service quality are relevant in predicting service attitude and service satisfaction. Moreover, service quality has a significant impact on both service attitude and service satisfaction as the structural coefficients for these paths are significant. Service satisfaction, in turn, has a significant impact on patronage intent. Service attitude does not directly impact patronage intent; rather, it has only an indirect effect through service satisfaction.

If the sample was representative of the target population, we could cautiously suggest the following marketing implications to the management of a bank. All the dimensions of service quality are relevant and should be emphasized. Marketing programs should be launched to enhance the customers' perceptions of tangibility, reliability, responsiveness, assurance, and

---

TABLE 22.7

Structural Model Coefficients

Dimensions of Service Quality		Second-Order Loading Estimates	T-values
TANG	γ_{11}	0.82	λ fixed to 1
REL	γ_{21}	0.85	13.15
RESP	γ_{31}	0.93	13.37
ASSU	γ_{41}	0.98	16.45
EMP	γ_{51}	0.93	15.18

Consequences of Service Quality		Structural Coefficient Estimates	
SQ→ATT	γ_{61}	0.60	10.25
SQ→SAT	γ_{71}	0.45	8.25
ATT→SAT	β_{76}	0.47	8.91
ATT→PAT	β_{86}	0.03	0.48
SAT→PAT	β_{87}	0.88	13.75

empathy. The indicators for each service quality dimension suggest how that dimension should be impacted by management action. Also, customer satisfaction with banking services is important in influencing patronage intent. Therefore, the bank should conduct customer satisfaction surveys at regular intervals, e.g., quarterly. This will help the bank to monitor customer satisfaction and take appropriate actions as needed to ensure that a high level of satisfaction is maintained.

ACTIVE RESEARCH

Redesigning Google

As the research director for Google, you are to develop a model that explains consumers' patronage of an Internet portal. Visit www.google.com and search the Internet to identify the factors that influence patronage of an Internet portal. Formulate a structural model and draw a path diagram.

As the director of marketing at Google, how would you use the structural model in redesigning the Google Web site?

Project Research

Structural Equation Modeling (SEM)

In the department store project, SEM can be used to develop a model that explains store preference in terms of respondents' evaluations of the store on the eight factors of the choice criteria. The endogenous construct will be store preference, measured by 10 indicator variables; each indicator will be preference for one of the 10 stores considered in the study. The exogenous construct will be store evaluation, which is a second-order construct with evaluation of stores on the eight factors of the choice criteria as the eight first-order factors. Thus the eight first-order factors are evaluations of stores on quality of merchandise, variety and assortment of merchandise, returns and adjustment policy, service of store personnel, prices, convenience of location, layout of store, and credit and billing policies. Each first-order factor is measured by 10 indicator variables, with each indicator representing the evaluation of one of the 10 stores on a particular aspect of the choice criteria.

Project Activities

SPSS Data File

SAS Data File

Download the SPSS or SAS data file *Sears Data 17* from the Web site for this book. This file contains the evaluation of Sears on the eight factors of the choice criteria (quality, variety and assortment, return policy, service of store personnel, fair prices, convenience of location, store layout, and credit and billing policies), the preference for Sears, importance attached to eight factors of the choice criteria, and agreement with the 21 lifestyle statements. The measurement of these variables is described in Chapter 1. The remaining variables have not been included to keep the number of variables below 50.

1. Formulate the measurement model. Draw a path diagram.
2. Estimate the measurement model on the data contained in *Sears Data 17*.
3. Asses the reliability and validity of the measurement model.
4. Formulate the structural model. Draw a path diagram.
5. Estimate the structural model on the data contained in *Sears Data 17*.
6. Asses the validity of the structural model.
7. Interpret the results. What are your conclusions and what recommendations will you make to Sears management? ■

Path Analysis

Path analysis (PA) can be viewed as a special case of structural equation modeling (SEM). We could think of PA as SEM with only single indicators for each of the variables in the causal model. In other words, path analysis is SEM with a structural model, but no measurement model. Other terms used to refer to path analysis include *causal modeling*, *analysis of covariance structures*, and *latent variable models*.[21]

Path analysis may also be viewed as an extension of the regression model. The PA model is depicted in a rectangle-and-arrow figure in which single-headed arrows indicate causation. A regression is done for each variable in the model as a dependent on others, which the model indicates are causes. The regression weights estimated by the model are compared with the observed correlation matrix for the variables, and a goodness-of-fit statistic is calculated. Path analysis calculates the strength of each relationship using only a correlation or covariance matrix as input. We illustrate PA with an example.

Illustrative Example of Path Analysis

Suppose we observe the following correlation matrix between three variables Y_1, X_1, and X_2.

	X_1	X_2	Y_1
X_1	1.0		
X_2	.40	1.0	
Y_1	.50	.60	1.0

The first step is to construct a path diagram, as in Figure 22.12. This is similar to that done in SEM for the structural model and should be specified by the researcher based on theory. Figure 22.12 portrays a simple model with two exogenous constructs X_1 and X_2, both causally related to the endogenous construct Y_1. The correlational path A is X_1 correlated with X_2. Path B is the effect of X_1 predicting Y_1, and path C shows the effect of X_2 predicting Y_1. The value for Y_1 can be modeled as:

$$Y_1 = b_1 X_1 + b_2 X_2$$

Note that this is similar to a regression equation. The direct and indirect paths in our model can now be identified.

Direct Paths	Indirect Paths
A = X_1 to X_2	AC = X_1 to Y_1 (via X_2)
B = X_1 to Y_1	AB = X_2 to Y_1 (via X_1)
C = X_2 to Y_1	

In PA, the simple or bivariate correlation between two variables is decomposed into the sum of the direct and indirect paths connecting these variables. In our illustrative example, the unique correlations among the three constructs can be shown to be composed of direct and indirect paths as follows:

$$\text{Corr}_{x_1,x_2} = A$$
$$\text{Corr}_{x_1,y_1} = B + AC$$
$$\text{Corr}_{x_2,y_1} = C + AB$$

The correlation of X_1 and X_2 is simply equal to A. The correlation of X_1 and Y_1 (Corr x_1,y_1) can be represented by two paths: B and AC. B represents the direct path from X_1 to Y_1. AC is a compound path that follows the curved arrow from X_1 to X_2 and then to Y_1. Similarly, the correlation of X_2 and Y_1 can be shown to consist of two causal paths: C and AB. Given our observed correlation matrix, these equations can become:

$$.40 = A$$
$$.50 = B + AC$$
$$.60 = C + AB$$

Substituting A = .40

$$.50 = B + .40C$$
$$.60 = C + .40B$$

Solving for B and C

$$B = .310$$
$$C = .476$$

The paths represent either correlational estimates or causal relationships between constructs and their interpretation is similar to that in SEM.

We conclude our discussion of SEM by giving examples in the areas of international marketing research and ethics.

FIGURE 22.12

Diagram for Path Analysis

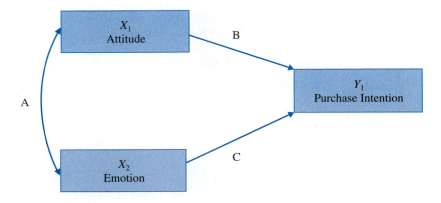

Real Research

The Path to International Success

A recent study sought to explain the internationalization of professional service firms. The underlying theoretical framework was based on attribution theory. The structural model posited that three causal constructs or factors (i.e., uniqueness of offering, financial resources, and competitive pricing) influenced cognitive social consequences (i.e., expectation of success) and the resulting behavioral consequence (i.e., international success). This model is shown in the accompanying diagram. The data were obtained from a sample of 152 U.S.-based professional service firms via a mail survey. First, a measurement model was specified and estimated using CFA. The results showed acceptable composite reliability and convergent and discriminant validity. Then, the structural model (see diagram) was estimated and found to be valid. The results of the structural model provided support for all the four hypotheses (H1 to H4), thereby providing support for the attribution theory framework. Several managerial implications were drawn. For example, the

Attribution Model of Internationalization of Professional Service Firms

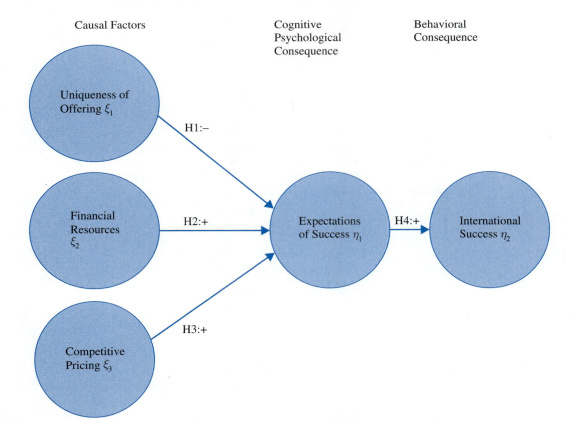

influence of cognitive psychological consequences on behavioral consequences means that managers who expect international success tend to be successful. Hence, professional service firms wishing to make greater inroads into the international marketplace may wish to search out and promote such managers.[22] ■

Real Research

Personal Values, Ethical Ideology, and Ethical Beliefs

The relationships among an individual's personal values, ethical ideology, and ethical beliefs were investigated using structural equation modeling. The data were collected in an Internet survey, and a final sample of 609 completed surveys was obtained. First, a measurement model was tested for key validity dimensions. Then, the hypothesized causal relationships were examined in several path models. The results indicated that individual differences in values directly and indirectly (through idealism) influence the judgment of ethically questionable consumer practices. The findings not only contributed to the theoretical understanding of ethical decision making but also had managerial implications. For example, understanding what underlies people's unethical attitudes and behavior would enable retailers to positively influence appropriate behavior of shoppers by appealing to personal values. This should result in a reduction of unethical behaviors such as shoplifting.[23] ■

Statistical Software

Several computer programs are available for SEM. The most widely used program is LISREL, an acronym for LInear Structural RELations. LISREL is a flexible program that can be used in a range of SEM applications normally encountered in marketing research. AMOS (Analysis of Moment Structures) is another program that is gaining in popularity because it is user-friendly and is available as an added module to SPSS. SAS offers the CALIS program. Another widely available program is EQS, an abbreviation for equations. LISREL, AMOS, and EQS are available with point-and-click interface. Mplus is another program that is also used for SEM. For applications commonly encountered in marketing research, these programs should produce similar results. Hence, the selection of a specific computer program for SEM should be made based on availability and the user's preference.[24]

LISREL

Because LISREL is a popular program, we give detailed instructions for conducting SEM using this software for the first-order factor model application that we have discussed. The data file can be downloaded from the Web site for this book.

```
!CFA-Lisrel
Raw Data from File CH 22 TAM.PSF

Latent Variables: PU PE INT
Relationships:

PU → PU1 PU2 PU3
PE → PE1 PE2 PE3
INT → INT1 INT2 INT3

Method of Estimation = Maximum Likelihood
Number of Decimals = 2
path diagram
Lisrel Output: SE TV MI EF FS RS SS SC AD=off IT=1300
End of Program

!SEM-Lisrel
Raw Data from File CH 22 TAM.PSF

Latent Variables: PU PE INT
Relationships:

PU1 = 1*PU
PU2 = PU
PU3 = PU
```

```
PE1 = 1* PE
PE2 = PE
PE3 = PE

INT1 = 1*INT
INT2 = INT
INT3 = INT
INT = PU PE
```

Method of Estimation = Maximum Likelihood

Number of Decimals = 2
path diagram
Lisrel Output: SE TV MI EF FS RS SS SC AD=off IT=1300
End of Program

SPSS Windows

AMOS provides you with powerful and easy-to-use structural equation modeling (SEM) software. Using AMOS, you specify, estimate, assess, and present your model in an intuitive path diagram to show hypothesized relationships among variables.

There are some distinctions of note when comparing the various SEM software packages. For example, AMOS varies from LISREL in how it approaches exogenous variables. LISREL (correctly) asks researchers to make a conceptual distinction between exogenous and endogenous variables prior to the testing of a model. AMOS simply treats any variables that do not have paths going to them as exogenous. As a result, LISREL by default allows all exogenous variables to freely covary with one another, while researchers using AMOS have to be proactive in establishing this set of relationships.

We give detailed instructions for conducting SEM using AMOS for the first-order factor model application that we have discussed. The data file can be downloaded from the Web site for this book.

```
'CFA

Sub Main ()
Dim sem As New AmosEngine

sem.Standardized
sem.TextOutput

sem.BeginGroup "CH 22 TAM.sav"

sem.Structure "PU1 = PU + (1) E1"
sem.Structure "PU2 = PU + (1) E2"
sem.Structure "PU3 = PU + (1) E3"
sem.Structure "PE1 = PE + (1) E4"
sem.Structure "PE2 = PE + (1) E5"
sem.Structure "PE3 = PE + (1) E6"
sem.Structure "INT1 = INT + (1) E7"
sem.Structure "INT2 = INT + (1) E8"
sem.Structure "INT3 = INT + (1) E9"

sem.Structure "PU (1)"
sem.Structure "PE (1)"
sem.Structure "INT (1)"

sem.Structure "PU ↔ PE"
sem.Structure "PU ↔ INT"
sem.Structure "PE ↔ INT"

End Sub
```

'SEM

Sub Main ()
Dim sem As New AmosEngine

sem.Standardized
sem.TextOutput

sem.BeginGroup "CH 22 TAM.sav"

sem.Structure "PU1 = (1) PU + (1) E1"
sem.Structure "PU2 = PU + (1) E2"
sem.Structure "PU3 = PU + (1) E3"
sem.Structure "PE1 = (1) PE + (1) E4"
sem.Structure "PE2 = PE + (1) E5"
sem.Structure "PE3 = PE + (1) E6"
sem.Structure "INT1 = (1) INT + (1) E7"
sem.Structure "INT2 = INT + (1) E8"
sem.Structure "INT3 = INT + (1) E9"

sem.Structure "INT = PU + PE + (1) ERR"

End Sub

SAS Learning Edition

The instructions given here and in all the data analysis chapters (14 to 22) will work with the SAS Learning Edition as well as with the SAS Enterprise Guide. SAS offers the CALIS procedure. We give detailed instructions for conducting SEM using the SAS Learning Edition for the first-order factor model application that we have discussed. The data file can be downloaded from the Web site for this book.

1. Select File>New>Code. (Note that SEM is not available as an SAS Learning Edition task and that SAS code needs to be submitted in order to run this analysis.)
2. Type the following SAS statements into the Code window and enter the physical location of dataset in the libname statement.

libname **<INSERT LOCATION OF DATA>**;

proc calis data = **<INSERT DATASET NAME>** cov;

Lineqs

    PE1 = a1 f_PE + e1,
    PE2 = a2 f_PE + e2,
    PE3 = a3 f_PE + e3,
    PU1 = a4 f_PU + e4,
    PU2 = a5 f_PU + e5,
    PU3 = a6 f_PU + e6,
    INT1 = a7 f_INT + e7,
    INT2 = a8 f_INT + e8,
    INT3 = a9 f_INT + e9;

Std

f_PE f_PU f_INT = **3 * 1.**,

e1-e9 = ev1-ev9;

Cov

f_PE f_PU = phi1,

f_PE f_INT = phi2,
f_PU f_INT = phi3;

run;

3. Select Code>Run Code on Local.

Decision Research The Situation

The soft drink market is one of the most popular but slowly growing markets in the United States. From 2002–2008, the average annual growth rate was estimated to be around 4.7 percent. Carbonated beverages hold the largest share of the market in soft drinks, followed by bottled water and then juices. Diet drinks as a whole have grown in popularity.

The top three companies in the soft drink market are Coca-Cola, PepsiCo., and Cadbury Schweppes. Coca-Cola has around 50 percent market share, Pepsi with 21 percent, and Cadbury Schweppes at 7 percent. These three companies control nearly 80 percent of the global market. Coca-Cola has attained this position due to the introduction of new products such as Diet Coke sweetened with SPLENDA brand sweetener, launched in 2005; Diet Black Cherry Vanilla Coke, launched in 2006; and Diet Coke Plus, launched in 2007 (www.dietcoke.com). With the new health front facing today's consumers, Muhtar Kent, president and chief executive officer of Coca-Cola, believed it was important from a marketing and managerial standpoint to sustain a strong diet drink image.

When Diet Coke was first introduced in 1982, consumers saw advertisements using celebrities to promote the new product. As time went on, a more body-conscious approach was taken in Diet Coke's advertising image. Consumers began to see advertisements of a construction worker being ogled by women working in an office, promoting the image of a healthier alternative to non-diet soft drinks. As competition has increased and Pepsi launched their advertising campaign of being the choice of the younger and "hipper" consumer, the Coca-Cola Company must reevaluate its current advertising campaign. Muhtar Kent is wondering whether a more product-focused advertising campaign that stresses the factors influencing consumers' choice of diet soft drink brands would be more effective.

The Marketing Research Decision

1. What theoretical framework can be used to explain consumers' attitudes, preferences, and consumption of diet soft drink brands?
2. What data should be collected and how should they be analyzed in determining what factors drive consumers' consumption of soft drink brands? Can SEM be used? If so how?

The Marketing Management Decision

1. Should Muhtar Kent change the advertising for Diet Coke to focus more on the factors influencing consumers' choice of diet soft drink brands?
2. Discuss how the marketing management decision action that you recommend to Muhtar Kent is influenced by the data analysis that you suggested earlier and by the likely findings.[25] ■

Summary

Structural equation modeling (SEM) is a procedure for estimating a series of dependence relationships among a set of concepts or constructs represented by multiple measured variables and incorporated into an integrated model. SEM is mainly used as a confirmatory, rather than exploratory, technique. Figure 22.13 gives a concept map for SEM.

It is very important that an SEM model be based on theory because all relationships must be specified before the SEM model can be estimated. A construct is an unobservable or latent variable that can be defined in conceptual terms but cannot be measured directly. Rather, a construct is measured approximately and indirectly by examining the consistency among multiple observed or measured variables. It is recommended that each construct be measured by using at least three observed variables. The steps involved in conducting SEM are (1) define the individual constructs, (2) specify the measurement model, (3) assess measurement model validity, (4) specify the structural model if the measurement model is valid, (5) assess structural model validity, and (6) draw conclusions and make recommendations if the structural model is valid.

FIGURE 22.13

A Concept Map for Structural Equation Modeling

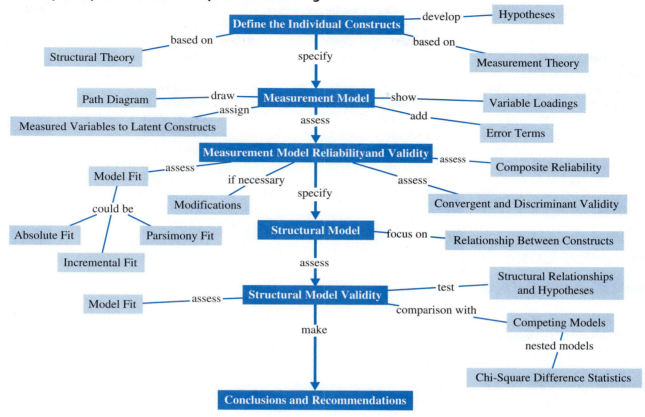

SEM analyzes covariance. Model fit is determined by comparing how closely the estimated covariance matrix, Σ_k, matches the observed covariance matrix S, i.e., the fit statistics are based on $|S - \Sigma_k|$. The various measures designed to assess fit consist of absolute fit, incremental fit, and parsimony fit indices. In absolute fit indices, each model is evaluated independently of other possible models. In contrast to the absolute fit indices, the incremental fit indices evaluate how well the specified model fits the sample data relative to some alternative model that is treated as a baseline model. The baseline model that is commonly used is the null model that is based on the assumption that the observed variables are uncorrelated. The parsimony fit indices are designed to assess fit in relation to model complexity and are useful in evaluating competing models. These indices are based on the parsimony ratio that is calculated as the ratio of degrees of freedom used by the model to the total degrees of freedom available.

In assessing the validity of the measurement model, it is useful to examine composite reliability and convergent and discriminant validity. Composite reliability (CR) is defined as the total amount of true score variance in relation to the total score variance. High factor loadings indicate that the observed variables converge on the same construct. Another measure that is used to assess convergent validity is the average variance extracted (AVE), which is defined as the variance in the indicators or observed variables that is explained by the latent construct. Cross-loadings indicate

lack of distinctiveness and present potential problems in establishing discriminant validity. Discriminant validity is established by showing that the average variance extracted is greater than the square of the correlations.

If the validity of the proposed measurement model is not satisfactory, then you can make use of the diagnostic information provided by CFA to make appropriate modifications. The diagnostic cues that can be used to make appropriate modifications include (1) the path estimates or loadings, (2) standardized residual, (3) modification indices, and (4) specification search. If the modifications are substantial, then you must modify the measurement theory, specify a new measurement model, and collect new data to test the new model.

Once the validity of the measurement model has been established, you can proceed with the specification of the structural model. In moving from the measurement model to the structural model, the emphasis shifts from the relationships between latent constructs and the observed variables to the nature and magnitude of the relationships between constructs. Assessing the validity of the structural model is similar to that for the measurement model and involves (1) examining the fit, (2) comparing the proposed structural model with competing models, and (3) testing structural relationships and hypotheses.

Several computer programs are available for SEM. The more popular ones include LISREL, AMOS, CALIS, and EQS.

Key Terms and Concepts

structural equation
modeling (SEM), 691
construct, 692
measurement error, 692
absolute fit indices, 693
average variance extracted (AVE), 693
chi-square difference
statistic ($\Delta\chi^2$), 693
composite reliability (CR), 693
confirmatory factor
analysis (CFA), 693
endogenous constructs, 693
estimated covariance matrix, 693
exogenous construct, 693

first-order factor model, 693
incremental fit indices, 693
measurement model, 693
modification index, 693
nested model, 693
nonrecursive model, 693
parsimony fit indices, 693
parsimony ratio, 694
path analysis (PA), 694
path diagram, 694
recursive model, 694
sample covariance matrix, 694
second-order factor model, 694

squared multiple correlations, 694
structural error, 694
structural model, 694
structural relationship, 694
unidimensionality, 694
model fit, 696
residuals, 696
model identification, 696
communality, 699
squared multiple correlations, 703
standardized residuals, 703
modification index, 703
specification search, 703

Suggested Cases, Video Cases, and HBS Cases

Running Case with Real Data

1.1 Dell

Data Analysis Cases with Real Data

3.2 IBM   3.3 Kimberly-Clark

Comprehensive Cases with Real Data

4.1 JPMorgan Chase   4.2 Wendy's

Video Case

23.1 Marriott

Live Research: Conducting a Marketing Research Project

1. The use of SEM may not be appropriate in some applied marketing research projects.
2. Even if a structural model is not being estimated, it may still be possible and desirable to specify and estimate a measurement

model and establish the composite reliability and convergent and discriminant validity of the scales and measures used.

3. If a structural model is estimated, it should be specified based on theory and the results discussed with the client.

Acronym

The two-part structural equation modeling can be summarized by the acronym

SEM:

S   tructural model
E   stimation and assessment of reliability and validity
M   easurement model

Exercises

Questions

1. What characteristics distinguish SEM from other multivariate techniques?
2. What is the role of theory in SEM?
3. What is a measurement model? Why is it estimated?

4. How is model fit assessed in SEM?
5. What are the similarities and differences between an absolute and incremental fit index?
6. What are the similarities and differences between a parsimony and incremental fit index?

7. What is confirmatory factor analysis? How is it similar to and different from exploratory factor analysis?
8. How do you assess the validity of a measurement model?
9. How do you establish convergent and discriminant validity in an SEM framework?
10. What is average variance extracted? Why is it useful to calculate this statistic?
11. What is a second-order factor model? How is it different from a first-order factor model?
12. What is a structural theory and how is it different from measurement theory?
13. How do we determine whether the difference between two structural path coefficients is significant?
14. What is a recursive model? Why is this aspect relevant in SEM?
15. SEM is similar to what other multivariate techniques? How is it similar?

Problems

1. Draw a path diagram with three exogenous constructs and one endogenous construct. The exogenous constructs are measured by 5, 4, and 3 observed variables or indicators. The endogenous construct is measured by 4 indicators. Two exogenous constructs are expected to be positively related and one negatively related to the endogenous construct. What are degrees of freedom of the associated measurement model?

Internet and Computer Exercises

1. Download the banking services data set from the Web site for this book. Estimate the measurement and structural models specified in this chapter. Do you get the same results given in this chapter?

2. Compare and contrast the following SEM software: LISREL, AMOS, and EQS. Which software is most user-friendly? Which is most useful? Why?

Activities

Role Playing

1. You work as a senior marketing research analyst with a major advertising agency. According to theory, advertising leads to awareness, which leads to understanding, which leads to preference, which leads to purchase intention. Draw a path diagram and explain this process to your boss, a group account manager and vice president in your agency (roles played by another student).

Fieldwork

1. Visit some of the marketing and other professors in your college. Ask them for papers they have published using SEM.

Write a simple description of the SEM analysis that was done in one of the papers.

Group Discussion

1. As a small group, discuss the similarities and differences between EFA and CFA? Which is more useful?

Dell Running Case

Review the Dell case, Case 1.1, and questionnaire given toward the end of the book. Go to the Web site for this book and download the Dell data file.

Develop an SEM explaining Dell satisfaction and loyalty (measured by Q4, Q5, and Q6) in terms of performance ratings on the first four items of Q8.

1. Specify the measurement model and draw a path diagram.
2. Estimate the measurement model and assess its reliability and validity.
3. Specify the structural model and draw a path diagram.
4. Estimate the structural model and assess its validity.
5. What are your conclusions? What recommendations would you make to Dell management?

"In any report or presentation, get right to the point in why these results matter to the firm. The tendency for beginners is to present all the answers and all the data, whether relevant or not. The role of the analyst is to boil, filter, and distill, so the audience receives the pure distillation."

Jerry Thomas, President/CEO, Decision Analyst, Inc.

Objectives   [After reading this chapter, the student should be able to:]

1. Discuss the basic requirements of report preparation, including report format, report writing, graphs, and tables.

2. Discuss the nature and scope of the oral presentation and describe the "Tell 'Em" and "KISS 'Em" principles.

3. Describe the approach to the marketing research report from the client's perspective and the guidelines for reading the research report.

4. Explain the reason for follow-up with the client and describe the assistance that should be given to the client and the evaluation of the research project.

5. Understand the report preparation and presentation process in international marketing research.

6. Identify the ethical issues related to the interpretation and reporting of the research process and findings to the client and the use of these results by the client.

7. Explain the use of the Internet and computers in report preparation and presentation.

Report Preparation and Presentation

Overview

Report preparation and presentation constitutes the sixth and final step in a marketing research project. It follows problem definition, approach development, research design formulation, fieldwork, and data preparation and analysis. This chapter describes the importance of this final step, as well as a process for report preparation and presentation. We provide guidelines for report preparation, including report writing and preparing tables and graphs. We discuss oral presentation of the report. Research follow-up, including assisting the client and evaluating the research process, is described. The special considerations for report preparation and presentation in international marketing research are discussed, and the relevant ethical issues identified. We conclude by discussing the use of software in report preparation and presentation.

To begin, we provide an illustrative example.

Real Research

Reporting the Friendly Skies

The task of marketing research is to assess information needs, to provide this information, and to help the decision maker in making the right decision. That is what United Airlines, the Chicago-based airline company, has understood with its ongoing in-flight customer satisfaction tracking program. Each month, 192,000 passengers among 900 flights are selected and surveyed, using a four-page scannable form. The survey covers the satisfaction of passengers on both "on-the-ground services" (flight reservation, airport service) and "in-the-air services" (flight attendants, meal, aircraft). The attendants distribute the forms early in the flight, so that passengers can take time to fill in the questionnaire.

Each month the internal department of marketing research at United issues a report summarizing customer satisfaction. The report is also posted on the Internet and available online to United managers all over the world. Because of the large size of the sample, the data are very reliable (representative) and all departments of the company use the report:

- The marketing department to make strategic planning, product positioning, and target marketing decisions;
- The finance department to measure the success of its product investments;

Monthly reports of customer satisfaction surveys have helped United Airlines to improve on-the-ground and in-the-air services.

- The airport department to evaluate ground service, including speed and efficiency of check-in (service representatives, waiting lines);
- The executive management to evaluate the performance of United, both internally in achieving its goals, and externally compared to the competition.

The result of this high-powered customer satisfaction report is that all departments at United Airlines are customer oriented. This helps the company to differentiate itself in an environment where all companies have the same schedules, the same service, and the same fares. In winter 2009, United Airlines reduced the prices of many of its routes when its surveys showed that many passengers were looking for low fares in an uncertain economy.[1] ■

The United Airlines example highlights the importance of regular reporting.

Importance of the Report and Presentation

report
A written and/or oral presentation of the research process, results, recommendations, and/or conclusions to a specific audience.

A **report** is a written and/or oral presentation of the research process, results, recommendations, and/or conclusions to a specific audience. For the following reasons, the report and its presentation are important parts of the marketing research project:

1. They are the tangible products of the research effort. After the project is complete and management has made its decision, there is little documentary evidence of the project other than the written report. The report serves as a historical record of the project.
2. Management decisions are guided by the report and the presentation. If the first five steps in the project are carefully conducted but inadequate attention is paid to the sixth step, the value of the project to management will be greatly diminished.
3. The involvement of many marketing managers in the project is limited to the written report and the oral presentation. These managers evaluate the quality of the entire project based on the quality of the report and presentation.
4. Management's decision to undertake marketing research in the future or to use the particular research supplier again will be influenced by the perceived usefulness of the report and the presentation.

The Report Preparation and Presentation Process

Figure 23.1 illustrates report preparation and presentation. The process begins by interpreting the results of data analysis in light of the marketing research problem, approach, research

FIGURE 23.1

The Report Preparation and Presentation Process

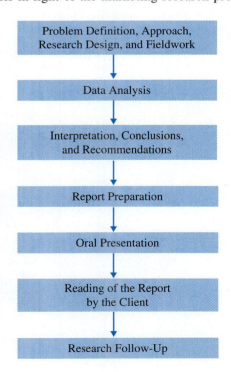

| Problem Definition, Approach, Research Design, and Fieldwork |
| Data Analysis |
| Interpretation, Conclusions, and Recommendations |
| Report Preparation |
| Oral Presentation |
| Reading of the Report by the Client |
| Research Follow-Up |

design, and fieldwork. Instead of merely summarizing the statistical results, the researcher should present the findings in such a way that they can be used directly as input into decision making. Wherever appropriate, conclusions should be drawn and recommendations made. Recommendations should be actionable. Before writing the report, the researcher should discuss the major findings, conclusions, and recommendations with the key decision makers. Discussions play a major role in ensuring that the report meets the client's needs and that the report is ultimately accepted. These discussions should confirm specific dates for the delivery of the written report and other data.

The entire marketing research project should be summarized in a single written report or in several reports addressed to different readers. Generally, an oral presentation supplements the written documents. The client should be given an opportunity to read the report. After that, the researcher should take necessary follow-up actions. The researcher should assist the client in understanding the report, implementing the findings, undertaking further research, and evaluating the research process in retrospect. The importance of the researcher being intimately involved in the report preparation and presentation process is highlighted by the following example.

Real Research Focus Group Moderators' Ghostwriters Can Shortchange Clients

Thomas Greenbaum, president of a market research company focusing on qualitative research, notes a disturbing trend in recent years in the focus group service sector. Greenbaum, of Groups Plus, Inc., of Wilton, Connecticut (www.groupsplus.com), asserts that some moderators of focus groups misrepresent their work to clients because their reports are actually written by ghostwriters who did not participate in the focus group sessions.

According to Greenbaum, perhaps more than half of moderators use ghostwriters to develop their reports for clients. Often, junior researchers learning the business or part-time employees write these ghostwritten reports. Greenbaum criticizes such ghostwriting because the nonverbal reactions of focus group participants, or group synergy, cannot always be accurately reported by those who merely listen to audiotapes or view videotapes of focus group sessions. Greenbaum calls upon moderators to be forthright with clients about the authorship of focus group reports, and calls upon clients to be more demanding of their contracted research teams.

"Although some people in the industry defend ghostwriting by saying they always review the reports before they are sent to the client, or perhaps even write certain key sections, this practice must be looked at carefully by clients who use focus group research," Greenbaum said. "If the clients know in advance that their reports will be written by someone else, it is clearly less of a problem, but they still do not get the best effort from their research consultants."

In addition to the likelihood of degrading a report, Greenbaum observes that the ghostwriting system delays the submission of the final report. "Moderators who write their own reports try to complete them within a week or 10 days of the last group, so the information is still fresh in their minds when they do the writing," Greenbaum said. "However, most moderators (using ghostwriters) are not able to provide clients with final reports for three to four weeks after the last group, due to the process they use with ghostwriters."[2] ■

Report Preparation

Researchers differ in the way they prepare a research report. The personality, background, expertise, and responsibility of the researcher, along with the decision maker (DM) to whom the report is addressed, interact to give each report a unique character. In short or repetitive projects, an extensive formal written report of the type we describe here may not be prepared. Nonetheless, there are guidelines for formatting and writing reports and designing tables and graphs that should be generally followed.[3]

Report Format

Report formats are likely to vary with the researcher or the marketing research firm conducting the project, the client for whom the project is being conducted, and the nature of the project itself. Hence, the following is intended as a guideline from which the researcher can develop a format for the research project at hand. Most formal research reports include most of the following elements:

I. Title page
II. Letter of transmittal
III. Letter of authorization
IV. Table of contents
V. List of tables
VI. List of graphs
VII. List of appendices
VIII. List of exhibits
IX. Executive summary
    a. Major findings
    b. Conclusions
    c. Recommendations

→ Prefatory Part

X. Problem definition
    a. Background to the problem
    b. Statement of the problem
XI. Approach to the problem
XII. Research design
    a. Type of research design
    b. Information needs
    c. Data collection from secondary sources
    d. Data collection from primary sources
    e. Scaling techniques
    f. Questionnaire development and pretesting
    g. Sampling techniques
    h. Fieldwork
XIII. Data analysis
    a. Methodology
    b. Plan of data analysis
XIV. Results
XV. Limitations and caveats
XVI. Conclusions and recommendations

→ Main Body

XVII. Exhibits
    a. Questionnaires and forms
    b. Statistical output
    c. Lists

→ Appended Part

This format closely follows the earlier steps of the marketing research process. The results may be presented in several chapters of the report. For example, in a national survey, data analysis may be conducted for the overall sample and then the data for each of the four geographic regions may be analyzed separately. If so, the results may be presented in five chapters instead of one.

Title Page

The title page should include the title of the report, information (name, address, email, and telephone) about the researcher or organization conducting the research, the name of the client for whom the report was prepared, and the date of release. The title should indicate the nature of the project, as illustrated in the following example.

Real Research   Global Guidelines on the Title Page

Use client language in title—avoid "research-eze":

- "Practices Followed in Selecting Long-Distance Carriers" is better than "Long-Distance Service Study"
- "Customers' Reactions to an Expanded Financial/Insurance Relationship" is better than "Relationship Study"

Letter of Transmittal

A formal report generally contains a letter of transmittal that delivers the report to the client and summarizes the researcher's overall experience with the project, without mentioning the findings. The letter should also identify the need for further action on the part of the client, such as implementation of the findings or further research that should be undertaken.

Letter of Authorization

A letter of authorization is written by the client to the researcher before work on the project begins. It authorizes the researcher to proceed with the project and specifies its scope and the terms of the contract. Often, it is sufficient to refer to the letter of authorization in the letter of transmittal. However, sometimes it is necessary to include a copy of the letter of authorization in the report.

Table of Contents

The table of contents should list the topics covered and the appropriate page numbers. In most reports, only the major headings and subheadings are included. The table of contents is followed by a list of tables, list of graphs, list of appendices, and list of exhibits.

Executive Summary

The executive summary is an extremely important part of the report, because this is often the only portion of the report that executives read. The summary should concisely describe the problem, approach, and research design that was adopted. A summary section should be devoted to the major results, conclusions, and recommendations. The executive summary should be written after the rest of the report has been completed.

Problem Definition

This section of the report gives the background to the problem, highlights the discussions with the decision makers and industry experts, and discusses the secondary data analysis, the qualitative research that was conducted, and the factors that were considered. Moreover, it should contain a clear statement of the management decision problem and the marketing research problem (see Chapter 2).

Approach to the Problem

This section should discuss the broad approach that was adopted in addressing the problem. This section should also contain a description of the theoretical foundations that guided the research, any analytical models formulated, research questions, hypotheses, and the factors that influenced the research design.

Research Design

The section on research design should specify the details of how the research was conducted (see Chapters 3 to 13). This should include the nature of the research design adopted, information needed, data collection from secondary and primary sources, scaling techniques, questionnaire development and pretesting, sampling techniques, and fieldwork. These topics should be presented in a nontechnical, easy-to-understand manner. The technical details should be included in an appendix. This section of the report should justify the specific methods selected.

Data Analysis

This section should describe the plan of data analysis and justify the data analysis strategy and techniques used. The techniques used for analysis should be described in simple, nontechnical terms.

Results

This section is normally the longest part of the report and may comprise several chapters. Often, the results are presented not only at the aggregate level but also at the subgroup (market segment, geographical area, etc.) level. The results should be organized in a coherent and logical way. For example, in a health care marketing survey of hospitals, the results were presented in four chapters. One chapter presented the overall results, another examined the differences between geographical regions, a third presented the differences between for-profit and nonprofit hospitals, and a fourth presented the differences according to bed capacity. The presentation of the results should be geared directly to the components of the marketing research problem and the information needs that were identified. The details should be presented in tables and graphs, with the main findings discussed in the text.

Limitations and Caveats

All marketing research projects have limitations caused by time, budget, and other organizational constraints. Furthermore, the research design adopted may be limited in terms of the various types of errors (see Chapter 3), and some of these may be serious enough to warrant discussion. This section should be written with great care and a balanced perspective. On one hand, the researcher must make sure that management does not overly rely on the results or use them for unintended purposes, such as projecting them to unintended populations. On the other hand, this section should not erode their confidence in the research or unduly minimize its importance.

Conclusions and Recommendations

Presenting a mere summary of the statistical results is not enough. The researcher should interpret the results in light of the problem being addressed to arrive at major conclusions. Based on the results and conclusions, the researcher may make recommendations to the decision makers. Sometimes marketing researchers are not asked to make recommendations because they research only one area but do not understand the bigger picture at the client firm. If recommendations are made, they should be feasible, practical, actionable, and directly usable as inputs into managerial decision making. The following example contains guidelines on conclusions and recommendations.

Real Research

Guidelines on Conclusions and Recommendations

Conclusions

- Conclusions

  Conclusions concerning, for example:

  - Customer behavior
  - Customer attitudes or perceptions
  - The nature of the markets studied

  Generally, in studies with samples designed to represent the market
  Avoid interesting results that are not relevant to the conclusions

- May be in the form of statement or paragraphs
- Use subheadings to identify conclusions covering different subjects or market segments

Recommendations

- Recommendations regarding actions that should be taken or considered in light of the research results:
  Add/drop a product
  What to say in advertising—advertising positioning
  Market segments to select as primary targets
  How to price product
  Further research that should be considered
- Should be related to the stated purpose of the research
- Sometimes omitted—e.g.:
  Client staff members want to author the recommendations
  Study designed merely to familiarize client with a market
- Most clients are interested in our suggestions, in spite of the fact that we may not be familiar with internal financial issues and other internal corporate factors.

Report Writing

Readers

A report should be written for a specific reader or readers: the marketing managers who will use the results. The report should take into account the readers' technical sophistication and interest in the project, as well as the circumstances under which they will read the report and how they will use it.

Technical jargon should be avoided. As expressed by one expert, "The readers of your reports are busy people; and very few of them can balance a research report, a cup of coffee, and a dictionary at one time."[4] Instead of technical terms such as *maximum likelihood, heteroscedasticity,* and *nonparametric,* use descriptive explanations. If some technical terms cannot be avoided, briefly define them in an appendix. When it comes to marketing research, people would rather live with a problem they cannot solve than accept a solution they cannot understand.

Often the researcher must cater to the needs of several audiences with different levels of technical sophistication and interest in the project. Such conflicting needs may be met by including different sections in the report for different readers, or by separate reports entirely.

Easy to Follow

The report should be easy to follow.[5] It should be structured logically and written clearly. The material, particularly the body of the report, should be structured in a logical manner so that the reader can easily see the inherent connections and linkages. Headings should be used for different topics and subheadings for subtopics.

A logical organization also leads to a coherent report. Clarity can be enhanced by using well-constructed sentences that are short and to the point. The words used should express precisely what the researcher wants to communicate. Difficult words, slang, and clichés should be avoided. An excellent check on the clarity of a report is to have two or three people who are unfamiliar with the project read it and offer critical comments. Several revisions of the report may be needed before the final document emerges.

Presentable and Professional Appearance

The appearance of a report is important. The report should be professionally reproduced with quality paper, typing, and binding. The typography should be varied. Variation in type size and skillful use of white space can greatly contribute to the appearance and readability of the report.

Objective

Objectivity is a virtue that should guide report writing. Researchers can become so fascinated with their project that they overlook their scientific role. The report should accurately present the methodology, results, and conclusions of the project, without slanting the findings to conform to the expectations of management. Decision makers are unlikely to receive with enthusiasm a report that reflects unfavorably on their judgment or actions. However, the researcher must have the courage to present and defend the results objectively. The rule is, "Tell it like it is."

Reinforce Text with Tables and Graphs

It is important to reinforce key information in the text with tables, graphs, pictures, maps, and other visual devices. Visual aids can greatly facilitate communication and add to the clarity and impact of the report. Guidelines for tabular and graphical presentation are discussed later.

Terse

A report should be terse and concise. Anything unnecessary should be omitted. If too much information is included, important points may be lost. Avoid lengthy discussions of common procedures. Yet brevity should not be achieved at the expense of completeness.

Guidelines for Tables

Statistical tables are a vital part of the report and deserve special attention. We illustrate the guidelines for tables using the data for U.S. automobile sales reported in Table 23.1. The numbers in parentheses in the following sections refer to the numbered sections of the table.

Title and Number

Every table should have a number (1a) and title (1b). The title should be brief yet clearly descriptive of the information provided. Arabic numbers are used to identify tables so that they can be referred to in the text.[6]

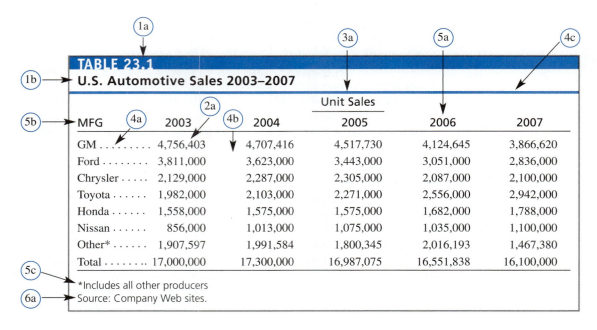

TABLE 23.1

U.S. Automotive Sales 2003–2007

			Unit Sales		
MFG	2003	2004	2005	2006	2007
GM	4,756,403	4,707,416	4,517,730	4,124,645	3,866,620
Ford	3,811,000	3,623,000	3,443,000	3,051,000	2,836,000
Chrysler	2,129,000	2,287,000	2,305,000	2,087,000	2,100,000
Toyota	1,982,000	2,103,000	2,271,000	2,556,000	2,942,000
Honda	1,558,000	1,575,000	1,575,000	1,682,000	1,788,000
Nissan	856,000	1,013,000	1,075,000	1,035,000	1,100,000
Other*	1,907,597	1,991,584	1,800,345	2,016,193	1,467,380
Total	17,000,000	17,300,000	16,987,075	16,551,838	16,100,000

*Includes all other producers
Source: Company Web sites.

Arrangement of Data Items

The arrangement of data items in a table should emphasize the most significant aspect of the data. Thus, when the data pertain to time, the items should be arranged by appropriate time period. When order of magnitude is most important, the data items should be arranged in that order (2a). If ease of locating items is critical, an alphabetical arrangement is most appropriate.

Basis of Measurement

The basis or unit of measurement should be clearly stated (3a).

Leaders, Rulings, and Spaces

Leaders, dots, or hyphens are used to lead the eye horizontally, impart uniformity, and improve readability (4a). Instead of ruling the table horizontally or vertically, white spaces (4b) are used to set off data items. Skipping lines after different sections of the data can also assist the eye. Horizontal rules (4c) are often used after the headings.

Explanations and Comments: Headings, Stubs, and Footnotes

Explanations and comments clarifying the table can be provided in the form of captions, stubs, and footnotes. Designations placed over the vertical columns are called *headings* (5a). Designations placed in the left-hand column are called *stubs* (5b). Information that cannot be incorporated in the table should be explained by footnotes (5c). Letters or symbols should be used for footnotes rather than numbers. The footnotes should come after the main table, but before the source note.

Sources of the Data

If the data contained in the table are secondary, the source of data should be cited (6a).

Guidelines for Graphs

As a general rule, graphic aids should be employed whenever practical. Graphical display of information can effectively complement the text and tables to enhance clarity of communication and impact. As the saying goes, a picture is worth a thousand words. The guidelines for preparing graphs are similar to those for tables. Therefore, this section focuses on the different types of graphical aids.[7] We illustrate several of these using the U.S. automobile sales data from Table 23.1.

Geographic and Other Maps

Geographic and other maps, such as product-positioning maps, can communicate relative location and other comparative information. Geographic maps can pertain to countries, states, counties, sales territories, and other divisions. For example, suppose the researcher wanted to present information on the relative number of Coca-Cola Company bottlers versus the bottlers for PepsiCo and other competitors for each state in the United States. This information could be effectively communicated in a map in which each state was divided into three areas, proportionate to the number of Coca-Cola, PepsiCo, and other bottlers, with each area in a different color. Chapter 21 showed examples of product-positioning maps derived by using MDS procedures (e.g., Figure 21.4).

Round or Pie Charts

In a **pie chart**, the area of each section, as a percentage of the total area of the circle, reflects the percentage associated with the value of a specific variable. A pie chart is not useful for displaying relationships over time or relationships among several variables. As a general guideline, a pie chart should not require more than seven sections.[8] Figure 23.2 shows a pie chart for U.S. automobile sales.

Line Charts

A **line chart** connects a series of data points using continuous lines. This is an attractive way of illustrating trends and changes over time. Several series can be compared on the same chart, and forecasts, interpolations, and extrapolations can be shown. If several series are displayed simultaneously, each line should have a distinctive color or form (see Figure 23.3).[9]

A **stratum chart** is a set of line charts in which the data are successively aggregated over the series. Areas between the line charts display the magnitudes of the relevant variables (see Figure 23.4).

Pictographs

A **pictograph** uses small pictures or symbols to display the data. As Figure 23.5 shows, pictographs do not depict results precisely. Hence, caution should be exercised when using them.[10]

Histograms and Bar Charts

A **bar chart** displays data in various bars that may be positioned horizontally or vertically. Bar charts can be used to present absolute and relative magnitudes, differences, and change. The **histogram** is a vertical bar chart in which the height of the bars represents the relative or cumulative frequency of occurrence of a specific variable (see Figure 23.6).

pie chart
A round chart divided into sections.

line chart
A chart that connects a series of data points using continuous lines.

stratum chart
A set of line charts in which the data are successively aggregated over the series. Areas between the line charts display the magnitudes of the relevant variables.

pictograph
A graphical depiction that makes use of small pictures or symbols to display the data.

bar chart
A chart that displays data in bars positioned horizontally or vertically.

histogram
A vertical bar chart in which the height of the bars represents the relative or cumulative frequency of occurrence.

FIGURE 23.2

Pie Chart of Auto Sales by Manufacturer (2007)

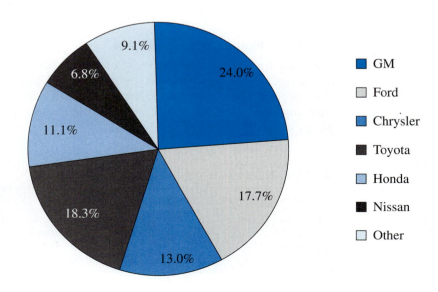

FIGURE 23.3

Line Chart of Auto Sales by Manufacturer (2003–2007)

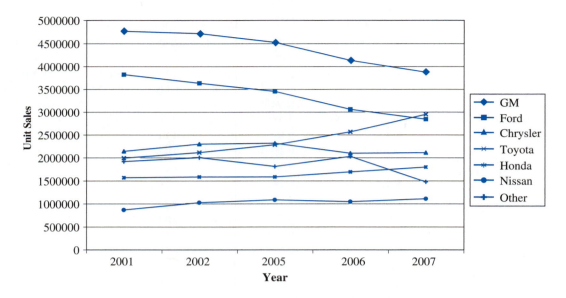

FIGURE 23.4

Stratum Chart of Auto Sales (2003–2007)

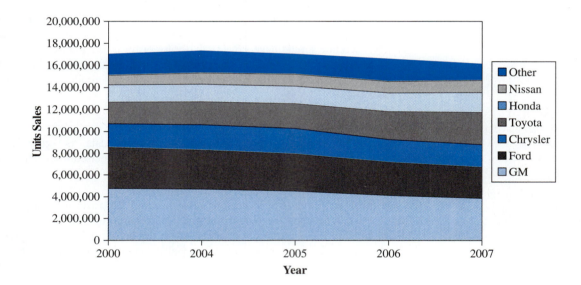

Schematic Figures and Flowcharts

Schematic figures and flowcharts take on a number of different forms. They can be used to display the steps or components of a process, as in Figure 23.1. Another useful form of these charts is classification diagrams. Examples of classification charts for classifying secondary data were provided in Chapter 4 (Figures 4.1 to 4.4). An example of a flowchart for questionnaire design was given in Chapter 10 (Figure 10.2).[11]

ACTIVE RESEARCH

Reporting Procter & Gamble

Visit www.pg.com and search for the company's latest annual report.

Critically evaluate the use of graphs in P&G's latest annual report. What additional graphs would you construct?

As the vice president of marketing, how useful do you find the graphs in P&G's latest annual report?

FIGURE 23.5

Pictograph of Auto Sales (2007)

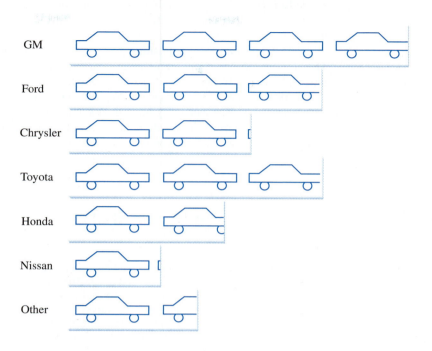

Each Symbol Equals 1,000,000 Units

FIGURE 23.6

Histogram of Auto Sales by Manufacturer (2007)

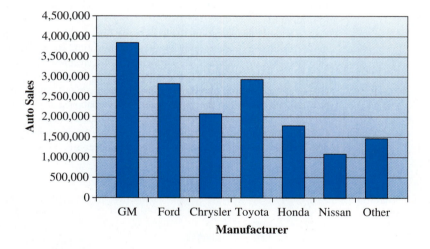

Report Distribution

The marketing research report should be distributed to appropriate personnel in the client organization. The report could be distributed in a variety of formats including hard copy and electronic. Increasingly, research reports are being published or posted directly to the Web. Normally, these reports are not located in publicly accessible areas but in locations that are protected by passwords or on corporate intranets. The various word-processing, spreadsheet, and presentation packages have the capability to produce material in a format that can be posted directly to the Web, thus facilitating the process.

There are a number of advantages to publishing marketing research reports on the Web. These reports can incorporate all kinds of multimedia presentations, including graphs, pictures, animation, audio, and full-motion video. The dissemination is immediate and the reports can be accessed by authorized persons online on a worldwide basis. These reports can be electronically searched to identify materials of specific interest. For example, a General Electric manager in Kuala Lumpur can electronically locate the portions of the report that pertain to Southeast Asia. Storage and future retrieval is efficient and effortless. It is easy to integrate these reports into the decision support system.

One good example of publishing marketing research reports on the Web is by accutips.com. They have published many marketing research reports on the Web. The reports published online deal with many different categories in marketing, such as case studies, market focus/trends, sales and marketing, data selection and mailing lists, creating successful direct mail, Web marketing, and e-marketing. You can easily go to their site at www.accutips.com and search in any of these categories. Furthermore, new Internet applications are allowing companies to share information with specific recipients within their organization.

Decision Research ## Subaru of America, Inc.: A Report on Reporting

The Situation

Tomohiko Ikeda, chairman, president, and CEO of Subaru of America, Inc, knows that customer loyalty is a big part of the automotive industry today, and Subaru has long been aware of this fact. Subaru, in the past, relied heavily on the traditional, paper-based customer response surveys. Short, follow-up purchase experience surveys and service experience surveys were mailed to customers within 7 to 14 days after purchase. These surveys entailed both multiple-choice questions and open-ended questions. The response rates from the mailings ranged from 30 to 45 percent. After all the data were collected from the mailings, dealerships received a Subaru Owner Loyalty Indicator (SOLI) rating quarterly report. These reports provided valuable information to the dealers, but they used to receive this information only four times a year. Upon receipt of this report that contained customer complaints, it was usually too late to resolve the problems.

To address this situation, the answer for Tomohiko Ikeda was the Internet, which would provide faster, more flexible service and information to dealers, field staff, and the management team. Subaru hired Data Recognition Corporation (DRC) of Minneapolis, Minnesota, to set up the program design and provide the ongoing service. The process begins by scanning the responses from customer survey forms using optical character recognition. Customer comments are captured and categorized. Next, all survey information is electronically added to the appropriate dealer's database using a customized program developed by DRC. The entire process is managed by DRC; hence, Subaru may concentrate on selling cars.

The Web-based reports give field managers an opportunity to see what is happening at their assigned dealerships. They can access up-to-the-minute reports on a specified dealership before meeting with the

Web-based reports have enabled field managers and dealers of Subaru of America to stay on top of where they are in terms of customer satisfaction.

dealer. This works well because the managers are able to access this information from anywhere as long as they can tap into the Internet.

Dealers are able to use the site to stay on top of where they are in terms of customer satisfaction. They can see their quality scores and check on a particular salesperson's performance. Dealers are able to take immediate action because of this new technology. This allows for better management, and in the long run, better performance from all employees. As dealers became more comfortable with the Web format, they began to request more detailed and timely reports. Due to this request, Subaru has recently begun to develop a series of reports called "Just-in-Time Reports." These reports provide immediate access to current performance rankings in addition to the quarterly rankings. This has become another tool for Subaru to help boost their sales and performance. This new technology and refocused goals on customer measurement and loyalty will help propel Subaru forward with an advantage over lagging competition.

The Marketing Research Decision

1. While Subaru management finds the report very useful, the dealers have a slightly different opinion. How should the report be modified to improve its usefulness to the dealers?
2. Discuss the role of the type of report you recommend in enabling Tomohiko Ikeda to make the dealer sales effort more effective.

The Marketing Management Decision

1. What should Tomohiko Ikeda do to make the dealer sales effort more effective?
2. Discuss how the marketing management decision action that you recommend to Tomohiko Ikeda is influenced by the type of report that you suggested earlier.[12] ■

Oral Presentation

The entire marketing research project should be presented to the management of the client firm. This presentation will help management understand and accept the written report. Any preliminary questions that the management may have can be addressed in the presentation. Because many executives form their first and lasting impressions about the project based on the presentation, its importance cannot be overemphasized.[13]

The key to an effective presentation is preparation. A written script or detailed outline should be prepared following the format of the written report. The presentation must be geared to the audience. For this purpose the researcher should determine their backgrounds, interests, and involvement in the project, as well as the extent to which they are likely to be affected by it. The presentation should be rehearsed several times before it is made to the management.

Visual aids, such as tables and graphs, should be displayed with a variety of media. Chalkboards enable the researcher to manipulate numbers. They are particularly useful in communicating answers to technical questions. Although not as flexible, magnetic boards and felt boards allow for rapid presentation of previously prepared material. Flip charts are large pads of blank paper mounted on an easel. Visual aids are drawn on the pages in advance, and the speaker flips through the pages during the presentation. Computer projectors can present simple charts as well as complex overlays produced by the successive addition of new images to the screen. Several computer programs are available for producing attractive presentations. Blu-ray and DVD players and large-screen projectors are particularly effective in presenting focus groups and other aspects of fieldwork that are dynamic in nature. PowerPoint and other software are very useful for making a visual presentation. Computer projectors attached to personal computers, which project the monitor image onto the screens, may also be employed. They can be used for making computer-controlled presentations or for presenting technical information such as analytical models.

It is important to maintain eye contact and interact with the audience during the presentation. Sufficient opportunity should be provided for questions, both during and after the presentation. The presentation should be made interesting and convincing with the use of appropriate stories, examples, experiences, and quotations. Filler words, such as "uh," "y'know," and "all right," should not be used. The **"Tell 'Em" principle** is effective for structuring a presentation. This principle states: (1) Tell 'em what you're going to tell 'em, (2) tell 'em, and (3) tell 'em what you've told 'em. Another useful guideline is the **"KISS 'Em" principle**, which states: Keep It Simple and Straightforward (hence the acronym KISS).

"Tell 'Em" principle
An effective guideline for structuring a presentation. This principle states (1) Tell 'em what you're going to tell 'em, (2) tell 'em, and (3) tell 'em what you've told 'em.

"KISS 'Em" principle
A principle of report presentation that states: Keep It Simple and Straightforward.

Body language should be employed. Descriptive gestures are used to clarify or enhance verbal communication. Emphatic gestures are used to emphasize what is being said. Suggestive gestures are symbols of ideas and emotions. Prompting gestures are used to elicit a desired response from the audience. The speaker should vary the volume, pitch, voice quality, articulation, and rate while speaking. The presentation should terminate with a strong closing. To stress its importance, the presentation should be sponsored by a top-level manager in the client's organization, as in the following example.

Real Research   Taking It to the Top

TNS Global (www.tns-global.com) conducted a research project to measure the relative effectiveness of television, print, and radio as advertising media for a client firm. In addition, the effectiveness of 10 TV commercials, radio commercials, and print ads was assessed. Given the nature of the project, the oral presentation of the report was particularly important in communicating the findings. A laptop computer and computer projector were used for showing the PowerPoint slides, and playing TV and radio commercials. A storyboard was used for showing the print ads. The presentation was made to the client's top corporate officers, consisting of the president, all vice presidents, and all assistant vice presidents, at one of their monthly meetings.[14] ∎

After the presentation, key executives in the client firm should be given time to read the report in detail. Some guidelines are available for report reading.

Reading the Research Report

Guidelines for reading the report and evaluating the marketing research project have been developed by the Advertising Research Foundation.[15]

Address the Problem

The reader should focus on the problem being addressed to determine if it has been clearly defined and that the relevant background information has been provided. The organization sponsoring the research, as well as the one conducting the research, should be clearly identified. The report should not assume that the reader has prior knowledge of the problem situation, but should give all the relevant information. A report that does not provide such information has missed the mark, as well as the readers.

Research Design

If readers in the target audience of the report cannot understand the research design procedure, the fault lies with the researcher. The research design should be clearly described in nontechnical terms. The report should include a discussion of the information needs, data-collection methods, scaling techniques, questionnaire design and pretesting, sampling techniques, and fieldwork. Justification should be provided for the specific methods used. Reports that do not contain, or otherwise make available, methodological details should be viewed with caution.

Execution of the Research Procedures

The reader should pay special attention to the manner in which the research procedures were executed. The people working on the project should be well qualified and properly trained. Proper supervision and control procedures should be followed. This is particularly important with respect to data collection, data preparation, and statistical analysis.

Numbers and Statistics

Numbers and statistics reported in tables and graphs should be examined carefully by the reader. Inappropriate numbers and statistics can be highly misleading. Consider, for example, percentages based on small samples or means reported for ordinal data. Unfortunately, the occurrence of these types of misleading statistics in reports is not uncommon.

Interpretation and Conclusions

The reader should evaluate the findings and assess if they have been reported in an objective and candid way. The interpretation of the basic results should be differentiated from the results per se. Any assumptions made in interpreting the results should be clearly identified. The limitations of the research should be discussed. Any conclusions or recommendations made without a specification of the underlying assumptions or limitations should be treated cautiously by the reader.

Generalizability

It is the responsibility of the researcher to provide evidence regarding the reliability, validity, and generalizability of the findings. The report should clearly identify the target population to which the findings apply. Factors that limit the generalizability of the findings, such as the nature and representativeness of the sample, mode and time of data collection, and various sources of error should be clearly identified. The reader should not attempt to generalize the findings of the report without explicit consideration of these factors.

Disclosure

Finally, the reader should carefully examine whether the spirit in which the report was written indicates an honest and complete disclosure of the research procedures and results. It is particularly important that procedures—for example, those used for the treatment of missing values, weighting, and so on—that call for subjective judgment on the part of the researcher be made known. If any negative or unexpected findings were obtained, they should be reported. The reader should feel free to ask for any relevant information that is not contained in the report.

A careful reading of the report using these guidelines will help the client to effectively participate in research follow-up.

Project Research | ## Report Preparation and Presentation

In the department store project, the formal report was prepared for the client's vice president of marketing. The writing of the report was influenced by the style preferences of the vice president for marketing and other key executives. The first volume, the main body of the report, had a title page, table of contents, executive summary, and details of problem definition, approach, research design, methodology used to analyze the data, results, limitations of the project, and conclusions and recommendations. Volume I had a nontechnical orientation and was easy to follow. Volume II contained a title page, list of figures, and all the figures and graphs. Finally, all the statistical details, including all the tables, were given in Volume III. In addition to the written report, an oral presentation of the entire project was made to the top management. Several of the recommendations made to management in the report were eventually implemented.

Project Activities

Read the Sears project write-ups in each chapter and consider all the analyses that you have done. Prepare an executive summary of the results for Sears' management. ■

Research Follow-Up

The researcher's task does not end with the oral presentation. Two other tasks remain. The researcher should help the client understand and implement the findings and take follow-up action. Secondly, while it is still fresh in the researcher's mind, the entire marketing research project should be evaluated.

Assisting the Client

After the client has read the report in detail, several questions may arise. Parts of the report, particularly those dealing with technical matters, may not be understood and the researcher should provide the help needed. Sometimes the researcher helps implement the findings. Often, the client retains the researcher to help with the selection of a new product or advertising agency, development of a pricing policy, market segmentation, or other marketing actions. An important reason for client follow-up is to discuss further research projects. For example, the researcher and management may agree to repeat the study after two years. Finally, the researcher should help the client firm make the information generated in the marketing research project a part of the firm's marketing (management) information system (MIS) or decision support system (DSS), as discussed in Chapter 1.

Evaluation of the Research Project

Although marketing research is scientific, it also involves creativity, intuition, and expertise. Hence, every marketing research project provides an opportunity for learning, and the researcher should critically evaluate the entire project to obtain new insights and knowledge. The key question to ask is, "Could this project have been conducted more effectively or efficiently?" This question, of course, raises several more specific questions. Could the problem have been defined differently so as to enhance the value of the project to the client or reduce the costs? Could a different approach have yielded better results? Was the best research design used? How about the mode of data collection? Should mall intercepts have been used instead of telephone interviews? Was the sampling plan employed the most appropriate? Were the sources of possible research design error correctly anticipated and kept under control, at least in a qualitative sense? If not, what changes could have been made? How could the selection, training, and supervision of field workers be altered to improve data collection? Was the data analysis strategy effective in yielding information useful for decision making? Were the conclusions and recommendations appropriate and useful to the client? Was the report adequately written and presented? Was the project completed within the time and budget allocated? If not, what went wrong? The insights gained from such an evaluation will benefit the researcher and the subsequent projects conducted.

Experiential Research

Brevity in Report Writing and Presentation

Ipsos Group SA is a leading global marketing research company. Go to www.ipsos-na.com/news/results.cfm, review the list of press releases in the archives, and choose a press release with data that can be rendered into a brief report. Use Excel to create a set of charts for your report and import the charts into PowerPoint. Some of the press releases already include PowerPoint slides; others include charts that can be readily imported into PowerPoint.

Can you make a compelling business presentation in 3 minutes? Select a topic from Ipsos' press release archive. Then, develop a 3-minute presentation using no more than five PowerPoint slides to explain (1) why this research finding matters to a firm in an industry of your choosing and (2) what this firm can do to take advantage of this finding.

Alternatively, you can create your report and presentation by using your analysis skills and the SPSS program.

Share your final presentation with a group of fellow students in a formal setting.

1. What was the most challenging part of preparing, rehearsing, and making this presentation?
2. What will you do differently in your next presentation as a result of what you have learned in this experiential learning exercise? ■

International Marketing Research

The guidelines presented earlier in the chapter apply to international marketing research as well, although report preparation may be complicated by the need to prepare reports for management in different countries and in different languages. In such a case, the researcher should prepare different versions of the report, each geared to specific readers. The different reports should be comparable, although the formats may differ. The guidelines for oral presentation are also similar to those given earlier, with the added proviso that the presenter should be sensitive to cultural norms. For example, making jokes, which is frequently done in the United States, is not appropriate in all cultures. Most marketing decisions are made from facts and figures arising out of marketing research. But these figures have to pass the test and limits of logic, subjective experience, and gut feelings of decision makers. The subjective experience and gut feelings of managers could vary widely across countries, necessitating that different recommendations be made for implementing the research findings in different countries. This is particularly important when making innovative or creative recommendations such as those pertaining to advertising campaigns.

Real Research   ## Camry Chicken Fries Ford

In 2008, Toyota announced it would build a hybrid version of its Camry sedan in Australia. The ad campaign designed for Toyota Camry in Australia was very different from the one used in Japan. "Why did the chicken cross the road?" Toyota asks in a continuing series of TV commercials aired recently in Australia. The answer: "To sell more Toyota Camrys, of course." The spots, showing an animated chicken trying to cross the road and getting its feathers blown off by a passing Camry, were created by Saatchi & Saatchi Advertising. When Bob Miller, Toyota's general manager for marketing, tried to explain the ad to their counterpart in Japan, they thought he was insane. Maybe so, but the commercial did unbelievably well. Hoary old joke that it was, the gag helped Toyota topple Ford's dominance in Australia. As a continuing series, the next ad showed the featherless chicken sitting on a pile of eggs in the middle of the road and hatching chicks as the Camry speeds past. Whereas such use of humor was offensive to the Japanese, it solicited a favorable response from the Australians. By customizing its advertising and marketing efforts in each culture, the Toyota company remained the biggest auto seller in Australia as of 2009, with some of the best-selling cars, such as the Camry.[16] ■

Ethics in Marketing Research

Report preparation and presentation involves many issues pertaining to research integrity. These issues include defining the marketing research problem to suit hidden agendas, compromising the research design, deliberately misusing statistics, falsifying figures, altering research results, misinterpreting the results with the objective of supporting a personal or corporate point of view, and withholding information.[17] A survey of 254 marketing researchers revealed that 33 percent of the respondents considered that the most difficult ethical problems they face encompass issues of research integrity. The researcher must address these issues when preparing the report and presenting the findings. The dissemination of the marketing research results to the client, and other stakeholders as may be appropriate, should be honest, accurate, and complete.

The researcher should be objective throughout all phases of the marketing research process. Some research procedures and analyses may not reveal anything new or significant. For example, the discriminant function may not classify better than chance (Chapter 18). Ethical dilemmas can arise in these instances if the researcher nevertheless attempts to draw conclusions from such analyses. Such temptations must be resisted to avoid unethical conduct.

Likewise, clients also have the responsibility for complete and accurate disclosure of the research findings and are obligated to use the research results in an ethical manner. For example, the public can be disadvantaged by a client who distorts the research findings to develop a biased advertising campaign that makes brand claims that have not been substantiated by marketing research. Such activities are condemned by the code of ethics of the American Marketing Association and other professional research associations (see Chapter 1).[18] Ethical issues also arise when client firms, such as tobacco companies, use marketing research findings to formulate questionable marketing programs.

Toyota launched a humorous advertising campaign to topple Ford's dominance in Australia. However, that campaign may not be successful in other countries.

Real Research   Tobacco Industry Is "Smoking Gun"

Examination of secondary data sources uncovered the facts that tobacco smoking is responsible for 30 percent of all cancer deaths in the United States and is a leading cause of heart disease, along with being associated with problems such as colds, gastric ulcers, chronic bronchitis, emphysema, and other diseases. Do tobacco companies share an ethical responsibility for this situation? Is it ethical for these companies to employ marketing research to create glamorous images for cigarettes that have a strong appeal to the target market? It is estimated that advertising by the tobacco industry based on systematic research has a part in creating more than 3,000 teenage smokers each day in the United States. Advertising for Camel cigarettes through the Old Joe cartoon advertisements increased Camel's share of the illegal children's cigarette market segment from 0.5 percent to 32.8 percent—representing sales estimates at $476 million per year. These detrimental effects are not limited to the United States. Not only is the tobacco industry enticing children to smoke, but it also targets other less informed populations such as Third World countries because this is a way for tobacco companies to replace those smokers that quit or die.

In 1998, a multistate tobacco agreement was set forth between major cigarette manufacturers and 46 state governments in an effort to prohibit cigarette makers from targeting children in their advertisements. In 2002, however, R.J. Reynolds Tobacco Holdings, Inc., was sued by California's attorney general for allegedly targeting youth with their tobacco advertisements in magazines such as *Rolling Stone* and *Sports Illustrated*. On September 21, 2004, the government opened arguments in its $280 billion civil racketeering lawsuit against the cigarette industry, with the future of big tobacco in the balance. In the biggest civil racketeering case in history, the Justice Department alleged massive, coordinated fraud to conceal tobacco's deadly and addictive nature. As of October 1, 2008, the United States government lawsuit in the United States District Court for the District of Columbia against various cigarette manufacturers, including Philip Morris International and others, such as Altria Group, Inc., was still pending.[19] ∎

ACTIVE RESEARCH

Gallup on Reports

Visit www.gallup.com and search for the recent reports posted on this Web site. What can you learn about report writing from these reports?

Critically evaluate, from a researcher's perspective, the format of one of the reports posted at www.gallup.com.

As the marketing manager for whom the report was meant, how useful do you find the report you considered?

Statistical Software

In addition to a number of specialized programs, the mainframe and microcomputer versions of the major statistical packages have reporting procedures. We discuss the use of SPSS and SAS in detail in the subsequent sections. Here, we briefly describe the use of MINITAB and EXCEL. MINITAB also has the capability to create graphs and charts and edit them for use in reports or professional presentations. Graphs can be created using GRAPH>PLOT, or GRAPH>CHART, or GRAPH>HISTOGRAM. Editing can be done using EDIT>EDIT LAST COMMAND DIALOG. Excel has extensive charting capabilities and, through Microsoft Office, provides a direct link to Word and PowerPoint for report preparation and presentation.

Other online and software packages are also available for efficiently producing graphs, charts, tables, and indeed entire reports by largely automating the process to make it more efficient. E-Tabs (www.e-tabs.com) is one example of a system designed for reporting continuous, tracking, syndicated, and customized projects and facilitating multilevel reporting. One of their products, E-Tabs Enterprise, automates the production of charts, graphs, summary tables, and reports directly from the research data and updates them automatically for every wave, region, or brand. This can significantly boost productivity for the time-consuming task of creating charts from ongoing tracking studies.

SPSS Windows

Whereas the normal graphs can be produced using the Base module of SPSS, for more extensive graphing, the DeltaGraph package can be used. This package has extensive graphing capabilities with 80 chart types and 200 chart styles.

Likewise, the SPSS TABLES program enables the researcher to create even complicated tables. For example, the results of multiple response tables can be condensed into a single table. The researcher can create a polished look by changing the column width, adding boldface, drawing lines, or aligning.

SPSS OLAP cubes are interactive tables that enable you to slice your data in different ways for data exploration and presentation.

SmartViewer enables the researcher to distribute reports, graphs, tables, even pivotal report cubes, over the Web. Company managers can be empowered to interact with the results by putting a report cube on the Web, intranet, or extranet. Thus, they can answer their own questions by drilling down for more detail and creating new views of the data.

SAS Enterprise Guide

SAS Learning Edition is especially useful for reporting. Results from SAS Learning Edition can be used to create a customized report that can be printed, exported, and shared with other applications. Multiple results can be added to reports with text and images and there is great flexibility in arranging the results in the report. When output included in customized reports is updated, the results in the report are automatically refreshed.

SAS Learning Edition provides comprehensive graphing capabilities. More than 80 chart types are available and can be created as ActiveX (dynamic or image), Jave Applets (dynamic or image), GIFs or JPEGs.

The OLAP Analyzer within SAS Learning Edition enables you to access and analyze data that is stored in an OLAP cube. You can slice and dice data as needed to explore the information, as well as drill through to underlying detailed data. Individual views on multidimensional information can be saved as bookmarks for easy reuse, and slices from multidimensional information can be provided to other analytical tasks.

The Document Builder within SAS Learning Edition can be used to combine the HTML results from multiple tasks in your project into a single document that can be shared with others. SAS Enterprise Guide also enables users to publish data and task results to predefined channels, which function as repositories to which users can subscribe. Any reports that are published to a channel will automatically be delivered to all of that channel's subscribers through e-mail or some other method.

Summary

Figure 23.7 gives a concept map of report preparation and presentation, the final step in the marketing research project. This process begins with interpretation of data analysis results and leads to conclusions and recommendations. Next, the formal report is written and an oral presentation made. After management has read the report, the researcher should conduct a follow-up, assisting management and undertaking a thorough evaluation of the marketing research project.

In international marketing research, report preparation may be complicated by the need to prepare reports for management in different countries and in different languages. Several ethical issues are pertinent, particularly those related to the interpretation and reporting of the research process and findings to the client and the use of these results by the client. The use of microcomputers and mainframes can greatly facilitate report preparation and presentation.

Key Terms and Concepts

report, 728
pie chart, 735
line chart, 735

stratum chart, 735
pictograph, 735
bar chart, 735

histogram, 735
"Tell 'Em" principle, 739
"KISS 'Em" principle, 740

Suggested Cases, Video Cases, and HBS Cases

Running Case with Real Data

1.1 Dell

Comprehensive Critical Thinking Cases

2.1 American Idol   2.2 Baskin-Robbins   2.3 Akron Children's Hospital

FIGURE 23.7

A Concept Map for Report Preparation and Presentation

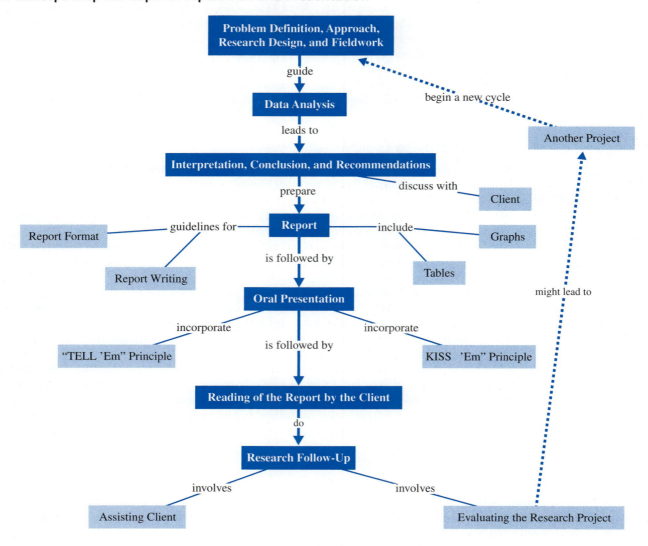

Data Analysis Cases with Real Data

3.1 AT&T   3.2 IBM   3.3 Kimberly-Clark

Comprehensive Cases with Real Data

4.1 JPMorgan Chase   4.2 Wendy's

Video Case

23.1 Marriott

Comprehensive Harvard Business School Cases

Case 5.1: The Harvard Graduate Student Housing Survey (9-505-059)

Case 5.2: BizRate.Com (9-501-024)

Case 5.3: Cola Wars Continue: Coke and Pepsi in the Twenty-First Century (9-702-442)

Case 5.4: TiVo in 2002 (9-502-062)

Case 5.5: Compaq Computer: Intel Inside? (9-599-061)

Case 5.6: The New Beetle (9-501-023)

Live Research: Conducting a Marketing Research Project

1. The individual parts of the report can be assigned to the teams with each team writing a specific part. Each team also prepares the PowerPoint slides for that part.
2. The project coordinators should be responsible for compiling the final report and the presentation.
3. Make liberal use of graphs.
4. Make a presentation of the project to the client with each team presenting its portion.

Acronyms

The guidelines for report writing may be expressed by the acronym

Report:

R eaders: written for specific readers
E asy to follow
P resentable and professional appearance
O bjective
R einforce text with tables and graphs
T erse: concise, yet complete

The guidelines for constructing tables may be described by the acronym

Tables:

T itle and number
A rrangement of data items
B asis of measurement
L eaders, rulings, spaces
E xplanations and comments: headings, stubs, and footnotes
S ources of data

The guidelines for constructing graphs may be described by the acronym

Graphs:

G eographic and other maps
R ound or pie chart
A ssembly or line charts
P ictographs
H istograms and bar charts
S chematic figures and flowcharts

The guidelines for making a presentation can be summarized by the acronym

Presentation:

P reparation
R ehearse your presentation
E ye contact
S tories, experiences, examples, and quotations
E quipment: multimedia
N o filler words
T ell 'Em principle
A udience analysis
T erminate with a strong closing
I nteract with the audience
O utline or script should be prepared
N umber one level manager should sponsor it

The guidelines for reading and evaluating a report may be specified by the acronym

Reading:

R esearch design
E xecution of the research procedures
A ddresses the problem
D isclosure
I nterpretation and conclusion
N umbers and statistics
G eneralizability

Exercises

Questions

1. Describe the process of report preparation.
2. Describe a commonly used format for writing marketing research reports.
3. Describe the following parts of a report: title page, table of contents, executive summary, problem definition, research design, data analysis, conclusions, and recommendations.
4. Why is the "limitations and caveats" section included in the report?
5. Discuss the importance of objectivity in writing a marketing research report.
6. Describe the guidelines for report writing.
7. How should the data items be arranged in a table?
8. What is a pie chart? For what type of information is it suitable? For what type of information is it not suitable?
9. Describe a line chart. What kind of information is commonly displayed using such charts?
10. Describe the role of pictographs. What is the relationship between bar charts and histograms?
11. What is the purpose of an oral presentation? What guidelines should be followed in an oral presentation?
12. Describe the "Tell 'Em" and "KISS 'Em" principles.
13. Describe the evaluation of a marketing research project in retrospect.

Problems

1. The following passage is taken from a marketing research report prepared for a group of printers and lithographers without much formal education who run a small family-owned business:

   To measure the image of the printing industry, two different scaling techniques were employed. The first was a series of semantic differential scales. The second consisted of a set of Likert scales. The use of two different techniques for measurement could be justified based on the need to assess the convergent validity of the findings. Data obtained using both these techniques were treated as interval scaled. Pearson product moment correlations were computed between the sets of ratings. The resulting correlations were high, indicating a high level of convergent validity.

   Rewrite this paragraph so that it is suitable for inclusion in the report.

2. Graphically illustrate the consumer decision-making process described in the following paragraph:

   The consumer first becomes aware of the need. Then the consumer simultaneously searches for information from several sources: retailers, advertising, word of mouth, and independent publications. After that, a criterion is developed for evaluating the available brands in the marketplace. Based on this evaluation, the most preferred brand is selected.

Internet and Computer Exercises

1. For the data given in Table 23.1, use a graphics package or a spreadsheet, such as Excel, to construct the following graphs:

   a. Pie chart
   b. Line chart
   c. Bar chart

2. Using one of the report-generation programs discussed in this chapter or a similar package, write a report explaining the data and the charts constructed in exercise 1 of this section.

3. Visit www.gallup.com to identify a recent report prepared by this company. How does the format of this report compare to the one in the book?

Activities

Role Playing

1. You are a researcher preparing a report for a high-tech firm on "The Demand Potential for Microcomputers in Europe." Develop a format for your report. How is it different from the one given in the book? Discuss your format with your boss (role enacted by a student in your class).

2. In Fieldwork Activity 2, suppose you were the researcher who wrote the report. Prepare an oral presentation of this report for senior marketing managers. Deliver your presentation to a group of students and ask them to critique it.

Fieldwork

1. Make a trip to your library. Read the latest annual reports of three different companies that are known for effective marketing (e.g., Coca-Cola, P&G, GE). Identify the strong and weak points of these reports.

2. Obtain a copy of a marketing research report from your library or a local marketing research firm. (Many marketing research firms will provide copies of old reports for educational purposes.) Critically evaluate this report.

Group Discussion

1. In a small group, discuss the following statement: "All the graphical aids are really very similar; therefore, it does not matter which ones you use."

2. "Writing a report that is concise and yet complete is virtually impossible because these two objectives are conflicting." Discuss.

3. "Writing reports is an art. Presenting reports is an art. Reading reports is an art. It is all a matter of art." Discuss in a small group.

Dell Running Case

Review the Dell case, Case 1.1, and questionnaire given toward the end of the book. Go to the Web site for this book and download the Dell data file.

1. Write a report for Dell management summarizing the results of your analyses. Prepare a set of charts using EXCEL.

2. What recommendations do you have for the management?

3. Can you make a compelling business presentation in 10 minutes? Develop a 10-minute presentation for Dell management using no more than 10 PowerPoint slides.

4. Share your final presentation with a group of fellow students (representing Dell management) in a formal setting.

   a. What was the most challenging part of preparing, rehearsing, and making this presentation?

   b. What will you do differently in your next presentation as a result of what you have learned in this exercise?

VIDEO CASE 23.1   Marriott: Marketing Research Leads to Expanded Offerings

With roots that go back to before the Great Depression, Marriott International (www.marriott.com) has come a long way from its founding by husband and wife John and Alice Marriott. As of 2009, Marriott had a presence in 66 countries with more than 3,100 properties.

This sustained vast expansion over the last several decades is due in large part to marketing research. Marriott began pioneering segmentation in the hospitality industry by expanding its product offering in the 1980s, both upward and downward in quality from its flagship Marriott brand. Marriott found from focus groups and survey research that it could have many types of hotels serving different market segments, and that these market segments, although all providing the same basic needs, would not compete with each other. Certain brands under the Marriott umbrella serve the business traveler. Courtyard by Marriott, with pricing and scaled-back service levels compared to the larger Marriott hotels, is targeted toward the price-sensitive frequent business traveler. Courtyard hotels—said to be designed for business travelers by business travelers—offer high-speed Internet access, ample workspace within the room, and other amenities that are appealing to the business traveler. Fairfield Inns are priced still more modestly to appeal to travelers who are even more price sensitive. Other brands under the Marriott flag, such as the Ramada line, serve more of a family-style vacation market, with a focus toward comfort and affordability.

However, differentiation is not based on service and pricing alone. Marketing research has revealed other attributes that are important. For example, a family or a basic business traveler on a budget might be looking for a convenient location in addition to affordability. Hence, Marriott places Fairfield Inns along interstates and highways, because these targeted groups travel by car. Convenient location becomes another attribute that adds value and enhances perception of the Marriott brand name.

When Marriott began its Fairfield Inn and Suites brand, it started simply as Fairfield Inn. Then, with marketing research (focus groups and surveys), Marriott found that its Fairfield Inn customers desired a luxury-class room within the value hotel of the Fairfield line. Responding to this, Marriott changed the name to Fairfield Inn and Suites and added high-class rooms that contain amenities such as a spa.

Analysis of internal secondary data identified a substantial number of travelers who stayed in Marriott hotels for more than a few nights. Focus groups and surveys revealed that these extended-stay travelers have different needs. They might need meeting space to conduct business, a kitchenette to dine in occasionally, or a suite space so that they do not get tired of seeing the same four walls around their beds when they come "home" in the evening after yet another day on the road. For these travelers, Marriott opened the Residence Inn line (a hotel line designed for an extended stay). Marriott found from subsequent marketing research that this segment had room to expand to a more value-priced line as well. Again, responding to this research, Marriott introduced TownePlace Suites (a value-priced extended-stay hotel line). Some of the guests at the Residence Inn or TownePlace Suites spend up to 6 months to a year at the same hotel.

At the high end, Marriott offers even fuller service and higher prices with its Hotel Resorts & Suites and its Renaissance upscale business properties. According to Marriott's research estimating potential demand, the size of this high-end segment is substantial. With all of these hotel lines, Marriott continues the commitment to quality that began with John and Alice. Knowing from research that all hotel residents desire quality, Marriott strives to provide this in all facets of the hotel service. One way in which Marriott demonstrates this is by empowering its customer service representatives to address customer problems.

Although each of the various Marriott brands has worked hard to carve out a niche for itself, they all share the Marriott brand identity—the key ingredient to their success. According to Gordon Lambourne, Vice President, Marketing and Public Relations, the Marriott brand identity is all about commitment to service excellence, a strong focus on employees that work in the hotels, taking care of the associates so that they can really focus on their jobs and provide a level of service that customers demand and expect today and that service is consistent throughout the world from Philadelphia to Hong Kong. Each of Marriott's hotels has a different personality with a distinct design and service level that make the guest feel like they are in London or Munich or Paris, but all these hotels have a common thread running through them that identifies them as Marriott hotels.

The numerous Marriott brands, rather than creating competition for each other, actually help bring in more business. According to Gordon Lambourne, each of the brands does an excellent job of going out to its particular segment. Each brand has its loyal following and markets itself independently and as a part of a portfolio of brands. There is some crossover, however, but Marriott views it as a great opportunity, to serve customers whose needs may change. So a customer looking for an extended stay might prefer the Residence Inn, but choose a full-service hotel such as the Renaissance for a shorter trip. So whatever happens, whatever that need might be, Marriott is well positioned to capture that customer and that piece of business.

Conclusion

Marriott has been highly successful in using marketing research to develop a segmentation strategy of targeting different customers with different needs by providing different products and options. The diverse offerings have helped Marriott appeal to an increasingly wide range of clients and win greater business. Continued reliance on marketing research will be critical to Marriott's success in the future.

Questions

1. Discuss the role that marketing research can play in helping Marriott formulate sound marketing strategies.
2. Marriott would like to further penetrate the non-business-travelers segment in the United States. Define the management decision problem.
3. Define an appropriate marketing research problem based on the management decision problem you have identified.
4. What type of research design should be adopted? Justify your recommendation.
5. Use the Internet to determine the market shares of the major hotel chains for the last calendar year.
6. What type of internal secondary data will be useful to Marriott?
7. What type of syndicate data will be useful to Marriott?
8. Discuss the role of qualitative research in helping Marriott further penetrate the non-business-travelers segment in the United States.
9. Marriott has developed a new hotel package for families on a vacation. It would like to determine consumers' response to this package before introducing it in the marketplace. If a survey is to be conducted to determine consumer preferences, which survey method should be used and why?

10. In what way could Marriott make use of experimentation? What specific experimental design would you recommend?
11. Illustrate the use of the primary scales for measuring consumer preferences for hotel chains.
12. Develop Likert, semantic differential, and Stapel scales for measuring consumer preferences for hotel chains.
13. Develop a questionnaire for assessing consumer preferences for hotels when on vacation.
14. What sampling plan should be adopted for the survey of question 9?
15. How should the sample size be determined for the survey of question 9?
16. How would you conduct the training and supervision of the fieldworkers for the survey of question 9?
17. According to Marriott's vice president of marketing and public relations, quality, price, service, amenities, comfort, and convenience are all independent variables that affect the preference for a hotel chain. Assume that in a survey of hotel chain, each of the independent variables is measured on a 7-point scale, with 1 = poor and 7 = excellent. Preference for hotel chain is also measured on a 7-point scale, with 1 = not at all preferred and 7 = greatly preferred. Each respondent rates Marriott and three competing hotel chains on all the independent variables as well as preference to stay there on a vacation. What statistical technique(s) would you use to answer the following questions:

  a. Is preference related to each of the independent variables considered individually? What is the nature of the relationship you expect?
  b. Is preference related to all the independent variables considered simultaneously?
  c. Do the respondents evaluate the hotel chains more favorable on quality than they do on price?
  d. The sample is divided into two groups: regular patrons of Marriott and patrons of other hotels. Do these two groups differ in terms of their ratings of Marriott on quality?
  e. Are the two groups of question d different in terms of income measured as high, medium, and low?
  f. Are the two groups of question d different in terms of quality, price, service, amenities, comfort, and convenience when all the independent variables are considered simultaneously?
  g. The sample is divided into three groups: heavy, medium, and light users of hotels. Do the three groups differ in terms of preference for Marriott?
  h. Are the three groups of question g different in terms of quality, price, service, amenities, comfort, and convenience when all the independent variables are considered simultaneously?
  i. Can the evaluation on quality, price, service, amenities, comfort, and convenience be represented by a reduced set of factors?
  j. Can the respondents be segmented based on their evaluations of hotels on quality, price, service, amenities, comfort, and convenience? How many segments should there be?
  k. What is the competitive positioning of the various hotel brands? What insights can be obtained?

l. About 13 percent of the respondents have missing values on one or more variables. How would you treat the missing values?

m. A question asked the respondents to check as many of the seven hotels that they had stayed in the past three years. How should the data for this question be coded?

18. Can the service quality model applied in the context of banking services in Chapter 22 be applied in the case of hotel services? Why or why not?

19. What charts and graphs would you use in preparing a report for Marriott?

20. If marketing research to determine consumer preferences for hotels was to be conducted in Latin America, how would the research process differ?

21. Discuss the ethical issues involved in researching consumer preferences for hotels.

References

1. www.marriott.com, accessed February 25, 2009.
2. www.hoovers.com, accessed February 25, 2009.
3. M. A. Baumann, "High-End Offerings the Result of In-Depth Research," *Hotel and Motel Management*, 219(9) (May 17, 2004): 36.

Chapter 24

"In international research, it is critical to take into account the environment and culture of the countries we are working in. This can mean not only adapting what we would normally do from our own perspective, but even going as far as to adapt our whole perspective."

Betty Fraley, Senior Vice President, Account Management, Burke, Inc.

Objectives [After reading this chapter, the student should be able to:]

1. Develop a framework for conducting international marketing research.

2. Explain in detail the marketing, governmental, legal, economic, structural, informational and technological, and sociocultural environmental factors and how they have an impact on international marketing research.

3. Describe the use of telephone, personal, and mail survey methods in different countries.

4. Discuss how to establish the equivalence of scales and measures, including construct, operational, scalar, and linguistic equivalence.

5. Describe the processes of back translation and parallel translation in translating a questionnaire into a different language.

6. Discuss the ethical considerations in international marketing research.

7. Explain the use of the Internet and computers in international marketing research.

International Marketing Research

Overview

This chapter discusses the environment in which international marketing research is conducted, focusing on the marketing, government, legal, economic, structural, informational and technological, and sociocultural environments.[1] Whereas discussions of how the six steps of the marketing research process should be implemented in an international setting took place in earlier chapters, here we present additional details on survey methods, scaling techniques, and questionnaire translation. The relevant ethical issues in international marketing research are identified and the use of the Internet and computers is discussed.

Real Research

IBM: Trekking on a Global Track

IBM (www.ibm.com), with 2008 revenues of $103.63 billion, conducts an international tracking study twice a year in 14 different languages across 27 different countries in Europe, North and South America, and Asia. The basic purpose of the study is to capture trend data on mainframe computing. It samples one out of every six sites where an IBM Enterprise Server is in use. The respondents surveyed are those responsible for IBM acquisition decisions at their respective companies. They are asked about their installed computing equipment, their future plans for acquiring equipment, and their views on various vendors. The survey allows IBM to track how it is doing on an ongoing basis. The questions are kept broad and are not used to determine a deeper understanding of customer wants but instead only to track overall trends. The information collected via this tracking survey becomes part of IBM's decision support system.

IBM utilizes the RONIN Corporation (www.ronin.com), a New Jersey–based research firm, to handle the interviewing and data collection process. RONIN conducts all interviews by telephone for this study at its international call center in London. Because the study is international, RONIN deals with such issues as accurate translations and receiving consistent results across countries and languages while rapidly turning results around. They must also communicate that results are representative only for specific countries, not for entire regions.

The results of such a study allow IBM to see how successful it is in penetrating key industries and how IBM equipment is used in large and small businesses across nations. These results are passed to the IBM sales force in each of the countries, where they provide their interpretation of the results and incorporate these results with their own field experiences to develop lists of the top 10 issues that they are experiencing in the field.

This tracking study is an example of problem identification research. IBM is seeking to identify possible problems, such as respondents indicating that they have no plans for future equipment acquisitions from IBM, problems with maintenance service, or low customer satisfaction. Any problems that are identified are investigated further by using problem-solving research with the objective of arriving at solutions. For example, low ratings on maintenance service, when investigated further, revealed that customers' expectations had increased, leading IBM to raise its service standards. The tracking study identified a new problem (or opportunity) when it revealed potential demand for Linux-driven mainframes. Based on subsequent problem solution research that investigated product preferences, in late January 2002, IBM introduced two new Linux-driven servers and a Linux-only mainframe computer that requires no traditional mainframe operating system. The eServer Z-Series uses the mainframe computer's ability to create up to hundreds of virtual Linux servers on only one physical box. IBM said the new mainframe will save energy and floor space and will reduce maintenance costs, thus addressing these needs identified in the tracking study. Non-Linux mainframe computers typically cost $750,000, whereas the new Z-Series mainframe computers cost $350,000. As of 2009, the IBM System Z10, is the new flagship of the eServer family that provides data protection and access for business continuity and efficiency.[2] ∎

International marketing research has enabled IBM to introduce innovative new products and services, such as the eServer Z-series, on a global basis.

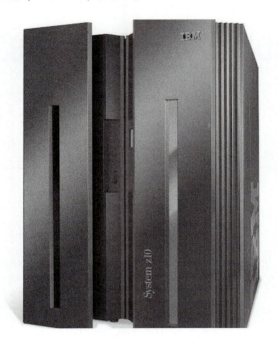

Real Research   Best in the West—And Around the World

As of 2009, Best Western International, Inc. (www.bestwestern.com), is the world's largest hotel brand with more than 4,000 independently owned and operated hotels in more than 80 countries. As the following chart shows, business travelers make up 36 percent of the market, the largest single share. Best Western has found, through survey research, that business travelers often resist trying less expensive hotels and appreciate the security of a well-known brand. This information has helped the chain attract business travelers.

Through secondary data analysis and surveys, Best Western has learned the sources of hotel business in different regions of the world and geared its marketing strategy accordingly (see the following table). For example, the chain emphasizes domestic business in North America, focuses on both domestic and international business in Europe, and emphasizes foreign business in the Far East, Australia, Africa, and the Middle East. The use of marketing research continues to prove successful for Best Western.[3]

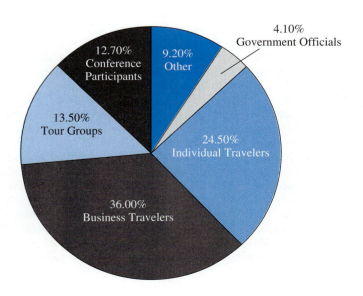

Sources of Worldwide Hotel Business by Region

Source of Hotel Business	All Hotels Worldwide	Africa/Middle East	Asia/Australia	North America	Europe
Domestic	50.7%	24.6%	35.0%	84.6%	47.3%
Foreign	49.3%	75.4%	65.0%	15.4%	52.7%
TOTAL	100.0%	100.0%	100.0%	100.0%	100.0% ■

Both these examples point to the fact that marketing research can contribute significantly to the formulation of successful international marketing strategies. The term *international marketing research* is used very broadly. It denotes research for true international products (international research), research carried out in a country other than the country of the research-commissioning organization (foreign research), research conducted in all or all important countries where the company is represented (multinational research), and research conducted in/across different cultures (cross-cultural research).

Marketing Research Goes International

In the 2000s, revenue generated outside the United States has become important to the top market research firms in the United States. Several of the top 50 research firms in the United States derive revenues from work done through subsidiaries, branch offices, and/or affiliates that are located outside the United States (see Chapter 1).[4]

Because overseas expansion is a hot topic in the 2000s, many marketers will begin to expand into the overseas market. This expansion is primarily due to economic integration and the lowering of trade barriers. Overseas expansion will mean increased opportunities for market research companies inside and outside of the United States. When consumers outside of the United States begin to spend their money, they give far greater attention to price and quality rather than to the country of origin. To many firms, regional markets represent the "international order of the day."[5]

As attractive as foreign markets are, companies must realize that setting up for operations in these markets does not guarantee success. Many economists warn that the economic conditions are, at best, sluggish. Others argue "that it is unrealistic to expect aggressive consumerism in the near future even in markets with a taste for foreign concepts." One of the greatest problems that many firms will face in foreign markets is "red tape." Many governments have implemented laws and policies that will protect their countries' businesses.

Since the demise of the Cold War, the world's economy is no longer a simple three-way battle between the United States, Japan, and Germany. Stiffer competition will force many companies inside of the United States to try to gain competitive advantages outside of the United States. Three massive markets have developed since the end of the Cold War, some of which will require significant amounts of market research before entrance into that market can occur. The three markets are the Americas, Europe, and the Pacific Rim nations.

Since the passage of the North American Free Trade Agreement (NAFTA), a "veritable free-market revolution" has begun to take place in Mexico.[6] The passage of NAFTA created the world's largest market. In other Latin American countries, trade barriers are being reduced. Companies entering these changing markets will be forced to change the ways in which they do business. Quality standards will increase and prices will become more competitive due to greater selection. As product choices widen, consumer awareness and sophistication will increase. Latin Americans will become shoppers, and companies will no longer hide behind the protective barriers of their countries and will face more competition due to the greater selection in the marketplace. As a result, market researchers will be faced with two significant challenges. First, as manufacturing and markets assume a regional focus, service providers will be forced to do the same to achieve consistent results and quality. Researchers, both those internal to product operations and their outside suppliers, must follow this trend for a regional, quality approach. A top-down approach to marketing research will result in company executives becoming increasingly involved in marketing research. Secondly, marketing researchers must remain flexible to handle local conditions.[7]

With the number of U.S. products that are currently available in Europe, one can see that many manufacturers and researchers will not have to radically alter their marketing plans and objectives. The formation of the European Union (EU) is perhaps the source of the greatest economic potential in the world. The western European market is roughly the size of the North American market, but the total size of the European market has been increasing due to the inclusion of new countries. However, companies must remain cognizant of the fact that there is a significantly lower level of disposable income. Therefore, they must find ways in which to cope with this particular problem. A particular opportunity that should be explored is the potential for smaller and medium-sized companies to expand in the European market.

Many believe that the Asian rim is the fastest growing part of the world. This growth is paced by a rapid rate of investment and an abundance of trained human capital. Countries that are included in the Asian rim range from Australia to Indonesia to India and China. This region's average real economic growth is more than 5 percent per year and is expected to continue through this decade. China is being called the next great mecca for marketing research because it has a consumer population of more than 1.2 billion. A few years ago, Gallup announced the formation of Gallup China, the first foreign marketing research firm in China. Gallup China will undoubtedly face many challenges in China, such as rapidly increasing competition, governmental regulation, and the forming of bonds with the Chinese people in order to be able to conduct successful research. Chinese research firms have begun to form within China, and American companies have begun to form alliances with these companies in order to penetrate the Chinese market. However, international marketing research can be very complex. We present a framework for understanding and dealing with the complexities involved.

A Framework for International Marketing Research

Conducting international marketing research is much more complex than domestic marketing research.[8] Although the six-step framework for domestic marketing research (Chapter 1) is applicable, the environment prevailing in the countries, cultural units, or international markets that are being researched influences the way the six steps of the marketing research process should be performed. Figure 24.1 presents a framework for conducting international marketing research.

The Environment

The differences in the environments of countries, cultural units, or foreign markets should be considered when conducting international marketing research. These differences may arise in the marketing environment, government environment, legal environment, economic environment, structural environment, informational and technological environment, and sociocultural environment, as shown in Figure 24.1.

Marketing Environment

The role of marketing in economic development varies in different countries. For example, developing countries are frequently oriented toward production rather than marketing. Demand typically exceeds supply, and there is little concern about customer satisfaction, especially when the level of competition is low. In assessing the marketing environment, the researcher should consider the variety and assortment of products available, pricing policies, government control of media, the public's attitude toward advertising, the efficiency of the distribution system, the level of marketing effort undertaken, and the unsatisfied needs and behavior of consumers. For example, surveys conducted in the United States usually involve questions on the variety and selection of merchandise. These questions would be inappropriate in some countries, such as in Africa, that are characterized by shortage economies. Likewise, questions about pricing may have to incorporate bargaining as an integral part of the exchange process. Questions about promotion should be modified as well. Television advertising, an extremely important promotion vehicle in the United States, is restricted or prohibited in some countries where TV stations are owned and operated by the government. Certain themes, words, and illustrations used in the United States are taboo in some countries. The types of retailers and intermediary institutions available, and the services these institutions offer, vary from country to country.

FIGURE 24.1

**A Framework
for International
Marketing
Research**

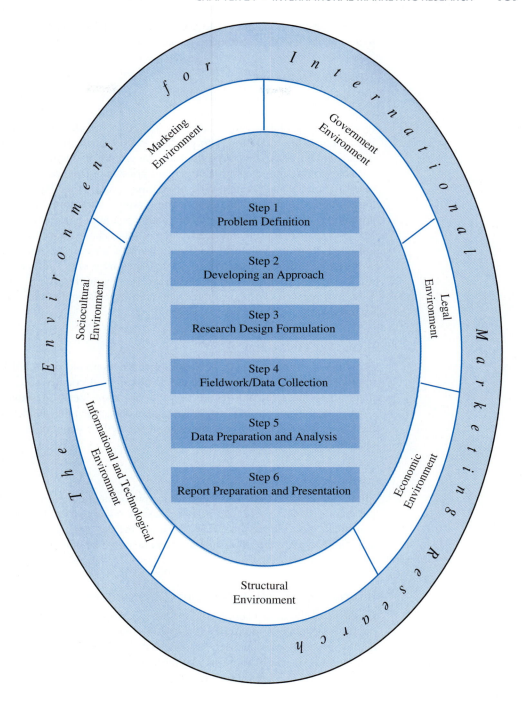

Government Environment

An additional relevant factor is the government environment. The type of government has a bearing on the emphasis on public policy, regulatory agencies, government incentives and penalties, and investment in government enterprises. Some governments, particularly in developing countries, do not encourage foreign competition. High tariff barriers create disincentives to the efficient use of marketing research approaches. Also, the role of government in setting market controls, developing infrastructure, and acting as an entrepreneur should be carefully assessed. The role of government is also crucial in many advanced countries, such as Germany and Japan, where government has traditionally worked with industry toward a common national industrial policy. At the tactical level, the government determines tax structures, tariffs, and product safety rules and regulations and often imposes special rules and regulations on foreign multinationals and their marketing practices. In many countries, the government may be an important member of the distribution channel. The government purchases essential products on a large scale and then sells them to the consumers, perhaps on a rationed basis.

Legal Environment

The legal environment encompasses common law, code law, foreign law, international law, transaction law, antitrust, bribery, and taxes. From the standpoint of international marketing research, particularly salient are laws related to the elements of the marketing mix. Product laws include those dealing with product quality, packaging, warranty and after-sales service, patents, trademarks, and copyright. Laws on pricing deal with price fixing, price discrimination, variable pricing, price controls, and retail price maintenance. Distribution laws relate to exclusive territory arrangements, type of channels, and cancellation of distributor or wholesaler agreements. Likewise, laws govern the type of promotional methods that can be employed. Although all countries have laws regulating marketing activities, some countries have only a few laws that are loosely enforced, whereas others have many complicated laws that are strictly enforced. In many countries, the legal channels are clogged and the settlement of court cases is prolonged. In addition, home-country laws may also apply while conducting business or marketing research in foreign countries. For example, a U.S. citizen is subject to certain U.S. laws regardless of the country where business is being done. These laws relate to national security, antitrust, and ethical considerations.

Economic Environment

Economic environmental characteristics include economic size (GDP), level, source, and distribution of income, growth trends, and sectoral trends. A country's stage of economic development determines the size, the degree of modernization, and the standardization of its markets. Consumer, industrial, and commercial markets become more standardized and consumers' work, leisure, and lifestyles become more homogenized by economic development and advances in technology.

Structural Environment

Structural factors relate to transportation, communication, utilities, and infrastructure. For example, mail service is inefficient in many developing countries. Personal contact with respondents is difficult, because city people work during the day and rural residents are inaccessible. Block statistics and maps are not available or can be obtained only with great difficulty. Many dwelling units are unidentified.

Informational and Technological Environment

Elements of the informational and technological environment include information and communication systems, computerization and the use of the Internet, use of electronic equipment, energy, production technology, science, and invention. For example, in India, South Korea, and many Latin American countries, advances in science and technology have not had a proportionate impact on the lifestyle of the common citizens, particularly those living in rural areas. Computers, the Internet, and electronic information transfer have yet to make an impact in rural areas. Information handling and record keeping are performed in the traditional way. This, again, has an impact on the type of information and how it can be solicited from consumers, businesses, and other enterprises.

Sociocultural Environment

Sociocultural factors include values, literacy, language, religion, communication patterns, and family and social institutions. Relevant values and attitudes toward time, achievement, work, authority, wealth, scientific method, risk, innovation, change, and the Western world should be considered. The marketing research process should be modified so that it does not conflict with the cultural values.[9] In some developing countries, as much as 50 percent of the population is illiterate. In tradition-directed, less developed societies, the ability of respondents to formulate opinions of their own seems to be all but absent; consequently, it is difficult to solicit information from these respondents. As a result, the sophisticated rating scales employed in the United States are not useful. Complexities are added by the fact that in a given nation or region there may be several distinct spoken languages and dialects.

A country with a homogeneous family structure is likely to be more culturally homogeneous than a country with multiple family structures. For example, Japan is culturally more homogeneous than either the United States or many African countries, which have many different kinds of family structures. The importance of designing products to be consistent with the sociocultural factors prevailing in a country is brought home by Universal Studios Japan.

Real Research   Universal Studios: Less Universal in Japan

When Universal Studios (www.universalstudios.com) decided to build a Universal Studios in Osaka, Japan, they relied heavily on focus groups, depth interviews, and survey research to understand the sociocultural environment in Japan. The research was done by their business partner Dentsu (www.dentsu.com). The American and Japanese ways of doing business had to be combined.

Marketing research helped to decide on food items, which allowed them to take the Japanese culture into account. The portions of the food were made smaller to accommodate the traditional Japanese servings, whereas American foods such as hot dogs and pizzas were made larger to create the American image. Pies were made less sweet and the barbeque sauce was made sweeter.

Universal also found out about souvenirs and merchandise preferences through focus groups and depth interviews. The Japanese buy more souvenirs for friends and coworkers. Candy, household items, and stationery products are very popular. There is a great teenage girl population in the market who like items with cartoons on them. Clothing is not as important in Japan as it is in other countries.

The focus group and depth interview findings were confirmed by survey research. Universal was able to adapt to the Japanese culture while keeping an American image. For example, the Wild Wild Wild West stunt show has all of the components of an American cowboy show, but the dialogue is in Japanese. The use of focus groups, depth interviews, and survey research helped Universal to launch successfully in Japan. Continued reliance on marketing research has resulted in Universal Studios Japan opening new attractions that successfully mold the American image to the Japanese culture and environment. For example, in 2008, the theme park opened a new musical show called Fantastic World that is about two white tigers who go on an adventure.[10] ■

Universal Studios was able to adapt to the Japanese culture while keeping an American image. This has been a key to its success in Japan.

Project Research   Project Activities

Read the Sears project write-ups in each chapter and consider all the analyses that you have done. Suppose Sears Holdings Corp. was interested in further expanding its business on an international level. Choose a country (other than the United States or your own country) and discuss environmental factors that would have to be considered and possible opportunities in light of these environmental factors. How should the research process be modified in conducting research in that country? ■

Each country's environment is unique, so international marketing research must take into consideration the environmental characteristics of the countries or foreign markets involved. The previous chapters in this text discussed how we can adapt the marketing research process to international situations. In the following sections, we provide additional details for implementing survey methods, scaling techniques, and questionnaire translation in international marketing research.[11]

Survey Methods

The following sections discuss the major interviewing methods in light of the challenges of conducting research in foreign countries, especially Europe and developing countries.[12]

Telephone Interviewing and CATI

In the United States and Canada, the telephone has achieved almost total penetration of households. As a result, telephone interviewing is the dominant mode of questionnaire administration. The same situation exists in some of the European countries. In Sweden, the number of telephones per 1,000 inhabitants exceeds 900, and in Stockholm the figure is even higher.[13] This, along with the low cost, has led to a sharp increase in the use of telephone interviews, which now account for 46 percent of the interviews conducted and constitute the dominant interviewing method. In countries such as The Netherlands, the number of telephone interviews exceeds the number of personal interviews.[14] Even in these countries, the sampling of respondents for telephone interviewing may pose serious problems. (See Chapter 6 for a discussion of the issues related to the selection of probability samples in telephone interviewing.)

In many of the other European countries, telephone (land line) penetration is still not complete. Telephone penetration in Great Britain is only about 80 percent (although cell phone penetration is higher), and many practitioners are still skeptical of the value of telephone interviewing, especially for voting-intention measurement. In Finland, only about 15 percent of interviews are administered over the telephone. In Portugal, telephone (land line) penetration is still not very high, although mobile phone penetration is one of the highest in Europe, reaching 128.8 per 100 inhabitants in 2008. For this reason, only 17 percent of interviews conducted are telephone interviews.[15]

In Hong Kong, 96 percent of households (other than on outlying islands and on boats) can be contacted by telephone. With some persistence, evening telephone interviewing can successfully achieve interviews with 70 to 75 percent of selected respondents. Residents are uninhibited about using telephones and relaxed about telephone interviews. Yet, given the face-to-face culture, this is not the most important mode of data collection.

In developing countries, only a few households have telephones. Telephone incidence is low in Africa. India is a predominantly rural society where the penetration of telephones is less than 10 percent of households in the villages. In Brazil, the proportion of households with telephones is low (less than 50 percent in large cities).[16] Even in countries such as Saudi Arabia, where telephone ownership is extensive, telephone directories tend to be incomplete and outdated. In many developing countries, telephone interviewing may present additional problems. Daytime calls to households may be unproductive, because social customs may prohibit the housewife from talking with strangers. This situation can be somewhat alleviated by using female telephone interviewers, but the employment of women creates many obstacles in such countries. In many cultures, face-to-face relationships are predominant. These factors severely limit the use of telephone interviewing.

Telephone interviews are most useful with relatively upscale consumers who are accustomed to business transactions by phone or consumers who can be reached by phone and can express themselves easily. With the decline of costs for international telephone calls, multicountry studies can be conducted from a single location. This greatly reduces the time and costs associated with the organization and control of the research project in each country. Furthermore, international calls obtain a high response rate, and the results have been found to be stable (i.e., the same results are obtained from the first 100 interviews as from the next 200 or 500). It is necessary to find interviewers fluent in the relevant languages, but for most European countries, this is not a problem.

Computer-assisted telephone interviewing (CATI) facilities are well developed in the United States and Canada and in some European countries, such as Germany. As the use of telephone interviewing is growing, they are becoming popular in other countries.[17]

In-Home Personal Interviews

In-home interviews require a large pool of qualified interviewers. Contractual arrangements with interviewers vary considerably. For example, in France, there are three categories of interviewers: interviewers with an annual guarantee for a specified duration, interviewers with an annual guarantee for an unspecified duration, and freelance interviewers with no salary guarantee. Overheads may also vary. In France, the employer and the interviewer must pay large social security contributions; in Belgium, the interviewers are self-employed and pay their own social security contributions. In the United Kingdom, although both the employer and the interviewer pay national insurance contributions, these tend to be small.

Due to high cost, the use of in-home personal interviews has declined in the United States and Canada, but this is the dominant mode of collecting survey data in many parts of Europe and the developing world. In-home personal interviewing is the dominant interviewing method in Switzerland.[18] In Portugal, face-to-face interviews are the majority of the total interviews conducted. Most of these surveys are done door to door, whereas some quick sociopolitical polls are carried out in the street using accidental routes. Likewise, in-home interviews are popular in many Latin American countries.

Real Research

Coke Tops in Americas and Around the World

In one of the research surveys conducted by the Gallup Organization, the objective was to assess consumers' recall of different ads they had seen in the past month. In-home personal surveys were conducted by Gallup and its affiliates in the United States, Canada, Uruguay, Chile, Argentina, Brazil, Mexico, and Panama. In all 7,498 people were surveyed. Unaided recall was used to get responses. Questions like, "What brands of soft drink advertisements seen in the past month first come to mind?" were asked. Results show that Coca-Cola ads are the choice of a new generation of both North and South Americans. Coca-Cola ads were among the top six ads mentioned in seven of the eight Western Hemisphere nations and were cited the most often in four countries. Ads of archrival Pepsi-Cola Co. were named among the top six in four countries, and McDonald's Corp. appeared in the top six in two countries. However, none of these three made it to the top six in Brazil. In 2008, Interbrand (www.interbrand.com), a brand consulting firm, named Coca-Cola the world's most valuable brand with a value of $66.667 billion. Whereas Coca-Cola may be the soft drink of choice in both North and South America, according to this firm, Coca-Cola is also the company of choice around the world.[19] ■

Mall Intercept and CAPI

In North America, many marketing research organizations have permanent facilities in malls, equipped with interviewing rooms, kitchens, observation areas, and other devices. Mall intercepts constitute about 15 percent of the interviews in Canada and 20 percent in the United States. Although mall intercepts are being conducted in some European countries, such as Sweden, they are not popular in Europe or developing countries. In contrast, central location/street interviews constitute the dominant method of collecting survey data in France and The Netherlands.

However, some interesting developments with respect to computer-assisted personal interviewing (CAPI) are taking place in Europe. Interviewing programs for the home computer have been developed and used in panel studies and at central locations using computer-assisted personal interviewing (CAPI).[20]

Mail Interviews

Because of low cost, mail interviews continue to be used in most developed countries where literacy is high and the postal system is well developed. Mail interviews constitute 6.2 percent of the interviews in Canada and 7 percent in the United States. In countries where the education level of the population is extremely high (Denmark, Finland, Iceland, Norway, Sweden, and The Netherlands), mail interviews are common.[21] In Africa, Asia, and South America, however, the use of mail surveys and mail panels is low because of illiteracy and the large proportion of the population living in rural areas. In Hong Kong, mail surveys have been tried with varied success. Mail surveys are, typically, more effective in industrial international marketing research, although it is difficult to identify the appropriate respondent within each firm and to personalize the address. Nevertheless, mail surveys are used internationally, as illustrated by the following example.

Real Research   Worldwide Achievers

Global Scan is a detailed survey conducted annually by Bates Asia, an operating company of the WPP Group (www.wpp.com), to measure the attitudes and behaviors of 15,000 respondents in 14 countries. The questionnaire contains 120 attitudinal statements and is customized for each country by insertion of attitudes, lifestyles, and purchases (both products and brands).

   The questionnaire is administered by mail, with local country offices responsible for distribution, meeting sampling requirements, and then transcribing the returned questionnaires to computer tape. Global Scan averages a 50 percent response rate.

   Bates claims that 95 percent of the combined population of all countries surveyed can be assigned to five segments. Based on the data, five lifestyle segments have emerged and have remained constant over time: strivers (26 percent), achievers (22 percent), pressured (13 percent), adapters (18 percent), and traditionals (16 percent). Thus, marketers have a common set of attitudes and behaviors for defining consumers all over the world. For example, the similarities between achievers in the United States, England, Australia, and Finland are greater than those between achievers and strivers in the United States. Global Scan collects detailed brand and category information on more than 1,000 products. Marketers can then use this information to develop specific strategies. Financial services company Fidelity Investments targeted the achievers on a global basis in 2009 because they tend to be heavy investors.[22] ■

Mail and Scanner Panels

Mail panels are extensively used in the United Kingdom, France, Germany, and The Netherlands. Mail and diary panels are also available in Finland, Sweden, Italy, Spain, and other European countries. Use of panels may increase with the advent of new technology. For example, in Germany, two agencies (Nielsen and GfK-Nurnberg) have installed fully electronic scanner test markets, based on the Behavior Scan model from the United States. Nielsen will use on-the-air television; GfK, cable. Panels of this kind have not yet been developed in Hong Kong or most of the developing countries. Mail panels are being gradually replaced by Internet panels in many parts of the world.[23]

Electronic Surveys

In the United States and Canada, the use of e-mail and the Internet is growing by leaps and bounds. As such, the use of these methods for conducting surveys is growing not only with business and institutional respondents, but also with households. Both these methods have become viable for conducting surveys related to a wide range of product categories and scenarios. The popularity of both e-mail and Internet surveys is also growing overseas. Both these types of surveys are increasingly being used in western Europe, where access to the Internet is freely available. However, in some parts of eastern Europe and in other developing countries, e-mail access is restricted and Internet availability is even poorer. Hence, these methods are not suitable for surveying the general population in these countries. However, surveys with business and institutional respondents may still be attempted, particularly using e-mail. E-mail surveys can be received and responded to by anyone with an e-mail address, whether or not they have access to the Internet. Multinational firms are using both e-mail and the Internet to survey their employees worldwide.

Real Research

Vovici: Enterprise Feedback Surveys for Enterprises

Vovici (www.vovici.com) products enable business professionals to quickly and easily obtain, analyze, and manage sophisticated enterprise feedback using intuitive Web-based software. Vovici was engaged by a global news agency. The worldwide chief information officers (CIO) organization needed support on an ongoing feedback process. The agency requirements included a survey software system capable of supporting high-volume traffic from more than 35 countries and 17,000 employees. The agency also required technical implementation support, training, and consulting support for questionnaire design and analysis.

Vovici implemented Vovici v4 Enterprise Edition, a customized survey product, at the agency's headquarters. The system was configured to support worldwide, multilingual surveys. In addition, Vovici's professional services organization provided the agency with an annual contract for research and consulting support to deploy the CIO survey three times throughout the year.

Vovici implemented its Vovici v4 Enterprise Edition software for use by 50 professionals spread across 33 countries responsible for data collection of its various Web sites. Each of the 50 could download Vovici v4 Enterprise Edition software in about 30 minutes. Each user could create a survey in a Microsoft Word document, convert it into a Vovici document, and, in about an hour, have a standard, 30-question survey ready to publish. Vovici provided the software company with a secure, password-accessed Web portal through which its employees could communicate and view survey data over the Internet just as they would if the data were housed on their desktops. Vovici staff also helped set up more complex surveys, such as those carried out in 22 countries in multiple languages, with the data compiled in separate tables depending on which site the respondent was visiting. In short, the solution offered by Vovici helped the client perform the survey twice as fast, more securely, and at a reduced cost. The Vovici v4 Enterprise Edition software and Vovici's professional services have formed the basis for the news agency's establishment of an internal business unit to consolidate Web surveys throughout the CIO organizations.[24] ∎

As was discussed and illustrated in Chapter 6, an important consideration in selecting the methods of administering questionnaires is to ensure equivalence and comparability across countries. Issues of equivalence are also salient in measurement and scaling.

ACTIVE RESEARCH

Johnson & Johnson Baby Products: No Child's Play

Visit www.jnj.com and search the Internet using a search engine as well as your library's online database to obtain information on how consumers select baby product brands in the United States. Obtain similar information for France.

What survey research techniques would you use to determine how consumers select baby product brands in France?

As the brand manager for Johnson & Johnson, how would you use information on how consumers select baby product brands to formulate marketing strategies that would increase your market share in France?

Measurement and Scaling

construct equivalence
Construct equivalence deals with the question of whether the marketing constructs have the same meaning and significance in different countries.

In international marketing research, it is critical to establish the equivalence of scales and measures used to obtain data from different countries. As illustrated in Figure 24.2, this requires an examination of construct equivalence, operational equivalence, measurement equivalence, and linguistic equivalence.[25]

Construct equivalence deals with the question of whether the marketing constructs (for example, opinion leadership, variety seeking, and brand loyalty) have the same meaning and significance in different countries. It focuses on the basic conceptual definition of the underlying

FIGURE 24.2

Scaling and Measurement Equivalence in International Marketing Research

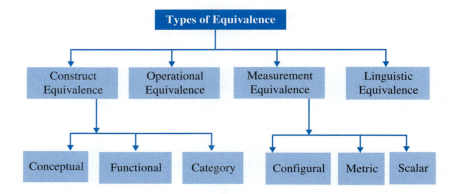

conceptual equivalence
Conceptual equivalence deals specifically with whether the interpretation of brands, products, consumer behavior, and the marketing effort is the same in different countries.

functional equivalence
Functional equivalence deals specifically with whether a given concept or behavior serves the same role or function in different countries.

category equivalence
Category equivalence deals specifically with whether the categories in which brands, products, and behavior are grouped is the same in different countries.

operational equivalence
A type of equivalence that measures how theoretical constructs are operationalized in different countries to measure marketing variables.

measurement equivalence
Measurement equivalence deals with the comparability of responses to particular (sets of) items. Measurement equivalence includes configural (structural), metric (measurement unit), and scalar equivalence.

configural equivalence
Configural equivalence concerns the relationships of measured items to the latent constructs and implies that the patterns of factor loadings should be the same across countries or cultural units.

metric equivalence
Metric equivalence refers to the unit of measurement; the factor loading should be the same.

construct. In many countries, the number of brands available in a given product category is limited. In some countries, the dominant brands have become generic labels symbolizing the entire product category. Consequently, a different perspective on brand loyalty may have to be adopted in these countries.

Construct equivalence is comprised of conceptual equivalence, functional equivalence, and category equivalence. **Conceptual equivalence** deals with the interpretation of brands, products, consumer behavior, and marketing effort. For example, promotional sales are an integral component of marketing effort in the United States. On the other hand, in countries with shortage economies, where the market is dominated by the sellers, consumers view sales with suspicion because they believe that the product being promoted is of poor quality. **Functional equivalence** examines whether a given concept or behavior serves the same role or function in different countries. For example, in many developing countries, bicycles are predominantly a means of transportation rather than of recreation. Marketing research related to the use of bicycles in these countries must examine different motives, attitudes, behaviors, and even different competing products than such research would in the United States. **Category equivalence** refers to the category in which stimuli like products, brands, and behaviors are grouped. In the United States, the category of the principal shopper in the household may be defined as either the male or female head of household. This category may be inappropriate in countries where routine daily shopping is done by a domestic servant. Furthermore, the category "household" itself varies across countries.

Operational equivalence concerns how theoretical constructs are operationalized to make measurements. In the United States, leisure may be operationalized as playing golf, tennis, or other sports; watching television; or basking in the sun. This operationalization may not be relevant in countries where people do not play these sports or do not have round-the-clock TV transmission. Lying in the sun is not normal behavior in countries with hot climates or where people have brown skin.

Measurement equivalence deals with the comparability of responses to particular (sets of) items. Measurement equivalence includes configural (structural), metric (measurement unit), and scalar equivalence. **Configural equivalence** concerns the relationships of measured items to the latent constructs (see Chapter 22). Technically, configural equivalence implies that the patterns of factor loadings should be the same across countries or cultural units. **Metric equivalence** refers to the unit of measurement; the factor loading should be the same. Metric equivalence suggests that the survey instruments (questionnaires) are measuring the same constructs to the same extent in different countries or cultures. **Scalar equivalence** refers to equivalence of both the unit of measurement and the constant in the equation between the construct and the items measuring the construct (the intercept) (see Chapter 22). The distinction is important because for some purposes (e.g., comparing structural relationships across groups) metric invariance is sufficient, whereas for other purposes (e.g., comparing means across groups) both metric and scalar equivalence are needed.

Finally, **linguistic equivalence** refers to both the spoken and the written language forms used in scales, questionnaires, and interviewing. The scales and other verbal stimuli should be translated so that they are readily understood by respondents in different countries and have equivalent meaning.[26]

scalar equivalence
Scalar equivalence refers to equivalence of both the unit of measurement and the constant in the equation between the construct and the items measuring the construct (the intercept).

linguistic equivalence
The equivalence of both spoken and written language forms used in scales and questionnaires.

back translation
A translation technique that translates a questionnaire from the base language by a translator whose native language is the one into which the questionnaire is being translated. This version is then retranslated back into the original language by a bilingual whose native language is the base language. Translation errors can then be identified.

parallel translation
A translation method in which a committee of translators, each of whom is fluent in at least two languages, discusses alternative versions of a questionnaire and makes modifications until consensus is reached.

ACTIVE RESEARCH

Gap Plugs the Gap in Casual Clothing

Visit www.gap.com and search the Internet using a search engine as well as your library's online database to obtain information on consumer preferences for casual clothing.

Which comparative scaling technique(s) would you use to measure consumer preferences for casual clothing in the United States and in rural Nigeria?

As the marketing manager for Gap, how would you use information on consumer preferences for casual clothing to increase your sales?

Questionnaire Translation

The questions may have to be translated for administration in different cultures. Direct translation, in which a bilingual translator translates the questionnaire directly from a base language to the respondent's language, is frequently used. However, if the translator is not fluent in both languages and not familiar with both cultures, direct translation of certain words and phrases may be erroneous. Procedures such as back translation and parallel translation have been suggested to avoid these errors. In **back translation**, the questionnaire is translated from the base language by a bilingual speaker whose native language is the language into which the questionnaire is being translated. This version is then retranslated back into the original language by a bilingual whose native language is the initial or base language. Translation errors can then be identified. Several repeat translations and back translations may be necessary to develop equivalent questionnaires, and this process can be cumbersome and time-consuming.[27]

An alternative procedure is **parallel translation**. A committee of translators, each of whom is fluent in at least two of the languages in which the questionnaire will be administered, discusses alternative versions of the questionnaire and makes modifications until consensus is reached. In countries where several languages are spoken, the questionnaire should be translated into the language of each respondent subgroup. It is important that any nonverbal stimuli (pictures and advertisements) also be translated using similar procedures. The following example underscores the importance of correct translation.

Real Research

Researchers Can Get No Self-Respect in Germany

A common questionnaire used to measure consumer values is the List of Values (LOV). In North America, it has revealed nine basic value segments held by consumers. The most widely held values of Americans are self-respect, security, and warm relationships with others. To conduct a comparative study in Germany, the LOV had to be translated into a German version (GLOV). Through the process of translation and back translation, a suitable form was created; however, some inconsistencies remained. For example, it was very difficult to translate the English concepts of "warm relationships with others" and "self-respect" into German. As a result, the data revealed that significantly fewer Germans than Americans hold these as their most important values. The researchers concluded that the imprecise translation was more responsible for these results than actual differences in value orientations. The table shows the distribution of the top three values for each culture, with the rank in parentheses.

Values	Germany	United States
Self-respect	13% (3)	21% (1)
Security	24 (2)	21 (2)
Warm relationships	8 (4)	16 (3)
Sense of belonging	29 (1)	8 (7)

Another recent study examined the significance of values in Chinese women's emerging roles. Based on six female role dimensions, the Chinese women were segmented into three groups. The groups were ideologues, traditionalists, and moderns, and they were found to have very different demographic and attitudinal characteristics. Characterized mainly by their performance outside the household, ideologues still endorse the idea of serving country and promoting national welfare. Ideologues tend to select brands that are given a seal of approval by an independent testing agency or a socially respected individual. The traditionalists are influenced by Confucianism, which values family relationships, loyalty, and harmony. Moderns desire to live for today without any concern for the more restrictive values that might be imposed by society or family. They are more apt to choose products that meet their own personal needs rather than the family's.[28] ■

Experiential Research

CIA on BRIC

You are to design a survey to determine people's attitudes toward globalization in the BRIC countries (Brazil, Russia, India, and China). Visit www.cia.gov and click on the World Factbook. From the Factbook, obtain information on each of these four countries. Based on the information you obtained, answer the following questions.

1. Which survey method should be used in each of these four countries? Why?
2. In what language should the questionnaire be administered in each of these four countries? If the questionnaire has to be translated, what translation issues are involved and how will you handle these issues. ■

Decision Research

Polo Ralph Lauren: Penetrating Europe

The Situation

Over the past 35 years, Polo Ralph Lauren Corporation (www.polo.com) has been able to redefine how American style and quality are perceived. It is a leader in the design, marketing, and distribution of premium lifestyle products in four categories (apparel, home, accessories, and fragrances) across a number of products, brands, and international markets. The company's brand names include Polo, Polo by Ralph Lauren, Ralph Lauren Purple Label, Polo Sport, Ralph Lauren, RALPH, Lauren, Polo Jeans Co, RL, Chaps, and Club Monaco. The group markets its products in the United States, Europe, and other foreign countries. In April 2008, Polo Ralph Lauren won the U.S. Olympic contract to outfit the 2008 U.S. Olympic Team.

In order to continue its growth and expansion into new horizons, Polo Ralph Lauren follows these key elements:

1. Extend Polo Ralph Lauren brands—While maintaining a consistent global image of the present brands, they will seek both to extend existing brands and to create new brands to address new and emerging markets and consumers.
2. Expand Polo's geographic coverage—In addition to the United States, there are international markets (e.g., Europe and Japan) that are underpenetrated and provide growth opportunities for the expansion of their American designs and lifestyle image.
3. Increase direct management—To continue to enhance their ability to control their brands, Polo Ralph Lauren will open more specialty stores, improve the merchandising in existing stores, and strategically acquire select licensees.
4. Enhance operations—Potential still exists for further significant margin expansion on the operations level.

Polo Ralph Lauren has recently completed a series of transactions to increase the direct management of its growing business in Japan. Under the agreement, the company will hold a 50 percent interest in its Japanese master license and will acquire an 18 percent stake in a company that will hold the sublicenses for Polo's men's, women's, and Polo Jeans businesses in Japan. Polo's total investment in the transactions was approximately $70 million, funded through Polo's available cash. Ralph Lauren, chairman and chief executive, would like to push harder in international markets, particularly into Europe.

The Marketing Research Decision

1. What type of marketing research should Polo Ralph Lauren undertake to successfully increase its penetration in Europe and how should such research be reported?
2. Discuss the role of the type of research you recommend in enabling Ralph Lauren to increase market share in Europe.

International marketing reasearch can help Polo Ralph Lauren increase its penetration in Europe.

The Marketing Management Decision

1. How should Ralph Lauren build an aggressive marketing strategy in Europe?
2. Discuss how the marketing management decision action that you recommend to Ralph Lauren is influenced by the research that you suggested earlier and by the findings of that research. ■

Ethics in Marketing Research

Ethical responsibilities for marketing research conducted abroad are very similar to that conducted domestically. For each of the six stages of the marketing research design process, the same four stakeholders (client, researcher, respondent, and public) must act honorably and respect their responsibilities to one another. As the following example indicates, the ethical constraints facing marketing researchers abroad are fairly similar to those at home. For all the similarities, some ethical issues become more difficult. Conducting marketing research in a foreign country can easily become a political issue. Researchers must be careful to adopt the ethical guidelines of not only the domestic country but the host country as well.

Real Research   ## Europeans Legislate Data Privacy

There is widespread implementation of data privacy laws in the European Union (EU). A prototype of the EU's data privacy laws is the United Kingdom's Data Protection Act (DPA), embodying eight guidelines.

1. Personal data will be obtained and processed fairly and lawfully.
2. Personal data will be held only for specified and lawful purposes.
3. Personal data will not be used for any reason other than the specified purpose.
4. Personal data for specified purposes will not be excessive in amount.
5. Personal data will be accurate and will be kept current.
6. Personal data will not be kept longer than necessary for the specified purpose.
7. Users of personal data must provide nondelayed access to personal data (at no expense) when individuals make requests to examine their personal data over reasonable intervals. Where appropriate, data users must correct or erase erroneous data.
8. Data users must take appropriate security measures against unauthorized access, alteration, disclosure, destruction, or loss of personal data.

As of October 31, 2003, European Union member states must comply with the Directive on Privacy and Electronic Communications, which sets EU standards for the protection of privacy and personal data in electronic communications. As of 2009, the European Commission has stated its desire to achieve bilateral and multilateral international cooperation efforts in complying with the Directive.[29] ■

Statistical Software

Software programs that can facilitate cross-cultural research, such as INTERVIEWER, should become more widely available in the future to meet the challenges of international marketing research. INTERVIEWER by Voxco of Montreal (Quebec), Canada (www.voxco.com), provides bilingual interviewing capability for computer-assisted telephone interviewing (CATI). With two keystrokes, operators can switch from a questionnaire written in English to the same questionnaire written in Spanish. This can even be done during the course of the interview in a matter of seconds. This feature markedly reduces the mental strain for bilingual interviewers. Such interviewing features prove useful in areas with nested cultures, such as in Miami, Los Angeles, or New York. In areas of the world where market areas spread beyond political or cultural boundaries, such as in Basel, Switzerland (near the three borders of Switzerland, France, and Germany), INTERVIEWER could be used with modification. Because of lower transnational telecommunication charges and political agreements permitting more open markets around the world, INTERVIEWER offered switching capability between most of the major languages as of 2009.

Summary

With the globalization of markets, international marketing research is burgeoning rapidly. The environment prevailing in the international markets being researched influences all six steps of the marketing research process. Important aspects of this environment include the marketing, government, legal, economic, structural, informational and technological, and sociocultural environment.

In collecting data from different countries, it is desirable to use survey methods with equivalent levels of reliability rather than the same method. It is critical to establish the equivalence of scales and measures in terms of construct equivalence, operational equivalence, measurement equivalence,

and linguistic equivalence. Figure 24.3 gives a concept map for types of equivalence. The questionnaire should be adapted to the specific cultural environment and should not be biased in favor of any one culture or language. Back translation and parallel translation are helpful in detecting translation errors.

The ethical concerns facing international marketing researchers are similar in many ways to the issues confronting domestic researchers. However, some of the responsibilities of the researchers become more difficult in the international arena. Specialized software has been developed to facilitate international marketing research.

FIGURE 24.3

A Concept Map for Types of Equivalence

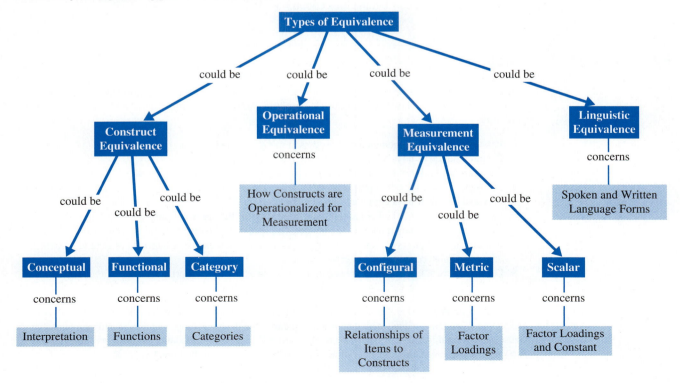

Key Terms and Concepts

construct equivalence, 763
conceptual equivalence, 764
functional equivalence, 764
category equivalence, 764

operational equivalence, 764
measurement equivalence, 764
configural equivalence, 764
metric equivalence, 764

scalar equivalence, 765
linguistic equivalence, 765
back translation, 765
parallel translation, 765

Suggested Cases, Video Cases, and HBS Cases

Running Case with Real Data

1.1 Dell

Comprehensive Critical Thinking Cases

2.1 American Idol   2.2 Baskin-Robbins   2.3 Akron Children's Hospital

Data Analysis Cases with Real Data

3.1 AT&T   3.2 IBM   3.3 Kimberly-Clark

Comprehensive Cases with Real Data

4.1 JPMorgan Chase   4.2 Wendy's

Video Cases

23.1 Marriott   24.1 Nivea

Comprehensive Harvard Business School Cases

Case 5.1: The Harvard Graduate Student Housing Survey (9-505-059)

Case 5.2: BizRate.Com (9-501-024)

Case 5.3: Cola Wars Continue: Coke and Pepsi in the Twenty-First Century (9-702-442)

Case 5.4: TiVo in 2002 (9-502-062)

Case 5.5: Compaq Computer: Intel Inside? (9-599-061)

Case 5.6: The New Beetle (9-501-023)

Live Research: Conducting a Marketing Research Project

1. If the project is a multicountry study, the students should be sensitized to the culture and environment of each country.
2. Comparable, rather than the same, procedures should be followed across countries.
3. If the project is a domestic study, discuss in class how the study would be conducted differently if it were conducted in a foreign

country, for example, China. Select a foreign country that is represented among the students. Students from that country can then lead the discussion on culture and environment.

Acronym

In international marketing research, the components of the environment may be summarized by the acronym

Culture:

C ultural and social (sociocultural) environment
U nsatisfied consumer needs: marketing environment
L egal environment
T echnological and information environment
U tilities: structural environment
R egulatory: government environment
E conomic environment

Exercises

Questions

1. Describe the aspects of the environment of each country that should be taken into account in international marketing research.
2. Describe the importance of considering the marketing environment in conducting international marketing research.
3. What is meant by the structural environment? How do the variables comprising the structural environment influence international marketing research?
4. What is meant by the informational and technological environment? How do the variables comprising the informational and technological environment influence international marketing research?
5. What is meant by the sociocultural environment? How do the variables comprising the sociocultural environment influence international marketing research?
6. Describe the status of telephone interviewing and CATI in foreign countries.
7. Describe the status of in-home personal interviewing in foreign countries.
8. Describe the status of mail interviewing in foreign countries.
9. How should the equivalence of scales and measures be established when the data are to be obtained from different countries or cultural units?
10. What problems are involved in the direct translation of a questionnaire into another language? How should these problems be addressed?

Problems

1. Develop a short questionnaire to measure consumers' attitudes toward air travel. Have some foreign students do a direct translation of this questionnaire into their native language, and then do a back translation. What translation errors occurred? Correct these errors.
2. Formulate a research design for assessing consumer preferences for designer jeans in the United States, Sweden, Hong Kong, and China. Identify the sources of secondary data, decide whether any qualitative research should be carried out, recommend which survey method to use in each country, recommend one or more scaling techniques, develop a questionnaire in English, and suggest appropriate sampling procedures for use in each country.

Internet and Computer Exercises

1. Identify several cultural issues pertaining to Europeans by visiting http://europa.eu.
2. By visiting the Web site of Kodak (www.kodak.com), what can you learn about the company's international marketing efforts? Write a brief report.
3. You have to prepare a plan for marketing Coke in France. Visit www.invest-in-france.org/north-america/en or www.afii.fr/NorthAmerica to find the relevant information.
4. How can General Motors benefit from NAFTA? Visit www.nafta-sec-alena.org to identify the relevant information.
5. Compile data on GDP, level of literacy, and percentage of households with telephones for 20 different countries. Using SPSS, SAS, MINITAB, or EXCEL, run a regression analysis with GDP as the dependent variable and the other two variables as the independent variables. Interpret your results.
6. Compile data on consumption and expenditures for the following categories in 30 different countries: (1) food and beverages, (2) clothing and footwear, (3) housing and home operations, (4) household furnishings, (5) medical care and health, (6) transportation, and (7) recreation. Using SPSS, SAS, or MINITAB, determine if these variables are correlated. Run a factor analysis. Interpret your results.
7. Visit the Web site of a foreign firm and then visit the Web site of a competing U.S. firm. For example, visit the Web site of Unilever (U.K.) (www.unilever.com) and P&G (U.S.) (www.pg.com). Compare the two sites. Which site is more useful for a marketing researcher?

Activities

Role Playing

1. You are the marketing research director for P&G for Europe. What challenges do you see in researching markets for household products in eastern European countries? Prepare a report for P&G management in the United States. Make a presentation to a group of students representing P&G management.
2. You are a project manager in the international marketing research department of the Coca-Cola Company. Your boss, the director of the international marketing research department, has assigned you to a project designed to measure consumer preference for soft drinks in the United States, United Kingdom, Hong Kong, and Brazil. Your immediate task is to recommend survey methods to be used in this project and discuss them with your boss (who happens to be a student in your class).

Fieldwork

1. Obtain the report of a marketing research project conducted in the United States from a local marketing research firm. Discuss how the research would be different if the same project were conducted in France.
2. Visit a local business with international operations. Discuss with them some possible international marketing research projects they could undertake.

Group Discussion

1. Some scholars have argued that the same standardized marketing strategy should be adopted for all foreign markets. Does this imply that the marketing research process should also be standardized and the same procedures followed no matter where the research is being conducted? Discuss this question in a small group.

2. Discuss the impact of the globalization of markets on marketing research.

Dell Running Case

Review the Dell case, Case 1.1, and questionnaire given toward the end of the book. Go to the Web site for this book and download the Dell data file.

1. If this survey were to be conducted in India rather than the United States, how would the research process be different?

2. What survey method would you use if the survey were to be conducted in India?

3. How will you manage the question translation into Hindi (a major language in India)?

4. Should the sample size in India be the same as the sample size in the United States? Should the same sampling procedures be used in the two countries?

Video Cases

VIDEO CASE 24.1   Nivea: Marketing Research Leads to Consistency in Marketing

Nivea (www.nivea.com), the skin care products company, is part of the German Beiersdorf conglomerate. As of 2009, Nivea's skin care product line is marketed in more than 150 countries. The product line has been around for about 10 decades, originating with a scientific breakthrough of the first skin cream that did not separate into water and oil. That, coupled with intelligent marketing based on marketing research, has led to a strong positive brand image, which accounts for much of Nivea's success.

Nivea, founded in 1911, began marketing in the 1920s when it changed its logo and began selling its product around the world. Early on, Nivea established its brand identity as a pure and gentle product that families could rely on. Early advertisements featured the Nivea Girl. In 1924, it broke from tradition and began advertising with the Nivea Boy. This helped Nivea convey the message that Nivea skin cream was for the entire family. Its brand image has transcended the decades with the help of a foundation built upon advertising that stresses family relationships and values.

In the 1970s, Nivea had to defend itself against true competition for the first time. It relied heavily on marketing research, which helped it to formulate a two-pronged response: (1) defense of its core business through a new advertising campaign—Crème de la Crème and (2) the introduction of new products, which helped keep the brand fresh and introduced new sources of sales.

In the 1980s, marketing research indicated that brand differentiation was becoming increasingly important. In response, Nivea began branding with sub-brands. These sub-brands included skin care, bath products, sun protection, baby care, facial care, hair care, and care for men. It used an umbrella strategy with the sub-brands, meaning that it used its core brand to encompass all of the sub-brands. The goal was to establish individual images that were distinct but consistent with Nivea's core image. Nivea focused on strengthening the brand name and linking the new sub-brands with the core brand's traditional values. The result was an explosion in sales.

Nivea was able to continue its success into the 1990s, and sales grew rapidly throughout the decade. The growth was due in large part to the introduction of new products, each based on extensive marketing research. The most successful products were its antiwrinkle cream and an entire line of cosmetics.

Nivea entered the new millennium as the number one skin care and cosmetics company in the world. However, Nivea, a nearly 100-year-old brand, found itself in need of a makeover to evolve its strongly entrenched brand image of being a mild, reliable family product. The company had to revamp its product portfolio and marketing and branding strategy in order to address the changing needs and aspirations of its consumers and to appeal to a younger, more modern audience. This initiative placed a great emphasis on marketing research to transform the Nivea brand into a new, youthful identity.

The launch of *Nivea Styling* is an example of how the old Nivea image had become a handicap. Marketing research revealed that Nivea was very strongly identified with richness and creaminess, whereas in styling products consumers look for long-lasting hold and funky hairstyles. Nivea had to convince customers that it was not only about mild and caring products, but could also fulfill the needs of the category, which meant long-lasting hold.

However, Nivea, did not want to restrict itself to an exclusively young audience, but sought to extend the Nivea legacy and the Nivea line of products to more mature women. The launch of *Nivea Vital*, a line of products for mature women, was not without its share of challenges. Older women had not been given due attention by most beauty products companies, and hence there was a lack of understanding of awareness about how older women feel about beauty and aging. The company relied on marketing research to fill this gap. An unprecedented ad campaign featuring a mature woman was planned. Nivea was fearful that showing an older woman in an ad campaign could negatively impact the brand, making it appear old and less modern, thereby losing the support of its younger consumers. Marketing research was used to carefully test the choice of the model for the ad, and her beauty and self-confidence helped Nivea prevent this harmful side effect to its brand image. The model, a 50-years old woman, turned out to be the perfect model for the brand, and the campaign had the opposite effect of what was feared. Consumers felt that Nivea, by daring to show a mature and beautiful model, was truly a modern brand.

The company still faces many challenges. Its greatest challenge is in the U.S. market, where the brand is not as strong as it is in other parts of the world. The U.S. market poses many obstacles because it is the largest and most dynamic market in the world. Nivea hopes to overcome these obstacles through the use of extensive marketing research. This research will lead Nivea to launch more products and to develop focused marketing strategies. Nivea seeks consistency in its marketing, which can be problematic when trying to communicate the same message across various cultures and countries. However, Nivea will do whatever it takes to maintain this consistency, because it believes it gives it an edge over competitors. It helps consumers relate all its products to its core brand and identity. Nivea will continue to rely on marketing research to retain and refine the consistency in its marketing across global markets.

Conclusion

Nivea, a large company, had to rely on marketing research to revamp its brand image to keep itself relevant and to appeal to consumers. The company's launch of *Nivea Vital* demonstrates that if researched well, a product line can significantly enhance a company's brand image, even though the product might not be targeted at the core target audience. In sum, the case shows the use of marketing research in some of the aspects of developing, sustaining, and evolving a brand.

Questions

1. Nivea would like to increase its share of the U.S. market. Define the management decision problem.
2. Define an appropriate marketing research problem based on the management decision problem identified in question 1.
3. Nivea would like to undertake research to understand the preferences of American consumers for skin care products. What type of research design should be adopted and why?
4. Discuss the role of qualitative research in understanding the preferences of American consumers for skin care products. Which qualitative research techniques should be used and why?
5. If a survey is to be conducted to understand the preferences of American consumers for skin care products, which survey method should be used and why?
6. Develop Likert, semantic differential, and Stapel scales for determining consumers' evaluation of skin care products.
7. Develop a sampling plan for administering the survey in question 5.
8. If Nivea were to conduct the survey in Singapore to understand the preferences of consumers for skin care products, which survey method should be used and why?

References

1. www.nivea.com, accessed February 20, 2009.
2. www.wikipedia.com, accessed February 20, 2009.
3. Anonymous, "World's Top 100 Brands—Are They Fact or Fiction," *Brand Strategy* (August 21, 2002): 10.

Case 1.1

Running Case with Real Data
Dell Direct

Dell Inc. is the world's number one direct-sale computer vendor and competes with Hewlett-Packard in that segment. Dell offers network servers, workstations, storage systems, and Ethernet switches for enterprise customers, in addition to a full line of desktop and notebook PCs designed for consumers. It also sells handheld computers and markets third-party software and peripherals. Dell's growing services unit provides systems integration, support, and training.

Michael Dell, the flamboyant founder and chairman of Dell, started college at the University of Texas as a pre-med student but found time to establish a business selling random-access memory (RAM) chips and disk drives for IBM PCs. Dell bought products at cost from IBM dealers, who were required at the time to order large monthly quotas of PCs from IBM. Dell then resold his stock through newspapers and computer magazines at 10 to 15 percent below retail. By April 1984, Dell was grossing about $80,000 a month—enough to persuade him to drop out of college. Soon he started making and selling IBM clones under the brand name PC's Limited. Dell sold his machines directly to consumers, rather than through retail outlets as most other manufacturers did. By eliminating the retail markup, Dell could sell PCs at about 40 percent of the price of an IBM.

Michael Dell renamed his company Dell Computer and added international sales offices in 1987. In 1988, the company started selling to larger customers, including government agencies. That year Dell Computer went public. In 1996, Dell started selling PCs and notebook computers through its Web site. This channel of order confirmation and shipping and handling is still the bread-and-butter means of addressing Dell's consumer and enterprise customers' requirements. In 1997, Dell entered the market for workstations and strengthened its consumer business by separating it from its small-business unit and launching a leasing program for consumers. In order to diversify its revenue sources, in 2001 Dell expanded its storage offerings when it agreed to resell systems from EMC. To grow its services unit, Dell acquired Microsoft software support specialist Plural in 2002.

Despite its success at grabbing PC market share, Dell continues to attack new markets. It has put increasing emphasis on server computers and storage devices for enterprises. Furthering its push beyond PCs, Dell has introduced a handheld computer, a line of Ethernet switches, and consumer electronics such as digital music players and LCD televisions. It originally partnered with

U.S. PC Shipment Estimates for Q3 2008

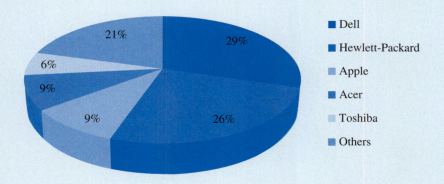

Dell—Financials—U.S. Dollars (in millions)

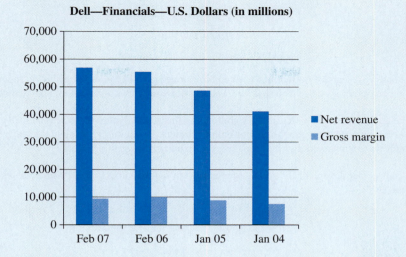

Lexmark to develop a line of Dell-branded printers, and it has formed additional partnerships to quickly grow its printing line. On the services front, Dell has mirrored its straightforward approach to hardware sales, embracing a fixed-price model for offerings such as data migration and storage systems implementation. Dell is currently looking to international revenue to supplant sales in the PC-saturated U.S. market. Sales inside the United States were about 53 percent of consolidated net revenue in fiscal 2008.

Dell has thrived as downward-spiraling prices and commoditization washed over the PC industry, benefiting the company's customers and bashing its competitors. Instead of battling the tide by attempting to erect proprietary systems, as HP and IBM often did, Dell used its low-cost, direct-sales model to ride the wave. In 2008, Dell announced PartnerDirect, a global program that brought their existing partner initiatives under one umbrella. Dell intends to expand the program globally. Continuing their strategy and efforts of better meeting customers' needs and demands, they began offering select products in retail stores in several countries in the Americas, Europe, and Asia during fiscal 2008. These actions represent the first steps in their retail strategy, which will allow them to extend their business model to reach customers that they have not been able to reach directly.

Of late, with all the brand equity Dell has built up, Dell Inc. is pushing into consumer products. Dell has recently made a move into manufacturing flat-screen TVs. With TVs that use the newest technology, Dell is now diversifying even further. The latest battle in the PC business isn't in computers but in printers. Dell is now waging war on HP's vaunted imaging and printing division, which produces

some 70 percent of HP's operating profit. In the case of printers, the printer cartridges is where HP has the biggest margins, and Dell seems to be focused on making inroads into this market, over which HP has had a strong hold.

With such an intense competition for market share and customer patronage, Dell is conducting a survey of recent purchasers of Dell PCs and notebooks. Dell wants to understand their consumers' primary usage of their computers for Internet and other usage. Based on that, Dell wants to understand the satisfaction that their consumers are deriving from Dell products. Dell wants to estimate their customers' probability of repeat buying of Dell products and the extent to which their current customers will recommend Dell to their friends and family. Finally, Dell wants to understand if there is any correlation on any of these identified usage factors and the underlying demographic aspects of the classification of their customers.

Questions

The questions are given in the Dell Running Case contained in the chapters.

References

1. www.gartner.com/it/page.jsp?id=777613, accessed November 18, 2008.
2. www.dell.com/downloads/global/corporate/sec/proxy08.pdf, accessed November 18, 2008.

Note: This case was prepared for class discussion purposes only and does not represent the views of Dell or their affiliates. The problem scenario is hypothetical and the name of the actual company has been disguised. However, the questionnaire and the data provided are real. Some questions have been deleted, while the data for other questions are not provided because of proprietary reasons.

DELL COMPUTERS
Internet Interview

Thank you for your interest in our study.

Burke is an independent marketing research firm that has been commissioned by DELL Computers to get the honest opinions of recent purchasers of DELL personal computer systems. You will be asked to offer your views about DELL and describe your Internet usage.

This survey should only take a few minutes of your time. By completing this survey, you will be automatically entered into a drawing for $100 gift certificates that can be used at a variety of major online retailers. If you don't complete the survey, you may qualify for the drawing by writing to the address contained on the email inviting you to participate in this project.

Unless you give us your permission at the end of the survey to release your name to DELL along with your responses, your individual responses will kept confidential.

INTERNET USAGE

Q1. Approximately how many total hours per week do you spend online? This would be the total from all the locations you might use.

Less than 1 hour	☐ —1
1 to 5 hours	☐ —2
6 to 10 hours	☐ —3
11 to 20 hours	☐ —4
21 to 40 hours	☐ —5
41 hours or more	☐ —6

Q2A. Following is a list of things people can do online. Please indicate which of these you have ever done on the Internet. *(Rotate responses.)*

Don't Know = 0

Ask First   **Yes**   **No**

_____ Communicated with others via newsgroups or chat rooms	☐ —1	☐ —2
_____ Looked for a job	☐ —1	☐ —2
_____ Planned or booked trips	☐ —1	☐ —2
_____ Downloaded a picture or graphic	☐ —1	☐ —2
_____ Downloaded sounds or audio clips	☐ —1	☐ —2
_____ Looked up information about a TV show or movie	☐ —1	☐ —2
_____ Downloaded a video clip	☐ —1	☐ —2

Q3. What other type of things do you use the Internet for? _____

DELL SATISFACTION AND LOYALTY

Q4. Overall, how satisfied are you with your DELL computer system?

Very satisfied	☐ —1
Somewhat satisfied	☐ —2
Somewhat dissatisfied	☐ —3
or Very dissatisfied	☐ —4

Q5. How likely would you be to recommend DELL to a friend or relative?

Definitely would recommend	☐ —1
Probably would	☐ —2
Might or might not	☐ —3
Probably would not	☐ —4
or Definitely would not recommend	☐ —5

Q6. If you could make your computer purchase decision again, how likely would you be to choose DELL?

Definitely would	☐ −1
Probably would	☐ −2
Might or might not	☐ −3
Probably would not	☐ −4
or Definitely would not	☐ −5

Q7. Deleted (Open ended) _____

COMPUTER MANUFACTURER IMPORTANCE/PERFORMANCE RATINGS

Q8. The following set of statements refers to personal computer manufacturers. For each statement, please first indicate to what extent you agree that **DELL Computers** meets that requirement.

To do this, please use a scale from 1 to 9, where a "1" means you **do not agree at all** with the statement, and a "9" means you **agree completely**. Of course, you may use any number between 1 and 9 that best describes how much you agree or disagree with the statement. Don't Know = 0

A. How much do you agree that **DELL Computers** does *(insert statement)*?

(Rotate statements.)

Ask First		Rating
_____	Make ordering a computer system easy	_____
_____	Let customers order computer systems customized to their specifications	_____
_____	Deliver its products quickly	_____
_____	Price its products competitively	_____
_____	Feature attractively designed computer system components	_____
_____	Have computers that run programs quickly	_____
_____	Have high-quality computers with no technical problems	_____
_____	Have high-quality peripherals (e.g., monitor, keyboard, mouse, speakers, disk drives)	_____
_____	"Bundle" its computers with appropriate software	_____
_____	"Bundle" its computers with Internet access	_____
_____	Allow users to easily assemble components	_____
_____	Have computer systems that users can readily upgrade	_____
_____	Offer easily accessible technical support	_____

Q9A. If the price of the DELL computer system you purchased had been **5%** higher, and all other personal computer prices had been the same, how likely would you have been to have purchased your DELL computer system?

Definitely would have purchased	☐ −1
Probably would have purchased	☐ −2
Might or might not have purchased	☐ −3
Probably would not have purchased	☐ −4
or Definitely would not have purchased	☐ −5

Q9B. If the price of the DELL computer system you purchased had been **10%** higher, and all other personal computer prices had been the same, how likely would you have been to have purchased your DELL computer system?

Definitely would have purchased	☐ −1
Probably would have purchased	☐ −2
Might or might not have purchased	☐ −3
Probably would not have purchased	☐ −4
or Definitely would not have purchased	☐ −5

EARLY ADOPTOR ATTRIBUTES

Q10. Following is a series of statements that people may use to describe themselves. Please indicate how much you agree or disagree that they describe you. To do this, please use a scale of 1 to 7 where a "1" means you **disagree completely** and a "7" means you **agree completely**. Of course, you may use any number between 1 and 7.

Don't Know = 0

The first/next statement is *(insert statement)*. What number from 1 to 7 best indicates how much you agree or disagree that this statement describes you?

Ask First		Rating
	Market Maven Items	
_____	I like introducing new brands and products to my friends	_____
_____	I like helping people by providing them with information about many kinds of products	_____
_____	People ask me for information about products, places to shop, or sales	_____
_____	My friends think of me as a good source of information when it comes to new products or sales	_____
	Innovativeness	
_____	I like to take a chance	_____
_____	Buying a new product that has not yet been proven is usually a waste of time and money	_____
_____	If people would quit wasting their time experimenting, we would get a lot more accomplished	_____
_____	I like to try new and different things	_____
_____	I often try new brands before my friends and neighbors do	_____
_____	I like to experiment with new ways of doing things	_____
	Opinion Leadership	
_____	When it comes to computer-related products, my friends are very likely to ask my opinion	_____
_____	I am often used as a source of advice about computer-related products by friends and neighbors	_____
_____	I often tell my friends what I think about computer-related products	_____

DEMOGRAPHICS

Q11. These next questions are about you and your household and will just be used to divide our interviews into groups. What was the last grade of school you completed?

Some High School or less   ☐ −1
High School Graduate   ☐ −2
Some College/Technical School   ☐ −3
College Graduate or higher   ☐ −4

Q12. Which of the following best describes your age?

18 to 19	☐ −1
20 to 24	☐ −2
25 to 29	☐ −3
30 to 34	☐ −4
35 to 39	☐ −5
40 to 44	☐ −6
45 to 49	☐ −7
50 to 54	☐ −8
55 to 59	☐ −9
60 to 64	☐ −10
65 to 69	☐ −11
70 to 74	☐ −12
75 to 79	☐ −13
80 or older	☐ −14

Q13. Which of the following best describes your household's total yearly income before taxes?

Under $20,000	☐ −1
$20,000–$29,999	☐ −2
$30,000–$49,999	☐ −3
$50,000–$74,999	☐ −4
$75,000–$99,999	☐ −5
$100,000 or over	☐ −6
No Answer − 0	

Q14. Are you . . . ?

Male	☐ −1
Female	☐ −2

This completes all the questions.
Thank you very much for your assistance with this interview!

Case 2.1

Comprehensive Critical Thinking Cases
American Idol: A Big Hit for Marketing Research?

"This could be more of a challenge than we previously thought," Melissa Marcello told her business associate, Julie Litzenberger. After nodding in agreement, Litzenberger put down her cup of coffee at the Vienna, Virginia, Starbucks coffee shop near her firm's headquarters.

Both Marcello and Litzenberger were far along their career paths as researchers in the winter of 2008 when they met at Starbucks. Marcello was CEO of research agency Pursuant, Inc. (www.pursuantresearch.com), and Litzenberger led the public relations division at marketing communications agency Sage Communications (www.sagecommunications.com). Both were based in the Washington, D.C., area.

Litzenberger took the last bite of her cinnamon scone before sipping her latte. She nodded again to Marcello across the table for two before answering. "Research studies that are the most successful in moving the needle are the studies where the research firm uses scientific and credible methods, poses the right questions, and provides the client company with the insights needed to sufficiently reduce risk in decision making," Litzenberger said. "In short, improving decision making is what effective marketing research is about."

Over the years, Marcello and Litzenberger had witnessed prospective client companies voicing resistance to pursuing marketing research. Skeptics of professional marketing research sometimes would say that they "already knew enough about customers to make decisions." Other times, skeptics would assail the sampling methods of studies in an attempt to dismiss the results. And in other instances, skeptics would merely claim that finding the answers to such questions about customers would be too expensive to obtain. In sum, professionally done marketing research was presented as being impractical.

Marcello and Litzenberger were attempting to overcome a challenge in client development. Specifically, they were attempting to obtain evidence to confront skeptics of professionally done marketing research without compromising the privacy of previous clients with whom they had worked. It

was inappropriate for them to share the results of previous studies with anyone other than the clients who had contracted them for those custom marketing research studies.

While considering dozens of ideas over the past three weeks of project development brainstorming sessions, Marcello and Litzenberger were now focused on one project for demonstrating the usefulness of marketing research to prospective clients. The research question was: "What still needs to be known about the viewers and voters for contestants of the popular TV show *American Idol*?"

American Idol (www.americanidol.com) is an annual televised singing competition, which began its first season in 2002. The program has always sought to discover the best young singer in the United States. Each year, a series of nationwide auditions are followed by a series of telecasts featuring the singers who advance to the next week's show based on public voting. Throughout the show's history, three judges have critiqued the singing of surviving contestants each week: record producer and bass player Randy Jackson, pop singer and dancer Paula Abdul, and the blunt-speaking music executive Simon Cowell. Good-guy Ryan Seacrest has hosted the show each year. Singer-songwriter and record producer Kara DioGuard was added as the fourth judge in the eight season.

In the spring of 2008, *American Idol* had reached an all-time peak, garnering as many as 28 million viewers for a single episode. Despite the sizable audience—composed of people from different demographics, from tweens to senior citizens—no third party had conducted a research study to gain more insight into who the viewers actually were or their motivations for voting for *American Idol* contestants.

"Are we kidding ourselves?" Marcello challenged Litzenberger. "Who would care about a study investigating *American Idol* viewers?"

"How about the sponsors of the show?" Litzenberger quickly countered. "Pepsi-Cola passed on sponsoring the show during its development, but Coca-Cola decided to take a risk and invested $10 million to become a sponsor in

American Idol's first season. That's a lot of cola and that was a lot of risk to take in the volatile world of broadcast television!"

"You're right," Marcello said. "I later read in *USA Today* that Kelly Clarkson might have been voted the first American Idol, but Coke was the real winner. So maybe Pepsi was the real loser. Coke and Ford now spend tens of millions each year not only to be sponsors, but also to have tie-in promotions, such as you might find at cokemusic.com."

"But just how durable is the show's concept?" Litzenberger asked after finishing her latte. "What if we find that voters are mostly pre-teen girls? What if we find that adults don't vote for the contestants or adults don't have confidence in the judge's opinions?"

"The news media should find such answers more delicious than that slice of pumpkin bread I am spying in that glass case over there by the cash register," Marcello said. "Journalists will almost always cover what they regard as relevant and quantifiable trends in popular culture."

Litzenberger leaned forward. "So how do you propose that we do such a study?"

"We've devoted hours to this question at my firm for better than a week. Here's our best thinking on it as of today," Marcello said. "We could place about six questions on Opinion Research Corporation's CARAVAN (www.opinionresearch.com) national omnibus telephone survey to find out more about who, among adults 18 or older living in the United States, watched and voted in the 2009 season of *American Idol*. Such an omnibus survey could be done by telephone during three days in April 2009."

"OK, but what about sampling?" Litzenberger said. "You know we might get attacked on this. It could be really expensive, too. Can we afford it?"

"If we do it this way, we can afford it," Marcello said. "It will run about $1,000 per question. We'll have the Opinion Research Corporation ask our questions along with those of other sponsoring companies to a randomly selected national sample of 1,045 adults comprised about evenly of men and women. With a total sample size of more than 1,000, we will be able to say with 95 percent certainty that the results would be accurate to within +/–3.0 percent. This exceeds acceptable standards for a survey about media preferences."

"So if only 10 percent of our sample reported voting for *American Idol* contestants, we would be able to say with 95 percent confidence that the actual percentage of the adult population who voted was somewhere between 7 and 13 percent?" Litzenberger asked.

"You've got it," Marcello affirmed. "Of course, it could be a lower or a much higher percentage. Nobody really knows now. Anybody who says otherwise is merely speculating."

Silence now overcame these two researchers as they reflected on the future courses of action they could take. They could drop the whole idea of demonstrating the usefulness of marketing research. They could pursue this *American Idol* study. If so, what questions should be asked to respondents and why. Should they continue to consider other ideas for such a study and pursue it later? What should they do? Why?

Critical Thinking Questions

1. Marcello and Litzenberger felt it was important to conduct this study because _____.
   (State the relevant background information used to justify their work.)
2. The main purpose of Marcello and Litzenberger's study was _____.
   (State as accurately as possible the purpose for doing the study.)
3. The key questions Marcello and Litzenberger are addressing are _____.
   (Identify the key questions in the minds of the case's protagonists.)
4. The methods used to answer their key questions were _____.
   (Describe the general approach used and include details that assist in evaluating the quality of the results; for example, sample size, etc.).
5. The most important information in this article is _____.
   (Identify the facts, observations, and/or data Marcello and Litzenberger are using to support their conclusions. Be quantitative.)
6. The results can be put into context by comparing them to _____.
   (Place the quantitative results into an easily understood context by expressing as percentages or by comparing them to an intuitively understood value; for example, twice the size of a football field.)
7. The main inferences/conclusions in this article are _____.
   (Identify the key conclusions the case protagonists present in the article.)
8. If we take this line of reasoning seriously, the implications are _____.
   (What consequences are likely to follow if people take Marcello and Litzenberger's reasoning seriously?)

Technical Questions

9. What steps of the six-step marketing research process are evident in this case?
10. What is the role of marketing research in marketing decision making suggested by this case?
11. Define the management decision problem confronting Melissa Marcello and Julie Litzenberger and a corresponding marketing research problem and show the linkages between the two.
12. If Marcello and Litzenberger decide to conduct this study, what research design should they adopt? Relate the different phases of the research design to specific aspects of the marketing research problem.
13. What kind of secondary and syndicated data would be helpful in addressing the questions raised by Marcello and Litzenberger? What is the role played by such data?
14. Discuss the role of qualitative research in gaining a better understanding of why people watch *American Idol*.
15. Is the telephone survey the most appropriate method in this case? If not, which survey method would you recommend?
16. Why did Marcello and Litzenberger not consider doing an experiment? What aspects of *American Idol* viewers should be researched by conducting an experiment?
17. Discuss the role of measurement and scaling in assessing the audience response to *American Idol*.

18. Critically evaluate the wording of the following question: "Who is your favorite American Idol?"
19. Describe the sampling process employed by Opinion Research Corporation's CARAVAN. (Hint: Visit www.opinionresearch.com.)
20. Is the sample size appropriate? Why or why not?
21. If you were the supervisor in charge of the CARAVAN telephone interviewers, what challenges would you face?
22. As part of the management team at Fox that produces *American Idol*, how would you evaluate the report produced by Marcello and Litzenberger? How will the proposed study help you make decisions about the show?

Reference

1. Adapted from Melissa Marcello and Julie Litzenberger, "Fascinating Findings" *Quirk's Marketing Research Review*, 21(3) (March 2007): 58–62.

The contribution of Professor Mark Peterson in developing this case is gratefully acknowledged.

Case 2.2

Baskin-Robbins: Can It Bask in the Good 'Ole Days?

It was early December 2008, and Baskin-Robbins Brand Officer Ken Kimmel had just returned from lunch. To his surprise, his walk from the parking lot to the Randolph, Massachusetts, headquarters building had quickly turned into a sprint. Kimmel was trying to avoid the chilly effects of a Nor'easter that was whipping most of New England with arctic winds.

Like the nasty weather that Kimmel had just escaped, the frozen-food retailing industry had become more hostile to Baskin-Robbins (www.baskinrobbins.com) in recent years. New entrants, such as Cold Stone Creamery founded in 1988, and others had popularized the in-store experience, with customers watching their ice cream creations being made before their eyes on cold stone slabs. For years, Baskin-Robbins had turned their back to Cold Stone Creamery's gains, in a similar way the Baskin-Robbins counter staff turned their back on customers to make a banana split. Cold Stone Creamery's sales were now almost 75 percent of Baskin-Robbins' sales.

In response, the Baskin-Robbins executive group along with Kimmel had recently moved to redesign stores, but it was not easy convincing the thousands of franchisees who ran the Baskin-Robbins stores to change. A store redesign could run up to $50,000 and was funded mostly by the franchisees. One aspect of the redesign resulted in lowering the ice cream cases to make it easier for children to look down into the ice cream bins.

Another change being considered was changing the Baskin-Robbins logo to coincide with the redesign of store interiors. The logo appears on napkins, cone wrappers, spoons, cups, uniforms, and signs at each Baskin-Robbins store. The estimated cost for making such a change was $5 million for Baskin-Robbins headquarters. Individual franchisees would have to invest about $10,000 for the logo change to be made inside the stores.

Later that afternoon, Kimmel's brand group was deep in discussion about whether to change the brand symbol of Baskin-Robbins at the same time stores would be redesigned.

"The context has changed since the mid-1980s," visiting retailing consultant Zack Wheatly said. "Customers are more demanding about the hospitality experience. They earn more money and they can buy comparable ice creams to Baskin-Robbins in grocery stores now."

Kimmel sensed it was time to mention recent strategy decisions by the Baskin-Robbins executive group.

"While our competitors are pushing this mix-in experience—a higher-priced theater experience—Baskin-Robbins has decided to focus on delivering a great value for our consumers in an accessible kind of environment," Kimmel responded. "The executive group has decided that we are going to focus on our new products as opposed to the theater of the business. As part of this new emphasis, we have recently begun highlighting innovations such as our own frozen coffee beverage—the Cappuccino Blast—and a fruit-based beverage—Bold Breezes. Carrying frozen custard is also on the horizon."

Marsha Davis, Kimmel's research director, took her turn in the conversation. "Is Baskin-Robbins such an established brand that the logo for Baskin-Robbins should not be overhauled?" Davis asked.

"I know what you are suggesting," Wheatly replied. "Conventional wisdom in this industry would say that one shouldn't tinker with an established brand."

"We have discussed this among ourselves here at headquarters with the CEO and other senior executives, and we have also invested in hearing from consultants in retailing communications," Kimmel said. "They think the decision to change the logo should be taken only after extensive deliberation and direct research with customers."

"Right," Wheatly said. "Analysts in the quick-service restaurant industry have reported in the trade journals that the new entrants have continued to grow faster than Baskin-Robbins—especially in the key metric of same-store sales compared to the previous year. What did the qualitative research say about the proposed new logos?"

Davis paused, dug in her briefcase, and removed the glossy printed versions of the old logo and the leading candidate among the proposed new logo. She put them both on the table facing the others.

"We talked with four focus groups in Chicago, LA, and New York, and they agreed that the Baskin-Robbins brand represented irresistible treats, smiles, and fun," Davis said. "They also liked this proposed logo that the senior executive group liked."

"So where do we go from here?" Kimmel asked.

"Because your management wants to make a change to the logo only if it is necessary, you should study your customers' attitude toward the new logo, so that you can explain whether a logo change is warranted," Wheatly said.

Everyone stopped talking to reflect on what was just said. After about 10 seconds, Kimmel raised an open hand to the group.

"Wait. This is beginning to remind me of the New Coke introduction," Kimmel said after some reflection. "Customers' subjective attachment to the old Coke was ignored, then. We need to ask about the old logo, too. Also, I know the senior executives want a clear margin of preference for the new logo. If the new logo is not preferred 2:1 in a head-to-head competition with the old one, we need to drop it."

Wheatly picked up the line of thought.

"OK, and now that you mention it, we also need to present the drawings of the new redesigned stores and have the customers respond to the old and new logos after understanding what our new stores will be like," Wheatly said.

"So restating our problem, I guess it sounds this way," Davis said. "Because management wants to make a change to the logo only if it is absolutely necessary, we should study our customers' attitudes toward the old logo and toward the new logo after showing them the drawings of the redesigned stores. Only then can we explain whether customers prefer the new logo 2:1 over the old logo."

The words seem to hang in the air in the conference room at Baskin-Robbins headquarters. The statement of the marketing research problem was sounding much improved to Kimmel. But he also had the following thoughts: (1) Given that Baskin-Robbins had moved to redesign store interiors, should the brand logo be changed to signal something new is happening at Baskin-Robbins? (2) If the logo is changed, would there be synergy between the logo change and the redesigned interiors? Synergistic results could be dramatic. A new look, a new menu, and a new strategy focused on delivering "irresistible treats, smiles, and fun" in an accessible way and at a reasonable price could check the momentum rival brands have developed by focusing on a high-end, in-store experience. Considering these elements, the strategic importance of the Baskin-Robbins' research project became more clear in Kimmel's mind.

But had they missed anything in their process of developing the statement of the research problem? Were they focused upon the right issue now? Should they continue to consider other logos for such a study? Should they just go ahead with the new logo because focus group participants had liked the new logo and the senior executives had, as well? What should they do? Why?

Critical Thinking Questions

1. Baskin-Robbins Brand Officer Ken Kimmel felt it was important to conduct this study because _____.
   (State the relevant background information used to justify their work.)

2. The main purpose of the Baskin-Robbins study was _____.
   (State as accurately as possible their reason for doing the study.)

3. The key questions the Baskin-Robbins brand team is addressing are _____.
   (Identify the key questions in the minds of the case protagonists.)

4. The methods used by Kimmel and his team to identify the marketing research problem were _____.
   (Describe the general approach used and include details that assist in evaluating the quality of the results.)

5. The most important understanding about Baskin-Robbins as an organization that led the firm to consider a new logo as part of problem definition was _____.
   (Identify the facts, observations, and/or data Kimmel and his team are using to support their conclusions. Be quantitative.)

6. The series of marketing research problem statements can be put into context by comparing each to _____.
   (Place the marketing research problem statements into other readily understood contexts.)

7. The main inferences/conclusions in this case pertaining to problem definition are _____.
   (Identify the key conclusions implied by the case.)

8. If we take this line of reasoning seriously, the implications for many other firms seeking to define the marketing research problem related to rebranding are _____.
   (What consequences are likely to follow if people take the brand team's reasoning seriously and apply them to other firms?)

Technical Questions

9. What is the role of marketing research in deciding whether to change the logo in this case?

10. Define the management decision problem confronting the Baskin-Robbins executive group, along with Kimmel, and a corresponding marketing research problem and show the linkages between the two.

11. What specific research question and hypothesis are suggested in this case?

12. If Kimmel decides to conduct a study to address the marketing research problem, what research design should be adopted? Relate the different phases of the research design to specific aspects of the marketing research problem.

13. What kind of secondary and syndicated data would be helpful in addressing the issue of changing the brand logo? What is the role played by such data?

14. Discuss the role of qualitative research in gaining a better understanding of the influence of the brand image on consumer selection of an ice cream brand.

15. Do you think that Kimmel should commission a survey in this case? If yes, which survey method would you recommend and why?

16. Can an experiment be conducted to address the issue of changing the brand logo? If yes, what experimental design would you recommend and why?

17. Discuss the role of measurement and scaling in assessing the consumer response to the old and new logos.

18. After showing the respondent the old and the new logos, the following question is asked: "Do you like the new logo better than the old logo?" Critically evaluate the wording of this question.

19. If mall-intercept interviews are to be conducted to determine consumers' preferences for ice cream brands, design a suitable sampling process. What should be the sample size and how should it be determined?

20. If you were the supervisor in charge of mall-intercept interviewing, what challenges would you face in training the interviewers?

21. How should the executive group, along with Kimmel, evaluate the marketing research report? How will the findings of marketing research help them make decisions about changing the brand logo?

References

1. Sherri Daye Scott, "Remaining Relevant," *QSR* (February 2006): 26–30.
2. David Colker, "Ice Cream Battle Getting Hotter," *Los Angeles Times* (November 5, 2005): C1.
3. www.baskinrobbins.com/about/OurHistory.aspx, accessed February 15, 2009.

The contribution of Professor Mark Peterson in developing this case is gratefully acknowledged.

Case 2.3

Kid Stuff? Determining the Best Positioning Strategy for Akron Children's Hospital

"I'm not sure we are getting anywhere in this meeting," Aaron Powell thought to himself as he pushed his chair away from the conference room table and slowly stood up to stretch his legs after an hour had already gone past.

Powell, Akron Children's Hospital's (ACH; akron-childrens.org) marketing director, stood to gaze out the conference room windows onto the two ribbons of train tracks that curled near the hospital on the north side of this midsized city in Northeast Ohio. He was thinking about how rival hospitals, such as Akron City Hospital, Akron General Medical Center, and St. Thomas Hospital, had recently hired marketing directors like himself. The urgency to advance Akron Children's Hospital's marketing effort was going to intensify in the next year.

Powell's meeting was going into its second hour. In addition to Powell, the meeting's participants were Mark Norton, the hospital operations officer (Powell's boss), and Janet Jones from the Cleveland-based Marcus Thomas communications and research agency (marcusthomasllc.com). One staff member from finance was there, along with the soon to be retiring public relations director for the hospital. In the past, both of these staffers would support whatever Norton proposed or liked. It now looked like Powell and Jones were on the other side of a divide about how to approach positioning Akron Children's Hospital in next year's advertising campaign. To make matters worse, Powell and Jones appeared to be outnumbered, and the tension in the room was palpable.

"Let me read the research problem statement all of us revised in the first hour of our meeting," Jones said. "Akron Children's Hospital board wants the hospital to become the preferred hospital in the high-growth areas of the region. Accordingly, we are studying positioning possibilities, so that the board can select the best positioning for next year's communications campaign intended to boost the number of patient cases 10 percent in the following year."

"That's it. That's what we want," Norton said. "But I don't think we have to pursue a research project with a survey that just may lead us to reinvent the wheel—and for $60,000, too."

"What wheel is that?" Powell asked, turning away from the window to face Norton.

"Aaron, you know as well as I do that this hospital is all about children. It's even in our name," Norton said. "Emphasize the kids. Whatever we do in the media should feature the kids. Just do some focus groups that will allow Marcus Thomas to get some ideas for their advertising about kids and our hospital. That should only cost about $20,000. But honestly, I am not sure we even need that."

"Mark, remember that McDonald's tends to emphasize kids, too, but adults are featured in their advertising most of the time," Powell said. "Marcus Thomas needs to cover the entire range of issues families consider when choosing a hospital for their kid. If we miss something important, one of the other hospitals in Akron might claim they are the better hospital when it comes to this."

"Aaron is making a good point," Jones said. "Right now, we don't know which positioning would help Akron Children's the most."

"So describe which paths we can pursue now," Norton said.

"Plan A—do focus groups only, as you suggested," Jones said. "Plan B—do focus groups with a follow-on survey. Plan C—do a survey with follow-on focus groups. And plan D—do no research."

"Tell me more about each of these," Norton said.

"In plan A, Marcus Thomas would conduct four focus groups, with an average of 10 respondents per group," Jones said. "We'll ask participants to discuss their experiences while at a hospital. Participants will be required to be the primary decision makers for health-care decisions within the family and have a child—newborns to 18 years old—with an acute condition and who had spent at least 3 consecutive days in a hospital. Because most health-care decision makers within a family tend to be women, most of the participants will be female between 25 and 54 years old with one or more children ranging from newborns to 18 years old."

"Cost?" Norton asked.

"About $20,000," Powell said.

Jones continued. "In plan B, we'll do plan A, plus a field survey to follow up on the issues we identify in the focus groups. First, we'll ask about unaided and aided awareness of hospitals in the region. Then, based on what we learn in the focus groups, we will identify the concepts of three positioning strategies and ask survey respondents which one they prefer most and which one they prefer next most. We'll be able to statistically determine the degree of preference among the positioning alternatives."

"The three strategies might be, one, Akron Children's Hospital has doctors who listen to you," Powell said. "Or, two, we know how to meet the unique needs of children, or, three, we use the latest advances in treating children."

"Cost?" Norton asked again.

"About $60,000," Powell said.

"What about plan C? Why does that make sense?" Norton asked.

"We can identify the best positioning strategy by conducting a survey. The salient aspects of this positioning strategy to the consumers can then be explored via focus groups. The cost will be the same as plan B; that is, $60,000," responded Jones.

"And plan D—no research. Turn our creative staff loose and hang on for the ride," Jones said with a wry smile.

Norton returned the smile and looked around the room. "Doesn't your firm do the advertising for the Ohio Lottery?" Norton asked. "With plan D, we might do better by playing the Ohio Lottery!"

Sensing the humor, everyone in the room laughed together. Finally, tension seemed to begin dissipating.

Norton nodded slowly. Powell nodded, too. However, the questions Powell was thinking about still remained. Which of the plans would Akron Children's Hospital pursue—plan A, plan B, plan C, or plan D? If money was invested, would it be a worthwhile investment? Would the idea of research being a "cost" (with no apparent return) persist in the minds of Norton and the other staff members long after this meeting? What could be done now to help Norton and the other executives view research as an investment (with an implied return)?

Critical Thinking Questions

1. Akron Children's Hospital Marketing Director Aaron Powell felt it was important to conduct this study because _____.
   (State the relevant background information used to justify their work.)
2. The main purpose of the Akron Children's Hospital study was _____.
   (State as accurately as possible the reason for doing the study.)
3. The key questions the Akron Children's Hospital employees address in the case are _____.
   (Identify the key questions in the minds of the case protagonists.)
4. The methods used by Powell and his team to answer the marketing research problem were _____.

(Describe the general approach used and include details that assist in evaluating the quality of the results.)
5. The most important understanding about Akron Children's Hospital as an organization that led the firm to consider the research about its positioning was _____.
   (Identify the facts, observations, and/or data Powell and his team are using to support their conclusions.)
6. The research design decision can be put into context by _____.
   (Place the research design decision into other readily understood contexts.)
7. The main inferences/conclusions in this case are _____.
   (Identify the key conclusions implied by the case.)
8. If we take this line of reasoning seriously, the implications for many other firms are _____.
   (What consequences are likely to follow if people take the marketing team's reasoning seriously and apply it to other firms?)

Technical Questions

9. What is the role of marketing research in determining the best positioning strategy for Akron Children's Hospital?
10. Define the management decision problem confronting Akron Children's Hospital and a corresponding marketing research problem and show the linkages between the two.
11. In this case, how do Norton and the finance people differ from the marketers (Powell and Jones) in their views about the roles of exploratory and conclusive designs?
12. In your opinion, what would be the best sequence for using exploratory and conclusive research in this case?
13. What kind of secondary and syndicated data would be helpful in determining a positioning strategy for Akron Children's Hospital? What is the role played by such data?
14. Discuss the role of qualitative research in gaining a better understanding of how households select a hospital for their children when in need of health care for acute cases.
15. Do you think that Norton should commission a survey in this case? If yes, which survey method would you recommend and why?
16. Can an experiment be conducted to address the issue of the best positioning strategy? If yes, what experimental design would you recommend and why?
17. Discuss the role of measurement and scaling in assessing households' preferences for hospitals for their children when in need of health care for acute cases.
18. Design a questionnaire to measure consumer preferences for children's hospitals.
19. If a mail survey is to be conducted to determine households' preferences for children's hospitals, design a suitable sampling process. What should the sample size be and how should it be determined?
20. How should Norton evaluate the marketing research report? How will the findings of marketing research help Akron Children's Hospital select an appropriate positioning strategy?

Reference

1. Adapted from Robin Segbers, "Adding a Human Touch," *Quirk's Marketing Research Review* (June 2006): 30–34.

The contribution of Professor Mark Peterson in developing this case is gratefully acknowledged.

Case 3.1

Data Analysis Cases with Real Data
AT&T Wireless: Ma Bell Becomes Ma Again

The wireless service provider market in the United States is extremely competitive. The wireless market for individuals and/or families (nonenterprise market) is the most competitive segment. In this segment, there are a few big wireless service providers (wireless carriers), four of which can be categorized as having substantial market share. There has been some consolidation. Although these acquisitions have somewhat changed the dynamics of the market, there are still many players. An oligopoly market is considered to have three to four players, and such markets are typically stable in terms of growth, technical innovation, and pricing policies. It seems that the wireless carrier market will require a few more years before it becomes an oligopoly. Also, the rate of innovation in wireless technologies is frantic. A pathbreaking technical innovation by one of the big players has the potential to change the industry dynamic.

The major players and the number of subscribers that they have are as follows:

1. AT&T (70.1 million subscribers). In 2004, Cingular Wireless acquired AT&T Wireless. That acquisition gave Cingular nationwide coverage. Then the BellSouth acquisition in 2006 gave AT&T 100 percent ownership of Cingular.
2. Verizon Wireless (65.7 million subscribers), formed by the union of Bell Atlantic Mobile, AirTouch Cellular, PrimeCo, and GTE Wireless. European wireless giant Vodafone has a 45 percent stake in Verizon Wireless.

3. Sprint Nextel (53.8 million subscribers).
4. T-Mobile (28 million subscribers).
5. AllTel Inc. (12 million subscribers). In 2007, Alltel completed its merger with an affiliate of TPG Capital and GS Capital Partners and ceased trading on the New York Stock Exchange.
6. US Cellular (6.1 million subscribers).

The growth in the number of subscribers and in revenues (which does not include roaming charges, etc.) over the last decade and a half has been nothing short of meteoric.

In the earlier years of this industry, pricing pressure and consolidation caused the smaller service providers to be acquired or to exit the market. This has somewhat eased the pressure on the larger players. Currently, it's unusual to find carriers competing aggressively on price alone. Instead, the bigger players seem to be trying to retain their most coveted customers under extended two-year contract renewals. Although carriers are offering more "anytime" minutes and monthly rollover minutes in their rate plans, as well as handset subsidies, larger carriers are experiencing growth in higher average revenue per user (ARPU), a key industry metric. In addition to voice, new data services such as WiFi, photo, video, and multimedia applications are fueling this ARPU growth. Industry analysts look for a growing subscriber base. However, even with increased ARPU, the net subscriber addition in this industry has been

Percentage of Subscribers (in millions)

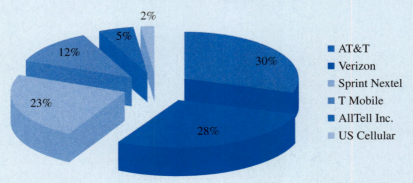

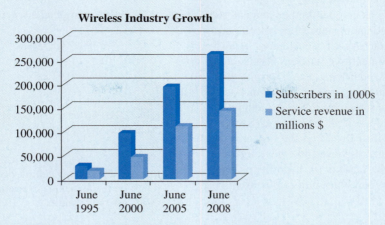

Wireless Industry Growth

somewhat low. Therefore, industry analysts are concerned whether the carriers can maintain high ARPU for long. Upgrades to enhance data networks and third-generation handsets with Web-based capability can potentially boost growth, but not at the same magnitude at which increased net new subscriber additions can drive higher revenue growth.

The current trend is for people to prefer using their wireless phone rather than their wireline phones at home. In the long term, this trend is considered a positive for the wireless industry. As a result, nationally, wireless carriers report higher minutes of use attributed to long-distance traffic. For instance, AT&T recently stated that wireless data usage is quadrupling every year. They have reported an increase in the same from 840MBPS in 2006 to 3800MBPS (megabit per second) in 2007.

A closely watched event in the industry was the acquisition of BellSouth by AT&T for $86 billion in 2006. It was widely expected that, following this merger, AT&T would slow its marketing and network capital expense in the short term to ensure that it would realize the synergies of this acquisition. Analysts watched to see whether AT&T would continue to grow even with this pricey acquisition, especially when compared to the growth they expected for its closest competitor, Verizon Wireless.

Given the myriad interfaces of the technologies, networks, and government licenses, the wireless carriers are competing and allied at the same time. Sprint PCS, which was not really considered a high-growth-potential carrier until recently, experienced 6.5 percent growth in 2004. Sprint accomplished this improvement by focusing on improved wireless services and by leasing its networks to other carriers. For example, currently, Virgin Mobile buys wholesale wireless service from Sprint and has been targeting the youth market to become the fastest-growing wireless company in the United States. Qwest buys wireless service from Sprint and resells it in different markets. On August 12, 2005, Sprint and Nextel completed their merger. The new company, called Sprint Nextel, is the third largest wireless carrier in the United States.

To increase market share, wireless service providers are trying hard to poach their competitors' customers by providing superior quality of services, appealing calling plans, and great customer support. In order to have a predictable stream of revenues, wireless service providers entice their new customers into signing moderate to long-term service commitments. Once these service contracts expire, customers can continue with their current wireless provider, move to a different provider, or stop using wireless service entirely. With the current changes in laws by the Federal Communications Commission (FCC), wireless customers can keep their existing phone numbers even if they are moving to a different provider. This has made it harder for wireless service providers to keep their current customers, who become enticed into moving to competitors because of appealing calling plans, superior customer service, free or subsidized upgrades to advanced cellular handsets, and so on.

Wireless carriers often use subscriber surveys to study strategies that can be implemented to maintain their current subscribers while attracting those from other carriers. Recently, *Consumer Reports* conducted a survey of more than 31,000 cell phone subscribers. One of the major findings was that fewer than 50 percent of respondents were highly satisfied with their cell phone service, and a significant number of them said they had no service or experienced a dropped call or poor connection at least once in the week before the survey was conducted. Another key finding was that "churn," the industry term for the number of subscribers who change carriers, remains high. On average, nearly 37 percent of cell phone users switch carriers each year, seeking better service or a better calling plan. A leading reason consumers used to be hesitant to do so was that they couldn't take their old numbers with them. With the aforementioned FCC ruling, subscribers are now aware that they have more choices and more freedom. Overall, 10 percent of subscribers had filed a billing problem with their carriers. Only 40 percent of those reporting problems said the company's response to a complaint was very helpful. These findings suggest that wireless carriers should focus on improving service quality so as to reduce dropped calls and should improve billing and customer service in order to increase subscriber satisfaction.

The acquisition of BellSouth in 2006 aided AT&T in becoming the biggest player in the industry. Like other carriers, AT&T tries to woo its competitors' customers. At the same time, AT&T is also under siege from its competitors, who are trying to attract AT&T's customers. AT&T believes that it provides competitive wireless service and appealing calling packages and pricing plans. Despite that, AT&T has experienced customer turnover. AT&T management wants to study the reasons why customers might be leaving and commissioned a telephone survey. (See the accompanying questionnaire.) Based on the outcome of this study, AT&T management believes that they might be able to better understand the reasons for losing their subscribers to their competitors and, thus, reduce this loss.

Questions

Chapter 14

1. Convert Year you were born (Q8) into age quartiles.
2. Recode Question 9 as follows. Recode Adults 18 Years of Age or Older (Q9(1)) by combining 3, 4, 5, and 6 into a single category labeled 3 Plus. Recode Teenagers 13 to 17 Years of Age (Q9(2)) by combining 2 and 3 into a single category labeled 2 Plus. Recode Children 12 Years Old and Younger (Q9(3)) by combining 2, 3, 4, 5, 6, and 7 into a single category labeled 2 Plus.
3. Recode "Highest Level of Education (Q10)" as follows: Combine (1) Some High School and (2) High School Graduate or GED into a single category labeled "High School or Less"; combine Vocational School (3) and Some College (4) into a single category labeled "No College Degree"; and combine Graduated from College (5), Some Graduate School (6), Graduate or Professional Degree (7) into a single category labeled "College Degree."
4. Recode Household Situation (Q11) by combining Two (2) and More Than Two (3) into a single category labeled "2 Plus."

Chapter 15

1. Run a frequency distribution for all variables except Identification Number (ID). Note that the demographic variables (Q8 to Q11) should be recoded as described in the questions for Chapter 14. What is the value of running such an analysis?
2. Cross-tabulate "Do you currently have a wireless service from a carrier other than AT&T Wireless" (Q3) with the recoded demographic variables (Q8 to Q11). Interpret the results.
3. Do those who currently have or do not have a wireless service from a carrier other than AT&T Wireless (Q3) differ in terms of the evaluations of AT&T on each of the attributes (Q7A through Q7K)? How would your analysis change if the evaluations (Q7A through Q7K) were treated as ordinal rather than interval?
4. Do the respondents evaluate AT&T more favorably on contract requirements (Q7E) than they do on coverage (Q7A)? Formulate the null and alternative hypotheses and conduct an appropriate test. How would your analysis change if these evaluations were treated as ordinal rather than interval?
5. Do the respondents evaluate AT&T more favorably on high-quality customer service (Q7I) than they do on lower prices (Q7K)? Formulate the null and alternative hypotheses and conduct an appropriate test. How would your analysis

change if these evaluations were treated as ordinal rather than interval?
6. Do the evaluations of AT&T on selection of phones (Q7G) exceed 5.0?

Chapter 16

1. Do the evaluations of AT&T on able to make or receive calls (Q7B) differ according to the recoded demographic characteristics (Q8 to Q11)?

Chapter 17

1. Regress "AT&T has calling plans that meet your needs" (Q7F) on the remaining evaluations (Q7A to Q7E, Q7G to Q7K). Interpret your results.

Chapter 18

1. Do those who currently have or do not have a wireless service from a carrier other than AT&T Wireless (Q3) differ in terms of the evaluations of AT&T on all of the attributes (Q7A through Q7K) when these variables are considered simultaneously? Run a two-group discriminant analysis and logistic regression and compare the results.

Chapter 19

1. Can the evaluations of AT&T on all of the attributes (Q7A through Q7K) be represented by a reduced set of factors? Conduct a principal components analysis using varimax rotation and save the factor scores.

Chapter 20

1. Cluster the respondents on the evaluations of AT&T on all of the attributes (Q7A through Q7K). Run a hierarchical clustering using Ward's method and squared euclidean distances. What should be the number of clusters?
2. Cluster the respondents on the evaluations of AT&T on all of the attributes (Q7A through Q7K) using K-means clustering and specify a four-cluster solution. Interpret the results.
3. Cluster the respondents on the factor scores of the evaluations of AT&T on all of the attributes (Q7A through Q7K) using K-means clustering and specify a four-cluster solution. Interpret the results. Compare the results to those arrived at by using the original variables.

Chapter 21

1. Construct 32 full profiles of wireless service providers using the following attributes and the levels: coverage area (M, H), voice quality (M, H), contract requirements (M, H), selection of phones (M, H), and customer service (M, H). Rate the 32 profiles in terms of your preference using a 7-point scale (1 = not at all preferred, 7 = greatly preferred). Calculate the part-worth functions and the relative importance of the attributes. Note that M = medium and H = high.

Chapter 23

1. Write a report for AT&T based on all the analyses that you have conducted. What would you recommend that AT&T do in order to increase customer retention?

Chapter 24

1. If the survey conducted by AT&T were to be conducted in China, how should the marketing research be conducted?

References

1. www.att.com/Investor/ATT_Annual/letter/page3.html, accessed November 18, 2008.
2. www.3g.co.uk/PR/May2006/3031.htm, accessed November 18, 2008.
3. nyse.10kwizard.com/cgi/convert?pdf=1&ipage=5671237&num=-2&pdf=1&xml=1&odef=8&dn=2&quest=1&rid=12, accessed November 18, 2008.
4. www.ctia.org/advocacy/research/index.cfm/AID/10323, financial data extracted from companies' annual reports, accessed November 18, 2008.
5. www.att.com/Investor/ATT_Annual/downloads/07_ATTar_FullFinalAR.pdf, accessed November 18, 2008.
6. www.att.com/Investor/ATT_Annual/2006/downloads/ATT_2006_Annual_Report.pdf, accessed November 18, 2008.
7. Shawn Young, "Cingular Swings to Profit as Sales Increase by 24%," *Wall Street Journal* (January 25, 2006): B2.

Note: This case was prepared for class discussion purposes only and does not represent the views of AT&T or their affiliates. The problem scenario is hypothetical and the name of the actual company has been disguised. However, the questionnaire and the data provided are real. Some questions have been deleted, while the data for other questions are not provided because of proprietary reasons.

AT&T WIRELESS
Customer Churn Survey—Fall 2008

(RECRUIT FROM LIST THOSE CHURNED JULY AND AUGUST 2008. FROM THOSE, RECRUIT/EXHAUST "NON-DISCLOSURE" RESPONDENTS FIRST, THEN RANDOMIZE CALLING BY "REASONS")
("RELOCATION" REASONS SHOULD NOT ANSWER—TRACK HOW MANY DO ANSWER AND ARE THE ACTUAL PERSON FROM THE LIST)

(ASK TO SPEAK TO PERSON ON LIST)

Hello, my name is _____ with _____. We are conducting a marketing research study with former customers of AT&T Wireless. Let me assure you this is not a sales call. We are only interested in your opinions. Your responses will be kept confidential. Would you have a few minutes to share your opinions?

1. Our records show that you recently discontinued your AT&T Wireless cellular service. Is this correct? (FYI: They may still have Clearwave broadband service)

   1. Yes (CONTINUE)
   2. No (THANK AND TERMINATE)

2. What is the primary reason you decided to discontinue service with AT&T Wireless?

   _____

3. Do you currently have wireless service from a carrier other than AT&T Wireless?

   1. Yes
   2. No

4. Who is your current wireless service provider? (IF REFUSED, SKIP TO Q6)(DO NOT READ LIST)

   1. Alltel
   2. AT&T
   3. BevComm
   4. Cellular One
   5. Hickory Tech
   6. Nextel
   7. Qwest
   8. Sprint
   9. T-Mobile
   10. US Cellular
   11. Verizon
   12. Other (SPECIFY) _____

5. Why did you select [COMPANY NAME] as your wireless service provider?

6. Next, I'm going to give you a series of reasons that may or may not have been important when you decided to cancel your service with AT&T Wireless. After each statement, please tell me if this was a <u>major</u> reason, a <u>minor</u> reason, or <u>not at all</u> a reason for canceling your service with AT&T Wireless.

	Major	Minor	Not at all
a) Their coverage area did not meet your needs	1	2	3
b) You had trouble making or receiving calls where you live and travel	1	2	3
c) You had trouble with dropped calls	1	2	3
d) You had problems with the voice quality of the calls you made or received	1	2	3
e) Their contract requirements were unappealing	1	2	3

	Major	Minor	Not at all
f) Their calling plans did not meet your needs	1	2	3
g) Their selection of phones did not meet your needs	1	2	3
h) They made errors on your billing statements	1	2	3
i) They did not provide high-quality customer service	1	2	3
j) Their stores were not conveniently located	1	2	3
k) (IF Q3 = NO) The service was too costly for your needs	1	2	3
(IF Q3 = YES) Their prices were too high			

7. Based on your experience with AT&T Wireless, please rate them on a brief list of attributes. Use a 0-to-10 scale where 0 means the statement does not describe AT&T Wireless and 10 means the statement describes AT&T Wireless very well. You may use any number from 0 to 10. Do you understand the scale? The first statement is (ROTATE). How would you rate AT&T Wireless?

Does not describe
company

Describes the
company well

0   1   2   3   4   5   6   7   8   9   10

Statement   **Rating**

a) The company's coverage area meets your needs

b) You are able to make or receive calls where you live and travel

c) You get few dropped calls

d) Voice quality of the calls is very good

e) Has favorable contract requirements

f) Has calling plans that meet your needs

g) Has a selection of phones that meet your needs

h) Has error-free billing statements

i) Provides high-quality customer service

j) Has conveniently-located stores

k) Has lower prices

These last questions are for classification purposes only.

8. In what year were you born? _____ (year)
   (DON'T READ) Refused (code = 9999)

9. Including yourself, how many in your household are . . . ? (IF NONE, ENTER 0)

   1. Adults 18 years of age and older   _____
   2. Teenagers 13 to 17 years of age   _____
   3. Children 12 years old and younger _____

10. What is your highest level of education?

   1. Some high school
   2. High school graduate or GED
   3. Vocational school
   4. Some college
   5. Graduated from college
   6. Some graduate school, or
   7. Graduate or professional degree
   8. (DO NOT READ) Refused

11. Which of the following best describes your household situation?

   1. Single income provider in your household
   2. Two income providers in your household
   3. More than two income providers in your household, or
   4. None of the above or other situation
   5. (DO NOT READ) Refused

(THANK RESPONDENT)

Case 3.2

IBM: The World's Top Provider of Computer Hardware, Software, and Services

International Business Machines (IBM, www.ibm.com) had been dubbed the proverbial "sinking ship" in the early nineties, but since then, due to the competent leadership of its management team, IBM has made a successful comeback. IBM, with $103.63 billion in revenue in 2008, is the world's top provider of computer hardware, software, and services. More than 50% of IBM's revenues in 2008 can be attributed to sales outside the U.S. Among the leaders in almost every market in which it competes, IBM makes mainframes and servers, storage systems, and peripherals in its hardware product stream. IBM's service arm is the largest in the world. It is also one of the largest providers of both software (ranking number two, behind Microsoft) and semiconductors. IBM has traditionally used acquisitions to augment its software and service businesses, while streamlining its hardware, software, and service operations. In 2007, for the fifteenth consecutive year, IBM was issued more U.S. patents (3,125) than any other company.

IBM has seen significant changes in recent years. It reorganized its hardware business, merging its desktop and laptop operations to concentrate on its leading enterprise server and storage products. Early in 2004, IBM announced that it would also combine its technology (microchips) and systems (servers, storage) groups. Late in 2004, IBM ended the year with an agreement to sell its PC business—a segment that had yielded little profit for the company in recent years—to China's Lenovo.

IBM's growing services business now accounts for almost half of its sales, even though it is traditionally seen as a provider of mainframe hardware. Looking to extend its lead, IBM acquired PricewaterhouseCoopers' consulting and IT services unit, PWC Consulting, for an estimated $3.5 billion in cash and stock. Presenting IBM with a significant integration challenge, the transaction also served the dual purpose of augmenting IBM's standard array of outsourcing, maintenance, and integration services, while moving the company into high-end management consulting.

IBM has largely used acquisitions to become a leader in yet another market—software—where it trails only Microsoft. A pioneer in server operating system (OS) software, IBM made an early move into messaging and network management software with its acquisitions of Lotus Development (1995) and Tivoli (1996). Its software operations now focused primarily on e-commerce infrastructure, IBM has continued its push beyond OS software, purchasing the database operations of Informix (2001) and application integration products from CrossWorlds Software (2002). In 2003, IBM acquired development tool maker Rational Software for $2.1 billion in cash, and it also acquired supply chain software developer Trigo Technologies early in 2004. In early 2005, Lenovo Group Limited completed the acquisition of IBM's Personal Computing Division. IBM's ownership in Lenovo upon closing is 18.9 percent. In the dynamic IT industry, companies need to continually reinvent themselves to bring long-term value for clients. IBM's strategy is to be the world leader in providing high-value solutions—focused on the enterprise and small and medium business clients. In 2007, IBM and Ricoh announced the formation of a joint venture company, the InfoPrint Solutions Company, based on IBM's Printing Systems Division.

In late 2007, IBM acquired Cognos for $5 billion. For IBM, the Cognos acquisition is a continuation of a "growth through mergers-and-acquisitions" effort it launched in February 2006. Since then, IBM has bought 23 software companies as part of its Information on Demand strategy, which combines software and services to help corporations get the most out of all the data they gather about customers and their own business operations.

IBM is one of the top *Fortune* 500 companies. Roughly half of IBM's revenues and profits come from its hardware and software products.

In order to compete with Microsoft, IBM, along with others like Sun, has supported the Linux platform in a big way. Also, the open source initiative that IBM and others have spearheaded is seen as an effective means of cornering Microsoft. To gain support in the developer community, IBM has fully supported Java in its flagship middleware software platform, Websphere, and also in its other parallel

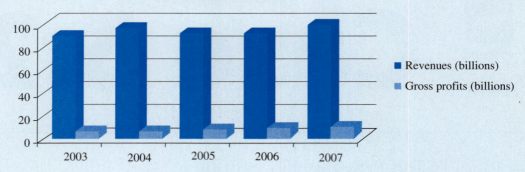

products such as Tivoli. IBM has almost the complete footprint in its product line in the hardware segment and software segment. The only area of software product that IBM conspicuously lacks is the ERP/CRM market, which is now being hotly contested by SAP and Oracle, especially after Oracle's buyout of PeopleSoft. But, even in this segment, IBM has made successful inroads using its Websphere middleware product, which is often preferred by some customers for their applications-integration requirement. Also, IBM's PWC is one of the major players in the ERP/CRM implementation-services market.

In order to maintain this lead, it is important for IBM to ensure that its customers—the managers and decision makers who make purchasing decisions—are satisfied with IBM's hardware and software products. IBM therefore conducted a survey-based study of decision makers in different roles in various companies. The survey participants chose a company, which they evaluated. The company chosen by the participants was IBM or a different company that competes with IBM in some way. The survey, named the IT Industry Customer Benchmark Survey, will be repeated each year. It will provide data on how IBM and its competitors are perceived by customers. The survey questionnaire follows and the data file can be downloaded from the Web site for this book. IBM's management team can use the results of the survey and its analysis to make strategic decisions to improve IBM's standing in the eyes of its customers.

Questions

Chapter 14

1. Run a frequency count on all the variables. Identify the variables with a large number of missing values. How should these missing values be treated?
2. Recode satisfaction (Q4) into two groups: $1-4 =$ Low Satisfaction and $5 =$ High Satisfaction.
3. Recode the Q2 variable to a different variable, "Q2_Recoded," so that the values 1 though 4 of variable Q2 are given value 1 in the variable "Q2_Recoded" and values 5 through 7 of variable Q2 are given value 2.
4. Recode the Q3 variable to a different variable, "Q3_Recoded." The 250 cases for company 55, Microsoft, should be recoded to 1, and the 109 cases for company 26, Compaq/Hewlett-

Packard, should be recoded to 2. All the firm variables for all the remaining cases should be recoded to value 999. The value 999 for the variable Q3_Recoded should be declared as a missing value.

Chapter 15

1. Conduct a frequency count of variables in this database.
2. In this survey, participants of what role (Q1) and what size of companies (Q2) are represented the highest? (Hint: Cross-tabulate variables Q1 and Q2.)
3. Conduct a cross-tabulation of IT role (Q1) with the dimensions of overall measures of the firm being evaluated (variables Q4, Q5, Q6, and Q7).
4. Do the top two companies in terms of frequency of responses (Q3_Recoded) differ on the dimensions of overall measures (Q4, Q5, Q6, and Q7)?
5. For Microsoft (the company with the highest frequency of selection based on Q3), how do the evaluations differ on ratings of "Overall Satisfaction," variable Q4, and "Overall Quality," variable Q7?

   (Hint: First, select the menu, Data → Select cases. Next, in the window that pops up, select variable "Q3" and then click the radio button for the option, "Select - If condition is satisfied." In the next window that pops up, select or type "Q3 = 55" and then click on the "Continue" button. This ensures that only the cases for Microsoft (company 55 per the code book) are selected. Next, execute a paired-samples T-test with "Q4 – Q7" as the paired variables.)
6. For Microsoft (the company with the highest frequency of selection based on Q3), how do the evaluations differ on ratings of "financially sound company," variable Q13, and "company I can trust," variable Q14?

   (Hint: See the hint to question 5.)
7. Is IBM seen as an ethical company?

   (Hint: First ensure that only the cases for IBM (Q3 = 44) are selected.

   Next, conduct a one-sample t test on the variable Q9 to check if the average value is greater than 3.)

Chapter 16

1. Does the evaluation of the IT company on dimensions of overall measures (Q4, Q5, Q6, and Q7) differ according to the role of the evaluator (Q1)? Interpret the results.
2. Conduct two-factor ANOVAs with Q1 and Q2_Recoded as factors and Q4, Q5, Q6, and Q7 as the dependent variables. Interpret the results.

3. Conduct two-factor ANOVAs with Q1 and Q2_Recoded as factors and Q18, Q20, and Q21 as the dependent variables. Interpret the results.

Chapter 17

1. Can the evaluation of the participant on "overall quality of the company in relation to prices" (Q7) be explained in terms of the participants' evaluation on sales and service support variables (Q22, Q23, Q24, Q25, and Q26) when these variables are considered simultaneously?
2. Can the likelihood of purchase from company being evaluated (Q18) be explained in terms of the participants' evaluation on sales and service support variables (Q22, Q23, Q24, Q25, and Q26) when these variables are considered simultaneously?
3. Can the likelihood of recommending the company being evaluated (Q20) be explained in terms of the participants' evaluation on sales and service support variables (Q22, Q23, Q24, Q25, and Q26) when these variables are considered simultaneously?
4. Can the likelihood of purchase from company being evaluated (Q18) be explained in terms of the participants' evaluation on dimensions of overall measures (Q4, Q5, Q6, and Q7)?
5. Create a correlation matrix of the following variables and interpret the results:
   • Variables Q4, Q5, Q6, and Q7
   • Variables Q18, Q19, Q20, and Q21
   • Variables Q22, Q23, Q24, Q25, and Q26

Chapter 18

1. Do survey participants who evaluated the companies with the two highest frequencies differ in terms of dimensions of overall measures (Q4, Q5, Q6, and Q7) when these variables are considered simultaneously?
   (Hint: First, select the menu, Data→ Select cases. Next, in the window that pops up, select variable "Q3_Recoded" and then click the radio button for the option, "Select - If condition is satisfied." In the next window that pops up, select or type "Q3_Recoded < 3" and then click on the "Continue" button. This selects only the cases with Microsoft and Compaq/Hewlett-Packard, the companies with the two highest frequencies. Next, conduct a discriminant analysis with Q3_Recoded as the grouping variable and variables Q4, Q5, Q6, and Q7 as independent variables.)
2. Do survey participants who belong to "Small" companies and "Large" companies (Q2_Recoded) differ in terms of dimensions of overall measures (Q4, Q5, Q6, and Q7) when these variables are considered simultaneously?
3. Do survey participants who have different IT roles (Q1) differ in terms of dimensions of overall measures (Q4, Q5, Q6, and Q7) when these variables are considered simultaneously?
4. Do survey participants who have different IT roles (Q1) differ in terms of sales and service support variables (Q22, Q23, Q24, Q25, and Q26) when these variables are considered simultaneously?
5. Do survey participants who have different IT roles (Q1) differ in terms of future trends variables (Q27A, Q27B, Q27C, Q27D, Q27E, Q27F, and Q27G) when these variables are considered simultaneously?

Chapter 19

1. Can the dimensions of overall measures (Q4, Q5, Q6, and Q7) be represented by a reduced set of variables?
   (Hint: Conduct a principal components analysis for variables Q4, Q5, Q6, and Q7 in the database. Use varimax rotation. Save the factor scores.)
2. Can the image variables (Q8, Q9, Q10, Q11, Q12, Q13, Q14, Q15, Q16, and Q17) be represented by a reduced set of variables?
3. Can the likelihood of purchase variables (Q18, Q19, Q20, and Q21) be represented by a reduced set of variables?
4. Can the sales and service support variables (Q22, Q23, Q24, Q25, and Q26) of the questionnaire be represented by a reduced set of variables?
5. Can the future trends variables (Q27A, Q27B, Q27C, Q27D, Q27E, Q27F, and Q27G) of the questionnaire be represented by a reduced set of variables?

Chapter 20

1. Can the survey participants be segmented on their evaluation of the dimensions of overall measures (Q4, Q5, Q6, and Q7)?
2. Can the survey participants be segmented on the factor scores of dimensions of overall measures (Q4, Q5, Q6, and Q7)?
3. Can the survey participants be segmented on the image variables (Q8 through Q17)?
4. Can the survey participants be segmented on the factor scores of the image variables (Q8 through Q17)?

Chapter 21

1. Provide similarity ratings on a 1 to 7 scale for all possible pairs of the following IT companies (use your impressions even if you are not familiar with them): Apple, Cisco, Compaq/HP, Dell, EMC, Gateway, IBM, Intel, Lucent, and Microsoft. Develop a two-dimensional MDS map. Interpret the dimensions and the map.
2. Construct 32 full profiles of IT companies using the following attributes and the levels: account management (M, H), quality of products (M, H), nontechnical customer service (M, H), training programs (M, H), and technical support (M, H). Rate the 32 profiles in terms of your preference using a 7-point scale (1 = not at all preferred, 7 = greatly preferred). Calculate the part-worth functions and the relative importance of the attributes. Note that M = medium and H = high.

Chapter 22

1. Develop an SEM model that posits image and sales and service support as exogenous constructs. To keep the model manageable, assume that image is measured by the five items of Q8 to Q12. Sales and service support is measured by the five items of Q22 to Q26. Image and sales and service support influence overall evaluation, which in turn determines likelihood of purchase. Overall evaluation is measured by the four "Overall Measures" items of Q4 to Q7. Likelihood of purchase is measured by four items of Q18 to Q21.

a. Specify the measurement model.
b. Estimate the measurement model and assess its reliability and validity.
c. Specify the structural model.
d. Estimate the structural model and assess its validity.
e. Draw conclusions and make recommendations.

Chapter 23

1. Write a report for IBM management summarizing the results of your analyses. What recommendations do you have for the management?

Chapter 24

1. If this survey were to be conducted in France rather than the United States, how would the research process be different?

References

1. www.ibm.com, accessed January 5, 2009.
2. Charles Forelle, "IBM Services Business Bounces Back," *Wall Street Journal* (October 18, 2005): A3, A14.
3. ftp://ftp.software.ibm.com/annualreport/2007/2007_ibm_annual.pdf, accessed November 18, 2008.
4. www.lenovo.com/news/us/en/2005/05/dayone.html, accessed November 18, 2008.
5. www-03.ibm.com/press/us/en/pressrelease/20965.wss, accessed November 18, 2008.
6. www.businessweek.com/technology/content/nov2007/tc20071112_678294.htm, accessed November 18, 2008.

Note: This case was prepared for class discussion purposes only and does not represent the views of IBM or their affiliates. The problem scenario is hypothetical and the name of the actual company has been disguised. However, the questionnaire and the data provided are real. Some questions have been deleted, while the data for other questions are not provided because of proprietary reasons.

2008 IT INDUSTRY CUSTOMER BENCHMARK SURVEY

INTRODUCTION

We are conducting a study to obtain a comprehensive view of your attitudes and perceptions about companies in the IT industry. You will be asked to evaluate the quality, products, and services of key companies in the IT field. We would like **you** to complete the online survey, as we are interested in **your** perspective and opinions. This survey is posted at:

http://survey.pearsonhighered.com/malhotra

The Web site will be available to you for the next several weeks—from today (May 8, 2008) through Friday, June 27, 2008.

We look forward to your feedback.

QUALIFICATION

1. Please select that option that best describes your role within your company. (Please select one to continue.) (Q1)

○ **IT Decision Maker** (e.g., CIO, CTO, VP of IT)—executive with primary authority and decision-making responsibility over your company's IT and the high level relationship with IT vendors (1)
○ **IT Influencer** (e.g. IT Director, Manager)—manager, with decision-making responsibility, who is responsible for the planning, design, and implementation of your company's IT and/or who manages the organizations that operate and maintain your company's IT (2)
○ **IT Staff**—staff member responsible for designing or maintaining the operations of your company's IT and troubleshooting problems (3)
○ Don't Know (9)

IF NOT ANSWERED: "You must answer this question to qualify for the survey."
IF DON'T KNOW: "You must be an IT Decision Maker, Influencer, or Staff to continue the survey."
ALLOW RESPONDENT TO GO BACK AND CHANGE ANSWER; IF STILL NOT ANSWERED OR DON'T KNOW, TERMINATE SURVEY.

2. How many employees are there in your organization? (Q2)

○ 1−49
○ 50−99
○ 100−499
○ 500−999
○ 1,000−4,999
○ 5,000−9,999
○ 10,000 or more
○ Don't Know (99)

IF DON'T KNOW OR NOT ANSWERED: "You must answer this question to qualify for the survey."
ALLOW RESPONDENT TO GO BACK AND CHANGE ANSWER; IF STILL NOT ANSWERED OR DON'T KNOW, TERMINATE SURVEY.

OVERALL MEASURES

3. Please select one of the following vendors that you want to evaluate. (Select one only) (Q3)

ADIC	Hyperion
Alcatel	IBM
3Com	Intel
Adaptec	JD Edwards
ADC	Linksys
Adobe	Lucent
Adtran	Maxtor
Apple	McAfee
Ariba	MetaSolv
Belkin	Microsoft
Black Box	Netgear
Cabletron/Enterasys	Nortel
Cisco	Novell
Compaq/Hewlett-Packard	Onyx
Computer Associates	Oracle
Corel Corporation	Peoplesoft
Datalink	Peregrine Systems
Dell	Quantum
E.piphany	SAP
EMC	Seagate
Exabyte	SMC
Extreme	Sun Microsystems
Fluke Networks	Sybase
Gateway	Symantec
Great Plains	Tivoli Systems
Hitachi	Toshiba

4. How would you rate your <u>overall satisfaction</u> of the selected company? (Q4)

	Very Satisfied 5	Satisfied 4	Neutral 3	Dissatisfied 2	Very Dissatisfied 1	Don't Know 9
Company Selected	O	O	O	O	O	O

5. Considering your own experiences and what you may have read or heard, how would you rate the <u>overall quality</u> of the products, services, and support provided by the selected company? (Q5)

	Excellent 5	Very Good 4	Good 3	Fair 2	Poor 1	Don't Know 9
Company Selected	O	O	O	O	O	O

6. Please evaluate the <u>total cost of ownership</u> for the company including acquisition costs as well as on-going costs. (Q6)

	Very High 5	High 4	Moderate 3	Low 2	Very Low 1	Don't Know 9
Company Selected	O	O	O	O	O	O

7. Considering the overall quality of the company in relation to its prices, how would you rate the <u>value</u> offered? (Q7)

	Excellent 5	Very Good 4	Good 3	Marginal 2	Poor 1	Don't Know 9
Company Selected	O	O	O	O	O	O

IMAGE

For each of the following statements, please indicate your level of agreement.

8. This company seems to care about the community and society. (Q8)

	Strongly Agree 5	Agree 4	Neither Agree Nor Disagree 3	Disagree 2	Strongly Disagree 1	Don't Know 9
Company Selected	O	O	O	O	O	O

9. This company is a highly ethical company. (Q9)

	Strongly Agree 5	Agree 4	Neither Agree Nor Disagree 3	Disagree 2	Strongly Disagree 1	Don't Know 9
Company Selected	O	O	O	O	O	O

10. This company is a leader in the IT industry. (Q10)

	Strongly Agree 5	Agree 4	Neither Agree Nor Disagree 3	Disagree 2	Strongly Disagree 1	Don't Know 9
Company Selected	O	O	O	O	O	O

11. This company is an innovative company. (Q11)

	Strongly Agree 5	Agree 4	Neither Agree Nor Disagree 3	Disagree 2	Strongly Disagree 1	Don't Know 9
Company Selected	O	O	O	O	O	O

12. This company has strong capable senior leaders. (Q12)

	Strongly Agree 5	Agree 4	Neither Agree Nor Disagree 3	Disagree 2	Strongly Disagree 1	Don't Know 9
Company Selected	O	O	O	O	O	O

13. This company is a financially sound company. (Q13)

	Strongly Agree 5	Agree 4	Neither Agree Nor Disagree 3	Disagree 2	Strongly Disagree 1	Don't Know 9
Company Selected	O	O	O	O	O	O

14. This company is a company I can trust. (Q14)

	Strongly Agree 5	Agree 4	Neither Agree Nor Disagree 3	Disagree 2	Strongly Disagree 1	Don't Know 9
Company Selected	O	O	O	O	O	O

15. This company has advertising I really like. (Q15)

	Strongly Agree 5	Agree 4	Neither Agree Nor Disagree 3	Disagree 2	Strongly Disagree 1	Don't Know 9
Company Selected	O	O	O	O	O	O

16. This company is well known for treating its employees well. (Q16)

	Strongly Agree 5	Agree 4	Neither Agree Nor Disagree 3	Disagree 2	Strongly Disagree 1	Don't Know 9
Company Selected	O	O	O	O	O	O

17. Compared to other companies, this company does its fair share to help the community and society. (Q17)

	Strongly Agree 5	Agree 4	Neither Agree Nor Disagree 3	Disagree 2	Strongly Disagree 1	Don't Know 9
Company Selected	O	O	O	O	O	O

LIKELIHOOD OF PURCHASE

18. How likely are you to continue purchasing from this company during the next year? (Q18)

	Extremely Likely 5	Very Likely 4	Somewhat Likely 3	Not Very Likely 2	Not At All Likely 1	Don't Know 9
Company Selected	O	O	O	O	O	O

19. As a percentage, how likely are you to continue purchasing from this company during the next year? As an example, if you know for sure that you will continue, then you would give a 100%. At the opposite extreme, a 0% chance means that you will not purchase from this company again. (Q19)

Percentage Likelihood to Continue

Company Selected   _____

20. If someone asked you to recommend an IT company, what is the likelihood that you would recommend this company? (Q20)

	Extremely Likely	Very Likely	Somewhat Likely	Not Very Likely	Not At All Likely	Don't Know
	5	4	3	2	1	9
Company Selected	O	O	O	O	O	O

21. All other factors staying the same, how likely are you to increase your current purchases of the products and services from this company? (Q21)

	Extremely Likely	Very Likely	Somewhat Likely	Not Very Likely	Not At All Likely	Don't Know
	5	4	3	2	1	9
Company Selected	O	O	O	O	O	O

SALES & SERVICE SUPPORT

22. Overall, how would you rate the quality of the account representative or team? (Q22)

	Excellent	Very Good	Good	Fair	Poor	Don't Know
	5	4	3	2	1	9
Company Selected	O	O	O	O	O	O

23. Overall, how would you rate the overall quality of the products or services purchased including availability, reliability, scalability, and security? (Q23)

	Excellent	Very Good	Good	Fair	Poor	Don't Know
	5	4	3	2	1	9
Company Selected	O	O	O	O	O	O

24. Overall, how would you rate the overall quality of nontechnical customer service? (Q24)

	Excellent	Very Good	Good	Fair	Poor	Don't Know
	5	4	3	2	1	9
Company Selected	O	O	O	O	O	O

25. Overall, how would you rate the overall quality of training or education programs? (Q25)

	Excellent	Very Good	Good	Fair	Poor	Don't Know
	5	4	3	2	1	9
Company Selected	O	O	O	O	O	O

26. Overall, how would you rate the overall quality of technical support? (Q26)

	Excellent	Very Good	Good	Fair	Poor	Don't Know
	5	4	3	2	1	9
Company Selected	O	O	O	O	O	O

FUTURE TRENDS

27. Now please think about your company in the next 3−6 months. (Q27A through Q27G)

	Extremely Likely	Very Likely	Somewhat Likely	Not Very Likely	Not At All Likely	Don't Know
	5	4	3	2	1	9
a. How likely is your company to increase IT spending overall?	O	O	O	O	O	O
b. How likely is your company to outsource existing IT services such as Web hosting or network performance monitoring?	O	O	O	O	O	O

	Extremely Likely	Very Likely	Somewhat Likely	Not Very Likely	Not At All Likely	Don't Know
c. How likely is your company to increase the current level of security measures around your IT structure?	○	○	○	○	○	○
d. How likely is your company to invest in Microsoft's .NET Web services?	○	○	○	○	○	○
e. How likely is your company to consider offering new Web services?	○	○	○	○	○	○
f. How likely is your company to adopt XML language in your company's internal applications?	○	○	○	○	○	○
g. How likely is your company to expand its usage of mobile and wireless devices?	○	○	○	○	○	○

INDUSTRY

28. Please select the industry that best classifies your organization. (Q28)

○ Consumer Packaged Goods
○ Financial Services
○ Health Care
○ Information Technology
○ Manufacturing/Industrial
○ Business Services
○ Telecommunications
○ Utilities
○ Other, please specify: [   ]
○ Don't Know

CLOSING

Your survey has been completed. Thank you for your participation.

Case 3.3

Kimberly-Clark: Competing Through Innovation

The diaper industry has always been in a stage of flux. Right from the beginning of the industry in the early 1960s, this industry has gone through periods of rapid growth and fierce competition. A brief outline of the diaper industry will be helpful in understanding its competitive nature. A new idea, the disposable diaper, revolutionized this industry in the late 1950s. This was the Procter & Gamble (P&G) brand, Pampers. Pampers was advertised to parents as a convenient method of keeping their children clean when they were traveling. However, P&G managed to create a whole new market with Pampers, which eventually led to the creation of a new section in grocery stores. P&G's Pampers had a meteoric growth in popularity and in revenues. Typically a growing industry attracts new players, and one of the companies to give P&G an early fight for market share was Kimberly-Clark (KC). With its Huggies brand that it introduced in the late 1970s, KC was able to successfully gain a share in this market. By the mid-nineties, KC had roughly a third of the disposable diapers market.

Not many other players (other than P&G and KC) have been able to penetrate the disposable diaper market. One of the important reasons for this barrier to entry is technology and innovation. P&G and KC have continuously made innovations and improved technology to make Pampers and Huggies, respectively, extra absorbent and extra convenient. Innovations ranged from creating new absorbent material to avoiding leakages to designing new delicate outer layers for diapers to reduce or avoid the occurrence of diaper rash in infants. In fact, P&G and KC have made so many innovations and have tried so hard to keep each other at bay that there was virtually a diaper-patents race between them for a few years. But, since the mid-eighties, P&G has been dominating the patents that have been filed in this industry.

Other big consumer–packaged goods companies (CPG) did eventually enter this market, such as Johnson & Johnson and Colgate-Palmolive in the mid-seventies. Despite their initial strengths, Colgate-Palmolive and Johnson & Johnson have now all but disappeared from the disposable diaper industry. One of the reasons for this might be attributed to the fact that both of these late entrants had to play catch-up with P&G and KC, who were both innovating rapidly. Perhaps because of the patents that P&G and KC had obtained, it became more difficult for Colgate-Palmolive and Johnson & Johnson to make comparatively superior products.

Because of its inherent nature, the disposable diaper is considered very wasteful and especially harmful to our environment. During the mid-eighties, the disposable industry became a target of the environmental lobby. To counter this problem, P&G increased its own lobbying efforts in Congress and other appropriate forums. P&G and KC, through their advertising, tried to soften this issue and to portray an image of a conscious corporate citizen. P&G eventually made further innovations to make their Pampers product more environmentally friendly.

KC became the dominant player in the disposable diaper market, overtaking P&G in revenues. In 2001, KC had roughly 46 percent of the market share, whereas P&G had 34 percent, mainly through its two product lines, Pampers and Luvs. P&G then, through some shrewd pricing strategies and promotions, seemed to have outmaneuvered KC. By 2003, KC's market share had decreased to around 44 percent and P&G's had increased to 38.5 percent.

In 2006, according to an online KC survey of mothers, 98 percent rated keeping their baby comfortable as an extremely or very important factor when choosing baby care products. In addition, 85 percent of moms said that their child's comfort needs change as they grow. Responding to these needs, KC introduced two new super premium diapers—Huggies Supreme Gentle Care and Huggies Supreme Natural Fit diapers. In North America, net sales increased nearly 5 percent, driven by a more than 6 percent sales volume increase reflecting higher sales of Huggies diapers. KC's earnings through the diapers sector went up from $3.6 billion in 2006 to $4.2 billion in 2007. Total revenues in 2008 amounted to $19.42 billion.

As of 2009, the global market of the disposable diaper industry was around $25 billion, and the economic recession of 2008–2009 seems to have intensified the competition between P&G and KC to capture/increase market share. In an effort to increase market share and customer satisfaction, KC initiated a customer survey. KC wanted to get specific information from potential customers to better understand the market segments and related demographics. Since the focus of a new campaign will be on direct mail, the survey concerns the evaluation of a mailer. The survey questionnaire follows and the data file is provided. Based on the results of this survey, KC management will devise further strategies.

Questions

Chapter 14

1. How would you treat missing values in the following variables that are to be treated as dependent variables: Mailer_Noticed (Q1), Mailer_Opened (Q2), and Likely_Purchase (Q3)?
2. How would you treat missing values in the following variables that are to be treated as independent variables: Info_New_Different (Q6), Info_Appropriate (Q7), Info_Believable (Q8), and Info_Understanding (Q9)?
3. Recode Diaper_Size (Q13) by combining Newborn, One, and Two into a single category and also combining Five, Six, and Some Other Size into a single category.
4. Recode the remaining demographic variables as follows: (a) Age_Range (Q15) categories should be Under 25, 26−30, 31−35, and 36+; (b) Marital_Status (Q16) should be recoded by combining Single, Divorced, Widowed, and Separated into a single category; (c) for Education (Q18), combine Grade School and Some High School into a single category as well as combine Graduated College and Post Graduate Work into another category; (d) Ethnic_Origin (Q19) should have Hispanic/Latino, Asian, and Some Other Race combined into a single category; and (e) Household_Income (Q20) should have the two highest income categories combined into a single category denoted by $50,000 or more.

Chapter 15

1. Calculate an overall rating score for Diaper Dash brand that is the sum of Overall_Quality (Q4a), Brand_I_Trust (Q4b), and Brand_I_Recommend (Q4c). Run a frequency distribution, calculate the summary statistics, and interpret the results.
2. Cross-tabulate Mailer_Noticed (Q1) and Mailer_Opened (Q2) against the original categorical demographic variables. What problems do you see? How could these problems have been averted?
3. Recode the purchase likelihood (Likely_Purchase, Q3) into two groups by combining codes 2, 3, 4, and 5 into a single category. Cross-tabulate the recoded purchase likelihood against the recoded categorical demographic variables.
4. Does the response to the mailer in terms of likelihood of purchase (Likely_Purchase, Q3) differ for respondents in Cell L and Cell M (Screening Q4)? How would your analysis change if this variable were treated as ordinal rather than interval scaled?
5. Do the responses to the mailer in terms of likelihood of purchase (Likely_Purchase, Q3) differ depending upon the gender of baby (boy vs. girl, Screening QH)? How would your analysis change if this variable were treated as ordinal rather than interval scaled?
6. Do the ratings of Diaper Dash (Overall_Quality (Q4a), Brand_I_Trust (Q4b), and Brand_I_Recommend (Q4c)) differ for respondents in Cell L and Cell M (Screening Q4)? How would your analysis change if these variables were treated as ordinal rather than interval scaled?
7. Do the ratings of Diaper Dash brand (Overall_Quality (Q4a), Brand_I_Trust (Q4b), and Brand_I_Recommend (Q4c)) differ depending upon the gender of baby (boy vs. girl, Screening QH)? How would your analysis change if these variables were treated as ordinal rather than interval scaled?
8. Do the respondents evaluate Diaper Dash higher on Brand_I_Trust (Q4b) than they do on Brand_I_Recommend (Q4c)? What analysis would you conduct if these variables were treated as ordinal rather than interval scaled?
9. Do the respondents evaluate the mailer higher on Info_Understanding (Q9) than they do on Info_New_Different (Q6)? What analysis would you conduct if these variables were treated as ordinal rather than interval scaled? Note that lower numbers indicate higher evaluations on these scales.

Chapter 16

1. Can the ratings of Diaper Dash brand (Overall_Quality (Q4a), Brand_I_Trust (Q4b), and Brand_I_Recommend (Q4c)) be explained in terms of the recoded demographic characteristics?
2. Can the message ratings (Info_New_Different (Q6), Info_Appropriate (Q7), Info_Believable (Q8), and Info_Understanding (Q9)) be explained in terms of the recoded demographic characteristics?

Chapter 17

1. Can each of the ratings of Diaper Dash brand (Overall_Quality (Q4a), Brand_I_Trust (Q4b), and Brand_I_Recommend (Q4c)) be explained in terms of message ratings (Info_New_Different (Q6), Info_Appropriate (Q7), Info_Believable (Q8), and Info_Understanding (Q9)) when responses to the message are considered simultaneously?
2. Can each of the mailer ratings (High_Quality_Brand (Q10a), Info_is_Informative (Q10b), and Info_I_Want (Q10c)) be explained in terms of message ratings (Info_New_Different (Q6), Info_Appropriate (Q7), Info_Believable (Q8), and Info_Understanding (Q9)) when responses to the mailer are considered simultaneously?
3. Can the Likely_Purchase (Likely_Purchase, Q3) be explained in terms of message ratings (Info_New_Different (Q6), Info_Appropriate (Q7), Info_Believable (Q8), and Info_Understanding (Q9)) when responses to the message are considered simultaneously? Interpret the results of your analysis.

Chapter 18

1. Recode the purchase likelihood (Likely_Purchase, Q3) into two groups by combining codes 2, 3, 4, and 5 into a single category. Run a two-group discriminant analysis with recoded Likely_Purchase as the dependent variable and responses to the message ratings (Info_New_Different (Q6), Info_Appropriate (Q7), Info_Believable (Q8), and Info_Understanding (Q9)) as the independent variables. Interpret the results.
2. Recode each of the ratings of Diaper Dash brand (Overall_Quality (Q4a), Brand_I_Trust (Q4b), and Brand_I_Recommend (Q4c)) into two groups (1 to 8 = Group 1, 9 and 10 = Group 2). Run three two-group discriminant analyses with message ratings (Info_New_Different (Q6), Info_Appropriate (Q7), Info_Believable (Q8), and Info_Understanding (Q9)) as the independent variables. Interpret the results.

3. Recode each of the ratings of Diaper Dash brand (Overall_Quality (Q4a), Brand_I_Trust (Q4b), and Brand_I_Recommend (Q4c)) into three groups (1 to 7 = Group 1, 8 and 9 = Group 2, and 10 = Group 3). Run three three-group discriminant analyses with message ratings (Info_New_Different (Q6), Info_Appropriate (Q7), Info_Believable (Q8), and Info_Understanding (Q9)) as the independent variables. Interpret the results.

Chapter 19

1. Factor analyze Diaper Dash brand ratings (Overall_Quality (Q4a), Brand_I_Trust (Q4b), and Brand_I_Recommend (Q4c)). Use principal components with varimax rotation. Interpret and explain the results.
2. Factor analyze the message ratings (Info_New_Different (Q6), Info_Appropriate (Q7), Info_Believable (Q8), and Info_Understanding (Q9)). Use principal components with varimax rotation. Interpret and explain the results.
3. Factor analyze the mailer ratings (High_Quality_Brand (Q10a), Info_is_Informative (Q10b), and Info_I_Want (Q10c)). Use principal components with varimax rotation. Interpret and explain the results.

Chapter 20

1. Cluster the respondents based on message ratings (Info_New_Different (Q6), Info_Appropriate (Q7), Info_Believable (Q8), and Info_Understanding (Q9)). Interpret the results.

Chapter 21

1. Construct 16 full profiles using the following attribute levels: style (print/colors, plain white), absorbency (regular, super absorbent), taping (regular tape, resealable tape), and leakage (regular, leak-proof). Rank the 16 full profiles in terms of preference. Calculate the part-worth functions and the importance of each attribute.

Chapter 22

1. Develop an SEM model that posits brand ratings (measured by items Q4a, Q4b, and Q4c), message ratings (measured by Q6, Q7, Q8, and Q9), and mailer ratings (measured by items Q10a, Q10b, and Q10c) as exogenous variables. These three exogenous variables determine mailer impressions (measured by Q1, Q2, and Q3).
   a. Specify the measurement model.
   b. Estimate the measurement model and assess its reliability and validity.
   c. Specify the structural model.
   d. Estimate the structural model and assess its validity.
   e. Draw conclusions and make recommendations.

Chapter 23

1. Write a report for Kimberly-Clark based on all the analyses that you have conducted. What would you recommend that Kimberly-Clark do in order to increase market share?

Chapter 24

1. If the survey conducted by Kimberly-Clark were to be conducted in Australia, how should the marketing research be conducted?

References

1. www.kimberly-clark.com, accessed January 12, 2009.
2. http://files.shareholder.com/downloads/KMB/0x0x172215/1bca372c-279a-47d8-bed3-dc9cd4e19a88/KMB_News_2006_8_23_Brands/Businesses.pdf, accessed November 18, 2008.
3. http://rkconline.net/AR/KimberlyClark07/PDF/AR07.pdf, accessed November 18, 2008.

Note: This case was prepared for class discussion purposes only and does not represent the views of Kimberly-Clark or their affiliates. The problem scenario is hypothetical and the name of the actual company has been disguised. However, the questionnaire and the data provided are real. Some questions have been deleted, while the data for other questions are not provided because of proprietary reasons.

DIRECT MAIL EVALUATION SCREENING INFORMATION QUESTIONNAIRE

Resp# (1−5)

Card 01 (6−7)

1. Enter Respondent Name: _____
2. Enter Respondent Phone Number beginning with the area code in this format (###)###-####.
   Phone #: _____

3. City

   ☐ 1 Littleton   ☐ 6 Lake Grove
   ☐ 2 Troy   ☐ 7 Puyallup   (21−22)
   ☐ 3 Downey   ☐ 8 Springfield
   ☐ 4 Memphis   ☐ 9 St. Peters
   ☐ 5 Burnsville   ☐ 10 Tallahassee

4. Cell Assignment

   ☐ 1 Cell L   (23)
   ☐ 2 Cell M

SCREENING INFORMATION

QG. Enter age of youngest child in diapers.

Age [   ] Months   (24−25)

QH. Gender of Baby

☐ 1 Boy   (26)
☐ 2 Girl

QI. Brand of diaper use most of the time

(27)	☐	Wet 'b Gone Ultra
(28)	☐	Wet 'b Gone Super
(29)	☐	Huggies Overnites
(30)	☐	Huggies Super
(31)	☐	Huggies (DK Type)
(32)	☐	Bottom's Dry Super
(33)	☐	Bottom's Dry Overnites
(34)	☐	Bottom's Dry Sensitive
(35)	☐	Bottom's Dry Sooper Dooper
(36)	☐	Bottom's Dry (DK Type)
(37)	☐	Diaper Duty (Any)
(38)	☐	Store Brand
(39)	☐	Other (Specify) _____

Supervisor Check Box

(40−43) other (39)=& DK

MAIN QUESTIONNAIRE

MAILER IMPRESSION

(Escort respondent to interviewing area. Pay careful attention to the Code. Make sure the respondent is evaluating the correct mail piece for the appropriate Code.)

In front of you is a mailer that you might receive in the mail at your home, about which we would like your opinions.

I'd like you to open and look through the mailer the way you would if you received this in the mail. Please let me know when you are finished.

(Allow respondent time to examine the mailer.)

Q1. Would you have noticed this mailer if it came to your home in the mail, or not?

Yes ☐−1
No ☐−2 (44)
Don't Know ☐−3

Q2. Would you have opened this mailer if it came to your home in the mail, or not?

Yes ☐−1
No ☐−2 (45)
Don't Know ☐−3

Q3. How likely are you to purchase this brand of diapers?
Would you say you . . . (read list)?

Definitely would purchase ☐−1
Probably would purchase ☐−2
Might or might not purchase ☐−3
Probably would not purchase ☐−4 (45)
Definitely would not purchase ☐−5
DK/Refuse ☐−6

BRAND RATINGS/MAIN IDEA

Q4. Now, I would like you to tell me what you think of Huggies diapers by rating Huggies on several characteristics using the scale from "1" to "10" with "1" being the lowest possible rating and "10" being the highest possible rating.

Of course, you can give any number from "1" to "10."

The <u>first/next characteristic</u> is (<u>characteristic</u>). Using the 1 to 10 scale, how would you rate Huggies for (<u>characteristic</u>)?

Clear initial DK's: Just based on anything you know about Huggies, how would you rate Huggies from the standpoint of (<u>characteristic</u>).

(Rotate attributes.)

		Lowest Rating									Highest Rating	DK

a. _____ Overall quality ☐−1 ☐−2 ☐−3 ☐−4 ☐−5 ☐−6 ☐−7 ☐−8 ☐−9 ☐−10 ☐−99 (47−48)

b. _____ Is a brand I trust ☐−1 ☐−2 ☐−3 ☐−4 ☐−5 ☐−6 ☐−7 ☐−8 ☐−9 ☐−10 ☐−99 (49−50)

c. _____ Is a brand I would recommend to others ☐−1 ☐−2 ☐−3 ☐−4 ☐−5 ☐−6 ☐−7 ☐−8 ☐−9 ☐−10 ☐−99 (51−52)

Q5. What, if anything, do you think is the main idea of this mailer?
What else? **(Probe until unproductive, allow for multiple responses. Record first mentions separately.) (Record on Open End Answer Sheet.)**

MESSAGE RATINGS

Q6. Thinking about the information in this mailer, how new and different would you consider this information to be? Would you say it is . . . (read list)?

Extremely New and Different ☐−1
Very New and Different ☐−2
Somewhat New and Different ☐−3 (53)
Slightly New and Different ☐−4
Not at All New and Different ☐−5
DK/Refuse ☐−6

Q7. How appropriate would you say the information in this mailer is for your baby? Would you say it is . . . (read list)?

Very appropriate ☐−1
Somewhat appropriate ☐−2
Neither appropriate nor inappropriate ☐−3
Somewhat inappropriate ☐−4 (54)
Very inappropriate ☐−5
DK/Refuse ☐−6

Q8. How believable is the information in this mailer? Would you say it is . . . (read list)?

Extremely Believable ☐−1
Very Believable ☐−2
Somewhat Believable ☐−3 (55)
Not Very Believable ☐−4
Not at All Believable ☐−5
DK/Refuse ☐−6

Q9. How easy or difficult to understand is the information in this mailer? Would you say it is . . . (read list)?

Very Easy ☐−1
Somewhat Easy ☐−2
Neither Easy nor Difficult ☐−3 (56)
Somewhat Difficult ☐−4
Very Difficult ☐−5
DK/Refuse ☐−6

MAILER RATINGS

(Hand respondent Agreement Card.)

Q10. I am going to read you several statements that may be used to describe this mailer. Using the phrases on this card, please tell me whether you agree strongly, agree somewhat, neither agree nor disagree, disagree somewhat, or disagree strongly that each of these statements describes the mailer.

The (first/next) statement is, the mailer (insert attribute).

Do you agree strongly, agree somewhat, neither agree nor disagree, disagree somewhat, or disagree strongly that the statement describes the product you tried for us?

(Clear initial DK's: Just based on any impression you may have about this product, how much do you agree or disagree that the product you tried for us (insert statement)?

(If necessary, clear further with: Is that (agree/disagree) strongly or somewhat?)

(Rotate attributes.)

	Agree Strongly	Agree Somewhat	Neither Agree nor Disagree	Disagree Somewhat	Disagree Strongly	DK
a. _____ Is for a high quality brand	□–5	□–4	□–3	□–2	□–1	□–9 (57)
b. _____ Is informative	□–5	□–4	□–3	□–2	□–1	□–9 (58)
c. _____ Has information I want to know	□–5	□–4	□–3	□–2	□–1	□–9 (59)

Q11. How likely would you be to use the coupons in the mailer? Would you say . . . (read list)?

Very Likely	□–1
Somewhat Likely	□–2
Neither Likely Nor Unlikely	□–3 (60)
Somewhat Unlikely	□–4
Very Unlikely	□–5
DK/Refuse	□–6

DEMOGRAPHICS

These next few questions are to help us divide our interviews into groups.
Please consider your (qualifying child age from QG) month old (qualifying child gender from QH) when answering these questions.

Q12. How sensitive would you say your child's skin is at the diaper area? Would you say it is . . . **(read list)**?

Very Sensitive	□–1
Somewhat Sensitive	□–2
A Little Sensitive	□–3 (61)
Not at All Sensitive	□–4
DK/Refused	□–5

Q13. What size disposable diaper does this child usually wear?

Newborn	□–1
One	□–2
Two	□–3
Three	□–4 (62)
Four	□–5
Five	□–6
Six	□–7
Some Other Size	□–8
DK/Refused	□–9

Q14. Is this your first baby, or not?

Yes	□–1
No	□–2 (63)
DK/Refused	□–3

Q15. Which of the following ranges best describes your age? **(Read list)**

Under 18	□–1
18–25	□–2
26–30	□–3
31–35	□–4 (64)
36–40	□–5
41–45	□–6
46+	□–7
DK/Refused	□–8

Q16. What is your marital status?

Single	☐−1
Married	☐−2
Divorced	☐−3 (65)
Widowed	☐−4
Separated	☐−5
DK/Refused	☐−6

Q17. Are you employed outside your home, or not? (**If yes**: "Is that full time or part time?")

YES, Part time	☐−1
YES, Full time	☐−2 (66)
NO, Not Employed	☐−3
DK/Refused	☐−4

Q18. What was the last grade of school you, yourself, completed?

Grade School	☐−1
Some High School	☐−2
Graduated High School/Technical School	☐−3
Some College	☐−4 (67)
Graduated College	☐−5
Post Graduate Work	☐−6
DK/Refused	☐−7

Q19. What is your ethnic origin?

White	☐−1
Black/African American	☐−2
Hispanic/Latino	☐−3 (68)
Asian	☐−4
Some Other Race	☐−5
DK/Refused	☐−6

Q20. What is your total yearly household income, before taxes?
(**Read list if necessary.**)

Under $15,000	☐−1
$15,000 and over but less than $25,000	☐−2
$25,000 and over but less than $35,000	☐−3
$35,000 and over but less than $50,000	☐−4 (69)
$50,000 and over but less than $75,000	☐−5
or, $75,000 or more	☐−6
DK/Refused	☐−7

THANK RESPONDENT FOR PARTICIPATING.

SPSS

SPSS Data File

S.sas.

SAS Data File

Case 4.1

Comprehensive Cases with Real Data

JPMorgan Chase: Chasing Growth Through Mergers and Acquisitions

JPMorgan Chase is a leading global financial services firm that provides broad-range investment banking, financial services for consumers, small business and commercial banking, financial transaction processing, asset management, and private equity services. As of 2009, JPMorgan Chase operates in more than 60 countries with more than 200,000 employees. JPMorgan Chase serves millions of U.S. consumers and many of the world's most prominent corporate, institutional, and government clients. JPMorgan Chase is a component of the Dow Jones Industrial Average.

With more than $2.3 trillion in assets, JPMorgan Chase is one of the largest banks in the United States. The company is not only doing well currently, with a promising future, but it also has a noteworthy history.

JPMorgan Chase & Co. was founded in New York in 1799. The firm is built on the foundation of nearly 1,000 predecessor institutions that have come together over the years to form today's company. Here are some highlights from its recent history and the key transactions leading up to the formation of JPMorgan Chase:

- In 1991, Chemical Banking Corp. combined with Manufacturers Hanover Corp., keeping the name

Chemical Banking Corp., then the second-largest banking institution in the United States.
- In 1995, First Chicago Corp. merged with National Bank of Detroit's parent NBD Bancorp., forming First Chicago NBD, the largest banking company based in the Midwest.
- In 1996, Chase Manhattan Corp. merged with Chemical Banking Corp., creating what was then the largest bank holding company in the United States.
- In 1998, Banc One Corp. merged with First Chicago NBD, taking the name Bank One Corp. Merging subsequently with Louisiana's First Commerce Corp., Bank One became the largest financial services firm in the Midwest, the fourth-largest bank in the United States, and the world's largest Visa credit card issuer.
- In 2000, JPMorgan & Co. merged with Chase Manhattan Corp., in effect combining four of the largest and oldest money center banking institutions in New York City (JPMorgan, Chase, Chemical, and Manufacturers Hanover) into one firm called JPMorgan Chase & Co.
- In 2004, JPMorgan Chase merged with Bank One.
- In 2008, JPMorgan Chase acquired Washington Mutual's deposits for $1.9 billion after the largest bank failure in U.S. history.

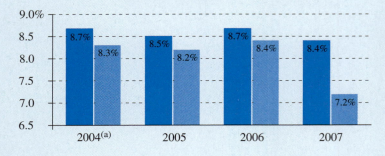

Peer Comparison of Tier 1 Capital Ratios

■ Tier 1 Capital Ratio—JPMorgan Chase

■ Tier 1 Capital Ratio Peers
(Bank of America, Citi, Wachovia, Wells Farg

(a) 2004 data are pro forma combined, reflecting the merger of JPMorgan Chase and Bank One

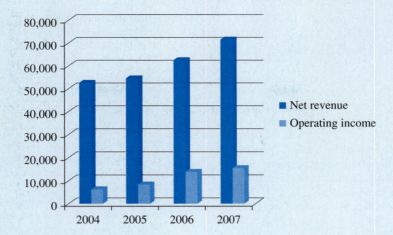

The acquisition of other companies is one of the primary methods that JPMorgan has used to grow its numbers and can be considered a strength in regard to how these mergers have combined to give rise to a broad range of commercial and investment banking capabilities.

JPMorgan achieved its best overall ranking ever in the 2008 *Institutional Investor* magazine's annual survey of U.S. equity analysts. The firm captured 38 spots—the most ever for JPMorgan—placing the team second overall in the survey, up from fourth place in 2007. One noteworthy ranking is that JPMorgan ranked #1 with their top 150 priority clients for the second year in a row.

In order to sustain growth that is so important in its strategic and long-term plans, JPMorgan Chase conducted a study to understand its consumers, their lifestyles, and potential for customer segmentation in terms of investment products and service needs. The questionnaire used follows and the data file can be downloaded from the Web site for this book. The outputs and the analyses of this study should help JPMorgan Chase carve its growth plan and its successful implementation.

Questions

Chapter 1

1. Discuss the role that marketing research can play in helping JPMorgan Chase formulate sound marketing strategies.

Chapter 2

1. Management would like to further expand JPMorgan Chase's market share in the consumer market. Define the management decision problem.
2. Define an appropriate marketing research problem based on the management decision problem you have identified.

Chapter 3

1. Formulate an appropriate research design for investigating the marketing research problem that you have defined in Chapter 2.

Chapter 4

1. Use the Internet to determine the market shares of the major banks for the last calendar year.
2. What type of syndicate data will be useful to JPMorgan Chase?

Chapter 5

1. Discuss the role of focus groups versus depth interviews in helping JPMorgan Chase expand its market share.

Chapter 6

1. If a survey is to be conducted to determine consumer preferences for banks, which survey method should be used and why?

Chapter 7

1. Discuss the role of preexperimental versus true experimental designs in helping JPMorgan Chase expand its product offerings.

Chapter 8

1. Illustrate the use of paired comparison and constant sum scales in measuring consumer preferences for banks. Should any of these scales be used?

Chapter 9

1. Develop a multi-item scale for measuring attitudes toward JPMorgan Chase bank.

Chapter 10

1. Critically evaluate the questionnaire developed for the JPMorgan Chase survey.

Chapters 11 and 12

1. What sampling plan should be adopted for the survey of Chapter 6? How should the sample size be determined?

Chapter 13

1. How would you supervise and evaluate fieldworkers for conducting the survey of Chapter 6?

Chapter 14

1. Many of the importance items have more than 10 percent missing values. Identify these items. How would you address these missing values?

2. Recode the following demographic characteristics into the categories specified: (a) Age (Q9) (27–57 = 1, 58–68 = 2, 69–75 = 3, 76–90 = 4); (b) Marital status (Q11) (now married = 1, all other, i.e., now not married = 2); (c) number of dependent children (Q12) (3–10 = 3); and (d) education (Q14) (combine some high school, high school graduate, and vocational or technical school into a single category, and also combine law school graduate, dental/medical school graduate, and doctorate into a single category).

3. Recode the advantage of using primary provider (Q5) into two categories (1–3 = 1 (small advantage), 4–5 = 2 (big advantage)).

4. Recode overall satisfaction with service provider (Q6_a) into three categories (2–4 = 1, 5 = 2, 6 = 3).

Chapter 15

1. Calculate an overall rating score for the primary financial provider by summing the ratings of all the 13 items in Q6 (Q6_a through Q6_m). Obtain a frequency distribution and summary statistics. Interpret the results.

2. Are the decision-making approaches (Q8) related to any of the demographic characteristics (Q9 through Q15, as recoded in Chapter 14)?

3. Is the recoded advantage of using primary provider (Recoded Q5) related to any of the recoded demographic characteristics?

4. Is the recoded advantage of using primary provider (Recoded Q5) related to any of the importance variables (Q1_a through Q1_l)? How would your analysis change if the importance variables were treated as ordinal rather than interval scaled?

5. Is the recoded advantage of using primary provider (Recoded Q5) related to any of the ratings of the primary financial provider (Q6_a through Q6_m)? How would your analysis change if the importance variables were treated as ordinal rather than interval scaled?

6. Is "the performance of investments with this provider" (Q1_a) more important than "online services offered" (Q1_e)? Formulate the null and alternative hypotheses and conduct an appropriate test. How would your analysis change if these variables were treated as ordinal rather than interval scaled?

7. Is the likelihood of "recommend your primary provider to someone you know" (Q2) lower than the likelihood of "continue to use your primary provider at least at the same level as up to now" (Q3)? Formulate the null and alternative hypotheses and conduct an appropriate test. How would your analysis change if these variables were treated as ordinal rather than interval scaled?

Chapter 16

1. Can the decision-making approaches (Q8) explain any of the importance variables (Q1_a through Q1_l)?

2. Is there a relationship between the importance variables considered individually (Q1_a through Q1_l) and the recoded demographic characteristics (Q9 through Q15)?

Chapter 17

1. Can the likelihood of "recommend your primary provider to someone you know" (Q2) be explained by the ratings of the primary financial provider (Q6_a through Q6_m) when these ratings are considered simultaneously?

2. Can the likelihood of "continue to use your primary provider at least at the same level as up to now" (Q3) be explained by the ratings of the primary financial provider (Q6_a through Q6_m) when these ratings are considered simultaneously?

Chapter 18

1. Is the recoded advantage of using primary provider (Recoded Q5) related to any of the importance variables (Q1_a through Q1_l) when they are considered simultaneously? Run a two-group discriminant analysis as well as logit analysis and compare the results.

2. Do the ratings of the primary financial provider (Q6_a through Q6_m) considered simultaneously explain who switched some assets from one investment/savings provider to another and who did not (Q7)? Run a two-group discriminant analysis as well as logit analysis and compare the results.

Chapter 19

1. Can the importance variables (Q1_a through Q1_l) be represented by a reduced set of factors? Conduct a principal components analysis using varimax rotation. Save the factor scores.

2. Can the ratings of the primary financial provider (Q6_a through Q6_m) be represented by a reduced set of factors? Conduct a principal components analysis using varimax rotation. Save the factor scores.

3. Can the likelihood of "recommend your primary provider to someone you know" (Q2) be explained by the factor scores of ratings of the primary financial provider (Q6_a through Q6_m) when these factor scores are considered simultaneously?

4. Can the likelihood of "continue to use your primary provider at least at the same level as up to now" (Q3) be explained by the factor scores of ratings of the primary financial provider (Q6_a through Q6_m) when these factor scores are considered simultaneously?

5. Do the factor scores of ratings of the primary financial provider (Q6_a through Q6_m) considered simultaneously explain who switched some assets from one investment/savings provider to another and who did not (Q7)?

6. Do the factor scores of ratings of the primary financial provider (Q6_a through Q6_m) considered simultaneously explain the various decision-making approaches (Q8)?

7. Do the factor scores of the importance variables (Q1_a through Q1_l) considered simultaneously explain the various decision-making approaches (Q8)?

Chapter 20

1. Cluster the respondents based on the importance variables (Q1_a through Q1_l). Use K-means clustering and specify a two-cluster solution. Interpret the resulting clusters.

2. Cluster the respondents based on the factor scores of the importance variables (Q1_a through Q1_l). Use K-means clustering and specify a two-cluster solution. Interpret the resulting clusters. Compare your results to those obtained by clustering on the original importance variables.

Chapter 21

1. Provide similarity ratings on a 1 to 7 scale for all possible pairs of the following financial services companies (use your

impressions even if you are not familiar with them): Bank of America, JPMorgan Chase, Citibank, Fidelity Investments, Goldman Sachs, SunTrust Bank, New York Life, T. Rowe Price, Vanguard, and Wells Fargo. Develop a two-dimensional MDS map. Interpret the dimensions and the map.

2. Construct 32 full profiles of financial services companies using the following attributes and the levels: performance of investments (M, H), fees or commissions (M, H), ability to resolve problems (M, H), quality of advice (M, H), and quality of service (M, H). Rate the 32 profiles in terms of your preference using a 7-point scale (1 = not at all preferred, 7 = greatly preferred). Calculate the part-worth functions and the relative importance of the attributes. Note that M = medium and H = high.

Chapter 22

Develop an SEM model that posits evaluation of the primary financial provider (measured by the first five items, a to e, of question 6) as an exogenous construct and patronage intent as an endogenous construct. Only the first five items of Q6 are considered to keep the model manageable. The endogenous construct is measured by Q2, Q3, Q4, and Q5.

1. Specify the measurement model.
2. Estimate the measurement model and assess its reliability and validity.
3. Specify the structural model.
4. Estimate the structural model and assess its validity.
5. Draw conclusions and make recommendations.

Chapter 23

1. Write a report for JPMorgan Chase based on all the analyses that you have conducted. What do you recommend that JPMorgan Chase do in order to continue to grow?

Chapter 24

1. If the survey conducted by JPMorgan Chase were to be conducted in Argentina, how should the marketing research be conducted?

References

1. www.jpmorganchase.com, accessed March 18, 2009.
2. www.jpmorganchase.com/cm/cs?pagename=Chase/Href& urlname=jpmc/about/history, accessed November 18, 2008.
3. www.jpmorganchase.com/cm/BlobServer?blobtable= Document&blobcol=urlblob&blobkey=name&blobheader= application/pdf&blobnocache=true&blobwhere=jpmc/about/ history/shorthistory.pdf, accessed November 18, 2008.
4. http://files.shareholder.com/downloads/ONE/46864433 4x0x184756/31e544ec-a273-4228-8c2a-8e46127783f8/ 2007ARComplete.pdf, accessed November 18, 2008.
5. http://investor.shareholder.com/JPMorganChase/press/ releases.cfm, accessed November 18, 2008.

Note: This case was prepared for class discussion purposes only and does not represent the views of JPMorgan Chase or their affiliates. The problem scenario is hypothetical and the name of the actual company has been disguised. However, the questionnaire and the data provided are real. Some questions have been deleted, while the data for other questions are not provided because of proprietary reasons.

ANNUAL FINANCIAL SERVICES SURVEY

Introduction

This survey asks some questions about financial services, i.e., about investments and banking. The **primary financial services provider** (company) is where you have the **largest** portion of your household's investments and savings/checking assets.

Your co-operation in answering these questions is greatly appreciated.

Part A. Financial Services Provider

1. If you were selecting a **primary financial provider (company) today**, how important would each of the following be to you? **(X ONE Box for EACH)**

	Extremely Important	Very Important	Somewhat Important	Somewhat Unimportant	Not Important At All
a. Performance of investments with this provider	5 ☐	4 ☐	3 ☐	2 ☐	1 ☐
b. Fees or commissions charged	5 ☐	4 ☐	3 ☐	2 ☐	1 ☐
c. Depth of products and services to meet the range of your investment needs	5 ☐	4 ☐	3 ☐	2 ☐	1 ☐
d. Ability to resolve problems.	5 ☐	4 ☐	3 ☐	2 ☐	1 ☐
e. Online services offered	5 ☐	4 ☐	3 ☐	2 ☐	1 ☐
f. Multiple providers' products to choose from.	5 ☐	4 ☐	3 ☐	2 ☐	1 ☐
g. Quality of advice	5 ☐	4 ☐	3 ☐	2 ☐	1 ☐
h. Knowledge of representatives or advisors you deal with	5 ☐	4 ☐	3 ☐	2 ☐	1 ☐
i. Representative knowing your overall situation and needs	5 ☐	4 ☐	3 ☐	2 ☐	1 ☐
j. Access to other professional resources	5 ☐	4 ☐	3 ☐	2 ☐	1 ☐
k. Degree to which my provider knows me	5 ☐	4 ☐	3 ☐	2 ☐	1 ☐
l. Quality of service.	5 ☐	4 ☐	3 ☐	2 ☐	1 ☐

	Extremely Likely	Very Likely	Somewhat Likely	Somewhat Unlikely	Very Unlikely
2. How **likely** are you to recommend your primary provider to someone you know? (**X ONE Box**)	5 ☐	4 ☐	3 ☐	2 ☐	1 ☐
3. How **likely** is it that you will continue to use your primary provider at least at the same level as up to now? (**X ONE Box**)	5 ☐	4 ☐	3 ☐	2 ☐	1 ☐
4. How **likely** is it that you or your household will **drop** or **replace** your primary provider? (**X ONE Box**)	5 ☐	4 ☐	3 ☐	2 ☐	1 ☐

	Very Big	Big	Some	Slight	None
5. How would you rate the **advantage** to you of using your primary provider rather than other financial services providers? (**X ONE Box**)	5 ☐	4 ☐	3 ☐	2 ☐	1 ☐

6. How would you rate the following elements of your **primary financial provider (company)?** If it is not applicable, select "NA." (**X ONE Box for EACH Statement**)

	Excellent	Very Good	Good	Fair	Poor	NA
a. Overall satisfaction with primary provider	6 ☐	5 ☐	4 ☐	3 ☐	2 ☐	1 ☐
b. Performance of investments with this provider	6 ☐	5 ☐	4 ☐	3 ☐	2 ☐	1 ☐
c. Fees or commissions charged	6 ☐	5 ☐	4 ☐	3 ☐	2 ☐	1 ☐
d. Depth of products and services to meet the range of your investments needs	6 ☐	5 ☐	4 ☐	3 ☐	2 ☐	1 ☐
e. Ability to resolve problems.	6 ☐	5 ☐	4 ☐	3 ☐	2 ☐	1 ☐
f. Online services offered	6 ☐	5 ☐	4 ☐	3 ☐	2 ☐	1 ☐
g. Multiple providers' products to choose from	6 ☐	5 ☐	4 ☐	3 ☐	2 ☐	1 ☐
h. Quality of advice	6 ☐	5 ☐	4 ☐	3 ☐	2 ☐	1 ☐
i. Knowledge of representatives or advisors you deal with	6 ☐	5 ☐	4 ☐	3 ☐	2 ☐	1 ☐
j. Representative knowing your overall situation and needs	6 ☐	5 ☐	4 ☐	3 ☐	2 ☐	1 ☐
k. Access to other professional resources	6 ☐	5 ☐	4 ☐	3 ☐	2 ☐	1 ☐
l. Degree to which my provider knows me	6 ☐	5 ☐	4 ☐	3 ☐	2 ☐	1 ☐
m. Quality of service.	6 ☐	5 ☐	4 ☐	3 ☐	2 ☐	1 ☐

7. During the past 12 months, have you or anyone in your household switched some assets (other than checking account assets) from one investment/savings **provider** to another? (Do NOT include switching money from one individual investment such as a stock or bond to another stock or bond within the same brokerage or investment company.) Please **exclude** assets in a 401(k), 403(b), 457, or similar defined contribution retirement accounts.

    1. ☐ Yes ⟶ (**Continue**)   2. ☐ No ⟶ (**Skip to Section IV**)

8. The following are some different approaches you and/or your household might take regarding advice and investment decision making. Please read each one and then answer the question below.
   1. Using a variety of online or offline information sources, you make your own investment decisions without the assistance of an investment professional or advisor.
   2. Using a variety of online or offline information sources, you make most of your own investment decisions but use an investment professional or advisor for specialized needs only (e.g., alternative investments or tax advice).
   3. You regularly consult with an investment professional or advisor and you may also get additional information yourself, but you make most of the final decisions.
   4. You rely upon an investment professional or advisor to make most or all your investment decisions.

   For the majority of your assets, which ONE of the previous approaches (1−4) BEST describes your preferred approach? (**Write in a number from 1–4.**)
   Number: _____

Your answers to the following questions will be used to help us interpret the information you have provided.

9. What is your age?

   Age: _____ years

10. Are you . . . ?

    1. ☐ Male   2. ☐ Female

11. What is your current marital status? **(X ONE Box)**

    1. ☐ Now married   3. ☐ Divorced   5. ☐ Single, never married
    2. ☐ Widowed   4. ☐ Separated   6. ☐ Living together, not married

12. How many people in your household are dependent children? **(Write In)** # _____

13. How many other dependents are you supporting (e.g., parents, grandparents)? **(Write In)** # _____

14. For the following type of financial transaction, please indicate who is <u>primarily</u> responsible, or if the responsibilities are shared. **(X ONE Box for Each)**

	Male Head of Household	Female Head of Household	Shared Equally	Other
Investment decision making	1 ☐	2 ☐	3 ☐	4 ☐

15. What is the highest level of education you have completed? **(X ONE Box)**

    01 ☐ Some high school   06 ☐ Some graduate school
    02 ☐ High school graduate   07 ☐ Master's degree
    03 ☐ Vocational or technical school/apprenticeship 08 ☐ Law school graduate
    04 ☐ Some college   09 ☐ Dental/medical school graduate
    05 ☐ College graduate   10 ☐ Doctorate

16. What is your retirement status? **(X ONE Box)**

    1. ☐ Retired   2. ☐ Semi-Retired   3. ☐ Not Retired

Case 4.2

Wendy's: History and Life After Dave Thomas

Wendy's/Arby's Group, Inc. (www.wendysarbys.com) is the number three hamburger chain by sales, which trail only those of McDonald's and Burger King. The Group is comprised of the Wendy's® and Arby's® brands, two companies distinguished by traditions of quality food and service. The company, with approximately $12 billion in system-wide sales in 2008, owns or franchises more than 10,000 restaurants.

Wendy's/Arby's Group, Inc., restaurants offer burgers and fries as well as alternative items such as baked potatoes, chili, and salads. Each Wendy's restaurant offers a standard menu featuring hamburgers and chicken breast sandwiches, prepared to order with the customer's choice of condiments, as well as chicken nuggets, chili, baked potatoes, french fries, salads, desserts, soft drinks, and children's meals. Arby's serves traditional fast food with items such as slow-roasted and freshly sliced roast beef sandwiches, Curly Fries, Jamocha shakes, Market Fresh sandwiches, and wraps and salads made with wholesome ingredients and served with the convenience of a drive-through.

Dave Thomas, the founder of Wendy's, began his fast-food career in 1956 when he and Phil Clauss opened a barbecue restaurant in Knoxville, Tennessee. He put his restaurant experience to use in 1969 by opening his first Wendy's restaurant, naming it after his daughter. Thomas limited the menu to cooked-to-order hamburgers, chili, and shakes, charging prices slightly higher than rivals Burger King and McDonald's. The restaurants were decorated with carpeting, wood paneling, and Tiffany-style lamps to reinforce the relatively upscale theme. In the early 1970s, the company began franchising to accelerate expansion. It also founded its Management Institute to train owners and managers in Wendy's operational techniques. The first non-U.S. Wendy's opened in Canada in 1975. Wendy's went public in 1976, and by the end of that year, it boasted a collection of 500 restaurants. Its first national commercial aired in 1977. Two years later, the chain added a salad bar to its menu.

Dave Thomas retired as chairman in 1982 and took the title of senior chairman. Wendy's launched an $8 million TV ad campaign featuring Clara Peller asking, "Where's the beef?" in 1984, and its market share jumped to 12 percent. When McDonald's and Burger King responded with their own campaigns, neither the introduction of a breakfast menu (1985), new products such as the Big Classic burger (1986), nor the SuperBar buffet (1987) could help reverse the erosion of the company's market share (down to 9 percent by 1987). With his honest demeanor and humble delivery, Thomas found an audience as Wendy's TV spokesperson in 1989. The company even attributed the rebound in earnings at the time to his appearances.

Wendy's reacted to growing concern about nutrition by introducing a grilled chicken sandwich in 1990. It also appealed to budget-conscious consumers with its 99-cent Super Value Menu. Wendy's had 4,000 restaurants by 1992, the same year it added packaged salads to its menu. The next year, high school dropout Thomas earned his diploma; his class voted him Most Likely to Succeed.

The death of Dave Thomas early in 2002 was a crushing blow to the company and a loss for the fast-food industry. Wendy's continued to perform well over the next three years, even after losing its founder, Dave Thomas. In November 2004, Wendy's decided to end its unsuccessful ad campaign featuring an Everyman-type character, an "unofficial spokesman" called Mr. Wendy, because the campaign drew attention away from the food. This marks an ongoing dilemma for Wendy's: how to brand the company in the post-Thomas era. The company initiated a series of ads featuring still images of Dave Thomas in late November 2005 to commemorate the chain's 35th anniversary, but the long-term question of its identity remains. During 2005, it started a campaign built around the call to action "Do What Tastes Right" that underscores Wendy's 35-year heritage of serving great tasting, high-quality food. It featured a variety of different style ads, matched to targeted audiences. Included were advertising that promoted specific menu items as well as executions that supported the Wendy's brand as a whole.

In mid-2006, Wendy's International, Inc., created a new area of marketing to lead innovation efforts for the Wendy's brand. The expanded role of Wendy's marketing department included the establishment of an Innovation and Strategy group comprised of Research and Development, Strategic Insights, & Innovation, and Operations Innovation.

Wendy rolled out its strategic growth plan in October 2007, and identified 10 imperatives for 2008. The imperatives are focused on "Doing What's Right for Customers." The 10 imperatives build on Wendy's "Recipe for Success," which is focused on revitalizing the Wendy's brand, streamlining and improving operations, reclaiming innovation leadership, strengthening franchisee commitment, capturing new opportunities (e.g., international growth), and embracing a performance driven culture.

In August 2008, Wendy's reached out to cash-strapped consumers with a trio of high-quality, signature sandwiches priced at 99 cents. It introduced a 99-cent Double Stack cheeseburger and plans to aggressively promote this menu option, along with the company's popular 99-cent Junior Bacon Cheeseburger and 99-cent Crispy Chicken Sandwich. On September 29, 2008, Triarc Companies, Inc., the franchisor of the Arby's restaurant system, completed its previously announced merger with Wendy's International, Inc. The combined company was renamed Wendy's/Arby's Group, Inc.

Wendy's is leading the way with some innovations such as fruit bowls and combo-meal flexibility. Wendy's is currently testing some new products, including a deli-style sandwich line using fresh-baked bread called frescata, and yogurt, granola, and mix-ins for its Frosty. Wendy's uses no preservatives in its bowls of pineapple, honeydew, cantaloupe, and grapes, which come with a low-fat, strawberry-flavored yogurt for dipping. Wendy's is also pinning hopes on a new double-sided grill to boost burger quality and speed of service, and said it may be ready to test breakfast in the next year or so. But Wendy's has a few hurdles to overcome. Rivals have caught up to the menu innovations of Wendy's. McDonald's has crested a youth wave with "I'm lovin' it" and music promotions. And, while Wendy's in the past came within a half share point of overtaking number two Burger King, Burger King now looks to have widened that gap, thanks to edgy marketing that's given it a cult following among the fast-food faithful. Wendy's advertising emphasized more clearly their points of differentiation from their competition, including higher quality, great taste, and fresh—never frozen—ground beef.

In order to survive the merciless fast-food industry, Wendy's conducted a survey. Wendy's wanted to study customer demographics and awareness of different competing fast-food chains; the satisfaction responses of consumers in terms of family orientation, comfort, price, quick service, healthy foods, cleanliness, and so on; and the patronage preferences of costumers in terms of eat-in or drive-through. The questionnaire used follows and the data obtained can be downloaded from the Web site for this book. Based on the data collected and analysis of this study, Wendy's intends to improve its service and brand orientation.

Questions

Chapter 1

1. Discuss the role that marketing research can play in helping a fast-food restaurant such as Wendy's formulate sound marketing strategies.

Chapter 2

1. Wendy's is considering further expansion in the United States. Define the management decision problem.
2. Define an appropriate marketing research problem based on the management decision problem you have identified.

Chapter 3

1. Formulate an appropriate research design for investigating the marketing research problem you have defined in Chapter 2.

Chapter 4

1. Use the Internet to determine the market shares of the major national fast-food chains for the last calendar year.
2. What type of syndicate data will be useful to Wendy's?

Chapter 5

1. Discuss the role of qualitative research in helping Wendy's expand further in the United States.

Chapter 6

1. Wendy's has developed a new fish sandwich with a distinctive Cajun taste. It would like to determine consumers' response to this new sandwich before introducing it in the marketplace. If a survey is to be conducted to determine consumer preferences, which survey method should be used and why?

Chapter 7

1. Discuss the role of experimentation in helping Wendy's determine its optimal level of advertising expenditures.

Chapter 8

1. Illustrate the use of primary type of scales in measuring consumer preferences for fast-food restaurants.

Chapter 9

1. Illustrate the use of Likert, semantic differential, and Stapel scales in measuring consumer preferences for fast-food restaurants.

Chapter 10

1. Develop a questionnaire for assessing consumer preferences for fast-food restaurants.

Chapters 11 and 12

1. What sampling plan should be adopted for the survey of Chapter 6? How should the sample size be determined?

Chapter 13

1. How should the fieldworkers be selected and trained to conduct the fieldwork for the survey in Chapter 6?

Chapter 14

1. How should the missing values be treated for the following demographic variables: education (D5), income (D6), employment status (D7), and marital status (D8)?

2. Recode payment method (D1) by combining Debit card, Check, and Other into one category.
3. Recode number of people living at home (D3A) as follows: for adults age 18+, four or more should be combined into one category labeled 4 plus; for each of the three remaining age groups (under 5, 6−11, and 12−17), two or more should be combined into a single category labeled 2 plus.
4. Recode education (D5) by combining the lowest two categories and labeling it completed high school or less.
5. Recode income (D6) by combining the highest three categories and labeling it $100,000 or more.
6. Recode employment status (D7) by combining homemaker, retired, and unemployed into a single category.
7. Classify respondents into light, medium, and heavy users of fast food based on a frequency distribution of S3A: In the past four weeks, approximately how many times, have you, yourself, eaten food from a fast-food restaurant? Use the following classification: 1−4 times = light, 5−8 times = medium, 9 or more times = heavy.

Chapter 15

1. Run a frequency distribution for all variables except respondent ID (respanid). Why is this analysis useful?
2. Cross-tabulate fast-food consumption classification (recoded S3A, see Chapter 14 questions) with the demographic characteristics (some recoded as specified in Chapter 14): age (S1), gender (S2), payment method (D1), number of people living at home (D3A), education (D5), income (D6), employment (D7), marital status (D8), and Region. Interpret the results.
3. Cross-tabulate payment method (recoded D1) with the remaining demographic characteristics (some recoded as specified in Chapter 14): age (S1), gender (S2), number of people living at home (D3A), education (D5), income (D6), employment (D7), marital status (D8), and Region. Interpret the results.
4. Cross-tabulate eating there more often, less often, or about the same as a year or so ago (q8_1, q8_7, q8_26, q8_36, q8_39) with the demographic characteristics (some recoded as specified in Chapter 14): age (S1), gender (S2), payment method (D1), number of people living at home (D3A), education (D5), income (D6), employment (D7), marital status (D8), and Region. Interpret the results.
5. Do the ratings on the psychographic statements (q14_1, q14_2, q14_3, q14_4, q14_5, q14_6, and q14_7) differ for males and females (S2)? How would your analysis differ if the ratings on the psychographic statements were treated as ordinal rather than interval scaled?
6. Do the respondents agree more with "I have been making an effort to look for fast-food choices that have better nutritional value than the foods I have chosen in the past" (q14_6) than they do with "I consider the amount of fat in the foods my kids eat at fast food restaurants" (q14_5)? How would your analysis differ if these ratings were treated as ordinal rather than interval scaled?

Chapter 16

1. Do the restaurant ratings (q9_1, q9_7, q9_26, q9_36, q9_39) differ for the various demographic characteristics (some recoded as specified in Chapter 14): age (S1), gender (S2), payment method (D1), number of people living at home (D3A), education (D5), income (D6), employment (D7), marital status (D8), and Region. Interpret the results.

2. Do the four groups defined by "the extent to which you find it difficult to make up your mind about which fast food restaurant to go to" (q13) differ in their restaurant ratings (q9_1, q9_7, q9_26, q9_36, q9_39)?

Chapter 17

1. Can each of the restaurant ratings (q9_1, q9_7, q9_26, q9_36, q9_39) be explained in terms of the ratings on the psychographic statement (q14_1, q14_2, q14_3, q14_4, q14_5, q14_6, and q14_7) when the statements are considered simultaneously?

Chapter 18

1. Can the males and females (S2) be differentiated based on the ratings on the psychographic statements (q14_1, q14_2, q14_3, q14_4, q14_5, q14_6, and q14_7) when the ratings are considered simultaneously? Run a two-group discriminant analysis. Then run a logit analysis. Compare the results from the two analyses.

Chapter 19

1. Factor analyze the psychographic statement (q14_1, q14_2, q14_3, q14_4, q14_5, q14_6, and q14_7). Use principal components analysis with varimax rotation. Interpret the factors.

Chapter 20

1. How would you cluster the respondents based on the psychographic statement (q14_1, q14_2, q14_3, q14_4, q14_5, q14_6, and q14_7)? Interpret the resulting clusters.

Chapter 21

1. Provide similarity ratings on a 1 to 7 scale for all possible pairs of the following brands of fast-food restaurants: Arby's, Burger King, Church's, Domino's Pizza, KFC, McDonald's, Pizza Hut, Subway, Taco Bell, and Wendy's. Develop a two-dimensional MDS map. Interpret the dimensions and the map.
2. Construct 36 full profiles of fast-food restaurants using the following attributes and the levels: price (L, M, H), quality (M, H), cleanliness (M, H), service (L, M, H). Note that L = low, M = medium, and H = high. Rate the 36 profiles in terms of your preference using a 7-point scale (1 = not at all preferred, 7 = greatly preferred). Calculate the part-worth functions and the relative importance of the attributes.

Chapter 22

Develop an SEM model that posits evaluation of fast-food restaurants and attitude toward healthy food as exogenous constructs and patronage of fast-food restaurants as an endogenous construct.

1. Develop three items to measure each of the three constructs.
2. Draw the path diagram of the measurement model.
3. What are degrees of freedom of the measurement model?
4. Draw the path diagram of the structural model.

Chapter 23

1. Write a report for Wendy's management summarizing the results of your analyses. What recommendations do you have for the management?

Chapter 24

1. If this survey were to be conducted in Malaysia rather than the United States, how would the research process be different?

2. Should the sample size in Malaysia be the same as the sample size in the United States? Should the same sampling procedures be used in the two countries?

References

1. www.wendys.com, accessed February 1, 2009.

2. www.wendysarbys.com/about, accessed November 18, 2008.

3. www.arbys.com/about, accessed November 18, 2008.

4. www.wendysarbys.com/about/our-brands, accessed November 18, 2008.

5. http://ir.wendysarbys.com/phoenix.zhtml?c=67548&p= irol-wendynewsArticle&ID=1200232&highlight=, accessed November 18, 2008.

6. http://ir.wendysarbys.com/phoenix.zhtml?c=67548&p= irol-wendynewsArticle&ID=1200436&highlight=3-year% 20combo, accessed November 18, 2008.

7. http://ir.wendysarbys.com/phoenix.zhtml?c=67548&p= irol-wendynewsArticle&ID=1200343&highlight=, accessed November 18, 2008.

8. http://ir.wendysarbys.com/phoenix.zhtml?c=67548&p= irol-wendynewsArticle&ID=1200327&highlight=, accessed November 18, 2008.

Note: This case was prepared for class discussion purposes only and does not represent the views of Wendy's or their affiliates. The problem scenario is hypothetical and the name of the actual company has been disguised. However, the questionnaire and the data provided are real. Some questions have been deleted, while the data for other questions are not provided because of proprietary reasons.

Region information is not indicated in the questionnaire but is coded in the data file as: 1 = Northeast, 2 = Midwest, 3 = South, and 4 = West.

ONLINE WENDY'S COMMITMENT STUDY QUESTIONNAIRE APRIL 1, 2008

RID_____

Thank you for participating in our survey.

S1. To begin, which of the following categories includes your age? (CHOOSE ONE RESPONSE ONLY.)

    1. Under 18   **[TERMINATE QS1]**
    2. 18−24
    3. 25−29
    4. 30−34
    5. 35−39
    6. 40−45
    7. 46 or older   **[TERMINATE QS1]**
    – Refused   **[TERMINATE QS1]**

S2. Are you . . . ? (CHOOSE ONE RESPONSE ONLY.)

    1. Male
    2. Female

S3. OMITTED

S3A. In the past four weeks, approximately how many times, have you, yourself, eaten food from a fast-food restaurant? **[ACCEPT WHOLE NUMBERS ONLY; DO NOT ACCEPT RANGE.] [RANGE: 0−99]**

_____

    & DK/refused   **[TERMINATE QS3A]**
                        [TERMINATE QS3A IF ZERO]

    1. OMITTED

    2. OMITTED

    3. OMITTED

3a. You have indicated that you have heard of these restaurants. When was the last time, if ever, that you, yourself, have eaten from each one? (PLEASE SELECT ONE TIMEFRAME FOR EACH RESTAURANT.) **[FORMAT AS GRID: INCLUDE RESPONSES FROM Q1].**

1. Within the past 4 weeks
2. More than 4 weeks to within the past 3 months
3. More than 3 months ago
4. Never

4. OMITTED

5. OMITTED

6. OMITTED

7. OMITTED

8. For each of the restaurants listed below, please indicate whether you, yourself, are eating from there more often, less often, or about the same frequency as a year or so ago. **[SHOW ONLY THOSE Q3a = 1 or 2]**

	More often	About the same	Less often
Insert brands	1	2	3

9. I'd like you to rate the restaurants you, yourself, have eaten from in the past three months using a 10-point scale, where "10" means you think it is perfect, and "1" means you think it is terrible. Now taking into account everything that you look for in a fast-food restaurant, how would you rate each of the following? **[SHOW Q3a = 1 or 2]**

Terrible (1)	2	3	4	5	6	7	8	9	Perfect (10)
○	○	○	○	○	○	○	○	○	○

10. OMITTED

11. OMITTED

12. OMITTED

13. Sometimes it is difficult for people to make up their minds about which fast-food restaurant to go to on a given visit. Think about when you go to a fast-food restaurant. In general, which of the following statements best describes the extent to which you find it difficult to make up your mind about which fast-food restaurant to go to? (CHOOSE ONE RESPONSE ONLY.)

1. I **always know** exactly which fast-food restaurant I am going to go to
2. I **usually know** exactly which fast-food restaurant I am going to go to
3. I'm **usually undecided** about which fast-food restaurant I am going to go to
4. I'm **always undecided** about which fast-food restaurant I am going to go to

14. Below is a list of statements that may or may not be used to describe you in general. Using the scale of Agree completely, Agree somewhat, Neither agree nor disagree, Disagree somewhat, and Disagree completely, please indicate how strongly you agree or disagree with each statement. (CHOOSE ONE RESPONSE FOR EACH STATEMENT.)

Disagree Completely	Disagree Somewhat	Neither Agree nor Disagree	Agree Somewhat	Agree Completely	N/A
○	○	○	○	○	○

1. I try to stay current on the latest health and nutrition information
2. I read nutritional labels on most products I buy
3. I am making more of an effort to find out about the nutritional content of the foods I eat at fast-food restaurants
4. I consider the amount of fat in the foods I eat at fast-food restaurants
5. I consider the amount of fat in the foods my kids eat at fast-food restaurants
6. I have been making an effort to look for fast-food choices that have better nutritional value than the foods I have chosen in the past
7. I am eating at fast-food restaurants less often out of concern for the high fat content in the foods at fast-food restaurants

These last few questions are for classification purposes only.

D1. Which of the following methods do you most often use when purchasing from fast-food restaurants? Do you pay . . . ? CHOOSE ONE RESPONSE ONLY.)

    1. Cash
    2. Credit card
    3. Debit card
    4. Check
    5. Other

D2. OMITTED

D3. OMITTED

D3A. How many people in each of the following age groups live in your home? (PLEASE ENTER A NUMBER FOR EACH AGE RANGE. ENTER "0" IF THERE IS NO ONE IN THAT RANGE IN YOUR HOUSEHOLD.)

    A. Adults age 18 + **[RANGE: 1–15]**
    B. Children under age 5 **[RANGE: 0–9]**
    C. Children age 6−11 **[RANGE: 0–9]**
    D. Children age 12−17 **[RANGE: 0–9]**

D4. OMITTED

D5. Which of the following best represents the last level of education that you, yourself, completed? (CHOOSE ONE RESPONSE ONLY.)

    1. Some high school or less
    2. Completed high school
    3. Some college
    4. Completed college
    5. Post graduate
    – Prefer not to answer

D6. Which of the following best describes your family's annual household income before taxes? (CHOOSE ONE RESPONSE ONLY.)

    1. Under $25,000
    2. $25,000 but under $50,000
    1. $50,000 but under $75,000
    2. $75,000 but under $100,000
    3. $100,000 but under $150,000
    4. $150,000 but under $200,000
    5. $200,000 or more
    – Prefer not to answer

D7. Which of the following best describes your employment status? (CHOOSE ONE RESPONSE ONLY.)

    1. Full-time
    2. Part-time
    3. Retired
    4. Student
    5. Homemaker
    6. Unemployed
    – Prefer not to answer

D8. Are you . . . ?

    1 Single, Separated, Divorced, Widowed
    0 Married/Living as Married
    – Prefer not to answer

Thank you for taking the time to participate in our research!

	Q1		Q1
Arby's	1	La Salsa	23
Atlanta Bread Company	2	Little Caesars	24
A&W	3	Long John Silvers	25
Baja Fresh	4	McDonald's	26
Blimpie	5	Panda Express	27
Boston Chicken/Market	6	Panera Bread	28
Burger King	7	Papa John's	41
Captain D's	8	Pick Up Stix	29
Carl's Jr.	9	Pizza Hut	30
Checker's Drive In	10	Popeye's	31
Chick-Fil-A	11	Quiznos	32
Chipotle Mexican Grill	12	Rally's	33
Church's	13	Rubio's	34
Del Taco	14	Sonic	35
Domino's Pizza	15	Subway	36
El Pollo Loco	16	Taco Bell	37
Grandy's	17	Taco Bueno	38
Green Burrito	18	Wendy's	39
Hardee's	19	Whataburger	40
In-N-Out Burger	20	OMITTED—OTHER	
Jack in the Box	21	SPECIFY	
KFC/Kentucky Fried Chicken	22	None	42

Case 5.1

Comprehensive Harvard Business School Cases

The Harvard cases are not printed in the book. Students can purchase these cases directly from Harvard Business Online at harvardbusinessonline.hbsp.harvard.edu.

Instructors can find the questions and answers for HBS cases in the *Instructor's Manual* and Instructor Resource Center on the Web site for this book.

Appendix
Statistical Tables

TABLE 1
Simple Random Numbers

Line/Col.	(1)	(2)	(3)	(4)	(5)	(6)	(7)	(8)	(9)	(10)	(11)	(12)	(13)	(14)
1	10480	15011	01536	02011	81647	91646	69179	14194	62590	36207	20969	99570	91291	90700
2	22368	46573	25595	85393	30995	89198	27982	53402	93965	34095	52666	19174	39615	99505
3	24130	48390	22527	97265	76393	64809	15179	24830	49340	32081	30680	19655	63348	58629
4	42167	93093	06243	61680	07856	16376	39440	53537	71341	57004	00849	74917	97758	16379
5	37570	39975	81837	16656	06121	91782	60468	81305	49684	60072	14110	06927	01263	54613
6	77921	06907	11008	42751	27756	53498	18602	70659	90655	15053	21916	81825	44394	42880
7	99562	72905	56420	69994	98872	31016	71194	18738	44013	48840	63213	21069	10634	12952
8	96301	91977	05463	07972	18876	20922	94595	56869	69014	60045	18425	84903	42508	32307
9	89579	14342	63661	10281	17453	18103	57740	84378	25331	12568	58678	44947	05585	56941
10	85475	36857	53342	53988	53060	59533	38867	62300	08158	17983	16439	11458	18593	64952
11	28918	69578	88231	33276	70997	79936	56865	05859	90106	31595	01547	85590	91610	78188
12	63553	40961	48235	03427	49626	69445	18663	72695	52180	20847	12234	90511	33703	90322
13	09429	93969	52636	92737	88974	33488	36320	17617	30015	08272	84115	27156	30613	74952
14	10365	61129	87529	85689	48237	52267	67689	93394	01511	26358	85104	20285	29975	89868
15	07119	97336	71048	08178	77233	13916	47564	81056	97735	85977	29372	74461	28551	90707
16	51085	12765	51821	51259	77452	16308	60756	92144	49442	53900	70960	63990	75601	40719
17	02368	21382	52404	60268	89368	19885	55322	44819	01188	65255	64835	44919	05944	55157
18	01011	54092	33362	94904	31273	04146	18594	29852	71685	85030	51132	01915	92747	64951
19	52162	53916	46369	58586	23216	14513	83149	98736	23495	64350	94738	17752	35156	35749
20	07056	97628	33787	09998	42698	06691	76988	13602	51851	46104	88916	19509	25625	58104
21	48663	91245	85828	14346	09172	30163	90229	04734	59193	22178	30421	61666	99904	32812
22	54164	58492	22421	74103	47070	25306	76468	26384	58151	06646	21524	15227	96909	44592
23	32639	32363	05597	24200	13363	38005	94342	28728	35806	06912	17012	64161	18296	22851
24	29334	27001	87637	87308	58731	00256	45834	15398	46557	41135	10307	07684	36188	18510
25	02488	33062	28834	07351	19731	92420	60952	61280	50001	67658	32586	86679	50720	94953
26	81525	72295	04839	96423	24878	82651	66566	14778	76797	14780	13300	87074	79666	95725
27	29676	20591	68086	26432	46901	20849	89768	81536	86645	12659	92259	57102	80428	25280
28	00742	57392	39064	66432	84673	40027	32832	61362	98947	96067	64760	64584	96096	98253
29	05366	04213	25669	26422	44407	44048	37937	63904	45766	66134	75470	66520	34693	90449
30	91921	26418	64117	94305	26766	25940	39972	22209	71500	64568	91402	42416	07844	69618
31	00582	04711	87917	77341	42206	35126	74087	99547	81817	42607	43808	76655	62028	76630
32	00725	69884	62797	56170	86324	88072	76222	36086	84637	93161	76038	65855	77919	88006
33	69011	65795	95876	55293	18988	27354	26575	08625	40801	59920	29841	80150	12777	48501
34	25976	57948	29888	88604	67917	48708	18912	82271	65424	69774	33611	54262	85963	03547

(continued)

TABLE 1
Simple Random Numbers (*continued*)

Line/Col.	(1)	(2)	(3)	(4)	(5)	(6)	(7)	(8)	(9)	(10)	(11)	(12)	(13)	(14)
35	09763	83473	73577	12908	30883	18317	28290	35797	05998	41688	34952	37888	38917	88050
36	91567	42595	27958	30134	04024	86385	29880	99730	55536	84855	29088	09250	79656	73211
37	17955	56349	90999	49127	20044	59931	06115	20542	18059	02008	73708	83517	36103	42791
38	46503	18584	18845	49618	02304	51038	20655	58727	28168	15475	56942	53389	20562	87338
39	92157	89634	94824	78171	84610	82834	09922	25417	44137	48413	25555	21246	35509	20468
40	14577	62765	35605	81263	39667	47358	56873	56307	61607	49518	89656	20103	77490	18062
41	98427	07523	33362	64270	01638	92477	66969	98420	04880	45585	46565	04102	46880	45709
42	34914	63976	88720	82765	34476	17032	87589	40836	32427	70002	70663	88863	77775	69348
43	70060	28277	39475	46473	23219	53416	94970	25832	69975	94884	19661	72828	00102	66794
44	53976	54914	06990	67245	68350	82948	11398	42878	80287	88267	47363	46634	06541	97809
45	76072	29515	40980	07391	58745	25774	22987	80059	39911	96189	41151	14222	60697	59583
46	90725	52210	83974	29992	65831	38857	50490	83765	55657	14361	31720	57375	56228	41546
47	64364	67412	33339	31926	14883	24413	59744	92351	97473	89286	35931	04110	23726	51900
48	08962	00358	31662	25388	61642	34072	81249	35648	56891	69352	48373	45578	78547	81788
49	95012	68379	93526	70765	10592	04542	76463	54328	02349	17247	28865	14777	62730	92277
50	15664	10493	20492	38301	91132	21999	59516	81652	27195	48223	46751	22923	32261	85653
51	16408	81899	04153	53381	79401	21438	83035	92350	36693	31238	59649	91754	72772	02338
52	18629	81953	05520	91962	04739	13092	97662	24822	94730	06496	35090	04822	86774	98289
53	73115	35101	47498	87637	99016	71060	88824	71013	18735	20286	23153	72924	35165	43040
54	57491	16703	23167	49323	45021	33132	12544	41035	80780	45393	44812	12515	98931	91202
55	30405	83946	23792	14422	15059	45799	22716	19792	09983	74353	68668	30429	70735	25499
56	16631	35006	85900	98275	32388	52390	16815	69293	82732	38480	73817	32523	41961	44437
57	96773	20206	42559	78985	05300	22164	24369	54224	35083	19687	11052	91491	60383	19746
58	38935	64202	14349	82674	66523	44133	00697	35552	35970	19124	63318	29686	03387	59846
59	31624	76384	17403	53363	44167	64486	64758	75366	76554	31601	12614	33072	60332	92325
60	78919	19474	23632	27889	47914	02584	37680	20801	72152	39339	34806	08930	85001	87820
61	03931	33309	57047	74211	63445	17361	62825	39908	05607	91284	68833	25570	38818	46920
62	74426	33278	43972	10119	89917	15665	52872	73823	73144	88662	88970	74492	51805	99378
63	09066	00903	20795	95452	92648	45454	69552	88815	16553	51125	79375	97596	16296	66092
64	42238	12426	87025	14267	20979	04508	64535	31355	86064	29472	47689	05974	52468	16834
65	16153	08002	26504	41744	81959	65642	74240	56302	00033	67107	77510	70625	28725	34191
66	21457	40742	29820	96783	29400	21840	15035	34537	33310	06116	95240	15957	16572	06004
67	21581	57802	02050	89728	17937	37621	47075	42080	97403	48626	68995	43805	33386	21597
68	55612	78095	83197	33732	05810	24813	86902	60397	16489	03264	88525	42786	05269	92532
69	44657	66999	99324	51281	84463	60563	79312	93454	68876	25471	93911	25650	12682	73572
70	91340	84979	46949	81973	37949	61023	43997	15263	80644	43942	89203	71795	99533	50501
71	91227	21199	31935	27022	84067	05462	35216	14486	29891	68607	41867	14951	91696	85065
72	50001	38140	66321	19924	72163	09538	12151	06878	91903	18749	34405	56087	82790	70925
73	65390	05224	72958	28609	81406	39147	25549	48542	42627	45233	57202	94617	23772	07896
74	27504	96131	83944	41575	10573	03619	64482	73923	36152	05184	94142	25299	94387	34925
75	37169	94851	39117	89632	00959	16487	65536	49071	39782	17095	02330	74301	00275	48280
76	11508	70225	51111	38351	19444	66499	71945	05422	13442	78675	84031	66938	93654	59894
77	37449	30362	06694	54690	04052	53115	62757	95348	78662	11163	81651	50245	34971	52974
78	46515	70331	85922	38329	57015	15765	97161	17869	45349	61796	66345	81073	49106	79860
79	30986	81223	42416	58353	21532	30502	32305	86482	05174	07901	54339	58861	74818	46942

(*continued*)

TABLE 1
Simple Random Numbers (*continued*)

Line/Col.	(1)	(2)	(3)	(4)	(5)	(6)	(7)	(8)	(9)	(10)	(11)	(12)	(13)	(14)
80	63798	64995	46583	09785	44160	78128	83991	42865	92520	83531	80377	35909	81250	54238
81	82486	84846	99254	67632	43218	50076	21361	64816	51202	88124	41870	52689	51275	83556
82	21885	32906	92431	09060	64297	51674	64126	62570	26123	05155	59194	52799	28225	85762
83	60336	98782	07408	53458	13564	59089	26445	29789	85205	41001	12535	12133	14645	23541
84	43937	46891	24010	25560	86355	33941	25786	54990	71899	15475	95434	98227	21824	19535
85	97656	63175	89303	16275	07100	92063	21942	18611	47348	20203	18534	03862	78095	50136
86	03299	01221	05418	38982	55758	92237	26759	86367	21216	98442	08303	56613	91511	75928
87	79626	06486	03574	17668	07785	76020	79924	25651	83325	88428	85076	72811	22717	50585
88	85636	68335	47539	03129	65651	11977	02510	26113	99447	68645	34327	15152	55230	93448
89	18039	14367	61337	06177	12143	46609	32989	74014	64708	00533	35398	58408	13261	47908
90	08362	15656	60627	36478	65648	16764	53412	09013	07832	41574	17639	82163	60859	75567
91	79556	29068	04142	16268	15387	12856	66227	38358	22478	73373	88732	09443	82558	05250
92	92608	82674	27072	32534	17075	27698	98204	63863	11951	34648	88022	56148	34925	57031
93	23982	25835	40055	67006	12293	02753	14827	23235	35071	99704	37543	11601	35503	85171
94	09915	96306	05908	97901	28395	14186	00821	80703	70426	75647	76310	88717	37890	40129
95	59037	33300	26695	62247	69927	76123	50842	43834	86654	70959	79725	93872	28117	19233
96	42488	78077	69882	61657	34136	79180	97526	43092	04098	73571	80799	76536	71255	64239
97	46764	86273	63003	93017	31204	36692	40202	35275	57306	55543	53203	18098	47625	88684
98	03237	45430	55417	63282	90816	17349	88298	90183	36600	78406	06216	95787	42579	90730
99	86591	81482	52667	61582	14972	90053	89534	76036	49199	43716	97548	04379	46370	28672
100	38534	01715	94964	87288	65680	43772	39560	12918	80537	62738	19636	51132	25739	56947

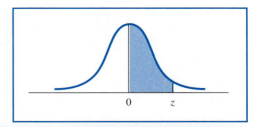

TABLE 2
Area Under the Normal Curve

Z	.00	.01	.02	.03	.04	.05	.06	.07	.08	.09
0.0	.0000	.0040	.0080	.0120	.0160	.0199	.0239	.0279	.0319	.0359
0.1	.0398	.0438	.0478	.0517	.0557	.0596	.0636	.0675	.0714	.0753
0.2	.0793	.0832	.0871	.0910	.0948	.0987	.1026	.1064	.1103	.1141
0.3	.1179	.1217	.1255	.1293	.1331	.1368	.1406	.1443	.1480	.1517
0.4	.1554	.1591	.1628	.1664	.1700	.1736	.1772	.1808	.1844	.1879
0.5	.1915	.1950	.1985	.2019	.2054	.2088	.2123	.2157	.2190	.2224
0.6	.2257	.2291	.2324	.2357	.2389	.2422	.2454	.2486	.2518	.2549
0.7	.2580	.2612	.2642	.2673	.2704	.2734	.2764	.2794	.2823	.2852
0.8	.2881	.2910	.2939	.2967	.2995	.3023	.3051	.3078	.3106	.3133
0.9	.3159	.3186	.3212	.3238	.3264	.3289	.3315	.3340	.3365	.3389
1.0	.3413	.3438	.3461	.3485	.3508	.3531	.3554	.3577	.3599	.3621
1.1	.3643	.3665	.3686	.3708	.3729	.3749	.3770	.3790	.3810	.3830
1.2	.3849	.3869	.3888	.3907	.3925	.3944	.3962	.3980	.3997	.4015
1.3	.4032	.4049	.4066	.4082	.4099	.4115	.4131	.4147	.4162	.4177
1.4	.4192	.4207	.4222	.4236	.4251	.4265	.4279	.4292	.4306	.4319
1.5	.4332	.4345	.4357	.4370	.4382	.4394	.4406	.4418	.4429	.4441
1.6	.4452	.4463	.4474	.4484	.4495	.4505	.4515	.4525	.4535	.4545
1.7	.4554	.4564	.4573	.4582	.4591	.4599	.4608	.4616	.4625	.4633
1.8	.4641	.4649	.4656	.4664	.4671	.4678	.4686	.4693	.4699	.4706
1.9	.4713	.4719	.4726	.4732	.4738	.4744	.4750	.4756	.4761	.4767
2.0	.4772	.4778	.4783	.4788	.4793	.4798	.4803	.4808	.4812	.4817
2.1	.4821	.4826	.4830	.4834	.4838	.4842	.4846	.4850	.4854	.4857
2.2	.4861	.4864	.4868	.4871	.4875	.4878	.4881	.4884	.4887	.4890
2.3	.4893	.4896	.4898	.4901	.4904	.4906	.4909	.4911	.4913	.4916
2.4	.4918	.4920	.4922	.4925	.4927	.4929	.4931	.4932	.4934	.4936
2.5	.4938	.4940	.4941	.4943	.4945	.4946	.4948	.4949	.4951	.4952
2.6	.4953	.4955	.4956	.4957	.4959	.4960	.4961	.4962	.4963	.4964
2.7	.4965	.4966	.4967	.4968	.4969	.4970	.4971	.4972	.4973	.4974
2.8	.4974	.4975	.4976	.4977	.4977	.4978	.4979	.4979	.4980	.4981
2.9	.4981	.4982	.4982	.4983	.4984	.4984	.4985	.4985	.4986	.4986
3.0	.49865	.49869	.49874	.49878	.49882	.49886	.49889	.49893	.49897	.49900
3.1	.49903	.49906	.49910	.49913	.49916	.49918	.49921	.49924	.49926	.49929
3.2	.49931	.49934	.49936	.49938	.49940	.49942	.49944	.49946	.49948	.49950
3.3	.49952	.49953	.49955	.49957	.49958	.49960	.49961	.49962	.49964	.49965
3.4	.49966	.49968	.49969	.49970	.49971	.49972	.49973	.49974	.49975	.49976
3.5	.49977	.49978	.49978	.49979	.49980	.49981	.49981	.49982	.49983	.49983
3.6	.49984	.49985	.49985	.49986	.49986	.49987	.49987	.49988	.49988	.49989
3.7	.49989	.49990	.49990	.49990	.49991	.49991	.49992	.49992	.49992	.49992
3.8	.49993	.49993	.49993	.49994	.49994	.49994	.49994	.49995	.49995	.49995
3.9	.49995	.49995	.49996	.49996	.49996	.49996	.49996	.49996	.49997	.49997

Entry represents area under the standard normal distribution from the mean to z.

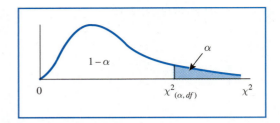

TABLE 3
Chi-Square Distribution

Degrees of Freedom	Upper Tail Areas (α)											
	.995	.99	.975	.95	.90	.75	.25	.10	.05	.025	.01	.005
1	—	—	0.001	0.004	0.016	0.102	1.323	2.706	3.841	5.024	6.635	7.879
2	0.010	0.020	0.051	0.103	0.211	0.575	2.773	4.605	5.991	7.378	9.210	10.597
3	0.072	0.115	0.216	0.352	0.584	1.213	4.108	6.251	7.815	9.348	11.345	12.838
4	0.207	0.297	0.484	0.711	1.064	1.923	5.385	7.779	9.488	11.143	13.277	14.860
5	0.412	0.554	0.831	1.145	1.610	2.675	6.626	9.236	11.071	12.833	15.086	16.750
6	0.676	0.872	1.237	1.635	2.204	3.455	7.841	10.645	12.592	14.449	16.812	18.548
7	0.989	1.239	1.690	2.167	2.833	4.255	9.037	12.017	14.067	16.013	18.475	20.278
8	1.344	1.646	2.180	2.733	3.490	5.071	10.219	13.362	15.507	17.535	20.090	21.955
9	1.735	2.088	2.700	3.325	4.168	5.899	11.389	14.684	16.919	19.023	21.666	23.589
10	2.156	2.558	3.247	3.940	4.865	6.737	12.549	15.987	18.307	20.483	23.209	25.188
11	2.603	3.053	3.816	4.575	5.578	7.584	13.701	17.275	19.675	21.920	24.725	26.757
12	3.074	3.571	4.404	5.226	6.304	8.438	14.845	18.549	21.026	23.337	26.217	28.299
13	3.565	4.107	5.009	5.892	7.042	9.299	15.984	19.812	22.362	24.736	27.688	29.819
14	4.075	4.660	5.629	6.571	7.790	10.165	17.117	21.064	23.685	26.119	29.141	31.319
15	4.601	5.229	6.262	7.261	8.547	11.037	18.245	22.307	24.996	27.488	30.578	32.801
16	5.142	5.812	6.908	7.962	9.312	11.912	19.369	23.542	26.296	28.845	32.000	34.267
17	5.697	6.408	7.564	8.672	10.085	12.792	20.489	24.769	27.587	30.191	33.409	35.718
18	6.265	7.015	8.231	9.390	10.865	13.675	21.605	25.989	28.869	31.526	34.805	37.156
19	6.844	7.633	8.907	10.117	11.651	14.562	22.718	27.204	30.144	32.852	36.191	38.582
20	7.434	8.260	9.591	10.851	12.443	15.452	23.828	28.412	31.410	34.170	37.566	39.997
21	8.034	8.897	10.283	11.591	13.240	16.344	24.935	29.615	32.671	35.479	38.932	41.401
22	8.643	9.542	10.982	12.338	14.042	17.240	26.039	30.813	33.924	36.781	40.289	42.796
23	9.260	10.196	11.689	13.091	14.848	18.137	27.141	32.007	35.172	38.076	41.638	44.181
24	9.886	10.856	12.401	13.848	15.659	19.037	28.241	33.196	36.415	39.364	42.980	45.559
25	10.520	11.524	13.120	14.611	16.473	19.939	29.339	34.382	37.652	40.646	44.314	46.928
26	11.160	12.198	13.844	15.379	17.292	20.843	30.435	35.563	38.885	41.923	45.642	48.290
27	11.808	12.879	14.573	16.151	18.114	21.749	31.528	36.741	40.113	43.194	46.963	49.645
28	12.461	13.565	15.308	16.928	18.939	22.657	32.620	37.916	41.337	44.461	48.278	50.993
29	13.121	14.257	16.047	17.708	19.768	23.567	33.711	39.087	42.557	45.722	49.588	52.336
30	13.787	14.954	16.791	18.493	20.599	24.478	34.800	40.256	43.773	46.979	50.892	53.672
31	14.458	15.655	17.539	19.281	21.434	25.390	35.887	41.422	44.985	48.232	52.191	55.003
32	15.134	16.362	18.291	20.072	22.271	26.304	36.973	42.585	46.194	49.480	53.486	56.328
33	15.815	17.074	19.047	20.867	23.110	27.219	38.058	43.745	47.400	50.725	54.776	57.648
34	16.501	17.789	19.806	21.664	23.952	28.136	39.141	44.903	48.602	51.966	56.061	58.964
35	17.192	18.509	20.569	22.465	24.797	29.054	40.223	46.059	49.802	53.203	57.342	60.275
36	17.887	19.233	21.336	23.269	25.643	29.973	41.304	47.212	50.998	54.437	58.619	61.581
37	18.586	19.960	22.106	24.075	26.492	30.893	42.383	48.363	52.192	55.668	59.892	62.883

(continued)

TABLE 3
Chi-Square Distribution (*continued*)

Degrees of Freedom	Upper Tail Areas (α)											
	.995	.99	.975	.95	.90	.75	.25	.10	.05	.025	.01	.005
38	19.289	20.691	22.878	24.884	27.343	31.815	43.462	49.513	53.384	56.896	61.162	64.181
39	19.996	21.426	23.654	25.695	28.196	32.737	44.539	50.660	54.572	58.120	62.428	65.476
40	20.707	22.164	24.433	26.509	29.051	33.660	45.616	51.805	55.758	59.342	63.691	66.766
41	21.421	22.906	25.215	27.326	29.907	34.585	46.692	52.949	56.942	60.561	64.950	68.053
42	22.138	23.650	25.999	28.144	30.765	35.510	47.766	54.090	58.124	61.777	66.206	69.336
43	22.859	24.398	26.785	28.965	31.625	36.436	48.840	55.230	59.304	62.990	67.459	70.616
44	23.584	25.148	27.575	29.787	32.487	37.363	49.913	56.369	60.481	64.201	68.710	71.893
45	24.311	25.901	28.366	30.612	33.350	38.291	50.985	57.505	61.656	65.410	69.957	73.166
46	25.041	26.657	29.160	31.439	34.215	39.220	52.056	58.641	62.830	66.617	71.201	74.437
47	25.775	27.416	29.956	32.268	35.081	40.149	53.127	59.774	64.001	67.821	72.443	75.704
48	26.511	28.177	30.755	33.098	35.949	41.079	54.196	60.907	65.171	69.023	73.683	76.969
49	27.249	28.941	31.555	33.930	36.818	42.010	55.265	62.038	66.339	70.222	74.919	78.231
50	27.991	29.707	32.357	34.764	37.689	42.942	56.334	63.167	67.505	71.420	76.154	79.490
51	28.735	30.475	33.162	35.600	38.560	43.874	57.401	64.295	68.669	72.616	77.386	80.747
52	29.481	31.246	33.968	36.437	39.433	44.808	58.468	65.422	69.832	73.810	78.616	82.001
53	30.230	32.018	34.776	37.276	40.308	45.741	59.534	66.548	70.993	75.002	79.843	83.253
54	30.981	32.793	35.586	38.116	41.183	46.676	60.600	67.673	72.153	76.192	81.069	84.502
55	31.735	33.570	36.398	38.958	42.060	47.610	61.665	68.796	73.311	77.380	82.292	85.749
56	32.490	34.350	37.212	39.801	42.937	48.546	62.729	69.919	74.468	78.567	83.513	86.994
57	33.248	35.131	38.027	40.646	43.816	49.482	63.793	71.040	75.624	79.752	84.733	88.236
58	34.008	35.913	38.844	41.492	44.696	50.419	64.857	72.160	76.778	80.936	85.950	89.477
59	34.770	36.698	39.662	42.339	45.577	51.356	65.919	73.279	77.931	82.117	87.166	90.715
60	35.534	37.485	40.482	43.188	46.459	52.294	66.981	74.397	79.082	83.298	88.379	91.952

For a particular number of degrees of freedom, entry represents the critical value of χ^2 corresponding to a specified upper tail area, α.

For larger values of degrees of freedom (DF), the expression $z = \sqrt{2\chi^2} - \sqrt{2(df) - 1}$ may be used and the resulting upper tail area can be obtained from the table of the standardized normal distribution.

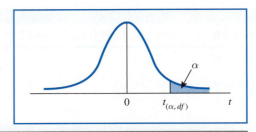

TABLE 4
t Distribution

Degrees of Freedom	Upper Tail Areas					
	.25	.10	.05	.025	.01	.005
1	1.0000	3.0777	6.3138	12.7062	31.8207	63.6574
2	0.8165	1.8856	2.9200	4.3027	6.9646	9.9248
3	0.7649	1.6377	2.3534	3.1824	4.5407	5.8409
4	0.7407	1.5332	2.1318	2.7764	3.7469	4.6041
5	0.7267	1.4759	2.0150	2.5706	3.3649	4.0322
6	0.7176	1.4398	1.9432	2.4469	3.1427	3.7074
7	0.7111	1.4149	1.8946	2.3646	2.9980	3.4995
8	0.7064	1.3968	1.8595	2.3060	2.8965	3.3554
9	0.7027	1.3830	1.8331	2.2622	2.8214	3.2498
10	0.6998	1.3722	1.8125	2.2281	2.7638	3.1693
11	0.6974	1.3634	1.7959	2.2010	2.7181	3.1058
12	0.6955	1.3562	1.7823	2.1788	2.6810	3.0545
13	0.6938	1.3502	1.7709	2.1604	2.6503	3.0123
14	0.6924	1.3450	1.7613	2.1448	2.6245	2.9768
15	0.6912	1.3406	1.7531	2.1315	2.6025	2.9467
16	0.6901	1.3368	1.7459	2.1199	2.5835	2.9208
17	0.6892	1.3334	1.7396	2.1098	2.5669	2.8982
18	0.6884	1.3304	1.7341	2.1009	2.5524	2.8784
19	0.6876	1.3277	1.7291	2.0930	2.5395	2.8609
20	0.6870	1.3253	1.7247	2.0860	2.5280	2.8453
21	0.6864	1.3232	1.7207	2.0796	2.5177	2.8314
22	0.6858	1.3212	1.7171	2.0739	2.5083	2.8188
23	0.6853	1.3195	1.7139	2.0687	2.4999	2.8073
24	0.6848	1.3178	1.7109	2.0639	2.4922	2.7969
25	0.6844	1.3163	1.7081	2.0595	2.4851	2.7874
26	0.6840	1.3150	1.7056	2.0555	2.4786	2.7787
27	0.6837	1.3137	1.7033	2.0518	2.4727	2.7707
28	0.6834	1.3125	1.7011	2.0484	2.4671	2.7633
29	0.6830	1.3114	1.6991	2.0452	2.4620	2.7564
30	0.6828	1.3104	1.6973	2.0423	2.4573	2.7500
31	0.6825	1.3095	1.6955	2.0395	2.4528	2.7440
32	0.6822	1.3086	1.6939	2.0369	2.4487	2.7385
33	0.6820	1.3077	1.6924	2.0345	2.4448	2.7333
34	0.6818	1.3070	1.6909	2.0322	2.4411	2.7284
35	0.6816	1.3062	1.6896	2.0301	2.4377	2.7238
36	0.6814	1.3055	1.6883	2.0281	2.4345	2.7195
37	0.6812	1.3049	1.6871	2.0262	2.4314	2.7154
38	0.6810	1.3042	1.6860	2.0244	2.4286	2.7116

(continued)

TABLE 4
t Distribution (*continued*)

Degrees of Freedom	.25	.10	.05	.025	.01	.005
			Upper Tail Areas			
39	0.6808	1.3036	1.6849	2.0227	2.4258	2.7079
40	0.6807	1.3031	1.6839	2.0211	2.4233	2.7045
41	0.6805	1.3025	1.6829	2.0195	2.4208	2.7012
42	0.6804	1.3020	1.6820	2.0181	2.4185	2.6981
43	0.6802	1.3016	1.6811	2.0167	2.4163	2.6951
44	0.6801	1.3011	1.6802	2.0154	2.4141	2.6923
45	0.6800	1.3006	1.6794	2.0141	2.4121	2.6896
46	0.6799	1.3002	1.6787	2.0129	2.4102	2.6870
47	0.6797	1.2998	1.6779	2.0117	2.4083	2.6846
48	0.6796	1.2994	1.6772	2.0106	2.4066	2.6822
49	0.6795	1.2991	1.6766	2.0096	2.4049	2.6800
50	0.6794	1.2987	1.6759	2.0086	2.4033	2.6778
51	0.6793	1.2984	1.6753	2.0076	2.4017	2.6757
52	0.6792	1.2980	1.6747	2.0066	2.4002	2.6737
53	0.6791	1.2977	1.6741	2.0057	2.3988	2.6718
54	0.6791	1.2974	1.6736	2.0049	2.3974	2.6700
55	0.6790	1.2971	1.6730	2.0040	2.3961	2.6682
56	0.6789	1.2969	1.6725	2.0032	2.3948	2.6665
57	0.6788	1.2966	1.6720	2.0025	2.3936	2.6649
58	0.6787	1.2963	1.6716	2.0017	2.3924	2.6633
59	0.6787	1.2961	1.6711	2.0010	2.3912	2.6618
60	0.6786	1.2958	1.6706	2.0003	2.3901	2.6603
61	0.6785	1.2956	1.6702	1.9996	2.3890	2.6589
62	0.6785	1.2954	1.6698	1.9990	2.3880	2.6575
63	0.6784	1.2951	1.6694	1.9983	2.3870	2.6561
64	0.6783	1.2949	1.6690	1.9977	2.3860	2.6549
65	0.6783	1.2947	1.6686	1.9971	2.3851	2.6536
66	0.6782	1.2945	1.6683	1.9966	2.3842	2.6524
67	0.6782	1.2943	1.6679	1.9960	2.3833	2.6512
68	0.6781	1.2941	1.6676	1.9955	2.3824	2.6501
69	0.6781	1.2939	1.6672	1.9949	2.3816	2.6490
70	0.6780	1.2938	1.6669	1.9944	2.3808	2.6479
71	0.6780	1.2936	1.6666	1.9939	2.3800	2.6469
72	0.6779	1.2934	1.6663	1.9935	2.3793	2.6459
73	0.6779	1.2933	1.6660	1.9930	2.3785	2.6449
74	0.6778	1.2931	1.6657	1.9925	2.3778	2.6439
75	0.6778	1.2929	1.6654	1.9921	2.3771	2.6430
76	0.6777	1.2928	1.6652	1.9917	2.3764	2.6421
77	0.6777	1.2926	1.6649	1.9913	2.3758	2.6412
78	0.6776	1.2925	1.6646	1.9908	2.3751	2.6403
79	0.6776	1.2924	1.6644	1.9905	2.3745	2.6395
80	0.6776	1.2922	1.6641	1.9901	2.3739	2.6387
81	0.6775	1.2921	1.6639	1.9897	2.3733	2.6379
82	0.6775	1.2920	1.6636	1.9893	2.3727	2.6371

(*continued*)

TABLE 4
t Distribution (*continued*)

Degrees of Freedom	Upper Tail Areas					
	.25	.10	.05	.025	.01	.005
83	0.6775	1.2918	1.6634	1.9890	2.3721	2.6364
84	0.6774	1.2917	1.6632	1.9886	2.3716	2.6356
85	0.6774	1.2916	1.6630	1.9883	2.3710	2.6349
86	0.6774	1.2915	1.6628	1.9879	2.3705	2.6342
87	0.6773	1.2914	1.6626	1.9876	2.3700	2.6335
88	0.6773	1.2912	1.6624	1.9873	2.3695	2.6329
89	0.6773	1.2911	1.6622	1.9870	2.3690	2.6322
90	0.6772	1.2910	1.6620	1.9867	2.3685	2.6316
91	0.6772	1.2909	1.6618	1.9864	2.3680	2.6309
92	0.6772	1.2908	1.6616	1.9861	2.3676	2.6303
93	0.6771	1.2907	1.6614	1.9858	2.3671	2.6297
94	0.6771	1.2906	1.6612	1.9855	2.3667	2.6291
95	0.6771	1.2905	1.6611	1.9853	2.3662	2.6286
96	0.6771	1.2904	1.6609	1.9850	2.3658	2.6280
97	0.6770	1.2903	1.6607	1.9847	2.3654	2.6275
98	0.6770	1.2902	1.6606	1.9845	2.3650	2.6269
99	0.6770	1.2902	1.6604	1.9842	2.3646	2.6264
100	0.6770	1.2901	1.6602	1.9840	2.3642	2.6259
110	0.6767	1.2893	1.6588	1.9818	2.3607	2.6213
120	0.6765	1.2886	1.6577	1.9799	2.3578	2.6174
130	0.6764	1.2881	1.6567	1.9784	2.3554	2.6142
140	0.6762	1.2876	1.6558	1.9771	2.3533	2.6114
150	0.6761	1.2872	1.6551	1.9759	2.3515	2.6090
∞	0.6745	1.2816	1.6449	1.9600	2.3263	2.5758

For a particular number of degrees of freedom, entry represents the critical value of *t* corresponding to a specified upper tail area α.

TABLE 5
F Distribution

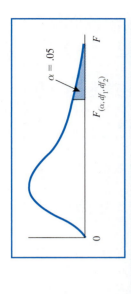

$\alpha = .05$

$F_{(\alpha, df_1, df_2)}$

Denominator df_2	Numerator df_1																		
	1	2	3	4	5	6	7	8	9	10	12	15	20	24	30	40	60	120	∞
1	161.4	199.5	215.7	224.6	230.2	234.0	236.8	238.9	240.5	241.9	243.9	245.9	248.0	249.1	250.1	251.1	252.2	253.3	254.3
2	18.51	19.00	19.16	19.25	19.30	19.33	19.35	19.37	19.38	19.40	19.41	19.43	19.45	19.45	19.46	19.47	19.48	19.49	19.50
3	10.13	9.55	9.28	9.12	9.01	8.94	8.89	8.85	8.81	8.79	8.74	8.70	8.66	8.64	8.62	8.59	8.57	8.55	8.53
4	7.71	6.94	6.59	6.39	6.26	6.16	6.09	6.04	6.00	5.96	5.91	5.86	5.80	5.77	5.75	5.72	5.69	5.66	5.63
5	6.61	5.79	5.41	5.19	5.05	4.95	4.88	4.82	4.77	4.74	4.68	4.62	4.56	4.53	4.50	4.46	4.43	4.40	4.36
6	5.99	5.14	4.76	4.53	4.39	4.28	4.21	4.15	4.10	4.06	4.00	3.94	3.87	3.84	3.81	3.77	3.74	3.70	3.67
7	5.59	4.74	4.35	4.12	3.97	3.87	3.79	3.73	3.68	3.64	3.57	3.51	3.44	3.41	3.38	3.34	3.30	3.27	3.23
8	5.32	4.46	4.07	3.84	3.69	3.58	3.50	3.44	3.39	3.35	3.28	3.22	3.15	3.12	3.08	3.04	3.01	2.97	2.93
9	5.12	4.26	3.86	3.63	3.48	3.37	3.29	3.23	3.18	3.14	3.07	3.01	2.94	2.90	2.86	2.83	2.79	2.75	2.71
10	4.96	4.10	3.71	3.48	3.33	3.22	3.14	3.07	3.02	2.98	2.91	2.85	2.77	2.74	2.70	2.66	2.62	2.58	2.54
11	4.84	3.98	3.59	3.36	3.20	3.09	3.01	2.95	2.90	2.85	2.79	2.72	2.65	2.61	2.57	2.53	2.49	2.45	2.40
12	4.75	3.89	3.49	3.26	3.11	3.00	2.91	2.85	2.80	2.75	2.69	2.62	2.54	2.51	2.47	2.43	2.38	2.34	2.30
13	4.67	3.81	3.41	3.18	3.03	2.92	2.83	2.77	2.71	2.67	2.60	2.53	2.46	2.42	2.38	2.34	2.30	2.25	2.21
14	4.60	3.74	3.34	3.11	2.96	2.85	2.76	2.70	2.65	2.60	2.53	2.46	2.39	2.35	2.31	2.27	2.22	2.18	2.13
15	4.54	3.68	3.29	3.06	2.90	2.79	2.71	2.64	2.59	2.54	2.48	2.40	2.33	2.29	2.25	2.20	2.16	2.11	2.07
16	4.49	3.63	3.24	3.01	2.85	2.74	2.66	2.59	2.54	2.49	2.42	2.35	2.28	2.24	2.19	2.15	2.11	2.06	2.01
17	4.45	3.59	3.20	2.96	2.81	2.70	2.61	2.55	2.49	2.45	2.38	2.31	2.23	2.19	2.15	2.10	2.06	2.01	1.96
18	4.41	3.55	3.16	2.93	2.77	2.66	2.58	2.51	2.46	2.41	2.34	2.27	2.19	2.15	2.11	2.06	2.02	1.97	1.92
19	4.38	3.52	3.13	2.90	2.74	2.63	2.54	2.48	2.42	2.38	2.31	2.23	2.16	2.11	2.07	2.03	1.98	1.93	1.88
20	4.35	3.49	3.10	2.87	2.71	2.60	2.51	2.45	2.39	2.35	2.28	2.20	2.12	2.08	2.04	1.99	1.95	1.90	1.84
21	4.32	3.47	3.07	2.84	2.68	2.57	2.49	2.42	2.37	2.32	2.25	2.18	2.10	2.05	2.01	1.96	1.92	1.87	1.81
22	4.30	3.44	3.05	2.82	2.66	2.55	2.46	2.40	2.34	2.30	2.23	2.15	2.07	2.03	1.98	1.94	1.89	1.84	1.78
23	4.28	3.42	3.03	2.80	2.64	2.53	2.44	2.37	2.32	2.27	2.20	2.13	2.05	2.01	1.96	1.91	1.86	1.81	1.76
24	4.26	3.40	3.01	2.78	2.62	2.51	2.42	2.36	2.30	2.25	2.18	2.11	2.03	1.98	1.94	1.89	1.84	1.79	1.73
25	4.24	3.39	2.99	2.76	2.60	2.49	2.40	2.34	2.28	2.24	2.16	2.09	2.01	1.96	1.92	1.87	1.82	1.77	1.71
26	4.23	3.37	2.98	2.74	2.59	2.47	2.39	2.32	2.27	2.22	2.15	2.07	1.99	1.95	1.90	1.85	1.80	1.75	1.69
27	4.21	3.35	2.96	2.73	2.57	2.46	2.37	2.31	2.25	2.20	2.13	2.06	1.97	1.93	1.88	1.84	1.79	1.73	1.67
28	4.20	3.34	2.95	2.71	2.56	2.45	2.36	2.29	2.24	2.19	2.12	2.04	1.96	1.91	1.87	1.82	1.77	1.71	1.65
29	4.18	3.33	2.93	2.70	2.55	2.43	2.35	2.28	2.22	2.18	2.10	2.03	1.94	1.90	1.85	1.81	1.75	1.70	1.64
30	4.17	3.32	2.92	2.69	2.53	2.42	2.33	2.27	2.21	2.16	2.09	2.01	1.93	1.89	1.84	1.79	1.74	1.68	1.62
40	4.08	3.23	2.84	2.61	2.45	2.34	2.25	2.18	2.12	2.08	2.00	1.92	1.84	1.79	1.74	1.69	1.64	1.58	1.51
60	4.00	3.15	2.76	2.53	2.37	2.25	2.17	2.10	2.04	1.99	1.92	1.84	1.75	1.70	1.65	1.59	1.53	1.47	1.39
120	3.92	3.07	2.68	2.45	2.29	2.17	2.09	2.02	1.96	1.91	1.83	1.75	1.66	1.61	1.55	1.50	1.43	1.35	1.25
∞	3.84	3.00	2.60	2.37	2.21	2.10	2.01	1.94	1.88	1.83	1.75	1.67	1.57	1.52	1.46	1.39	1.32	1.22	1.00

(continued)

TABLE 5
F Distribution (continued)

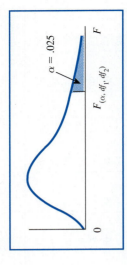

$\alpha = .025$

$F_{(\alpha, df_1, df_2)}$

Denominator df_2	\multicolumn{19}{c	}{Numerator df_1}
	1	2	3	4	5	6	7	8	9	10	12	15	20	24	30	40	60	120	∞
1	647.8	799.5	864.2	899.6	921.8	937.1	948.2	956.7	963.3	968.6	976.7	984.9	993.1	997.2	1001	1006	1010	1014	1018
2	38.51	39.00	39.17	39.25	39.30	39.33	39.36	39.37	39.39	39.40	39.41	39.43	39.45	39.46	39.46	39.47	39.48	39.49	39.50
3	17.44	16.04	15.44	15.10	14.88	14.73	14.62	14.54	14.47	14.42	14.34	14.25	14.17	14.12	14.08	14.04	13.99	13.95	13.90
4	12.22	10.65	9.98	9.60	9.36	9.20	9.07	8.98	8.90	8.84	8.75	8.66	8.56	8.51	8.46	8.41	8.36	8.31	8.26
5	10.01	8.43	7.76	7.39	7.15	6.98	6.85	6.76	6.68	6.62	6.52	6.43	6.33	6.28	6.23	6.18	6.12	6.07	6.02
6	8.81	7.26	6.60	6.23	5.99	5.82	5.70	5.60	5.52	5.46	5.37	5.27	5.17	5.12	5.07	5.01	4.96	4.90	4.85
7	8.07	6.54	5.89	5.52	5.29	5.12	4.99	4.90	4.82	4.76	4.67	4.57	4.47	4.42	4.36	4.31	4.25	4.20	4.14
8	7.57	6.06	5.42	5.05	4.82	4.65	4.53	4.43	4.36	4.30	4.20	4.10	4.00	3.95	3.89	3.84	3.78	3.73	3.67
9	7.21	5.71	5.08	4.72	4.48	4.32	4.20	4.10	4.03	3.96	3.87	3.77	3.67	3.61	3.56	3.51	3.45	3.39	3.33
10	6.94	5.46	4.83	4.47	4.24	4.07	3.95	3.85	3.78	3.72	3.62	3.52	3.42	3.37	3.31	3.26	3.20	3.14	3.08
11	6.72	5.26	4.63	4.28	4.04	3.88	3.76	3.66	3.59	3.53	3.43	3.33	3.23	3.17	3.12	3.06	3.00	2.94	2.88
12	6.55	5.10	4.47	4.12	3.89	3.73	3.61	3.51	3.44	3.37	3.28	3.18	3.07	3.02	2.96	2.91	2.85	2.79	2.72
13	6.41	4.97	4.35	4.00	3.77	3.60	3.48	3.39	3.31	3.25	3.15	3.05	2.95	2.89	2.84	2.78	2.72	2.66	2.60
14	6.30	4.86	4.24	3.89	3.66	3.50	3.38	3.29	3.21	3.15	3.05	2.95	2.84	2.79	2.73	2.67	2.61	2.55	2.49
15	6.20	4.77	4.15	3.80	3.58	3.41	3.29	3.20	3.12	3.06	2.96	2.86	2.76	2.70	2.64	2.59	2.52	2.46	2.40
16	6.12	4.69	4.08	3.73	3.50	3.34	3.22	3.12	3.05	2.99	2.89	2.79	2.68	2.63	2.57	2.51	2.45	2.38	2.32
17	6.04	4.62	4.01	3.66	3.44	3.28	3.16	3.06	2.98	2.92	2.82	2.72	2.62	2.56	2.50	2.44	2.38	2.32	2.25
18	5.98	4.56	3.95	3.61	3.38	3.22	3.10	3.01	2.93	2.87	2.77	2.67	2.56	2.50	2.44	2.38	2.32	2.26	2.19
19	5.92	4.51	3.90	3.56	3.33	3.17	3.05	2.96	2.88	2.82	2.72	2.62	2.51	2.45	2.39	2.33	2.27	2.20	2.13
20	5.87	4.46	3.86	3.51	3.29	3.13	3.01	2.91	2.84	2.77	2.68	2.57	2.46	2.41	2.35	2.29	2.22	2.16	2.09
21	5.83	4.42	3.82	3.48	3.25	3.09	2.97	2.87	2.80	2.73	2.64	2.53	2.42	2.37	2.31	2.25	2.18	2.11	2.04
22	5.79	4.38	3.78	3.44	3.22	3.05	2.93	2.84	2.76	2.70	2.60	2.50	2.39	2.33	2.27	2.21	2.14	2.08	2.00
23	5.75	4.35	3.75	3.41	3.18	3.02	2.90	2.81	2.73	2.67	2.57	2.47	2.36	2.30	2.24	2.18	2.11	2.04	1.97
24	5.72	4.32	3.72	3.38	3.15	2.99	2.87	2.78	2.70	2.64	2.54	2.44	2.33	2.27	2.21	2.15	2.08	2.01	1.94
25	5.69	4.29	3.69	3.35	3.13	2.97	2.85	2.75	2.68	2.61	2.51	2.41	2.30	2.24	2.18	2.12	2.05	1.98	1.91
26	5.66	4.27	3.67	3.33	3.10	2.94	2.82	2.73	2.65	2.59	2.49	2.39	2.28	2.22	2.16	2.09	2.03	1.95	1.88
27	5.63	4.24	3.65	3.31	3.08	2.92	2.80	2.71	2.63	2.57	2.47	2.36	2.25	2.19	2.13	2.07	2.00	1.93	1.85
28	5.61	4.22	3.63	3.29	3.06	2.90	2.78	2.69	2.61	2.55	2.45	2.34	2.23	2.17	2.11	2.05	1.98	1.91	1.83
29	5.59	4.20	3.61	3.27	3.04	2.88	2.76	2.67	2.59	2.53	2.43	2.32	2.21	2.15	2.09	2.03	1.96	1.89	1.81
30	5.57	4.18	3.59	3.25	3.03	2.87	2.75	2.65	2.57	2.51	2.41	2.31	2.20	2.14	2.07	2.01	1.94	1.87	1.79
40	5.42	4.05	3.46	3.13	2.90	2.74	2.62	2.53	2.45	2.39	2.29	2.18	2.07	2.01	1.94	1.88	1.80	1.72	1.64
60	5.29	3.93	3.34	3.01	2.79	2.63	2.51	2.41	2.33	2.27	2.17	2.06	1.94	1.88	1.82	1.74	1.67	1.58	1.48
120	5.15	3.80	3.23	2.89	2.67	2.52	2.39	2.30	2.22	2.16	2.05	1.94	1.82	1.76	1.69	1.61	1.53	1.43	1.31
∞	5.02	3.69	3.12	2.79	2.57	2.41	2.29	2.19	2.11	2.05	1.94	1.83	1.71	1.64	1.57	1.48	1.39	1.27	1.00

(continued)

TABLE 5
F Distribution (continued)

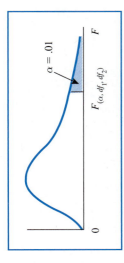

$\alpha = .01$

$F_{(\alpha, df_1, df_2)}$

Denominator df_2	Numerator df_1																		
	1	2	3	4	5	6	7	8	9	10	12	15	20	24	30	40	60	120	∞
1	4052	4999.5	5403	5625	5764	5859	5928	5982	6022	6056	6106	6157	6209	6235	6261	6287	6313	6339	6366
2	98.50	99.00	99.17	99.25	99.30	99.33	99.36	99.37	99.39	99.40	99.42	99.43	99.45	99.46	99.47	99.47	99.48	99.49	99.50
3	34.12	30.82	29.46	28.71	28.24	27.91	27.67	27.49	27.35	27.23	27.05	26.87	26.69	26.60	26.50	26.41	26.32	26.22	26.13
4	21.20	18.00	16.69	15.98	15.52	15.21	14.98	14.80	14.66	14.55	14.37	14.20	14.02	13.93	13.84	13.75	13.65	13.56	13.46
5	16.26	13.27	12.06	11.39	10.97	10.67	10.46	10.29	10.16	10.05	9.89	9.72	9.55	9.47	9.38	9.29	9.20	9.11	9.02
6	13.75	10.92	9.78	9.15	8.75	8.47	8.26	8.10	7.98	7.87	7.72	7.56	7.40	7.31	7.23	7.14	7.06	6.97	6.88
7	12.25	9.55	8.45	7.85	7.46	7.19	6.99	6.84	6.72	6.62	6.47	6.31	6.16	6.07	5.99	5.91	5.82	5.74	5.65
8	11.26	8.65	7.59	7.01	6.63	6.37	6.18	6.03	5.91	5.81	5.67	5.52	5.36	5.28	5.20	5.12	5.03	4.95	4.86
9	10.56	8.02	6.99	6.42	6.06	5.80	5.61	5.47	5.35	5.26	5.11	4.96	4.81	4.73	4.65	4.57	4.48	4.40	4.31
10	10.04	7.56	6.55	5.99	5.64	5.39	5.20	5.06	4.94	4.85	4.71	4.56	4.41	4.33	4.25	4.17	4.08	4.00	3.91
11	9.65	7.21	6.22	5.67	5.32	5.07	4.89	4.74	4.63	4.54	4.40	4.25	4.10	4.02	3.94	3.86	3.78	3.69	3.60
12	9.33	6.93	5.95	5.41	5.06	4.82	4.64	4.50	4.39	4.30	4.16	4.01	3.86	3.78	3.70	3.62	3.54	3.45	3.36
13	9.07	6.70	5.74	5.21	4.86	4.62	4.44	4.30	4.19	4.10	3.96	3.82	3.66	3.59	3.51	3.43	3.34	3.25	3.17
14	8.86	6.51	5.56	5.04	4.69	4.46	4.28	4.14	4.03	3.94	3.80	3.66	3.51	3.43	3.35	3.27	3.18	3.09	3.00
15	8.68	6.36	5.42	4.89	4.56	4.32	4.14	4.00	3.89	3.80	3.67	3.52	3.37	3.29	3.21	3.13	3.05	2.96	2.87
16	8.53	6.23	5.29	4.77	4.44	4.20	4.03	3.89	3.78	3.69	3.55	3.41	3.26	3.18	3.10	3.02	2.93	2.84	2.75
17	8.40	6.11	5.18	4.67	4.34	4.10	3.93	3.79	3.68	3.59	3.46	3.31	3.16	3.08	3.00	2.92	2.83	2.75	2.65
18	8.29	6.01	5.09	4.58	4.25	4.01	3.84	3.71	3.60	3.51	3.37	3.23	3.08	3.00	2.92	2.84	2.75	2.66	2.57
19	8.18	5.93	5.01	4.50	4.17	3.94	3.77	3.63	3.52	3.43	3.30	3.15	3.00	2.92	2.84	2.76	2.67	2.58	2.49
20	8.10	5.85	4.94	4.43	4.10	3.87	3.70	3.56	3.46	3.37	3.23	3.09	2.94	2.86	2.78	2.69	2.61	2.52	2.42
21	8.02	5.78	4.87	4.37	4.04	3.81	3.64	3.51	3.40	3.31	3.17	3.03	2.88	2.80	2.72	2.64	2.55	2.46	2.36
22	7.95	5.72	4.82	4.31	3.99	3.76	3.59	3.45	3.35	3.26	3.12	2.98	2.83	2.75	2.67	2.58	2.50	2.40	2.31
23	7.88	5.66	4.76	4.26	3.94	3.71	3.54	3.41	3.30	3.21	3.07	2.93	2.78	2.70	2.62	2.54	2.45	2.35	2.26
24	7.82	5.61	4.72	4.22	3.90	3.67	3.50	3.36	3.26	3.17	3.03	2.89	2.74	2.66	2.58	2.49	2.40	2.31	2.21
25	7.77	5.57	4.68	4.18	3.85	3.63	3.46	3.32	3.22	3.13	2.99	2.85	2.70	2.62	2.54	2.45	2.36	2.27	2.17
26	7.72	5.53	4.64	4.14	3.82	3.59	3.42	3.29	3.18	3.09	2.96	2.81	2.66	2.58	2.50	2.42	2.33	2.23	2.13
27	7.68	5.49	4.60	4.11	3.78	3.56	3.39	3.26	3.15	3.06	2.93	2.78	2.63	2.55	2.47	2.38	2.29	2.20	2.10
28	7.64	5.45	4.57	4.07	3.75	3.53	3.36	3.23	3.12	3.03	2.90	2.75	2.60	2.52	2.44	2.35	2.26	2.17	2.06
29	7.60	5.42	4.54	4.04	3.73	3.50	3.33	3.20	3.09	3.00	2.87	2.73	2.57	2.49	2.41	2.33	2.23	2.14	2.03
30	7.56	5.39	4.51	4.02	3.70	3.47	3.30	3.17	3.07	2.98	2.84	2.70	2.55	2.47	2.39	2.30	2.21	2.11	2.01
40	7.31	5.18	4.31	3.83	3.51	3.29	3.12	2.99	2.89	2.80	2.66	2.52	2.37	2.29	2.20	2.11	2.02	1.92	1.80
60	7.08	4.98	4.13	3.65	3.34	3.12	2.95	2.82	2.72	2.63	2.50	2.35	2.20	2.12	2.03	1.94	1.84	1.73	1.60
120	6.85	4.79	3.95	3.48	3.17	2.96	2.79	2.66	2.56	2.47	2.34	2.19	2.03	1.95	1.86	1.76	1.66	1.53	1.38
∞	6.63	4.61	3.78	3.32	3.02	2.80	2.64	2.51	2.41	2.32	2.18	2.04	1.88	1.79	1.70	1.59	1.47	1.32	1.00

For a particular combination of numerator and denominator degrees of freedom, entry represents the critical values of F corresponding to a specified upper tail area α.

Notes

Chapter 1

1. Information from www.defense-aerospace.com; www.boeing.com/flash.html; and www.harrisinteractive.com.

2. www.satmetrix.com, accessed February 4, 2009; Joe Flint, "How NBC Defies Network Norms—To Its Advantage," *Wall Street Journal* (May 20, 2002): A1, A10; Michael Freeman, "NBC: No Laughing Matter," *Electronic Media,* 21(1), January 7, 2002; and Jack Neff, "Marketers Use Recipio to Tap Users' View," *Advertising Age,* 72(7) (February 12, 2001): 24.

3. Gina Chon, "Free Preview—WSJ.com," Business Financial News, Business News Online & Personal Finance News at WSJ.com, online.wsj.com/article/SB116313070935919553.html, accessed May 13, 2008; Paul Gu, Paul, "Scion Marketing—ScionWiki," www.scionwiki.com/Scion, accessed May 13, 2008; Nielsen Buzzmetrics, "Case Study: Scion—A Word-of-Mouth Research & Planning Firm," www.nielsenbuzzmetrics.com/files/uploaded/NBZM_Scion_Case_Study.pdf, accessed May 12, 2008; L. Guyer, "Scion Connects in Out of Way Places," *Advertising Age,* 76(8) (2005): 38; www.attik.com/articles/designinm102203.html, accessed March 10, 2005; and www.scion.com/about/about_faq.html, accessed March 3, 2005.

4. Bruce Horovitz, "USATODAY.com—Fast Food Could Soon Mean Fast Fruit as Chains Test Dishes," USATODAY.com, www.usatoday.com/money/industries/food/2004-11-07-fresh-fruit_x.htm, accessed May 13, 2008; Sandelman & Associates, "Fast-Food Users Increasingly Satisfied According to Sandelman & Associates; Chains Responding to Consumers' Desires for Healthier Fare," *Business Wire* (February 7, 2005); S. Gray, "Fast Fruit? At Wendy's and McDonald's, It's a Main Course," *Wall Street Journal* (February 9, 2005): B1.

5. For the strategic role of marketing research, see "SMART—Strategic Marketing and Research Techniques—Survey Market Research," www.s-m-a-r-t.com, accessed May 13, 2008; Sid Simmons and Angela Lovejoy, "Oh No, the Consultants Are Coming!" *International Journal of Market Research,* 45(3) (2003): 355–371; Denise Jarratt and Ramzi Fayed, "The Impact of Market and Organizational Challenges on Marketing Strategy Decision Making," *Journal of Business Research,* 51(1) (January 2001): 61–72; and Lexis F. Higgins, "Applying Principles of Creativity Management to Marketing Research Efforts in High-Technology Markets," *Industrial Marketing Management,* 28(3) (May 1999): 305–317.

6. The AMA definition is reported in "New Marketing Research Definition Approved," *Marketing News,* 21 (January 2, 1987). See also Michelle Wirth Fellman, "An Aging Profession," *Marketing Research,* Chicago (Spring 2000): 33–35; and Lawrence D. Gibson, "Quo Vadis, Marketing Research?" *Marketing Research,* Chicago (Spring 2000): 36–41.

7. For a historical discussion and an assessment of marketing research, see Stephen Brown, "Always Historicize! Researching Marketing History in a Post Historical Epoch," *Marketing Theory,* 1(1) (September 2001): 49–89; L. McTier Anderson, "Marketing Science: Where's the Beef?" *Business Horizons,* 37 (January/February 1994): 8–16; Alvin J. Silk, "Marketing Science in a Changing Environment," *Journal of Marketing Research,* 30 (November 1993): 401–404; and Frank M. Bass, "The Future of Research in Marketing: Marketing Science," *Journal of Marketing Research,* 30 (February 1993): 1–6.

8. "Identifying Opportunities and Marketing," *Marketing* (January 10, 2007), geo.international.gc.ca/can-am/sell2/sell2usgov/IdentifyingOpps-en.asp, accessed May 13, 2008; Gordon A. Wyner, "Learn and Earn Through Testing on the Internet," *Marketing Research* (Fall 2000): 3; and Jerry W. Thomas, "How, When and Why to Do Market Research," *Nation's Restaurant News,* 31(19) (May 12, 1997): 84, 136.

9. Herbert A. Simon, "Decision Making and Problem Solving," http://dieoff.org/page163.htm, accessed November 28, 2008; Peter H. Gray, "A Problem-Solving Perspective on Knowledge Management Practices," *Decision Support Systems,* Amsterdam (May 2001): 87; G. H. van Bruggen, A. Smidts, and B. Wierenga, "The Powerful Triangle of Marketing Data, Managerial Judgment, and Marketing Management Support Systems," *European Journal of Marketing,* 35(7/8) (2001): 796–816; and Barry de Ville, "Intelligent Tools for Marketing Research: Case-Based Reasoning," *Marketing Research: A Magazine of Management & Applications,* 9(2) (Summer 1997): 38–40.

10. Catherine Boal, "Kellogg Rolls Out New Cereal and Snacking Options," *Bakery & Snacks* (February 12, 2007), www.bakeryandsnacks.com/news/ng.asp?id=74110-kellogg-leatherhead-breakfast-snacks, accessed May 14, 2008; "Kellogg Company—Get the Facts on Cereal Eaters' Secrets," Kellogg Company (January 23, 2007), http://investor.kelloggs.com/releasedetail.cfm?releaseid=125378, accessed May 14, 2008; Anonymous, "Kellogg's Crunchy Nut Gets Ready for Adult Breakfast," *Grocer,* 224(7524) (October 6, 2001): 53; and www.kelloggs.com.

11. "Marriott International—SWOT Framework Analysis from Report Buyer," Report Buyer, www.reportbuyer.com/leisure_media/company_reports_leisure_media/marriott_international_swot_framework_analysis.html, accessed May 14, 2008; and Sanjit Sengupta, Robert E. Krapfel, and Michael A. Pusateri, "The Marriott Experience," *Marketing Management,* 6(2) (Summer 1997): 33.

12. For the relationship among information processing, marketing decisions, and performance, see "Performance Marketing," Performance Marketing, www.callpm.com/home/outPerform/index.php, accessed May 15, 2008; William D. Neal, "Getting Serious About Marketing Research," *Marketing Research,* 14(2) (2002): 24–28; and William D. Neal, "Advances in Marketing Segmentation," *Marketing Research* Chicago (Spring 2001): 14–18.

13. "Motrin," *Advertising Age,* 72(11) (March 12, 2001): 44; and "J.J. Unit Purchases St. Joseph's Aspirin of Schering-Plough," *Wall Street Journal,* 236 (120) (December 20, 2000): 20.

14. For the role of marketing research in marketing management, see "Marketing Research," QuickMBA: Accounting, Business Law, Economics, Entrepreneurship, Finance, Management, Marketing, Operations, Statistics, Strategy, www.quickmba.com/marketing/research, accessed May 15, 2008; Victoria Brooks, "Exploitation to Engagement: The Role of Market Research in Getting Close to Niche Markets," *International Journal of Market Research,* 45(3) (2003), 337–354; Naresh K. Malhotra, "The Past, Present, and Future of the Marketing Discipline," *Journal of the Academy of Marketing Science,* 27 (Spring 1999): 116–119; Naresh K. Malhotra, Mark Peterson, and Susan Kleiser, "Marketing Research: A State-of-the-Art Review and Directions for the Twenty-First Century," *Journal of the Academy of Marketing Science,* 27 (Spring 1999): 160–183; and Siva K. Balasubramanian, "The New Marketing Research Systems—How to Use Strategic Database Information for Better Marketing," *Journal of the Academy of Marketing Science,* 24(2) (Spring 1996): 179–181.

15. Naresh K. Malhotra and Mark Peterson, "Marketing Research in the New Millennium: Emerging Issues and Trends," *Market Intelligence and Planning,* 19 (4) (2001): 216–235; David Smith and Andy Dexter, "Whenever I Hear the Word 'Paradigm' I Reach for My Gun: How to Stop Talking and Start Walking: Professional Development Strategy and Tactics for the 21st Century Market Researcher," *International Journal of Market Research,* 43(3) (Third Quarter 2001): 321–340; and Naresh K. Malhotra, "Shifting Perspective on the Shifting Paradigm in Marketing Research," *Journal of the Academy of Marketing Science,* 20 (Fall 1992): 379–387.

16. Information from www.powerdecisions.com/success-new-product-development.cfm and www.powerdecisions.com/marketing-research-company.cfm, accessed November 28, 2008.

17. Formal approaches, such as the Bayesian approach, are available for assessing the cost and value of information obtained by conducting marketing research. See, for example, Chih-Ming Lee, "A Bayesian Approach to Determine the Value of Information in the Newsboy Problem," *International Journal of Production Economics* 112 (March) (2008): 391–402.

18. A complete listing and description of the individual firms in the marketing research industry is provided in *The GreenBook International Directory of Marketing Research Companies and Services* (New York Chapter, American Marketing Association, annually); see www.greenbook.org.

19. Jack Honomichl, "Honomichl Top 50: Annual Business Report on the Marketing Research Industry," *Marketing News* (June 15, 2005): H1–H59.

20. For a historical note and future directions in syndicated services, see Mike Penford, "Continuous Research—Art Nielsen to AD 2000," Journal of the Market Research Society, 36 (January 1994): 19–28; and the Nielsen Web site (www. nielsen.com).

21. www.marketresearchcareers.com, accessed January 2, 2009; Laura Lake, "Market Research Manager—Marketing Career Profile," Marketing, http://marketing.about.com/od, accessed May 15, 2008; and Thomas C. Kinnear and Ann R. Root, *1988 Survey of Marketing Research,* Chicago: American Marketing Association.

22. "Market Research Careers, Jobs, and Training Information," Careers, Career Information, Job Search, Descriptions, Education and Job Search Guide, www.careeroverview.com/market-research-careers.html, accessed May 15, 2008; Sarah Nonis and Gail Hudson, "The Second Course in Business Statistics and Its Role in Undergraduate Marketing Education," *Journal of Marketing Education,* 21 (December 1999): 232–241; and Ralph W. Giacobbe and Madhav N. Segal, "Rethinking Marketing Research Education: A Conceptual, Analytical, and Empirical Investigation," *Journal of Marketing Education,* 16 (Spring 1994): 43–58.

23. See www.time.com/time/2002/globalinfluentials/gbikim.html and www.samsung.com, accessed November 28, 2008.

24. "Decision Support Systems Resources," DSSResources.com, http://dssresources.com, accessed May 17, 2008; O. I. Larichev, A. V. Kortnev, and D. Yu Kochin, "Decision Support System for Classification of a Finite Set of Multicriteria Alternatives," *Decision Support Systems,* 33(1) (May 2002): 13–21; Jehoshua Eliashberg, Jedid-jah Jonker, Mohanbir S. Sawhney, and Berend Wierenga, "MOVIEMOD: An Implementable Decision-Support System for Prerelease Market Evaluation of Motion Pictures," *Marketing Science,* 19(3), (2000): 226–243.

25. Sanjay K. Rao, "A Marketing Decision Support System for Pricing New Pharmaceutical Products," *Marketing Research,* Chicago (Winter 2000): 22–29.

26. "Neural Network—Wikipedia, the Free Encyclopedia," Wikipedia, http://en.wikipedia.org/wiki/Neural_network#Neural_network_software, accessed May 20, 2008; R. Jeffery Thieme, "Artificial Neural Network Decision Support Systems for New Product Development Project Selection," *Journal of Marketing Research* (November 2000): 499–507.

27. "Federal Express Tracks Customers on the Move," Business Intelligence and Enterprise Reporting—Information Builders, www.informationbuilders.com/applications/fedex.html, accessed May 20, 2008; Anonymous, "FedEx Ground Receives Wireless Industry Award for New System That Captures Digital Signatures at Package Delivery," *Businesswire* (December 10, 2001); Aisha Williams, "FedEx Delivers Information Right to Customers' Hands," *Information Week* (March 19, 2001): 33; and www.fedex.com.

28. David Gikandi, "International Marketing Research on the Web," www.4hb.com/0111intlmarkresrce.html, accessed May 20, 2008; Allyson Stewart, "Do Your International Homework First," *Marketing News,* 33(1), (January 4, 1999): 25.

29. See "Starbucks Voted Top Brand in Japan's Restaurant Industry," Business Services Industry, http://archive.japantoday.com/jp/news/299435, accessed May 20, 2008; www.intage.co.jp/express/micjapancom; and www.intage.co.jp/express/micjapancom/special/0009/si0009_1.html.

30. "AMA Statement of Ethics," American Marketing Association, www.marketingpower.com/content435.php, accessed May 20, 2008; "BMA Code of Ethics," Business Marketing Association, www.marketing.org/i4a/pages/index.cfm?pageid=3286, accessed May 20, 2008; Naresh K. Malhotra and Gina Miller, "Social Responsibility and the Marketing Educator: A Focus on Stakeholders, Ethical Theories, and Related Codes of Ethics," *Journal of Business Ethics,* 19 (1999): 211–224.

31. See www.samsonite.com/global/history_90now.jsp, accessed November 28, 2008; and Bob Bengan, "Easing Travel Restrictions," www.quirks.com/articles/a1992/19920201.aspx?searchID=12356947&sort=9, accessed May 21, 2008.

32. Information about the software cited in this book, if not referenced, can be obtained from recent issues of *Marketing News and Marketing Research: A Magazine of Management & Applications,* published by the American Marketing Association, or from a software vendor directory.

Chapter 2

1. Corporate Design Foundation, "Harley-Davidson: Marketing an American Icon," www.cdf.org/issue_journal/harley-davidson_marketing_an_american_icon.html, accessed May 21, 2008; Marilyn Alva, "Hog Maker Gets (Financial) Motor Running," *Investor's Business Daily* (January 28, 2002): A9; Ian Murphy, "Aided by Research, Harley Goes Whole Hog," *Marketing News* (December 2, 1996): 16–17; and www.harleydavidson.com, accessed February 4, 2009.

2. "Marketing Profs Knowledge Exchange: Money Spent, Marketing Research, Decision-Making," www.marketingprofs.com/ea/qst_question.asp?qstID=11527, accessed May 22, 2008; Jagdish N. Sheth and Rajendra S. Sisodia, "Marketing Productivity: Issues and Analysis," *Journal of Business Research,* 55(5) (May 2002): 349; Lawrence D. Gibson (1998), "Defining Marketing Problems," *Marketing Research,* 10(1): 4–12; and Patrick Butler, "Marketing Problem: From Analysis to Decision," *Marketing Intelligence & Planning,* 12(2) (1994): 4–12.

3. "Research to Aid Decision-Making—How to Evaluate Market Research Reports Tutorials from KnowThis.com," www.knowthis.com/tutorials/marketing/how-to-evaluate-market-research-reports/1.htm, accessed May 22, 2008; Molly Inhofe Rapert, "The Strategic Implementation Process: Evoking Strategic Consensus Through Communication," *Journal of Business Research,* 55(4) (April 2002): 301; and David Smith and Andy Dexter, "Quality in Marketing Research: Hard Frameworks for Soft Problems," *Journal of the Market Research Society,* 36(2) (April 1994): 115–132.

4. Greg W. Marshall, "Selection Decision Making by Sales Managers and Human Resource Managers: Decision Impact, Decision Frame and Time of Valuation," *The Journal of Personal Selling and Sales Management* (Winter 2001): 19–28; and Berend Wierenga and Gerrit H. van Bruggen, "The Integration of Marketing Problem Solving Modes and Marketing Management Support Systems," *Journal of Marketing,* 61(3) (July 1997): 21–37.

5. Anonymous, "How to Decide Who Should Get What Data," *HR Focus* (May 2001): 7; R. P. Hamlin, "A Systematic Procedure for Targeting Marketing Research," *European Journal of Marketing,* 34(9/10) (2000): 1038–1052; and Mary J. Cronin, "Using the Web to Push Key Data to Decision Makers," *Fortune,* 36(6) (September 29, 1997): 254.

6. Copernicus Marketing Consulting, "Auditing a Marketing Program," www.copernicusmarketing.com/univers/audit.shtml, accessed May 22, 2008; "The Marketing Audit," www.marketingaudit.com, accessed May 22, 2008; Neil A. Morgan, "Marketing Productivity, Marketing Audits, and Systems for Marketing Performance Assessment: Integrating Multiple Perspectives," *Journal of Business Research,* 55(5) (May 2002): 363; Merrilyn Astin Tarlton, "Quick Marketing Audit," *Law Practice Management,* 23(6) (September 1997): 18, 63; and Leonard L. Berry, Jeffrey S. Conant, and A. Parasuraman, "A Framework for Conducting a Services Marketing Audit," *Journal of the Academy of Marketing Science,* 19 (Summer 1991): 255–268.

7. "Clash Resolution—Decision Making—Corporate Culture Change Management," www.cmd-hmc.com/clash-motivation-decision-making-sites.htm, accessed May 22, 2008; Ram Charan, "Conquering a Culture of Indecision," *Harvard Business Review* (April 2001): 74; and Saviour L. S. Nwachukwu and Scott J. Vitell, Jr., "The Influence of Corporate Culture on Managerial Ethical Judgments," *Journal of Business Ethics,* 16(8) (June 1997): 757–776.

8. Ellen Neuborne and Stephanie Anderson Forest, "Look Who's Picking Levi's Pocket," *Business Week* (September 8, 1997): 68, 72.

9. Analysys Mason, "Expert Interview Surveys," www.analysysmason.com/Research/Custom-research/Expert-interview-surveys, accessed May 23, 2008; "Individual In-Depth Interview, Expert Interview," www.szondaipsos.hu/en/modszereink/melyinterju/melyinterjuen, accessed May 23, 2008; "Optimizing the Use of Experts," www.zyen.com/Knowledge/Research/Research%20into%20optimising%20the%20use%20of%20experts.pdf, accessed May 23, 2008; and J. Scott Armstrong, "Prediction of Consumer Behavior by Experts and Novices," *Journal of Consumer Research,* 18 (September 1991): 251–256.

10. Kenneth Hein, "Cherry Coke Gets Fresh Jay-Z Remix," www.brandweek.com/bw/news/recent_display.jsp?vnu_content_id=1003538680, accessed May 23, 2008; Joanne Lutynec, "Jay-Z Helps Relaunch Cherry Coke—Slashfood," www.slashfood.com/2007/02/12/jay-z-helps-relaunch-cherry-coke, accessed May 23, 2008; and Hank Kim, "Freeman Sets Goals for Cherry Coke," *Adweek* (August 24, 1998).

11. Information from http://classwork.busadm.mu.edu/Durvasula/Mark142/MktRes%20at%20P&G.doc; www.pg.com/products/usa_product_facts.jhtml, accessed November 28, 2008.

12. Anonymous, "Movers, Shakers, and Decision Makers 2002," *Financial Planning* (January 1, 2002): 1; and Mary T. Curren, Valerie S. Folkes, and Joel H. Steckel, "Explanations for Successful and Unsuccessful Marketing Decisions: The Decision Maker's Perspective," *Journal of Marketing,* 56 (April 1992): 18–31.

13. Michael J. Hennel, "Forecasting Demand Begins with Integration," *B to B,* 87(11) (November 11): 9; and C. L. Jain, "Myths and Realities of Forecasting," *Journal of Business Forecasting,* 9 (Fall 1990): 18–22.

14. See http://emergemarketing.com/15.0.0.1.0.0.shtml; and www.smartecarte.com/about/index.html, accessed January 2, 2009.

15. Pat Cavill, "Marketing Plan Worksheet," units.sla.org/chapter/cwcn/wwest/v1n3/cavilb13.htm, accessed May 26, 2008; Ray Suutari, "Playing the Decision-Making Game," *CMA Management,* 75(7), (October 2001): 14–17; Lehman Benson III and Lee Roy Beach, "The Effect of Time Constraints on the Prechoice Screening of Decision Options," *Organizational Behavior & Human Decision Processes,* 67(2) (August 1996): 222–228; and Ron Sanchez and D. Sudharshan, "Real-Time Market Research," *Marketing Intelligence and Planning,* 11 (1993): 29–38.

16. Based on a marketing research project conducted by the author. See also Darren W. Dahl, "The Influence and Value of Analogical Thinking During New Product Ideation," *Journal of Marketing Research,* 39(1) (February 2002): 47–60; and "Identifying Constraints in Your Opportunity Pipeline," www.avidian.com/identifying_constraints_in_your_salesOpportunity_pipeline.aspx, accessed May 26, 2008.

17. "'Got Milk?' From Memorable to Motivational. How Research Helped Re-Focus One of America's Most Visible Advertising Campaigns," www.harrisinteractive.com/about/pubs/HI_BSC_CASESTUDY_Milk.pdf, accessed May 26, 2008; Hillary Chura and Stephanie Thompson, "Bozell Moving Beyond Mustaches in Milk Ads," *Advertising Age,* 70(43) (October 18, 1999): 81; and www.gotmilk.com/story.html, accessed January 16, 2001.

18. R. Jeffery Thieme, "Artificial Neural Network Decision Support Systems for the New Product Development Project Selection," *Journal of Marketing Research,* Chicago (November 2000): 499–507; and Stephen M. Heyl, "Decision Matrix Points the Way to Better Research ROI," *Marketing News,* 31(19) (September 15, 1997): 18, 30.

19. See www.sportseconomics.com/services/CS_marketing.html.

20. Utpal M. Dholakia, "Concept Discovery, Process Explanation, and Theory Deepening in E-Marketing," Marketing Theory,

http://mtq.sagepub.com/cgi/content/abstract/5/1/117, accessed May 26, 2008; Gary L. Lilien, "Bridging the Marketing Theory," *Journal of Business Research,* 55(2) (February 2002): 111; and Shelby D. Hunt, "For Reason and Realism in Marketing," *Journal of Marketing,* 56 (April 1992): 89–102.

21. A positivist perspective on research is used here. Positivism encompasses logical positivism, logical empiricism, and all forms of falsificationism. This is the dominant perspective adopted in commercial marketing research. More recently, a relativist perspective has been offered. See, for example, Jillian Dawes and Reva Berman Brown, "Postmodern Marketing: Research Issues for Retail Financial Services," *Qualitative Market Research,* 3(2) (2000): 90–98; and Shelby D. Hunt, *A General Theory of Competition* (Thousand Oaks, CA: Sage, 2000).

22. Mika Boedeker, "New-Type and Traditional Shoppers: A Comparison of Two Major Consumer Groups," *International Journal of Retail & Distribution Management,* 23(3) (1995): 17–26; and Naresh K. Malhotra, "A Threshold Model of Store Choice," *Journal of Retailing* (Summer 1983): 3–21.

23. Scott M. Smith, "Introduction to Marketing Models," http://marketing.byu.edu/htmlpages/courses/693r/modelsbook/chapter1.html, accessed May 26, 2008; Martin Callingham and Tim Baker, "We Know What They Think, But Do We Know What They Do?" *International Journal of Market Research,* 44(3) (2002): 299–334; Naresh K. Malhotra and Lan Wu, "Decision Models and Descriptive Models: Complementary Roles," *Marketing Research,* 13(4) (December 2001): 43–44; and Peter S. H. Leeflang, "Building Models for Marketing Decisions: Past, Present and Future," *International Journal of Research in Marketing* (September 2000): 105.

24. The integrated role of theory, models, research questions, and hypotheses in marketing research can be seen in Arne Nygaard and Robert Dahlstrom, "Role Stress and Effectiveness in Horizontal Alliances," *Journal of Marketing,* 66 (April 2002): 61–82; and Joseph C. Nunes, "A Cognitive Model of People's Usage Estimations," *Journal of Marketing Research,* 37(4) (November 2000): 397–409. See also "Hypotheses," www.socialresearchmethods.net/kb/hypothes.php, accessed May 26, 2008.

25. "How to Create Brand Loyalty Among Today's Consumers," Business Market Research Reports, www.bharatbook.com/detail.asp?id=46953, accessed May 27, 2008; Deepak Sirdeshmukh, "Consumer Trust, Value, and Loyalty in Relational Exchanges," *Journal of Marketing,* 66(1) (January 2002): 15–37.

26. "Comfort Food Consumption Varies with Gender, Emotions, Says Study," www.foodnavigator-usa.com/news/ng.asp?id=64039-comfort-foods-snack-foods-gender, accessed May 29, 2008; Brian Wansink and Cynthia Sangerman, "The Taste of Comfort," *American Demographics,* 22(7) (July 2000): 66–67; and Anonymous, "Comfort Food," *Potentials,* 35(1) (January 2002): 12.

27. Sonia Reyes, "Heinz Builds on EZ Squirt Success with Adult-Skewing Kick'rs Line," *Brandweek,* 43(3) (January 21, 2002): 4; and "ConAgra, Heinz Rule Mexican Frozens," *Frozen Food Age,* 45(11) (June 1997): 16.

28. John B. Ford, "Special Issue on Cross-Cultural Issues in Marketing Research," www.amsreview.org/articles/ford05-2007.pdf, accessed May 29, 2008; Paul Westhead, "International Market Selection Strategies Selected by 'Micro' and 'Small' Firms," *Omega,* 30(1), (February 2002): 51; and Susan P. Douglas and C. Samuel Craig, *International Marketing Research* (Englewood Cliffs, NJ: Prentice Hall, 1983).

29. Sonoo Singh, "Unilever Picks Global Brand Director for Surf," *Marketing Week* (March 7, 2002): 7; and David Kilburn, "Unilever Struggles with Surf in Japan," *Advertising Age* (May 6, 1991).

30. J. Pierre Brans, "Ethics and Decisions," *European Journal of Operational Research,* 136(2) (January 16, 2002): 340; and G. R. Laczniak and P. E. Murphy, *Ethical Marketing Decisions, the Higher Road* (Boston, MA: Allyn & Bacon, 1993).

31. See www.kelloggs.com, accessed January 9, 2009; and Nicci Pugh, "Kellogg to Stop Marketing Unhealthy Products to Under-12s," Food

Business Review, www.food-business-review.com/article_news. asp?guid=9136E134-CA24-4E88-A387-06A07F62CA8D, accessed May 29, 2008.

Chapter 3

1. www.starbucks.com, accessed January 8, 2009; Brad Broberg, "Ben Packard, Starbucks' Boss for Environment," *Puget Sound Business Journal* (Seattle), www.bizjournals.com/seattle/stories/2008/02/18/focus6.html, accessed May 29, 2008; Report of the Starbucks Coffee Company, www.edf.org/documents/523_starbucks.pdf, accessed May 29, 2008; and Marianne Wilson, "More Than Just Causes," *Business and Industry* 76 (August 2000): 37–54.

2. "What Is Exploratory Research?" Market Research Portal, www.marketresearchworld.net/index.php?option=content&task=view&id=798&Itemid=, accessed May 31, 2008; I. M. Halman, "Evaluating Effectiveness of Project Start-Ups: An Exploratory Study," *International Journal of Project Management* 20(1) (January 2002): 81; and Thomas T. Semon, "Marketing Research Needs Basic Research," *Marketing News* 28(6) (March 14, 1996): 12.

3. "ESOMAR—Market Research Glossary C," www.esomar.org/index.php/glossary-c.html, accessed May 31, 2008; Sharlene Hesse-Biber, *Emergent Methods in Social Research: Theories, Methods, and Methodologies* (Thousand Oaks, CA: Sage Publications, 2006); John W. Creswell, *Research Design: Qualitative, Quantitative, and Mixed Method Approaches*, 2nd ed. (Thousand Oaks, CA: Sage Publications, 2002); Hanjoon Lee, Jay D. Lindquist, and Frank Acito, "Managers' Evaluation of Research Design and Its Impact on the Use of Research: An Experimental Approach," *Journal of Business Research* 39(3) (July 1997): 231–240; and R. Dale Wilson, "Research Design: Qualitative and Quantitative Approaches," *Journal of Marketing Research* 33(2) (May 1996): 252–255.

4. For examples of exploratory research, see Paul Ellis and Anthony Pecotich, "Social Factors Influencing Export Initiation in Small and Medium-Sized Enterprises," *Journal of Marketing Research* 38(1) (February 2001): 119–130; and Ellen Bolman Pullins, "An Exploratory Investigation of the Relationship of Sales Force Compensation and Intrinsic Motivation," *Industrial Marketing Management*, 30(5) (July 2001): 403. See also, Joseph A. Maxwell, *Qualitative Research Design*, 2nd ed. (Thousand Oaks, CA: Sage Publications, 2004).

5. www.waterpik.com; www.innovationfocus.com/success/index.asp, accessed January 12, 2009.

6. For an example of descriptive research, see William T. Robinson, "Is the First to Market the First to Fail?" *Journal of Marketing Research*, 39(1) (February 2002): 120–128.

7. "Patient, Physician, Employee, and Community Healthcare Perception Research, Customized Marketing, Health Risk Assessments, Health Status Measurements," www.prconline.com, accessed June 1, 2008; Jeff Goldsmith, "Integrating Care: A Talk with Kaiser Permanente's David Lawrence," *Health Affairs*, 21(1) (January/February 2002): 39–48; and Julie T. Chyna, "Is Your Culture E-Compatible?" *Healthcare Executive*, 17(1) (January/February 2002): 53.

8. William M. Mason, "Cohort Analysis," Center for Population Research, www.ccpr.ucla.edu/ccprwpseries/ccpr_005_01.pdf, accessed June 1, 2008; Nicholas H. Wolfinger, "Cohort Analysis," repositories.cdlib.org/ccpr/olwp/CCPR-005-01, accessed June 1, 2008; Ellen Perecman, *A Handbook for Social Science Field Research* (Thousand Oaks, CA: Sage Publications, 2006); John Creswell, *Research Design: Qualitative, Quantitative, and Mixed Method Approaches*, 2nd ed. (Thousand Oaks, CA: Sage Publications, 2002); Ranjita Misra and B. Panigrahi, "Changes in Attitudes Toward Women: A Cohort Analysis," *International Journal of Sociology & Social Policy*, 15(6) (1995): 1–20; and Norval D. Glenn, *Cohort Analysis* (Beverly Hills: Sage Publications, 1981).

9. Joseph O. Rentz, Fred D. Reynolds, and Roy G. Stout, "Analyzing Changing Consumption Patterns with Cohort Analysis," *Journal of Marketing Research*, 20 (February 1983): 12–20. See also, Joseph O. Rentz and Fred D. Reynolds, "Forecasting the Effects of an Aging Population on Product Consumption: An Age-Period-Cohort Framework," *Journal of Marketing Research* (August 1991): 355–360.

10. Stephanie Kang, "Michelle Wie Wins a Deal Helping Nike Target Women Golfers," *Wall Street Journal* (October 5, 2005): B1, B5; and Anonymous, "Ways to Use Golf," *Incentive* (January 2001): 2–7.

11. For recent applications of panel data, see Jack K. H. Lee, K. Sudhir, and Joel H. Steckel, "A Multiple Ideal Point Model: Capturing Multiple Preference Effects from Within an Ideal Point Framework," *Journal of Marketing Research,* 39(1) (February 2002): 73–86. For a basic treatment, see Gregory B. Markus, *Analyzing Panel Data* (Beverly Hills: Sage Publications, 1979).

12. Table 3.6 can also be viewed as a transition matrix. It depicts the brand-buying changes from period to period. Knowing the proportion of consumers who switch allows for early prediction of the ultimate success of a new product or change in market strategy.

13. Aric Rindfleisch, Alan J. Malter, Shankar Ganesan, and Christine Moorman, "Cross-Sectional Versus Longitudinal Survey Research: Concepts, Findings, and Guidelines," *Journal of Marketing Research,* 45(3) (June 2008): 261–279; "Panel Data," Data and Statistical Services, dss.princeton.edu/online_help/analysis/panel.htm, June 3, 2008; David de Vaus, *Research Design*, 4 vols. (Thousand Oaks, CA: Sage Publications, 2005); E. K. F. Leong, M. T. Ewing, and L. F. Pitt, "Australian Marketing Managers' Perceptions of the Internet: A Quasi-Longitudinal Perspective," *European Journal of Marketing*, 37(3/4) (2003): 554–571; Kurt Brannas, "A New Approach to Modeling and Forecasting Monthly Guest Nights in Hotels," *International Journal of Forecasting*, 18(1) (January–March 2002): 19; and Seymour Sudman and Robert Ferber, *Consumer Panels* (Chicago: American Marketing Association, 1979): 19–27.

14. Joshua Clinton, "Panel Bias from Attrition and Conditioning: A Case Study of the Knowledge Networks Panel," www.knowledgenetworks.com/insights/docs/Panel%20Effects.pdf, accessed June 3, 2008; John Brewer, *Foundations of MultiMethod Research* (Thousand Oaks, CA: Sage Publications, 2005); Toon W. Taris, *A Primer in Longitudinal Data Analysis* (Thousand Oaks, CA: Sage Publications, 2001); G. J. Van Den Berg, M. Lindeboom, and G. Ridder, "Attrition in Longitudinal Panel Data and the Empirical Analysis of Dynamic Labour Market Behaviour," *Journal of Applied Econometrics*, 9(4), (October–December 1994): 421–435; and Russell S. Winer, "Attrition Bias in Econometric Models Estimated with Panel Data," *Journal of Marketing Research*, 20 (May 1983): 177–186.

15. Denise Oliveri, "Consumer Panels: Are They Legitimate and Time Worthy?" Consumer Education @ Suite101.com, consumereducation.suite101.com/article.cfm/consumer_panels, accessed June 4, 2008; Jack K. H. Lee, K. Sudhir, and Joel H. Steckel, "A Multiple Ideal Point Model: Capturing Multiple Preference Effects from Within an Ideal Point Framework," *Journal of Marketing Research,* 39(1) (February 2002): 73–86; and Laszlo Maytas and Patrick Sevestre, eds., *The Econometrics of Panel Data, A Handbook of the Theory with Applications* (Norwell: Kluwer Academic Publishers, 1996).

16. "Causal Research: Descriptive vs. Causal Research," spsp.clarion.edu/mm/RDE3/C6/CausalvsDescriptiveAct.html, accessed June 3, 2008; Grant F. Gould and James L. Gould, *Chance and Causation: To Experimental Design and Statistica* (New York: W. H. Freeman, 2001); John Hulland, Yiu Ho, and Shunyin Lam, "Use of Causal Models in Marketing Research: A Review," *International Journal of Research in Marketing,* 13(2) (April 1996): 181–197.

17. "Discover Which Marketing Programs Really Work," www.marketingexperiments.com, accessed June 4, 2008; Russell S. Winer, "Experimentation in the 21st Century: The Importance of External Validity," *Academy of Marketing Science Journal*, Greenvale (Summer 1999): 349–158.

18. Heather Leigh, "One Louder: Market Research . . . What Does Microsoft Look For?" blogs.msdn.com/heatherleigh/archive/2004/03/18/92232.aspx, accessed June 4, 2008; www.microsoft.com/usabilty/default.htm, accessed January 8, 2008.

19. "Citi Financial Education Program," www.citi.com/citigroup/ financialeducation/highlights070501.htm, accessed June 4, 2008; Jack Willoughby, "Exit Citigroup Smiling," *Barron's,* 82(11) (March 18, 2002): 1; and Sabra Brock, Sara Lipson, and Ron Levitt, "Trends in Marketing Research and Development at Citicorp/Citibank," *Marketing Research: A Magazine of Management and Applications,* 1(4) (December 1989).

20. "Learning Resources: Statistics: Power from Data! Non-Sampling Error," www.statcan.ca/english/edu/power/ch6/nonsampling/ nonsampling.htm#response, accessed June 4, 2008; Madhu Viswanathan, *Measurement Error and Research Design* (Thousand Oaks, CA: Sage Publications, 2005); Eunkyu Lee, "Are Consumer Survey Results Distorted? Systematic Impact of Behavioral Frequency and Duration on Survey Response Errors," *Journal of Marketing Research* (February 2000): 125–133; and Solomon Dutka and Lester R. Frankel, "Measuring Response Error," *Journal of Advertising Research,* 37(1) (January/February 1997): 33–39.

21. Alison Stein Wellner, "The American Family in the 21st Century," *American Demographics,* 23(8) (August 2001): 20; Rebecca P. Heath, "Life on Easy Street," *American Demographics,* 19(4) (April 1997): 32–38; and *Marketing News* (April 10, 1987): 3.

22. "Survey Sampling Methods," StatPac Survey Software—Comprehensive Statistical Reports, www.statpac.com/surveys/sampling.htm, accessed June 4, 2008; Pritbhushan Sinha, "Determination of Reliability of Estimations Obtained with Survey Research: A Method of Simulation," *International Journal of Market Research,* 42(3) (Summer 2000): 311–318; Margret R. Rollere, "Control Is Elusive in Research Design," *Marketing News,* 31(19) (September 15, 1997): 17; and Tom Corlett, "Sampling Errors in Practice," *Journal of Market Research Society,* 38(4) (October 1996): 307–318.

23. "Program Evaluation and Review Technique (PERT): A Planning and Control Tool for Occupational Field Studies," Public STINET (Scientific and Technical Information Network), http://stinet.dtic. mil/oai/oai?verb=getRecord&metadataPrefix=html&identifier= ADA024131, accessed June 6, 2008; I. M. Premachandra, "An Approximation of the Activity Duration Distribution in PERT," *Computers and Operations Research,* New York (April 2001): 443; and Zedan Hatush and Martin Skitmore, "Assessment and Evaluation of Contractor Data Against Client Goals Using PERT Approach," *Construction Management & Economics,* 15(4) (July 1997): 327–340. See also, Michael Bamberger, *Real World Evaluation* (Thousand Oaks, CA: Sage Publications, 2006).

24. Saabira Chaudhuri, "Marketing Tuesday: McDonalds Caters to Local Palates | Fast Company," www.fastcompany.com/blog-post/ marketing-tuesday-mcdonalds-caters-local-palates, accessed June 7, 2008; Carl Rohde and Ole Christensen, "Understanding European Youth," *Quirk's Marketing Research Review* (November 2000), article number 0630 at www.quirks.com/articles/article_print.asp?arg_ articleid=630.

25. Neil C. Herndon Jr., "An Investigation of Moral Values and the Ethical Content of the Corporate Culture: Taiwanese Versus U.S. Sales People," *Journal of Business Ethics,* 30(1) (March 2001): 73–85; and Betsy Peterson, "Ethics Revisited," *Marketing Research: A Magazine of Management & Applications,* 8(4) (Winter 1996): 47–48.

26. Liz Clarke, "NASCAR's New Marketing Strategy Is the Latest Buzz," www.washingtonpost.com/wp-dyn/content/article/ 2007/05/25/AR2007052502411.html, accessed June 6, 2008; Leigh Somerville, "In the Driver's Seat: NASCAR Seeks Diversification," *The Business Journal,* 5(49) (August 8, 2003): 11; and "NASCAR, Nextel Buckle Up as Partners for Top Racing Series," *Knight Ridder Tribune Business News* (June 20, 2003): 1.

Chapter 4

1. "Secondary Data Research," Data and Information Services Center Home Page, www.disc.wisc.edu/types/secondary.htm, accessed June 8, 2008; Marc Riedel, *Research Strategies for Secondary Data* (Thousand Oaks, CA: Sage Publications, 2005); Niall Ó Dochartaigh, *The Internet Research Handbook: A Practical Guide for Students and Researchers in the Social Sciences* (Thousand Oaks, CA: Sage Publications, 2002); Stephen B. Castleberry, "Using Secondary Data in Marketing Research: A Project that Melds Web and Off-Web Sources," *Journal of Marketing Education,* 23(3) (December 2001): 195–203; and Gordon L. Patzer, *Using Secondary Data in Marketing Research* (Westport, CT, Greenwood Publishing Group, 1995).

2. "Boston Market 'Times' New Strategy," www.brandweek.com/bw/ news/recent_display.jsp?vnu_content_id=1002275549, accessed June 7, 2008; Ron Ruggless, "Boston Market Rolls Out Latest Fast-Casual Rotisserie Grill Unit," *Nation's Restaurant News,* 37(49) (December 8, 2003): 1; Anonymous, "HMR: Designed to Beat Eating Out," *Grocer,* 224(7505) (May 26, 2001): 52–53; and www.bostonmarket.com/4_company/news_110601.htm.

3. "The Aging American Workforce: Get Ready," www.aarp.org/ money/careers/employerresourcecenter/trends/ a2004-07-22-agingworkforce.html, accessed June 6, 2008; Amy Garber, "McDonald's Unveils Technology Upgrades to Improve Service," *Nation's Restaurant News,* 38(13) (March 29, 2004): 6; Steven M. Barney, "A Changing Workforce Calls for Twenty-First Century Strategies," *Journal of Healthcare Management,* 47(2) (March/April 2002): 81–84; and www.elotouch.com/pdfs/ marcom/regal.pdf.

4. For recent applications of secondary data, see Mark B. Houston, "Assessing the Validity of Secondary Data Proxies for Marketing Constructs," *Journal of Business Research,* 57(2) (2004): 154–161; Masaaki Kotabe, "Using Euromonitor Database in International Marketing Research," *Journal of the Academy of Marketing Science,* 30(2) (Spring 2002): 172; and Paul A. Bottomley and Stephen J. S. Holden, "Do We Really Know How Consumers Evaluate Brand Extensions? Empirical Generalizations Based on Secondary Analysis of Eight Studies," *Journal of Marketing Research,* 38(4) (November 2001): 494–500.

5. Dave Andrews, "How Nielsen TV Ratings Work," www.helium.com/ items/990477-how-nielsen-tv-ratings-work, accessed June 8, 2008; Kevin Downey, "Calm After the Nielsen Storm," *Broadcasting & Cable,* 134(29) (July 19, 2004): 10; Meg James, "Nielsen Rolls Out People Meters: The TV Ratings Firm Switches to the New Devices in L.A. Despite Continued Criticism," *Los Angeles Times* (July 8, 2004): C1; Anonymous, "Nielsen Ratings," *Adweek,* 43(4) (January 21, 2002): B1; Claude Brodesser, "Nielsen Under Fire on Hispanic Sample," *Mediaweek* (July 21, 1997): 15; and www.acnielsen.com/ services/media/trad, accessed January 26, 2002.

6. Linda Rosencrance, "E-Commerce Sales to Boom for Next 5 Years: Forecasts Project Online Sales of $215B to $335B Annually by 2012," www.computerworld.com/action/article.do?command= viewArticleBasic&articleId=9061108, accessed September 24, 2008; and Antonio A. Prado, "E-Tail Revenue Numbers Seldom Add Up," *Investor's Business Daily,* 18(201) (January 25, 2002): A6.

7. "ROI Case Study SPSS American Airlines," Nucleus Research, www. spss.pl/dodatki/download/American%20Airlines_Nucleus%20Reseach %20report.pdf, accessed December 1, 2008; Terry Maxon, "American Airlines to Join Swiss Air Lines in Marketing Partnership," *Knight Ridder Tribune Business News* (March 27, 2002): 1; Peter Keating, "The Best Airlines to Fly Today," *Money* (November 1997): 118–128.

8. "DMA Database Marketing Seminar," www.the-dma.org/seminars/ database, accessed June 8, 2008; Ronald G. Drozdenko and Perry D. Drake, *Optimal Database Marketing* (Thousand Oaks, CA: Sage Publications, 2002); Bill Donaldson and George Wright, "Sales Information Systems: Are They Being Used for More Than Simple Mail Shots?" *Journal of Database Management,* 9(3) (2002): 276–284; and Drayton Bird, "Database Marketing Gets Vote over Management Consultants," *Marketing* (March 7, 2002): 18.

9. Eric Morath, "Chrysler Creates Online Forum for Buyer Feedback," CRM Daily, www.crm-daily.com/news/Chrysler-Implements- Online-Feedback/story.xhtml?story_id=010000102NOK, accessed June 8, 2008; Jean Halliday, "Carmakers Learn to Mine Databases," *Advertising Age* (April 2000): S6–S8; and www.chrysler.com, accessed January 27, 2009.

10. "J.D. Power and Associates Reports: Caterpillar and Cummins Rank Highest in Heavy-Duty Truck Engine Customer Satisfaction," www.theautochannel.com/news/2007/10/16/067401.html, accessed June 9, 2008; www.cat.com/cda/components/fullArticleNoNav?id= 224609; and www.dbmarketing.com/articles/Art125.htm.

11. "Sources for Market Research Data (2008)," www.business.gov/ guides/advertising/market_research, accessed June 9, 2008; and Keith Malo, "Corporate Strategy Requires Market Research," *Marketing News,* 36(2) (January 21, 2002): 14.

12. www.census.gov/compendia/statab, accessed June 9, 2008; Bob Brewin, "U.S. Census Bureau Plans for First Paperless Tally in 2010," *Computerworld,* 36(12) (March 18, 2002): 5; Cynthia Etkin, "Historical United States Census Data Browser," *Library Journal,* 125(7) (April 15, 2000): 58; and www.census.gov.

13. http://factfinder.census.gov/jsp/saff/SAFFInfo.jsp?geo_id= 01000US&_geoContext=01000US&_street=&_county=&_cityTown= &_state=&_zip=&_pageId=sp4_decennial&_submenuId=&_ci_nbr= null, accessed June 9, 2008; and Katarzyna Dawidowska, "The Census Bureau Century," *American Demographics,* 24(3) (March 2002): 12.

14. One such firm is Nielsen's Claritas (www.claritas.com). See David Wren, "San Diego's Claritas Studies Myrtle Beach, SC, Demographics by Zip Code," *Knight Ridder Tribune Business News* (May 7, 2002): 1.

15. David Minckler, "U.S. Minority Population Continues to Grow," www. america.gov/st/diversity-english/2008/May/20080513175840zjsredna0. 1815607.html, accessed June 9, 2008; "Minorities Now Make Up Majority in Orange Co., Calif.," Dow Jones Newswires (September 30, 2004); Robert J. Samuelson, "Can America Assimilate?" *Newsweek,* 137(15) (April 9, 2001): 42; and www.census. gov, accessed January 28, 2002.

16. Ephraim Schwartz, "Dawn of a New Database," *InfoWorld,* 24(11) (March 18, 2002): 32; and Carol Post, "Marketing Data Marts Help Companies Stay Ahead of the Curve and in Front of the Competition," *Direct Marketing,* 59(12) (April 1997): 42–44.

17. "Internet Marketing | Database Development | Kent," www.buzzinfly. co.uk, accessed June 9, 2008; and Darla Martin Tucker, "Technology: Online Database Set to Debut This Summer," *The Business Press* (March 18, 2002): 8.

18. Jody Dodson, "Dos, Don'ts of Online Research," *Advertising Age's Business Marketing* (August 1999): 8.

19. www.infousa.com/direct_marketing.htm, accessed January 20, 2009; Anonymous, "InfoUSA.com Provides Fee Internet Database," *Direct Marketing* (January 2000): 15–16; and Mary Ellen Bates, "American Business Information: Here, There, and Everywhere," *Database,* 20(2) (April/May 1997): 45–50.

20. David Wilson, "Bibliographic/Database," http://wiki.services. openoffice.org/wiki/Bibliographic_Database, accessed June 12, 2008; Carol Tenopir, "Links and Bibliographic Databases," *Library Journal,* 126(4) (March 1, 2001): 34–35; and Greg R. Notess, "The Internet as an Online Service: Bibliographic Databases on the Net," *Database,* 19(4) (August/September 1996): 92–95.

21. "About PIMS Database," www.pimsonline.com/about_pims_ db.htm, accessed December 2, 2008. For applications of the PIMS database, see David Besanko, David Dranove, and Mark Shanley, "Exploiting a Cost Advantage and Coping with a Cost Disadvantage," *Management Science,* 47(2) (February 2001): 221; and Venkatram Ramaswamy, Hubert Gatignon, and David J. Reibstein, "Competitive Marketing Behavior," *Journal of Marketing,* 58 (April 1994): 45–56.

22. Karl Greenberg, "New Campbell Soup Ads Will Focus On Health, One NFL Player," MediaPost Publications Home Page, http:// publications.mediapost.com/index.cfm?fuseaction=Articles.showArticl eHomePage&art_aid=81944, accessed June 12, 2008; "The MonitorTM Service," brochure prepared by Yankelovich and Partners (http://www.yankelovich.com); and Gail Pitts, "Too Bad We Can't Eat the Campbell's Soup Web Site," *Knight Ridder Tribune Business News* (February 6, 2002): 1.

23. SRI Consulting Business Intelligence (SRIC-BI), "VALS," www.sricbi.com/VALS, accessed June 12, 2008; Julie Napoli,

"The Net Generation: An Analysis of Lifestyles, Attitudes and Media Habits," *Journal of International Consumer Marketing* (2001): 21; and Leon G. Schiffman and Leslie Lazar Kanuk, *Consumer Behavior,* 9th ed. (Upper Saddle River, NJ: Prentice Hall, 2007).

24. Cheong Yunjae and John D. Leckenby, "Advertising Evaluation: An Evaluation of Advertising Media Spending Efficiency Using Data Envelopment Analysis," www.ciadvertising.org/studies/reports/ measurement/AAA2006_Cheong_Leckenby_AnEvaluationofAd_ DEA.pdf, accessed June 12, 2008; and William D. Wells, "Recognition, Recall, and Rating Scales," *Journal of Advertising Research,* 40(6) (November/December 2000): 14–20.

25. "Top 5 Women's Accessories," www.npd.com, accessed June 20, 2005; and "NPD Fashion World Reveals That Women Secretly Like Shopping for Swimwear: Two New NPD Fashion World Reports Examine the Swimwear Market and Shopping Experience," www.npd.com, accessed January 23, 2002.

26. Nielsen Media Research, "Television Audience Measurement Terms," www.nielsenmedia.ca/English/NMR_U_PDF/TV%20Terms.pdf, accessed June 13, 2008; Allison Romano, "New to Nielsen's Numbers," *Broadcasting and Cable,* 132(5) (February 4, 2002): 29; John Gill, "Managing the Capture of Individual Viewing Within a Peoplemeter Service," *International Journal of Market Research,* 42(4) (2000): 431–438; and Steve Wilcox, "Sampling and Controlling a TV Audience Measurement Panel," *International Journal of Market Research,* 42(4) (Winter 2000): 413–430.

27. http://searchenginewatch.com/reports/article.php/3099931; www.centerformediaresearch.com/cfmr_brief.cfm?fnl=041201; www.cimwessex.co.uk/pdf/2004_november.pdf, accessed December 2, 2008.

28. www.hitwise.com, accessed February 4, 2009.

29. "Panel Surveys," www.gfk.si/eng/3_1_panel.php, accessed June 13, 2008; J. M. Dennis, "Are Internet Panels Creating Professional Respondents?" *Marketing Research,* 13(2) (2001): 34–38; Eunkyu Lee, Michael Y. Hu, and Rex S. Toh, "Are Consumer Survey Results Distorted? Systematic Impact of Behavioral Frequency and Duration on Survey Response Errors," *Journal of Marketing Research,* 37(1) (February 2000): 125–133; "Why Consumer Mail Panel Is the Superior Option" (Chicago: Market Facts, Inc., undated); and John H. Parfitt and B. J. K. Collins, "Use of Consumer Panels for Brand -Share Predictions," *Journal of Market Research Society,* 38(4) (October 1996): 341–367.

30. Kevin J. Clancy, "Brand Confusion," *Harvard Business Review,* 80(3) (March 2002): 22; and Seymour Sudman, "On the Accuracy of Recording of Consumer Panels II," *Learning Manual* (New York: Neal-Schumen Publishers, 1981).

31. "Targeted Promotions Using Scanner Panel Data," www. ingentaconnect.com/content/mcb/096/1997/00000006/00000006/ art00003;jsessionid=60wq46oo0on9.alexandra, accessed May 15, 2008; Harald J. Van Heerde, "The Estimation of Pre-and Post-Promotion Dips with Store Level Scanner Data," *Journal of Marketing Research,* 37(3) (August 2000): 383–396; and Randolph F. Bucklin and Sunil Gupta, "Commercial Use of UPC Scanner Data: Industry and Academic Perspectives," *Marketing Science,* 18(3) (1999): 247–273. A study investigating the accuracy of UPC scanner pricing systems found that both underring and overring rates were significantly higher than retailers' expectations: Ronald C Goodstein, "UPC Scanner Pricing Systems: Are They Accurate?" *Journal of Marketing,* 58 (April 1994): 20–30.

32. William J.Hawkes, "The Use of Scanner Data in Reconciling Time-Series," Georgraphic Price Comparisons, www.ottawagroup.org/ Ottawa/ottawagroup.nsf/home/Meeting+4/$file/1998%204th%20 Meeting%20-%20Hawkes%20William%20-%20The%20Use%20of% 20Scanner%20Data%20in%20Reconciling%20Timeseries%20 (Consumer%20Price%20Index)%20and%20Geographic%20(Place- to-Place)%20Price%20Comparisons.pdf, accessed June 15, 2008; Martin Natter, "Real World Performance of Choice-Based Conjoint Models," *European Journal of Operational Research,* 137(2)

(March 1, 2002): 448; and Marcel Corstjens and Rajiv Lal, "Building Store Loyalty Through Store Brands," *Journal of Marketing Research,* 37(3) (August 2000): 281–291.

33. It is possible to combine store-level scanner data with scanner panel data to do an integrated analysis. See Tulin Erdem, Glenn Mayhew, and Baohong Sun, "Understanding Reference-Price Shoppers: A Within- and Cross-Category Analysis," *Journal of Marketing Research,* 38(4) (November 2001): 445–457; and Gary J Russell and Wagner A Kamakura, "Understanding Brand Competition Using Micro and Macro Scanner Data," *Journal of Marketing Research,* 31 (May 1994): 289–303.

34. Jack K. H. Lee, K. Sudhir, and Joel H. Steckel, "A Multiple Ideal Point Model: Capturing Multiple Preference Effects from Within an Ideal Point Framework," *Journal of Marketing Research,* 39(1) (February 2002): 73–86; and Anonymous, "Cereals: A Key Meal— But When?" *Grocer,* 224(7507) (June 9, 2001): 72.

35. Examples of applications of scanner data include Katherine W. Lemon and Stephen M. Nowlis, "Developing Synergies Between Promotions and Brands in Different Price-Quality Tiers," *Journal of Marketing Research,* 39(2) (May 2002): 171–185; and Pradeep K. Chintagunta, "Investigating Category Pricing Behavior at a Retail Chain," *Journal of Marketing Research,* 39(2) (May 2002): 141–154.

36. Anonymous, "Study of Online Shopping in U.S. Released by comScore Networks," *Internet Business News* (January 21, 2002); and ashford.com, accessed January 2, 2009.

37. "Single-Source Information: An Agile Practice for Effective Documentation," www.agilemodeling.com/essays/singleSourceInformation.htm, accessed December 16, 2008. For applications of single-source data, see Bruce Fox, "Retailers Integrate Space Planning with Key Business Functions," *Stores,* 83(12) (December 2001): 59–60; Michael Darkow, "Compatible or Not? Results of a Single Source Field Experiment Within a TV Audience Research Panel," *Marketing & Research Today,* 24(3) (August 1996): 150–161; and John Deighton, Caroline M. Henderson, and Scott A. Neslin, "The Effects of Advertising on Brand Switching and Repeat Purchasing," *Journal of Marketing Research,* 31 (February 1994): 28–43.

38. Stephanie Thompson, "Diet V8 Splash Carves Niche in Juice Category for Adults," *Advertising Age,* 71(13) (March 27, 2000): 24; Joanne Lipman, "Single-Source Ad Research Heralds Detailed Look at Household Habits," *Wall Street Journal* (February 16, 1988): 39; www.cbs.com; and www.v8juice.com, accessed January 10, 2009.

39. "ALLTEL Communications," www.claritas.com/claritas/Default.jsp?ci=2&pn=cs_alltel, accessed June 16, 2008; and www.clusterbigip1.claritas.com/claritas/Default.jsp?main=2&submenu=ce&subcat=ce2, accessed November 12, 2008.

40. For an example of international marketing research based on secondary data, see Sherriff T. K. Luk, "The Use of Secondary Information Published by the PRC Government," *Market Research Society, Journal of the Market Research Society* (July 1999): 355–365.

41. Peter M. Chisnall, "Marketing Research: State of the Art Perspectives," *International Journal of Market Research,* 44 (1) (First Quarter 2002): 122–125.

42. David Smith, "A Deficit of Consumer Loyalty," *Management Today* (July 1996): 22; and "Europeans More Active as Consumers," *Marketing News* (October 6, 1991).

43. "Network TV Audience Trends," http://journalism.org/node/1178, accessed June 17, 2008; John Consoli, "Network Report Card," *Mediaweek,* 14(17) (April 26, 2004): SR3–5; Dan Trigoboff, "Saying No to Nielsen," *Broadcasting & Cable,* 132(5) (February 4, 2002): 33; and Alan Bunce, "Faced with Lower Ratings, Networks Take Aim at Nielsen; The Big Three Consider a Competing Ratings Service," *Christian Science Monitor* (March 20, 1997).

44. Sandra O'Loughlin, "Strategy: Flagging Tommy Goes Back to Roots," www.allbusiness.com/marketing-advertising/branding-brand-development/4673957-1.html, accessed June 17, 2008; Tara Croft, "Tommy Hilfiger Seeks Targets," *The Daily Deal,* New York (May 9, 2003); and tommyhilfiger.com/info/press-release.jhtml?id=701245.

Chapter 5

1. "Baby Boomers at Mid-life," ssw.unc.edu/CARES/boom28.pdf, accessed June 19, 2008; Carol Hymowitz, "The Baby-Boomer Fashion Crisis," *Wall Street Journal* (Eastern edition), 246(143) (December 31, 2005): 5; Gloria F. Mazzella, "Show and Tell Focus Groups Reveal Core Boomer Values," *Marketing News* (September 23, 1996); and www.honda.com, accessed January 11, 2006.

2. David Warschawski, "Effective Branding Means Sensitivity to Customer Feelings and Experience," *Boston Business Journal* (July 9, 2004), http://boston.bizjournals.com/boston/stories/2004/07/12/focus3.html; Kenneth Wade, "Focus Groups' Research Role Is Shifting," *Marketing News,* 36(5) (March 4, 2002): 47; and Rana Dogar, "Marketing to the Sense," *Working Woman* (April 1997): 32–35.

3. Uwe Flick, *An Introduction to Qualitative Research*, 3rd ed. (Thousand Oaks, CA: Sage Publications, 2006); Kathryn C. Rentz, "Reflexive Methodology: New Vistas for Qualitative Research," *The Journal of Business Communication,* 39(1) (January 2002): 149–156; David J. Carson, Audrey Gilmore, Chad Perry, and Kjell Gronhaug, *Qualitative Marketing Research* (Thousand Oaks, CA: Sage Publications, 2001).

4. Clara E. Hill, Sarah Knox, Barbara J. Thompson, Elizabeth Nutt Williams, Shirley A. Hess, and Nicho Ladany, "Consensual Qualitative Research: An Update," *Journal of Counseling Psychology,* 52(2) (April 2005): 196–205; Paul ten Have, *Understanding Qualitative Research and Ethnomethodology* (Thousand Oaks, CA: Sage Publications, 2004); Timothy Bock and John Sergeant, "Small Sample Market Research," *International Journal of Market Research,* 44(2) (2002): 235–244; Gill Ereaut, Mike Imms, and Martin Callingham, *Qualitative Market Research: Principle & Practice,* 7 vols. (Thousand Oaks, CA: Sage Publications, 2002); and Shay Sayre, *Qualitative Methods for Marketplace Research* (Thousand Oaks, CA: Sage Publications, 2001).

5. A positivist perspective on research is being adopted here. Positivism encompasses logical positivism, logical empiricism, and all forms of falsificationism. This is the dominant perspective in commercial marketing research. A relativist perspective has been offered. See, for example, Richard R. Wilk, "The Impossibility and Necessity of Re-Inquiry: Finding Middle Ground in Social Science," *Journal of Consumer Research,* 28(2) (September 2001): 308–312; and Shelby D. Hunt, *A General Theory of Competition* (Thousand Oaks, CA: Sage Publications, 2000). See also, Alexandra J. Kenyon, "Exploring Phenomenological Research," *International Journal of Market Research,* 46(4) (2004): 427–441.

6. Michael Lutz, "Kellogg's Agrees to Make Foods for Children Healthier," www.associatedcontent.com/article/281293/kelloggs_agrees_to_make_foods_for_children.html?cat=35, accessed June 23, 2008; B. Light, "Kellogg's Goes Online for Consumer Research," *Packaging Digest* (July 2004): 40; and www.buzzback.com, accessed March 30, 2005.

7. Sharlene Nagy Hesse-Biber, *The Practice of Qualitative Research* (Thousand Oaks, CA: Sage Publications, 2006); Gill Ereaut, Mike Imms, and Martin Callingham, *Qualitative Market Research: Principle & Practice,* 7 vols. (Thousand Oaks, CA: Sage Publications, 2002); and John Gill and Phil Johnson, *Research Methods for Managers*, 3rd ed. (Thousand Oaks, CA: Sage Publications, 2002).

8. Clive Seale, *Qualitative Research Practice* (Thousand Oaks, CA: Sage Publications, 2004); Michael Bloor, Jane Frankland, Michelle Thomas, and Kate Robson, *Focus Groups in Social Research* (Thousand Oaks, CA: Sage Publications, 2001).

9. Carter Mcnamara, "Basics of Conducting Focus Groups," www.managementhelp.org/evaluatn/focusgrp.htm, accessed June 23, 2008; Barry E. Langford, Gerald Schoenfeld, and George Izzo, "Nominal Grouping Sessions vs. Focus Groups," *Qualitative Market Research,* 5(1) (2002): 58–70; Richard A. Krueger and Mary Anne Casey, *Focus Groups: A Practical Guide for Applied Research,* 3rd ed. (Thousand Oaks, CA: Sage Publications, 2000).

10. The group size of 8–12 is based on rules of thumb. For more discussion, see Edward F. Fern, *Advanced Focus Group Research* (Thousand Oaks, CA: Sage Publications, 2001); and Robert Blackburn, "Breaking Down the Barriers: Using Focus Groups to Research Small and Medium-Sized Enterprises," *International Small Business Journal,* 19(1) (October–December 2000): 44–67.

11. Thomas L. Greenbaum, "'The Focus Group Report," *Quirk's Marketing Research Review,* www.groupsplus.com/pages/qmr1297.htm, accessed June 23, 2008; Claudia Puchta, *Focus Group Practice* (Thousand Oaks, CA: Sage Publications, 2004); Catherine Forrest, "Research with a Laugh Track," *Marketing News,* 36(5) (March 4, 2002): 48; Gloria F. Mazella, "Show-and-Tell Focus Groups Reveal Core Boomer Values," *Marketing News,* 31(12) (June 9, 1997): H8.

12. "How to Get More Out of Your Focus Groups," www.mnav.com/getmore.htm, accessed June 23, 2008; Colin MacDougall, "Planning and Recruiting the Sample for Focus Groups and In-Depth Interviews," *Qualitative Health Research,* 11(1) (January 2001): 117–126; Hazel Kahan, "A Professional Opinion," *American Demographics (Tools Supplement)* (October 1996): 1–19.

13. Janine Morgan Traulsen, Anna Birna Almarsdottir, and Ingunn Bjornsdottir, "Interviewing the Moderator: An Ancillary Method to Focus Groups," *Qualitative Health Research,* 14(5) (May 2004): 714; Jonathan Hall, "Moderators Must Motivate Focus Group," *Marketing News,* 34(9) (September 11, 2000): 26–27; and Thomas L. Greenbaum, *Moderating Focus Groups: A Practical Guide for Group Facilitation* (Thousand Oaks, CA: Sage Publications, 1999). Adapted from Donald A. Chase, "The Intensive Group Interviewing in Marketing," *MRA Viewpoints* (1973).

14. Norman K. Denzin, *The Sage Handbook of Qualitative Research,* 3rd ed. (Thousand Oaks, CA: Sage Publications, 2005); Edward F. Fern, *Advanced Focus Group Research* (Thousand Oaks, CA: Sage Publications, 2001); Richard A. Krueger, *Developing Questions for Focus Groups* (Newbury Park, CA: Sage Publications, 1997); and Martin R. Lautman, "Focus Group: Theory and Method," in Andrew Mitchell, ed., *Advances in Consumer Research* (Pittsburgh: Association for Consumer Research, 1982), 9: 22.

15. David Silverman, *Qualitative Research: Theory, Method, and Practice,* 2nd ed. (Thousand Oaks, CA: Sage Publications, 2004); Becky Ebenkamp, "The Focus Group Has Spoken," *Brandweek,* 42(17) (April 23, 2001): 24; and David L. Morgan, *The Focus Group Guidebook* (Newbury Park, CA: Sage Publications, 1997).

16. Claudia Puchta, *Focus Group Practice* (Thousand Oaks, CA: Sage Publications, 2004); Anonymous, "Focus Groups: A Practical Guide for Applied Research," *International Journal of Public Opinion Research,* 13(1) (Spring 2001): 85; and Richard A. Krueger and Mary Anne Casey, *Focus Groups: A Practical Guide for Applied Research,* 3rd ed. (Thousand Oaks, CA: Sage Publications, 2000).

17. Stephanie Thompson, "Kraft Does The 'Twist': Kool-Aid Effort Touts Interactive Powder Mixes," *Advertising Age,* http://findarticles.com/p/articles/mi_hb6398/is_200101/ai_n25595928, accessed June 23, 2008; Anonymous, "Kool-Aid Serves Up Promotional Magic," *Marketing Magazine,* 108(34) (October 6–13, 2003); Joan Raymond, "All Smiles," *American Demographics,* 23(3) (March 2001): S18; and Stephanie Thompson, "Kraft Does the 'Twist,'" *Advertising Age,* 72(4) (January 22, 2001): 8.

18. Ronald E. Goldsmith, "The Focus Group Research Handbook," *The Service Industries Journal,* 20(3) (July 2000): 214–215; and Thomas L. Greenbaum, *The Handbook for Focus Group Research* (Newbury Park, CA: Sage Publications, 1997).

19. Don Akchin, "Quick & Dirty Research," *Nonprofit World,* Madison (May/June 2001): 3–33; and "How Nonprofits Are Using Focus Groups," *Nonprofit World,* 14(5) (September/October 1996): 37.

20. Donna J. Reid and Fraser J. Reid, "Online Focus Groups," *International Journal of Market Research,* 47(2) (2005): 131–162; Henrietta O'Connor and Clare Madge, "Focus Groups in Cyberspace: Using the Internet for Qualitative Research," *Qualitative Market Research,* 6(2) (2003): 133–143; Robert V. Kozinets, "The Field Behind the Screen: Using Netnography for Marketing Research Online Communities," *Journal of Marketing Research,* 39(1) (February 2002): 61–72; Thomas L Greenbaum, "Focus Groups vs. Online," *Advertising Age,* Chicago (February 14, 2000): 34; Judith Langer, "'On' and 'Offline' Focus Groups: Claims, Questions," *Marketing News,* 34(12) (June 5, 2000): H38.

21. Daren Fonda, "The Shrinking SUV," *Time,* 164(9) (August 30, 2004): 65; Chuck Moozakis, "Nissan Wants to Be Like Dell—Automaker Says It Can Achieve Build-to-Order via the Web in 18 Months; Experts Are Skeptical," *InternetWeek* (January 7, 2002): 11; Jean Halliday, "Makers Use Web to Help Design Cars," *Automotive News* (5860) (February 7, 2001): 22; and www.nissandriven.com.

22. David Stokes and Richard Bergin, "Methodology or 'Methodolatry': An Evaluation of Focus Groups and Depth Interviews," *Qualitative Market Research: An International Journal,* 9(1) (2006): 26–37; Richard Poppy Brech, "Research Proves the Obvious," *Marketing* (March 21, 2002): 48. For a recent application of depth interviews, see Jodie L. Ferguson, Kofi Q. Dadzie, and Wesley J. Johnston, "Country-of-Origin Effects in Service Evaluation in Emerging Markets: Some Insights from Five West African Countries," *The Journal of Business & Industrial Marketing,* 23(6) (2008): 429.

23. Naomi R Henderson, "The Power of Probing," *Marketing Research,* 19(4) (Winter 2007): 38; Shay Sayre, *Qualitative Methods for Marketplace Research* (Thousand Oaks, CA: Sage Publications, 2001); and "Looking for a Deeper Meaning," *Marketing* (Market Research Top 75 Supplement) (July 17, 1997): 16–17.

24. Edward C. Baig, "One Smart Card for All Your Debts," *USA Today* (February 6, 2002): D7.

25. Tomaz Kolar, "Linking Customers and Products by Means-End Chain Analysis," *Management,* 12(2) (November 2007): 69–78; and Klaus G. Grunert and Suzanne C. Grunert, "Measuring Subjective Meaning Structures by Laddering Method: Theoretical Considerations and Methodological Problems," *International Journal of Research in Marketing,* 12(3) (October 1995): 209–225. This example is derived from Jeffrey F. Durgee, "Depth-Interview Techniques for Creative Advertising," *Journal of Advertising Research,* 25 (December 1985–January 1986): 29–37.

26. R. Kenneth Wade, "Focus Groups' Research Role Is Shifting," *Marketing News,* 36(5) (March 4, 2002): 47; Brian Wansink, "New Techniques to Generate Key Marketing Insights," *Marketing Research,* 12(2) (Summer 2000): 28–36; and Richard A. Feder, "Depth Interviews Avoid Turmoil of Focus Groups," *Advertising Age,* 68(16) (April 21, 1997): 33.

27. Ginny Parker, "Sony Unveils Smaller Version of PlayStation 2 Game Console," *Wall Street Journal* (Eastern edition) (September 22, 2004): D4; Robert A. Guth, "PlayStation 2 Helps Sony Beat Forecasts," *Wall Street Journal* (January 28, 2002): A12; and Brian Wansink, "New Techniques to Generate Key Marketing Insights," *Marketing Research,* 12 (Summer 2000): 28–36.

28. Clive Boddy, "Projective Techniques in Market Research: Valueless Subjectivity or Insightful. Reality?" *International Journal of Market Research,* 47(3) (2005): 239–254; Gill Ereaut, Mike Imms, and Martin Callingham, *Qualitative Market Research: Principle & Practice,* 7 vols. (Thousand Oaks, CA: Sage Publications, 2002); and H. H. Kassarjian, "Projective Methods," in R. Ferber, ed., *Handbook of Marketing Research* (New York: McGraw-Hill, 1974): 85–100.

29. Joerg Koenigstorfer, Andrea Groeppel-Klein and Stefan Pla, "The Motivations Underlying the Use of Technological Innovations: New Insights from Projective Techniques," *International Journal of Business Environment,* 2(2) (2008): 215–241; Judith Lynne Zaichowsky, "The Why of Consumption: Contemporary Perspectives and Consumer Motives, Goals, and Desires," *Academy of Marketing Science,* 30(2) (Spring 2002): 179; and Sidney J. Levy, "Interpreting Consumer Mythology: Structural Approach to Consumer Behavior Focuses on Story Telling," *Marketing Management,* 2(4) (1994): 4–9.

30. Anouk Hofstede, Joris van Hoof, Natascha Walenberg, and Menno de Jong, "Projective Techniques for Brand Image Research; Two Personification-Based Methods Explored," *Qualitative Market Research,* 10(3) (2007): 300; Miriam Catterall, "Using Projective

Techniques in Education Research," *British Educational Research Journal,* 26(2) (April 2000): 245–256; Marilyn M. Kennedy, "So How'm I Doing?" *Across the Board,* 34(6) (June 1997): 53–54; and G. Lindzey, "On the Classification of Projective Techniques," *Psychological Bulletin* (1959): 158–168.

31. Ellen Byron, "How P&G Led Also-Ran to Sweet Smell of Success," *Wall Street Journal* (September 4, 2007): B2; Kerri Walsh, "Soaps and Detergents," *Chemical Week,* 164(3) (January 23, 2002): 24–26; and "Interpretation Is the Essence of Projective Research Techniques," *Marketing News* (September 28, 1984): 20. For a theoretical discussion, see William S. Maki, "A Database of Associative Strengths from the Strength-Sampling Model: A Theory-Based Supplement to the Nelson, Mcevoy, and Schreiber Word Association Norms," *Behavior Research Methods,* 40(1) (February 2008): 232–235.

32. J. Dee Hill, "7-Eleven Hopes Hosiery Has Legs," *Adweek,* 22(42) (October 16, 2000): 12; Ronald B. Lieber, "Storytelling: A New Way to Get Close to Your Customer," *Fortune* (February 3, 1997); and www.dupont.com. See also, Barbara Czarniawska, *Narratives in Social Science Research* (Thousand Oaks, CA: Sage Publications, 2004).

33. Sally Squires, "You Know You Crave It," *The Washington Post* (June 22, 2004): F1; Amy Zuber, "McD Unveils New Brands, Tries to Reverse 'McSlide,' " *Nation's Restaurant News,* 35(46) (November 12, 2001): 1–2; David Kilburn, "Haagen-Dazs Is Flavor of Month," *Marketing Week,* 20(23) (September 4, 1997): 30; and S. Bhargava, "Gimme a Double Shake and a Lard on White," *Business Week* (March 1, 1993): 59.

34. Debby Andrews, "Playing a Role," *Business Communication Quarterly,* 64(1) (March 2001): 7–8; "Role Playing for Better Service," *Lodging Hospitality,* 53(2) (February 1997): 16.

35. Kevin Smith, "Apartment, Townhouse Area Offers Upscale Living in Rancho Cucamonga, Calif.," *Knight Ridder Tribune Business News* (May 17, 2002): 1; and Jerome R. Corsi, "Adapting to Fit the Problem: Impact Research Takes a Different Approach to Marketing," *Rocky Mountain Business Journal,* 36(26) (March 25, 1985): 1.

36. Sharon Begley, "Afraid to Fly After 9/11, Some Took a Bigger Risk—In Cars," *Wall Street Journal* (Eastern edition) (March 23, 2004): B1; Edward H. Phillips, "Fear of Flying," *Aviation Week & Space Technology,* 154(3) (January 15, 2001): 419; "Fear of Flying," *The Economist,* 339(7966) (May 18, 1996): 30; www.airlines.org; and www.airsafe.com. For a theoretical perspective, see Vincent-Wayne Mitchell and Greg Harris, "The Importance of Consumers' Perceived Risk in Retail Strategy," *European Journal of Marketing,* 39(7/8) (2005): 821–837.

37. Gill Ereaut, Mike Imms, and Martin Callingham, *Qualitative Market Research: Principle & Practice,* 7 vols. (Thousand Oaks, CA: Sage Publications, 2002); David Bakken, "State of the Art in Qualitative Research," *Marketing Research: A Magazine of Management & Applications,* 8(2) (Summer 1996): 4–5; Elaine Cibotti and Eugene H. Fram, "The Shopping List Studies and Projective Techniques: A 40-Year View," *Marketing Research: A Magazine of Management & Applications,* 3(4) (December 1991): 14–22; and Maison Haire, "Projective Techniques in Marketing Research," *Journal of Marketing,* 14 (April 1950): 649–656.

38. John Gill and Phil Johnson, *Research Methods for Managers,* 3rd ed. (Thousand Oaks, CA: Sage Publications, 2002); and Sajeev Varki, Bruce Cooil, and Roland T. Rust, "Modeling Fuzzy Data in Qualitative Marketing Research," *Journal of Marketing Research,* 37(4) (November 2000): 480–489.

39. www.just-the-facts.com/Consulting2.asp

40. These steps are taken from Matthew B. Miles and A. Michael Huberman, *Qualitative Data Analysis,* 2nd ed. (Newbury Park, CA: Sage Publications, 1994). See also, Lyn Richards, *Handling Qualitative Data: A Practical Guide* (Thousand Oaks, CA: Sage Publications, 2005); and Janet Heaton, *Reworking Qualitative Data* (Thousand Oaks, CA: Sage Publications, 2004).

41. Clive R. Boddy, "Projective Techniques in Taiwan and Asia–Pacific Market Research," *Qualitative Market Research,* 10(1) (2007): 48; Alan S. Zimmerman and Michael Szenberg, "Implementing

International Qualitative Research: Techniques and Obstacles," *Qualitative Market Research,* 3(3) (2000): 158–164; and Jeffery S. Nevid, "Multicultural Issues in Qualitative Research," *Psychology & Marketing* (July 1999): 305–325.

42. Raymond Boudon, *The European Tradition in Qualitative Research,* 4 vols. (Thousand Oaks, CA: Sage Publications, 2003); and Thomas L. Greenbaum, "Understanding Focus Group Research Abroad," *Marketing News,* 30(12) (June 3, 1996): H14, H36.

43. www.pbelisle.com , accessed February 4, 2009; and www.quirks. com/articles/article.asp?arg_ArticleId=1121

44. Svend Brinkmann and Steinar Kvale, "Confronting the Ethics of Qualitative Research," *Journal of Constructivist Psychology,* 18(2) (March 2005): 157–181; Connie Rate Bateman, "Framing Effects Within the Ethical Decision-Making Process of Consumers," *Journal of Business Ethics,* 36(1/2) (March 2002): 119–138; and Melanie Mauthner, *Ethics in Qualitative Research* (Thousand Oaks, CA: Sage Publications, 2002).

45. Angela Galloway, "Mudslinging, Attacks . . . Then It Could Get Nasty," *Seattle Post-Intelligencer* (September 3, 2004), http:// seattlepi.nwsource.com/local/189286_nasty03.html; and Evan Thomas, "Calling All Swing States," *Newsweek,* 136(21) (November 20, 2000): 110–120.

46. Lotus Web site: www.lotus.com; and www-3.ibm.com/software/ swnews/swnews.nsf/n/jmae5n7sjh?OpenDocument&Site=default

Chapter 6

1. Anonymous, "Partisans: Don't Shoot the Pollster," *New York Times* (Late edition, East Coast) (September 29, 2004); and Humphrey Taylor, John Bremer, Cary Overmeyer, Jonathan W. Siegel, and George Terhanian, "Using Internet Polling to Forecast the 2000 Elections," *Marketing Research,* 13 (Spring 2001): 26–30.

2. Anonymous, "Canon Logs Record Profit, Sales in '01," *Jiji Press English News Service* (January 31, 2002): 1; and Johnny K. Johansson and Ikujiro Nonaka, "Market Research the Japanese Way," *Harvard Business Review* (May–June 1987): 16–18.

3. Surveys are commonly used in marketing research. See, for example, Aric Rindfleisch, Alan J. Malter, Shankar Ganesan, and Christine Moorman, "Cross-Sectional Versus Longitudinal Survey Research: Concepts, Findings, and Guidelines," *Journal of Marketing Research,* 45(3) (June 2008): 261–279; and Naresh K. Malhotra and Daniel McCort, "A Cross-Cultural Comparison of Behavioral Intention Models: Theoretical Consideration and an Empirical Investigation," *International Marketing Review,* 18(3) (2001): 235–269. See also, Lawrence A. Crosby, Sheree L. Johnson, and Richard T. Quinn, "Is Survey Research Dead?" *Marketing Management,* 11(3) (2002): 24–29.

4. Rajesh Nakwah, "Getting Good Feedback," *Quirk's Marketing Research Review* (November 2000).

5. Linda Borque, *How to Conduct Telephone Surveys,* 2nd ed. (Thousand Oaks, CA: Sage Publications, 2002); David W. Glasscoff, "Measuring Clinical Performance: Comparison and Validity of Telephone Survey and Administrative Data," *Marketing Health Services,* 22(1) (Spring 2002): 43–44; and Niki Thurkow, "The Effects of Group and Individual Monetary Incentives on Productivity of Telephone Interviewers," *Journal of Organizational Behavior Management,* 20(2) (2000): 3.

6. Leigh Dyer, "Maya Angelou Sells Lines to Hallmark," *Knight Ridder Tribune Business News* (February 1, 2002): 1.

7. www.mediamark.com. See also, Floyd J. Fowler, Jr., *Survey Research Methods,* 3rd ed. (Thousand Oaks, CA: Sage Publications, 2001).

8. Carolyn Folkman Curasi, "A Critical Exploration of Face-to-Face Interviewing vs. Computer-Mediated Interviewing," *International Journal of Market Research,* 43(4) (2001): 361–375; Karen V. Fernandez, "The Effectiveness of Information and Color in Yellow Pages Advertising," *Journal of Advertising,* 29(2) (Summer 2000): 61–73; and A. J. Bush, and J. F. Hair, Jr., "An Assessment of the Mall-Intercept as a Data Collection Method," *Journal of Marketing Research* (May 1985): 158–167.

9. Rebecca Gardyn, "Same Name, New Number," *American Demographics,* 23(3) (March 2001): 6.

10. www.touchscreenresearch.com.au/Testimonials.htm; www.kioskbusiness.com/KB_BS_04/KB_BS_04_02.html; and http://www.etf.com

11. Mail surveys are common in institutional and industrial marketing research. See, for example, Duane P. Bachmann, John Elfrink, and Gary Vazzana, "E-Mail and Snail Mail Face Off in Rematch," *Marketing Research,* 11(4) (1999/2000): 10–15.

12. Linda Borque, *How to Conduct Self-Administered and Mail Surveys,* 2nd ed. (Thousand Oaks, CA: Sage Publications, 2002); Jack Schmid, "Assigning Value to Your Customer List," *Catalog Age,* 18(5) (April 2001): 69; and Rob Yoegei, "List Marketers Head to Cyberspace," *Target Marketing,* 20(8) (August 1997): 54–55.

13. Michael Straus, "Charlotte Art Museum Uses Research to Light Path to 21st Century," *Quirks* (February 1998), www.quirks.com/articles/article.asp?arg_ArticleId=311; and www.mintmuseum.org/mmcd/index.htm.

14. Katja Lozar Manfreda, Michael Bosnjak, Jernej Berzelak, Iris Haas, and Vasja Vehovar, "Web Surveys Versus Other Survey Modes," *International Journal of Market Research,* 50(1), 2008: 79–104; Bert Weijters, Niels Schillewaert, and Maggie Geuens, "Assessing Response Styles Across Modes of Data Collection," *Journal of the Academy of Marketing Science,* 36(3) (September 2008): 409; Shintaro Okazaki, "Assessing Mobile-Based Online Surveys," *International Journal of Market Research,* 49(5) (2007): 651–675; Niels Schillewaert and Pascale Meulemeester, "Comparing Response Distributions of Offline and Online Data Collection Methods," *International Journal of Market Research,* 47(2) (2005): 163–178; Janet Ilieva, Steve Baron, and Nigel Healey, "Online Surveys in Marketing Research: Pros and Cons," *International Journal of Market Research,* 44(3) (2002): 361–376; and Peter Kellner, "Can Online Polls Produce Accurate Findings?" *International Journal of Market Research,* 46(1) (2004): 3–19.

15. http://weblogs.jupiterresearch.com/analysts/laszlo/archives/002560.html; and www.sony.com; www.sonymusic.com/shop/index.html

16. Luigi Anolli, Daniela Villani, and Giuseppe Riva, "Personality of People Using Chat: An On-Line Research," *CyberPsychology & Behavior,* 8(1) (February 2005): 89–95; Steven K. Thompson, *Sampling* (New York: John Wiley & Sons, 2002); and Terry L. Childers and Steven J. Skinner, "Theoretical and Empirical Issues in the Identification of Survey Respondents," *Journal of the Market Research Society,* 27 (January 1985): 39–53.

17. J. N. K. Rao and Sharon Lohr, "Estimation in Multiple-Frame Surveys," *Journal of the American Statistical Association,* 101(475) (September 2006): 1019–1030; Gregory B. Murphy, "The Effects of Organizational Sampling Frame Selection," *Journal of Business Venturing,* 17(3) (May 2002): 237; and Wayne Smith, Paul Mitchell, Karin Attebo, and Stephen Leeder, "Selection Bias from Sampling Frames: Telephone Directory and Electoral Rolls Compared to Door-to-Door Population Census: Results from the Blue Mountain Eye Study," *Australian & New Zealand Journal of Public Health,* 21(2) (April 1997): 127–133.

18. Timothy R. Graeff, "Uninformed Response Bias in Telephone Surveys," *Journal of Business Research,* 55(3) (March 2002): 251; and Scott Keeter, "Estimating Telephone Noncoverage Bias with a Telephone Survey," *Public Opinion Quarterly,* 59(2) (Summer 1995): 196–217.

19. Anonymous, "Random Sampling," *Marketing News,* 36(3) (February 4, 2002): 7; Dana James, "Old, New Make Up Today's Surveys," *Marketing News* (June 5, 2000): 4; David Wilson, "Random Digit Dialing and Electronic White Pages Samples Compared: Demographic Profiles and Health Estimates," *Australian and New Zealand Demographic Profiles and Health Estimates,* 23(6) (December 1999): 627–633; Johnny Blair and Ronald Czaja, "Locating a Special Population Using Random Digit Dialing," *Public Opinion Quarterly,* 46 (Winter 1982): 585–590; and E. L. Landon, Jr., and S. K. Banks, "Relative Efficiency and Bias of Plus-One Telephone Sampling," *Journal of Marketing Research,* 14 (August 1977): 294–299.

20. Ron Czaja, *Designing Surveys: A Guide to Decisions and Procedures* (Thousand Oaks, CA: Sage Publications, 2004); Sherry Chiger, "Benchmark 2002: Lists and E-Lists," *Catalog Age,* 19(3) (March 1, 2002): 41–45; David O. Schwartz, "Mailing List Owners and the Millennium," *Marketing News,* 31(11) (May 26, 1997): 4; Paul M. Biner and Deborah L. Barton, "Justifying the Enclosure of Monetary Incentives in Mail Survey Cover Letters," *Psychology and Marketing* (Fall 1990): 153–162; and "Lists Make Targeting Easy," *Advertising Age* (July 9, 1984): 20.

21. B. Zafer Erdogan, "Increasing Mail Survey Response Rates from an Industrial Population: A Cost Effectiveness Analysis of Four Follow-Up Techniques," *Industrial Marketing Management,* 31(1) (January 2002): 65; Jack Edmonston, "Why Response Rates Are Declining," *Advertising Age's Business Marketing,* 82(8) (September 1997): 12; Raymond Hubbard and Eldon L. Little, "Promised Contributions to Charity and Mail Survey Responses: Replications with Extension," *Public Opinion Quarterly,* 52 (Summer 1988): 223–230; and Paul L. Erdos and Robert Ferber, ed., "Data Collection Methods: Mail Surveys," *Handbook of Marketing Research* (New York: McGraw-Hill, 1974): 102.

22. Eunkyu Lee, "Are Consumer Survey Results Distorted? Systematic Impact of Behavioral Frequency and Duration on Survey Response Errors," *Journal of Marketing Research,* 37(1) (February 2000): 125–133.

23. Robert M. Groves and Emilia Peytcheva, "The Impact of Nonresponse Rates on Nonresponse Bias," *Public Opinion Quarterly,* 72(2) (Summer 2008): 167–189; Anton Korinek, Johan A. Mistiaen, and Martin Ravallion, "An Econometric Method of Correcting for Unit Nonresponse Bias in Surveys," *Journal of Econometrics,* 136(1) (January 2007): 213–235; and Edward Blair and George M. Zinkhan, "Nonresponse and Generalizability in Academic Research," *Journal of the Academy of Marketing Science,* 34(1) (December 2006): 4–7.

24. Robert M. Groves, "Nonresponse Rates and Nonresponse Bias in Household Surveys," *Public Opinion Quarterly,* 70(5), 2006: 646–675; Abhijit Roy and Paul Berger, "E-Mail and Mixed Mode Database Surveys Revisited: Exploratory Analyses of Factors Affecting Response Rates," *The Journal of Database Marketing & Customer Strategy Management,* 12(2,1) (January 2005): 153–171; Jamie Smith, "How to Boost DM Response Rates Quickly," *Marketing News,* 35(9) (April 23, 2001): 5; Richard Colombo, "A Model for Diagnosing and Reducing Nonresponse Bias," *Journal of Advertising Research* (January/April 2000): 85–93; Barbara Bickart, "The Distribution of Survey Contact and Participation in the United States: Constructing a Survey-Based Estimate," *Journal of Marketing Research* (May 1999): 286–294; William L. Nicholls II, "Highest Response," *Marketing Research: A Magazine of Management & Applications,* 8(1) (Spring 1996): 5–7; Jeannine M. James and Richard Bolstein, "The Effect of Monetary Incentives and Follow-Up Mailings on the Response Rate and Response Quality in Mail Surveys," *Public Opinion Quarterly,* 54 (Fall 1990): 346–361; and Julie Yu and Harris Cooper, "A Quantitative Review of Research Design Effects on Response Rates to Questionnaires," *Journal of Marketing Research,* 20 (February 1983): 36–44.

25. Floyd J. Fowler, Jr., *Survey Research Methods,* 3rd ed. (Thousand Oaks, CA: Sage Publications, 2001); Pamela G. Guengel, Tracy R. Berchman, and Charles F. Cannell, *General Interviewing Techniques: A Self-Instructional Workbook for Telephone and Personal Interviewer Training* (Ann Arbor, MI: Survey Research Center, University of Michigan, 1983).

26. Timothy R. Graeff, "Uninformed Response Bias in Telephone Surveys," *Journal of Business Research,* 55(3) (March 2002): 251; Eleanor Singer, "Experiments with Incentives in Telephone Surveys," *Public Opinion Quarterly,* 64(2) (Summer 2000): 171–188; Charles F. Cannell, Peter U. Miller, Lois Oksenberg, and Samuel Leinhardt, eds., "Research on Interviewing Techniques," *Sociological Methodology* (San Francisco: Jossey-Bass, 1981);

and Peter U. Miller, and Charles F. Cannell, "A Study of Experimental Techniques for Telephone Interviewing," *Public Opinion Quarterly*, 46 (Summer 1982): 250–269.

27. Duane P. Bachmann, John Elfrink, and Gary Vazzana, "E-Mail and Snail Mail Face Off in Rematch," *Marketing Research,* 11 (Winter 1999/Spring 2000): 10–15.

28. Arlene Fink, *How to Conduct Surveys: A Step-by-Step Guide*, 3rd ed. (Thousand Oaks, CA: Sage Publications, 2005); Mark McMaster, "E-Marketing Poll Vault," *Sales and Marketing Management,* 153(8) (August 2001): 25; and Arlene Fink, *A Survey Handbook* (Thousand Oaks, CA: Sage Publications, 1995).

29. Bruce Keillor, "A Cross-Cultural/Cross-National Study of Influencing Factors and Socially Desirable Response Biases," *International Journal of Market Research,* 43(1) (First Quarter 2001): 63–84; Maryon F. King, "Social Desirability Bias: A Neglected Aspect of Validity Testing," *Psychology & Marketing* (February 2000): 79; and Deniz Ones, Angelika D. Reiss, and Chockalingam Viswesvaran, "Role of Social Desirability in Personality Testing for Personnel Selection: The Red Herring," *Journal of Applied Psychology,* 81(6) (December 1996): 660–679.

30. Uwe Peter Kanning and Susanne Kuhne, "Social Desirability in a Multimodal Personnel Selection Test Battery," *European Journal of Work and Organizational Psychology,* 15(3) (September 2006): 241; Anonymous, "Random Sampling: Homework—Yeah Right," *Marketing News,* 36(6) (March 18, 2002): 4; Gerald Vinten, "The Threat in the Question," *Credit Control,* 18(1) (1997): 25–31; and Priya Raghubir and Geeta Menon, "Asking Sensitive Questions: The Effects of Type of Referent and Frequency Wording in Counterbiasing Method," *Psychology & Marketing,* 13(7) (October 1996): 633–652.

31. Heath McDonald and Stewart Adam, "A Comparison of Online and Postal Data Collection Methods in Marketing Research," *Marketing Intelligence and Planning,* 21(2) (2003): 85–95.

32. Alan Wilson and Nial Laskey, "Internet-Based Marketing Research: A Serious Alternative to Traditional Research Methods?" *Marketing Intelligence and Planning,* 21(2) (2003): 79–84; Cihan Cobanoglu, Bill Warde, and Patrick J. Moreo, "A Comparison of Mail, Fax, and Web-Based Survey Methods," *International Journal of Market Research,* 43(4) (Fourth Quarter 2001): 441–452; Sophie K. Turley, "A Case of Response Rate Success," *Journal of the Market Research Society* (July 1999): 301–309; and Stanley L. Payne, "Combination of Survey Methods," *Journal of Marketing Research* (May 1964): 62.

33. www.nielsenbuzzmetrics.com, accessed, January 10, 2009.

34. Andrew J. Milat, "Measuring Physical Activity in Public Open Space—An Electronic Device Versus Direct Observation," *Australian and New Zealand Journal of Public Health,* 26(1) (February 2002): 1; Stephen B. Wilcox, "Trust, But Verify," *Appliance Manufacturer,* 46(1) (January 1998): 8, 87; and Langbourne Rust, "How to Reach Children in Stores: Marketing Tactics Grounded in Observational Research," *Journal of Advertising Research,* 33 (November/December 1993): 67–72.

35. Beth Kurcina, "Use Videos to Obtain Crucial POP Info," *Marketing News,* 34(24) (November 20, 2000): 16; A. V. Seaton, "Unobtrusive Observational Measures as a Qualitative Extension of Visitor Surveys at Festivals and Events: Mass Observation Revisited," *Journal of Travel Research,* 35(4) (Spring 1997): 25–30; and Fred N. Kerlinger, *Foundations of Behavioral Research*, 3rd ed. (New York: Holt, Rinehart & Winston, 1986): 538.

36. www.inc.com/magazine/20040601/microsoft.html; and http://brand.blogs.com/mantra/market_research/http://www.gartner.com.

37. Erwin Ephron, "Nielsen's Secret Passive Meter," *Mediaweek,* 10(36) (September 18, 2000): 32; and Laurence N. Gold, "Technology in Television Research: The Meter," *Marketing Research: A Magazine of Management & Applications,* 6(1) (Winter 1994): 57–58.

38. Rik Pieters, Edward Rosbergen, and Michel Wedel, "Visual Attention to Repeated Print Advertising: A Test of Scanpath Theory," *Journal of Marketing Research,* 36(4) (November 1999): 424–438; J. Edward Russo and France Leclerc, "An Eye-Fixation Analysis of Choice Processes for Consumer Nondurables," *Journal of Consumer Research,* 21 (September 1994): 274–290.

39. For applications of GSR, see Gary H. Anthes, "Smile, You're on Candid Computer," *Computerworld,* 35(49) (December 3, 2001): 50; Priscilla A. LaBarbera and Joel D. Tucciarone, "GSR Reconsidered: A Behavior-Based Approach to Evaluating and Improving the Sales Potency of Advertising," *Journal of Advertising Research,* 35(5) (September/October 1995): 33–53; and Piet Vanden Abeele and Douglas L. Maclachlan, "Process Tracing of Emotional Responses to TV Ads: Revisiting the Warmth Monitor," *Journal of Consumer Research,* 20 (March 1994): 586–600.

40. N'Gai Croal, "Moviefone Learns to Listen," *Newsweek,* 135(19) (May 8, 2000): 84; S. Gregory, S. Webster, and G. Huang, "Voice Pitch and Amplitude Convergence as a Metric of Quality in Dyadic Interviews," *Language & Communication,* 13(3) (July 1993): 195–217; and Glen A. Buckman, "Uses of Voice-Pitch Analysis," *Journal of Advertising Research,* 20 (April 1980): 69–73.

41. John M. Rose and Iain R. Black, "Means Matter, But Variance Matters Too: Decomposing Response Latency Influences on Variance Heterogeneity in Stated Preference Experiments," *Marketing Letters,* 17(2006): 295–310; Rinus Haaijer, "Response Latencies in the Analysis of Conjoint Choice Experiments," *Journal of Marketing Research* (August 2000): 376–382; Nicholas Vasilopoulos, "The Influence of Job Familiarity and Impression Management on Self-Report Measure Scale Scores and Response Latencies," *Journal of Applied Psychology,* 85(1) (February 2000): 50; John N. Bassili and B. Stacey Scott, "Response Latency as a Signal to Question Problems in Survey Research," *Public Opinion Quarterly,* 60(3) (Fall 1996): 390–399; and David A. Aaker, Richard P. Bagozzi, James M. Carman, and James M. MacLachlan, "On Using Response Latency to Measure Preference," *Journal of Marketing Research,* 17 (May 1980): 237–244.

42. Joseph Rydholm, "Design Inspiration," *Marketing Research Review* (January 2000), www.newellrubbermaid.com, accessed June 3, 2001. See also, Bella Dicks, *Qualitative Research and Hypermedia: Ethnography for the Digital Age* (Thousand Oaks, CA: Sage Publications, 2005); and D. Soyini Madison, *Critical Ethnography: Method, Ethics, and Performance* (Thousand Oaks, CA: Sage Publications, 2005).

43. Les Carlson, "Use, Misuse, and Abuse of Content Analysis for Research on the Consumer Interest," *Journal of Consumer Affairs,* 42(1) (Spring 2008): 100–105; Daniel Riffe, Stephen Lacy, and Frederick Fico, *Media Messages: Using Quantitative Content Analysis in Research* (Routledge, 2005); G. Harris and S. Attour, "The International Advertising Practices of Multinational Companies: A Content Analysis Study," *European Journal of Marketing,* 37(1/2) (2003): 154–168; Kimberly A. Neuendorf, *The Content Analysis Guidebook* (Thousand Oaks, CA: Sage Publications, 2002); and Cheng Lu Wang, "A Content Analysis of Connectedness vs. Separateness Themes Used in U.S. and PRC Print Advertisements," *International Marketing Review,* 18(2) (2001): 145.

44. Laurel Wentz, "2002 Lookout: Global," *Advertising Age,* 23(1) (January 7, 2002): 8; Michael Maynard, "Girlish Images Across Cultures: Analyzing Japanese Versus U.S. *Seventeen* Magazine Ads," *Journal of Advertising,* 28(1) (Spring 1999): 39–48; Subir Sengupta, "The Influence of Culture on Portrayals of Women in Television Commercials: A Comparison Between the United States and Japan," *International Journal of Advertising,* 14(4) (1995): 314–333; Charles S. Madden, Marjorie J. Caballero, and Shinya Matsukubo, "Analysis of Information Content in U.S. and Japanese Magazine Advertising," *Journal of Advertising,* 15(3) (1986): 38–45; and adv.asahi.com.

45. www.expedia.com, accessed, January 8, 2009; and Ruby Bayan, "Privacy Means Knowing Your Cookies," *Link-Up,* 18(1) (January/February 2001): 22–23.

46. Gerald Berstell and Denise Nitterhouse, "Looking Outside the Box," *Marketing Research: A Magazine of Management & Applications,* 9(2) (Summer 1997): 4–13.

47. "Cattle Outlook: Heifer Weights Increase, Beef Demand Projections Down" (September 5, 2008), www.cattlenetwork.com/content. asp?contentid=250409, accessed September 26, 2008; Kendra Parker, "How Do You Like Your Beef?" *American Demographics,* 22(1) (January 2000): 35–37; and www.beef.org.

48. Barbara Benson, "Market Researcher Wins Clients with Documentaries," *Crain's New York Business,* 17(17) (April 23, 2001): 31.

49. Bruce Keillor, "A Cross-Cultural/Cross-National Study of Influencing Factors and Socially Desirable Response Bias," *International Journal of Market Research* (First Quarter 2001): 63–84; C. L. Hung, "Canadian Business Pursuits in the PRC, Hong Kong and Taiwan, and Chinese Perception of Canadians as Business Partners," *Multinational Business Review,* 6(1) (Spring 1998): 73–82; and C. Min Han, Byoung-Woo Lee, and Kong-Kyun Ro, "The Choice of a Survey Mode in Country Image Studies," *Journal of Business Research,* 29(2) (February 1994): 151–162.

50. Richard Linnett, "Reebok Re-Brands for Hip-Hop Crowd," *Advertising Age,* 73(4) (January 28, 2002): 3–4.

51. Steve Jarvis, "CMOR Finds Survey Refusal Rate Still Rising," *Marketing News,* 36(3) (February 4, 2002): 4.

52. Marla Royne Stafford and Thomas F. Stafford, "Participant Observation and the Pursuit of Truth: Methodological and Ethical Considerations," *Journal of the Market Research Society,* 35 (January 1993): 63–76.

53. Guilherme D. Pires, "Ethnic Marketing Ethics," *Journal of Business Ethics,* 36(1/2) (March 2002): 111–118; and C. N. Smith and J. A. Quelch, *Ethics in Marketing* (Homewood, IL: Richard D. Irwin, 1993).

54. Renee Boucher Ferguson, "Automating the Back Office; Netledger, Microsoft Aim Updates at Smaller Firms," *eWeek* (August 4, 2003): 1.

Chapter 7

1. Booth Moore, "Fashion Notes: Those '70s Bags Are Back in LeStyle, with a New Range of Looks," *The Los Angeles Times* (Record edition) (December 21, 2001): E.2; "LeSportsac Announces Latest International Expansion," *Showcase,* 20(6) (December 1995): 67; and "Surveys Help Settle Trade Dress Infringement Case," *Quirk's Marketing Research Review* (October/November 1987): 16, 17, 33.

2. Michelle L. Kirsche, "POPAI Study Confirms Importance of POP Ads," *Drug Store News,* 26(13) (October 11, 2004): 4–5; Anonymous, "In-Store Promo Drives Soda Sales, Study Says," *Drug Store News,* 23(18) (December 17, 2001): 81; Robert Dwek, "Prediction of Success," *Marketing* (POP & Field Marketing Supplement) (April 17, 1997): 12–13; and "POP Radio Test Airs the Ads in Store," *Marketing News* (October 24, 1986): 16.

3. Rafael Moreno and Rafael Martínez, "Causality as Validity: Some Implications for the Social Sciences," *Quality & Quantity,* 42(5) (October 2008): 597–604; Madhu Viswanathan, *Measurement Error and Research Design* (Thousand Oaks, CA: Sage Publications, 2003); Michael Sobel, "Causal Inference in the Social Sciences," *Journal of the American Statistical Association,* 95(450) (June 2000): 647–651; and R. Barker Bausell, *Conducting Meaningful Experiments* (Thousand Oaks, CA: Sage Publications, 1994).

4. James J. Heckman, "The Scientific Model of Causality," *Sociological Methodology,* 35(1) (2007): 1–98; Grant F. Gould and James L. Gould, *Chance and Causation: To Experimental Design and Statistica* (New York: W. H. Freeman, 2001); and Robert F. Boruch, *Randomized Experiments for Planning and Evaluation* (Thousand Oaks, CA: Sage Publications, 1994).

5. Thomas Lee, "Experts Say Point-of-Purchase Advertising Can Influence Shoppers' Choices," *Knight Ridder Tribune Business News* (January 19, 2002): 1; and Michele Witthaus, "POP Stars," *Marketing Week,* 20(16) (July 17, 1997): 37–41.

6. Madhu Viswanathan, *Measurement Error and Research Design* (Thousand Oaks, CA: Sage Publications, 2005); John Liechty, Venkatram Ramaswamy, and Steven H. Cohen, "Choice Menus for Mass Customization: An Experimental Approach for Analyzing Customer Demand with an Application to a Web-Based Information Service," *Journal of Marketing Research,* 38(2) (May 2001): 183–196; Gordon A. Wyner, "Experimental Design," *Marketing Research: A Magazine of Management & Applications,* 9(3) (Fall 1997): 39–41; and Steven R. Brown and Lawrence E. Melamed, *Experimental Design and Analysis* (Newbury Park, CA: Sage Publications, 1990).

7. Paul W. Farris, "Overcontrol in Advertising Experiments," *Journal of Advertising Research* (November/December 2000): 73–78.

8. "FSI Coupons Deliver 257 Billion Consumer Offers Totaling over $320 Billion in Consumer Incentives in 2007," www.tns-mi.com/news/01092008.htm, accessed October 1, 2008; "CPGs Change Coupon Media Mix & Purchase Requirements," *NCH Marketing Services Press Release* (March 15, 2002): 1–4; John Fetto, "Redeeming Value," *American Demographics,* 23(10) (October 2001): 25; Uri Ben-Zion, "The Optimal Face Value of a Discount Coupon," *Journal of Economics and Business,* 51(2) (March/April 1999): 159–164; and Robert W. Shoemaker and Vikas Tibrewala, "Relating Coupon Redemption Rates to Past Purchasing of the Brand," *Journal of Advertising Research,* 25 (October/November 1985): 40–47.

9. In addition to internal and external validity, there also exist construct and statistical conclusion validity. Construct validity addresses the question of what construct, or characteristic, is in fact being measured and is discussed in Chapter 9 on measurement and scaling. Statistical conclusion validity addresses the extent and statistical significance of the covariation that exists in the data and is discussed in the chapters on data analysis. See Kimberli R. H Treadwell, "Demonstrating Experimenter 'Ineptitude' as a Means of Teaching Internal and External Validity," *Teaching of Psychology,* 35(3) (August 2008): 184–188; and Richard R. Klink and Daniel C. Smith, "Threats to the External Validity of Brand Extension Research," *Journal of Marketing Research,* 38(3) (August 2001): 326–335.

10. Hart Blanton and James Jaccard, "Representing Versus Generalizing: Two Approaches to External Validity and Their Implications for the Study of Prejudice," *Psychological Inquiry,* 19(2) (2008): 99–105; Gilles Laurent, "Improving the External Validity of Marketing Models: A Plea for More Qualitative Input," *International Journal of Research in Marketing,* 17(2) (September 2000): 177; Prashant Bordia, "Face-to-Face Computer-Mediated Communication: A Synthesis of the Experimental Literature," *Journal of Business Communication,* 34(1) (January 1997): 99–120; David M. Bowen, "Work Group Research: Past Strategies and Future Opportunities," *IEEE Transactions on Engineering Management,* 42(1) (February 1995): 30–38; and John G. Lynch, Jr., "On the External Validity of Experiments in Consumer Research," *Journal of Consumer Research,* 9 (December 1982): 225–244.

11. Russell Winer, "Experimentation in the 21st Century: The Importance of External Validity," *Academy of Marketing Science,* 27(3) (Summer 1999): 349–358; Chris Argyris, "Actionable Knowledge: Design Causality in the Service of Consequential Theory," *Journal of Applied Behavioral Science,* 32(4) (December 1966): 390–406; John G. Lynch, Jr., "The Role of External Validity in Theoretical Research," B. J. Calder, L. W. Phillips, and Alice Tybout, "Beyond External Validity," and J. E. McGrath and D. Brinberg, "External Validity and the Research Process," *Journal of Consumer Research* (June 1983): 109–124.

12. Paul Berger and Robert Maurer, *Experimental Design with Applications in Management, Engineering and the Sciences* (Boston: Boston University Press, 2002). See also Utpal M. Dholakia and Vicki G. Morwitz, "The Scope and Persistence of Mere-Measurement Effects: Evidence from a Field Study of Customer Satisfaction Measurement," *Journal of Consumer Research,* 29 (2) (2002): 159–47.

13. Dylan S. Small, Thomas R. Ten Have and Paul R. Rosenbaum, "Randomization Inference in a Group-Randomized Trial of Treatments for Depression: Covariate Adjustment, Noncompliance, and Quantile Effects," *Journal of the American Statistical Association,* 103(481) (March 2008): 271–279; James Breaugh,

"Rethinking the Control of Nuisance Variables in Theory Testing," *Journal of Business & Psychology,* 20(3) (Spring 2006): 429–443; Paul R. Rosenbaum, "Attributing Effects to Treatment in Matched Observational Studies," *Journal of the American Statistical Association,* 97(457) (March 2002): 183–192; and Lloyd S. Nelson, "Notes on the Use of Randomization in Experimentation," *Journal of Quality Technology,* 28(1) (January 1996): 123–126.

14. Reuven Glick, Xueyan Guo and Michael Hutchison, "Currency Crises, Capital-Account Liberalization, and Selection Bias," *The Review of Economics & Statistics,* 88(4) (November 2006): 698–714; Paul R. Rosenbaum, "Attributing Effects to Treatment in Matched Observational Studies," *Journal of the American Statistical Association,* 97(457) (March 2002): 183–192; Marcus Selart, "Structure Compatibility and Restructuring in Judgment and Choice," *Organizational Behavior & Human Decision Processes,* 65(2) (February 1996): 106–116; and R. Barker Bausell, *Conducting Meaningful Experiments* (Thousand Oaks, CA: Sage Publications, 1994).

15. Beomsoo Kim, "Virtual Field Experiments for a Digital Economy: A New Research Methodology for Exploring an Information Economy," *Decision Support Systems,* 32(3) (January 2002): 215; Eleni Chamis, "Auto Dealers Test Online Sales in 90-Day Experiment," *Washington Business Journal,* 19(54) (May 11, 2001): 15; Betsy Spethmann, "Choosing a Test Market," *Brandweek,* 36(19) (May 8, 1995): 42–43; and Andrew M. Tarshis, "Natural Sell-in Avoids Pitfalls of Controlled Tests," *Marketing News* (October 24, 1986): 14.

16. Other experimental designs are also available. See, Connie M. Borror, "Evaluation of Statistical Designs for Experiments Involving Noise Variables," *Journal of Quality Technology,* 34(1) (January 2002): 54–70; and Donald T. Campbell and M. Jean Russo, *Social Experimentation* (Thousand Oaks, CA: Sage Publications, 1999).

17. For an application of the Solomon four-group design, see Joe Ayres, "Are Reductions in CA an Experimental Artifact? A Solomon Four-Group Answer," *Communication Quarterly,* 48(1) (Winter 2000): 19–26.

18. Manuel M. Ramos-Álvarez, Berenice Valdés-Conroy, and Andrés Catena, "Criteria of the Peer-Review Process for Publication of Experimental and Quasiexperimental Research in Psychology," *International Journal of Clinical and Health Psychology,* 6(3) (2006): 773–787; Duncan Simester, "Implementing Quality Improvement Programs Designed to Enhance Customer Satisfaction: Quasi Experiments in the United States and Spain," *Journal of Marketing Research,* 37(1) (February 2000): 102–112; and C. Moorman, "A Quasi Experiment to Assess the Consumer and Informational Determinants of Nutrition Information-Processing Activities—The Case of the Nutrition Labeling and Education Act," *Journal of Public Policy and Marketing,* 15(1) (Spring 1996): 28–44.

19. Roger Baron, "Knowing When to Advertise Is Key," *TelevisionWeek,* 23(34) (August 23, 2004): 21; Fred S. Zufryden, "Predicting Trial, Repeat, and Sales Response from Alternative Media Plans," *Journal of Advertising Research,* 40(6) (November/December 2000): 65–72; Leonard M. Lodish, Magid M. Abraham, Jeanne Livelsberger, Beth Lubetkin, et al., "A Summary of Fifty-Five In-Market Experimental Estimates of the Long-Term Effects of TV Advertising," *Marketing Science* (Summer 1995): G133–G140; and Lakshman Krishnamurthi, Jack Narayan, and S. P. Raj, "Intervention Analysis of a Field Experiment to Assess the Buildup Effect of Advertising," *Journal of Marketing Research,* 23 (November 1986): 337–345.

20. See, for example, Anthony Vagnoni, "Fear of Funny Abating," *Advertising Age,* 73(10) (March 11, 2002): 8–9; and M. G. Weinberger, H. Spotts, L. Campbell, and A. L. Parsons, "The Use and Effect of Humor in Different Advertising Media," *Journal of Advertising Research,* 35(3) (May/June 1995): 44–56.

21. For a recent application of factorial designs, see Chang Chung-Chau and Chou Yu-Jen, "Goal Orientation and Comparative Valence in Persuasion," *Journal of Advertising,* 37(1) (Spring 2008): 73–87.

22. Michelle L. Roehm, Ellen Bolman Pullins, and Harper A. Roehm, Jr., "Designing Loyalty-Building Programs for Packaged Goods Brands," *Journal of Marketing Research,* 39(2) (May 2002): 202–213.

23. See Aradhna Krishna and M. Utku Ünver, "Improving the Efficiency of Course Bidding at Business Schools: Field and Laboratory Studies," *Marketing Science,* 27(2) (March/April 2008): 262–282; and Niraj Dawar, "Impact of Product Harm Crises on Brand Equity: The Moderating Role of Consumer Expectations," *Journal of Marketing Research,* 37(2) (May 2000): 215–226.

24. Chris T. Allen, "A Theory-Based Approach for Improving Demand Artifact Assessment in Advertising Experiments," *Journal of Advertising,* 33(2) (Summer 2004): 63–73; J. Perrien, "Repositioning Demand Artifacts in Consumer Research," *Advances in Consumer Research,* 24 (1997): 267–271; and T. A. Shimp, E. M. Hyatt, and D. J. Snyder, "A Critical Appraisal of Demand Artifacts in Consumer Research," *Journal of Consumer Research,* 18(3) (December 1991): 272–283.

25. Chezy Ofir and Itamar Simonson, "In Search of Negative Customer Feedback: The Effect of Expecting to Evaluate on Satisfaction Evaluations," *Journal of Marketing Research,* 38(2) (May 2001): 170–182; and Gilles Laurent, "Improving the External Validity of Marketing Models: A Plea for More Qualitative Input," *International Journal of Research in Marketing,* 17(2, 3) (September 2000): 177.

26. Karen Blumenschein, "Hypothetical Versus Real Willingness to Pay in the Health Care Sector: Results from a Field Experiment," *Journal of Health Economics,* 20(3) (May 2001): 441; and Richard M. Alston and Clifford Nowell, "Implementing the Voluntary Contribution Game: A Field Experiment," *Journal of Economic Behavior & Organization,* 31(3) (December 1996): 357–368.

27. Grant F. Gould and James L. Gould, *Chance and Causation: To Experimental Design and Statistica* (New York: W. H. Freeman, 2001); and Hurbert M. Blalock, Jr., *Causal Inferences in Nonexperimental Research* (Chapel Hill: University of North Carolina Press, 1964).

28. In some situations, surveys and experiments can complement each other and may both be used. For example, the results obtained in laboratory experiments may be further examined in a field survey.

29. Natalie Zmuda and Emily Bryson York, "McD's Tries to Slake Consumer Thirst for Wider Choice of Drinks," *Advertising Age,* 79(23) (June 9, 2008): 1, 45; and Peter Romeo, "Testing, Testing," *Restaurant Business,* 97(2) (January 15, 1998): 12.

30. Gunter J. Hitsch, "An Empirical Model of Optimal Dynamic Product Launch and Exit Under Demand Uncertainty," *Marketing Science,* 25(1) (January–February 2006): 25–50.

31. Anonymous, "P&G Wields Axe on Failing Brands," *Grocer,* 224(7509) (June 23, 2001): 18; and Tara Parker-Pope, "Frito-Lay to Begin Selling Wow! Chips Made with Olestra Later This Month," *Wall Street Journal* (February 10, 1998): B2. See also, Jack Neff, "Will P&G Use Canada as Testing Ground?" *Advertising Age,* 79(20) (May 19, 2008): 41.

32. Anonymous, "Vaseline to Back Dermacare with Llm Ads Activity," *Marketing* (January 10, 2002): 4; and Sean Mehegan, "Vaseline Ups Ante via AntiBacterial," *Brandweek,* 38(21) (May 26, 1997): 1, 6.

33. Anonymous, "Simulated Test Marketing," *Sloan Management Review,* 36(2) (Winter 1995): 112.

34. Frank S. Costanza, "Exports Boost German Jewelry Industry," *National Jeweler,* 45(8) (April 16, 2001): 57; and David Woodruff and Karen Nickel, "When You Think Deluxe, Think East Germany," *Business Week,* May 26, 1997: 124E2.

35. David E. Hansen, "Knowledge Transfer in Online Learning Environments," *Journal of Marketing Education,* 30(2) (August 2008): 93–105; Anonymous, "The Disclosure Dilemma," *Workspan,* 45(1) (January 2002): 72; and Bernd H. Schmitt, "Contextual Priming of Visual Information in Advertisements," *Psychology & Marketing,* 11(1) (January/February 1994): 1–14.

36. "Nike Earnings Jump 15%," money.cnn.com, accessed June 27, 2005; Marlene de Laine, *Fieldwork, Participation and Practice: Ethics and Dilemmas in Qualitative Research* (Thousand Oaks, CA: Sage Publications, 2001); and Betsy Peterson, "Ethics, Revisited,"

Marketing Research: A Magazine of Management & Applications, 8(4) (Winter 1996): 47–48.

37. Fara Warner, "Levi's Fashions a New Strategy," *Fast Company,* 64 (November 2002): 48, www.fastcompany.com/magazine/64/smartcompany.html.

Chapter 8

1. "2008 Fortune 500: Wal-Mart's No. 1," http://money.cnn.com/magazines/fortune/rankings, accessed October 2, 2008.

2. David J. Bortholomew, *Measurement* (Thousand Oaks, CA: Sage Publications, 2006); Gordon A. Wyner, "The Right Side of Metrics," *Marketing Management,* 13(1) (2004): 8–9; Ken Gofton, "If It Moves, Measure It," *Marketing* (Marketing Technique Supplement) (September 4, 1997): 17; and Jum C. Nunnally, *Psychometric Theory,* 2nd ed. (New York: McGraw-Hill, 1978): 3.

3. Christof Schuster and David A. Smith, "Estimating with a Latent Class Model the Reliability of Nominal Judgments upon Which Two Raters Agree," *Educational and Psychological Measurement,* 66(5) (October 2006): 739; and Stanley S. Stevens, "Mathematics, Measurement and Psychophysics," in Stanley S. Stevens, ed., *Handbook of Experimental Psychology* (New York: John Wiley, 1951).

4. Alessandra Giovagnoli, Johnny Marzialetti, and Henry P. Wynn, "A New Approach to Inter-Rater Agreement Through Stochastic Orderings: The Discrete Case," *Metrika,* 67(3) (April 2008): 349–370; Sharon E. Kurpius, *Testing and Measurement* (Thousand Oaks, CA: Sage Publications, 2002); Helen M. Moshkovich, "Ordinal Judgments in Multiattribute Decision Analysis," *European Journal of Operational Research,* 137(3) (March 16, 2002): 625; Wade D. Cook, Moshe Kress, and Lawrence M. Seiford, "On the Use of Ordinal Data in Data Envelopment Analysis," *Journal of the Operational Research Society,* 44(2) (February 1993): 133–140; and William D. Perreault, Jr., and Forrest W. Young, "Alternating Least Squares Optimal Scaling: Analysis of Nonmetric Data in Marketing Research," *Journal of Marketing Research,* 17 (February 1980): 1–13.

5. Merja Halme, "Dealing with Interval Scale Data in Data Envelopment Analysis," *European Journal of Operational Research,* 137(1) (February 16, 2002): 22; and Michael Lynn and Judy Harris, "The Desire for Unique Consumer Products: A New Individual Difference Scale," *Psychology & Marketing,* 14(6) (September 1997): 601–616.

6. www.fifa.com, accessed October 2, 2008.

7. For a discussion of these scales, refer to Delbert C. Miller and Neil J. Salkind, *Handbook of Research Design and Social Measurement,* 6th ed. (Thousand Oaks, CA: Sage Publications, 2002); Taiwo Amoo, "Overall Evaluation Rating Scales: An Assessment," *International Journal of Market Research* (Summer 2000): 301–311; and C. H. Coombs, "Theory and Methods of Social Measurement," L. Festinger and D. Katz, eds., *Research Methods in the Behavioral Sciences* (New York: Holt, Rinehart & Winston, 1953).

8. However, there is some controversy regarding this issue. See, Jordan J. Louviere and Towhidul Islam, "A Comparison of Importance Weights and Willingness-to-Pay Measures Derived from Choice-Based Conjoint, Constant Sum Scales and Best–Worst Scaling," *Journal of Business Research,* 61(9) (September 2008): 903–911; Donald T. Campbell and M. Jean Russo, *Social Measurement* (Thousand Oaks, CA: Sage Publications, 2001); and T. Amoo, "Do the Numeric Values Influence Subjects' Responses to Rating Scales," *Journal of International Marketing and Marketing Research* (February 2001): 41.

9. Anonymous, "Competition Between Coca-Cola and Pepsi to Start," *Asiainfo Daily China News* (March 19, 2002): 1; Leah Rickard, "Remembering New Coke," *Advertising Age,* 66(16) (April 17, 1995): 6; and "Coke's Flip-Flop Underscores Risks of Consumer Taste Tests," *Wall Street Journal* (July 18, 1985): 25.

10. However, it is not necessary to evaluate all possible pairs of objects. Procedures such as cyclic designs can significantly reduce the number of pairs evaluated. A treatment of such procedures may be found in Albert C. Bemmaor and Udo Wagner, "A Multiple-Item

Model of Paired Comparisons: Separating Chance from Latent Performance," *Journal of Marketing Research,* 37(4) (November 2000): 514–524; and Naresh K. Malhotra, Arun K. Jain, and Christian Pinson, "The Robustness of MDS Configurations in the Case of Incomplete Data," *Journal of Marketing Research,* 25 (February 1988): 95–102.

11. For an advanced application involving paired comparison data, see Albert C. Bemmaor and Udo Wagner, "A Multiple-Item Model of Paired Comparisons: Separating Chance from Latent Performance," *Journal of Marketing Research,* 37(4) (November 2000): 514–524.

12. For the assumption of transitivity, see Alex Voorhoeve and Ken Binmore, "Transitivity, the Sorites Paradox, and Similarity-Based Decision-Making," *Erkenntnis,* 64(1) (January 2006): 101–114; and Dragan Miljkovic, "Rational Choice and Irrational Individuals or Simply an Irrational Theory: A Critical Review of the Hypothesis of Perfect Rationality," *Journal of Socio-Economics,* 34(5) (October 2005): 621–634. For Thurstone scaling, see Madhu Viswanathan, *Measurement Error and Research Design* (Thousand Oaks, CA: Sage Publications, 2005); Donald T. Campbell and M. Jean Russo, *Social Measurement* (Thousand Oaks, CA: Sage Publications, 2001); Rensis Likert, Sydney Roslow, and Gardner Murphy, "A Simple and Reliable Method of Scoring the Thurstone Attitude Scales," *Personnel Psychology,* 46(3) (Autumn 1993): 689–690; and L. L. Thurstone, *The Measurement of Values* (Chicago: University of Chicago Press, 1959). For an application of the case V procedure, see Naresh K. Malhotra, "Marketing Linen Services to Hospitals: A Conceptual Framework and an Empirical Investigation Using Thurstone's Case V Analysis," *Journal of Health Care Marketing,* 6 (March 1986): 43–50.

13. www.oceanspray.com, accessed October 2, 2008; Heather Todd, "It's Tea Time in the Juice Isle," *Beverage World,* 123(1740) (July 15, 2004): 12; Anonymous, "Cranberry Juice in a Can," *Grocer,* 225(7538) (January 26, 2002): 64; and The Beverage Network, www.bevnet.com.

14. Paul A. Bottomley, "Testing the Reliability of Weight Elicitation Methods: Direct Rating Versus Point Allocation," *Journal of Marketing Research,* 37(4) (November 2000): 508–513; and Michael W. Herman and Waldemar W. Koczkodaj, "A Monte Carlo Study of Pairwise Comparison," *Information Processing Letters,* 57(1) (January 15, 1996): 25–29.

15. www.corebrand.com/brandpower/index.html, accessed May 15, 2005.

16. Keith Chrzan and Natalia Golovashkina, "An Empirical Test of Six Stated Importance Measures," *International Journal of Market Research,* 48(6) (2006): 717–740; Tony Siciliano, "Magnitude Estimation," *Quirk's Marketing Research Review* (November 1999); Noel M. Noel and Nessim Hanna, "Benchmarking Consumer Perceptions of Product Quality with Price: An Exploration," *Psychology & Marketing,* 13(6) (September 1996): 591–604; and Jan-Benedict E. M. Steenkamp and Dick R. Wittink, "The Metric Quality of Full-Profile Judgments and the Number of Attribute Levels Effect in Conjoint Analysis," *International Journal of Research in Marketing,* 11(3) (June 1994): 275–286.

17. Roger Calantone, "Joint Ventures in China: A Comparative Study of Japanese, Korean, and U.S. Partners," *Journal of International Marketing,* 9(1) (2001): 1–22; Joseph Marinelli and Anastasia Schleck, "Collecting, Processing Data for Marketing Research Worldwide," *Marketing News* (August 18, 1997): 12, 14; and Naresh K. Malhotra, "A Methodology for Measuring Consumer Preferences in Developing Countries," *International Marketing Review,* 5 (Autumn 1988): 52–66.

18. Anonymous, "Nissan Europe Reports May Sales," www.theautochannel.com/news/2005/06/07/116354.html, accessed June 27, 2005; and Anonymous, "Sales Down But Profits Up for Nissan," *Northern Echo* (January 31, 2002): 14.

19. Gael McDonald, "Cross-Cultural Methodological Issues in Ethical Research," *Journal of Business Ethics,* 27(1/2) (September 2000): 89–104; and I. P. Akaah, "Differences in Research Ethics Judgments Between Male and Female Marketing Professionals," *Journal*

of Business Ethics, 8 (1989): 375–381. See also, Anusorn Singhapakdi, Scott J. Vitell, Kumar C. Rallapalli, and Kenneth L. Kraft, "The Perceived Role of Ethics and Social Responsibility: A Scale Development," *Journal of Business Ethics,* 15(11) (November 1996): 1131–1140.

20. Hilary Cassidy, "New Balance Ages Up; IMG Skates Off with Disson," *Brandweek,* 42(2) (January 8, 2001): 8.

Chapter 9

1. www.mta.nyc.ny.us/nyct/index.html, accessed February 16, 2009; Daniel Sforza, "Chief of New York–New Jersey Transit System Says Ridership Merits Upgrade," *Knight Ridder Tribune Business News* (October 26, 2004): 1; Anonymous, "Planned Rail Projects Still Moving Forward," *New York Construction News* (March 20, 2002): 10; and Heidi Tolliver, "A Tale of Four Cities: How Paris, London, Florence and New York Measure—and React—to What Riders Want," *Mass Transit,* XXII (2) (March/April 1996): 22–30, 107.

2. www.mcdonalds.com, accessed February 16, 2009; Anonymous, "McDonald's July Sales Top Forecasts, Europe Strong," http://today.reuters.com/news/newsarticle.aspx?type=comktNews&storyid=URI:2005-08-08T154826Z_01_N08317024_RTRIDST_0_LEISURE-MCDONALDS-SALES-UPDATE-4.XML&src=CNN, accessed August 11, 2005; Bob Sperber, "McDonald's Targets Adults with 'Trust' Effort,'" *Brandweek,* 43(14) (April 8, 2002): 6; William Murphy and Sidney Tang, "Continuous Likeability Measurement," *Marketing Research: A Magazine of Management & Applications,* 10(2) (Summer 1998): 28–35; and www.perceptionanalyzer.com.

3. Scott D. Swain, Danny Weathers, Ronald W. Niedrich, "Assessing Three Sources of Misresponse to Reversed Likert Items," *Journal of Marketing Research,* 45(1) (February 2008): 116–131; David J. Bortholomew, *Measurement* (Thousand Oaks, CA: Sage Publications, 2006); Taiwoo Amoo and Hershey H. Friedman, "Overall Evaluation Rating Scales: An Assessment," *International Journal of Market Research,* 42(3) (Summer 2000): 301–310; G. Albaum, "The Likert Scale Revisited—An Alternate Version," *Journal of the Market Research Society,* 39(2) (April 1997): 331–348; C. J. Brody and J. Dietz, "On the Dimensionality of 2-Question Format Likert Attitude Scales," *Social Science Research,* 26(2) (June 1997): 197–204; and Rensis Likert, "A Technique for the Measurement of Attitudes," *Archives of Psychology,* 140 (1932).

4. However, when the scale is multidimensional, each dimension should be summed separately. See Karin Braunsberger, R. Brian Buckler, and David J. Ortinau, "Categorizing Cognitive Responses: An Empirical Investigation of the Cognitive Intent Congruency Between Independent Raters and Original Subject Raters," *Journal of the Academy of Marketing Science,* 33(4) (September 2005): 620–632; Jeffrey M. Stanton, "Issues and Strategies for Reducing the Length of Self-Report Scales," *Personnel Psychology,* 55(1) (Spring 2002): 167–194; and Jennifer L. Aaker, "Dimensions of Brand Personality," *Journal of Marketing Research,* 34 (August 1997): 347–356.

5. Naresh K. Malhotra, Sung Kim, and James Agarwal, "Internet Users' Information Privacy Concerns (IUIPC): The Construct, the Scale, and a Causal Model," *Information Systems Research,* 15(4) (December 2004): 336–355.

6. Rajesh Sethi, Daniel C. Smith, and C. Whan Park, "Cross-Functional Product Development Teams, Creativity, and the Innovativeness of New Consumer Products," *Journal of Marketing Research,* 38(1) (February 2001): 73–85; and T. A. Chandler and C. J. Spies, "Semantic Differential Comparisons of Attributions and Dimensions Among Respondents from Seven Nations," *Psychological Reports,* 79(3, part 1) (December 1996): 747–758.

7. Sharon E. Kurpius, *Testing and Measurement* (Thousand Oaks, CA: Sage Publications, 2002); Delbert C. Miller and Neil J. Salkind, *Handbook of Research Design and Social Measurement,* 6th ed. (Thousand Oaks, CA: Sage Publications, 2002); and William O. Bearden and Richard G. Netemeyer, *Handbook of Marketing Scales: Multi-Item Measures for Marketing and Consumer Behavior Research* (Thousand Oaks, CA: Sage Publications, 1999).

8. Naresh K. Malhotra, "A Scale to Measure Self-Concepts, Person Concepts and Product Concepts," *Journal of Marketing Research,* 18 (November 1981): 456–464. See also, Stuart Van Auken, Thomas E. Barry, Richard P. Bagozzi, "A Cross-Country Construct Validation of Cognitive Age," *Journal of the Academy of Marketing Science,* 34(3) (Summer 2006): 439–455.

9. However, there is little difference in the results based on whether the data are ordinal or interval. See, Shizuhiko Nishisato, *Measurement and Multivariate Analysis* (New York: Springer-Verlag, 2002); and John Gaiton, "Measurement Scales and Statistics: Resurgence of an Old Misconception," *Psychological Bulletin,* 87 (1980): 564–567.

10. Chezy Ofir, "In Search of Negative Customer Feedback: The Effect of Expecting to Evaluate on Satisfaction Evaluations," *Journal of Marketing Research* (May 2001): 170–182; Timothy H. Reisenwitz and G. Joseph Wimbish, Jr., "Over-the-Counter Pharmaceuticals: Exploratory Research of Consumer Preferences Toward Solid Oral Dosage Forms," *Health Marketing Quarterly,* 13(4) (1996): 47–61; and S. Malhotra, S. Van Auken, and S. C. Lonial, "Adjective Profiles in Television Copy Testing," *Journal of Advertising Research* (August 1981): 21–25.

11. Michael K. Brady, "Performance Only Measurement of Service Quality: A Replication and Extension," *Journal of Business Research,* 55(1) (January 2002): 17; Jan Stapel "About 35 Years of Market Research in the Netherlands," *Markonderzock Kwartaalschrift,* 2 (1969): 3–7.

12. John Dawes, "Do Data Characteristics Change According to the Number of Scale Points Used?" *International Journal of Market Research,* 50(1) (2008): 61–77; Eugene W. Anderson, "Foundations of the American Customer Satisfaction Index," *Total Quality Management,* 11(7) (September 2000): 5869–5882; A. M. Coleman, C. E. Norris, and C. C. Peterson, "Comparing Rating Scales of Different Lengths—Equivalence of Scores from 5-Point and 7-Point Scales," *Psychological Reports,* 80(2) (April 1997): 355–362; Madhubalan Viswanathan, Mark Bergen, and Terry Childers, "Does a Single Response Category in a Scale Completely Capture a Response?" *Psychology & Marketing,* 13(5) (August 1996): 457–479; and Eli P. Cox III, "The Optimal Number of Response Alternatives for a Scale: A Review," *Journal of Marketing Research,* 17 (November 1980): 407–422.

13. Yadolah Dodge, "On Asymmetric Properties of the Correlation Coefficient in the Regression Setting," *The American Statistician,* 55(1) (February 2001): 51–54; D. F. Alwin, "Feeling Thermometers Versus 7-Point Scales—Which Are Better," *Sociological Methods & Research,* 25(3) (February 1997): 318–340; M. M. Givon and Z. Shapira, "Response to Rating Scales: A Theoretical Model and Its Application to the Number of Categories Problem," *Journal of Marketing Research* (November 1984): 410–419; and D. E. Stem, Jr., and S. Noazin, "The Effects of Number of Objects and Scale Positions on Graphic Position Scale Reliability," in R. F. Lusch, et al., *1985 AMA Educators' Proceedings* (Chicago: American Marketing Association, 1985): 370–372.

14. Bradford S. Jones, "Modeling Direction and Intensity in Semantically Balanced Ordinal Scales: An Assessment of Congressional Incumbent Approval," *American Journal of Political Science,* 44(1) (January 2000): 174; D. Watson, "Correcting for Acquiescent Response Bias in the Absence of a Balanced Scale—An Application to Class-Consciousness," *Sociological Methods & Research,* 21(1) (August 1992): 52–88; and H. Schuman and S. Presser, *Questions and Answers in Attitude Surveys* (New York: Academic Press, 1981): 179–201.

15. Palmer Morrel-Samuels, "Getting the Truth into Workplace Surveys," *Harvard Business Review,* 80(2) (February 2002): 111; and G. J. Spagna, "Questionnaires: Which Approach Do You Use?" *Journal of Advertising Research* (February/March 1984): 67–70.

16. John Kulas, Alicia Stachowski, and Brad Haynes, "Middle Response Functioning in Likert Responses to Personality Items," *Journal of Business & Psychology,* 22(3) (March 2008): 251–259; Janet McColl-Kennedy, "Measuring Customer Satisfaction: Why, What

and How," *Total Quality Management,* 11(7) (September 2000): 5883–5896; Kathy A. Hanisch, "The Job Descriptive Index Revisited: Questions About the Question Mark," *Journal of Applied Psychology,* 77(3) (June 1992): 377–382; and K. C. Schneider, "Uninformed Response Rate in Survey Research," *Journal of Business Research* (April 1985): 153–162.

17. For the effect of verbal description on scale perception, see Justin Kruger and Patrick Vargas, "Consumer Confusion of Percent Differences," *Journal of Consumer Psychology,* 18(1) (January 2008): 49–61; T. Amoo, "Do Numeric Values Influence Subjects' Responses to Rating Scales," *Journal of International Marketing and Market Research* (February 2001): 41; K. M. Gannon and T. M. Ostrom, "How Meaning Is Given to Rating Scales—The Effects of Response Language on Category Activation," *Journal of Experimental Social Psychology,* 32(4) (July 1996): 337–360; and H. H. Friedman and J. R. Leefer, "Label Versus Position in Rating Scales," *Journal of the Academy of Marketing Science* (Spring 1981): 88–92.

18. D. F. Alwin, "Feeling Thermometers Versus 7-Point Scales—Which Are Better," *Sociological Methods & Research,* 25(3) (February 1997): 318–340.

19. For recent constructions of multi-item scales, see John R. Rossiter, "The C-OAR-SE Procedure for Scale Development in Marketing," *International Journal of Research in Marketing,* 19(4) (2002): 305–335; Tom Brown, "The Customer Orientation of Service Workers: Personality Trait Effects on Self- and Supervisor-Performance Ratings," *Journal of Marketing Research,* 39(1) (February 2002): 110–119; and Charla Mathwick, Naresh K. Malhotra, and Edward Rigdon, "Experiential Value: Conceptualization, Measurement and Application in the Catalog and Internet Shopping Environment," *Journal of Retailing,* 77 (2001): 39–56.

20. For example, see Blair Kidwell, David M. Hardesty and Terry L. Childers, "Consumer Emotional Intelligence: Conceptualization, Measurement, and the Prediction of Consumer Decision Making," *Journal of Consumer Research,* 35(1) (June 2008): 154–166; Elena Delgado-Ballester, Jose Luis Munuera-Alemán, and Marí Jesús Yagüe-Guillén, "Development and Validation of a Brand Trust Scale," *International Journal of Market Research,* 45(1) (2003): 35–53; Leisa Reinecke Flynn and Dawn Pearcy, "Four Subtle Sins in Scale Development: Some Suggestions for Strengthening the Current Paradigm," *International Journal of Market Research,* 43(4) (Fourth Quarter 2001): 409–423; and Maryon F. King, "Social Desirability Bias: A Neglected Aspect of Validity Testing," *Psychology & Marketing,* 17(2) (February 2000): 79.

21. Stephania H. Davis, "Smart Products for Smart Marketing," *Telephony,* 234(9) (March 2, 1998): 66; and Erin Anderson, Wujin Chu, and Barton Weitz, "Industrial Purchasing: An Empirical Exploration of the Buyclass Framework," *Journal of Marketing,* 51 (July 1987): 71–86.

22. See Naresh K. Malhotra, Sung Kim, and James Agarwal, "Internet Users' Information Privacy Concerns (IUIPC): The Construct, the Scale, and a Causal Model," *Information Systems Research,* 15(4) (December 2004): 336–355; Walter C. Borman, "An Examination of the Comparative Reliability, Validity, and Accuracy of Performance Ratings Made Using Computerized Adaptive Rating Scales," *Journal of Applied Psychology,* 86(5) (October 2001): 965; and Eric A. Greenleaf, "Improving Rating Scale Measures by Detecting and Correcting Bias Components in Some Response Styles," *Journal of Marketing Research,* 29 (May 1992): 176–188.

23. Bruce Thompson, *Score Reliability: Contemporary Thinking on Reliability Issues* (Thousand Oaks, CA: Sage Publications, 2002); Pritibhushan Sinha, "Determination of Reliability of Estimations Obtained with Survey Research: A Method of Simulation," *International Journal of Market Research,* 42(3) (Summer 2000): 311–317; E. J. Wilson, "Research Design Effects on the Reliability of Rating Scales in Marketing—An Update on Churchill and Peter," *Advances in Consumer Research,* 22 (1995): 360–365; William D. Perreault, Jr., and Laurence E. Leigh, "Reliability of Nominal Data Based on Qualitative Judgments," *Journal of Marketing Research,* 25 (May 1989): 135–148; and J. Paul Peter, "Reliability: A Review of Psychometric Basics and Recent Marketing Practices," *Journal of Marketing Research,* 16 (February 1979): 6–17.

24. Michael C. Sturman, Robin A. Cheramie, and Luke H. Cashen, "The Impact of Job Complexity and Performance Measurement on the Temporal Consistency, Stability, and Test–Retest Reliability of Employee Job Performance Ratings," *Journal of Applied Psychology,* 90(2) (2005): 269–283; Madhu Viswanathan, *Measurement Error and Research Design* (Thousand Oaks, CA: Sage Publications, 2005); Donald T. Campbell and M. Jean Russo, *Social Measurement* (Thousand Oaks, CA: Sage Publications, 2001); and Simon S. K. Lam and Ka S. Woo, "Measuring Service Quality: A Test-Retest Reliability Investigation of SERVQUAL," *Journal of the Market Research Society,* 39(2) (April 1997): 381–396.

25. David Hunt, *Measurement and Scaling in Statistics* (London, UK: Edward Arnold, 2001); David Armstrong, Ann Gosling, John Weinman, and Theresa Marteau, "The Place of Inter-Rater Reliability in Qualitative Research: An Empirical Study," *Sociology: The Journal of the British Sociological Association,* 31(3) (August 1997): 597–606; and M. N. Segal, "Alternate Form Conjoint Reliability," *Journal of Advertising Research,* 4 (1984): 31–38.

26. Niels G. Waller, "Commingled Samples: A Neglected Source of Bias in Reliability Analysis," *Applied Psychological Measurement,* 32(3) (May 2008): 211–223; Adam Duhachek, Anne T. Coughlan, and Dawn Iacobucci, "Results on the Standard Error of the Coefficient Alpha Index of Reliability," *Marketing Science,* 24(2) (Spring 2005): 294–301; Robert A. Peterson, "A Meta-Analysis of Chronbach's Coefficient Alpha," *Journal of Consumer Research,* 21 (September 1994): 381–91; and L. J Cronbach, "Coefficient Alpha and the Internal Structure of Tests," *Psychometrika,* 16 (1951): 297–334.

27. Patrick Y. K. Chau and Kai Lung Hui, "Identifying Early Adopters of New IT Products: A Case of Windows 95," *Information & Management,* 33(5) (May 28, 1998): 225–230.

28. Pierre Chandon, Vicki G. Morwitz, and Werner J. Reinartz, "Do Intentions Really Predict Behavior? Self-Generated Validity Effects in Survey Research," *Journal of Marketing,* 69(2) (April 2005): 1–14; Gilad Chen, "Validation of a New General Self-Efficacy Scale," *Organizational Research Methods,* 4(1) (January 2001): 62–83; D. G. Mctavish, "Scale Validity–A Computer Content-Analysis Approach," *Social Science Computer Review,* 15(4) (Winter 1997): 379–393; and J. Paul Peter, "Construct Validity: A Review of Basic Issues and Marketing Practices," *Journal of Marketing Research,* 18 (May 1981): 133–145.

29. For further details on validity, see Blair Kidwell, David M. Hardesty, and Terry L. Childers, "Consumer Emotional Intelligence: Conceptualization, Measurement, and the Prediction of Consumer Decision Making," *Journal of Consumer Research,* 35(1) (June 2008): 154–166; Bruce L. Alford and Brian T. Engelland, "Measurement Validation in Marketing Research: A Review and Commentary," *Journal of Business Research,* 57(2) (2004): 95–97; Bruce Keillor, "A Cross-Cultural/Cross-National Study of Influencing Factors and Socially Desirable Response Biases," *International Journal of Market Research* (First Quarter 2001): 63–84; M. Joseph Sirgy, Dhruv Grewal, Tamara F. Mangleburg, Jae-ok Park, et al., "Assessing the Predictive Validity of Two Methods of Measuring Self-Image Congruence," *Journal of the Academy of Marketing Science,* 25(3) (Summer 1997): 229–241; and Rosann L. Spiro and Barton A. Weitz, "Adaptive Selling: Conceptualization, Measurement, and Nomological Validity," *Journal of Marketing Research,* 27 (February 1990): 61–69.

30. For a discussion of generalizability theory and its applications in marketing research, see Karen L. Middleton, "Socially Desirable Response Sets: The Impact of Country Culture," *Psychology and Marketing* (February 2000): 149; Shuzo Abe, Richard P. Bagozzi, and Pradip Sadarangani, "An Investigation of Construct Validity and Generalizability of the Self-Concept: Self-Consciousness in Japan and the United States," *Journal of International Consumer*

Marketing, 8(3, 4) (1996): 97–123; and Joseph O. Rentz, "Generalizability Theory: A Comprehensive Method for Assessing and Improving the Dependability of Marketing Measures," *Journal of Marketing Research,* 24 (February 1987): 19–28.

31. Matthew Myers, "Academic Insights: An Application of Multiple-Group Causal Models in Assessing Cross-Cultural Measurement Equivalence," *Journal of International Marketing,* 8(4) (2000): 108–121; and Timothy R. Hinkin, "A Review of Scale Development Practices in the Study of Organizations," *Journal of Management,* 21(5) (1995): 967–988.

32. Stuart Van Auken, Thomas E. Barry, and Richard P. Bagozzi, "A Cross-Country Construct Validation of Cognitive Age," *Journal of the Academy of Marketing Science* 34(3) (Summer 2006): 439–455; Alan Page Fiske, "Using Individualism and Collectivism to Compare Cultures—A Critique of the Validity and Measurement of the Constructs: Comment on Oyserman," *Psychological Bulletin,* 128(1) (January 2002): 78; Michael R. Mullen, George R. Milne, and Nicholas M. Didow, "Determining Cross-Cultural Metric Equivalence in Survey Research: A New Statistical Test," *Advances in International Marketing,* 8 (1996): 145–157; and E. Gencturk, T. L. Childers, and R. W. Ruekert, "International Marketing Involvement—The Construct, Dimensionality, and Measurement," *Journal of International Marketing,* 3(4) (1995): 11–37.

33. Alan L. Unikel, "Imitation Might Be Flattering, But Beware of Trademark Infringement," *Marketing News,* 21(19) (September 11, 1997): 20-21; and Betsy Mckay, "Xerox Fights Trademark Battle," *Advertising Age International* (April 27, 1992).

34. Denny Hatch, "How Truthful Is Your Offer?" *Target Marketing,* 24(4) (April 2001): 94.

35. Andrea L. Stape, "Job-Search Site Monster Gets Ready to Make Noise," *Knight Ridder Tribune Business News* (August 28, 2003): 1.

Chapter 10

1. www.census.gov/acs, accessed July 13, 2005; and Patricia Kelly, "Questionnaire Design, Printing, and Distribution," *Government Information Quarterly,* 17(2) (2000): 147.

2. Thomas Obrey, "Proving Web Site Value: It's More Than a Pretty (User) Face," *Customer Inter@ction Solutions,* 22(5) (November 2003): 52; and Marshall Rice, "What Makes Users Revisit a Web Site?" *Marketing News,* 31 (March 17, 1997): 12.

3. S. L. Payne, *The Art of Asking Questions* (Princeton, NJ: Princeton University Press, 1951): 141. See also, Thomas T. Semon, "Consider Context of Questionnaires as Survey Results Can Be Affected," *Marketing News,* 39(12) (July 2005): 8–18; Michael Schrage, "Survey Says," *Adweek Magazines' Technology Marketing,* 22(1) (January 2002): 11; and Bill Gillham, *Developing a Questionnaire* (New York: Continuum International Publishing Group, 2000).

4. These guidelines are drawn from several books on questionnaire design. See, for example, Marco Vriens, "Split-Questionnaire Designs: A New Tool in Survey Design and Panel Management," *Marketing Research,* 13(2) (Summer 2001): 14–19; Stephen Jenkins, "Automating Questionnaire Design and Construction," *Journal of the Market Research Society* (Winter 1999–2000): 79–95; Bill Gillham, *Developing a Questionnaire* (New York: Continuum International Publishing Group, 2000); Robert A. Peterson, *Constructing Effective Questionnaires* (Thousand Oaks, CA: Sage Publications, 2000); Howard Schuman and Stanley Presser, *Questions & Answers in Attitude Survey* (Thousand Oaks, CA: Sage Publications, 1996); Arlene Fink, *How to Ask Survey Questions* (Thousand Oaks, CA: Sage Publications, 1995); and Floyd J. Fowler, Jr., *Improving Survey Questions* (Thousand Oaks, CA: Sage Publications, 1995).

5. Bruce H Clark, "Bad Examples," *Marketing Management,* 12(6) (2003): 34–38; Darlene B. Bordeaux, "Interviewing—Part II: Getting the Most Out of Interview Questions," *Motor Age,* 121(2) (February 2002): 38–40; Thomas T. Semon, "Better Questions Means More Honesty," *Marketing News,* 34(17) (August 14, 2000): 10; and Thomas T. Semon, "Asking 'How Important' Is Not Enough," *Marketing News,* 31(16) (August 4, 1997): 19.

6. Benjamin Healey, Terry Macpherson, and Bart Kuijten, "An Empirical Evaluation of Three Web Survey Design Principles," *Marketing Bulletin* (16) (May 2005): 1–9; Jennifer Hess, "The Effects of Person-Level Versus Household-Level Questionnaire Design on Survey Estimates and Data Quality," *Public Opinion Quarterly,* 65(4) (Winter 2001): 574–584; John N. Bassili and B. Stacey Bassili, "Response Latency as a Signal to Question Problems in Survey Research," *Public Opinion Quarterly,* 60(3) (Fall 1996): 390–399.

7. Timothy R. Graeff, "Reducing Uninformed Responses: The Effects of Product-Class Familiarity and Measuring Brand Knowledge on Surveys," *Psychology & Marketing,* 24(8) (August 2007): 681–702; Timothy R. Graeff, "Uninformed Response Bias in Telephone Surveys," *Journal of Business Research,* 55(3) (March 2002): 251; Rachel Miller, "Counting the Cost of Response Rates," *Marketing* (January 18, 2001): 37–38; Arthur Sterngold, Rex H. Warland, and Robert O. Herrmann, "Do Surveys Overstate Public Concerns?" *Public Opinion Quarterly,* 58(20) (Summer 1994): 255–263; and D. I. Hawkins and K. A. Coney, "Uninformed Response Error in Survey Research," *Journal of Marketing Research* (August 1981): 373.

8. Barbel Knauper, "Filter Questions and Question Interpretation: Presuppositions at Work," *Public Opinion Quarterly,* 62(1) (Spring 1998): 70–78; and George F. Bishop, Robert W. Oldendick, and Alfred J. Tuchfarber, "Effects of Filter Questions in Public Opinion Surveys," *Public Opinion Quarterly,* 46 (Spring 1982): 66–85.

9. Timothy R. Graeff, "Reducing Uninformed Responses: The Effects of Product-Class Familiarity and Measuring Brand Knowledge on Surveys," *Psychology & Marketing,* 24(8) (August 2007): 681–702; and Timothy R. Graeff, "Uninformed Response Bias in Telephone Surveys," *Journal of Business Research,* 55(3) (March 2002): 251.

10. Karin Braunsberger, Roger Gates, and David J. Ortinau, "Prospective Respondent Integrity Behavior in Replying to Direct Mail Questionnaires: A Contributor in Overestimating Nonresponse Rates," *Journal of Business Research,* 58(3) (March 2005): 260–267; Eunkyu Lee, Michael Y. Hu, and Rex S. Toh, "Are Consumer Survey Results Distorted? Systematic Impact of Behavioral Frequency and Duration on Survey Response Errors," *Journal of Marketing Research,* 37(1) (February 2000): 125–133; Solomon Dutka and Lester R. Frankel "Measuring Response Error," *Journal of Advertising Research,* 37(1) (January/February 1997): 33–39; and Terry Haller, *Danger: Marketing Researcher at Work* (Westport, CT: Quorum Books, 1983): 149.

11. "Questionnaire Design," www.quickmba.com/marketing/research/qdesign, accessed February 10, 2008; Ursula Grandcolas, Ruth Rettie, and Kira Marusenko, "Web Survey Bias: Sample or Mode Effect?" *Journal of Marketing Management,* 19(5/6) (July 2003): 541–561; George D. Gaskell, "Telescoping of Landmark Events: Implications for Survey Research," *Public Opinion Quarterly,* 64(1) (Spring 2000): 77–89; Geeta Menon, Priya Raghubir, and Norbert Schwarz, "Behavioral Frequency Judgments: An Accessibility-Diagnosticity Framework," *Journal of Consumer Research,* 22(2) (September 1995): 212–228; and William A. Cook, "Telescoping and Memory's Other Tricks," *Journal of Advertising Research* (February/March 1987): 5–8.

12. Roger Tourangeau and Ting Yan, "Sensitive Questions in Surveys," *Psychological Bulletin,* 133(5) (September 2007): 859–883; R. P. Hill, "Researching Sensitive Topics in Marketing—The Special Case of Vulnerable Populations," *Journal of Public Policy & Marketing,* 14(1) (Spring 1995): 143–148.

13. Duane P. Bachmann, John Elfrink, and Gary Vazzana, "E-Mail and Snail Mail Face Off in Rematch," *Marketing Research,* 11(4) (Winter 1999/Spring 2000): 10–15; Patrick Hanrahan, "Mine Your Own Business," *Target Marketing* (February 2000): 32; Roger Tourangeau and Tom W. Smith, "Asking Sensitive Questions: The Impact of Data-Collection Mode, Question Format, and Question Context," *Public Opinion Quarterly,* 60(20) (Summer 1996): 275–304; and Kent H. Marquis, et al., *Response Errors in Sensitive Topic Survey: Estimates, Effects, and Correction Options* (Santa Monica, CA: Rand Corporation, 1981).

14. "The Questionnaire Design Process," http://profitmatters.ca/Articles/ Questionnaire%20Design.pdf, accessed February 11, 2008; Hans Baumgartner and Jan-Benedict E. M. Steenkamp, "Response Styles in Marketing Research: A Cross-National Investigation," *Journal of Marketing Research,* 38(2) (May 2001): 143–156; and Priya Raghubir and Geeta Menon, "Asking Sensitive Questions: The Effects of Type of Referent and Frequency Wording in Counterbiasing Methods," *Psychology & Marketing,* 13(7) (October 1996): 633–652.

15. For applications, see Ernest R. Larkins, Evelyn C. Hume, and Bikramjit S. Garcha, "The Validity of the Randomized Response Method in Tax Ethics Research," *Journal of Applied Business Research,* 13(3) (Summer 1997): 25–32; Brian K. Burton and Janet P. Near, "Estimating the Incidence of Wrongdoing and Whistle-Blowing: Results of a Study Using Randomized Response Technique," *Journal of Business Ethics,* 14 (January 1995): 17–30; and D. E. Stem, Jr., and R. K. Steinhorst, "Telephone Interview and Mail Questionnaire Applications of the Randomized Response Model," *Journal of the American Statistical Association* (September 1984): 555–564.

16. Mildred L. Patten, *Questionnaire Research: A Practical Guide* (Los Angeles: Pyrczak Publishing, 2001); and Lynn M. Newman, "That's a Good Question," *American Demographics,* (Marketing Tools) (June 1995): 10–13.

17. John W. Mullins, "Discovering 'Unk-Unks,' " *MIT Sloan Management Review,* 48(4) (Summer 2007): 17–21; Karin Braunsberger, R. Brian Buckler, and David J. Ortinau, "Categorizing Cognitive Responses: An Empirical Investigation of the Cognitive Intent Congruency Between Independent Raters and Original Subject Raters," *Journal of the Academy of Marketing Science,* 33(4) (Fall 2005): 620–632; Roel Popping, *Computer-Assisted Text Analysis* (Thousand Oaks, CA: Sage Publications, 2000); and Serge Luyens, "Coding Verbatims by Computers," *Marketing Research: A Magazine of Management & Applications,* 7(2) (Spring 1995): 20–25.

18. Based on a marketing research project conducted by the author. See also, Steven G. Rogelberg, "Attitudes Toward Surveys: Development of a Measure and Its Relationship to Respondent Behavior," *Organizational Research Methods,* 4(1) (January 2001): 3–25.

19. Anne-Marie Pothas, "Customer Satisfaction: Keeping Tabs on the Issues That Matter," *Total Quality Management,* 12(1) (January 2001): 83; and Kevin W. Mossholder, Randall P. Settoon, Stanley G. Harris, and Achilles A. Armenakis, "Measuring Emotion in Open-Ended Survey Responses: An Application of Textual Data Analysis," *Journal of Management,* 21(2) (1995): 335–355.

20. Michael Russell, Michael J. Fischer, Carol M. Fischer, and Kathleen Premo, "Exam Question Sequencing Effects on Marketing and Management Sciences Student Performance," *Journal for Advancement of Marketing Education,* 3 (Summer 2003): 1–10; Debra Javeline, "Response Effects in Polite Cultures," *Public Opinion Quarterly,* 63(1) (Spring 1999): 1–27; and Jon A. Krosnick and Duane F. Alwin, "An Evaluation of a Cognitive Theory of Response-Order Effects in Survey Measurement," *Public Opinion Quarterly* (Summer 1987): 201–219. Niels J. Blunch, "Position Bias in Multiple-Choice Questions," *Journal of Marketing Research,* 21 (May 1984): 216–220, has argued that position bias in multiple-choice questions cannot be eliminated by rotating the order of the alternatives. This viewpoint is contrary to the common practice.

21. Carol W. DeMoranville and Carol C. Bienstock, "Question Order Effects in Measuring Service Quality," *International Journal of Research in Marketing,* 20(3) (2003): 217–231; Bobby Duffy, "Response Order Effects—How Do People Read?" *International Journal of Market Research,* 45(4) (2003): 457–466; Eleanor Singer, "Experiments with Incentives in Telephone Surveys," *Public Opinion Quarterly,* 64(2) (Summer 2000): 171–188; and Howard Schuman and Stanley Presser, *Questions & Answers in Attitude Survey* (Thousand Oaks, CA: Sage Publications, 1996).

22. "Marketing—Controlling Questions," www.studentzone.cz/ dokumenty_down.php?id=112&db=1, accessed February 12, 2008;

Karen Blumenschein, "Hypothetical Versus Real Willingness to Pay in the Health Care Sector: Results from a Field Experiment," *Journal of Health Economics,* 20(3) (May 2001): 441; Joseph A. Herriges and Jason F. Shogren, "Starting Point Bias in Dichotomous Choice Valuation with Follow-Up Questioning," *Journal of Environmental Economics & Management,* 30(1) (January 1996): 112–131; and R. W. Mizerski, J. B. Freiden, and R. C. Green, Jr., "The Effect of the 'Don't Know' Option on TV Ad Claim Recognition Tests," *Advances in Consumer Research,* 10 (Association for Consumer Research, 1983): 283–287.

23. Marco Vriends, Michel Wedel, and Zsolt Sandor, "Split-Questionnaire Design," *Marketing Research,* 13(2) (2001): 14–19; Frederick G. Conrad, "Clarifying Question Meaning in a Household Telephone Survey," *Public Opinion Quarterly,* 64(1) (Spring 2000): 1–27; Michael McBurnett, "Wording of Questions Affects Responses to Gun Control Issue," *Marketing News,* 31(1) (January 6, 1997): 12; and M. Wanke, N. Schwarz, and E. Noelle-Neumann, "Asking Comparative Questions: The Impact of the Direction of Comparison," *Public Opinion Quarterly,* 59(3) (Fall 1995): 347–372.

24. "A Global Perspective," www.quirks.com/articles/a2000/ 20001102.aspx?searchID=3330564, accessed February 12, 2008; and Joseph Rydholm, "Syndicated Survey Monitors Airline Performance Around the World," *Quirk's Marketing Research Review* (November, 2000), www.quirks.com/articles/ article_ print.asp?arg_articleid=623, accessed March 23, 2001.

25. Richard Colombo, "A Model for Diagnosing and Reducing Nonresponse Bias," *Journal of Advertising Research,* 40(1/2) (January/April 2000): 85–93; G. S. Omura, "Correlates of Item Nonresponse," *Journal of the Market Research Society* (October 1983): 321–330; and S. Presser, "Is Inaccuracy on Factual Survey Items Item-Specific or Respondent-Specific?" *Public Opinion Quarterly* (Spring 1984): 344–355.

26. Christopher R. Bollinger, "Estimation with Response Error and Nonresponse: Food-Stamp Participation in the SIPP," *Journal of Business & Economic Statistics,* 19(2) (April 2001): 129–141; John Dawes, "The Impact of Question Wording Reversal on Probabilistic Estimates of Defection/Loyalty for a Subscription Product," *Marketing Bulletin,* 11 (May 2000): 1–9; and Nancy Johnson Stout, "Questionnaire Design Workshop Helps Market Researchers Build Better Surveys," *Health Care Strategic Management,* 12(7) (July 1994): 10–11.

27. Bill Gillham, *Developing a Questionnaire* (New York: Continuum International Publishing Group, 2000); and Lida C. Saltz, "How to Get Your News Release Published," *Journal of Accountancy,* 182(5) (November 1996): 89–91.

28. Michael J. Baker, "Data Collection—Questionnaire Design," *Marketing Review,* 3(3) (July 2003): 343–367; Mick P. Couper, "Web Surveys: A Review of Issues and Approaches," *Public Opinion Quarterly,* 64(4) (Winter 2000): 464–494; Brad Edmondson, "How to Spot a Bogus Poll," *American Demographics,* 8(10) (October 1996): 10–15; and John O'Brien, "How Do Market Researchers Ask Questions?" *Journal of the Market Research Society,* 26 (April 1984): 93–107.

29. Peter M. Chisnall, "Marketing Research: State of the Art Perspectives," *International Journal of Market Research,* 44(1) (First Quarter 2002): 122–125; and Paul R. Abramson and Charles W. Ostrom, "Question Wording and Partisanship," *Public Opinion Quarterly,* 58(1) (Spring 1994): 21–48.

30. Craig Charney, "Top 10 Ways to Get Misleading Poll Results," *Campaigns & Elections* 28(7) (July 2007): 66–67; Bob Becker, "Take Direct Route When Data Gathering," *Marketing News,* 33(20) (September 27, 1999): 29–30; and "Don't Lead: You May Skew Poll Results," *Marketing News,* 30(12) (June 3, 1996): H37.

31. Svend Brinkmann, "Could Interviews Be Epistemic? An Alternative to Qualitative Opinion Polling," *Qualitative Inquiry,* 13(8) (December 2007): 1116–1138; Bill Gillham, *Developing a Questionnaire* (New York: Continuum International Publishing Group, 2000); Raymond J. Adamek, "Public Opinion and Roe v. Wade:

Measurement Difficulties," *Public Opinion Quarterly,* 58(3) (Fall 1994): 409–418; and E. Noelle-Neumann and B. Worcester, "International Opinion Research," *European Research* (July 1984): 124–131.

32. Sandra Chen, Blake Poland, and Harvey A. Skinner, "Youth Voices: Evaluation of Participatory Action Research," *Canadian Journal of Program Evaluation,* 22(1) (March 2007): 125; Ming Ouyand, "Estimating Marketing Persistence on Sales of Consumer Durables in China," *Journal of Business Research,* 55(4) (April 2002): 337; Jacob Jacoby and George J. Szybillo, "Consumer Research in FTC Versus Kraft (1991): A Case of Heads We Win, Tails You Lose?" *Journal of Public Policy & Marketing,* 14(1) (Spring 1995): 1–14; and E. D. Jaffe and I. D. Nebenzahl, "Alternative Questionnaire Formats for Country Image Studies," *Journal of Marketing Research* (November 1984): 463–471.

33. Nancy A. Glassman and Myron Glassman, "Screening Questions," *Marketing Research,* 10(3) (1998): 25–31; Howard Schuman and Stanley Presser, *Questions & Answers in Attitude Survey* (Thousand Oaks, CA: Sage Publications, 1996); and Jon A. Krosnick and Duane F. Alwin, "An Evaluation of a Cognitive Theory of Response-Order Effects in Survey Measurement," *Public Opinion Quarterly* (Summer 1987): 201–219.

34. Rating a brand on specific attributes early in a survey may affect responses to a later overall brand evaluation. For example, see "Survey Design Workshop," www2.oeas.ucf.edu/oeas2/pdf/SurveyDesignWorkshop.pdf, accessed February 16, 2008; Larry M. Bartels, "Question Order and Declining Faith in Elections," *Public Opinion Quarterly,* 66(1) (Spring 2002): 67–79; and Barbara A. Bickart, "Carryover and Backfire Effects in Marketing Research," *Journal of Marketing Research,* 30 (February 1993): 52–62.

35. "Qualities of a Good Question," www.statpac.com/surveys/question-qualities.htm, accessed February 16, 2008: Peter D. Watson, "Adolescents' Perceptions of a Health Survey Using Multimedia Computer-Assisted Self-Administered Interview," *Australian and New Zealand Journal of Public Health,* 25(6) (December 2001): 520; Fern K. Willits and Bin Ke, "Part-Whole Question Order Effects: Views of Rurality," *Public Opinion Quarterly,* 59(3) (Fall 1995): 392–403; and Donald J. Messmer and Daniel J. Seymour, "The Effects of Branching on Item Nonresponse," *Public Opinion Quarterly,* 46 (Summer 1982): 270–277.

36. David Zatz, "Create Effective E-Mail Surveys," *HRMagazine,* 45(1) (January 2000): 97–103; and George R. Milne, "Consumer Participation in Mailing Lists: A Field Experiment," *Journal of Public Policy & Marketing,* 16(2) (Fall 1997): 298–309.

37. Jon Van, "New Technology, Fast Internet Connections Give Researchers Easy Data Access," *Knight Ridder Tribune Business News* (February 3, 2002): 1; "A World Press Model Debuts," *Graphic Arts Monthly,* 66(6) (June 1994): 66.

38. Johnny Blair and K. P. Srinath, "A Note on Sample Size for Behavior Coding Pretests," *Field Methods,* 85(11) (February 2008): 20; Frederick G. Conrad, "Clarifying Questions Meaning in a Household Telephone Survey," *Public Opinion Quarterly,* 64(1) (Spring 2000): 1–27; E. Martin and A. E. Polivka, "Diagnostics for Redesigning Survey Questionnaires—Measuring Work in the Current Population Survey," *Public Opinion Quarterly,* 59(4) (Winter 1995): 547–567; Adamantios Diamantopoulos, Nina Reynolds, and Bodo B. Schlegelmilch, "Pretesting in Questionnaire Design: The Impact of Respondent Characteristics on Error Detection," *Journal of the Market Research Society,* 36 (October 1994): 295–314; and Ruth M Bolton, "Pretesting Questionnaires: Content Analyses of Respondents' Concurrent Verbal Protocols," *Marketing Science,* 12(3) (1993): 280–303.

39. "Pretesting the Questionnaire," http://writing.colostate.edu/guides/research/survey/com4a3.cfm, accessed February 16, 2008; Bill Gillham, *Developing a Questionnaire* (New York: Continuum International Publishing Group, 2000); and Nina Reynolds, A. Diamantopoulos, and Bodo B. Schlegelmilch, "Pretesting in Questionnaire Design: A Review of the Literature and Suggestions

for Further Research," *Journal of the Market Research Society,* 35 (April 1993): 171–182.

40. H. Lee Murphy, "Survey Software Gets Simpler, More Effective," *Marketing News,* 35 (January 29, 2001): 4–6.

41. Donald J. MacLaurin and Tanya L. MacLaurin, "Customer Perceptions of Singapore's Theme Restaurants," *Cornell Hotel and Restaurant Administration Quarterly,* 41(3) (June 2000): 75–85; and www.visitsingapore.com, accessed November 22, 2008.

42. M. Evans, M. Robling, F. Maggs Rapport, H. Houston, P. Kinnersley, and C. Wilkinson, "It Doesn't Cost Anything Just to Ask, Does It? The Ethics of Questionnaire-Based Research," http://jme.bmj.com/cgi/content/abstract/28/1/41, accessed February 18, 2008; John Tsalikis and Bruce Seaton, "Business Ethics Index: Measuring Consumer Sentiments Toward Business Ethical Practices," *Journal of Business Ethics,* 64(4) (April 2006): 317–326; Janet K. Mullin Marta, Anusorn Singhapakdi, Ashraf Attia, and Scott J. Vitell, "Some Important Factors Underlying Ethical Decisions of Middle-Eastern Marketers," *International Marketing Review* 21(1) (2004): 53; Mark A. Davis, "Measuring Ethical Ideology in Business Ethics: A Critical Analysis of the Ethics Position Questionnaire," *Journal of Business Ethics,* 32(1) (July 2001): 35–53; and R. W. Armstrong, "An Empirical Investigation of International Marketing Ethics: Problems Encountered by Australian Firms," *Journal of Business Ethics,* 11 (1992): 161–171.

43. "Delta Airlines: Change the Experience/Experience Change," www.experientia.com/blog/delta-airlines-change-the-experience-experience-change, accessed February 18, 2008; Trebor Banstetter, "Delta Flights from Dallas/Fort Worth Airport Will Pilot Food Sales," *Knight Ridder Tribune Business News* (July 9, 2003): 1; and Joseph Rydholm, "A Global Perspective," *Quirks Marketing Research Review* (November 2000), www.quirks.com/articles/article.asp?arg_ArticleId=623.

Chapter 11

1. "Federal Duck Stamp Program Unveils Marketing Plan for 2007–2008 Artist-Signed Pane of One," *US Fed News Service, Including US State News* (Washington, D.C.) (April 2007); and Joseph Rydholm, "Focus Groups Shape Ads Designed to Expand Market for Federal Duck Stamp Program," *Quirk's Marketing Research Review* (March 2000), www.quirks.com/articles/article_print.asp?arg_articleid=566, accessed January 30, 2002.

2. Shane Schick, "IT Managers Stress Skills Help," *Computer Dealer News,* 17(3) (February 2, 2001): 1–2; and www.comscore.com/solutions/surveysite.asp, accessed October 4, 2008.

3. Thomas T. Semon, "Nonresponse Bias Affects All Survey Research," *Marketing News,* 38(12) (July 2004): 7(1); Anonymous, "Random Sampling," *Marketing News* (July 16, 2001): 10; Steve Wilcox, "Sampling and Controlling a TV Audience Measurement Panel," *International Journal of Market Research,* 42(4) (Winter 2000): 413–430; Donald P. Green, Alan S. Gerber, and Suzanna L De Boef, "Tracking Opinion over Time: A Method for Reducing Sampling Error," *Public Opinion Quarterly,* 63(2) (July 1999), 178–192; V. Verma and T. Le, "An Analysis of Sampling Errors for the Demographic and Health Surveys," *International Statistical Review,* 64(3) (December 1966): 265–294; and H. Assael and J. Keon, "Nonsampling vs. Sampling Errors in Sampling Research," *Journal of Marketing* (Spring 1982): 114–123.

4. "Federal Assistance: Illustrative Simulations of Using Statistical Population Estimates for Reallocating Certain Federal Funding: GAO-06-567," *GAO Reports* (July 2006): 1–42; Bob Brewin, "U.S. Census Bureau Plans for First Paperless Tally in 2010," *Computerworld,* 36(12) (March 18, 2002): 5; Simon Marquis, "I'm a Research Addict But Even I Can See the Census Is a Waste," *Marketing* (May 10, 2001): 22; and "Frequently Asked Questions About Census 2000," *Indiana Business Review,* 72(8) (Summer 1997): 10.

5. Janusz L. Wywial, "Sampling Design Proportional to Order Statistic of Auxiliary Variable," *Statistical Papers,* 49(2) (April 2008): 277–289; Anonymous, "Random Sampling: Bruised, Battered,

Bowed," *Marketing News,* 36(5) (March 4, 2002): 12; Steve Wilcox, "Sampling and Controlling a TV Audience Measurement Panel," *International Journal of Market Research,* 42(4) (200): 413–430; Arlene Fink, *How to Sample in Surveys* (Thousand Oaks, CA: Sage Publications, 1995); Martin R. Frankel, "Sampling Theory," in Peter H. Rossi, James D. Wright, and Andy B. Anderson, eds., *Handbook of Survey Research* (Orlando, FL: Academic Press, 1983): 21–67; and R. M. Jaeger, *Sampling in Education and the Social Sciences* (New York: Longman, 1984): 28–29.

6. "Sampling Methods," www.statpac.com/surveys/sampling.htm, accessed February 18, 2008; Jerome P. Reiter, "Topics in Survey Sampling/Finite Population Sampling and Inference: A Prediction Approach," *Journal of the American Statistical Association,* 97(457) (March 2002): 357–358; Gary T. Henry, *Practical Sampling* (Thousand Oaks, CA: Sage Publications, 1995); and Seymour Sudman, "Applied Sampling," in Peter H. Rossi, James D. Wright, and Andy B. Anderson, eds., *Handbook of Survey Research* (Orlando, FL: Academic Press, 1983): 145–194.

7. Gordon A. Wyner, "Survey Errors," *Marketing Research,* 19(1) (April 2007): 6–8; Mick P. Couper, "Web Surveys: A Review of Issues and Approaches," *Public Opinion Quarterly,* 64(4) (Winter 2000): 464–494; and Wayne Smith, Paul Mitchell, Karin Attebo, and Stephen Leeder, "Selection Bias from Sampling Frames: Telephone Directory and Electoral Roll Compared with Door-to-Door Population Census: Results from the Blue Mountain Eye Study," *Australian & New Zealand Journal of Public Health,* 21(2) (April 1997): 127–133.

8. For the effect of sample frame error on research results, see Gregory B. Murphy, "The Effects of Organizational Sampling Frame Selection," *Journal of Business Venturing,* 17(3) (May 2002): 237; and Kelly E. Fish, James H. Barnes, and Benjamin F. Banahan III, "Convenience or Calamity: Pharmaceutical Study Explores the Effects of Sample Frame Error on Research Results," *Journal of Health Care Marketing,* 14 (Spring 1994): 45–49.

9. "Florida Tourism Industry Flying High Going into Summer," www.usatoday.com/travel/destinations/2005-05-29-florida-tourism_x.htm, accessed February 18, 2008; Sean Mussenden, "Florida Tourism Leaders Say Industry Is Recovering Slowly," *Knight Ridder Tribune Business News* (March 22, 2002): 1; "The Many Faces of Florida," *Association Management* (A Guide to Florida Supplement) (April 1997): 3; and "Florida Travel Habits Subject of Phone Survey," *Quirk's Marketing Research Review* (May 1987): 10, 11, 31, 56, 60.

10. Linda Ritchie, "Empowerment and Australian Community Health Nurses Work with Aboriginal Clients: The Sociopolitical Context," *Qualitative Health Research,* 11(2) (March 2001): 190–205.

11. "2012 Olympics Offers Key Corporate Opportunities." *Marketing Week,* 30(17), April 2007: 40; Kindred SSIs in China Collaborate on Groundbreaking 2008 Summer Olympics and Media Effectiveness Project, online at www.surveysampling. com/? q=en/about/news/aug2608, accessed October 4, 2008; Anonymous, "2004 Olympics—Spectators Very Satisfied, Says Survey," (August 25, 2004) at www. greekembassy.org/Embassy/Content/en/Article.aspx?office=3&folder =200&article =13944; and Kate Maddox, "XIX Winter Olympics: Marketing Hot Spot," *B to B,* 87(2) (February 11, 2002): 1–2.

12. Steven K. Thompson, *Sampling* (New York: John Wiley & Sons, 2002); Seymour Sudman, "Sampling in the Twenty-First Century," *Academy of Marketing Science Journal,* 27(2) (Spring 1999): 269–277; and Leslie Kish, *Survey Sampling* (New York: John Wiley & Sons, 1965): 552.

13. Patricia M. Getz, "Implementing the New Sample Design for the Current Employment Statistics Survey," *Business Economics,* 35(4) (October 2000): 47–50; "Public Opinion: Polls Apart," *The Economist,* 336(7927) (August 12, 1995): 48; and Seymour Sudman, "Improving the Quality of Shopping Center Sampling," *Journal of Marketing Research,* 17 (November 1980): 423–431.

14. For a recent application of snowball sampling, see Elizabeth Hemphill, Steve Dunn, Hayley Barich, and Rebecca Infante, "Recruitment and Retention of Rural General Practitioners: A Marketing Approach

Reveals New Possibilities," *Australian Journal of Rural Health,* 15(6) (December 2007): 360–367; Francis Piron, "China's Changing Culture: Rural and Urban Customers' Favorite Things," *Journal of Consumer Marketing,* 23(6) (June 2006): 327; and Gary L. Frankwick, James C. Ward, Michael D. Hutt, and Peter H. Reingen, "Evolving Patterns of Organizational Beliefs in the Formation of Strategy," *Journal of Marketing,* 58 (April 1994): 96–110.

15. If certain procedures for listing members of the rare population are followed strictly, the snowball sample can be treated as a probability sample. See, S. Sampath, *Sampling Theory and Methods* (Boca Raton, FL: CRC Press, 2000); Gary T. Henry, *Practical Sampling* (Thousand Oaks, CA: Sage Publications, 1995); and Graham Kalton and Dallas W. Anderson, "Sampling Rare Populations," *Journal of the Royal Statistical Association* (1986): 65–82.

16. Lisa Maher, "Risk Behaviors of Young Indo-Chinese Injecting Drug Users in Sydney and Melbourne," *Australian & New Zealand Journal of Public Health* (February 2001): 50–54.

17. When the sampling interval, *i,* is not a whole number, the easiest solution is to use as the interval the nearest whole number below or above *i.* If rounding has too great an effect on the sample size, add or delete the extra cases. See, Julie W. Pepe, University of Central Florida, Orlando, Florida, "Demonstrating Systematic Sampling," www2.sas.com/proceedings/sugi22/POSTERS/PAPER213. PDF, accessed February 20, 2008.

18. For recent applications of systematic random sampling, see Phyllis MacFarlane, "Structuring and Measuring the Size of Business Markets," *International Journal of Market Research,* 44(1) (First Quarter 2002): 7–30; Hailin Qu and Isabella Li, "The Characteristics and Satisfaction of Mainland Chinese Visitors to Hong Kong," *Journal of Travel Research,* 35(4) (Spring 1997): 37–41; and Goutam Chakraborty, Richard Ettenson, and Gary Gaeth, "How Consumers Choose Health Insurance," *Journal of Health Care Marketing,* 14 (Spring 1994): 21–33.

19. Ed Garsten, "Poll: Phone Ban Support Tepid," *Chicago Tribune* (July 23, 2001): 9.

20. For a recent application of stratified random sampling, see Sofronija Miladinoski, PhD, "Sample Size Determination in International Marketing Research Studies," http://isi.cbs.nl/iamamember/CD2/pdf/922.PDF, accessed February 20, 2008; Gunnar Kjell, "The Level-Based Stratified Sampling Plan," *Journal of the American Statistical Association,* 95(452) (December 2000): 1185–1191; and Samaradasa Weerahandi and Soumyo Moitra, "Using Survey Data to Predict Adoption and Switching for Services," *Journal of Marketing Research,* 32 (February 1995): 85–96.

21. Anonymous, "Charge, Losses Stifle Growth," *Business Insurance,* 36(6) (February 11, 2002): 2; and Joanne Gallucci, "Employees with Home Internet Access Want Online Retirement Plans, CIGNA Retirement & Investment Services Study Reveals," *PR Newswire* (June 27, 2000).

22. Jeff D. Opdyke and Carrick Mollenkamp, "Yes, You Are 'High Net Worth,' " *Wall Street Journal* (May 21, 2002): D1, D3; and Thomas J. Stanley and Murphy A. Sewall, "The Response of Affluent Consumers to Mail Surveys," *Journal of Advertising Research* (June/July 1986): 55–58.

23. M. Farrelly, K. Davis, et al., "Evidence of a Dose-Response Relationship Between 'Truth' Antismoking Ads and Youth Smoking Prevalence," *American Journal of Public Health,* 95(3) (2005): 425–431; and www.thetruth.com/index.cfm?seek=aboutUs, accessed April 13, 2005.

24. Geographic clustering of rare populations, however, can be an advantage. See, Poduri S. Rao, *Sampling Methodologies with Applications* (Boca Raton, FL: CRC Press, 2001); John B. Carlin, "Design of Cross-Sectional Surveys Using Cluster Sampling: An Overview with Australian Case Studies," *Australian & New Zealand Journal of Public Health,* 23(5) (October 1999): 546–551; James C. Raymondo, "Confessions of a Nielsen Household," *American Demographics,* 19(3) (March 1997): 24–27; and Seymour Sudman, "Efficient Screening Methods for the Sampling of Geographically Clustered

Special Populations," *Journal of Marketing Research,* 22 (February 1985): 20–29. For estimation issues, see N. Nematollahi, M. Salehi, and R. A. Saba, "Two-Stage Cluster Sampling with Ranked Set Sampling in the Secondary Sampling Frame," *Communications in Statistics: Theory & Methods*, 37(15) (September 2008): 2404–2415.

25. J. Walker, "A Sequential Discovery Sampling Procedure," *The Journal of the Operational Research Society,* 53(1) (January 2002): 119; June S. Park, Michael Peters, and Kwei Tang, "Optimal Inspection Policy in Sequential Screening," *Management Science,* 37(8) (August 1991): 1058–1061; and E. J. Anderson, K. Gorton, and R. Tudor, "The Application of Sequential Analysis in Market Research," *Journal of Marketing Research,* 17 (February 1980): 97–105.

26. For more discussion of double sampling, see Ken Brewer, *Design and Estimation in Survey Sampling* (London, UK: Edward Arnold, 2001); John Shade, "Sampling Inspection Tables: Single and Double Sampling," *Journal of Applied Statistics,* 26(8) (December 1999): 1020; David H. Baillie, "Double Sampling Plans for Inspection by Variables When the Process Standard Deviation Is Unknown," *International Journal of Quality & Reliability Management,* 9(5) (1992): 59–70; and Martin R. Frankel and Lester R. Frankel, "Probability Sampling," in Robert Ferber, ed., *Handbook of Marketing Research* (New York: McGraw-Hill, 1974): 2–246.

27. Charles J. Whalen, "Jobs: The Truth Might Hurt," *Business Week,* 3725 (March 26, 2001): 34.

28. For the use of different nonprobability and probability sampling techniques in cross-cultural research, see Sofronija Miladinoski, PhD, "Sample Size Determination in International Marketing Research Studies," http://isi.cbs.nl/iamamember/CD2/pdf/922. PDF, accessed February 20, 2008; Naresh K. Malhotra and Mark Peterson, "Marketing Research in the New Millennium: Emerging Issues and Trends," *Market Intelligence and Planning,* 19(4) (2001): 216–235; Naresh K. Malhotra, James Agarwal, and Mark Peterson, "Cross-Cultural Marketing Research: Methodological Issues and Guidelines," *International Marketing Review,* 13(5) (1996): 7–43; and Samiee Saeed and Insik Jeong, "Cross-Cultural Research in Advertising: An Assessment of Methodologies," *Journal of the Academy of Marketing Science,* 22 (Summer 1994): 205–215.

29. Sunil Erevelles, "The Use of Price and Warranty Cues in Product Evaluation: A Comparison of U.S. and Hong Kong Consumers," *Journal of International Consumer Marketing,* 11(3) (1999): 67; Taylor Humphrey, "Horses for Courses: How Survey Firms in Different Countries Measure Public Opinion with Different Methods," *Journal of the Market Research Society,* 37(3) (July 1995): 211–219; and B. J. Verhage, U. Yavas, R. T. Green, and E. Borak, "The Perceived Risk Brand Loyalty Relationship: An International Perspective," *Journal of Global Marketing,* 3(3) (1990): 7–22.

30. Jamal A. Al-Khatib, Stacy M. Volimers, and Liu Yusin, "Business-to-Business Negotiating in China: The Role of Morality," *Journal of Business & Industrial Marketing*, 22(2) (2007): 84–96; Aileen Smith, "Ethics-Related Responses to Specific Situation Vignettes: Evidence of Gender-Based Differences and Occupational Socialization," *Journal of Business Ethics,* 28(1) (November 2000): 73–86; Satish P. Deshpande, "Managers' Perception of Proper Ethical Conduct: The Effect of Sex, Age, and Level of Education," *Journal of Business Ethics,* 16(1) (January 1997): 79–85; and I. P. Akaah, "Differences in Research Ethics Judgments Between Male and Female Marketing Professionals," *Journal of Business Ethics,* 8 (1989): 375–381.

31. Thomas S. Mulligan, "Marketing; No Breaking for Commercials; MTV Networks and Others Weave Ads into Shows' Story Lines to Keep Viewers Tuned In," *Los Angeles Times* (January 2008): C.1; Catherine Belton, Brian Bremner, Kerry Capell, Manjeet Kripalani, Tom Lowry, and Dexter Roberts, "MTV's World," *Business Week* (3770) (February 18, 2002): 81; and Gordon Masson, "MTV Availability Reaches 100 Million Mark in Europe," *Billboard,* 113(29) (July 21, 2001): 10–11.

Chapter 12

1. *Bicycling, Bicycling* Magazine's 2008 Semiannual Study of U.S. Retail Bicycle Stores (2008).

2. A discussion of the sampling distribution may be found in any basic statistics textbook. For example, see Mark L. Berenson, Timothy Krehbiel, and David M. Levine, *Basic Business Statistics: Concepts and Applications,* 11th ed. (Upper Saddle River, NJ: Prentice Hall, 2009).

3. Other statistical approaches are also available. However, a discussion of these is beyond the scope of this book. The interested reader is referred to Andrew J. Rohm, George R. Milne, and Mark A. McDonald, "A Mixed-Method Approach for Developing Market Segmentation Typologies in the Sports Industry," *Sport Marketing Quarterly* 15(1) (2006): 29–39; Marion R. Reynolds, Jr., "EWMA Control Charts with Variable Sample Sizes and Variable Sampling Intervals," *IIE Transactions,* 33(6) (June 2001): 511–530; S. Sampath, *Sampling Theory and Methods* (Boca Raton, FL: CRC Press, 2000); L. Yeh and L. C. Van, "Bayesian Double-Sampling Plans with Normal Distributions," *Statistician,* 46(2) (1997): 193–207; W. G. Blyth and L. J. Marchant, "A Self-Weighing Random Sampling Technique," *Journal of the Market Research Society,* 38(4) (October 1996): 473–479; Clifford Nowell and Linda R. Stanley, "Length-Biased Sampling in Mall Intercept Surveys," *Journal of Marketing Research,* 28 (November 1991): 475–479; and Raphael Gillett, "Confidence Interval Construction by Stein's Method: A Practical and Economical Approach to Sample Size Determination," *Journal of Marketing Research,* 26 (May 1989): 237.

4. Trevor Sharot, "The Design and Precision of Data-Fusion Studies," *International Journal of Market Research*, 49(4) (2007): 449–470; Ken Kelley, "Sample Size Planning for the Coefficient of Variation from the Accuracy in Parameter Estimation Approach," *Behavior Research Methods*, 39(4) (November 2007): 755–766; Steven K. Thompson, *Sampling* (New York: John Wiley & Sons, 2002); Melanie M. Wall, "An Effective Confidence Interval for the Mean with Samples of Size One and Two," *The American Statistician,* Alexandria (May 2001): 102–105; and Siu L. Chow, *Statistical Significance* (Thousand Oaks, CA: Sage Publications, 1996).

5. Richard L. Valliant, Alan H. Dorfman, and Richard M. Royall, *Finite Population Sampling and Inference: A Prediction Approach* (New York: John Wiley & Sons, 2000).

6. "City of Los Angeles Internet Services Project: Market Analysis and Best Practices Report," *e-Government Services Project Reports* (October 29, 1999), www.ci.la.ca.us/311/marketanalysis.pdf, accessed April 8, 2001.

7. See, for example, "Introduction to the Sampling Theory," www.rocw. raifoundation.org/management/mba/Managinginformation/lecture%20notes/lecture-24.pdf, accessed February 23, 2008; S. Sampath, *Sampling Theory and Methods* (Boca Raton, FL: CRC Press, 2000); Nigel Bradley, "Sampling for Internet Surveys: An Examination of Respondent Selection for Internet Research," *Market Research Society,* 41(4) (October 1999): 387–395; C. J. Adcock, "Sample Size Determination—A Review," *Statistician,* 46(2) (1997): 261–283; and Seymour Sudman, "Applied Sampling," in Peter H. Rossi, James D. Wright, and Andy B. Anderson, eds., *Handbook of Survey Research* (Orlando, FL: Academic Press, 1983): 145–194.

8. Adjusting for incidence and completion rates is discussed in Poduri S. Rao, *Sampling Methodologies with Applications* (Boca Raton, FL: CRC Press, 2001); Barbara Bickart, "The Distribution of Survey Contact and Participation in the United States: Constructing a Survey-Based Estimate," *Journal of Marketing Research,* 36(2) (May 1999): 286–294; Don A. Dillman, Eleanor Singer, Jon R. Clark, and James B. Treat, "Effects of Benefits Appeals, Mandatory Appeals, and Variations in Statements of Confidentiality on Completion Rates for Census Questionnaires," *Public Opinion Quarterly,* 60(3) (Fall 1996): 376–389; and Louis G. Pol and Sukgoo Pak, "The Use of Two-Stage Survey Design in Collecting Data from Those Who Have Attended Periodic or Special Events," *Journal of the Market Research Society,* 36 (October 1994): 315–326. For a recent marketing application, see Michael Lewis, "The Effect of

Shipping Fees on Customer Acquisition, Customer Retention, and Purchase Quantities," *Journal of Retailing*, 82(1) (March 2006): 13–23.

9. Judith Green, "Jacksonville Symphony Sets Big Anniversary Fest," *The Atlanta Journal–Constitution* (February 20, 2000): K7; Nevin J. Rodes, "Marketing a Community Symphony Orchestra," *Marketing News*, 30(3) (January 29, 1996): 2; and "Sales Makes Sweet Music," *Quirk's Marketing Research Review* (May 1988): 10–12.

10. Robert M. Groves, Stanley Presser, and Sarah Dipko, "The Role of Topic Interest in Survey Participation Decisions," *Public Opinion Quarterly*, 68(1) (April 2004), 2–31; Patrick Van Kenhove, "The Influence of Topic Involvement on Mail-Survey Response Behavior," *Psychology & Marketing*, 19(3) (March 2002): 293; M. R. Fisher, "Estimating the Effect of Nonresponse Bias on Angler Surveys," *Transactions of the American Fisheries Society*, 125(1) (January 1996): 118–126; and Charles Martin, "The Impact of Topic Interest on Mail Survey Response Behaviour," *Journal of the Market Research Society*, 36 (October 1994): 327–338.

11. "Customer Satisfaction Surveys: Maximizing Survey Responses," www.customer-feedback-surveys.net/maximize.asp, accessed February 16, 2008; Dirk Heerwegh, "Effects of Personal Salutations in E-Mail Invitations to Participate in a Web Survey," *Public Opinion Quarterly*, 69(4) (Winter 2005): 588–598; Simone M. Cummings, "Reported Response Rates to Mailed Physician Questionnaires," *Health Services Research*, 35(6) (February 2001): 1347–1355; A. Hill, J. Roberts, P. Ewings, and D. Gunnell, "Nonresponse Bias in a Lifestyle Survey," *Journal of Public Health Medicine*, 19(2) (June 1997): 203–207; and Stephen W. McDaniel, Charles S. Madden, and Perry Verille, "Do Topic Differences Affect Survey Nonresponse?" *Journal of the Market Research Society* (January 1987): 55–66.

12. For minimizing the incidence of nonresponse and adjusting for its effects, see Katja Lozar Manfreda, Michael Bosnjak, Jernej Berzelak, Iris Haas, and Vasja Vehovar, "Web Surveys Versus Other Survey Modes," *International Journal of Market Research*, 50(1) (2008): 79–104; Eunkyu Lee, Michael Y. Hu, and Rex S. Toh, "Respondent Non-Cooperation on Surveys and Diaries: An Analysis of Item Non-Response and Panel Attrition," *International Journal of Market Research*, 46(3) (2004): 311–326; Richard Colombo, "A Model for Diagnosing and Reducing Nonresponse Bias," *Journal of Advertising Research*, 40(1/2) (January/April 2000): 85–93; H. C. Chen, "Direction, Magnitude, and Implications of Nonresponse Bias in Mail Surveys," *Journal of the Market Research Society*, 38(3) (July 1996): 267–276; and Michael Brown, "What Price Response?" *Journal of the Market Research Society*, 36 (July 1994): 227–244.

13. Steve Jarvis, "CMOR Finds Survey Refusal Rate Still Rising," *Marketing News*, 36(3) (February 4, 2002): 4; Artur Baldauf, "Examining Motivations to Refuse in Industrial Mail Surveys," *Journal of the Market Research Society*, 41(3) (July 1999): 345–353; Reg Baker, "Nobody's Talking," *Marketing Research: A Magazine of Management & Applications*, 8(1) (Spring 1996): 22–24; and Jolene M. Struebbe, Jerome B. Kernan, and Thomas J. Grogan, "The Refusal Problem in Telephone Surveys," *Journal of Advertising Research* (June/July 1986): 29–38.

14. Mike Brennan, Susan Benson, and Zane Kearns, "The Effect of Introductions on Telephone Survey Response Rates," *International Journal of Market Research*, 47(1) (2005): 65–74; Van Kenhove, "The Influence of Topic Involvement on Mail-Survey Response Behavior," *Psychology & Marketing*, 19(3) (March 2002): 293; Robert M. Groves, "Leverage-Saliency Theory of Survey Participation: Description and an Illustration," *Public Opinion Quarterly*, 64(3) (Fall 2000): 299–308; S. A. Everett, J. H. Price, A. W. Bedell, and S. K. Telljohann," The Effect of a Monetary Incentive in Increasing the Return Rate of a Survey of Family Physicians," *Evaluation and the Health Professions*, 20(2) (June 1997): 207–214; J. Scott Armstrong and Edward J. Lusk, "Return Postage in Mail Surveys: A Meta-Analysis," *Public Opinion Quarterly* (Summer 1987): 233–248; and Julie Yu and Harris

Cooper, "A Quantitative Review of Research Design Effects on Response Rates to Questionnaires," *Journal of Marketing Research*, 20 (February 1983): 36–44.

15. Paul D. Larson and Garland Chow, "Total Cost/Response Rate Trade-Offs in Mail Survey Research: Impact of Follow-Up Mailings and Monetary Incentives" *Industrial Marketing Management*, 32(7) (October 2003): 533; Ali Kanso, "Mail Surveys: Key Factors Affecting Response Rates," *Direct Marketing and Survey Research* (2000): 3–16; Steven G. Rogelberg, "Attitudes Toward Surveys: Development of a Measure and Its Relationship to Respondent Behavior," *Organizational Research Methods*, 4(1) (January 2001): 3–25; and Edward F. Fern, Kent B. Monroe, and Ramon A. Avila, "Effectiveness of Multiple Request Strategies: A Synthesis of Research Results," *Journal of Marketing Research*, 23 (May 1986): 144–153.

16. Dale S. Rose, Stuart D. Sidle, and Kristin H. Griffith, "A Penny for Your Thoughts: Monetary Incentives Improve Response Rates for Company-Sponsored Employee Surveys," *Organizational Research Methods* 10(2) (April 2007): 225–240; Kasper M. Hansen, "The Effects of Incentives, Interview Length, and Interviewer Characteristics on Response Rates in a CATI-Study," *International Journal of Public Opinion Research*, 19(1) (April 2007): 112–121; J. Saunders, D. Jobber, and V. Mitchell, "The Optimum Prepaid Monetary Incentives for Mail Surveys," *Journal of the Operational Research Society* 57(10) (October 2006): 1224–1230; Cihan Cobanoglu and Nesrin Cobanoglu, "The Effect of Incentives in Web Surveys: Application and Ethical Considerations," *International Journal of Market Research*, 45(4) (2003): 475–488; Michael J. Shaw, "The Use of Monetary Incentives in a Community Survey: Impact on Response Rates, Date, Quality, and Cost," *Health Services Research*, 35(6) (February 2001): 1339–1346; Sheldon Wayman, "The Buck Stops Here When It Comes to Dollar Incentives," *Marketing News*, 31(1) (January 6, 1997): 9; and Paul M. Biner and Heath J. Kidd, "The Interactive Effects of Monetary Incentive Justification and Questionnaire Length on Mail Survey Response Rates," *Psychology & Marketing*, 11(5) (September/October 1994): 483–492.

17. Christopher McCarty, Mark House, Jeffrey Harman, and Scott Richards, "Effort in Phone Survey Response Rates: The Effects of Vendor and Client-Controlled Factors," *Field Methods*, 18(2) (May 2006): 172; and B. Zafer Erdogan, "Increasing Mail Survey Response Rates from an Industrial Population: A Cost-Effectiveness Analysis of Four Follow-up Techniques," *Industrial Marketing Management*, 31(1) (January 2002): 65.

18. Daniel M. Ladik, Franois A. Carrillat, and Paul J. Solomon, "The Effectiveness of University Sponsorship in Increasing Survey Response Rate," *Journal of Marketing Theory & Practice*, 15(3) (July 2007): 263–271; John Byrom, "The Effect of Personalization on Mailed Questionnaire Response Rates," *International Journal of Market Research* (Summer 2000): 357–359; D. A. Dillman, E. Singer, J. R. Clark, and J. B. Treat, "Effects of Benefits Appeals, Mandatory Appeals, and Variations in Statements of Confidentiality on Completion Rates for Census Questionnaires," *Public Opinion Quarterly*, 60(3) (Fall 1996): 376–389; P. Gendall, J. Hoek, and D. Esslemont, "The Effect of Appeal, Complexity, and Tone in a Mail Survey Covering Letter," *Journal of the Market Research Society*, 37(3) (July 1995): 251–268; and Thomas V. Greer and Ritu Lohtia, "Effects of Source and Paper Color on Response Rates in Mail Surveys," *Industrial Marketing Management*, 23 (February 1994): 47–54.

19. Anonymous, "Arbitron Dip Again," *Mediaweek*, 14(21) (May 24, 2004): 26.

20. Scott Keeter, "Consequences of Reducing Nonresponse in a National Telephone Survey," *Public Opinion Quarterly*, 64(2) (Summer 2000): 125–148; G. L. Bowen, "Estimating the Reduction in Nonresponse Bias from Using a Mail Survey as a Backup for Nonrespondents to a Telephone Interview Survey," *Research on Social Work Practice*, 4(1) (January 1994): 115–128; and R. A. Kerin and R. A. Peterson, "Scheduling Telephone Interviews," *Journal of Advertising Research* (May 1983): 44.

21. Robert M. Groves, "Nonresponse Rates and Nonresponse Bias in Household Surveys," *Public Opinion Quarterly*, 70(5) (2006): 646–675; Karin Braunsberger, Roger Gates, and David J. Ortinau, "Prospective Respondent Integrity Behavior in Replying to Direct Mail Questionnaires: A Contributor in Overestimating Nonresponse Rates," *Journal of Business Research*, 58(3) (March 2005): 260–267; Richard Colombo, "A Model for Diagnosing and Reducing Nonresponse Bias," *Journal of Advertising Research* (January/April 2000): 85–93; and M. L. Rowland and R. N. Forthofer, "Adjusting for Nonresponse Bias in a Health Examination Survey," *Public Health Reports,* 108(3) (May/June 1993): 380–386.

22. Katharine G. Abraham, Aaron Maitland, and Suzanne M. Bianchi, "Nonresponse in the American Time Use Survey," *Public Opinion Quarterly*, 70(5) (2006): 676–703; Michael D. Larsen, "The Psychology of Survey Response," *Journal of the American Statistical Association,* 97(457) (March 2002): 358–359; and E. L. Dey, "Working with Low Survey Response Rates—The Efficacy of Weighting Adjustments," *Research in Higher Education,* 38(2) (April 1997): 215–227.

23. Mark Jurkowitz, "TV Networks Hope to Avoid Exit Poll Errors in Calling Presidential Race," *Knight Ridder Tribune Business News* (November 2, 2004): 1; Marc L. Songini "Reliability a Tossup in E-Voting Exit Poll," *Computerworld*, 40(46) (November 2006): 1–3; Kevin J. Flannelly, "Reducing Undecided Voters and Other Sources of Error in Election Surveys," *International Journal of Market Research,* 42(2) (Spring 2000): 231–237; and John Maines, "Taking the Pulse of the Voter," *American Demographics* (November 1992): 20.

24. Martijn G. de Jong, Jan-Benedict E. M. Steenkamp, Jean-Paul Fox, and Hans Baumgartner, "Using Item Response Theory to Measure Extreme Response Style in Marketing Research: A Global Investigation," *Journal of Marketing Research,* 45(1) (February 2008): 104–115; Rana Sobh and Chad Perry, "Research Design and Data Analysis in Realism Research," *European Journal of Marketing,* 40(11) (January 2006): 1194; Clyde Tucker, J. Michael Brick, and Brian Meekins, "Household Telephone Service and Usage Patterns in the United States in 2004: Implications for Telephone Samples," *Public Opinion Quarterly*, 71(1) (April 2007): 3–22; R. C. Kessler, R. J. Little, and R. M. Grover, "Advances in Strategies for Minimizing and Adjusting for Survey Nonresponse," *Epidemiologic Reviews,* 17(1) (1995): 192–204; and James C. Ward, Bertram Russick, and William Rudelius, "A Test of Reducing Callbacks and Not-at-Home Bias in Personal Interviews by Weighting At-Home Respondents," *Journal of Marketing Research,* 2 (February 1985): 66–73.

25. R. M. Groves and E. Peytcheva, "The Impact of Nonresponse Rates on Nonresponse Bias: A Meta-Analysis," *Public Opinion Quarterly* 72(2) (Summer 2008): 167–189; Ken Brewer, *Design and Estimation in Survey Sampling* (London: Edward Arnold, 2001); Jun Sao, "Variance Estimation for Survey Data with Composite Imputation and Nonnegligible Sampling Fractions," *Journal of American Statistical Association* (March 1999): 254–265; J. W. Drane, D. Richter, and C. Stoskopf, "Improved Imputation of Nonresponse to Mailback Questionnaires," *Statistics in Medicine,* 12(3–4) (February 1993): 283–288; and William M. Campion, "Multiple Imputation for Nonresponse in Surveys," *Journal of Marketing Research,* 26(4) (November 1989): 485–486.

26. David Ketchum, "The China Travel Market Takes Off," *Upstream*, www.aboutupstream.com/blogs/david-ketchum/2006/10/01/the-china-travel-market-takes-off, accessed February 27, 2008; and Charles Hutzler, "Boeing Sees Strong Chinese Demand," *Wall Street Journal* (November 2, 2004): D.4. See also, Karen S. Lyness and Marcia Brumit Kropf, "Cultural Values and Potential Nonresponse Bias: A Multilevel Examination of Cross-National Differences in Mail Survey Response Rates," *Organizational Research Methods,* 10(2) (2007): 210–224.

27. H. Baumgartner and J.B.E.M. Steenkamp, "Response Styles in Marketing Research: A Cross-National Investigation," *Journal of Marketing Research*, 38(2) (May 2001): 143–156; and Anne-Wil Harzing, "Cross-National Industrial Mail Surveys; Why Do

Response Rates Differ Between Countries?" *Industrial Marketing Management*, 29(3) (May 2000): 243–254.

28. William F. Christensen and Lindsay W. Florence, "Predicting Presidential and Other Multistage Election Outcomes Using State-Level Pre-Election Polls," *The American Statistician,* 62(1) (February 2008): 1; Humphrey Taylor, "Using Internet Polling to Forecast the 2000 Elections," *Marketing Research*, 13(1) (Spring 2001): 26–30; and Vicki G. Morwitz and Carol Pluzinski, "Do Polls Reflect Opinions or Do Opinions Reflect Polls? The Impact of Political Polling on Voters' Expectations, Preferences, and Behavior," *Journal of Consumer Research,* 23(1) (June 1996): 53–67.

29. Based on www.pg.com, accessed January 20, 2009; Vanessa L. Facenda, "P&G Sees Valuable Assets in $86M Charmin Relaunch," *Brandweek*, 48(37) (October 15, 2007), online at www.brandweek. com/bw/esearch/searchResult.jsp?keyword=p%26g+cHARMIN&searc hType=ARTICLE_SEARCH&exposeNavigation=true&kw=&searchT ype=ARTICLE_SEARCH&action=Submit&searchInterface=Keyword &matchType=mode%2Bmatchallpartial&an=brandweek& x=44&y=7, accessed February 16, 2009; and Jack Neff, "P&G Brings Potty to Parties," *Advertising Age*, 74(7) (February 17, 2003): 22.

Chapter 13

1. www.cmor.org, accessed January 20, 2009; Steve Jarvis, "CMOR Finds Survey Refusal Rate Still Rising," *Marketing News* (February 4, 2002): 4; Reg Baker, "Nobody's Talking," *Marketing Research: A Magazine of Management & Applications,* 8(1) (Spring 1996): 22–24; and "Study Tracks Trends in Refusal Rates," *Quirk's Marketing Research Review* (August/September 1989): 16–18, 42–43.

2. Carolyn Folkman Curasi, "A Critical Exploration of Face-to-Face Interviewing vs. Computer-Mediated Interviewing," *International Journal of Market Research,* 43(4) (Fourth Quarter 2001): 361–375; Gale D. Muller and Jane Miller, "Interviewers Make the Difference," *Marketing Research: A Magazine of Management & Applications,* 8(1) (Spring 1996): 8–9; and "JDC Interviews Michael Redington," *Journal of Data Collection,* 25 (Spring 1985): 2–6.

3. Greg Guest, Arwen Bunce, and Laura Johnson, "How Many Interviews Are Enough? An Experiment with Data Saturation and Variability," *Field Methods*, 18(1) (February 2006): 59–83; Jaber F. Gubrium and James A. Holstein, *Handbook of Interview Research: Context and Method* (Thousand Oaks, CA: Sage Publications, 2001); and James H. Frey and Sabine M. Oishi, *How to Conduct Interviews by Telephone and in Person* (Thousand Oaks, CA: Sage Publications, 1995).

4. Curt J. Dommeyer, "The Effects of the Researcher's Physical Attractiveness and Gender on Mail Survey Response," *Psychology & Marketing*, 25(1) (January 2008): 47–70; Joshua M. Sacco, Christine R. Scheu, Ann Marie Ryan, and Neal Schmitt, "An Investigation of Race and Sex Similarity Effects in Interviews: A Multilevel Approach to Relational Demography," *Journal of Applied Psychology*, 88(5) (2003): 852–865; Susan C. McCombie, "The Influences of Sex of Interviewer on the Results of an AIDS Survey in Ghana," *Human Organization,* 61(1) (Spring 2002): 51–55; Joseph A. Catina, Diane Binson, Jesse Canchola, Lance M. Pollack, et al., "Effects of Interviewer Gender, Interviewer Choice, and Item Wording on Responses to Questions Concerning Sexual Behavior," *Public Opinion Quarterly,* 60(3) (Fall 1996): 345–375; Philip B. Coulter, "Race of Interviewer Effects on Telephone Interviews," *Public Opinion Quarterly,* 46 (Summer 1982): 278–284; and Eleanor Singer, Martin R. Frankel, and Marc B. Glassman, "The Effect of Interviewer Characteristics and Expectations on Response," *Public Opinion Quarterly,* 47 (Spring 1983): 68–83.

5. Kasper M. Hansen, "The Effects of Incentives, Interview Length, and Interviewer Characteristics on Response Rates in a CATI-Study," *International Journal of Public Opinion Research,* 19(1) (April 2007): 112–121; Jessica Clark Newman, "The Differential Effects of Face-to-Face and Computer Interview Models," *American Journal of Public Health,* 92(2) (February 2002): 294–297; Darren W. Davis, "Nonrandom Measurement Error and Race of Interviewer Effects

Among African Americans," *Public Opinion Quarterly,* 61(1) (Spring 1997): 183–207; and Raymond F. Barker, "A Demographic Profile of Marketing Research Interviewers," *Journal of the Market Research Society* (UK) (July 29, 1987): 279–292.

6. Richard G. Starr and Karen V. Fernandez, "The Mindcam Methodology: Perceiving Through the Native's Eye," *Qualitative Market Research: An International Journal,* 10(2) (April 2007): 168–182; Anonymous, "Dextra Hands Out Vital Interview Advice," *Management Services,* 46(2) (February 2002): 6; M. K. Kacmar and W. A. Hochwarter, "The Interview as a Communication Event: A Field Examination of Demographic Effects on Interview Outcomes," *Journal of Business Communication,* 32(3) (July 1995): 207–232; and Martin Collins and Bob Butcher, "Interviewer and Clustering Effects in an Attitude Survey," *Journal of the Market Research Society* (UK) 25 (January 1983): 39–58.

7. "Interviewer Training" www.fcsm.gov/working-papers/spwp27_5.pdf, accessed March 1, 2008; Jennie Lai and Charles Shuttles, "Improving Cooperation of Asian Households Through Cultural Sensitivity Training for Field Interviewers," *Conference Papers—American Association for Public Opinion Research* (2004); Anonymous, "Renewing Your Interviewing Skills," *Healthcare Executive,* 17(1) (January/February 2002): 29; Pamela Kiecker and James E. Nelson, "Do Interviewers Follow Telephone Survey Instructions?" *Journal of the Market Research Society,* 38(2) (April 1996): 161–176; Gale D. Muller and Jane Miller, "Interviewers Make the Difference," *Marketing Research,* 8(1) (1996): 8–9; and P. J. Guenzel, T. R. Berkmans, and C. F. Cannell, *General Interviewing Techniques* (Ann Arbor, MI: Institute for Social Research, 1983).

8. Steven G. Rogelberg and Jeffrey M. Stanton, "Introduction Understanding and Dealing with Organizational Survey Nonresponse," *Organizational Research Methods,* 10(2) (April 2007): 195–209; Brent Robertson, "The Effect of an Introductory Letter on Participation Rates Using Telephone Recruitment," *Australian and New Zealand Journal of Public Health,* 24(5) (October 2000): 552; Karl Feld, "Good Introductions Save Time, Money," *Marketing News,* 34(5) (February 28, 2000): 19–20; and Mick P. Couper, "Survey Introductions and Data Quality," *Public Opinion Quarterly* (Summer 1997): 317–338.

9. This procedure is similar to that followed by Burke Marketing Research, Cincinnati, Ohio.

10. Raj Sethuraman, Roger A. Kerin, and William L. Cron, "A Field Study Comparing Online and Offline Data Collection Methods for Identifying Product Attribute Preferences Using Conjoint Analysis," *Journal of Business Research,* 58(5) (May 2005): 602–610; Darlene B. Bordeaux, "Interviewing—Part II: Getting the Most out of Interview Questions," *Motor Age,* 121(2) (February 2002): 38–40; "Market Research Industry Sets Up Interviewing Quality Standards," *Management-Auckland,* 44(2) (March 1997): 12; and "JDC Interviews Michael Redington," *Journal of Data Collection,* 25 (Spring 1985): 2–6.

11. This section follows closely the material in *Interviewer's Manual,* rev. ed. (Ann Arbor, MI: Survey Research Center, Institute for Social Research, University of Michigan); and P. J. Guenzel, T. R. Berkmans, and C. F. Cannell, *General Interviewing Techniques* (Ann Arbor, MI: Institute for Social Research). See also, Raj Sethuraman, Roger A. Kerin, and William L. Cron, "A Field Study Comparing Online and Offline Data Collection Methods for Identifying Product Attribute Preferences Using Conjoint Analysis," *Journal of Business Research,* 58(5) (May 2005): 602–610.

12. For an extensive treatment of probing, see Naomi R. Henderson, "The Power of Probing," *Marketing Research,* 19(4) (January 2007): 38–39; Jaber F. Gubrium and James A. Holstein, *Handbook of Interview Research: Context and Method* (Thousand Oaks, CA: Sage Publications, 2001); and *Interviewer's Manual,* rev. ed. (Ann Arbor, MI: Survey Research Center, Institute for Social Research, University of Michigan): 15–19.

13. Ding Hooi Ting, "Further Probing of Higher Order in Satisfaction Construct," *International Journal of Bank Marketing,* 24(2/3) (2006): 98–113; and *Interviewer's Manual,* rev. ed. (Ann Arbor, MI: Survey Research Center, Institute for Social Research, University of Michigan): 16.

14. Ara C. Trembly, "Poor Data Quality: A $600 Billion Issue," *National Underwriter,* 106(11) (March 18, 2002): 48; "Market Research Industry Sets Up Interviewing Quality Standards," *Management-Auckland,* 44(2) (March 1997): 12; and Jean Morton-Williams and Wendy Sykes, "The Use of Interaction Coding and Follow-Up Interviews to Investigate Comprehension of Survey Questions," *Journal of the Market Research Society,* 26 (April 1984): 109–127.

15. Statement of Matthew L. Myers, President, Campaign for Tobacco-Free Kids, "New CDC Global Survey Finds Tobacco Taking Massive Toll on World's Children," *PR Newswire* (New York) (January 2008); and John Anderson, *Behavioral Risk Factors Surveillance System User's Guide* (Atlanta: U.S. Department of Health and Human Services, Centers for Disease Control and Prevention, 1998).

16. Nick Sparrow, "Quality Issues in Online Research," *Journal of Advertising Research,* 47(2) (June 2007): 179–182; Dominique Cri and Andrea Micheaux, "From Customer Data to Value: What Is Lacking in the Information Chain?" *Journal of Database Marketing & Customer Strategy Management,* 13(4) (July 2006): 282–299; John Pallister, "Navigating the Righteous Course: A Quality Issue," *Journal of the Market Research Society,* 41(3) (July 1999): 327–343; and Martin Collins and Bob Butcher, "Interviewer and Clustering Effects in an Attitude Survey," *Journal of the Market Research Society* (UK), 25 (January 1983): 39–58.

17. Tammie Frost-Norton, "The Future of Mall Research: Current Trends Affecting the Future of Marketing Research in Malls," *Journal of Consumer Behaviour,* 4(4) (June 2005): 293–301; Nigel G. Fielding, *Interviewing,* 4 vols. (Thousand Oaks, CA: Sage Publications, 2003); David E. Harrison and Stefanie I. Krauss, "Interviewer Cheating: Implications for Research on Entrepreneurship in Africa, *Journal of Developmental Entrepreneurship* (Norfolk), 7(3) (October 2002): 319; J. E. Nelson and P. L. Kiecker, "Marketing Research Interviewers and Their Perceived Necessity of Moral Compromise," *Journal of Business Ethics* (1996); and Donald S. Tull and Larry E. Richards, "What Can Be Done About Interviewer Bias," in Jagdish Sheth, ed., *Research in Marketing* (Greenwich, CT: JAI Press, 1980): 143–162.

18. Derek S. Chapman and Patricia M. Rowe, "The Impact of Videoconference Technology, Interview Structure, and Interviewer Gender on Interviewer Evaluations in the Employment Interview: A Field Experiment," *Journal of Occupational and Organizational Psychology* (September 2001); Carla Johnson, "Making Sure Employees Measure Up," *HRMagazine,* 46(3) (March 2001): 36–41; and Elaine D. Pulakos, Neal Schmitt, David Whitney, and Matthew Smith, "Individual Differences in Interviewer Ratings: The Impact of Standardization, Consensus Discussion, and Sampling Error on the Validity of a Structured Interview," *Personnel Psychology,* 49(1) (Spring 1996): 85–102.

19. Katja Lozar Manfreda, Michael Bosnjak, Jernej Berzelak, Iris Haas, and Vasja Vehovar, "Web Surveys Versus Other Survey Modes," *International Journal of Market Research,* 50(1) 2008: 79–114; Ian Alam, "Fieldwork and Data Collection in Qualitative Marketing Research," *Qualitative Market Research: An International Journal,* 8(1) (January 2005): 97; Jamie Smith, "How to Boost DM Response Rates Quickly," *Marketing News,* 35(9) (April 23, 2001): 5; Sophie K. Turley, "A Case of Response Rate Success," *Journal of Market Research Society,* 41(3) (July 1999): 301–309; and Jack Edmonston, "Why Response Rates Are Declining," *Advertising Age's Business Marketing,* 82(8) (September 1997): 12.

20. Jami A. Fullerton, "Brand America: Can Advertising Help Improve America's Image Abroad?" *American Academy of Advertising Conference Proceedings* (2007): 189; Carter Dougherty, "European Union Asks U.S. to Follow Rules, End Exports Spat," *Knight Ridder Tribune Business News* (January 26, 2002): 1; Laurel Wentz, "Poll: Europe Favors U.S. Products," *Advertising Age* (September 23, 1991); and www.npes.org/membersonly/INTERNATIONAL-TRADE-FAX-2001.pdf, accessed July 6, 2008.

21. Thomas H. Davenport, Jeanne G. Harris, George L. Jones, Katherine N. Lemon, et al., "HBR Case Study: The Dark Side of Customer Analytics," *Harvard Business Review,* 85(5) (May 2007): 37; Jamal A. Al-Khatib, Angela D'Auria Stanton, and Mohammed Y. A. Rawwas, "Ethical Segmentation of Consumers in Developing Countries: A Comparative Analysis," *International Marketing Review,* 22(2) (2005): 225–246; Stephanie Stahl, "Ethics and the No-Fear Generation," *Information Week* (880) (March 18, 2002): 8; and James E. Nelson and Pamela L. Kiecker, "Marketing Research Interviewers and Their Perceived Necessity of Moral Compromise," *Journal of Business Ethics,* 15(10) (October 1996): 1107–1117.

22. www.gallup.com, accessed February 18, 2009.

23. "Nissan Taps into TV Shows for Interactive Ad Campaign," *Precision Marketing* (March 2004): P3; and Michael McCarthy, "Nissan Xterra Discover Extra Success," *USA Today Online,* www.usatoday.com/money/index/2001-02-26-ad-track-nissan.htm#more, accessed February 26, 2001.

Chapter 14

1. Rick L Andrews, Imran S. Currim, "An experimental investigation of scanner data preparation strategies for consumer choice models" *International Journal of Research in Marketing (Amsterdam),* 22(3) (September 2005): 319; Ara C. Trembly, "Poor Data Quality: A $600 Billion Issue," *National Underwriter,* 106 (11) (March 18, 2002): 48; Kevin T. Higgins, "Never Ending Journey," *Marketing Management,* 6 (1) (Spring 1997): 4–7; and Joann Harristhal, "Interviewer Tips," *Applied Marketing Research,* 28 (Fall 1988): 42–45.

2. Bruce Keillor, Deborah Owens, and Charles Pettijohn, "A Cross-Cultural/Cross-National Study of Influencing Factors and Socially Desirable Response Biases," *International Journal of Market Research,* 43(1) (First Quarter 2001): 63–84; and Kofi Q. Dadzie, "Demarketing Strategy in Shortage Marketing Environment," *Journal of the Academy of Marketing Science* (Spring 1989): 157–165. See also, Shizuhiko Nishisato, *Measurement and Multivariate Analysis* (New York: Springer-Verlag, 2002).

3. Stephen Jenkins, "Automating Questionnaire Design and Construction," *Journal of the Market Research Society,* 42(1) (Winter 1999–2000): 79–95; Arlene Fink, *How to Analyze Survey Data* (Thousand Oaks, CA: Sage Publications, 1995); and Pamela L. Alreck and Robert B. Settle, *The Survey Research Handbook,* 2nd ed. (Homewood, IL: Irwin Professional Publishing, 1994).

4. Shu-pei Tsai, "Investigating Archetype-Icon Transformation in Brand Marketing," *Marketing Intelligence & Planning,* 24(6) (2006): 648; Ide Kearney, "Measuring Consumer Brand Confusion to Comply with Legal Guidelines," *International Journal of Market Research,* 43(1) (First Quarter 2001): 85–91; and Serge Luyens, "Coding Verbatims by Computer," *Marketing Research: A Magazine of Management & Applications,* 7(2) (Spring 1995): 20–25.

5. Yvette C. Hammett, "Voters in Hillsborough County, Florida, Try Out Touch-Screen Voting Machines," *Knight Ridder Tribune Business News* (April 3, 2002): 1; Tim Studt, "Exclusive Survey Reveals Move to High-Tech Solutions," *Research & Development,* 43(3) (March 2001): 37–38; and Norman Frendberg, "Scanning Questionnaires Efficiently," *Marketing Research: A Magazine of Management & Application,* 5(2) (Spring 1993): 38–42.

6. www.princess.com, accessed January 8, 2009; Emily Rogers, "Princess Cruises to Target Wider Market," *Marketing* (December 2004): 6; Joseph Rydholm, "Scanning the Seas," *Qurik's Marketing Research Review* (May 1993); and "Optical Scanning Takes a Cruise," *Marketing News,* 25(22) (October 1991): 15.

7. Refer to the guides and manuals available for these software packages.

8. John E. Overall and Scott Tonidandel, "A Two-Stage Analysis of Repeated Measurements with Dropouts and/or Intermittent Missing Data," *Journal of Clinical Psychology,* 62(3) (March 2006): 285–291; Roger Sapsford, *Data Collection and Analysis,* 2nd ed. (Thousand Oaks, CA: Sage Publications, 2006); Atai Winkler and Paul McCarthy, "Maximising the Value of Missing Data," *Journal of Targeting, Measurement and Analysis for Marketing* (London),

13(2) (February 2005): 168; Dwayne Ball, "Statistical Analysis with Missing Data," *JMR, Journal of Marketing Research,* 40(3) (August 2003): 374; Marco Vriens and Eric Melton, "Managing Missing Data," *Marketing Research,* 14(3) (2002): 12–17; Paul D. Allison, *Missing Data* (Thousand Oaks, CA: Sage Publications, 2001); Byung-Joo Lee, "Sample Selection Bias Correction for Missing Response Observations," *Oxford Bulletin of Economics and Statistics,* 62(2) (May 2000): 305; and Naresh K. Malhotra, "Analyzing Marketing Research Data with Incomplete Information on the Dependent Variable," *Journal of Marketing Research,* 24 (February 1987): 74–84.

9. A meaningful and practical value should be imputed. The value imputed should be a legitimate response code. For example, a mean of 3.86 may not be practical if only single-digit response codes have been developed. In such cases, the mean should be rounded to the nearest integer. See, Natalie J. Allen, Helen Williams, David J. Stanley, and Sarah J. Ross, "Assessing Dissimilarity Relations Under Missing Data Conditions: Evidence From Computer Simulations," *Journal of Applied Psychology,* 92(5) (September 2007): 1414–1426.

10. Robert Zeithammer and Peter Lenk, "Bayesian Estimation of Multivariate-Normal Models When Dimensions Are Absent," *Quantitative Marketing & Economics,* 4(3) (September 2006): 241–264; Raymond A. Kent, "Cases as Configurations: Using Combinatorial and Fuzzy Logic to Analyse Marketing Data," *International Journal of Market Research,* 47(2) (2005): 205–228; Kevin M. Murphy, "Estimation and Inference in Two-Step Econometric Models," *Journal of Business & Economic Statistics,* 20(1) (January 2002): 88–97; Ali Kara, Christine Nielsen, Sundeep Sahay, and Nagaraj Sivasubramaniam, "Latent Information in the Pattern of Missing Observations in Global Mail Surveys," *Journal of Global Marketing,* 7(4) (1994): 103–126; and Naresh K. Malhotra, "Analyzing Marketing Research Data with Incomplete Information on the Dependent Variable," *Journal of Marketing Research,* 24 (February 1987): 74–84.

11. Some weighting procedures require adjustments in subsequent data analysis techniques. See, John Dawes, "Do Data Characteristics Change According to the Number of Scale Points Used?" *International Journal of Market Research,* 50(1) (2008): 61–77; Clyde Tucker, J. Michael Brick, and Brian Meekins, "Household Telephone Service and Usage Patterns in the United States in 2004: Implications for Telephone Samples," *Public Opinion Quarterly,* 71(1) (April 2007): 3–22; David J. Bartholomew, *The Analysis and Interpretation of Multivariate Data for Social Scientists* (Boca Raton, FL: CRC Press, 2002); Llan Yaniv, "Weighting and Trimming: Heuristics for Aggregating Judgments Under Uncertainty," *Organizational Behavior & Human Decision Processes,* 69(3) (March 1997): 237–249; and Humphrey Taylor, "The Very Different Methods Used to Conduct Telephone Surveys of the Public," *Journal of the Market Research Society,* 39(3) (July 1997): 421–432.

12. Fevzi Akinci and Bernard J. Healey, "The Role of Social Marketing in Understanding Access to Primary Health Care Services: Perceptions and Experiences," *Health Marketing Quarterly,* 21(4) (January 2004): 3–30; Michael Bradford, "Health Care Access Services for Expats Gain in Popularity," *Business Insurance,* 36(1) (January 7, 2002): 19–20; and Arch G. Woodside, Robert L. Nielsen, Fred Walters, and Gale D. Muller, "Preference Segmentation of Health Care Services: The Old-Fashioneds, Value Conscious, Affluents, and Professional Want-It-Alls," *Journal of Health Care Marketing* (June 1988): 14–24. See also, Rama Jayanti, "Affective Responses Toward Service Providers: Implications for Service Encounters," *Health Marketing Quarterly,* 14(1) (1996): 49–65.

13. See, Richard Arnold Johnson and Dean W. Wichern, *Applied Multivariate Statistical Analysis* (Paramus, NJ: Prentice Hall, 2001); B. Swift, "Preparing Numerical Data," in Roger Sapsford and Victor Jupp, eds., *Data Collection and Analysis* (Thousand Oaks, CA: Sage Publications, 1996); and Ronald E. Frank, "Use of Transformations," *Journal of Marketing Research* (August 1966): 247–253, for specific transformations frequently used in marketing research.

14. Bivariate techniques have been included here with multivariate techniques. Whereas bivariate techniques are concerned with pairwise relationships, multivariate techniques examine more complex simultaneous relationships among phenomena. See, Wayne S. DeSarbo, Robert E. Hausman, and Jeffrey M. Kukitz, "Restricted Principal Components Analysis for Marketing Research," *Journal of Modeling in Management,* 2(3) (2007): 305; John Spicer, *Making Sense of Multivariate Data Analysis: An Intuitive Approach* (Thousand Oaks, CA: Sage Publications, 2004); and Wayne S. DeSarbo, Robert E. Hausman, and Jeffrey M. Kukitz, "Restricted Principal Components Analysis for Marketing Research," *Journal of Modeling in Management,* 2(3) (2007): 305.

15. Wayne S. DeSarbo, "The Joint Spatial Representation of Multiple Variable Batteries Collected in Marketing Research," *Journal of Marketing Research,* 38(2) (May 2001): 244–253; and J. Douglass Carroll and Paul E. Green, "Psychometric Methods in Marketing Research: Part II: Multidimensional Scaling," *Journal of Marketing Research,* 34(2) (May 1997): 193–204.

16. Roger Slavens, "Haagen-Dazs Tastes Success with Creme de la Creme Campaign," *B to B,* 92(1) (January 2007): 23; Stephanie Thompson, "Haagen-Dazs Goes for Mass, Not Class," *Advertising Age* (Midwest Edition), 75(12) (March 22, 2004): 4–5; David Kilburn, "Haagen-Dazs Is Flavor of Month," *Marketing Week,* 20(23) (September 4, 1997): 30; Mark Maremont, "They're All Screaming for Haagen Dazs," *Business Week* (October 14, 1991); and www.dairyfoods.com/articles/2001/0901/0901market.htm, accessed August 3, 2007.

17. Sara Dolnicar and Bettina Grün, "Cross-Cultural Differences in Survey Response Patterns," *International Marketing Review* 24(2) (2007): 127; Gael McDonald, "Cross-Cultural Methodological Issues in Ethical Research," *Journal of Business Ethics,* 27(1/2) (September 2000): 89–104; Pertti Alasuutari, *Researching Culture* (Thousand Oaks, CA: Sage Publications, 1995); and C. T. Tan, J. McCullough, and J. Teoh, "An Individual Analysis Approach to Cross-Cultural Research," in Melanie Wallendorf and Paul Anderson, eds., *Advances in Consumer Research,* vol. 14 (Provo, UT: Association for Consumer Research, 1987): 394–397.

18. See, for example, John A. McCarty, Martin I. Horn, Mary Kate Szenasy, and Jocelyn Feintuch, "An Exploratory Study of Consumer Style: Country Differences and International Segments," *Journal of Consumer Behaviour,* 6(1) (February 2007): 48; Robert G. Tian, "Cross-Cultural Issues in Internet Marketing," *Journal of American Academy of Business,* 1(2) (March 2002): 217–224; Lisa D. Spiller and Alexander J. Campbell, "The Use of International Direct Marketing by Small Businesses in Canada, Mexico, and the United States: A Comparative Analysis," *Journal of Direct Marketing,* 8 (Winter 1994): 7–16; and Meee-Kau Nyaw and Ignace Ng, "A Comparative Analysis of Ethical Beliefs: A Four-Country Study," *Journal of Business Ethics,* 13 (July 1994): 543–556.

19. Rosemary Barnes, "Downsizing, Increased Competition Has Employees Working Longer, Feeling Anger," *Knight Ridder Tribune Business News* (May 8, 2004): 1; and Willie E. Hopkins and Shirley A. Hopkins, "The Ethics of Downsizing: Perception of Rights and Responsibilities," *Journal of Business Ethics,* 18(2) (January 1999): 145–154.

20. Based on Valerie Seckler, "Banana Republic Ads Go Refined, Contemporary for Fall," *WWD: Women's Wear Daily,* 194(17) (July 2007): 3; Michael Barbaro and Hillary Chura, "Gap Is in Need of a Niche," *New York Times,* 156(53837) (January 27, 2001): B1(2); and Alice Z. Cuneo, "Calhoun Takes Up Challenge to Revamp Banana Republic," *Advertising Age,* 74(24) (June 16, 2003): 22.

21. The help of Pamela Prentice of SAS in writing these and the SAS instructions in all the chapters (14 to 22) is gratefully acknowledged.

Chapter 15

1. John B. Ford, Michael S. LaTour, and Irvine Clarke, "A Prescriptive Essay Concerning Sex Role Portrayals in International Advertising Contexts," *American Business Review,* 22(1) (January 2004): 42; Laura M. Milner, "Sex-Role Portrayals and the Gender of Nations," *Journal of Advertising,* 29(1) (Spring 2000): 67–79; and Mary C. Gilly, "Sex Roles in Advertising: A Comparison of Television Advertisements in Australia, Mexico, and the United States," *Journal of Marketing,* 52 (April 1988): 75–85.

2. Cherie Keen, Martin Wetzels, Ko de Ruyter, and Richard Feinberg, "E-tailers Versus Retailers: Which Factors Determine Consumer Preferences," *Journal of Business Research,* 57(7) (July 2004): 685; Charla Mathwick, Naresh K. Malhotra, and Edward Rigdon, "The Effect of Dynamic Retail Experiences on Experiential Perceptions of Value: An Internet and Catalog Comparison," *Journal of Retailing,* 78(2002): 51–60; and Troy A. Festervand, Don R. Snyder, and John D. Tsalikis, "Influence of Catalog vs. Store Shopping and Prior Satisfaction on Perceived Risk," *Journal of the Academy of Marketing Science* (Winter 1986): 28–36.

3. Max Chafkin, "Gold-Medal Marketing," *Inc.,* 29(4) (April 2007): 35–36; and Lisa Deply Neirotti, Heather A. Bosetti, and Kenneth C. Teed, "Motivation to Attend the 1996 Summer Olympic Games," *Journal of Travel Research,* 39(3) (February 2001): 327–331.

4. See any introductory statistics book for a more detailed description of these statistics; for example, Mark L. Berenson, Timothy Krehbiel, and David M. Levine, *Basic Business Statistics: Concepts and Applications,* 11th ed. (Upper Saddle River, NJ: Prentice Hall, 2009).

5. For our purposes, no distinction will be made between formal hypothesis testing and statistical inference by means of confidence intervals. See, for example, Denis Larocque and Ronald H. Randles, "Confidence Intervals for a Discrete Population Median." *American Statistician,* 62(1) (February 2008): 32–39.

6. Excellent discussions of ways to analyze cross-tabulations can be found in William E. Wagner, *Using SPSS for Social Statistics and Research Methods* (Thousand Oaks, CA: Pine Forge Press, 2007); Bryan E. Denham, "Advanced Categorical Statistics: Issues and Applications in Communication Research," *Journal of Communication,* 52(1) (March 2002): 162; and O. Hellevik, *Introduction to Causal Analysis: Exploring Survey Data by Crosstabulation* (Beverly Hills, CA: Sage Publications, 1984).

7. Donelda S. McKechnie, Jim Grant, Victoria Korepina, and Naila Sadykova, "Women: Segmenting the Home Fitness Equipment Market," *Journal of Consumer Marketing,* 24(1) (2007): 18–26; Ran Kivetz and Itamar Simonson, "Earning the Right to Indulge: Effort as a Determinant of Customer Preferences Toward Frequency Program Rewards," *Journal of Marketing Research,* 39(2) (May 2002): 155–170; and Lawrence F. Feick, "Analyzing Marketing Research Data with Association Models," *Journal of Marketing Research,* 21 (November 1984): 376–386. For a recent application, see Wagner A. Kamakura and Michel Wedel, "Statistical Data Fusion for Cross-Tabulation," *Journal of Marketing Research,* 34(4) (November 1997): 485–498.

8. R. Mark Sirkin, *Statistics for the Social Sciences,* 3rd ed. (Thousand Oaks, CA: Sage Publications, 2005); and Daniel B. Wright, *First Steps in Statistics* (Thousand Oaks, CA: Sage Publications, 2002).

9. James J. Higgins, *Introduction to Modern Nonparametric Statistics* (Pacific Grove, CA: Duxbury, 2002); and Marjorie A. Pett, *Nonparametric Statistics for Health Care Research* (Thousand Oaks, CA: Sage Publications, 1997). For a more extensive treatment, see H. O. Lancaster, *The Chi-Squared Distribution* (New York: John Wiley & Sons, 1969). For a recent application, see Eric W. T. Ngai, Vincent C. S. Heung, Y. H. Wong, and Fanny K. Y. Chan, "Consumer Complaint Behaviour of Asians and non-Asians About Hotel Services: An Empirical Analysis," *European Journal of Marketing,* 41(11/12) (2007): 1375–1392.

10. Mark L. Berenson, Timothy Krehbiel, and David M. Levine, *Basic Business Statistics: Concepts and Applications,* 11th ed. (Upper Saddle River, NJ: Prentice Hall, 2009).

11. Some statisticians, however, disagree. They feel that a correction should not be applied. See, for example, John E. Overall, "Power of Chi-Square Tests for 2 × 2 Contingency Tables with Small Expected Frequencies," *Psychological Bulletin* (January 1980): 132–135. See also, Roger R. Betancourt, Monica Cortinas, Margarita Elorz, and Jose Miguel Mugica, "The Demand for and the Supply of

Distribution Services: A Basis for the Analysis of Customer Satisfaction in Retailing," *Quantitative Marketing and Economics*, 5(3) (September 2007): 293–312.

12. Significance tests and confidence intervals are also available for either lambda-asymmetric or lambda-symmetric. See, L. A. Goodman and W. H. Kruskal, "Measures of Association for Cross-Classification: Appropriate Sampling Theory," *Journal of the American Statistical Association,* 88 (June 1963): 310–364.

13. Andy Fields, *Discovering Statistics Using SPSS,* 2nd ed. (Thousand Oaks, CA: Sage Publications, 2005); John M. Hoenig, "The Abuse of Power: The Pervasive Fallacy of Power Calculation for Data Analysis," *The American Statistician,* 55(1) (February 2001): 19–24; and Michael Cowles and Caroline Davis, "On the Origins of the 0.05 Level of Statistical Significance," *American Psychologist* (May 1982): 553–558. See also, Thomas T. Semon, "Stat Tests for Survey Data Don't Tell Full Story," *Marketing News,* 40(2) (February 2006): 6.

14. Technically, a null hypothesis cannot be accepted. It can be either rejected or not rejected. This distinction, however, is inconsequential in applied research.

15. The condition when the variances cannot be assumed to be equal is known as the Behrens-Fisher problem. There is some controversy over the best procedure in this case. For a recent example, see Bertil Hultén, "Customer Segmentation: The Concepts of Trust, Commitment and Relationships," *Journal of Targeting, Measurement and Analysis for Marketing,* 15(4) (September 2007): 256–269.

16. Rajesh Iyer and Jacqueline K. Eastman, "The Elderly and Their Attitudes Toward the Internet: The Impact on Internet Use, Purchase, and Comparison Shopping," *Journal of Marketing Theory & Practice,* 14(1) (January 2006): 57–66; Susan Chandler, "Some Retailers Begin to Cater to Growing Group of Aging Shoppers," *Knight Ridder Tribune Business News* (March 17, 2001): 1; and James R. Lumpkin and James B. Hunt, "Mobility as an Influence on Retail Patronage Behavior of the Elderly: Testing Conventional Wisdom," *Journal of the Academy of Marketing Science* (Winter 1989): 1–12.

17. Paula Schleis, "Startup Bets on Super Bowl: Local Entrepreneurs Hope Pricey 15-Second Ad Draws Viewers to New Web Site," *McClatchy–Tribune Business News* (January 2008); Nat Ives, "In a TV World Filled with Clutter, Some Commercials Are Running Longer, Hoping to Be Noticed," *New York Times* (July 28, 2004): C.11; Larry Dunst, "Is It Possible to Get Creative in 15 Seconds?" *Advertising Age,* 64(50) (November 29, 1993): 18; and Jerry A. Rosenblatt and Janet Mainprize, "The History and Future of 15-Second Commercials: An Empirical Investigation of the Perception of Ad Agency Media Directors," in William Lazer, Eric Shaw, and Chow-Hou Wee, eds., *World Marketing Congress, International Conference Series,* vol. IV (Boca Raton, FL: Academy of Marketing Science, 1989): 169–177.

18. Rajiv Grover and Marco Vriens, *The Handbook of Marketing Research: Uses, Misuses, and Future Advances* (Thousand Oaks, CA: Sage Publications, 2006); Gopal K. Kanji, *100 Statistical Tests: New Edition* (Thousand Oaks, CA: Sage Publications, 1999); and Donald L. Harnett, *Statistical Methods,* 3rd ed. (Reading, MA: Addison-Wesley, 1982).

19. James J. Higgins, *Introduction to Modern Nonparametric Statistics* (Pacific Grove, CA: Duxbury, 2002); and Marjorie A. Pett, *Nonparametric Statistics for Health Care Research* (Thousand Oaks, CA: Sage Publications, 1997). For an application, see Peter J. Danaher, "Modeling Page Views Across Multiple Websites with an Application to Internet Reach and Frequency Prediction," *Marketing Science,* 26(3) (June 2007): 42.

20. There is some controversy over whether nonparametric statistical techniques should be used to make inferences about population parameters.

21. The t test in this case is equivalent to a chi-square test for independence in a 2×2 contingency table. The relationship is $\chi^2_{0.95(1)} = t^2_{0.05(n_1+n_2-2)}$. For large samples, the t distribution approaches the normal distribution and so the t test and the z test are equivalent.

22. Sheree R. Curry, "Drawing a Prize Ad Client," *TelevisionWeek,* 23(24) (June 14, 2004): 12; and James R. Krum, Pradeep A. Rau,

and Stephen K. Keiser, "The Marketing Research Process: Role Perceptions of Researchers and Users," *Journal of Advertising Research* (December/January 1988): 9–21.

23. Reinhard Bergmann, "Different Outcomes of the Wilcoxon-Mann-Whitney Test from Different Statistics Packages," *The American Statistician,* 54(1) (February 2000): 72–77. For an application, see Christina Sichtmann and Susanne Stingel, "Limit Conjoint Analysis and Vickrey Auction as Methods to Elicit Consumers' Willingness-to-Pay: An Empirical Comparison," *European Journal of Marketing* (Bradford), 41(11/12) (2007): 1359.

24. "General Mills and Curves International Partnership Delivers New Weight Management Food Brand," (May 8, 2007), www. midatlanticcurves.com/curves_cereal.htm, accessed September 5, 2007.

25. William Bailey, "Data Use: Nonparametric Tests: Sturdy Alternatives," www.quirks.com/articles/a2002/20020509.aspx?searchID=3435634, accessed March 23, 2008; Marjorie A. Pett, *Nonparametric Statistics for Health Care Research* (Thousand Oaks, CA: Sage Publications, 1997); and J. G. Field, "The World's Simplest Test of Significance," *Journal of the Market Research Society* (July 1971): 170–172.

26. Roger Strange, "Branding and the Externalisation of Production," *International Marketing Review,* 23(6) (2006): 578; Louella Miles, "Finding a Balance in Global Research," *Marketing* (November 29, 2001): 33; and Leslie de Chernatony, Chris Halliburton, and Ratna Bernath, "International Branding: Demand or Supply Driven," *International Marketing Review,* 12(2) (1995): 9–21.

27. Nick Ellis and Matthew Higgins, "Recatechizing Codes of Practice in Supply Chain Relationships: Discourse, Identity and Otherness," *Journal of Strategic Marketing,* 14(4) (December 2006): 387–412; Mark Dolliver, "Keeping Honest Company," *Adweek,* 41(28) (July 10, 2000): 29; Lawrence B. Chonko, *Ethical Decision Making in Marketing* (Thousand Oaks, CA: Sage Publications, 1995); and G. R. Laczniak and P. E. Murphy, "Fostering Ethical Marketing Decisions," *Journal of Business Ethics,* 10 (1991): 259–271.

Chapter 16

1. Youcheng Wang, "Web-Based Destination Marketing Systems: Assessing the Critical Factors for Management and Implementation," *The International Journal of Tourism Research,* 10(1) (February 2008): 55; "Turkish Tourism Minister Wants Tax Plan Scrapped," (April 10, 2008), www.eturbonews.com/2094/turkish-tourism-minister-wants-tax-plan-scrap, accessed October 16, 2008; Bob McKercher and Donna Y. Y. Wong, "Understanding Tourism Behavior: Examining the Combined Effects of Prior Visitation History and Destination Status," *Journal of Travel Research,* 43(2) (November 2004): 17; and Seyhmus Baloglu and Mehmet Mangaloglu, "Tourism Destination Images of Turkey, Egypt, Greece, and Italy as Perceived by U.S.-Based Tour Operators and Travel Agents," *Tourism Management,* 22(1) (February 2001): 1–9.

2. Jesse W. J. Weltevreden and Ron A. Boschma, "Internet Strategies and Performance of Dutch Retailers," *Journal of Retailing & Consumer Services,* 15(3) (May 2008): 163–178; "Over 875 Million Consumers Have Shopped Online—The Number of Internet Shoppers Up 40% in Two Years," www.nielsen.com/media/2008/pr_080128b.html, accessed October 16, 2008; "Statistics: U.S. Online Shoppers," (June 29, 2005), www.shop.org/learn/stats_usshop_general.asp; Ellen Garbarino and Michal Strahilevitz, "Gender Differences in the Perceived Risk of Buying Online and the Effects of Receiving a Site Recommendation," *Journal of Business Research,* 57(7) (July 2004): 768; Richard Burnett, "As Internet Sales Rise, So Do Shoppers' Complaints," *Knight Ridder Tribune Business News* (December 20, 2001): 1; and Pradeep Korgaonkar and George P. Moschis, "The Effects of Perceived Risk and Social Class on Consumer Preferences for Distribution Outlets," in Paul Bloom, Russ Winer, Harold H. Kassarjian, Debra L. Scammon, Bart Weitz, Robert Spekman, Vijay Mahajan, and Michael Levy, eds., *Enhancing Knowledge Development in Marketing,* Series No. 55 (Chicago: American Marketing Association, 1989): 39–43.

3. For recent applications of ANOVA, see Sadrudin A. Ahmed and Alain d'Astous, "Antecedents, Moderators and Dimensions of

Country-of-Origin Evaluations," *International Marketing Review* (London), 25(1) (2008): 75; Joffre Swait and Tülin Erdem, "Brand Effects on Choice and Choice Set Formation Under Uncertainty" *Marketing Science,* 26(5) (October 2007): 679–700; and Stephen M. Nowlis, Naomi Mandel, and Deborah Brown McCabe, "The Effect of a Delay Between Choice and Consumption on Consumption Enjoyment," *Journal of Consumer Research*, 31 (December 2004), 502–510.

4. R. Mark Sirkin, *Statistics for the Social Sciences,* 3rd ed. (Thousand Oaks, CA: Sage Publications, 2005); Denis G. Janky, "Sometimes Pooling for Analysis of Variance Hypothesis Tests: A Review and Study of a Split-Plot Model," *The American Statistician,* 54(4) (November 2000): 269–279; Wade C. Driscoll, "Robustness of the ANOVA and Tukey-Kramer Statistical Tests," *Computers & Industrial Engineering,* 31(1, 2) (October 1996): 265–268; and Richard K. Burdick, "Statement of Hypotheses in the Analysis of Variance," *Journal of Marketing Research* (August 1983): 320–324.

5. The F test is a generalized form of the t test. If a random variable is t distributed with n degrees of freedom, then t^2 is F distributed with 1 and n degrees of freedom. Where there are two factor levels or treatments, ANOVA is equivalent to the two-sided t test.

6. Although computations for the fixed-effects and random-effects models are similar, interpretations of results differ. A comparison of these approaches is found in J. Rick Turner and Julian Thayer, *Introduction to Analysis of Variance: Design, Analysis, and Interpretation* (Thousand Oaks, CA: Sage Publications, 2001); and Amir Erez, Matthew C. Bloom, and Martin T. Wells, "Using Random Rather Than Fixed Effects Models in Meta-Analysis: Implications for Situational Specificity and Validity Generalization," *Personnel Psychology,* 49(2) (Summer 1996): 275–306. See also, J. Rick Turner and Julian F. Thayer, *Introduction to Analysis of Variance: Design, Analysis, and Interpretation* (Thousand Oaks, CA: Sage Publications, 2001).

7. Allen Hall and Lisa Berardino, "Teaching Professional Behaviors: Differences in the Perceptions of Faculty, Students, and Employers," *Journal of Business Ethics* (63) (2006): 407–415.

8. We consider only the full factorial designs, which incorporate all possible combinations of factor levels.

9. Anthony Pecotich and Steven Ward, "Global Branding, Country of Origin and Expertise: An Experimental Evaluation," *International Marketing Review,* 24(3) (2007): 271; Michael A. Kamins, Xavier Dreze, and Valerie S. Folkes, "Effects of Seller-Supplied Prices on Buyers' Product Evaluations: Reference Prices in an Internet Auction Context," *Journal of Consumer Research*, 30 (March 2004): 622–628; James Jaccard, *Interaction Effects in Factorial Analysis of Variance* (Thousand Oaks, CA: Sage Publications, 1997); and Jerome L. Mayers, *Fundamentals of Experimental Design,* 3rd ed. (Boston: Allyn & Bacon, 1979).

10. Andy Fields, *Discovering Statistics Using SPSS,* 2nd ed. (Thousand Oaks, CA: Sage Publications, 2005); and Shizuhiko Nishisato, *Measurement and Multivariate Analysis* (New York: Springer-Verlag New York, 2002).

11. Durairaj Maheswaran and Cathy Yi Chen, "Nation Equity: Incidental Emotions in Country-of-Origin Effects," *Journal of Consumer Research,* 33(3) (December 2006): 370–376; Kalpesh Kaushik Desai, "The Effects of Ingredient Branding Strategies on Host Brand Extendibility," *Journal of Marketing,* 66(1) (January 2002): 73–93; and Paul Chao, "The Impact of Country Affiliation on the Credibility of Product Attribute Claims," *Journal of Advertising Research* (April/May 1989): 35–41. Hudson's in this study has been replaced by Best Buy and the prices have also been adjusted to reflect those of digital TVs.

12. Although this is the most common way in which analysis of covariance is performed, other situations are also possible. For example, covariate and factor effects may be of equal interest, or the set of covariates may be of major concern. For recent applications, see Trevor Sharot, "The Design and Precision of Data-Fusion Studies," *International Journal of Market Research,* 49(4) (2007): 449–470; and Lisa E. Bolton and Americus Reed, "Sticky Priors: The Perseverance of Identity Effects on Judgment," *Journal of Marketing Research*, 41 (November 2004): 397–410.

13. For a more detailed discussion, see Marija Norusis, *SPSS 13.0 Statistical Procedures Companion* (Paramus, NJ: Prentice Hall); J. Rick Turner and Julian Thayer, *Introduction to Analysis of Variance: Design, Analysis, and Interpretation* (Thousand Oaks, CA: Sage Publications, 2001); Stanton A. Glantz and Bryan K. Slinker, *Primer of Applied Regression and Analysis of Variance* (Blacklick, OH: McGraw-Hill, 2000); and A. R. Wildt and O. T. Ahtola, *Analysis of Covariance* (Beverly Hills, CA: Sage Publications, 1978).

14. Shi Zhang and Bernd H. Schimitt, "Creating Local Brands in Multilingual International Markets," *Journal of Marketing Research,* 38(3) (August 2001): 313–325; U. N. Umesh, Robert A. Peterson, Michelle McCann-Nelson, and Rajiv Vaidyanathan, "Type IV Error in Marketing Research: The Investigation of ANOVA Interactions," *Journal of the Academy of Marketing Science,* 24(1) (Winter 1996): 17–26; William T. Ross, Jr., and Elizabeth H. Creyer, "Interpreting Interactions: Raw Means or Residual Means," *Journal of Consumer Research,* 20(2) (September 1993): 330–338; and J. H. Leigh and T. C. Kinnear, "On Interaction Classification," *Educational and Psychological Measurement,* 40 (Winter 1980): 841–843.

15. James Jaccard, *Interaction Effects in Factorial Analysis of Variance* (Thousand Oaks, CA: Sage Publications, 1997).

16. This formula does not hold if repeated measurements are made on the dependent variable. See, Edward F. Fern and Kent B. Monroe, "Effect-Size Estimates: Issues and Problems in Interpretation," *Journal of Consumer Research,* 23(2) (September 1996): 89–105; and David H. Dodd and Roger F. Schultz, Jr., "Computational Procedures for Estimating Magnitude of Effect for Some Analysis of Variance Designs," *Psychological Bulletin* (June 1973): 391–395.

17. The ω^2 formula is attributed to Hays. See, W. L. Hays, *Statistics for Psychologists* (New York: Holt, Rinehart & Winston, 1963).

18. Richard Arnold Johnson and Dean W. Wichern, *Applied Multivariate Statistical Analysis* (Paramus, NJ: Prentice Hall, 2001); Edward F. Fern and Kent B. Monroe, "Effect-Size Estimates: Issues and Problems in Interpretation," *Journal of Consumer Research,* 23(2) (September 1996): 89–105; and Jacob Cohen, *Statistical Power Analysis for the Behavioral Sciences* (Mahwah, NJ: Lawrence Erlbaum Associates, 1988).

19. Carmen Ximnez and Javier Revuelta, "Extending the CLAST Sequential Rule to One-Way ANOVA Under Group Sampling," *Behavior Research Methods,* 39(1) (February 2007): 86–100; J. Rick Turner and Julian F. Thayer, *Introduction to Analysis of Variance: Design, Analysis, and Interpretation* (Thousand Oaks, CA: Sage Publications, 2001); John W. Neter, *Applied Linear Statistical Models,* 4th ed. (Burr Ridge, IL: Irwin, 1996); and B. J. Winer, Donald R. Brown, and Kenneth M. Michels, *Statistical Principles in Experimental Design,* 3rd ed. (New York: McGraw-Hill, 1991).

20. It is possible to combine between-subjects and within-subjects factors in a single design. See, for example, Franziska Vlckner and Julian Hofmann, "The Price-Perceived Quality Relationship: A Meta-Analytic Review and Assessment of Its Determinants," *Marketing Letters,* 18(3) (July 2007): 181–196; and Rohini Ahluwalia, H. Rao Unnava, and Robert E. Burnkrant, "The Moderating Role of Commitment on the Spillover Effect of Marketing Communications," *Journal of Marketing Research,* 38(4) (November 2001): 458–470.

21. www.marriott.com, accessed January 20, 2009; and Glenn Haussman, "Desks Become Important Aspect in Laptop Culture," www.hotelinteractive.com/news/articleView.asp?articleID=46, accessed May 23, 2007.

22. See James R. Schott, "Some High-Dimensional Tests for a One-Way MANOVA," *Journal of Multivariate Analysis,* 98(9) (October 2007): 1825–1839; Soyoung Kim and Stephen Olejnik, "Bias and Precision of Measures of Association for a Fixed-Effect Multivariate Analysis of Variance Model," *Multivariate Behavioral Research,* 40(4) (October 2005): 401–421; Paul M. Herr and Christine M. Page, "Asymmetric Association of Liking and Disliking Judgments: So What's Not to Like?" *Journal of Consumer Research,* 30 (March 2004), 588–601; and J. H. Bray and S. E. Maxwell, *Multivariate Analysis of Variance* (Beverly Hills, CA: Sage

Publications, 1985). For a recent application of MANOVA, see Rongrong Zhou and Michel Tuan Pham, "Promotion and Prevention Across Mental Accounts: When Financial Products Dictate Consumers' Investment Goals," *Journal of Consumer Research*, 31 (June 2004): 125–135.

23. Oliver M. Freestone and Peter J. McGoldrick, "Ethical Positioning and Political Marketing: The Ethical Awareness and Concerns of UK Voters," *Journal of Marketing Management,* 23(7/8) (September 2007): 651–673; Allan J. Kimmel and N. Craig Smith, "Deception in Marketing Research: Ethical, Methodological, and Disciplinary Implications," *Psychology and Marketing*, 18(7) (July 2001): 663–689; and Ishmael P. Akaah, "A Cross-National Analysis of the Perceived Commonality of Unethical Practices in Marketing Research," in William Lazer, Eric Shaw, and Chow-Hou Wee, eds., *World Marketing Congress*, International Conference Series, vol. IV (Boca Raton, FL: Academy of Marketing Science, 1989): 2–9.

24. Dane Peterson, Angela Rhoads, and Bobby C. Vaught, "Ethical Beliefs of Business Professionals: A Study of Gender, Age and External Factors," *Journal of Business Ethics,* 31(3) (June 2001): 1; and Ishmael P. Akaah, "Differences in Research Ethics Judgments Between Male and Female Marketing Professionals," *Journal of Business Ethics*, 8 (1989): 375–381.

Chapter 17

1. Ann Harrington and Petra Bartosiewicz, "Who's Up? Who's Down?" *Fortune,* 150(8) (October 18, 2004): 181–186; Christine Bittar, "Avon Refreshed 'Let's Talk' Campaign—Goes Global for Skincare Line Debut," *Brandweek*, 43(7) (February 18, 2002): 4; Joanne Wojcik, "Avon's Benefits Booklet Presents Easily Understood Information to All Levels of the Corporation," *Business Insurance*, 35(47) (November 19, 2001): 14; and Cyndee Miller, "Computer Modeling Rings the Right Bell for Avon," *Marketing News* (May 9, 1988): 14.

2. Kate Maddox, "Online Ad Sales Expected to Keep Growing in '05," *B to B*, 89(11) (October 11, 2004): 12; and Pradeep K. Korgaonkar and Allen E. Smith, "Shopping Orientation, Demographic, and Media Preference Correlates of Electronic Shopping," in Kenneth D. Bahn, ed., *Developments in Marketing Science*, vol. 11 (Blacksburg, VA: Academy of Marketing Science, 1988): 52–55.

3. Peter Y. Chen and Paula M. Popovich, *Correlation: Parametric and Nonparametric Measures* (Thousand Oaks, CA: Sage Publications, 2002); Philip Bobko, Philip L. Roth, and Christopher Bobko, "Correcting the Effect Size of *d* for Range Restriction and Unreliability," *Organizational Research Methods*, 4(1) (January 2001): 46–61; Michael E. Doherty and James A. Sullivan, "rho = ρ," *Organizational Behavior & Human Decision Processes*, 43(1) (February 1989): 136–144; W. S. Martin, "Effects of Scaling on the Correlation Coefficient: Additional Considerations," *Journal of Marketing Research*, 15 (May 1978): 304–308; and K. A. Bollen and K. H. Barb, "Pearson's *R* and Coarsely Categorized Measures," *American Sociological Review*, 46 (1981): 232–239.

4. Trevor Cox and Joao Branco, *Introduction to Multivariate Analysis* (New York: Oxford University Press, 2002).

5. Although the topic is not discussed here, partial correlations can also be helpful in locating intervening variables and making certain types of causal inferences.

6. "Global Gallery," *Advertising Age*, 78(9) (February 2007): S-10; Ronald E. Goldsmith, "The Impact of Corporate Credibility and Celebrity Credibility on Consumer Reaction to Advertisements and Brands," *Journal of Advertising*, 29(3) (Fall 2000): 43–54; and Ken Kasriel, "Hungary's Million-Dollar Slap," *Advertising Age* (June 8, 1992).

7. Another advantage to tau is that it can be generalized to a partial correlation coefficient. James J. Higgins, *Introduction to Modern Nonparametric Statistics* (Pacific Grove, CA: Duxbury, 2002); Marjorie A. Pett, *Nonparametric Statistics for Health Care Research* (Thousand Oaks, CA: Sage Publications, 1997); and Sidney Siegel

and N. J. Castellan, *Nonparametric Statistics,* 2nd ed. (New York: McGraw-Hill, 1988).

8. In a strict sense, the regression model requires that errors of measurement be associated only with the criterion variable and that the predictor variables be measured without error. For serially correlated errors, see Richard A. Berk, *Regression* (Thousand Oaks, CA: Sage Publications 2003); and Eugene Canjels and Mark W. Watson, "Estimating Deterministic Trends in the Presence of Serially Correlated Errors," *Review of Economic and Statistics*, 79(2) (May 1997): 184–200. See also, John Fox, *Applied Regression Analysis and Generalized Linear Models*, 2nd ed. (Thousand Oaks, CA: Sage Publications, 2008).

9. See any text on regression, such as Leo H. Kahane, *Regression Basics,* 2nd ed. (Thousand Oaks, CA: Sage Publications, 2007).

10. Technically, the numerator is $b - \beta$. However, since it has been hypothesized that $\beta = 0.0$, it can be omitted from the formula.

11. The larger the *SEE*, the poorer the fit of the regression.

12. The assumption of fixed levels of predictors applies to the "classical" regression model. It is possible, if certain conditions are met, for the predictors to be random variables. However, their distribution is not allowed to depend on the parameters of the regression equation. See, Paul D. Allison, *Fixed Effects Regression Models* (Thousand Oaks, CA: Sage Publications, 2009); and N. R. Draper and H. Smith, *Applied Regression Analysis*, 3rd ed. (New York: John Wiley & Sons, 1998).

13. For an approach to handling the violations of these assumptions, see Duncan K. H. Fong and Wayne S. DeSarbo, "A Bayesian Methodology for Simultaneously Detecting and Estimating Regime Change Points and Variable Selection in Multiple Regression Models for Marketing Research," *Quantitative Marketing and Economics,* 5(4) (December 2007): 427–453; Arnold Zellner, "Further Results on Baysian Method of Moments Analysis of the Multiple Regression Model," *International Economic Review*, 42(1) (February 2001): 121–140; Gary S. Dispensa, "Use Logistic Regression with Customer Satisfaction Data," *Marketing News*, 31(1) (January 6, 1997): 13; and S. K. Reddy, Susan L. Holak, and Subodh Bhat, "To Extend or Not to Extend: Success Determinants of Line Extensions," *Journal of Marketing Research,* 31 (May 1994): 243–262.

14. Teresa da Silva Lopes and Mark Casson, "Entrepreneurship and the Development of Global Brands," *Business History Review*, 81(4) (January 2007): 651–680; Ying Fan, "The National Image of Global Brands," *Journal of Brand Management*, 9(3) (January 2002): 180–192; Naveen Donthu, Sungho Lee, and Boonghee Yoo, "An Examination of Selected Marketing Mix Elements and Brand Equity," *Academy of Marketing Science*, 28(2) (Spring 2000): 195–211; and Nancy Giges, "Europeans Buy Outside Goods, But Like Local Ads," *Advertising Age International* (April 27, 1992).

15. For other recent applications of multiple regression, see Anne-Sophie Binninger, "Exploring the Relationships Between Retail Brands and Consumer Store Loyalty," *International Journal of Retail & Distribution Management,* 36(2) (2008): 94; Ahmet H. Kirca, Satish Jayachandran, and William O. Bearden, "Market Orientation: A Meta-Analytic Review and Assessment of Its Antecedents and Impact on Performance," *Journal of Marketing,* 69 (April 2005), 24–41; and Pierre Chandon, Vicki G. Morwitz, and Werner J. Reinartz, "Do Intentions Really Predict Behavior? Self-Generated Validity Effects in Survey Research," *Journal of Marketing,* 69 (April 2005), 1–14.

16. Yet another reason for adjusting R^2 is that, as a result of the optimizing properties of the least-squares approach, it is a maximum. Thus, to some extent, R^2 always overestimates the magnitude of a relationship.

17. If R_{pop}^2 is zero, then the sample R^2 reflects only sampling error, and the *F* ratio will tend to be equal to unity.

18. Another approach is the hierarchical method, in which the variables are added to the regression equation in an order specified by the researcher.

19. R. Mark Sirkin, *Statistics for the Social Sciences,* 3rd ed. (Thousand Oaks, CA: Sage Publications, 2005); Julie R. Irwin and Gary H. McClelland, "Misleading Heuristics and Moderated Multiple Regression Models," *Journal of Marketing Research,* 38(1) (February 2001): 100–109; A. C. Atkinson, S. J. Koopman, and N. Shephard, "Detecting Shocks: Outliers and Breaks in Time Series," *Journal of Econometrics,* 80(2) (October 1997): 387–422; George C. S. Wang and Charles K. Akabay, "Autocorrelation: Problems and Solutions in Regression Modeling," *Journal of Business Forecasting Methods & Systems,* 13(4) (Winter 1994–1995): 18–26; David Belsley, *Conditioning Diagnostics: Collinearity and Weak Data in Regression* (New York: John Wiley & Sons, 1980); and David Belsley, Edwin Kuh, and Roy E. Walsh, *Regression Diagnostics* (New York: John Wiley & Sons, 1980).

20. The Durbin-Watson test is discussed in virtually all regression text-books, for example, Paul D. Allison, *Fixed Effects Regression Models* (Thousand Oaks, CA: Sage Publications, 2009). See also, George E. Halkos and Ilias S. Kevork, "A Comparison of Alternative Unit Root Tests," *Journal of Applied Statistics,* 32(1) (January 2005): 45–60.

21. M. Mondello and P. Rishe, "Ticket Price Determination in Professional Sports: An Empirical Analysis of the NBA, NFL, NHL, and Major League Baseball," *Sport Marketing Quarterly,* 13 (2004): 104–112.

22. Ronen Meiri and Jacob Zahavi, "Using Simulated Annealing to Optimize the Feature Selection Problem in Marketing Applications," *European Journal of Operational Research,* 171(3) (June 2006): 842–858; Edward J. Fox and Stephen J. Hoch, "Cherry-Picking," *Journal of Marketing,* 69 (January 2005): 46–62; Neal Schmitt, "Estimates for Cross-Validity for Stepwise Regression and with Predictor Selection," *Journal of Applied Psychology,* 84(1) (February 1999): 50; and Shelby H. McIntyre, David B. Montgomery, V. Srinivasan, and Barton A. Weitz, "Evaluating the Statistical Significance of Models Developed by Stepwise Regression," *Journal of Marketing Research,* 20 (February 1983): 1–11.

23. Murray Forseter and David Q. Mahler, "The Roper Starch Report," *Drug Store News* (2000): 46–63; and Glen R. Jarboe and Carl D. McDaniel, "A Profile of Browsers in Regional Shopping Malls," *Journal of the Academy of Marketing Science* (Spring 1987): 46–53.

24. Possible procedures are given in Raj Echambadi and James D. Hess, "Mean-Centering Does Not Alleviate Collinearity Problems in Moderated Multiple Regression Models," *Marketing Science,* 26(3) (June 2007): 438–445; Rajesh Sethi, Daniel C. Smith, and C. Whan Park, "Cross-Functional Product Development Teams, Creativity, and the Innovations of New Consumer Products," *Journal of Marketing Research,* 38(1) (February 2001): 73–85; Terry Grapentine, "Path Analysis vs. Structural Equation Modeling," *Marketing Research,* 12(3) (Fall 2000): 12–20; George C. S. Wang, "How to Handle Multicollinearity in Regression Modeling," *Journal of Business Forecasting Methods & Systems,* 15(1) (Spring 1996): 23–27; Charlotte H. Mason and William D. Perreault, Jr., "Collinearity, Power, and Interpretation of Multiple Regression Analysis," *Journal of Marketing Research,* 28 (August 1991): 268–280; R. R. Hocking, "Developments in Linear Regression Methodology: 1959–1982," *Technometrics,* 25 (August 1983): 219–230; and Ronald D. Snee, "Discussion," *Technometrics,* 25 (August 1983): 230–237.

25. Nedret Billor, "An Application of the Local Influence Approach to Ridge Regression," *Journal of Applied Statistics,* 26(2) (February 1999): 177–183; R. James Holzworth, "Policy Capturing with Ridge Regression," *Organizational Behavior & Human Decision Processes,* 68(2) (November 1996): 171–179; Albert R. Wildt, "Equity Estimation and Assessing Market Response," *Journal of Marketing Research,* 31 (February 1994): 437–451; and Subhash Sharma and William L. James, "Latent Root Regression: An Alternative Procedure for Estimating Parameters in the Presence of Multicollinearity," *Journal of Marketing Research* (May 1981): 154–161.

26. Only relative importance can be determined, because the importance of an independent variable depends upon all the independent variables in the regression model.

27. Andy Fields, *Discovering Statistics Using SPSS,* 2nd ed. (Thousand Oaks, CA: Sage Publications, 2005); McKee J. McClendon, *Multiple Regression and Causal Analysis* (Prospect Heights, IL: Waveland Press, 2002); Robert Rugimbana, "Predicting Automated Teller Machine Usage: The Relative Importance of Perceptual and Demographic Factors," *International Journal of Bank Marketing,* 13(4) (1995): 26–32; Paul E. Green, J. Douglas Carroll, and Wayne S. DeSarbo, "A New Measure of Predictor Variable Importance in Multiple Regression," *Journal of Marketing Research* (August 1978): 356–360; and Barbara Bund Jackson, "Comment on 'A New Measure of Predictor Variable Importance in Multiple Regression,' " *Journal of Marketing Research* (February 1980): 116–118.

28. In the rare situation in which all the predictors are uncorrelated, simple correlations = partial correlations = part correlations = betas. Hence, the squares of these measures will yield the same rank order of the relative importance of the variables.

29. Tom Logue, "Minor League, Major Loyalty: Michigan Baseball Team Surveys Its Fans," *Quirk's Marketing Research Review,* www.quirks.com/articles/article.asp?arg_ArticleId=616, accessed December 8, 2008.

30. For further discussion on dummy variable coding, see J. Mauro, C. Hernandez, and J. Afonso Mazzon, "Adoption of Internet Banking: Proposition and Implementation of an Integrated Methodology Approach," *International Journal of Bank Marketing,* 25(3) (2007): 72–82; Stanton A. Glantz and Bryan K. Slinker, *Primer of Applied Regression and Analysis of Variance* (Blacklick, OH: McGraw-Hill, 2000); and Jacob Cohen and Patricia Cohen, *Applied Multiple Regression Correlation Analysis for the Behavioral Sciences,* 2nd ed. (Hillsdale, NJ: Lawrence Erlbaum Associates, 1983): 181–222.

31. Mark M. H. Goode and Lloyd C. Harris, "Online Behavioural Intentions: An Empirical Investigation of Antecedents and Moderators," *European Journal of Marketing* (Bradford), 41(5/6) (2007): 512; Herman Aguinis, James C. Beaty, Robert J. Boik, and Charles A. Pierce, "Effect Size and Power in Assessing Moderating Effects of Categorical Variables Using Multiple Regression: A 30-Year Review," *Journal of Applied Psychology,* 90(1) (2005): 94–107; and Stanton A. Glantz and Bryan K. Slinker, *Primer of Applied Regression and Analysis of Variance* (Blacklick, OH: McGraw-Hill, 2000). For an application, see Michael J. Barone, Kenneth C. Manning, and Paul W. Miniard, "Consumer Response to Retailers' Use of Partially Comparative Pricing," *Journal of Marketing,* 68 (July 2004): 37–47.

32. Anonymous, "World Airline Performance: Asia Pacific–Transpacific Recovery Continues," *Interavia,* 58(671) (May/June 2003): 35; Jens Flottau, "Asian Carriers Advised to Seek New Formulas," *Aviation Week & Space,* 155(23) (December 3, 2001): 45; and Andrew Geddes, "Asian Airlines Try Loyalty Offers," *Advertising Age* (December 14, 1992).

33. Tim Barnett and Sean Valentine, "Issue Contingencies and Marketers' Recognition of Ethical Issues, Ethical Judgments and Behavioral Intentions," *Journal of Business Research* 57(4) (April 2004): 338; Denise E. DeLorme, George M. Zinkhan, and Warren French, "Ethics and the Internet: Issues Associated with Qualitative Research," *Journal of Business Ethics,* 33(4) (October 2001): 2; and I. P. Akaah and E. A. Riordan, "The Incidence of Unethical Practices in Marketing Research: An Empirical Investigation," *Journal of the Academy of Marketing Science,* 18 (1990): 143–152.

Chapter 18

1. Lu Qiang and Sridhar Moorthy, "Coupons Versus Rebates," *Marketing Science,* 26(1) (February 2007): 67–82; Joe Michaelree, "Incentive Programs Mean More Than Money to Retailers," *Agri Marketing,* 42(5) (June 2004): 32; Donald R. Lichtenstein, Scot Burton, and Richard G. Netemeyer, "An Examination of Deal Proneness Across Sales Promotion Types: A Consumer Segmentation Perspective," *Journal of Retailing,* 73(2) (Summer 1997): 283–297; and Marvin A. Jolson, Joshua L. Wiener, and

Richard B. Rosecky, "Correlates of Rebate Proneness," *Journal of Advertising Research* (February/March 1987): 33–43.

2. A detailed discussion of discriminant analysis may be found in Geoffrey J. McLachlan, *Discriminant Analysis and Statistical Pattern Recognition* (Hoboken, NJ: John Wiley & Sons, 2004); E. K. Kemsley, *Discriminant Analysis and Class Modeling of Spectroscopic Data* (New York: John Wiley & Sons, 1998); Jacques Tacq, *Multivariate Analysis Techniques in Social Science Research* (Thousand Oaks, CA: Sage Publications, 1997); William D. Neal, "Using Discriminant Analysis in Marketing Research: Part I," *Marketing Research*, 1(3) (1989): 79–81; William D. Neal, "Using Discriminant Analysis in Marketing Research: Part 2," *Marketing Research*, 1(4) (1989): 55–60; and P. A. Lachenbruch, *Discriminant Analysis* (New York: Hafner Press, 1975). For a recent application, see Chezy Ofir, "Reexamining Latitude of Price Acceptability and Price Thresholds: Predicting Basic Consumer Reaction to Price," *Journal of Consumer Research*, 30 (March 2004): 612–621.

3. See, Richard Arnold Johnson and Dean W. Wichern, *Applied Multivariate Statistical Analysis* (Paramus, NJ: Prentice Hall, 2001); and W. R. Klecka, *Discriminant Analysis* (Beverly Hills, CA: Sage Publications, 1980).

4. Robert Ping, "Second-Order Latent Variables: Interactions, Specification, Estimation, and an Example," American Marketing Association, *Conference Proceedings* (Chicago), 18 (January 2007): 286; Sung-Joon Yoon and Jong-Whan Kang, "Validation of Marketing Performance Model for Service Industries in Korea," *Services Marketing Quarterly* (Binghamton), 26(4) (2005): 57; Philip Hans Franses, "A Test for the Hit Rate in Binary Response Models," *International Journal of Market Research,* 42(2) (Spring 2000): 239–245; Vincent-Watne Mitchell, "How to Identify Psychographic Segments: Part 2," *Marketing Intelligence & Planning,* 12(7) (1994): 11–16; and M. R. Crask and W. D. Perreault, Jr., "Validation of Discriminant Analysis in Marketing Research," *Journal of Marketing Research,* 14 (February 1977): 60–68.

5. Strictly speaking, before testing for the equality of group means, the equality of group covariance matrices should be tested. Box's M test can be used for this purpose. If the equality of group covariance matrices is rejected, the results of discriminant analysis should be interpreted with caution. In this case, the power of the test for the equality of group means decreases.

6. See, Nessim Hanna, "Brain Dominance and the Interpretation of Advertising Messages," *International Journal of Commerce & Management,* 9(3/4) (1999): 19–32; Lillian Fok, John P. Angelidis, Nabil A. Ibrahim, and Wing M. Fok, "The Utilization and Interpretation of Multivariate Statistical Techniques in Strategic Management," *International Journal of Management,* 12(4) (December 1995): 468–481; and D. G. Morrison, "On the Interpretation of Discriminant Analysis," *Journal of Marketing Research,* 6 (May 1969): 156–163.

7. Bob Miodonski, "Retaining Good Employees Starts at the Top," *Contractor*, 51(10) (October 2004): 7–8; and Edward F. Fern, Ramon A. Avila, and Dhruv Grewal, "Salesforce Turnover: Those Who Left and Those Who Stayed," *Industrial Marketing Management* (1989): 1–9.

8. For the validation of discriminant analysis, see Sung-Joon Yoon and Jong-Whan Kang, "Validation of Marketing Performance Model for Service Industries in Korea" *Services Marketing Quarterly* (Binghamton), 26(4) (2005): 57; and Werner J. Reinartz and V. Kumar, "On the Profitability of Long-Life Customers in a Noncontractual Setting: An Empirical Investigation and Implications for Marketing," *Journal of Marketing,* 64(4) (October 2000): 17–35.

9. Joseph F. Hair, Jr., William C. Black, Barry J. Babin, and Ralph E. Anderson, *Multivariate Data Analysis with Readings,* 7th ed. (Upper Saddle River, NJ: Prentice Hall, 2010). See also, J. J. Glen, "Classification Accuracy in Discriminant Analysis: A Mixed Integer Programming Approach," *The Journal of the Operational Research Society,* 52(3) (March 2001): 328.

10. "Making a Meal of Couch Potatoes and Doughnuts," *Marketing Week* (March 2004): 28; Nick Goodway, "ITV on a Winner with 42 Percent Surge in Profits," *Knight Ridder Tribune Business News* (September 9, 2004): 1; and Don R. Rahtz, M. Joseph Sirgy, and Rustan Kosenko, "Using Demographics and Psychographic Dimensions to Discriminate Between Mature, Heavy, and Light Television Users: An Exploratory Analysis," in Kenneth D. Bahn, ed., *Developments in Marketing Science,* vol. 11 (Blacksburg, VA: Academy of Marketing Science, 1988): 2–7.

11. Richard A. Johnson and Dean W. Wichern, *Applied Multivariate Statistical Analysis,* 5th ed. (Upper Saddle River, NJ: Prentice Hall, 2002). For recent applications, see Rachel S. Duffy, "Towards a Better Understanding of Partnership Attributes: An Exploratory Analysis of Relationship Type Classification," *Industrial Marketing Management*, 37(2) (April 2008): 228–244; and Aviv Shoham and Ayalla Ruvio, "Opinion Leaders and Followers: A Replication and Extension," *Psychology & Marketing*, 25(3) (March 2008): 280–297.

12. Jan Tudor, "Valuation of the Health Services Industry," *Weekly Corporate Growth Report* (1133) (March 26, 2001): 11237–11238; Kathryn H. Dansky and Diane Brannon, "Discriminant Analysis: A Technique for Adding Value to Patient Satisfaction Surveys," *Hospital & Health Services Administration,* 41(4) (Winter 1996): 503–513; and Jeen-Su Lim and Ron Zallocco, "Determinant Attributes in Formulation of Attitudes Toward Four Health Care Systems," *Journal of Health Care Marketing* (June 1988): 25–30.

13. Richard A. Johnson and Dean W. Wichern, *Applied Multivariate Statistical Analysis,* 5th ed. (Upper Saddle River, NJ: Prentice Hall, 2002); and Joseph F. Hair, Jr., William C. Black, Barry J. Babin, and Ralph E. Anderson, *Multivariate Data Analysis with Readings*, 7th ed. (Upper Saddle River, NJ: Prentice Hall, 2010).

14. For a discussion of the logit model, see Naresh K. Malhotra, "The Use of Linear Logit Models in Marketing Research," *Journal of Marketing Research* (February 1983): 20–31. For a comparison of OLS regression, discriminant, logit, and probit models, see Naresh K. Malhotra, "A Comparison of the Predictive Validity of Procedures for Analyzing Binary Data," *Journal of Business and Economic Statistics,* 1 (October 1983): 326–336.

15. Timothy J. Richards, "A Nested Logit Model of Strategic Promotion," *Quantitative Marketing and Economics* (Dordrecht), 5(1) (March 2007): 63–91; S. Sriram, Pradeep K. Chintagunta, and Ramya Neelamegham, "Effects of Brand Preference, Product Attributes, and Marketing Mix Variables in Technology Product Markets." *Marketing Science*, 25(5) (June 2006): 440; and Naresh K. Malhotra, "The Use of Linear Logit Models in Marketing Research," *Journal of Marketing Research* (February 1983): 20–31.

16. "2005 Global Citizenship Report," www.hp.com/hpinfo/globalcitizenship/gcreport/index.html; and Charlotte Klopp and John Sterlicchi, "Customer Satisfaction Just Catching On in Europe," *Marketing News* (May 28, 1990).

17. Madhav N. Segal and Ralph W. Giacobbe, "Ethical Issues in Australian Marketing Research Services: An Empirical Investigation," *Services Marketing Quarterly* (Binghamton), 28(3) (2007): 33; Charles H. Schwepker, Jr., and Michael D. Hartline, "Managing the Ethical Climate of Customer-Contact Service Employees," *Journal of Service Research,* 7(4) (May 2005): 377–396; Roger J. Volkema, "Demographic, Cultural, and Economic Predictors of Perceived Ethicality of Negotiation Behavior: A Nine-Country Analysis," *Journal of Business Research* 57(1) (January 2004): 69; and Paul R. Murphy, Jonathan E. Smith, and James M. Daley, "Executive Attitudes, Organizational Size and Ethical Issues: Perspectives on a Service Industry," *Journal of Business Ethics,* 11 (1992): 11–19.

Chapter 19

1. Charles Blankson, Julian Ming-Sung Cheng; and Nancy Spears, "Determinants of Banks Selection in USA, Taiwan and Ghana," *International Journal of Bank Marketing,* 25(7) (2007): 469–489; Barbara R. Lewis and Sotiris Spyrakopoulos, "Service Failures and Recovery in Retail Banking: The Customers' Perspective,"

The International Journal of Bank Marketing, 19(1) (2001): 37–48; and James M. Sinukula and Leanna Lawtor, "Positioning in the Financial Services Industry: A Look at the Decomposition of Image," in Jon M. Hawes and George B. Glisan, eds., *Developments in Marketing Science,* vol. 10 (Akron, OH: Academy of Marketing Science, 1987): 439–442.

2. For a detailed discussion of factor analysis, see John C. Loehlin, *Latent Variable Models: An Introduction to Factor, Path, and Structural Equation Analysis* (Mahwah, NJ: Lawrence Erlbaum Associates, 2004); Jacques Tacq, *Multivariate Analysis Techniques in Social Science Research* (Thousand Oaks, CA: Sage Publications, 1997); George H. Dunteman, *Principal Components Analysis* (Newbury Park, CA: Sage Publications, 1989); Marcel Croon, *Methods for Correlational Research: Factor Analysis, Path Analysis, and Structural Equation Modeling* (Harlow: Pearson Custom Publishing, 2008); and Robert Cudeck and Robert C. MacCallum, *Factor Analysis at 100: Historical Developments and Future Directions* (Mahwah, NJ: Lawrence Erlbaum Associates, 2007).

3. See, Robert Cudeck and Robert C. MacCallum, *Factor Analysis at 100: Historical Developments and Future Directions* (Mahwah, NJ: Lawrence Erlbaum Associates, 2007); Marjorie A. Pett, Nancy Lackey, and John Sullivan, *Making Sense of Factor Analysis: The Use of Factor Analysis for Instrument Development in Health Care Research* (Thousand Oaks, CA: Sage Publications, 2006); A. Adam Ding, "Prediction Intervals, Factor Analysis Models, and High-Dimensional Empirical Linear Prediction," *Journal of the American Statistical Association,* 94(446) (June 1999): 446–455; and W. R. Dillon and M. Goldstein, *Multivariate Analysis: Methods and Applications* (New York: John Wiley & Sons, 1984): 23–99.

4. For recent applications of factor analysis, see Leo Huang, "Exploring the Determinants of E-Loyalty Among Travel Agencies," *Service Industries Journal,* 28(2) (March 2008): 239–254; Rajdeep Grewal, Raj Mehta, and Frank R. Kardes, "The Timing of Repeat Purchases of Consumer Durable Goods: The Role of Functional Bases of Consumer Attitudes," *Journal of Marketing Research,* 41 (February 2004), 101–115; and Yuhong Wu, Sridhar Balasubramanian, and Vijay Mahajan, "When Is a Preannounced New Product Likely to Be Delayed?" *Journal of Marketing,* 68 (April 2004), 101–113.

5. Dennis Child, *The Essentials of Factor Analysis,* 3rd ed. (New York: Continuum, 2006); David J. Bartholomew and Martin Knott, *Latent Variable Models and Factor Analysis* (London: Edward Arnold Publishers, 1999); Joseph F. Hair, Jr., William C. Black, Barry J. Babin, and Ralph E. Anderson, *Multivariate Data Analysis with Readings,* 7th ed. (Upper Saddle River, NJ: Prentice Hall, 2010); and Alexander Basilevsky, *Statistical Factor Analysis & Related Methods: Theory & Applications* (New York: John Wiley & Sons, 1994).

6. Factor analysis is influenced by the relative size of the correlations rather than the absolute size.

7. See, Jianan Wu, Wayne DeSarbo, Pu-Ju Chen, and Yao-Yi Fu, "A Latent Structure Factor Analytic Approach for Customer Satisfaction Measurement," *Marketing Letters,* 17(3) (July 2006): 221–237; Pamela W. Henderson, Joan L. Giese, and Joseph Cote, "Impression Management Using Typeface Design," *Journal of Marketing,* 68 (October 2004), 60–72; Wagner A. Kamakura and Michel Wedel, "Factor Analysis and Missing Data," *Journal of Marketing Research,* 37(4) (November 2000): 490–498; Sangit Chatterjee, Linda Jamieson, and Frederick Wiseman, "Identifying Most Influential Observations in Factor Analysis," *Marketing Science* (Spring 1991): 145–160; and Frank Acito and Ronald D. Anderson, "A Monté Carlo Comparison of Factor Analytic Methods," *Journal of Marketing Research,* 17 (May 1980): 228–236.

8. Other methods of orthogonal rotation are also available. The quartimax method minimizes the number of factors needed to explain a variable. The equamax method is a combination of varimax and quartimax.

9. Haesun Park, "US Retailers' Cooperation with Manufacturer Promotional Support," *Journal of Fashion Marketing and Management,* 8(4) (2004): 412–424; Jorge M. Silva-Risso, Randolph E. Bucklin, and Donald G. Morrison, "A Decision Support System for Planning Manufacturers' Sales Promotion Calendars," *Marketing Science,* 18(3) (1999): 274; and Ronald C. Curhan and Robert J. Kopp, "Obtaining Retailer Support for Trade Deals: Key Success Factors," *Journal of Advertising Research* (December 1987–January 1988): 51–60.

10. www.att.com, accessed October 22, 2008; and Peter Tat, William A. Cunningham III, and Emin Babakus, "Consumer Perceptions of Rebates," *Journal of Advertising Research* (August/September 1988): 45–50.

11. "New Volkswagen Beetle," www.motortrend.com/new_cars/04/volkswagen/beetle/index.html, accessed October 21, 2008; Lillie Guyer, "Fitting in at VW: Try 'Raumwunder,' " *Advertising Age,* 77(16) (April 2006): S-8(2); Don Hammonds, "Volkswagen's New Beetle Acquits Itself Well in Sporting World," *Knight Ridder Tribune Business News* (July 23, 2004): 1; and "Return of the Beetle," *The Economist,* 346(8050) (January 10, 1998).

12. Terri Rittenburg, Sean Valentine, and James Faircloth, "An Ethical Decision-Making Framework for Competitor Intelligence Gathering," *Journal of Business Ethics,* 70(3) (February 2007): 235–245; Erin Stout, "Are Your Salespeople Ripping You Off?" *Sales and Marketing Management,* 153(2) (February 2001): 56–62; David J. Fritzsche, "Ethical Climates and the Ethical Dimension of Decision Making," *Journal of Business Ethics,* 24(2) (March 2000): 125–140; and Ishmael P. Akaah and Edward A. Riordan, "The Incidence of Unethical Practices in Marketing Research: An Empirical Investigation," *Journal of the Academy of Marketing Science,* 18(1990): 143–152.

13. www.tiffany.com, accessed January 7, 2009; "Retail Brief: Tiffany & Co.," *Wall Street Journal,* Eastern Edition (May 15, 2003): D.4; and D. E. LeGer, "Tiffany & Co. Offers Homier Look at Miami-Area Store," *Knight Ridder Tribune Business News* (Washington) (April 24, 2003), p. 1.

Chapter 20

1. Roger Slavens, "Haagen-Dazs Tastes Success with Creme de la Creme Campaign," *B to B,* 92(1) (January 2007): 23; Sam Solley, "Haagen-Dazs," *Marketing* (June 16, 2004): 22; Emma Reynolds, "Is Haagen-Dazs Shrewd to Drop Its Sexy Image?" *Marketing* (September 6, 2001): 17; Liz Stuart, "Haagen-Dazs Aims to Scoop a Larger Share," *Marketing Week,* 19(46/2) (February 21, 1997): 26; and Dwight J. Shelton, "Birds of a Geodemographic Feather Flock Together," *Marketing News* (August 28, 1987): 13.

2. For recent applications of cluster analysis, see Francesca Bassi, "Latent Class Factor Models for Market Segmentation: An Application to Pharmaceuticals," *Statistical Methods and Applications,* 16(2) (January 2007): 279–287; Charla Mathwick and Edward Rigdon, "Play, Flow, and the Online Search Experience," *Journal of Consumer Research,* 31 (September 2004): 324–332; and Maureen Morrin, Jacob Jacoby, Gita Venkataramani Johar, Xin He, Alfred Kuss, and David Mazursky, "Taking Stock of Stockbrokers: Exploring Momentum Versus Contrarian Investor Strategies and Profiles," *Journal of Consumer Research,* 29 (September 2002), 188–198.

3. Overlapping clustering methods that permit an object to be grouped into more than one cluster are also available. See, Bruce Curry, Fiona Davies, Martin Evans, Luiz Moutinho, and Paul Phillips, "The Kohonen Self-Organising Map as an Alternative to Cluster Analysis: An Application to Direct Marketing," *International Journal of Market Research,* 45(2) (February 2003): 191–211; and Anil Chaturvedi, J. Douglass Carroll, Paul E. Green, and John A. Rotondo, "A Feature-Based Approach to Market Segmentation via Overlapping K-Centroids Clustering," *Journal of Marketing Research,* 34 (August 1997): 370–377.

4. Excellent discussions on the various aspects of cluster analysis may be found in János Abonyi and Balázs Feil, *Cluster Analysis for Data Mining and System Identification* (Basel: Birkhäuser, 2007); Leonard Kaufman and Peter J. Rousseeuw, *Finding Groups in Data: An Introduction to Cluster Analysis* (Hoboken, NJ: John Wiley & Sons, 2005); Brian S. Everitt, Sabine Landau, and Morven Leese, *Cluster*

Analysis, 4th ed. (Oxford, UK: Oxford University Press, 2001); and H. Charles Romsburg, *Cluster Analysis for Researchers* (Melbourne: Lulu.com, 2004).

5. Jafar Ali, "Micro-Market Segmentation Using a Neural Network Model Approach," *Journal of International Consumer Marketing* (2001): 7; Vicki Douglas, "Questionnaires Too Long? Try Variable Clustering," *Marketing News,* 29(5) (February 27, 1995): 38; and Girish Punj and David Stewart, "Cluster Analysis in Marketing Research: Review and Suggestions for Application," *Journal of Marketing Research,* 20 (May 1983): 134–148.

6. For the use of cluster analysis for segmentation, see Angela Brandt, *Cluster Analysis for Market Segmentation* (Ottawa: Library and Archives Canada, 2006); Arthur W. Allaway, Richard M. Gooner, David Berkowitz, and Lenita Davis, "Deriving and Exploring Behavior Segments Within a Retail Loyalty Card Program," *European Journal of Marketing,* 40(11/12) (2006): 1317–1339; George Arimond, "A Clustering Method for Categorical Data in Tourism Market Segmentation Research," *Journal of Travel Research,* 39(4) (May 2001): 391–397; William D. Neal, "Advances in Market Segmentation," *Marketing Research* (Spring 2001): 14– 18; and Mark Peterson and Naresh K. Malhotra, "A Global View of Quality of Life: Segmentation Analysis of 165 Countries," *International Marketing Review,* 17(1) (2000): 56–73.

7. Kenneth F. Hyde, "Contemporary Information Search Strategies of Destination-Naive International Vacationers," *Journal of Travel & Tourism Marketing,* 21(2/3) (2006): 63–76; Tom J. Brown, Hailin Qu, and Bongkosh Ngamsom Rittichainuwat, "Thailand's International Travel Image: Mostly Favorable," *Cornell Hotel and Restaurant Administration Quarterly,* 42(2) (April 2001): 85–95; Chul-Min Mo, Mark E. Havitz, and Dennis R. Howard, "Segmenting Travel Markets with the International Tourism Role (ITR) Scale," *Journal of Travel Research,* 33(1) (Summer 1994): 24–31; and George P. Moschis and Daniel C. Bello, "Decision-Making Patterns Among International Vacationers: A Cross-Cultural Perspective," *Psychology & Marketing* (Spring 1987): 75–89.

8. Petrua C. Caragea and Richard L. Smith, "Asymptotic Properties of Computationally Efficient Alternative Estimators for a Class of Multivariate Normal Models," *Journal of Multivariate Analysis,* 98(104) (August 2007): 1417–1440; Rajan Sambandam, "Cluster Analysis Gets Complicated," *Marketing Research,* 15(1) (2003): 16–21; and Brian S. Everitt, Sabine Landau, and Morven Leese, *Cluster Analysis,* 4th ed. (Oxford, UK: Oxford University Press, 2001).

9. For a detailed discussion on the different measures of similarity and formulas for computing them, see Eric T. Bradlow, "Subscale Distance and Item Clustering Effects in Self-Administered Surveys: A New Metric," *Journal of Marketing Research* (May 2001): 254–261; Victor Chepoi and Feodor Dragan, "Computing a Median Point of a Simple Rectilinear Polygon," *Information Processing Letters,* 49(6) (March 22, 1994): 281–285; and H. Charles Romsburg, *Cluster Analysis for Researchers* (Melbourne: Krieger Publishing, 1990).

10. For further discussion of the issues involved in standardization, see S. Dolnicar, "A Review of Unquestioned Standards in Using Cluster Analysis for Data-Driven Market Segmentation," http://ro.uow.edu.au/cgi/viewcontent.cgi?article=1286&context=commpapers, accessed April 20, 2008; and H. Charles Romsburg, *Cluster Analysis for Researchers* (Melbourne: Krieger Publishing, 1990).

11. Brian Everitt, Sabine Landau, and Morven Leese, *Cluster Analysis,* 4th ed. (Oxford, UK: Oxford University Press, 2001); and G. Milligan, "An Examination of the Effect of Six Types of Error Perturbation on Fifteen Clustering Algorithms," *Psychometrika,* 45 (September 1980): 325–342.

12. Brian Everitt, Sabine Landau, and Morven Leese, *Cluster Analysis,* 4th ed. (Oxford, UK: Oxford University Press, 2001).

13. For a formal discussion of reliability, validity, and significance testing in cluster analysis, see Stuart J. Barnes, Hans H. Bauer, Marcus M. Neumann, and Frank Huber, "Segmenting Cyberspace: A Customer Typology for the Internet," *European Journal of Marketing,* 41(1/2)

(2007): 71–93; Paul Bottomley and Agnes Nairn, "Blinded by Science: The Managerial Consequences of Inadequately Validated Cluster Analysis Solutions," *International Journal of Market Research,* 46(2) (2004): 171–187; Michael J. Brusco, J. Dennis Cradit, and Stephanie Stahl, "A Simulated Annealing Heuristic for a Bicriterion Partitioning Problem in Market Segmentation," *Journal of Marketing Research,* 39(1) (February 2002): 99–109; Hui-Min Chen, "Using Clustering Techniques to Detect Usage Patterns in a Web-Based Information System," *Journal of the American Society for Information Science and Technology,* 52(11) (September 2001): 888; S. Dibbs and P. Stern, "Questioning the Reliability of Market Segmentation Techniques," *Omega,* 23(6) (December 1995): 625–636; G. Ray Funkhouser, "A Note on the Reliability of Certain Clustering Algorithms," *Journal of Marketing Research,* 30 (February 1983): 99–102; T. D. Klastorin, "Assessing Cluster Analysis Results," *Journal of Marketing Research,* 20 (February 1983): 92–98; and S. J. Arnold, "A Test for Clusters," *Journal of Marketing Research,* 16 (November 1979): 545–551.

14. Finfacts Team, "European Investment Monitor: UK Leads in Foreign Direct Investment Projects in 2007; Ireland Had 80 Projects Compared with 123 for 10th Ranking Netherlands," (June 5, 2008), www.finfacts.com/irishfinancenews/article_1013823.shtml, accessed October 22, 2008; John Saunders and Rosalind H. Forrester, "Capturing Learning and Applying Knowledge: An Investigation of the Use of Innovation Teams in Japanese and American Automotive Firms," *Journal of Business Research,* 47(1) (January 2000): 35; Peter Doyle, John Saunders, and Veronica Wong, "International Marketing Strategies and Organizations: A Study of U.S., Japanese, and British Competitors," in Paul Bloom, Russ Winer, Harold H. Kassarjian, Debra L. Scammon, Bart Weitz, Robert E. Spekman, Vijay Mahajan, and Michael Levy, eds., *Enhancing Knowledge Development in Marketing,* Series No. 55 (Chicago: American Marketing Association, 1989): 100–104.

15. George P. Moschis, Danny N. Bellenger, and Carolyn Folkman Curasi, "What Influences the Mature Consumer?" *Marketing Health Services* (Chicago), 23(4) (January 2003): 16; Alfred Lin, Leslie A. Lenert, Mark A. Hlatky, Kathryn M. McDonald, et al., "Clustering and the Design of Preference-Assessment Surveys in Healthcare," *Health Services Research,* 34(5) (December 1999): 1033–1045; Edward J. Holohean, Jr., Steven M. Banks, and Blair A. Maddy, "System Impact and Methodological Issues in the Development of an Empirical Typology of Psychiatric Hospital Residents," *Journal of Mental Health Administration,* 22(2) (Spring 1995): 177–188; and Arch G. Woodside, Robert L. Nielsen, Fred Walters, and Gale D. Muller, "Preference Segmentation of Health Care Services: The Old-Fashioneds, Value Conscious, Affluents, and Professional Want-It-Alls," *Journal of Health Care Marketing* (June 1988): 14–24.

16. www.sony.com, accessed January 22, 2009; Rufus Jay, "Can Sony Regain Market Domination by Making Content Its King?" *Marketing Week,* 31(12) (March 2008): 6; Tobi Elkin, "Sony Marketing Aims at Lifestyle Segments," *Advertising Age* (Midwest Region Edition), 73(11) (March 18, 2002): 3, 72; Tobi Elkin, "Sony Ad Campaign Targets Boomers-Turned-Zoomers," *Advertising Age,* 73(42) (October 21, 2002): 6; and Steve Smith, "Upbeat Nishida Outlines New Plans for Sony," *TWICE,* 17(14) (June 17, 2002): 1, 26.

17. "Variable Selection in Clustering for Marketing Segmentation Using Genetic Algorithms," *Expert Systems with Applications: An International Journal Archive,* 34(1) (January 2008): 502–510; Stuart J. Barnes, Hans H. Bauer, Marcus M. Neumann, and Frank Huber, "Segmenting Cyberspace: A Customer Typology for the Internet," *European Journal of Marketing,* 41(1/2) (2007): 71–23; Brian Everitt, Sabine Landau, and Morven Leese, *Cluster Analysis,* 4th ed. (Oxford, UK: Oxford University Press, 2001); and Vicki Douglas, "Questionnaire Too Long? Try Variable Clustering," *Marketing News,* 29(5) (February 27, 1995): 38.

18. www.nikon.com, accessed October 22, 2008; Todd A. Mooradian, Kurt Matzler, and Lisa Szykman, "Empathetic Responses to Advertising: Testing a Network of Antecedents and Consequences,"

Marketing Letters (Boston), 19(2) (June 2008): 79–92; Thorolf Helgesen, "The Power of Advertising Myths and Realities," *Marketing & Research Today,* 24(2) (May 1996): 63–71; and David A. Aaker, Douglas M. Stayman, and Richard Vezina, "Identifying Feelings Elicited by Advertising," *Psychology & Marketing* (Spring 1988): 1–16.

19. Gergory M. Pickett, "The Impact of Product Type and Parity on the Informational Content of Advertising," *Journal of Marketing Theory and Practice,* 9(3) (Summer 2001): 32–43; Fred Zandpour and Katrin R. Harich, "Think and Feel Country Clusters: A New Approach to International Advertising Standardization," *International Journal of Advertising,* 15(4) (1996): 325–344; and Nancy Giges, "World's Product Parity Perception High," *Advertising Age* (June 20, 1988).

20. John P. Fraedrich, Jr., Neil C. Herndon, Jr., and Quey-Jen Yeh, "An Investigation of Moral Values and the Ethical Content of the Corporate Culture," *Journal of Business Ethics,* 30(1) (March 2001): 73–85; Ishmael P. Akaah, "Organizational Culture and Ethical Research Behavior," *Journal of the Academy of Marketing Science,* 21(1) (Winter 1993): 59–63; and R. E. Reidenbach and D. P. Robin, "Some Initial Steps Toward Improving the Measurement of Ethical Evaluations of Marketing Activities," *Journal of Business Ethics,* 7 (1988): 871–879.

Chapter 21

1. "SIC 2086 Bottled and Canned Soft Drinks and Carbonated Waters," www.encyclopedia.com/doc/fullarticle/1G2-3434500049.html, accessed October 23, 2008; Andrea Foote, "Another Wake Up Call," *Beverage World,* 124(3) (March 2005): 4; Dean Foust, "Things Go Better with . . . Juice; Coke's New CEO Will Have to Move Quickly to Catch Up in Noncarbonated Drink," *Business Week* (3883) (May 17, 2004): 81; and Paul E. Green, Frank J. Carmone, Jr., and Scott M. Smith, *Multidimensional Scaling: Concepts and Applications* (Boston: Allyn & Bacon, 1989): 16–17.

2. www.printronix.com, accessed January 9, 2009.

3. For a review of MDS studies in marketing research, see Wayne S. DeSarbo and Jianan Wu, "The Joint Spatial Representation of Multiple Variable Batteries Collected in Marketing Research," *Journal of Marketing Research,* 38(2) (May 2001): 244; Rick L. Andrews and Ajay K. Manrai, "MDS Maps for Product Attributes and Market Response: An Application to Scanner Panel Data," *Marketing Science,* 18(4) (1999): 584–604; Tammo H. A. Bijmolt and Michel Wedel, "A Comparison of Multidimensional Scaling Methods for Perceptual Mapping," *Journal of Marketing Research,* 36(2) (May 1999): 277–285; J. Douglass Carroll and Paul E. Green, "Psychometric Methods in Marketing Research: Part II, Multidimensional Scaling," *Journal of Marketing Research,* 34 (February 1997): 193–204; and Lee G. Cooper, "A Review of Multidimensional Scaling in Marketing Research," *Applied Psychological Measurement,* 7 (Fall 1983): 427–450.

4. An excellent discussion of the various aspects of MDS may be found in Ingwer Borg and Patrick J. F. Groenen, *Modern Multidimensional Scaling: Theory and Applications*, 2nd ed. (New York: Springer, 2005); Joseph B. Kruskal and Myron Wish, *Multidimensional Scaling* (Newbury Park, CA: Sage Publications, 2005); Paul E. Green and Yoram Wind, *Marketing Research and Modeling: Progress and Prospects: A Tribute to Paul E. Green* (New York: Springer, 2005); Iain Pardoe, "Multidimensional Scaling for Selecting Small Groups in College Courses," *The American Statistician,* 58(4) (November 2004): 317–321; Tammo H. A. Bijmolt, "A Comparison of Multidimensional Methods for Perceptual Mapping," *Journal of Marketing Research,* 36(2) (May 1999): 277–285; and Mark L. Davison, *Multidimensional Scaling* (Melbourne: Krieger Publishing, 1992).

5. The data are commonly treated as symmetric. For an asymmetric approach, see Wayne S. DeSarbo and Rajdeep Grewal, "An Alternative Efficient Representation of Demand-Based Competitive Asymmetry," *Strategic Management Journal,* 28(7) (July 2007): 755–766; and Wayne S. Desarbo and Ajay K. Manrai, "A New Multidimensional Scaling Methodology for the Analysis of Asymmetric Proximity Data in Marketing Research," *Marketing Science,* 11(1) (Winter 1992): 1–20. For other approaches to MDS data, see Kim Juvoung, "Incorporating

Context Effects in the Multidimensional Scaling of 'Pick Any/N' Choice Data," *International Journal of Research in Marketing,* 16(1) (February 1999): 35–55; and Tammo H. A. Bijmolt and Michel Wedel, "The Effects of Alternative Methods of Collecting Similarity Data for Multidimensional Scaling," *International Journal of Research in Marketing,* 12(4) (November 1995): 363–371.

6. See, Ingwer Borg and Patrick J. F. Groenen, *Modern Multidimensional Scaling: Theory and Applications*, 2nd ed. (New York: Springer, 2005); Trevor F. Cox and Michael A. Cox, *Multidimensional Scaling,* 2nd ed. (New York: Chapman & Hall, 2000); Tammo H. A. Bijmolt and Michel Wedel, "A Comparison of Multidimensional Scaling Methods for Perceptual Mapping," *Journal of Marketing Research,* 36(2) (1999): 277–285; Jan-Benedict SteenKamp and Hans C. M. van Trijp, "Task Experience and Validity in Perceptual Mapping: A Comparison of Two Consumer-Adaptive Techniques," *International Journal of Research in Marketing,* 13(3) (July 1996): 265–276; and Naresh K. Malhotra, Arun K. Jain, and Christian Pinson, "The Robustness of MDS Configurations in the Case of Incomplete Data," *Journal of Marketing Research,* 25 (February 1988): 95–102.

7. See, Trevor F. Cox and Michael A. Cox, *Multidimensional Scaling,* 2nd ed. (New York: Chapman & Hall, 2000). For an application, see Alain d'Astous and Lilia Boujbel, "Positioning Countries on Personality Dimensions: Scale Development and Implications for Country Marketing," *Journal of Business Research*, 60(3) (March 2007): 231–239.

8. Kruskal's stress is probably the most commonly used measure for lack of fit. See, Joseph B. Kruskal and Myron Wish, *Multidimensional Scaling* (Newbury Park, CA: Sage Publications, 2005). For the original article, see J. B. Kruskal, "Multidimensional Scaling by Optimizing Goodness of Fit to a Nonmetric Hypothesis," *Psychometrika,* 29 (March 1964): 1–27.

9. Wayne S. DeSarbo, "The Joint Spatial Representation of Multiple Variable Batteries Collected in Marketing Research," *Journal of Marketing Research,* 38(2) (May 2001): 244–253; J. Douglass Carroll and Paul E. Green, "Psychometric Methods in Marketing Research: Part II, Multidimensional Scaling," *Journal of Marketing Research,* 34 (February 1997): 193–204; and Naresh K. Malhotra, "Validity and Structural Reliability of Multidimensional Scaling," *Journal of Marketing Research,* 24 (May 1987): 164–173.

10. See, for example, Wayne S. DeSarbo and Rajdeep Grewal, "An Alternative Efficient Representation of Demand-Based Competitive Asymmetry," *Strategic Management Journal*, 28(7) (July 2007): 755–766; Jack K. H. Lee, K. Sudhir, and Joel H. Steckel, "A Multiple Ideal Point Model: Capturing Multiple Preference Effects from Within an Ideal Point Framework," *Journal of Marketing Research,* 39(1) (February 2002): 73–86; Wayne S. DeSarbo, M. R. Young, and Arvind Rangaswamy, "A Parametric Multidimensional Unfolding Procedure for Incomplete Nonmetric Preference/Choice Set Data Marketing Research," *Journal of Marketing Research,* 34(4) (November 1997): 499–516; and David B. Mackay, Robert F. Easley, and Joseph L. Zinnes, "A Single Ideal Point Model for Market Structure Analysis," *Journal of Marketing Research,* 32(4) (November 1995): 433–443. See also, George Balabanis and Adamantios Diamantopoulos, "Domestic Country Bias, Country-of-Origin Effects, and Consumer Ethnocentrism: A Multidimensional Unfolding Approach," *Journal of the Academy of Marketing Science*, 32 (Winter 2004): 80–95.

11. Paul Ferris, "All the Right Designs," *Marketing,* 109(15) (April 26, 2004): 3; Gaby Odekerken-Schroder, Hans Ouwersloot, Jos Lemmink, and Janjaap Semeijn, "Consumers' Trade-Off Between Relationship, Service Package and Price: An Empirical Study in the Car Industry," *European Journal of Marketing*, 37(1/2) (2003): 219–244; and Ian P. Murphy, "Downscale Luxury Cars Drive to the Heart of Baby Boomers," *Marketing News,* 30(21) (October 1997): 1, 19.

12. For recent applications of correspondence analysis, see Monica Gomez and Natalia Rubio Benito, "Manufacturer's Characteristics That Determine the Choice of Producing Store Brands," *European Journal of Marketing*, 42(1/2) (2008): 154–177; J. Jeffrey Inman, Venkatesh Shankar, and Rosellina Ferraro, "The Roles of Channel-Category

Associations and Geodemographics in Channel Patronage," *Journal of Marketing*, 68 (April 2004): 51–71; Naresh K. Malhotra and Betsy Charles, "Overcoming the Attribute Prespecification Bias in International Marketing Research by Using Nonattribute Based Correspondence Analysis," *International Marketing Review,* 19(1) (2002): 65–79; and Ken Reed, "The Use of Correspondence Analysis to Develop a Scale to Measure Workplace Morale from Multi-Level Data," *Social Indicators Research,* 57(3) (March 2002): 339. See also, David B. Whitlark and Scott M. Smith, "Using Correspondence Analysis to Map Relationships," *Marketing Research*, 13(3) (2001): 22–27.

13. See, David J. Bartholomew, *Analysis of Multivariate Social Science Data,* 2nd ed. (Boca Raton, FL: CRC Press, 2008); Jorg Blasius and Michael L. Greenacre, *Visualization of Categorical Data* (McLean, VA: Academic Press, 1998); Michael J. Greenacre, *Correspondence Analysis in Practice* (New York: Academic Press, 1993); Michael J. Greenacre, "The Carroll-Green-Schaffer Scaling in Correspondence Analysis: A Theoretical and Empirical Appraisal," *Journal of Marketing Research,* 26 (August 1989): 358–365; Michael J. Greenacre, *Theory and Applications of Correspondence Analysis* (New York: Academic Press, 1984); and Donna L. Hoffman and George R. Franke, "Correspondence Analysis: Graphical Representation of Categorical Data in Marketing Research," *Journal of Marketing Research,* 23 (August 1986): 213–227.

14. Ingwer Borg and Patrick J. F. Groenen, *Modern Multidimensional Scaling: Theory and Applications*, 2nd ed. (New York: Springer, 2005); Tammo H. A. Bijmolt and Michel Wedel, "A Comparison of Multidimensional Scaling Methods for Perceptual Mapping," *Journal of Marketing Research,* 36(2) (May 1999): 277–285; and John R. Hauser and Frank S. Koppelman, "Alternative Perceptual Mapping Techniques: Relative Accuracy and Usefulness," *Journal of Marketing Research,* 16 (November 1979): 495–506. Hauser and Koppelman conclude that factor analysis is superior to discriminant analysis. See also, Ingwer Borg and Patrick J. Groenen, *Modern Multidimensional Scaling Theory and Applications* (New York: Springer-Verlag, 1996).

15. For applications and issues in conjoint analysis, see Erik Mønness and Shirley Coleman, "Comparing a Survey and a Conjoint Study: The Future Vision of Water Intermediaries," *Journal of Applied Statistics*, 35(1) (January 2008): 19–30; Ulrich R. Orth and Keven Malkewitz, "Holistic Package Design and Consumer Brand Impressions," *Journal of Marketing*, 72(3) (July 2008): 64–81; Raghuram Iyengar, Kamel Jedidi, and Rajeev Kohli, "A Conjoint Approach to Multipart Pricing," *Journal of Marketing Research*, 45(2) (May 2008): 195–210; Michael Yee, Ely Dahan, John R. Hauser, and James Orlin, "Greedoid-Based Noncompensatory Inference," *Marketing Science*, 26(4) (July 2007): 532; Theodoros Evgeniou, Constantinos Boussios, and Giorgos Zacharia, "Generalized Robust Conjoint Estimation," *Marketing Science*, 24(3) (June 2005): 415–429; John R. Hauser and Olivier Toubia, "The Impact of Utility Balance and Endogeneity in Conjoint Analysis," *Marketing Science*, 24(3) (June 2005): 498–507; John C. Liechty, Duncan K. H. Fong, and Wayne S. DeSarbo, "Dynamic Models Incorporating Individual Heterogeneity: Utility Evolution in Conjoint Analysis," *Marketing Science*, 24(2) (March 2005): 285–293; Ming Ding, Rajdeep Grewal, and John Liechty, "Incentive-Aligned Conjoint Analysis," *Journal of Marketing Research*, 42 (February 2005): 67–82; Eric T. Bradlow, Ye Hu, and Teck-Hua Ho, "A Learning-Based Model for Imputing Missing Levels in Partial Conjoint Profiles," *Journal of Marketing Research*, 41 (November 2004): 369–381; Joseph W. Alba and Alan D. J. Cooke, "When Absence Begets Inference in Conjoint Analysis," *Journal of Marketing Research*, 41 (November 2004): 382–387; Eric T. Bradlow, Ye Hu, and Teck-Hua Ho, "Modeling Behavioral Regularities of Consumer Learning in Conjoint Analysis," *Journal of Marketing Research*, 41 (November 2004): 392–396; and Olivier Toubia, John R. Hauser, and Duncan I. Simester, "Polyhedral Methods for Adaptive Choice-Based Conjoint Analysis," *Journal of Marketing Research*, 41 (February 2004): 116–131.

16. Muriel Wilson-Jeanselme and Jonathan Reynolds, "The Advantages of Preference-Based Segmentation: An Investigation of Online Grocery Retailing," *Journal of Targeting, Measurement & Analysis for Marketing*, 14(4) (July 2006): 297–308; Marsha A. Dickson, Sharron J. Lennon, Catherine P. Montalto, Doug Shen, and Li Zhang, "Chinese Consumer Market Segments for Foreign Apparel Products," *The Journal of Consumer Marketing* (Santa Barbara), 21(4/5) (2004): 301; Marco Vriens, "Linking Attributes, Benefits, and Consumer Values," *Marketing Research*, 12(3) (Fall 2000): 4–10; and Judith Thomas Miller, James R. Ogden, and Craig A. Latshaw, "Using Trade-Off Analysis to Determine Value-Price Sensitivity of Custom Calling Features," *American Business Review,* 16(1) (January 1998): 8–13. For an overview of conjoint analysis in marketing, see J. Douglass Carroll and Paul E. Green, "Psychometric Methods in Marketing Research: Part I, Conjoint Analysis," *Journal of Marketing Research,* 32 (November 1995): 385–391; and Paul E. Green and V. Srinivasan, "Conjoint Analysis in Marketing: New Developments with Implications for Research and Practice," *Journal of Marketing,* 54 (October 1990): 3–19.

17. Reinhold Hatzinger and Josef A. Mazanec, "Measuring the Part Worth of the Mode of Transport in a Trip Package: An Extended Bradley Terry Model for Paired-Comparison Conjoint Data," *Journal of Business Research*, 60(12) (December 2007): 1290–1302; John C. Liechty, Duncan K. H. Fong, and Wayne S. DeSarbo, "Dynamic Models Incorporating Individual Heterogeneity: Utility Evolution in Conjoint Analysis," *Marketing Science*, 24(2) (March 2005): 285–293; Peter H. Bloch, Frederic F. Brunel, and Todd J. Arnold, "Individual Differences in the Centrality of Visual Product Aesthetics: Concept and Measurement," *Journal of Consumer Research*, 29 (March 2003): 551–565; Zsolt Sandor and Michel Wedel, "Designing Conjoint Choice Experiments Using Managers' Prior Beliefs," *Journal of Marketing Research*, 38(4) (November 2001): 430–444; S. R. Jaeger, D. Hedderley, and H. J. H. MacFie, "Methodological Issues in Conjoint Analysis: A Case Study," *European Journal of Marketing*, 35(11) (2001): 1217–1239; V. Srinivasan, "Predictive Validation of Multiattribute Choice Models," *Marketing Research*, 11(4) (Winter 1999/ Spring 2000): 28–34; Dick R. Wittink, Marco Vriens, and Wim Burhenne, "Commercial Uses of Conjoint Analysis in Europe: Results and Critical Reflections," *International Journal of Research in Marketing,* 11(1) (January 1994): 41–52; and Dick R. Wittink and Philippe Cattin, "Commercial Use of Conjoint Analysis: An Update," *Journal of Marketing,* 53 (July 1989): 91–97. For using conjoint analysis to measure price sensitivity, see "Multistage Conjoint Methods to Measure Price Sensitivity," *Sawtooth News,* 10 (Winter 1994/1995): 5–6.

18. These three attributes are a subset of attributes identified in the literature. See, Rune Lines and Jon M. Denstadli, "Information Overload in Conjoint Experiments," *International Journal of Market Research,* 46(3) (2004): 297–310.

19. C. Jansson, B. Bointon, and N. Marlow, "An Exploratory Conjoint Analysis Study of Consumers' Aesthetic Responses of Point-of-Purchase Materials," *The International Review of Retail, Distribution and Consumer Research*, 13(1) (January 2003): 59–76; Martin Wetzels, "Measuring Service Quality Trade-Offs in Asian Distribution Channels: A Multilayer Perspective," *Total Quality Management,* 11(3) (May 2000): 307–318; and Gerard H. Loosschilder, Edward Rosbergen, Marco Vriens, and Dick R. Wittink, "Pictorial Stimuli in Conjoint Analysis to Support Product Styling Decisions," *Journal of the Market Research Society,* 37 (January 1995): 17–34.

20. See, Klaus G. Grunert, Lars Esbjerg, Tino Bech-Larsen, Karen Bruns, and Hans Juhl, "Consumer Preferences for Retailer Brand Architectures: Results from a Conjoint Study," *International Journal of Retail & Distribution Management*, 34(8) (2006): 597–608; Olivier Toubia, John R. Hauser, and Duncan I. Simester, "Polyhedral Methods for Adaptive Choice-Based Conjoint Analysis," *Journal of Marketing Research*, 41(1) (February 2004): 116–131; Paul E. Green, Abba M. Krieger, and Yoram Wind, "Thirty Years of Conjoint Analysis: Reflections and Prospects," *Interfaces*, 31(3) (May/June 2001): S56; J. Douglass Carroll and Paul E. Green, "Psychometric Methods

in Marketing Research: Part I, Conjoint Analysis," *Journal of Marketing Research,* 32 (November 1995): 385–391; Warren F. Kuhfeld, Randall D. Tobias, and Mark Garratt, "Efficient Experimental Designs with Marketing Applications," *Journal of Marketing Research,* 31 (November 1994): 545–557; Sidney Addleman, "Orthogonal Main-Effect Plans for Asymmetrical Factorial Experiments," *Technometrics,* 4 (February 1962): 21–36; and Paul E. Green, "On the Design of Choice Experiments Involving Multifactor Alternatives," *Journal of Consumer Research,* 1 (September 1974): 61–68.

21. Raghuram Iyengar, Kamel Jedidi, and Rajeev Kohli, "A Conjoint Approach to Multipart Pricing," *Journal of Marketing Research,* 45(2) (May 2008): 195–210; Rinus Haaijer, Wagner Kamakura, and Michel Wedel, "Response Latencies in the Analysis of Conjoint Choice Experiments," *Journal of Marketing Research,* 37(3) (August 2000): 376–382; and J. Douglass Carroll and Paul E. Green, "Psychometric Methods in Marketing Research: Part I, Conjoint Analysis," *Journal of Marketing Research,* 32 (November 1995): 385–391.

22. R. Helm, M. Steiner, A. Scholl, and L. Manthey, "A Comparative Empirical Study on Common Methods for Measuring Preferences," *International Journal of Management and Decision Making,* 9(3) (2008): 242–265; Min Ding, "An Incentive-Aligned Mechanism for Conjoint Analysis," *Journal of Marketing Research* (Chicago), 44(2) (May 2007): 214; Zsolt Sandor and Michel Wedel, "Designing Conjoint Choice Experiments Using Managers' Prior Beliefs," *Journal of Marketing Research,* 38(4) (November 2001): 430–444; and Arun K. Jain, Franklin Acito, Naresh K. Malhotra, and Vijay Mahajan, "A Comparison of the Internal Validity of Alternative Parameter Estimation Methods in Decompositional Multiattribute Preference Models," *Journal of Marketing Research* (August 1979): 313–322.

23. Theodoros Evgeniou, Constantinos Boussios, and Giorgos Zacharia, "Generalized Robust Conjoint Estimation," *Marketing Science,* 24(3) (June 2005): 415–429; Neeraj Arora and Greg M. Allenby, "Measuring the Influence of Individual Preference Structures in Group Decision Making," *Journal of Marketing Research,* 36(4) (November 1999): 476–487; J. Douglass Carroll and Paul E. Green, "Psychometric Methods in Marketing Research: Part I, Conjoint Analysis," *Journal of Marketing Research,* 32 (November 1995): 385–391; and Frank J. Carmone and Paul E. Green, "Model Misspecification in Multiattribute Parameter Estimation," *Journal of Marketing Research,* 18 (February 1981): 87–93.

24. Dilip Chhajed and Kilsun Kim, "The Role of Inclination and Part Worth Differences Across Segments in Designing a Price-Discriminating Product Line," *International Journal of Research in Marketing,* 21(3) (September 2004): 313. For a recent application of conjoint analysis using OLS regression, see Rinus Haaijer, Wagner Kamakura, and Michel Wedel, "The 'No-Choice' Alternative to Conjoint Choice Experiments," *International Journal of Market Research,* 43(1) (First Quarter 2001): 93–106; Amy Ostrom and Dawn Iacobucci, "Consumer Trade-Offs and the Evaluation of Services," *Journal of Marketing,* 59 (January 1995): 17–28; and Peter J. Danaher, "Using Conjoint Analysis to Determine the Relative Importance of Service Attributes Measured in Customer Satisfaction Surveys," *Journal of Retailing,* 73(2) (Summer 1997): 235–260.

25. Min Ding, Rajdeep Grewal, and John Liechty, "Incentive-Aligned Conjoint Analysis," *Journal of Marketing Research* (Chicago), 42(1) (February 2005): 67; William L. Moore, "A Cross-Validity Comparison of Rating-Based and Choice-Based Conjoint Analysis Models," *International Journal of Research in Marketing,* 21(3) (2004): 299–312; Rick L. Andrews, Asim Ansari, and Imran S. Currim, "Hierarchical Bayes Versus Finite Mixture Conjoint Analysis: A Comparison of Fit, Prediction and Partworth Recovery," *Journal of Marketing Research,* 39(1) (February 2002): 87–98; J. Douglass Carroll and Paul E. Green, "Psychometric Methods in Marketing Research: Part I, Conjoint Analysis," *Journal of Marketing Research,* 32 (November 1995): 385–391; Naresh K. Malhotra, "Structural Reliability and Stability of Nonmetric Conjoint Analysis," *Journal of Marketing Research,* 19 (May 1982): 199–207; Thomas W. Leigh, David B. MacKay, and John O. Summers,

"Reliability and Validity of Conjoint Analysis and Self-Explicated Weights: A Comparison," *Journal of Marketing Research,* 21 (November 1984): 456–462; and Madhav N. Segal, "Reliability of Conjoint Analysis: Contrasting Data Collection Procedures," *Journal of Marketing Research,* 19 (February 1982): 139–143.

26. Rosanna Garcia, Paul Rummel, and John Hauser, "Validating Agent-Based Marketing Models Through Conjoint Analysis," *Journal of Business Research,* 60(8) (August 2007): 848–857; Michael Yee, Ely Dahan, John R. Hauser, and James Orlin, "Greedoid-Based Noncompensatory Inference," *Marketing Science,* 26(4) (August 2007): 532–549; Jay Palmer, "The Best Notebook Computers," *Barron's,* 80(46) (November 13, 2000): V16–V17; William L. Moore, "Using Conjoint Analysis to Help Design Product Platforms," *The Journal of Product Innovation Management,* 16(1) (January 1999): 27–39; and Del I. Hawkins, Roger J. Best, and Kenneth A. Coney, *Consumer Behavior Implications for Marketing Strategy,* 7th ed. (Boston: McGraw-Hill, 1998).

27. Frenkel Ter Hofstede, Youngchan Kim, and Michel Wedel, "Bayesian Prediction in Hybrid Conjoint Analysis," *Journal of Marketing Research,* 39(2) (May 2002): 253–261; Terry G. Vavra, Paul E. Green, and Abba M. Krieger, "Evaluating EZPass," *Marketing Research,* 11(2) (Summer 1999): 4–14; Clark Hu and Stephen J. Hiemstra, "Hybrid Conjoint Analysis as a Research Technique to Measure Meeting Planners' Preferences in Hotel Selection," *Journal of Travel Research,* 35(2) (Fall 1996): 62–69; Paul E. Green and Abba M. Krieger, "Individualized Hybrid Models for Conjoint Analysis," *Management Science,* 42(6) (June 1996): 850–867; and Paul E. Green, "Hybrid Models for Conjoint Analysis: An Expository Review," *Journal of Marketing Research,* 21 (May 1984): 155–169.

28. Jayson L. Lusk, Deacue Fields, and Walt Prevatt, "An Incentive Compatible Conjoint Ranking Mechanism," *American Journal of Agricultural Economics,* 90(2) (May 2008): 487–498; Anonymous, "Enhancing Adjuvants Give Drastic Advance to Fusilade," *Farmers Guardian* (July 18, 2003): 27; Kevin J. Boyle, "A Comparison of Conjoint Analysis Response Formats," *American Journal of Agricultural Economics,* 83(2) (May 2001): 441–454; Dale McDonald, "Industry Giants," *Farm Industry News,* 34(3) (February 2001): 6; and Diane Schneidman, "Research Method Designed to Determine Price for New Products, Line Extensions," *Marketing News* (October 23, 1987): 11.

29. Chris Wright, "Asian Automakers Add European Style to Boost Sales," *Automotive News,* 78(6100) (June 28, 2004): 28; Anonymous, "US's Newest Automaker Brings European Micro Car to the US," *Octane Week,* 19(43) (November 29, 2004): 1; and "Luxury Car Makers Assemble World View," *Corporate Location* (January/February 1997): 4.

30. Anonymous, "Lever Faberge Plans Major Softener Launch," *Marketing Week* (September 9, 2004): 5; Sukanya Jitpleecheep, "Thailand's Detergent Market Growth Rate Slows," *Knight Ridder Tribune Business News* (May 24, 2002): 1; Linda Grant, "Outmarketing P & G," *Fortune,* 137(1) (January 12, 1998): 150–152; and David Butler, "Thai Superconcentrates Foam," *Advertising Age* (January 18, 1993).

31. Katharina J. Srnka, "Culture's Role in Marketers' Ethical Decision Making: An Integrated Theoretical Framework," *Academy of Marketing Science Review* (2004): 1; Dane Peterson, Angela Rhoads, and Bobby C. Vaught, "Ethical Beliefs of Business Professionals: A Study of Gender, Age and External Factors," *Journal of Business Ethics,* 31(3) (June 2001): 1; and S. J. Vitell and F. N. Ho, "Ethical Decision Making in Marketing: A Synthesis and Evaluation of Scales Measuring the Various Components of Decision Making in Ethical Situations," *Journal of Business Ethics,* 16(7) (May 1997): 699–717.

Chapter 22

1. The help of Professor James Agarwal with the banking service application and Professor Sung Kim with the TAM application is gratefully acknowledged. The material presented in this chapter is drawn from several sources on SEM. Special mention is made of

K. A. Bollen, *Structural Equation Modeling with Latent Variables* (New York: John Wiley & Sons, 1989) and Joseph F. Hair, William C. Black, Barry J. Babin, Rolph E. Anderson, and Ronald L. Tatham, *Multivariate Data Analysis*, 6th ed. (Upper Saddle River, NJ: Prentice Hall, 2006).

2. Naresh K. Malhotra, Sung Kim, and James Agarwal, "Internet Users' Information Privacy Concerns (IUIPC): The Construct, the Scale, and a Causal Model," *Information Systems Research*, 15(4) (December 2004): 336–355.

3. Good sources for introduction to SEM include J. L. Arbuckle, *AMOS 6.0 User's Guide* (Chicago, IL: 2005); K. A. Bollen, *Structural Equations with Latent Variables* (New York: John Wiley & Sons, 1989); Rick Hoyle, *Structural Equation Modeling: Concepts, Issues and Applications* (Thousand Oaks, CA: Sage Publications, 1995); R. B. Kline, *Principles and Practice of Structural Equation Modeling*, 2nd ed. (New York: Guilford Press, 2005); and Donna Harrington, *Confirmatory Factor Analysis* (New York; Oxford University Press, 2008).

4. For a history of SEM, see W. T. Bielby and R. M. Hauser, "Structural Equation Models," *Annual Review of Sociology*, 3 (1977): 137–161; K. A. Bollen, *Structural Equations with Latent Variables* (New York: John Wiley & Sons, 1989); and R. J. Epstein, *A History of Econometrics* (Amsterdam: Elsevier, 1987).

5. R. A. Berk, "Causal Inference for Sociological Data," in N. J. Smelser, ed., *Handbook of Sociology* (Newbury Park, CA: Sage Publications, 1988).

6. J. C. Anderson and D. W. Gerbing, "Structural Equation Modeling in Practice: A Review and Recommended Two-Step Approach," *Psychological Bulletin,* 103(1988): 411–423.

7. Typically, we assume reflective measurement theory. This theory posits that latent constructs cause the observed variables, and the inability to fully explain the observed variables results in errors. Therefore, the arrows are drawn from the latent constructs to the observed variables. An alternative approach that is sometimes used is formative measurement theory, where the observed variables cause the construct. Formative constructs are not considered latent. Reflective measurement theory is commonly used in marketing and the social sciences and hence is the approach adopted here.

8. For more discussion, see R. Cudek, "Analysis of Correlation Matrices Using Covariance Structure Models," *Psychological Bulletin*, 2 (1989): 317–327.

9. MLE is the most widely used estimation approach and is the default option in most SEM programs. However, alternative methods such as weighted least squares (WLS), generalized least squares (GLS), and asymptotically distribution free (ADF) are also available.

10. Joseph F. Hair, William C. Black, Barry J. Babin, Rolph E. Anderson, and Ronald L. Tatham, *Multivariate Data Analysis*, 6th ed. (Upper Saddle River, NJ: Prentice Hall, 2006).

11. Donna Harrington, *Confirmatory Factor Analysis* (New York: Oxford University Press, 2008); D. L. Jackson, "Sample Size and Number of Parameter Estimates in Maximum Likelihood Confirmatory Factor Analysis: A Monte Carlo Investigation," *Structural Equation Modeling,* 8(2) (2001): 205–223; D. Kaplan, "Statistical Power in Structural Equation Modeling," in R. Hoyle, ed., *Structural Equation Modeling: Concepts, Issues, and Applications* (Thousand Oaks, CA: Sage Publications, 1995): 100–117; and L. T. Hu and P. M. Bentler, "Cutoff Criteria for Fit Indexes in Covariance Structure Analysis: Conventional Criteria Versus New Alternatives," *Structural Equation Modeling*, 6 (1999): 1–55.

12. L. Hu, and P. M. Bentler, "Fit Indices in Covariance Structure Modeling: Sensitivity to Underparameterized Model Misspecification," *Psychological Methods*, 3(4) (1998): 424–453; L. Hu and P. M. Bentler, "Cutoff Criteria for Fit Indexes in Covariance Structure Analysis: Conventional Criteria Versus New Alternatives," *Structural Equation Modeling*, 6(1) (1999): 1-55; H. W. Marsh, J. R. Balla, and R. P. McDonald, "Goodness of Fit Indexes in Confirmatory Factor Analysis: The Effect of Sample Size," *Psychological Bulletin*, 103 (1988): 391–410; H. W. Marsh, J. W. Balla, and K.Hau, "An Evaluation of Incremental Fit Indices: A Clarification of Mathematical and Empirical Properties," in G. A. Marcoulides and R. E. Schumacker, eds., *Advanced Structural Equation Modeling: Issues and Techniques* (Mahwah, NJ: Erlbaum, 1996): 315–353; J. Nevitt and G. R. Hancock, "Improving the Root Mean Squared Error of Approximation for Nonnormal Conditions in Structural Equation Modeling," *Journal of Experimental Education,* 68 (2000): 51–268; and H. W. Marsh and K-T Hau, "Assessing Goodness of Fit: Is Parsimony Always Desirable?" *Journal of Experimental Education*, 64 (1996): 364–390.

13. W. W. Chin, A. Gopal, and W. D. Salisbury, "Advancing the Theory of Adaptive Structuration: The Development of a Scale to Measure Faithfulness of Appropriation," *Information Systems Research*, 8(4) (1997): 342–367.

14. C. Fornell and D. F. Larcker, "Evaluating Structural Equation Models with Unobservable Variables and Measurement Error," *Journal of Marketing Research,* 18 (February 1981): 39–50.

15. R. C. MacCallum, M. Roznowski, and L. B. Necowitz, "Model Modifications in Covariance Structure Analysis: The Problem of Capitalization on Chance," *Psychological Bulletin*, 111 (1992) : 490–504.

16. R. C. MacCallum, M. W. Browne, and L. Cai, "Testing Differences Between Nested Covariance Structure Models: Power Analysis and Null Hypotheses," *Psychological Methods*, 11 (2006): 19–35.

17. A. Boomsma, "Reporting Analyses of Covariance Structures," *Structural Equation Modeling*, 7 (2000): 461–483; and R. P. McDonald and M-H Ho, "Principles and Practice in Reporting Structural Equation Analyses," *Psychological Methods*, 7 (2002): 64–82.

18. Timothy A. Brown, *Confirmatory Factor Analysis for Applied Research* (New York: Guilford Press, 2006); A. E. Hurley et al., "Exploratory and Confirmatory Factor Analysis: Guidelines, Issues, and Alternatives," *Journal of Organizational Behavior*, 18 (1997): 667–683.

19. F. D. Davis, R. P. Bagozzi, and P. R. Warshaw, "User Acceptance of Computer Technology: A Comparison of Two Theoretical Models," *Management Science*, 35 (August 1989): 982–1003; Sung Kim and Naresh K. Malhotra, "A Longitudinal Model of Continued IS Use: An Integrative View of Four Mechanisms Underlying Post-Adoption Phenomena," *Management Science,* 51(5) (May 2005): 741–755; and Naresh K. Malhotra, Sung Kim, and Ashutosh Patil, "Common Method Variance in IS Research: A Comparison of Alternative Approaches and a Reanalysis of Past Research," *Management Science,* (December 2006): 1865–1883.

20. A. Parasuraman, V. A. Zeithaml, and L. L. Berry "SERVQUAL: A Multiple Item Scale for Measuring Consumer Perceptions of Service Quality," *Journal of Retailing*, 64(1) (1988): 12–40.

21. Marcel Croon, *Methods for Correlational Research: Factor Analysis, Path Analysis, and Structural Equation Modeling* (Harlow: Pearson Custom Publishing, 2008); K. A. Bollen "Total, Direct, and Indirect Effects in Structural Equation Models," in C. C. Clogg, ed., *Sociological Methodology* (Washington, DC: American Sociological Association, 1987): 37–69; L. Kelm, "Path Analysis," in L. G. Grimm and P. R. Yarnold, eds., *Reading and Understanding Multivariate Statistics* (Washington, DC: American Psychological Association, 2000): 65–97; and John C. Loehlin, *Latent Variable Models: An Introduction to Factor, Path, and Structural Analysis,* 3rd ed. (Mahwah, NJ:. Lawrence Erlbaum Associates, 1998).

22. Kathryn T. Cort, David A. Griffith, and D. Steven White, "An Attribution Theory Approach for Understanding the Internationalization of Professional Service Firms," *International Marketing Review*, 24(1) (2007): 9–25.

23. Sarah Steenhaut and Patrick van Kenhove, "An Empirical Investigation of the Relationships Among a Consumer's Personal Values, Ethical Ideology and Ethical Beliefs," *Journal of Business Ethics,* 64(2006): 137–155.

24. R. B. Kline, "Software Programs for Structural Equation Modeling: Amos, EQS, and LISREL," *Journal of Psychoeducational Assessment*, 16 (1998): 302–323; B. M. Byrne, *Structural Equation Modeling with LISREL, PRELIS, and SIMPLIS: Basic Concepts,*

Applications and Programming (Mahwah, NJ: Larence Erlbaum Associates, 1998).

25. www.dietcoke.com and www.thecoca-colacompany.com, accessed January 7, 2009.

Chapter 23

1. Stephen Shaw, *Airline Marketing and Management* (Surrey, UK: Ashgate Publishing, Ltd., 2007); Christine Tatum, "United Airlines Banks on New Network, Customer Data to Fill More Seats," *Knight Ridder Tribune Business News* (April 1, 2002): 1; and Joseph Rydholm, "Surveying the Friendly Skies," *Marketing Research* (May 1996).

2. Kenneth Hein, "Marketers Use Hypnosis to Mine Deep Thoughts," *Adweek*, 49(10) (March 2008): 4; Gill Ereaut, Mike Imms, and Martin Callingham, *Qualitative Market Research: Principles & Practice*, 7 vols. (Thousand Oaks, CA: Sage Publications, 2002); Thomas L. Greenbaum, *The Handbook for Focus Group Research* (Thousand Oaks, CA: Sage Publications, 1997); and Thomas L. Greenbaum, "Using 'Ghosts' to Write Reports Hurts Viability of Focus Group," *Marketing News*, 27(19) (September 13, 1993): 25.

3. "Macy's Finds Perfect Fit with Information Builders Webfocus," *Worldwide Databases*, 18(4) (April 2006): 2; Anonymous, "Research Reports," *Barron's*, 82(14) (April 8, 2002): 30; Edward R. Tufte, *Visual Explanations: Images and Quantities, Evidence and Narrative* (Cheshire, CT: Graphic Press, 1997); and Arlene Fink, *How to Report on Surveys* (Thousand Oaks, CA: Sage Publications, 1995).

4. "What You Say," *Advertising Age*, 79(14) (April 2008): 4; Harry F. Wolcott, *Writing Up Qualitative Research*, 2nd ed. (Thousand Oaks, CA: Sage Publications, 2001); and S. H. Britt, "The Writing of Readable Research Reports," *Journal of Marketing Research* (May 1971): 265. See also, Simon Mort, *Professional Report Writing* (Brookfield, VT: Ashgate Publishing, 1995); and David I. Shair, "Report Writing," *HR Focus*, 71(2) (February 1994): 20.

5. "New International Aims for Young Readers with Quick Response Codes in News Stories," *Marketing Week*, 31(11) (March 2008): 13; George S. Low, "Factors Affecting the Use of Information in the Evaluation of Marketing Communications Productivity," *Academy of Marketing Science Journal*, 29(1) (Winter 2001): 70–88; and Ann Boland, "Got Report-O-Phobia? Follow These Simple Steps to Get Those Ideas onto Paper," *Chemical Engineering*, 103(3) (March 1996): 131–132.

6. Gabriel Tanase, "Real-Life Data Mart Processing," *Intelligent Enterprise*, 5(5) (March 8, 2002): 22–24; L. Deane Wilson, "Are Appraisal Reports Logical Fallacies?" *Appraisal Journal*, 64(2) (April 1996): 129–133; John Leach, "Seven Steps to Better Writing," *Planning*, 59(6) (June 1993): 26–27; and A. S. C. Ehrenberg, "The Problem of Numeracy," *American Statistician*, 35 (May 1981): 67–71.

7. Joshua Dean, "High-Powered Charts and Graphs," *Government Executive*, 34(1) (January 2002): 58; and Neal B. Kauder, "Pictures Worth a Thousand Words," *American Demographics* (Tools Supplement) (November/December 1996): 64–68.

8. Ann Michele Gutsche, "Visuals Make the Case," *Marketing News*, 35(20) (September 24, 2001): 21–22; and Sue Hinkin, "Charting Your Course to Effective Information Graphics," *Presentations*, 9(11) (November 1995): 28–32.

9. Michael Lee, "It's All in the Charts," *Malaysian Business* (February 1, 2002): 46; Mark T. Chen, "An Innovative Project Report," *Cost Engineering*, 38(4) (April 1996): 41–45; and Gene Zelazny, *Say It with Charts: The Executive's Guide to Visual Communication*, 3rd ed. (Burr Ridge, IL: Irwin Professional Publishing, 1996).

10. N. I. Fisher, "Graphical Assessment of Dependence: Is a Picture Worth 100 Tests?" *The American Statistician*, 55(3) (August 2001): 233–239; and Patricia Ramsey and Louis Kaufman, "Presenting Research Data: How to Make Weak Numbers Look Good," *Industrial Marketing*, 67 (March 1982): 66, 68, 70, 74.

11. Irvine Clarke III, Theresa B. Flaherty, and Michael Yankey, "Teaching the Visual Learner: The Use of Visual Summaries in Marketing Education." *Journal of Marketing Education*, 28(3) (December 2006): 218–226; Anonymous, "Flow Chart," *B-to-B*,

87(4) (April 8, 2002): 16; and Sharon Johnson and Michael Regan, "A New Use for an Old Tool," *Quality Progress*, 29(11) (November 1996): 144. For a recent example, see Naresh K. Malhotra and Daniel McCort, "An Information Processing Model of Consumer Behavior: Conceptualization, Framework and Propositions," *Asian Journal of Marketing*, 8(2) (2000–2001): 5–32.

12. Diana T. Kurylko, "Subaru Will Broaden Marketing Strategy," *Automotive News*, 79(6133) (February 2005): 57; and Terry Box, "Subaru's Expansion Route Includes Solo Dealerships, Sporty Vehicles," *Knight Ridder Tribune Business News* (August 16, 2003): 1.

13. Lori Desiderio, "At the Sales Presentation: Ask and Listen," *ID*, 38(4) (April 2002): 55; and Charles R. McConnell, "Speak Up: The Manager's Guide to Oral Presentations," *The Health Care Manager*, 18(3) (March 2000): 70–77.

14. Information provided by Roger L. Bacik, senior vice president, Atlanta.

15. Janet Moody, "Showing the Skilled Business Graduate: Expanding the Tool Kit," *Business Communication Quarterly*, 65(1) (March 2002): 21–36; David Byrne, *Interpreting Quantitative Data* (Thousand Oaks, CA: Sage Publications, 2002); and Lawrence F. Locke, Stephen Silverman, and Wannen W. Spirduso, *Reading and Understanding Research* (Thousand Oaks, CA: Sage Publications, 1998).

16. "Toyota Takes 'Intuitive' Approach to Camry Push in Australia, New Zealand," *Media: Asia's Media & Marketing Newspaper* (September 2006): 8; Richard Blackburn, "Toyota to Build Hybrid Camry in Australia," www.smh.com.au/news/motors/toyota-to-build-hybrid-camry-in-australia/2008/06/10/1212863606689.html, accessed October 27, 2008; Anonymous, "Toyota Remains Top Auto Seller in Australia," *Jiji Press English News Service* (May 5, 2004): 1; Anonymous, "Toyota Camry," *Consumer Reports*, 67(4) (April 2002): 67; Ross Garnaut, "Australian Cars in a Global Economy," *Australian Economic Review*, 30(4) (December 1997): 359–373; and Geoffrey Lee Martin, "Aussies Chicken Fries Ford," *Advertising Age* (January 18, 1993).

17. Milton Liebman, "Beyond Ethics: Companies Deal with Legal Attacks on Marketing Practices," *Medical Marketing and Media*, 37(2) (February 2002): 74–77; and Ralph W. Giacobbe, "A Comparative Analysis of Ethical Perceptions in Marketing Research: USA vs. Canada," *Journal of Business Ethics*, 27 (3) (October 2000): 229–245.

18. Mark Dolliver, "Ethics, or the Lack Thereof," *Adweek*, 43(14) (April 1, 2002): 29; and Andrew Crane, "Unpacking the Ethical Product," *Journal of Business Ethics*, 30(4) (April 2001): 361–373.

19. Michelle Inness, Julian Barling, Keith Rogers, and Nick Turner, "De-Marketing Tobacco Through Price Changes and Consumer Attempts to Quit Smoking," *Journal of Business Ethics* 77(4) (February 2008): 405; "Department of Justice (DOJ) Tobacco Lawsuit," www.altria.com/media/03_06_03_04_05_doj.asp, accessed October 27, 2008; Kelly Rayburn, "U.S. Case Against Tobacco to Open; Civil Racketeering Lawsuit Is the Biggest in History; Diverging from Other Suits," *The Wall Street Journal* (Eastern edition) (September 20, 2004): B.2; Gordon Fairclough, "Case on Children and Tobacco Ads Commences Today," *The Wall Street Journal* (April 22, 2002): B8; and S. Rapp, "Cigarettes: A Question of Ethics," *Marketing News* (November 5, 1992): 17.

Chapter 24

1. See, Martijn G. de Jong, Jan-Benedict E. M. Steenkamp, Jean-Paul Fox, and Hans Baumgartner, "Using Item Response Theory to Measure Extreme Response Style in Marketing Research: A Global Investigation." *Journal of Marketing Research*, 45(1) (February 2008): 104–105; Trevor Denton, "Indexes of Validity and Reliability for Cross-Societal Measures," *Cross-Cultural Research* (Thousand Oaks), 42(2) (May 2008): 118; Robert H. Ross, S. Allen Broyles, and Thaweephan Leingpibul, "Alternative Measures of Satisfaction in Cross-Cultural Settings," *The Journal of Product and Brand Management*, 17(2) (2008): 82; Naresh K. Malhotra, "Cross-Cultural Marketing Research in the Twenty-First Century," *International Marketing Review*, 18(3) (2001): 230–234; Susan P. Douglas,

"Exploring New Worlds: The Challenge of Global Marketing," *Journal of Marketing,* 65(1) (January 2001): 103–107; Naresh K. Malhotra, James Agarwal, and Mark Peterson, "Cross-Cultural Marketing Research: Methodological Issues and Guidelines," *International Marketing Review,* 13(5) (1996): 7–43; Naresh K. Malhotra, "Administration of Questionnaires for Collecting Quantitative Data in International Marketing Research," *Journal of Global Marketing,* 4(2) (1991): 63–92; and Naresh K. Malhotra, "Designing an International Marketing Research Course: Framework and Content," *Journal of Teaching in International Business,* 3 (1992): 1–27.

2. Anonymous, "Company Spotlight: IBM Global Services," *MarketWatch: Technology,* 7(4) (April 2008): 76–80; and Joseph Rydholm, "A Global Enterprise," *Quirk's Marketing Research Review* (November 1997).

3. Anonymous, "Best Western International to Celebrate April Fools' Day with 'Funny' Online Promotion for Race Fans," *Business Wire* (February 2008); Anonymous, "Best Western Grows to 4,000," *Arizona Business Gazette* (August 16, 2001): 2; Anonymous, "Best Western Quantifies Guest Quality Measures," *Lodging Hospitality,* 57(3) (March 1, 2001): 34; "Hotel Chains Capitalize on International Travel Market," *Hotels and Restaurants International* (June 1989): 81S–86S; and "Target Marketing Points to Worldwide Success," *Hotels and Restaurants International* (June 1989): 87S.

4. Jack Honomichl, "Honomichl Top 50: Annual Business Report on the Marketing Research Industry," *Marketing News* (June 15, 2005): H1–H59.

5. Jan-Benedict E. M. Steenkamp, "Moving Out of the U.S. Silo: A Call to Arms for Conducting International Marketing Research," *Journal of Marketing,* 69(4) (October 2005): 6; Dave Crick, "Small High-Technology Firms and International High-Technology Markets," *Journal of International Marketing,* 8(2) (2000): 63–85; Associated Press, "Regional Markets Are International Order of the Day," *Marketing News* (March 1, 1993): IR–10; and Thomas T. Semon, "Red Tape Is Chief Problem in Multinational Research," *Marketing News* (March 1, 1993): 7.

6. John F. Tanner, Jr., Christophe Fournier, Jorge A. Wise, Sandrine Hollet, and Juliet Poujol, "Executives' Perspectives of the Changing Role of the Sales Profession: Views from France, the United States, and Mexico," *The Journal of Business & Industrial Marketing,* 23(3) (2008): 193; Ren Bautista, Mario Callegaro, Jos Alberto Vera, and Francisco Abundi, "Studying Nonresponse in Mexican Exit Polls," *International Journal of Public Opinion Research,* 19(4) (January 2007): 492–503; and Doreen Hemlock, "Mexican Companies Establish Offices in United States Due to NAFTA," *Knight Ridder Tribune Business News* (January 24, 2002): 1.

7. See, Naresh K. Malhotra, "Cross-Cultural Marketing Research in the Twenty-First Century," *International Marketing Review,* 18(3) (2001): 230–234.

8. For a recent example of international marketing research, see Naresh K. Malhotra and Betsy Charles, "Overcoming the Attribute Prespecification Bias in International Marketing Research by Using Nonattribute Based Correspondence Analysis," *International Marketing Review,* 19(1) (2002): 65–79.

9. Naresh K. Malhotra and Daniel McCort, "A Cross-Cultural Comparison of Behavioral Intention Models: Theoretical Consideration and an Empirical Investigation," *International Marketing Review,* 18(3) (2001): 235–269.

10. Anonymous, "Universal Studios Japan Visitors Up 3.5 Pct in Summer Vacation," *Jiji Press English News Service* (September 1, 2004): 1; and Natasha Emmons, "Universal Studios Japan Employs Aid of Focus Groups for Cultural Ideas," *Amusement Business,* 113(12) (March 26, 2001): 28.

11. See, Alex Rialp Criado and Josep Rialp Criado, "International Marketing Research: Opportunities and Challenges in the 21st Century," *Advances in International Marketing,* (17) (2007): 1–13; and Dana James, "Dark Clouds Should Part for International Marketers," *Marketing News,* 36(1) (January 7, 2002): 9–10.

12. Peter M. Chisnall, "International Marketing Research," *International Journal of Market Research,* 49(1) (2007): 133–135; Ming-Huei Hsieh, "Measuring Global Brand Equity Using Cross-National Survey Data," *Journal of International Marketing,* 12(2) (2004): 28–57; Naresh K. Malhotra, "Cross-Cultural Marketing Research in the Twenty-First Century," *International Marketing Review,* 18(3) (2001): 230–234; Susan P. Douglas, "Exploring New Worlds: The Challenge of Global Marketing," *Journal of Marketing,* 65(1) (January 2001): 103–107; and Naresh K. Malhotra, James Agarwal, and Mark Peterson, "Cross-Cultural Marketing Research: Methodological Issues and Guidelines," *International Marketing Review,* 13(5) (1996): 7–43.

13. Robert F. Belli, "Event History Calendars and Question List Surveys: A Direct Comparison of Interviewing Methods," *Public Opinion Quarterly,* 65(1) (Spring 2001): 45–74; and Thomas T. Semon, "Select Local Talent When Conducting Research Abroad," *Marketing News,* 31(19) (September 15, 1997): 28.

14. Michael A. Einhorn, "International Telephony: A Review of the Literature," *Information Economics and Policy,* 14(1) (March 2002): 51; and Humphrey Taylor, "The Very Different Methods Used to Conduct Telephone Surveys of the Public," *Journal of the Market Research Society,* 39(3) (July 1997): 421–432.

15. "Portugal: Mobile Phones in Schools," (September 29, 2008) at www.comminit.com/en/node/278880/36, accessed October 28, 2008; Peter M. Chisnall, "International Market Research," *International Journal of Market Research,* 42(4) (Winter 2000): 495–497; Clive Fletcher, "Just How Effective Is a Telephone Interview," *People Management,* 3(13) (June 26, 1997): 49; and Minoo Farhangmehr and Paula Veiga, "The Changing Consumer in Portugal," *International Journal of Research in Marketing,* 12(5) (December 1995): 485–502.

16. Norman Lerner, "Latin America and Mexico: A Change in Focus," *Telecommunications,* 34(3) (March 2000): 51–54; Peter H. Wertheim and Dayse Abrantes, "Brazil: New Take on Telecom," *Data Communications,* 26(5) (April 1997): 42; and P. Pinheiro de Andrade, "Market Research in Brazil," *European Research* (August 1987): 188–197.

17. Brad Frevert, "Is Global Research Different?" *Marketing Research,* 12(1) (Spring 2000): 49–51; and Karen Fletcher, "Jump on the Omnibus," *Marketing* (June 15, 1995): 25–28.

18. Robert B. Young and Rajshekhar G. Javalgi, "International Marketing Research: A Global Project Management Perspective," *Business Horizons,* 50(2) (April 2007): 113–122; Anonymous, "Searching for the Pan-European Brand (Part 1 of 2)," *Funds International* (March 1, 1999): 8; and Naresh K. Malhotra, James Agarwal, and Mark Peterson, "Cross-Cultural Marketing Research: Methodological Issues and Guidelines," *International Marketing Review,* 13(5) (1996): 7–43.

19. www.interbrand.com, accessed January 18, 2006; Patricia Sellers, "The New Coke Faces Reality," *Fortune,* 150(11) (November 29, 2004): 44–45; Anonymous, "Coca-Cola Listed as One of 10 Most Respected Firms," *Businessworld* (January 23, 2002): 1; Jonathan Holburt, "Global Tastes, Local Trimmings," *Far Eastern Economic Review,* 160(1) (December 26, 1996–January 2, 1997): 24; and Julie Skur Hill, "Coke Tops in Americas," *Advertising Age* (November 12, 1990).

20. Ase Hedberg, "The Rise of the Technophile," *Marketing Week,* 23(49) (January 25, 2001): 40; and Peter Jones and John Polak, "Computer-Based Personal Interviewing: State-of-the-Art and Future Prospects," *Journal of the Market Research Society,* 35(3) (July 1993): 221–223.

21. Cihan Cobanoglu, "A Comparison of Mail, Fax, and Web-Based Survey Methods," *International Journal of Market Research,* 43(4) (Fourth Quarter 2001): 441–454; Paul Lewis, "Do Your Homework!" *Successful Meetings,* 46(3) (March 1997): 120–121; T. Vahvelainen, "Marketing Research in the Nordic Countries," *European Research* (April 1985): 76–79; and T. Vahvelainen, "Marketing Research in Finland," *European Research* (August 1987): 62–66.

22. Geoffrey A. Fowler, "WPP, Bates Firm to Focus on Asia," *The Wall Street Journal* (December 12, 2003): B2; Mark Peterson and Naresh

K. Malhotra, "A Global View of Quality of Life: Segmentation Analysis of 165 Countries," *International Marketing Review,* 17(1) (2000): 56–73; Lewis C. Winters, "International Psychographics," *Marketing Research: A Magazine of Management & Applications,* 4(3) (September 1992): 48–49; and "We Are the World," *American Demographics* (May 1990): 42–43.

23. Kai Arzheimer, "Research Note: The Effect of Material Incentives on Return Rate, Panel Attrition and Sample Composition of a Mail Panel Survey," *International Journal of Public Opinion Research,* 11(4) (Winter 1999): 368–377; Kevin J. Clancy, "Brand Confusion," *Harvard Business Review,* 80(3) (March 2002): 22; Jorge Zamora, "Management of Respondents' Motivation to Lower the Desertion Rates in Panels in Emerging Countries: The Case of Talca, Chile," *Marketing & Research Today,* 25(3) (August 1997): 191–198; and "TSMS and AGB Set Up Ad Effectiveness Panel," *Marketing Week,* 18(27) (September 22, 1995): 15.

24. www.Vovici.com/survey/news/studies/ace_study.html

25. Christina Giannakopoulou, George Siomkos, and Aikaterini Vassilikopoulou, "The Input of Psychology in Methodological Considerations of Cross Cultural Marketing Research," *European Journal of Scientific Research,* 20(2) (April 2008): 249–254; Subhas Sharma and Danny Weathers, "Assessing Generalizability of Scales Used in Cross-National Research," *International Journal of Research in Marketing,* 20(3) (2003): 287–295; Hans Baumgartner and Jan-Benedict E. M. Steenkamp, "Response Styles in Marketing Research: A Cross-National Investigation," *Journal of Marketing Research,* 38 (2) (2001): 143–146; Matthew B. Myers, "Academic Insights: An Application of Multiple-Group Causal Models in Assessing Cross-Cultural Measurement Equivalence," *Journal of International Marketing,* 8(4) (2000): 108–121; and Naresh K. Malhotra, James Agarwal, and Mark Peterson, "Cross-Cultural Marketing Research: Methodological Issues and Guidelines," *International Marketing Review,* 13(5) (1996): 7–43.

26. Trevor Denton, "Indexes of Validity and Reliability for Cross-Societal Measures," *Cross-Cultural Research,* 42(2) (May 2008): 118; Nancy Wong, Aric Rindfleisch, James E. Burroughs, Jan-Benedict E. M. Steenkamp, and William O. Bearden, "Do Reverse-Worded Items Confound Measures in Cross-Cultural Consumer Research? The Case of the Material Values Scale," *Journal of Consumer Research,* 30(1) (2003): 72–91; Bruce Keillor, Deborah Owens, and Charles Pettijohn, "A Cross-Cultural/Cross-National Study of Influencing Factors and Socially Desirable Response Biases," *International Journal of Market Research,* 43(1) (2001): 63–84; and Gael McDonald, "Cross-Cultural Methodological Issues in Ethical Research," *Journal of Business Ethics,* 27(1/2) (September 2000): 89–104.

27. Martijn G. de Jong, Jan-Benedict E. M. Steenkamp, Jean-Paul Fox, and Hans Baumgartner, "Using Item Response Theory to Measure Extreme Response Style in Marketing Research: A Global Investigation," *Journal of Marketing Research,* 45(1) (February 2008): 104–105; Orlando Behling and Kenneth S. Law, *Translating Questionnaires and Other Research Instruments: Problems and Solutions* (Thousand Oaks, CA: Sage Publications, 2000); Naresh K. Malhotra and Daniel McCort, "A Cross-Cultural Comparison of Behavioral Intention Models: Theoretical Consideration and an Empirical Investigation," *International Marketing Review,* 18(3) (2001): 235–269; and Naresh K. Malhotra, James Agarwal, and Mark Peterson, "Cross-Cultural Marketing Research: Methodological Issues and Guidelines," *International Marketing Review,* 13(5) (1996): 7–43.

28. Jenny S. Y. Lee, Oliver H. M. Yau, Raymond P. M. Chow, Leo Y. M. Sin, and Alan C. B. Tse, "Changing Roles and Values of Female Consumers in China," *Business Horizons,* 47(3) (May/June 2004): 17; Leo Yat-ming Sin and Oliver Hon-ming Yau, "Female Role Orientation and Consumption Values: Some Evidence from Mainland China," *Journal of International Consumer Marketing,* 13(2) (2001): 49–75; John Shannon, "National Values Can Be Exported," *Marketing Week,* 19(45) (February 7, 1997): 20; and S. C. Grunert and G. Scherhorn, "Consumer Values in West Germany: Underlying Dimensions and Cross-Cultural Comparison with North America," *Journal of Business Research,* 20 (1990): 97–107. See also, H. C. Triandis, *Culture and Social Behavior* (New York: McGraw-Hill, 1994).

29. Jonathan Armstrong, "Privacy in Europe: The New Agenda," *Journal of Internet Law,* 8(5) (November 2004): 3–7; Heather R. Goldstein, "International Personal Data Safe Harbor Program Launched," *Intellectual Property & Technology Law Journal,* 13(4) (April 2001): 24–25; Rebecca Sykes, "Privacy Debates Get More Complicated Overseas," *InfoWorld,* 19(44) (November 3, 1997): 111; and Simon Chadwick, "Data Privacy Legislation All the Rage in Europe," *Marketing News,* 27(17) (August 16, 1993): A7.

Photo Credits

Chapter 1, 2 NKM Photo, Naresh K. Malhotra; 4 Shutterstock; 6 McDonalds Corp.; 24 AP Wide World Photos; 27 Samsonite Corporation; 31 kkgas/istockphoto.com

Chapter 2, 34 NKM Photo, Naresh K. Malhotra; 36 Harley-Davidson Motor Company; 45 National Fluid Milk Processor Promotion Board; 50 Jason Aron/Shutterstock; 58 Frank LaBua/Pearson Education/PH College; 64 kkgas/istockphoto.com

Chapter 3, 68 NKM Photo, Naresh K. Malhotra; 70 Shutterstock; 79 Shutterstock; 90 Demetrio Carrasco © Dorling Kindersley; 91 Shutterstock; 96 kkgas/istockphoto.com

Chapter 4, 98 NKM Photo, Naresh K. Malhotra; 99 Boston Market Corporation; 116 AP Wide World Photos; 118 AP Wide World Photos; 129 Rod Gonzalez; 134 kkgas/istockphoto.com

Chapter 5, 136 NKM Photo, Naresh K. Malhotra; 138 American Honda Motor Co. Inc.; 141 E & L Marketing Research; 155 Photos.com; 168 Christopher Lewis Cotrell/Ashley Fisher; 174 kkgas/istockphoto.com

Chapter 6, 176 NKM Photo, Naresh K. Malhotra; 177 Shutterstock; 181 Burke, Inc.; 183 E & L Marketing Research; 184 TouchScreen Solutions Pty. Ltd (incorporating TouchScreen Research) www.touchscreenresearch. com.au; 209 Emma Hockly; 214 kkgas/istockphoto.com

Chapter 7, 216 Lynd Bacon; 217 Kathy Ringrose/Pearson Education/PH College; 238 Frank LaBua/Pearson Education/ PH College; 242 Shutterstock; 246 kkgas/istockphoto.com

Chapter 8, 248 NKM Photo, Naresh K. Malhotra; 250 Paul Sakuma/AP Wide World Photos; 263 Northpoint/ Nissan North America, Inc.; 265 Dan Crosley; 270 kkgas/istockphoto.com

Chapter 9, 272 NKM Photo, Naresh K. Malhotra; 274 Shutterstock; 275 Copyright 2002 MSInteractive LLC; 293 Pearson Education/PH College; 298 kkgas/istockphoto. com; 298 Used with permission of eGO Vehicles, LLC

Chapter 10, 300 NKM Photo, Naresh K. Malhotra; 329 Shutterstock; 334 kkgas/istockphoto.com

Chapter 11, 336 NKM Photo, Naresh K. Malhotra; 338 U.S. Fish and Wildlife Service; 347 Shutterstock; 368 kkgas/istockphoto.com

Chapter 12, 370 Survey Sampling Inc.; 372 Shutterstock; 391 © Teri Stratford. All rights reserved; 397 kkgas/istockphoto.com

Chapter 13, 400 NKM Photo, Naresh K. Malhotra; 412X Pearson Education/PH College; 416 kkgas\istockphoto.com

Chapter 14, 418 NKM Photo, Naresh K. Malhotra; 438 Sergio Piumatti

Chapter 15, 448 NKM Photo, Naresh K. Malhotra; 450 © Jimmy Dorantes/Latin Focus.com; 482 Pearson Education/PH College

Chapter 16, 496 NKM Photo, Naresh K. Malhotra; 498 Shutterstock; 518 Shutterstock

Chapter 17, 528 NKM Photo, Naresh K. Malhotra; 530 Photo reprinted by permission of Retail Forward, Inc.; 556 Shutterstock

Chapter 18, 569 Corbis RF; 592 Boston Market Corporation

Chapter 19, 602 SDR Consulting; 603 Beaura Kathy Ringrose/Pearson Education/PH College; 622 Shutterstock

Chapter 20, 628 NKM Photo, Naresh K. Malhotra; 629 Beaura Kathy Ringrose/Kathy Ringrose; 646 Used by Permission of Sony Electronics Inc.

Chapter 21, 656 NKM Photo, Naresh K. Malhotra; 658 Frank LaBua/Pearson Education/PH College; 682 Kathy Ringrose

Chapter 22, 690 NKM Photo, Naresh K. Malhotra; 691 Shutterstock; 711 iStockPhoto

Chapter 23, 726 NKM Photo, Naresh K. Malhotra; 727 Shutterstock; 739 Shutterstock; 743 Toyota Motor Corporation—License and Trademark Dept.; 749 kkgas/istockphoto.com

Chapter 24, 752 Burke, Inc.; 754 Courtesy of International Business Machines Corporation. Unauthorized use not permitted; 759 Alamy Images; 767 Tony Reeves/www.movie-locations.com; 772 kkgas/istockphoto.com

Index

Subject Index

A

Absolute fit indices, 693, 699
Acquiescence bias (yea-saying), 316
Acronyms
  ANALYSIS, 688
  ANCOVA, 524
  ANOVA, 524
  CLUSTERING, 653
  C TABULATIONS, 491
  CULTURE, 769
  DEPTH, 171
  DESIGN, 93
  DISCRIMINANT, 599
  FACTOR, 626
  FOCUS GROUPS, 171
  FOUR, 267
  FREQUENCIES, 491
  GRAPHS, 747
  PRESENTATION, 747
  PRETEST, 331
  PROBLEM, 43, 62
  PROJECTIVE, 171
  QUESTIONAIRE, 331
  RATING, 295
  READING, 747
  REGRESSION, 565
  REPORT, 747
  REPRODUCE, 331
  RESEARCH, 29
  SAMPLE, 365
  SCALES, 267
  SCALING, 688
  SECOND, 132
  SEM, 724
  SIZE, 393
  STEP, 626
  TABLES, 747
  THREATS, 244
  TRAIN, 414
  VESTS, 414
Adjusted goodness-of-fit index (AGFI),
  699, 700
Adjusted R^2, 546
Advertising effectiveness, assessing, 659
Advertising evaluation surveys, 116–117
After-only design, 227
Agglomeration schedule, 632
Agglomerative clustering, 634, 636
Aggregate-level analysis, 665
Akaike Information Criterion (AIC),
  636, 644
Alternative-forms reliability, 287
Alternative hypothesis (H_1),
  457–458, 472
American Community Survey, 302
*American Marketing Association
  Bibliography Series,* 109
AMOS, 720–721
Analysis of covariance (ANCOVA),
  225–226, 499–500
  structures, 694, 716–718

Analysis of variance (ANOVA), 499–500
  assumptions in, 508
  F test, 516
  interpretation, issues in
    interactions, 513–515
    multiple comparisons, 516
    relative importance of factors,
      515–516
  n-way, 508–512
  repeated measures, 516–518
  software used in, 520
  See also One-way analysis of variance;
    SAS; SPSS
Analysis sample, 573
Analyst, 19, 20
*Annual Survey of Market Research
  Professionals,* 20
A posteriori contrasts, 516
A priori contrasts, 516
A priori determination, 611, 612
A priori knowledge, 663
Area sampling, 354
Art of Asking Questions, The (Payne), 303
ASCII text, 187
Assistant director of research, 20
Association techniques, 158
Assurance (ASSU), 692, 710, 712,
  714, 715
Asymmetric lambda, 469–470
Attitude scale construction, 659
Attitude toward service (ATT),
  714, 715
Attribute levels, 670
Audimeter, 199
Audit
  defined, 201
  described, 122
  pantry, 201
  problem, 38–39
  retailer and wholesale, 122–123
  services, 115, 122–123
Average linkage, 635
Average variance extracted (AVE), 693,
  702, 709
Awareness (AWA) in IUIPC, 706
Axioms, 51

B

Bachelor's degrees, 19
Back translation, 765
Backward elimination, 553
Badness-of-fit indices, 699–700
Balanced scales, 280–281
Bar charts, 735, 737
Bartlett's test of sphericity, 606
Bayesian approach, 341–342
Benefit segmentation, 631
Beta coefficient, 541
Beta weight, 541, 555
Between-people variation, 517
Between-subjects design, 516
Bibliographic databases, 112

Binary logit model
  concept map for, 598
  estimating the binary logit model,
    589–590
  formulate the problem, 589
  illustrative application of logistic
    regression, 591–592
  interpretation of coefficients
    and validation, 590
  model fit, 590
  significance testing, 590
  steps involved in, 588
Binomial test, 478
Bivariate correlation, 530
Bivariate cross-tabulation, 462–463
Bivariate regression, 536–545
  model, 536, 537, 539–540
  statistics associated with, 537
Bivariate regression, conducting, 537, 538
  assumptions, 545
  check prediction accuracy, 544–545
  concept map for, 564
  decomposition of total variation in, 542
  determine strength and significance
    of association, 542–544
  estimate standardized regression
    coefficient, 541
  estimate the parameters, 540–541
  formulate the regression model,
    539–540
  plot the scatter diagram, 537–539
  test for significance, 541–542
Branching questions, 319–320
Branded marketing research products, 18
Brand-switching matrix, 79, 80
Broad statement, 49
Budgeting and scheduling, 87–88
Business America, 110
Business Conditions Digest, 110
Business data, general, 108–110
Business Index, 109
Business Information Sources, 109
Business Periodical Index, 109
Business Statistics, 110
Buyer behavior, 45, 631
Buying power index (BPI), 126

C

Candor, in seven Cs, 40
Canonical correlation, 572
Canonical loadings, 578
Careers in marketing research, 19–21
  job descriptions, 20
  positions available in, 19
  preparing for, 20
  success in, 20–21
  trends in, 20
Cartoon tests, 161
Cases
  comprehensive cases with real data,
    808–820
  comprehensive critical thinking cases,
    780–787

Selected Formulas

Chapter 12: Sampling: Final and Initial Sample Size Determination

TABLE 12.1
Symbols for Population Parameters and Sample Statistics

Variable	Population	Sample
Mean	μ	$\overline{X}$
Proportion	π	p
Variance	σ^2	s^2
Standard deviation	σ	s
Size	N	n
Standard error of the mean	$\sigma_{\overline{x}}$	$s_{\overline{x}}$
Standard error of the proportion	σ_p	s_p
Standardized variate (z)	$\dfrac{X - \mu}{\sigma}$	$\dfrac{X - \overline{X}}{s}$
Coefficient of variation (CV)	$\dfrac{\sigma}{\mu}$	$\dfrac{s}{\overline{X}}$

Page 373: Mean:

$$\overline{X} = \frac{\left(\sum_{i=1}^{n} X_i\right)}{n}$$

Page 374: Standard error of the mean and the proportion:

Mean

$$\sigma_{\overline{x}} = \frac{\sigma}{\sqrt{n}}$$

Proportion

$$\sigma_p = \sqrt{\frac{\pi(1-\pi)}{n}}$$

Estimate of the population standard deviation:

$$s = \sqrt{\frac{\sum_{i=1}^{n}(X_i - \overline{X})^2}{n-1}} \quad \text{or} \quad s = \sqrt{\frac{\sum_{i=1}^{n} X_i^2 - \dfrac{\left(\sum_{i=1}^{n} X_i\right)^2}{n}}{n-1}}$$

In cases where σ is estimated by s, the standard error of the mean becomes

$$s_{\overline{x}} = \frac{s}{\sqrt{n}}$$

Estimate of the standard error of the proportion:

$$\text{est. } s_p = \sqrt{\frac{p(1-p)}{n}}$$

Computing z values:

$$z = \frac{\overline{X} - \mu}{\sigma_{\overline{x}}} \quad \text{and} \quad z = \frac{p - \pi}{\sigma_p}$$

Finite population correction factor:

$$\sqrt{\frac{N-n}{N-1}}$$

In this case

$$\sigma_{\overline{x}} = \frac{\sigma}{\sqrt{n}}\sqrt{\frac{N-n}{N-1}} \quad \text{and} \quad \sigma_p = \sqrt{\frac{\pi(1-\pi)}{n}}\sqrt{\frac{N-n}{N-1}}$$

Page 377: Determining the sample size using the formula for the standard deviation of the mean:

$$n = \frac{\sigma^2 z^2}{D^2}$$

Applying the finite population correction:

$$n_c = nN/(N + n - 1)$$

where

n = sample size without fpc
n_c = sample size with fpc

Page 378: Specifying precision in relative rather than absolute terms by specifying that the estimate be within plus or minus R percentage points of the mean:

$$D = R\mu$$

In these cases, the sample size may be determined by

$$n = \frac{\sigma^2 z^2}{D^2} = \frac{CV^2 z^2}{R^2}$$

where the coefficient of variation $CV = (\sigma/\mu)$ would have to be estimated.

Page 379: Determining the sample size using the formula for the standard error of the proportion:

$$n = \frac{\pi(1-\pi)z^2}{D^2}$$

Page 383: Considering completion rates when calculating final sample size:

In general, if there are c qualifying factors with an incidence of $Q_1, Q_2, Q_3, \ldots, Q_c$, each expressed as a proportion,

$$\text{Incidence rate} = Q_1 \times Q_2 \times Q_3 \ldots \times Q_c$$

$$\text{Initial sample size} = \frac{\text{Final sample size}}{\text{Incidence} \times \text{Completion rate}}$$

Response rates:

$$\text{Response Rate} = \frac{\text{Number of Completed Interviews}}{\text{Number of Eligible Units in Sample}}$$

Chapter 14: Data Preparation

Page 433: Standardization:

Standardized scores, z_i, may be obtained as:

$$z_i = (X_i - \overline{X})/s$$

Chapter 15: Frequency Distribution, Cross-Tabulation, and Hypothesis Testing

Page 455: Range:

$$\text{Range} = X_{\text{largest}} - X_{\text{smallest}}$$

Page 456: Coefficient of variation:

$$CV = \frac{s}{\overline{X}}$$

Page 467: Calculating the expected cell frequency under the null hypothesis:

$$f_e = \frac{n_r n_c}{n}$$

where

n_r = total number in the row
n_c = total number in the column
n = total sample size

Calculating the chi-square statistic:

$$\chi^2 = \sum_{\substack{\text{all} \\ \text{cells}}} \frac{(f_o - f_e)^2}{f_e}$$

where

f_o = observed frequency
f_e = expected frequency

Page 468: Phi coefficient:

$$\phi = \sqrt{\frac{\chi^2}{n}}$$

Page 469: Contingency coefficient:

$$C = \sqrt{\frac{\chi^2}{\chi^2 + n}}$$

Relationship between Cramer's V and the phi correlation coefficient for a table with r rows and c columns:

$$V = \sqrt{\frac{\phi^2}{\min(r-1), (c-1)}} \quad \text{or} \quad V = \sqrt{\frac{\chi^2/n}{\min(r-1), (c-1)}}$$

Page 473: Hypothesis test of means for two independent samples:

$$H_0: \mu_1 = \mu_2$$
$$H_1: \mu_1 \neq \mu_2$$

Computing a pooled variance estimate from two sample variances:

$$s^2 = \frac{\sum_{i=1}^{n_1}(X_{i1} - \bar{X}_1)^2 + \sum_{i=1}^{n_2}(X_{i2} - \bar{X}_2)^2}{n_1 + n_2 - 2} \quad \text{or}$$

$$s^2 = \frac{(n_1 - 1)s_1^2 + (n_2 - 1)s_2^2}{n_1 + n_2 - 2}$$

The standard deviation of the test statistic can be estimated as:

$$s_{\bar{X}_1 - \bar{X}_2} = \sqrt{s^2\left(\frac{1}{n_1} + \frac{1}{n_2}\right)}$$

The appropriate value of t can be calculated as:

$$t = \frac{(\bar{X}_1 - \bar{X}_2) - (\mu_1 - \mu_2)}{s_{\bar{X}_1 - \bar{X}_2}}$$

Page 474: Computing the F statistic:

$$F_{(n_1 - 1), (n_2 - 1)} = \frac{s_1^2}{s_2^2}$$

where

$$n_1 = \text{size of sample 1}$$
$$n_2 = \text{size of sample 2}$$
$$n_1 - 1 = \text{degrees of freedom for sample 1}$$
$$n_2 - 1 = \text{degrees of freedom for sample 2}$$
$$s_1^2 = \text{sample variance for sample 1}$$
$$s_2^2 = \text{sample variance for sample 2}$$

Page 475: Test statistic for two independent samples:

$$z = \frac{P_1 - P_2}{s_{P_1 - P_2}}$$

Standard error of the difference in the two proportions:

$$s_{P_1 - P_2} = \sqrt{p(1 - p)\left[\frac{1}{n_1} + \frac{1}{n_2}\right]}$$

where

$$p = \frac{n_1 P_1 + n_2 P_2}{n_1 + n_2}$$

Page 476: Paired samples t test:

$$H_0: \mu_D = 0$$
$$H_1: \mu_D \neq 0$$

$$t_{n-1} = \frac{\bar{D} - \mu_D}{\frac{s_D}{\sqrt{n}}}$$

where

$$\bar{D} = \frac{\sum_{i=1}^{n} D_i}{n}$$

$$s_D = \sqrt{\frac{\sum_{i=1}^{n}(D_i - \bar{D})^2}{n - 1}}$$

$$s_{\bar{D}} = \frac{s_D}{\sqrt{n}}$$

Page 478: Kolmogorov-Smirnov test statistic:

$$K = \text{Max} \, |A_i - O_i|$$

Chapter 16: Analysis of Variance and Covariance

Page 501: Total variation in Y, denoted by SS_y:

$$SS_y = SS_{between} + SS_{within}$$

Page 502: The total variation in Y may be decomposed as:

$$SS_y = SS_x + SS_{error}$$

where

$$SS_y = \sum_{i=1}^{N}(Y_i - \bar{Y})^2$$

$$SS_x = \sum_{j=1}^{c} n(\bar{Y}_j - \bar{Y})^2$$

$$SS_{error} = \sum_{j}^{c} \sum_{i}^{n}(Y_{ij} - \bar{Y}_j)^2$$

$$Y_i = \text{individual observation}$$
$$\bar{Y}_j = \text{mean for category } j$$
$$\bar{Y} = \text{mean over the whole sample, or grand mean}$$
$$Y_{ij} = i\text{th observation in the } j\text{th category}$$

Page 503: Measuring the strength of the effects of X on Y:

$$\eta^2 = \frac{SS_x}{SS_y} = \frac{(SS_y - SS_{error})}{SS_y}$$

Using the F statistic to test whether SS_x and SS_{error} come from the same source of variation:

$$F = \frac{SS_x/(c - 1)}{SS_{error}/(N - c)} = \frac{MS_x}{MS_{error}}$$

Page 509: Measuring the strength of the joint effect of two factors:

$$\text{multiple } \eta^2 = \frac{(SS_{x_1} + SS_{x_2} + SS_{x_1 x_2})}{SS_y}$$

The significance of the overall effect may be tested by an F test, as follows:

$$F = \frac{(SS_{x_1} + SS_{x_2} + SS_{x_1 x_2})/df_n}{SS_{error}/df_d}$$

$$= \frac{SS_{x_1, x_2, x_1 x_2}/df_n}{SS_{error}/df_d} = \frac{MS_{x_1, x_2, x_1 x_2}}{MS_{error}}$$

where

$$df_n = \text{degrees of freedom for the numerator}$$
$$= (c_1 - 1) + (c_2 - 1) + (c_1 - 1)(c_2 - 1)$$
$$= c_1 c_2 - 1$$
$$df_d = \text{degrees of freedom for the denominator}$$
$$= N - c_1 c_2$$
$$MS = \text{mean square}$$

Measuring the significance of the interaction effect:

$$F = \frac{SS_{x_1 x_2}/df_n}{SS_{error}/df_d} = \frac{MS_{x_1 x_2}}{MS_{error}}$$

where

$$df_n = (c_1 - 1)(c_2 - 1)$$
$$df_d = N - c_1 c_2$$

Page 510: The significance of the main effect of each factor may be tested as follows for X_1:

$$F = \frac{SS_{x_1}/df_n}{SS_{error}/df_d} = \frac{MS_{x_1}}{MS_{error}}$$

where

$$df_n = c_1 - 1$$
$$df_d = N - c_1 c_2$$

Page 515: Calculating omega squared:

$$\omega_x^2 = \frac{SS_x - (df_x \times MS_{error})}{SS_{total} + MS_{error}}$$

Selected Formulas (continued)

Chapter 17: Correlation and Regression

Page 530: Product moment correlation, r, can be calculated as:

$$r = \frac{\sum_{i=1}^{n}(X_i - \bar{X})(Y_i - \bar{Y})}{\sqrt{\sum_{i=1}^{n}(X_i - \bar{X})^2 \sum_{i=1}^{n}(Y_i - \bar{Y})^2}}$$

Division of the numerator and denominator by $n - 1$ gives:

$$r = \frac{\sum_{i=1}^{n}\dfrac{(X_i - \bar{X})(Y_i - \bar{Y})}{n - 1}}{\sqrt{\sum_{i=1}^{n}\dfrac{(X_i - \bar{X})^2}{n - 1} \sum_{i=1}^{n}\dfrac{(Y_i - \bar{Y})^2}{n - 1}}} = \frac{COV_{xy}}{s_x s_y}$$

Page 532: Expressing r in terms of the decomposition of the total variation:

$$r^2 = \frac{\text{Explained variation}}{\text{Total variation}} = \frac{SS_x}{SS_y}$$

$$= \frac{\text{Total variation} - \text{Error variation}}{\text{Total variation}} = \frac{SS_y - SS_{error}}{SS_y}$$

Page 533: Testing the statistical significance of the relationship between two variables measured by using r:

$$t = r\left[\frac{n - 2}{1 - r^2}\right]^{1/2}$$

Page 534: Calculating the partial correlation coefficient:

$$r_{xy.z} = \frac{r_{xy} - (r_{xz})(r_{yz})}{\sqrt{1 - r_{xz}^2}\sqrt{1 - r_{yz}^2}}$$

Page 535: Part correlation coefficient:

$$r_{y(x.z)} = \frac{r_{xy} - r_{xz}r_{yz}}{\sqrt{1 - r_{xz}^2}}$$

Page 537: Bivariate regression analysis:

Bivariate regression model. The basic regression equation is $Y_i = \beta_0 + \beta_1 X_i + e_i$, where Y = dependent or criterion variable, X = independent or predictor variable, β_0 = intercept of the line, β_1 = slope of the line, and e_i is the error term associated with the ith observation.

Estimated or predicted value. The estimated or predicted value of Y_i is $\hat{Y}_i = a + bx$, where $\hat{Y}_i$ is the predicted value of Y_i, and a and b are estimators of β_0 and β_1, respectively.

t statistic. A t statistic with $n - 2$ degrees of freedom can be used to test the null hypothesis that no linear relationship exists between X and Y, or

$$H_0: \beta_1 = 0, \text{ where } t = \frac{b}{SE_b}.$$

Page 540: Estimating the parameters:
In most cases, β_0 and β_1 are unknown and are estimated from the sample observations using the equation

$$\hat{Y}_i = a + bx_i$$

where $\hat{Y}_i$ is the estimated or predicted value of Y_i, and a and b are estimators of β_0 and β_1, respectively. The slope, b, may be computed in terms of the covariance between X and Y, (COV_{xy}), and the variance of X as:

$$b = \frac{COV_{xy}}{s_x^2} = \frac{\sum_{i=1}^{n}(X_i - \bar{X})(Y_i - \bar{Y})}{\sum_{i=1}^{n}(X_i - \bar{X})^2} = \frac{\sum_{i=1}^{n}X_iY_i - n\bar{X}\bar{Y}}{\sum_{i=1}^{n}X_i^2 - n\bar{X}^2}$$

The intercept, a, may then be calculated using:

$$a = \bar{Y} - b\bar{X}$$

Page 541: Relationship between the standardized and nonstandardized regression coefficients:

$$B_{yx} = b_{yx}(s_x/s_y)$$

Page 542: Decomposition of total variation:

$$SS_y = SS_{reg} + SS_{res}$$

where

$$SS_y = \sum_{i=1}^{n}(Y_i - \bar{Y})^2$$

$$SS_{reg} = \sum_{i=1}^{n}(\hat{Y}_i - \bar{Y})^2$$

$$SS_{res} = \sum_{i=1}^{n}(Y_i - \hat{Y}_i)^2$$

The strength of association may then be calculated as follows:

$$r^2 = \frac{SS_{reg}}{SS_y} = \frac{SS_y - SS_{res}}{SS_y}$$

Page 543: Test for the significance of the coefficient of determination:
The hypotheses in this case are:

$$H_0: R^2_{pop} = 0$$
$$H_1: R^2_{pop} > 0$$

The appropriate test statistic is the F statistic:

$$F = \frac{SS_{reg}}{SS_{res}/(n - 2)}$$

Page 544: Calculating the standard error of estimate, SEE:

$$SEE = \sqrt{\frac{\sum_{i=1}^{n}(Y_i - \hat{Y})^2}{n - 2}} \quad \text{or} \quad SEE = \sqrt{\frac{SS_{res}}{n - 2}}$$

or more generally, if there are k independent variables,

$$SEE = \sqrt{\frac{SS_{res}}{n - k - 1}}$$

Page 546: General form of the multiple regression model:

$$Y = \beta_0 + \beta_1 X_1 + \beta_2 X_2 + \beta_3 X_3 + \cdots + \beta_k X_k + e$$

which is estimated by the following equation:

$$\hat{Y} = a + b_1 X_1 + b_2 X_2 + b_3 X_3 + \cdots + b_k X_k$$

Page 548: Measuring the strength of association (also called the coefficient of multiple determination):

$$R^2 = \frac{SS_{reg}}{SS_y}$$

Page 549:
R^2 adjusted for the number of independent variables and the sample size:

$$\text{Adjusted } R^2 = R^2 - \frac{k(1 - R^2)}{n - k - 1}$$

Significance testing using an F statistic:

$$F = \frac{SS_{reg}/k}{SS_{res}/(n - k - 1)}$$

$$= \frac{R^2/k}{(1 - R^2)/(n - k - 1)}$$

This has an F distribution with k and $(n - k - 1)$ degrees of freedom.

Page 550: Incremental F statistic:

$$F = \frac{SS_{x_i}/1}{SS_{res}/(n - k - 1)}$$

This has an F distribution with 1 and $(n - k - 1)$ degrees of freedom.